NICHOLSON
LONDON
STREETFINDER

CONTENTS

Nicholson
HarperCollins*Publishers*
77-85 Fulham Palace Road
London W6 8JB

Generated from the Bartholomew London Digital Database.

London Underground Map by permission of London Regional Transport
LRT Registered User Number 93/1496

Printed and bound in Italy by Amilcare Pizzi spa, Milan.

Great care has been taken throughout this atlas to be accurate, but the publishers cannot accept responsibility for any errors which appear or their consequences. Queries or information regarding the London Streetfinder should be addressed to the Publishing Manager, Nicholson, HarperCollins*Publishers*, 77-85 Fulham Palace Road, Hammersmith, London W6 8JB

Paperback edition ISBN 0 7028 1903 4 MNM 93/1/135 E/J6020
Spiral bound edition ISBN 0 7028 1905 0 ENM 93/1/150 E/J6022

Nicholson
An Imprint of Bartholomew
A Division of HarperCollins*Publishers*

First Published 1993. Copyright © Nicholson 1993

KEY TO MAP PAGES

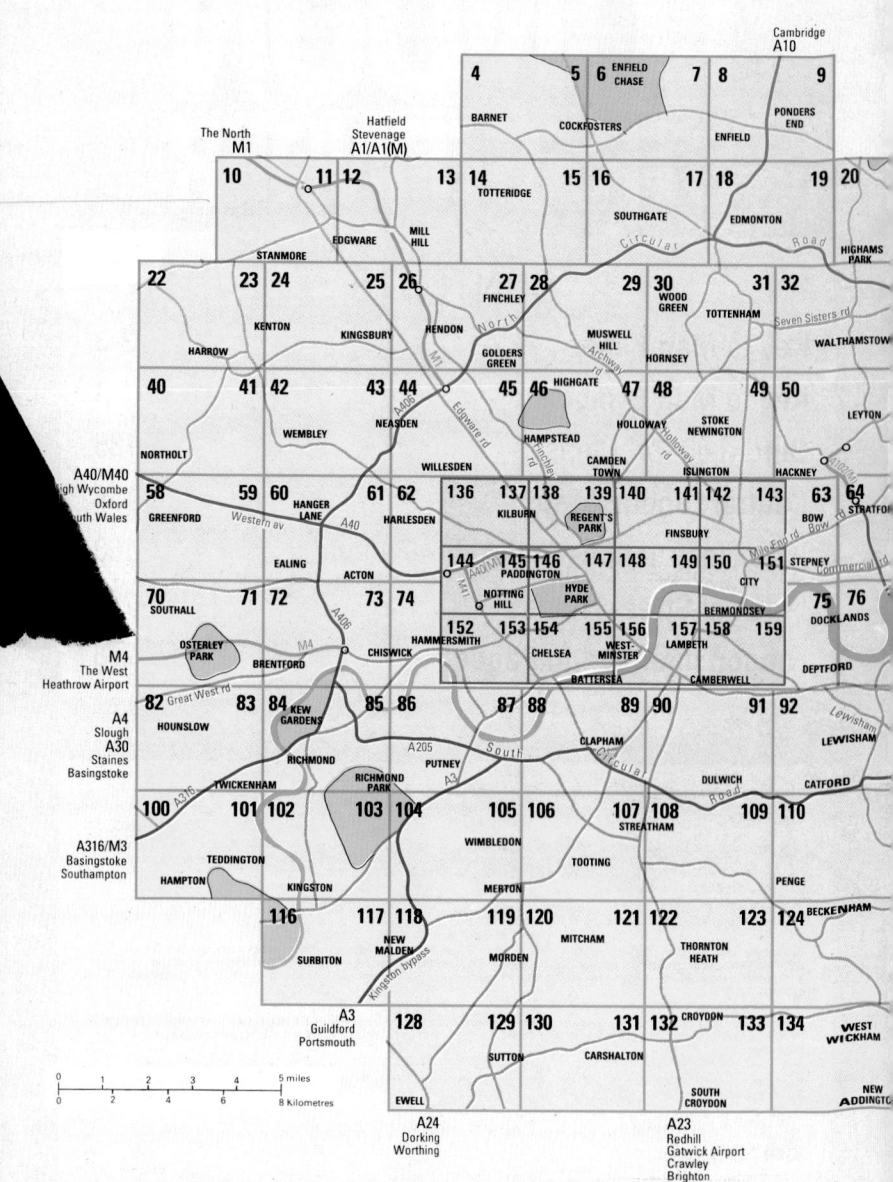

Cambridge
A10

| 4 | 5 | 6 ENFIELD CHASE | 7 | 8 | 9 |

BARNET   COCKFOSTERS   ENFIELD   PONDERS END

The North
M1

Hatfield
Stevenage
A1/A1(M)

| 10 | 11 12 | 13 14 | 15 16 | 17 18 | 19 20 |

TOTTERIDGE   SOUTHGATE   EDMONTON   HIGHAMS PARK

EDGWARE   MILL HILL

STANMORE   Circular   Road

| 22 | 23 24 | 25 26 | 27 28 | 29 30 | 31 32 |

KENTON   KINGSBURY   HENDON   FINCHLEY   WOOD GREEN   TOTTENHAM   Seven Sisters rd

HARROW   GOLDERS GREEN   MUSWELL HILL   HORNSEY   WALTHAMSTOW

North

| 40 | 41 42 | 43 44 | 45 46 | 47 48 | 49 50 |

WEMBLEY   NEASDEN   HIGHGATE   HOLLOWAY   STOKE NEWINGTON   LEYTON

NORTHOLT   HAMPSTEAD   CAMDEN TOWN   ISLINGTON   HACKNEY

A40/M40
High Wycombe
Oxford
South Wales

WILLESDEN

| 58 | 59 60 | 61 62 | 136 | 137 138 | 139 140 | 141 142 | 143 | 63 64 |

GREENFORD   Western av   HANGER LANE   HARLESDEN   KILBURN   REGENT'S PARK   FINSBURY   BOW   STRATFORD

EALING   A40   ACTON

| 70 | 71 72 | 73 74 | 144 | 145 146 | 147 148 | 149 150 | 151 | 75 76 |

SOUTHALL   PADDINGTON   NOTTING HILL   HYDE PARK   CITY   STEPNEY   BERMONDSEY   DOCKLANDS

| 152 | 153 154 | 155 156 | 157 158 | 159 |

HAMMERSMITH   CHELSEA   WEST-MINSTER   LAMBETH   CAMBERWELL

M4
The West
Heathrow Airport

OSTERLEY PARK   CHISWICK   BATTERSEA   DEPTFORD

| 82 | 83 84 | 85 86 | 87 88 | 89 90 | 91 92 |

A4
Slough
A30
Staines
Basingstoke

HOUNSLOW   KEW GARDENS   CLAPHAM   LEWISHAM

BRENTFORD   PUTNEY   DULWICH   CATFORD

RICHMOND   South

TWICKENHAM   RICHMOND PARK

| 100 | 101 102 | 103 104 | 105 106 | 107 108 | 109 110 |

A316/M3
Basingstoke
Southampton

TEDDINGTON   WIMBLEDON   STREATHAM

HAMPTON   KINGSTON   MERTON   TOOTING   PENGE

| 116 | 117 118 | 119 120 | 121 122 | 123 124 |

SURBITON   NEW MALDEN   MORDEN   MITCHAM   THORNTON HEATH   BECKENHAM

Kingston bypass

A3
Guildford
Portsmouth

| 128 | 129 130 | 131 132 | 133 134 |

SUTTON   CARSHALTON   CROYDON   WEST WICKHAM

EWELL   SOUTH CROYDON   NEW ADDINGTON

A24
Dorking
Worthing

A23
Redhill
Gatwick Airport
Crawley
Brighton

0 1 2 3 4   5 miles
0 2   4   6   8 kilometres

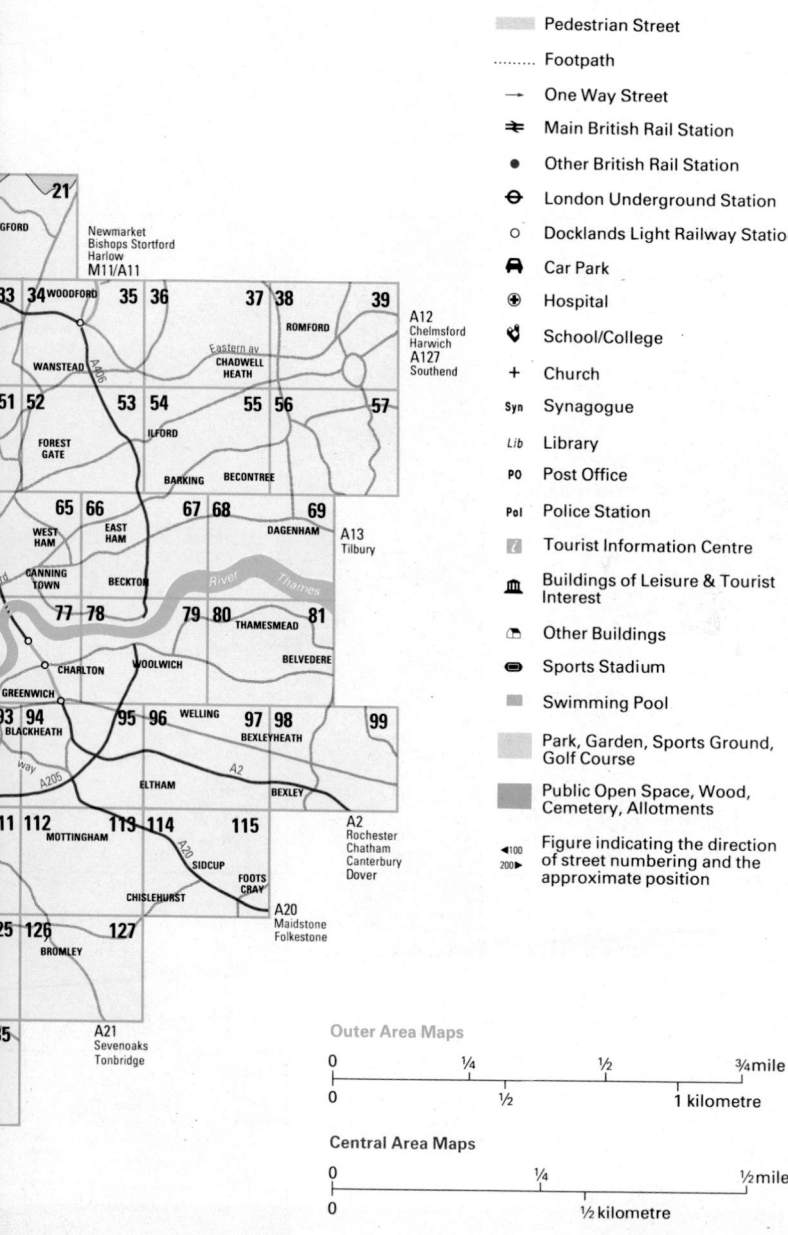

MAP SYMBOLS

	Street Market
	Pedestrian Street
....	Footpath
→	One Way Street
⇌	Main British Rail Station
•	Other British Rail Station
⊖	London Underground Station
○	Docklands Light Railway Station
🚗	Car Park
⊕	Hospital
⚐	School/College
+	Church
Syn	Synagogue
Lib	Library
PO	Post Office
Pol	Police Station
ℹ	Tourist Information Centre
🏛	Buildings of Leisure & Tourist Interest
▭	Other Buildings
⬭	Sports Stadium
▦	Swimming Pool
	Park, Garden, Sports Ground, Golf Course
	Public Open Space, Wood, Cemetery, Allotments
◄100 200►	Figure indicating the direction of street numbering and the approximate position

Outer Area Maps

```
0            ¼            ½            ¾mile
├────────────┼────────────┼────────────┤
0                 ½                 1 kilometre
```

Central Area Maps

```
0                  ¼                  ½mile
├──────────────────┼──────────────────┤
0                ½ kilometre
```

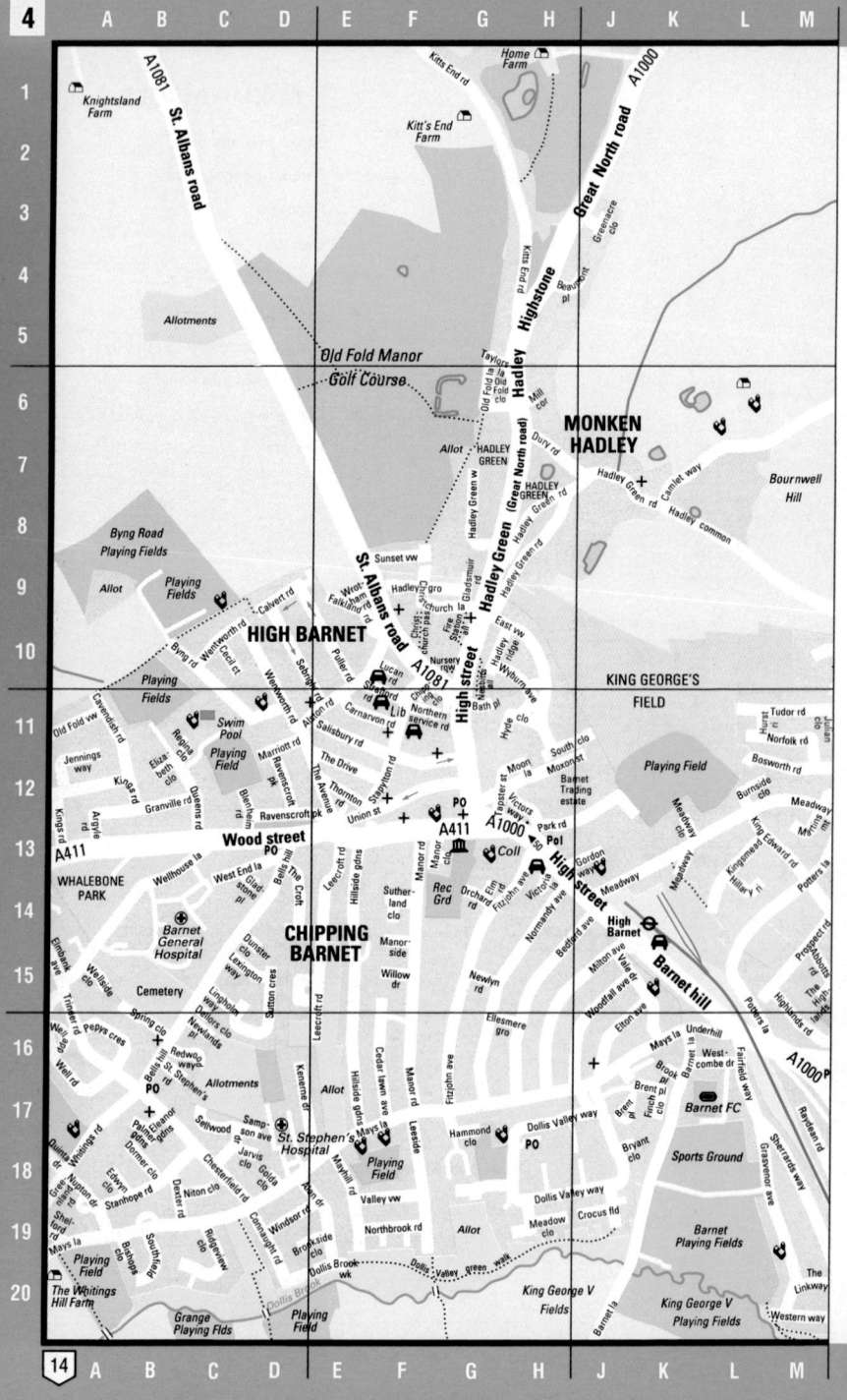

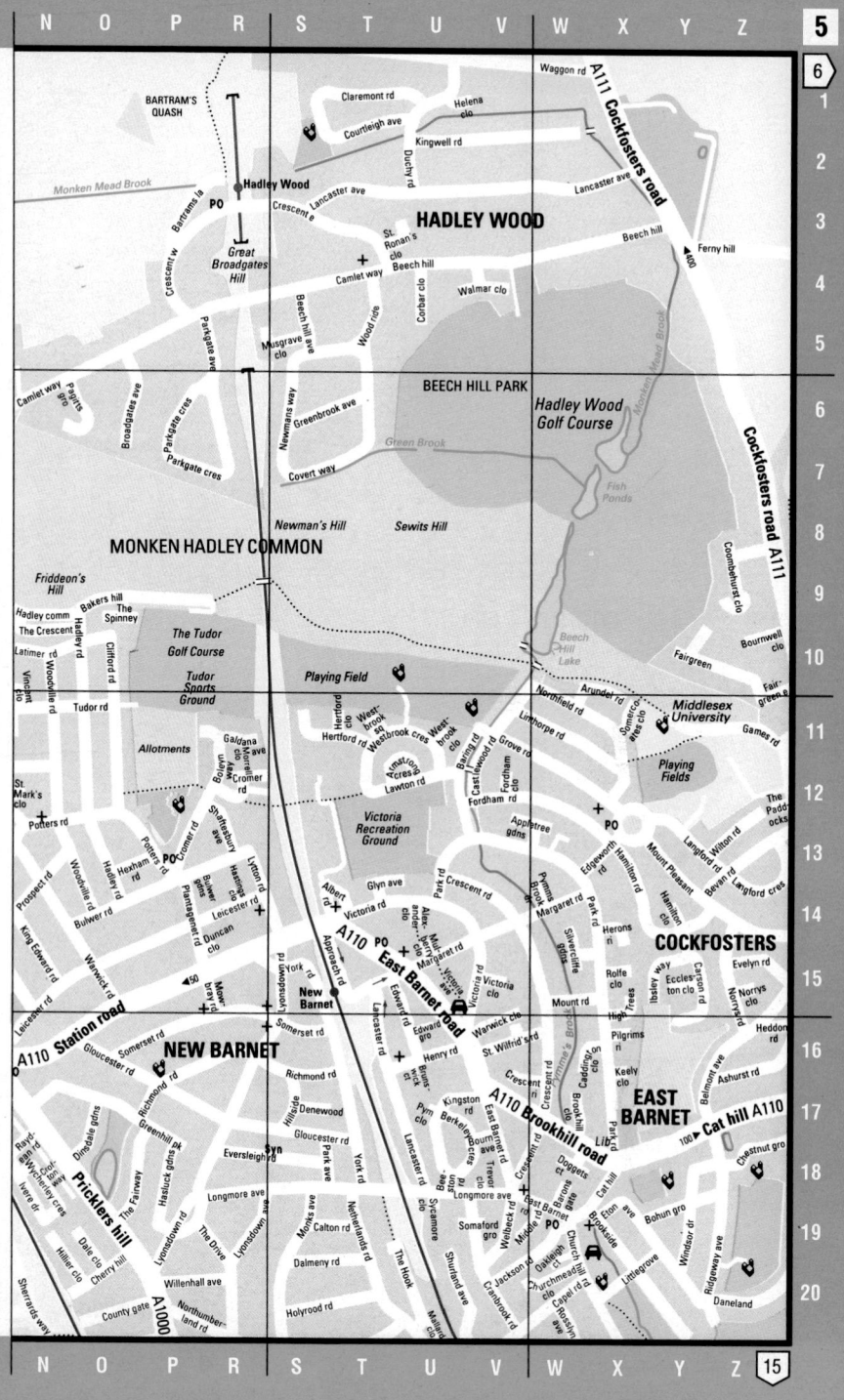

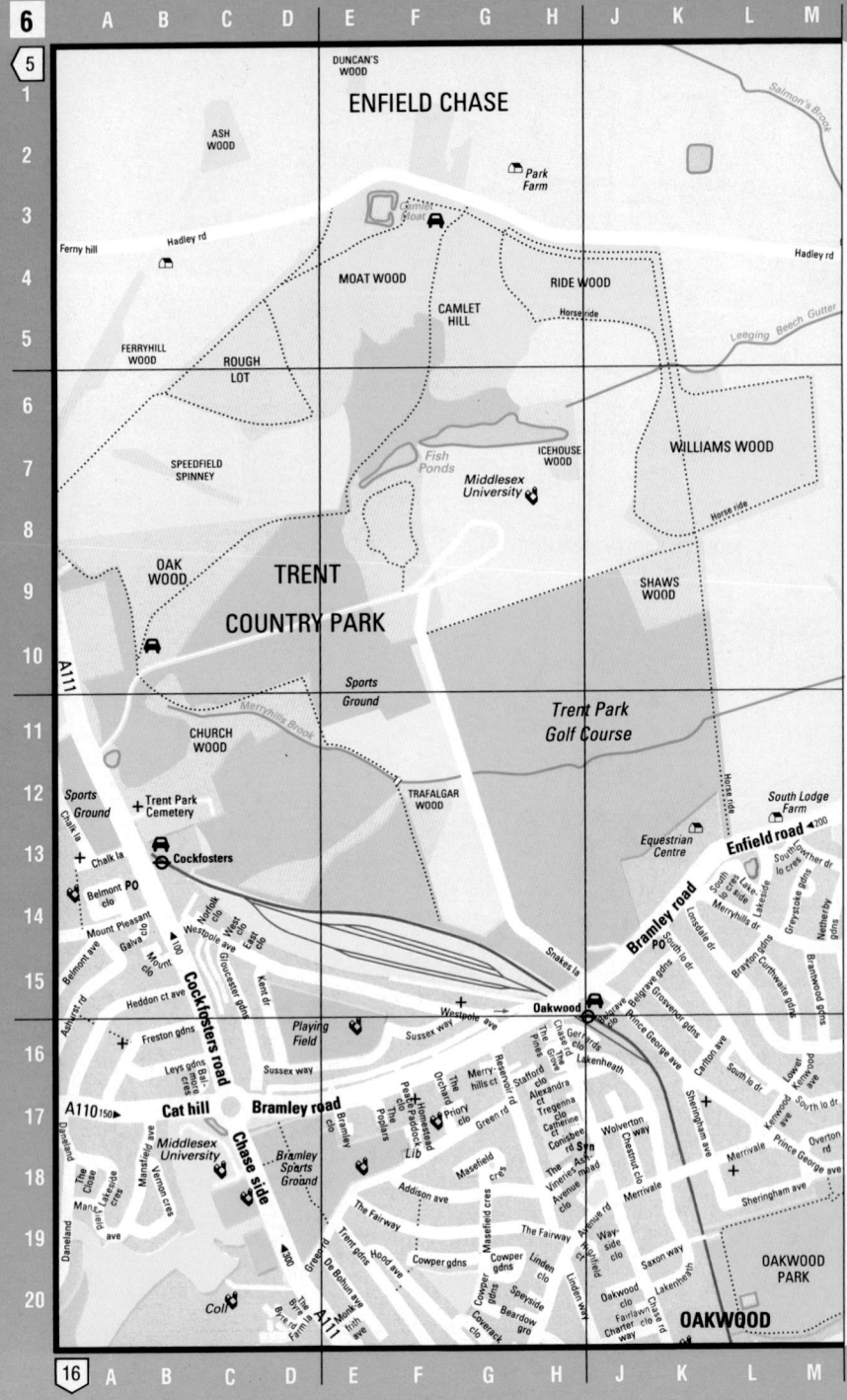

DUNCAN'S WOOD

ENFIELD CHASE

ASH WOOD

Park Farm

Ferny hill   Hadley rd   Hadley rd

Camlet Moat

MOAT WOOD   RIDE WOOD

CAMLET HILL   Horse ride

FERRYHILL WOOD   ROUGH LOT   Leeging Beech Gutter

SPEEDFIELD SPINNEY   Fish Ponds   ICEHOUSE WOOD   WILLIAMS WOOD

Middlesex University

OAK WOOD   SHAWS WOOD

TRENT

COUNTRY PARK   Horse ride

A111

Sports Ground

Merryhills Brook   CHURCH WOOD   Trent Park Golf Course

Sports Ground   Trent Park Cemetery   TRAFALGAR WOOD

Chalk la   Chalk la   Cockfosters   South Lodge Farm

Belmont PO clo   Equestrian Centre   Enfield road   ◄200

Mount Pleasant   Galva clo   Norfolk clo   West clo   South at Lake side   Lakeside   Southowther dr lo cres   Greyscote gdns

Belmont ave   Mount   East clo   Merryhills dr   South lo dr   Braylon gdns   Cumhealia gdns   Netherby gdns

Ashurst rd   Heddon ct ave   Kent dr   Westpole ave   Snakes la   Bramley road PO   Lessdale dr   Grosvenor gdns   Bramwood gdns

Freston gdns   Westpole ave   Oakwood   Badgeve   Prince George ave   Carlton ave   Kenwood gdns   Lower

Cockfosters road   Leys gdns Dal- more cres   Playing Field   Sussex way   Gerrards   Chase clo   Lakenheath   Kenwood   South lo dr   Overton

A110 ◄150   Cat hill   Bramley road   Sussex way   The Orchard   Merry hills ct clo   Stafford clo   The Glebe The Pines   South ave   Merrivale   Overton ave

Middlesex University   Chase side   Bramley   Homestead Paddock   Priory clo   Alexandra ct   Tregenna clo   Wolverton way   Sheringham ave   Prince George ave

Mansfield ave   Venton cres   Bramley Sports Ground   The Poplars   Stafford   Green rd   Catherine clo   Conisbee Avenue clo rd   Ash mead   Chestnut clo   Sheringham ave

Daneland   The Chase   Leaside cres   Addison ave   Masefield cres   The Viners   Merrivale

Mano Plain ave   The Fairway   Masefield cres   The Fairway   Way- side clo

Coll   The Brian Farm la   A111   De Bohun ave   Trent gdns   Hood ave   Cowper gdns   Cowper gdns   Linden clo   Speyside   Oakwood clo   Saxon way   Lakenheath   OAKWOOD PARK

Monk frith way   Cowper gdns   Beardow gro   Linden way   Charter clo   way   OAKWOOD

Coveback clo

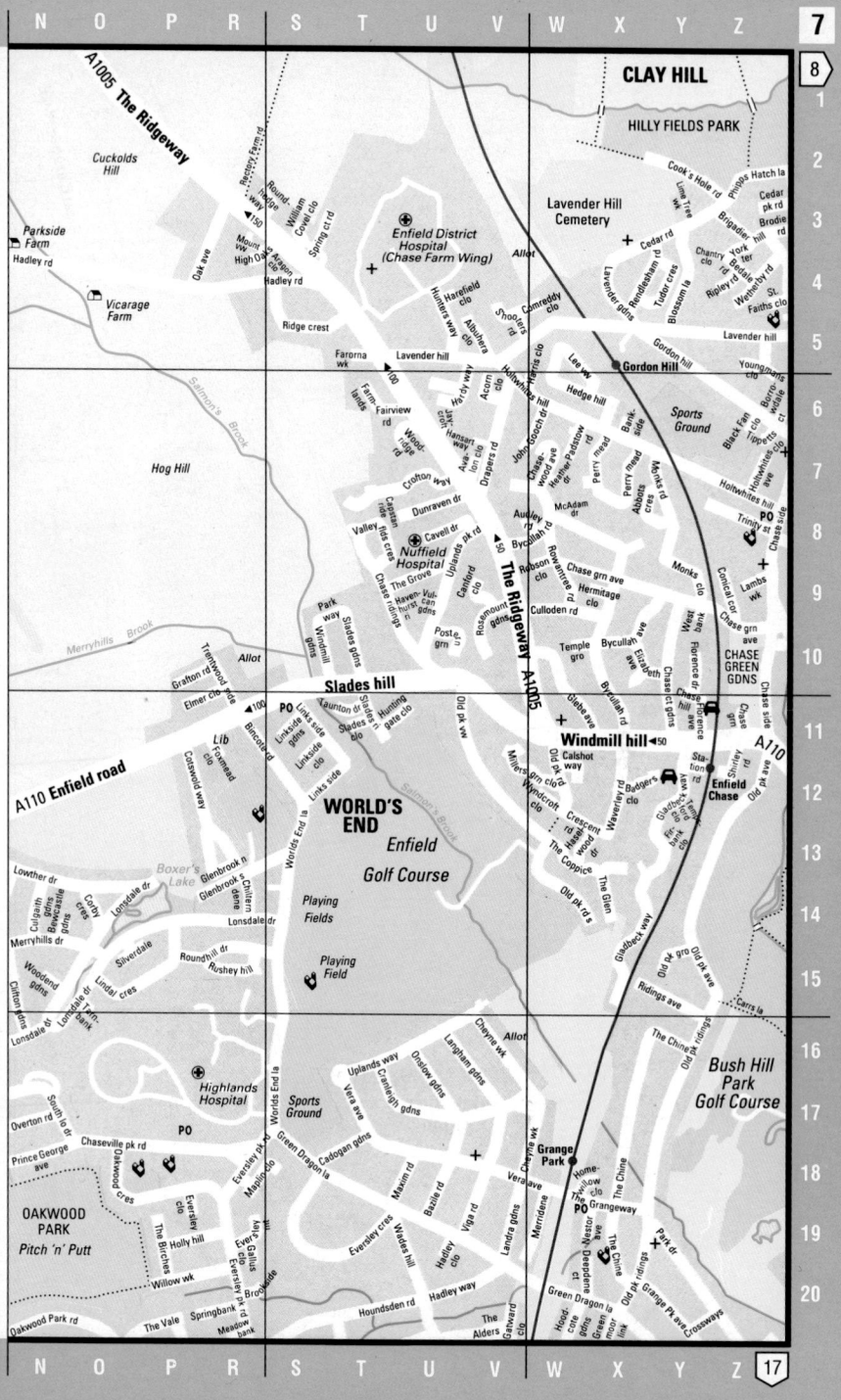

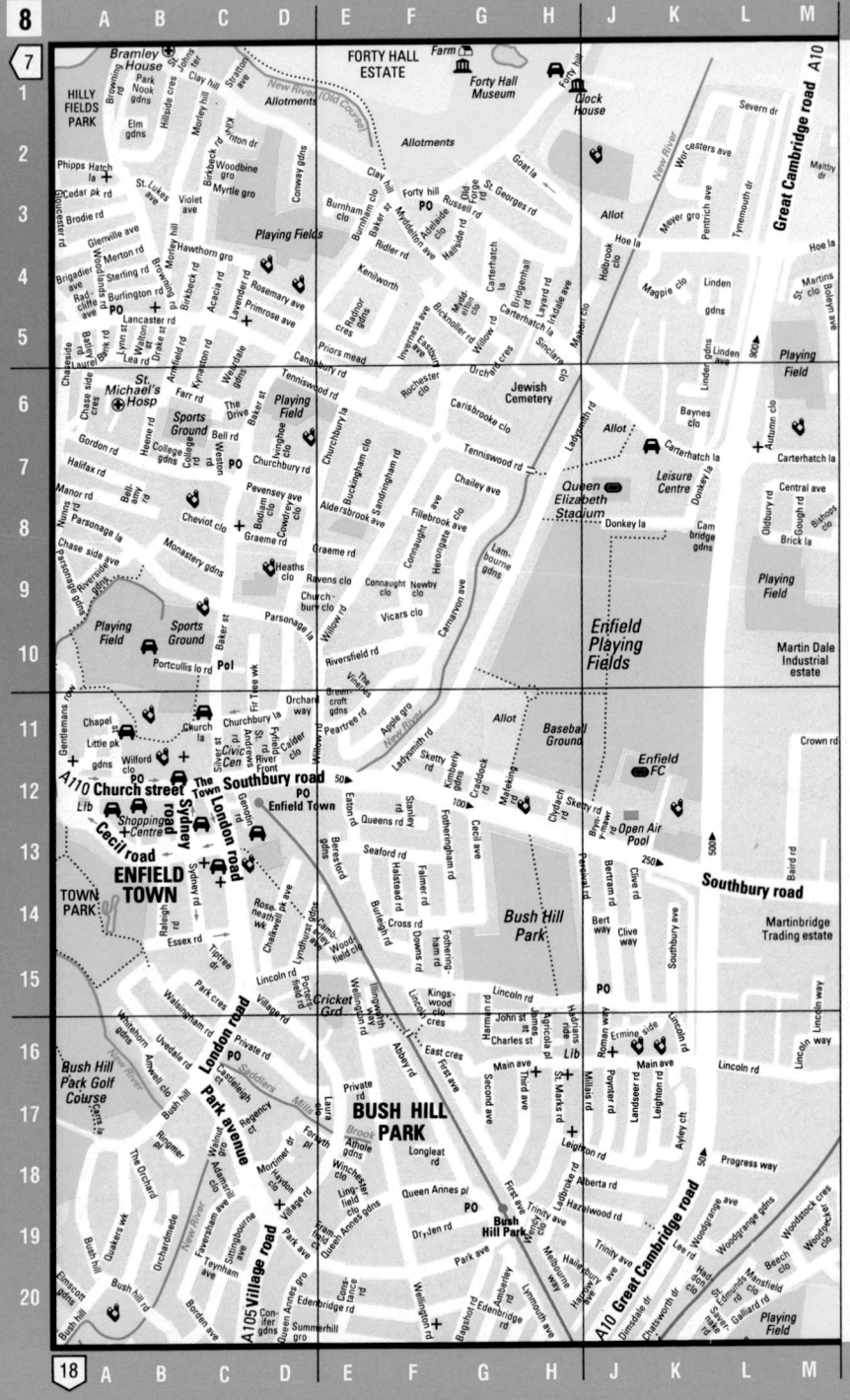

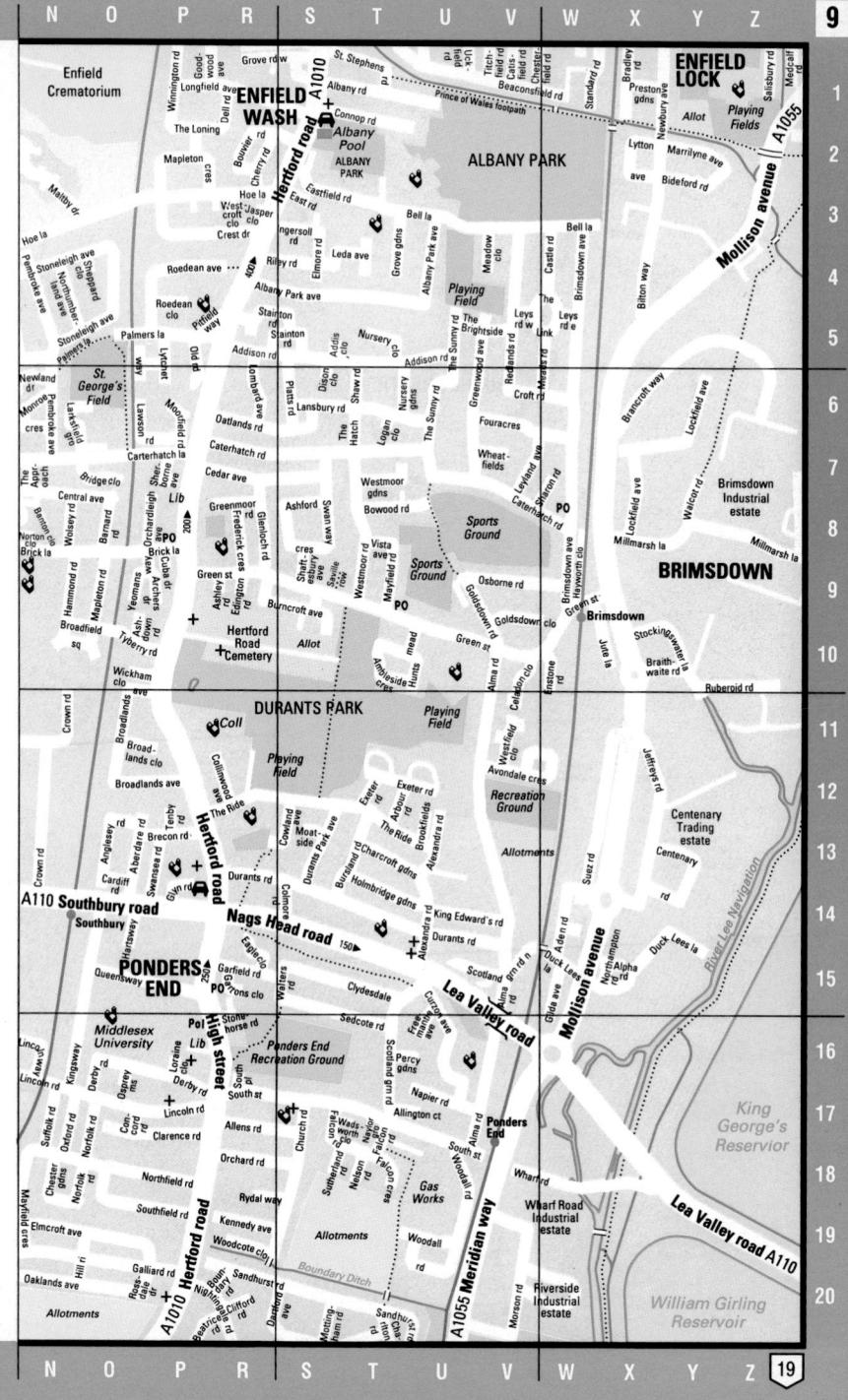

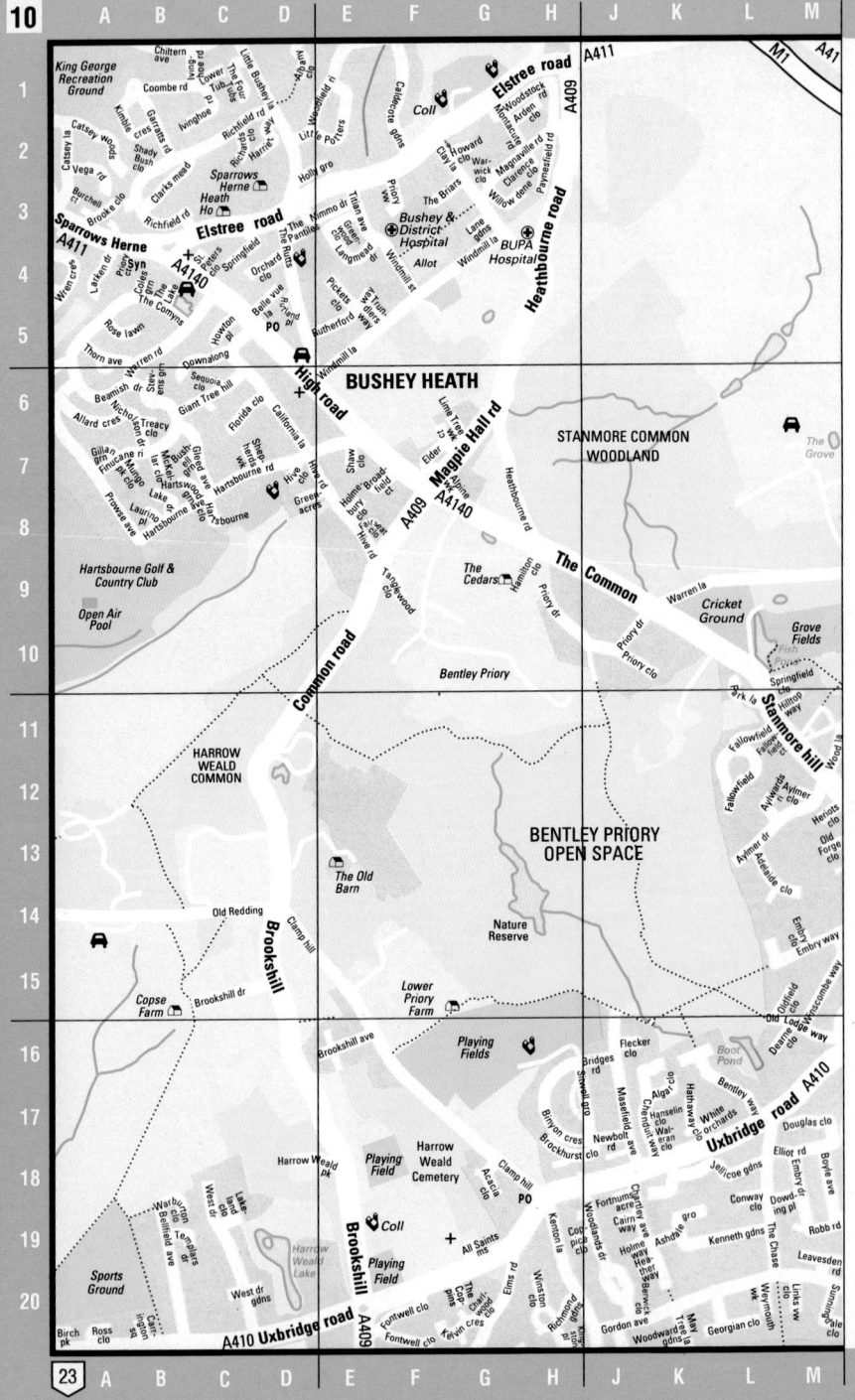

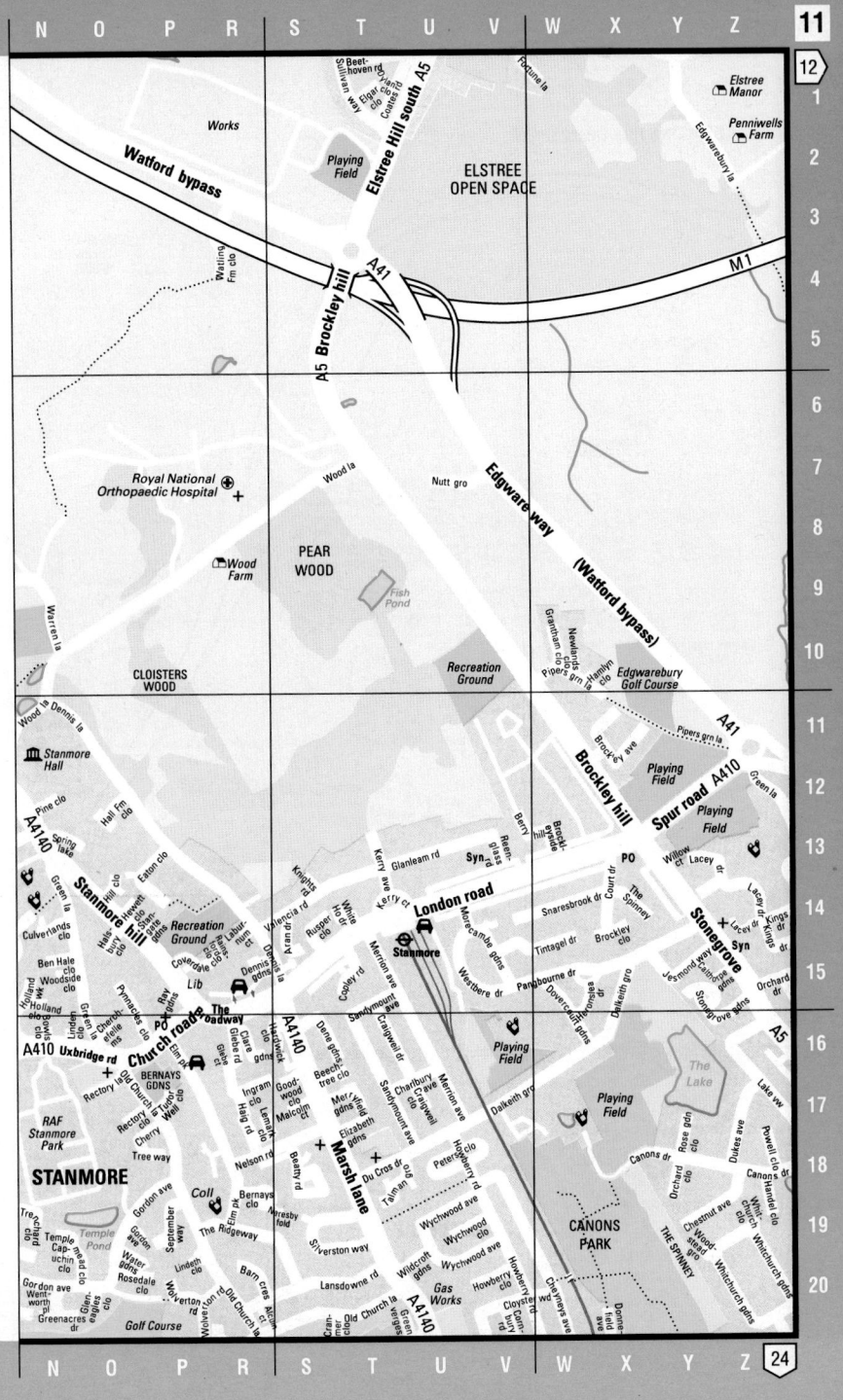

Elstree Manor

Penniwells Farm

Works

Watford bypass

Playing Field

Elgar clo
Coates clo
Beethoven ra
Elstree hill south A5

ELSTREE OPEN SPACE

Fortune la

Edgwarebury la

M1

Watling Fm clo

A41

A5 Brockley hill

Edgware way

Wood la

Nutt gro

(Watford bypass)

Royal National Orthopaedic Hospital

PEAR WOOD

Wood Farm

Fish Pond

Warren la

CLOISTERS WOOD

Recreation Ground

Newlands clo
Grantham clo
Hamlyn clo
Pipers grn la

Edgwarebury Golf Course

A41

Wood la Dennis la

Stanmore Hall

Pipers grn la

Brockley

Brockley hill

Playing Field

Spur road A410

Green la

Playing Field

Pine clo
Hall Fm clo

A4140

Spring lake

Stanmore hill

Hill clo
Eaton clo
Green la

Recreation Ground

Hall
Hewett
Sheridan
arbur
num

Knights

Kerry ave
Glanleam rd

White
Rusper
clo

Aran dr

Syn.
Berry ct
Reeth gdns
Brockhill avde
Brocki hill gro

PO
Court dr
Willow Ct
Lacey
The Spinney

Lacey dr
Kings dr

Pine clo
Hall Fm clo
Culverlands clo
Ben Hale clo
Woodside clo
Holland clo
Bowls gdns
Linden
Pennacks clo

Coverdale rd
Dennis gdns
Valencia rd

Copley rd

London road
Stanmore

Morecambe gdns

Snaresbrook dr

Westbere dr
Brockley clo
Pangbourne dr

Tintagel gro

Stonegrove

Jesmond way
Stonegrove gdns

Syn
Orchard dr

A5

Lib

PO
The Broadway

A410 Uxbridge rd Church road

BERNAYS GDNS

RAF Stanmore Park

STANMORE

Hardwick
Glebe rd
Clare gdns
Ingram clo
Heig rd
Lenton clo
Cherry
Tree way
Nelson rd
Bernays clo
Wenlock

Dene gdns
Goodwood clo
Malcolm rd
Beech tree clo

A4140

Marsh lane

Elizabeth clo
Du Cros dr
Tasman
Taunan

Peters clo

Craigweil dr
Sandymount ave
Charlbury cres
Sandymount ave
Cripwell dr
Merrion ave

Playing Field

Dalkeith gro
Horncastle gdns

Playing Field

Canons dr

Orchard clo
Rose gdn
Duke ave
Powell clo

Lake vw

Canon Handel clo

The Lake

Gordon ave
Coll
Treeuchladd clo
Temple Capuchin clo
Gordon ave
Wentworth
Greenacres dr
Golf Course

September way
Water gdns
Rosedale clo
Eagles clo
Lindlen clo

The Ridgeway
Barn cres
Wolverton rd
Old Church la

Silverston way
Lansdowne rd

Wychwood ave
Wychwood clo
Wildcroft gdns
Wychwood ave

Cranmer clo
Old Church la A4140
Green verges

Gas Works

CANONS PARK

THE SPINNEY

Chestnut ave
Wood side gro
Whitchurch gdns

Howberry rd
Cloyster wd
Howberry clo
Chgivers ansla
Dennis field ave
Whitchurch gdns

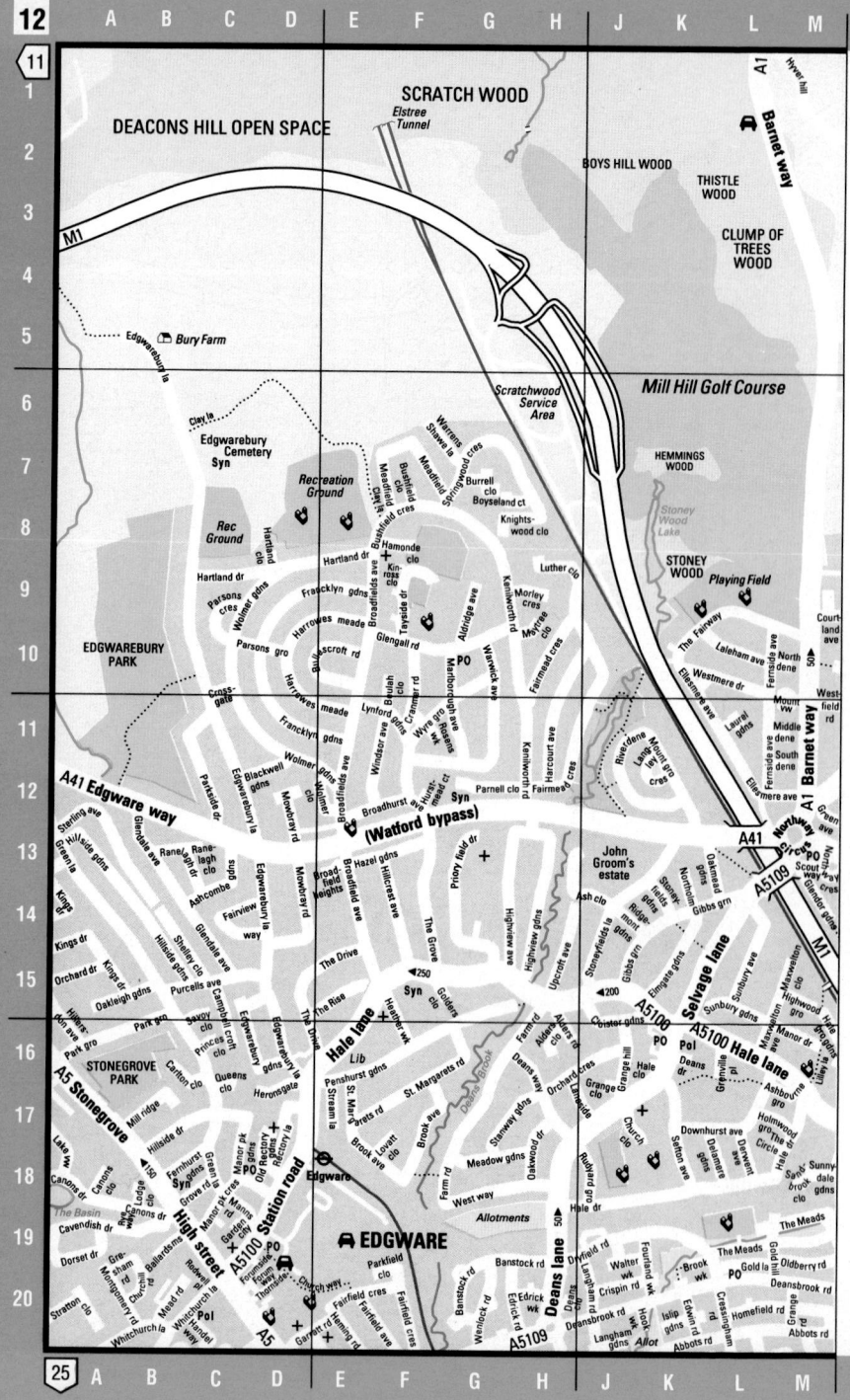

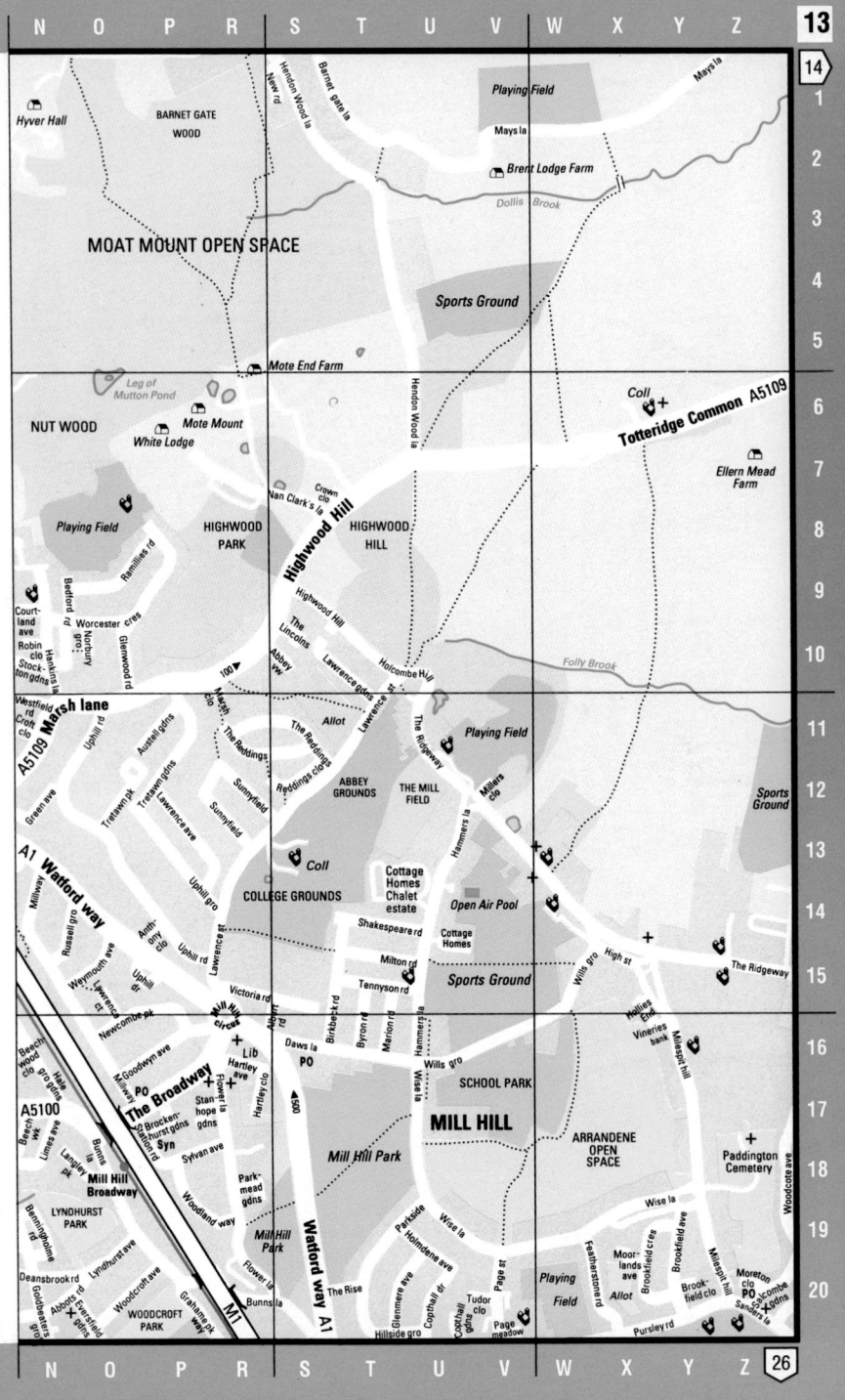

Hyver Hall

Playing Field

Mays la

BARNET GATE WOOD

New rd

Hendon Wood la

Barnet gate la

Mays la

Brent Lodge Farm

Dollis Brook

MOAT MOUNT OPEN SPACE

Sports Ground

Mote End Farm

Hendon Wood la

Coll

Totteridge Common A5109

Leg of Mutton Pond

NUT WOOD

Mote Mount

White Lodge

Ellern Mead Farm

Playing Field

HIGHWOOD PARK

Crown clo

Nan Clark's la

HIGHWOOD HILL

Highwood Hill

Highwood Hill

Courtland ave

Robin clo

Stockton gdns

Bedford rd

Worcester gdns

Norbury gdns

Ramillies rd

Glenwood rd

cres

The Lincolns

Abbey Vw

Lawrence gdns

Holcombe Hill

Folly Brook

100▶

Westfield rd

Croft clo

A5109 Marsh lane

Uphill rd

Nash clo

Ausell gdns

Tretawn gdns

Tretawn gdns

Lawrence ave

Sunnyfield

Sunnyfield

Allot

The Reddings

The Reddings

Reddings clo

Lawrence

The Ridgeway

Playing Field

Millers clo

Sports Ground

Green ave

A1 Watford way

Millway

Russell gro

Weymouth ave

Uphill gro

Anthony rd

Uphill gr

Uphill gro

Coll

COLLEGE GROUNDS

ABBEY GROUNDS

THE MILL FIELD

Hammers la

Cottage Homes Chalet estate

Open Air Pool

The Ridgeway

Lawrence

Victoria rd

Shakespeare rd

Cottage Homes

Milton rd

Tennyson rd

Sports Ground

Wills gro

High st

Mill Hill circus

Lib

PO

Daws la

PO

Birkbeck rd

Byron rd

Marion rd

Hammers la

Wills gro

Hollies bank

Vineries bank

Milespit hill

Beechwood clo

Goodwyn ave

Flower la

Stanhope gdns

Hartley ave

Hartley clo

The Broadway

PO

Brockenhurst gdns

Sylvan ave

Parkmead gdns

Woodland way

500

Wise la

SCHOOL PARK

MILL HILL

ARRANDENE OPEN SPACE

Featherstone rd

Moorlands clo

Brookfield cres

Brookfield ave

Milespit hill

Moreton clo

Paddington Cemetery

Woodcote ave

A5100

Beech wk

Limes ave

Langley pk

Mill Hill Broadway

LYNDHURST PARK

Benningholme rd

Deansbrook rd

Lyndhurst ave

Lyndhurst ave

Graham's rd

Grahame pk way

Bunns la

Bunns la

WOODCROFT PARK

Goodbeaters gro

Eversfield gdns

Mill Hill Park

The Rise

Hillside gro

Glenmere ave

Copthall dr

Copthall gdns

Tudor clo

Page meadow

Watford way A1

Parkside

Holmdene ave

Wise la

Page st

Playing Field

Allot

Brookfield clo

Sanders la

PO

Pursley rd

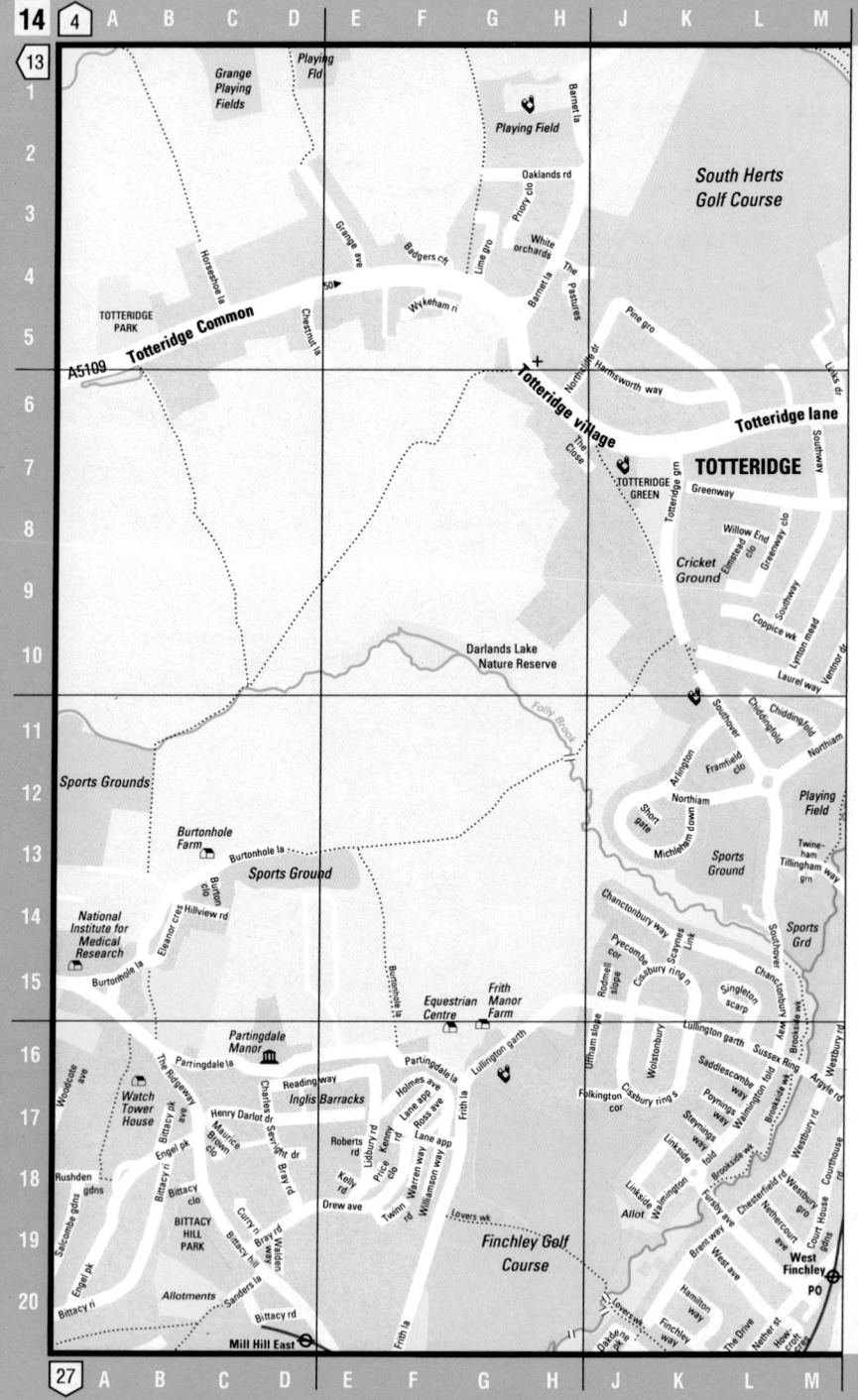

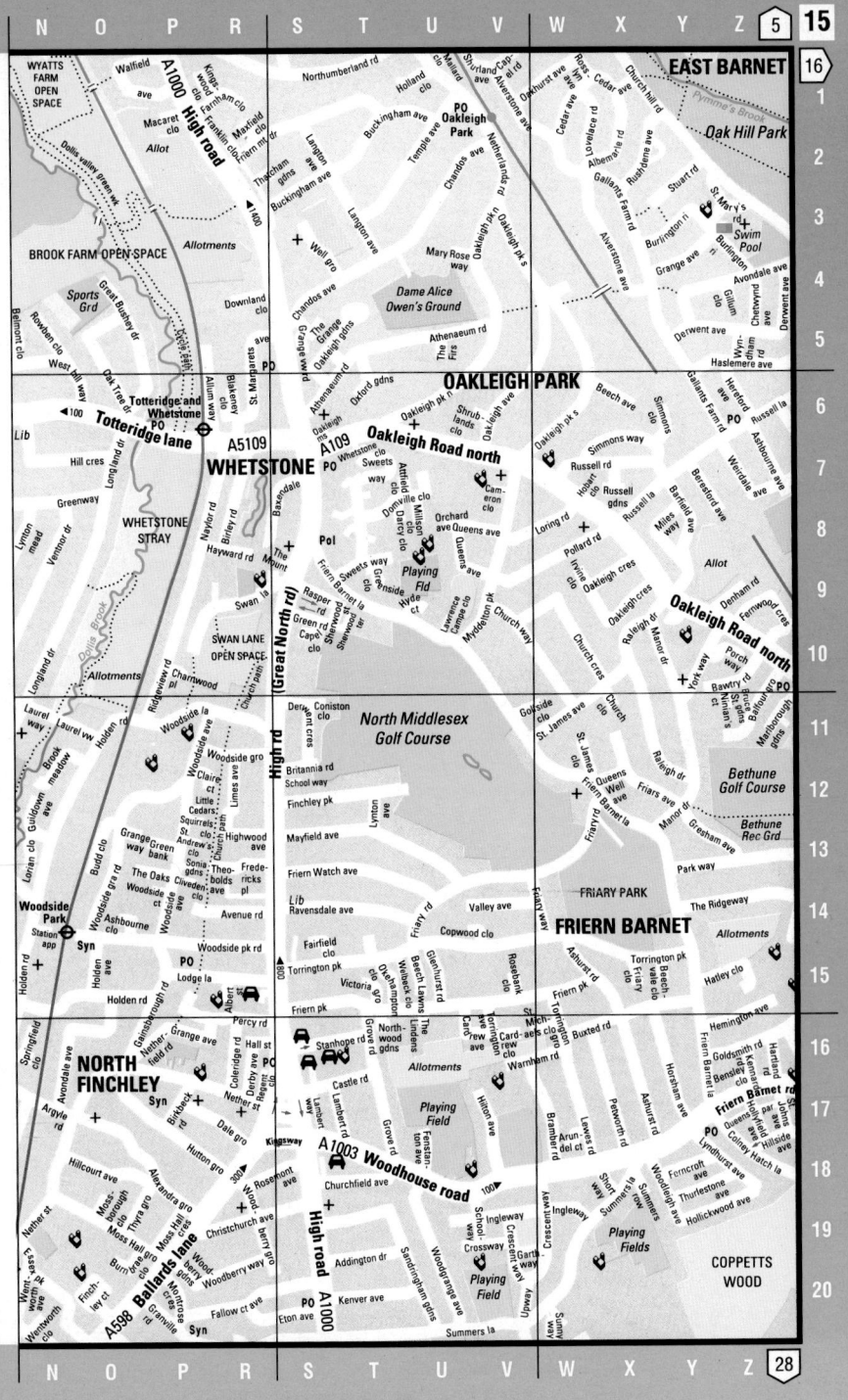

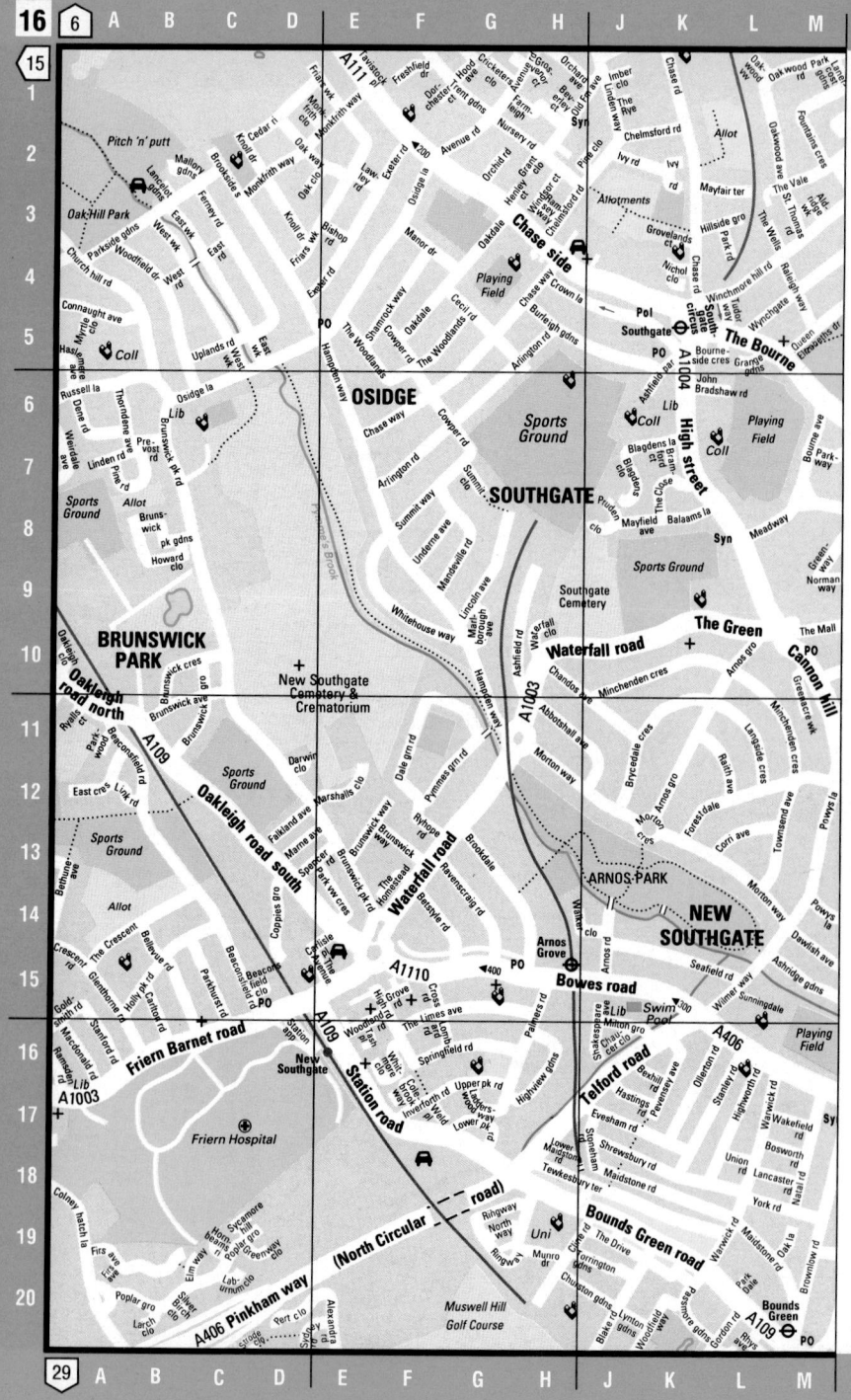

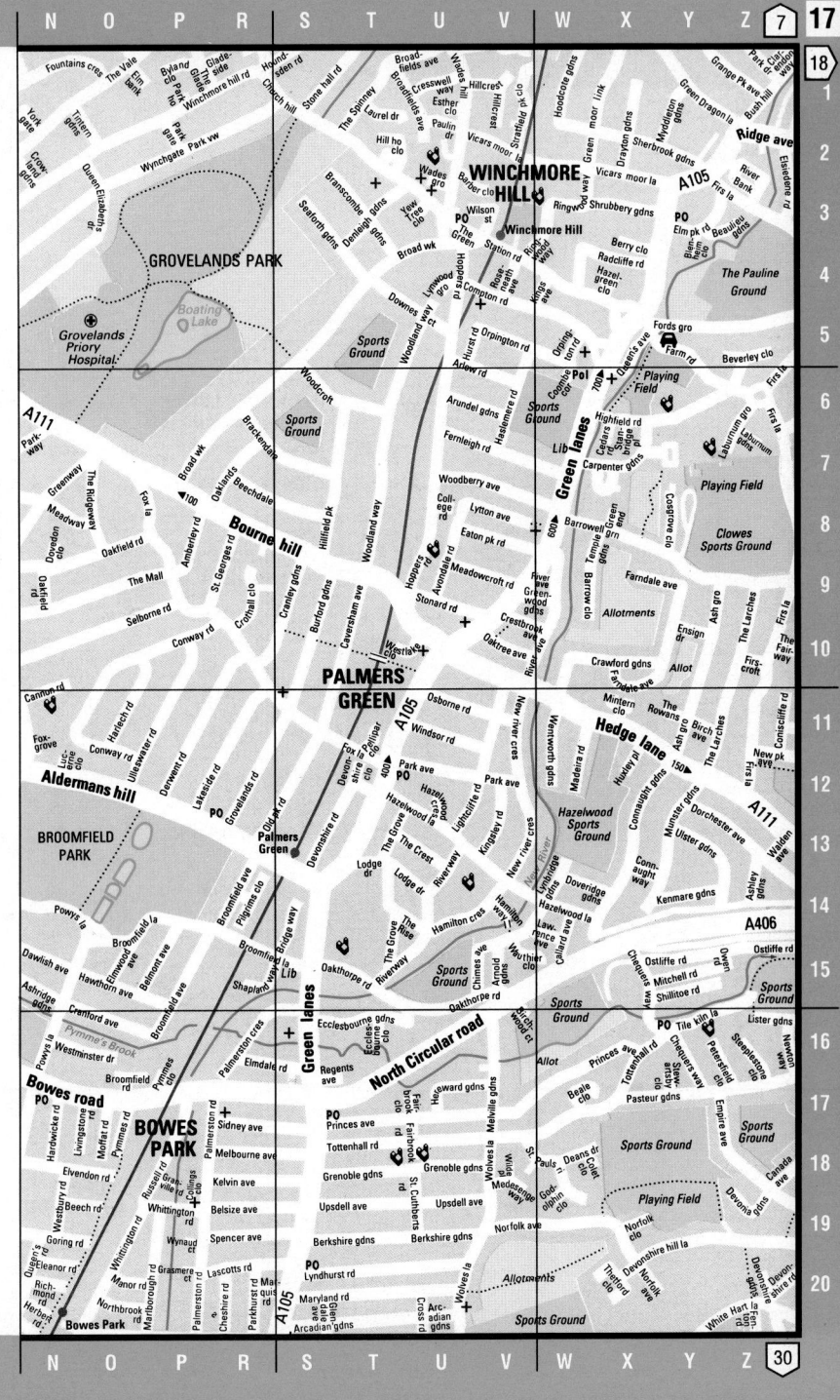

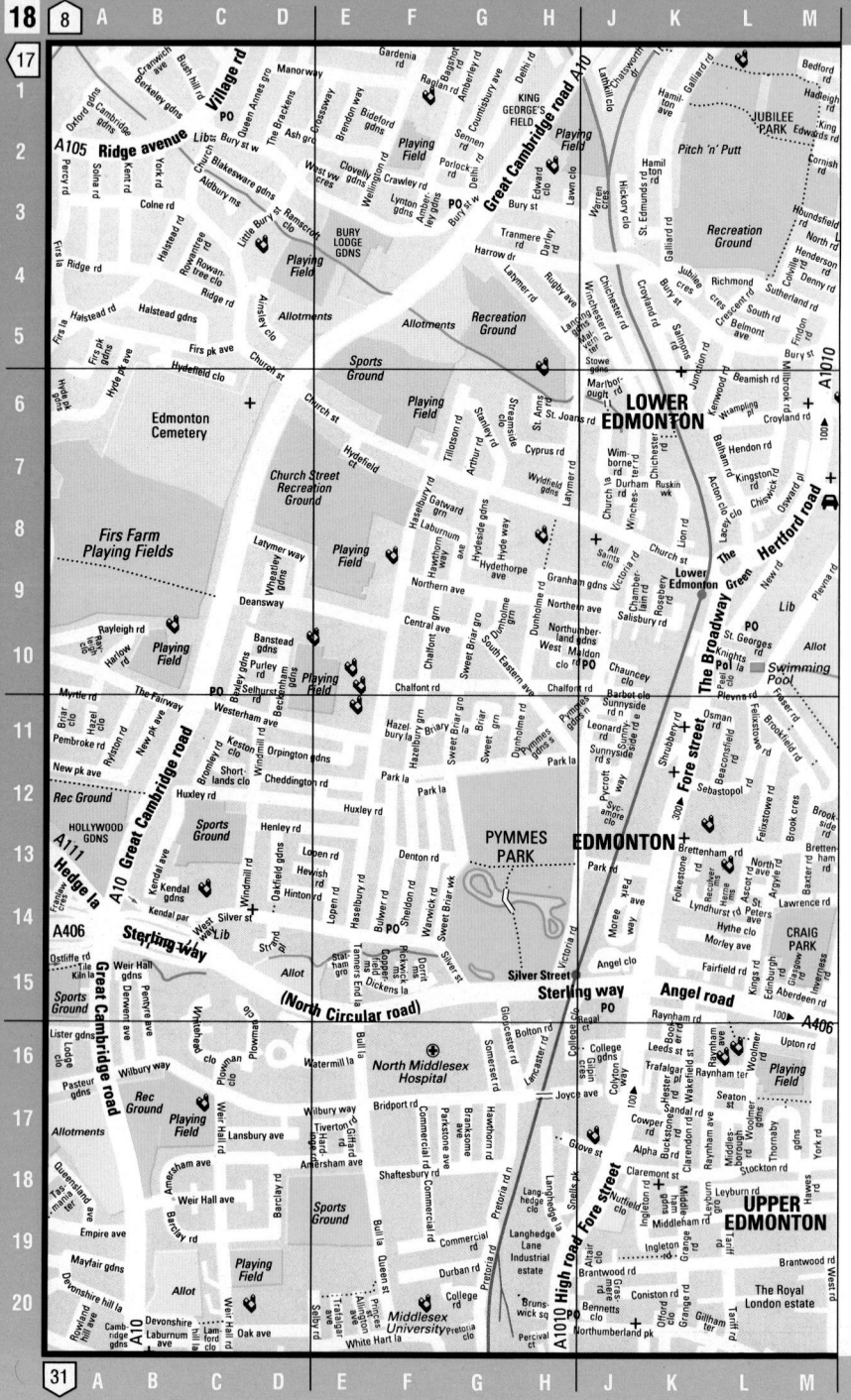

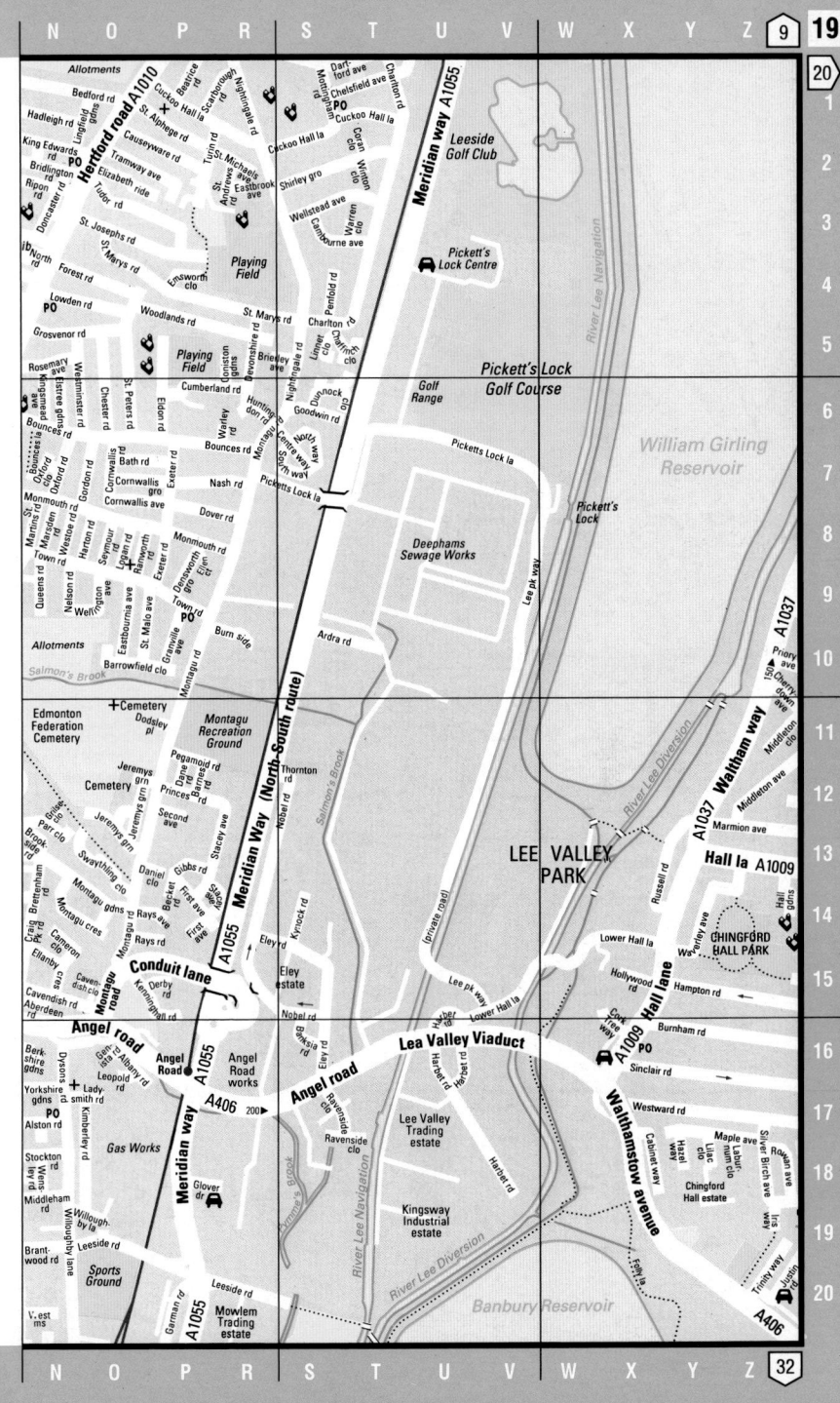

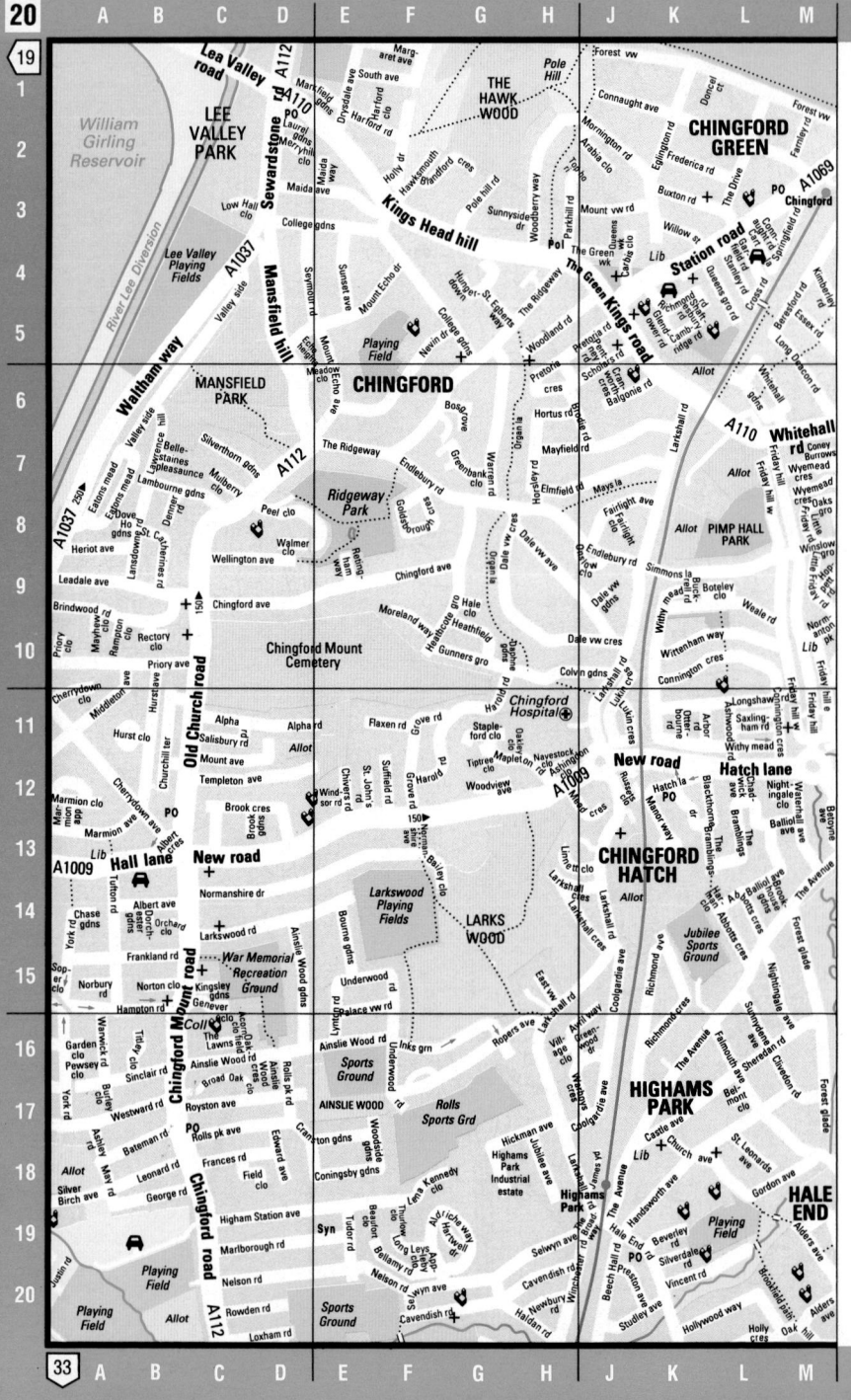

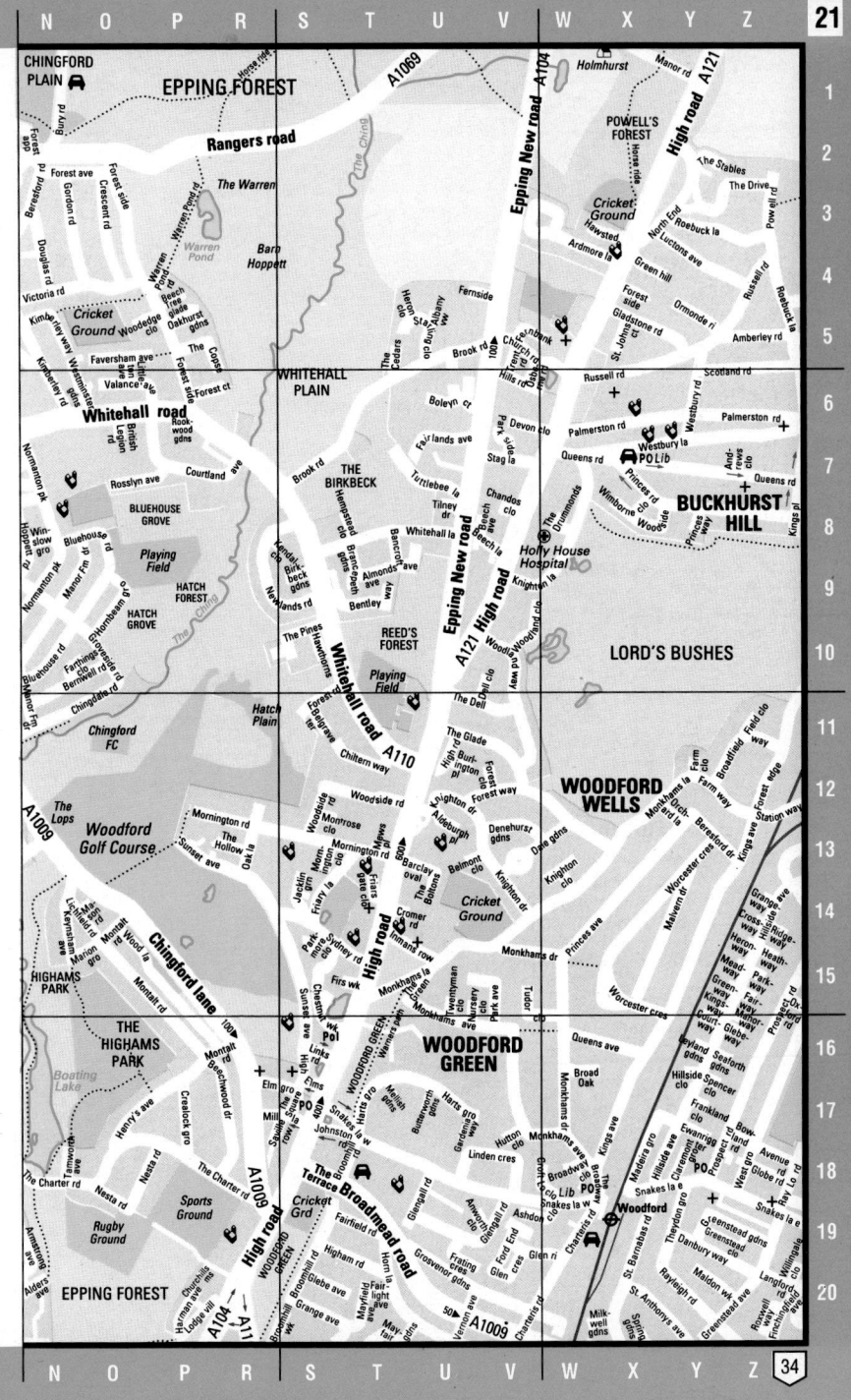

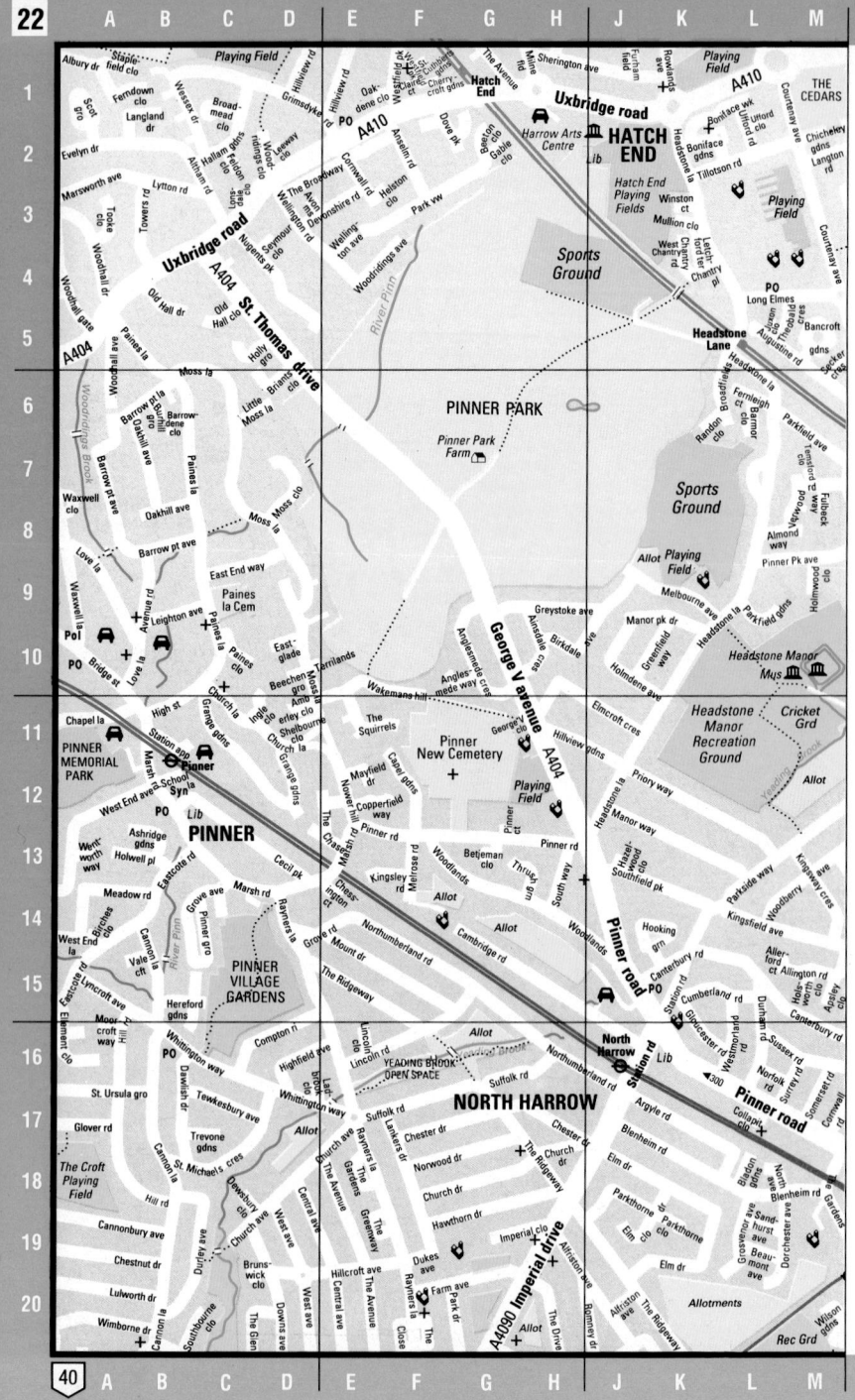

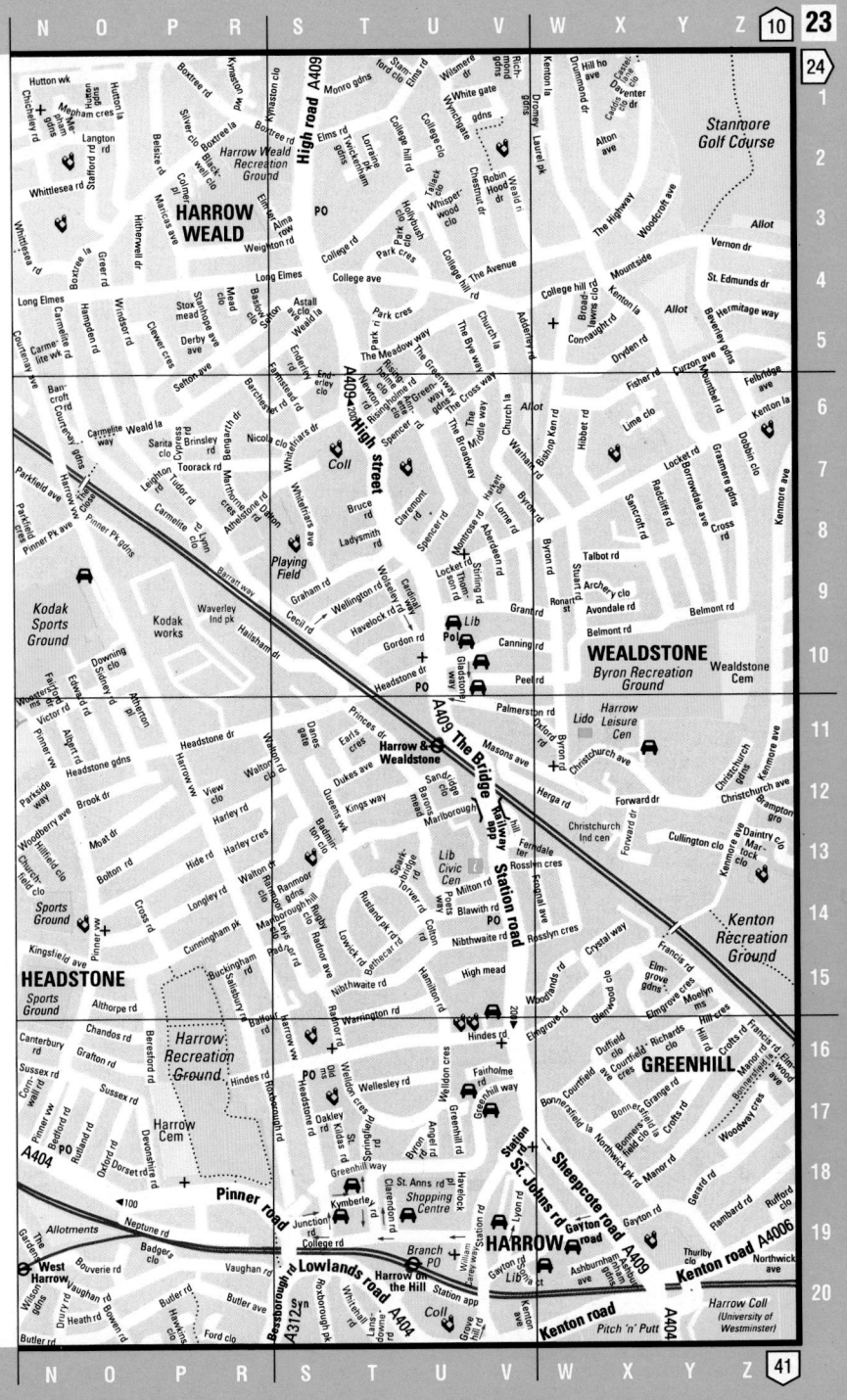

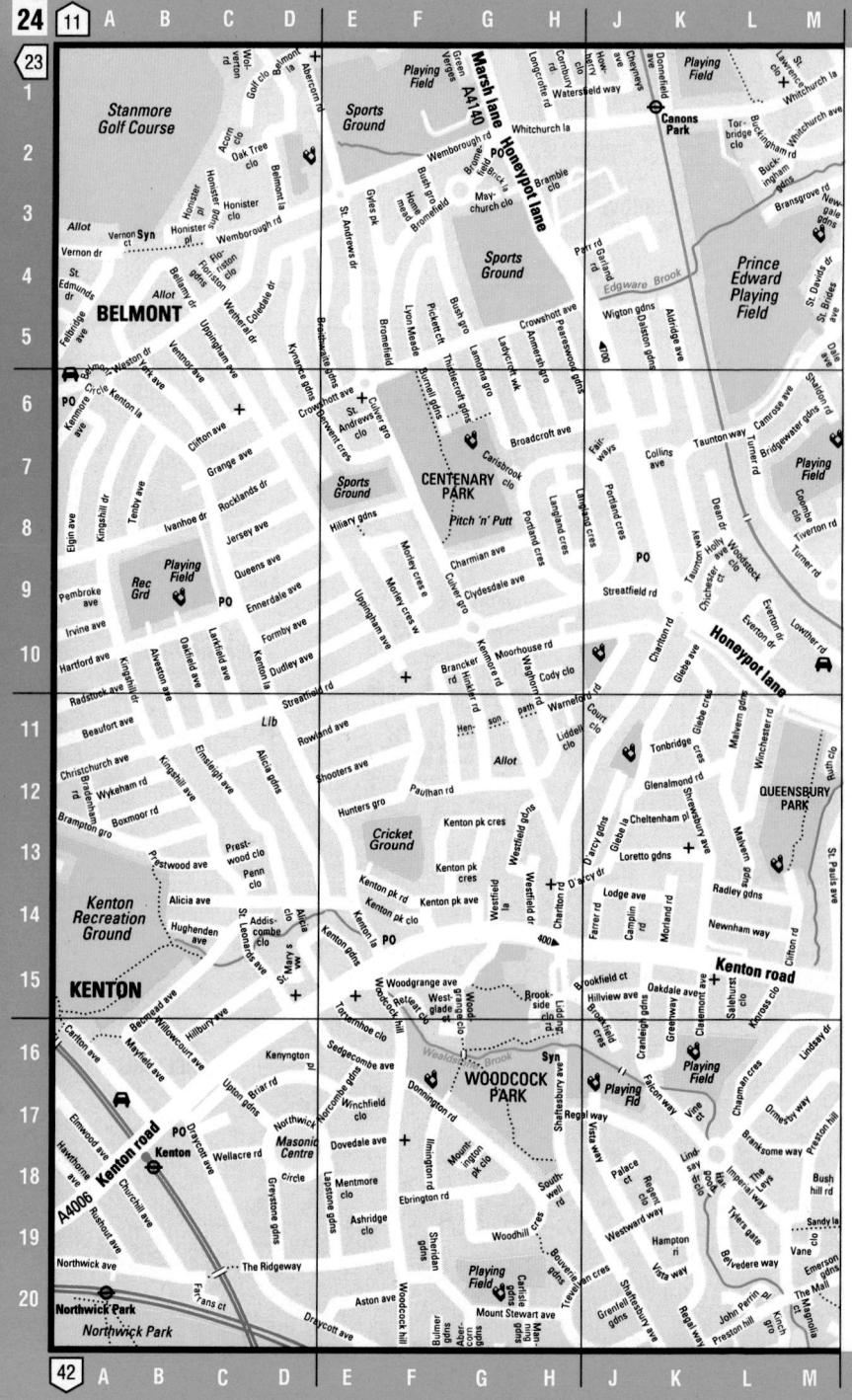

A B C D E F G H J K L M

1
2
3
4
5
6
7
8
9
10
11
12
13
14
15
16
17
18
19
20

Stanmore
Golf Course

Wol-
verton
rd
Golf clo
Belmont ct

Acorn gdns
Oak Tree clo

Honeypot lane
Honister rd
Honister clo
Honister ct
Honister rd
Belmont la

Wemborough rd

Green Verges
Brick la

Marsh lane A410
Whitchurch la
Longcroft rd
Cornbury rd
Watersfield way
Howberry
Chepping
Dennefield
ave

Playing
Field

St.
Lawrence clo
Whitchurch ave
Whitchurch ave

Canons
Park

Tor-
bridge
clo

Buckingham rd
Buck-
ingham gdns

Bransgrove rd
Newgate gdns

Prince
Edward
Playing
Field

St. Davids clo
St. Birdes

Allot
Vernon dr
St. Edmunds dr

Vernon
Syn
ct

Florston ct
Bellamy rd
Uppingham ave

BELMONT

Feltham dr
Weston dr
Vernon ave

Ryefield ave
Coledale dr
Beacondale ave
Kynance gdns

St. Andrews dr

Gyles pk
Playing
Field

Sports
Ground

Sports
Ground

Sports
Ground

Wemborough rd

Hem mead
Bromefield

Bush gro
Maychurch clo

Bramble clo

Lyon Meade
Pickett cft
Bush gro

Perr rd
Garland ave

Edgware Brook

Wigton gdns
Dalston gdns
Aldridge ave

Shelton clo
Dale rd

PO
Circle Kenton la
Kenmore ave

Clifton ave
Grange ave

Rocklands dr

Crowshott ave
Berwen gdns

St.
Andrews
clo
Culver gro

Thedacroft gdns
Burrell gdns

Lamorna gro
Lancraft wk
Ammash rd

Crowshott ave
Pearswood gdns

Carisbrook clo
Broadcroft ave

Fair-
webys
Collins
ave

Taunton way
Turner rd

Camrose gdns
Bridgewater gdns
Playing
Field

Elgin ave
Kingshill dr
Tenby ave

Ivanhoe dr
Jersey ave

Sports
Ground
Hilary gdns

CENTENARY
PARK

Pitch 'n' Putt

Langland cres
Portland cres

Portland cres

Dean dr
Taunton ave
Chichester dr
Holly ave
Woodcock
clo

Everton
clo
Tiverton rd
Turner rd

Pembroke
ave

Rec
Grd
Playing
Field
PO

Queens ave

Ennerdale ave

Charmian ave

Clydesdale ave

Morley cres e
Culver gro
Morley cres w
Uppingham ave

PO
Streatfield rd

Chanton rd
Glebe cres

Honeypot lane

Everton dr
Lowther rd

Irvine ave
Hartford ave

Kingshill dr
Alweston ave
Oakfield rd
Larkfield rd

Formby ave
Kenton la
Dudley rd

Brancker rd
Hinkler rd

Moorhouse rd
Kenmore rd
Wagborth

Cody clo

Radstock ave
Beaufort ave

Streatfield rd
Lib
Rowland ave

Hen-
son
path

Liddell
clo
Warnefod
Court
clo

Glebe gdns
Malvern gdns
Winchester rd

Christchurch
pl
Wykeham ave

Elmsleigh ave
Kingshill ave

Alicia gdns

Shooters gro
Allot

Tonbridge cres

Radley gdns
Streatbury ave
Bush clo
St. Pauls ave

QUEENSBURY
PARK

Brampton gro
Boxmoor rd

Hunters gro
Paulhan rd

Glenalmond rd

Glebe la
Cheltenham pl

Kenton pk cres

Prest-
wood clo
Pestwood ave

Penn
clo

Cricket
Ground

Kenton pk rd
Kenton pk
cres
Kenton pk clo
Kenton pk ave

Westfield gdns

Westfield
la

D'arcy gdns
D'arcy dr

Farrer rd

Loretto gdns

Lodge ave
Camplin rd
Morland rd

Newnham way

Kenton
Recreation
Ground

Alicia ave

Hughenden
ave
Addiscombe
clo
St. Leonards ave

Alicia
clo
Allan
St. Mary's
ave

Kenton gdns

Charlton rd
Westfield rd

Clifton rd

KENTON

Bacmead ave
Kenton
gdns
PO

Woodgrange ave
Woodcote ave
Retreat clo
Woodgrange
hill

Kenton road

Kenton road

West-
glade
Brook-
side clo

Brookfield ct
Hillview ave
Oakdale ave

Greenway
Claremont
cres

Salehurst rd
Kinross clo

Carlton ave
Mayfield ave
Killowcourt ave
Hillbury ave

Kenyngton pl

Sedgecombe ave

Tollerton clo

Weedacre Brook

Lipton
Syn
Playing
Fld

Cranleigh gdns
Falcon way

Playing
Field

Chapman cres

Lindsay dr

A4006
Kenton road

Elmwood ave
Hawthorne ave
Mayfield ave

Upton gdns
Briar rd

Northwick
Masonic
Centre
circle

Winchfield clo
Donnington rd
Shaftesbury ave

WOODCOCK
PARK

Regal way
Regal vista way

Vine
ct

Brantsome way

Ormesby way

Preston rd
Bush
hill rd

PO
Kenton
Wellacre rd
Draycott rd
Greystone gdns

Dovedale ave
Lapstone gdns

Ilmington rd
Mount
Ington
clo

South-
well rd

Palace
ct
Regent
clo
Lindsay
The Leys

Tyler's gate

Sandy la

Churchill rd
The Ridgeway

Mentmore
clo
Ashridge clo

Ebrington rd

Woodhill cres

Westward way

Hampton
ri
Vista way

Vane
clo
Belvedere way
Emerson rd
The Mall
Magnolia

Northwick ave
Frans ct

Sheridan gdns

Playing
Field

Carlisle gdns
Manning gdns

Bowens
way
Trevellan cres

Shaftesbury cres
John Perrin pl

Regal way
Grenfell gdns

Preston hill
Kinch
gro

Northwick Park
Northwick Park

Aston ave
Draycott ave

Woodcock hill

Mount Stewart ave
Aber-
ford gdns
Bulmer gdns

A B C D E F G H J K L M

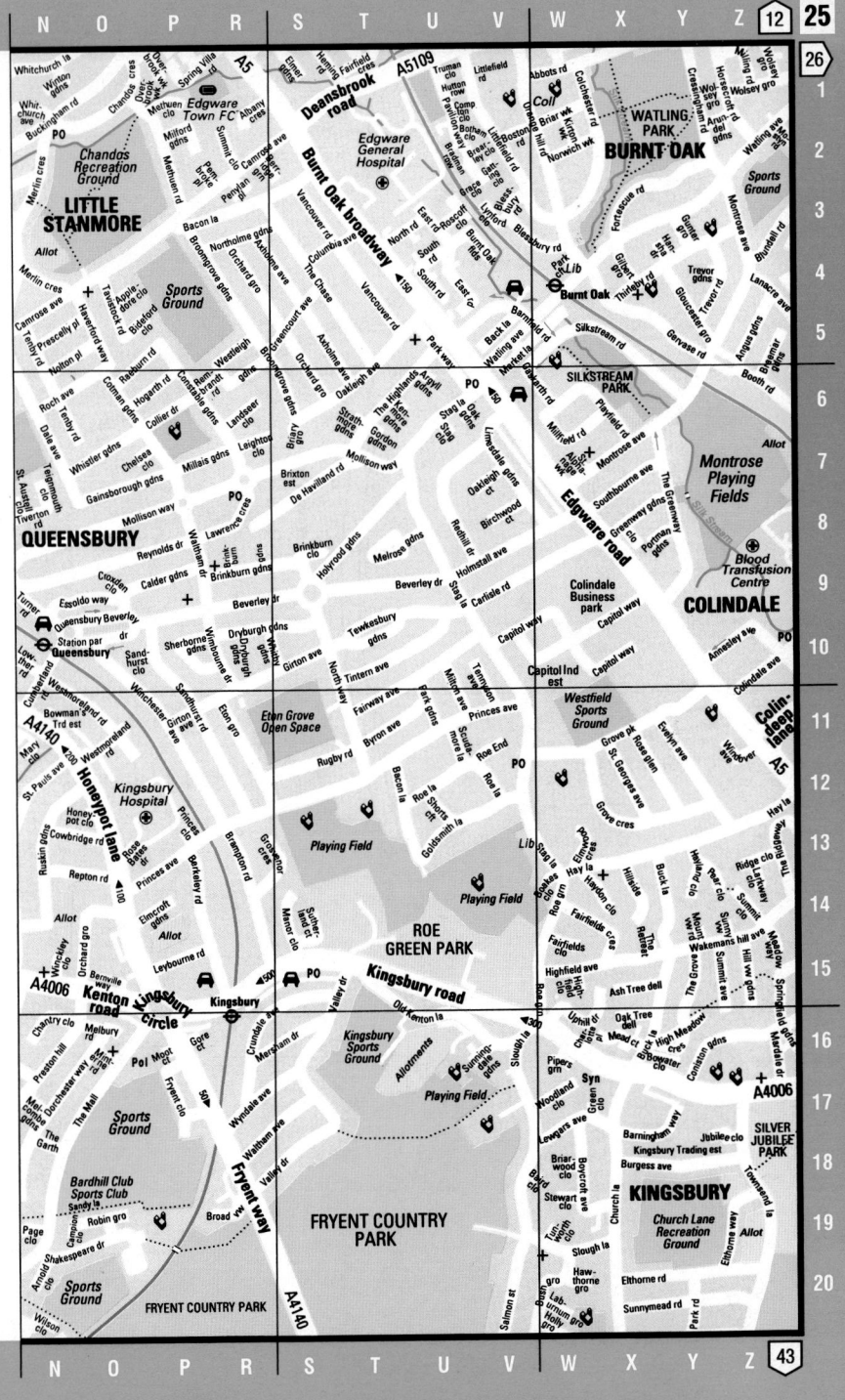

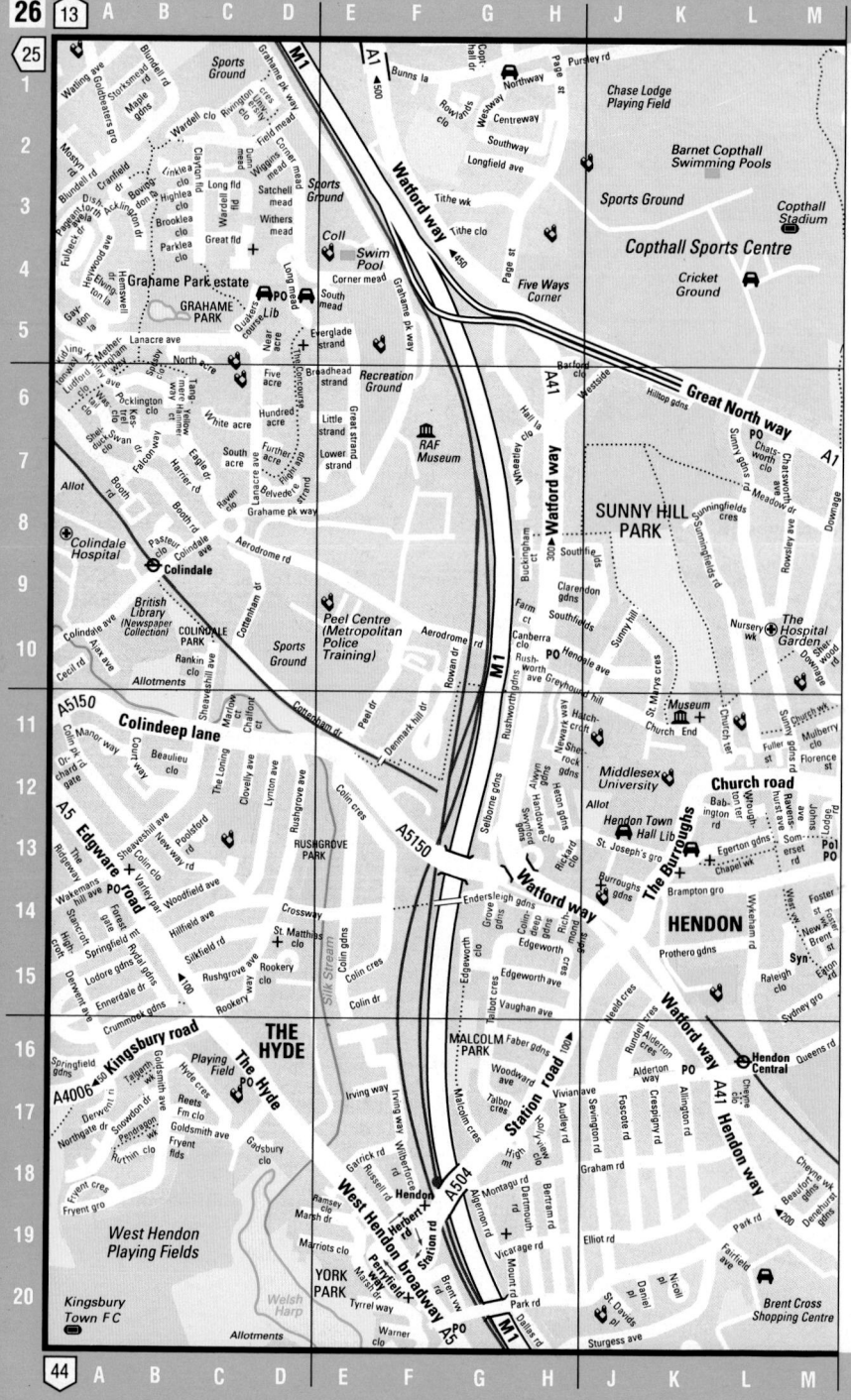

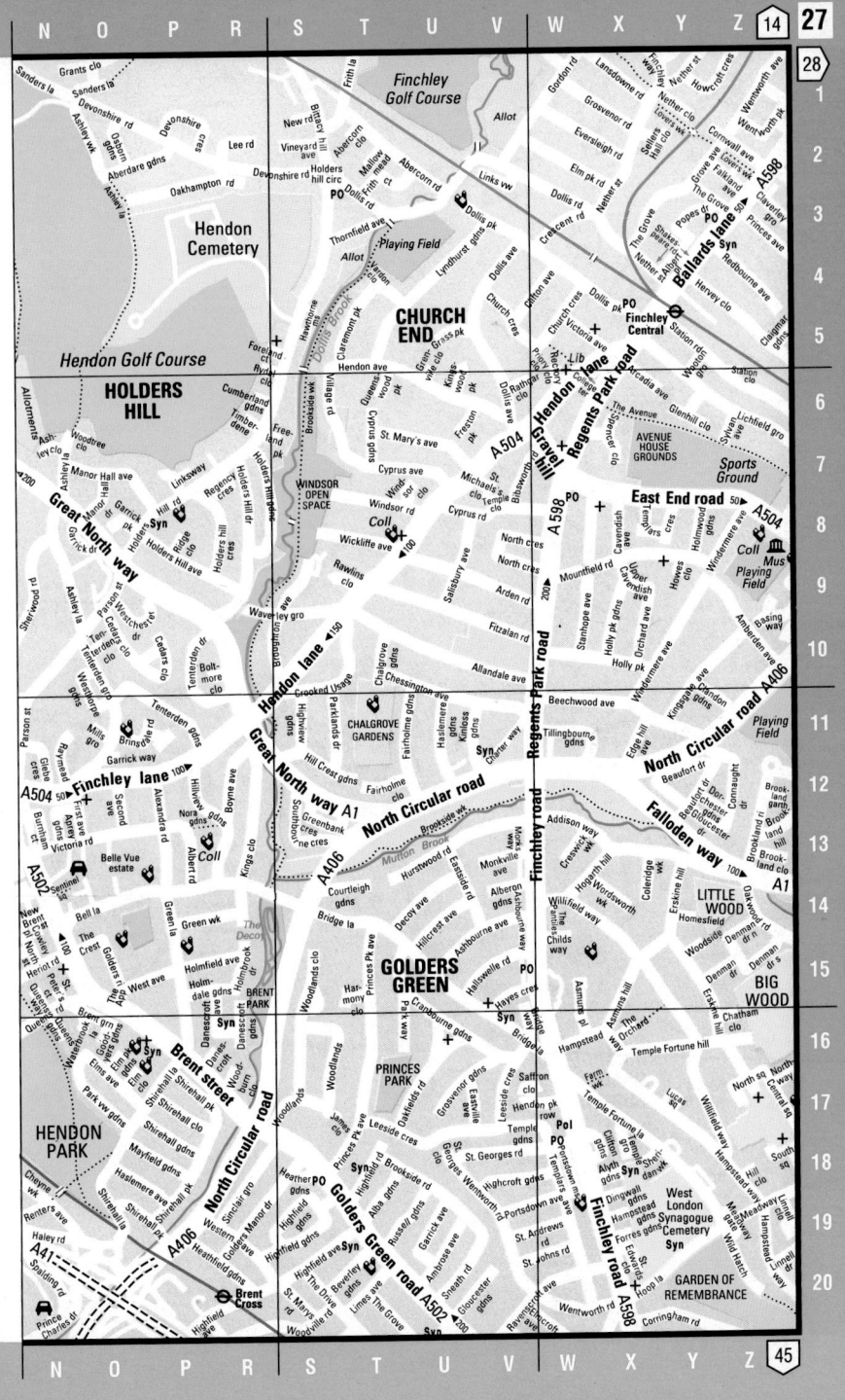

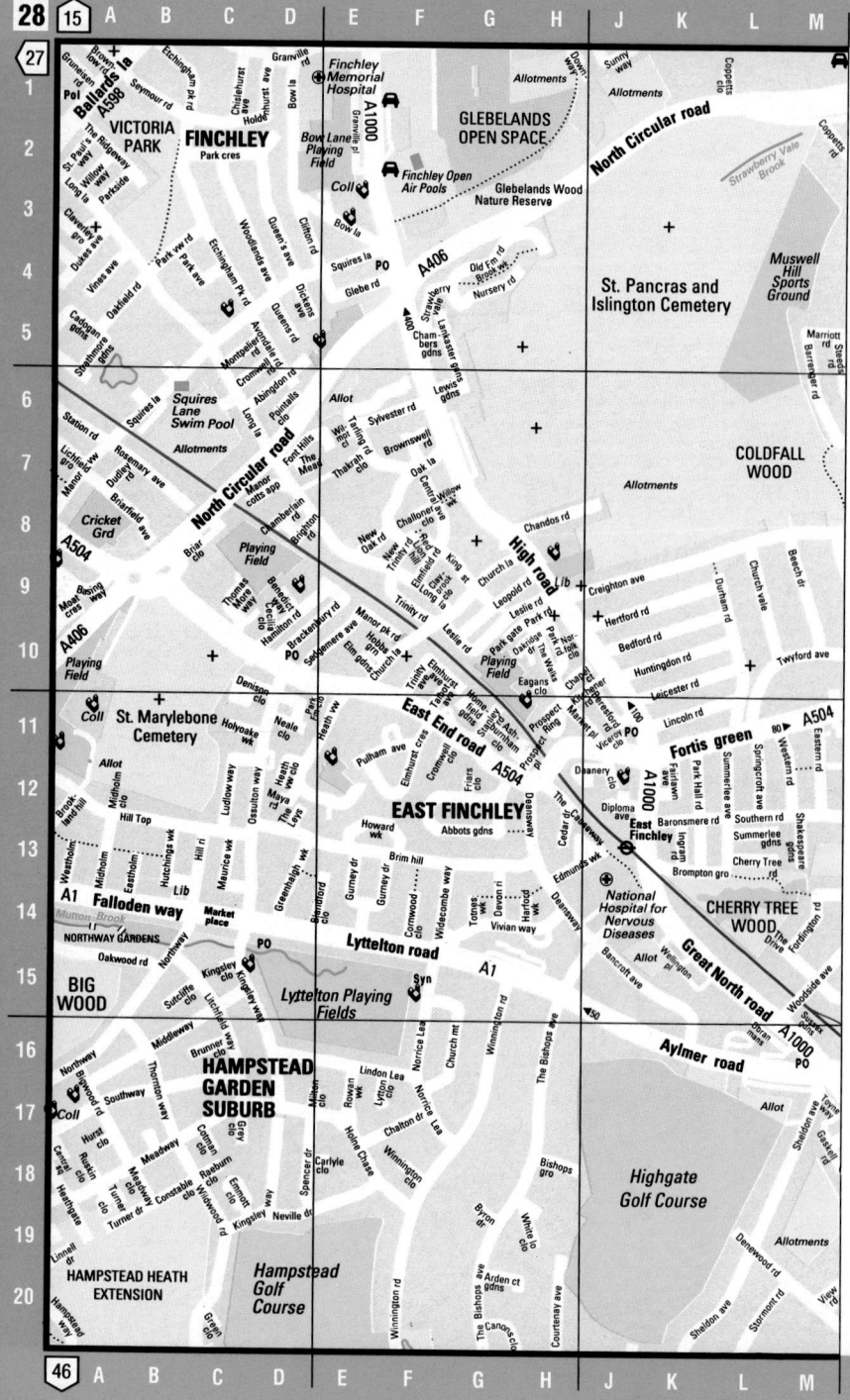

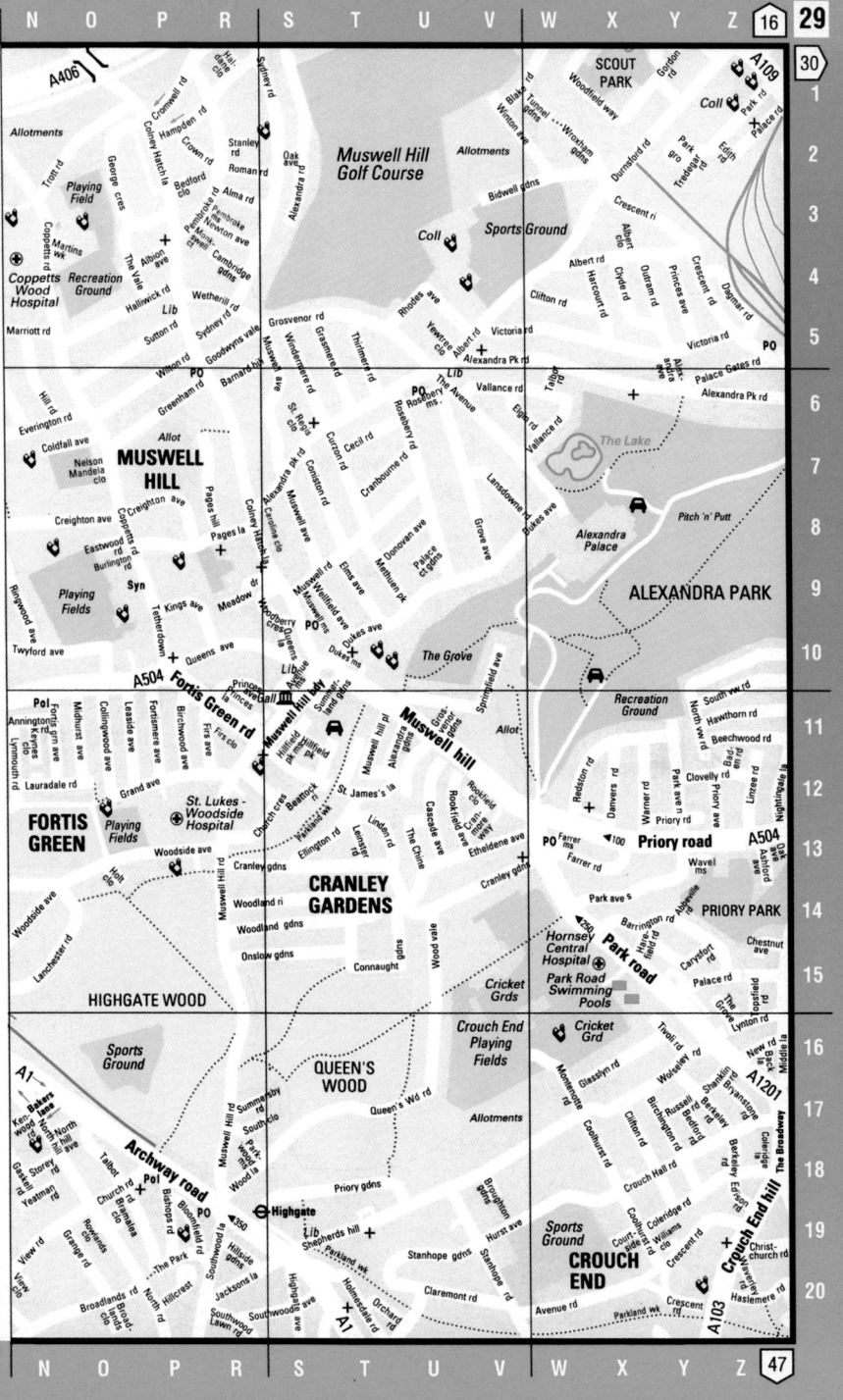

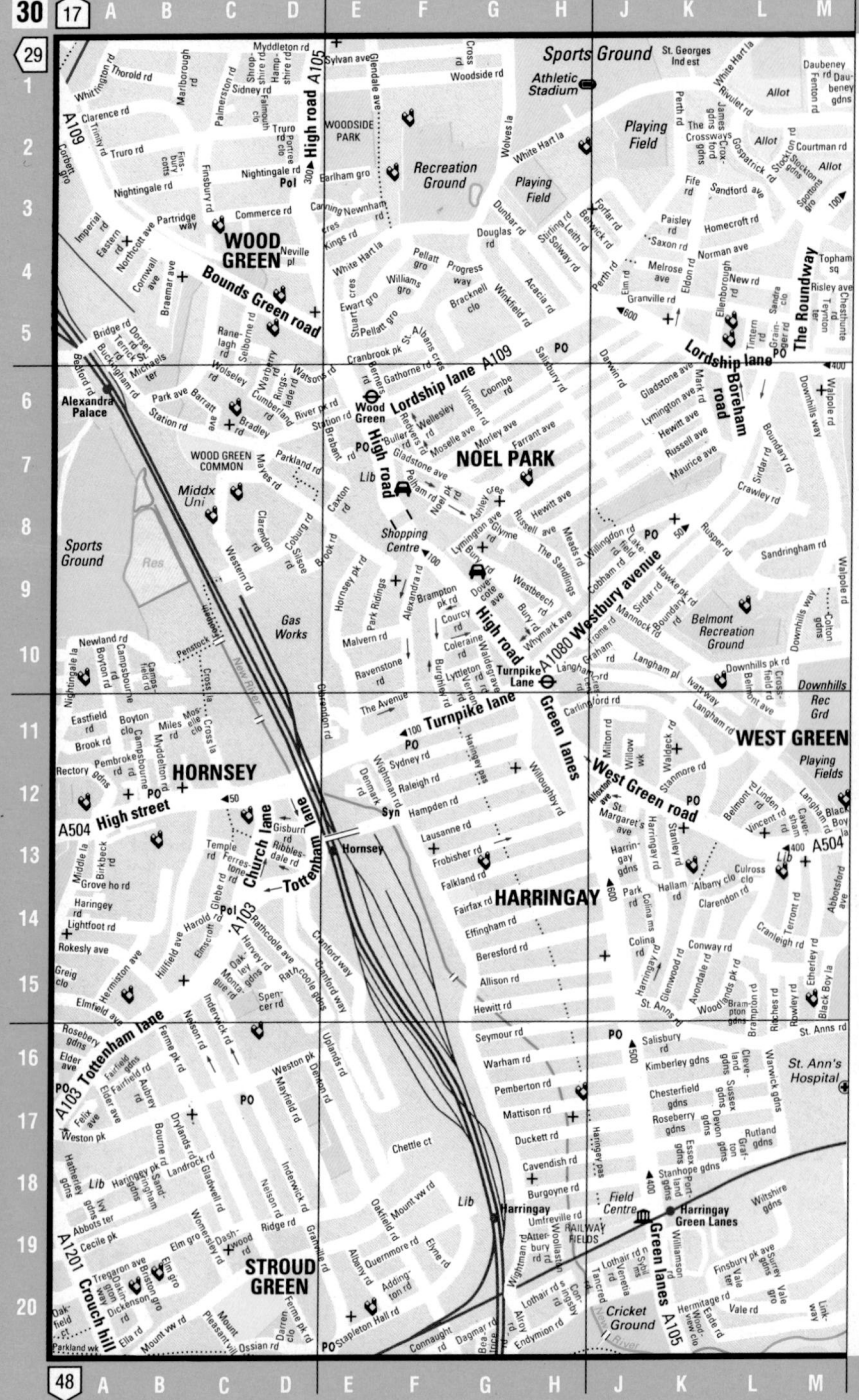

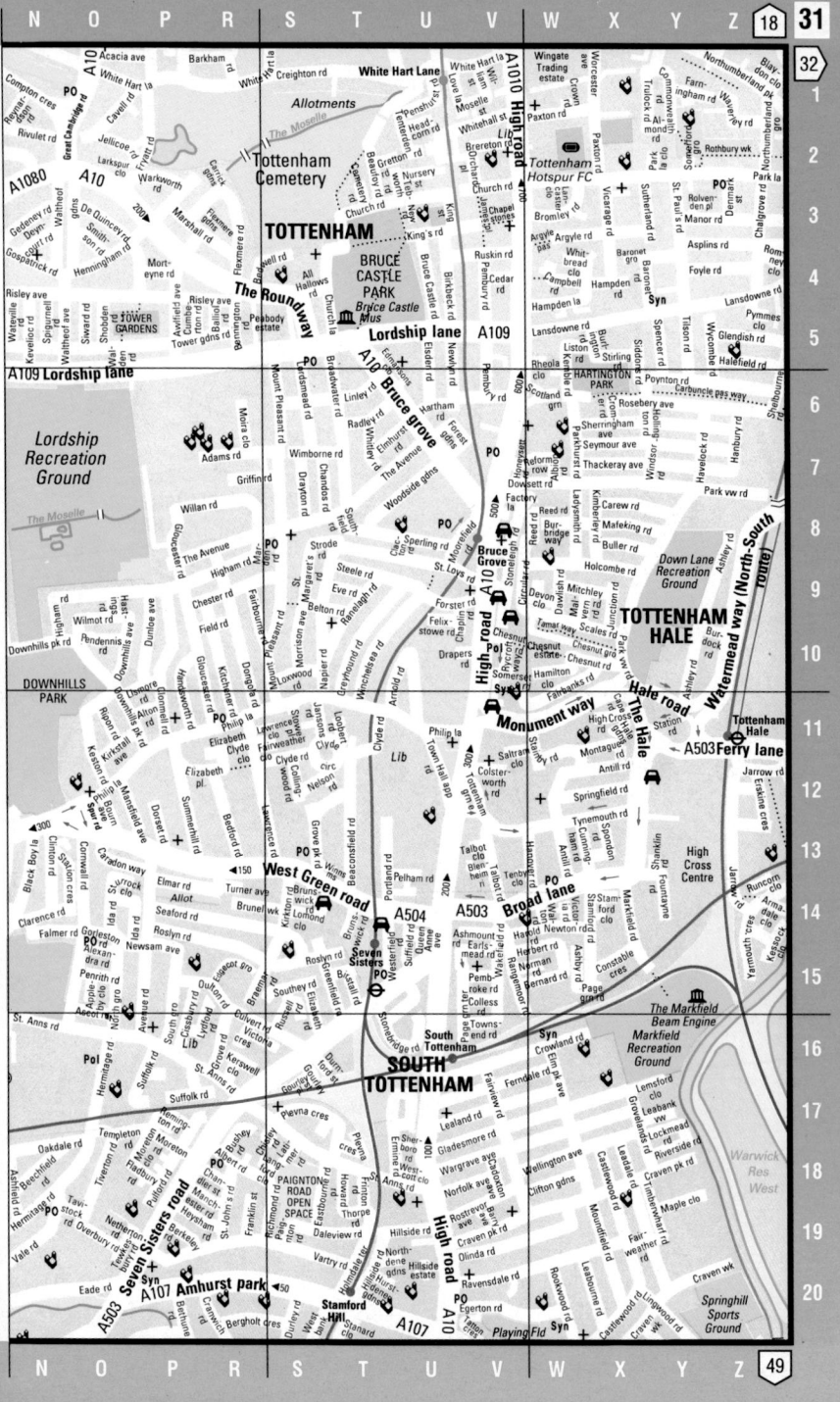

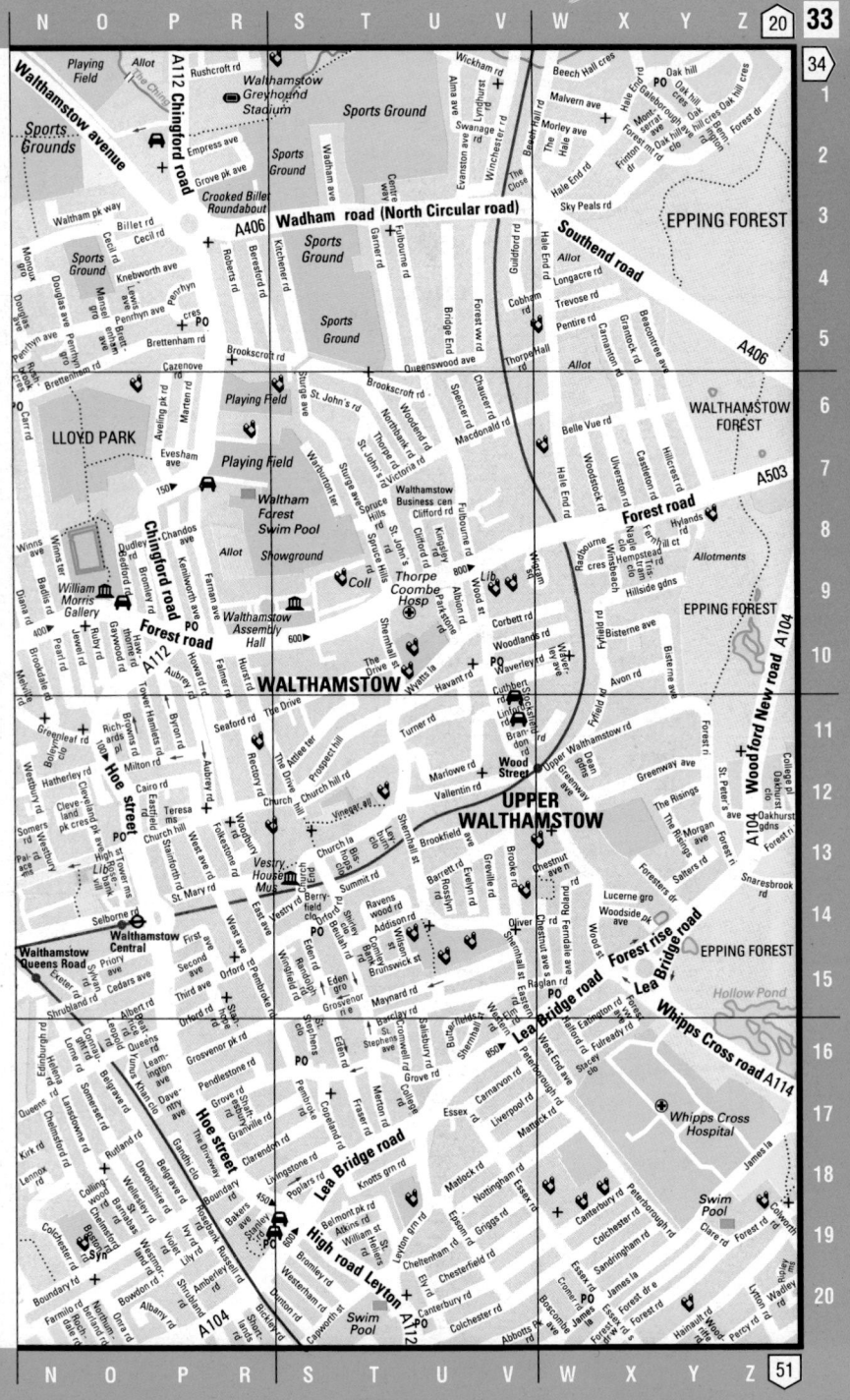

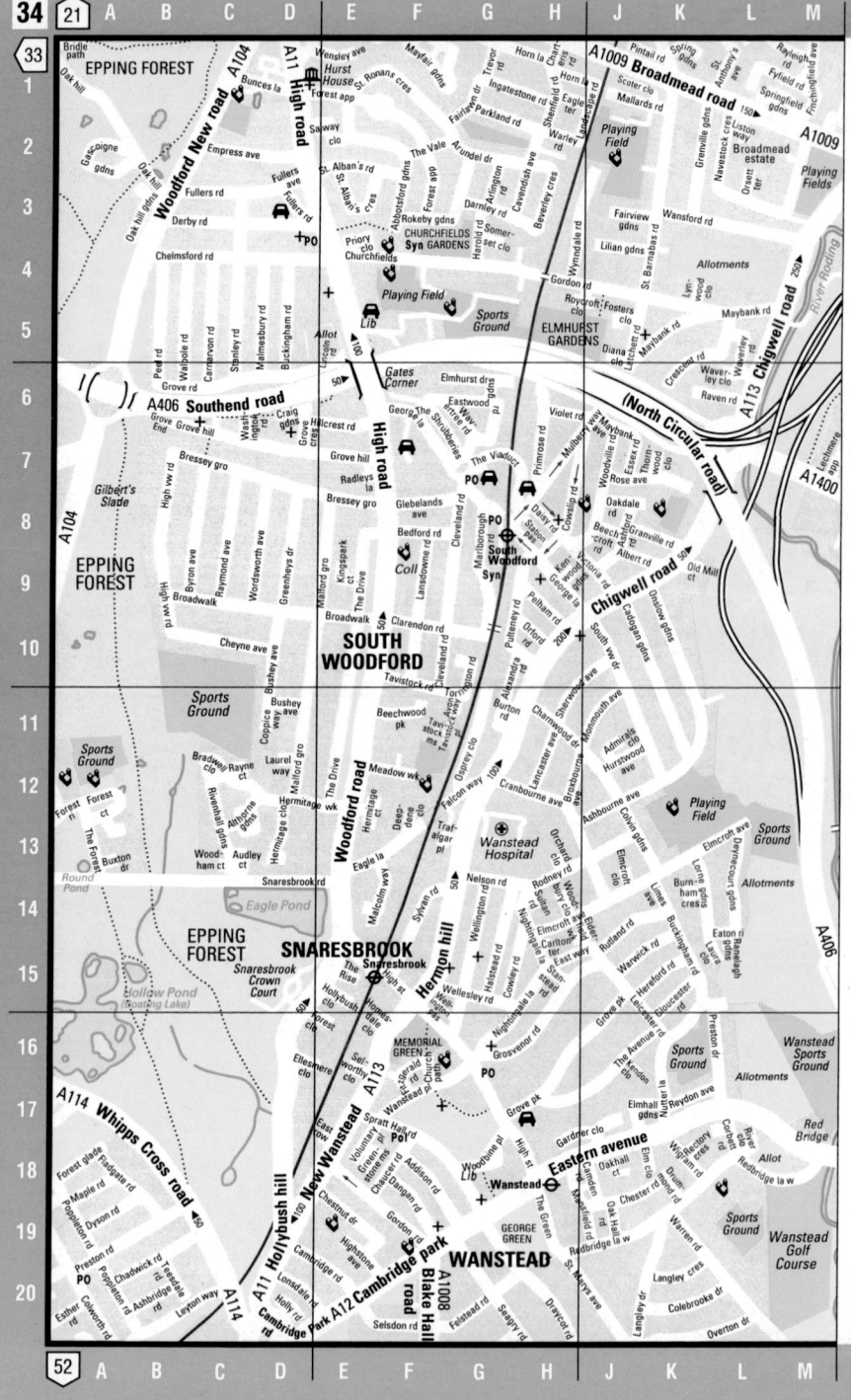

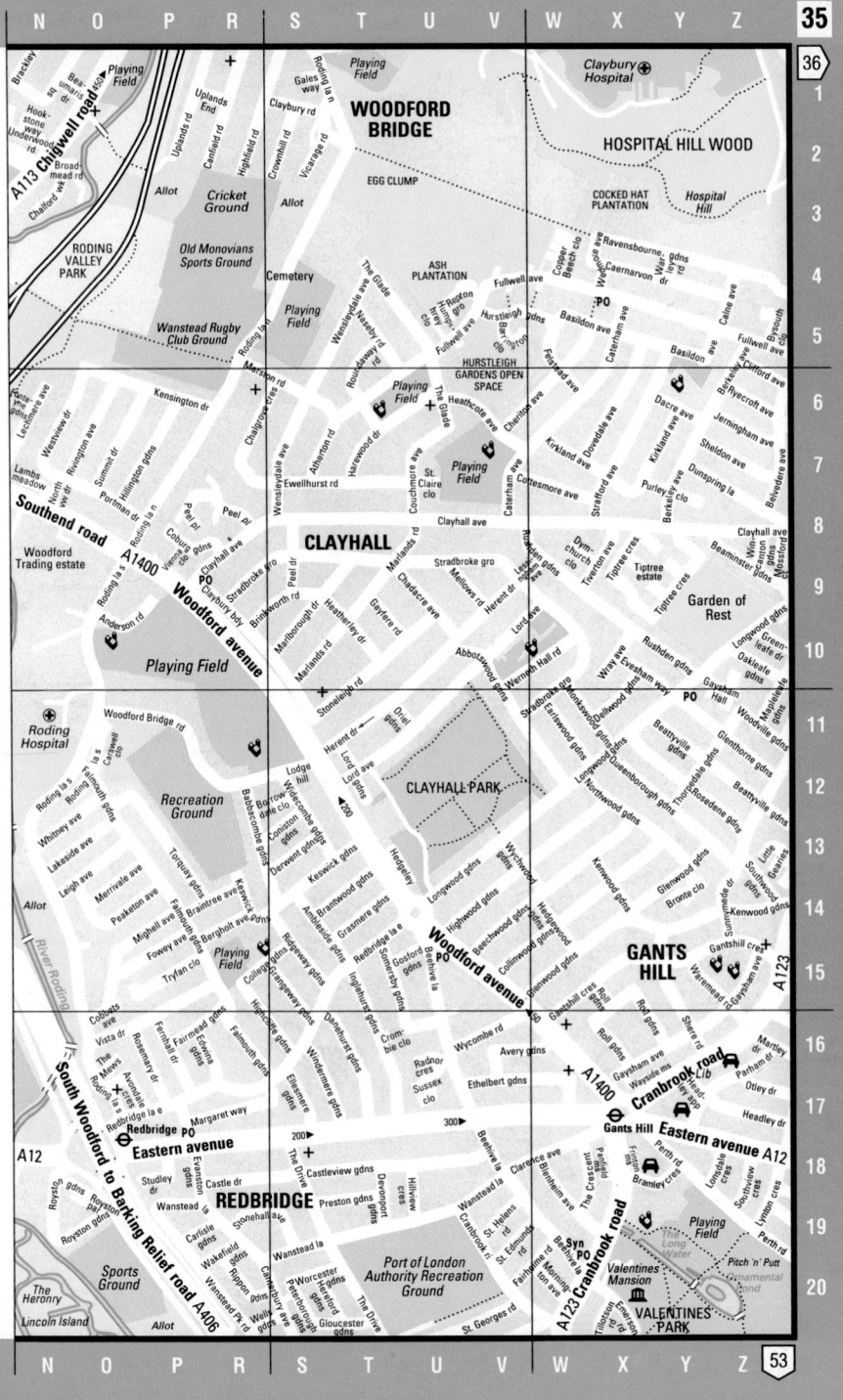

Brackley st
Bess
umarsh dr
Hook-
stone
way
Underwood
rd
A113 Chigwell road
Chalford way
Broad-
mead rd

Playing
Field

Uplands End
Claybury rd
Uplands rd
Canfield rd
Highfield rd
Crownhill rd
Vicarage rd

Gales way
Roding la

Playing
Field

**WOODFORD
BRIDGE**

Claybury
Hospital

HOSPITAL HILL WOOD

EGG CLUMP

RODING
VALLEY
PARK

Cricket
Ground

Allot

Allot

ASH
PLANTATION

COCKED HAT
PLANTATION

Hospital
Hill

Ravensbourne, gdns
Copper
Beech clo
Caernarvon dr

Cerne ave

Old Monovians
Sports Ground

Cemetery

Playing
Field

The Glade

Wheatlands ave
Naseby rd

Fullwell ave

PO

Hurstleigh gdns
Barrington
Fullwell ave

Fensted ave

Basildon ave

Catenham ave

Fullwell
ave

Basildon
ave

Wanstead Rugby
Club Ground

Merston rd

Roding la n

HURSTLEIGH
GARDENS OPEN
SPACE

Kensington dr

Chalgrove cres

Playing
Field

The Glade

Heathcote ave

Cheriton rd

Clifford ave
Ryecroft ave
Dacre ave
Berkeley ave
Jerningham ave

Lambs
meadow

Rangoon
gdns ave
Lanrhmore ave
Westview dr
Rowington dr
Summit dr
Hillington gdns
Portman la n
Roding la n

Peel pl
Coburg gdns
Venetia gdns
Peel pl
Peel pl

Atherton rd
Ewellhurst rd
Harwood dr

St.
Claire
clo
Couchmore ave
Caterham ave
Cottesmore ave

Wensleydale ave

Strafford ave
Doverdale ave
Kirkland ave
Sheldon ave
Purley gro
Berkeley clo
Dunspring la
Belvedere ave

Southend road

A1400

Woodford
Trading estate

CLAYHALL

Clayhall ave

Clayhall ave
Beaminster gdns
Winchester gdns
Mossford
la

PO
Claybury bdy
Stradbrokes gdns
Peel clo

Marlands rd

Stradbroke gro

Dym-
church
clo
Tiverton ave
Tiptree cres
Tiptree
estate

Anderson rd

Woodford avenue

Brinkworth rd
Marlborough rd
Heatherley dr
Gayfere rd

Mellows rd
Herent dr

Lord ave

Chadacre ave

Garden of
Rest

Rushden gdns

Playing Field

Marlands rd
Stoneleigh rd

Abbotswood gdns
Werneth Hall rd

Wray ave
Evesham way

Longwood gdns
Greenleafe dr
Oakleafe
gdns

**Roding
Hospital**

Woodford Bridge rd

Recreation
Ground

Lodge
Hill

Borrowdale
dale clo
Coniston gdns
Derwent gdns

Oriel
gdns

Herent dr
Lord ave
Lord ave

Stradbroke gro
Dellwood gdns
Meadway
Eastwood gdns

Longwood gdns
Northwood gdns
Queenborough gdns
Thorndale gdns
Rosedene gdns

PO

Gaysham
Hall
Woodville gdns
Maplestead gdns
Beattyville gdns
Glenthorne gdns
Beattyville
gdns

Roding la s
Falmouth gdns
Roding la s
Whitney ave
Lakeside ave
Leigh ave

Merrivale ave
Peaketon ave
Mighell ave
Fowey ave
Bergholt ave
Tryfan clo

Torquay gdns
Keswick gdns

Babbacombe gdns

Keswick gdns
Brantwood gdns
Grasmere gdns
Ambleside gdns
Redbridge la e

Hedgley

Longwood gdns
Highwood gdns
Hedgemoor
Beechwood gdns
Collingwood gdns
Glenwood gdns
Bronte clo
Summerdale dr
Kenwood gdns

Little
gdns
Southwood
clo

Playing
Field

Ridgeway gdns
Collingtree gdns
Grangeway gdns
Inglehurst gdns
Redbridge la e
Somersby gdns
Beehive la

Gosford gdns

Woodford avenue

Blenwood gdns
Gantshill cres
Gantshill cres

Gantshill cres

**GANTS
HILL**

Gaysham ave

A123

Colbets
ave
Vista dr
The
Mews
Rosemary dr
Fernhall dr
Fairmead gdns
Edina
gdns
Falmouth gdns

Wycombe rd
Avery gdns

Radnor
cres
Sussex
gdns

Crom-
bie clo

Ethelbert gdns

A1400
Gaysham ave
Warside ave
Meads la
Perth rd

Martley
dr
Parham st
Otley dr

Headley dr

South Woodford to Barking Relief road A406

Redbridge PO
Roding la s
Redbridge la e
Margaret way

Royston
gdns
Royston gdns
Royston gdns

Studley dr
Evanston gdns
Wanstead
Carlisle
gdns
Wakefield
gdns
Pappon
rd
Wanstead Pk

Castle dr
Preston gdns
Stonehall ave
Wanstead la

Worcester
Hereford
gdns
Peterborough rd
Churchdown
Welby
gdns
Gloucester
gdns

A12

Eastern avenue

Hillcrest
dr
Castleview gdns

Devonport
gdns

The Drive

The Drive

REDBRIDGE

Cranbrook road

Gants Hill

Lib

Eastern avenue A12

Lonsdale
cres
Southview
cres
Lyttan rd

Playfield ave
Frinton gdns
Clarence ave
Bramley cres
Beehive la
Wanstead la
St. Helens
Cranbrook la
St. Edmunds

The Crescent
Clarence ave
Blenheim ave
Perth rd

A123 Cranbrook road

Playing
Field

Perth rd

Sports
Ground

The Heronry

Lincoln Island

Allot

Carlisle
gdns

Castleton

Worcester
Hereford
gdns

**Port of London
Authority Recreation
Ground**

Gloucester
gdns

St. Georges
rd

Syn
PO

Fairholme av
Morning-
ton ave

Valentines
Mansion

**VALENTINES
PARK**

Tillotson gdns

Long
Water

Ornamental
Pond

Pitch 'n' Putt

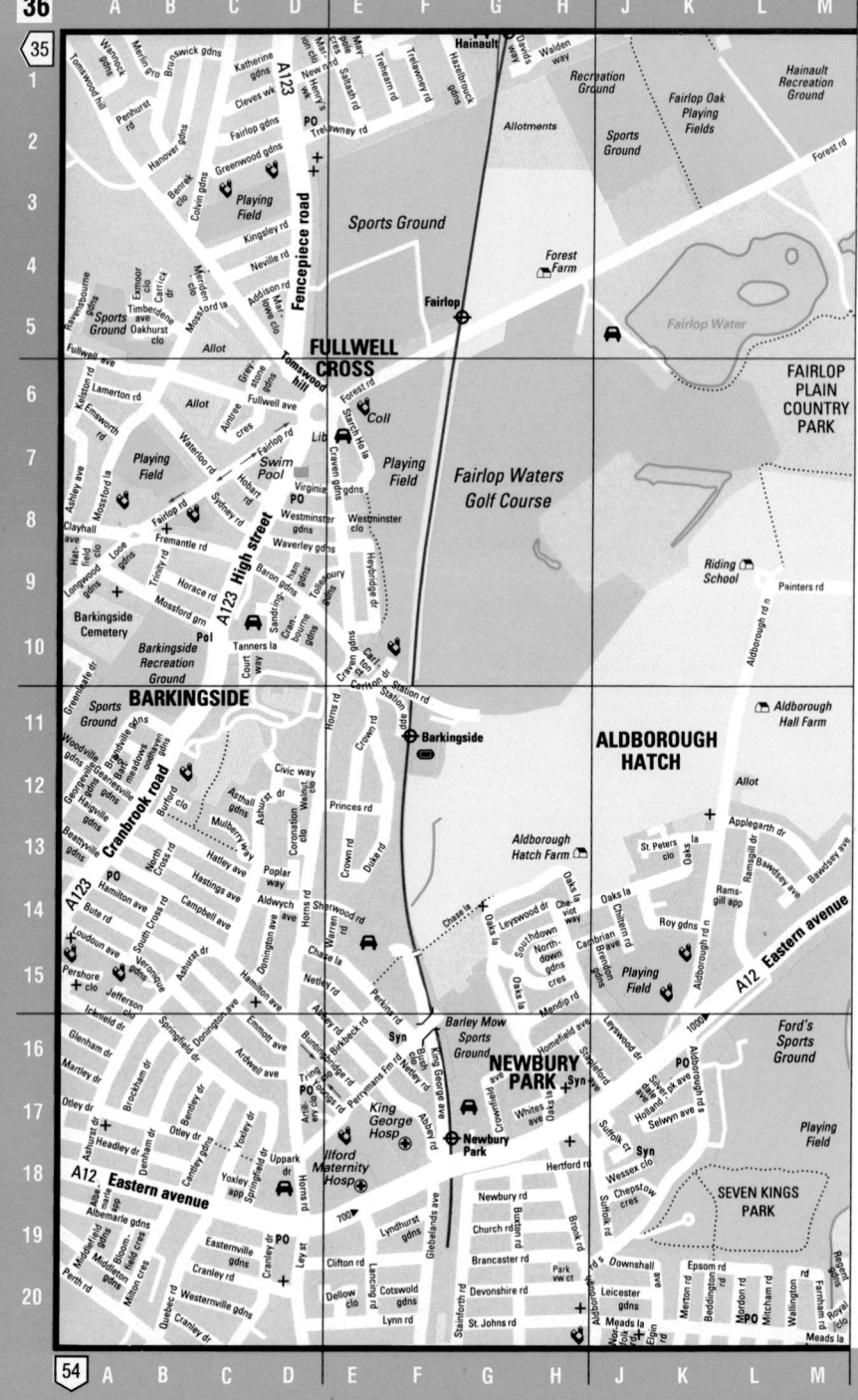

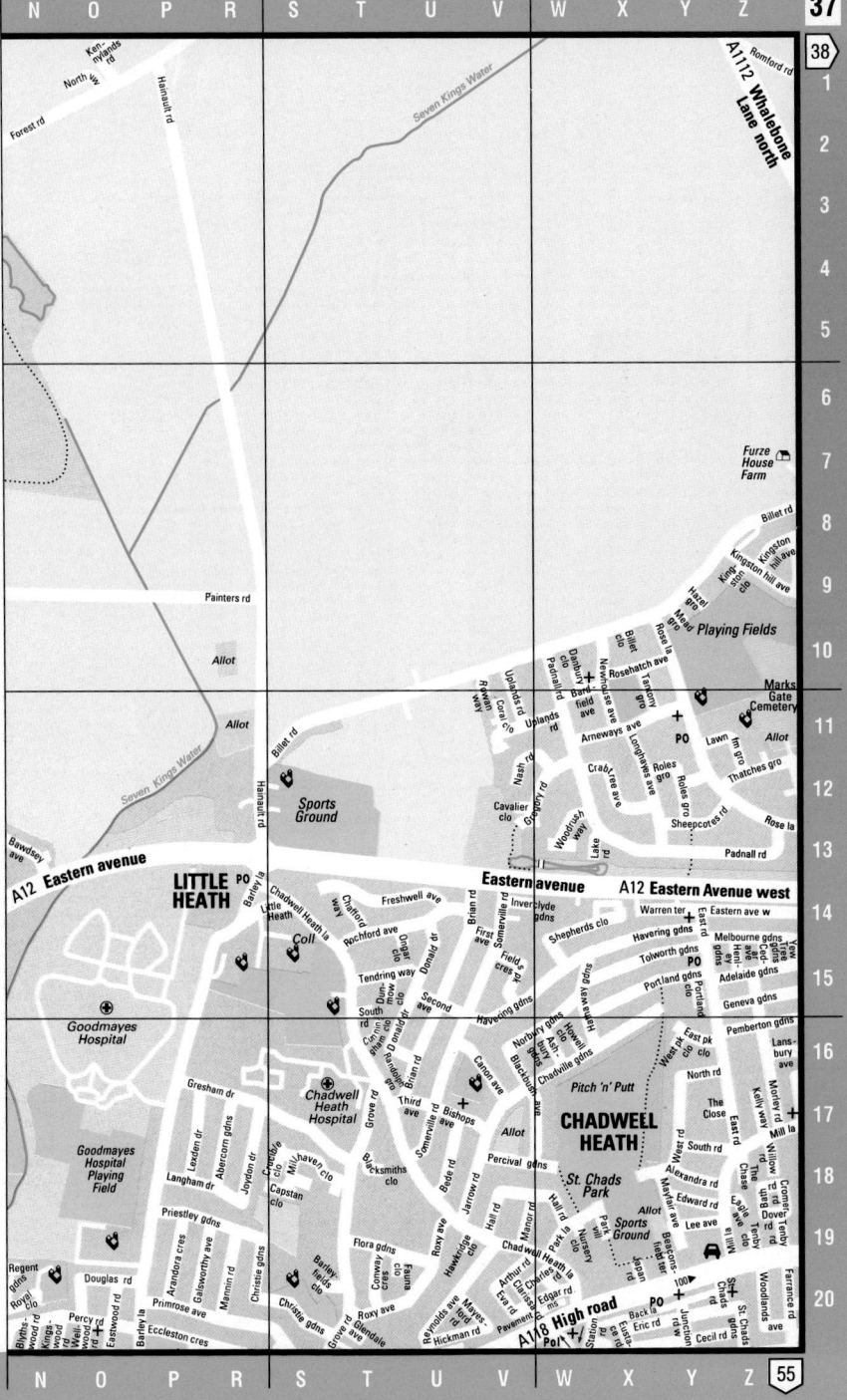

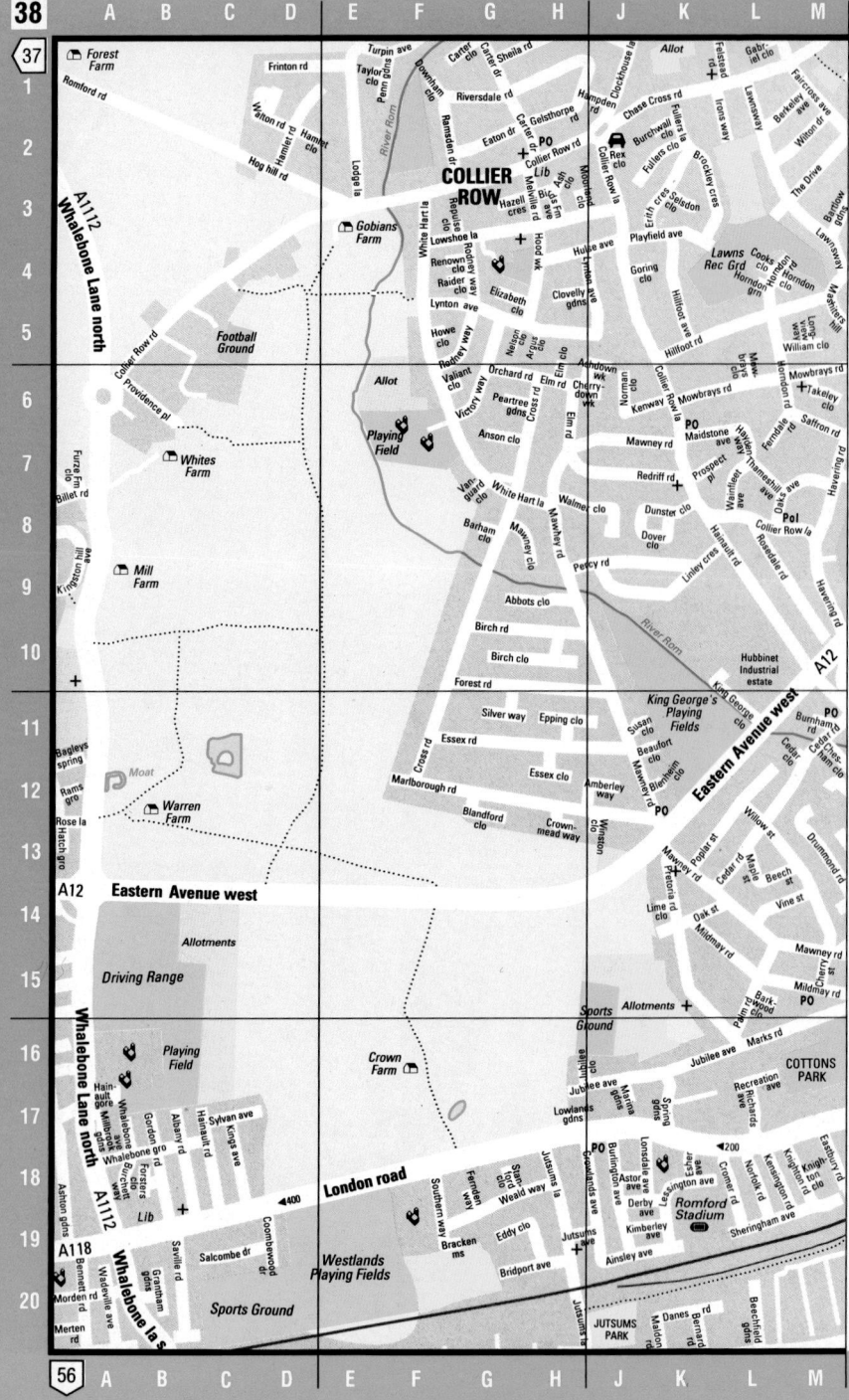

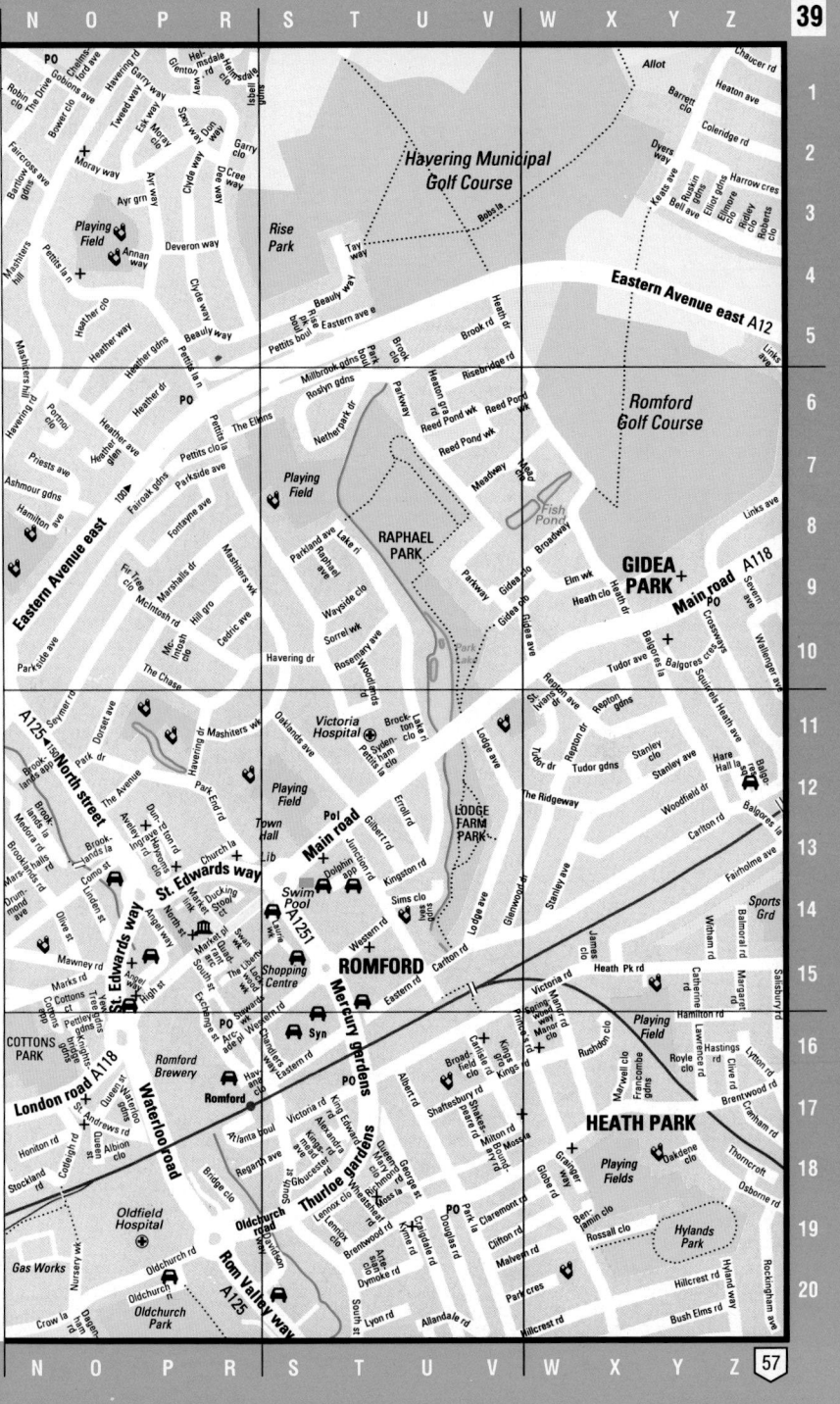

1
2
3
4
5
6
7
8
9
10
11
12
13
14
15
16
17
18
19
20

PO
Chainsw
ford ave
Gobions ave
Havering
Tweed way
Glenton
rd
Helmsdale
rd
Hemsdale
rd

Robin
clo
The Drive
Bower clo
Esk way
Moray
clo
Spey way
Garry way
Don way

Garry clo
Cree way
Dee way

Barrow
ave gdns
Faircross ave

Moray way
Ayr grn
Clyde way
Ayr way

Playing
Field
Annan
way
Deveron way
Clyde way

Mashiters
hill
Pettits la n

Rise
Park
Tay
way
Beauly wy

Havering Municipal
Golf Course

Allot
Heaton ave
Barrett
clo
Coleridge rd

Dyers
way
Ruskin
gdns
Harrow cres

Keats ave
Bell ave
Elliot gdns
Elphine
clo
Ridley
clo
Roberts
clo

Eastern Avenue east A12

Heather clo
Heather way

Heather gdns

Beauly way
Rise
la n
Eastern ave e
Pettits boul

Millbrook gdns
Roslyn gdns
Netherpark dr
Parkway

Brook rd
Heath clo
Brook dr
Risebridge rd

Reed Pond wk
Reed Pond wk

Links ave

PO
Heather dr
Pettits

The Elms
Pettits clo
Parkside ave

Romford
Golf Course

Priests ave
Heather
glen
Fairoak gdns

Fontayne ave

Playing
Field

Heaton way
Meadway

Broadway
Fish
Pond

GIDEA
PARK
Main road A118

Ashmour gdns
Hamilton ave

Eastern Avenue east

Fir Tree
clo
McIntosh rd
Mashiters dr

Mashiters wk

Parkland ave
Lake ri
Raphael
ave

RAPHAEL
PARK

Gidea clo
Elm wk
Heath clo

Severn
ave
PO

Marshalls dr
Hill gro
Cedric ave

Wayside clo
Sorrel wk

Parkway
Gidea clo
Gidea ave

Tudor ave
Balgores
la
Crossways
Squirrels Heath ave
Wallenger ave

Mc
Intosh
clo
The Chase

Havering dr
Rosemary wk
Woodlands

Park
la

St Ivans dr
Repton ave
Repton gdns

Parkside ave

A1251
Seymer rd
Havering dr
Mashiters wk

Oaklands ave

Victoria
Hospital
Brockton la
Syden-
ham ri
Lodge ave

Tudor dr
Tudor gdns

Stanley
ave
Hare
Hall la
Balgores
la

North street
Park-
lands av
Park dr
Dorset av
The Avenue
Park End rd

Playing
Field

Pettits la s

Errol rd

The Ridgeway

Glenwood av
Woodfield dr
Balgores
la

Brook
la
Medora
rd
Brook-
lands la
Dun-
croft
Ingrid rd

Town
Hall
Main road
Gilbert rd
Junction rd
Kingston rd

LODGE
FARM
PARK

Carlton rd
Fairholme ave

Aveley
rd

Brook-
lands la
Como rd

St. Edwards way
Church
la

Lib
Dolphin
app
Sims clo

Stanley ave
James
la

Sports
Grd
Balmoral rd

Drum-
mond
ave
Linden st
Olive st

Angel way
Ducking
Stool
Church st

Swim
Pool

Western rd

Ives
clo
Lodge ave

Carlton rd

Victoria rd
Heath Pk rd

Withom rd
Margaret rd
Salisbury rd

Mawney rd
Marks rd
Cottons
ct
Pettley
South st
Mkts pl
The Liberty
Market pl

ROMFORD
Mercury gardens

Eastern rd

Heath clo
Catherine rd

Lawrence rd
Hastings rd
Clive rd
Lyon rd

COTTONS
PARK
Marks
rd
High st
Exchange st

Shopping
Centre
PO
Syn
Broad-
field rd
Crisbet rd
Kings rd

Royle rd
Brentwood rd

London road A118
Honiton rd
Romford
Brewery
Hav-
Eastern rd

Albert rd
Shaftesbury rd
Shaftes-
peare rd

Victoria rd
Manor
way
Manor
clo

Rushden clo

Marvell clo
Frencombe gdns
Hamilton rd

Playing
Field

HEATH PARK
Oakdele clo

Thorncroft
Cornham rd

Waterloo road
Romford
Andrews rd
Queen st
Albion st

Regarth ave
Bridge clo
Victoria rd
King Edwards rd
Alexandra rd
Gloucester av

King George av
Richmond rd
Mawney rd

Milton rd
Bryant
Mossford
way

Grainger way
Benjamin clo
Rossall clo

Hillcrest rd
Hyland way

Osborne rd

Stockland
rd
Codeogh rd
Queen

Oldfield
Hospital
Bridge clo

Oldchurch
road

South st
Lennox clo
Lennox
Brentwood rd

George st
Rose gdns
Angel clo
Dymoke rd

Crigdale rd
PO
Park la
Claremont rd
Clifton rd
Malvern rd

Park cres

Hylands
Park

Hyland rd
Bush Elms rd
Rockingham ave

Gas Works

Oldfield
Hospital

Oldchurch
Park

Oldchurch
rd
A125
Rom Valley way

Crow la
Lyon rd
Allandale rd

Hillcrest rd

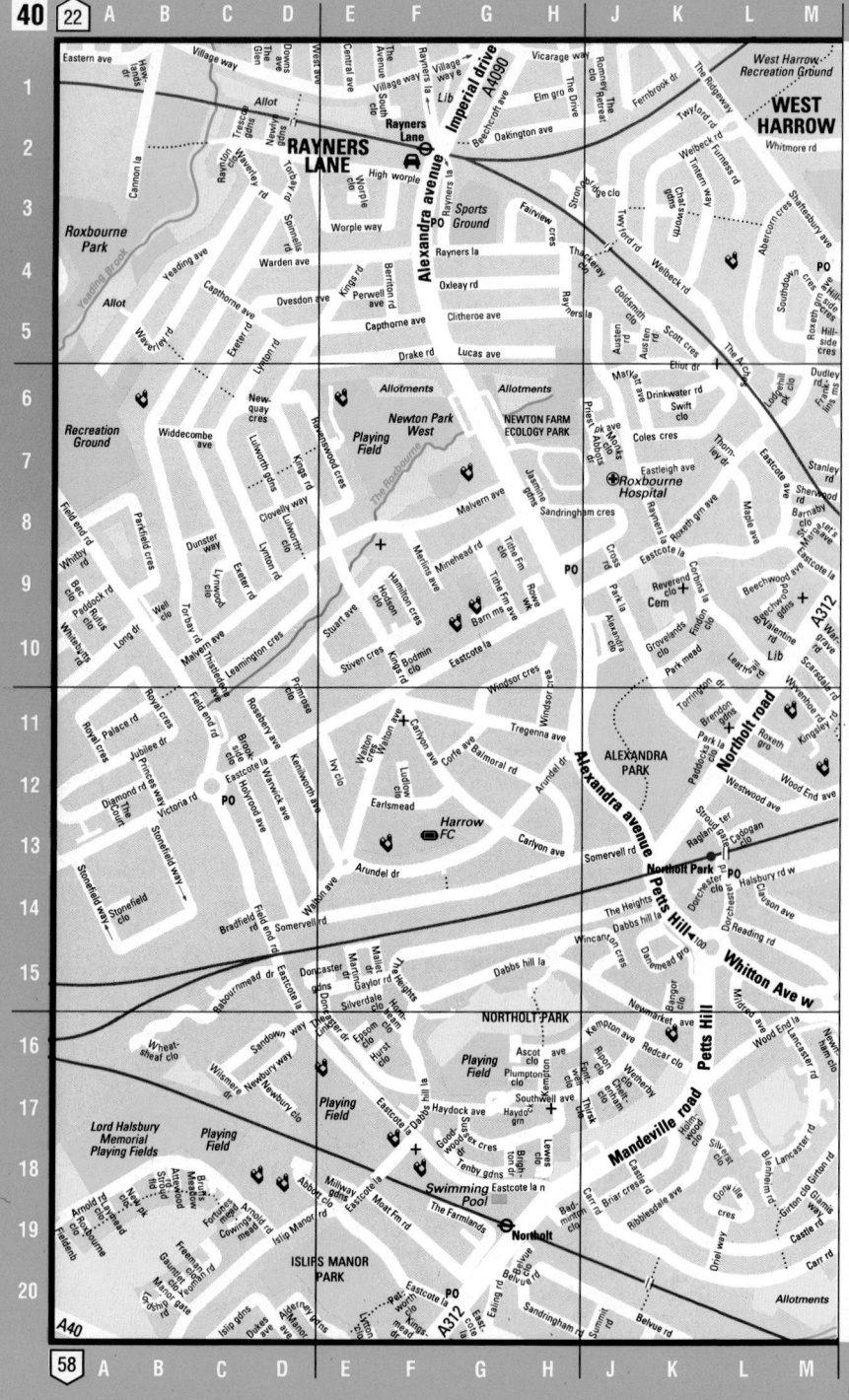

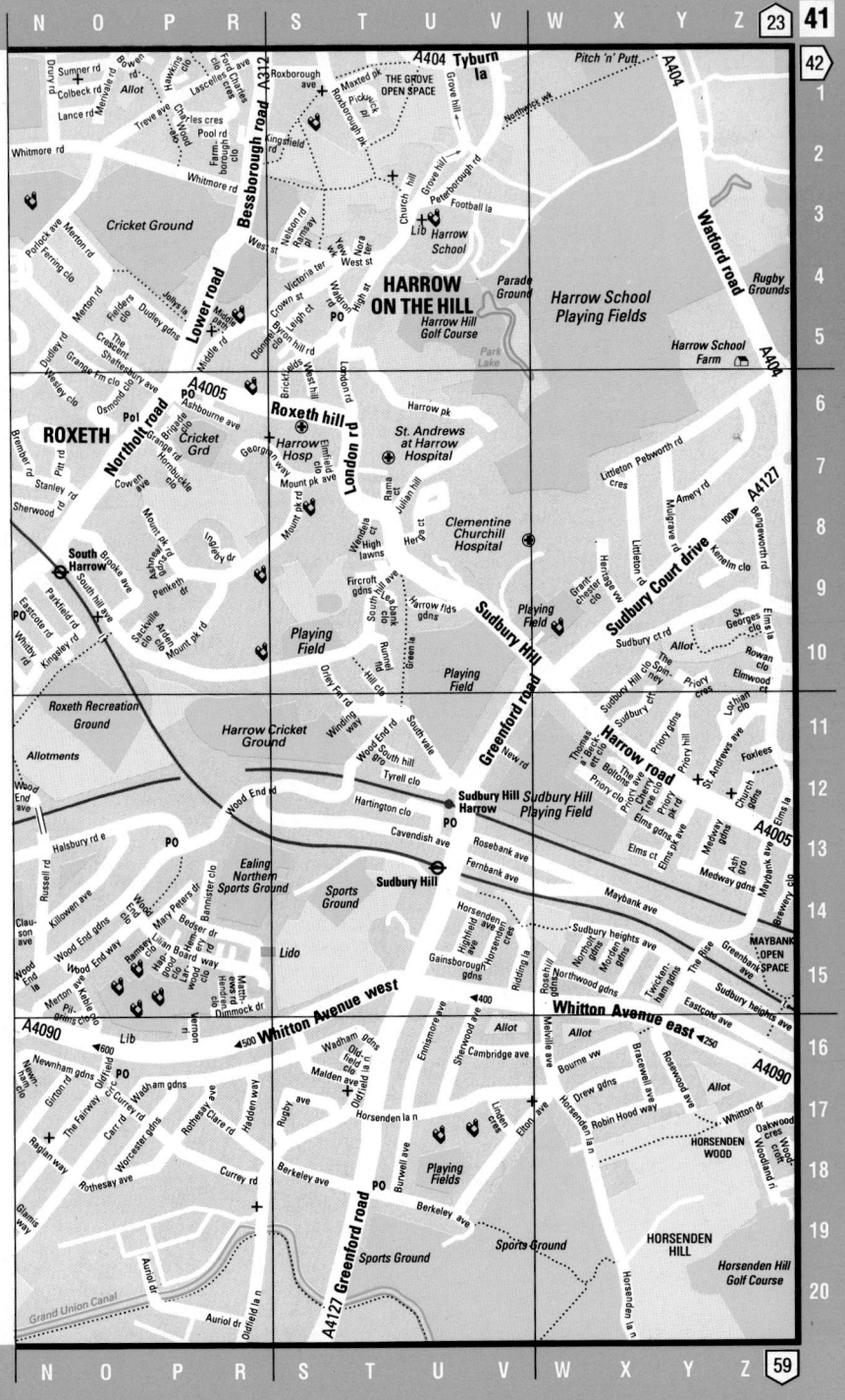

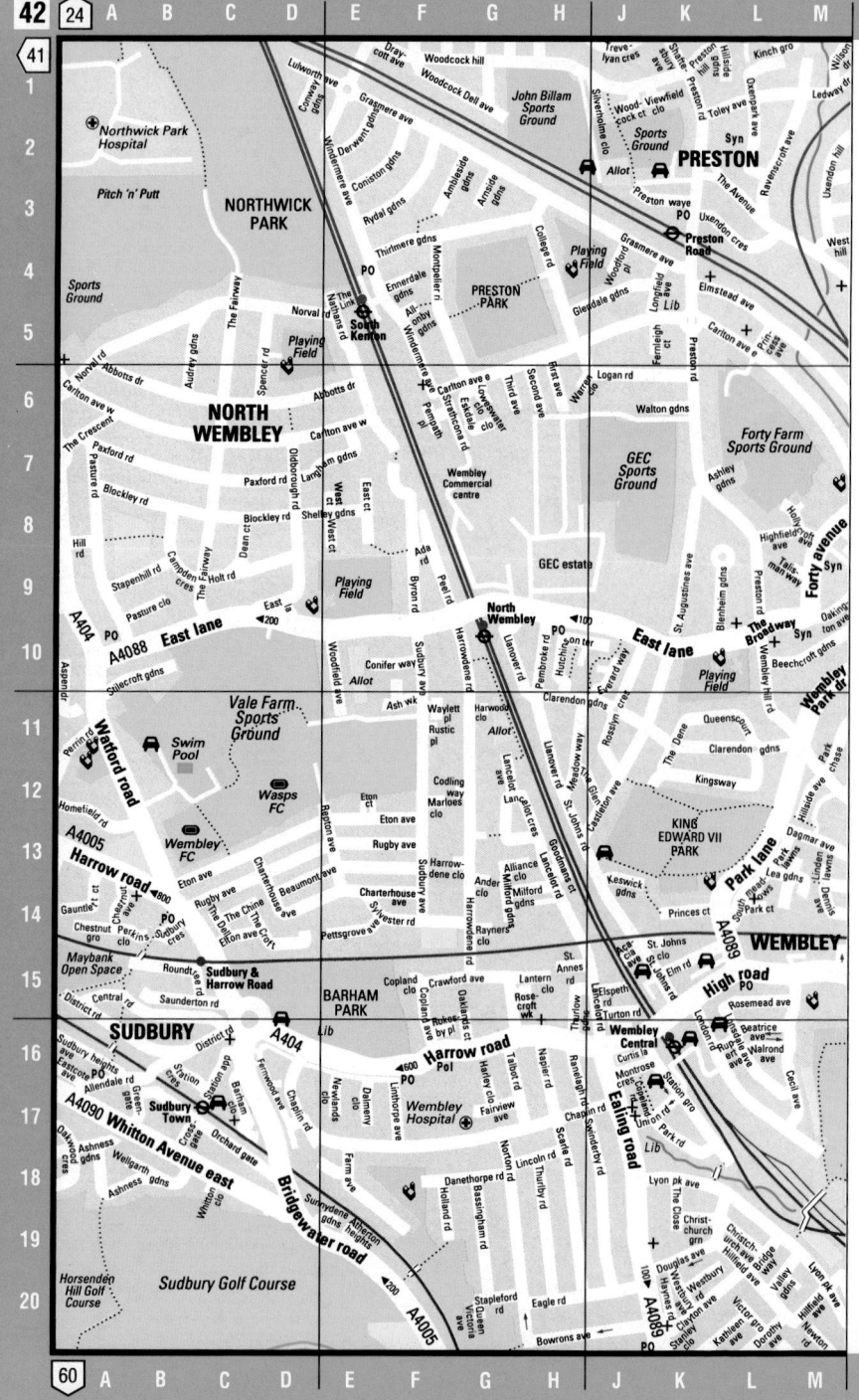

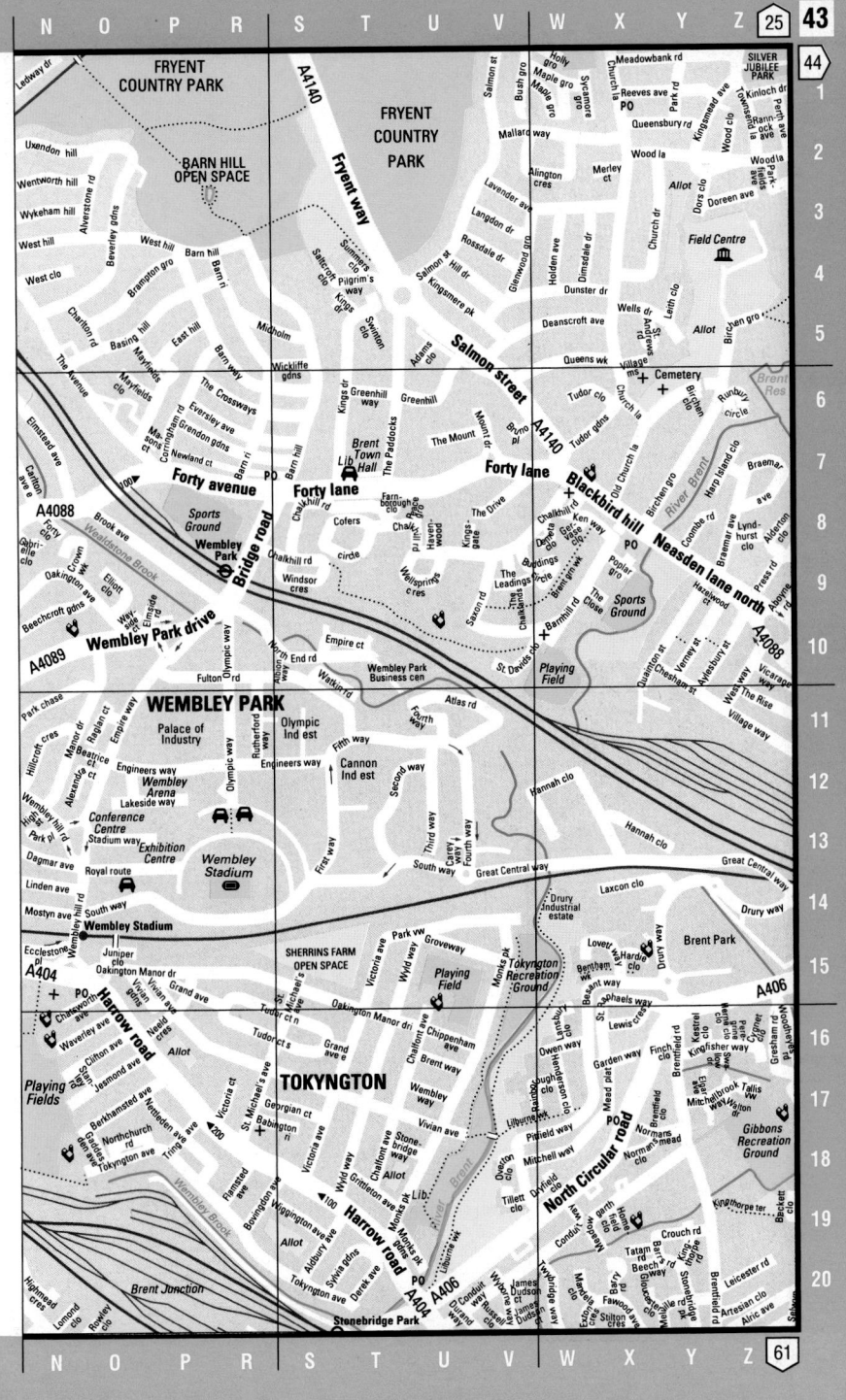

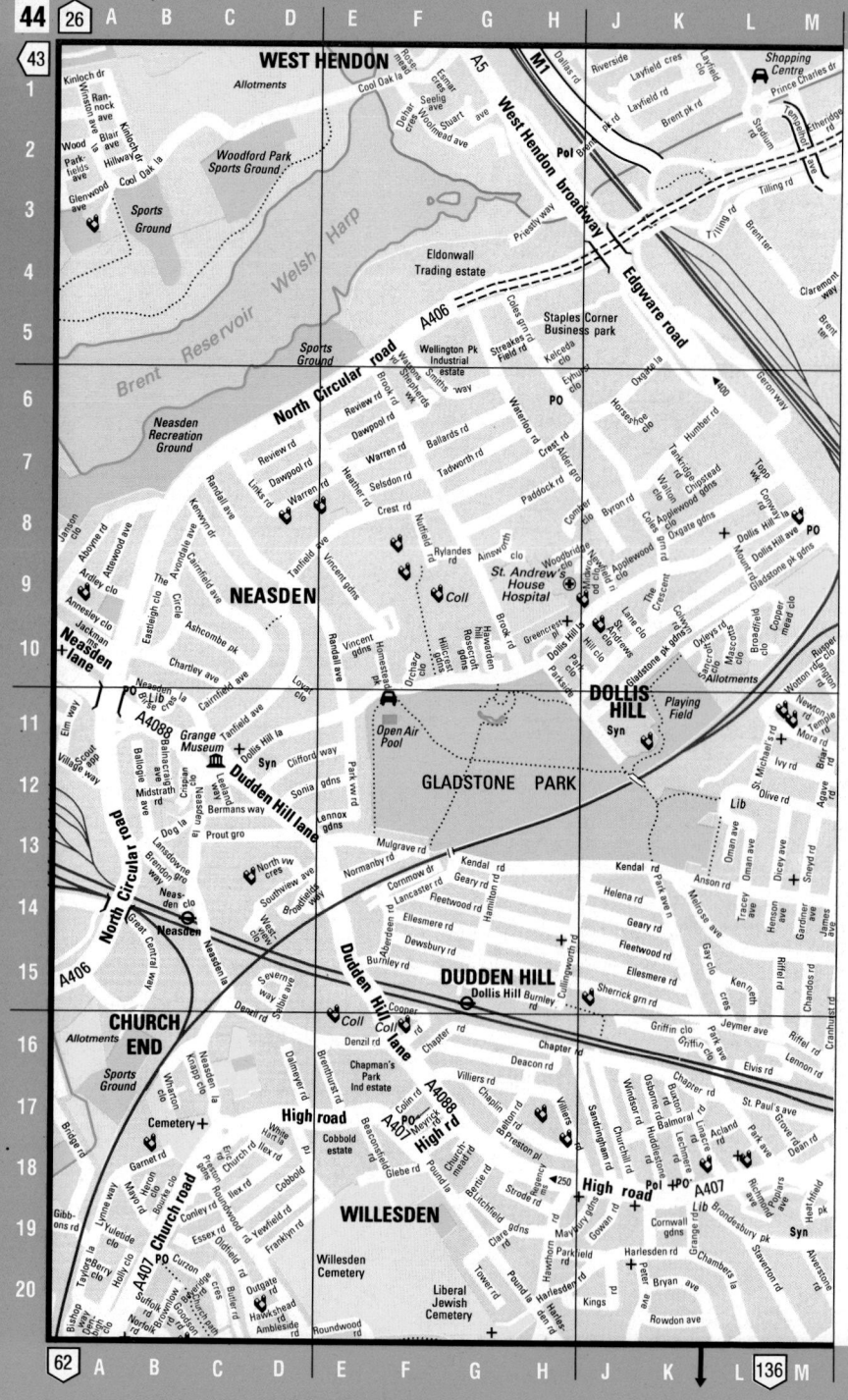

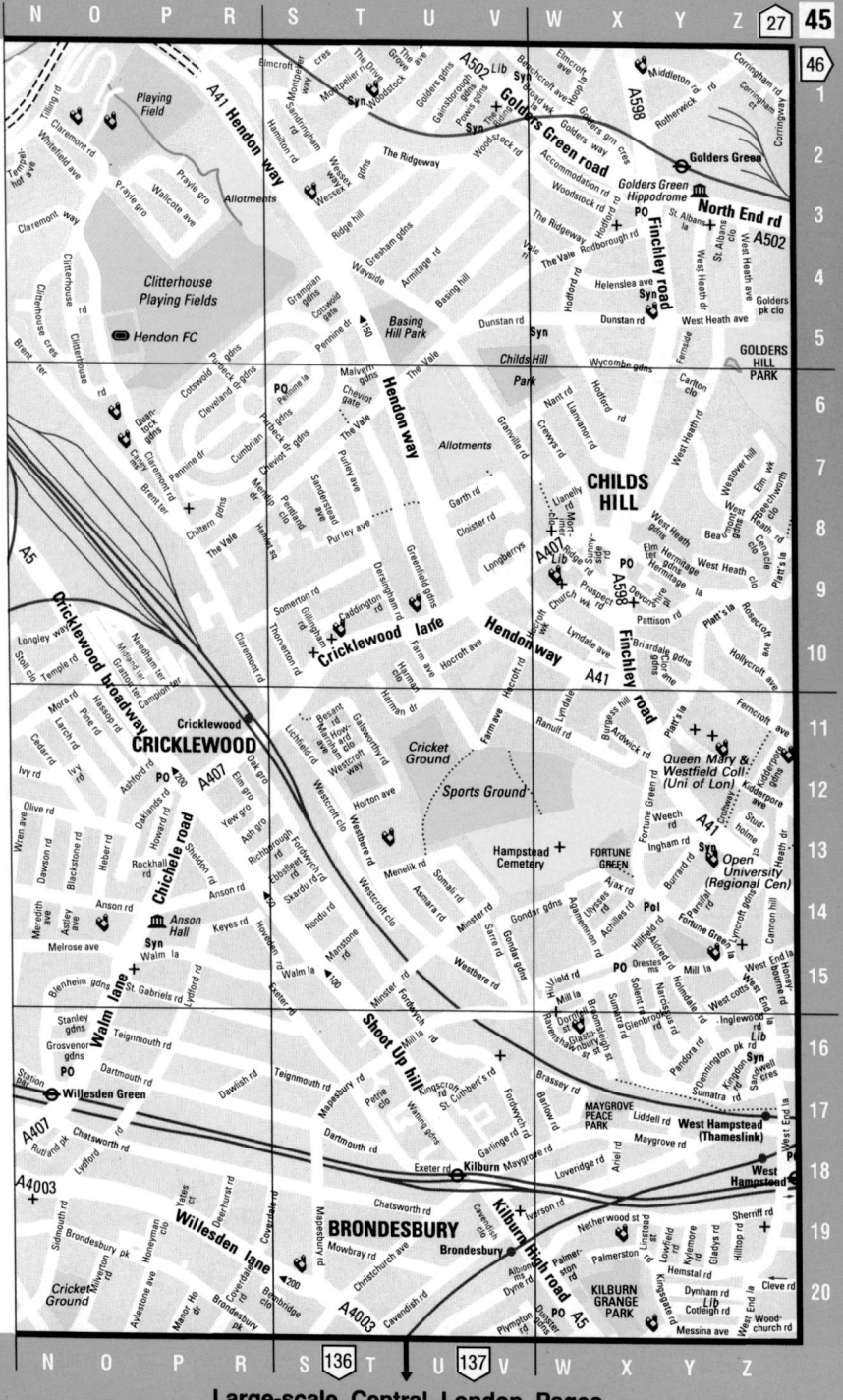

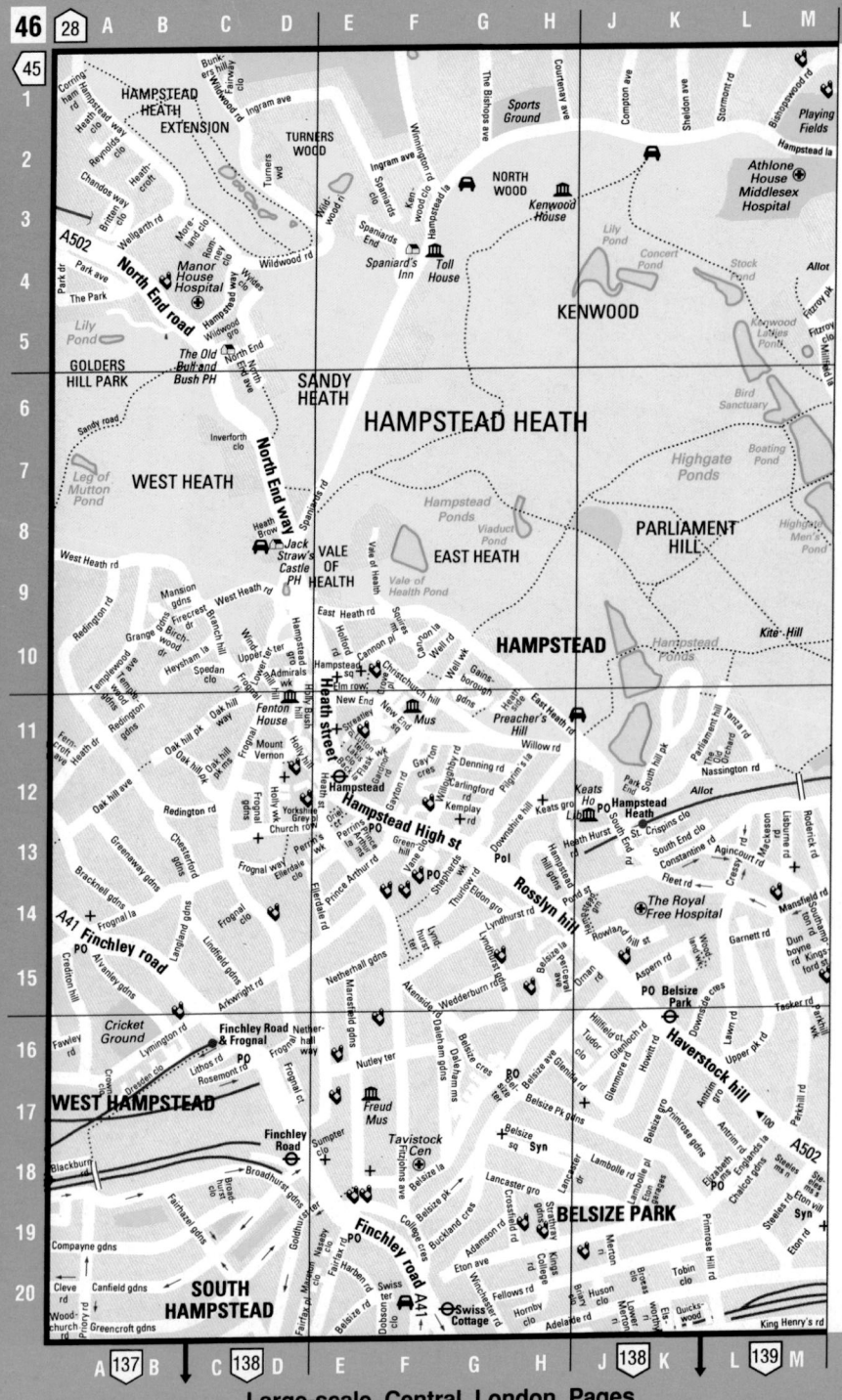

A B C D E F G H J K L M

HAMPSTEAD
HEATH
EXTENSION

TURNERS
WOOD

The Bishops ave

Sports
Ground

Courtenay ave

Compton ave

Sheldon av

Stormont rd

Playing
Fields

Corringham rd

Reynolds clo

Chandos way

Britten clo

Wellgarth rd

Ingram ave

Wildwood rd

NORTH
WOOD

Kenwood
House

Lily
Pond

Concert
Pond

Stock
Pond

Athlone
House
Middlesex
Hospital

A502

North End road

Manor
House Hospital

Spaniards clo

Spaniard's
Inn

Toll
House

KENWOOD

Kenwood
Ladies
Pond

Fitzroy
clo

Allot

GOLDERS
HILL PARK

The Old
Bull and
Bush PH

North End

SANDY
HEATH

Bird
Sanctuary

HAMPSTEAD HEATH

Sandy road

WEST HEATH

North End way

Leg of
Mutton
Pond

Inverforth
clo

Hampstead
Ponds

Highgate
Ponds

Boating
Pond

West Heath rd

Heath
Brow

Jack
Straw's
Castle
PH

VALE
OF
HEALTH

Viaduct
Pond

EAST HEATH

PARLIAMENT
HILL

Highgate
Men's
Pond

Mansion
gdns

West Heath rd

East Heath rd

Vale of Health Pond

Hampstead
Ponds

Kite Hill

Redington rd

Firecrest dr

Branch hill

HAMPSTEAD

TemPlewood
ave

Grange &
wood dr

Heysham la

Spedan
clo

Upper ter

Admirals
wk

New End

Well rd

Gains-borough gdns

East Heath rd

Nassington rd

Redington gdns

Oak hill pk

Fenton
House

Heath street

Christchurch hill

Mus

Preacher's
Hill

South hall pk

Parliament hill

Tanza rd

Redington rd

Oak hill pk

Oak hill clo

Mount
Vernon

Holly wk

Frognal gdns

New End

Willow rd

Keats
Ho

Hampstead
Heath

Allot

Chesterford gdns

Yorkshire
Grey
Church row

Perrins la

Hampstead
High st

Gayton rd

Denning rd

Keats gro

PO

Keats
Libn

St. Crispin's clo

Constantine rd

Agincourt rd

Roderick rd

Greenaway gdns

Frognal rise

Ellerdale rd

Prince Arthur rd

Shepherds

Carlingford rd

Kemplay rd

Downshire hill

Heath Hurst rd

South End

Fleet rd

Lisburne rd

Mansfield rd

A41 Finchley road

Bracknell gdns

Frognal la

Frognal clo

Lindfield gdns

Frognal

Netherhall gdns

Arkwright rd

Green-croft
hill

Prince
Arthur
rd

Lyndhurst
rd

Pilgrim's la

Pond st

The Royal
Free Hospital

Rowland

South hill

Aspern rd

Garnett rd

Dun
boyne
rd

Kings
ford

Cricket
Ground

Fawley
rd

Crossfield rd

Lymington rd

Finchley Road
& Frognal

PO

Nether-hall
way

Lithos rd

Frognal
ct

Nutley ter

Rosemont rd

Wedderburn rd

Akenside rd

Dacham ms

Belsize
cres

Date
Ham ms

Tudor

Hilling
don rd

Gleneloch rd

Glenmore rd

Belsize ave

PO

Belsize
Park

Lawn rd

Upper pk rd

Tasker rd

WEST HAMPSTEAD

Blackburn rd

Finchley
Road

Broadhurst gdns

Fairhazel gdns

Goldhurst ter

Sumpter
clo

Freud
Mus

Nasmyth
rd

Tavistock
Cen

Belsize pk

Lancaster gro

College cres

PO

Belsize
sq

Syn

Crossfield rd

Adamson rd

Stratford gdns

Belsize gro

Lambolle rd

Lambolle
pl

Primrose gdns

Antrim rd

Antrim gro

Primrose Hill rd

BELSIZE PARK

Elizabeth
clo

Eton Coll gdns

Strathray gdns

Chalcot gdns

Steeles rd

Eton rd

A502

Parkhill rd

Compayne gdns

Canfield gdns

Cleve
rd

Wood-church rd

Priory rd

Greencroft gdns

Fairfax pl

Maygrove rd

Fairfax rd

Harben rd

Swiss
ter
clo

Finchley road A41

Belsize rd

Dobson
clo

Swiss
Cottage

Eton ave

Buckland cres

Eton College

Fellows rd

Hornby
clo

Adelaide rd

SOUTH
HAMPSTEAD

Merton

Huson
clo

Tobin
clo

Lower
Merton
rise

Eton
av

Syn

Quickswood

King Henry's rd

A 137 B C 138 D E F G H J 138 K L 139 M

Large-scale Central London Pages

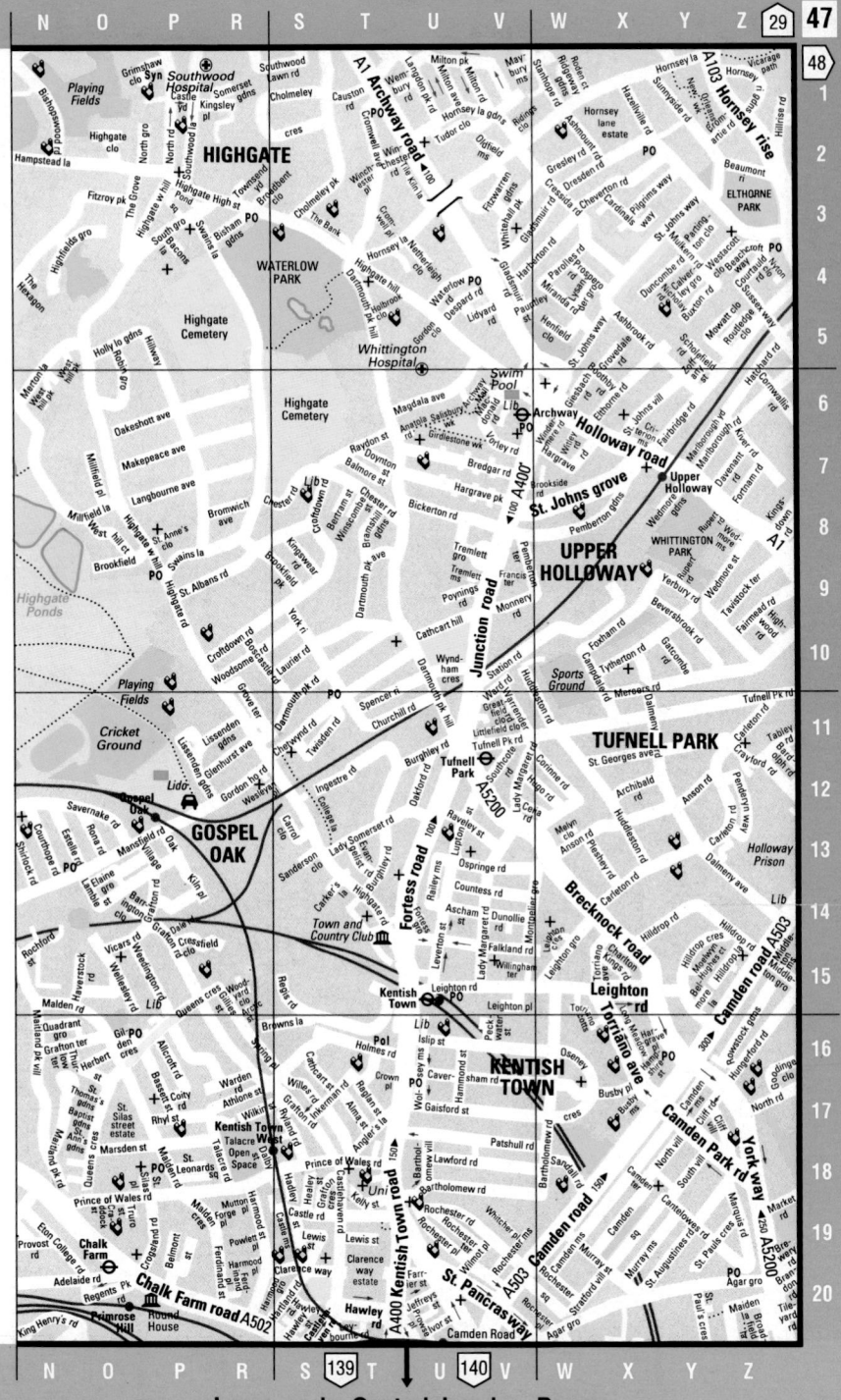

Large-scale Central London Pages

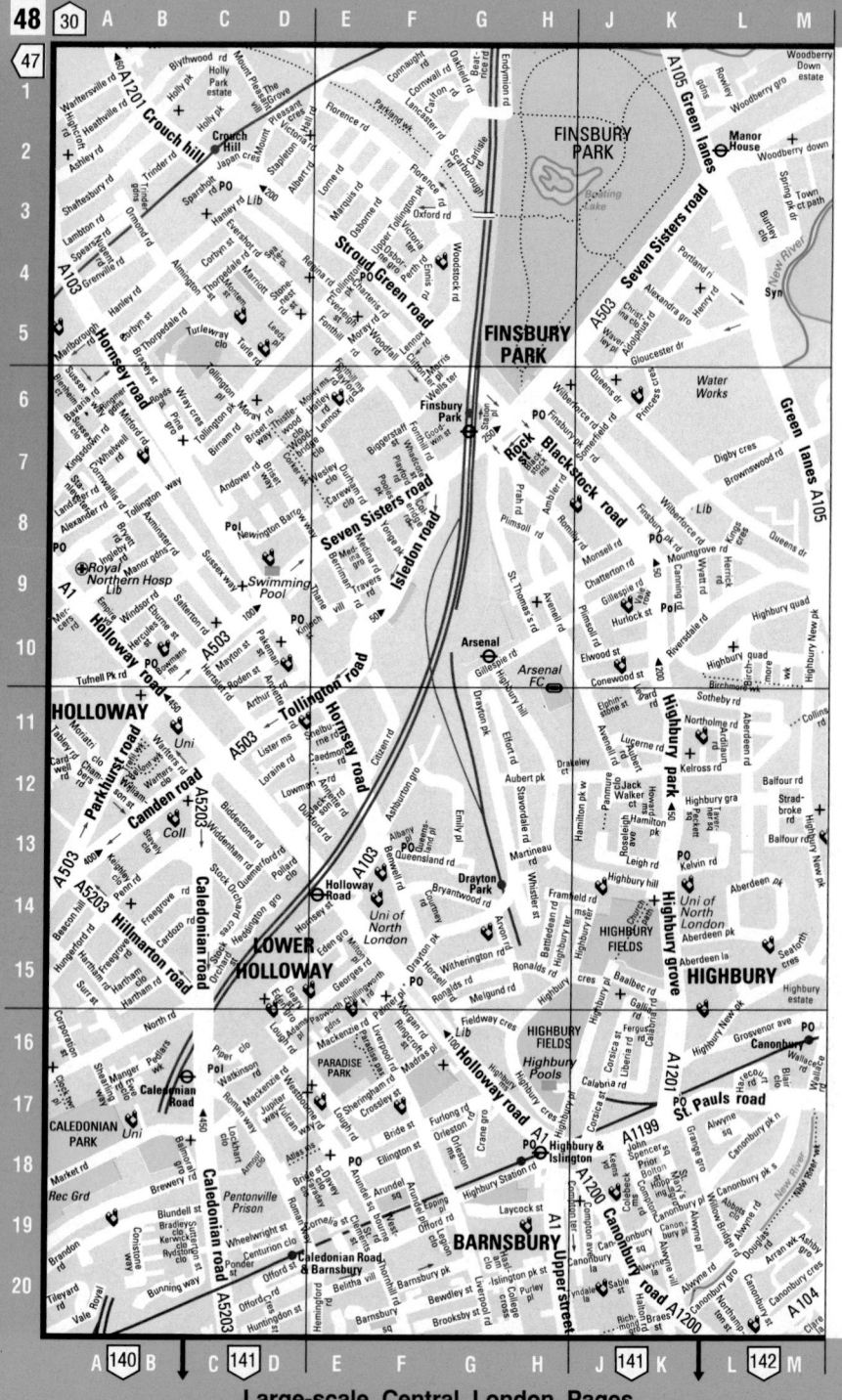

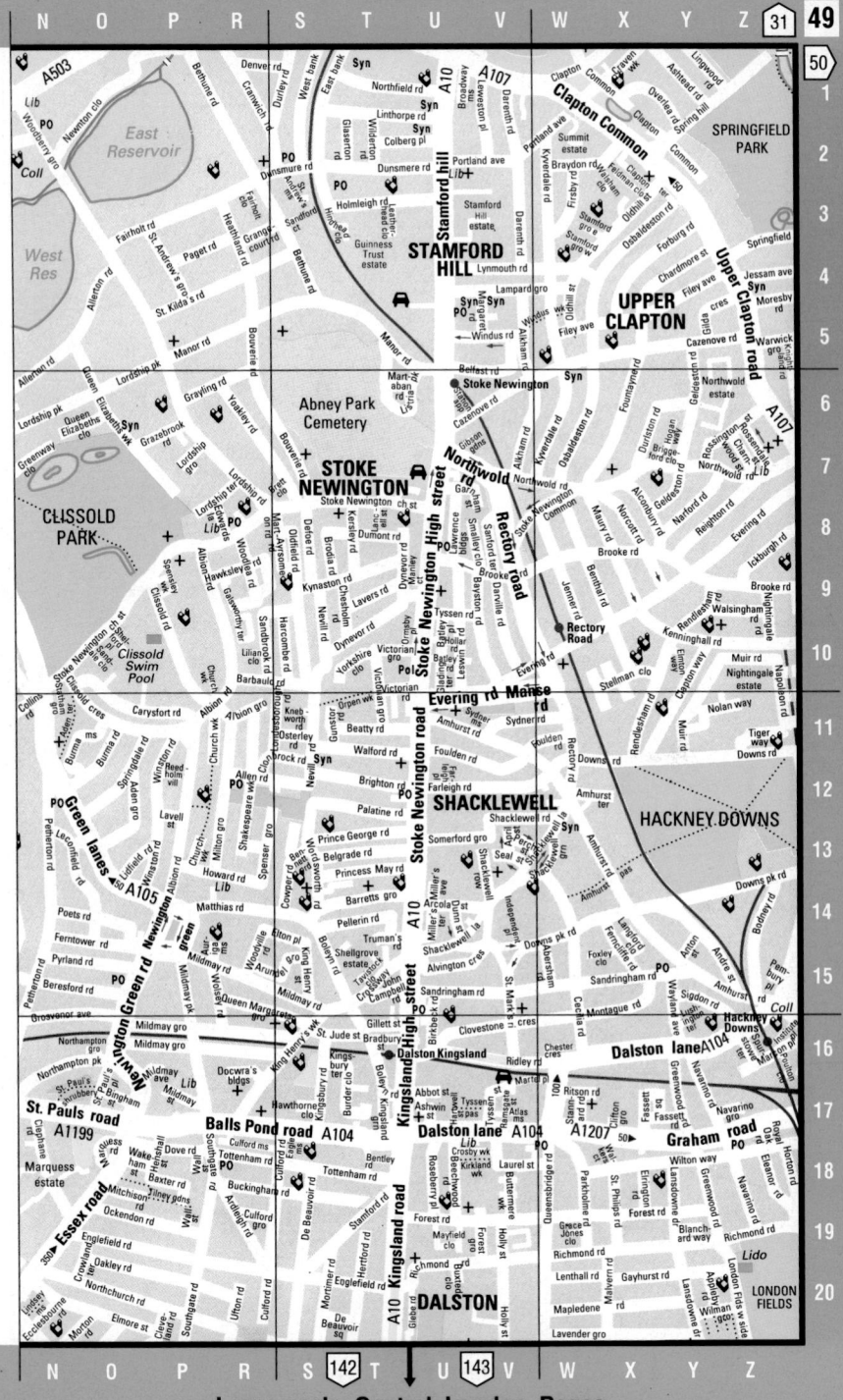

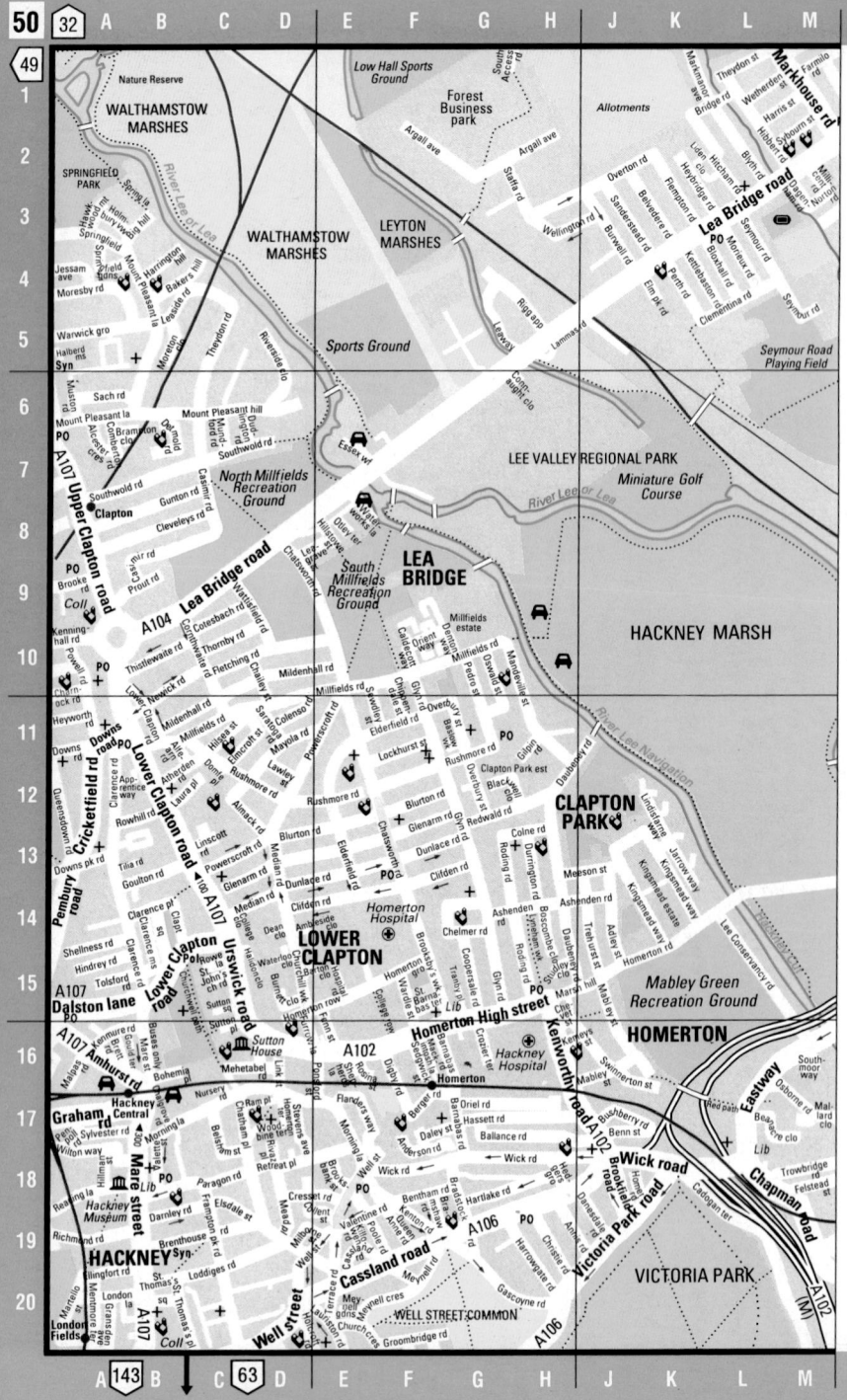

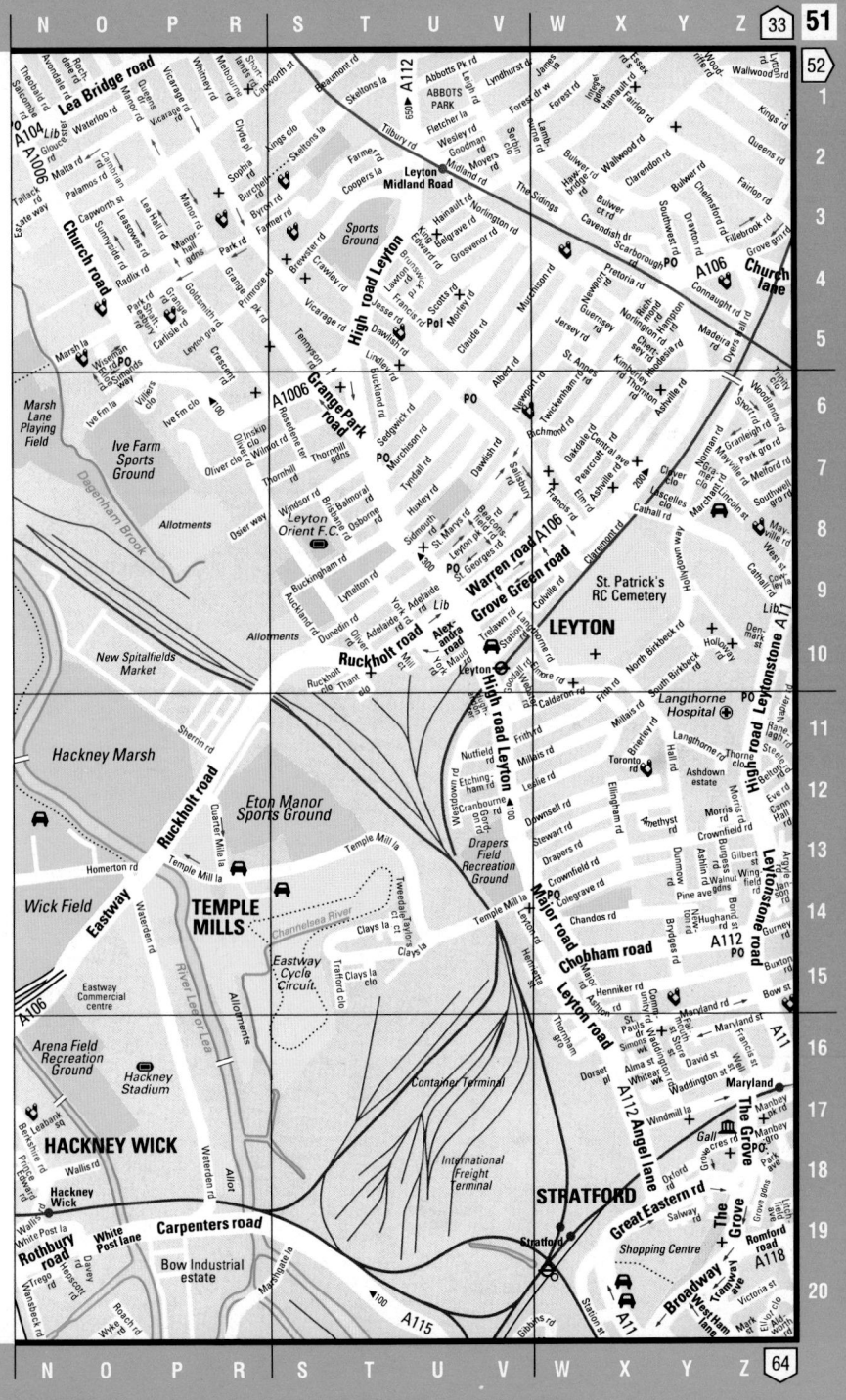

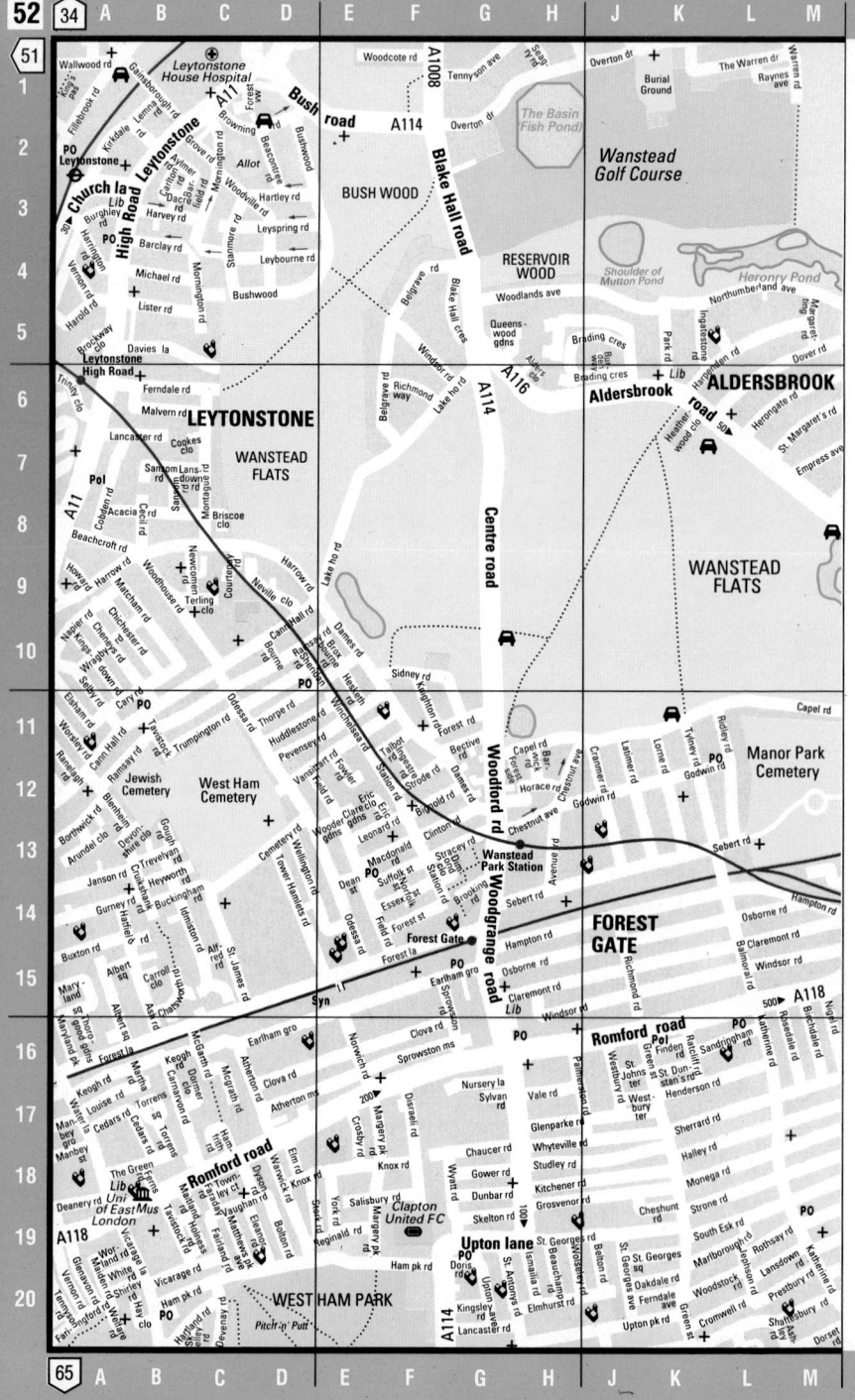

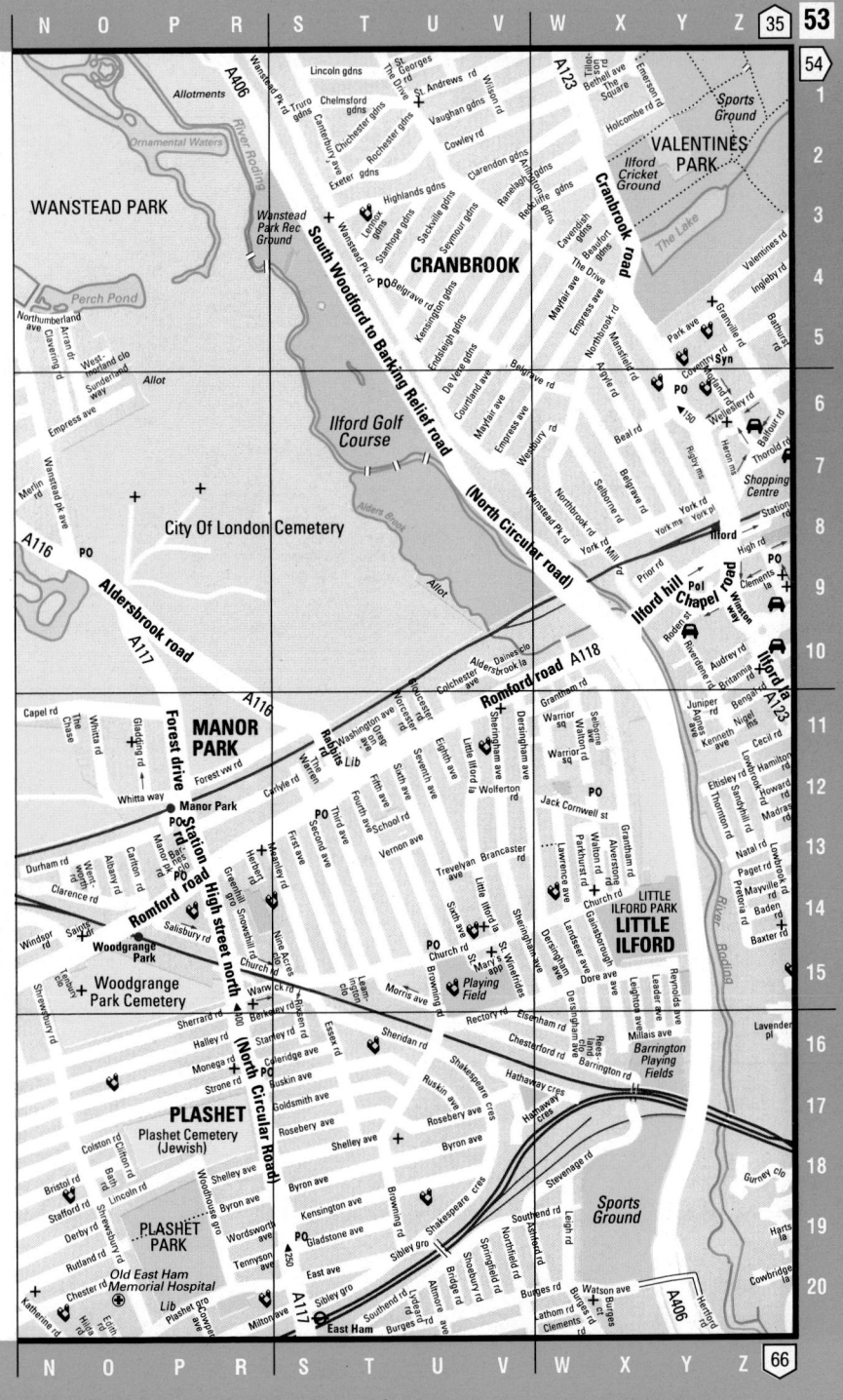

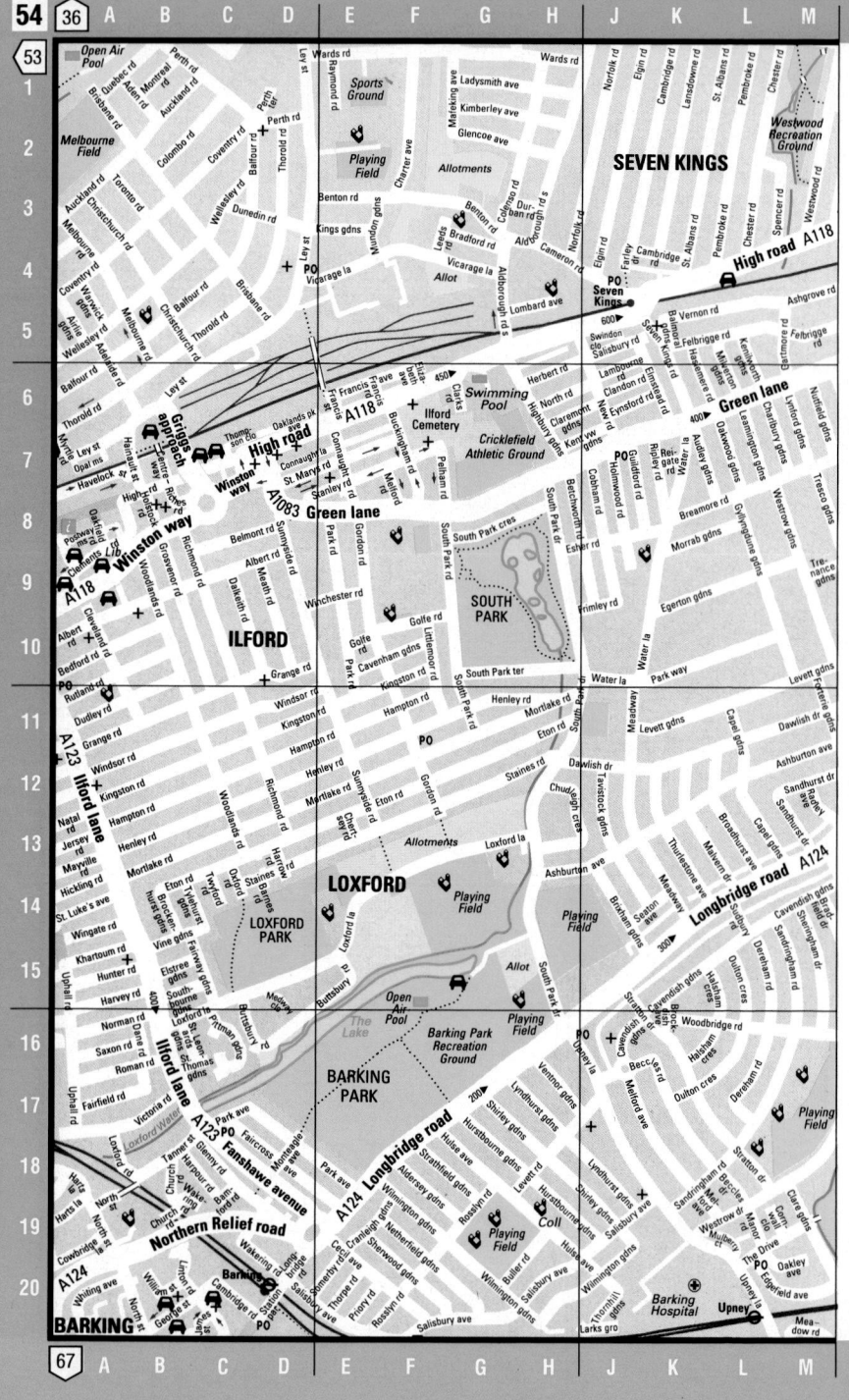

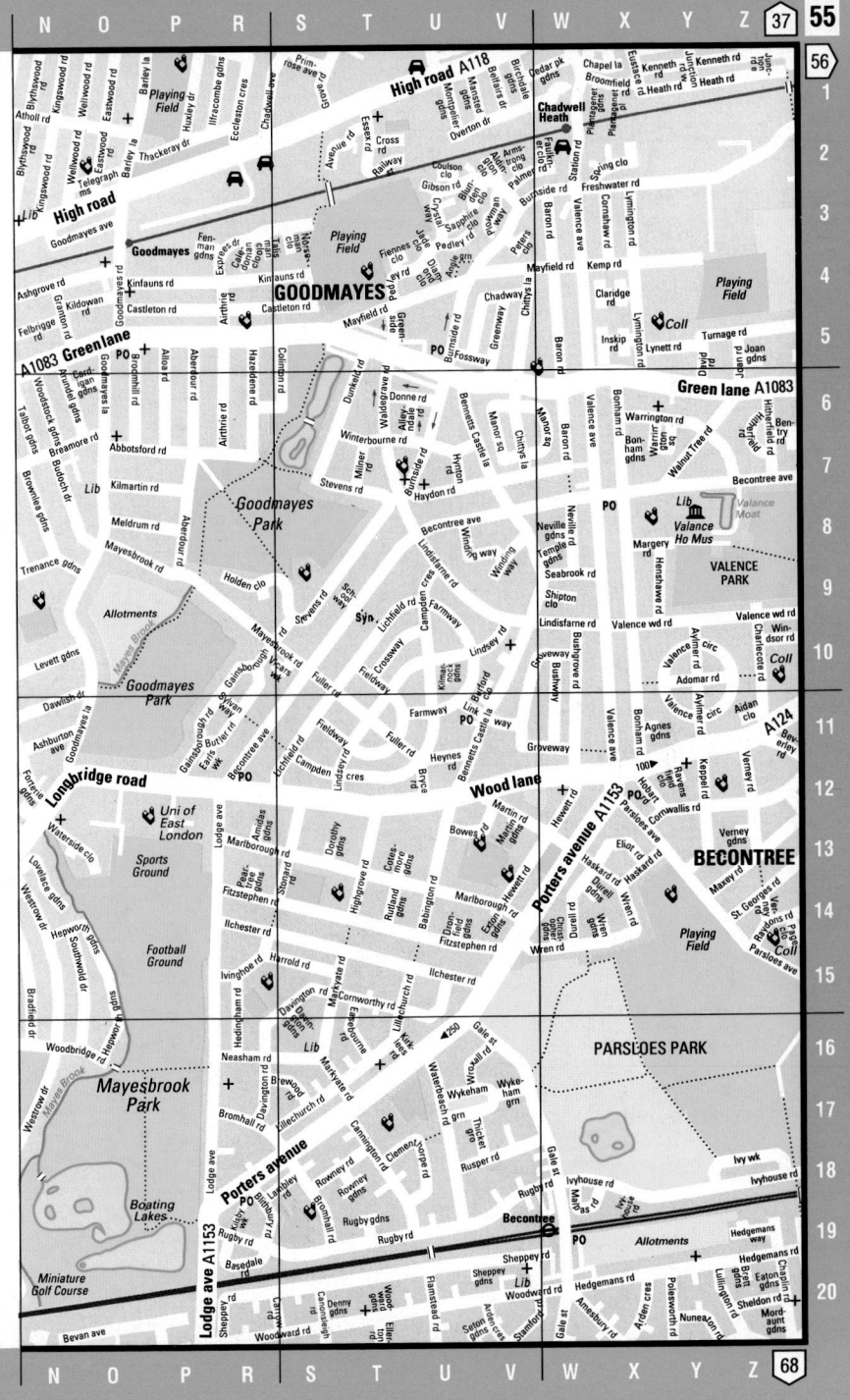

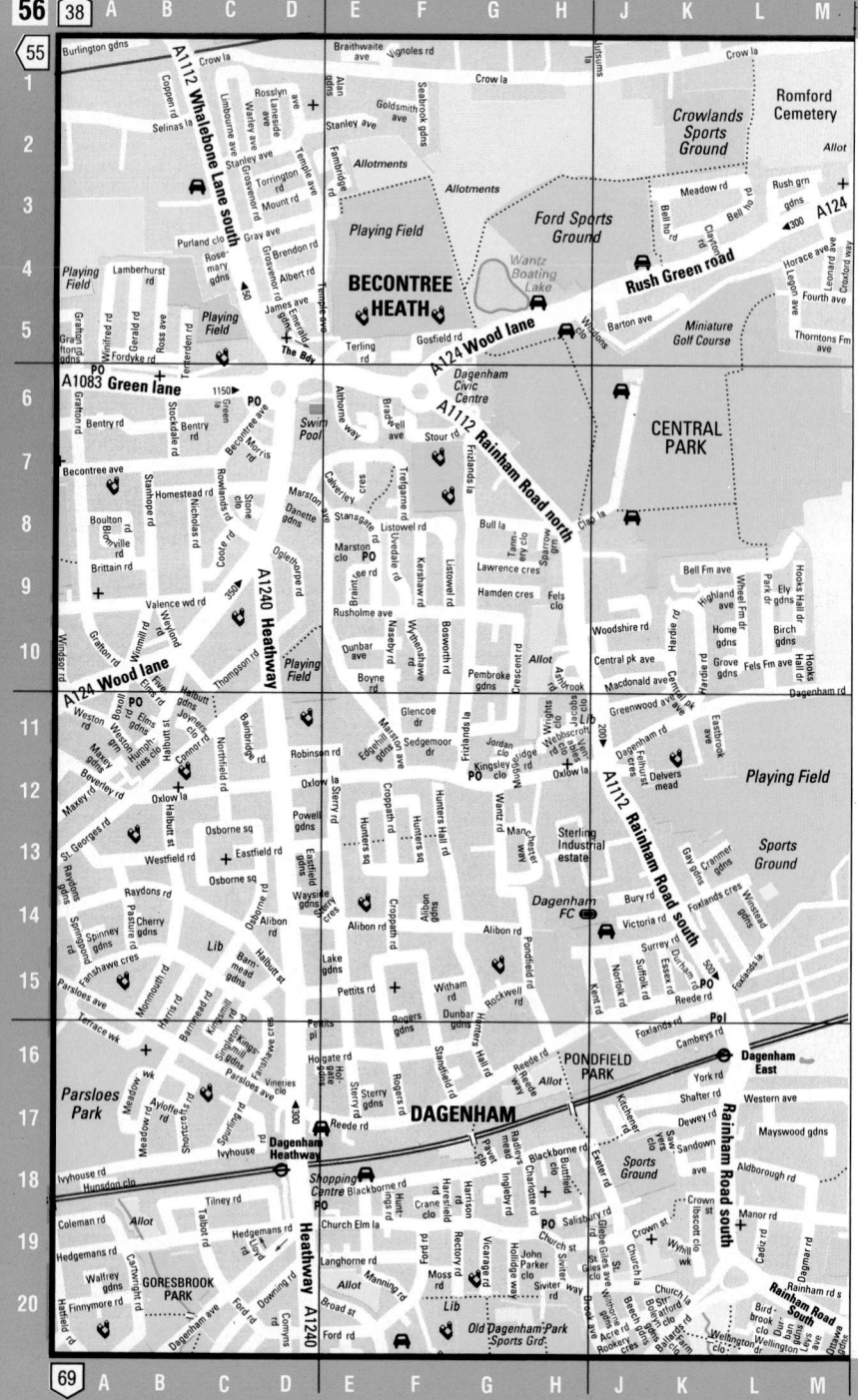

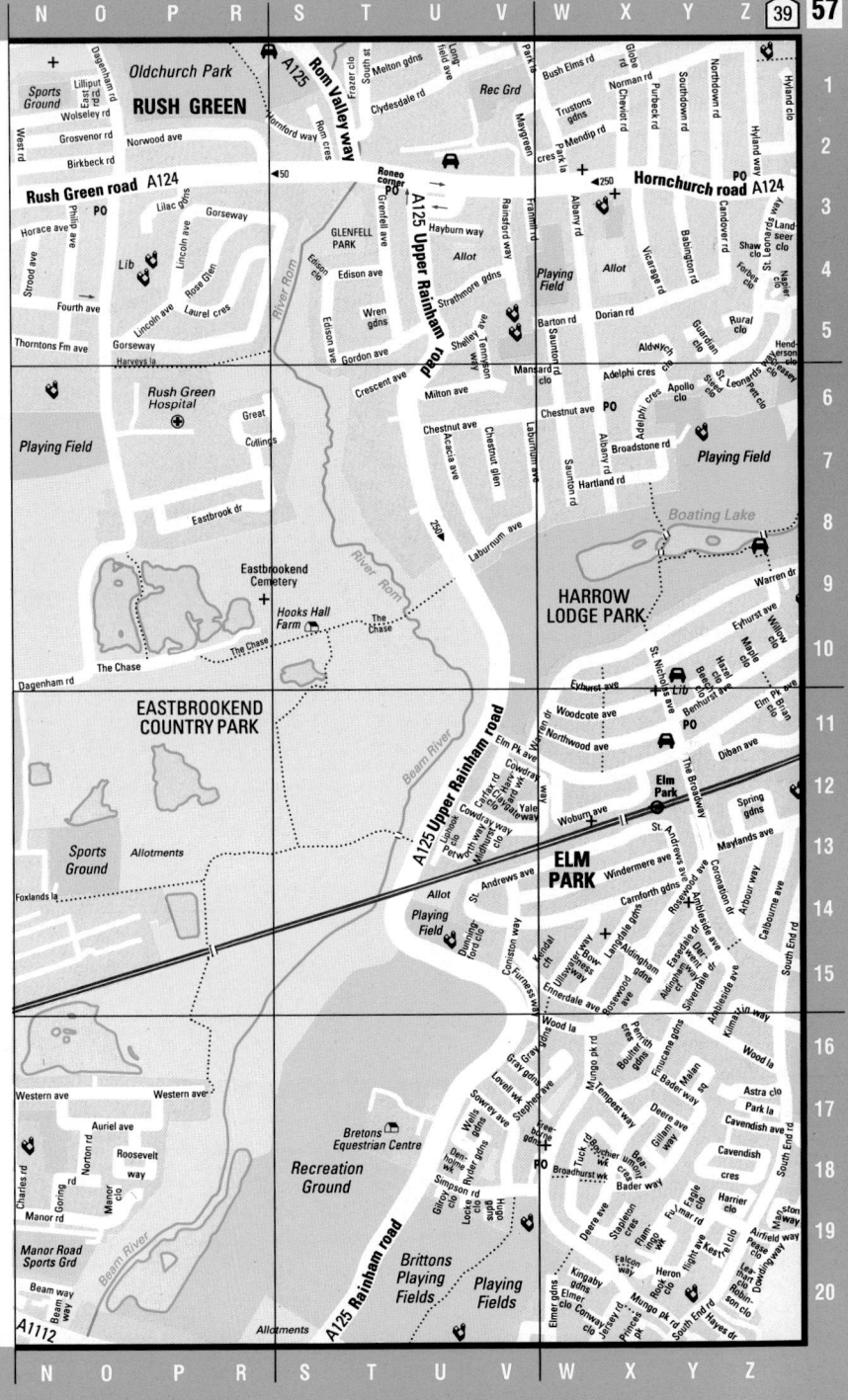

N O P R S T U V W X Y Z

1
2
3
4
5
6
7
8
9
10
11
12
13
14
15
16
17
18
19
20

Oldchurch Park
Sports Ground
RUSH GREEN
Dagenham rd
Lilliput rd
East rd
Wolseley rd
Grosvenor rd
Birkbeck rd
West rd
Norwood ave

Rush Green road A124
Horace ave
Philip rd
PO
Lilac gdns
Gorseway
Lincoln gdns
Strood ave
Lib
Rose Glen
Lincoln rd
Laurel cres
Fourth ave
Gorseway
Thorntons Fm ave
Harveys la

Rom Valley way
A125
Rom cres
Hornford way
Crazel rd old

Melton gdns
Melton st
Long Elm ave
Clydesdale rd
Maygreen

Rec Grd
Park la
Bush Elms rd
Globe rd
Northdown rd
Southdown rd
Hyland clo
Normar rd
Chevlot rd
Purbeck rd
Hyland clo
Trustons gdns
cres

◄50
Roneo corner
A125
Grenfell ave
Hayburn way
Rainsford way
Framstn
Mendip rd
cres
+
◄250
Hornchurch road A124
Landover rd
PO
Landseer clo
Shaw clo
GLENFELL PARK
Edison clo
Edison ave
Wren gdns
Strathmore gdns
Allot
Albany rd
Vicarage rd
Babington rd
Forbes rd
Napier clo

A125 Upper Rainham road
River Rom
Edison ave
Gordon ave
Shelley way
Tennyson way
Barton rd
Saunton rd
Mansard clo
Dorian rd
Guardian clo
Rural clo
Aldwych
Henderson clo
Hen

Crescent rd
Milton ave
Adelphi cres
Adelphi clo
Apollo clo
St. Leonards clo
Grove

Great Cullings
Chestnut ave
Chestnut ave
PO
Albany rd
Broadstone rd
St. Loard

Rush Green Hospital
Rush Green
Acacia ave
Chestnut glen
Laburnum ave
Saunton rd
Hartland rd
Playing Field

Playing Field
Eastbrook dr

Boating Lake
Warren dr

River Rom
HARROW LODGE PARK
Eyhurst ave
Willow
Maple

Eastbrookend Cemetery
Hooks Hall Farm
The Chase
The Chase
The Chase
Dagenham rd

St. Nicholas ave
Lib
Benhurst ave
PO
Eyhurst ave
Elm clo
Diban ave

EASTBROOKEND COUNTRY PARK
Beam River
A125 Upper Rainham road
Woodcote ave
Northwood ave
Cowdray way
Carter clo
Gateway
Yale
Perworth way
Midhurst way

Elm Park
Woburn ave
The Broadway
Spring gdns
St. Andrews rd
Maylands ave

Sports Ground
Allotments
Foxlands la
St. Andrews ave
Coniston way
Furness clo
Kendal clo
Dunnings ford clo
Allot
Playing Field
Langdale gdns
Bow
Galloway
Rossonare
Ennerdale ave
Windermere ave
Carnforth gdns
Ridgeway
Aldingham gdns
Coronation dr
Arbour way
Calbourne dr
South End rd
Ambleside dr
Easedale dr
Aldergrove
Silverdale dr

ELM PARK

Western ave
Western ave
Auriel ave
Roosevelt way
Norton rd
Goring rd
Manor clo
Manor rd

Wood la
Gray gdns
Gray gdns
Lovell wk
Sowrey ave
Stephens ave
Penrith gdns
Baxter gdns
Finucane gdns
Bader way
Malin sq
Ambleside
Killmartin
Wood la
Astra clo
Park la
Cavendish ave
Cavendish cres
South End rd

Charles rd
Manor rd
Manor Road Sports Grd
Beam way
Beam River

Bretons Equestrian Centre
Recreation Ground
Wells gdns
Denholme way
Locke gdns
Gilroy gdns
Ryder gdns
Simpson rd
Hugo gdns
Treebye gdns
PO
Tuck rd
Broadhurst wk
Beer
urchment
Bader way
Bader way
Deere ave
Stapleton rd
Gillam way
Tempest way
Beyher
Deere ave
Harrier clo
Airfield way
Kest
Sston way

A125 Rainham road
Brittons Playing Fields
Playing Fields
Allotments
A1112
Elmer gdns
Kingaby gdns
Elmer rd
Conways rd
Jersey rd
Princes rd
Mungo pk rd
Falcon way
Heron way
Eagle
Fulmar rd
Robin clo
Kingfisher rd
Lea
clo
South End rd
South End
Hayes clo

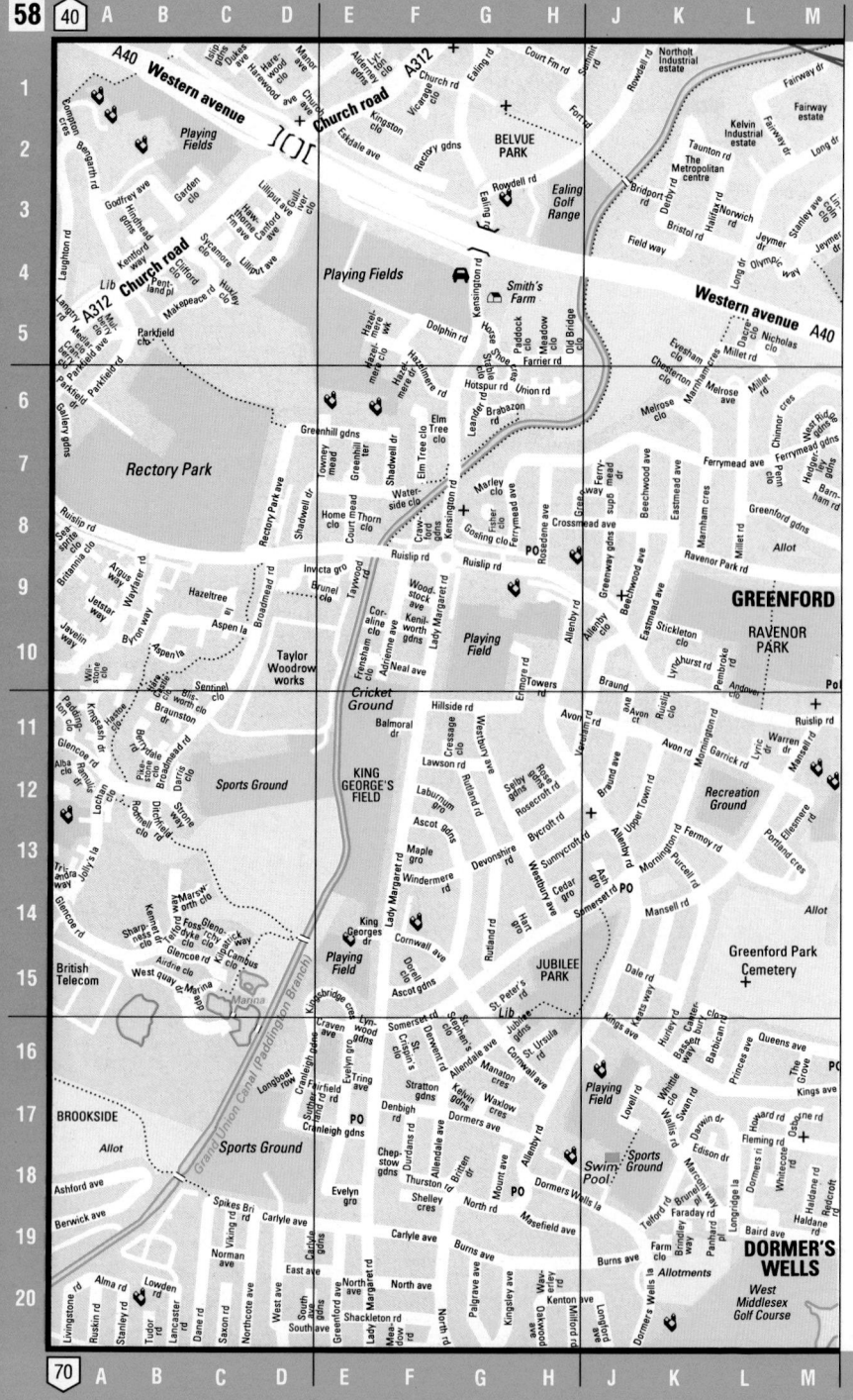

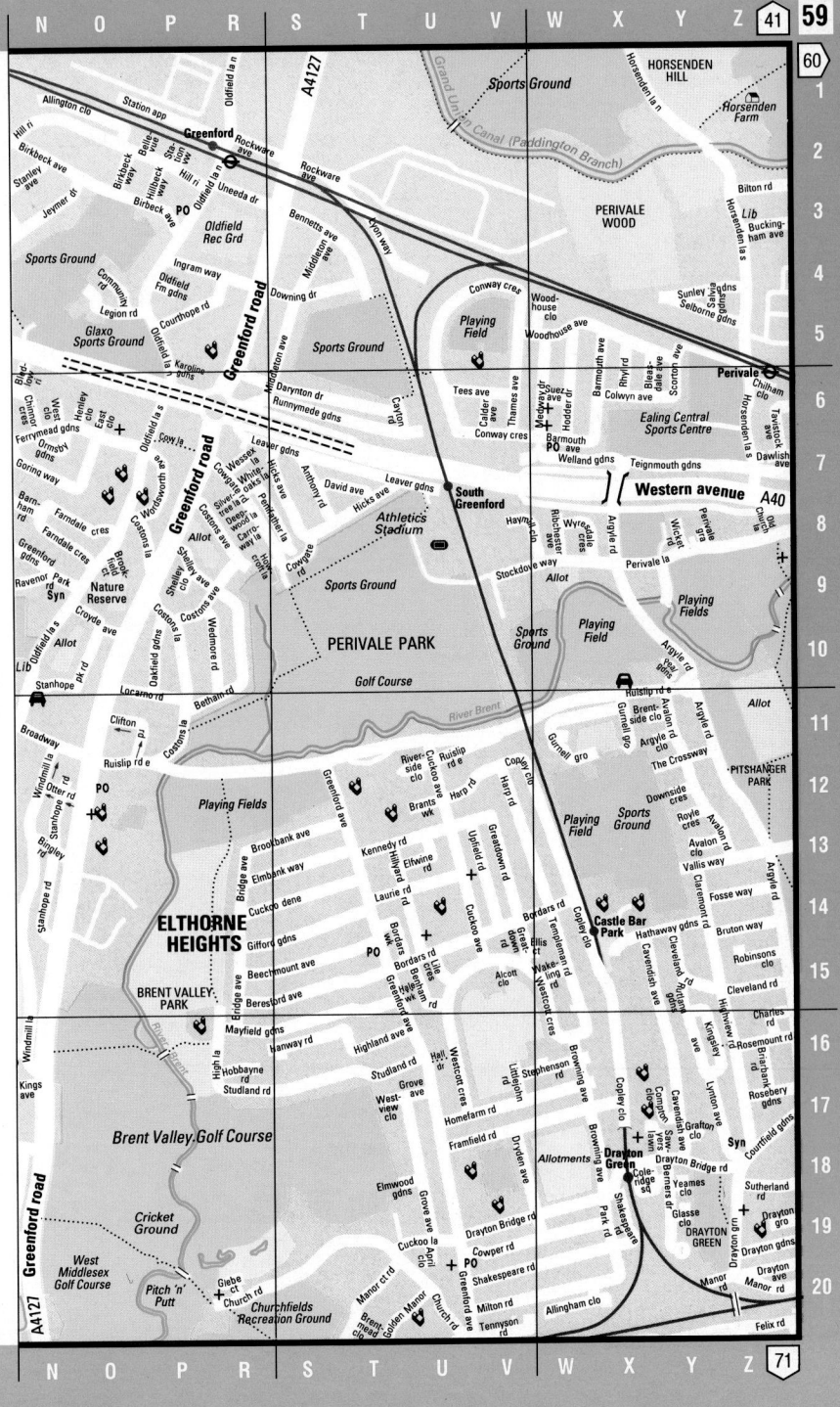

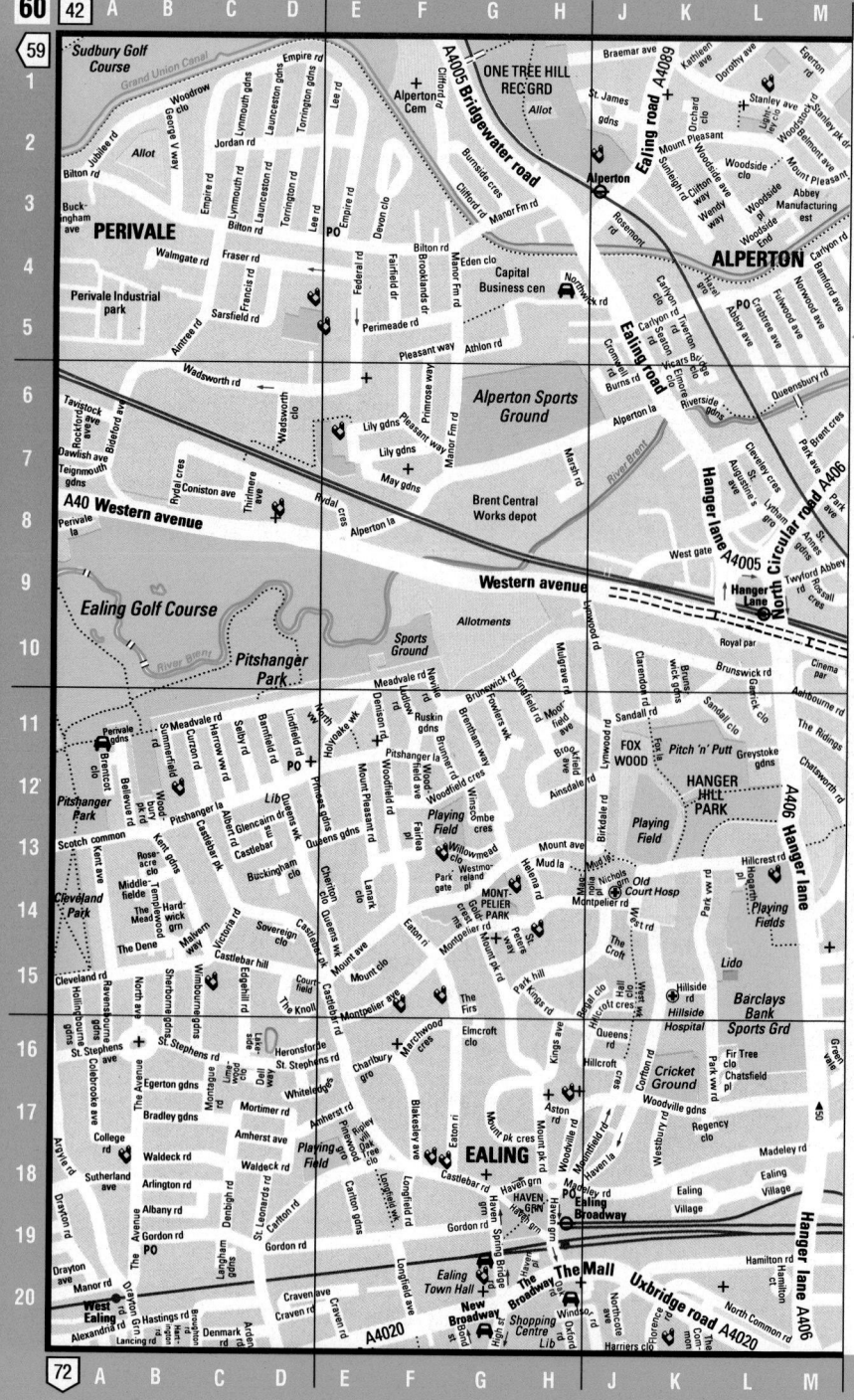

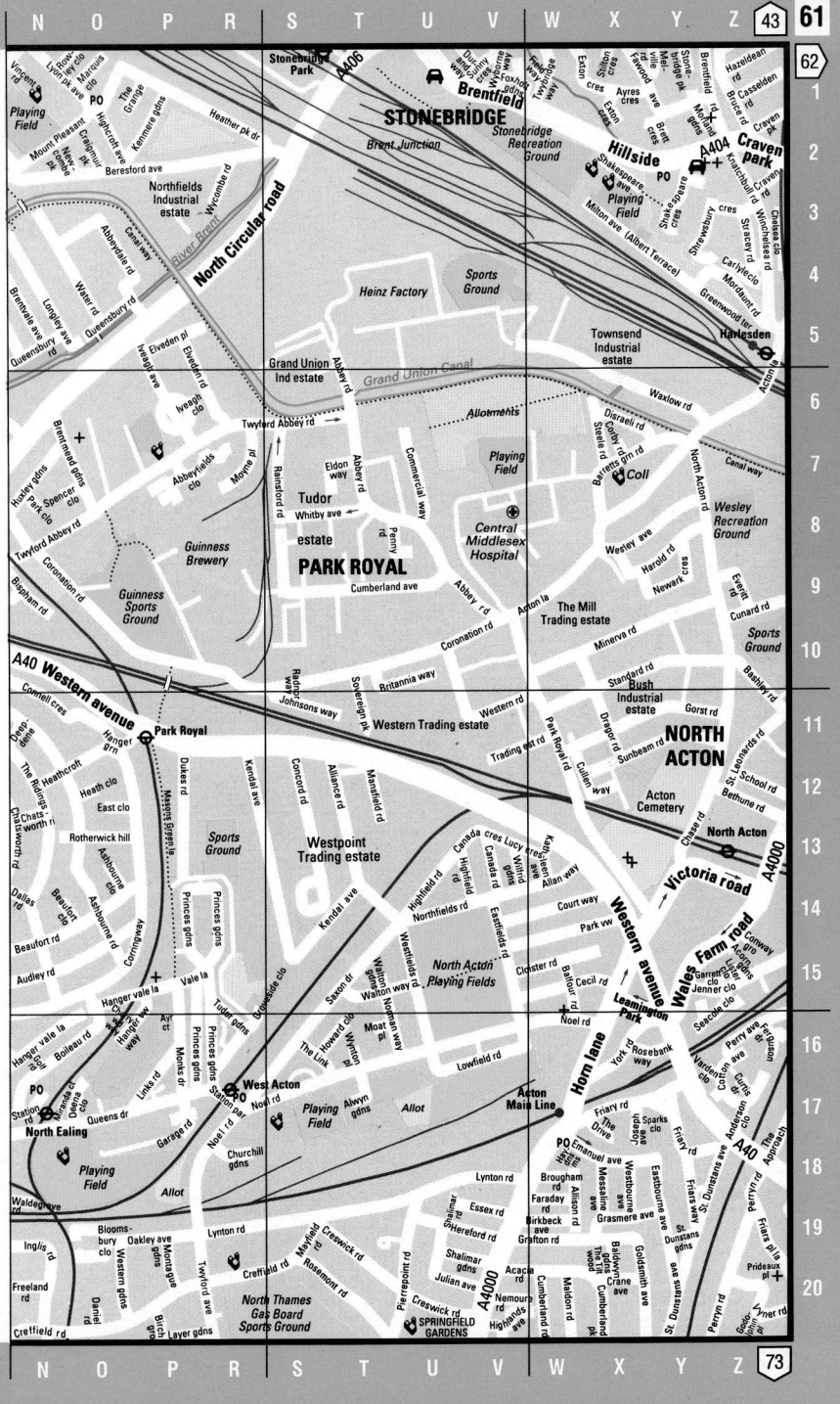

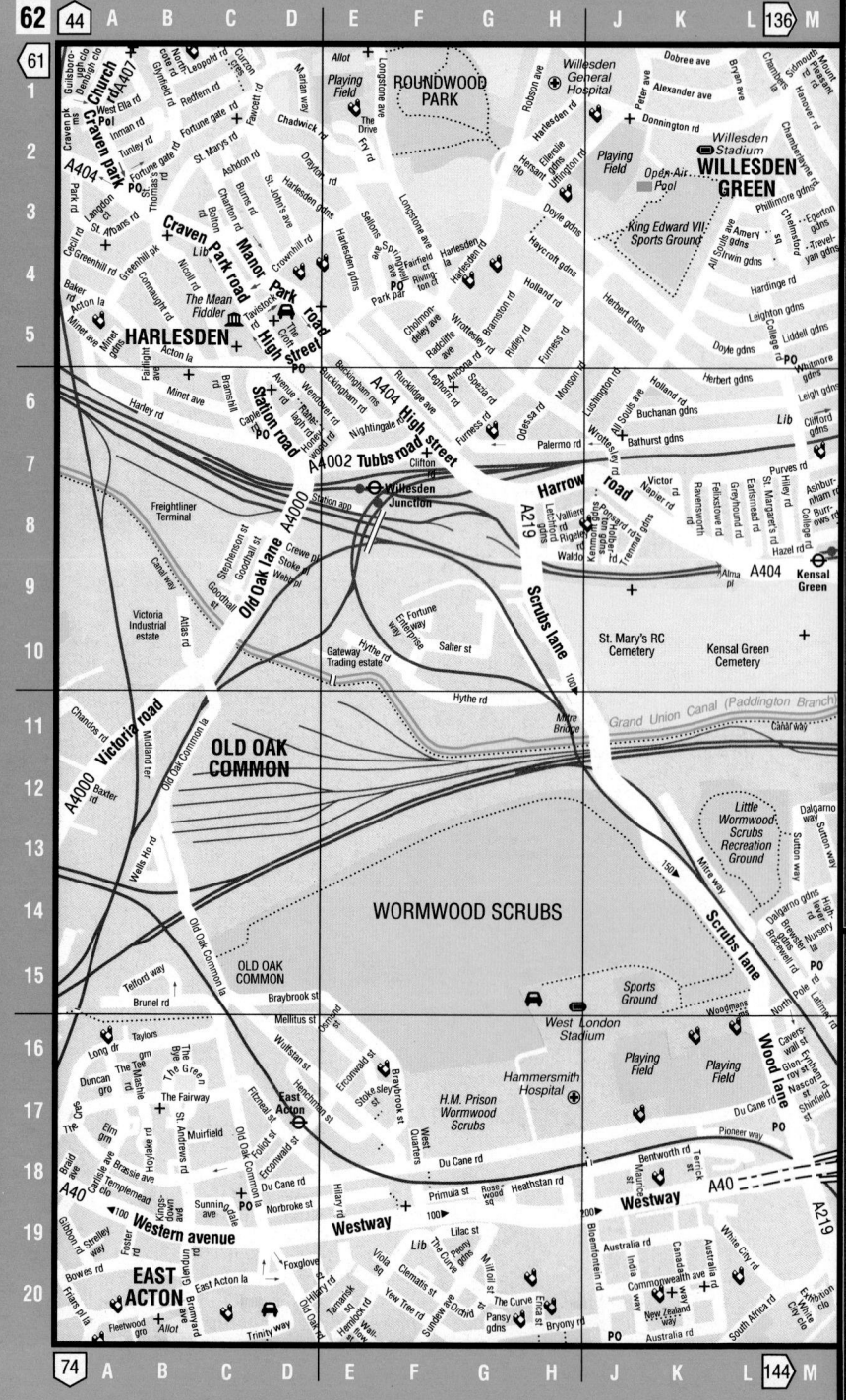

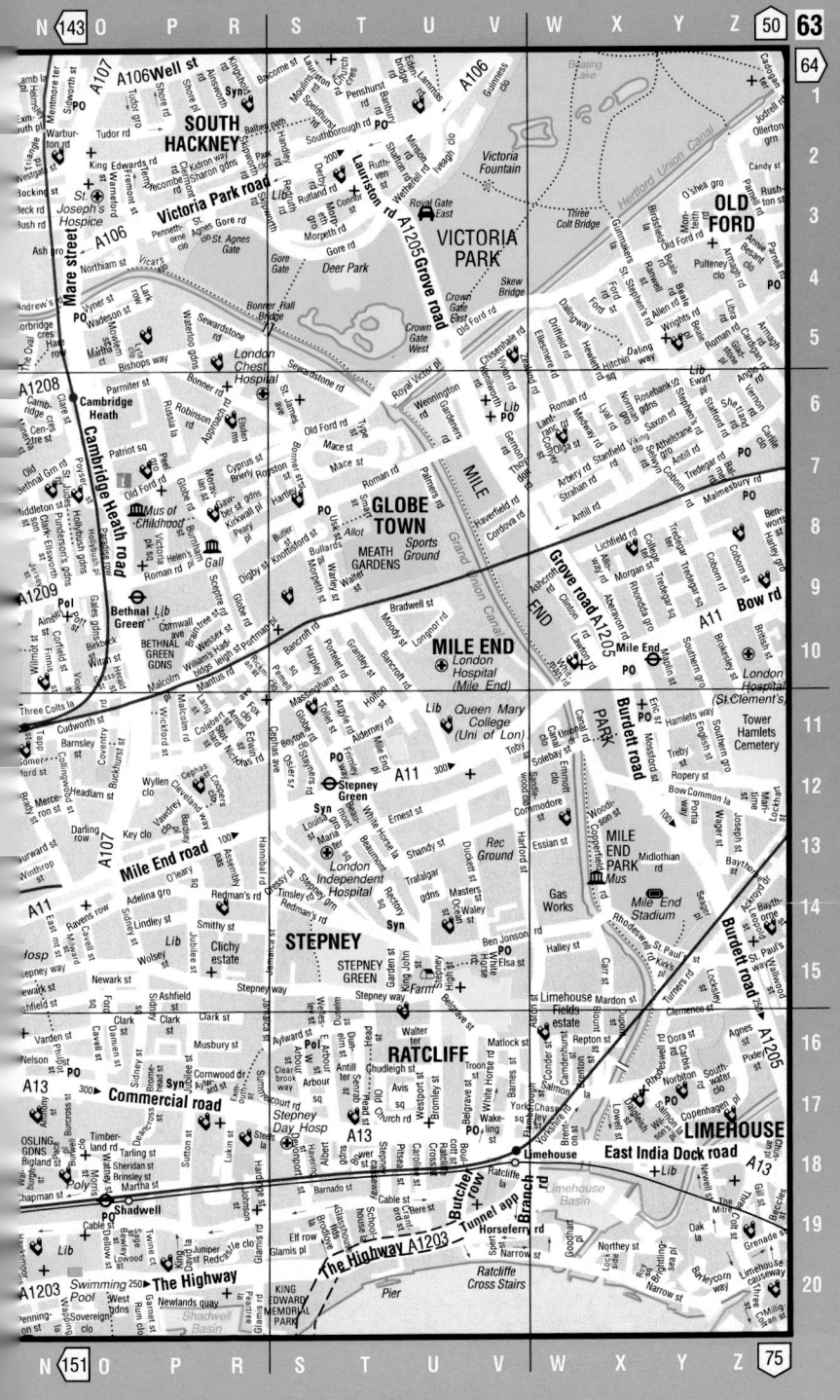

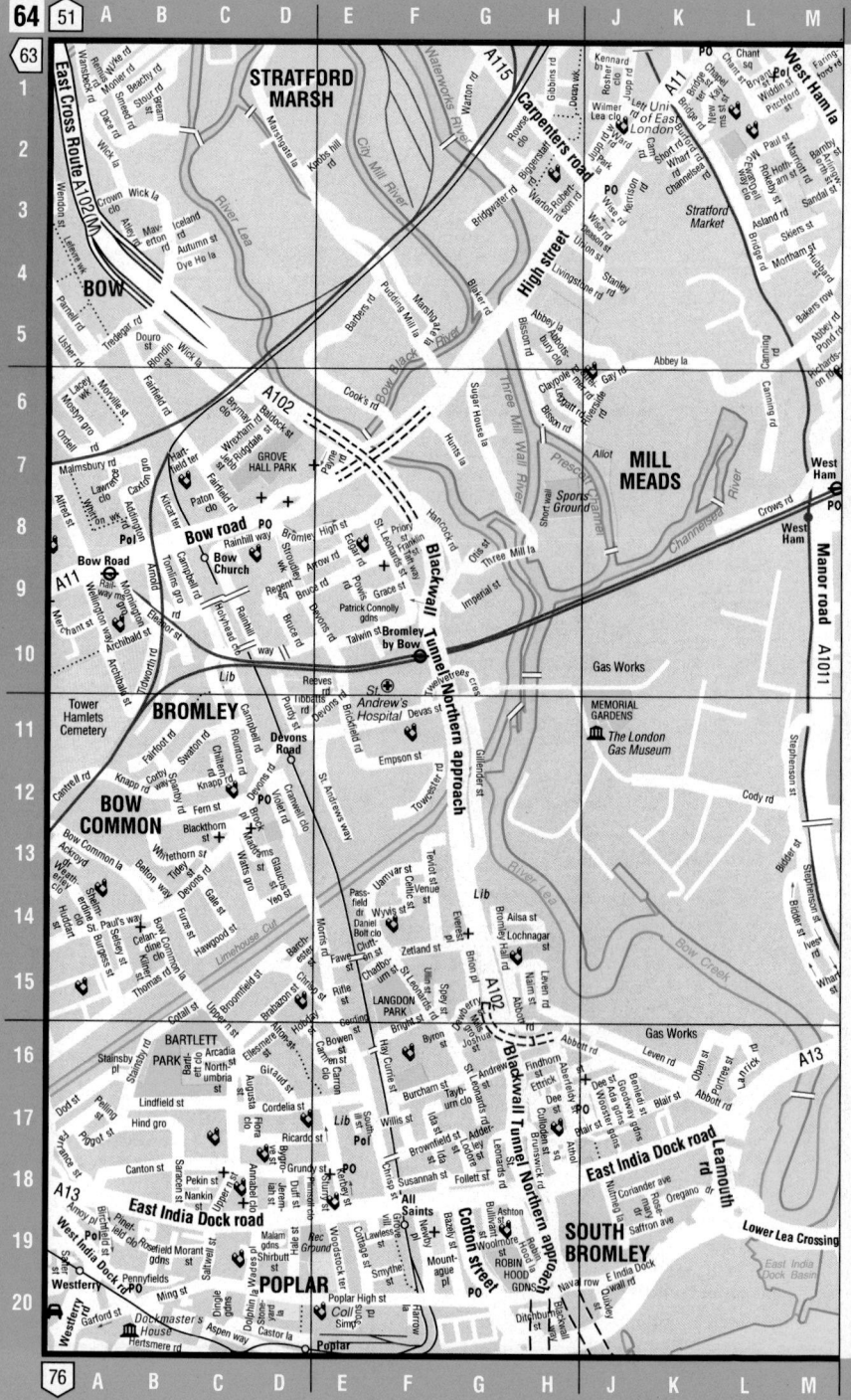

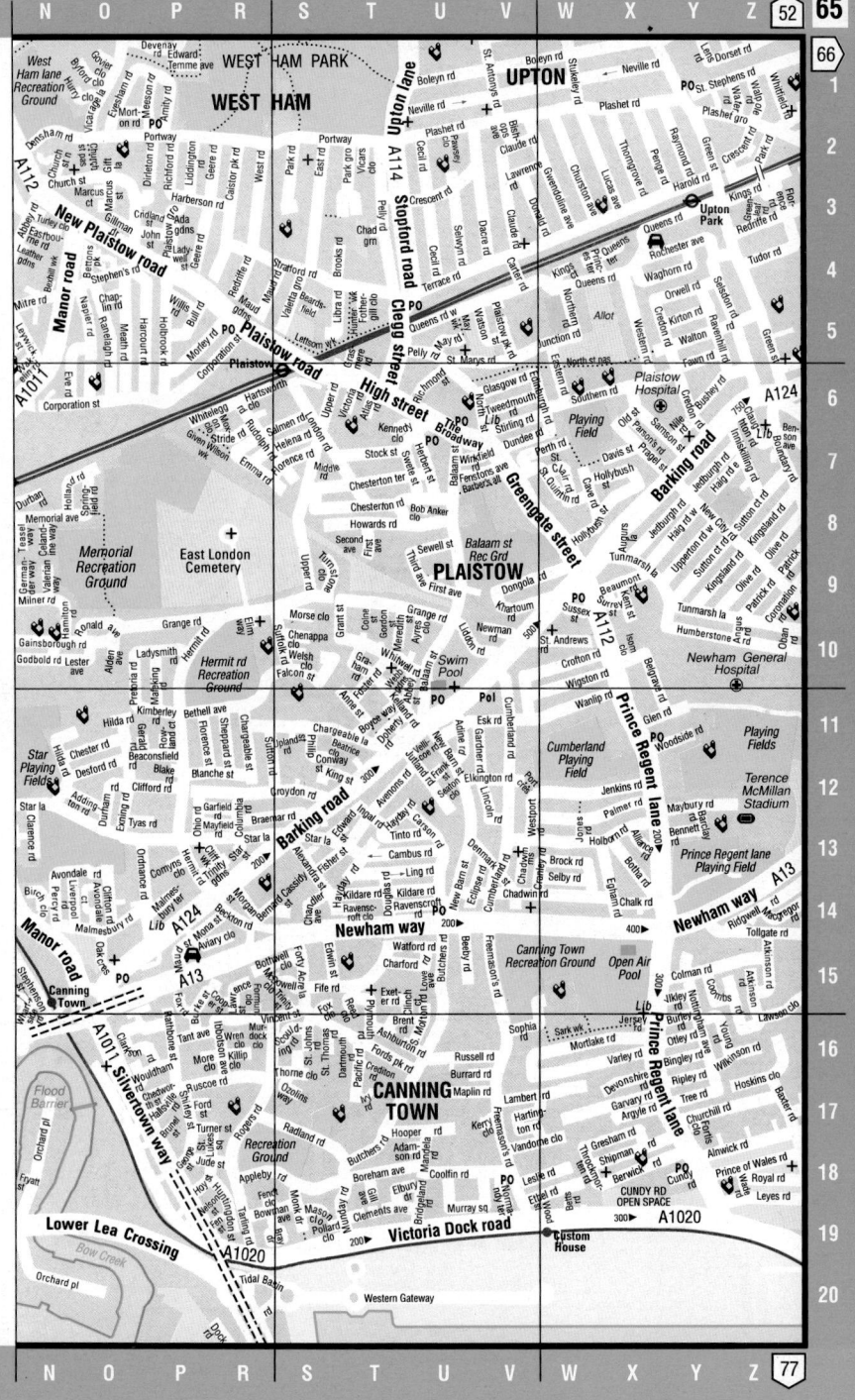

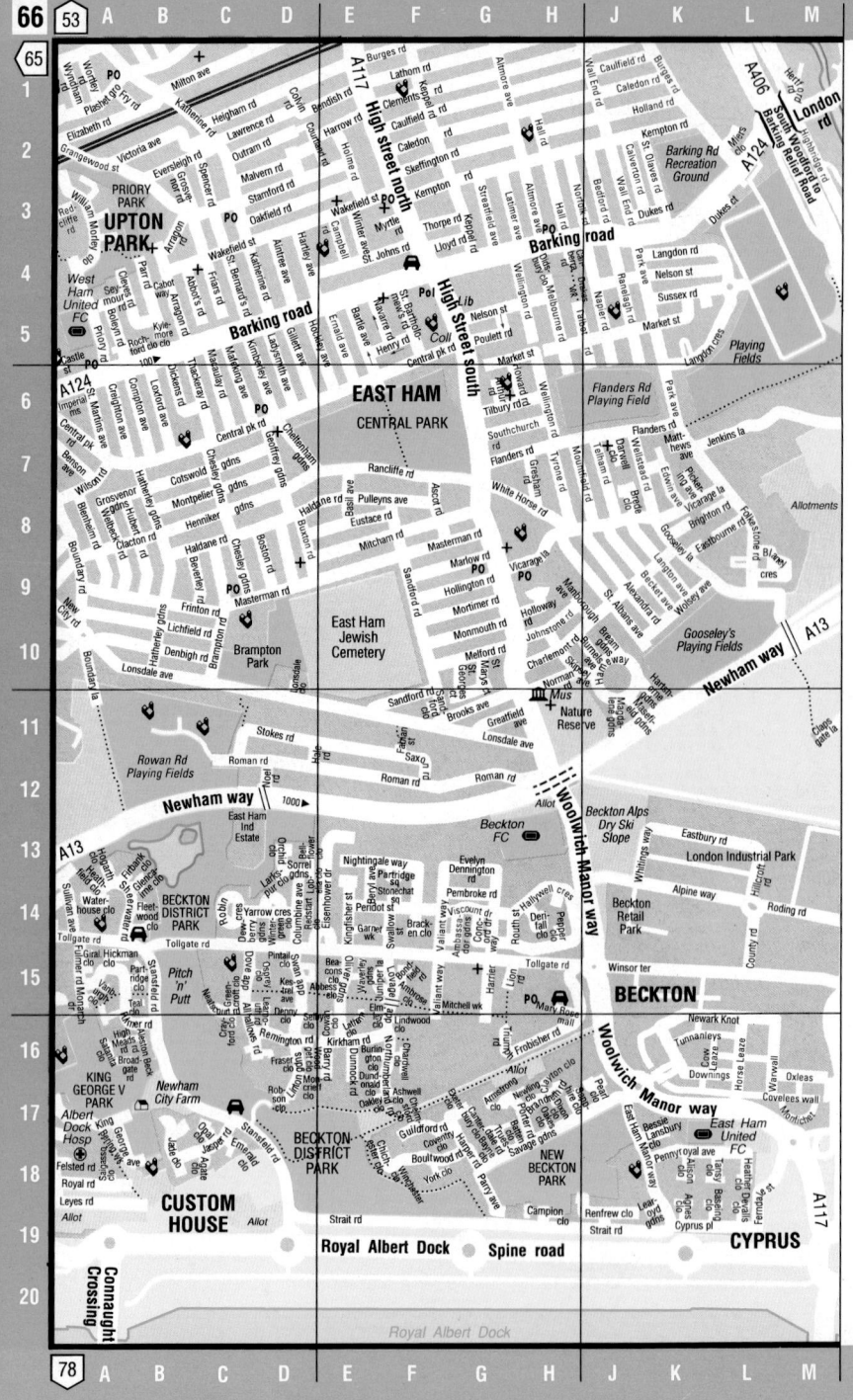

68

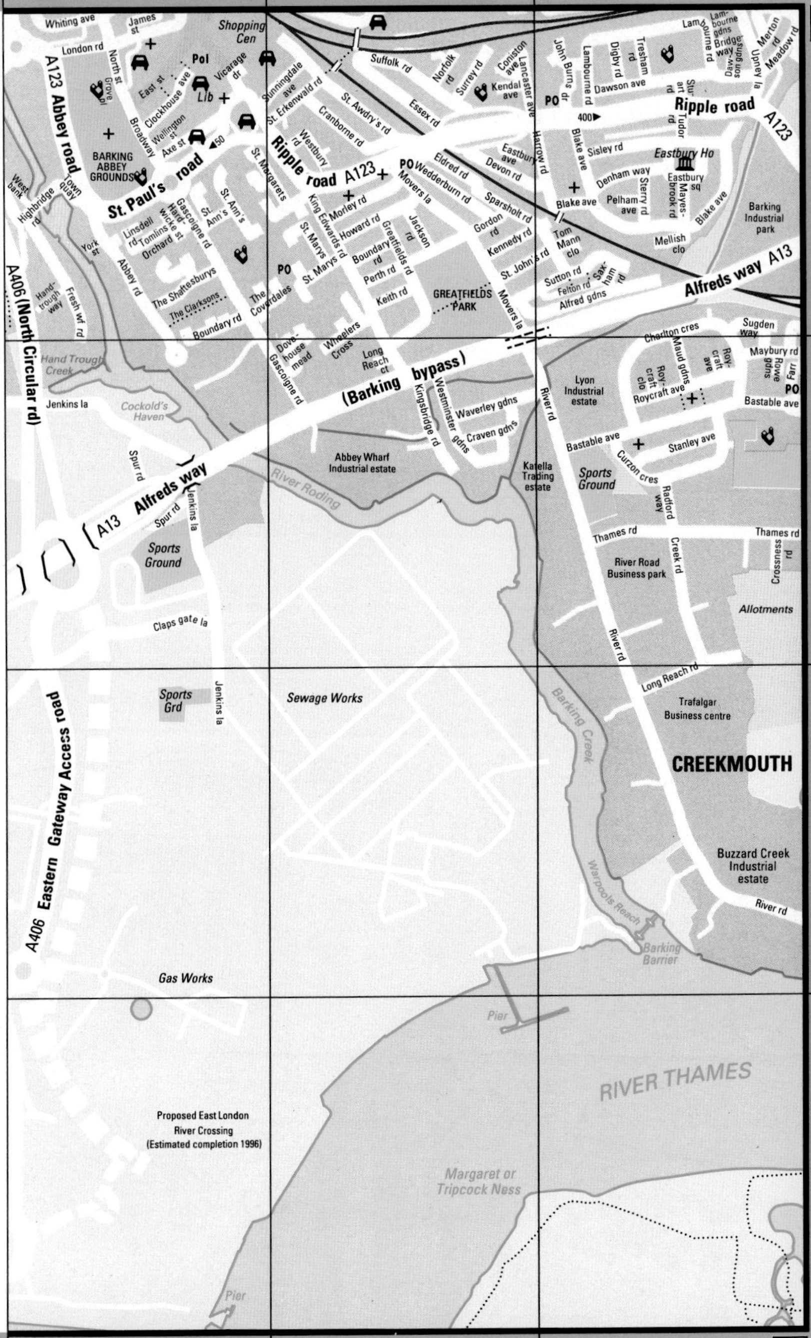
1
2
3
4
5
6
7
8
9
10
11
12
13
14
15
16
17
18
19
20
Whiting ave
James st
Shopping Cen
London rd
Pol
Lib
A123 Abbey road
North st
Grove pl
East st
Clockhouse ave
Vicarage dr
Wellington st
Broadway
Axe st
50
BARKING ABBEY GROUNDS
St. Paul's road
West bank
Town quay
Highbridge rd
York st
Linsdell rd
Tomlins Orchard
Hardwicke st
Gascoigne rd
St. Ann's
St. Ann's
St. Margarets
Abbey rd
The Shaftesburys
The Clarksons
The Coverdales
Boundary rd
A406 (North Circular rd)
Hand-trough way
Fresh wf rd
Sunningdale ave
St. Erkenwald rd
Cranborne rd
St. Awdry's rd
Westbury rd
Ripple road A123
King Edwards rd
Morley rd
St. Marys
St. Marys
Howard rd
Boundary rd
Perth rd
Greatfields rd
Jackson rd
Keith rd
PO
GREATFIELDS PARK
Suffolk rd
Essex rd
Norfolk rd
Surrey rd
Coniston ave
Kendal ave
Lancaster ave
PO
Wedderburn rd
Movers la
Eldred rd
Devon rd
Eastbury ave
Sparsholt rd
Gordon rd
Kennedy rd
St. John's rd
Movers la
Harrow rd
John Burns dr
Lambourne rd
Digby rd
Tresham rd
Lambourne rd
Lambourne gdns
Bridge way
Upney la
Merton rd
Meadow rd
Dawson ave
Sturt rd
Tudor rd
Ripple road
A123
PO
400
Blake ave
Sisley rd
Eastbury Ho
Denham way
Sterry rd
Pelham ave
Eastbury sq
Mayesbrook rd
Blake ave
Blake ave
Barking Industrial park
Tom Mann clo
Mellish clo
Sutton rd
Saxham rd
Felton rd
Alfred gdns
Alfreds way A13
Sugden way
Charlton cres
Maud gdns
Roycraft ave
Roycraft clo
Roycraft ave
Maybury rd
Rowe gdns
PO
Bastable ave
Hand Trough Creek
Jenkins la
Cockold's Haven
Dovehouse mead
Wheelers Cross
Long Reach ct
Gascoigne rd
(Barking bypass)
Kingsbridge rd
Westminster gdns
Waverley gdns
Craven gdns
River rd
Lyon Industrial estate
Bastable ave
Stanley ave
Curzon cres
Spur rd
Abbey Wharf Industrial estate
Katella Trading estate
Sports Ground
Alfreds way
A13
Spur rd
Jenkins la
River Roding
Radford way
Thames rd
Thames rd
Creek rd
Crossness rd
Sports Ground
River Road Business park
Allotments
Claps gate la
River rd
Long Reach rd
Sports Grd
Jenkins la
Sewage Works
Trafalgar Business centre
Barking Creek
CREEKMOUTH
A406 Eastern Gateway Access road
Buzzard Creek Industrial estate
River rd
Warpools Reach
Barking Barrier
Gas Works
Pier
RIVER THAMES
Proposed East London River Crossing (Estimated completion 1996)
Margaret or Tripcock Ness
Pier

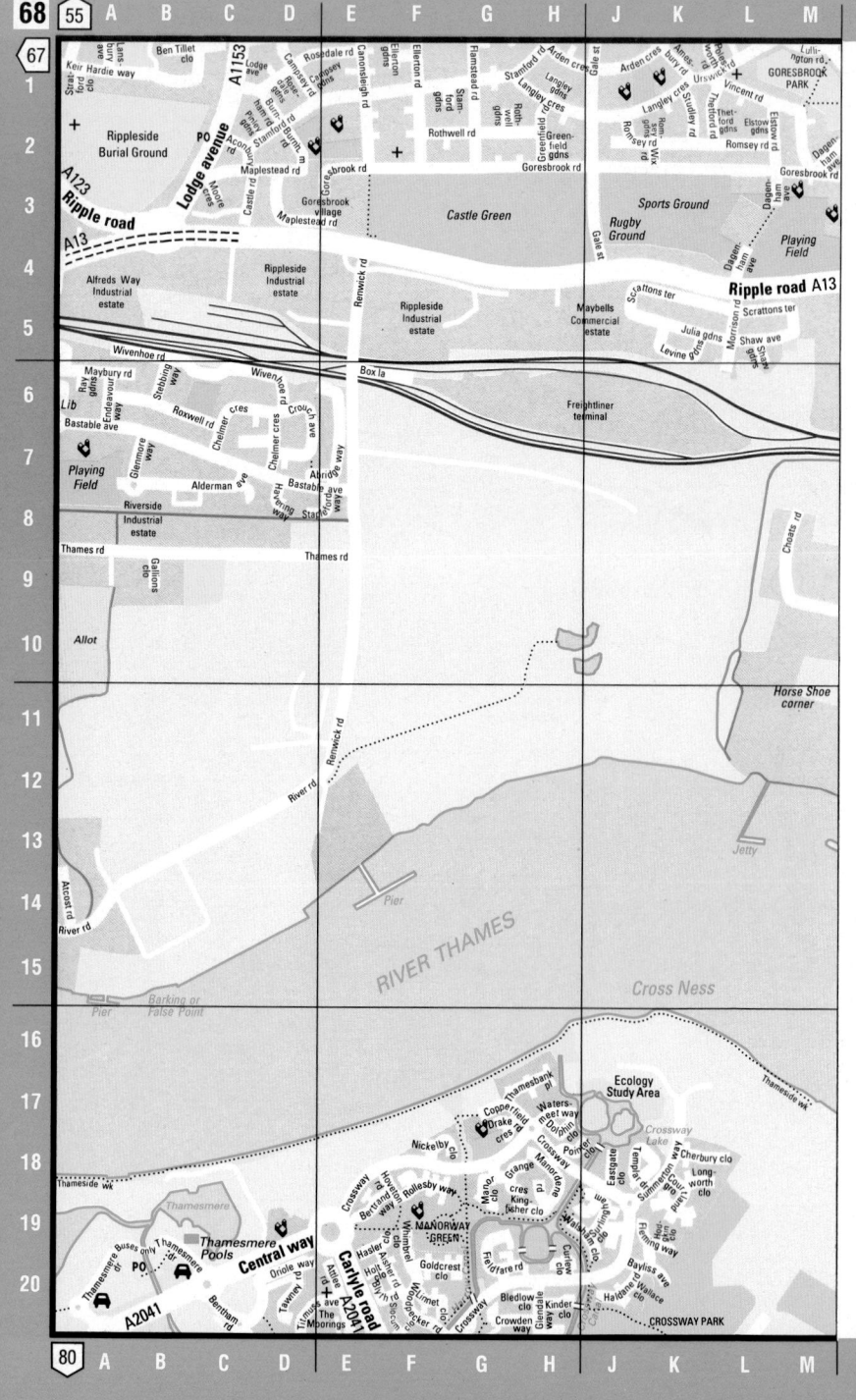

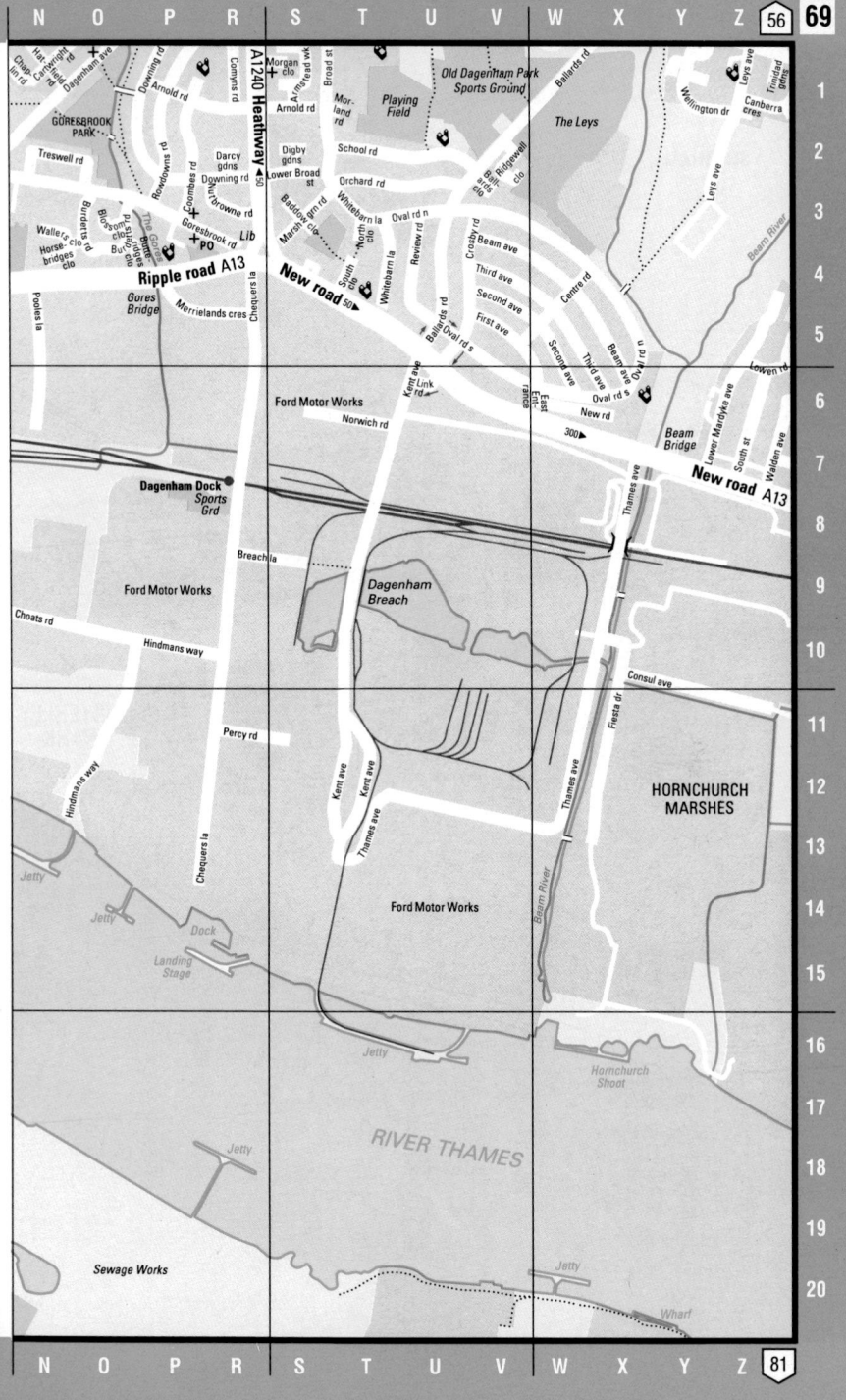

Cranworth rd
Hat
Dege land rd
Dagenham ave
Downing rd
Arnold rd
Comyns rd
Morgan clo
Armstead wk
Broad st
Old Dagenham Park
Sports Ground
Ballards rd
Leys ave
Trinidad gdns
Canberra cres

GORESBROOK PARK
Treswell rd
Rowdowns rd
Darcy gdns
Arnold rd
Morland rd
Playing Field
School rd
The Leys
Wellington dr
Leys ave

A1240 Heathway
Coombes rd
Rowdowns rd
Downing rd
Dbrowne rd
Digby gdns
Lower Broad st
Orchard rd
Whitebarn la
Oval rd n
Ballards clo
Beam Ridgewell clo

Waller rd
Burdetts rd
Blossom clo
The Gores
Bungalows
Butts rd
Goresbrook rd
Lib
Marsh clo
Baddow grn rd
North clo
Review rd
Crosby rd
Beam ave
Third ave

Horse bridges clo
clo
PO
New road
Whitebarn la
Oval rd n
Ballards rd
Oval rd s
Second ave
First ave
Centre rd
Beam ave
Third ave
Oval rd n

Ripple road A13
Gores Bridge
Merrielands cres
Chelsea la
50
Kent ave
Link rd
Second ave
East End
Beam ave
Third ave
Oval rd s
Lowen rd

Pooles la
Ford Motor Works
Norwich rd
300
New rd
New road A13
Beam Bridge
Lower Mardyke ave
South st
Walden ave

Dagenham Dock
Sports Grd
Thames ave
Breach la
Dagenham Breach

Ford Motor Works
Choats rd
Hindmans way
Consul ave
Fiesta dr

Percy rd
Kent ave
Kent ave
Thames ave
HORNCHURCH MARSHES

Hindmans way
Chequers la
Thames ave
Beam River

Ford Motor Works

Jetty
Jetty
Dock
Landing Stage

Jetty
Hornchurch Shoot

Jetty

RIVER THAMES

Sewage Works
Jetty
Wharf

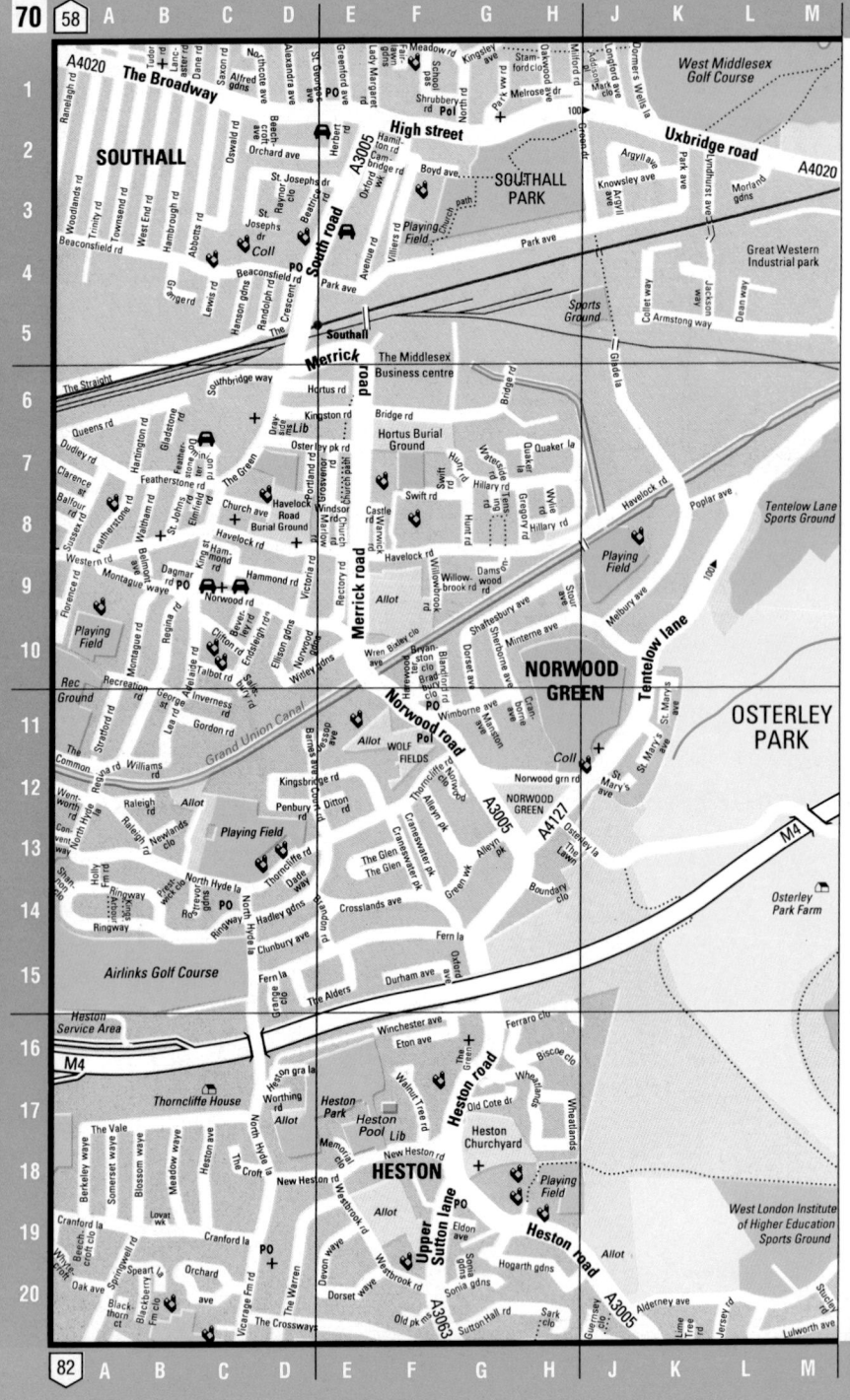

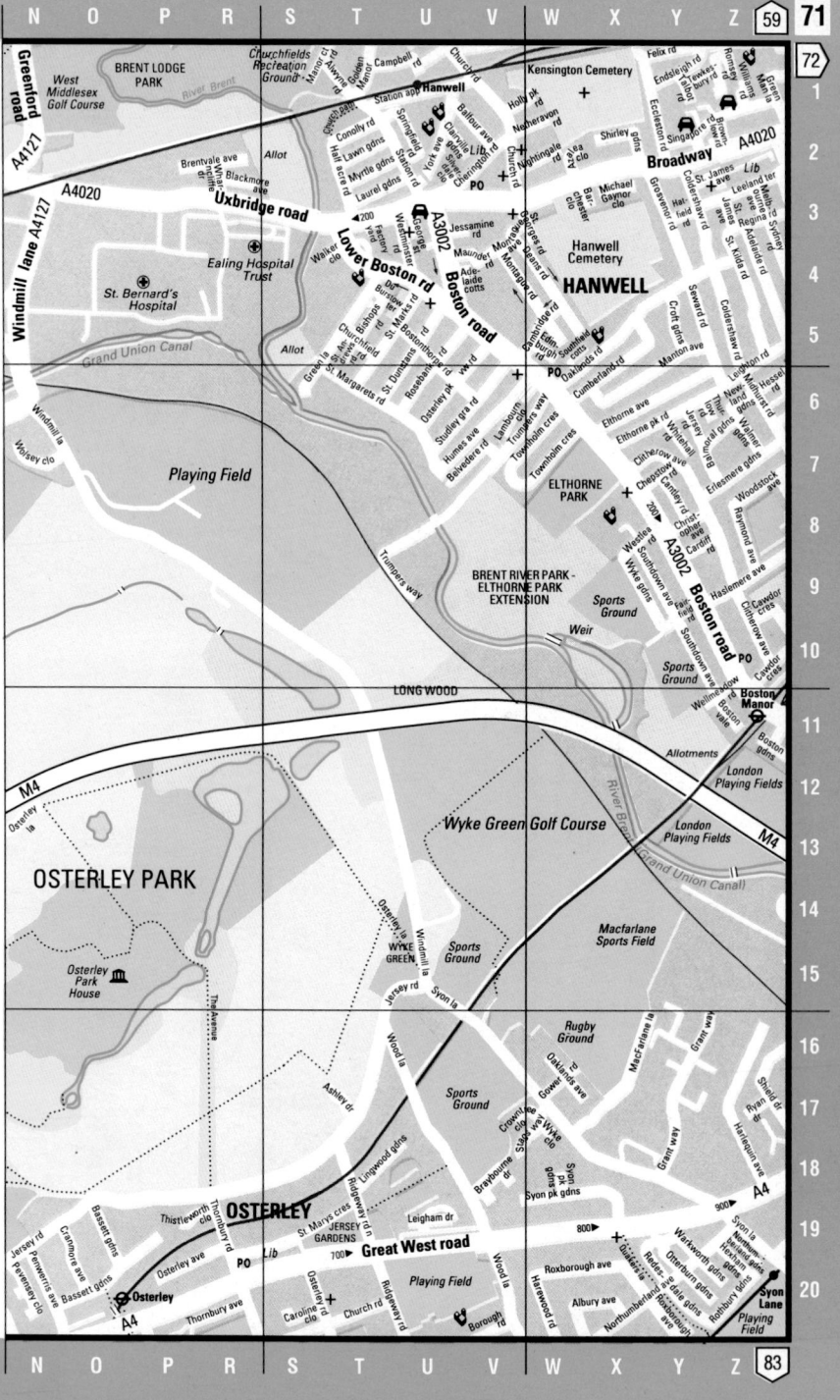

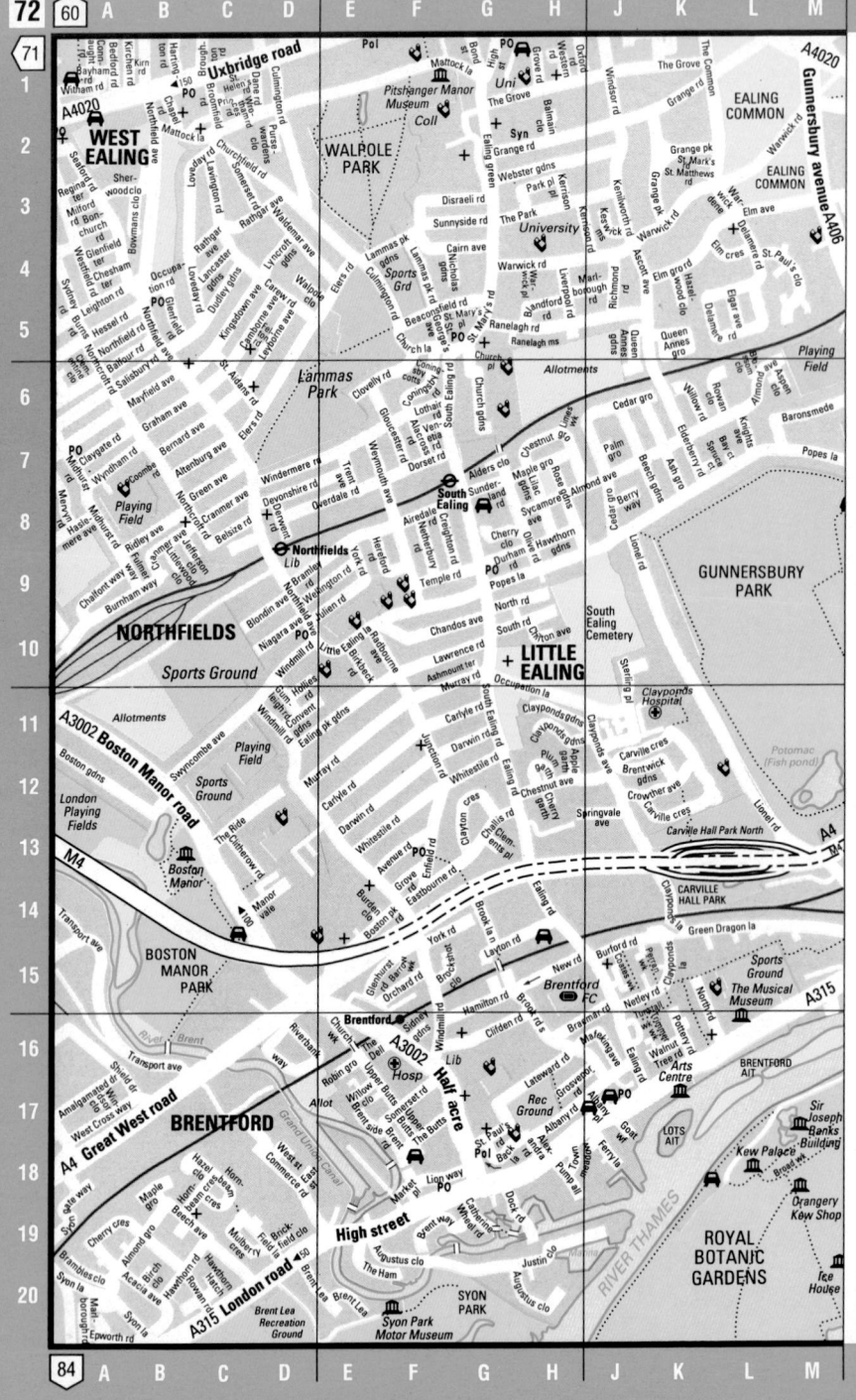

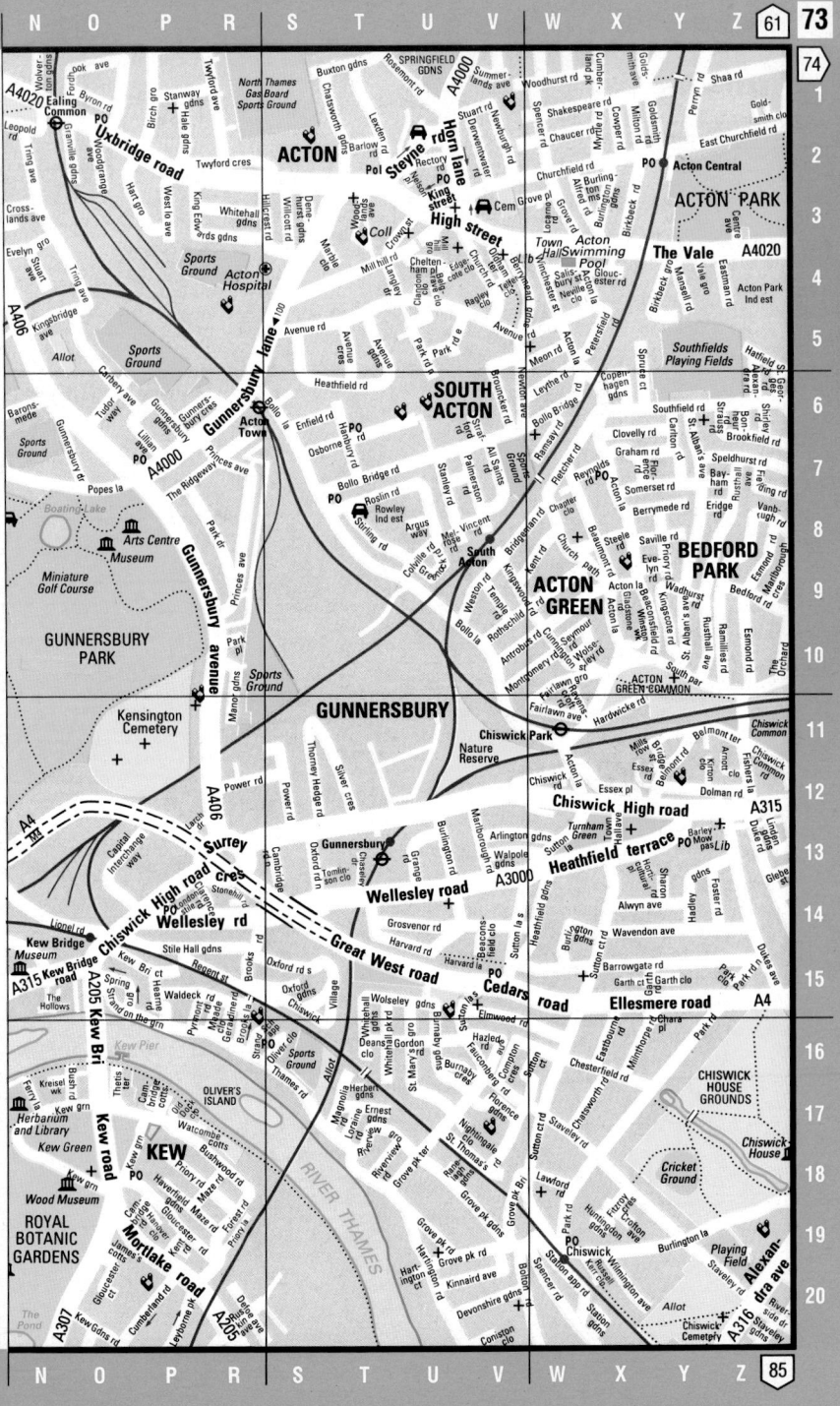

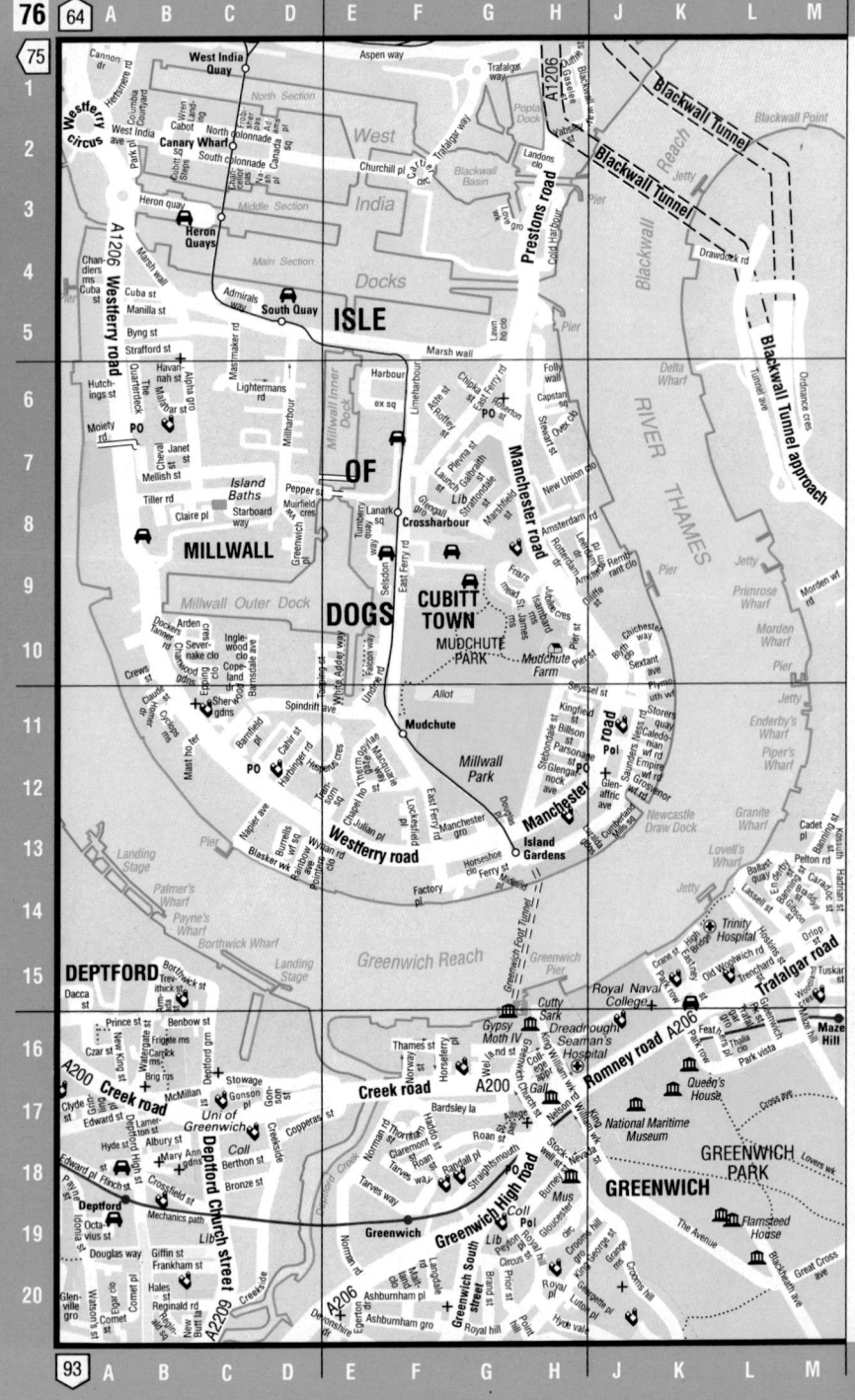

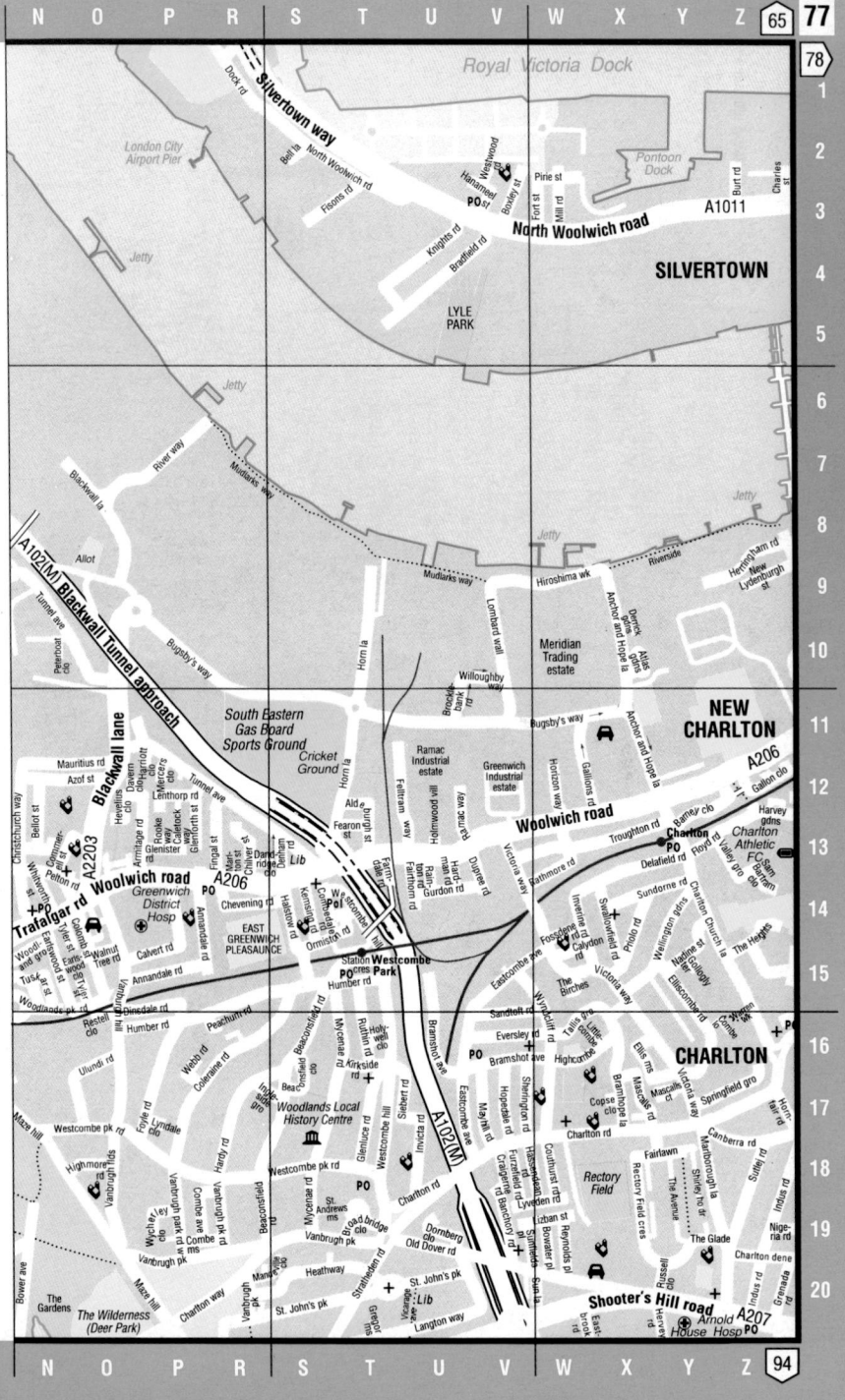

Royal Victoria Dock

1

Pontoon
Dock

2

London City
Airport Pier

Silvertown way

Dock rd

Bell la

North Woolwich rd

Fisons rd

Hanameel st

Pirie st

Westwood

Fort st

Mill rd

Burt rd

Charles st

PO

Blakeley st

3

Jetty

Knights rd

Bradfield rd

North Woolwich road

A1011

SILVERTOWN

4

LYLE
PARK

5

6

Jetty

River way

Mudlarks way

7

Blackwall la

Allot

8

A102(M) Blackwall Tunnel approach

Tunnel ave

Peterston clo

Bugsby's way

Mudlarks way

Hiroshima wk

Jetty

Riverside

Jetty

Henningham rd
New
Lydenburgh st

9

Horn la

Brockle-
bank rd

Willoughby
way

Derrick
gdns
Atlas
gdns

Anchor and Hope la

Meridian
Trading
estate

10

South Eastern
Gas Board
Sports Ground

Cricket
Ground

Horn la

Ramac
Industrial
estate

Feathers
pl

Greenwich
Industrial
estate

Bugsby's way

Horizon way

Anchor and Hope la

Gallions rd

**NEW
CHARLTON**

A206

Gallion clo

11

Blackwall lane

Mauritius rd

Azof st

Hevelius
clo

Dawen clo

Mercers clo

Marriott clo

Lenthorp rd

Tunnel ave

Woolwich road

Ald...burgh st

Fearon st

Fathom way

Hollowmount

Rain-
ton rd

Harding-
man rd

Dupree rd

Victoria way

Woolwich road

Troughton rd

Barney clo

Floyd rd

Harvey
gdns

**Charlton
Athletic
FC**

12

Christchurch way

Bellot st

Pelton rd

A2203

Armitage rd

Rooke
way

Brooke way

Glenister rd

Glenforth st

Fingal st

Denham
st

Mauritius
clo

David
Lib

Dares
rd

Farm-
dale rd

Kemsing rd

Westmoor st

Farm-
dale rd

Gurdon rd

Bathmore rd

Inverine rd

Charlton
PO

Delafield rd

Sundorne rd

Wellington gdns

Charlton Church la

Maryon rd

The Heights

13

Woolwich road

Trafalgar rd

A2203

Greenwich
District
Hosp

Chevening rd

Calvert rd

Annandale rd

EAST
GREENWICH
PLEASAUNCE

Ormiston rd

Vanbrugh
hill

Fossdene rd

Swallowfield rd

Pound
clo

Calydon
rd

Victoria way

Elliscombe rd

Combedale rd

Wyndcliff
rd

14

Woodlands
PO

Tusk ...
wood

Walnut
Tree rd

Humber rd

**Westcombe
Park**

PO cres

Station

Humber rd

The
Birches

Eastcombe ave

15

Restell
clo

Humber rd

Peachum rd

Dinsdale rd

Sandtoft rd

Wyndcliff rd

Falls gro

Wenlock
ter

Wyberton
ter

CHARLTON

16

Ulundi rd

Westcombe pk rd

Webb rd

Coleraine rd

Beaconsfield rd

Mycenae rd

Ruthin clo

Holly-
well clo

Kirkside
rd

Beaconfield

PO

Eversley rd

Bramshot ave

Highcombe

Shrimpton
...

Shirington rd

Braembope la

Hopedale rd

Mascalls rd

Highcombe

Copse clo

Charlton rd

Ellis me

Victoria way

Springfield gro

Hornfair rd

17

Maze hill

Highmore
rd

Vanbrugh flds

Foyle rd

Lyndale ave

Hardy rd

Westcombe pk rd

Glenluce rd

Siebert rd

Invicta rd

A102(M)

Charlton rd

Eastcombe ave

Sherington rd

Coulhurst rd

Fairlawn

Rectory Field cres

The Avenue

Shirley ho st

Marlborough la

Canberra rd

Sutlej rd

18

Wychely
clo

Combedale
rd

Combe
ave

Beaconfield

St
Andrews
ms

Broad
bridge

Woodlands Local
History Centre

PO

Charlton rd

Furzefield rd

Craigdale rd

Lyveden rd

Slumbridge
rd

Bowater pl

Bankhurst rd

Lizban st

**Rectory
Field**

Reynolds pl

Nigeria rd

19

The
Gardens

Bower ave

Maze hill

Charlton way

Vanbrugh pk

St. John's pk

Heathway

Mangrove
way

Vanbrugh pk

Strathbeden rd

St. John's pk

Dornberg
clo

Old Dover rd

Russell pl

Indus rd

The Glade

Charlton dene

Granada rd

20

*The Wilderness
(Deer Park)*

Vanbrugh
pk

Vicarage
way

:Lib

St. John's pk

Langton way

Shooter's Hill road

East
brook rd

Hervey rd

Arnold
House Hosp

A207

PO

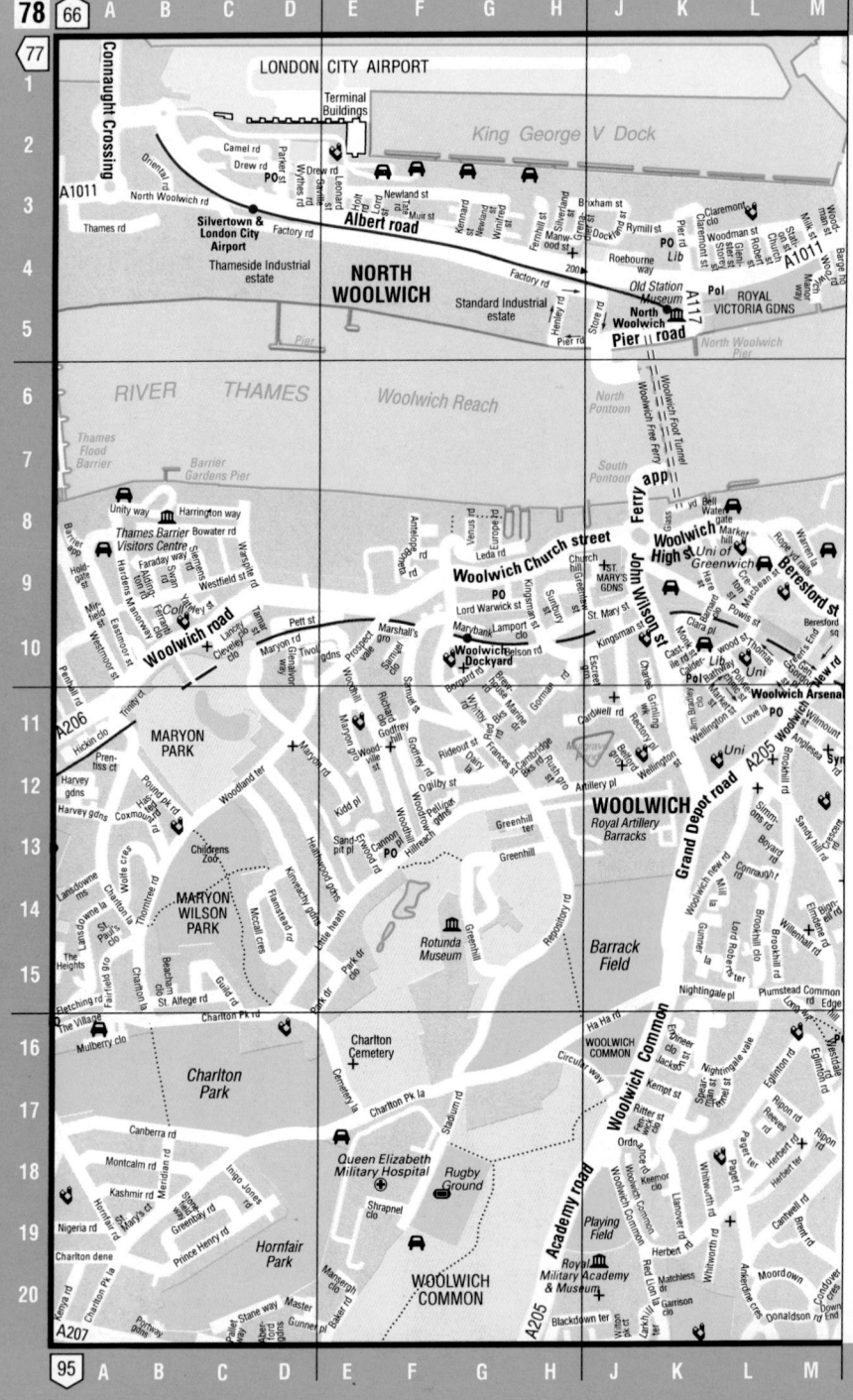

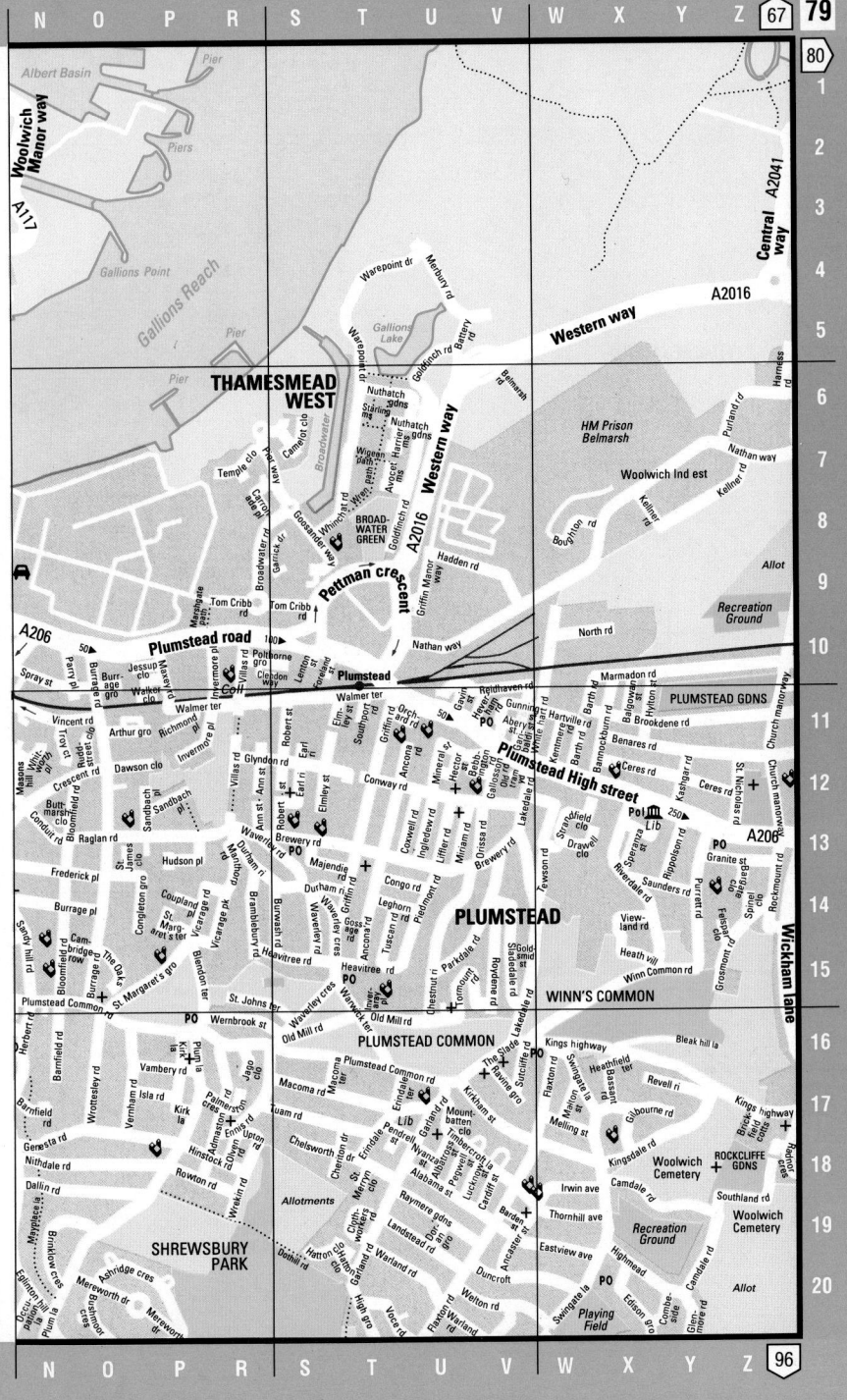

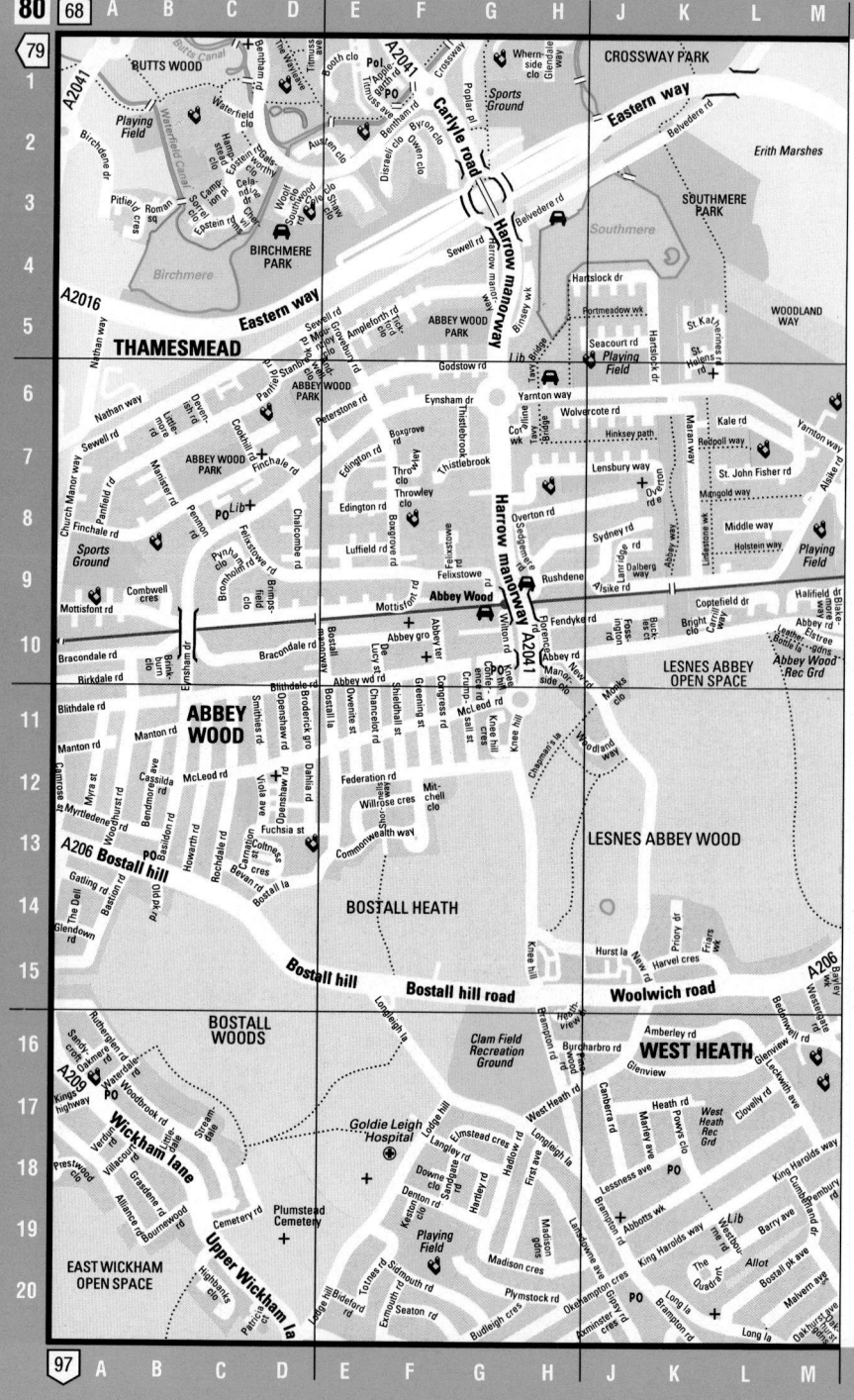

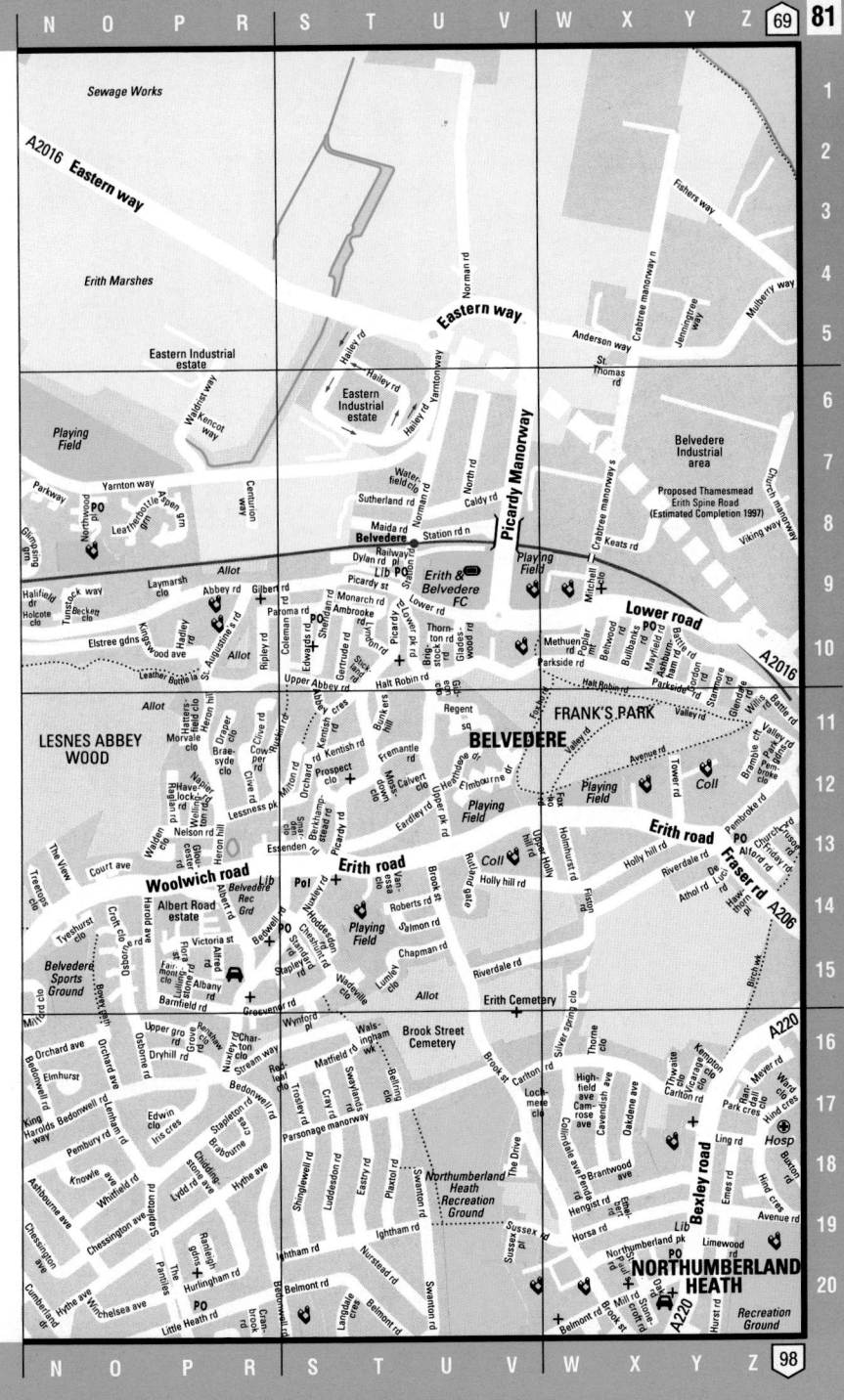

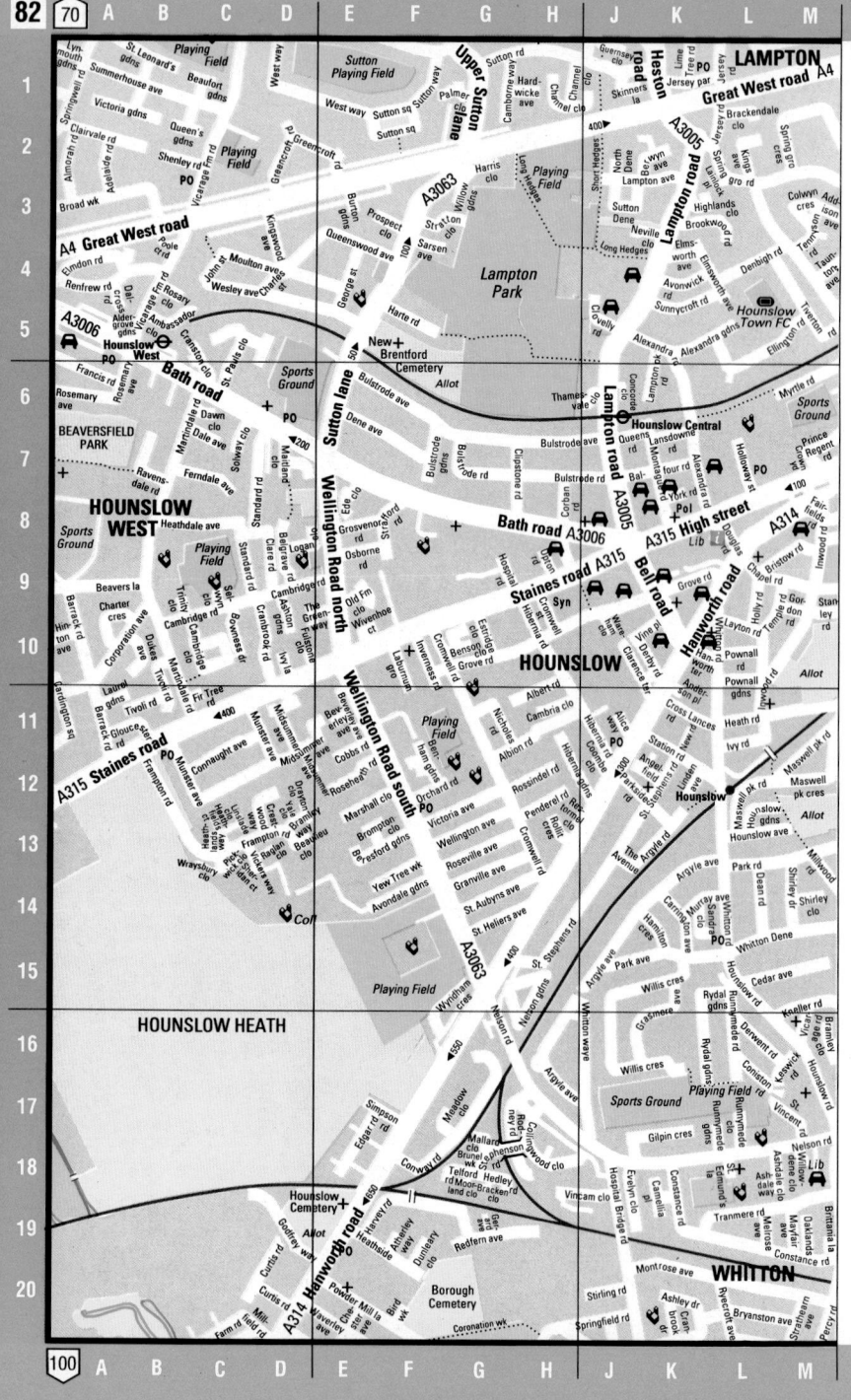

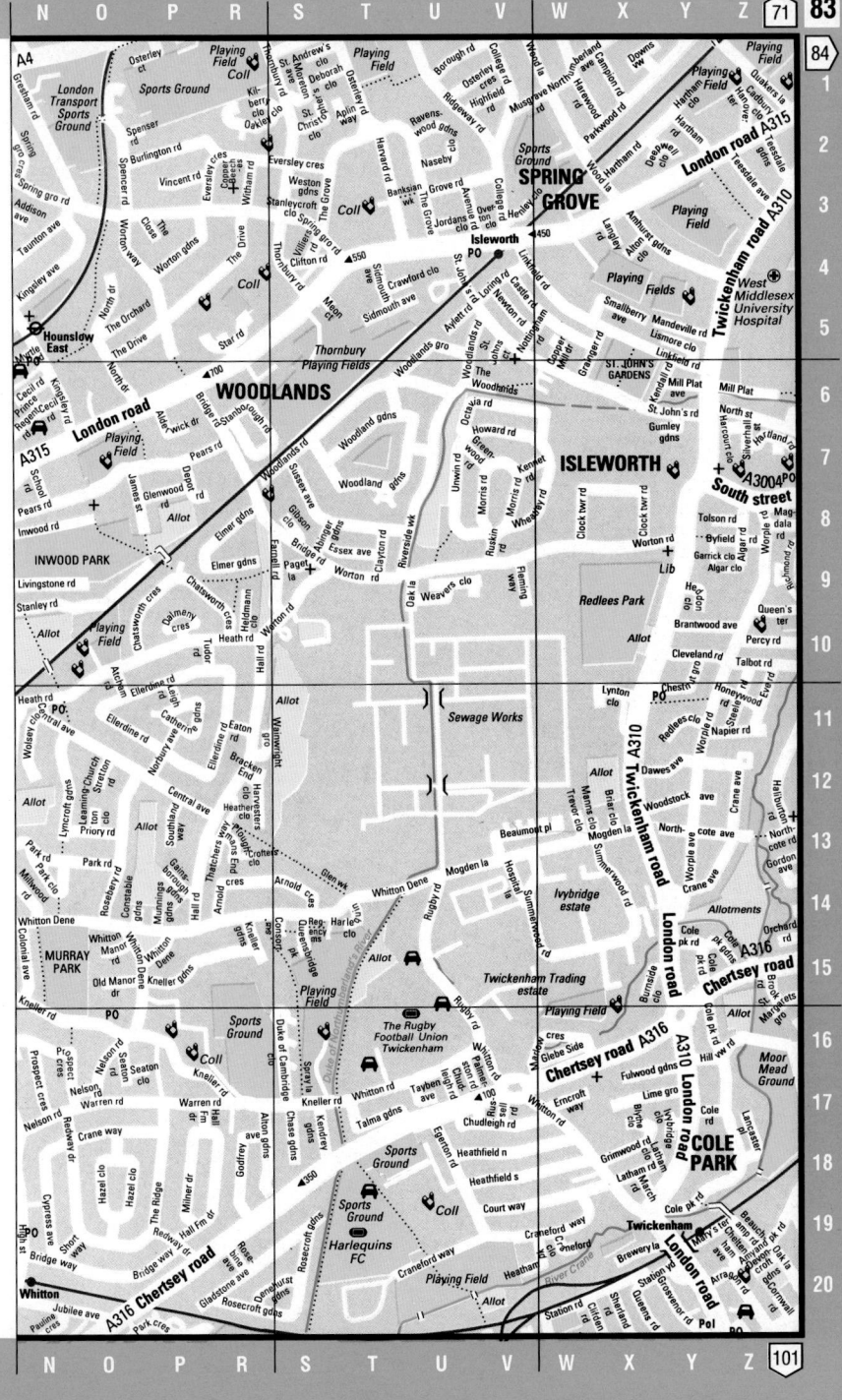

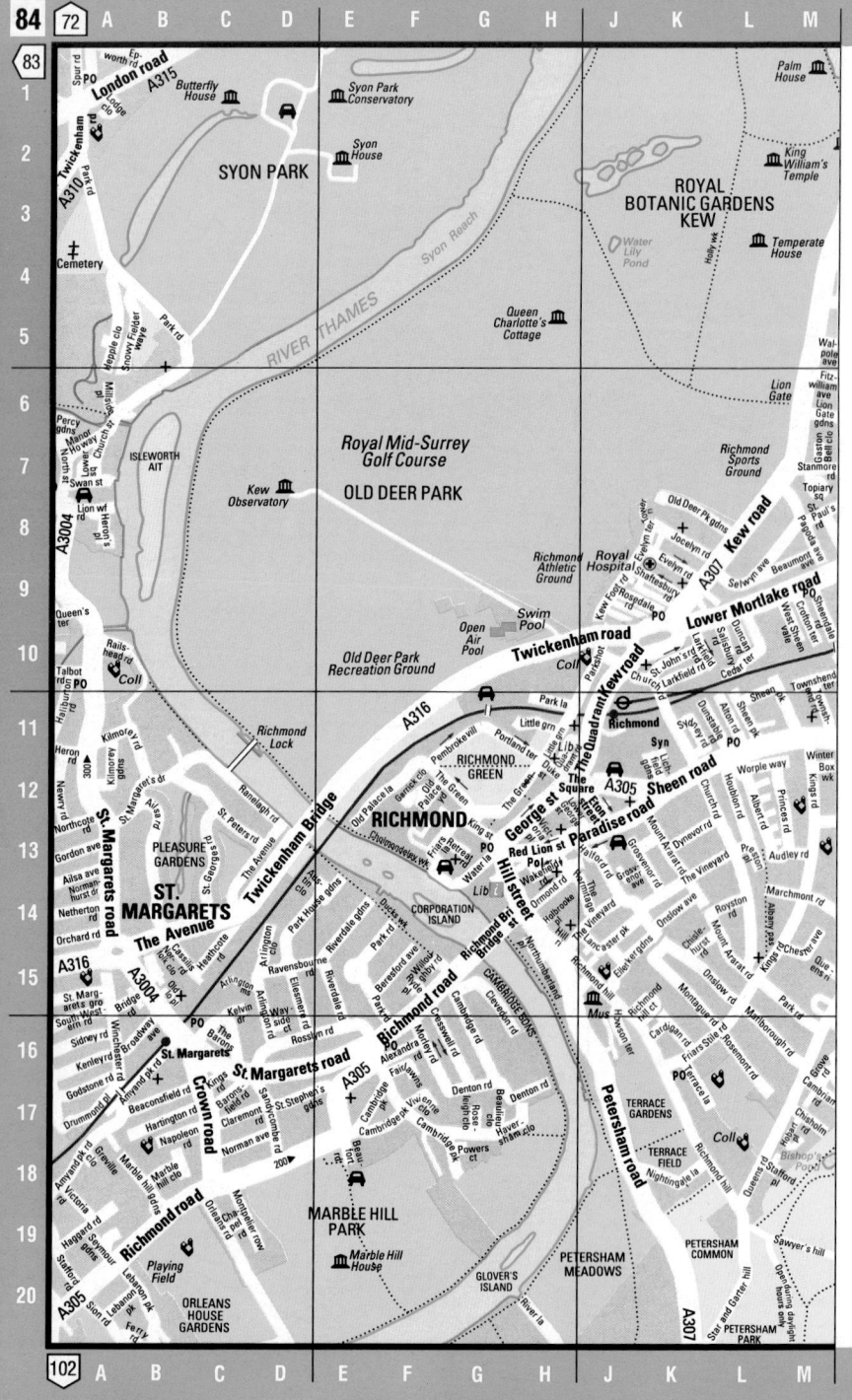

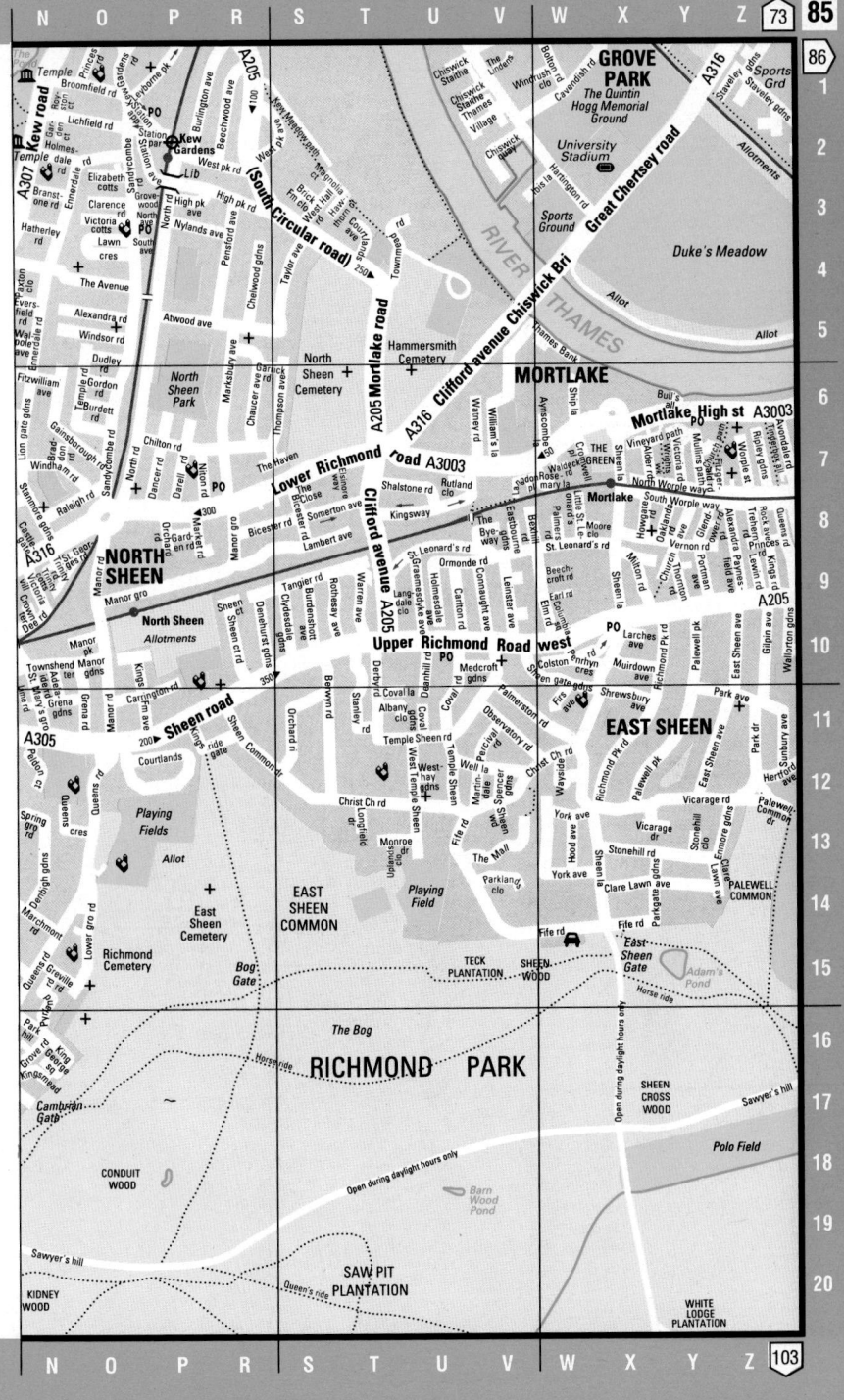

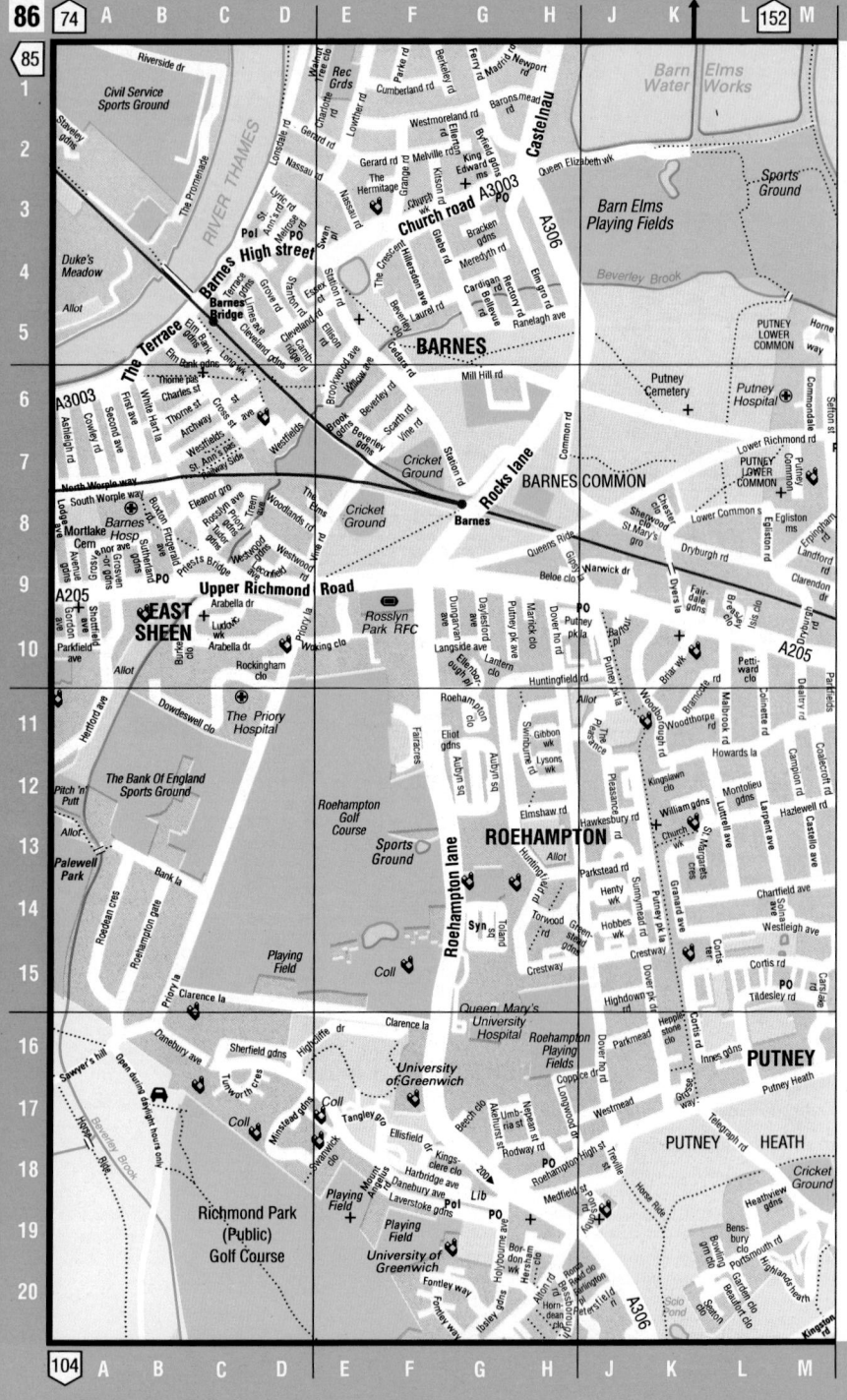

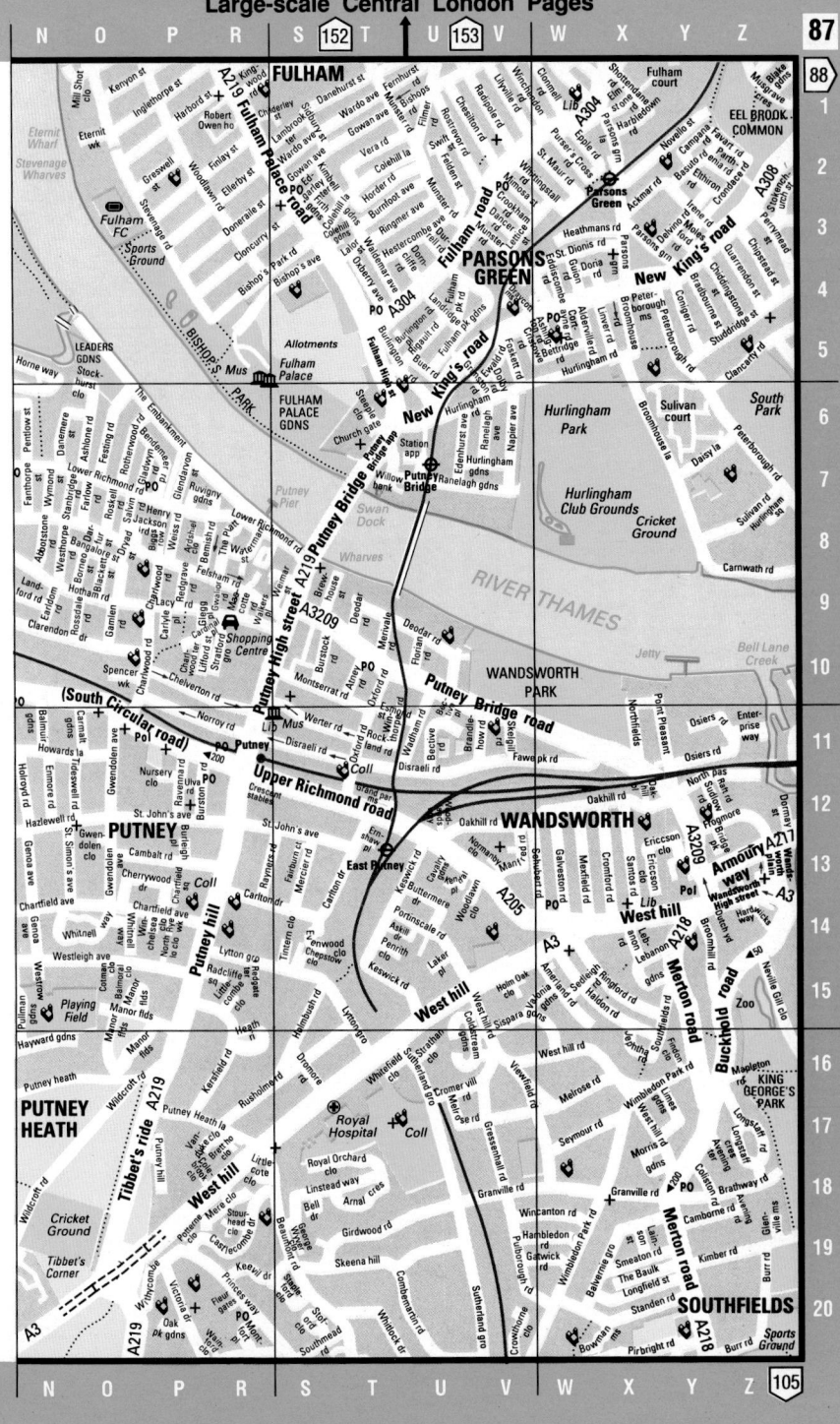

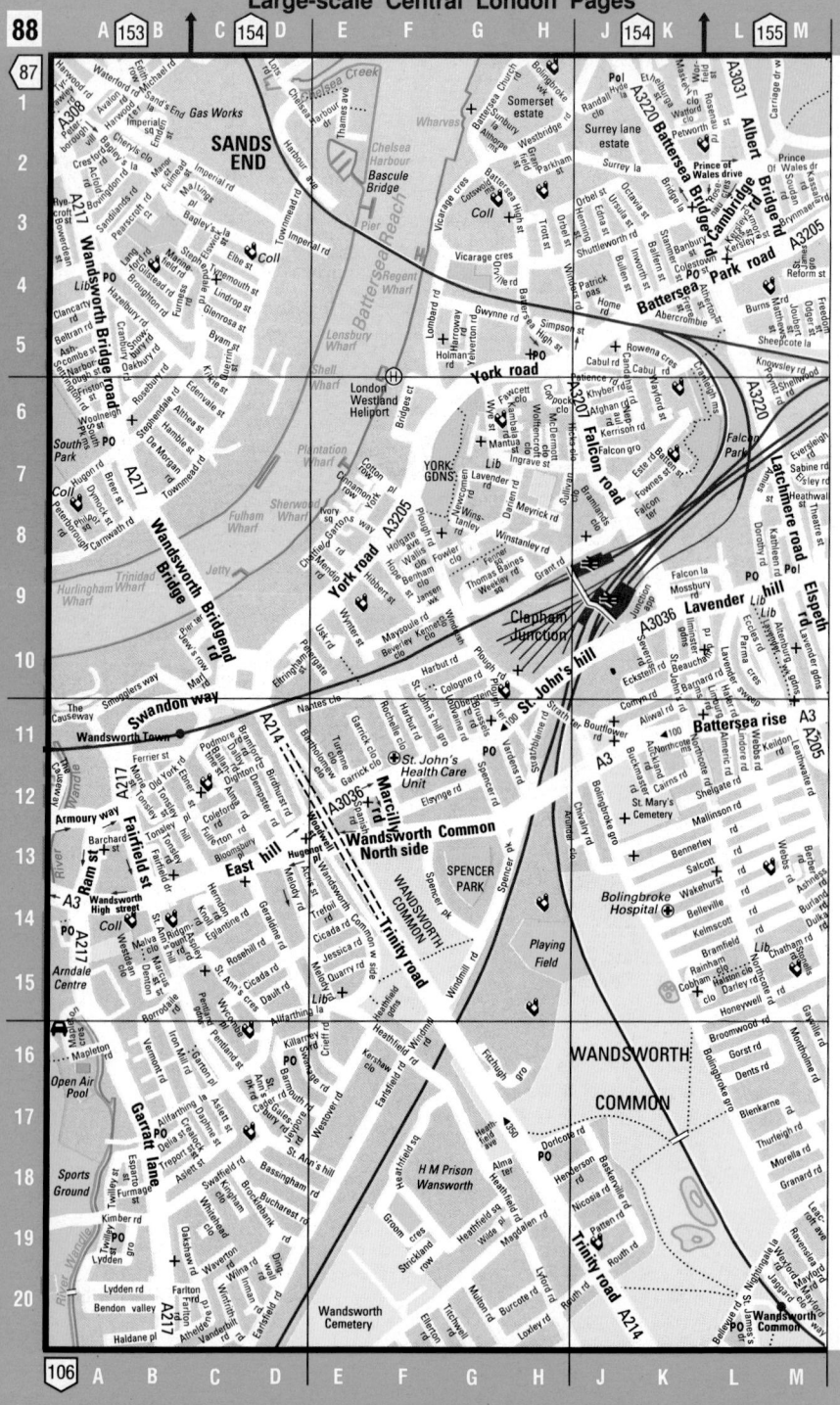

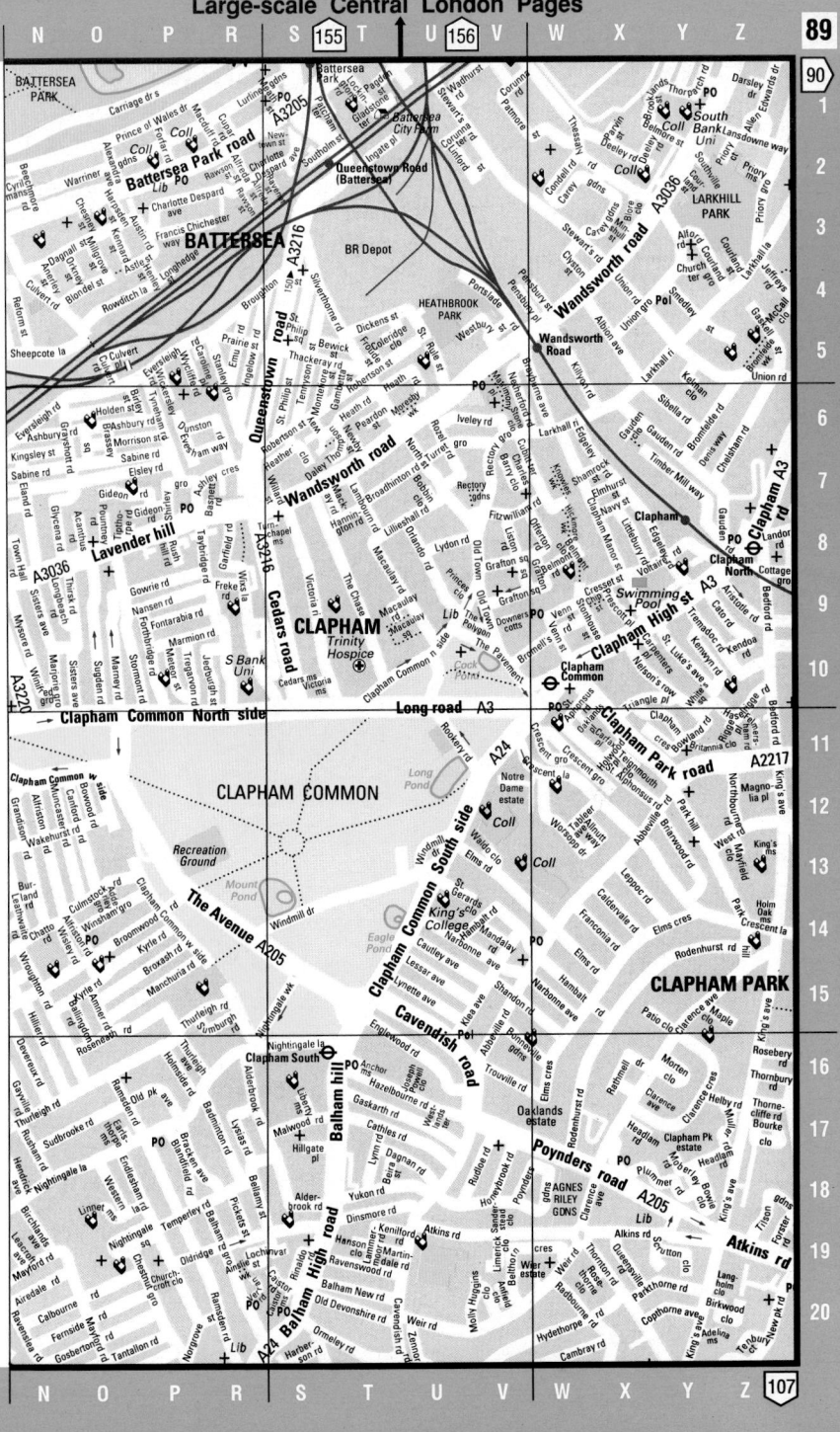

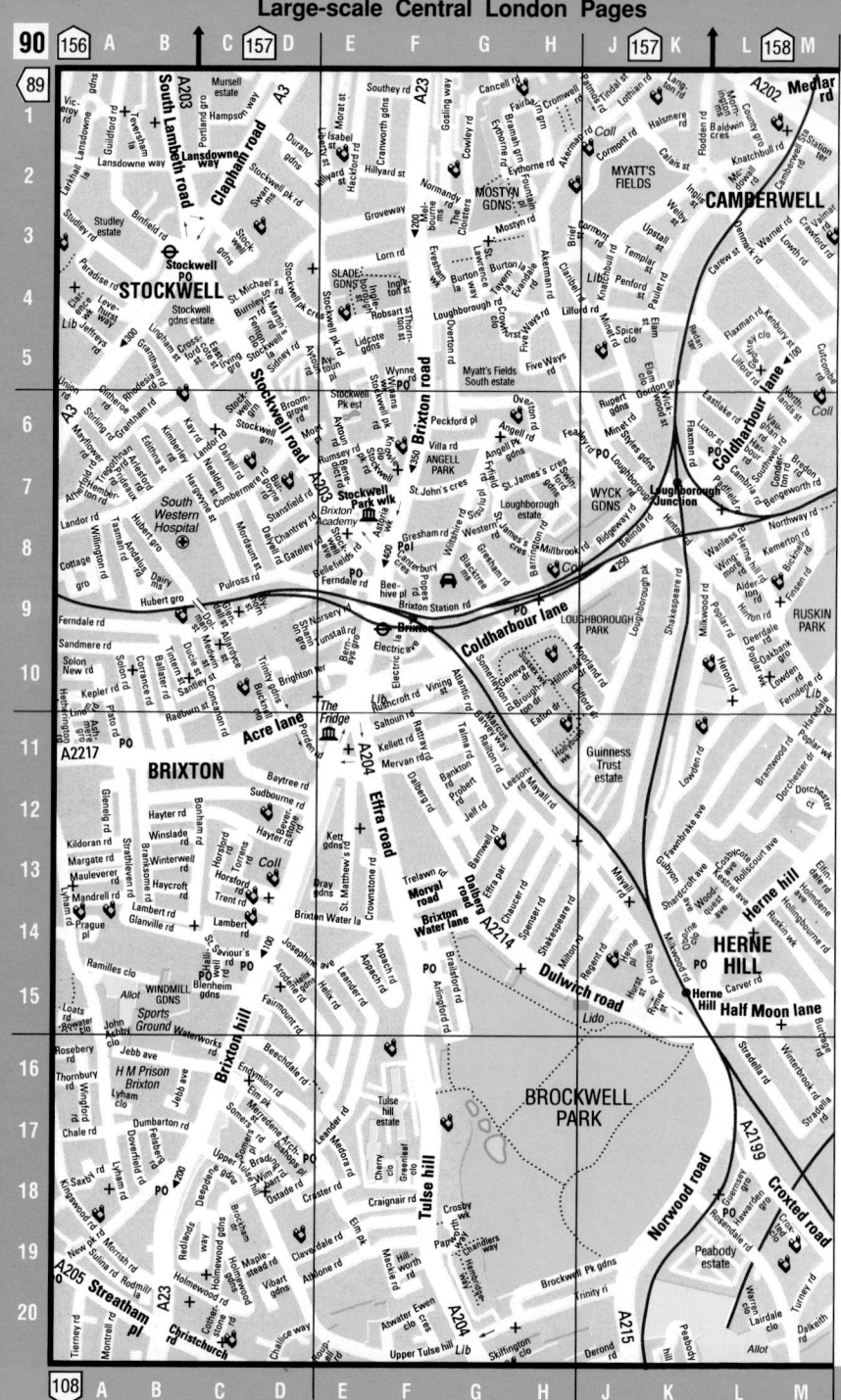

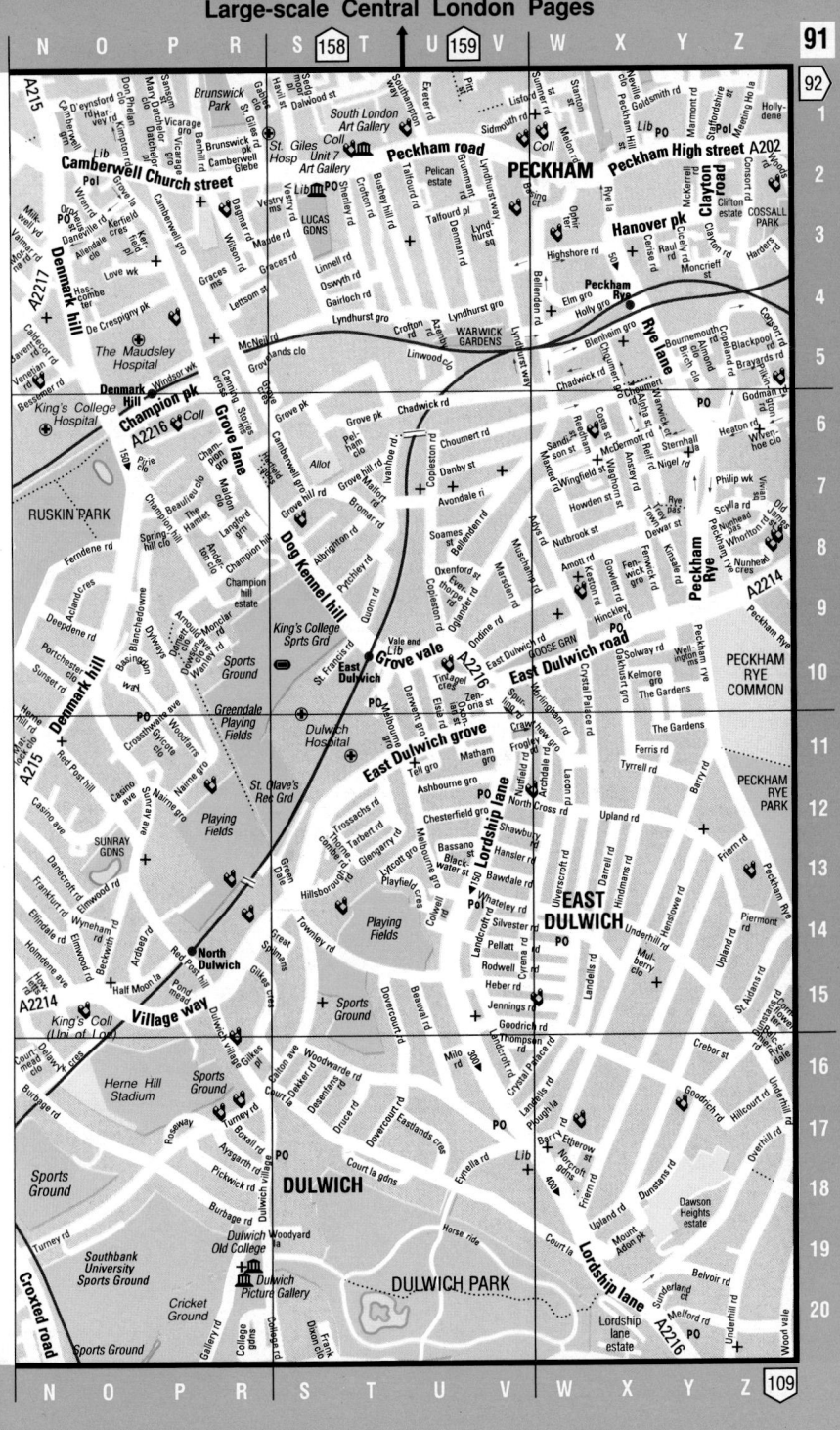

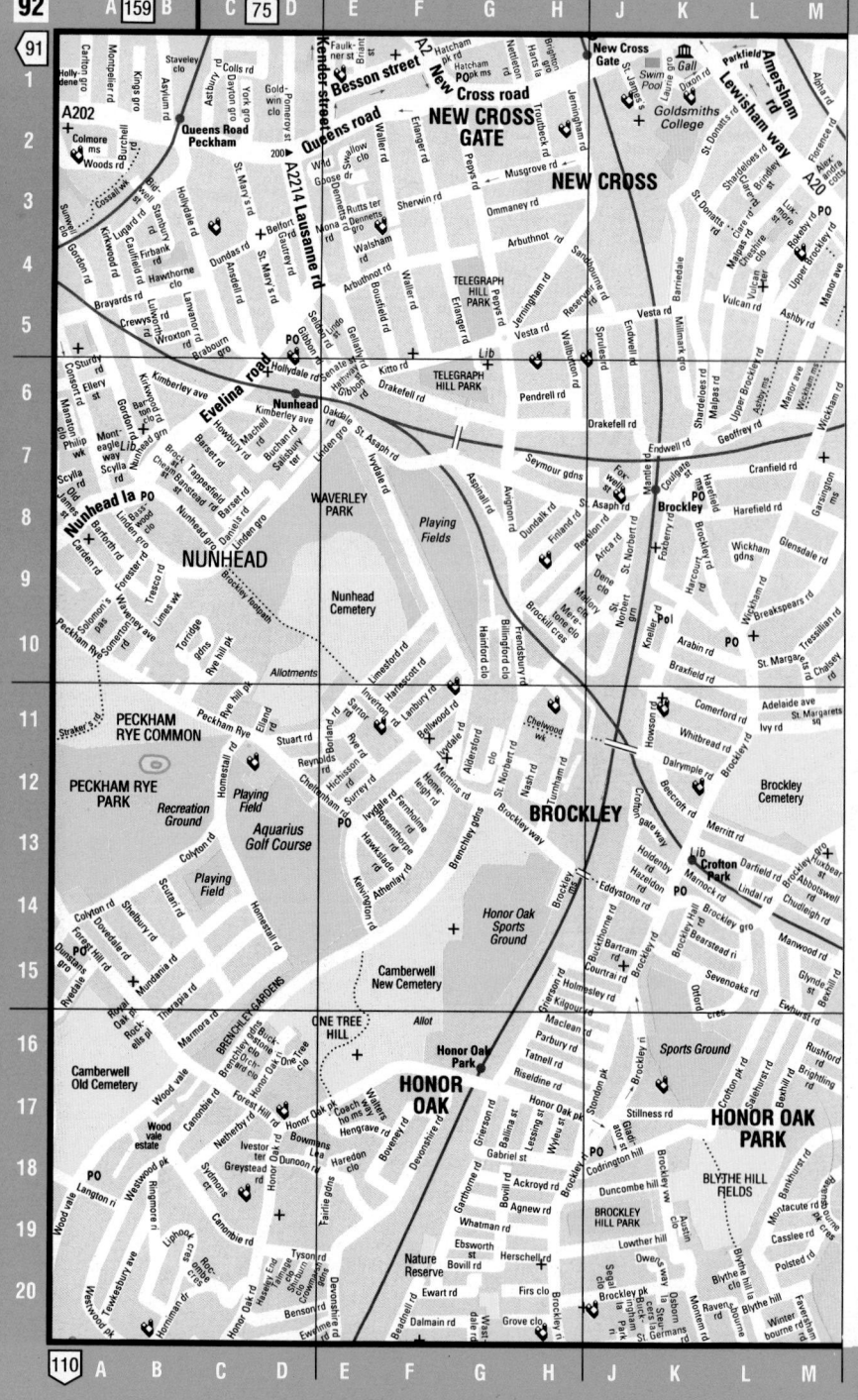

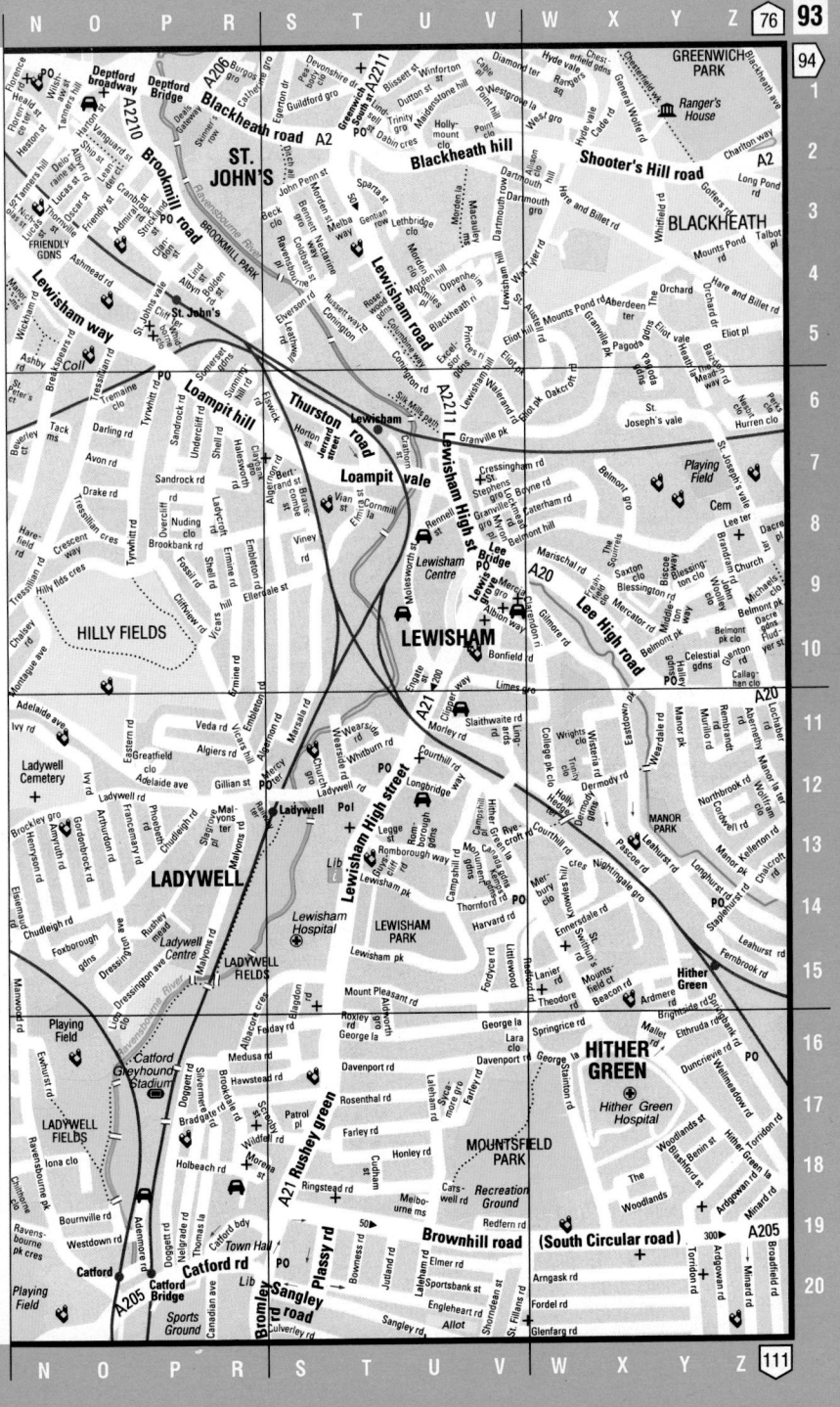

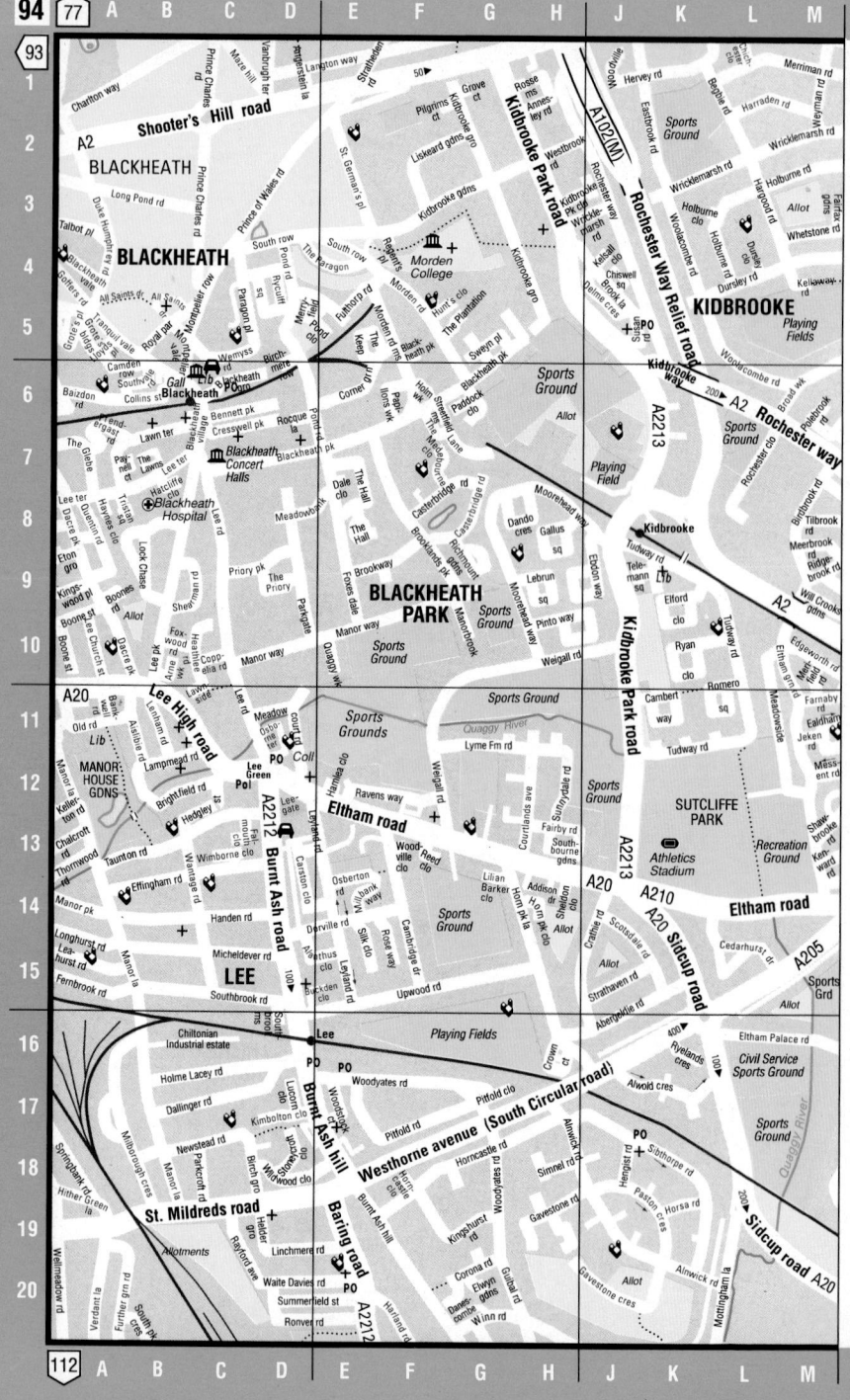

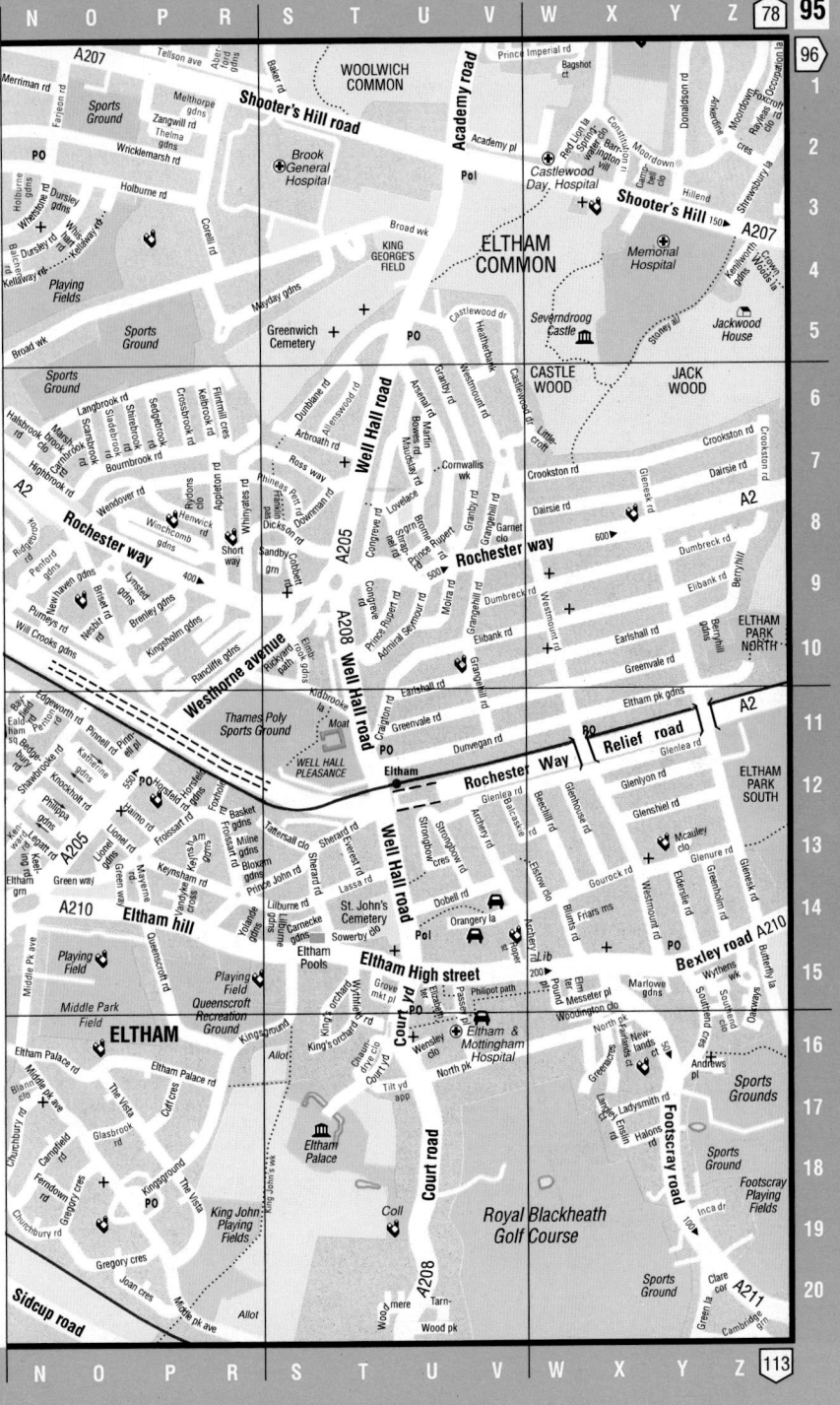

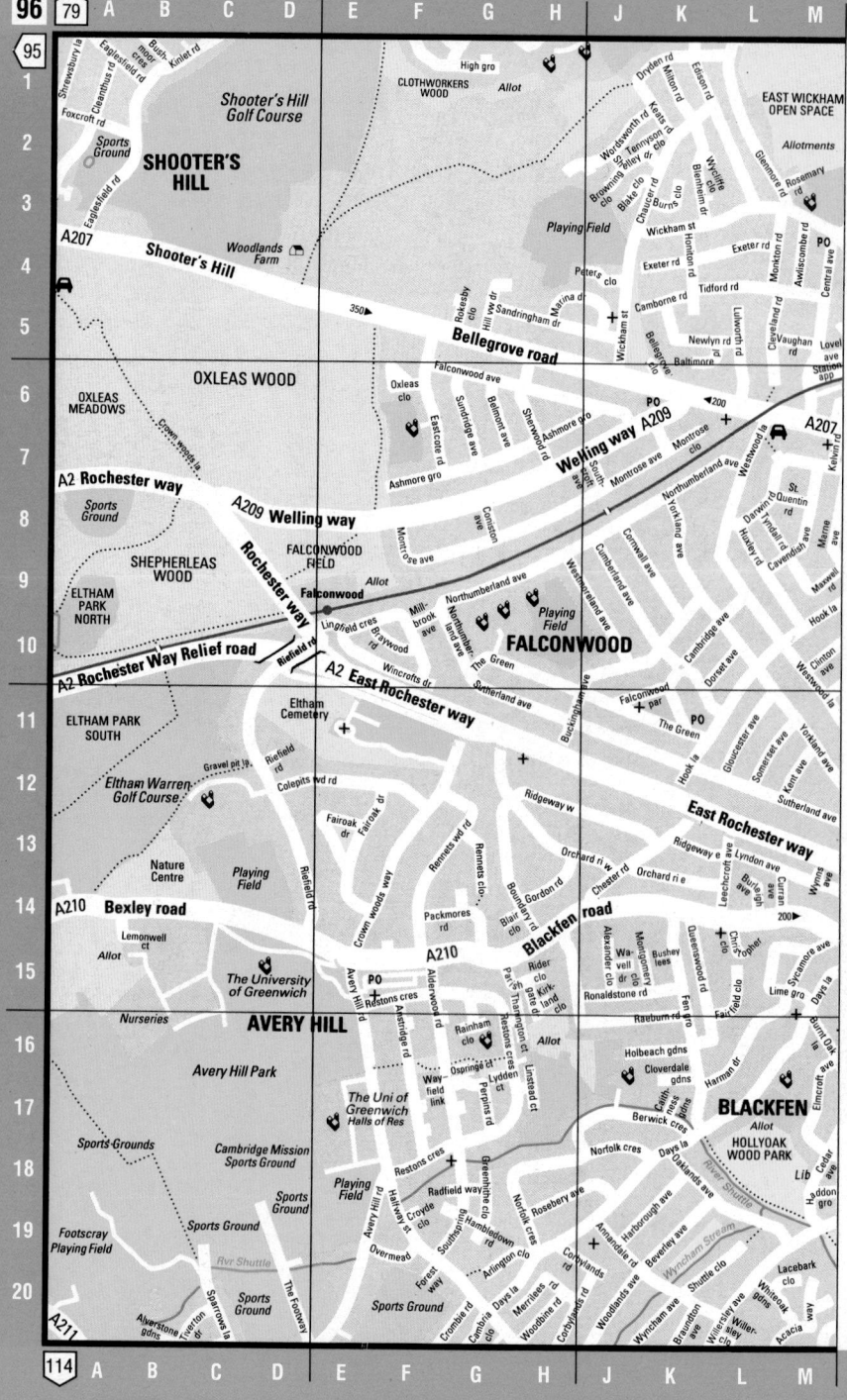

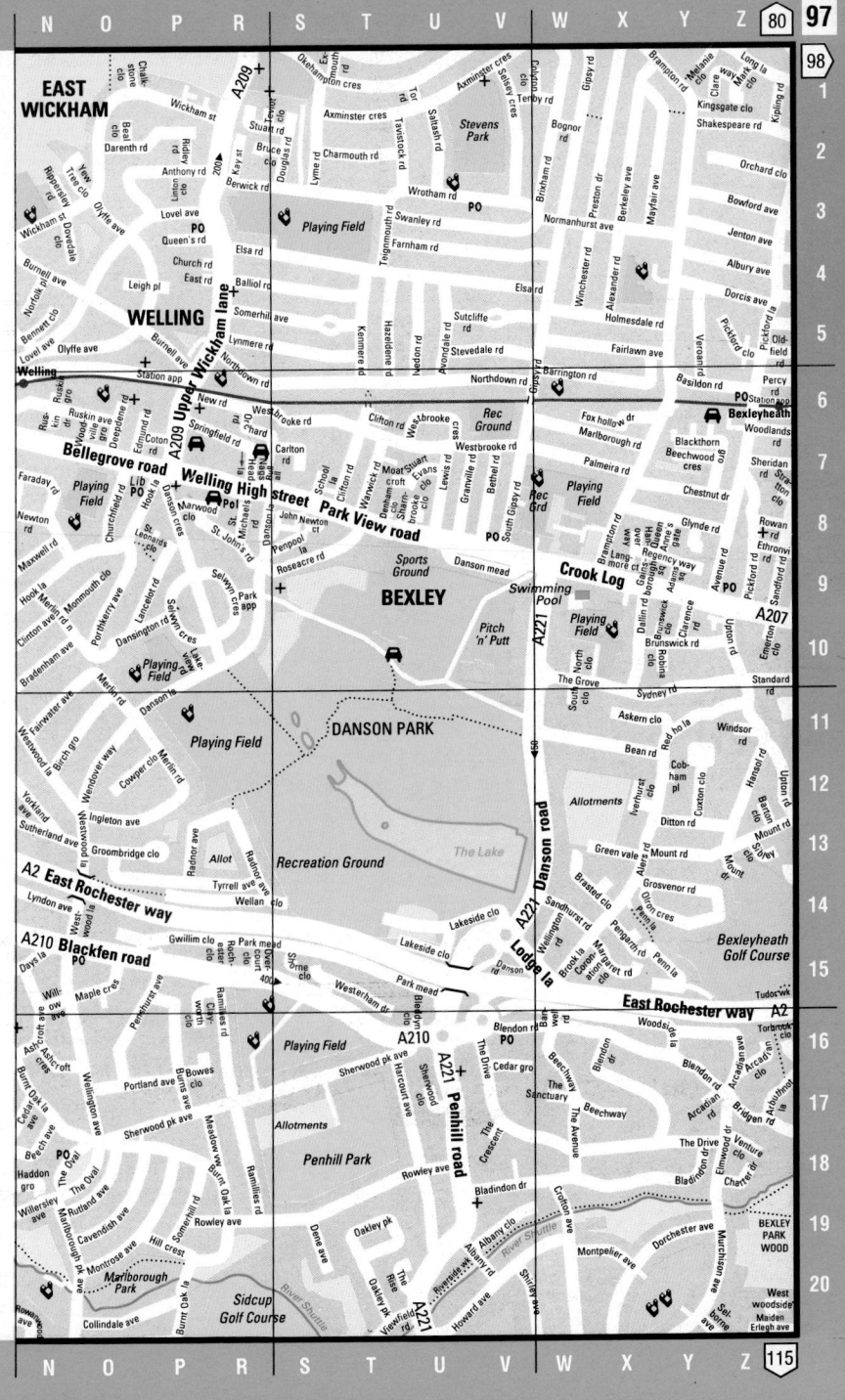

81
97

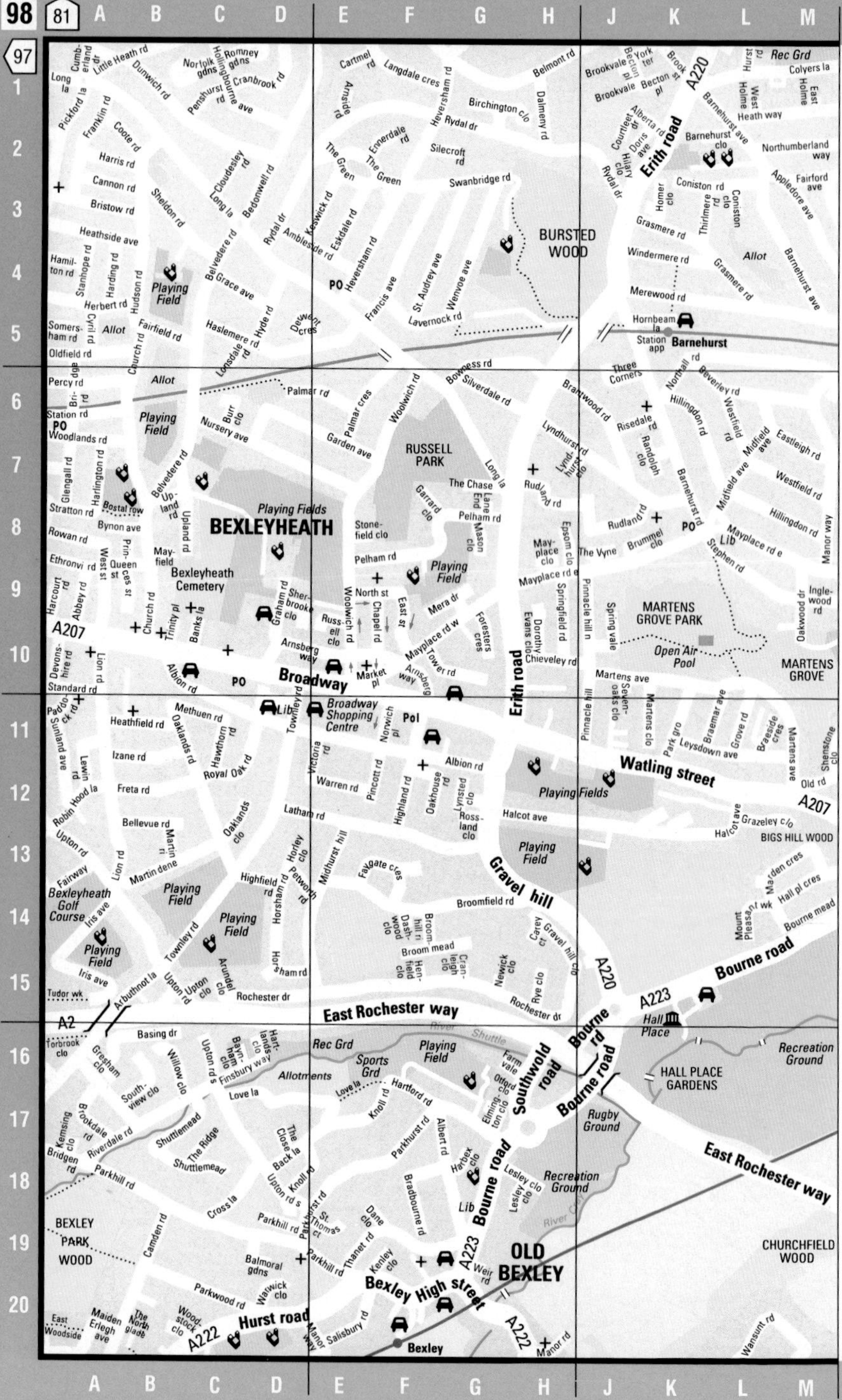
A B C D E F G H J K L M
1 2 3 4 5 6 7 8 9 10 11 12 13 14 15 16 17 18 19 20
Long la
Cumberland dr
Little Heath rd
Dunwich rd
Norfolk gdns
Romney gdns
Hollingbourne ave
Penshurst rd
Cranbrook rd
Cartmel rd
Langdale cres
Heversham rd
Belmont rd
Brookvale
Becton pl
York ter
Brook st
Becton pl
A220
Hurst rd
Rec Grd
Colyers la
Pickford la
Franklin rd
Coote rd
Harris rd
Cannon rd
Bristow rd
Sheldon rd
Cloudesley rd
Long la
Bedonwell rd
Arnside rd
Birchington clo
Dalmeny rd
Rydal dr
Ennerdale rd
Silecroft rd
The Green
Swanbridge rd
Alberta rd
Courtleet dr
Doris ave
Hilary clo
Rydal dr
Erith road
Barnehurst ave
Holme
Heath way
East Holme
Barnehurst clo
Northumberland way
Fairford ave
Appledore ave
Coniston rd
Homer clo
Thirlmere rd
Coniston clo
Grasmere rd
Heathside ave
Hamilton rd
Stanhope rd
Harding rd
Hudson rd
Playing Field
Belvedere rd
Grace ave
Rydal dr
Ambleside rd
Keswick rd
Eskdale rd
Heversham rd
PO
BURSTED WOOD
Windermere rd
Allot
Barnehurst ave
Grasmere rd
Herbert rd
Cyril rd
Somersham rd
Allot
Fairfield rd
Haslemere rd
Hyde rd
Derwent cres
Francis ave
St. Audrey ave
Wenvoe ave
Lavernock rd
Merewood rd
Hornbeam la
Station app
Barnehurst
Oldfield rd
Church rd
Lonsdale rd
Bowness rd
Silverdale rd
Three Corners
Northall rd
Beverley rd
Percy rd
Bridge rd
Allot
Palmar rd
Palmar cres
Woolwich rd
Brantwood rd
Hillingdon rd
Westfield rd
Station rd
PO
Woodlands rd
Playing Field
Burr clo
Nursery ave
Garden ave
RUSSELL PARK
Risedale rd
Randolph clo
Lyndhurst rd
Lyndhurst clo
Midfield ave
Eastleigh rd
Glengall rd
Harlington rd
Belvedere rd
Upland rd
Long la
The Chase
Lane End
Rudland rd
Barnehurst rd
Midfield ave
Westfield rd
Stratton rd
Bostal row
Bynon ave
Playing Fields
BEXLEYHEATH
Garrard clo
Pelham rd
Mason clo
Stonefield clo
Rudland rd
PO
Hillingdon rd
Rowan rd
Ethronvi rd
West st
Princes st
Queen st
Mayfield
Upland rd
Bexleyheath Cemetery
Pelham rd
Playing Field
Mayplace clo
Epsom clo
The Vyne
Brummel clo
Lib
Mayplace rd e
Stephen rd
Manor way
Harcourt rd
Abbey rd
Church rd
Trinity pl
Banks la
Graham rd
Sherbrooke clo
North st
Woolwich rd
Chapel rd
East st
Mera dr
Mayplace rd e
Springfield rd
Pinnacle hill n
Spring vale
MARTENS GROVE PARK
Inglewood rd
Oakwood dr
A207
Russell clo
Arnsberg way
Mayplace rd w
Tower rd
Foresters cres
Dorothy Evans clo
Open Air Pool
Devonshire rd
Lion rd
Broadway
Market pl
Arnsberg way
Erith road
Chieveley rd
MARTENS GROVE
Albion rd
PO
Standard rd
Martens ave
Sevenoaks clo
Paddock rd
Methuen rd
Townley rd
Broadway Shopping Centre
Lib
Pol
Pinnacle hill
Martens clo
Braemar ave
Grove rd
Braeside cres
Heathfield rd
Oaklands rd
Hawthorn rd
Norwich pl
Park gro
Leysdown ave
Martens ave
Shenstone clo
Sunland ave
Lewin rd
Izane rd
Royal Oak rd
Victoria rd
Albion rd
Watling street
Warren rd
Pincott rd
Highland rd
Oakhouse rd
Lynsted clo
Old rd
Robin Hood la
Freta rd
Playing Fields
A207
Latham rd
Rossland clo
Halcot ave
Halcot ave
Grazeley clo
Bellevue rd
Martin ri
Oaklands clo
BIGS HILL WOOD
Upton rd
Lion rd
Horley clo
Midhurst hill
Falgate cres
Playing Field
Gravel hill
Marden cres
Fairway
Martin dene
Highfield rd
Horsham rd
Petworth rd
Hall pl cres
Bexleyheath Golf Course
Playing Field
Playing Field
Broomfield rd
Mount Pleasant wk
Bourne mead
Iris ave
Dashwood clo
Broomhill ri
Carey ct
Gravel hill clo
Playing Field
Townley rd
Broom mead
Henfield clo
Cranleigh clo
Newick clo
A220
Bourne road
Iris ave
Arundel clo
Horsham rd
Rye clo
A223
Tudor wk
Arbuthnot la
Upton rd
Upton clo
Rochester dr
Rochester dr
A2
East Rochester way
Bourne rd
Hall Place
Basing dr
Upton rd s
Baynham clo
Hartlands clo
Rec Grd
River Shuttle
Playing Field
Torbrook clo
Gresham clo
Willow clo
Finsbury way
Sports Grd
Farm vale
Southwold road
Recreation Ground
HALL PLACE GARDENS
Allotments
Otford clo
Bourne road
Southview clo
Love la
Love la
Hartford rd
Knoll rd
Elmington clo
Rugby Ground
Kemsing clo
Brookdale rd
Riverdale rd
Shuttlemead
The Ridge
The Close
Back la
Parkhurst rd
Albert rd
East Rochester way
Bridgen rd
Shuttlemead
Harbex clo
Bourne road
Lesley clo
Recreation Ground
Parkhill rd
Upton rd s
Knoll rd
Bradbourne rd
Lesley clo
Cross la
Parkhurst rd
St. Thomas ct
Dane clo
Lib
River Cray
BEXLEY PARK WOOD
Camden rd
Parkhill rd
CHURCHFIELD WOOD
Thanet rd
Balmoral gdns
Parkhill rd
Kenley clo
A223
Weir rd
OLD BEXLEY
Parkwood rd
Warwick clo
Bexley High street
East Woodside
Maiden Erlegh ave
The North glade
Woodstock clo
Hurst road
A222
Manor way
Salisbury rd
A222
Manor rd
Wansunt rd
Bexley

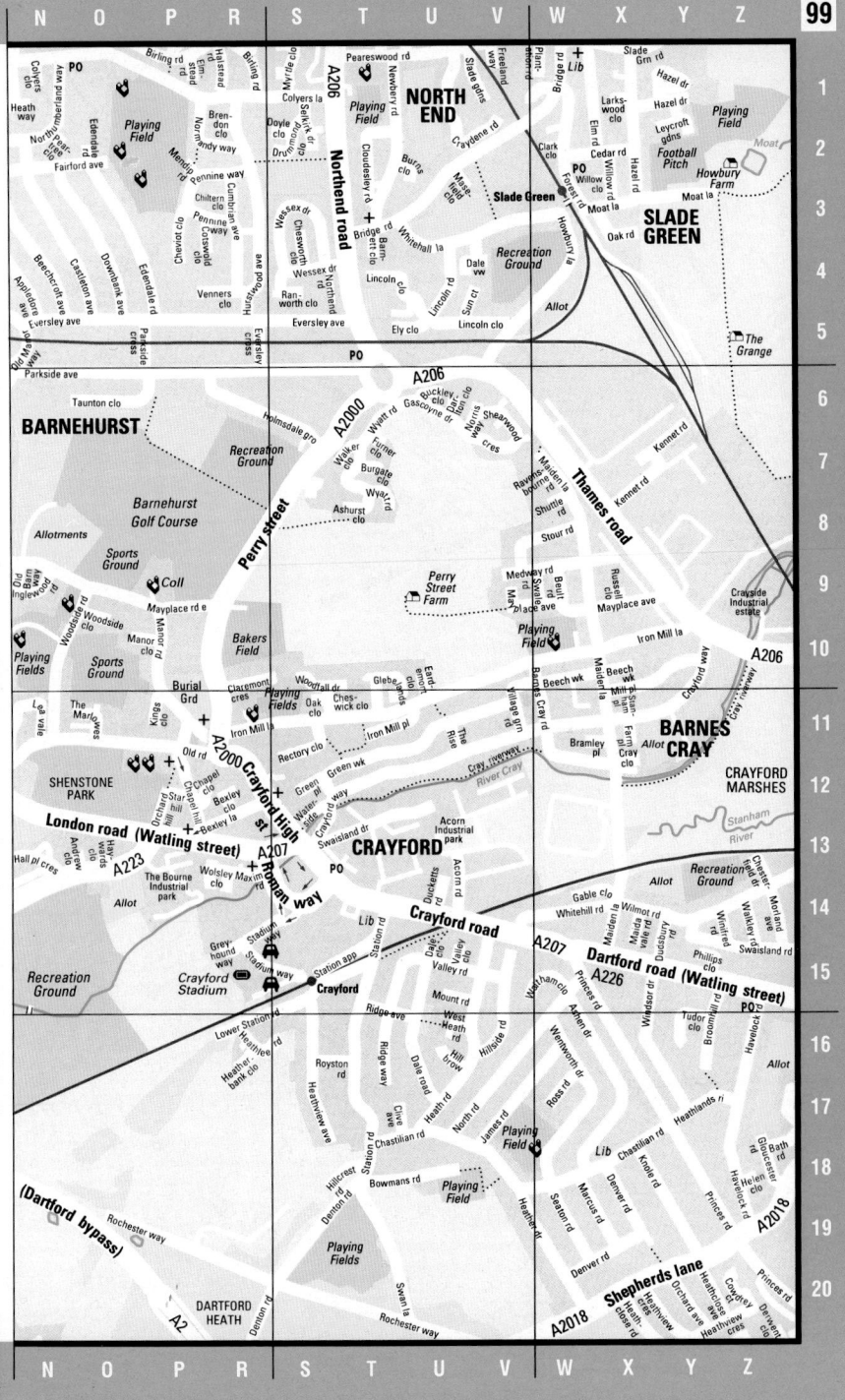

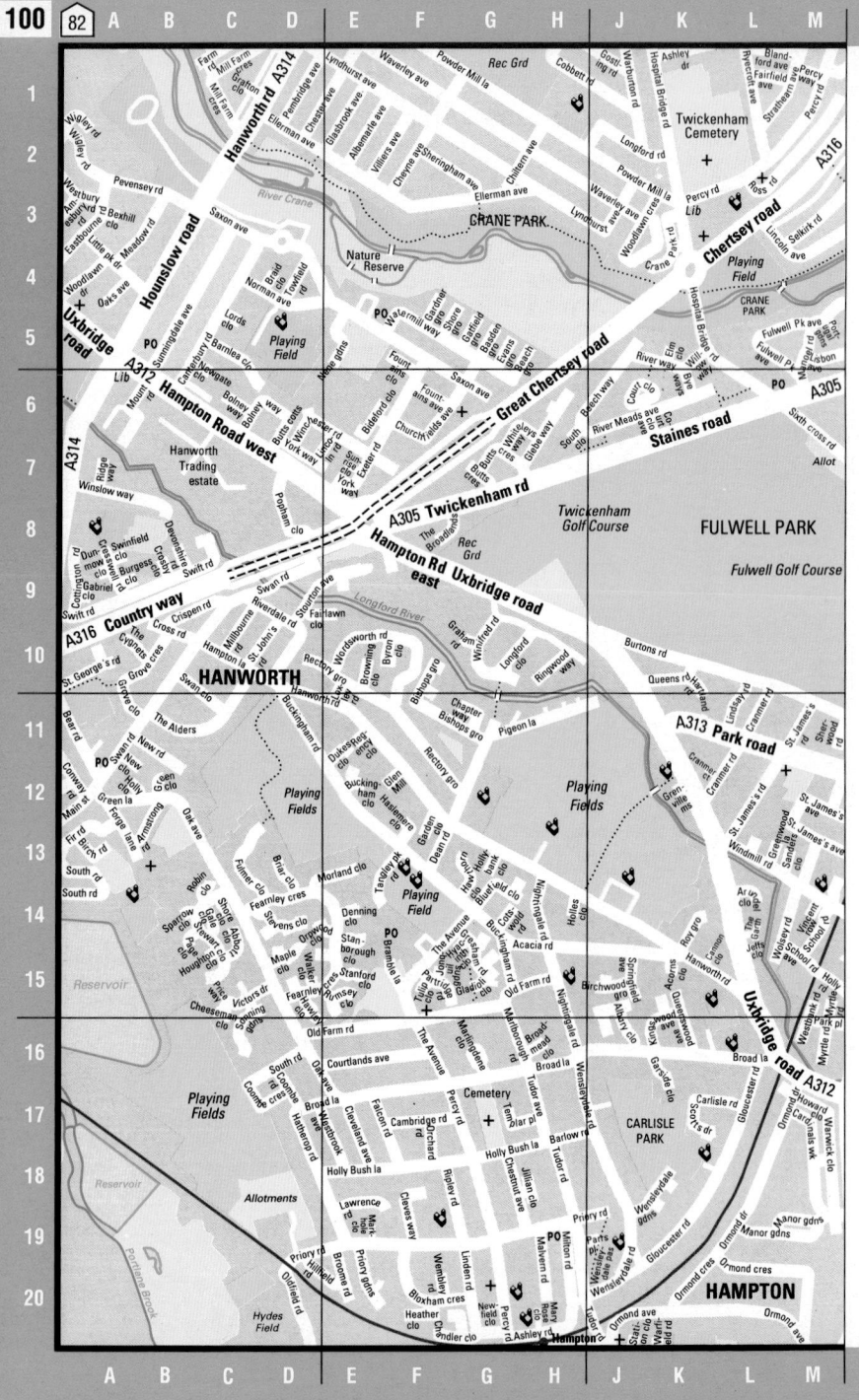

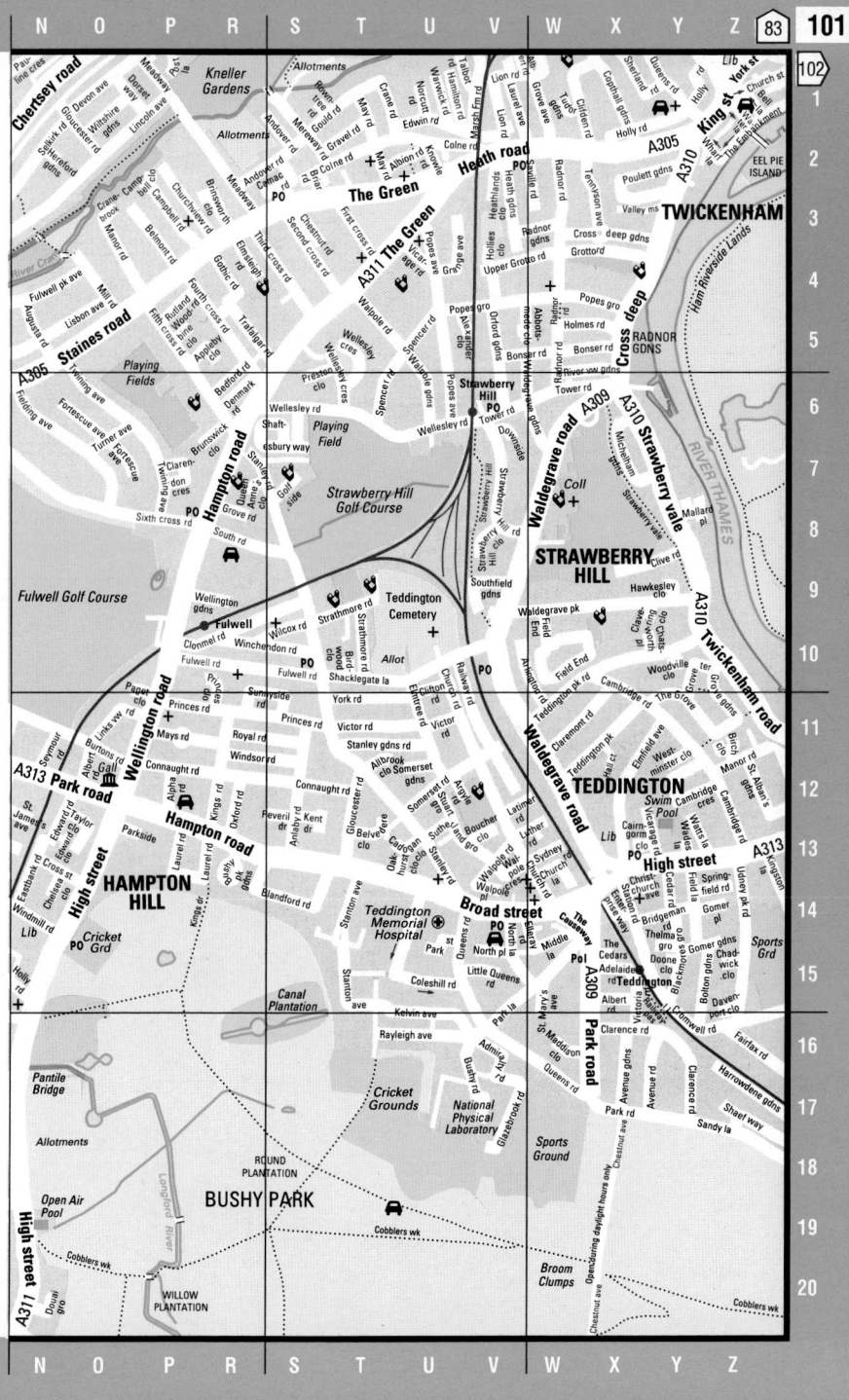

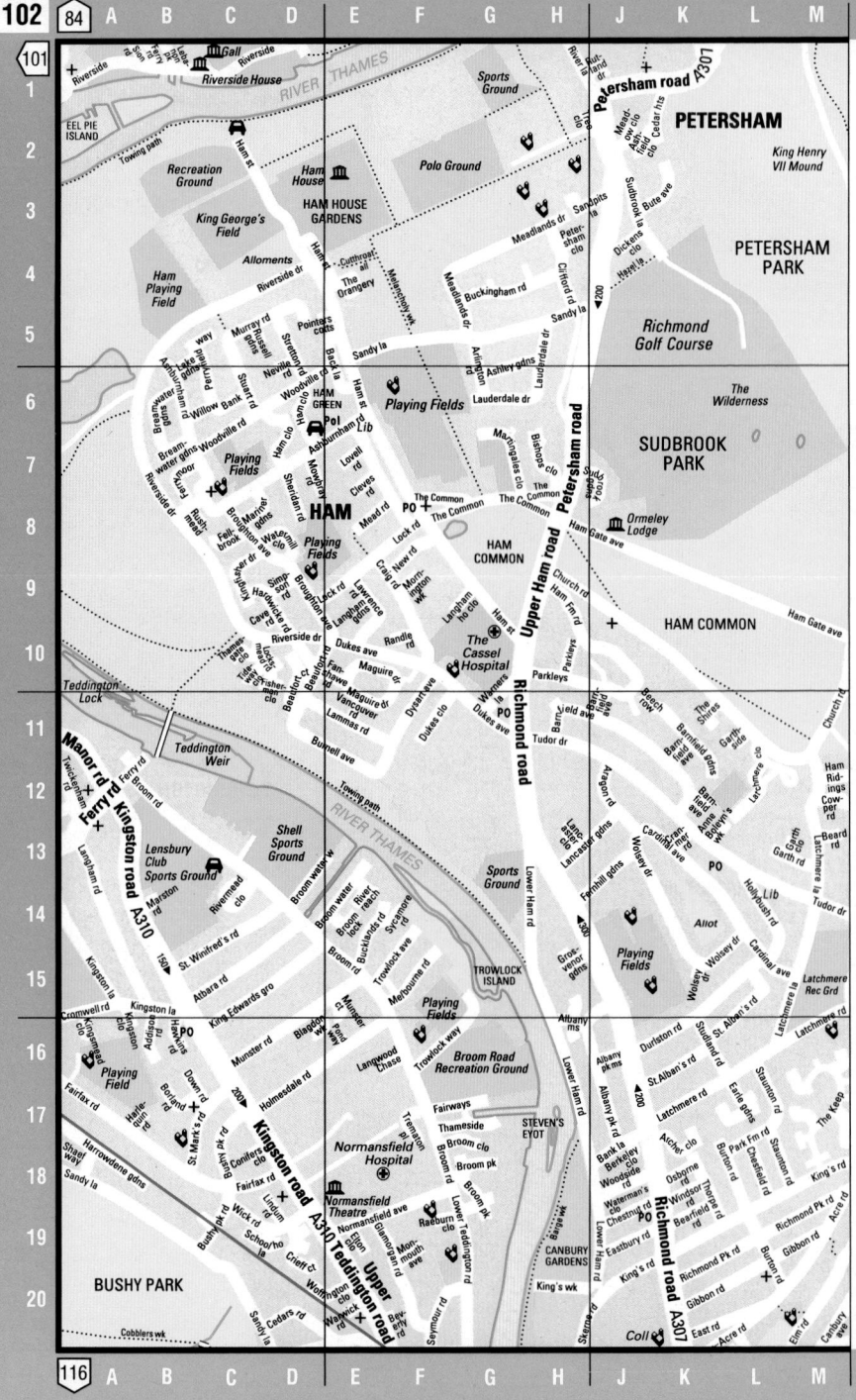

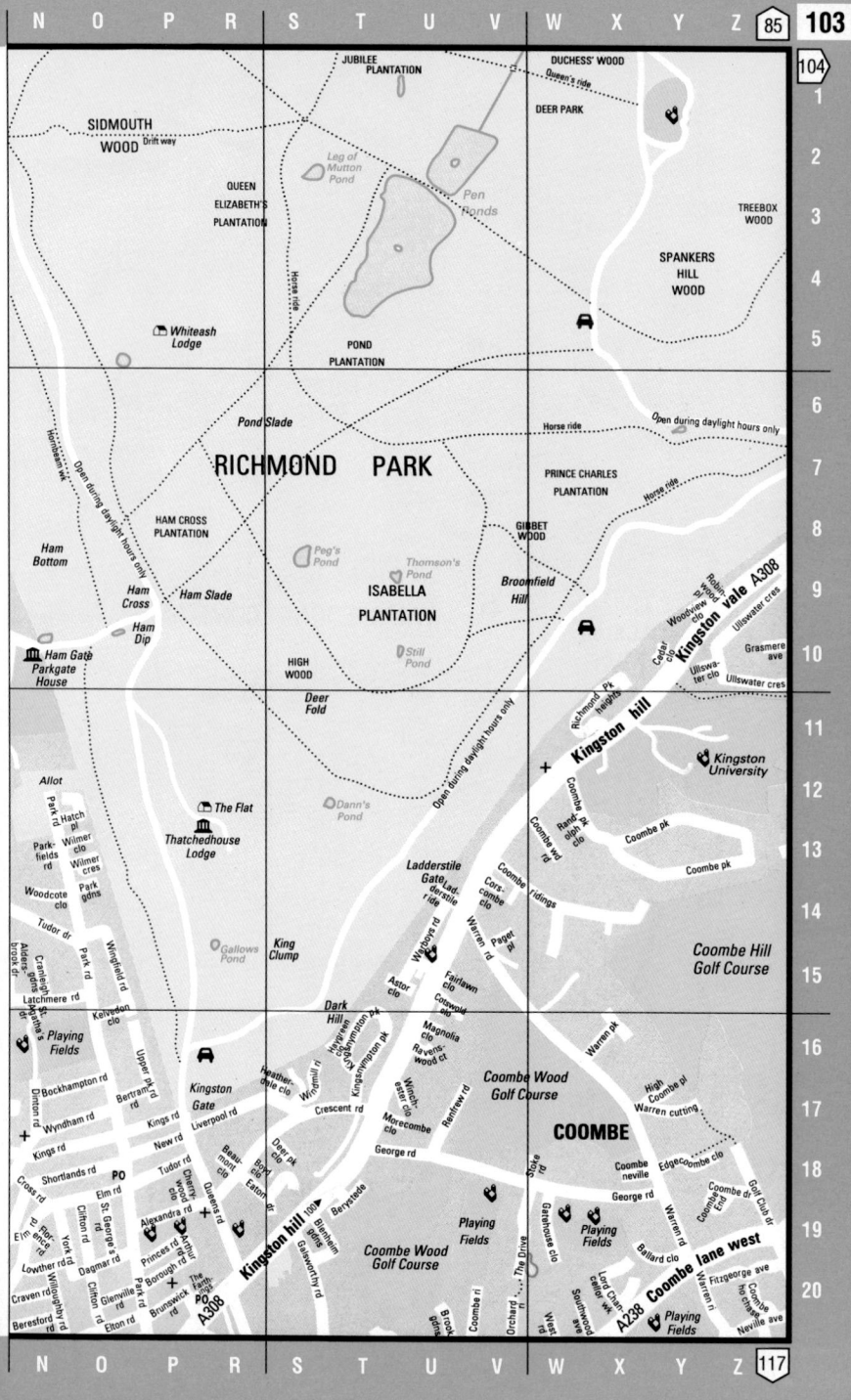

N O P R S T U V W X Y Z

DUCHESS' WOOD

JUBILEE
PLANTATION

Queen's ride

DEER PARK

SIDMOUTH
WOOD   Drift way

QUEEN
ELIZABETH'S
PLANTATION

Leg of
Mutton
Pond

Pen
Ponds

TREEBOX
WOOD

SPANKERS
HILL
WOOD

Whiteash
Lodge

POND
PLANTATION

Horse ride

Pond Slade

Horse ride

Open during daylight hours only

Hornbeam wk

RICHMOND   PARK

PRINCE CHARLES
PLANTATION

Horse ride

Open during daylight hours only

HAM CROSS
PLANTATION

GIBBET
WOOD

Ham
Bottom

Peg's
Pond

Thomson's
Pond

ISABELLA

Broomfield
Hill

Kingston vale A308

Ham
Cross

Ham Slade

PLANTATION

Cedar clo
Woodview clo
Rodney
clo

Ullswater clo

Grasmere
ave

Ham
Dip

HIGH
WOOD

Still
Pond

Ulls-
water clo

Ullswater cres

Ham Gate
Parkgate
House

Deer
Fold

Richmond Pk
heights

Kingston hill

Open during daylight hours only

Kingston
University

Allot

Park rd

Hatch
pl

Dann's
Pond

Kingston hill

Coombe vd

Rand-
olph
clo

Park-
fields
rd

Wilmer
clo

Wilmer
cres

Thatchedhouse
Lodge

The Flat

Coombe pk

Coombe pk

Woodcote
clo

Park
gdns

Ladderstile
Gate

Coombe ridings

Coombe
clo

Tudor dr

Wingfield rd

Gallows
Pond

King
Clump

Ladd-
erstile
ride

Warren rd

Paget pl

Corscombe
clo

Coombe Hill
Golf Course

Aldersgrove
av

Cranleigh
gdns

Park rd

Latchmere rd

Webb's rd

Astor
clo

Fairlawn
clo

St
Augustine's

Playing
Fields

Dark
Hill

Hargwyne rd

Kingswinston
pk

Cotswold
clo

Bockhampton rd

Upper pk rd

Bertram
rd

Kingston
Gate

Kings rd

Liverpool rd

Magnolia
clo

Ravenswood ct

Coombe Wood
Golf Course

High
Coombe pl

Warren cutting

Wyndham rd

Kings rd

New rd

Windmill ri

heatherdale clo

Crescent rd

Winchester
clo

Morecombe
clo

Renfrew rd

Warren pk

COOMBE

Edgecoombe clo

Dulton rd

Shortlands rd

Tudor rd

PO

Beaumont
rd

Cherrywood
clo

Eaton
clo

George rd

The Drive

Coombe
neville

Warren rd

Coombe dr

Coombe la west

Golf Club dr

Cross rd

Elm rd

Clifton rd

Alexandra rd

Arthur rd

Borough rd

Bensryde

Bintham
gdns

Coombe ri

Playing
Fields

George rd

Playing
Fields

Elm
grove

York rd

Dagmar rd

Princes rd

Park rd

The
Broadway

Grasvenor rd

Brook
rd

Garehouse
clo

Lord Chan's
cellor wk

Ballard rd

Fitzgeorge ave

Coombe
house cres

Lowther rd

Glenville rd

Clifton rd

Brunswick
rd

PO

Kingston hill

Coombe Wood
Golf Course

Stoke
rd

Southwood
rd

A238 Coombe lane west

Coombe
Neville ave

Craven rd

Willoughby rd

Elton rd

A308

Orchard
rd

West
rd

Playing
Fields

Beresford rd

Dark
pk
rd

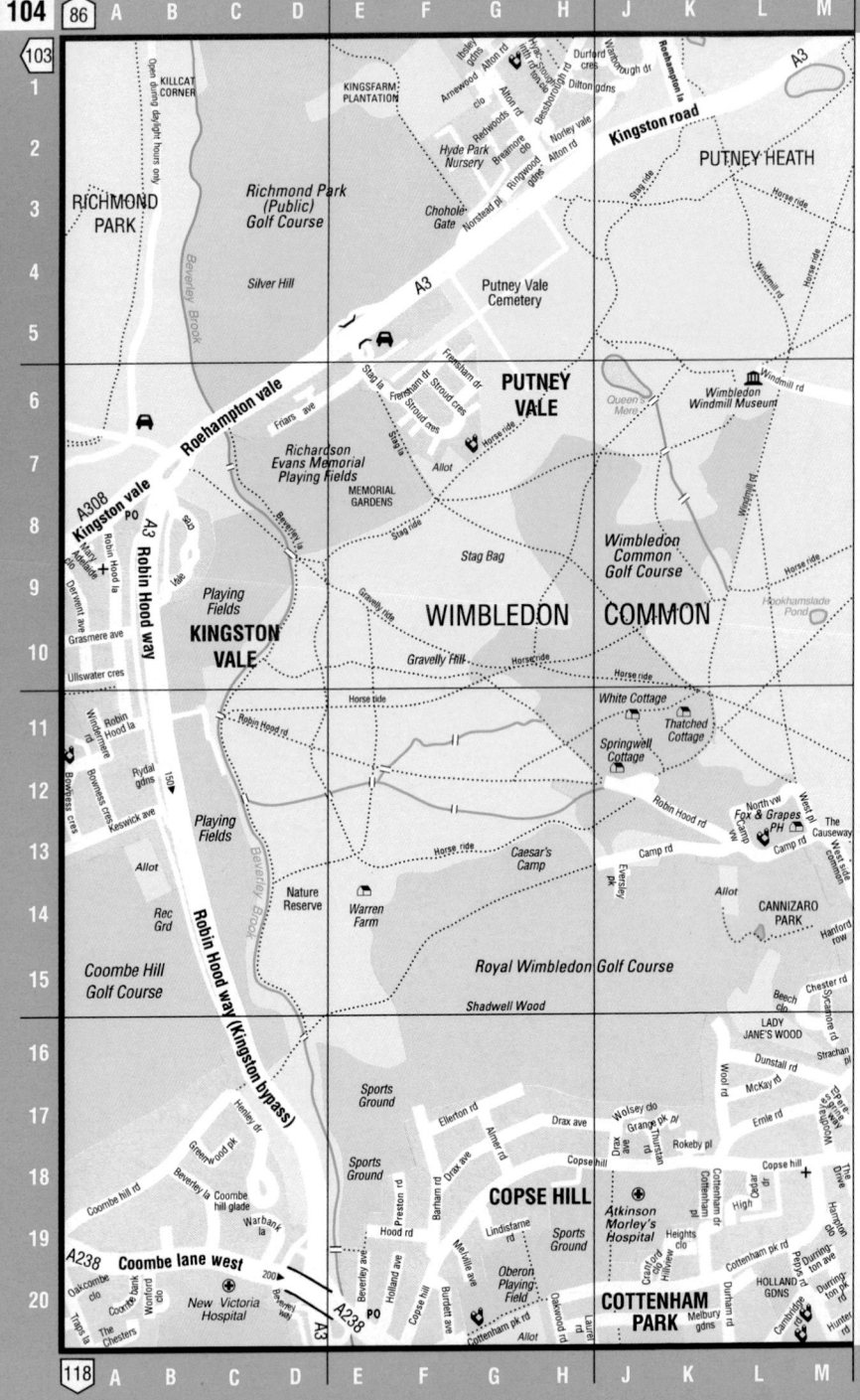

A B C D E F G H J K L M

A3

KILLCAT
CORNER

Open during daylight hours only

RICHMOND
PARK

Beverley Brook

KINGSFARM
PLANTATION

Richmond Park
(Public)
Golf Course

Silver Hill

Ibsley
gdns

Arnewood
clo

Alton rd

Durford
cres

Wansborough dr

Dilton
vale

Dilton gdns

Redwoods

Breamore clo

Morley vale

Alton cl

Kingston road

PUTNEY HEATH

Hyde Park
Nursery

Ringwood
gdns

Chohole
Gate

Norstead pl

Horse ride

A3

Putney Vale
Cemetery

Horse ride

Westmead

Horse ride

Roehampton vale

Friars ave

Stag la

Frenstam dr

Stroud cres

Stroud cres

PUTNEY
VALE

Queen's
Mere

Wimbledon
Windmill Museum

Windmill rd

A308
Kingston vale

PO

SPO

Richardson
Evans Memorial
Playing Fields

Stag la

Horse ride

Allot

MEMORIAL
GARDENS

Stag ride

Wimbledon
Common
Golf Course

Horse ride

Hookhamslade
Pond

Mary Adelaide

Robin Hood la

A3 Robin Hood way

Beverley la

Playing
Fields

Stag Bag

WIMBLEDON   COMMON

Derwent rise

Grasmere ave

KINGSTON
VALE

Gravelly ride

Gravelly Hill

Horse ride

Ullswater cres

Horse ride

Robin Hood rd

White Cottage

Thatched
Cottage

Robin
Hood la

Rydal gdns

150

Springwell
Cottage

North vw

Fox & Grapes
PH

West pl

The
Causeway

West side common

Windmill rd

Bowness cres

Keswick ave

Beverley Brook

Playing
Fields

Horse ride

Caesar's
Camp

Robin Hood rd

Camp rd

Eversley pk

Camp rd

Allot

Horse ride

CANNIZARO
PARK

Hanford
row

Allot

Rec
Grd

Nature
Reserve

Warren
Farm

Royal Wimbledon Golf Course

Beech
Clo

Chester rd

Sycamore clo

Coombe Hill
Golf Course

Robin Hood way (Kingston bypass)

Shadwell Wood

LADY
JANE'S WOOD

Dunstall rd

Strachan
clo

Wool rd

McKay rd

Stephen Ludgate Fitzgerald rd

Henley dr

Greenwood pk

Sports
Ground

Ellerton rd

Almer rd

Drax ave

Wolsey clo

Grange pk pl

Rokeby pl

Ernle rd

Copse hill

Coombe hill rd

Beverley la

Coombe
hill glade

Sports
Ground

Barnam rd

Drax ave

Drax clo

Dunstan
rd

Cottenham
dr

High

Cedar rd

Copse hill

The Harman
Wools

A238 Coombe lane west

Oakcombe clo

Coombe
Woods

Warbank
la

New Victoria
Hospital

200

Beverley ave

Beverley ave

A3

A238

PO

COPSE HILL

Lindisfarne
rd

Atkinson
Morley's
Hospital

Heights
clo

Craxford
clo

Hillvew

Cottenham pk rd

HOLLAND
GDNS

Cambridge rd

Durrington ave

The Chesters

Traps la

Preston rd

Hood rd

Melville ave

Beverley ave

Copse hill

Burfelt rd

Oberon
Playing
Field

Cottenham pk rd

Sports
Ground

Oakwood rd

Lauren

Durham rd

COTTENHAM
PARK

Melbury
gdns

Peppys clo

Durrington ave

Hunters clo

Allot

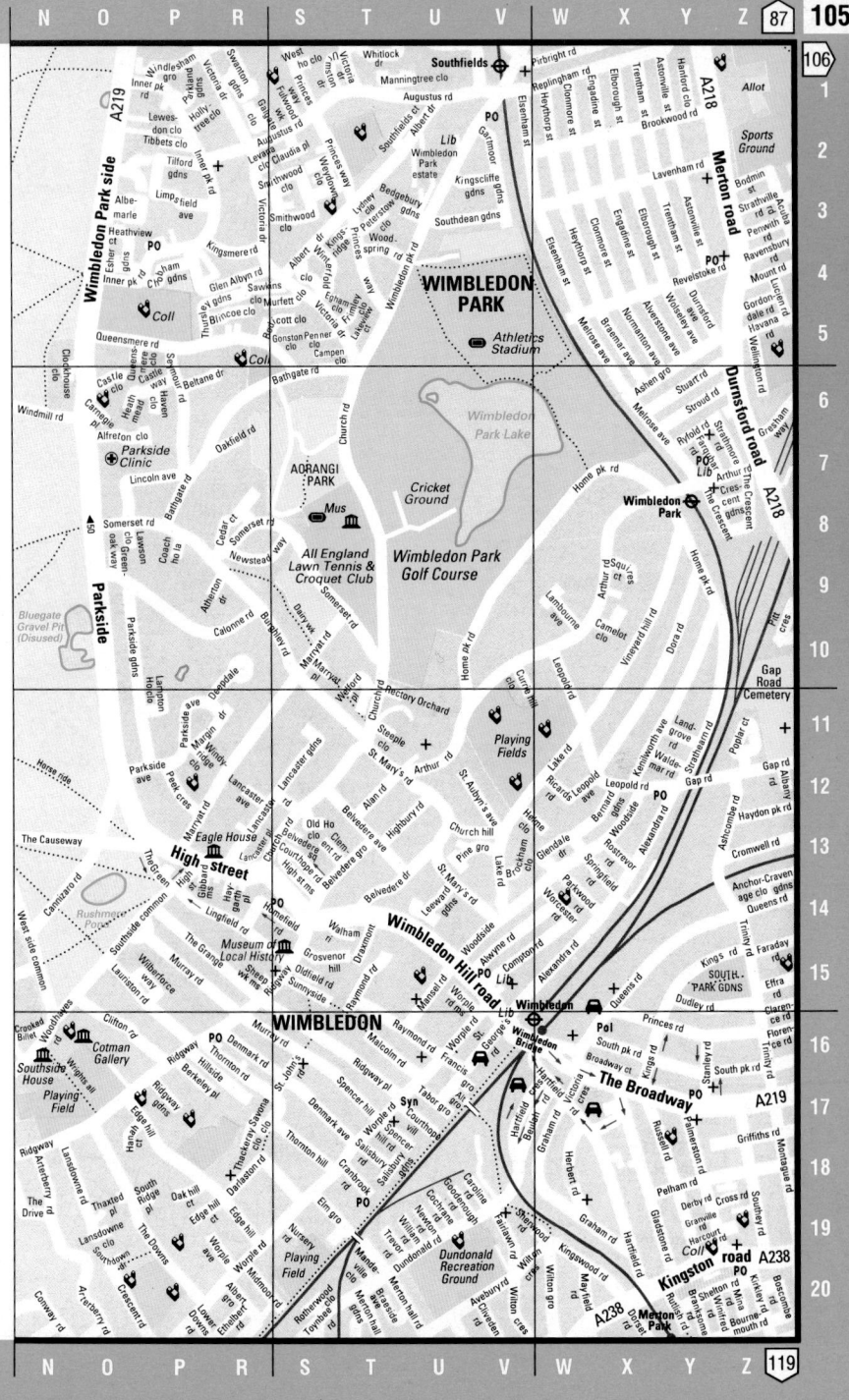

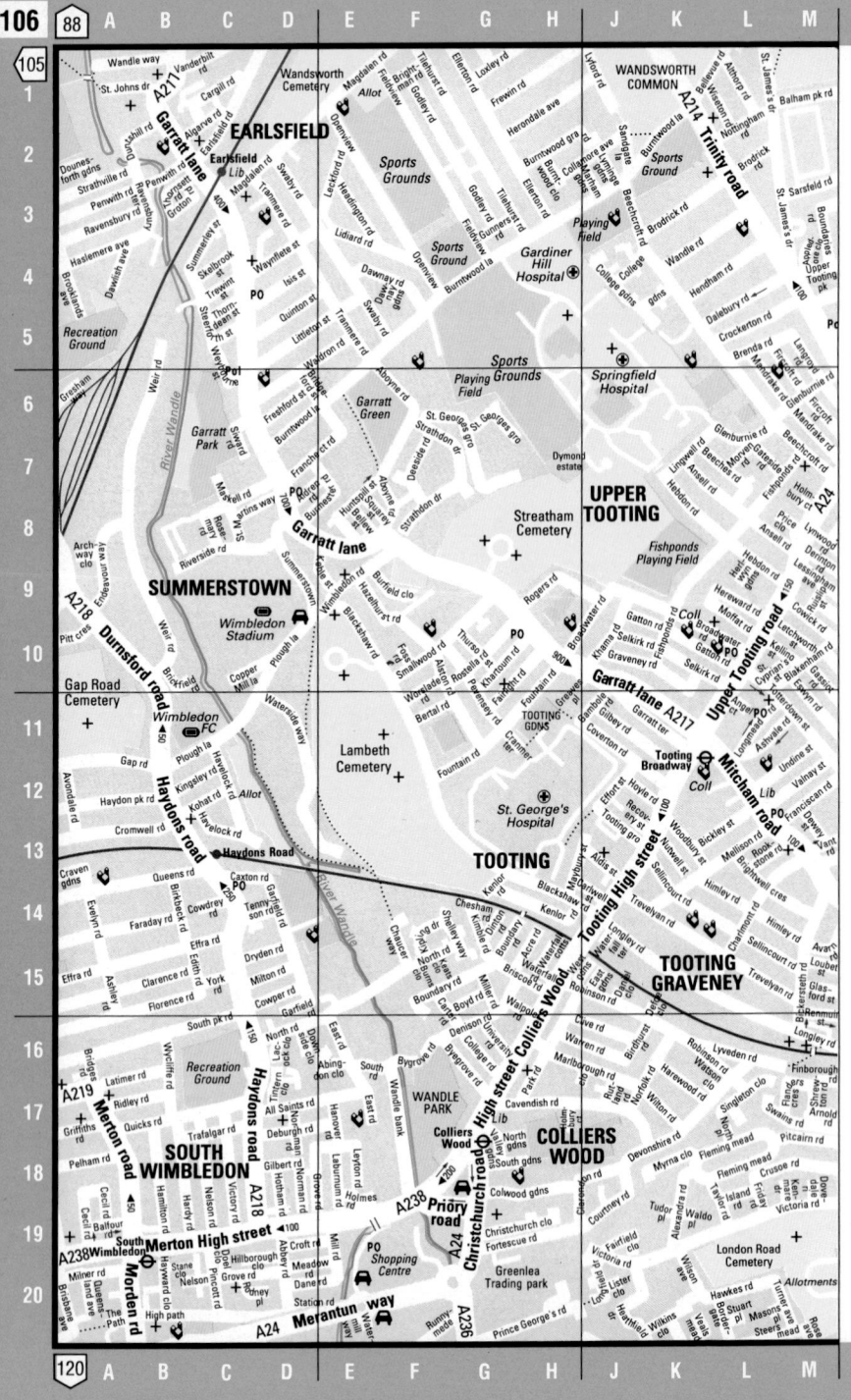

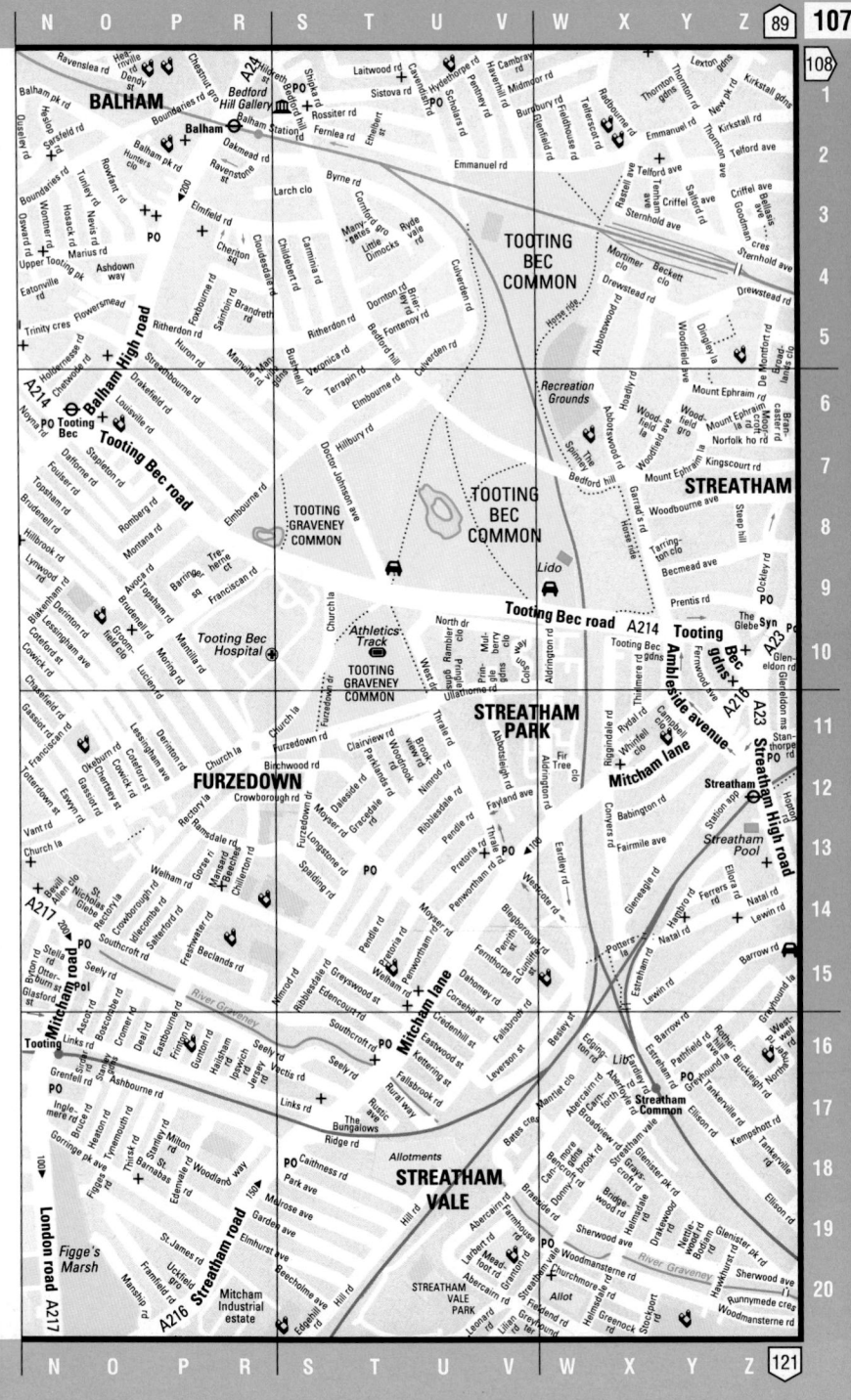

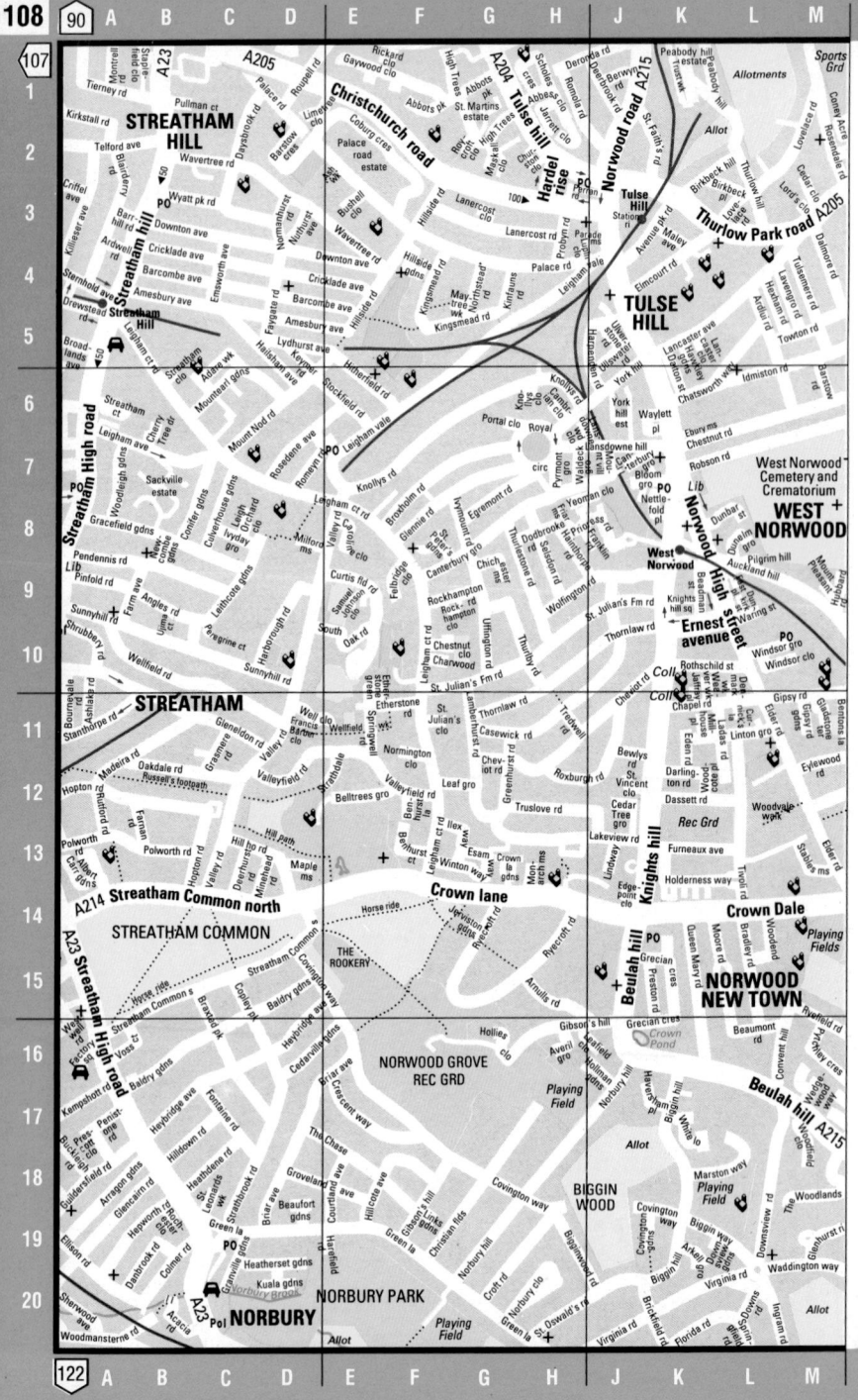

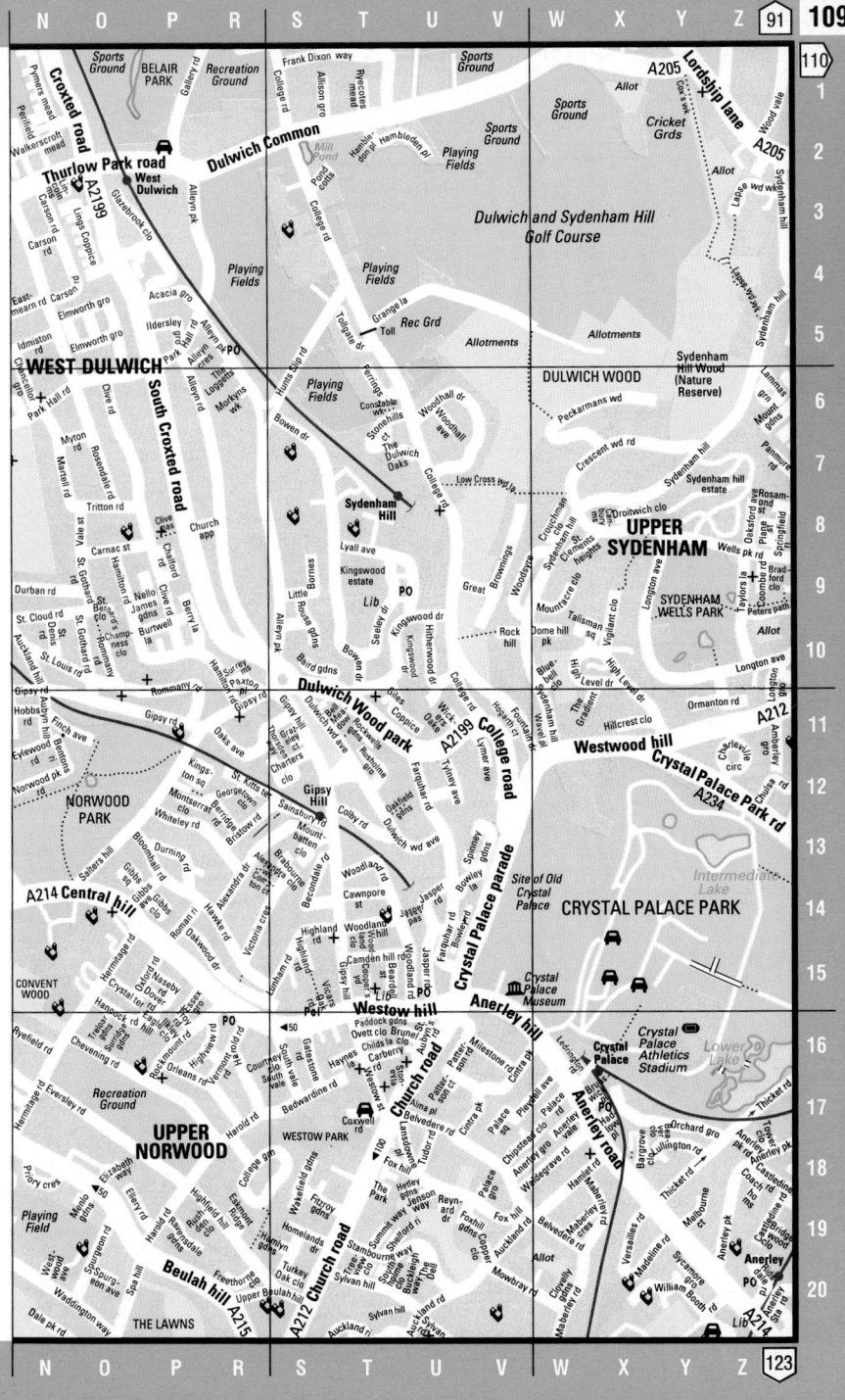

Grid columns (top and bottom): N O P R S T U V W X Y Z
Grid rows: 1–20

Major place names:
- Croxted road
- BELAIR PARK
- Dulwich Common
- Sports Ground / Recreation Ground / Playing Fields
- Thurlow Park road
- West Dulwich
- A2199
- WEST DULWICH
- South Croxted road
- Dulwich and Sydenham Hill Golf Course
- A205 / Lordship lane
- Cricket Grds
- DULWICH WOOD
- Sydenham Hill Wood (Nature Reserve)
- Sydenham Hill
- UPPER SYDENHAM
- SYDENHAM WELLS PARK
- Kingswood estate
- Dulwich Wood park
- College road
- Westwood hill
- Crystal Palace Park rd
- A212 / A234
- NORWOOD PARK
- Gipsy Hill
- A214 Central hill
- CONVENT WOOD
- CRYSTAL PALACE PARK
- Intermediate Lake
- Site of Old Crystal Palace
- Crystal Palace Museum
- Westow hill
- Anerley hill
- Crystal Palace parade
- UPPER NORWOOD
- Church road
- Crystal Palace
- Crystal Palace Athletics Stadium
- Lower Lake
- Anerley road
- Anerley
- Beulah hill
- A215
- THE LAWNS
- A212
- A214

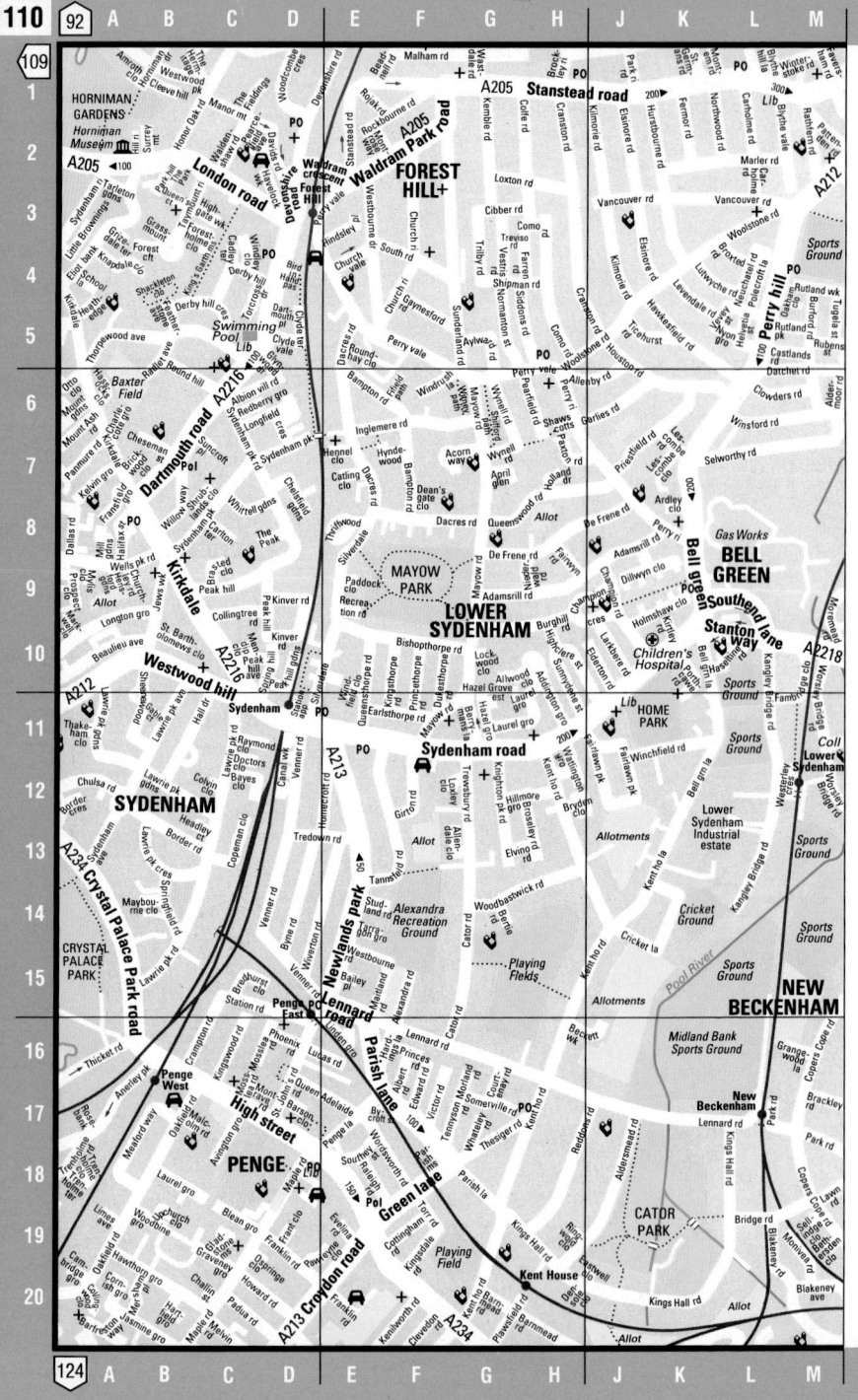

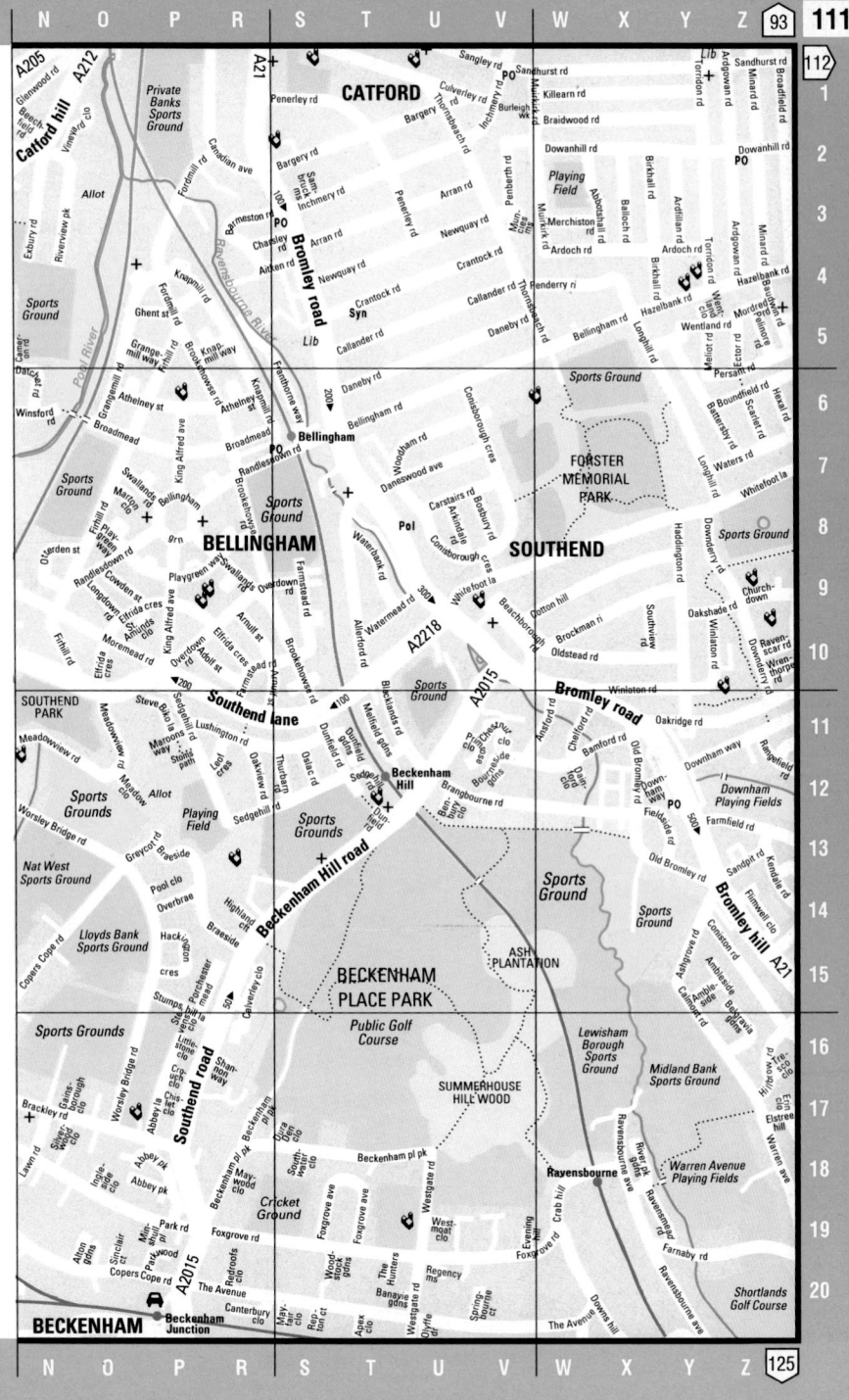

A205 A212 A21

Glenwood rd Catford hill Beech rd Vineys rd Private Banks Sports Ground Penerley rd Sangley rd Sandhurst rd Lib Torridon rd Ardgowan rd Sandhurst rd Minard rd Broadfield rd

CATFORD

Killearn rd Culverley rd Burleigh wk Inchmery rd Thornsbeach rd Braidwood rd

Ferdhill rd Canadian ave Bargery rd Bargery rd Dowanhill rd Dowanhill rd PO Allot Perceval av Sm. brook Inchmery rd Penberth rd Playing Field Birkhall rd Balloch rd Ardfillan rd Ardgowan rd Minard rd

Exbury rd Riverview pk Charsley rd Arran ave Arran rd Newquay rd Muirkirk rd Mina mead rd Merchiston rd Ardoch rd Ardroch rd Torridon rd Birkhall rd Hazelbank rd

Sports Ground Croft Kneymill rd Ghent st Ainten rd Newquay rd Crantock rd Crantock rd Callander rd Renderry ri Thornsbeach rd Hazelbank rd Wentland rd Mordred rd Ellington Mellmore

Syn Lib Callander rd Callander rd Daneby rd Bellingham rd Longhill rd Persant rd Ector rd

Winsford rd Atheley st Grangemill rd Ghent st Broadhouse rd Atheley rd Daneby rd Sports Ground Boundfield rd Hexal rd Scarlet rd Battersby rd

Broadmead Swallands rd King Alfred ave Bellingham rd Woodham rd **Bellingham** Conborough cres **FORSTER MEMORIAL PARK** Waters rd Whitefoot la

Sports Ground Finhill rd Swallands Randlesdown rd PO Daneswood ave Carstairs rd Bradbury rd Sports Ground

Olverden st Maroons Cowden st Longdown grn Playgreen way Swallands rd **BELLINGHAM** Sports Ground Pol Conaborough rd Whitefoot la **SOUTHEND** Haddington rd Downderry rd Churchdown

Randlesdown ave King Alfred ave Efrida cres Overdown rd Arnulf st Beachborough Dotton hill Oakshade rd Downderry rd Ravenscar rd Wrencroft

Frihill rd Elfrida Amulds Moremead rd Efrida cres Brookehaven rd A2218 Watermead rd Allerford rd Whitefoot la Brockman ri Oldstead rd Southview rd Winlaton rd

Elfrida cres Farmstead rd Blacklands rd Sports Ground **Bromley road** Winlaton rd Oakridge rd

SOUTHEND PARK Meadowview rd Steve Biko la Sedgehill rd Lushington rd **Southend Lane** Dunfield rd A2015 Banford rd Ansford rd Chelford rd Old Bromley rd Downham way Rangefield rd

Sports Grounds Maroons Meadow clo Oakview rd Thurbarn rd Sedge Priestfield rd Ben Bourne gdns Downham way PO Farmfield rd Downham Playing Fields

Worsley Bridge rd Greycot rd Braeside Playing Field Sedgehill rd Sports Grounds **Beckenham Hill** Brangbourne rd Old Bromley rd

Nat West Sports Ground Pool clo Overbrae Highland Braeside **Beckenham Hill road** Sports Ground Sports Ground Coniston rd Flinwell clo Kendale rd

Lloyds Bank Sports Ground Hack cres Calverley clo ASH PLANTATION Conston rd Ambleside Bolgavia gdns

Copers Cope rd Stumps Porchester sch mead **BECKENHAM PLACE PARK** Lewisham Borough Sports Ground Midland Bank Sports Ground Amblecroft Calmont rd

Sports Grounds Little stone Cranbo **Southend road** Shannon way Public Golf Course SUMMERHOUSE HILL WOOD Hillcrest clo Erin clo

Brackley rd Gainsborough clo Worsley Bridge rd Chislet clo Beckenham pl pk Ravensbourne rd Elstree rd Elstree hill Warren rd

Lawn rd Silver wood Ingle clo Beckenham pl Beckenham pl pk Ravensbourne rd **Ravensbourne** Warren Avenue Playing Fields

Alton gdns Sinclair clo Park rd May-wood clo Cricket Ground Foxgrove ave West-moat clo Evening Foxgrove rd Crab hill River pk Ravensbourne ave Farnaby rd

BECKENHAM **Beckenham Junction** A2015 The Avenue Canterbury clo May-fair ct Rep. ton ct Apex clo Foxgrove rd Wood-stock rd Banavie rd The Hunters Regency ms Spring-bourne Dylfe rd Downs clo The Avenue Downs rd Ravensbourne ave **Shortlands Golf Course**

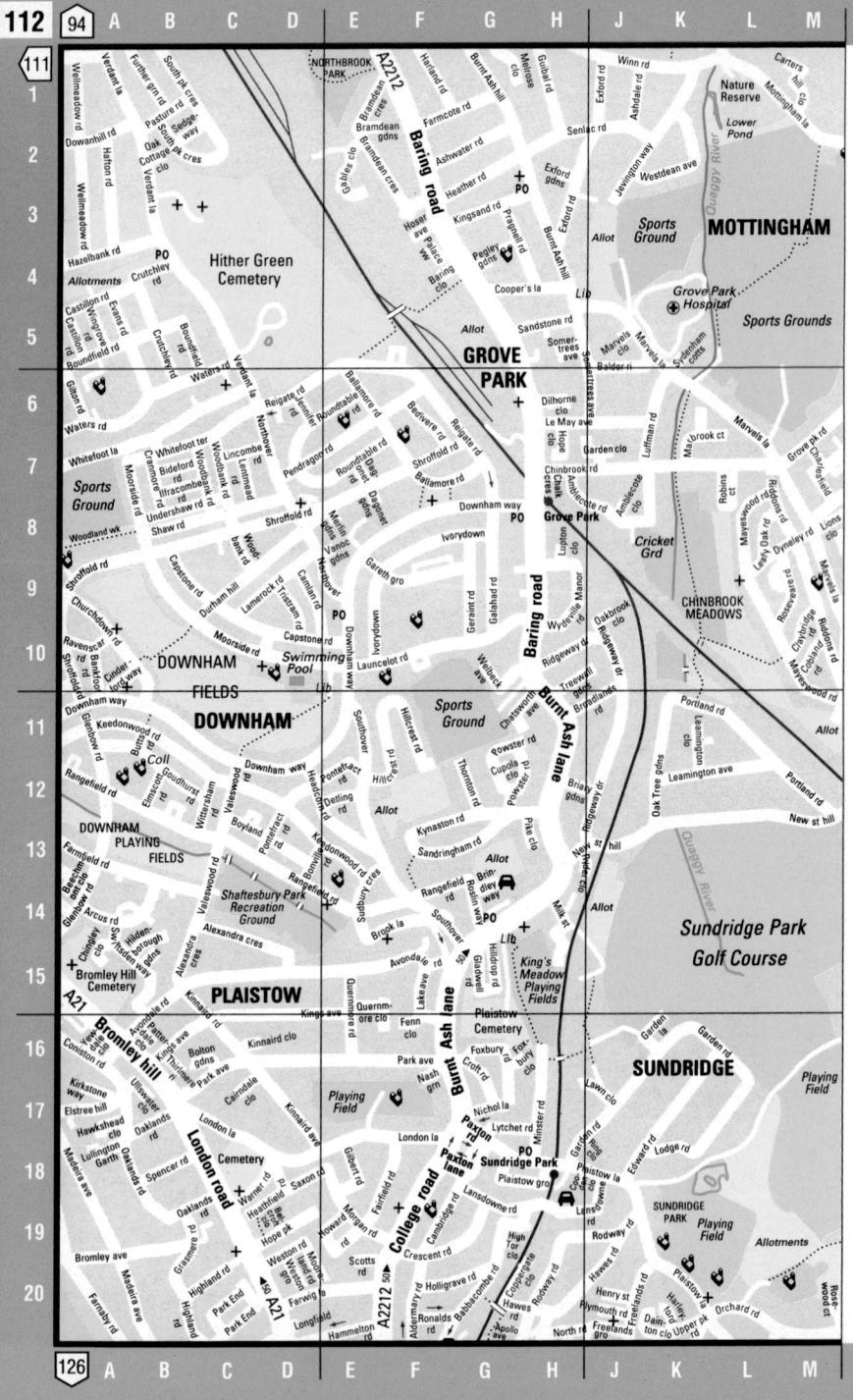

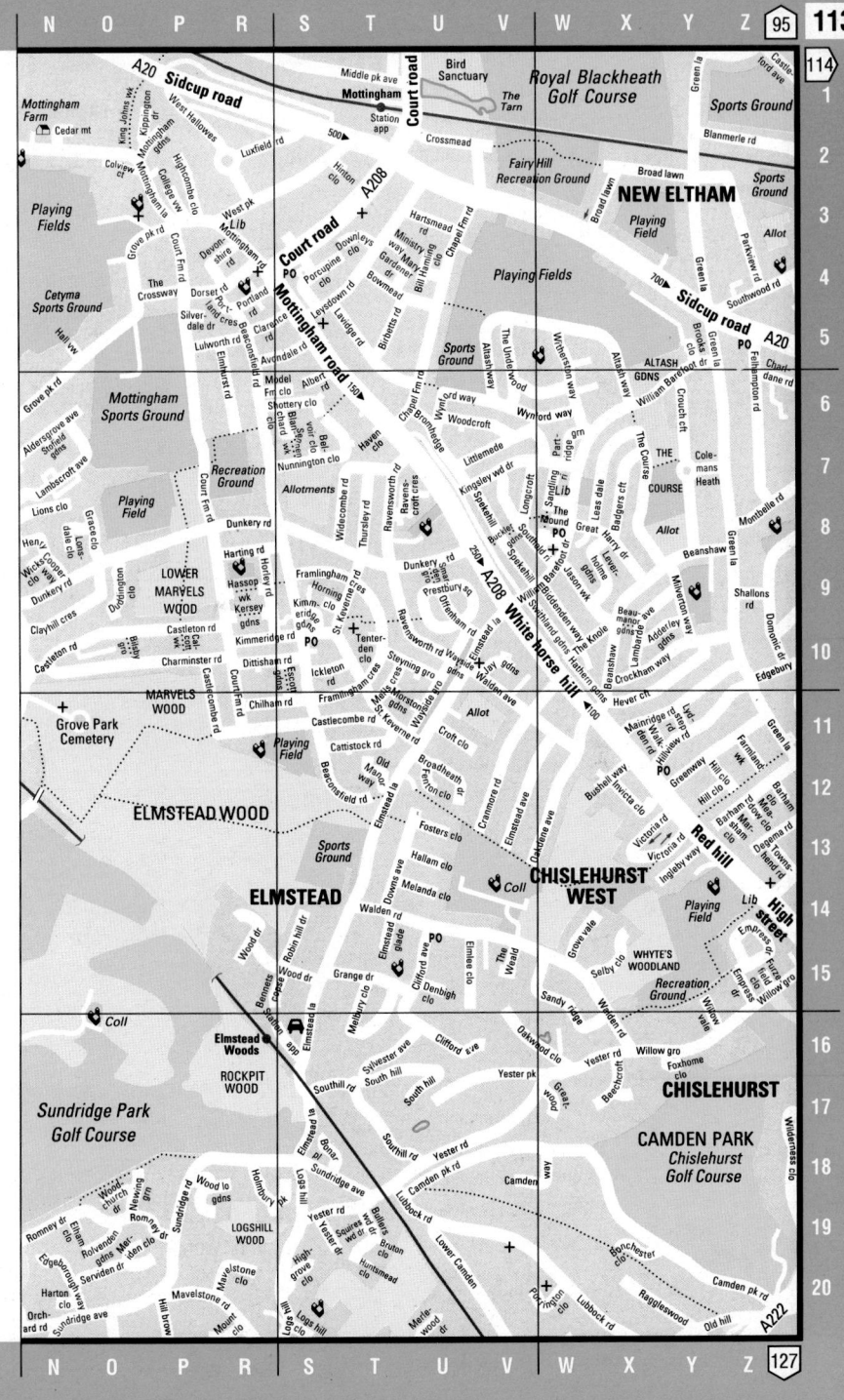

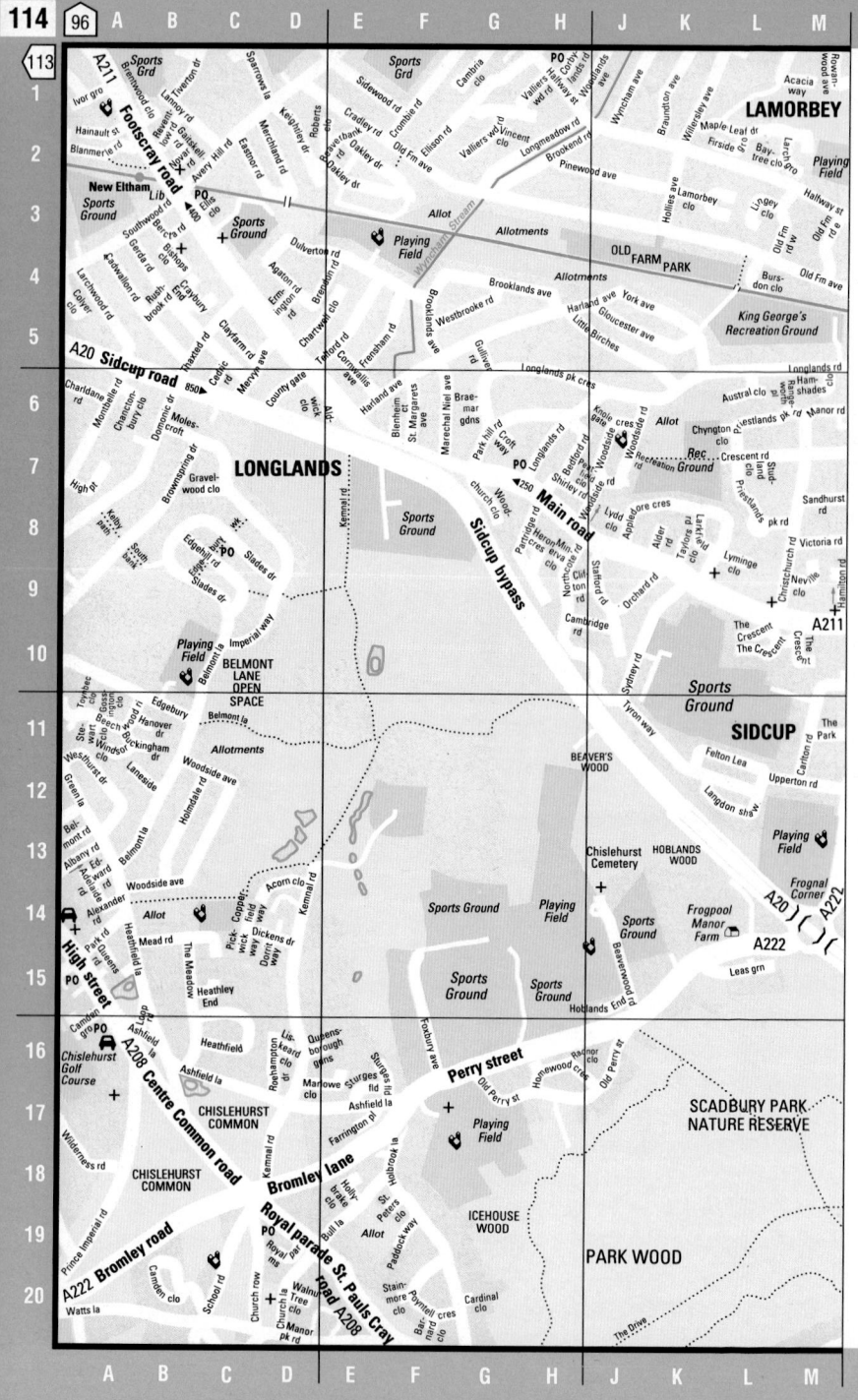

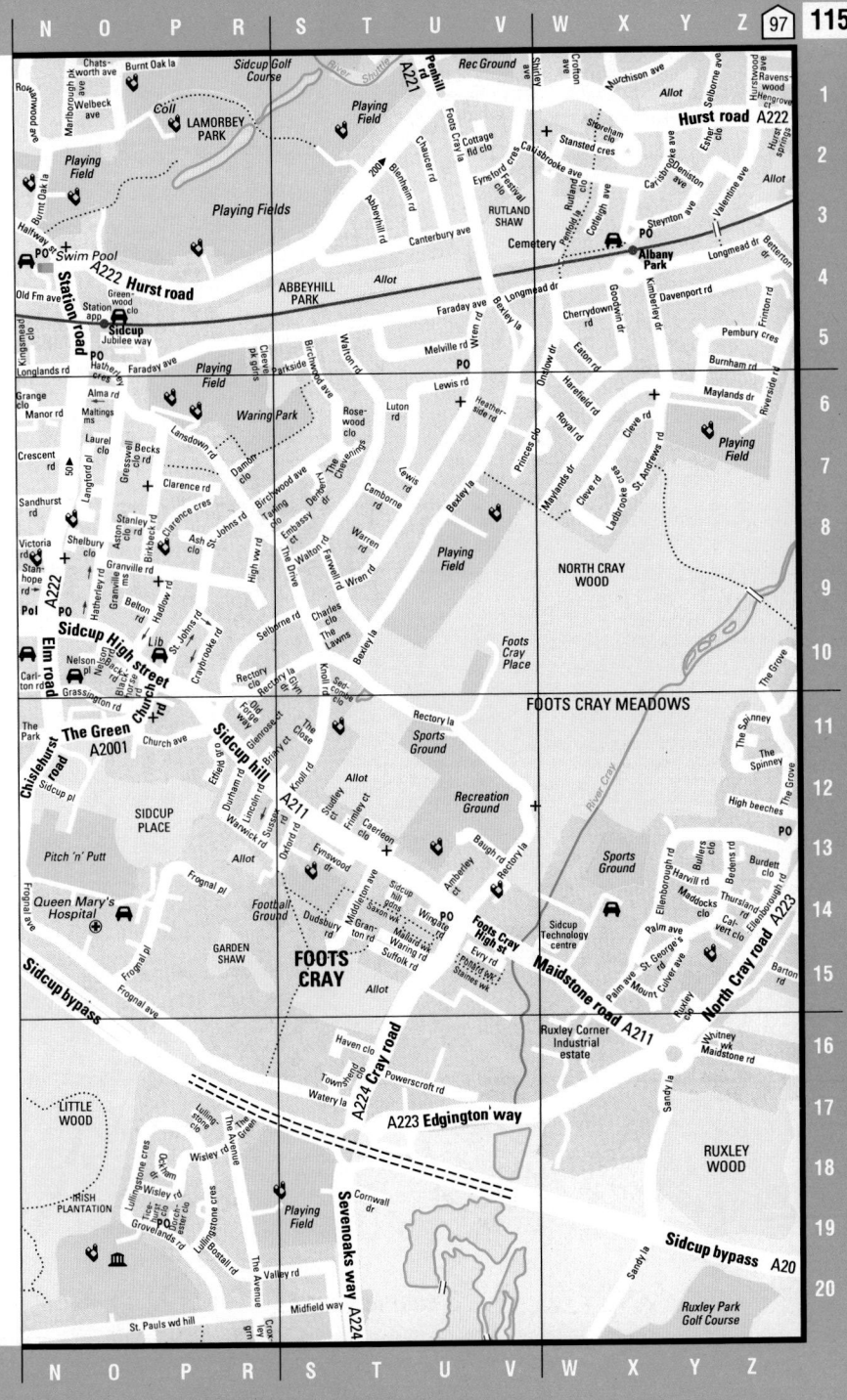

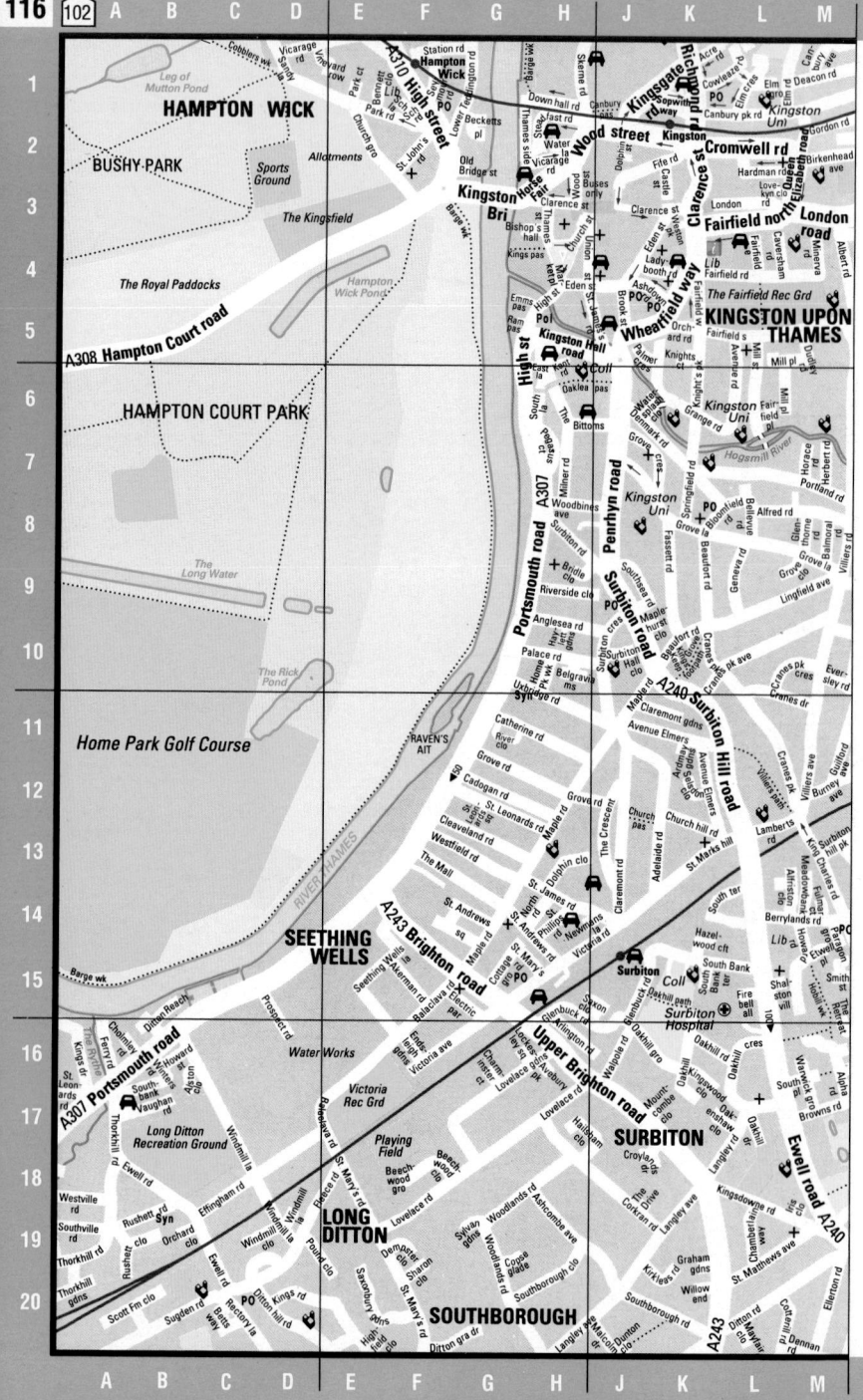

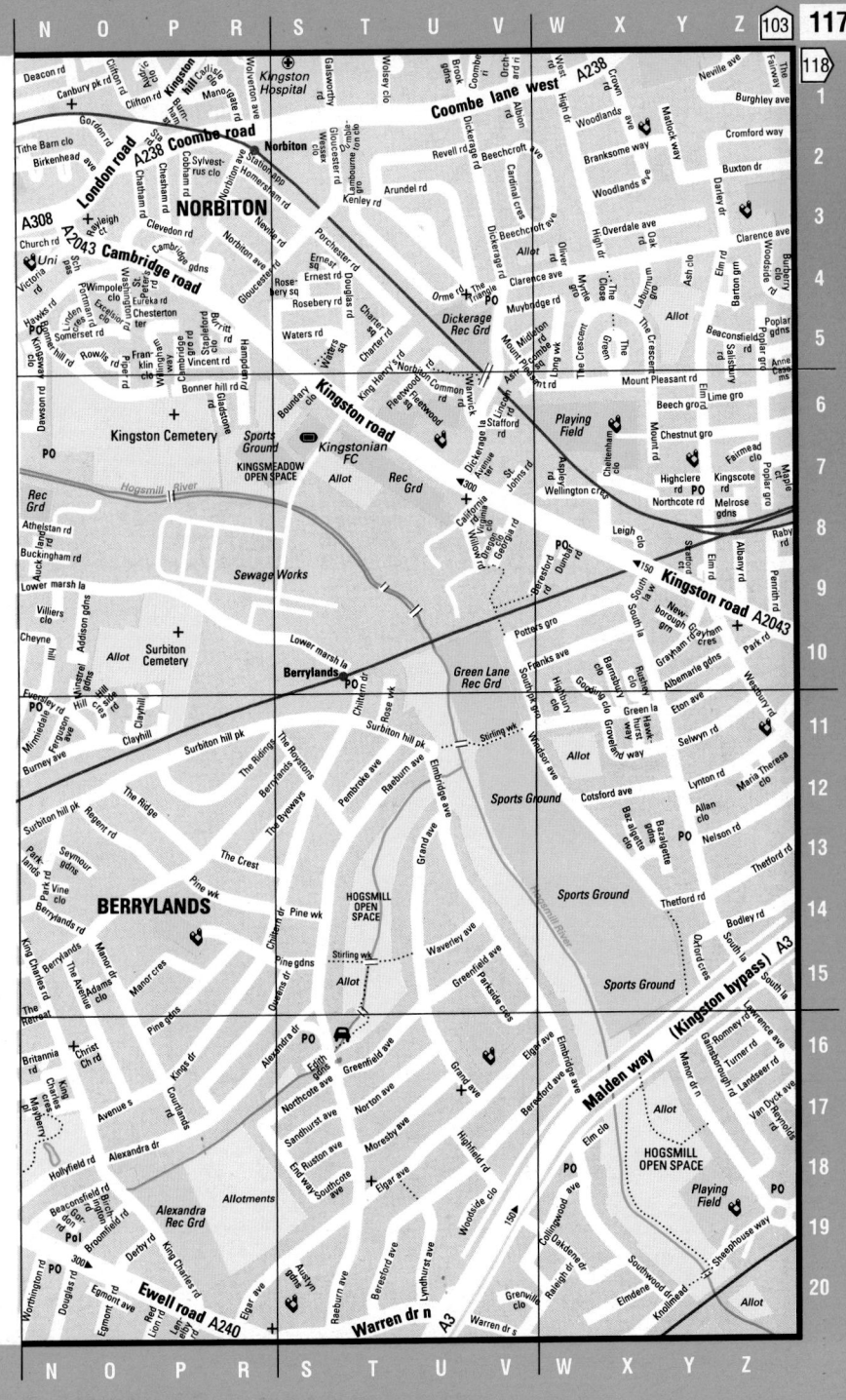

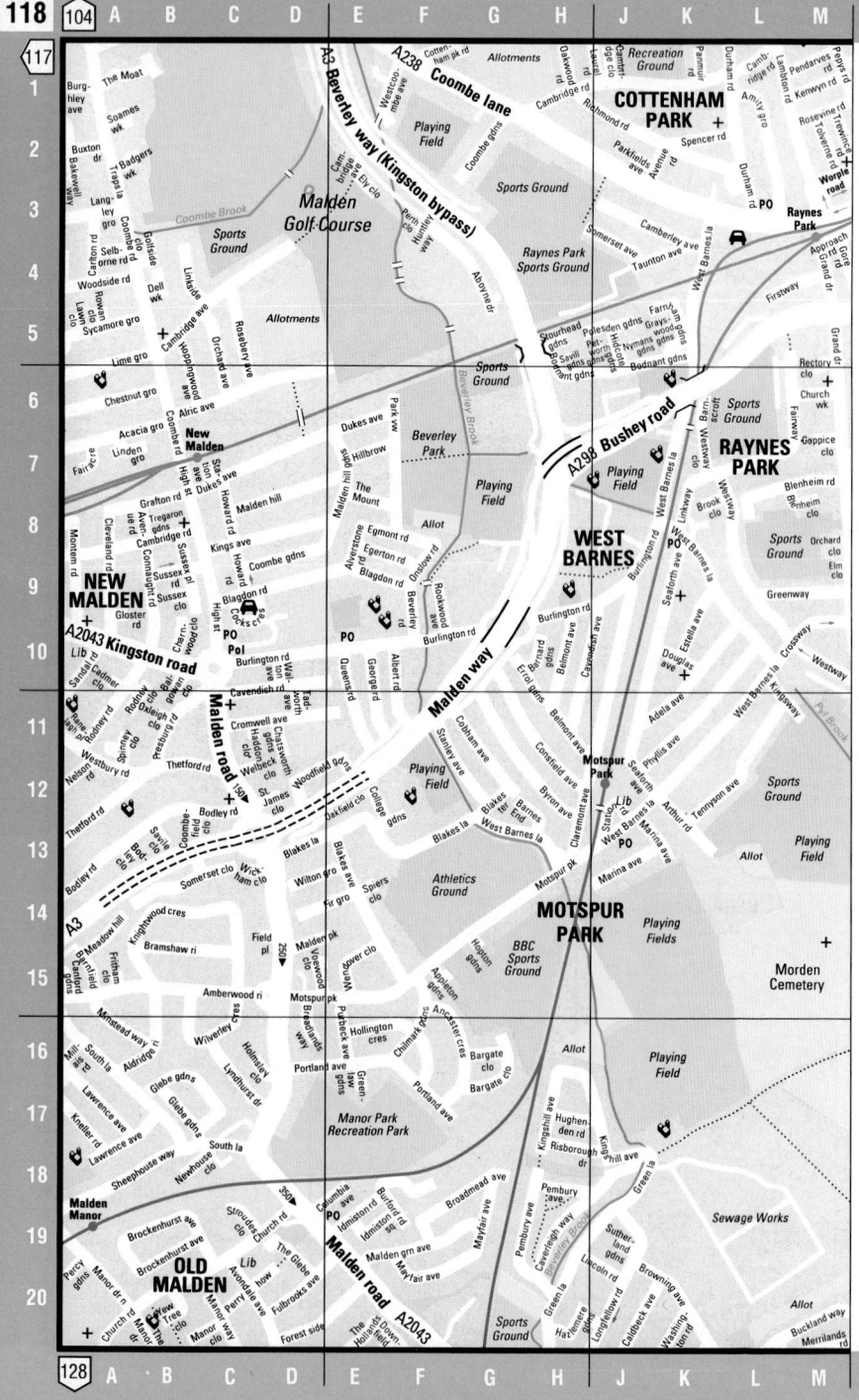

A B C D E F G H J K L M

A238 Cottenham pk rd
A3 Beverley way (Kingston bypass)
Coombe lane
Allotments
Oakwood rd
Camb-ridge ho
Panmuir rd
Durham rd
Recreation Ground
Pendarves rd
Popys rd
Kenwyn rd
Rosevine rd
Trewince rd
Towlmore rd
Worple road

COTTENHAM PARK
Richmond rd
Cambridge rd
Camberley ho
Spencer rd
Amity gro
Durham rd
PO
Raynes Park

Burghley ave
The Moat
Soames wk
Badgers wk
Bakewell way
Malden Golf Course
Coombe gdns
Playing Field
Parkfields ave
Avenue rd
Approach rd
Gore Grand rd

Buxton dr
Langley gro
Carlton rd
Selborne rd
Guilside rd
Linkside ave
Sports Ground
Coombe Brook
Sports Ground
Camberley ave
Taunton ave
West Barnes la
Firstway

Woodside rd
Rowan clo
Dell wk
Sycamore gro
Allotments
Rosebery ave
Beverley Brook
Stourhead gdns
Polesden gdns
Savill gdns
Nymans gdns
Grays-wood gdns
Bodnant gdns
Grand dr
Rectory clo

Lime gro
Chestnut gro
Acacia gro
Hoppingwood ave
Orchard ave
Alric ave
Sports Ground
Church wk
Goppice clo
Fairway

NEW MALDEN
Linden gro
Farrs
Grafton rd
Tregaron gdns
Cambridge rd
Sta. High st
Howard rd
Malden hill
Dukes ave
Park way
Hillbrow
Dukes ave
Beverley Park
A298 Bushey road
Playing Field
Barn croft
Sports Ground
RAYNES PARK

Montem rd
Cleveland rd
Connaught rd
Avon gdns
Sussex rd
Sussex pl
Sussex clo
Kings ave
Coombe gdns
The Mount
Malden hill
Egmont rd
Egerton rd
Onslow rd
Allot
Alverstone rd
Playing Field
West Barnes la
West Barnes la
Westway
Brook clo
Blenheim rd
Priheim clo
Sports Ground
Orchard clo
Elm clo
Greenway

NEW MALDEN
Gloster rd
A2043 Kingston road
Lib PO Pol
Charnock
Blagdon rd
Blagdon rd
Clooks cres
Beverley rd
Rookwood ave
Burlington rd
Burlington rd
Malden way
WEST BARNES
Seaforth ave
Burlington gdns
Estella ave
Douglas ave
Crossway
Westway

Sandal rd
Cadmer rd
Rodney rd
Oswlight rd
Presburg rd
PO
Burlington rd
Wilton rd
Tudor rd
Queensel
Albert rd
George rd
Errol gdns
Belmont ave
Cavendish ho
Bynard rd
Belmont ave
Adela ave
West Barnes la
Kingsway
Pyl Brook

Raite rd
Rodney rd
Westbury rd
Nelson rd
Thetford rd
Cromwell ave
Haddon gdns
Welbeck rd
Woodfield gro
St. James clo
Cobham ave
Stanley ave
Consfield ave
Motspur Park
Phyllis ave
Seaforth
Arthur rd
Tennyson ave
Sports Ground
Playing Field

Thetford rd
Bodley rd
Savile gdns Bdy
Coombe Piley
Bodley rd
Blakes la
Somerset clo
Wickham clo
Oakfield rd
College gdns
Blakes ter End
Barnes End
West Barnes la
Byron ave
Claremont ave
Station Lib
West Barnes la
PO
Marina ave
Allot

A3
Meadow hill
Knightwood cres
Bramshaw ri
Field pl
Malden pk
250m
Blakes la
Wilton rd
Spiers clo
Fir gro
Athletics Ground
Motspur pk
Hogbon gdns
MOTSPUR PARK
BBC Sports Ground
Playing Fields
Allot
Morden Cemetery

Millstead way
South la
Aldridge ri
Holmesley clo
Lyndhurst dr
Amberwood ri
Wiverley clo
Motspurpk
Voluwood clo
Dower clo
Broadlands way
Purbeck clo
Hollington cres
Ancaster cres
Chilmark gdns
Green law gdns
Bargate clo
Portland rd
Bargate clo
Allot
Playing Field

Lawrence ave
Kneller rd
Lawrence ave
Glebe gdns
Glebe gdns
South la
Sheephouse way
Newhouse clo
Manor Park Recreation Park
Portland ave
Kingshill ave
Hughenden rd
Risborough dr
Kings la
Green la

Malden Manor
Brockenhurst ave
Brockenhurst ave
560
Columbia ave
Stroudor clo
Church rd
The Glebe
Idmiston rd
Idmiston rd
Malden grn ave
PO
Mayfair ave
Broadmead rd
Pembury ave
Pembury ave
Caversleigh way
Sutherland gdns
Lincoln rd
Browning ave
Sewage Works

Percy gdns
Manor dr n
Avondale how
Perry la
Yew Tree clo
Manor way
Fulbrooks ave
Forest side
OLD MALDEN
Church rd
The Manor
Malden road A2043
The Down Holland field
Green la
Hazelmead
Longfellow rd
Caldbeck ave
Washington rd
Allot
Buckland la
Merrilands rd

Sports Ground

A B C D E F G H J K L M

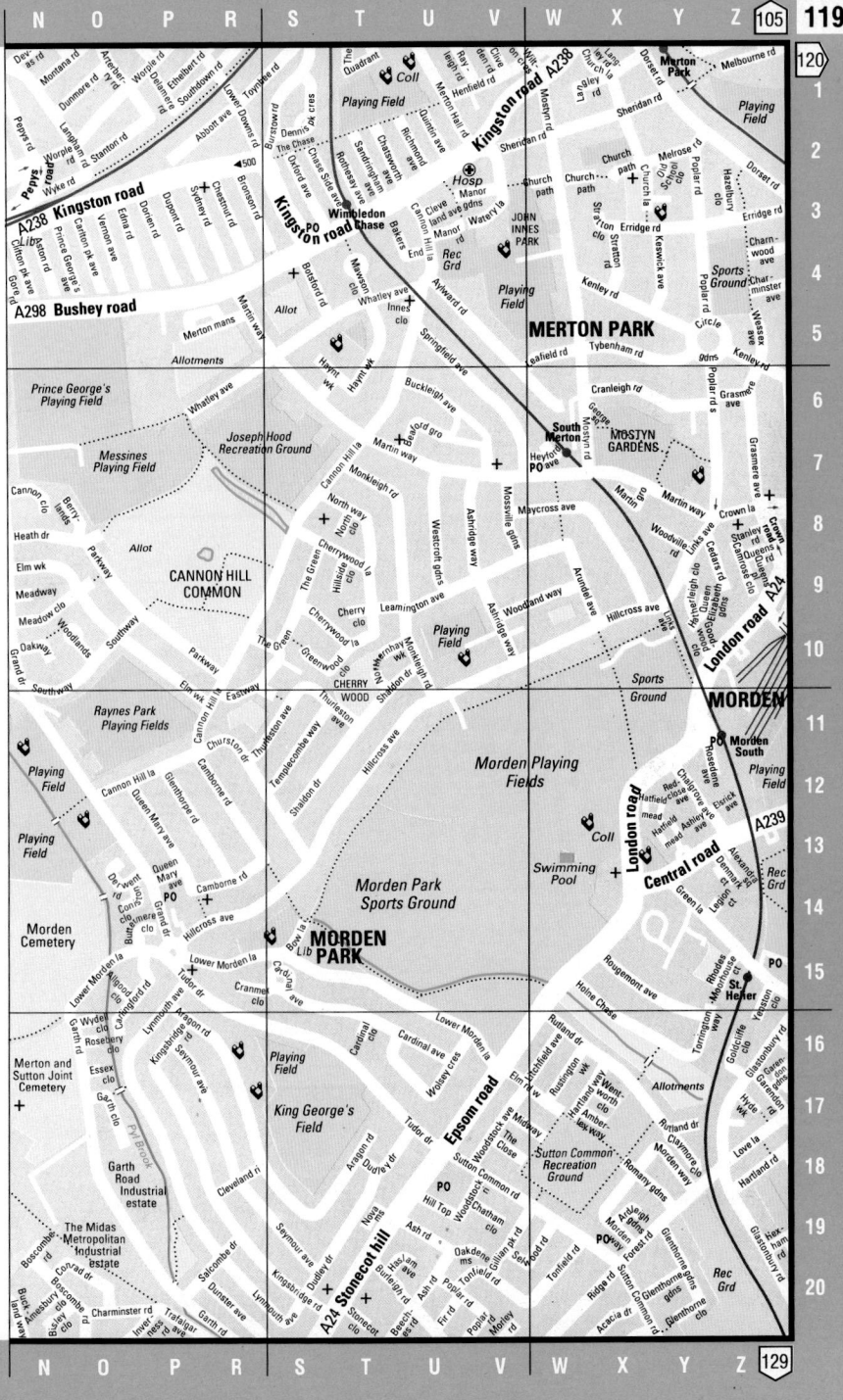

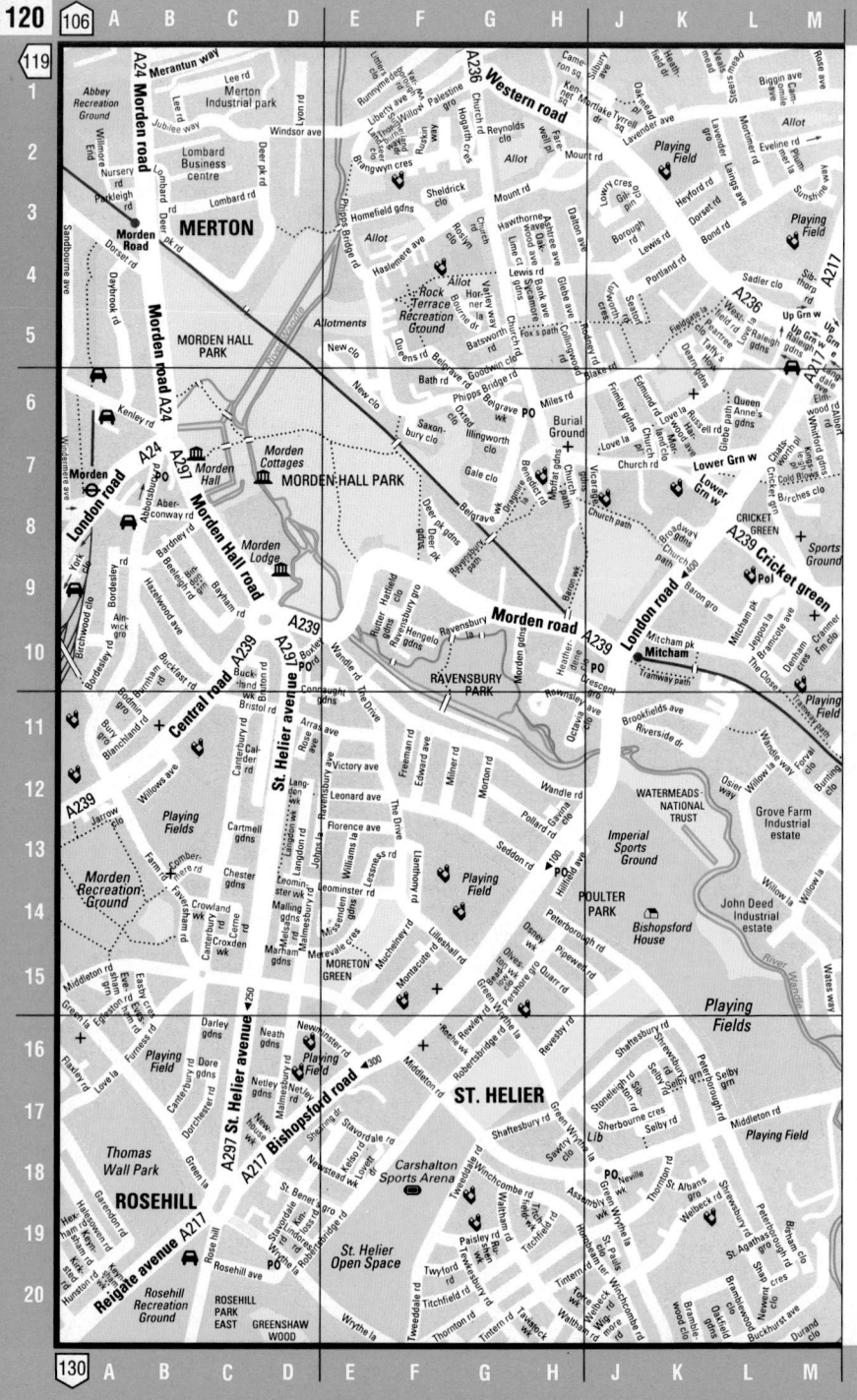

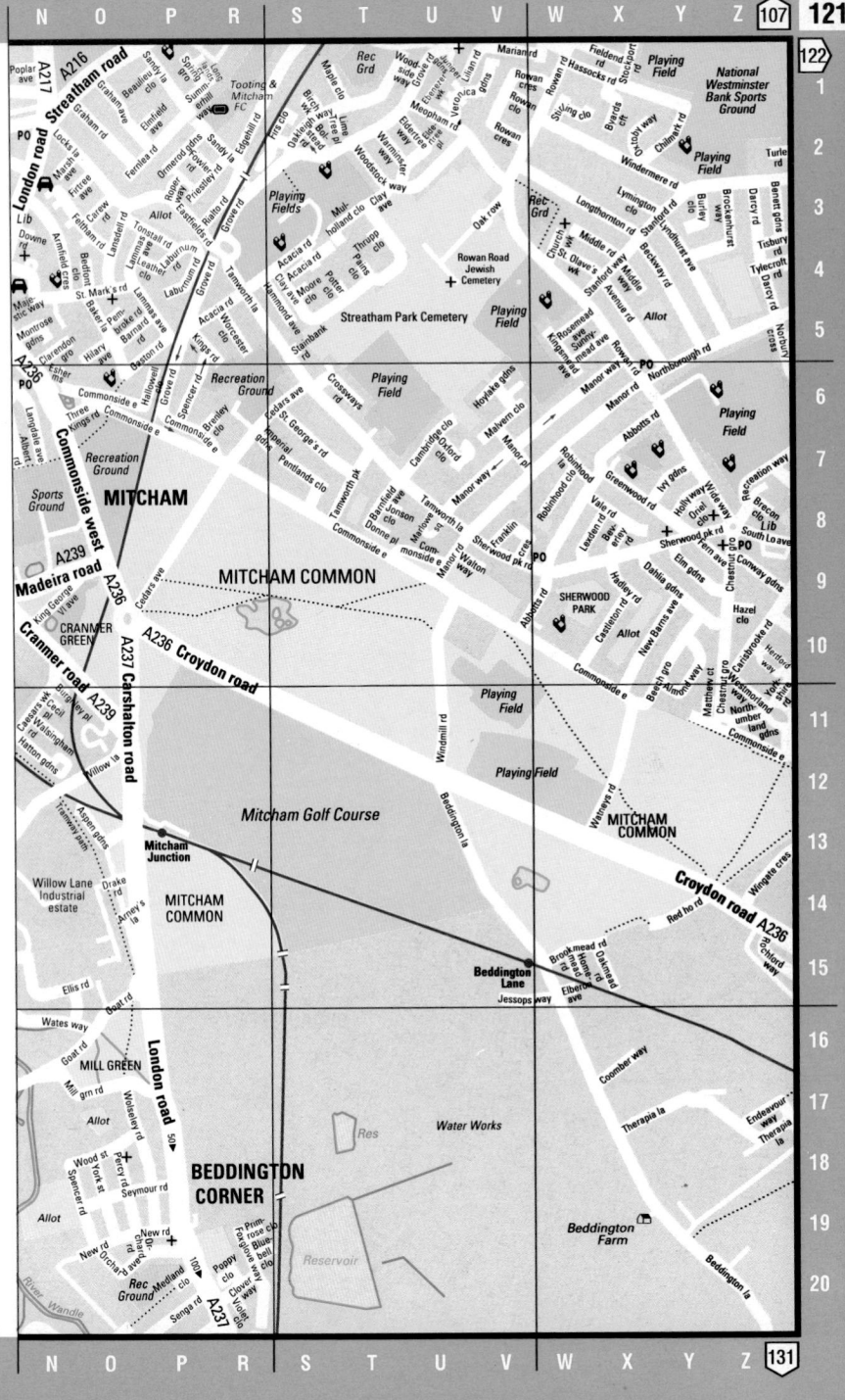

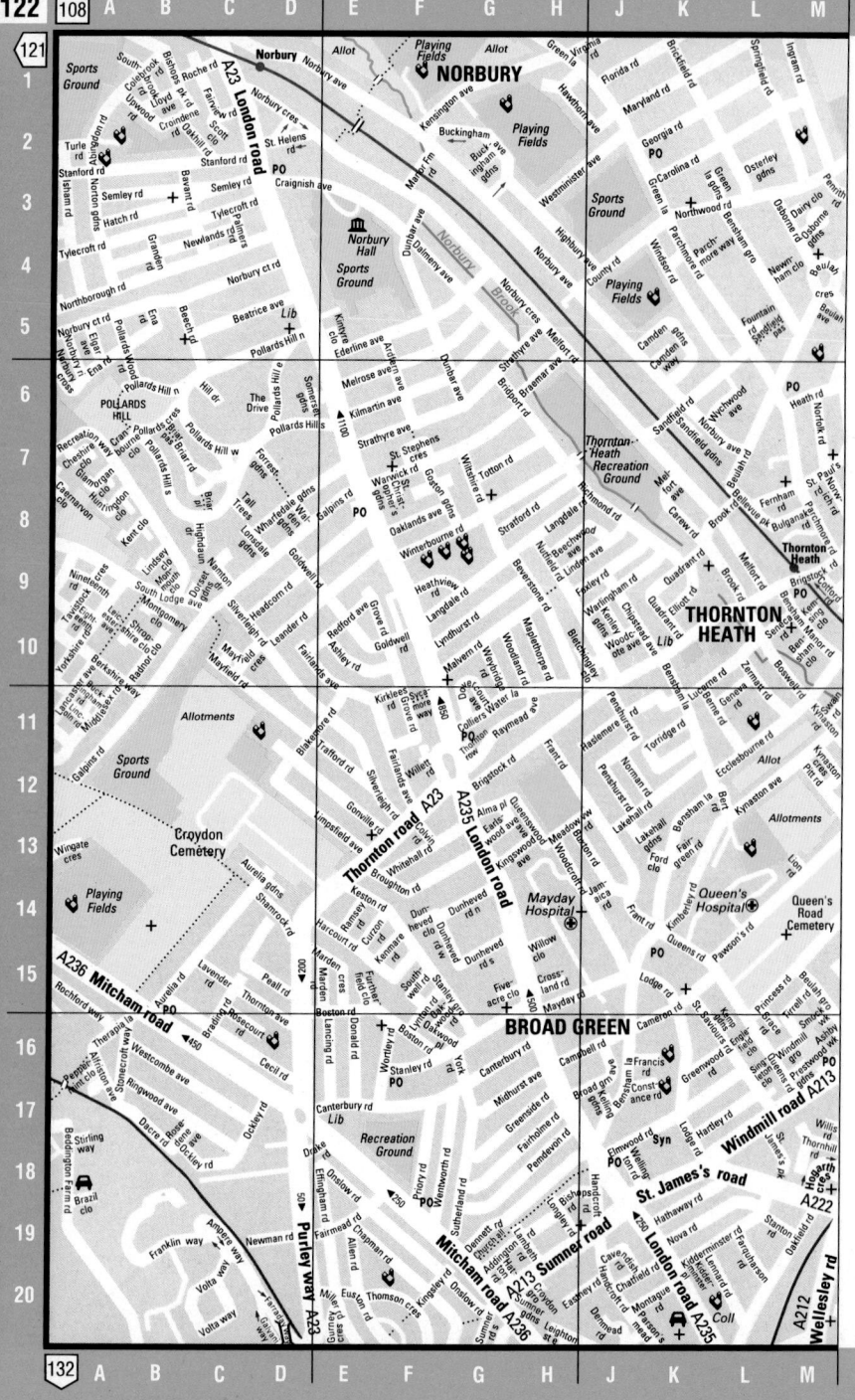

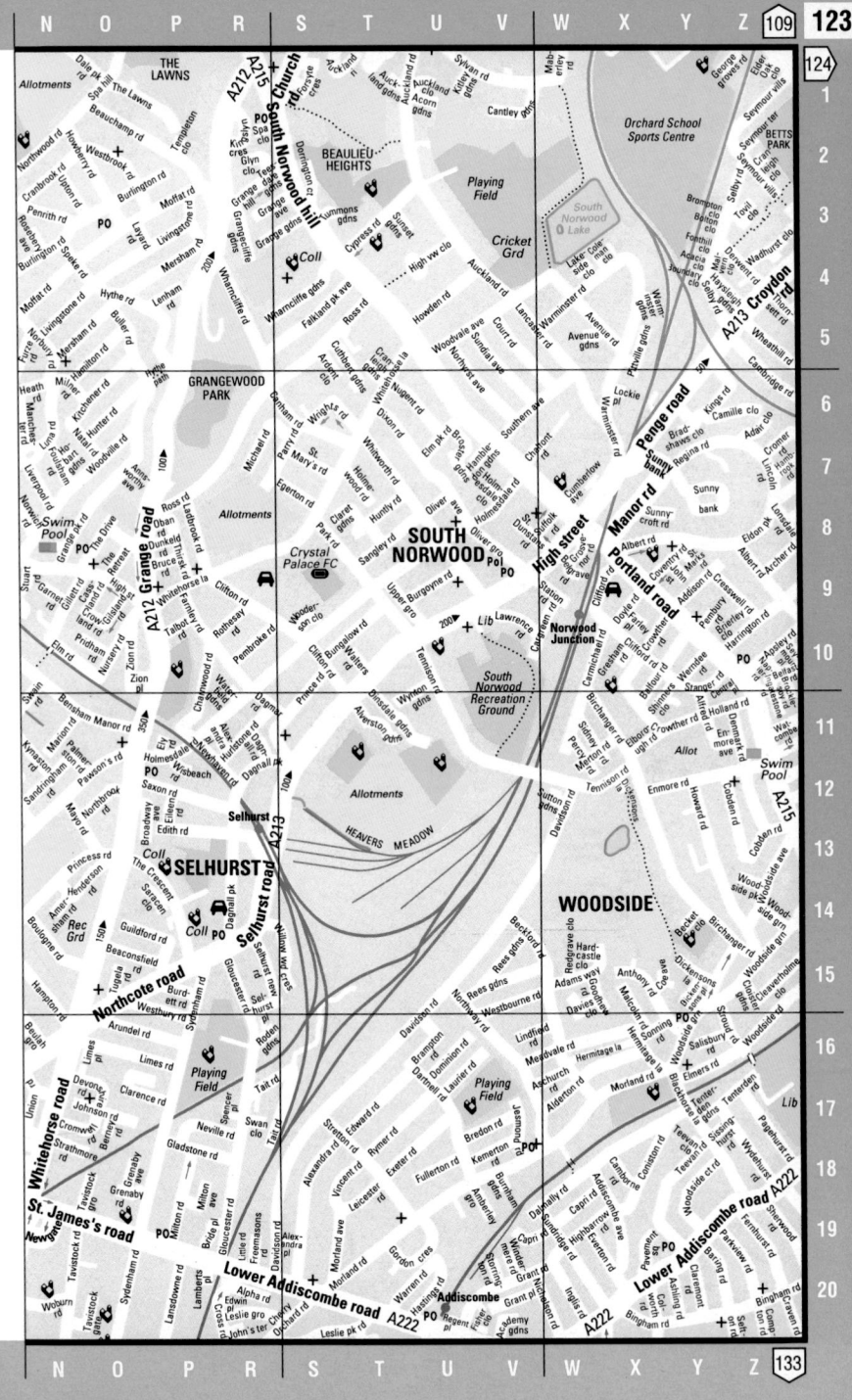

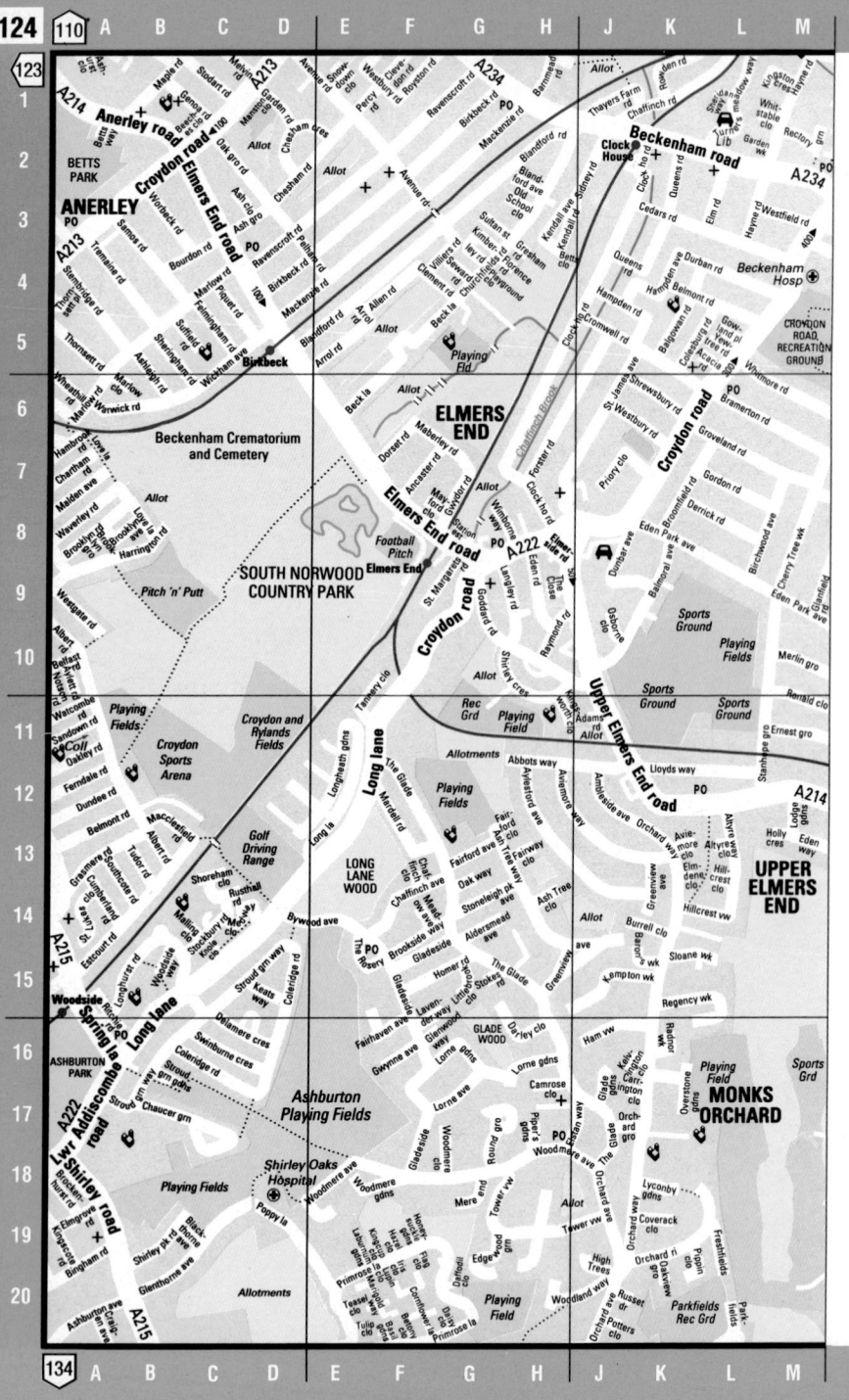

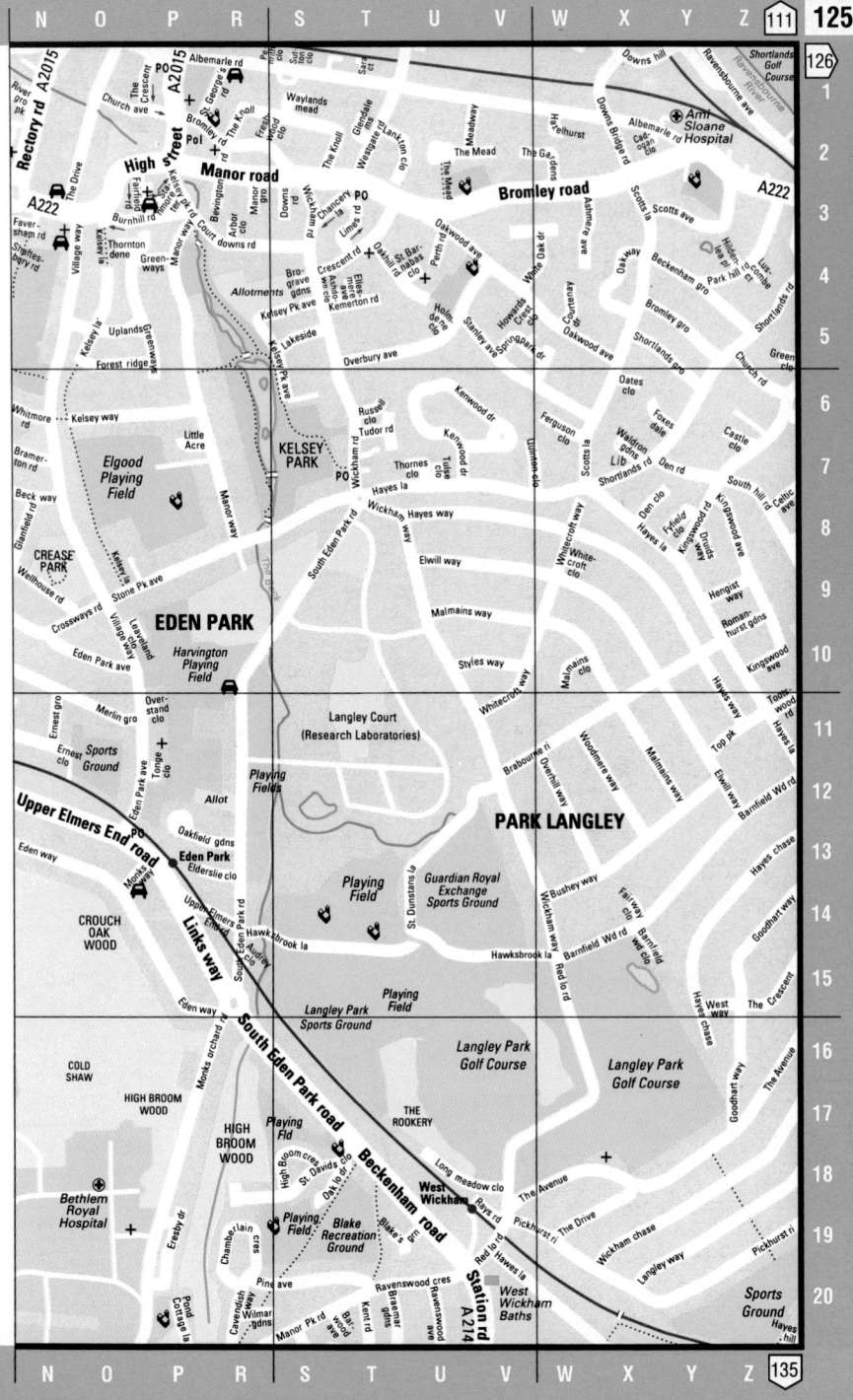

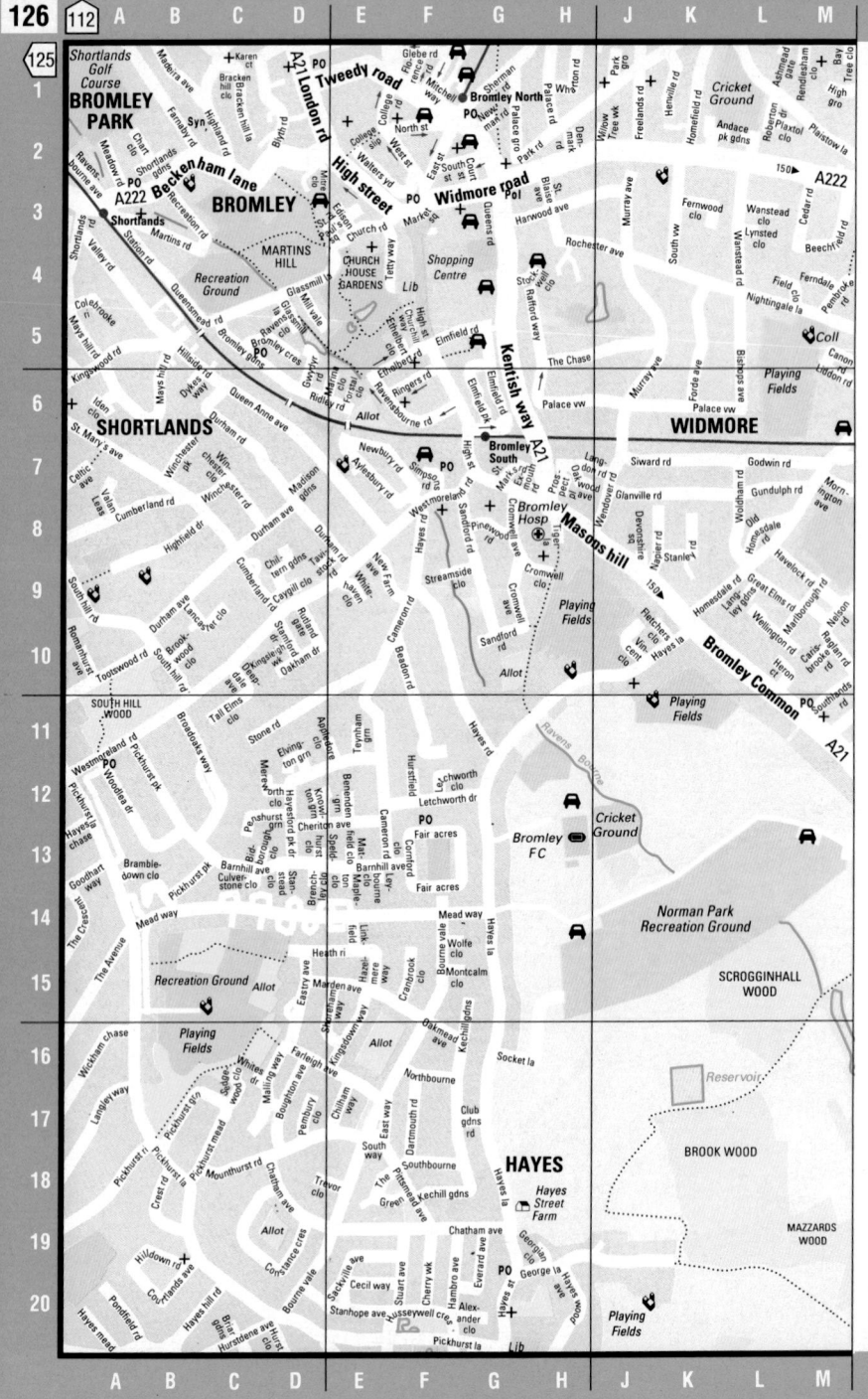

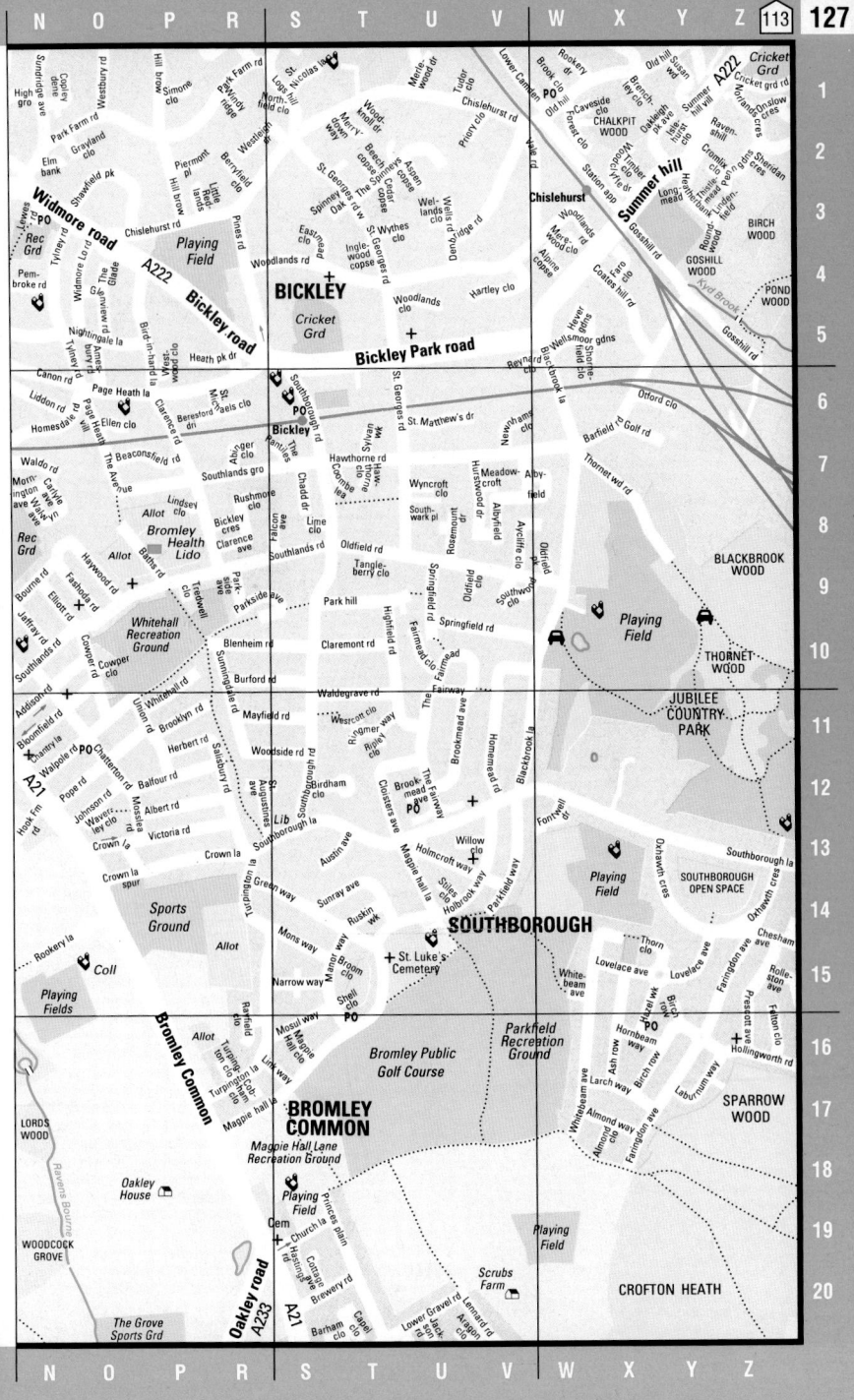

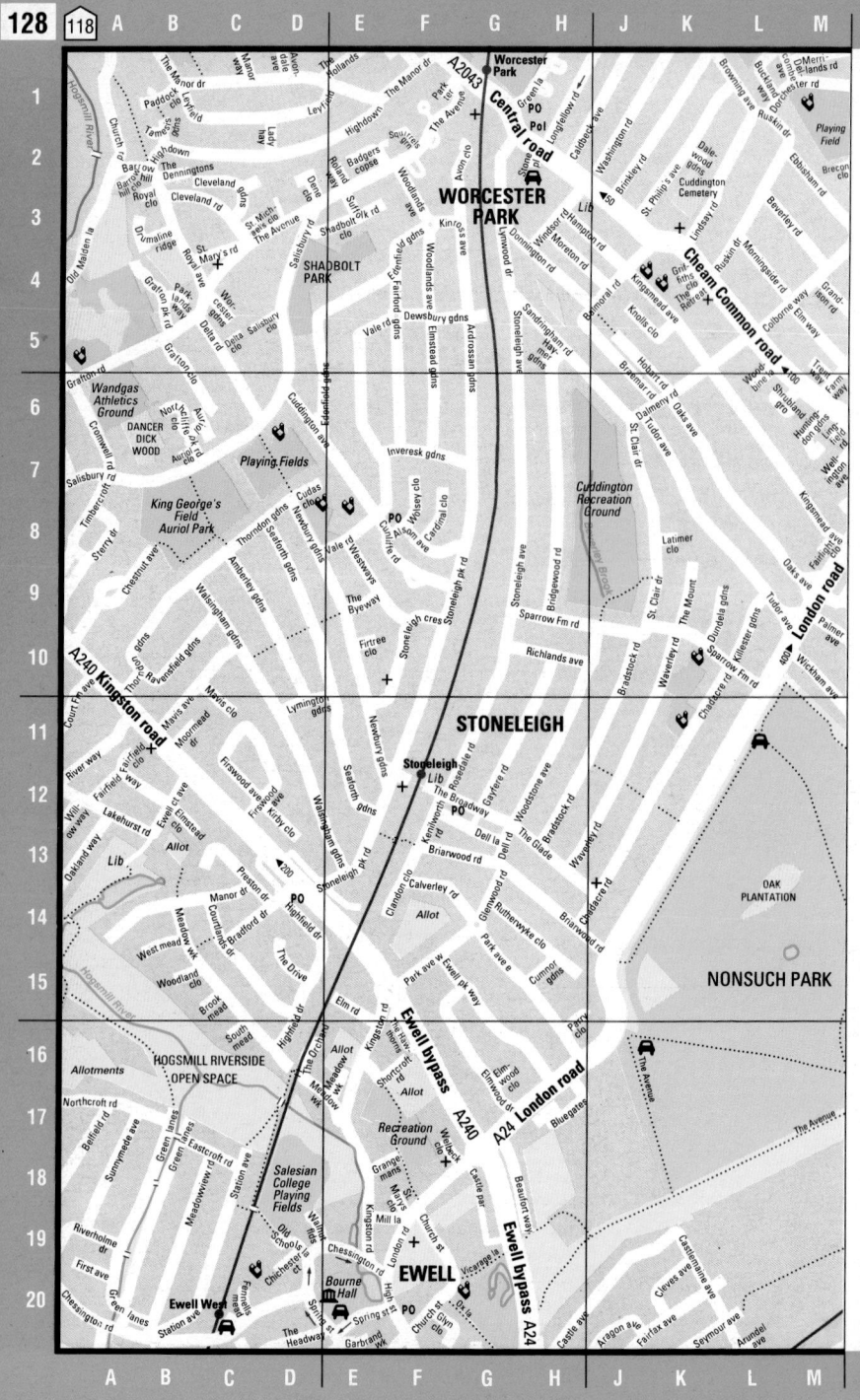

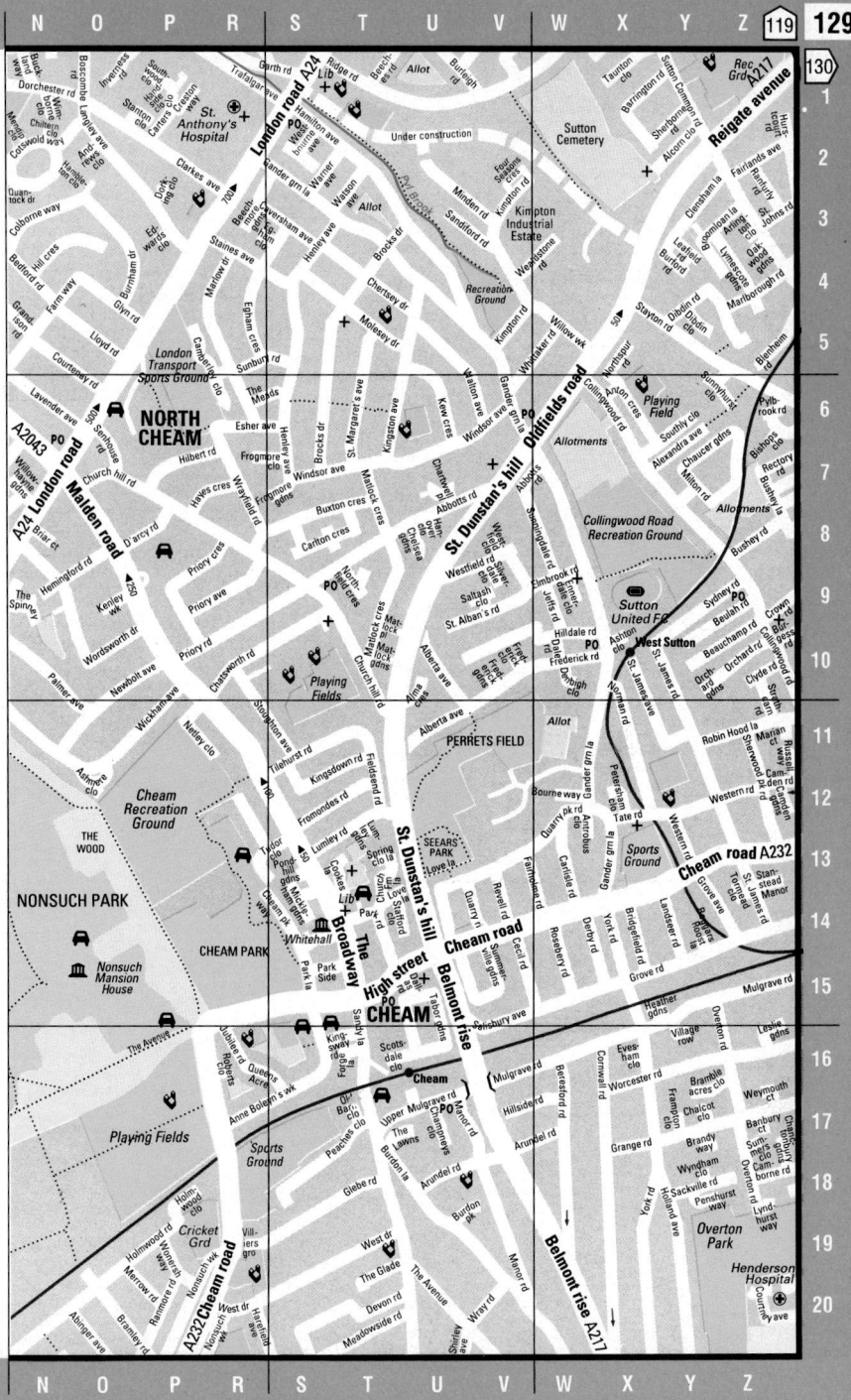

Map labels

Rec Grd A217

Reigate avenue

Taunton clo
Barrington la
Sherborne rd
Alcorn clo
Hurst court
Farlands ave
Hurst court

Sutton Cemetery

Garth rd
Ridge rd
Beech rd
Allot
Burleigh
A24
Lib
London road
PO
Hamilton rd
West
borne rd
Warner
Watson
Under construction

Fore
Seasons
clo
Kimpton rd
Oldham la
Atting rd
St. Johns rd

Boscombe rd
Langland rd
Inverness
South
wood
Creston way
Trafalgar ave

Dorchester rd
Wire
land
way
Chiltern clo
Cotswold way

St. Anthony's Hospital

Clarkes ave
Caversham ave
Henley ave
Kander grn la

Denham la
Leafield
Limesdale gdns
Oak
wood
gdns

Colborne way
And
rews
clo
Ed
wards
clo

Quan-
tock way

Beech-
more
ave
Delis-
Hoe
Henley ave
Shan-
non clo
Allot
Sandiford rd
Minden rd

Kimpton Industrial Estate
Weirstone

Burford
Marlborough rd

Bedford hill cres
Burnham dr
Glyn rd

Staines ave
Merlow dr
Egham cres

Brocks dr
Chertsey rd

Recreation Ground

Kimpton rd
Stayton rd

Didin rd
Didin
clo
Blenheim

Grand-
ison rd
Farm way

Lloyd rd

Courtenay rd

London Transport
Sports Ground

Sunbury rd
Molesey dr

Whitaker rd
Willow wk
50w
Northspur rd

Lavender ave
The Meads

NORTH CHEAM
A2043
PO
Seahouse
clo
Esher ave

Kew cres
Gander la

Windsor ave
PO
Oldfields road
Collingwood rd

Playing Field

Sunnyhurst
clo
Pyl-
brook rd

Willow
hayne
clo
Church hill rd
Hilbert rd

Hayes cres
Wayfield rd
Frogmore gdns
St. Margaret's ave
Kingston la

Windsor ave
Cherwell clo

St. Dunstan's hill
West
Abbotts rd

Allotments
Southly clo
Bishops
Rectory rd

Alexandra ave
Chaucer gdns
Milton rd

A24 London road
Malden road
D'arcy rd

Buxton cres
Chelsea rd

Collingwood Road Recreation Ground
Allotments
Bushey rd

Priory cres
Carlton cres

Westfield rd
Silver-
dale rd
Saltash clo

Emard rd
Elmbrook rd

Hemingford rd
Kenley wk
250

Priory ave
North-
field cres

Matlock cres
St. Alban's rd

Frederick clo
Dale rd
Frost
clo
Ashton rd
Sydney rd
PO
Beulah rd

Sutton United FC
Crown Rd
Garth Rd

The Spinney

Wordsworth dr
Newbolt ave
Priory rd
Chatsworth rd

Matlock gdns
Church hill rd
Alberta ave

Hildale rd
Denbigh clo
West Sutton
PO
St. James rd
Beauchamp rd
Orchard rd

Orch-
ard
clo
Clyde rd
Stretton Rd

Palmer ave

PO
Playing Fields

Alma cres
Alberta ave

PERRETS FIELD
Allot
Newman rd
St. James rd

Robin Hood la
Marian
Russell
Camden rd

Ashmere clo

Wickham ave

Netley clo

Tilehurst rd
Kingsdown rd
Fieldsend rd

Bourne way
Quarry pk rd
Peter-sham rd
Antrobus rd
Western rd
Sherwood rd
Cam-
den Clo

Cheam Recreation Ground
THE WOOD

Stoughton clo
A190

Fromondes rd
Lumley rd

Tate rd
Gander la
Carlisle rd

Sports Ground
Western rd
Landseer rd
Bridgefield rd

Cheam road A232

NONSUCH PARK

Taylor clo
The Pond gdns
Mickleham way
Cookes clo
Spring la
Love la

St. Dunstan's hill
SEEARS PARK
Love la
Quarry la
Revell rd
Summer gdns
Fairholme rd
York rd
Derby rd
Rosebery rd

Stan-
stead Manor

Nonsuch Mansion House

Lib
Stafford rd
Park rd

Cheam road
Cecil rd
Grove rd

CHEAM PARK
Whitehall
Park la
Park Side

The Broadway
High street
Belmont rise
CHEAM
PO

Mulgrave rd
Heather gdns
Village row
Overton rd
Leafie gdns

Mulgrave rd

The Avenue
Queens Acre
Anne Boleyn's wk
Kingsway rd
Scots-dale clo
Tabor gdns
Salisbury ave

Eves-
ham clo
Cornwall rd
Worcester rd
Bramble acres clo
Chalcot clo
Frampton clo
Weymouth ct
Banbury ct

Hillside rd
(Mulgrave rd)
Grange rd
Brandy way
Sum-
mer
clo
Cam-
borne rd

Playing Fields

Roberts
Bar-
rett
clo
Upper Mulgrave rd
PO
The Lawns
Peaches clo
Manor rd
Arundel rd

Wyndham clo
York rd
Holland ave
Sackville rd
Penshurst way

Lynd-hurst way

Sports Ground

Holm-
wood rd
Glebe rd
Burdon la

Burdon pk
Arundel rd

Overton Park

Cricket Grd
Villiers gro

West dr
Burdon la

Belmont rise A217

Merrow rd
Ramore rd
Nonsuch rd
West dr
Hereford rd

The Glade
Devon rd
Meadowside rd

Manor rd
Wilbury rd

Henderson Hospital
Courtney ave

A232 Cheam road
Abinger ave
Bramley rd

Row numbers down right side: 1 2 3 4 5 6 7 8 9 10 11 12 13 14 15 16 17 18 19 20

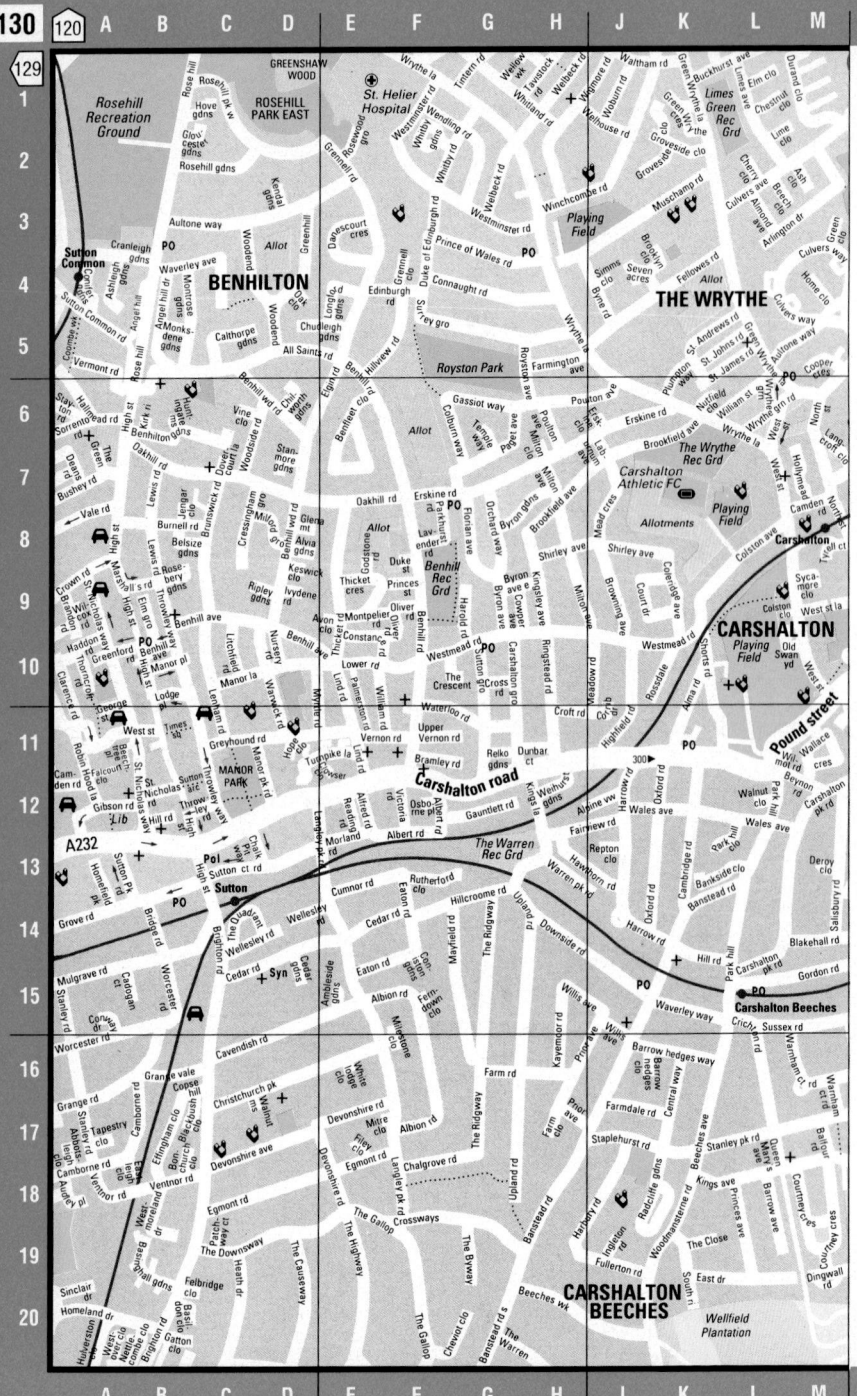

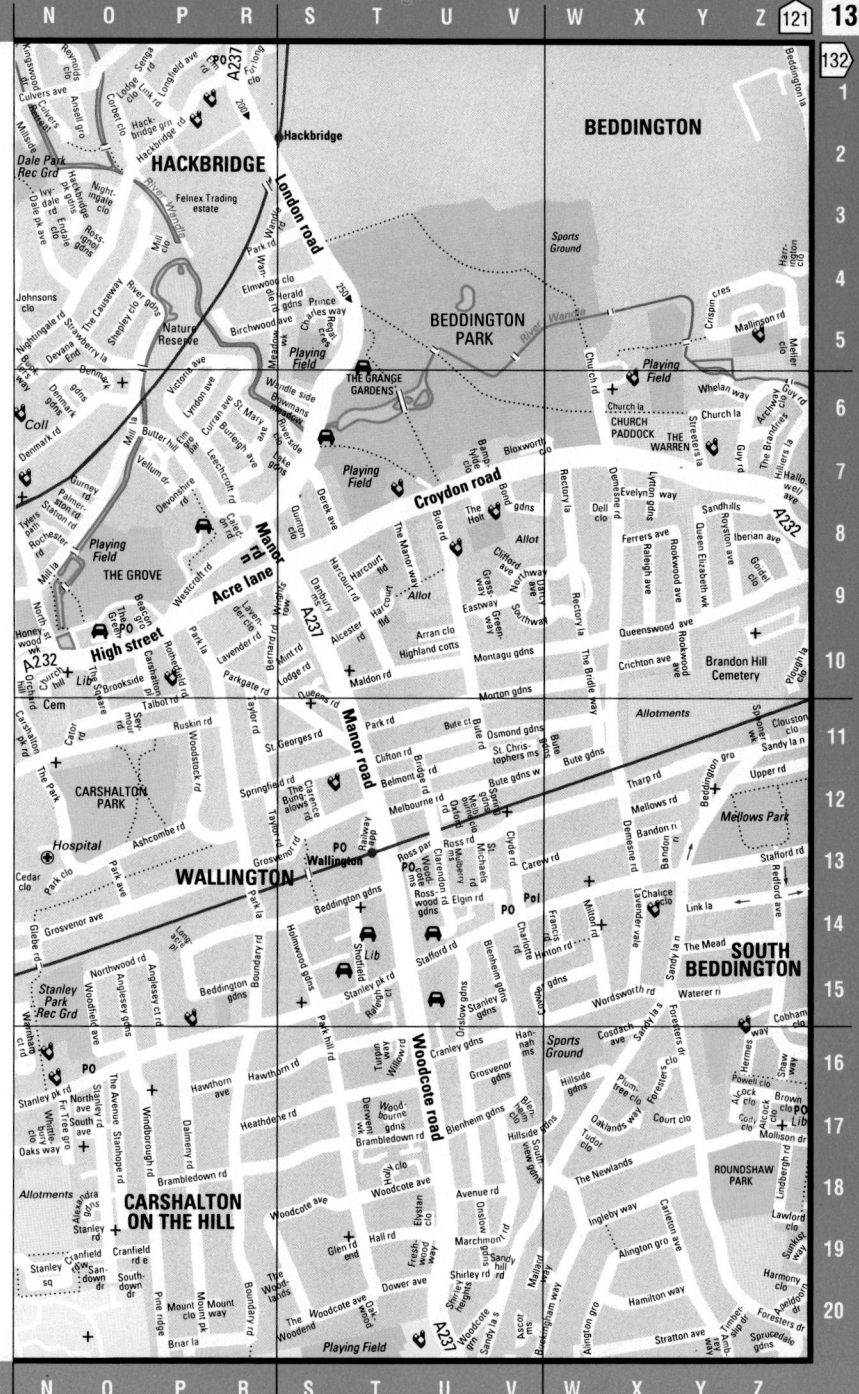

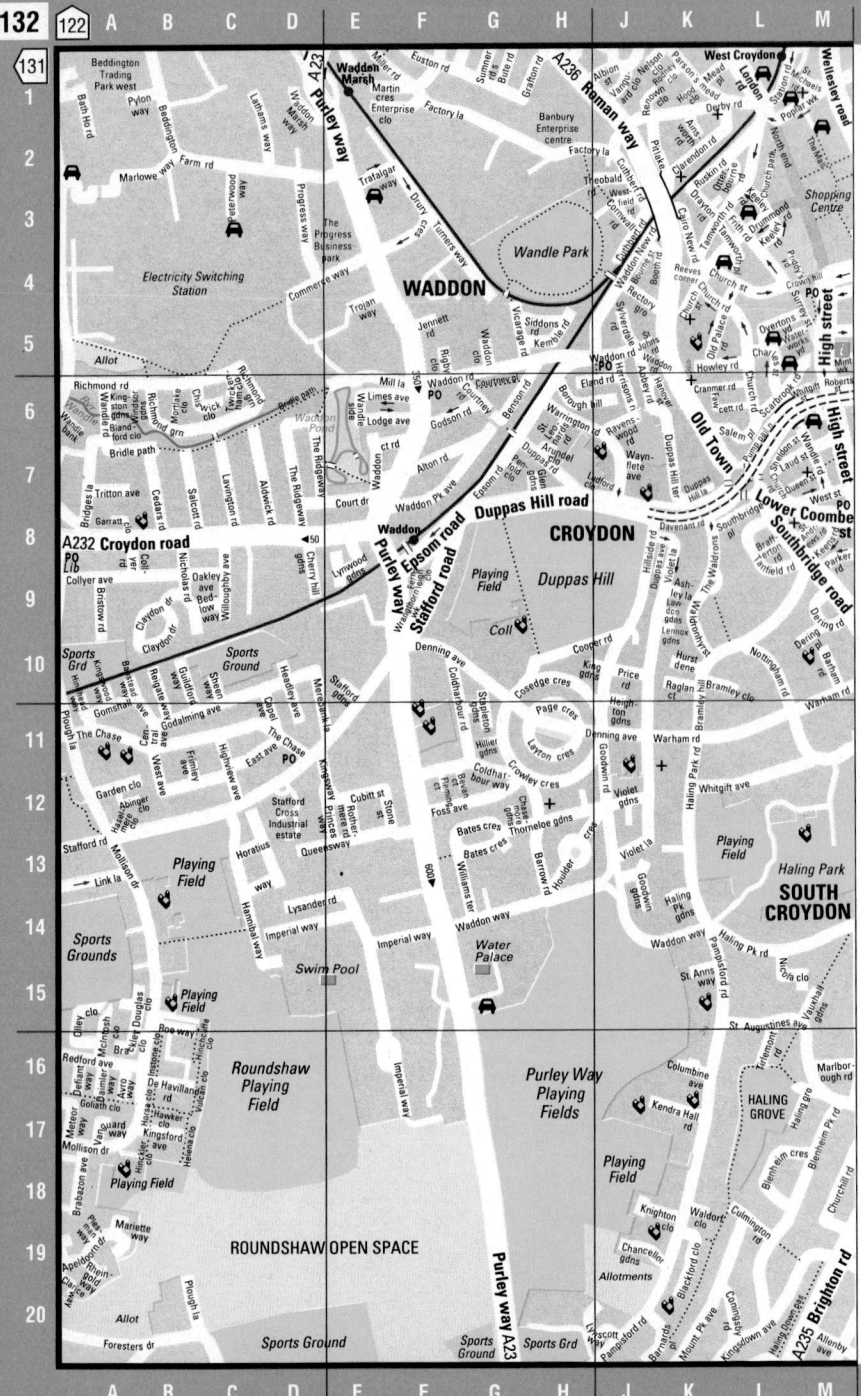

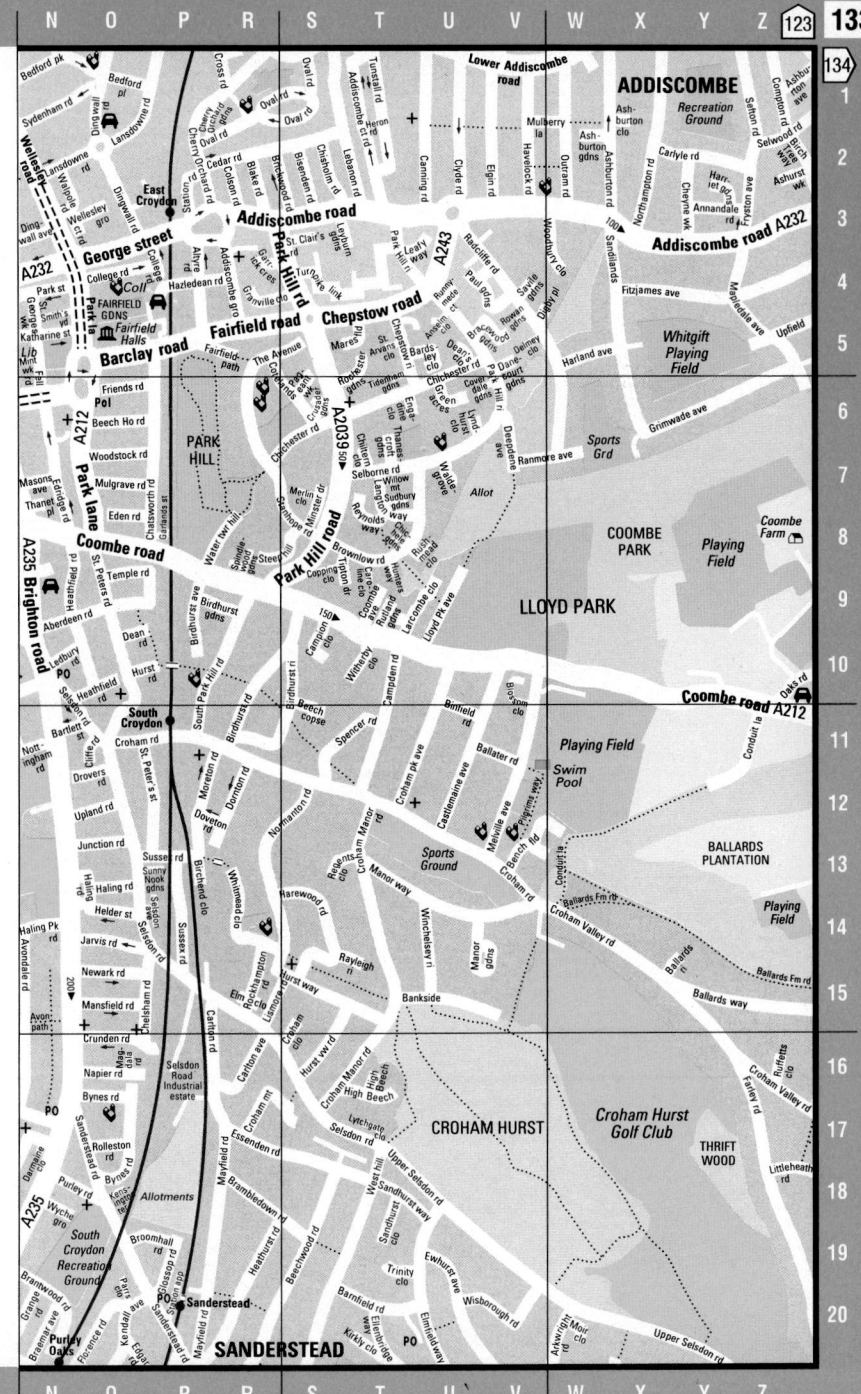

134

ADDISCOMBE

Lower Addiscombe road

Recreation Ground

Ashburton clo

Carlyle rd

Selwood rd

Ashurst wk

Addiscombe road A232

Fitzjames ave

Whitgift Playing Field

Upfield

Masons ave

Thanet rd

Park lane

Eden rd

Coombe road

A235 Brighton road

Aberdeen rd

Ledbury rd

Heathfield rd

Woodstock rd

Mulgrave rd

Chatsworth rd

PARK HILL

Watertwr hill

Steephill

Park Hill road

Birdhurst gdns

Dean rd

Hurst rd

South Park Hill rd

Birdhurst rd

Birdhurst rd

150

Cranston clo

Witney clo

Campden rd

Beech Copse

Spencer rd

Binfield clo

Coombe Park

Playing Field

Coombe Farm

LLOYD PARK

Sports Grd

Ranmore ave

Grimwade ave

Allot

Walde grove

Coombe road A212

Oaks rd

Conduit la

Playing Field

Swim Pool

BALLARDS PLANTATION

Playing Field

Ballards Fm rd

South Croydon

Croham rd

St. Peter's st.

Moreton rd

Dornton rd

Normanton rd

Croham pk ave

Castlemaine ave

Melville ave

Ballater rd

Croham rd

Croham Valley rd

Ballards way

Bartlett rd

Drovers rd

Cliffe rd

Upland rd

Junction rd

Sussex rd

Sunny Nook gdns

Birchend clo

Whinmead clo

Harewood rd

Croham Manor rd

Regents clo

Manor way

Sports Ground

Winchelsey ri

Manor gdns

Nottingham rd

Haling rd

Helder st

Jarvis rd

Newark rd

Selsdon rd

Sussex rd

Rayleigh ri

Hurst way

Croham clo

Winchelsey ri

Bankside

Avondale rd

Haling Pk rd

200

Avon path

Mansfield rd

Crunden rd

Napier rd

Bynes rd

Chelsham rd

Carlton rd

Elm Rockhampton rd

Selsdon Road Industrial estate

Mayfield rd

Brambledown rd

Carlton ave

Hurst vw rd

Croham mt

High Beech

Selsdon rd

Lytchgate clo

Upper Selsdon rd

CROHAM HURST

Croham Hurst Golf Club

THRIFT WOOD

Tuffetts clo

Farley rd

Croham Valley rd

Littleheath rd

PO

Sanderstead rd

Rolleston rd

Bynes rd

Kenley rd

Allotments

South Croydon Recreation Ground

Damsel rd

Purley rd

Wyche gro

Broomhall rd

Heathurst rd

Beechwood rd

West hill

Sandhurst way

Sandhurst clo

Ewhurst rd

Trinity clo

Wisborough rd

Upper Selsdon rd

Purley Oaks

Braemar ave

Brantwood rd

Grange rd

Florence rd

Kendall ave

Edgehill rd

Mayfield rd

Glossop rd

Sanderstead

Essenden rd

West hill

Selsdon rd

Barnfield rd

Ellenbridge way

Kirkly clo

Enmore clo

PO

Moir clo

Arkwright

SANDERSTEAD

Addiscombe road

Cross rd

Oval rd

Oval rd

Tunstall rd

Addiscombe rd

Heron rd

Canning rd

Clyde rd

Elgin rd

Havelock rd

Outram rd

Ashburton gdns

Ashburton rd

Northampton rd

Cheyne wk

Annandale rd

Sandilands

Maycliffe rd

Cross rd

Cherry Orchard rd

Cedar rd

Brecon

Bisenden rd

Chisholm rd

Lebanon rd

Park Hill ri

Leafy way

A243

Ratcliffe rd

Rusby

Paul gdns

Savile gdns

Brockenbury rd

Rowan

Deney rd

Deepdene

Woodbury clo

Harland ave

East Croydon

Lansdowne rd

Wellesley rd

George street

College rd

Coll

Park st

Smith's

Katharine st

Lib

Mkt

Barclay road

A212

Pol

Beech Ho rd

Friends rd

Fairfield path

The Avenue

Cherry Orchard rd

Park cres

Rochester rd

Engadine

Tidenham gdns

Chichester rd

St Arvans rd

Bards

Cavendale

Chepstow rd

Caveside clo

Dane court gdns

St. Clair's gdns

Lynburn gdns

Turnpike link

Gonville rd

Hazledean rd

Aldrie rd

Colson rd

Fairfield rd

Chepstow road

Mares

Dean's

Thames

Chilton rd

Selborne rd

Merlin clo

Sandpipe

Minster dr

Reynolds way

Brownlow rd

Colgreen

Tryon ct

Coombe

Croham

Humber

Colenso rd

Larcombe clo

Lloyd Pk ave

Willow

Sudbury gdns

Langton way

Chilham

FAIRFIELD GDNS

Fairfield Halls

A2039

George street

A2039

A232

Addiscombe road

Fairfield road

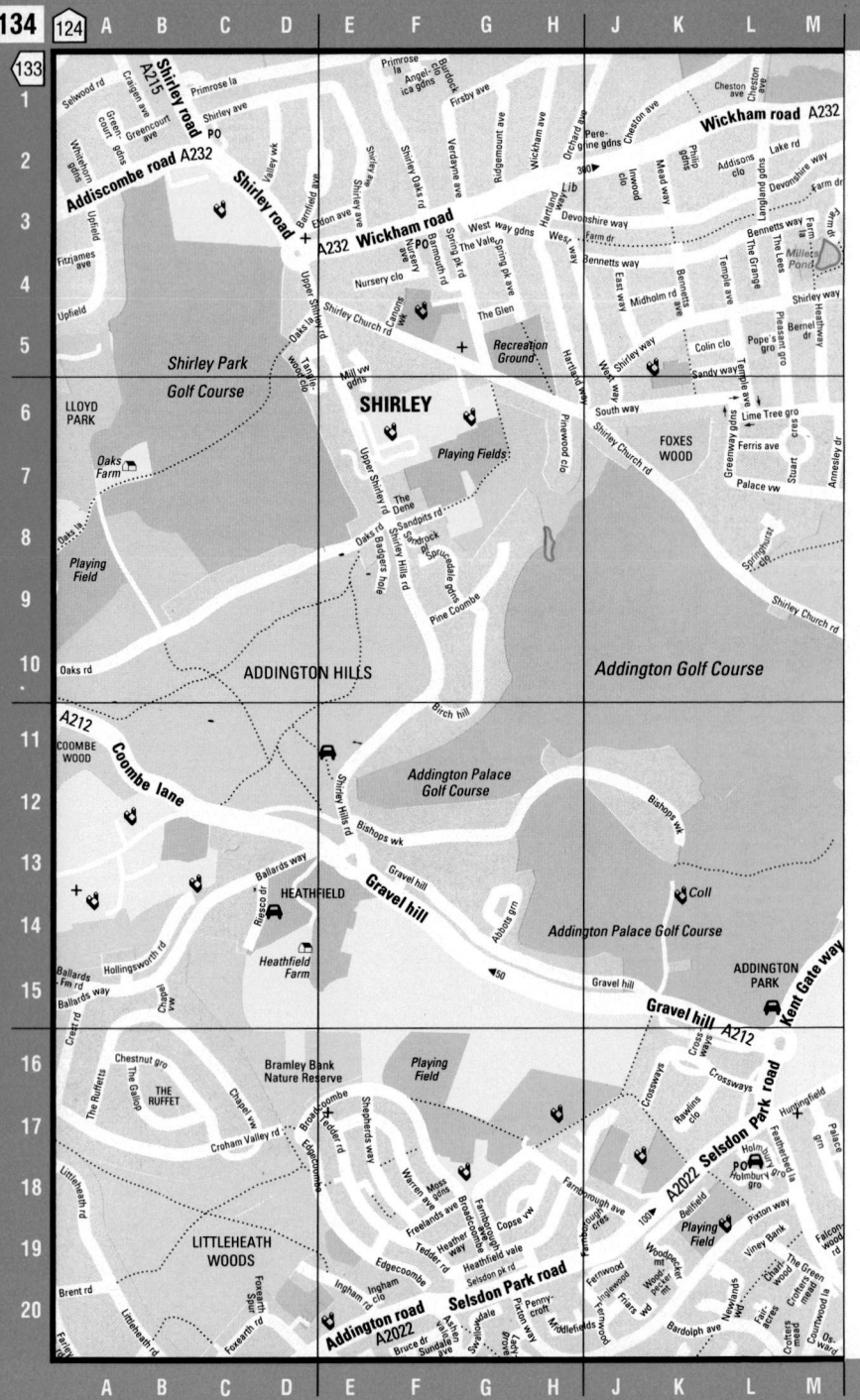

A B C D E F G H J K L M

Selwood rd
Shirley road A215
Cragen ave
Primrose la
Green court
Greencourt gdns
Shirley ave
Whitehorn ave
Shirley road
PO
Valley wk
Bamfield ave
Upfield
Fitzjames ave
Upfield

Addiscombe road A232
Shirley road
Eldon ave

A232 Wickham road
PO
Shirley Church rd
Oaks la
Temple wood clo

Primrose la
Angel-ica gdns
Burdock
Firsby ave
Wickham ave
Orchard ave
Peregrine gdns
Cheston ave
Cheston ave

Wickham road A232
Philip gdns
Addisons clo
Lake rd
Devonshire way

Verdayne ave
Ridgemount
Shirley Oaks rd
West way gdns
The Valley
West way
Hartland
Devonshire way
Farm dr
Inwood clo
Mead way
Bennetts way
The Lees
Farm dr
Millers Pond
The Grange

Nursery clo
Spring pk rd
Barmouth rd
Canons wk
West way
East way
Bennetts way
Midholm rd
Temple ave
Shirley way
Bernel Heathway

SHIRLEY
Mill vw gdns
Upper Shirley rd
Canons wk
Recreation Ground
West way
South way
Shirley way
Colin clo
Sandy way
Pope s grn
Pleasant gro
Lime Tree gro
Bernel av

Shirley Park
Golf Course

LLOYD PARK
Oaks Farm

Oaks la

Playing Field

Playing Fields
Upper Shirley rd
The Dene
Sandpits rd
Oaks rd
Badgers hole
Shirley Hills rd
Spindrock
Sprucedale gdns
Pine Coombe
Pinewood clo
Shirley Church rd
South way
FOXES WOOD
Palace vw
Greenway gdns
Ferris ave
Stuart
Springhurst clo
Amnesley dr
Shirley Church rd

Oaks rd

ADDINGTON HILLS

Addington Golf Course

A212
COOMBE WOOD
Coombe lane
Birch hill

Addington Palace Golf Course

Bishops wk

Ballards way
Resco dr
HEATHFIELD
Shirley Hills rd
Bishops wk
Gravel hill
Gravel hill
Coll

+
Ballards Fm rd
Ballards way
Crest rd
Chapel vw
Hollingsworth rd
Heathfield Farm
Abbots grn
50
Gravel hill
Addington Palace Golf Course

ADDINGTON PARK
Gravel hill A212
Kent Gate way

The Ruffets
The Gallop
THE RUFFET
Chestnut gro
Chapel vw
Croham Valley rd
Brookcoombe
Edgecoombe
Bramley Bank Nature Reserve
Playing Field
Shepherds way
Crossways
Crossways
Rawlins clo
Crossways
Selsdon Park road
Huntingfield
Palace grn
Littleheath rd
Shepherds way
Warren ave
Moss
Freelands gro
Farnborough ave
Holmbury gro
A2022
PO
Benfield
Holmbury gro
Feathbed la
Pixton way

LITTLEHEATH WOODS
Ingham clo
Tedder rd
Heather rd
Edgecoombe
Farnborough
Broadcoombe
Copse vw
Farnborough vale
Farnborough cres
Woodcote
Fernwood
Playing Field
Woodpecker mt
Hecter rd
Viney Bank
Chart wood
The Green

Brent rd
Foxearth Spur
Forearth rd
Addington road A2022
Ingham
Bruce dr
Ashlen
Sundale
ave
Edgecoombe
Selsdon Park rd
Ashen
dale
Picton way
Penny
croft
Mady
grove
Ingledow
Friars wd
Middleton
Newlands
Fair
acres
Crothers
mead
Courtwood la
Os-ward
Falcon-wood ct
Crothers wd
Falon rd
Brent rd
Fairby
Littleheath rd
Forearth rd
Bardolph ave

A B C D E F G H J K L M

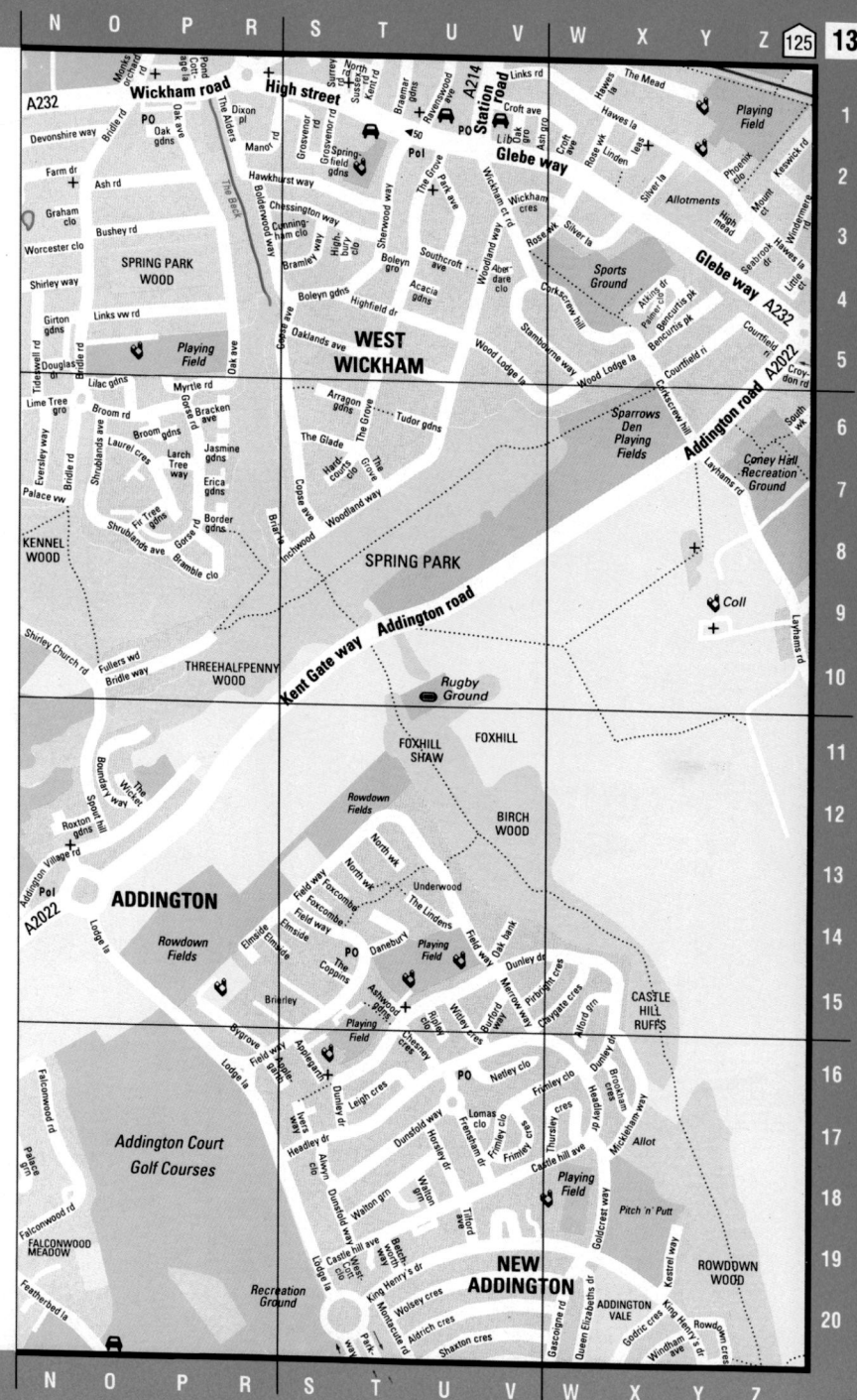

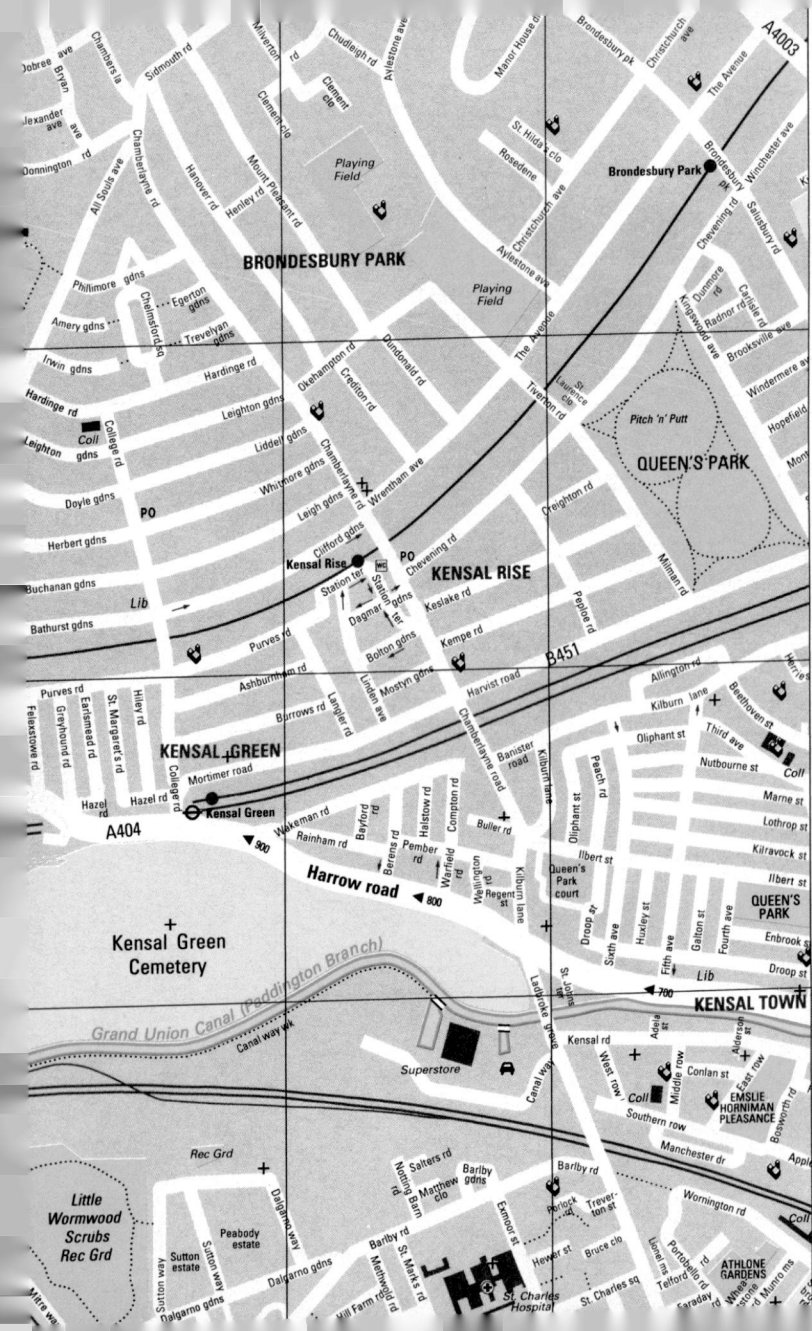

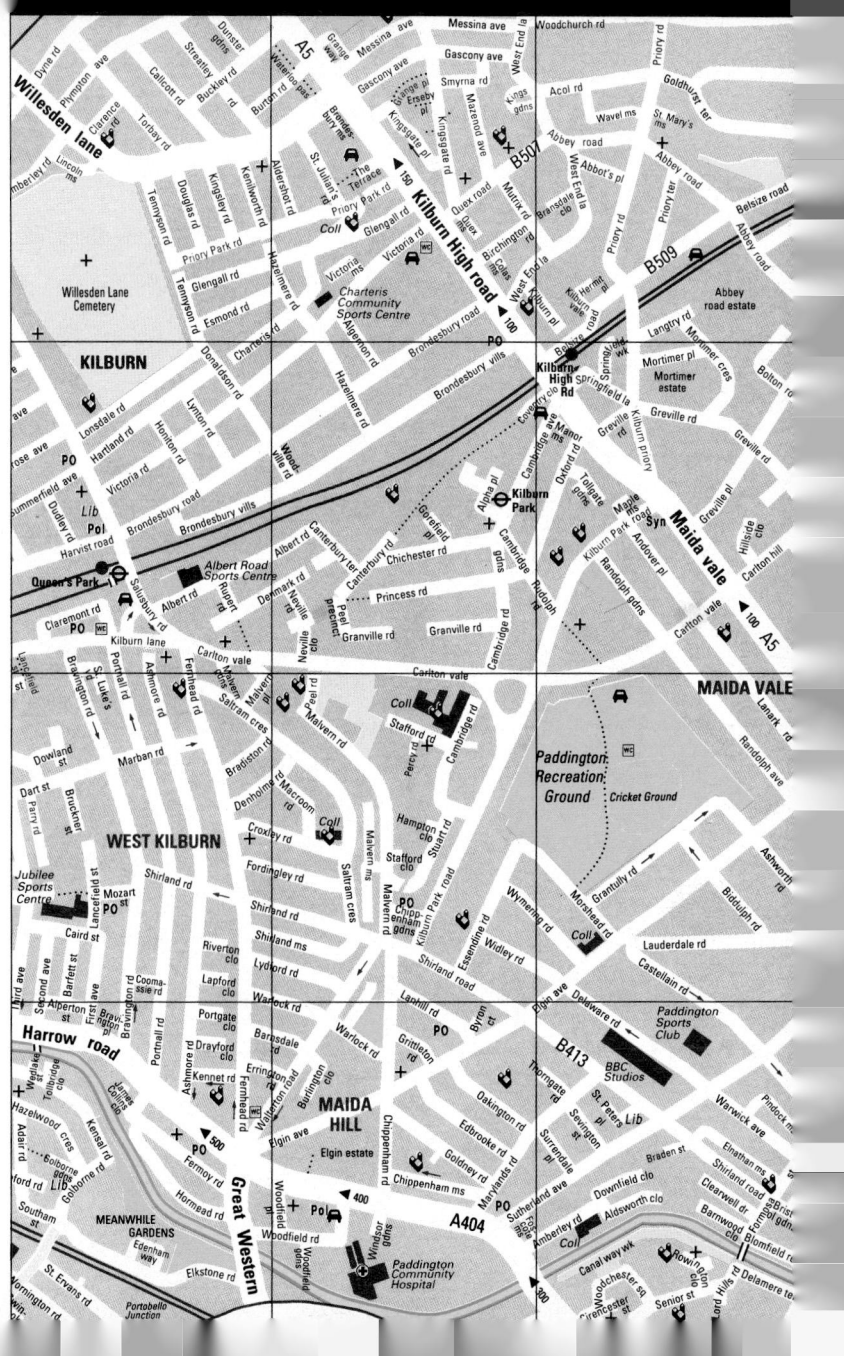

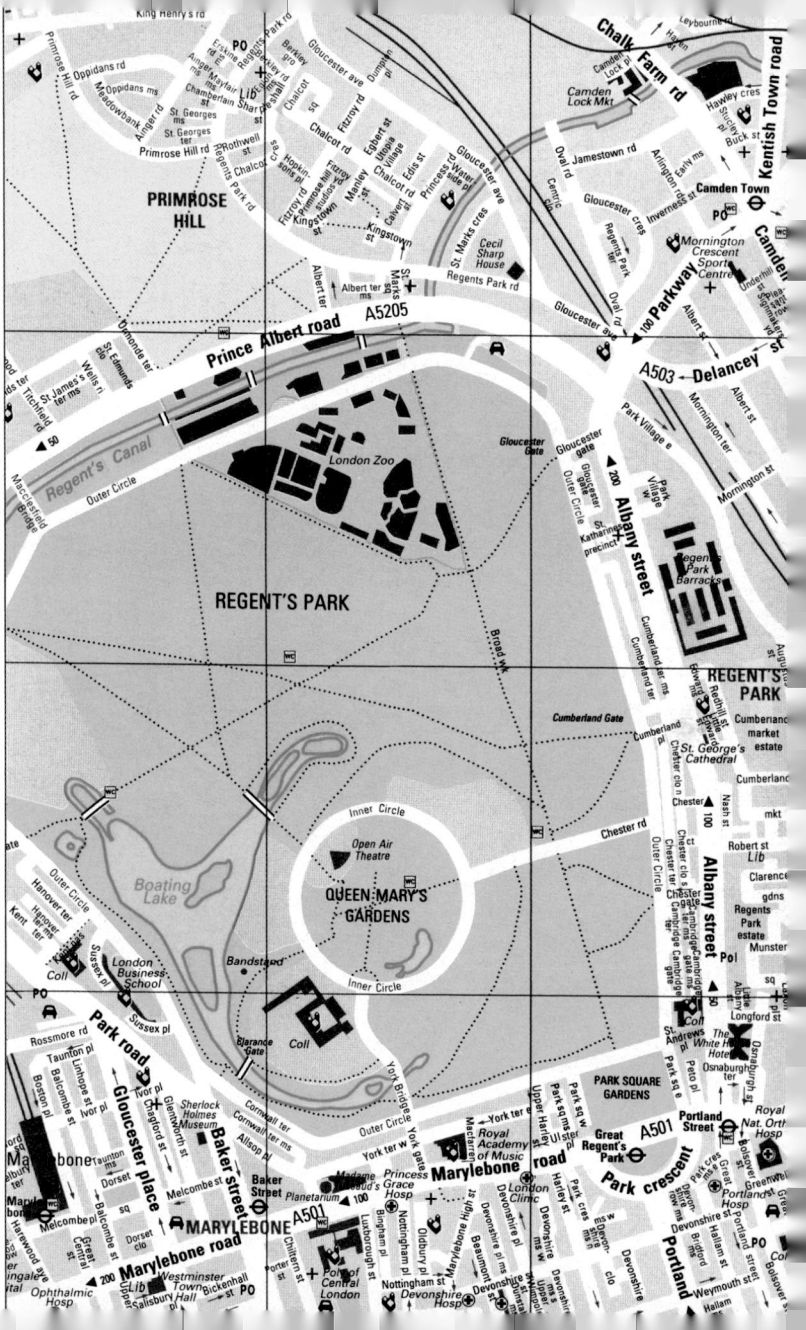

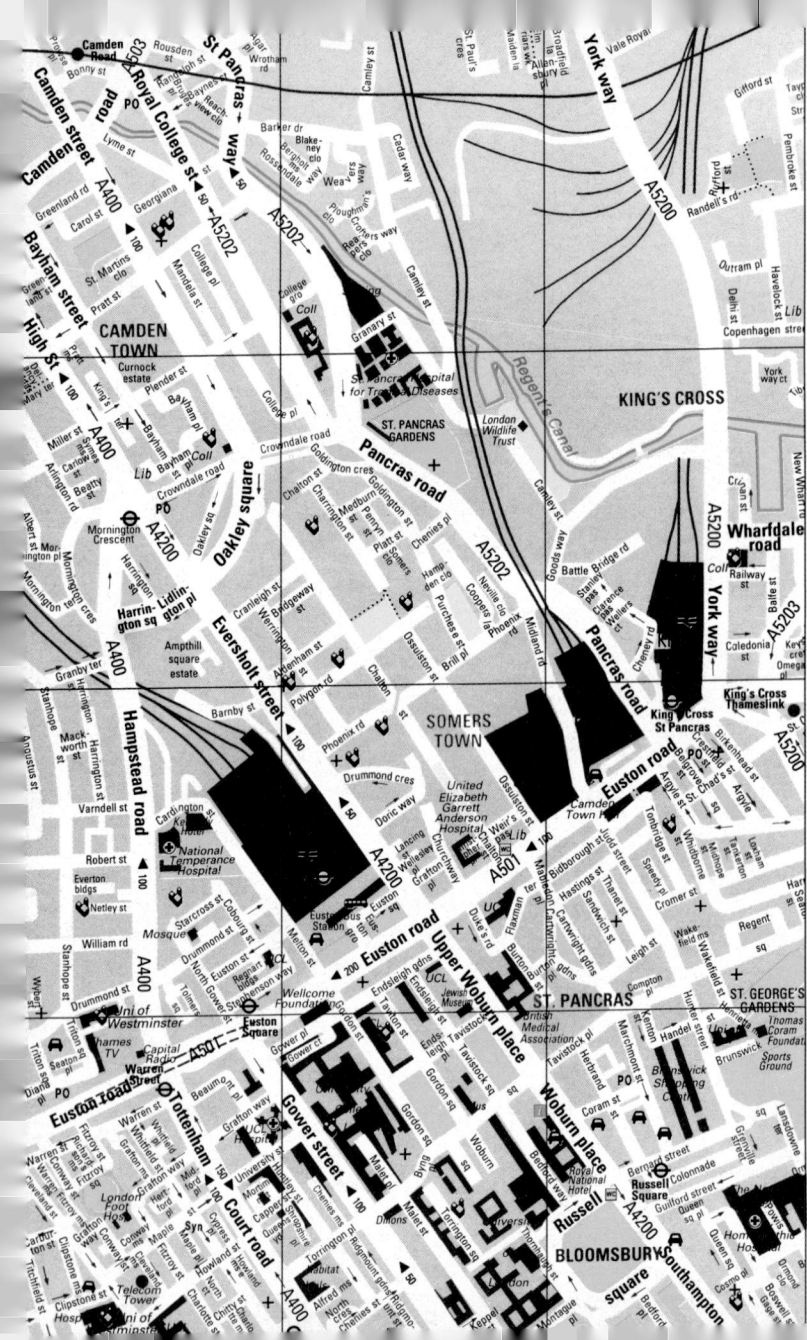

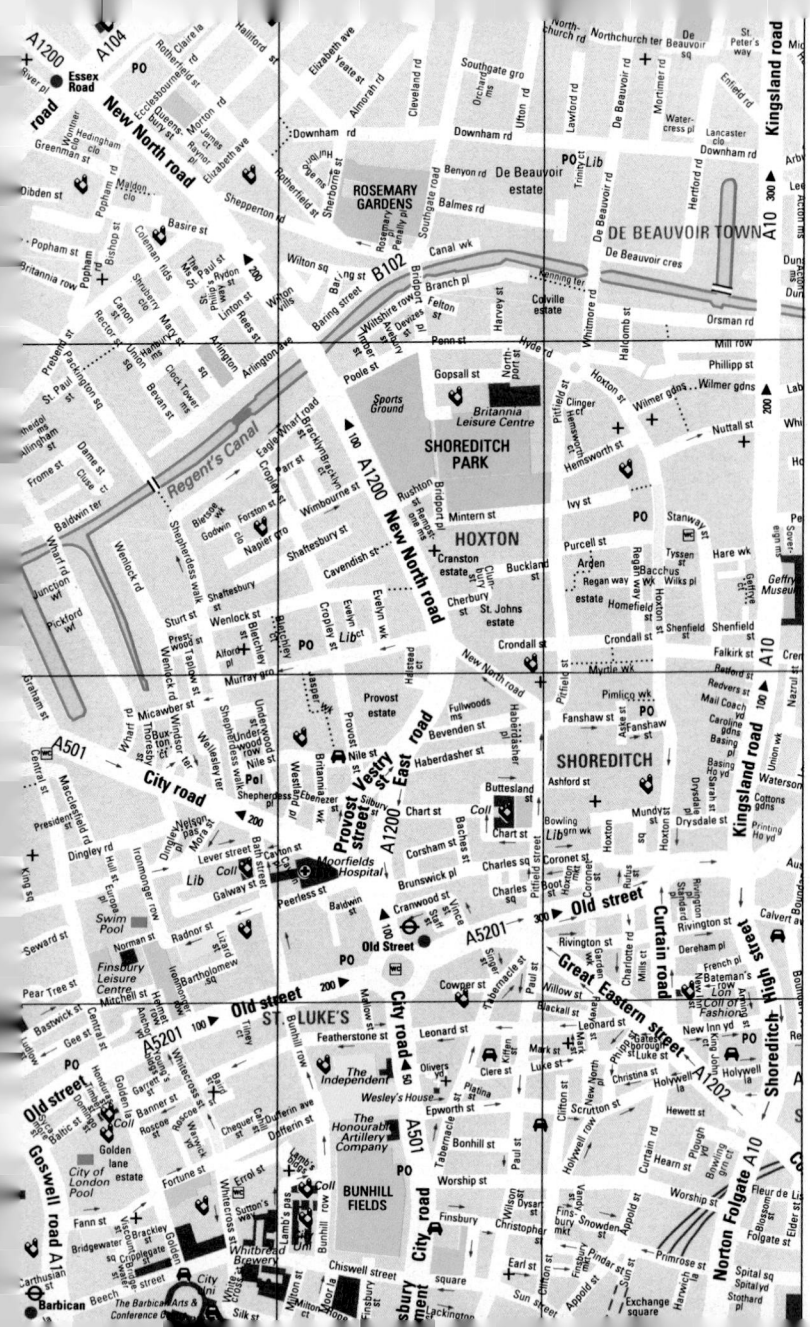

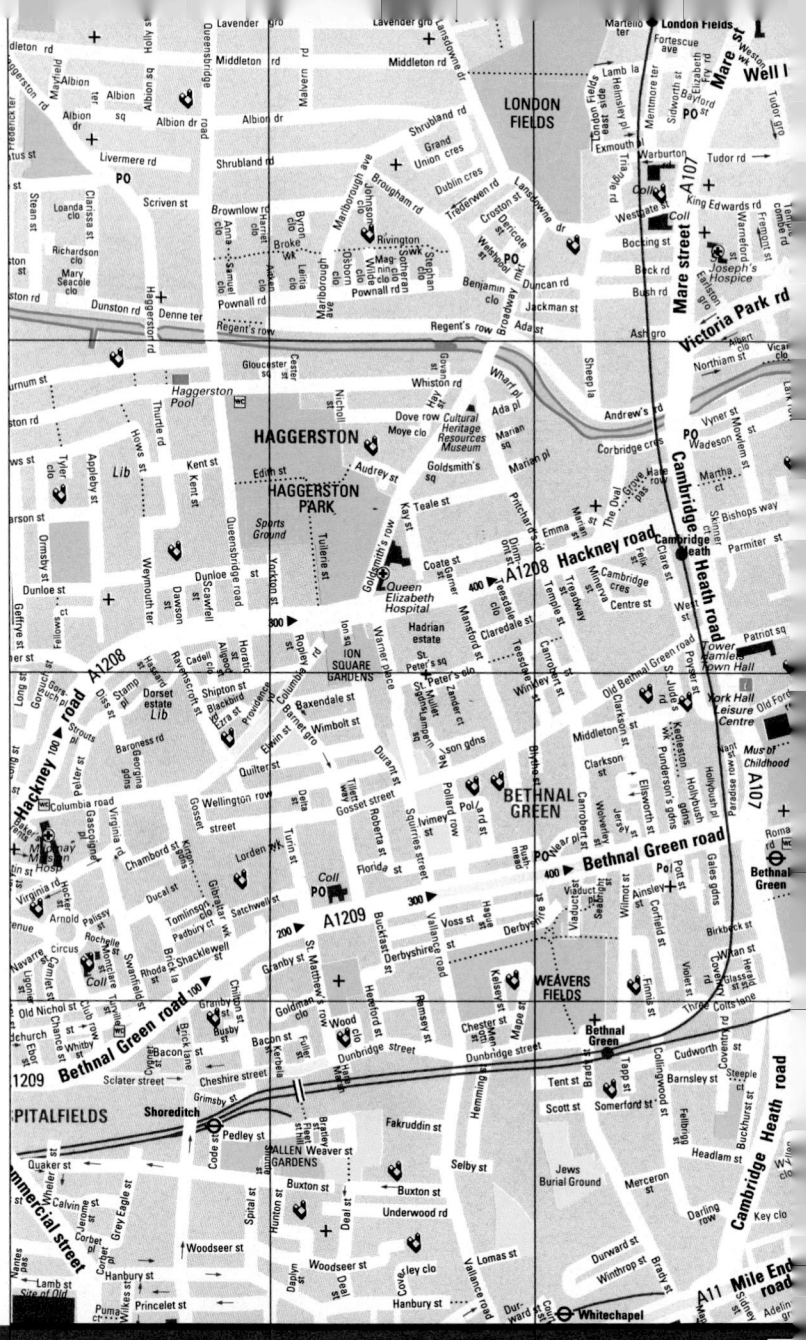

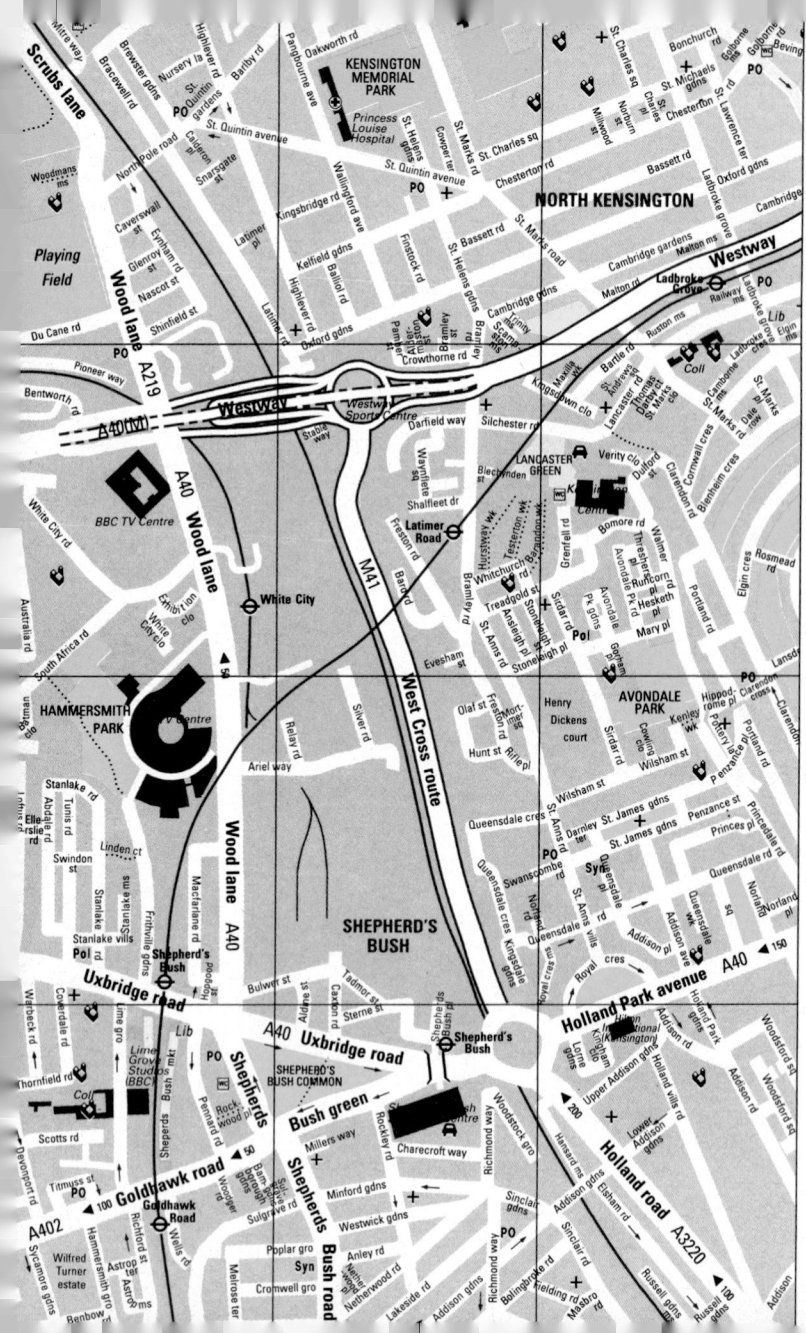

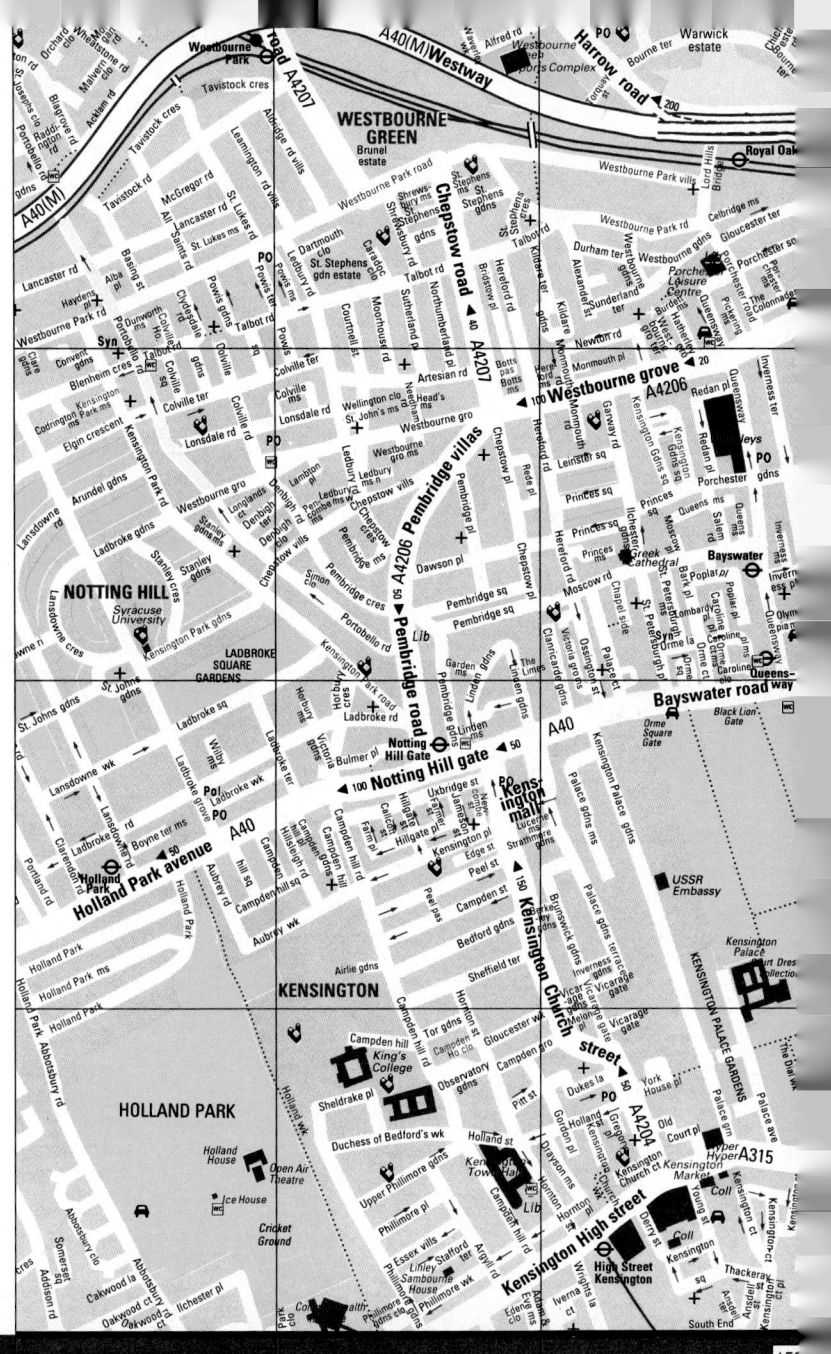

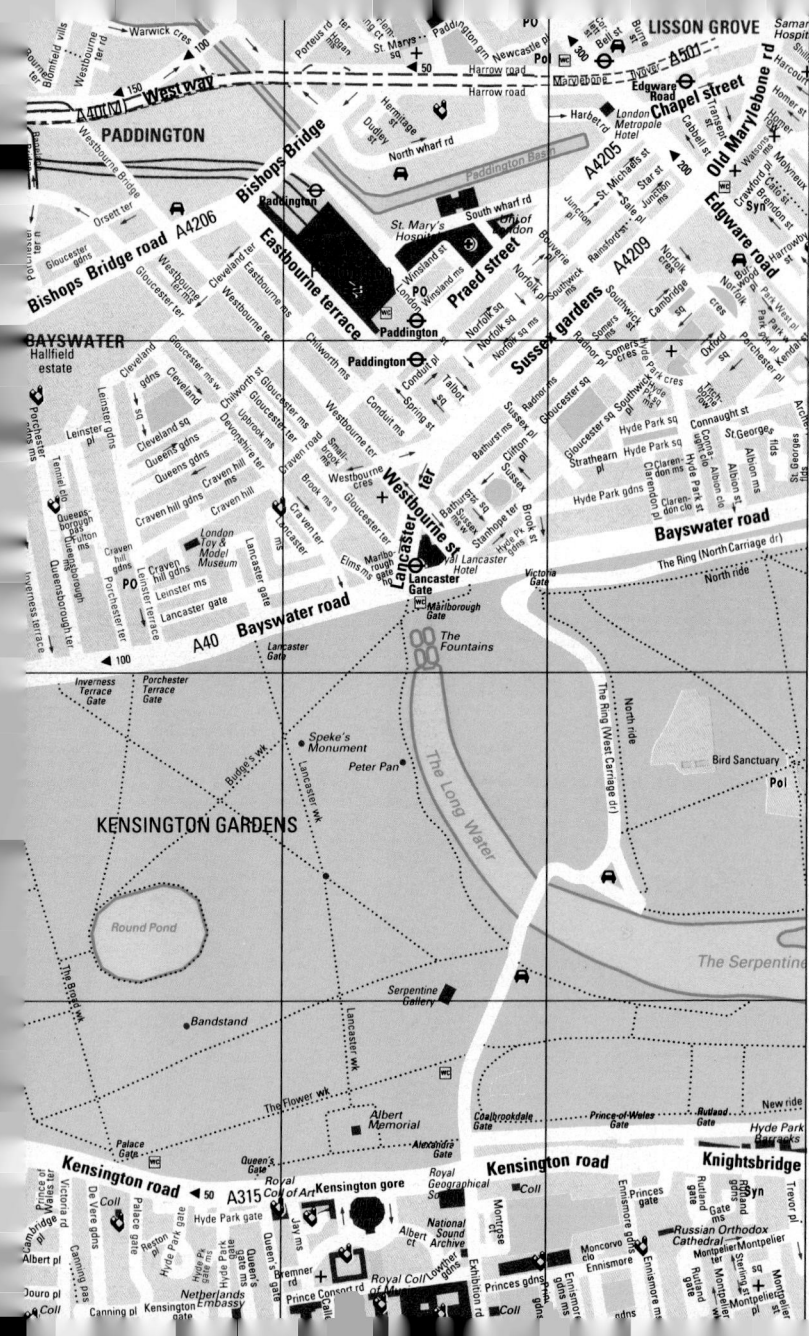

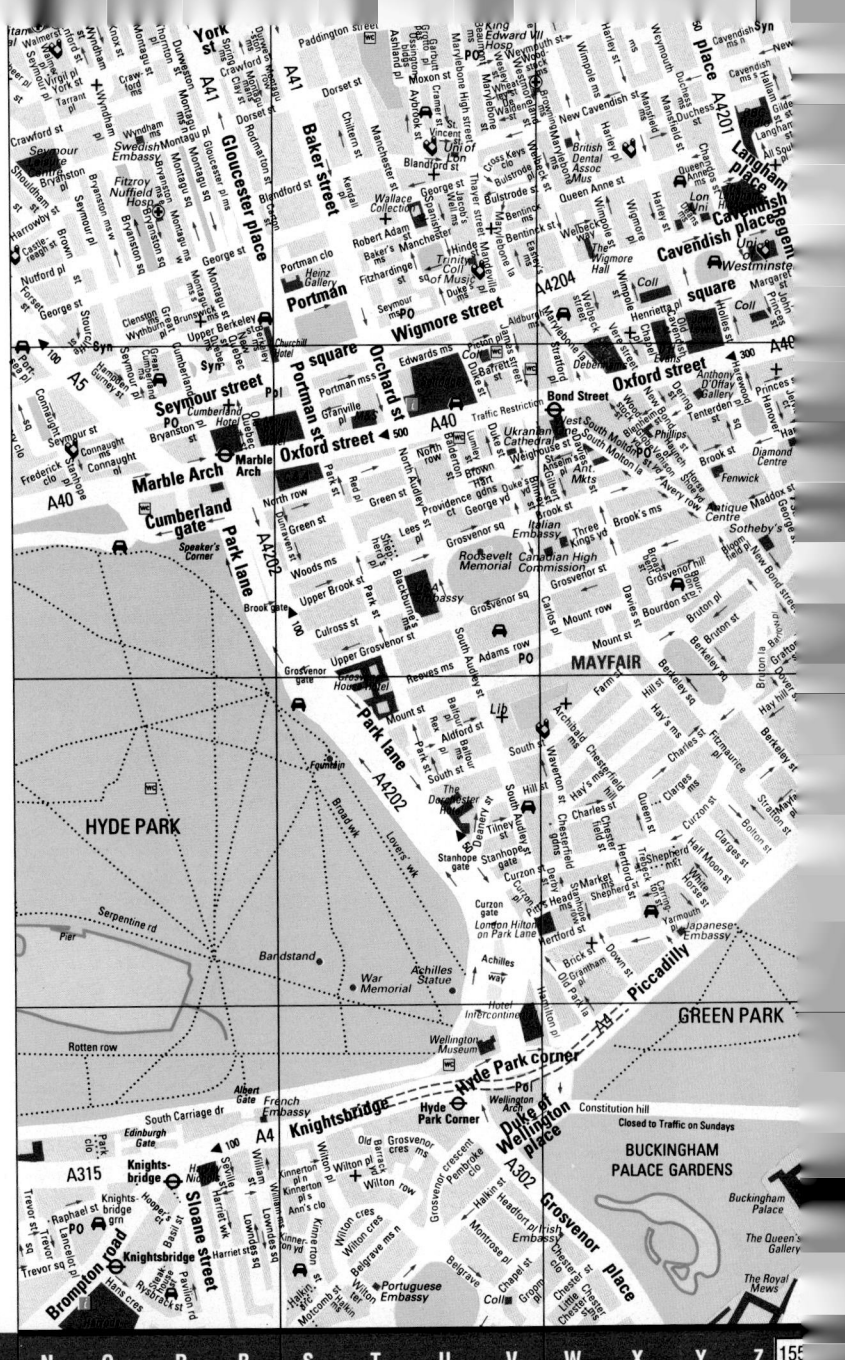

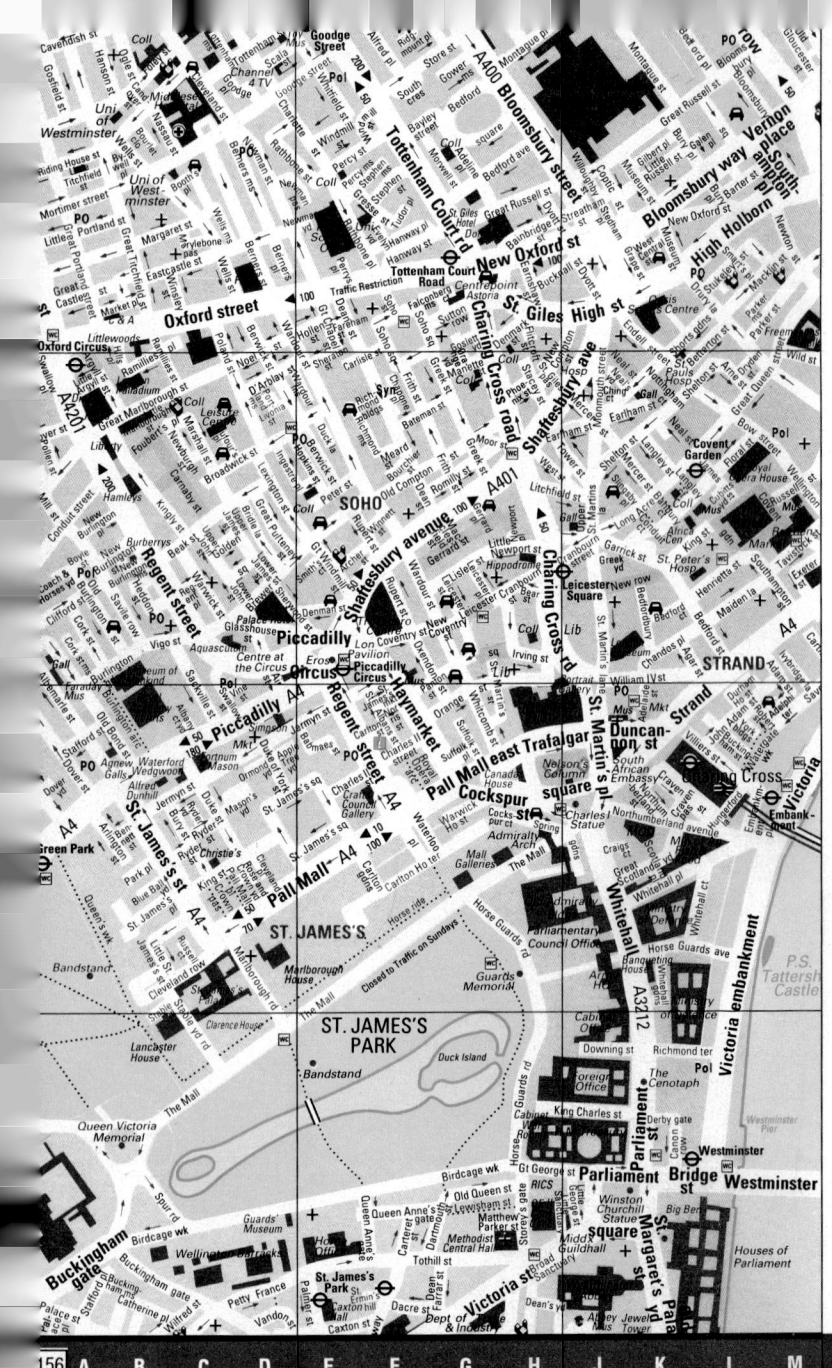

Drake Procter
High Holborn
Holborn
LINCOLN'S INN FIELDS
HOLBORN
Old Curiosity Shop
Kingsway
Inn road
Chancery Lane
A40
Holborn
Andrew Shoe la
Holborn Viaduct
Farringdon st
Stonecutter st
Newgate st
New Fetter la
Fetter Lane
Strand • Fleet street
Aldwych
Strand
Temple
Aldwych
Lancaster pl
Victoria embankment
City Thameslink
New Bridge st
Queen Victoria st
Blackfri
Upper Thames st
Waterloo Bridge
Cleopatra's Needle
H.Q.S. Wellington
H.M.S. President
RIVER THAMES
Blackfriars Bridge
Charing Cross Pier
Festival Pier
Hungerford Bridge
Queen Elizabeth
Hayward Gallery
Upper Ground
Stamford street
Blackfriars road
Southwark st
Bankside Gallery
Express Newspapers
Hopton st
A3200
Colombo Street Sports & Community Centre
A301
Tenison way
Waterloo East
British Library (India Records)
Union street
JUBILEE GARDENS
York road
The Cut
Waterloo road
A201 Blackfriars road
Surrey row
Pocock st
Great Suffolk st
Florence Nightingale Museum
Addington st
A3036
Westminster Bridge rd
Lambeth North
Bridge A302
Peabody square
St. Georges circus
Borough road
Westminster Bridge rd
Southwark

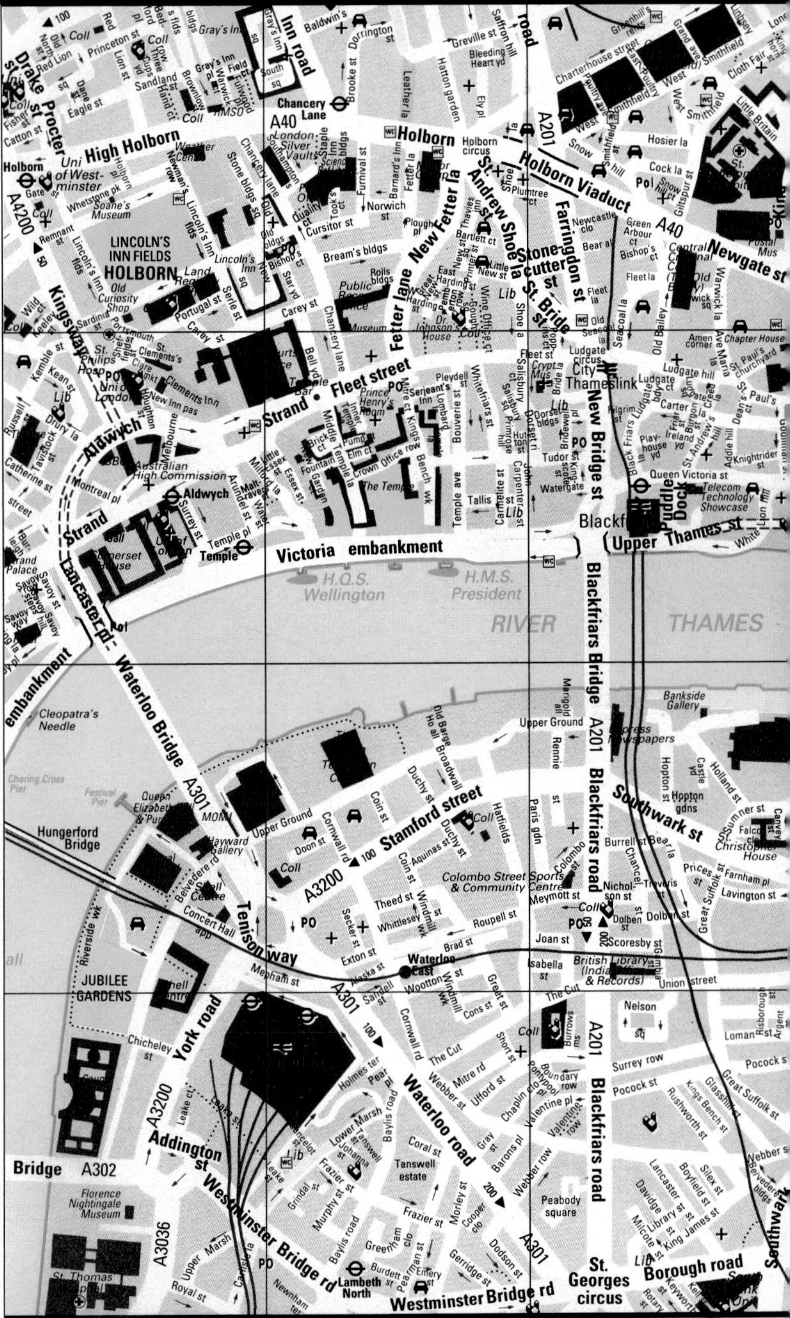

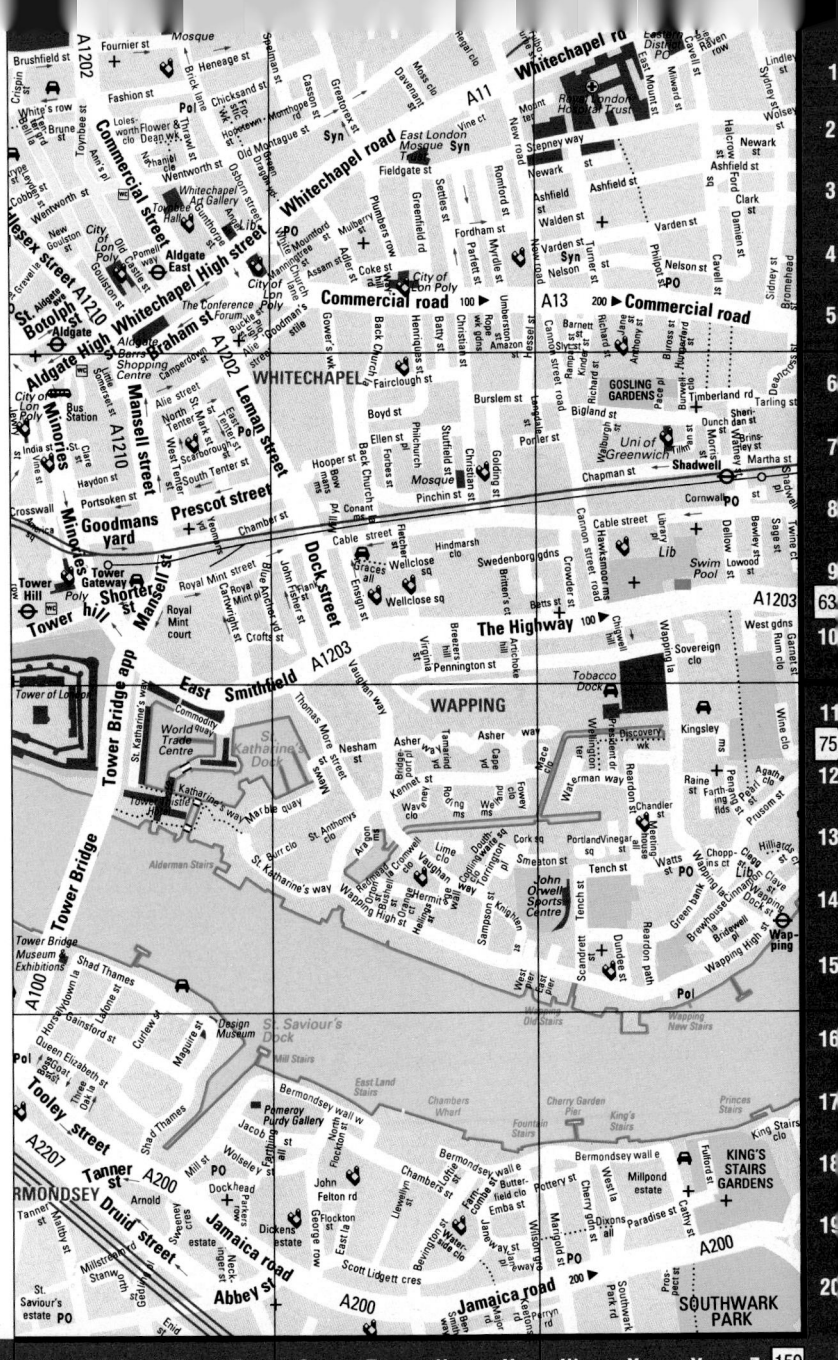

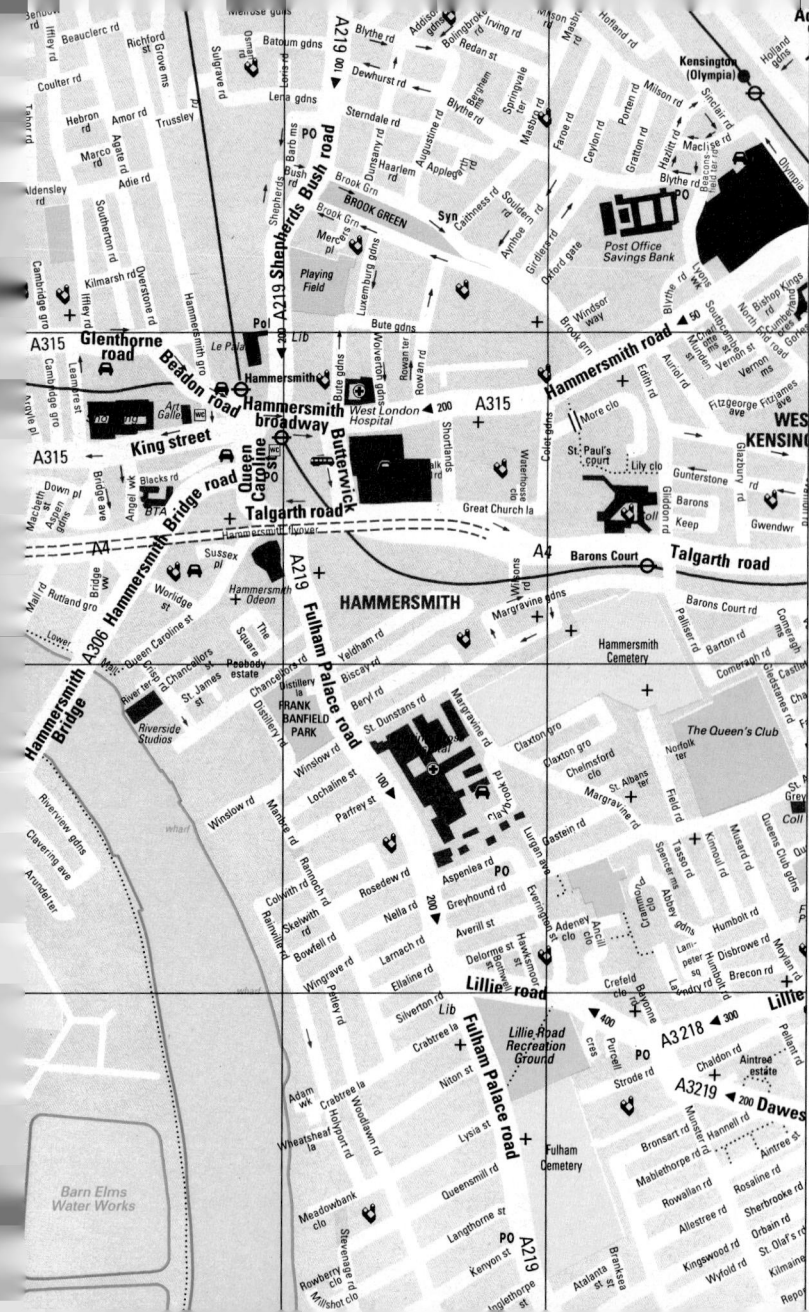

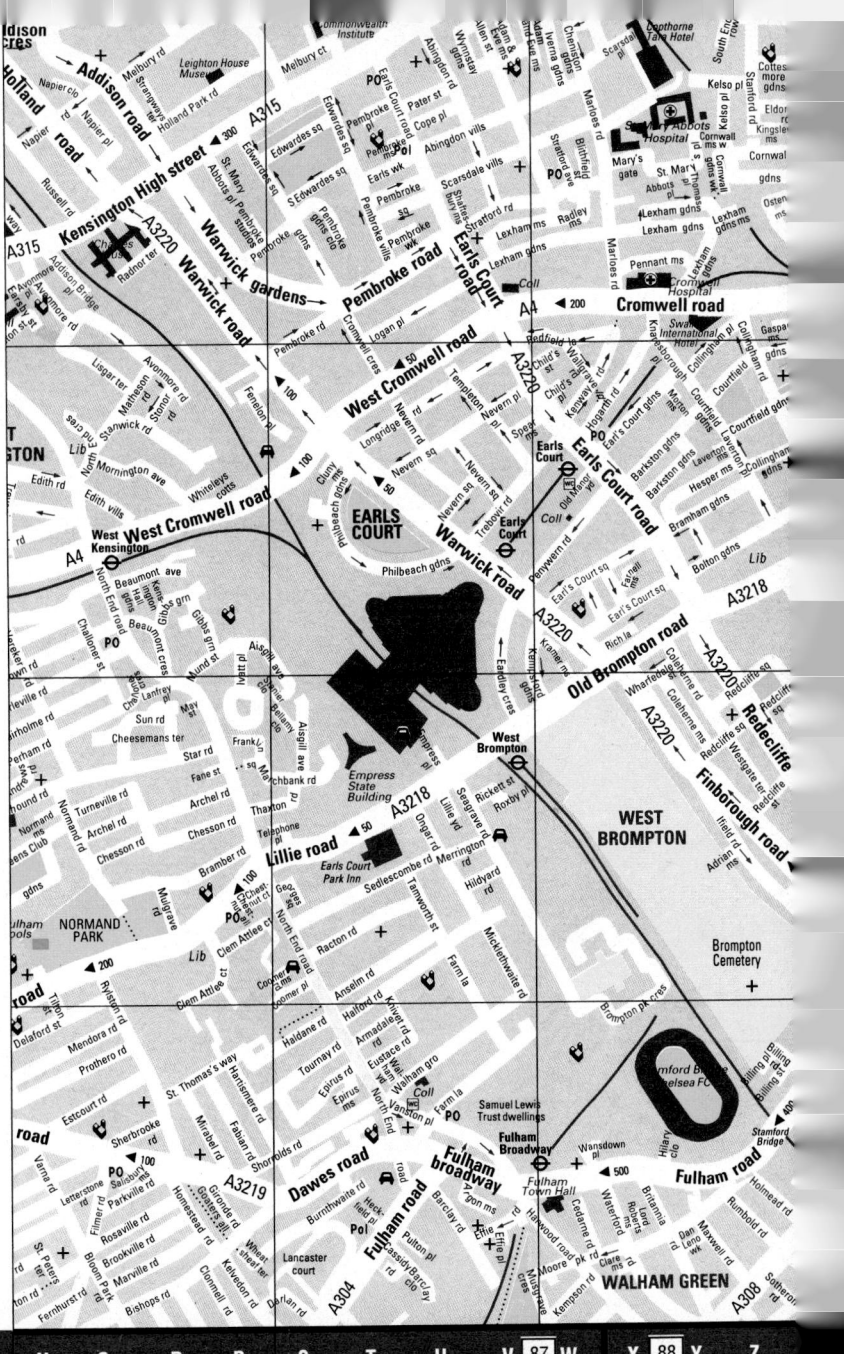

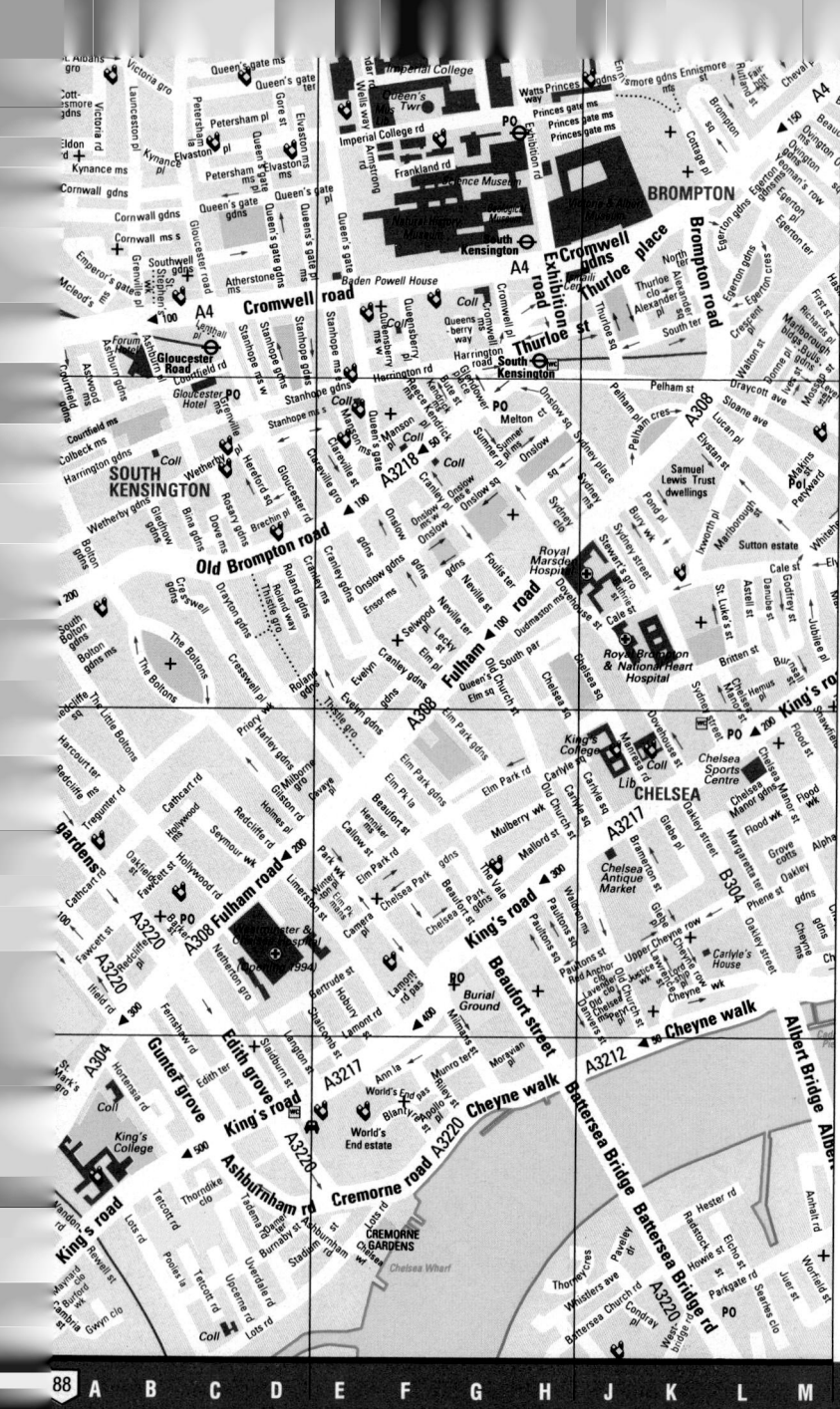

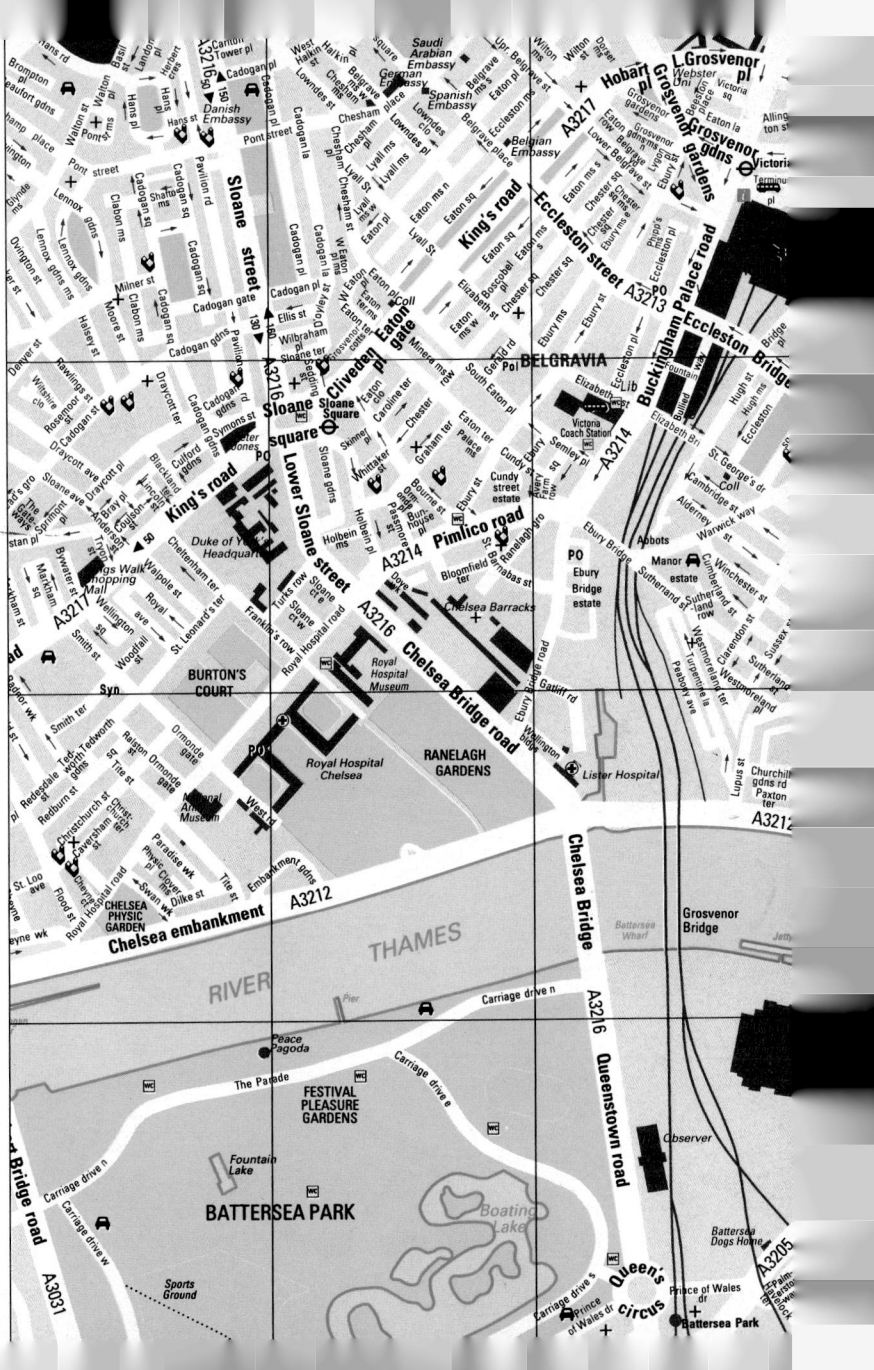

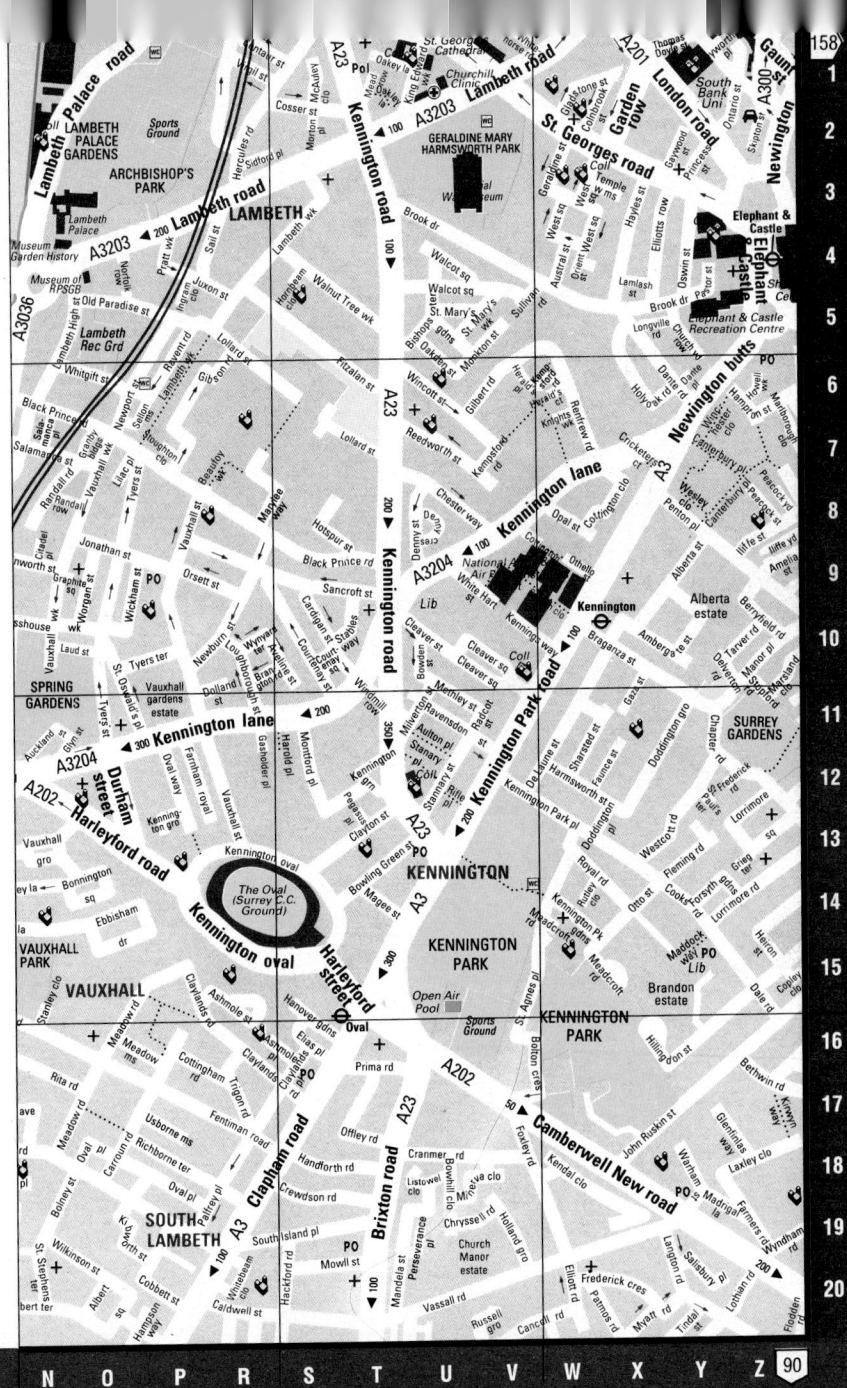

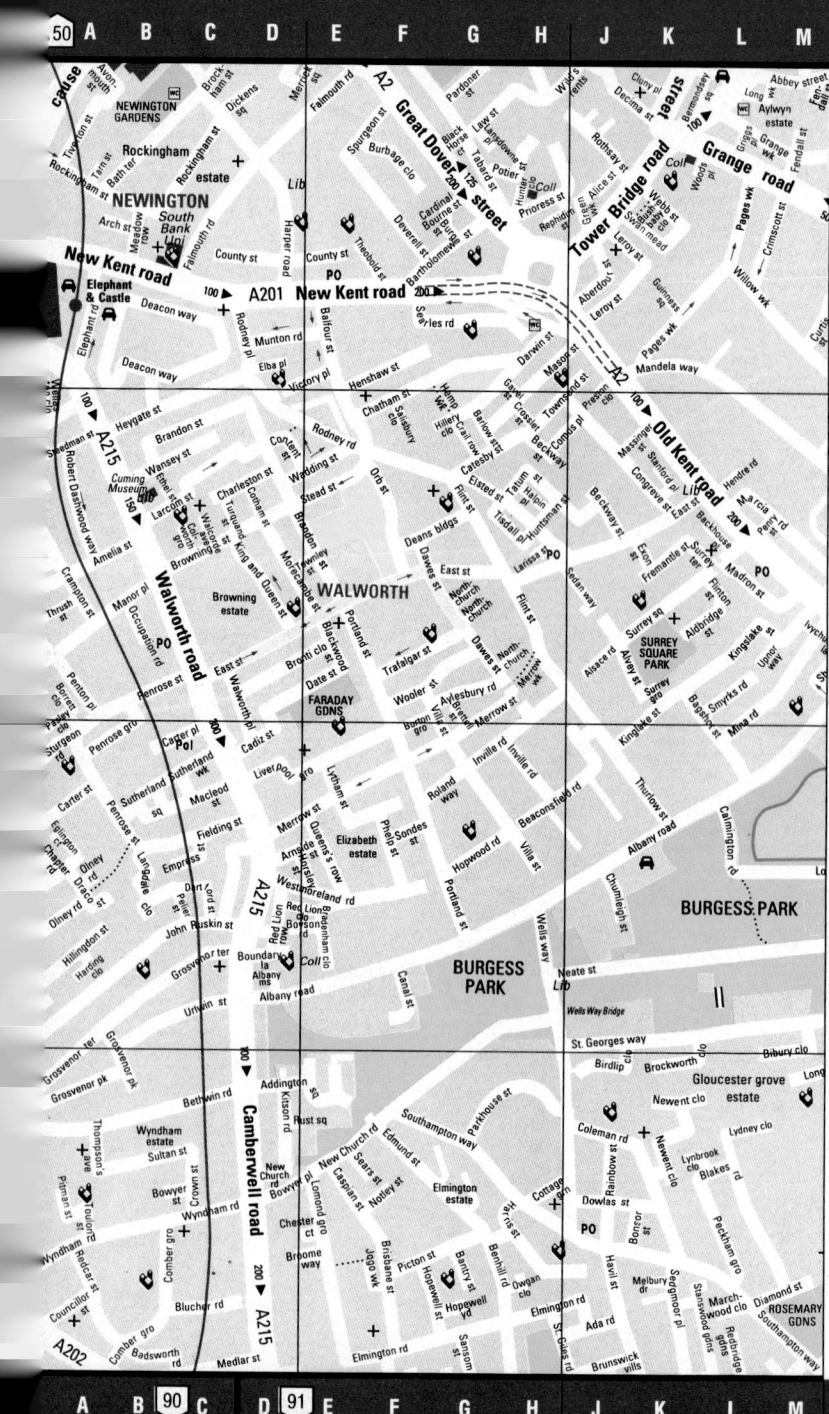

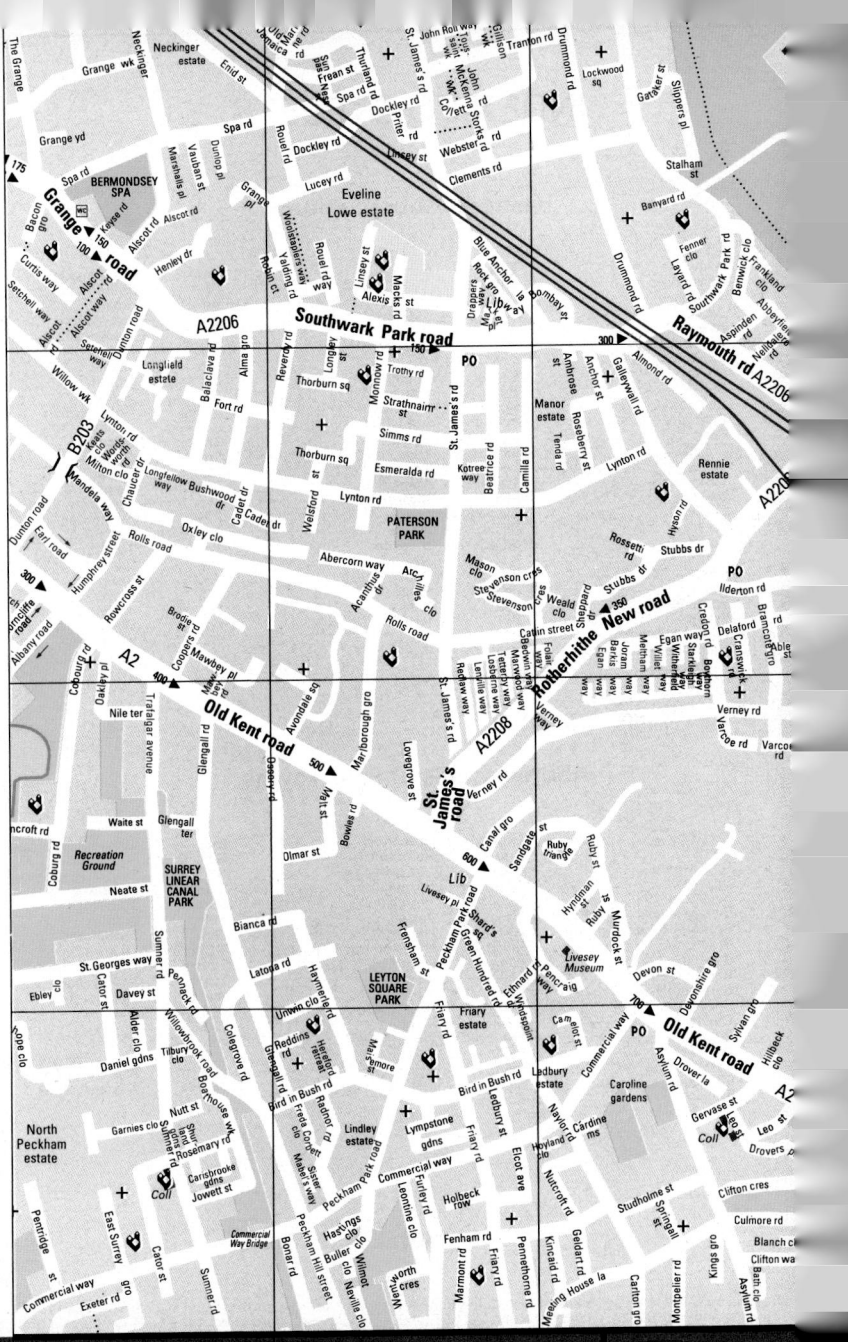

INDEX TO STREETS

General Abbreviations

All	Alley	Flds	Fields	Prom	Promenade
Allot	Allotments	Fm	Farm	Pt	Point
App	Approach	Gdn	Garden	Rd	Road
Arc	Arcade	Gdns	Gardens	Rec	Recreation
Ave	Avenue	Gra	Grange	Res	Reservoir
Bdy	Broadway	Grd	Ground	Ri	Rise
Bldgs	Buildings	Grn	Green	Rvr	River
Boul	Boulevard	Gro	Grove	S	South
Bri	Bridge	Ho	House	Sch	School
Cem	Cemetery	Hosp	Hospital	RUFC	Rugby Union
Cen	Central, Centre	Ind	Industrial		Football Club
Cft	Croft	Junct	Junction	Shop	Shopping
Ch	Church	La	Lane	Sq	Square
Circ	Circus	Lo	Lodge	St	Street
Clo	Close	Mans	Mansions	St	Saint
Coll	College	Mkt	Market	Sta	Station
Cotts	Cottages	Ms	Mews	Swim	Swimming
Cres	Crescent	Mt	Mount	Ter	Terrace
Ct	Court	Mus	Museum	Trd	Trading
Cts	Courts	N	North	Vill	Villas
Dr	Drive	PH	Public House	Vw	View
E	East	Par	Parade	W	West
Embk	Embankment	Pas	Passage	Wd	Wood
Est	Estate	Pk	Park	Wf	Wharf
FC	Football Club	Pl	Place	Wk	Walk
Fld	Field	Prec	Precinct	Yd	Yard

Abbreviations of Post Towns

Bark	Barking	Grnf	Greenford	Sid	Sidcup
Barn	Barnet	Hmptn	Hampton	Sthl	Southall
Beck	Beckenham	Har	Harrow	S Croy	South Croydon
Belv	Belvedere	Horn	Hornchurch	Stan	Stanmore
Bex	Bexley	Houns	Hounslow	Surb	Surbiton
Bexh	Bexleyheath	Ilf	Ilford	Sutt	Sutton
B Wd	Boreham Wood	Islw	Isleworth	Ted	Teddington
Brent	Brentford	Kings T	Kingston upon Thames	T Ditt	Thames Ditton
Brom	Bromley	Loug	Loughton	Th Hth	Thornton Heath
Buck H	Buckhurst Hill	Mitch	Mitcham	Twick	Twickenham
Cars	Carshalton	Mord	Morden	Wall	Wallington
Chis	Chislehurst	N Mal	New Malden	Wat	Watford
Croy	Croydon	Nthlt	Northolt	Well	Welling
Dag	Dagenham	Pnr	Pinner	Wem	Wembley
Dart	Dartford	Pur	Purley	W Wick	West Wickham
E Mol	East Molesey	Rain	Rainham	Wdf Grn	Woodford Green
Edg	Edgeware	Rich	Richmond	Wor Pk	Worcester Park
Enf	Enfield	Rom	Romford		
Felt	Feltham	Ruis	Ruislip		

Notes

Each street name is followed by its Postal District (or, if outside the London Postal District, by its Post Town), and then by a page and map square where the name can be found. For example **Oxford st W1 147 S7** will be found in the Postal District of **W1** on page **147** in square **S7**.

Name	Page	Grid
Abbess clo E6	66	D15
Abbess clo SW2	108	H1
Abbeville rd N8	29	Y14
Abbeville rd SW4	89	V16
Abbey ave Wem	60	L5
Abbey cres Belv	81	S11
Abbey gdns NW8	138	C9
Abbey gdns W6	152	K14
Abbey gro SE2	80	F10
Abbey la E15	64	H5
Abbey la Beck	111	P17
Abbey Manufacturing est Wem	60	M3
Abbey Orchard st SW1	156	G1
Abbey pk Beck	111	P18
Abbey rd E15	64	M5
Abbey rd NW6	137	W2
Abbey rd NW8	138	B7
Abbey rd SE2	80	H10
Abbey rd SW19	106	D19
Abbey rd Bark	67	N2
Abbey rd Belv	80	M10
Abbey rd Bexh	98	A9
Abbey rd Croy	132	J5
Abbey rd Enf	8	F16
Abbey rd Ilf	36	D15
Abbey Road est NW8	137	Y5
Abbey st E13	65	U11
Abbey st SE1	151	R20
Abbey ter SE2	80	F10
Abbey vw NW7	13	S10
Abbey way SE2	80	K9
Abbey Wharf Industrial est Bark	67	T7
Abbey Wood rd SE2	80	E10
Abbeydale rd Wem	61	O3
Abbeyfield rd SE16	159	Z5
Abbeyfields clo NW10	61	P7
Abbeyhill rd Sid	115	T13
Abbot st E8	49	U17
Abbots clo N1	48	L18
Abbots cres Enf	7	X8
Abbots dr Har	40	J7
Abbots gdns N2	28	F13
Abbots grn Croy	134	G14
Abbots la SE1	50	K14
Abbots Manor est SW1	155	X8
Abbots pk SW2	108	F1
Abbot's pl NW6	137	W3
Abbot's pl W8	153	X3
Abbot's rd E6	66	C4
Abbots ter N8	30	A19
Abbots way Beck	124	H11
Abbotsbury clo E15	64	H5
Abbotsbury clo W14	145	N19
Abbotsbury rd W14	145	N16
Abbotsbury rd Mord	120	B8
Abbotsford ave N15	30	M14
Abbotsford gdns Wdf Grn	34	F3
Abbotshall ave N14	16	H11
Abbotshall rd SE6	111	W3
Abbotsleigh clo Sutt	130	A17
Abbotsleigh rd SW16	107	X17
Abbotsmede clo Twick	101	W5
Abbotstone rd SW15	87	N8
Abbotswell rd SE4	92	M13
Abbotswood gdns Ilf	35	V10
Abbotswood rd SW16	107	X5
Abbott ave SW20	119	R2
Abbott clo Hmptn	100	C14
Abbott clo Nthlt	40	D18
Abbott rd E14	64	H15
Abbotts clo Rom	38	G9
Abbotts cres E4	20	L14
Abbotts dr Wem	42	A6
Abbotts Park rd E10	51	U1
Abbotts rd Barn	4	M15
Abbotts rd Mitch	121	V10
Abbotts rd Sthl	70	C4
Abbotts rd Sutt	129	U8
Abbotts wk Bexh	80	J19
Abchurch la EC4	150	F8
Abdale rd W12	144	A13
Aberavon rd E3	63	X9
Abercairn rd SW16	107	V19
Aberconway rd Mord	120	B8
Abercorn clo NW7	27	T2
Abercorn clo NW8	138	C11
Abercorn cres Har	40	L4
Abercorn gdns Har	24	G20
Abercorn gdns Rom	37	R18
Abercorn pl NW8	138	A12
Abercorn rd NW7	27	U2
Abercorn rd Stan	24	D1
Abercorn way SE1	159	S9
Abercrombie st SW11	88	K5
Aberdare clo W Wick	135	V4
Aberdare gdns NW6	138	A1
Aberdare gdns NW7	27	O2
Aberdare rd Enf	9	O13
Aberdeen la N5	48	K15
Aberdeen pk N5	48	K14
Aberdeen Park ms N5	48	L14
Aberdeen pl NW8	138	F17
Aberdeen rd N5	48	L11
Aberdeen rd N18	18	M15
Aberdeen rd NW10	44	E14
Aberdeen rd Croy	133	N9
Aberdeen rd Har	23	V8
Aberdeen ter SE3	93	X4
Aberdour rd Ilf	55	P5
Aberdour st SE1	158	J4
Aberfeldy st E14	64	H16
Aberford gdns SE18	95	R11
Aberfoyle rd SW16	107	X17
Abergeldie rd SE12	94	J16
Abernethy rd SE13	93	Z11
Abersham rd E8	49	W14
Abery st SE18	79	V11
Abingdon clo SW19	106	E16
Abingdon clo N3	28	D6
Abingdon rd SW16	122	A4
Abingdon rd W8	153	U1
Abingdon rd SW1	156	K1
Abingdon vill W8	153	U2
Abinger ave Sutt	129	N20
Abinger clo Brom	127	R7
Abinger clo Wall	132	A12
Abinger gdns Islw	83	S8
Abinger gro SE8	75	Y16
Abinger rd W4	74	C8
Ablett st SE16	159	Z10
Aboyne dr SW20	118	G4
Aboyne rd NW10	43	Z9
Aboyne rd SW17	106	F6
Abridge way Bark	68	D7
Acacia ave N17	31	O1
Acacia ave Brent	72	B19
Acacia ave Horn	57	U7
Acacia ave Wem	42	J14
Acacia clo SE20	123	Y4
Acacia clo Stan	10	G18
Acacia dr Sutt	119	X20
Acacia gdns NW8	138	G8
Acacia gdns W Wick	135	T4
Acacia gro SE21	109	P4
Acacia gro N Mal	118	A7
Acacia pl NW8	138	H7
Acacia rd E11	52	A8
Acacia rd E17	32	K19
Acacia rd N22	30	H4
Acacia rd NW8	138	G8
Acacia rd SW16	108	B20
Acacia rd W3	61	V20
Acacia rd Beck	124	L5
Acacia rd Enf	8	C4
Acacia rd Hmptn	100	G14
Acacia rd Mitch	121	R5
Acacia way Sid	96	M20
Academy gdns Croy	123	V20
Academy pl SE18	95	V2
Academy rd SE18	95	V2
Acanthus dr SE1	159	T9
Acanthus rd SW11	89	O8
Accommodation rd NW11	45	W2
Acfold rd SW6	88	A2
Achilles clo SE1	159	U9
Achilles rd NW6	45	X14
Achilles st SE14	75	X20
Achilles way W1	147	V15
Acklam rd W10	145	O2
Acklington dr NW9	26	A3
Ackmar rd SW6	87	X3
Ackroyd dr E3	63	Z14
Ackroyd rd SE23	92	H18
Acland cres SE5	91	N9
Acland rd NW2	44	L17
Acol rd NW6	137	W1
Aconbury rd Dag	68	C2
Acorn clo E4	20	C16
Acorn clo Chis	114	D13
Acorn clo Enf	7	V6
Acorn clo Stan	24	C2
Acorn gdns SE19	123	U1
Acorn gdns W3	61	Z15
Acorn Industrial pk Dart	99	U13
Acorn rd Dart	99	U13
Acorn wk SE16	75	X4
Acorn way SE23	110	F7
Acorns the Hmptn	100	K15
Acre la SW2	90	C11
Acre rd SW19	106	H17
Acre rd Dag	56	J20
Acre rd Kings T	116	K1
Acris st SW18	88	D13
Acton clo N9	18	L7
Acton la NW10	61	V9
Acton la W3	73	W4
Acton la W4	73	X7
Acton ms E8	142	M3
Acton Park Industrial est W3	73	Z4
Acton st WC1	141	N13
Acuba rd SW18	105	Z3
Ada gdns E14	64	J17
Ada gdns E15	65	P3
Ada pl E2	143	V7
Ada rd SE5	158	J20
Ada rd Wem	42	F8
Ada st E8	143	V5
Adair clo SE25	123	Z6
Adair rd W10	137	N18
Adam & Eve ms W8	153	S1
Adam st WC2	148	M10
Adam wk SW6	152	E17
Adams clo NW9	43	U5
Adams clo Surb	117	O15
Adams ct EC2	150	H5
Adams pl E14	76	D2
Adams pl N7	48	D16
Adams rd N17	31	R7
Adams rd Beck	124	J11
Adams row W1	147	V10
Adams sq Bexh	97	Y9
Adamson rd E16	65	T18
Adamson rd NW3	46	G19
Adamsrill clo Enf	8	C18
Adamsrill rd SE26	110	G9
Adare wk SW16	108	C6
Adderley gdns SE9	113	X10
Adderley gro SW11	89	O13
Adderley rd Har	23	V5
Adderley st E14	64	G17
Addington dr N12	15	S19
Addington gro SE26	110	H10
Addington rd E3	64	B8
Addington rd E16	65	R12
Addington rd N4	30	F19
Addington rd Croy	122	G19
Addington rd S Croy	134	E20
Addington rd W Wick	135	T9
Addington sq SE5	158	D16
Addington st SE1	157	T9
Addington Village rd Croy	135	N14
Addis clo Enf	9	S5
Addiscombe ave Croy	123	W18
Addiscombe clo Har	24	D14
Addiscombe Court rd Croy	133	T1
Addiscombe gro Croy	133	R4
Addiscombe rd Croy	133	R3
Addison ave N14	6	F18
Addison ave W11	144	L14
Addison ave Houns	82	M3
Addison Bridge pl W14	153	N4
Addison cres W14	152	M1
Addison dr SE12	94	H14
Addison gdns W14	152	G1
Addison gdns Surb	117	N10
Addison gro W4	74	C9
Addison pl W11	144	K14
Addison pl Sthl	70	J1
Addison rd E11	34	F18
Addison rd E17	33	T14
Addison rd SE25	123	Y9
Addison rd W14	153	O1
Addison rd Brom	127	N11
Addison rd Enf	9	R5
Addison rd Ilf	36	C5
Addison rd Tedd	102	B16
Addison way NW11	27	W13
Addisons clo Croy	134	L2
Addle hill EC4	149	Z7
Addle st EC2	150	C3
Adela av N Mal	118	K11
Adela st W10	136	K16
Adelaide ave SE4	92	L11
Adelaide clo Enf	8	F3
Adelaide clo Stan	10	L13
Adelaide cotts W7	71	V4
Adelaide gdns Rom	37	Y15
Adelaide gro W12	74	H3
Adelaide rd E10	51	T10
Adelaide rd NW3	138	F1
Adelaide rd W13	71	Z3
Adelaide rd Chis	114	A13
Adelaide rd Houns	82	A3
Adelaide rd Ilf	54	A5
Adelaide rd Rich	85	N10
Adelaide rd Sthl	70	B11
Adelaide rd Surb	116	K13
Adelaide rd Tedd	101	X15
Adelaide st WC2	148	K11
Adelina gro E1	143	Z20
Adelina ms SW12	89	Y20
Adeline pl WC1	148	G3
Adelphi cres Horn	57	X6
Adelphi ter WC2	148	M11
Aden gro N16	49	O12
Aden rd Enf	9	W14
Aden rd Ilf	54	B1
Aden ter N16	49	N11
Adeney clo W6	152	J14
Adenmore rd SE6	93	O19
Adie rd W6	152	B3
Adine rd E13	65	U11
Adler st E1	151	T4
Adley st E5	50	J14
Admaston rd SE18	79	R18
Admiral pl SE16	75	W1
Admiral Seymour rd SE9	95	T10
Admiral st SE8	93	O3
Admirals clo E18	34	J12
Admirals wk NW3	46	D10
Admirals way E14	76	C4
Admiralty rd Tedd	101	V16
Adolf st SE6	111	P10
Adolphus rd N4	48	J5
Adolphus st SE8	75	Z18
Adomar rd Dag	55	Y10
Adpar st W2	138	G19
Adrian ms SW10	153	Y13
Adrienne ave Sthl	58	F10
Adys rd SE15	91	W8
Aerodrome rd NW4	26	F9
Aerodrome rd NW9	26	C8
Affleck st N1	141	O10
Afghan rd SW11	88	J6
Agamemnon rd NW6	45	W14
Agar gro NW1	47	W20
Agar pl NW1	140	D1
Agar st WC2	148	K10
Agate clo E16	66	C18
Agate rd W6	152	B3
Agatha clo E1	151	Z12
Agaton rd SE9	114	D4
Agave rd NW2	44	M12
Agdon st EC1	141	X15
Agincourt rd NW3	46	L13
Agnes ave Ilf	53	Y11
Agnes clo E6	66	K18

Name	Page	Grid
Agnes gdns Dag	55	X11
Agnes rd W3	74	C4
Agnes st E14	63	Z16
Agnew rd SE23	92	H18
Agricola pl Enf	8	H16
Aidan clo Dag	55	Z11
Ailsa ave Twick	84	A13
Ailsa rd Twick	84	B12
Ailsa st E14	64	H14
Ainger ms NW3	139	P1
Ainger rd NW3	139	O2
Ainsdale cres Pnr	22	H9
Ainsdale rd W5	60	H12
Ainsley ave Rom	38	J19
Ainsley clo N9	18	D4
Ainsley st E2	143	X14
Ainslie wk SW12	89	R19
Ainslie Wood cres E4	20	D16
Ainslie Wood gdns E4	20	D14
Ainslie Wood rd E4	20	C16
Ainsworth clo NW2	44	G8
Ainsworth rd E9	63	R1
Ainsworth rd Croy	132	K2
Ainsworth way NW8	138	A4
Aintree ave E6	66	D4
Aintree cres Ilf	36	C7
Aintree est SW6	152	M17
Aintree rd Grnf	60	B5
Aintree st SW6	152	M18
Air st W1	148	D10
Airdrie clo N1	141	N1
Airdrie clo Hayes	58	N15
Airedale ave W4	74	D12
Airedale rd SW12	89	N20
Airedale rd W5	72	F8
Airfield way Horn	57	Z19
Airlie gdns W8	145	T15
Airlie gdns Ilf	54	A5
Airthrie rd Ilf	55	R6
Aisgill ave W14	153	R10
Aisher rd SE28	68	E19
Aislibie rd SE12	94	B11
Aitken clo E8	143	S4
Aitken clo SE6	111	R4
Ajax ave NW9	26	A10
Ajax rd NW6	45	X14
Akehurst st SW15	86	G17
Akenside rd NW3	46	F15
Akerman rd SW9	90	H3
Akerman rd Surb	116	F15
Alabama st SE18	79	U18
Alacross rd W5	72	F7
Alan dr Barn	4	D18
Alan gdns Rom	56	E1
Alan rd SW19	105	T12
Alanthus clo SE12	94	D15
Alaska st SE1	149	T15
Alba clo Hayes	58	A12
Alba gdns NW11	27	T19
Alba pl W11	145	O4
Albacore cres SE13	93	R16
Albany clo N15	30	K13
Albany clo SW14	85	T11
Albany clo Bex	97	V19
Albany clo (Bushey) Wat	10	D1
Albany ctyd W1	148	C11
Albany cres Edg	25	U9
Albany ms SE5	158	D14
Albany ms Kings T	102	H16
Albany Park ave Enf	9	R4
Albany Park rd Kings T	102	J17
Albany pas Rich	84	L14
Albany pl N7	48	F13
Albany pl Brent	72	J17
Albany rd E10	33	O20
Albany rd E12	53	O13
Albany rd E17	32	K18
Albany rd N4	30	E19
Albany rd N18	19	O16
Albany rd SE5	158	D15
Albany rd SW19	105	Z12
Albany rd W13	60	B18
Albany rd Belv	81	P15
Albany rd Bex	97	V19
Albany rd Brent	72	H17
Albany rd Chis	114	A13
Albany rd Enf	9	S1
Albany rd Horn	57	W3
Albany rd N Mal	117	Z8
Albany rd Rom	38	B17
Albany st NW1	139	X8
Albany vw Buck H	21	U5
Albatross st SE18	75	U18
Albatross way SE16	75	T6
Albemarle SW19	105	O3
Albemarle app Ilf	36	A18
Albemarle gdns Ilf	36	A19
Albemarle gdns N Mal	117	Y10
Albemarle rd Barn	15	W2
Albemarle rd Beck	125	P1
Albemarle st W1	148	A10
Albemarle ave Twick	100	E2
Alberon gdns NW11	27	V14
Albert ave E4	20	B14
Albert bri SW3	154	M15
Albert bri SW11	154	M16
Albert Bridge rd SW11	154	M17
Albert Carr gdns SW16	108	A13
Albert clo E9	143	Y6
Albert clo N22	29	X3
Albert ct SW7	146	F19
Albert cres E4	20	B13
Albert dr SW19	105	S4
Albert embk SE1	156	M8
Albert gdns E1	63	S18
Albert gro SW20	105	R20
Albert pl N3	27	Y4
Albert pl W8	146	A20
Albert rd E10	51	V6
Albert rd E16	78	E3
Albert rd E17	33	O15
Albert rd E18	34	J8
Albert rd N4	48	D3
Albert rd N15	31	R18
Albert rd N22	29	V5
Albert rd NW4	27	P13
Albert rd NW6	137	P10
Albert rd NW7	13	R16
Albert rd SE9	113	S6
Albert rd SE20	110	F16
Albert rd SE25	123	X8
Albert rd W5	60	C12
Albert rd Barn	5	S13
Albert rd Belv	81	R14
Albert rd Bex	98	F17
Albert rd Brom	127	P12
Albert rd Dag	56	D4
Albert rd Hmptn	101	O12
Albert rd Har	23	N11
Albert rd Houns	82	H11
Albert rd Ilf	54	A10
Albert rd Kings T	116	M4
Albert rd Mitch	120	M6
Albert rd N Mal	118	F10
Albert rd Rich	84	L12
Albert rd Rom	39	U17
Albert rd Sutt	130	F12
Albert rd Tedd	101	X15
Albert rd Twick	101	W1
Albert Road est Bark	81	P14
Albert sq E15	52	A15
Albert sq SW8	157	O20
Albert st N12	15	R15
Albert st NW1	139	Y5
Albert ter NW1	139	S5
Albert ter NW10	61	X4
Albert Terrace ms NW1	139	T5
Alberta ave Sutt	129	U10
Alberta est SE17	157	Y9
Alberta rd Enf	8	J18
Alberta rd Erith	98	J2
Alberta st SE17	157	Y9
Albion ave N10	29	P4
Albion ave SW8	89	X5
Albion clo W2	146	L8
Albion clo Rom	39	O18
Albion dr E8	143	N2
Albion gdns W6	74	J10
Albion gro N16	49	R11
Albion ms N1	141	T3
Albion ms NW6	45	V20
Albion ms W2	146	L7
Albion pl EC1	141	X20
Albion pl EC2	150	F2
Albion rd E17	33	U9
Albion rd N16	49	P8
Albion rd N17	31	W7
Albion rd Bexh	98	B10
Albion rd Houns	82	G11
Albion rd Kings T	117	V1
Albion rd Sutt	130	E15
Albion rd Twick	101	T2
Albion sq E8	143	O2
Albion st SE16	75	R5
Albion st W2	146	L8
Albion st Croy	132	J1
Albion ter E8	143	N1
Albion Villas rd SE26	110	C6
Albion way EC1	150	A2
Albion way SE13	93	V9
Albion way Wem	43	S10
Albrighton rd SE22	91	S8
Albuhera clo Enf	7	V5
Albury ave Bexh	97	Z4
Albury ave Islw	71	W20
Albury clo Hmptn	100	J15
Albury dr Pnr	22	A1
Albury st SE8	76	B17
Albyfield Brom	127	V7
Albyn rd SE8	93	O2
Alcester cres E5	50	A6
Alcester rd Wall	131	S10
Alcock clo Wall	131	Z17
Alconbury rd E5	49	X7
Alcorn clo Sutt	129	Y2
Alcott clo W7	59	V15
Alcuin ct Stan	11	R20
Aldborough rd Dag	56	L18
Aldborough Road north Ilf	36	K15
Aldborough Road south Ilf	54	G4
Aldbourne rd W12	74	F3
Aldbridge st SE17	158	K9
Aldburgh ms W1	147	V5
Aldbury ave Wem	43	S19
Aldbury ms N9	18	C3
Aldebert ter SW8	156	M20
Aldeburgh pl Wdf Grn	21	U12
Aldeburgh st SE10	77	T12
Alden ave E15	65	O10
Aldenham st NW1	140	D10
Aldensley rd W6	152	A3
Alder gro SE15	159	O16
Alder gro NW2	44	H7
Alder rd SW14	85	X7
Alder rd Sid	114	K8
Alderbrook rd SW12	89	R16
Alderbury rd SW13	74	H17
Aldergrove gdns Houns	82	A5
Alderman ave Bark	68	C7
Aldermanbury EC2	150	D4
Aldermanbury sq EC2	150	D3
Aldermans hill N13	17	N12
Alderman's wk EC2	150	K3
Aldermary rd Brom	112	F20
Aldermaston st W10	144	G6
Aldermoor rd SE6	110	M6
Alderney ave Houns	70	J20
Alderney gdns Nthlt	40	D20
Alderney rd E1	63	T11
Alderney st SW1	155	Y8
Alders the N21	7	V20
Alders the Felt	100	B11
Alders the Houns	70	D15
Alders the W Wick	135	R1
Alders ave Wdf Grn	20	M20
Alders clo E11	52	H5
Alders clo W5	72	G7
Alders clo Edg	12	H16
Alders rd Edg	12	H15
Aldersbrook ave Enf	8	E8
Aldersbrook dr Kings T	103	N15
Aldersbrook la E12	53	U10
Aldersbrook rd E11	52	J6
Aldersbrook rd E12	53	V10
Aldersey gdns Bark	54	F18
Aldersford clo SE4	92	G12
Aldersgate st EC1	150	A1
Aldersgrove ave SE9	113	N7
Aldershot rd NW6	137	S3
Aldersmead ave Croy	124	G14
Aldersmead rd Beck	110	J17
Alderson st W10	136	L16
Alderton cres NW4	26	K16
Alderton rd SE24	90	L9
Alderton rd Croy	123	W17
Alderton way NW4	26	J16
Alderville rd SW6	87	W5
Alderwick dr Houns	83	P6
Alderwood rd SE9	96	F15
Aldford st W1	147	U11
Aldgate EC3	150	M6
Aldgate ave E1	151	N5
Aldgate High st EC3	151	N6
Aldine st W12	144	E16
Aldingham ct Horn	57	X15
Aldingham gdns Horn	57	X15
Aldington clo Dag	55	V2
Aldington rd SE18	78	B9
Aldis st SW17	106	J13
Aldred rd NW6	45	X14
Aldren rd SW17	106	D7
Aldrich cres Croy	135	U20
Aldriche way E4	20	F19
Aldridge ave Edg	12	G10
Aldridge ave Stan	24	K5
Aldridge ri N Mal	118	A16
Aldridge Road vill W11	145	R2
Aldridge wk N14	16	M3
Aldrington rd SW16	107	W12
Aldsworth clo W9	137	X19
Aldwick clo SE9	114	E6
Aldwick rd Croy	132	D7
Aldworth gro SE13	93	T15
Aldworth rd E15	51	Z20
Aldwych WC2	149	O7
Aldwych ave Ilf	36	D14
Aldwych clo Horn	57	X5
Alers rd Bexh	97	X13
Aleston Beck rd E16	66	B16
Alexander ave NW10	136	A2
Alexander clo Barn	5	U14
Alexander clo Brom	126	G20
Alexander clo Sid	96	J14
Alexander clo Twick	101	V5
Alexander pl SW7	154	J4
Alexander rd N19	48	A8
Alexander rd Bexh	97	X5
Alexander rd Chis	114	A14
Alexander sq SW3	154	K4
Alexander st W2	145	W4
Alexandra ave N22	29	Y5
Alexandra ave SW11	89	O2
Alexandra ave W4	73	Z20
Alexandra ave Har	40	F4
Alexandra ave Sthl	70	D1
Alexandra ave Sutt	129	X7
Alexandra clo Har	40	J9
Alexandra cotts SE14	92	M3
Alexandra ct Har	14	H17
Alexandra ct Wem	43	N12
Alexandra cres Brom	112	B15
Alexandra dr SE19	109	R14
Alexandra dr Surb	117	O18
Alexandra gdns N10	29	T12
Alexandra gdns W4	74	A19
Alexandra gdns Cars	131	N19
Alexandra gdns Houns	82	K5
Alexandra gro N4	48	K4
Alexandra gro N12	15	P18
Alexandra Park rd N22	29	V5
Alexandra pl NW8	138	C3
Alexandra pl SE25	123	R11
Alexandra pl Croy	123	S19
Alexandra rd E6	66	J9
Alexandra rd E10	51	U10
Alexandra rd E17	32	M19
Alexandra rd E18	34	G11
Alexandra rd N8	30	F9
Alexandra rd N10	16	E20
Alexandra rd N15	27	P12
Alexandra rd NW4	27	P12
Alexandra rd NW8	138	D2
Alexandra rd SE26	110	F15

Alexandra rd SW14	85	Z8
Alexandra rd SW19	105	W15
Alexandra rd W4	73	Z5
Alexandra rd Brent	72	H17
Alexandra rd Croy	123	S18
Alexandra rd Enf	9	U14
Alexandra rd Houns	82	J5
Alexandra rd Kings T	103	P19
Alexandra rd Mitch	106	K19
Alexandra rd Rich	85	N5
Alexandra rd Rom	39	S17
Alexandra rd Rom	37	Y18
(Chadwell Heath)		
Alexandra rd Twick	84	F16
Alexandra sq Mord	119	Z13
Alexandra st E16	65	S13
Alexandra st SE14	75	X18
Alexandra wk SE19	109	R13
Alexandria rd W13	60	A20
Alexis st SE16	159	T5
Alfearn rd E5	50	B11
Alford grn Croy	135	W15
Alford pl N1	142	D10
Alford rd SW8	89	Y3
Alford rd Erith	81	Z13
Alfoxton ave N15	30	J12
Alfred ms W1	140	E20
Alfred pl WC1	148	F1
Alfred rd E15	52	C15
Alfred rd SE25	123	Y11
Alfred rd W2	145	V1
Alfred rd W3	73	W3
Alfred rd Belv	81	P15
Alfred rd Kings T	116	L8
Alfred rd Sutt	130	E12
Alfred st E3	64	A8
Alfreda gdns Bark	89	R2
Alfreds gdns Bark	67	W5
Alfreds rd Bark	67	P8
Alfreds Way Bark	68	A4
Alfreds Way		
Industrial est Bark		
Alfreton clo SW19	105	O7
Alfriston ave Croy	122	A16
Alfriston ave Har	24	H19
Alfriston clo Surb	116	M13
Alfriston rd SW11	89	N12
Algar clo Islw	83	Y9
Algar clo Stan	10	K17
Algar rd Islw	83	Z9
Algarve rd SW18	106	C2
Algernon rd NW4	26	G18
Algernon rd NW6	137	T5
Algernon rd SE13	93	R11
Algiers rd SE13	93	P11
Alibon gdns Dag	56	F14
Alibon rd Dag	56	C14
Alice st SE1	158	J2
Alice way Houns	82	J11
Alicia ave Har	24	B14
Alicia clo Har	24	D14
Alicia gdns Har	24	D11
Alie st E1	151	P6
Alington cres NW9	43	W2
Alington gro Wall	131	W20
Alison clo E6	66	K18
Aliwal rd SW11	88	K11
Alkerden rd W4	74	B13
Alkham rd N16	49	V5
All Hallows rd N17	31	S4
All Saints clo N9	18	J9
All Saints dr SE3	94	B5
All Saints ms Stan	10	G19
All Saints rd SW19	106	D17
All Saints rd W3	73	V7
All Saints rd W11	145	P3
All Saints rd Sutt	130	D5
All Saints st N1	141	N7
All Souls ave NW10	136	B3
All Souls pl W1	147	Z3
Allan clo N Mal	117	Y12
Allan way W3	60	W13
Allandale ave N3	27	V10
Allandale rd Horn	39	U20
Allard cres (Bushey)	10	A6
Wat		
Allardyce st SW4	90	C9
Allbrook clo Tedd	101	T12
Allcroft rd NW5	47	P16

Allen Edwards dr	156	J19
SW8		
Allen rd E3	63	Y5
Allen rd N16	49	R12
Allen rd Beck	124	E4
Allen rd Croy	122	E19
Allen st W8	153	V1
Allenby ave S Croy	132	M20
Allenby clo Grnf	58	J10
Allenby rd SE23	110	H6
Allenby rd Sthl	58	H18
Allendale ave Sthl	58	F18
Allendale clo SE5	91	O3
Allendale clo SE26	110	G13
Allendale rd Grnf	42	A17
Allens rd Enf	9	R17
Allensbury pl NW1	140	H1
Allenswood rd SE9	95	T6
Allerford ct Har	22	L14
Allerford rd SE6	111	T9
Allerton rd N16	49	N6
Allestree rd SW6	152	L19
Alleyn cres SE21	109	P5
Alleyn pk SE21	109	P3
Alleyn pk Sthl	70	F12
Alleyn rd SE21	109	P6
Alleyndale rd Dag	55	T6
Allfarthing la SW18	88	B17
Allgood clo Mord	119	O15
Allgood st E2	143	R10
Allhallows la EC4	150	E10
Allhallows rd E6	66	C15
Alliance clo Wem	42	G13
Alliance rd E13	65	X13
Alliance rd SE18	80	A18
Alliance rd W3	61	T12
Allingham clo W7	59	W20
Allingham st N1	142	A7
Allington ave N17	18	E20
Allington clo Grnf	59	N1
Allington ct Enf	9	T17
Allington rd NW4	26	K17
Allington rd W10	136	K11
Allington rd Har	22	M15
Allington st SW1	155	Z2
Allison clo SE10	93	W2
Allison gro SE21	109	S1
Allison rd N8	30	G15
Allison rd W3	61	W18
Allitsen rd NW8	138	J9
Allnutt way SW4	89	W12
Alloa rd SE8	75	U13
Alloa rd Ilf	55	P5
Allonby gdns Wem	42	F5
Alloway rd E3	63	X8
Allsop pl NW1	139	R18
Allum way N20	15	P6
Allwood clo SE26	110	G10
Alma ave E4	33	U1
Alma cres Sutt	129	U10
Alma gro SE1	159	R6
Alma pl SE19	109	U17
Alma pl Th Hth	122	G12
Alma rd N10	29	R3
Alma rd SW18	88	C12
Alma rd Cars	130	K11
Alma rd Enf	9	U17
Alma rd Sid	115	O6
Alma rd Sthl	58	A20
Alma row Har	23	S3
Alma sq NW8	138	C11
Alma st E15	51	X16
Alma st NW5	47	T17
Alma ter SW18	88	G18
Almack rd E5	50	C12
Almeida st N1	141	W2
Almer rd SW20	104	G17
Almeric rd SW11	88	L11
Almington st N4	48	B4
Almond ave W5	72	H8
Almond ave Cars	130	L3
Almond clo SE15	91	Y5
Almond clo Brom	127	W18
Almond gro Brent	72	B19
Almond rd N17	31	Y2
Almond rd SE16	159	X6
Almond way Brom	127	W17
Almond way Har	22	L8
Almond way Mitch	121	Y11

Almonds ave Buck H	21	T9
Almorah rd N1	142	F2
Almorah rd Houns	82	A3
Alnwick gro Mord	120	A10
Alnwick rd E16	65	Y18
Alnwick rd SE12	94	H17
Alperton la Grnf	60	E8
Alperton la Wem	60	J6
Alperton st W10	137	N16
Alpha clo NW1	138	M15
Alpha gro E14	76	B6
Alpha pl NW6	137	V8
Alpha pl SW3	154	M12
Alpha rd E4	20	C11
Alpha rd N18	18	J17
Alpha rd SE14	92	M1
Alpha rd Croy	123	R20
Alpha rd Enf	9	X15
Alpha rd Surb	116	M16
Alpha rd Tedd	101	P12
Alpha st SE15	91	X6
Alpine copse Brom	127	W4
Alpine rd SE16	75	S12
Alpine vw Sutt	130	H12
Alpine wk Stan	10	G7
Alpine way E6	66	K14
Alric ave NW10	43	Z20
Alric ave N Mal	118	B6
Alroy rd N4	30	H20
Alsace rd SE17	158	J10
Alscot rd SE1	159	N5
Alscot way SE1	159	O5
Alsike rd SE2	80	J9
Alsike rd Erith	80	M7
Alsom ave Wor Pk	128	F8
Alston clo Surb	116	B17
Alston rd N18	19	N17
Alston rd SW17	106	F10
Alston rd Barn	4	D11
Alt gro SW19	105	U17
Altair clo N17	18	J19
Altash way SE9	113	V5
Altenburg ave W13	72	B7
Altenburg gdns SW11	88	M9
Altham rd Pnr	22	C2
Althea st SW6	88	B6
Althorne gdns E18	34	C12
Althorne way Dag	56	E6
Althorpe rd SW17	106	L1
Althorpe rd Har	23	O15
Altmore ave E6	53	U20
Alton ave Stan	23	X2
Alton clo Islw	83	X4
Alton gdns Beck	111	N19
Alton gdns Twick	83	R17
Alton rd N17	31	P11
Alton rd SW15	104	H2
Alton rd Croy	132	F7
Alton rd Rich	84	L11
Alton st E14	64	D16
Altyre clo Beck	124	L13
Altyre rd Croy	133	P4
Altyre way Beck	124	L12
Alvanley gdns NW6	46	A15
Alverston gdns SE25	123	T11
Alverstone ave SW19	105	X5
Alverstone ave Barn	15	V1
Alverstone gdns SE9	96	B20
Alverstone rd E12	53	X13
Alverstone rd NW2	44	M19
Alverstone rd N Mal	118	E9
Alverstone rd Wem	43	O3
Alverton st SE8	75	X15
Alveston ave Har	24	B10
Alvey st SE17	158	J9
Alvia gdns Sutt	130	D8
Alvington cres E8	49	U15
Alwold cres SE12	94	J17
Alwyn ave W4	73	X14
Alwyn clo Croy	135	S17
Alwyn gdns NW4	26	H12
Alwyn gdns W3	61	T17
Alwyne la N1	48	L19
Alwyne pl N1	48	K19
Alwyne rd N1	48	K20
Alwyne rd SW19	105	V15
Alwyne rd W7	71	T1
Alwyne sq N1	48	L17

Alwyne vill N1	48	K19
Alyth gdns NW11	27	X18
Amalgamated dr	72	A17
Brent		
Amazon st E1	151	V5
Ambassador clo	82	B5
Houns		
Ambassador gdns E6	66	G14
Amber ave E17	32	J3
Amberden ave N3	27	Z9
Ambergate st SE17	157	X10
Amberley ct Sid	115	U13
Amberley gdns Enf	18	F3
Amberley gdns	128	C8
Epsom		
Amberley gro SE26	109	Z11
Amberley gro Croy	123	V18
Amberley rd E10	33	P20
Amberley rd N13	17	P8
Amberley rd SE2	80	K16
Amberley rd W9	137	W19
Amberley rd Buck H	21	Z5
Amberley rd Enf	18	G1
Amberley way Mord	119	W17
Amberley way Rom	38	J12
Amberwood ri N Mal	118	C15
Amblecote clo SE12	112	J8
Amblecote rd SE12	112	H7
Ambler rd N4	48	H8
Ambleside Brom	111	Y15
Ambleside ave SW16	107	Y10
Ambleside ave Beck	124	J12
Ambleside ave Horn	57	Y14
Ambleside clo E9	50	D14
Ambleside cres Enf	9	T10
Ambleside gdns Ilf	35	S14
Ambleside gdns Sutt	130	E15
Ambleside gdns Wem	42	F3
Ambleside rd NW10	44	D20
Ambleside rd Bexh	98	D3
Ambrey way Wall	131	Y20
Ambrooke rd Belv	81	S9
Ambrosden ave SW1	156	C3
Ambrose ave NW11	27	U20
Ambrose clo E6	66	F15
Ambrose st SE16	159	W6
Amelia st SE17	157	Z9
Amen corner EC4	149	Y6
America sq EC3	151	N8
America st SE1	150	B15
Amerland rd SW18	87	W15
Amersham ave N18	18	B18
Amersham gro SE14	75	Y18
Amersham rd SE14	92	L1
Amersham rd Croy	123	N14
Amersham vale SE14	75	Y19
Amery gdns NW10	136	A5
Amery rd Har	41	Y7
Amesbury ave SW2	108	B4
Amesbury clo Wor Pk	119	N20
Amesbury rd Brom	127	O5
Amesbury rd Dag	55	W20
Amesbury rd Felt	100	A3
Amethyst rd E15	51	X13
Amherst ave W13	60	C17
Amherst rd W13	60	D17
Amhurst gdns Islw	83	X3
Amhurst pk N16	31	P20
Amhurst pas E8	49	W14
Amhurst rd E8	49	W13
Amhurst rd N16	49	U11
Amhurst ter E8	49	W12
Amidas gdns Dag	55	R13
Amiel st E1	63	R11
Amies st SW11	88	L7
Amity gro SW20	118	L1
Amity rd E15	65	P2
Amner rd SW11	89	O15
Amor rd W6	152	B2
Amott rd SE15	91	W8
Amoy pl E14	64	A18
Ampere way Croy	122	C19
Ampleforth rd SE2	80	C15
Ampthill Square est	140	C10
NW1		
Ampton pl WC1	141	O14
Ampton st WC1	141	O14
Amroth clo SE23	110	A1

Amsterdam rd E14	76	J8
Amwell clo Enf	8	B16
Amwell st EC1	141	T14
Amyand Park rd Twick	83	Z19
Amyruth rd SE4	93	N13
Anatola rd N19	47	U6
Ancaster cres N Mal	118	F15
Ancaster rd Beck	124	F7
Ancaster st SE18	79	V19
Anchor & Hope la SE7	77	X9
Anchor ms SW12	89	T16
Anchor st SE16	159	W6
Anchor yd EC1	142	B16
Anchorage clo SW19	105	Y14
Ancill clo W6	152	J14
Ancona rd NW10	62	G6
Ancona rd SE18	79	T15
Andace Park gdns Brom	126	K2
Andalus rd SW9	90	B8
Ander clo Wem	42	G13
Anderson clo W3	61	Z17
Anderson pl Houns	82	K10
Anderson rd E9	50	F17
Anderson rd Wdf Grn	35	O9
Anderson st SW3	155	O8
Anderson way Belv	81	W5
Anderton clo SE5	91	R8
Andover clo Grnf	58	L10
Andover pl NW6	137	X9
Andover rd N7	48	C7
Andover rd Twick	101	R3
Andre st E8	49	Y15
Andrew clo Dart	99	N13
Andrew st E14	64	G16
Andrews clo Buck H	21	Y7
Andrews clo Wor Pk	129	O2
Andrews pl SE9	95	Y16
Andrew's rd E8	143	X7
Andwell clo SE2	80	E6
Anerley gro SE19	109	V18
Anerley hill SE19	109	V15
Anerley pk SE20	109	Y19
Anerley Park rd SE20	109	Z17
Anerley rd SE19	109	W17
Anerley rd SE20	124	A1
Anerley Station rd SE20	109	Z20
Anerley st SW11	89	N4
Anerley vale SE19	109	W17
Anfield clo SW12	89	V19
Angel all E1	151	R3
Angel clo N18	18	J15
Angel ct EC2	150	G5
Angel ct SW17	106	L11
Angel hill Sutt	130	B5
Angel Hill dr Sutt	130	B5
Angel la E15	51	X17
Angel ms N1	141	U9
Angel pas EC4	150	F10
Angel rd N18	18	K15
Angel rd Har	23	U17
Angel Road works N18	19	R16
Angel st EC1	150	A4
Angel wk W6	152	B8
Angel way Rom	39	P14
Angelfield Houns	82	K12
Angelica gdns Croy	134	F1
Angell Park gdns SW9	90	G6
Angell rd SW9	90	G6
Angerstein la SE3	94	D1
Angle grn Dag	55	V4
Angler's la NW5	47	T17
Angles rd SW16	108	B9
Anglesea rd SE18	78	M11
Anglesea rd Kings T	116	H9
Anglesey Court rd Cars	131	P15
Anglesey gdns Cars	131	O15
Anglesey rd Enf	9	O13
Anglesmede cres Pnr	22	G10
Anglesmede way Pnr	22	F10
Anglo rd E3	63	Z6
Angus gdns NW9	25	Z5
Angus rd E13	65	Z10
Angus st SE14	75	X19
Anhalt rd SW11	154	M18
Ankerdine cres SE18	78	L19
Anlaby rd Tedd	101	S13
Anley rd W14	144	F20
Anmersh gro Stan	24	H5
Ann la SW10	154	F16
Ann st SE18	79	R13
Anna clo E8	143	R4
Annabel clo E14	64	D18
Annan way Rom	39	O4
Annandale rd SE10	77	P15
Annandale rd W4	74	B12
Annandale rd Croy	133	Y3
Annandale rd Sid	96	J19
Anne Boleyn's wk Kings T	102	K13
Anne Boleyn's wk Sutt	129	R17
Anne Case ms N Mal	117	Z5
Anne st E13	65	T11
Annesley ave NW9	25	Y10
Annesley clo NW10	44	A9
Annesley dr Croy	134	M7
Annesley rd SE3	94	H2
Annette clo Har	23	U6
Annette rd N7	48	D10
Annie Besant clo E3	63	Z3
Anning st EC2	142	M15
Annington rd N2	29	N11
Annis rd E9	50	H19
Ann's clo SW1	147	S19
Ann's pl E1	151	O3
Annsworthy ave Th Hth	123	O7
Ansdell rd SE15	92	C4
Ansdell st W8	145	Z20
Ansdell ter W8	145	Y20
Ansell gro Cars	131	N1
Ansell rd SW17	106	K7
Anselm clo Croy	133	U5
Anselm rd SW6	153	T15
Anselm rd Pnr	22	F2
Ansford rd Brom	111	W11
Ansleigh pl W11	144	H10
Anson rd Rom	38	G7
Anson rd N7	47	W13
Anson rd NW2	44	K13
Anstey rd SE15	91	X7
Anstice clo W4	74	C20
Anstridge rd SE9	96	F15
Antelope rd SE18	78	F8
Anthony clo NW7	13	O14
Anthony rd SE25	123	X15
Anthony rd Grnf	59	S7
Anthony rd Well	97	P2
Anthony st E1	151	X5
Antill rd E3	63	W8
Antill rd N15	31	X12
Antill ter E1	63	T16
Anton cres Sutt	129	X6
Anton st E8	49	Y15
Antrim gro NW3	46	L17
Antrim rd NW3	46	L17
Antrobus clo Sutt	129	W12
Antrobus rd W4	73	V11
Anworth clo Wdf Grn	21	U18
Apeldoorn dr Wall	131	Z20
Apex clo Beck	111	T20
Aplin way Islw	83	S1
Apollo ave Brom	112	G20
Apollo clo Horn	57	Y6
Apollo pl SW10	154	F17
Appach rd SW2	90	F14
Apple garth Brent	72	H12
Apple gro Enf	8	F11
Apple Tree yd SW1	148	D12
Appleby clo E4	20	F19
Appleby clo N15	31	O15
Appleby clo Twick	101	P5
Appleby clo E8	49	Y20
Appleby rd E16	65	R18
Appleby st E2	143	O7
Appledore ave Bexh	98	M3
Appledore clo SW17	106	M4
Appledore clo Brom	126	D11
Appledore clo Edg	25	O4
Appledore cres Sid	114	J8
Appleford rd W10	136	M18
Applegarth Croy	135	S16
Applegarth dr Ilf	36	L13
Applegarth rd SE28	80	E1
Applegarth rd W14	152	G3
Appleton gdns N Mal	118	F15
Appleton rd SE9	95	R8
Appleton sq Mitch	106	J20
Appletree gdns Barn	5	V12
Applewood clo NW2	44	J8
Appold st EC2	142	J20
Apprentice way E5	50	B12
Approach the NW4	27	O15
Approach the W3	61	Z18
Approach the Enf	9	N7
Approach rd E2	63	R6
Approach rd SW20	118	M4
Approach rd Barn	5	S14
Aprey gdns NW4	27	N12
April clo W7	59	U19
April glen SE23	110	G7
April st E8	49	V13
Apsley clo Har	22	M15
Apsley rd SE25	123	Z10
Apsley rd N Mal	117	W7
Aquila st NW8	138	H8
Aquinas st SE1	149	U13
Arabella dr SW15	86	C9
Arabia clo E4	20	J2
Arabin rd SE4	92	K10
Aragon ave Epsom	128	J20
Aragon clo Brom	127	U20
Aragon clo Enf	7	S4
Aragon ms E1	151	T13
Aragon rd Kings T	102	J12
Aragon rd Mord	119	T18
Aran dr Stan	11	S14
Arandora cres Rom	37	P20
Arbery rd E3	63	W7
Arbor clo Beck	125	R3
Arbor rd E4	20	K11
Arbour rd Enf	9	T12
Arbour sq E1	63	S17
Arbour way Horn	57	Z14
Arbroath rd SE9	95	S7
Arbuthnot la Bex	97	Z17
Arbuthnot rd SE14	92	E4
Arbutus st E8	142	M3
Arcade the EC2	150	J3
Arcade pl Rom	39	R16
Arcadia ave N3	27	X6
Arcadia st E14	64	C16
Arcadian ave Bex	97	Z17
Arcadian clo Bex	97	Z16
Arcadian gdns N22	17	S20
Arcadian rd Bex	97	Y17
Arch st SE1	158	B3
Archangel st SE16	75	U5
Archbishops pl SW2	90	D17
Archdale rd SE22	91	W12
Archel rd W14	153	O13
Archer clo Kings T	102	K17
Archer rd SE25	123	Z9
Archer st W1	148	E9
Archers dr Enf	9	P9
Archery clo W2	146	M7
Archery clo Har	23	W9
Archery rd SE9	95	V12
Arches the Har	40	L5
Archibald ms W1	147	W11
Archibald rd N7	47	X12
Archibald st E3	64	A10
Archway clo SW19	106	A8
Archway clo Wall	131	Z6
Archway mall N19	47	V6
Archway rd N6	29	O18
Archway rd N19	47	T1
Archway st SW13	86	B7
Arcola st E8	49	U14
Arctic st NW5	47	R15
Arcus rd Brom	112	A14
Ardbeg rd SE24	91	O14
Arden clo Har	41	P10
Arden clo (Bushey) Wat	10	H2
Arden Court gdns N2	28	G19
Arden cres E14	76	B10
Arden cres Dag	55	V20
Arden est N1	142	J9
Arden rd N3	27	V9
Arden rd W13	60	C20
Ardent clo SE25	123	S5
Ardfern ave SW16	122	F5
Ardfillan rd SE6	111	Y3
Ardgowan rd SE6	93	Y19
Ardilaun rd N5	48	L11
Ardleigh gdns Sutt	119	X19
Ardleigh rd E17	32	M5
Ardleigh rd N1	49	R18
Ardleigh ter E17	32	M5
Ardley clo NW10	44	A9
Ardley clo SE6	110	K8
Ardlui rd SE27	108	L5
Ardmay gdns Surb	116	K12
Ardmere rd SE13	93	X15
Ardmore la Buck H	21	W4
Ardoch rd SE6	111	W4
Ardra rd N9	19	S10
Ardrossan gdns Wor Pk	128	G5
Ardshiel clo SW15	87	P8
Ardwell ave Ilf	36	C16
Ardwell rd SW2	108	A4
Ardwick rd NW2	45	X11
Argall ave E10	50	F2
Argent st SE1	149	Z16
Argon ms SW6	153	U18
Argus clo Rom	38	H5
Argus way W3	73	U8
Argus way Nthlt	58	A9
Argyle ave Houns	82	J15
Argyle clo W13	59	X11
Argyle pas N21	31	W3
Argyle pl W6	152	A7
Argyle rd E1	63	T11
Argyle rd E15	51	Z13
Argyle rd E16	65	X17
Argyle rd N12	14	M16
Argyle rd N17	31	W3
Argyle rd N18	18	L14
Argyle rd W13	59	X8
Argyle rd Barn	4	A12
Argyle rd Har	22	J17
Argyle rd Houns	82	K13
Argyle rd Ilf	53	X6
Argyle rd Tedd	101	U12
Argyle sq WC1	140	L12
Argyle st WC1	140	K12
Argyll ave Sthl	70	J2
Argyll gdns Edg	25	U6
Argyll rd W8	145	V19
Argyll st W1	148	A6
Arica rd SE4	92	J9
Ariel rd NW6	45	X18
Ariel way W12	144	E12
Aristotle rd SW4	89	Z9
Arkell gro SE19	108	K19
Arkindale rd SE6	111	U8
Arkley cres E17	32	L16
Arkley rd E17	32	L16
Arklow rd SE14	75	Y17
Arkwright rd NW3	46	C15
Arkwright rd S Croy	133	W20
Arlesford rd SW9	90	B7
Arlingford rd SW2	90	F15
Arlington N12	14	K12
Arlington ave N1	142	D6
Arlington clo Sid	96	G19
Arlington clo Sutt	129	Z3
Arlington clo Twick	84	D15
Arlington dr Cars	130	L3
Arlington gdns W4	73	V13
Arlington gdns Ilf	53	V2
Arlington ms Twick	84	C15
Arlington rd N14	16	E7
Arlington rd NW1	139	X3
Arlington rd W13	60	B18
Arlington rd Rich	102	G5
Arlington rd Surb	116	H16
Arlington rd Tedd	101	W10
Arlington rd Twick	84	D15
Arlington rd Wdf Grn	34	G3
Arlington sq N1	142	C5
Arlington st SW1	148	B13
Arlington way EC1	141	V12
Arlow rd N21	17	U5
Armada st SE8	76	B15
Armadale clo N17	31	Z14
Armadale rd SW6	153	T16
Armagh rd E3	63	Y4
Armfield cres Mitch	121	N4
Armfield rd Enf	8	B6
Arminger rd W12	74	K3

Street	No.	Ref	Street	No.	Ref	Street	No.	Ref	Street	No.	Ref
Armitage rd NW11	45	U4	Arundel gdns Edg	25	Y2	Ashby rd N15	31	W15	Ashmill st NW1	138	L19
Armitage rd SE10	77	O13	Arundel gdns Ilf	55	N5	Ashby rd SE4	92	M5	Ashmole pl SW8	157	R16
Armour clo N7	48	D18	Arundel gro N16	49	R15	Ashby st EC1	141	Y14	Ashmole st SW8	157	R15
Armoury way SW18	87	Y13	Arundel pl N1	48	F18	Ashby wk Croy	122	M16	Ashmore gro Well	96	F7
Armstead wk Dag	69	S1	Arundel rd Barn	5	W10	Aschurch gro W12	74	G7	Ashmore rd W9	137	P17
Armstrong ave	21	N19	Arundel rd Croy	123	O16	Aschurch Park vill	74	F7	Ashmount rd N15	31	U14
Wdf Grn			Arundel rd Kings T	117	T3	W12			Ashmount rd N19	47	W2
Armstrong clo E6	66	G17	Arundel rd Sutt	129	U18	Aschurch ter W12	74	F7	Ashmount ter W5	72	F10
Armstrong clo Dag	55	V2	Arundel sq N7	48	E18	Ashcombe ave Surb	116	H18	Ashmour gdns Rom	39	N7
Armstrong cres Barn	5	T12	Arundel st WC2	149	R8	Ashcombe gdns Edg	12	L12	Ashneal gdns Har	41	P9
Armstrong rd SW7	154	E2	Arundel ter SW13	152	A14	Ashcombe pk NW2	44	C10	Ashness gdns Grnf	42	A17
Armstrong rd W3	74	D2	Arvon rd N5	48	G14	Ashcombe rd SW19	105	Y13	Ashness rd SW11	88	M13
Armstrong rd Felt	100	B13	Ascalon st SW8	156	B20	Ashcombe rd Cars	131	O13	Ashridge clo Har	24	E19
Armstrong way Sthl	70	K5	Ascham end E17	32	K3	Ashcombe sq N Mal	117	V6	Ashridge cres SE18	79	O19
Arnal cres SW18	87	T18	Ascham st NW5	47	U14	Ashcombe rd SW6	88	A15	Ashridge gdns N13	16	M14
Arne st WC2	148	L6	Aschurch rd Croy	123	V17	Ashcroft ave Sid	97	N16	Ashridge gdns Pnr	22	B13
Arne wk SE3	94	B10	Ascot clo Nthlt	40	H16	Ashcroft cres Sid	97	N16	Ashridge way Mord	119	V8
Arneway st SW1	156	G4	Ascot gdns Sthl	58	F12	Ashcroft rd E3	63	W9	Ashtead rd E5	49	Y1
Arneways ave Rom	37	W11	Ascot ms Wall	131	V20	Ashdale clo Twick	82	M18	Ashton clo Sutt	129	X10
Arnewood clo SW15	104	F1	Ascot rd E6	66	F7	Ashdale gro Stan	10	K19	Ashton gdns Houns	82	D9
Arney's la Mitch	121	O14	Ascot rd N15	31	O16	Ashdale rd SE12	112	J2	Ashton gdns Rom	38	W18
Arngask rd SE6	93	W20	Ascot rd N18	18	L14	Ashdale way Twick	82	L18	Ashton rd E15	51	W15
Arnold circ E2	143	N14	Ascot rd SW17	107	N16	Ashdon clo Wdf Grn	21	V19	Ashton st E14	64	G18
Arnold clo Har	25	N20	Ascott ave W5	72	J4	Ashdon rd NW10	62	C2	Ashtree ave Mitch	120	H3
Arnold cres Islw	83	R14	Ash clo SE20	124	C3	Ashdown clo Beck	125	S4	Ashurst clo SE20	124	A1
Arnold est SE1	151	P18	Ash clo Cars	130	M2	Ashdown rd SE20	124	B5	Ashurst clo Dart	99	T8
Arnold gdns N13	17	V15	Ash clo Edg	12	J13	Ashdown rd Kings T	116	J4	Ashurst dr Ilf	36	A18
Arnold rd E3	64	B9	Ash clo N Mal	117	Y4	Ashdown wk Rom	38	J6	Ashurst rd N12	15	W15
Arnold rd N15	31	T11	Ash clo Rom	38	H3	Ashdown way SW17	107	O4	Ashurst rd Barn	5	Z16
Arnold rd SW17	106	M17	Ash clo Sid	115	P8	Ashen dr Dart	99	W15	Ashurst wk Croy	133	Z2
Arnold rd Dag	69	P1	Ash gro E8	143	X5	Ashen gro SW19	105	X6	Ashvale rd SW17	106	L11
Arnold rd Nthlt	40	A19	Ash gro N13	17	Y11	Ashen vale S Croy	134	F20	Ashville rd E11	51	X7
Arnos gro N14	16	K12	Ash gro NW2	45	R13	Ashenden rd E5	50	G14	Ashwater rd SE12	112	F2
Arnos rd N11	16	J15	Ash gro SE20	124	C3	Asher way E1	151	T11	Ashwell clo E6	66	F17
Arnott clo W4	73	Z11	Ash gro W5	72	K7	Ashfield clo Beck	102	J2	Ashwin st E8	49	U17
Arnould ave SE5	91	P9	Ash gro Enf	18	D2	Ashfield la Chis	114	B16	Ashwood gdns Croy	135	T15
Arnsberg way Bexh	98	D10	Ash gro Sthl	58	J13	Ashfield par N14	16	J6	Ashwood rd E4	20	L11
Arnside gdns Wem	42	G3	Ash gro Wem	41	Z13	Ashfield rd N4	31	N18	Ashworth rd W9	137	Z13
Arnside rd Bexh	98	E1	Ash gro W Wick	135	V2	Ashfield rd N14	16	H10	Aske st N1	142	K12
Arnside st SE17	158	D12	Ash rd E15	52	B15	Ashfield rd W3	74	C1	Askern clo Bexh	97	X11
Arnulls rd SW16	108	H15	Ash rd Croy	135	O3	Ashfield st E1	151	W3	Askew cres W12	74	F4
Arodene rd SW2	90	D14	Ash rd Sutt	119	U19	Ashford ave N8	29	Z13	Askew rd W12	74	E4
Arragon gdns SW16	108	A18	Ash Tree clo Croy	124	H14	Ashford ave Hayes	58	A18	Askham rd W12	74	F3
Arragon gdns W Wick	135	S6	Ash Tree dell NW9	25	X15	Ashford cres Enf	9	S8	Askill dr SW15	87	T14
Arragon rd E6	66	B4	Ash Tree way Croy	124	G13	Ashford rd E6	53	V19	Asland rd E15	64	L3
Arragon rd Twick	83	Y20	Ash wk SW2	108	E3	Ashford rd E18	34	J8	Aslett st SW18	88	C18
Arran clo Wall	131	U10	Ash wk Wem	42	F11	Ashford rd NW2	45	O12	Asmara rd NW2	45	U14
Arran dr E12	53	N5	Ashbourne ave E18	34	J12	Ashford st N1	142	J12	Asmuns hill NW11	27	X16
Arran rd SE6	111	S3	Ashbourne ave N20	15	Z6	Ashgrove rd Brom	111	Y15	Asmuns pl NW11	27	W15
Arran wk N1	48	M19	Ashbourne ave NW11	27	V15	Ashgrove rd Ilf	54	M4	Aspen clo W5	72	M6
Arras ave Mord	120	D11	Ashbourne ave Bexh	81	N18	Ashingdon clo E4	20	H12	Aspen copse Brom	127	U2
Arrol rd Beck	124	E5	Ashbourne ave Har	41	P6	Ashington rd SW6	87	W5	Aspen dr Wem	42	A10
Arrow rd E3	64	D9	Ashbourne clo N12	15	O14	Ashlake rd SW16	108	A11	Aspen gdns W6	152	A8
Arsenal rd SE9	95	U6	Ashbourne clo W5	61	O13	Ashland pl W1	147	T1	Aspen gdns Mitch	121	N12
Arterberry rd SW20	105	N18	Ashbourne gro NW7	12	L16	Ashleigh gdns Sutt	130	A4	Aspen grn Erith	81	P7
Artesian clo NW10	43	Z20	Ashbourne gro SE22	91	U12	Ashleigh rd SE20	124	B5	Aspen la Nthlt	58	B10
Artesian clo Horn	39	T19	Ashbourne gro W4	74	B14	Ashleigh rd SW14	86	A6	Aspen way E14	64	C20
Artesian rd W2	145	U6	Ashbourne rd W5	60	M11	Ashley ave Ilf	36	A8	Aspenlea rd W6	152	G14
Arthingworth st E15	64	E13	Ashbourne rd Mitch	107	O17	Ashley ave Mord	119	Y13	Aspern rd NW3	46	J15
Arthur gro SE18	79	O11	Ashbourne way NW11	27	V14	Ashley clo NW4	27	N7	Aspinall rd SE4	92	G7
Arthur rd E6	66	G6	Ashbridge rd E11	34	B20	Ashley cres N22	30	G8	Aspinden rd SE16	159	Y5
Arthur rd N7	48	D11	Ashbridge st NW8	138	K18	Ashley cres SW11	89	R8	Aspley rd SW18	88	C14
Arthur rd N9	18	G7	Ashbrook rd N19	47	X5	Ashley dr Islw	71	S17	Asplins rd N17	31	Y4
Arthur rd SW19	105	U12	Ashbrook rd Dag	56	H10	Ashley dr Twick	82	K20	Assembly pas E1	63	R13
Arthur rd Kings T	103	P19	Ashburn gdns SW7	154	A5	Ashley gdns N13	17	Z14	Assembly wk Cars	120	H18
Arthur rd N Mal	118	K12	Ashburn pl SW7	154	B5	Ashley gdns SW1	156	C3	Astall clo Har	23	S4
Arthur rd Rom	37	V19	Ashburnham ave Har	23	W19	Ashley gdns SW7	154	D5	Astbury rd SE15	92	C2
Arthur st EC4	150	G9	Ashburnham clo N2	28	G11	Ashley gdns Rich	102	G6	Aste st E14	76	F6
Arthurdon rd SE4	93	O12	Ashburnham gdns Har	23	X19	Ashley gdns Wem	42	K7	Astell st SW3	154	L9
Artichoke hill E1	151	V10	Ashburnham pl SE10	76	E20	Ashley la NW4	27	N9	Asthall gdns Ilf	36	C12
Artillery clo Ilf	36	D17	Ashburnham pl SE10	76	E20	Ashley la Croy	132	K9	Astle st SW11	89	O4
Artillery la E1	150	L2	Ashburnham rd	136	D11	Ashley pl SW1	156	B3	Astley ave NW2	45	N14
Artillery pl SE18	78	H12	NW10			Ashley rd E4	20	A17	Aston ave Har	24	E20
Artillery pl SW1	156	E2	Ashburnham rd	154	C17	Ashley rd E7	52	M20	Aston clo Sid	115	O8
Artillery row SW1	156	E2	SW10			Ashley rd N17	31	Y11	Aston rd SW20	119	N4
Artizan st E1	150	M4	Ashburnham rd Belv	81	X10	Ashley rd N19	48	A2	Aston rd W5	60	H17
Arundel ave Epsom	128	L20	Ashburnham rd Rich	102	B5	Ashley rd SW19	106	A15	Aston st E14	63	W16
Arundel ave Mord	119	W9	Ashburton ave Croy	133	Z1	Ashley rd Enf	9	R9	Astonville st SW18	105	X1
Arundel clo E15	52	A13	Ashburton ave Ilf	54	H13	Ashley rd Hmptn	100	G20	Astor ave Rom	38	J18
Arundel clo SW11	88	H12	Ashburton clo Croy	133	X1	Ashley rd Th Hth	122	E10	Astor clo Kings T	103	T15
Arundel clo Bex	98	C15	Ashburton gdns Croy	133	W2	Ashley wk NW7	27	N1	Astra clo Horn	57	Z17
Arundel clo Croy	132	H7	Ashburton gro N7	48	F12	Ashlin rd E15	51	Y13	Astrop ms W6	144	B20
Arundel clo Hmptn	100	L14	Ashburton rd E16	65	T16	Ashling rd Croy	123	Y20	Astrop ter W6	144	B20
Arundel ct N12	15	W17	Ashburton rd Croy	133	W2	Ashlone rd SW15	87	N7	Astwood ms SW7	154	A5
Arundel dr Har	40	E13	Ashbury gdns Rom	37	W16	Ashmead N14	6	H18	Asylum rd SE15	159	X16
Arundel dr Wdf Grn	34	G2	Ashbury rd SW11	89	N6	Ashmead gate Brom	126	L1	Atalanta st SW6	152	J20
Arundel gdns N21	17	U6	Ashby gro N1	48	M19	Ashmead rd SE8	93	O4	Atbara rd Tedd	102	C15
Arundel gdns W11	145	N8	Ashby ms SE4	92	L6	Ashmere ave Beck	125	W3	Atcham rd Houns	83	O10
						Ashmere clo Sutt	129	O12			
						Ashmere gro SW2	90	A11			

Name	Page	Grid
Atcost rd Bark	68	A14
Atheldene rd SW18	88	C20
Athelney st SE6	111	O6
Athelstan rd Kings T	117	N8
Athelstane gro E3	63	Y7
Athelstone rd Har	23	R8
Athenaeum rd N20	15	S6
Athenlay rd SE15	92	E14
Atherden rd E5	50	B12
Atherfold rd SW9	90	A7
Atherley way Houns	82	F19
Atherstone ms SW7	154	C4
Atherton dr SW19	105	P9
Atherton heights Wem	42	E19
Atherton ms E7	52	D17
Atherton pl Har	23	O10
Atherton rd E7	52	C16
Atherton rd SW13	74	F19
Atherton rd Ilf	35	S7
Atherton st SW11	88	L4
Athlon rd Wem	60	G5
Athlone rd SW2	90	D19
Athlone st NW5	47	R17
Athol rd Erith	81	Y14
Athol sq E14	64	H17
Athole gdns Enf	8	E17
Atholl rd Ilf	55	N1
Atkins dr W Wick	135	X4
Atkins rd E10	33	S19
Atkins rd SW12	89	Z19
Atkinson rd E16	65	Z15
Atlanta boul Rom	39	R17
Atlantic rd SW9	90	G10
Atlas gdns SE7	77	X10
Atlas ms E8	49	V17
Atlas ms N7	48	D18
Atlas rd E13	65	T6
Atlas rd NW10	62	B9
Atlas rd Wem	43	U11
Atley rd E3	64	B3
Atney rd SW15	87	T10
Atterbury rd N4	30	H19
Atterbury st SW1	156	J8
Attewood ave NW10	44	A9
Attewood rd Nthlt	40	B18
Attfield clo N20	15	U7
Attlee rd SE28	68	E20
Attlee ter E17	33	S12
Attneave st WC1	141	S15
Atwater clo SW2	90	F20
Atwood ave Rich	85	P5
Atwood rd W6	74	K10
Aubert pk N5	48	H12
Aubert rd N5	48	J11
Aubrey pl NW8	138	B10
Aubrey rd E17	33	P10
Aubrey rd N8	30	B16
Aubrey rd W8	145	R13
Aubrey wk W8	145	R14
Aubyn hill SE27	109	N11
Aubyn sq SW15	86	G12
Auckland clo SE19	123	U1
Auckland gdns SE19	123	T1
Auckland hill SE27	108	L9
Auckland ri SE19	109	S20
Auckland rd E10	51	S9
Auckland rd SE19	109	U20
Auckland rd SW11	88	K11
Auckland rd Ilf	54	A3
Auckland rd Kings T	117	N9
Auckland st SE11	157	N15
Audley ct E18	34	C13
Audley gdns Ilf	54	K7
Audley pl Sutt	130	A18
Audley rd NW4	26	H17
Audley rd W5	61	N15
Audley rd Enf	7	V8
Audley rd Rich	84	M13
Audrey clo Beck	125	R14
Audrey gdns Wem	42	B6
Audrey rd Ilf	53	Y10
Audrey st E2	143	T7
Audric clo Kings T	117	O1
Augurs la E13	65	X8
Augusta la Twick	101	N5
Augusta st E14	64	D16
Augustine rd W14	152	G3
Augustine rd Har	22	L5
Augustus clo Brent	72	E19
Augustus rd SW19	105	R2
Augustus st NW1	139	Z10
Aulton pl SE11	157	U11
Aultone way Cars	130	L5
Aultone way Sutt	130	B3
Aurelia gdns Croy	122	B15
Aurelia rd Croy	122	B15
Auriel ave Dag	57	O17
Auriga ms N16	49	P14
Auriol clo Wor Pk	128	B7
Auriol dr Grnf	41	O19
Auriol-Park rd Wor Pk	128	B6
Auriol rd W14	152	K6
Austell gdns NW7	13	O11
Austen clo SE28	80	D2
Austen rd Har	40	J5
Austin ave Brom	127	S13
Austin clo SE23	92	K19
Austin clo Twick	84	D13
Austin Friars EC2	150	H4
Austin rd SW11	89	P3
Austin st E2	142	M13
Austral clo SE8	114	L6
Austral st SE11	157	W4
Australia rd W12	144	A10
Austyn gdns Surb	117	S20
Autumn clo Enf	8	L7
Autumn st E3	64	B4
Avalon clo W13	59	Y13
Avalon clo Enf	7	V7
Avalon rd SW6	88	A1
Avalon rd W13	59	Y11
Avarn rd SW17	106	M14
Ave Maria la EC4	149	Y6
Avebury pk Surb	116	H16
Avebury rd SW19	105	V20
Avebury st N1	142	F5
Aveley rd Rom	39	O13
Aveline st SE11	157	R10
Aveling Park rd E17	33	P7
Avenell rd N5	48	H9
Avening rd SW18	87	Z18
Avening ter SW18	87	Y17
Avenons rd E13	65	T12
Avenue the E4	20	J19
Avenue the E11	34	J16
Avenue the N3	27	X6
Avenue the N8	30	E11
Avenue the N10	29	U6
Avenue the N11	16	E15
Avenue the N17	31	P8
Avenue the NW6	136	H6
Avenue the SE7	77	Y18
Avenue the SE10	76	K19
Avenue the SW4	89	P13
Avenue the W4	74	A7
Avenue the W13	60	B19
Avenue the Barn	4	E12
Avenue the Beck	111	P20
Avenue the Bex	97	W17
Avenue the Brom	127	O7
Avenue the Cars	131	O16
Avenue the Croy	133	R5
Avenue the Epsom	128	J16
Avenue the Hmptn	100	F14
Avenue the Har	23	V4
Avenue the Houns	82	J13
Avenue the Islw	71	R15
Avenue the Orp	115	R17
Avenue the (Church end) Pnr	22	E18
Avenue the (Royston Parke rd) Pnr	22	G1
Avenue the Rich	85	O4
Avenue the Rom	39	O12
Avenue the Surb	117	N15
Avenue the Sutt	129	U19
Avenue the Twick	84	B14
Avenue the Wem	42	L3
Avenue the W Wick	125	V18
Avenue the Wor Pk	128	C3
Avenue clo N14	6	H18
Avenue clo NW8	138	M6
Avenue cres W3	73	T5
Avenue Elmers Surb	116	K12
Avenue gdns SE25	123	W5
Avenue gdns SW14	86	A9
Avenue gdns W3	73	T5
Avenue gdns Tedd	101	X17
Avenue ms N10	29	S10
Avenue Park rd SE27	108	J4
Avenue rd E7	52	H13
Avenue rd N6	29	W20
Avenue rd N12	15	R14
Avenue rd N14	16	F2
Avenue rd N15	31	P16
Avenue rd NW3	138	G1
Avenue rd NW8	138	H4
Avenue rd NW10	62	D6
Avenue rd SE20	124	D1
Avenue rd SE25	123	W5
Avenue rd SW16	121	X4
Avenue rd SW20	118	J3
Avenue rd W3	73	S5
Avenue rd Beck	124	F2
Avenue rd Belv	81	X12
Avenue rd Bexh	97	Y9
Avenue rd Brent	72	E13
Avenue rd Erith	81	Z19
Avenue rd Islw	83	U3
Avenue rd Kings T	116	L5
Avenue rd N Mal	118	A8
Avenue rd Pnr	22	B9
Avenue rd Rom (Chadwell Heath)	55	S2
Avenue rd Sthl	70	E4
Avenue rd Tedd	101	X17
Avenue rd Wall	131	U18
Avenue rd Wdf Grn	21	Z18
Avenue south Surb	117	O17
Avenue ter N Mal	117	V7
Averil gro SW16	108	H16
Averill st W6	152	G15
Avery Farm row SW1	155	V16
Avery gdns Ilf	35	V16
Avery Hill rd SE9	114	B3
Avery row W1	147	X8
Aviary clo E16	65	P14
Aviemore clo Beck	124	K13
Aviemore way Beck	124	H12
Avignon rd SE4	92	G8
Avington gro SE20	110	C18
Avington way SE15	63	T17
Avis sq E1	143	U3
Avoca rd SW17	107	O9
Avocet ms SE28	79	T7
Avon clo Sutt	130	D9
Avon clo Wor Pk	128	F2
Avon ct Grnf	58	J11
Avon ms Pnr	22	D3
Avon path S Croy	133	N15
Avon pl SE1	150	C19
Avon rd E17	33	X10
Avon rd SE4	93	O7
Avon rd Grnf	58	H11
Avon way E18	34	F11
Avondale ave N12	15	N17
Avondale ave NW2	44	B9
Avondale ave Barn	5	Z4
Avondale ave Wor Pk	118	C19
Avondale clo E16	65	O14
Avondale cres Enf	9	V12
Avondale cres Ilf	35	Z6
Avondale gdns Houns	82	E14
Avondale Park gdns W11	144	K9
Avondale Park rd W11	144	K9
Avondale ri SE15	91	U7
Avondale rd E16	65	N13
Avondale rd E17	51	N1
Avondale rd N3	28	D5
Avondale rd N13	17	U9
Avondale rd N15	30	K15
Avondale rd SE9	113	R5
Avondale rd SW14	85	Z6
Avondale rd SW19	106	A12
Avondale rd Brom	112	B16
Avondale rd Har	23	W9
Avondale rd S Croy	133	N14
Avondale rd Well	97	U5
Avondale sq SE1	159	S11
Avonley rd SE14	75	S19
Avonmore pl W14	153	N4
Avonmore rd W14	153	N5
Avonmouth st SE1	158	A1
Avonwick rd Houns	82	K4
Avril way E4	20	H16
Avro way Wall	132	A16
Awlfield ave N17	31	P5
Awliscombe rd Well	96	M4
Axe st Bark	67	P3
Axholme ave Edg	25	R4
Axminster cres Well	97	S2
Axminster rd N7	48	B8
Aybrook st W1	147	U2
Aycliffe clo Brom	127	V8
Aycliffe rd W12	74	F2
Aylesbury rd SE17	158	G10
Aylesbury rd Brom	126	E7
Aylesbury st EC1	141	W17
Aylesbury st NW10	43	Y10
Aylesford ave Beck	124	H12
Aylesford st SW1	156	F11
Aylestone ave NW6	136	F1
Aylett rd SE25	124	A10
Aylett rd Islw	83	U5
Ayley cft Enf	8	K17
Aylmer clo Stan	10	M12
Aylmer dr Stan	10	L13
Aylmer rd E11	52	B2
Aylmer rd N2	28	K16
Aylmer rd W12	74	C6
Aylmer rd Dag	55	Y9
Ayloffe rd Dag	56	B17
Aylward rd SE23	110	G5
Aylward rd SW20	119	U4
Aylward st E1	63	P17
Aylwards ri Stan	10	L12
Aylwyn est SE1	158	M1
Aynhoe rd W14	152	H4
Aynscombe la SW14	85	W6
Ayr ct W3	61	P16
Ayr grn Rom	39	O3
Ayr way Rom	39	P3
Ayres clo E13	65	U10
Ayres cres NW10	61	X1
Ayres st SE1	150	C16
Ayrsome rd N16	49	S8
Aysgarth rd SE21	91	R17
Aytoun pl SW9	90	E5
Aytoun rd SW9	90	D5
Azalea clo W7	71	W2
Azenby rd SE15	91	U4
Azof st SE10	77	N12

B

Name	Page	Grid
Baalbec rd N5	48	J15
Babbacombe gdns Ilf	35	R12
Babbacombe rd Brom	112	G20
Babington ri Wem	43	R17
Babington rd NW4	26	K12
Babington rd SW16	107	X12
Babington rd Dag	55	U14
Babington rd Horn	57	Y4
Babmaes st SW1	148	E11
Bacchus wk N1	142	K9
Baches st N1	142	G13
Back Church la E1	151	T5
Back hill EC1	141	T19
Back la N8	29	Z16
Back la NW3	46	E12
Back la Bex	98	D18
Back la Brent	72	G18
Back la Edg	25	V5
Back la Rich	102	E5
Back la Rom	37	X20
Back rd Sid	115	O10
Back st W3	73	U2
Backhouse pl SE17	158	L7
Bacon gro SE1	159	N4
Bacon la NW9	25	T12
Bacon la Edg	25	P3
Bacon st E1	143	P16
Bacon st E2	143	R16
Bacons la N6	47	P4
Baddow clo Dag	69	S3
Baden pl SE1	150	F17
Baden rd N8	29	Z12
Baden rd Ilf	53	Z14
Bader way Rain	57	X18
Badgers clo Enf	7	X12
Badgers clo Har	23	O19
Badgers copse Wor Pk	128	E2
Badgers cft N20	14	F4
Badgers cft SE9	113	X8

Name		
Badgers hole Croy	134	E8
Badgers wk N Mal	118	A2
Badlis rd E17	33	N9
Badminton clo Har	23	S12
Badminton clo Nthlt	40	H19
Badminton rd SW12	89	R17
Badsworth rd SE5	158	B20
Bagley's la SW6	88	A2
Bagleys spring Rom	38	A11
Bagshot cl SE18	95	W1
Bagshot rd Enf	18	F1
Bagshot st SE17	158	L10
Bailey clo E4	20	F13
Bailey pl SE26	110	E15
Bainbridge rd Dag	56	C11
Bainbridge st WC1	148	H4
Baird ave Sthl	58	L19
Baird clo NW9	25	V18
Baird gdns SE19	109	S10
Baird rd Enf	8	M13
Baizdon rd SE3	93	Y5
Baker la Mitch	121	O5
Baker rd NW10	62	A4
Baker rd SE18	95	S1
Baker st NW1	139	R18
Baker st W1	147	S2
Baker st Enf	8	C10
Bakers ave E17	33	R19
Bakers end SW20	119	U3
Bakers hill E5	50	B4
Bakers hill Barn	5	O9
Bakers la N6	29	N17
Baker's ms W1	147	T4
Baker's rents E2	143	N13
Bakers row E15	64	M5
Baker's row EC1	141	T18
Bakewell way N Mal	118	A2
Balaam st E13	65	U10
Balaams la N14	16	K8
Balaclava rd SE1	159	R6
Balaclava rd Surb	116	F15
Balben path E9	63	R2
Balcaskie rd SE9	95	V12
Balchen st SE3	95	N4
Balchier rd SE22	91	Z15
Balcombe st NW1	139	N17
Balcorne st E9	63	R1
Balder ri SE12	112	J5
Balderton st W1	147	U7
Baldock st E3	64	D6
Baldry gdns SW16	108	B16
Baldwin cres SE5	90	L1
Baldwin st EC1	142	E14
Baldwin ter N1	142	A8
Baldwin's gdns EC1	149	S1
Baldwyn gdns W3	61	X19
Balfe st N1	140	M10
Balfern gro W4	74	C14
Balfern st SW11	88	K14
Balfour ave W7	71	V2
Balfour gro N20	15	Z15
Balfour ms W1	147	U11
Balfour pl SW15	86	J10
Balfour pl W1	147	U11
Balfour rd N5	48	M12
Balfour rd SE25	123	X11
Balfour rd SW19	106	A19
Balfour rd W3	61	W15
Balfour rd W13	72	A6
Balfour rd Brom	127	O12
Balfour rd Cars	130	M17
Balfour rd Har	23	R16
Balfour rd Houns	82	J7
Balfour rd Ilf	53	Z7
Balfour rd Sthl	70	A8
Balfour st SE17	158	E4
Balgonie rd E4	20	J6
Balgores cres Rom	39	Y10
Balgores la Rom	39	X10
Balgores sq Rom	39	Z12
Balgowan clo N Mal	118	B10
Balgowan rd Beck	124	K5
Balgowan st SE18	79	X11
Balham gro SW12	89	R18
Balham High rd SW12	89	S20
Balham High rd SW17	107	O6
Balham hill SW12	89	T17
Balham New rd SW12	89	S19
Balham Park rd SW12	106	M1
Balham rd N9	18	L7
Balham Station rd SW12	107	R2
Ballamore rd Brom	112	E6
Ballance rd E9	50	G17
Ballantine st SW18	88	C11
Ballard clo Kings T	103	X19
Ballards clo Dag	69	V3
Ballards Farm rd S Croy	133	Z15
Ballards la N3	27	Y4
Ballards la N12	15	O20
Ballards ms Edg	12	B19
Ballards ri S Croy	133	X14
Ballards rd NW2	44	F7
Ballards rd Dag	69	U5
Ballards way Croy	134	D13
Ballards way S Croy	133	Y15
Ballast quay SE10	76	L13
Ballater rd SW2	90	B10
Ballater rd S Croy	133	V11
Ballina st SE23	92	G17
Ballingdon rd SW11	89	O15
Balliol ave E4	20	L14
Balliol rd N17	31	R5
Balliol rd W10	144	E4
Balliol rd Well	97	R4
Balloch rd SE6	111	X3
Ballogie ave NW10	44	B12
Balls Pond rd N1	49	P17
Balmain clo W5	72	H2
Balmer rd E3	63	Z7
Balmes rd N1	142	G3
Balmoral ave Beck	124	K9
Balmoral clo SW15	87	O15
Balmoral dr Sthl	58	E11
Balmoral gdns W13	71	Y7
Balmoral gdns Bex	98	D19
Balmoral gdns Ilf	54	K5
Balmoral gro N7	48	C18
Balmoral ms W12	74	D7
Balmoral rd E7	52	L14
Balmoral rd E10	51	T8
Balmoral rd NW2	44	K17
Balmoral rd Har	40	G11
Balmoral rd Kings T	116	M8
Balmoral rd Rom	39	Z14
Balmoral rd Wor Pk	128	H5
Balmore cres Barn	6	C16
Balmore st N19	47	T7
Balmuir gdns SW15	87	N11
Balnacraig ave NW10	44	B11
Balniel gate SW1	156	G10
Baltic ct SE16	75	U5
Baltic st EC1	142	A18
Baltimore pl Well	96	K5
Balvernie gro SW18	87	W20
Bamborough gdns W12	74	A6
Bamford ave Wem	60	M4
Bamford rd Bark	54	C18
Bamford rd Brom	111	W11
Bampfylde clo Wall	131	V7
Bampton rd SE23	110	E6
Banavie gdns Beck	111	T20
Banbury ct WC2	148	K8
Banbury ct Sutt	129	Z17
Banbury Enterprise cen Croy	132	H2
Banbury rd E9	63	T1
Banbury rd E17	32	H3
Banbury st SW11	88	K4
Banchory rd SE3	77	V18
Bancroft ave N2	28	J15
Bancroft ave Buck H	21	T8
Bancroft gdns Har	22	M5
Bancroft rd E1	63	S10
Bancroft rd Har	23	N6
Bandon ri Wall	131	X13
Bangalore st SW15	87	N8
Bangor clo Nthlt	40	K15
Banim st W6	74	K10
Banister rd W10	136	H12
Bank the N6	47	S3
Bank ave Mitch	120	H4
Bank end SE1	150	D12
Bank la SW15	86	B13
Bank la Kings T	102	J18
Bankfoot rd Brom	112	A10
Bankhurst rd SE6	92	M18
Banks la Bexh	98	C10
Banksia rd N18	19	S16
Banksian wk Islw	83	T3
Bankside SE1	150	B11
Bankside Enf	7	X6
Bankside S Croy	133	T15
Bankside clo Cars	130	K13
Bankton rd SW2	90	G11
Bankwell rd SE13	94	A11
Banner st EC1	142	B17
Banning st SE10	76	L14
Bannister clo Grnf	41	P14
Bannockburn rd SE18	79	X12
Banstead gdns N9	18	D10
Banstead rd Cars	130	H19
Banstead Road south Sutt	130	G20
Banstead st SE15	92	B7
Banstead way Wall	132	A10
Banstock rd Edg	12	G20
Banton clo Enf	9	N8
Bantry st SE5	158	G19
Banwell rd Bex	97	W16
Banyard rd SE16	159	X3
Baptist gdns NW5	47	N17
Barandon wk W11	144	H9
Barb ms W6	152	E3
Barbauld rd N16	49	R10
Barber clo N21	17	U3
Barber's all E13	65	V7
Barbers rd E15	64	E5
Barbican rd Grnf	58	L16
Barbon clo WC1	141	N20
Barbot clo N9	18	J10
Barchard st SW18	88	A13
Barchester clo W7	71	W3
Barchester rd Har	23	R6
Barchester st E14	64	D14
Barclay clo SW6	153	U20
Barclay Oval Wdf Grn	21	T13
Barclay rd E11	52	B4
Barclay rd E13	65	Y12
Barclay rd E17	33	T16
Barclay rd N18	18	B18
Barclay rd SW6	153	U18
Barclay rd Croy	133	O5
Barcombe ave SW2	108	B4
Bard rd W10	144	F9
Barden st SE18	79	V19
Bardfield ave Rom	37	W11
Bardney rd Mord	120	B8
Bardolph ave Croy	134	K20
Bardolph rd N7	47	Z11
Bardsey pl E1	63	P13
Bardsley clo Croy	133	U5
Bardsley la SE10	76	F17
Barfett st W10	137	N15
Barfield ave N20	15	Y7
Barfield rd E11	52	C3
Barfield rd Brom	127	W7
Barford clo NW4	26	H5
Barford st N1	141	V6
Barforth rd SE15	92	A8
Barfreston way SE20	110	A20
Bargate clo SE18	79	Z13
Bargate clo N Mal	118	G16
Barge House rd E16	78	M4
Barge wk Kings T	102	H19
Bargery rd SE6	111	S2
Bargrove clo SE20	109	X18
Barham clo Brom	127	S20
Barham clo Chis	113	Z12
Barham clo Rom	38	G8
Barham clo Wem	42	C17
Barham rd SW20	104	F19
Barham rd Chis	113	Y13
Barham rd S Croy	132	M10
Baring clo SE12	112	F4
Baring rd SE12	94	E19
Baring rd Barn	5	U12
Baring rd Croy	123	Y19
Baring st N1	142	E15
Bark pl W2	145	Y9
Barker dr NW1	140	D2
Barker st SW10	154	B14
Barkham rd N17	31	P1
Barking Industrial pk Bark	67	Z4
Barking rd E6	66	C5
Barking rd E13	65	S13
Barking rd E16	65	S13
Barkis way SE16	159	X10
Barkston gdns SW5	153	X7
Barkwood clo Rom	38	L15
Barlborough st SE14	75	S19
Barlby gdns W10	136	G18
Barlby rd W10	144	D1
Barley la Ilf	55	O2
Barley Mow pas W4	73	Y13
Barleycorn way E14	63	Y20
Barleyfields clo Rom	37	S19
Barlow pl W1	147	Z10
Barlow rd NW6	45	W17
Barlow rd W3	73	T2
Barlow rd Hmptn	100	H17
Barlow st SE17	158	G6
Barmeston rd SE6	111	R3
Barmor clo Har	22	L6
Barmouth ave Grnf	59	W7
Barmouth rd SW18	88	D16
Barmouth rd Croy	134	F3
Barn cres Stan	11	R19
Barn hill Wem	43	P4
Barn ms Har	40	G9
Barn ri Wem	43	R4
Barn way Wem	43	R5
Barnabas rd E9	50	G16
Barnaby clo Har	40	M8
Barnard clo SE18	78	K9
Barnard clo Chis	114	F20
Barnard gdns N Mal	118	H10
Barnard hill N10	29	R6
Barnard ms SW11	88	K10
Barnard rd SW11	88	K10
Barnard rd Enf	9	O8
Barnard rd Mitch	121	O5
Barnardo dr Ilf	36	L16
Barnardo st E1	63	S18
Barnard's Inn EC1	149	U3
Barnards pl S Croy	132	J20
Barnby st E15	64	M2
Barnby st NW1	140	C11
Barnehurst ave Bexh	98	M4
Barnehurst ave Erith	98	K1
Barnehurst clo Erith	98	K2
Barnehurst rd Bexh	98	K7
Barnes ave SW13	74	G18
Barnes ave Sthl	70	D11
Barnes clo E12	53	P13
Barnes Craig rd Dart	99	W10
Barnes end N Mal	118	H12
Barnes High st SW13	86	C4
Barnes rd N18	19	P12
Barnes rd Ilf	54	D14
Barnes st E14	63	V17
Barnet Gate la Barn	3	S1
Barnet gro E2	143	S11
Barnet hill Barn	4	K15
Barnet la N20	14	H1
Barnet la Barn	4	K16
Barnet Trading est Barn	4	H12
Barnet way NW7	12	M12
Barnett clo Erith	99	T4
Barnett st E1	151	W5
Barney clo SE7	77	Y12
Barnfield N Mal	118	A15
Barnfield ave Croy	134	D3
Barnfield ave Kings T	102	H11
Barnfield ave Mitch	121	T8
Barnfield gdns Kings T	102	K11
Barnfield pl E14	76	C11
Barnfield rd SE18	79	N17
Barnfield rd W5	60	D11
Barnfield rd Belv	81	P15
Barnfield rd Edg	25	V5
Barnfield rd S Croy	133	S19
Barnfield Wood clo Beck	125	X14
Barnfield Wood rd Beck	125	W14
Barnham rd Grnf	58	M7
Barnham st SE1	150	L16
Barnhill ave Brom	126	C13

Name	Page	Grid
Barnhill rd Wem	43	W10
Barningham way NW9	25	X17
Barnlea clo Felt	100	C5
Barnmead gdns Dag	56	C15
Barnmead rd Beck	110	G20
Barnmead rd Dag	56	B16
Barnsbury clo N Mal	117	X10
Barnsbury pk N1	48	F20
Barnsbury rd N1	141	S7
Barnsbury sq N1	141	S1
Barnsbury st N1	141	T2
Barnsbury ter N1	141	R1
Barnscroft SW20	118	K6
Barnsdale ave E14	76	C10
Barnsdale rd W9	137	R16
Barnsley st E1	143	Y17
Barnwell rd SW2	90	G13
Barnwood clo W9	137	Y19
Baron gdns Ilf	36	D9
Baron gro Mitch	120	K9
Baron rd Dag	55	W3
Baron st N1	141	T9
Baroness rd E2	143	O12
Baronet gro N17	31	X4
Baronet rd N17	31	X4
Barons the Twick	84	C16
Barons Court rd W14	152	L10
Barons gate Barn	5	W18
Barons Keep W14	152	L8
Barons mead Har	23	U12
Barons pl SE1	149	V18
Barons wk Croy	124	K14
Baronsfield rd Twick	84	C17
Baronsmead rd SW13	86	G1
Baronsmede W5	72	L6
Baronsmere rd N2	28	K12
Barrack rd Houns	82	A9
Barratt ave N22	30	C6
Barratt way Har	23	R9
Barrenger rd N10	28	M5
Barrett clo Rom	39	Y1
Barrett rd E17	33	U13
Barrett st W1	147	V6
Barretts Green rd NW10	61	X7
Barretts gro N16	49	T14
Barrhill rd SW2	108	A3
Barriedale SE14	92	K5
Barrier app SE7	78	A8
Barringer sq SW17	107	P9
Barrington clo NW5	47	O14
Barrington clo Ilf	35	V5
Barrington rd E12	53	W16
Barrington rd N8	29	X14
Barrington rd SW9	90	H8
Barrington rd Bexh	97	W6
Barrington rd Sutt	129	R8
Barrington vill SE18	95	X2
Barrow ave Cars	130	L18
Barrow clo N21	17	W9
Barrow Hedges clo Cars	130	K16
Barrow Hedges way Cars	130	J16
Barrow hill Wor Pk	128	A2
Barrow Hill clo WorPk	128	A3
Barrow Hill rd NW8	138	K10
Barrow Point ave Pnr	22	A7
Barrow Point la Pnr	22	A6
Barrow rd SW16	107	X16
Barrow rd Croy	132	H13
Barrow wk Brent	72	F15
Barrowdene clo Pnr	22	B6
Barrowell grn N21	17	W8
Barrowfield clo N9	19	O10
Barrowgate rd W4	73	X15
Barrs rd NW10	43	X19
Barry ave N15	31	V19
Barry ave Bexh	80	L19
Barry rd E6	66	E16
Barry rd NW10	43	X20
Barry rd SE22	91	W17
Barset rd SE15	92	C7
Barson clo SE20	110	D17
Barston rd SE27	108	M6
Barstow cres SW2	108	D2
Barter st WC1	148	L3
Barth rd SE18	79	W12
Bartholomew clo EC1	150	A2
Bartholomew clo SW18	88	D11
Bartholomew la EC2	150	F5
Bartholomew pl EC1	150	A1
Bartholomew rd NW5	47	U18
Bartholomew sq EC1	142	C15
Bartholomew st SE1	158	F4
Bartholomew vill NW5	47	U18
Bartle ave E6	66	E5
Bartle rd W11	144	K6
Bartlett clo E14	64	C16
Bartlett ct EC4	149	V4
Bartlett st S Croy	133	N11
Bartlow gdns Rom	38	M3
Barton ave Rom	56	J5
Barton clo E9	50	D15
Barton clo SE15	92	B6
Barton clo Bexh	97	Z12
Barton grn N Mal	117	Z4
Barton meadows Ilf	36	A12
Barton rd W14	152	L10
Barton rd Horn	57	W5
Barton rd Sid	115	Z15
Barton st SW1	156	J1
Bartram rd SE4	92	J14
Bartrams la Barn	5	P3
Barwick rd E7	52	H12
Barwood ave W Wick	125	S20
Basden gro Felt	100	G5
Basedale rd Dag	55	R19
Baseing clo E6	66	L18
Bashley rd NW10	61	Z10
Basil ave E6	66	E8
Basil gdns Croy	124	F20
Basil st SW3	155	O1
Basildon ave Ilf	35	W5
Basildon clo Sutt	130	B20
Basildon rd SE2	80	B13
Basildon rd Bexh	97	Y6
Basing ct SE15	91	V2
Basing dr Bex	98	B16
Basing hill NW11	45	V5
Basing hill Wem	43	O5
Basing House yd E2	142	L12
Basing pl E2	142	L12
Basing st W11	145	O4
Basing way N3	27	Z10
Basingdon way SE5	91	O10
Basinghall ave EC2	150	E3
Basinghall gdns Sutt	130	B19
Basinghall st EC2	150	E3
Basire st N1	142	C4
Baskerville rd SW18	88	J18
Basket gdns SE9	95	R12
Baslow clo Har	23	R4
Baslow wk E5	50	G11
Basnett rd SW11	89	R8
Bassano st SE22	91	U13
Bassant rd SE18	79	X16
Bassein Park rd W12	74	E7
Bassett gdns Islw	71	N20
Bassett rd W10	144	G4
Bassett st NW5	47	P16
Bassett way Grnf	58	K16
Bassingham rd SW18	88	D18
Bassingham rd Wem	42	G18
Basswood clo SE15	92	B8
Bastable ave Bark	67	W7
Bastion rd SE2	80	A14
Bastwick st EC1	142	A16
Basuto rd SW6	87	Y2
Batavia rd SE14	75	W20
Batchelor st N1	141	T7
Bateman rd E4	20	B18
Bateman st W1	148	F7
Bateman's row EC2	142	L15
Bates cres SW16	107	V17
Bates cres Croy	132	G13
Bath clo SE15	159	Z20
Bath ct EC1	141	T17
Bath House rd Croy	132	A1
Bath pl Barn	8	G11
Bath rd E7	53	O18
Bath rd N9	19	O7
Bath rd W4	74	C10
Bath rd Dart	99	Z18
Bath rd Houns	82	C6
Bath rd Mitch	120	F6
Bath rd Rom	37	Z18
Bath st EC1	142	D13
Bath ter SE1	158	B2
Bathgate rd SW19	105	P8
Baths rd Brom	127	P8
Bathurst gdns NW10	136	A10
Bathurst ms W2	146	H7
Bathurst st W2	146	G8
Batley pl N16	49	U10
Batley rd N16	49	U10
Batley rd Enf	8	A5
Batman clo W12	144	A11
Batoum gdns W6	152	D1
Batson st W12	74	H5
Batsworth rd Mitch	120	G5
Batten clo E6	66	H17
Batten st SW11	88	K7
Battersby rd SE6	111	Y6
Battersea bri SW3	154	H16
Battersea bri SW11	154	J17
Battersea Bridge rd SW11	154	K18
Battersea Church rd SW11	154	H20
Battersea High st SW11	88	G2
Battersea Park rd SW8	156	A18
Battersea Park rd SW11	89	P2
Battersea ri SW11	88	L11
Battersea rd SE28	79	U5
Battishill st N1	141	W2
Battle Bridge la SE1	150	J14
Battle Bridge rd NW1	140	J9
Battle rd Belv	81	Y10
Battle rd Erith	81	Z11
Battledean rd N5	48	H15
Batty st E1	151	U5
Baudwin rd SE6	111	Z4
Baugh rd Sid	115	V13
Baulk the SW18	87	X19
Bavant rd SW16	122	B3
Bavaria rd N19	48	A6
Bavent rd SE5	91	N5
Bawdale rd SE22	91	V13
Bawdsey ave Ilf	36	L13
Bawtree rd SE14	75	W18
Bawtry rd N20	15	Y10
Baxendale N20	15	S8
Baxendale st E2	143	S11
Baxter rd E16	65	Z17
Baxter rd N1	49	P18
Baxter rd N18	18	M13
Baxter rd NW10	62	A12
Baxter rd Ilf	53	Z14
Bay ct W5	72	L7
Bay Tree clo Brom	126	M1
Bayes clo SE26	110	C12
Bayfield rd SE9	95	N11
Bayford rd NW10	136	F13
Bayford st E8	143	Y2
Bayham pl NW1	140	C6
Bayham rd W4	73	Y7
Bayham rd W13	72	A1
Bayham rd Mord	120	C9
Bayham st NW1	140	A4
Bayley st WC1	148	F2
Bayley wk SE2	80	M15
Baylis rd SE1	149	T20
Bayliss ave SE28	68	J19
Bayne clo E6	66	G17
Baynes clo Enf	8	K6
Baynes st NW1	140	C1
Baynham clo Bex	98	C16
Bayonne rd W6	152	K16
Bayston rd N16	49	V9
Bayswater rd W2	146	D10
Baythorne st E3	63	Z13
Baytree clo Sid	114	L2
Baytree rd SW2	90	D12
Bazalgette clo N Mal	117	X13
Bazalgette gdns N Mal	117	X13
Bazely st E14	64	G19
Bazile rd N21	7	U19
Beach gro Felt	100	G5
Beacham clo SE7	78	B15
Beachborough rd Brom	111	V9
Beachcroft rd E11	52	A8
Beachcroft way N19	47	Z4
Beachy rd E3	64	B1
Beacon gro Cars	131	O9
Beacon hill N7	48	A14
Beacon rd SE13	93	X15
Beacons clo E6	66	E15
Beaconsfield clo N11	16	C15
Beaconsfield clo SE3	77	S17
Beaconsfield clo W4	73	V14
Beaconsfield rd E10	51	V8
Beaconsfield rd E16	65	O12
Beaconsfield rd E17	32	M19
Beaconsfield rd N9	18	L12
Beaconsfield rd N11	16	A11
Beaconsfield rd N15	31	T13
Beaconsfield rd NW10	44	E17
Beaconsfield rd SE3	77	R19
Beaconsfield rd SE9	113	R5
Beaconsfield rd SE17	158	H12
Beaconsfield rd W4	73	X9
Beaconsfield rd W5	72	F5
Beaconsfield rd Brom	127	O7
Beaconsfield rd Croy	123	O14
Beaconsfield rd Enf	9	V1
Beaconsfield rd N Mal	117	Y5
Beaconsfield rd Sthl	70	A4
Beaconsfield rd Surb	117	N18
Beaconsfield rd Twick	84	B17
Beaconsfield ter Rom	37	X19
Beaconsfield Terrace rd W14	152	L3
Beacontree ave E17	33	X5
Beacontree rd E11	52	D2
Beadlow clo Cars	120	G15
Beadman st SE27	108	K9
Beadnell rd SE23	110	E1
Beadon rd W6	152	C6
Beadon rd Brom	126	F10
Beaford gro SW20	119	U7
Beak st W1	148	C8
Beal clo Well	97	O2
Beal rd Ilf	53	X7
Beale clo N13	17	W17
Beale pl E3	63	Y5
Beale rd E3	63	Y4
Beam ave Dag	69	V4
Beam way Dag	57	N20
Beaminster gdns Ilf	35	Y8
Beamish dr (Bushey) Wat	10	A6
Beamish rd N9	18	L6
Bean rd Bexh	97	X11
Beanacre clo E9	50	L17
Beanshaw SE9	113	X10
Bear all EC4	149	W4
Bear gdns SE1	150	B12
Bear la SE1	149	X13
Bear rd Felt	100	A11
Bear st WC2	148	H9
Beard rd Kings T	102	M13
Beardell st SE19	109	T15
Beardow gro N14	6	G20
Beardsfield E13	65	S4
Bearfield rd Kings T	102	K19
Bearstead ri SE4	92	K14
Beatrice ave SW16	122	C5
Beatrice ave Wem	42	L16
Beatrice clo E13	65	S11
Beatrice ct Wem	43	N11
Beatrice rd E17	33	O15
Beatrice rd N4	48	G1
Beatrice rd N9	19	P1
Beatrice rd SE1	159	V8
Beatrice rd Sthl	70	D3
Beatson wk SE16	75	U1
Beatty rd N16	49	S12
Beatty rd Stan	11	S18
Beatty st NW1	140	A8
Beattyville gdns Ilf	35	X11
Beauchamp pl SW3	154	M2

Name	Page	Grid
Beauchamp rd E7	52	H19
Beauchamp rd SE19	123	O1
Beauchamp rd SW11	88	K10
Beauchamp rd Sutt	129	Y10
Beauchamp rd Twick	83	Z19
Beauclerc rd W6	152	A1
Beaufort ave Har	24	A11
Beaufort clo E4	20	E18
Beaufort clo SW15	86	L20
Beaufort clo W5	61	N14
Beaufort clo Rom	38	J31
Beaufort ct Rich	102	D11
Beaufort dr NW11	27	Y12
Beaufort gdns NW4	26	M18
Beaufort gdns SW3	155	N1
Beaufort gdns SW16	108	D18
Beaufort gdns Hours	82	C1
Beaufort gdns Ilf	53	W4
Beaufort rd W5	61	N14
Beaufort rd Kings T	116	K8
Beaufort rd Rich	102	D10
Beaufort rd Twick	84	E18
Beaufort st SW3	154	E12
Beaufort way Epsom	128	H18
Beaufoy rd N17	31	T2
Beaufoy wk SE11	157	P7
Beaulieu ave SE26	110	A10
Beaulieu clo NW9	26	B12
Beaulieu clo SE5	91	P7
Beaulieu clo Hours	82	D13
Beaulieu clo Mitch	121	O1
Beaulieu clo Twick	84	G17
Beaulieu gdns N21	17	Y3
Beauly way Rom	39	P5
Beaumanor gdns SE9	113	X9
Beaumaris dr Wdf Grn	35	O1
Beaumont ave W14	153	O9
Beaumont ave Har	22	L19
Beaumont ave Rich	84	M9
Beaumont ave Wem	42	D14
Beaumont clo Kings T	103	R18
Beaumont cres W14	153	O10
Beaumont cres Rain	57	X18
Beaumont gdns NW3	45	Y8
Beaumont gro E1	63	T12
Beaumont ms W1	147	V1
Beaumont pl W1	140	C17
Beaumont pl Barn	4	H4
Beaumont pl Islw	83	V13
Beaumont ri N19	47	Z2
Beaumont rd E10	51	S1
Beaumont rd E13	65	X9
Beaumont rd SE19	108	L16
Beaumont rd SW19	87	S18
Beaumont rd W4	73	X8
Beaumont sq E1	63	T13
Beaumont st W1	139	V19
Beauval rd SE22	91	U15
Beaver clo SE20	109	Y17
Beaverbank rd SE9	114	D2
Beavers la Hours	82	A9
Beaverwood rd Chis	114	J14
Beavor la W6	74	G12
Bebbington rd SE18	79	V12
Bec clo Ruis	40	A9
Beccles dr Bark	54	J16
Beccles st E14	63	Z19
Beck clo SE13	93	S3
Beck la Beck	124	E6
Beck rd E8	143	X4
Beckenham gdns N9	18	D11
Beckenham gro Brom	125	X4
Beckenham Hill rd SE6	111	U12
Beckenham Hill rd Beck	111	R14
Beckenham la Brom	126	B3
Beckenham Place pk Beck	111	R18
Beckenham rd Beck	124	K2
Beckenham rd W Wick	125	T18
Becket ave E6	66	K9
Becket clo SE25	123	Y14
Becket rd N18	19	P14
Becket st SE1	150	E20
Beckett clo NW10	43	Z19
Beckett clo SW16	107	X4
Beckett clo Belv	81	N9
Beckett wk Beck	110	H16
Becketts pl Kings T	116	G2
Beckford rd Croy	123	V14
Becklow rd W12	74	E5
Becks rd Sid	115	O7
Beckton Retail pk E6	66	J14
Beckton rd E16	65	R14
Beckway rd SW16	121	X4
Beckway st SE17	158	H6
Beckwith rd SE24	91	O14
Beclands rd SW17	107	P15
Becmead ave SW16	107	Y9
Becmead ave Har	24	B16
Becondale rd SE19	109	S14
Becontree ave Dag	55	R12
Bective pl SW15	87	U11
Bective rd E7	52	G11
Bective rd SW15	87	U11
Becton pl Erith	98	J1
Bedale rd Enf	7	Z4
Bedale st SE1	150	F13
Beddington Farm rd Croy	122	A17
Beddington gdns Cars	131	P15
Beddington gdns Wall	131	S14
Beddington gro Wall	131	Y12
Beddington la Croy	121	U12
Beddington rd Ilf	36	K20
Beddington Trading Park west Croy	132	A1
Bede rd Rom	37	U18
Bedens rd Sid	115	Y13
Bedfont clo Mitch	121	O4
Bedford ave Barn	4	H15
Bedford ave WC1	148	G3
Bedford clo N10	29	P3
Bedford ct WC2	148	K9
Bedford gdns W8	145	U15
Bedford hill SW12	107	S1
Bedford pk Croy	133	N1
Bedford pl WC1	140	K20
Bedford pl Croy	133	O1
Bedford rd E6	66	J3
Bedford rd E17	33	O8
Bedford rd E18	34	F8
Bedford rd N2	28	J10
Bedford rd N8	29	Y17
Bedford rd N9	18	M1
Bedford rd N15	31	R12
Bedford rd N22	30	A5
Bedford rd NW7	13	N9
Bedford rd SW4	89	Z9
Bedford rd W4	73	Z9
Bedford rd W13	72	A1
Bedford rd Har	23	N17
Bedford rd Ilf	54	A10
Bedford rd Sid	114	H7
Bedford rd Twick	101	R6
Bedford rd Wor Pk	129	N4
Bedford row WC1	149	P1
Bedford sq WC1	148	G2
Bedford way WC1	140	H18
Bedfordbury WC2	148	K9
Bedgebury gdns SW19	105	T3
Bedgebury rd SE9	95	N11
Bedivere rd Brom	112	F6
Bedlow way Croy	132	C9
Bedonwell rd SE2	80	M15
Bedonwell rd Bexh	81	R17
Bedser dr Grnf	41	P14
Bedwardine rd SE19	109	S17
Bedwell rd N17	31	R4
Bedwell rd Belv	81	R14
Bedwin way SE16	159	V10
Beeby rd E16	65	U14
Beech ave N20	15	X6
Beech ave W3	74	B3
Beech ave Brent	72	E18
Beech ave Buck H	21	V8
Beech ave Sid	97	N18
Beech clo N9	8	M19
Beech clo SW15	86	G17
Beech clo SW19	104	L15
Beech clo Cars	130	L3
Beech clo Horn	57	Y10
Beech copse Brom	127	T2
Beech copse S Croy	133	S10
Beech dr N2	28	M8
Beech gdns W5	72	J7
Beech gdns Dag	56	J20
Beech gro Mitch	121	X11
Beech gro N Mal	117	Y6
Beech Hall cres E4	33	W1
Beech Hall rd E4	33	V2
Beech hill Barn	5	T4
Beech Hill ave Barn	5	S4
Beech la Buck H	21	V8
Beech Lawns N12	15	U15
Beech rd N11	17	N19
Beech rd SW16	122	B5
Beech row Rich	102	J11
Beech st EC2	142	B20
Beech Tree glade E4	21	P4
Beech wk NW7	13	N17
Beech wk Dart	99	W10
Beech way NW10	43	X20
Beech way Twick	100	H6
Beechcroft Chis	113	X17
Beechcroft ave NW11	45	V1
Beechcroft ave Bexh	99	N4
Beechcroft ave Har	40	G2
Beechcroft ave N Mal	117	O2
Beechcroft ave Sthl	70	D2
Beechcroft clo Houns	70	D3
Beechcroft gdns Wem	42	L10
Beechcroft rd E18	34	J8
Beechcroft rd SW14	85	W9
Beechcroft rd SW17	106	J3
Beechdale N21	17	R7
Beechdale rd SW2	90	D16
Beechen gro Pnr	22	D10
Beeches ave Cars	130	K17
Beeches clo SE20	124	B2
Beeches rd SW17	106	K7
Beeches rd Sutt	129	T1
Beeches wk Cars	130	H19
Beechfield gdns Rom	38	L20
Beechfield rd N4	31	N18
Beechfield rd SE6	111	N2
Beechfield rd Brom	126	M4
Beechhill rd SE9	95	W12
Beechmont clo Brom	112	A14
Beechmore gdns Sutt	129	R3
Beechmore rd SW11	89	N2
Beechmount ave W7	59	R15
Beecholme clo Mitch	107	S20
Beechtree clo Stan	11	S16
Beechtree pl Sutt	130	A11
Beechvale clo N12	15	X15
Beechway Bex	97	W16
Beechwood ave N3	27	W11
Beechwood ave Grnf	58	J9
Beechwood ave Har	40	L9
Beechwood ave Rich	85	R2
Beechwood ave Th Hth	122	H8
Beechwood clo NW7	13	N16
Beechwood clo Surb	116	F18
Beechwood cres Bexh	97	Y7
Beechwood dr Wdf Grn	21	P16
Beechwood gdns Har	40	L9
Beechwood gdns Ilf	35	V15
Beechwood gro Surb	116	F18
Beechwood pk E18	34	E11
Beechwood ri Chis	114	A11
Beechwood rd E8	49	U18
Beechwood rd N8	29	Y11
Beechwood rd S Croy	133	S19
Beechworth clo NW3	45	Z8
Beecroft rd SE4	92	K12
Beehive la Ilf	35	U15
Beehive pl SW9	90	E9
Beeleigh rd Mord	120	B8
Beeston pl SW1	155	Y2
Beeston rd Barn	5	U18
Beethoven rd Borwd	11	T1
Beethoven st W10	136	L11
Beeton clo Pnr	22	G2
Begbie rd SE3	94	K1
Beggars Roost la Sutt	129	Y14
Beira st SW12	89	T18
Belcroft clo Brom	112	D19
Belfairs dr Rom	55	V1
Belfast rd N16	49	U5
Belfast rd SE25	123	Z10
Belfield rd Epsom	128	A17
Belfont wk N7	48	B12
Belford gro SE18	78	J11
Belfort rd SE15	92	D4
Belgrade rd N16	49	S13
Belgrave clo N14	6	J16
Belgrave clo W3	73	U4
Belgrave gdns N14	6	J15
Belgrave gdns NW8	138	A7
Belgrave Mews north SW1	147	T20
Belgrave Mews south SW1	155	V1
Belgrave Mews west SW1	155	T1
Belgrave pl SW1	155	V2
Belgrave rd E10	51	V3
Belgrave rd E11	52	F6
Belgrave rd E13	65	X10
Belgrave rd E17	33	O16
Belgrave rd SE25	123	W8
Belgrave rd SW1	156	B7
Belgrave rd SW13	74	E20
Belgrave rd Houns	82	D8
Belgrave rd Ilf	53	T4
Belgrave rd Mitch	120	F5
Belgrave sq SW1	147	U19
Belgrave st E1	63	U15
Belgrave ter Wdf Grn	21	S11
Belgrave wk Mitch	120	G6
Belgrave yd SW1	155	X2
Belgravia gdns Brom	111	Z16
Belgravia ms Kings T	116	H10
Belgrove st WC1	140	L12
Belinda rd SW9	90	J8
Belitha vill N1	48	E20
Bell ave Rom	39	Y3
Bell dr SW18	87	S18
Bell Farm ave Dag	56	K9
Bell grn SE26	110	K10
Bell Green la SE26	110	K10
Bell House rd Rom	56	K3
Bell Inn yd EC3	150	H7
Bell la E1	151	N2
Bell la E16	77	S2
Bell la NW4	27	N14
Bell la Enf	9	U3
Bell la Twick	101	Z1
Bell meadow SE19	109	S11
Bell rd Enf	8	C7
Bell rd Houns	82	J9
Bell st NW1	146	J1
Bell Water gate SE18	78	K8
Bell yd WC2	149	S6
Bellamy clo W14	153	S11
Bellamy dr Stan	24	B4
Bellamy rd E4	20	E19
Bellamy rd Enf	8	B7
Bellamy st SW12	89	R18
Bellasis ave SW2	107	Z3
Belle Staines Pleasaunce E4	20	B7
Belle Vue est NW4	27	O13
Belle Vue la (Bushey) Wat	10	D5
Belle Vue rd E17	33	W6
Bellefields rd SW9	90	D8
Bellegrove clo Well	96	K5
Bellegrove rd Well	96	G5
Bellenden rd SE15	91	W4
Belleville rd SW11	88	K14
Bellevue pk Th Hth	122	L8
Bellevue rd N11	16	B14
Bellevue rd SW13	86	G4
Bellevue rd SW17	106	K1
Bellevue rd W13	60	B12
Bellevue rd Bexh	98	B12
Bellevue rd Kings T	116	L8
Bellew st SW17	106	E8
Bellfield Croy	134	K18
Bellfield ave Har	10	B18

Name	Page	Grid
Bellflower clo E6	66	D13
Bellingham grn SE6	111	P8
Bellingham rd SE6	111	T6
Bellot st SE10	77	N13
Bellring clo Belv	81	T16
Bells hill Barn	4	B16
Belltrees gro SE28	108	E12
Bellwood rd SE15	92	F11
Belmarsh rd SE28	79	V6
Belmerton st N1	141	N3
Belmont ave N9	18	L5
Belmont ave N13	17	O15
Belmont ave N17	30	L10
Belmont ave Barn	5	Y17
Belmont ave N Mal	118	H11
Belmont ave Sthl	70	B8
Belmont ave Well	96	G6
Belmont ave Wem	60	M2
Belmont circle Har	24	A6
Belmont clo E4	20	L17
Belmont clo N20	15	N5
Belmont clo SW4	89	W8
Belmont clo Barn	6	A14
Belmont clo Wdf Grn	21	U13
Belmont gro SE13	93	X7
Belmont hill SE13	93	V8
Belmont la SW4	114	A13
Belmont la Stan	24	D2
Belmont pk SE13	93	X10
Belmont Park clo SE13	93	Z10
Belmont Park rd E10	33	S19
Belmont ri Sutt	129	T15
Belmont rd N15	30	L12
Belmont rd N17	30	M11
Belmont rd SE25	124	A13
Belmont rd SW4	89	W8
Belmont rd W4	73	Y12
Belmont rd Beck	124	K4
Belmont rd Chis	114	A13
Belmont rd Erith	81	S20
Belmont rd Har	23	W9
Belmont rd Ilf	54	C8
Belmont rd Twick	101	P3
Belmont rd Wall	131	T12
Belmont st NW1	47	P9
Belmont ter W4	73	Y11
Belmore la N7	47	Y15
Belmore st SW8	89	X1
Beloe clo SW15	86	H9
Belsham st E9	50	C17
Belsize ave N13	17	P18
Belsize ave NW3	46	H17
Belsize ave W13	72	C8
Belsize cres NW3	46	G16
Belsize gdns Sutt	130	B8
Belsize gro NW3	46	K17
Belsize la NW3	46	F18
Belsize pk NW3	46	F19
Belsize Park gdns NW3	46	H17
Belsize rd NW6	137	W6
Belsize rd Har	23	P2
Belsize sq NW3	46	H17
Belsize ter NW3	46	H17
Belson rd SE18	78	G10
Beltane dr SW19	105	P6
Belthorn cres SW12	89	V20
Belton rd E7	52	J19
Belton rd E11	51	Z12
Belton rd N17	31	S9
Belton rd NW2	44	G17
Belton rd Sid	115	O9
Belton way E3	64	B13
Beltran rd SW6	88	A5
Beltwood rd Belv	81	X10
Belvedere ave SW19	105	T12
Belvedere ave Ilf	35	Z7
Belvedere bldgs SE1	149	Z18
Belvedere clo Tedd	101	T13
Belvedere dr SW19	105	T12
Belvedere gro SW19	105	S14
Belvedere Industrial est Belv	81	Y7
Belvedere rd E10	50	K3
Belvedere rd SE1	149	P14
Belvedere rd SE2	80	G3
Belvedere rd SE19	109	U17
Belvedere rd W7	71	U7
Belvedere rd Bexh	98	B7
Belvedere sq SW19	105	S13
Belvedere strand NW9	26	D7
Belvedere way Har	24	L19
Belvoir clo SE9	113	S7
Belvoir rd SE22	91	Y19
Belvue clo Nthlt	40	H19
Belvue rd Nthlt	40	G20
Bembridge clo NW6	45	R20
Bemerton st N1	141	N3
Bemish rd SW15	87	P8
Bemsted rd E17	32	M9
Ben Hale clo Stan	11	N15
Ben Jonson rd E1	63	V15
Ben Smith way SE16	151	U20
Ben Tillet clo Bark	68	B1
Benares rd SE18	79	X11
Benbow rd W6	144	A20
Benbow st SE8	76	B16
Benbury clo Brom	111	U12
Bench fld S Croy	133	V13
Bencroft rd SE16	107	W18
Bendall ms NW1	138	M20
Bendemeer rd SW15	87	O6
Bendish rd E6	66	E1
Bendmore ave SE2	80	B13
Bendon valley SW18	88	A20
Benedict clo SW9	90	E7
Benedict rd Mitch	120	H7
Benedict way N2	28	D9
Benenden grn Brom	126	E12
Benett gdns SW16	121	Z3
Benfleet clo Sutt	130	E6
Bengal rd Ilf	53	Z11
Bengarth dr Har	23	R7
Bengarth rd Nthlt	58	A2
Bengeworth rd SE5	90	L7
Bengeworth rd Har	41	Z8
Benham clo SW11	88	F9
Benham gdns Houns	82	F11
Benham rd W7	59	U15
Benhill ave Sutt	130	B10
Benhill rd SE5	158	H19
Benhill rd Sutt	130	E5
Benhill Wood rd Sutt	130	C5
Benhilton gdns Sutt	130	B6
Benhurst ave Horn	57	Y11
Benhurst ct SW16	108	F13
Benhurst la SW16	108	E13
Benin st SE13	93	Y18
Benjamin clo E8	143	U5
Benjamin clo Horn	39	W19
Benjamin st EC1	141	W20
Benledi st E14	64	J16
Benn st E9	50	J17
Bennerley rd SW11	88	K13
Bennets copse Chis	113	S15
Bennet clo Kings T	116	E2
Bennett clo Well	97	N5
Bennett gro SE13	93	S3
Bennett pk SE3	94	C6
Bennett rd E13	65	Y13
Bennett rd N16	49	S13
Bennett rd Rom	38	A19
Bennett st SW1	148	B13
Bennett st W4	74	B15
Bennetts ave Croy	134	K4
Bennetts ave Grnf	59	S3
Bennetts Castle la Dag	55	U6
Bennetts clo N17	18	J20
Bennetts way Croy	134	J4
Benningholme rd Edg	13	N18
Bennington rd N17	31	R5
Bennington rd Wdf Grn	33	Y2
Benrek clo Ilf	36	B3
Bensbury clo SW15	86	L19
Bensham clo Th Hth	122	M10
Bensham gro Th Hth	122	L3
Bensham la Croy	122	J17
Bensham la Th Hth	122	K10
Bensham Manor rd Th Hth	122	M9
Bensley clo N11	15	Y16
Benson ave E6	65	Z7
Benson clo Houns	82	G10
Benson rd SE23	92	D20
Benson rd Croy	132	G6
Benthal rd N16	49	W9
Bentham rd E9	50	F18
Bentham rd SE28	68	C20
Bentham wk NW10	43	W15
Bentinck ms W1	147	V4
Bentinck st W1	147	V4
Bentley dr Ilf	36	B17
Bentley rd N1	49	T18
Bentley way Stan	10	L17
Bentley way Wdf Grn	21	T9
Benton rd Ilf	54	E3
Bentons la SE27	108	M11
Bentons ri SE27	109	N11
Bentry clo Dag	55	Z6
Bentworth rd W12	144	A6
Benwell rd N7	48	F13
Benwick clo SE16	159	Z5
Benworth st E3	63	Z8
Benyon rd N1	142	G3
Berber rd SW11	88	M13
Bercta rd SE9	114	B3
Bere st E1	63	U19
Berens rd NW10	136	F14
Beresford ave N20	15	Y7
Beresford ave W7	59	R15
Beresford ave Surb	117	T20
Beresford ave Twick	61	O2
Beresford ave Wem	61	O2
Beresford dr Brom	127	P6
Beresford dr Wdf Grn	21	Y13
Beresford gdns Enf	8	E13
Beresford gdns Houns	82	E13
Beresford rd E4	20	M5
Beresford rd E17	33	R4
Beresford rd N2	28	J11
Beresford rd N5	49	N15
Beresford rd N8	30	G15
Beresford rd Har	23	P16
Beresford rd Kings T	103	N20
Beresford rd N Mal	117	W9
Beresford rd Sutt	129	W16
Beresford sq SE18	78	M10
Beresford st SE18	78	M9
Berestede rd W6	74	E13
Bergen sq SE16	75	X7
Berger rd E9	50	F17
Berghem ms W14	152	G2
Bergholt ave Ilf	35	R14
Bergholt cres N16	31	R20
Bergholt ms NW1	140	E2
Bering wk E16	66	A17
Berkeley ave Bexh	97	X3
Berkeley ave Grnf	41	S18
Berkeley ave Ilf	35	Y8
Berkeley ave Rom	38	L2
Berkeley clo Kings T	102	J18
Berkeley cres Barn	5	U17
Berkeley gdns W8	145	V14
Berkeley ms W1	147	R5
Berkeley pl SW19	105	P16
Berkeley rd E12	53	R16
Berkeley rd N8	29	Y17
Berkeley rd N15	31	P19
Berkeley rd NW9	25	P13
Berkeley rd SW13	86	F1
Berkeley sq W1	147	Y10
Berkeley st W1	147	Z11
Berkeley waye Houns	70	A18
Berkhampstead rd Belv	81	S13
Berkhamsted ave Wem	43	O17
Berkley gro NW1	139	S1
Berkley rd NW1	139	R1
Berkshire gdns N13	17	S19
Berkshire gdns N18	19	N16
Berkshire rd E9	51	N17
Berkshire way Mitch	122	A10
Bermans way NW10	43	V15
Bermondsey sq SE1	150	J15
Bermondsey Wall east SE16	151	U18
Bermondsey Wall west SE16	151	S17
Bernard ave W13	72	B7
Bernard Cassidy st E16	65	R14
Bernard gdns SW19	105	W12
Bernard rd N15	31	V15
Bernard rd Rom	38	K20
Bernard rd Wall	131	R10
Bernard st WC1	140	K18
Bernays gdns SW9	90	E10
Bernays gro SW9	90	E10
Berne rd Th Hth	122	K11
Berner dr Croy	134	M5
Berners dr W13	59	Y18
Berners ms W1	148	D2
Berners pl W1	148	D4
Berners rd N1	141	V7
Berners rd N22	30	E5
Berners st W1	148	D4
Berney rd Croy	123	O17
Bernville way Har	25	O15
Bernwell rd E4	21	N10
Berridge grn Edg	25	R2
Berridge rd SE19	109	R12
Berriman rd N7	48	E8
Berriton rd Har	40	F4
Berry clo N21	17	X4
Berry clo NW10	44	A19
Berry hill Stan	11	V12
Berry la SE21	109	P9
Berry pl EC1	141	Y15
Berry st EC1	141	Y17
Berry way W5	72	J8
Berrydale rd Hayes	58	B11
Berryfield clo E17	33	S14
Berryfield clo Brom	127	R2
Berryfield rd SE17	157	Z9
Berryhill SE9	95	Z9
Berryhill gdns SE9	95	Y10
Berrylands SW20	119	N8
Berrylands Surb	117	N15
Berrylands Surb	116	L14
Berrymans la SE26	110	G11
Berrymead gdns W3	73	V4
Berrymede rd W4	73	X8
Bert la Th Hth	122	L12
Bertal rd SW17	106	F11
Berthon st SE8	76	C18
Bertie rd NW10	44	G18
Bertie rd SE26	110	G14
Bertram rd NW4	26	H18
Bertram rd Enf	8	J13
Bertram rd Kings T	103	O17
Bertram st N19	47	S8
Bertrand st SE13	93	S7
Bertrand way SE28	68	E19
Berwick ave Hayes	58	A19
Berwick clo Stan	10	J20
Berwick cres Sid	96	J17
Berwick rd E16	65	X18
Berwick rd N22	30	H3
Berwick rd Well	97	R3
Berwick st W1	148	D5
Berwyn ave Houns	82	K3
Berwyn rd SE24	108	J1
Berwyn rd Rich	85	S10
Beryl ave E6	66	E14
Beryl rd W6	152	F11
Berystede Kings T	103	T18
Besant rd NW2	45	S11
Besant way NW10	43	W15
Besley st SW16	107	W16
Bessborough gdns SW1	156	G9
Bessborough pl SW1	156	F10
Bessborough rd SW15	86	H20
Bessborough rd Har	41	R3
Bessborough st SW1	156	F9
Bessemer rd SE5	91	N6
Bessie Lansbury clo E6	66	K17
Besson st SE14	92	E1
Bestwood st SE8	75	U12
Betchworth rd Ilf	54	H7
Betchworth way Croy	135	T19
Betham rd Grnf	59	P11
Bethecar rd Har	23	T15
Bethel rd Well	97	V7
Bethell ave E16	65	P11
Bethell ave Ilf	53	W1

Name	Page	Grid
Bethersden clo Beck	110	M19
Bethnal Green rd E1	143	N17
Bethnal Green rd E2	143	W14
Bethune ave N11	16	A14
Bethune rd NW10	61	Z12
Bethwin rd SE5	157	Z16
Betjeman clo Pnr	22	G13
Betony clo Croy	124	F20
Betoyne ave E4	20	M12
Betstyle rd N11	16	F14
Betterton dr Sid	115	Z3
Betterton st WC2	148	K6
Bettons pk E15	65	O4
Bettridge rd SW6	87	W5
Betts clo Beck	124	H4
Betts rd E16	65	W18
Betts st E1	151	W9
Betts way SE20	124	A2
Betts way Surb	116	C20
Beulah ave Th Hth	122	M5
Beulah clo Edg	12	F11
Beulah cres Th Hth	122	M4
Beulah gro Croy	122	M15
Beulah hill SE19	108	J15
Beulah rd E17	33	S14
Beulah rd SW19	105	V17
Beulah rd Sutt	129	Y9
Beulah rd Th Hth	122	L7
Beult rd Dart	99	W9
Bevan ave Bark	55	N20
Bevan ct Croy	132	G12
Bevan rd SE2	80	C13
Bevan rd Barn	5	Y13
Bevan st N1	142	B6
Bevenden st N1	142	G12
Beveridge rd NW10	44	C20
Beverley SW20	104	E20
Beverley ave Houns	82	E11
Beverley ave Sid	96	K19
Beverley clo N21	17	Y5
Beverley clo SW11	88	F10
Beverley clo SW13	86	F5
Beverley ct N14	16	H1
Beverley ct SE4	34	N7
Beverley cres Wdf Grn	34	H3
Beverley dr Edg	25	O9
Beverley gdns NW11	27	S20
Beverley gdns SW13	86	E6
Beverley gdns Stan	23	Y4
Beverley gdns Wem	43	O4
Beverley la Kings T	104	B18
Beverley rd E4	20	K19
Beverley rd E6	66	C9
Beverley rd SW13	86	E6
Beverley rd W4	74	D13
Beverley rd Bexh	98	K5
Beverley rd Dag	55	Z11
Beverley rd Kings T	102	F20
Beverley rd Mitch	121	X8
Beverley rd N Mal	118	F9
Beverley rd Sthl	70	C10
Beverley rd Wor Pk	128	L3
Beverley way SW20	118	E1
Beverley way N Mal	118	E1
Beversbrook rd N19	47	X9
Beverstone rd SW2	90	D12
Beverstone rd Th Hth	122	H9
Bevill Allen clo SW17	107	N14
Bevin way WC1	141	S11
Bevington rd W10	144	M1
Bevington rd Beck	125	R3
Bevington st SE16	151	U19
Bevis Marks EC3	150	L5
Bewcastle gdns Enf	7	N14
Bewdley st N1	48	F20
Bewick st SW8	89	S5
Bewley st E1	151	Z8
Bewlys rd SE27	108	J11
Bexhill clo Felt	100	A3
Bexhill rd N11	16	J16
Bexhill rd SE4	92	M17
Bexhill rd SW14	85	V8
Bexhill wk E15	65	N4
Bexley gdns N9	18	C11
Bexley High st Bex	98	E19
Bexley la Dart	99	P13
Bexley la Sid	115	T10
Bexley rd SE9	95	V15
Bexley rd Erith	81	Y19
Beynon rd Cars	130	M12
Bianca rd SE15	159	R14
Bibsworth rd N3	27	V7
Bibury clo SE15	158	M15
Bicester rd Rich	85	R8
Bickenhall st W1	139	P20
Bickersteth rd SW17	106	M16
Bickerton rd N19	47	U8
Bickley cres Brom	127	R8
Bickley Park rd Brom	127	T5
Bickley rd E10	33	R20
Bickley rd Brom	127	P4
Bickley st SW17	106	K13
Bicknell st SE5	90	M8
Bicknoller rd Enf	8	F5
Bidborough clo Brom	126	C13
Bidborough st WC1	140	J14
Biddenden way SE9	113	W9
Bidder st E16	64	M13
Biddestone rd N7	48	C12
Biddulph rd W9	137	Y14
Bideford ave Grnf	60	A7
Bideford clo Edg	25	O5
Bideford clo Felt	100	E6
Bideford gdns Enf	18	E2
Bideford rd Brom	112	B7
Bideford rd Enf	9	Y3
Bideford rd Well	80	E20
Bidwell gdns N11	29	V3
Bidwell st SE15	92	B3
Big hill E5	50	B3
Biggerstaff rd E15	64	H2
Biggerstaff st N4	48	E7
Biggin ave Mitch	120	L1
Biggin hill SE19	108	K19
Biggin way SE19	108	K19
Bigginwood rd SW16	108	H19
Biggs row SW15	87	P8
Bigland st E1	151	W6
Bignell rd SE18	78	M14
Bignold rd E7	52	F12
Bigwood rd NW11	28	A16
Bill Hamling clo SE9	113	P4
Billet clo Rom	37	X10
Billet rd E17	32	F5
Billet rd Rom	37	S11
Billing pl SW10	153	Z16
Billing rd SW10	153	Z16
Billing st SW10	153	Z17
Billingford clo SE4	92	G10
Billington rd SE14	75	T20
Billiter sq EC3	150	K7
Billiter st EC3	150	L7
Billson st E14	76	H11
Bilsby gro SE9	113	O10
Bilton rd Grnf	59	Z3
Bilton way Enf	9	X4
Bina gdns SW5	154	C8
Bincote rd Enf	7	N11
Binden rd W12	74	E7
Bindon grn Mord	120	B9
Binfield rd SW4	90	B3
Binfield rd S Croy	133	U10
Bingfield st N1	141	N3
Bingham pl W1	139	T19
Bingham rd Croy	123	X20
Bingham st N1	49	O17
Bingley rd E16	65	X16
Bingley rd Grnf	59	N13
Binney st W1	147	V8
Binns rd W4	74	A14
Binsey wk SE2	80	G5
Binyon cres Stan	10	H17
Birbetts rd SE9	113	T5
Birch ave N13	17	Y11
Birch clo E16	65	N14
Birch clo SE15	91	Y5
Birch clo Brent	72	B19
Birch clo Rom	38	G10
Birch clo Tedd	101	Z11
Birch gdns Dag	56	L10
Birch gro SE12	94	C18
Birch gro W3	61	P20
Birch gro Well	97	N12
Birch hill Croy	134	F11
Birch pk Har	10	A20
Birch rd Felt	100	A13
Birch rd Rom	38	G10
Birch row Brom	127	X17
Birch Tree way Croy	133	Z2
Birch wk Erith	81	Z15
Birch wk Mitch	121	S1
Birchanger rd SE25	123	W11
Birchdale gdns Rom	55	V1
Birchdale rd E7	52	M15
Birchdene dr SE28	80	A2
Birchen clo NW9	43	Y6
Birchen gro NW9	43	X8
Birchend clo S Croy	133	P13
Birches the N21	7	P19
Birches the SE7	77	W15
Birches clo Mitch	120	M7
Birches clo Pnr	22	A14
Birchfield st E14	64	A18
Birchin la EC3	150	G7
Birchington clo Bexh	98	G1
Birchington rd N8	29	X17
Birchington rd NW6	137	V4
Birchington rd Surb	117	O18
Birchlands ave SW12	89	N18
Birchmere row SE3	94	D6
Birchmore wk N5	48	L10
Birchwood ave N10	29	P11
Birchwood ave Beck	124	L8
Birchwood ave Sid	115	S5
Birchwood ave Wall	131	R5
Birchwood clo Mord	120	A10
Birchwood ct N13	17	V16
Birchwood ct Edg	25	V8
Birchwood dr NW3	46	B10
Birchwood gro Hmptn	100	J15
Birchwood rd SW17	107	R12
Bird in Bush rd SE15	159	S17
Bird wk Twick	82	F20
Bird-in-hand la Brom	127	P5
Bird-in-hand pas SE23	110	D4
Birdbrook clo Dag	56	L20
Birdbrook rd SE3	94	M8
Birdcage wk SW1	148	B19
Birdham clo Brom	127	S12
Birdhurst ave S Croy	133	P9
Birdhurst gdns S Croy	133	P9
Birdhurst ri S Croy	133	S10
Birdhurst rd SW18	88	D12
Birdhurst rd SW19	106	J16
Birdhurst rd S Croy	133	R11
Birdlip clo SE15	158	J16
Birds Farm ave Rom	38	H3
Birdsfield la E3	63	X3
Birdwood clo Tedd	101	T10
Birkbeck ave W3	61	W19
Birkbeck ave Grnf	59	N2
Birkbeck gdns Wdf Grn	21	S9
Birkbeck gro W3	73	X5
Birkbeck hill SE21	108	K3
Birkbeck pl SE21	108	K3
Birkbeck rd E8	49	U16
Birkbeck rd N8	30	A13
Birkbeck rd N12	15	P17
Birkbeck rd N17	31	U4
Birkbeck rd NW7	13	S16
Birkbeck rd SW19	106	B14
Birkbeck rd W3	73	X3
Birkbeck rd W5	72	E10
Birkbeck rd Beck	124	D4
Birkbeck rd Enf	8	C3
Birkbeck rd Ilf	36	E16
Birkbeck rd Rom	57	N2
Birkbeck rd Sid	115	O8
Birkbeck st E2	143	Y15
Birkbeck way Grnf	59	O3
Birkdale ave Pnr	22	H10
Birkdale clo SE2	80	A10
Birkdale rd W5	60	J13
Birkenhead ave Kings T	116	M2
Birkenhead st WC1	140	L11
Birkhall rd SE6	111	X2
Birkwood clo SW12	89	Y20
Birley rd N20	15	R8
Birley st SW11	89	O6
Birling rd Erith	99	P1
Birnam rd N4	48	C7
Birse cres NW10	44	B11
Birstall rd N15	31	T15
Biscay rd W6	152	F11
Biscoe clo Houns	70	H16
Biscoe way SE13	93	Y9
Bisenden rd Croy	133	S2
Bisham clo Cars	120	M19
Bisham gdns N6	47	R3
Bishop Ken rd Har	23	W7
Bishop Kings rd W14	152	M5
Bishop rd N14	16	E3
Bishop st N1	142	B4
Bishop way NW10	44	A20
Bishop's ave E13	65	V2
Bishops ave SW6	87	S4
Bishops ave Brom	126	L5
Bishops ave Rom	37	U17
Bishops ave the N2	46	G1
Bishops bri W2	146	D3
Bishops Bridge rd W2	146	A5
Bishops clo E17	33	T13
Bishops clo SE9	114	B4
Bishops clo Barn	4	B19
Bishops clo Enf	8	M8
Bishops clo Rich	102	H7
Bishops clo Sutt	129	Z7
Bishop's ct EC4	149	X4
Bishop's ct WC2	149	S4
Bishops gro N2	28	H18
Bishops gro Hmptn	100	F11
Bishop's Hall Kings T	116	G3
Bishop's Park rd SW6	87	R4
Bishops Park rd SW16	122	B1
Bishops rd N6	29	P18
Bishops rd SW6	153	O20
Bishops rd W7	71	T5
Bishops rd Croy	122	H18
Bishops ter SE11	157	U5
Bishops wk Croy	134	E12
Bishops way E2	143	Y8
Bishopsford rd Mord	120	D17
Bishopsgate EC2	150	J5
Bishopsgate churchyard EC2	150	J3
Bishopsthorpe rd SE26	110	F10
Bishopswood rd N6	46	M2
Bisley clo Wor Pk	119	N20
Bispham rd NW10	61	N9
Bisson rd E15	64	H5
Bisterne ave E17	33	X10
Bittacy clo NW7	14	B18
Bittacy hill NW7	14	C19
Bittacy Park ave NW7	14	B17
Bittacy ri NW7	14	A20
Bittacy rd NW7	14	D20
Bittern st SE1	150	A18
Bittoms the Kings T	116	H6
Bixley clo Sthl	70	F10
Black Boy la N15	30	M15
Black Fan clo Enf	7	Z7
Black Friars la EC4	149	X7
Black Horse ct SE1	158	G2
Black Lion la W6	74	F12
Black Prince rd SE11	157	N6
Black Swan yd SE1	150	K17
Blackall st EC2	142	H16
Blackberry Farm clo Houns	70	B20
Blackbird hill NW9	43	W7
Blackbird yd E2	143	R11
Blackborne rd Dag	56	E18
Blackburn rd NW6	46	A18
Blackburne's ms W1	147	T9
Blackbush ave Rom	37	V16
Blackbush clo Sutt	130	B17
Blackdown ter SE18	78	H20
Blackett st SW15	87	O9
Blackfen rd Sid	96	H14
Blackford clo S Croy	132	K20
Blackfriars bri EC4	149	X9
Blackfriars bri SE1	149	X10
Blackfriars rd SE1	149	X12
Blackheath ave SE10	76	L19
Blackheath gro SE3	94	C6

Name	Page	Ref
Blackheath hill SE10	93	U2
Blackheath pk SE3	94	D7
Blackheath ri SE13	93	U5
Blackheath rd SE10	93	R1
Blackheath vale SE3	94	A4
Blackheath village SE3	94	C7
Blackhorse la E17	32	F6
Blackhorse la Croy	123	Y16
Blackhorse rd E17	32	G12
Blackhorse rd SE8	75	X15
Blackhorse rd Sid	115	O10
Blackland ter SW3	155	P7
Blacklands rd SE6	111	T10
Blackmore ave Sthl	71	R3
Blackmores gro Tedd	101	Y15
Blackpool rd SE15	91	Z5
Blacks rd W6	152	C18
Blackshaw rd SW17	106	E9
Blacksmiths clo Rom	37	T18
Blackstock ms N4	48	H7
Blackstock rd N4	48	H7
Blackstock rd N5	48	H7
Blackstone rd NW2	45	N14
Blackwall la SE10	77	O12
Blackwall Tunnel E14	76	J2
Blackwall Tunnel app SE10	76	L5
Blackwall Tunnel Northern app E3	64	F8
Blackwall Tunnel Northern app E14	64	H16
Blackwall way E14	64	H20
Blackwater st SE22	91	U13
Blackwell clo E5	50	G12
Blackwell clo Har	23	P2
Blackwell gdns Edg	12	C12
Blackwood st SE17	158	E9
Bladindon dr Bex	97	V18
Bladon gdns Har	22	L18
Blagdens clo N14	16	J7
Blagdens la N14	16	J7
Blagdon rd SE13	93	S15
Blagdon rd N Mal	118	C9
Blagdon wk Tedd	102	D16
Blagrove rd W10	145	N2
Blair ave NW9	44	A2
Blair clo N1	48	M16
Blair clo Sid	96	G14
Blair st E14	64	J17
Blairderry rd SW2	108	A12
Blake ave Bark	67	W2
Blake clo Well	96	J3
Blake gdns SW6	87	Z1
Blake Hall cres E11	52	G4
Blake Hall rd E11	34	F20
Blake rd E16	65	P12
Blake rd N11	29	V1
Blake rd Croy	133	R2
Blake rd Mitch	120	J6
Blakehall rd Cars	130	M14
Blakemore rd Th Hth	122	D11
Blakemore way Belv	80	M9
Blakeney ave Beck	110	M20
Blakeney clo NW1	15	N6
Blakeney clo NW1	140	E2
Blakeney rd Beck	110	L19
Blakenham rd SW17	106	M10
Blaker rd E15	64	G14
Blakes ave N Mal	118	E13
Blake's grn W Wick	125	T19
Blakes la N Mal	118	D13
Blakes rd SE15	158	L17
Blakes ter N Mal	118	G12
Blakesley ave W5	72	E5
Blakesware gdns N9	18	C2
Blanch clo SE15	159	Z19
Blanchard rd SE9	113	S6
Blanchard way E8	49	Y19
Blanche st E16	65	P12
Blanchedowne SE5	91	O9
Blanchland rd Mord	120	A11
Blandfield rd SW12	89	P17
Blandford ave Beck	124	H2
Blandford ave Twick	100	L1
Blandford clo N2	28	E14
Blandford clo Croy	132	A6
Blandford clo Rom	38	G12
Blandford cres E4	20	F3
Blandford cres E4	24	A8
Blandford rd W4	72	A8
Blandford rd W5	72	H5
Blandford rd Beck	124	D5
Blandford rd Sthl	70	F10
Blandford rd Tedd	101	S14
Blandford sq NW1	138	M18
Blandford st W1	147	R3
Blaney cres E6	66	L8
Blanmerle rd SE9	113	Y2
Blann clo SE9	95	N17
Blantyre st SW10	154	F17
Blashford st SE13	93	Y18
Blasker wk E14	76	C13
Blawith rd Har	23	U14
Blaydon clo N17	31	Z1
Bleak Hill la SE18	79	Y16
Blean gro SE20	110	C18
Bleasdale ave Grnf	59	X6
Blechynden st W10	144	H8
Blechynden st W11	144	H8
Bleddyn clo Sid	97	U15
Bledlow clo SE28	68	G20
Bledlow ri Grnf	59	N6
Bleeding Heart yd EC1	149	V1
Blegborough rd SW16	107	V14
Blendon dr Bex	97	W16
Blendon rd Bex	97	V16
Blendon ter SE18	79	P15
Blenheim ave Ilf	35	W18
Blenheim clo N21	17	Y4
Blenheim clo SW20	118	M7
Blenheim clo Rom	38	K12
Blenheim clo Wall	131	V17
Blenheim ct N19	48	A6
Blenheim ct Sid	114	F6
Blenheim cres W11	144	L8
Blenheim cres S Croy	132	L18
Blenheim dr Well	96	K3
Blenheim gdns NW2	45	N15
Blenheim gdns SW2	90	C15
Blenheim gdns Kings T	103	S19
Blenheim gdns Wall	131	V14
Blenheim gdns Wem	42	L9
Blenheim gro SE15	91	W5
Blenheim Park rd S Croy	132	M18
Blenheim ri N15	31	V13
Blenheim rd E6	66	A8
Blenheim rd E15	52	A12
Blenheim rd E17	32	G10
Blenheim rd NW8	138	C7
Blenheim rd SW20	118	M7
Blenheim rd W4	74	B8
Blenheim rd Barn	4	C12
Blenheim rd Brom	127	R10
Blenheim rd Har	22	J17
Blenheim rd Nthlt	40	L18
Blenheim rd Sid	115	T2
Blenheim rd Sutt	129	Z5
Blenheim st W1	147	X7
Blenheim ter NW8	138	B9
Blenkarne rd SW11	88	L17
Blessbury rd Edg	25	V3
Blessington clo SE13	93	Y9
Blessington rd SE13	93	X9
Bletchingley clo Th Hth	122	H10
Bletchley ct N1	142	E10
Bletchley st N1	142	D10
Bletsoe wk N1	142	C8
Blincoe clo SW19	105	R5
Blissett st SE10	93	T1
Blisworth clo Hayes	58	B11
Blithbury rd Dag	55	R18
Blithdale rd SE2	80	A11
Blithfield st W8	153	W3
Blockley rd Wem	42	A7
Bloemfontein ave W12	74	J3
Bloemfontein rd W12	62	J19
Blomfield rd W9	137	Z19
Blomfield st EC2	150	H3
Blomfield vill W2	146	A1
Blomville rd Dag	56	A8
Blondel st SW11	89	O5
Blondin ave W5	72	C10
Blondin st E3	64	B5
Bloom gro SE27	108	J7
Bloom Park rd SW6	153	O19
Bloomburg st SW1	156	D6
Bloomfield cres Ilf	36	A19
Bloomfield pl W1	147	Y9
Bloomfield rd N6	29	P18
Bloomfield rd SE18	79	N15
Bloomfield rd Brom	127	N11
Bloomfield rd Kings T	116	K8
Bloomfield ter SW1	155	U9
Bloomhall rd SE19	109	O13
Bloomsbury clo W5	61	O19
Bloomsbury pl W5	88	C13
Bloomsbury pl WC1	148	L1
Bloomsbury sq WC1	148	L1
Bloomsbury st WC1	148	H2
Bloomsbury way WC1	148	K3
Blore clo SW8	89	X3
Blossom clo W5	72	L5
Blossom clo Dag	69	O3
Blossom clo S Croy	133	V10
Blossom la Enf	7	Y5
Blossom st E1	142	M19
Blossom waye Houns	70	B18
Blount st E14	63	X16
Bloxam gdns SE9	95	R13
Bloxhall rd E10	50	L4
Bloxham cres Hmptn	100	F20
Bloxworth clo Wall	131	V7
Blucher rd SE5	158	C19
Blue Anchor la SE16	159	V4
Blue Anchor yd E1	151	R9
Blue Ball yd SW1	148	B14
Bluebell clo SE26	109	W10
Bluebell clo Wall	121	R19
Bluefield clo Hmptn	100	G14
Bluegates Epsom	128	H17
Bluehouse rd E4	21	N10
Blundell rd Edg	25	Z4
Blundell st N7	48	B19
Blunden clo Dag	55	U3
Blunts rd SE9	95	W14
Blurton rd E5	50	D13
Blyth clo E14	76	J10
Blyth rd E17	50	L2
Blyth rd Brom	126	D2
Blythe clo Twick	83	X17
Blythe hill SE6	92	L20
Blythe Hill la SE6	92	L19
Blythe rd W14	152	F1
Blythe st E2	143	V12
Blythe vale SE6	92	L18
Blythswood rd Ilf	55	N2
Blythwood rd N4	48	B1
Boadicea st N1	141	N5
Boakes clo NW9	25	V14
Boathouse wk SE15	159	P17
Bob Anker clo E13	65	U8
Bobbin clo SW4	89	U7
Bobs la Rom	39	V3
Bockhampton rd Kings T	103	N17
Bocking st E8	143	X4
Boddicott clo SW19	105	R5
Bodiam clo Enf	8	D8
Bodiam rd SW16	107	Y19
Bodley clo N Mal	118	B13
Bodley rd N Mal	117	Z14
Bodmin clo Har	40	F10
Bodmin gro Mord	120	A11
Bodmin st SW18	105	Z3
Bodnant gdns SW20	118	H5
Bodney rd E8	49	Z14
Boevey path Belv	81	O15
Bognor rd Well	97	W2
Bohemia pl E8	50	B16
Bohun gro Barn	5	X19
Boileau rd SW13	74	H18
Boileau rd W5	61	O16
Bolden st SE8	93	R4
Bolderwood way W Wick	135	R3
Boleyn ave Enf	8	M4
Boleyn clo E17	33	N11
Boleyn ct Buck H	21	U6
Boleyn gdns Dag	56	J20
Boleyn gdns W Wick	135	S4
Boleyn gro W Wick	135	T4
Boleyn rd E6	66	A5
Boleyn rd E7	65	U1
Boleyn rd N16	49	S14
Boleyn way Barn	5	R12
Bolina rd SE16	75	R14
Bolingbroke gro SW11	88	J12
Bolingbroke rd W14	152	G1
Bolingbroke wk SW11	88	H1
Bollo Bridge rd W3	73	T7
Bollo la W3	73	S6
Bollo la W3	73	U9
Bolney st SW8	157	N19
Bolney way Felt	100	C6
Bolsover st W1	139	Z18
Bolstead rd Mitch	121	S2
Boltmore clo NW4	27	R10
Bolton clo SE20	123	Y3
Bolton cres SE5	157	V16
Bolton gdns NW10	136	F10
Bolton gdns SW5	153	Y9
Bolton gdns Brom	112	C16
Bolton gdns Tedd	101	Y15
Bolton Gardens ms SW10	154	A10
Bolton rd E15	52	D19
Bolton rd N18	18	H16
Bolton rd NW8	137	Z6
Bolton rd NW10	62	C3
Bolton rd W4	73	V19
Bolton rd Har	23	O13
Bolton st W1	147	Z13
Boltons the SW10	154	B10
Boltons the Wem	41	X12
Boltons the Wdf Grn	21	U14
Bombay st SE16	159	W5
Bomore rd W11	144	K8
Bonar pl Chis	113	S18
Bonar rd SE15	159	S19
Bonchester clo Chis	113	X19
Bonchurch clo Sutt	130	B17
Bonchurch rd W10	144	L1
Bonchurch rd W13	72	A3
Bond ct EC4	150	E7
Bond gdns Wall	131	V7
Bond rd Mitch	120	K4
Bond st E15	51	Z14
Bond st W5	60	G20
Bondfield rd E6	66	F15
Bondway SW8	156	L13
Boneta rd SE18	78	F8
Bonfield rd SE13	93	V10
Bonham gdns Dag	55	X7
Bonham rd SW2	90	C12
Bonham rd Dag	55	X6
Bonheur rd W4	73	Z6
Bonhill st EC2	142	G18
Boniface gdns Har	22	K2
Boniface wk Har	22	K2
Bonner Hill rd Kings T	117	N5
Bonner rd E2	63	P6
Bonner st E2	63	S7
Bonnersfield clo Har	23	X17
Bonnersfield la Har	23	W17
Bonneville gdns SW4	89	V16
Bonnington sq SW8	157	N13
Bonny st NW1	140	A1
Bonser rd Twick	101	V5
Bonsor st SE5	158	K18
Bonville rd Brom	112	D13
Booker clo N18	18	K16
Boone st SE13	94	A10
Boones rd SE13	94	A9
Boot st N1	142	J14
Booth clo SE28	80	E1
Booth rd NW9	25	Z6
Booth rd Croy	132	J4
Boothby rd N19	47	W6

Name	Pg	Ref
Booth's pl W1	148	C3
Bordars rd W7	59	T15
Bordars wk W7	59	T14
Borden ave Enf	8	C20
Border cres SE26	110	A12
Border gdns Croy	135	P8
Border rd SE26	110	B13
Bordergate Mitch	106	L20
Bordesley rd Mord	120	A10
Bordon wk SW15	86	H19
Boreham ave E16	65	T18
Boreham rd N22	30	L6
Borer's pas E1	150	L4
Borgard rd SE18	78	F11
Borland rd SE15	92	E11
Borland rd Tedd	102	B17
Borneo st SW15	87	N9
Borough High st SE1	150	B19
Borough hill Croy	132	H6
Borough rd SE1	149	X20
Borough rd Islw	83	U1
Borough rd Kings T	103	P20
Borough rd Mitch	120	J3
Borrett clo SE17	158	A10
Borrodaile rd SW18	88	B15
Borrowdale ave Har	23	Y7
Borrowdale clo Ilf	35	R12
Borrowdale ct Enf	7	Z6
Borthwick rd E15	52	A13
Borthwick st SE8	76	B15
Borwick ave E17	32	L10
Bosbury rd SE6	111	V8
Boscastle rd NW5	47	R10
Boscobel pl SW1	155	V4
Boscobel st NW8	138	G19
Boscombe ave E10	33	W20
Boscombe clo E5	50	H14
Boscombe rd SW17	107	O16
Boscombe rd SW19	105	Z20
Boscombe rd W12	74	H4
Boscombe rd Wor Pk	119	N19
Bosgrove E4	20	G6
Boss st SE1	151	N16
Bostal row Bexh	98	A8
Bostall hill SE2	80	A13
Bostall Hill rd SE2	80	F15
Bostall la SE2	80	D14
Bostall Manorway SE2	80	E10
Bostall Park ave Bexh	80	L20
Bostall rd Orp	115	P19
Boston gdns W4	74	C16
Boston gdns Brent	71	Z11
Boston Manor rd Brent	72	A11
Boston pl NW1	139	N17
Boston rd E6	66	D8
Boston rd E17	33	O19
Boston rd W7	71	U4
Boston rd Croy	122	E15
Boston vale W7	71	Z11
Bostonthorpe rd W7	71	U5
Boswell clo Th Hth	122	M10
Boswell st WC1	140	M20
Bosworth clo E17	32	K5
Bosworth rd N11	16	L17
Bosworth rd W10	136	M18
Bosworth rd Barn	4	L12
Bosworth rd Dag	56	F9
Boteley clo E4	20	K9
Botha rd E13	65	X13
Botham clo Edg	25	U2
Bothwell clo E16	65	R15
Bothwell st W6	152	H15
Botolph la EC3	150	H9
Botsford rd SW20	119	S4
Botts ms W2	145	V6
Botts pas W2	145	V6
Boucher clo Tedd	101	V13
Bouchier wk Rain	57	W17
Boughton ave Brom	126	D17
Boughton rd SE28	79	W8
Boulcott st E1	63	V18
Boulogne rd Croy	123	N14
Boulter gdns Rain	57	X16
Boulton rd Dag	56	A8
Boultwood rd E6	66	F18
Bounces la N9	19	N6
Bounces rd N9	19	N6
Boundaries rd SW12	106	M3
Boundary clo SE20	123	Y4
Boundary clo Kings T	117	S6
Boundary clo Sthl	70	H14
Boundary la E13	66	A10
Boundary la SE17	158	D14
Boundary rd E13	65	Z7
Boundary rd E17	32	M20
Boundary rd N9	9	R20
Boundary rd N22	30	L7
Boundary rd NW8	138	A5
Boundary rd SW19	106	F15
Boundary rd Bark	67	P5
Boundary rd Cars	131	R15
Boundary rd Rom	39	V18
Boundary rd Sid	96	H14
Boundary rd Wall	81	H19
Boundary row SE1	149	W17
Boundary st E2	142	H6
Boundary way Croy	135	O11
Boundfield rd SE6	111	Y6
Bounds Green rd N11	16	J18
Bounds Green rd N22	30	C4
Bourchier st W1	148	F7
Bourdon pl W1	147	Y9
Bourdon rd SE20	124	B4
Bourdon st W1	147	X10
Bourke clo NW10	44	B19
Bourke clo SW4	89	Z17
Bourlet clo W1	148	B2
Bourn ave N15	31	O12
Bourn ave Barn	5	V17
Bournbrook rd SE3	95	O7
Bourne Ho N14	16	L5
Bourne ave N14	16	M7
Bourne dr Mitch	120	G5
Bourne est EC1	141	S19
Bourne gdns E4	20	E14
Bourne hill N13	17	R8
Bourne Industrial pk Dart	99	P13
Bourne mead Bex	98	M14
Bourne rd E7	52	D10
Bourne rd N8	30	B17
Bourne rd Bex	98	G18
Bourne rd Brom	127	N9
Bourne rd SW1	155	U7
Bourne st Croy	132	J4
Bourne ter W2	145	X1
Bourne vale Brom	126	D20
Bourne vw Grnf	41	W16
Bourne way Sutt	129	W12
Bournemouth rd SE15	91	Y5
Bournemouth rd SW19	105	Z20
Bourneside cres N14	16	K5
Bourneside gdns SE6	111	V12
Bournevale rd SW16	108	A11
Bournewood rd SE18	80	B19
Bournville rd SE6	93	N19
Bournwell clo Barn	5	Z10
Bousfield rd SE14	92	E4
Boutflower rd SW11	88	J11
Bouverie gdns Har	24	H19
Bouverie pl W2	146	H4
Bouverie rd N16	49	R5
Bouverie rd Har	23	N19
Bouverie st EC4	149	U7
Bouvier rd Enf	9	Y8
Boveney rd SE23	92	F18
Bovill rd SE23	92	G19
Bovingdon ave Wem	43	R19
Bovingdon la NW9	26	B3
Bovingdon rd SW6	88	A3
Bow Common la E3	63	Y12
Bow Industrial est E15	51	P19
Bow la EC4	150	C7
Bow la N12	28	E3
Bow la Mord	119	S14
Bow rd E3	63	Z9
Bow st E15	51	Z15
Bow st WC2	148	L7
Bowater clo NW9	25	X16
Bowater clo SW2	90	A15
Bowater pl SE3	77	W19
Bowater rd SE18	78	C8
Bowden st SE11	157	U10
Bowditch SE8	75	Y12
Bowdon rd E17	33	O20
Bowen dr SE21	109	S6
Bowen rd Har	23	O20
Bowen st E14	64	E16
Bower ave SE10	77	N20
Bower clo Rom	39	N2
Bower st E1	63	T18
Bowerdean st SW6	88	A3
Bowerman ave SE14	75	X17
Bowes clo Sid	97	P16
Bowes rd N11	16	H15
Bowes rd N13	17	N16
Bowes rd W3	62	A20
Bowes rd Dag	55	U13
Bowfell rd W6	152	E15
Bowford ave Bexh	97	Z3
Bowhill clo SW9	157	U18
Bowie clo SW4	89	Y18
Bowland rd SW4	89	Y11
Bowland rd Wdf Grn	21	Z17
Bowles rd SE1	159	T13
Bowley la SE19	109	U14
Bowley rd SE19	109	U15
Bowling Green clo SW15	86	L19
Bowling Green ct EC2	142	L19
Bowling Green la EC1	141	U17
Bowling Green pl SE1	150	F17
Bowling Green st SE11	157	T14
Bowling Green wk N1	142	J13
Bowls clo Stan	11	N16
Bowman ave E16	65	R19
Bowman ms SW18	87	W20
Bowmans clo W13	72	B4
Bowmans lea SE23	92	D17
Bowmans meadow Wall	131	R6
Bowmans ms E1	151	S6
Bowmans ms N7	48	B10
Bowmans rd Dart	99	T18
Bowman's Trading est NW9	25	N11
Bowmead SE9	113	T4
Bowness cres SW15	104	A12
Bowness dr Houns	82	C9
Bowness rd SE6	93	T20
Bowness rd Bexh	98	G6
Bowness way Horn	57	W15
Bowood rd SW11	89	O12
Bowood rd Enf	9	T8
Bowrons ave Wem	42	H20
Bowyer pl SE5	158	D18
Bowyer st SE5	158	B18
Box la Bark	68	E6
Boxall rd SE21	91	R17
Boxgrove rd SE2	80	F7
Boxley rd Mord	120	D10
Boxley st E16	77	V3
Boxmoor rd Har	24	A12
Boxoll rd Dag	56	A11
Boxtree la Har	23	O4
Boxtree rd Har	23	P1
Boxworth gro N1	141	R4
Boyard rd SE18	78	L13
Boyce way E13	65	T11
Boycroft ave NW9	25	W18
Boyd ave Sthl	70	F3
Boyd clo Kings T	103	R18
Boyd rd SW19	106	G15
Boyd st E1	151	T6
Boyfield st SE1	149	Y18
Boyland rd Brom	112	C12
Boyle ave Stan	10	M18
Boyle st W1	148	A9
Boyne ave NW4	27	R12
Boyne rd SE13	93	V7
Boyne rd Dag	56	E10
Boyne Terrace ms W11	145	O13
Boyseland ct Edg	12	G7
Boyson rd SE17	158	D14
Boythorn way SE16	159	Y10
Boyton clo E1	63	S11
Boyton clo N8	30	A11
Boyton rd N8	30	A10
Brabant ct EC3	150	H8
Brabant rd N22	30	E7
Brabazon ave Wall	132	A18
Brabazon rd Nthlt	58	G6
Brabazon st E14	64	D15
Brabourn gro SE15	92	C5
Brabourne clo SE19	109	S13
Brabourne cres Bexh	81	P18
Brabourne ri Beck	125	V2
Bracewell ave Grnf	41	X16
Bracewell rd W10	144	B1
Bracewood gdns Croy	133	U5
Bracey st N4	48	B5
Bracken ave SW12	89	P17
Bracken ave Croy	135	P6
Bracken clo E6	66	F14
Bracken clo Twick	82	G18
Bracken end Islw	83	R12
Bracken gdns SW13	86	G3
Bracken Hill clo Brom	126	C1
Bracken Hill la Brom	126	C1
Bracken ms Rom	38	F19
Brackenbury gdns W6	74	K7
Brackenbury rd N2	28	D10
Brackenbury rd W6	74	K7
Brackendale N21	17	R6
Brackendale clo Houns	82	L2
Brackens the Enf	18	D2
Brackley clo Wall	132	A16
Brackley rd W4	74	B12
Brackley rd Beck	110	M17
Brackley sq Wdf Grn	35	O1
Brackley st EC1	142	B19
Brackley ter W4	74	B13
Bracklyn ct N1	142	E7
Bracklyn st N1	142	E7
Bracknell clo N22	30	F5
Bracknell gdns NW3	46	A13
Bracondale rd SE2	80	A10
Brad st SE1	149	U15
Bradbourne rd Bex	99	F18
Bradbourne st SW6	87	Y4
Bradbury clo Sthl	70	F10
Bradbury st N16	49	T16
Braddon rd Rich	85	N7
Braddyll st SE10	76	M14
Braden st W9	137	X18
Bradenham ave Well	97	N10
Bradenham clo SE17	158	E13
Bradenham rd Har	24	A12
Bradfield dr Bark	54	M14
Bradfield rd E16	77	U4
Bradfield rd Ruis	40	C14
Bradford clo SE26	109	Z9
Bradford dr Epsom	128	C14
Bradford rd W3	74	A4
Bradford rd Ilf	54	G4
Bradgate SE6	93	P17
Brading cres E11	52	H5
Brading rd SW2	90	D17
Brading rd Croy	122	C16
Bradiston rd W9	137	R12
Bradley clo N1	141	U8
Bradley clo N7	48	B19
Bradley gdns W13	60	B17
Bradley rd N22	30	C6
Bradley rd SE19	108	L14
Bradley rd Enf	9	X1
Bradman row Edg	25	U2
Bradmead SW8	156	A20
Bradmore Park rd W6	74	K10
Bradshaws clo SE25	123	Y6
Bradstock rd E9	50	G18
Bradstock rd Epsom	128	H13
Bradwell ave Dag	56	E6
Bradwell clo E18	34	C12
Bradwell st E1	63	T9
Brady st E1	143	W17
Braemar ave N22	30	B5
Braemar ave NW10	43	Z9
Braemar ave SW19	105	X5
Braemar ave Bexh	98	K11
Braemar ave S Croy	133	N20
Braemar ave Th Hth	122	H6
Braemar ave Wem	60	J1

Street	Page	Grid
Braemar gdns NW9	25	Z6
Braemar gdns Sid	114	G6
Braemar gdns W Wick	125	T20
Braemar rd E13	65	R12
Braemar rd N15	31	R15
Braemar rd Brent	72	H16
Braemar rd Wor Pk	128	J5
Braes st N1	48	K20
Braeside Beck	111	P13
Braeside ave SW19	105	T20
Braeside cres Bexh	98	L11
Braeside rd SW16	107	V18
Braesyde clo Belv	81	R11
Brafferton rd Croy	132	L8
Braganza st SE17	157	W10
Braham st E1	151	P5
Braid ave W3	62	A18
Braid clo Felt	100	D4
Braidwood rd SE6	111	W2
Braidwood st SE1	150	K14
Brailsford rd SW2	90	G14
Braintree ave Ilf	35	P14
Braintree rd Dag	56	E9
Braintree st E2	63	P10
Braithwaite ave Rom	56	E1
Braithwaite gdns Stan	24	D5
Braithwaite rd Enf	9	X10
Bramah grn SW9	90	G1
Bramalea clo N6	29	O18
Bramber rd N12	15	W17
Bramber rd W14	153	R13
Bramble Acres clo Sutt	129	Y16
Bramble clo Croy	135	P8
Bramble clo Stan	24	H3
Bramble cft Erith	81	Z12
Bramble la Hmptn	100	E14
Bramblebury rd SE18	79	R14
Brambledown clo W Wick	126	A13
Brambledown rd Cars	131	P18
Brambledown rd S Croy	133	R18
Brambledown rd Wall	131	T17
Brambles clo Islw	72	A19
Bramblewood clo Cars	120	L20
Bramblings the E4	20	L13
Bramcote ave Mitch	120	L10
Bramcote gro SE16	159	Z10
Bramcote rd SW15	86	K11
Bramdean cres SE12	112	E2
Bramdean gdns SE12	112	E2
Bramerton rd Beck	124	L6
Bramerton st SW3	154	J12
Bramfield rd SW11	88	L14
Bramford ct N14	16	K7
Bramford rd SW18	88	D11
Bramham gdns SW5	153	Y8
Bramhope la SE7	77	X17
Bramlands clo SW11	88	J7
Bramley clo E17	32	J8
Bramley clo N14	6	E17
Bramley clo S Croy	132	K10
Bramley clo Twick	82	M16
Bramley cres Ilf	35	X18
Bramley hill S Croy	132	K11
Bramley pl Dart	99	W11
Bramley rd N14	6	D10
Bramley rd W5	72	D9
Bramley rd W10	144	H16
Bramley rd Sutt	130	F11
Bramley rd (Cheam) Sutt	129	O20
Bramley st W1	144	G6
Bramley way Hours	82	D13
Bramley way W Wick	135	S4
Brampton clo E5	50	B6
Brampton gdns N15	30	L15
Brampton gro NW4	26	K14
Brampton gro Har	23	Z12
Brampton gro Wem	30	A9
Brampton Park rd N8	30	F9
Brampton rd E6	66	C10
Brampton rd N15	30	L16
Brampton rd NW9	25	R13
Brampton rd SE2	80	H15
Brampton rd Bexh	97	X1
Brampton rd Croy	123	U16
Bramshaw ri N Mal	118	B14
Bramshaw rd E9	50	G18
Bramshill gdns NW5	47	T8
Bramshill rd NW10	62	C6
Bramshot ave SE7	77	U16
Bramston rd NW10	62	G5
Brancaster rd E12	53	V13
Brancaster rd SW16	107	Z6
Brancaster Ilf	36	G19
Brancepeth gdns Buck H	21	T8
Branch hill NW3	46	C9
Branch pl N1	142	G5
Branch rd E14	63	V19
Brancker rd Har	24	F10
Brancroft way Enf	9	X6
Brand st SE10	76	G20
Brandlehow rd SW15	87	U11
Brandon est SE17	157	X15
Brandon rd E17	33	V11
Brandon rd N7	47	Z20
Brandon rd Sthl	70	D14
Brandon st SE17	158	A9
Brandon st SE17	158	B6
Brandram rd SE13	93	Z8
Brandreth rd E6	66	H17
Brandreth rd SW17	107	R5
Brandries the Wall	131	Z7
Brandville gdns Ilf	36	A12
Brandy way Sutt	129	Y17
Brangbourne rd Brom	111	U12
Brangton rd SE11	157	R10
Brangwyn cres SW19	120	E2
Branksea st SW6	152	K19
Branksome ave N18	18	G17
Branksome rd SW2	90	B13
Branksome rd SW19	105	Y20
Branksome way Har	24	L17
Branksome way N Mal	117	W2
Branscombe gdns N21	17	S3
Branscombe st SE13	93	S7
Bransdale clo NW6	137	W3
Bransgrove rd Edg	24	M3
Branstone rd Rich	85	N3
Brants wk W7	59	U12
Brantwood ave Erith	81	W18
Brantwood ave Islw	83	Y10
Brantwood gdns Enf	6	M15
Brantwood gdns Ilf	35	S14
Brantwood rd N17	18	J19
Brantwood rd SE24	90	L12
Brantwood rd Bexh	98	H6
Brantwood rd S Croy	133	N19
Brassey rd NW6	45	W16
Brassey sq SW11	89	O7
Brassie ave W3	62	A18
Brasted clo SE26	110	C9
Brasted clo Bexh	97	W13
Brathway rd SW18	87	Y18
Bratley st E1	143	S17
Braund ave Grnf	58	J10
Braundton ave Sid	114	K2
Braunston dr Hayes	58	B11
Bravington pl W9	137	O10
Bravington rd W9	137	N10
Braxfield rd SE4	92	K10
Braxted pk SW16	108	A1
Bray dr E16	65	S19
Bray rd NW7	14	D19
Brayards rd SE15	91	Z5
Braybourne dr Islw	71	V18
Braybrook st W12	62	D15
Brayburne ave SW4	89	V5
Braydon rd N16	49	W2
Brayfield ter N1	141	S17
Brayton gdns Enf	6	L15
Braywood rd SE9	96	E10
Brazil clo Croy	122	A18
Breach la Dag	69	R8
Bread st EC4	150	C6
Breakspears rd SE4	92	L9
Bream gdns E6	66	J10
Bream st E3	64	B1
Breamore clo SW15	104	G2
Breamore rd Ilf	54	K8
Bream's bldgs EC4	149	T4
Breamwater gdns Rich	102	B7
Brearley clo Edg	25	V2
Breasley clo SW15	86	L9
Brechin pl SW7	154	D8
Brecknock rd N7	47	W13
Brecknock rd N19	47	W13
Brecon clo Mitch	121	Z8
Brecon clo Wor Pk	128	M2
Brecon rd W6	152	L15
Brecon rd Enf	9	P13
Brede clo E6	66	J8
Bredgar rd N19	47	V7
Bredhurst clo SE20	110	C15
Bredon rd SE5	90	M7
Bredon rd Croy	123	U17
Breer st SW6	88	A7
Breezers hill E1	151	U10
Brember rd Har	41	N7
Bremner rd SW7	146	E20
Brenchley clo Brom	126	D14
Brenchley clo Chis	127	X1
Brenchley gdns SE23	92	C16
Brenda rd SW17	106	L5
Brendon ave NW10	44	B13
Brendon clo Erith	99	R2
Brendon gdns Har	40	K11
Brendon gdns Ilf	36	J15
Brendon rd SE9	114	D4
Brendon rd Dag	56	D4
Brendon st W1	146	M3
Brendon way Enf	18	E2
Brenley clo Mitch	121	R6
Brenley gdns SE9	95	P9
Brent cres NW10	60	M7
Brent Cross Shopping cen NW4	26	M20
Brent grn NW4	27	N15
Brent Green w Wem	43	W9
Brent lea Brent	72	D19
Brent Park rd NW4	44	J2
Brent pl Barn	4	K17
Brent rd E16	65	T16
Brent rd SE18	78	M19
Brent rd Brent	72	F17
Brent rd S Croy	134	A19
Brent st NW4	27	P16
Brent ter NW2	44	L3
Brent View rd NW9	26	G20
Brent way N3	14	K19
Brent way Brent	72	F19
Brent way Wem	43	U16
Brentcot clo W13	60	A12
Brentfield NW10	61	V1
Brentfield clo NW10	43	X17
Brentfield rd NW10	43	V16
Brentham way W5	60	G11
Brenthouse rd E9	50	B19
Brenthurst rd NW10	44	E16
Brentmead clo W7	59	T20
Brentmead gdns NW10	61	N6
Brenton st E14	63	W17
Brentside Brent	72	E17
Brentside clo W13	59	X11
Brentvale ave Sthl	71	P2
Brentvale ave Wem	61	N4
Brentwick gdns Brent	72	J12
Brentwood clo SE9	114	A1
Brentwood rd Rom	39	T19
Brereton rd N17	31	V2
Bressenden pl SW1	156	A1
Bressey ave E18	34	B7
Brett clo N16	49	S7
Brett cres N16	61	Y2
Brett gdns Dag	55	Z19
Brett House clo SW15	87	R17
Brett rd E8	50	A16
Brettell st SE17	158	D18
Brettenham ave E17	33	O5
Brettenham rd E17	33	N6
Brettenham rd N18	18	K13
Brewer st W1	148	D9
Brewery clo Wem	41	Z14
Brewery la Twick	83	X19
Brewery rd N7	47	Z19
Brewery rd SE18	79	S18
Brewery rd Brom	127	S20
Brewhouse la E1	151	Y14
Brewhouse rd SE18	78	G10
Brewhouse st SW15	87	S9
Brewhouse wk SE16	75	V3
Brewood rd Dag	55	R16
Brewster gdns W10	144	B13
Brewster rd E10	51	S4
Brian clo Horn	57	Z11
Brian rd Rom	37	U17
Briant st SE14	75	S20
Briants clo Pnr	22	D6
Briar ave SW16	108	D19
Briar clo N2	28	C8
Briar clo N13	18	A11
Briar clo Hmptn	100	D13
Briar clo Islw	83	X12
Briar ct Sutt	129	N8
Briar cres Nthlt	40	J18
Briar gdns Brom	126	C20
Briar la Cars	131	P20
Briar la Croy	135	R8
Briar pas SW16	122	B7
Briar pl SW16	122	C8
Briar rd NW2	44	M12
Briar rd SW16	122	B7
Briar rd Har	24	C17
Briar rd Twick	101	S2
Briar wk SW15	86	K10
Briar wk Edg	25	W2
Briarbank rd W13	59	Z16
Briardale gdns NW3	45	X10
Briarfield av N3	28	A8
Briars the (Bushey) Wat	10	F3
Briarwood clo NW9	25	W18
Briarwood rd SW4	89	Y12
Briarwood rd Epsom	128	F13
Briary clo NW3	46	J20
Briary ct Sid	115	R11
Briary gdns Brom	112	H12
Briary gro Edg	25	S7
Briary la N9	18	F11
Brick ct EC4	149	S19
Brick Farm clo Rich	85	S3
Brick la E1	143	P16
Brick la E2	143	P15
Brick la Enf	8	M8
Brick la Stan	24	G2
Brick st W1	147	W15
Brickfield clo Brent	72	D19
Brickfield cotts SE18	79	Z17
Brickfield rd E3	64	E11
Brickfield rd SW19	106	B10
Brickfield rd Th Hth	108	J20
Brickfields Har	41	S6
Brickwood clo SE26	110	B7
Brickwood rd Croy	133	R2
Bride la EC4	149	W6
Bride pl Croy	123	P19
Bride st N7	48	D18
Bridewell pl E1	151	Y14
Bridewell pl EC4	149	W7
Bridford ms W1	139	Y19
Bridge the Har	23	U11
Bridge ave W6	152	B8
Bridge ave W7	59	R15
Bridge clo Enf	9	O7
Bridge clo Rom	39	R18
Bridge end E17	33	U5
Bridge la NW11	27	S14
Bridge la SW11	88	K2
Bridge pk SW18	87	Y13
Bridge pl SW1	155	Z5
Bridge rd E6	53	U20
Bridge rd E15	64	K1
Bridge rd E17	50	K1
Bridge rd N22	30	A5
Bridge rd NW10	44	A17
Bridge rd Beck	110	L19
Bridge rd Bexh	98	A6
Bridge rd Erith	99	T3
Bridge rd Houns	83	P6
Bridge rd Islw	83	S8
Bridge rd Sthl	70	E6
Bridge rd Sutt	130	B14
Bridge rd Twick	84	B15

Bridge rd Wall	131	U12
Bridge rd Wem	43	R9
Bridge st W4	73	X11
Bridge st Pnr	22	A10
Bridge st Rich	84	G14
Bridge ter E15	64	K1
Bridge vw W6	152	B9
Bridge way N13	17	S14
Bridge way NW11	27	V16
Bridge way Twick	83	N19
Bridge way Wem	42	L19
Bridge yd SE1	150	H13
Bridgefield rd Sutt	129	X14
Bridgefoot SE1	156	L13
Bridgeford st SW18	106	D6
Bridgeland rd E16	65	U19
Bridgeman rd N1	141	O1
Bridgeman rd W4	73	V8
Bridgeman rd Tedd	101	X14
Bridgeman st NW8	138	J9
Bridgen rd Bex	97	Z17
Bridgend rd SW18	88	C9
Bridgenhall rd Enf	8	H4
Bridgeport pl E1	151	L12
Bridges ct SW11	88	F6
Bridges la Croy	132	A8
Bridges rd SW19	106	A16
Bridges rd Stan	10	J16
Bridgewater gdns Edg	24	L7
Bridgewater rd Wem	42	D18
Bridgewater sq EC2	142	A19
Bridgewater st EC2	142	B20
Bridgeway Bark	67	Y1
Bridgeway st NW1	140	D10
Bridgewood clo SE20	109	Z19
Bridgewood rd SW16	107	X18
Bridgewood rd Wor Pk	128	H9
Bridgwater rd E15	64	G3
Bridle clo Kings T	116	H9
Bridle la W1	148	D8
Bridle path Croy	132	A2
Bridle path Wdf Grn	34	A1
Bridle rd Croy	135	N7
Bridle way Croy	135	O10
Bridle way the Wall	131	W10
Bridlington rd N9	19	N2
Bridport ave Rom	38	G19
Bridport pl N1	142	G4
Bridport rd N18	18	E17
Bridport rd Grnf	58	J3
Bridport rd Th Hth	122	G6
Bridstow pl W2	145	V5
Brief st SE5	90	H3
Brierley rd Croy	135	R15
Brierley ave N9	19	R5
Brierley clo SE25	123	V9
Brierley rd E11	51	X11
Brierley rd SW12	107	V18
Brierly gdns E2	63	R7
Brig ms SE8	76	B16
Brigade clo Har	41	P6
Brigadier ave Enf	8	A4
Brigadier hill Enf	7	Z3
Briggeford clo E5	49	X7
Bright clo Belv	80	K10
Bright st E14	64	F16
Brightfield rd SE12	94	B12
Brightling rd SE4	92	M16
Brightlingsea pl E14	63	X20
Brighton ave E17	32	L16
Brighton dr Nthlt	40	H18
Brighton gro SE14	92	H1
Brighton rd E6	66	K8
Brighton rd N2	28	D8
Brighton rd N16	49	T12
Brighton rd S Croy	132	M20
Brighton rd Surb	116	F14
Brighton rd Sutt	130	C14
Brighton ter SW9	90	D10
Brightside the Enf	9	U5
Brightside rd SE13	93	Y16
Brightwell cres SW17	106	L13
Brigstock rd Belv	81	U10
Brigstock rd Th Hth	122	G12
Brill pl NW1	140	G10
Brim hill N2	28	F13
Brimpsfield clo SE2	80	D9
Brimsdown ave Enf	9	W9
Brimsdown Industrial est Enf	9	Y7
Brindley st SE14	92	L3
Brindley way Brom	112	G14
Brindley way Sthl	58	K19
Brindwood rd E4	20	A9
Brinkburn clo SE2	80	B10
Brinkburn clo Edg	25	S8
Brinkburn gdns Edg	25	P9
Brinkley rd Wor Pk	128	J3
Brinklow cres SE18	79	N19
Brinkworth rd Ilf	35	R9
Brinsdale rd NW4	27	O11
Brinsley rd Har	23	P6
Brinsley st E1	151	Z7
Brinsworth clo Twick	101	R3
Brion pl E14	64	G14
Brisbane ave SW19	106	A20
Brisbane rd E10	51	S8
Brisbane rd Ilf	54	A1
Brisbane st SE5	158	F18
Briscoe clo E11	52	C8
Briscoe rd SW19	106	G15
Briset rd SE9	95	O9
Briset st EC1	141	X19
Briset way N7	48	L19
Bristol gdns W9	137	Z20
Bristol ms W9	138	A19
Bristol rd E7	53	N18
Bristol rd Grnf	58	K3
Bristol rd Mord	120	C11
Bristow rd SE19	109	R13
Bristow rd Bexh	98	A3
Bristow rd Croy	132	A9
Bristow rd Houns	82	L9
Britannia clo SW4	89	Y11
Britannia rd N12	15	S12
Britannia rd SW6	153	X18
Britannia rd Ilf	53	Z10
Britannia rd Surb	117	N16
Britannia row N1	142	A4
Britannia st WC1	141	N12
Britannia wk N1	142	E12
Britannia way NW10	61	T10
British gro W4	74	E12
British Grove pas W4	74	E14
British Legion rd E4	21	O6
British st E3	63	Z10
Brittain rd Dag	56	A9
Britten clo NW11	46	A3
Britten dr Sthl	58	G18
Britten st SW3	154	L10
Britten's ct E1	151	V9
Britton st EC1	141	W19
Brixham gdns Ilf	54	J14
Brixham rd Well	97	W3
Brixham st E16	78	H3
Brixton est Edg	25	S7
Brixton hill SW2	90	C16
Brixton rd SW9	157	T19
Brixton Station rd SW9	90	F9
Brixton Water la SW2	90	F14
Broad Green ave Croy	122	J17
Broad la N15	31	V14
Broad la Hmptn	100	D17
Broad Lawn SE9	113	X2
Broad Oak Wdf Grn	21	W16
Broad Oak clo E4	20	C17
Broad Sanctuary SW1	148	H19
Broad st Dag	56	E20
Broad st Tedd	101	V14
Broad Street ave EC2	150	J3
Broad vw NW9	25	P19
Broad wk N21	17	P7
Broad wk NW1	139	V10
Broad wk SE3	94	M6
Broad wk W1	147	S12
Broad wk Houns	82	A3
Broad wk Rich	72	M18
Broad wk the W8	146	A15
Broad Walk la NW11	45	W1
Broad yd EC1	141	W19
Broadbent clo N6	47	R3
Broadbent st W1	147	X9
Broadbridge clo SE3	77	T19
Broadcoombe S Croy	134	D17
Broadcroft ave Stan	24	G7
Broadfield clo NW2	44	L10
Broadfield clo Rom	39	U16
Broadfield ct (Bushey) Wat	10	E7
Broadfield heights Edg	12	E13
Broadfield la NW1	140	J1
Broadfield rd SE6	93	Z19
Broadfield sq Enf	9	N10
Broadfield way Buck H	21	Y12
Broadfields Har	22	L6
Broadfields ave N21	17	T1
Broadfields ave Edg	12	E12
Broadfields way NW10	44	D14
Broadgate rd E16	66	B16
Broadgates ave Barn	5	D7
Broadhead strand NW9	26	D6
Broadheath dr Chis	113	U12
Broadhinton rd SW4	89	T7
Broadhurst ave Edg	12	E12
Broadhurst ave Ilf	54	L13
Broadhurst clo NW6	46	C18
Broadhurst gdns NW6	46	D18
Broadhurst wk Rain	57	W18
Broadlands the Felt	100	F8
Broadlands ave E5	108	A5
Broadlands ave Enf	9	O11
Broadlands clo N6	29	O20
Broadlands clo SW16	107	Z6
Broadlands clo Enf	9	O11
Broadlands rd N6	29	O20
Broadlands rd Brom	112	H11
Broadlands way N Mal	118	D15
Broadlawns ct Har	23	W5
Broadley st NW8	138	J20
Broadley ter NW1	138	L18
Broadmead SE6	111	O6
Broadmead ave Wor Pk	118	F18
Broadmead clo Hmptn	100	H16
Broadmead clo Pnr	22	C1
Broadmead est Wdf Grn	34	L2
Broadmead rd Hayes	58	B12
Broadmead rd Nthlt	58	D9
Broadmead rd Wdf Grn	21	T18
Broadoaks way Brom	126	B11
Broadstone Ho Horn	57	X7
Broadview rd SW16	107	W17
Broadwalk E18	34	B9
Broadwall SE1	149	U17
Broadwater rd N17	31	T5
Broadwater rd SE28	79	R9
Broadwater rd SW17	106	H10
Broadway E15	51	Y20
Broadway SW1	156	F1
Broadway Bark	67	P2
Broadway Bexh	98	D10
Broadway Grnf	59	N11
Broadway Rom	39	W8
Broadway the E4	20	J19
Broadway the E13	65	U6
Broadway the N8	29	Z18
Broadway the N9	18	K10
Broadway the NW7	13	O17
Broadway the SW19	105	X17
Broadway the W5	60	H19
Broadway the W13	71	V2
Broadway the Dag	56	D5
Broadway the Epsom	128	F12
Broadway the Har	23	U6
Broadway the Horn	57	Y12
Broadway the Pnr	22	D3
Broadway the Sthl	70	B1
Broadway the Stan	11	R15
Broadway the Sutt	129	T14
Broadway the Wem	42	L16
Broadway the Wdf Grn	21	W18
Broadway ave Croy	123	O13
Broadway ave Twick	84	B16
Broadway clo Wdf Grn	21	W18
Broadway ct SW19	105	W16
Broadway gdns Mitch	120	K8
Broadway mkt E8	143	V5
Broadway ms E5	49	U1
Broadwick st W1	148	C7
Brocas clo NW3	46	K20
Brock pl E3	64	D12
Brock rd E13	65	W13
Brock st SE15	92	B7
Brockdish ave Bark	54	K15
Brockenhurst ave Wor Pk	118	B19
Brockenhurst gdns NW7	13	P17
Brockenhurst gdns Ilf	54	B14
Brockenhurst rd Croy	124	A18
Brockenhurst way SW16	121	Z3
Brockham clo SW19	105	V13
Brockham cres Croy	135	X16
Brockham dr SW2	90	C18
Brockham dr Ilf	36	B17
Brockham st SE1	158	C1
Brockhurst clo Stan	10	H17
Brockill cres SE4	92	H9
Brocklebank rd SE7	77	U11
Brocklebank rd SW18	88	D18
Brocklehurst st SE14	75	T18
Brocklesby rd SE25	123	Z10
Brockley ave Stan	11	X11
Brockley clo Stan	11	X14
Brockley cres Rom	38	K2
Brockley footpath SE15	92	C9
Brockley gro SE4	92	K14
Brockley Hall rd SE4	92	K15
Brockley hill Stan	11	S5
Brockley ms SE4	92	H14
Brockley pk SE23	92	J20
Brockley ri SE23	110	H1
Brockley rd SE4	92	K8
Brockley vw SE23	92	K15
Brockley way SE4	92	G12
Brockleyside Stan	11	W13
Brockman ri Brom	111	W10
Brocks dr Sutt	129	S7
Brockshot clo Brent	72	F15
Brockton clo Rom	39	U11
Brockway clo E11	52	A5
Brockwell Park gdns SE24	90	H19
Brockworth clo SE15	158	K16
Broderick gro SE2	80	D11
Brodia rd N16	49	S8
Brodie rd E4	20	H6
Brodie rd Enf	7	Z3
Brodie st SE1	159	P10
Brodlove la E1	63	S19
Brodrick rd SW17	106	K3
Brograve gdns Beck	125	S4
Broke wk E8	143	S4
Brokesley st E3	63	Z10
Bromar rd SE5	91	T7
Brome rd SE9	95	U8
Bromefield Stan	24	F3
Bromehead st E1	151	Z5
Bromell's rd SW4	89	V10
Bromfelde rd SW4	89	Y6
Bromfelde wk SW4	89	Z5
Bromfield st N1	141	U7
Bromhall rd Dag	55	R17
Bromhedge SE9	113	U6
Bromholm rd SE2	80	C9
Bromley ave Brom	112	A19
Bromley common Brom	126	K10
Bromley cres Brom	126	C5
Bromley gdns Brom	126	C5
Bromley gro Brom	125	X5
Bromley Hall rd E14	64	G14
Bromley High st E3	64	D8

Name	Map	Ref
Bromley hill Brom	111	Y14
Bromley la Chis	114	D18
Bromley rd E10	33	S19
Bromley rd E17	33	O9
Bromley rd N17	31	W3
Bromley rd N18	18	C12
Bromley rd SE6	93	R20
Bromley av Beck	125	V3
Bromley av (BR1) Brom	111	X11
Bromley av (BR2) Brom	125	V3
Bromley rd Chis	114	A19
Bromley st E1	63	U17
Brompton clo SE20	123	Y3
Brompton clo Houns	82	E13
Brompton gro N2	28	K13
Brompton Park cres SW6	153	X16
Brompton pl SW3	155	N1
Brompton rd SW3	147	N20
Brompton sq SW3	154	L1
Bromwich av N6	47	R8
Bromyard av W3	62	C20
Brondesbury ms NW6	137	T2
Brondesbury pk NW2	44	L19
Brondesbury pk NW6	136	J1
Brondesbury rd NW6	137	O8
Brondesbury vill NW6	137	P8
Bronsart rd SW6	152	K18
Bronson rd SW20	119	R3
Bronte clo Ilf	35	Y14
Bronti clo SE17	158	D10
Bronze st SE8	76	C18
Brook av Dag	56	J20
Brook av Edg	12	E17
Brook av Wem	43	O8
Brook clo SW20	118	K8
Brook clo Chis	127	W1
Brook clo Rom	39	U5
Brook cres E4	20	C12
Brook cres N9	18	M13
Brook dr SE11	157	U3
Brook dr Har	23	N12
Brook gdns E4	20	D13
Brook gdns SW13	86	E6
Brook gdns Kings T	103	U20
Brook grn W6	152	E3
Brook la SE3	94	J4
Brook la Bex	97	W15
Brook la Brom	112	E14
Brook Lane north Brent	72	G14
Brook mead Epsom	128	C15
Brook meadow N12	15	N12
Brook Mews north W2	146	E8
Brook pl Barn	4	K16
Brook rd N8	30	A11
Brook rd N22	30	D9
Brook rd NW2	44	E6
Brook rd Buck H	21	S7
Brook rd Ilf	36	H19
Brook rd Rom	39	V5
Brook rd Th Hth	122	L8
Brook rd Twick	83	Z15
Brook Road south Brent	72	H15
Brook st W1	147	W8
Brook st W2	146	H8
Brook st Belv	81	U13
Brook st Erith	98	K1
Brook st Kings T	116	J5
Brook wk N2	28	G4
Brook wk Edg	12	K19
Brookbank av W7	59	R13
Brookbank rd SE13	93	P8
Brookdale N11	16	G13
Brookdale rd E17	33	O10
Brookdale rd SE6	93	R16
Brookdale rd Bex	98	A17
Brookdene rd SE18	79	X11
Brooke av Har	41	O8
Brooke clo (Bushey) Wat	10	A3
Brooke rd E5	49	Z9
Brooke rd E17	33	V13
Brooke rd N16	49	V9
Brooke st EC1	149	T2
Brookehowse rd SE6	111	P5
Brookend rd Sid	114	H2
Brookfield N6	47	O9
Brookfield av E17	33	U13
Brookfield av NW7	13	Y19
Brookfield av Beck	60	H11
Brookfield av Sutt	130	H8
Brookfield clo NW7	13	Y20
Brookfield ct Grnf	59	O8
Brookfield ct Har	24	H15
Brookfield cres NW7	13	X20
Brookfield cres Har	24	J15
Brookfield pk NW5	47	R8
Brookfield path Wdf Grn	20	L19
Brookfield rd E9	50	J18
Brookfield rd N9	18	L11
Brookfield rd W4	73	Z7
Brookfields Enf	9	U13
Brookfields ave Mitch	120	J11
Brookhill clo SE18	78	L14
Brookhill clo Barn	5	W17
Brookhill rd SE18	78	M12
Brookhill rd Barn	5	W17
Brookhouse gdns E4	20	M14
Brooking rd E7	52	G14
Brookland clo NW11	27	Z13
Brookland garth NW11	27	Z12
Brookland hill NW11	27	Z13
Brookland ri NW11	27	Z13
Brooklands app Rom	39	N12
Brooklands ave SW19	106	A4
Brooklands av Sid	114	G4
Brooklands dr Grnf	60	F4
Brooklands la Rom	39	N12
Brooklands pk SE3	94	F8
Brooklands rd Rom	39	N13
Brooklands st SW8	89	X1
Brooklea clo NW9	26	B3
Brooklyn av SE25	124	B8
Brooklyn clo Cars	130	J3
Brooklyn gro SE25	124	A8
Brooklyn rd SE25	124	A8
Brooklyn rd Brom	127	P11
Brookmead av Brom	127	U12
Brookmead rd Croy	121	W15
Brookmill rd SE8	93	P2
Brooks av E6	66	G11
Brooks clo SE9	113	Y5
Brooks la W4	73	R16
Brook's ms W1	147	X8
Brooks rd E13	65	T4
Brooks rd W4	73	R15
Brooksbank st E9	50	E18
Brooksby st N1	48	F20
Brooksby's wk E9	50	F14
Brookscroft rd E17	33	R5
Brookshill Har	10	D14
Brookshill av Har	10	E16
Brookshill dr Har	10	C15
Brookside N21	7	R20
Brookside Barn	5	X19
Brookside Cars	131	O10
Brookside clo Barn	4	D19
Brookside clo Har	40	C11
Brookside clo (Kenton) Har	24	H15
Brookside rd N9	18	M12
Brookside rd N19	47	W7
Brookside rd NW11	27	T18
Brookside south Barn	16	C2
Brookside wk N3	27	S6
Brookside wk N12	14	L17
Brookside wk NW4	27	U13
Brookside wk NW11	27	U13
Brookside way Croy	124	F14
Brooksville av NW6	136	L6
Brookvale Erith	98	J1
Brookview rd SW16	107	U11
Brookville rd SW6	153	O19
Brookway SE3	94	E9
Brookwood av SW13	86	E6
Brookwood clo Brom	126	B10
Brookwood rd SW18	105	X2
Brookwood rd Houns	82	K3
Broom clo Brom	127	T15
Broom clo Tedd	102	F17
Broom gdns Croy	135	O6
Broom Lock Tedd	102	E14
Broom mead Bexh	98	F14
Broom pk Tedd	102	G18
Broom rd Croy	135	O6
Broom rd Tedd	102	B12
Broom water Tedd	102	D14
Broom Water west Tedd	102	D14
Broome rd Hmptn	100	E19
Broome way SE5	158	E19
Broomfield E17	32	M20
Broomfield av N13	17	P16
Broomfield la N13	17	O14
Broomfield rd N13	17	O16
Broomfield rd W13	72	C1
Broomfield rd Beck	124	K8
Broomfield rd Bexh	98	G14
Broomfield rd Rich	85	N1
Broomfield rd Rom	55	W1
Broomfield rd Surb	117	O19
Broomfield st E14	64	C15
Broomgrove gdns Edg	25	P4
Broomgrove rd SW9	90	D6
Broomhall rd S Croy	133	O19
Broomhill ri Bexh	98	F14
Broomhill rd SW18	87	Y14
Broomhill rd Dart	99	Y16
Broomhill rd Ilf	55	O5
Broomhill wk Wdf Grn	21	S20
Broomhill wk Wdf Grn	21	R20
Broomhouse la SW6	87	X6
Broomhouse rd SW6	87	X4
Broomloan la Sutt	129	Y4
Broomsleigh st NW6	45	W15
Broomwood rd SW11	104	J10
Broseley gro SE26	110	H12
Broster gdns SE25	123	U6
Brough clo SW8	156	L19
Brougham rd E8	143	T3
Brougham rd W3	61	W18
Broughton av N3	27	S10
Broughton av Rich	102	G18
Broughton dr SW9	90	H10
Broughton gdns N6	29	V18
Broughton rd SW6	88	B4
Broughton rd W13	60	C20
Broughton rd Th Hth	122	E13
Broughton st SW8	89	R4
Brouncker rd W3	73	V6
Brown clo Wall	131	Z17
Brown Hart gdns W1	147	U7
Brown st W1	147	N4
Brownfield st E14	64	F17
Brownhill rd SE6	93	U19
Browning av W7	59	W16
Browning av Sutt	130	J9
Browning av Wor Pk	118	J19
Browning clo W9	138	D17
Browning clo Hmptn	100	E10
Browning clo Well	96	J3
Browning est SE17	158	C9
Browning ms W1	147	W2
Browning rd E11	52	C2
Browning rd E12	53	U15
Browning rd Enf	8	A1
Browning st SE17	158	C8
Brownlow ms WC1	141	P17
Brownlow rd E8	143	R3
Brownlow rd N3	28	A1
Brownlow rd N11	16	M20
Brownlow rd NW10	44	B20
Brownlow rd W13	71	Z2
Brownlow rd Croy	133	S8
Brownlow st WC1	149	P1
Brown's bldgs EC3	150	K6
Browns la NW5	47	R16
Browns rd E17	33	O11
Browns rd Surb	116	M17
Brownspring dr SE9	114	B8
Brownswell rd N2	28	F7
Brownswood rd N4	48	L7
Broxash rd SW11	89	P14
Broxbourne av E18	34	H12
Broxbourne rd E7	52	E10
Broxholm rd SE27	108	F8
Broxted rd SE6	110	L4
Broxwood way NW8	138	M6
Bruce Castle rd N17	31	U4
Bruce clo W10	136	J20
Bruce clo Well	97	R2
Bruce dr S Croy	134	F20
Bruce gdns N20	15	Z10
Bruce gro N17	31	T6
Bruce rd E3	64	D9
Bruce rd NW10	61	Z1
Bruce rd SE25	123	P8
Bruce rd Har	23	T7
Bruce rd Mitch	107	N17
Bruckner st W10	137	N12
Brudenell rd SW17	107	N8
Bruffs meadow Nthlt	40	C18
Bruges pl NW1	140	C1
Brummell clo Bexh	98	J8
Brune st E1	151	N2
Brunel clo SE19	109	T16
Brunel clo Nthlt	58	D9
Brunel est W2	145	T2
Brunel pl Sthl	58	K18
Brunel rd SE16	75	P6
Brunel rd W3	62	B15
Brunel rd E16	65	P17
Brunel wk N15	31	R14
Brunel wk Twick	82	G18
Brunner clo NW11	28	C16
Brunner rd E17	32	K16
Brunner rd W5	60	F11
Bruno pl Wem	43	V6
Brunswick av N11	16	B11
Brunswick clo Bexh	97	X10
Brunswick clo Pnr	22	C19
Brunswick clo Twick	101	P7
Brunswick ct SE1	150	L17
Brunswick ct Barn	5	U16
Brunswick cres N11	16	B11
Brunswick gdns W5	60	K10
Brunswick gdns W8	145	W14
Brunswick gdns Ilf	36	B1
Brunswick gro N11	16	B11
Brunswick ms W1	147	P5
Brunswick pk SE5	91	R2
Brunswick Park gdns N11	16	B8
Brunswick Park rd N11	16	B6
Brunswick pl N1	142	F14
Brunswick pl SE19	109	W17
Brunswick quay SE16	75	U9
Brunswick rd E10	51	U4
Brunswick rd E14	64	H17
Brunswick rd N15	31	S14
Brunswick rd W5	60	G11
Brunswick rd Bexh	97	X10
Brunswick rd Kings T	103	P20
Brunswick rd Sutt	130	C8
Brunswick sq N17	18	H20
Brunswick sq WC1	140	L16
Brunswick st E17	33	T15
Brunswick vill SE5	158	J20
Brunswick way N11	16	E13
Brushfield st E1	151	N1
Brussels rd SW11	88	G11
Bruton clo Chis	113	T19
Bruton la W1	147	Z11
Bruton pl W1	147	Y10
Bruton rd Mord	120	D11
Bruton st W1	147	Y10
Bruton way W13	59	Y14
Bryan av NW10	136	A1
Bryan rd SE16	75	X5
Bryanston av Twick	82	L20
Bryanston clo Sthl	70	F19
Bryanston Mews east W1	147	P3
Bryanston Mews west W1	147	O3
Bryanston pl W1	147	N2
Bryanston sq W1	147	P3
Bryanston st W1	147	P7

Name	Page	Grid
Bryanstone rd N8	29	Z17
Bryant clo Barn	4	J17
Bryant st E15	64	L1
Bryantwood rd N7	48	F14
Bryce rd Dag	55	U12
Brycedale cres N14	16	J12
Bryden clo SE26	110	H12
Brydges rd E15	51	Y14
Bryett rd N7	48	B8
Brymay clo E3	64	C6
Bryn-y-Mawr rd Enf	8	J13
Brynmaer rd SW11	88	M3
Bryony rd W12	62	H20
Buchan rd SE15	92	D7
Buchanan gdns NW10	136	A9
Bucharest rd SW18	88	D18
Buck la NW9	25	X16
Buckden clo SE12	94	D15
Buckfast st E2	143	T14
Buckhold rd SW18	87	Y16
Buckhurst ave Cars	130	K1
Buckhurst st E1	143	Z18
Buckingham ave N20	15	S3
Buckingham ave Grnf	59	Z3
Buckingham ave Th Hth	122	F2
Buckingham ave Well	96	H11
Buckingham clo W5	60	C13
Buckingham clo Enf	8	E8
Buckingham clo Hmptn	100	E12
Buckingham ct NW4	26	H8
Buckingham dr Chis	114	B11
Buckingham gdns Edg	24	L2
Buckingham gdns Th Hth	122	G2
Buckingham gate SW1	148	A20
Buckingham ms NW10	62	E6
Buckingham ms SW1	148	B20
Buckingham Palace rd SW1	155	X6
Buckingham rd E10	51	S9
Buckingham rd E11	34	K14
Buckingham rd E15	52	B14
Buckingham rd E18	34	D6
Buckingham rd N1	49	R18
Buckingham rd N22	30	A5
Buckingham rd NW10	62	E6
Buckingham rd Edg	24	L2
Buckingham rd Hmptn	100	D11
Buckingham rd Har	23	R15
Buckingham rd Ilf	54	F6
Buckingham rd Kings T	117	N8
Buckingham rd Mitch	122	A10
Buckingham rd Rich	102	G4
Buckingham st WC2	148	L11
Buckingham way Wall	131	V20
Buckland cres NW3	46	F19
Buckland rd E10	51	T6
Buckland st N1	142	H9
Buckland wk Mord	120	C10
Buckland way Wor Pk	118	M20
Bucklands rd Tedd	102	E15
Buckle st E1	151	R5
Buckleigh ave SW20	119	U6
Buckleigh rd SW16	107	Z16
Buckleigh way SE19	109	U20
Buckler gdns SE9	113	V8
Bucklers way Cars	131	O5
Bucklersbury EC4	150	E6
Buckles ct Belv	80	K10
Buckley clo Dart	99	U6
Buckley rd NW6	137	P2
Buckmaster rd SW11	88	J11
Bucknall st WC2	148	H5
Bucknell clo SW2	90	D10
Buckrell rd E4	20	K9
Buckstone clo SE23	92	D16
Buckstone rd N18	18	K18
Buckters rents SE16	75	W2
Buckthorne rd SE4	92	J15
Budd clo N12	15	O13
Buddings circ Wem	43	V9
Budge's wk W2	146	D12
Budleigh cres Well	80	G20
Budoch dr Ilf	55	N7
Buer rd SW6	87	U5
Bugsby's way SE7	77	W11
Bugsby's way SE10	77	P10
Bulganak rd Th Hth	122	L8
Bulinga st SW1	156	H6
Bull all Well	97	R7
Bull la N18	18	E16
Bull la Chis	114	E19
Bull la Dag	56	G8
Bull rd E15	65	P5
Bull Wharf la EC4	150	C9
Bullards pl E2	63	S8
Bullbanks rd Belv	81	X10
Bullen st SW11	88	J4
Buller clo SE15	159	S19
Buller rd N17	31	X8
Buller rd N22	30	E7
Buller rd NW10	136	G13
Buller rd Bark	54	G20
Buller rd Th Hth	123	O5
Bullers clo Sid	115	Y13
Bullers Wood dr Chis	113	T19
Bullescroft rd Edg	12	D10
Bullied way SW1	155	Y6
Bullivant st E14	64	G18
Bull's all SW14	85	X6
Bulls gdns SW3	154	M5
Bulmer gdns Har	24	F20
Bulmer pl W11	145	T12
Bulstrode ave Houns	82	E6
Bulstrode gdns Houns	82	E4
Bulstrode pl W1	147	V3
Bulstrode rd Houns	82	G7
Bulstrode st W1	147	V3
Bulwer Court rd E11	51	X3
Bulwer gdns Barn	5	R13
Bulwer rd E11	51	W2
Bulwer rd N18	18	E14
Bulwer rd Barn	5	O14
Bulwer st W12	144	D15
Bunces la Wdf Grn	34	C1
Bungalow rd SE25	123	S10
Bungalows the SW16	107	T17
Bungalows the Wall	131	S12
Bunhill row EC1	142	E16
Bunhouse pl SW1	155	U8
Bunkers hill NW11	46	C1
Bunkers hill Belv	81	T11
Bunning way N7	48	B20
Bunns la NW7	13	O17
Bunting clo Mitch	120	M12
Buntingbridge rd Ilf	36	D16
Bunyan rd E17	32	J10
Burbage clo SE1	158	F2
Burbage rd SE21	91	R18
Burbage rd SE24	90	M15
Burberry clo N Mal	117	Z4
Burbridge way N17	31	W8
Burcham st E14	64	F17
Burcharbro rd SE2	80	H16
Burchell ct (Bushey) Wat	10	A3
Burchell rd E10	51	R3
Burchell rd SE15	92	A2
Burchett way Rom	38	B18
Burchwall clo Rom	38	J2
Burcote rd SW18	88	H20
Burden clo Brent	72	E14
Burden way E11	52	J5
Burdenshott ave Rich	85	S9
Burder clo N1	49	T17
Burdett ave SW20	104	F20
Burdett clo Sid	115	Z13
Burdett ms W2	145	X5
Burdett rd E3	63	X11
Burdett rd E14	63	Z15
Burdett rd Croy	123	P15
Burdett rd Rich	85	O6
Burdett st SE1	149	T20
Burdetts rd Dag	69	O3
Burdock clo Croy	134	F1
Burdock rd N17	31	Y10
Burdon la Sutt	129	T17
Burdon pk Sutt	129	U18
Burfield clo SW17	106	E9
Burford clo Dag	55	V10
Burford clo Ilf	36	B12
Burford gdns N13	17	S9
Burford rd E15	64	K2
Burford rd SE6	110	M5
Burford rd Brent	72	J15
Burford rd Brom	127	R10
Burford rd Sutt	129	Y4
Burford rd Wor Pk	118	E18
Burford wk SW6	154	A20
Burford way Croy	135	V15
Burgate clo Dart	99	T7
Burge st SE1	158	G3
Burges ct E6	53	X20
Burges rd E6	66	E1
Burgess ave NW9	25	X18
Burgess clo Felt	100	A9
Burgess hill NW2	45	X11
Burgess rd E15	51	Y13
Burgess rd Sutt	129	Z9
Burgess st E14	64	A14
Burgh st N1	141	Z8
Burghill rd SE26	110	H9
Burghley ave N Mal	117	Z1
Burghley pl Mitch	121	N11
Burghley rd E11	52	A3
Burghley rd N8	30	F10
Burghley rd NW5	47	T14
Burghley rd SW19	105	R9
Burgon st EC4	149	Y7
Burgos gro SE10	93	R1
Burgoyne rd N4	30	H18
Burgoyne rd SE25	123	V9
Burgoyne rd SW9	90	D7
Burhill gro Pnr	22	B6
Burke clo SW15	86	B10
Burke st E16	65	P16
Burland rd SW11	88	M14
Burleigh ave Sid	96	L13
Burleigh ave Wall	131	R6
Burleigh gdns N14	16	H5
Burleigh pl SW15	87	P13
Burleigh rd Enf	8	E14
Burleigh rd Sutt	119	T19
Burleigh st WC2	149	N9
Burleigh wk SE6	111	V1
Burley clo E4	20	A17
Burley clo SW16	121	Y3
Burley rd E16	65	Y16
Burlington arc W1	148	B11
Burlington ave Rich	85	P2
Burlington ave Rom	38	J17
Burlington clo E6	66	E16
Burlington clo W9	137	S17
Burlington gdns W1	148	A10
Burlington gdns W3	73	X3
Burlington gdns W4	73	W14
Burlington gdns Rom	56	A1
Burlington la W4	74	A18
Burlington ms W3	73	W3
Burlington pl SW6	87	U5
Burlington pl Wdf Grn	21	U11
Burlington ri Barn	15	X4
Burlington rd N10	29	O9
Burlington rd N17	31	X5
Burlington rd SW6	87	T5
Burlington rd W4	73	U13
Burlington rd Enf	8	A4
Burlington rd Islw	83	O2
Burlington rd N Mal	118	C10
Burlington rd Th Hth	123	N4
Burma ms N16	49	N11
Burma rd N16	49	O12
Burmester rd SW17	106	D8
Burn side N9	19	R9
Burnaby cres W4	73	U16
Burnaby gdns W4	73	U15
Burnaby st SW10	154	D19
Burnbrae clo N12	15	O19
Burnbury rd SW12	107	V1
Burncroft ave Enf	9	R9
Burne st NW1	146	K1
Burnell ave Rich	102	D11
Burnell ave Well	97	N4
Burnell gdns Stan	24	F6
Burnell rd Sutt	130	B8
Burnels ave E6	66	J10
Burnett clo E9	50	D15
Burney ave Surb	116	M12
Burney st SE10	76	H18
Burnfoot ave SW6	87	T3
Burnham clo Enf	8	E3
Burnham ct NW4	27	N12
Burnham cres E11	34	K14
Burnham dr Wor Pk	129	O4
Burnham gdns Croy	123	V18
Burnham rd E4	19	X16
Burnham rd Dag	68	D2
Burnham rd Mord	120	B10
Burnham rd Rom	38	M11
Burnham rd Sid	115	Y5
Burnham st E2	63	P8
Burnham st Kings T	117	P1
Burnham way W13	72	A9
Burnhill rd Beck	125	O3
Burnley rd NW10	44	E15
Burnley rd SW9	90	C4
Burns ave Sid	97	P16
Burns ave Sthl	58	G19
Burns clo SW19	106	F15
Burns clo Erith	99	U2
Burns clo Well	96	K3
Burns rd NW10	62	C3
Burns rd SW11	88	L4
Burns rd W13	72	A5
Burns rd Wem	60	J6
Burnsall st SW3	154	M10
Burnside clo SE16	75	U2
Burnside clo Barn	4	L12
Burnside clo Twick	83	X15
Burnside cres Wem	60	G2
Burnside rd Dag	55	U7
Burnt Ash hill SE12	94	D17
Burnt Ash la Brom	112	H11
Burnt Ash rd SE12	94	D13
Burnt Oak bdy Edg	25	S2
Burnt Oak flds Edg	25	V4
Burnt Oak la Sid	96	M16
Burnthwaite rd SW6	153	S19
Burntwood clo SW18	106	H2
Burntwood Grange rd SW18	106	H2
Burntwood la SW17	106	D7
Buross st E1	151	Y5
Burr clo E1	151	S13
Burr clo Bexh	98	C6
Burr rd SW18	87	Z20
Burrage gro SE18	79	O10
Burrage pl SE18	79	N14
Burrage rd SE18	79	O10
Burrard rd E16	65	U16
Burrard rd NW6	45	Y13
Burrell clo Croy	124	K14
Burrell clo Edg	12	G7
Burrell st SE1	149	X13
Burrells Wharf sq E14	76	D13
Burritt rd Kings T	117	R5
Burroughs the NW4	26	J14
Burroughs gdns NW4	26	J13
Burrows ms SE1	149	W16
Burrows rd NW10	136	D11
Burrsdon clo Sid	114	L4
Bursland rd Enf	9	S13
Burslem st E1	151	V6
Burstock rd SW15	87	S10
Burston rd SW15	87	P12
Burstow rd SW20	119	S2
Burt rd E16	77	Z3
Burtley clo N4	48	L3
Burton clo NW7	14	C13
Burton gdns Houns	82	E3
Burton gro SE17	158	F11
Burton la SW9	90	G4
Burton pl WC1	140	H15
Burton rd E18	34	G11
Burton rd NW6	137	P2
Burton rd Kings T	102	L18
Burton st WC1	140	H15
Burtonhole la NW7	14	A15
Burtons rd Hmptn	100	J10
Burtwell la SE27	109	P10
Burwash rd SE18	79	S14
Burwell ave Grnf	41	T18
Burwell clo E1	151	Y6
Burwell rd E10	50	J3

Name	Page	Ref
Burwood pl W2	146	L4
Bury clo SE16	75	T2
Bury ct EC3	150	L5
Bury gro Mord	120	A11
Bury gro WC1	148	K2
Bury rd E4	21	N2
Bury rd N22	30	G8
Bury rd Dag	56	J14
Bury rd EC3	150	L5
Bury st N9	18	H3
Bury st SW1	148	C12
Bury Street west N9	18	C2
Bury wk SW3	154	J7
Busby ms NW5	47	X15
Busby pl NW5	47	X17
Busby st E2	143	R16
Bush clo Ilf	36	F16
Bush Elms rd Horn	57	W1
Bush gro NW9	25	W20
Bush gro Stan	24	F2
Bush hill N21	8	B17
Bush Hill rd N21	8	A20
Bush Hill rd Har	24	M18
Bush Industrial est NW10	61	X10
Bush la EC4	150	E9
Bush rd E8	143	X5
Bush rd SE8	75	T11
Bush rd Rich	73	N16
Bushbaby clo SE1	158	K3
Bushberry rd E9	50	J17
Bushell clo SW2	108	E3
Bushell grn (Bushey) Wat	10	B7
Bushell st E1	151	T14
Bushell way Chis	113	W12
Bushey Hill rd SE5	91	T2
Bushey la Sutt	129	Z7
Bushey Lees Sid	96	K15
Bushey rd E13	65	Y6
Bushey rd N15	31	R18
Bushey rd SW20	118	J7
Bushey rd Croy	135	O3
Bushey rd Sutt	129	Z8
Bushey way Beck	125	W14
Bushfield clo Edg	12	F7
Bushfield cres Edg	12	E8
Bushgrove rd Dag	55	W10
Bushmoor cres SE18	79	O20
Bushnell rd SW17	107	S5
Bushway Dag	55	W10
Bushwood E11	52	C4
Bushwood dr SE1	159	P8
Bushwood rd Rich	73	R17
Bushy Park gdns Tedd	101	R13
Bushy Park rd Tedd	102	C19
Bushy rd Tedd	101	V16
Butcher row E1	63	U19
Butcher row E14	63	U19
Butchers rd E16	65	T18
Bute ave Rich	102	J3
Bute ct Wall	131	U11
Bute gdns W6	152	E6
Bute gdns Wall	131	W11
Bute Gardens west Wall	131	V12
Bute rd Croy	132	G1
Bute rd Ilf	36	A14
Bute rd Wall	131	U8
Bute st SW7	154	G6
Butler ave Har	23	R20
Butler pl SW1	156	E11
Butler rd NW10	44	C20
Butler rd Dag	55	P11
Butler rd Har	23	N20
Butler st E2	63	S8
Butter hill Cars	131	P6
Butter hill Wall	131	P6
Butterfield clo SE16	151	V18
Butterfields E17	33	U16
Butterfly la SE9	95	Z15
Butteridges clo Dag	69	Y8
Buttermere clo Mord	119	O14
Buttermere dr SW15	87	U13
Buttermere wk E8	49	V18
Butterwick W6	152	E7
Butterworth gdns Wdf Grn	21	U17
Buttesland st N1	142	H12
Buttfield clo Dag	56	H18
Buttmarsh clo SE18	79	N12
Butts the Brent	72	F17
Butts cres Felt	100	D7
Butts cotts Felt	100	G7
Butts rd Brom	112	B11
Buttsbury rd Ilf	54	C15
Buxted clo E8	49	U19
Buxted rd N12	15	W16
Buxted rd SE22	91	S8
Buxton cres Sutt	129	S8
Buxton dr E11	34	A13
Buxton dr N Mal	117	Z2
Buxton gdns W3	73	S1
Buxton rd E4	20	K3
Buxton rd E6	66	D8
Buxton rd E15	51	Z15
Buxton rd E17	32	K14
Buxton rd N19	47	Y5
Buxton rd NW2	44	K17
Buxton rd SW14	86	B8
Buxton rd Erith	81	Z18
Buxton rd Ilf	36	G18
Buxton rd Th Hth	122	H13
Buxton st E1	143	S19
Buzzard Creek Industrial est Bark	67	Y13
Byam st SW6	88	C5
Byards cft SW16	121	X2
Bycroft rd Sthl	58	H13
Bycroft st SE20	110	E17
Bycullah ave Enf	7	X10
Bycullah rd Enf	7	V8
Bye the W3	62	B16
Bye way the Har	23	U5
Bye Ways Twick	100	K6
Byegrove rd SW19	106	F16
Byeway the SW14	85	V8
Byeway the Epsom	128	E9
Byeways the Surb	117	R13
Byfeld gdns SW13	86	G2
Byford rd Islw	83	Y8
Byford clo E15	65	N1
Bygrove Croy	135	R16
Bygrove st E14	64	D17
Byland clo N21	17	P1
Byne rd SE26	110	D14
Byne rd Cars	130	J4
Bynes rd S Croy	133	O16
Byng pl WC1	140	G18
Byng rd Barn	4	B10
Byng st E14	76	B5
Bynon ave Bexh	98	A8
Byre the N14	6	D20
Byre rd N14	6	D20
Byrne rd SW12	107	S2
Byron ave E12	53	R18
Byron ave E18	34	B9
Byron ave NW9	25	T11
Byron ave N Mal	118	H12
Byron ave Sutt	130	G9
Byron Avenue east Sutt	130	G9
Byron clo E8	143	S4
Byron clo SE28	80	F2
Byron clo Hmptn	100	E10
Byron ct W9	137	V16
Byron dr N2	28	G18
Byron gdns Sutt	130	G8
Byron Hill rd Har	41	S5
Byron rd E10	51	R3
Byron rd E17	33	P11
Byron rd NW2	44	J8
Byron rd NW7	13	T16
Byron rd W5	73	O1
Byron rd Har	23	U18
Byron rd (Wealdstone) Har	23	V7
Byron rd Wem	42	F9
Byron st E14	64	F16
Byron way Nthlt	58	B10
Bysouth clo Ilf	35	Z5
Bythorn st SW9	90	D9
Byton rd SW17	107	N15
Byward st EC3	150	K10
Bywater pl SE16	75	W2
Bywater st SW3	155	N8
Byway the Sutt	130	G19
Bywell pl W1	148	B3
Bywood ave Croy	124	D14

C

Name	Page	Ref
Cabbell st NW1	146	L2
Cabinet way E4	19	X17
Cable pl SE10	93	V1
Cable st E1	151	T8
Cabot sq E14	76	B2
Cabot way E6	66	B4
Cabul rd SW11	88	J5
Cadbury clo Islw	83	Z1
Caddington clo Barn	5	W17
Caddington rd NW2	45	T9
Caddis clo Stan	23	X1
Cade rd SE10	93	X2
Cadell clo E2	143	P10
Cader rd SW18	88	D17
Cadet dr SE1	159	R8
Cadet pl SE10	76	M13
Cadiz rd Dag	56	L19
Cadiz st SE17	158	D11
Cadley ter SE23	110	C4
Cadmer clo N Mal	118	A10
Cadogan clo Beck	125	X2
Cadogan clo Har	40	L13
Cadogan clo Tedd	101	T13
Cadogan ct Sutt	130	B15
Cadogan gdns E18	34	J9
Cadogan gdns N3	28	A5
Cadogan gdns N21	7	S18
Cadogan gdns SW3	155	P4
Cadogan gate SW1	155	R5
Cadogan la SW1	155	S2
Cadogan pl SW1	155	R1
Cadogan rd Surb	116	G12
Cadogan sq SW1	155	P3
Cadogan st SW3	155	N7
Cadogan ter E9	50	K18
Cadoxton ave N15	31	V18
Cadwallon rd SE9	114	A4
Caedmon rd N7	48	E12
Caerleon clo Sid	115	T13
Caernarvon clo Mitch	122	A7
Caernarvon dr Ilf	35	X4
Caesars wk Mitch	121	N11
Cahill st EC1	142	D17
Cahir st E14	76	D11
Caird st W10	137	N15
Cairn ave W5	72	G4
Cairn way Stan	10	J19
Cairndale clo Brom	112	C17
Cairnfield ave NW2	44	C9
Cairngorm clo Tedd	101	X13
Cairns rd SW11	88	K12
Cairo New rd Croy	132	K3
Cairo rd E17	33	O12
Caistor ms SW12	89	S20
Caistor Park rd E15	65	R3
Caistor rd SW12	89	S18
Caithness gdns Sid	96	K17
Caithness rd W14	152	G4
Caithness rd Mitch	107	S18
Calabria rd N5	48	J17
Calais st SE5	90	K2
Calbourne ave Horn	57	Z14
Calbourne rd SW12	89	N20
Calcott wk SE9	113	P10
Caldbeck ave Wor Pk	128	H2
Caldecot rd SE5	91	N5
Caldecote gdns (Bushey) Wat	10	F1
Caldecott way E5	50	F10
Calder clo Enf	8	D11
Calder gdns Edg	25	P9
Calder rd Mord	120	C11
Calderon pl W10	144	C2
Calderon rd E11	51	W11
Caldervale rd SW4	89	X13
Calderwood st SE18	78	K10
Caldwell st SW9	157	R20
Caldy rd Belv	81	U8
Cale st SW3	154	J9
Caleb st SE1	150	B17
Caledon rd E6	66	F2
Caledon rd Wall	131	R8
Caledonia st N1	140	L19
Caledonian clo Ilf	55	R4
Caledonian rd N1	141	N8
Caledonian rd N7	48	C14
Caledonian Wharf rd E14	76	J11
Caletock way SE10	77	P13
California la (Bushey) Wat	10	D6
California rd N Mal	117	U8
Callaghan clo SE13	93	Z10
Callander rd SE6	111	T5
Callard ave N13	17	W15
Callcott rd NW6	137	P1
Callcott st W8	145	T12
Callendar rd SW7	146	E20
Callis rd E17	32	L18
Callow st SW3	154	E12
Calmington rd SE5	158	L12
Calmont rd Brom	111	Y15
Calne ave Ilf	35	Z5
Calonne rd SW19	105	R10
Calshot st N1	141	O10
Calshot way Enf	7	W11
Calthorpe gdns Edg	11	Y15
Calthorpe gdns Sutt	130	C5
Calthorpe st WC1	141	P17
Calton ave SE21	91	S16
Calton rd Barn	5	S19
Calverley rd Beck	111	R15
Calverley cres Dag	56	E7
Calverley gro N19	47	Y4
Calverley rd Epsom	128	F13
Calvert ave E2	142	M14
Calvert clo Belv	81	T12
Calvert clo Sid	115	Y14
Calvert rd SE10	77	P15
Calvert rd Barn	4	D9
Calvert st NW1	139	T4
Calverton rd E6	66	J2
Calvin st E1	143	N19
Calydon rd SE7	77	W14
Calypso way SE16	75	Y9
Cam rd E15	64	J2
Camac rd Twick	101	R3
Cambalt rd SW15	87	O13
Camberley ave SW20	118	J3
Camberley ave Enf	8	E14
Camberley clo Sutt	129	R5
Cambert way SE3	94	K11
Camberwell Church st SE5	91	N2
Camberwell Glebe SE5	91	R2
Camberwell grn SE5	91	N1
Camberwell gro SE5	91	P3
Camberwell New rd SE5	157	V17
Camberwell rd SE5	158	D17
Camberwell Station rd SE5	90	M2
Cambeys rd Dag	56	K16
Camborne ave W13	72	C5
Camborne ms W11	144	L6
Camborne rd SW18	87	Y18
Camborne rd Croy	123	X18
Camborne rd Mord	119	R12
Camborne rd Sid	115	T7
Camborne rd Sutt	129	Z18
Camborne rd Well	96	J5
Camborne way Houns	82	G2
Cambourne ave N9	19	S3
Cambray rd SW12	107	V1
Cambria clo Houns	82	H11
Cambria clo Sid	114	G1
Cambria rd SE5	90	L7
Cambria st SW6	154	A20
Cambrian ave Ilf	36	H14
Cambrian clo SE27	108	H6
Cambrian rd E10	51	O2
Cambrian rd Rich	84	M17
Cambridge ave NW6	137	O9
Cambridge ave W10	41	V16
Cambridge ave N Mal	118	B5
Cambridge ave Rom	96	K10
Cambridge Barracks rd SE18	78	H12

Name	Page	Grid
Cambridge clo SW20	118	J1
Cambridge clo Houns	82	C10
Cambridge cotts Rich	73	P17
Cambridge cres E2	143	X9
Cambridge cres Tedd	101	Y12
Cambridge dr SE12	94	F14
Cambridge gdns N10	29	R4
Cambridge gdns N13	18	A2
Cambridge gdns N17	18	A20
Cambridge gdns N21	18	A2
Cambridge gdns NW6	137	V9
Cambridge gdns W10	144	H5
Cambridge gdns Enf	8	K8
Cambridge gdns Kings T	117	P4
Cambridge gate NW1	139	Y15
Cambridge Gate ms NW1	139	Y15
Cambridge grn SE9	95	Z20
Cambridge gro SE20	110	A19
Cambridge gro W6	152	A5
Cambridge Grove rd Kings T	117	P6
Cambridge Heath rd E1	143	Z19
Cambridge Heath rd E2	143	Y7
Cambridge pk E11	34	E20
Cambridge pk Twick	34	E17
Cambridge Park rd E11	34	D20
Cambridge pl W8	146	A19
Cambridge rd E4	20	K5
Cambridge rd E11	34	D19
Cambridge rd NW6	137	U12
Cambridge rd SE20	123	Z5
Cambridge rd SW11	88	L3
Cambridge rd SW13	86	D5
Cambridge rd SW20	118	H1
Cambridge rd W7	71	W5
Cambridge rd Bark	54	C20
Cambridge rd Brom	112	F19
Cambridge rd Cars	130	K13
Cambridge rd Hmptn	100	F17
Cambridge rd Houns	82	B10
Cambridge rd Ilf	54	K4
Cambridge rd Kings T	117	O4
Cambridge rd Mitch	121	U7
Cambridge rd N Mal	118	B8
Cambridge rd Rich	73	O18
Cambridge rd Sid	114	H9
Cambridge rd Sthl	70	E2
Cambridge rd Tedd	101	X10
Cambridge rd Twick	84	G15
Cambridge Road north W4	73	S13
Cambridge row SE18	79	N14
Cambridge sq W2	146	K5
Cambridge st SW1	155	Y7
Cambridge ter NW1	139	Y14
Cambridge Terrace ms NW1	139	Y14
Cambus clo Hayes	58	C15
Cambus rd E16	65	T13
Camdale rd E8	79	X18
Camden clo Chis	114	B19
Camden gdns Th Hth	122	J5
Camden gro Chis	114	A16
Camden High st NW1	139	Z4
Camden Hill rd SE19	109	T15
Camden Lock pl NW1	139	X1
Camden ms NW1	141	W9
Camden pas N1	141	W7
Camden rd E11	34	J18
Camden rd E17	32	L17
Camden rd N7	47	Y16
Camden rd NW1	140	A3
Camden rd Bex	98	B19
Camden rd Cars	130	M8
Camden rd Sutt	129	Z12
Camden row SE3	94	A6
Camden sq NW1	47	X19
Camden st NW1	140	A1
Camden ter NW1	47	X18
Camden wk N1	141	X6
Camden way Chis	113	V18
Camden way Th Hth	122	K6
Camdenhurst st E14	63	W16
Camel rd E16	78	C2
Camellia pl Twick	82	K8
Camellia st SW8	156	K20
Camelot clo SE28	79	S7
Camelot clo SW19	105	X10
Camelot st SE15	159	W16
Camera pl SW10	154	E14
Cameron clo N18	19	N14
Cameron clo N20	15	V7
Cameron rd SE6	111	N5
Cameron rd Brom	126	E12
Cameron rd Croy	122	K16
Cameron rd Ilf	54	H4
Cameron sq Mitch	120	H1
Camilla rd SE16	159	V8
Camille clo SE25	123	Y6
Camlan rd Brom	112	D9
Camlet st E2	143	N15
Camlet way Barn	4	K8
Camley st NW1	140	F1
Camomile ave Mitch	120	M1
Camomile st EC3	150	K4
Camp rd SW19	104	J13
Camp vw SW19	104	L13
Campana rd SW6	87	Y2
Campbell ave Ilf	36	B14
Campbell clo SE18	95	X3
Campbell clo SW16	107	X11
Campbell clo Twick	101	O3
Campbell cft Edg	12	C15
Campbell rd E3	64	B8
Campbell rd E6	66	E3
Campbell rd E17	32	M12
Campbell rd N17	31	W4
Campbell rd W7	71	T1
Campbell rd Croy	122	H16
Campbell rd Twick	101	P3
Campdale rd N7	47	W10
Campden cres Dag	55	S11
Campden cres Wem	42	B8
Campden gro W8	145	V16
Campden hill W8	145	V16
Campden Hill gdns W8	145	S13
Campden Hill pl W11	145	S13
Campden Hill rd W8	145	T13
Campden Hill sq W8	145	R13
Campden House clo W8	145	U16
Campden S Croy	133	T10
Campden st W8	145	U14
Campen clo SW19	105	S5
Camperdown st E1	151	P6
Campfield rd SE9	95	N18
Campion clo E6	66	H19
Campion clo Croy	133	S10
Campion clo Har	25	N19
Campion pl SE28	80	C3
Campion rd SW15	86	M12
Campion rd Islw	83	X1
Campion ter NW2	45	P11
Camplin rd Har	24	J14
Camplin st SE14	75	Z20
Campsbourne rd N8	30	A10
Campsey gdns Dag	68	D1
Campsey rd Dag	68	D1
Campsfield rd N8	30	B10
Campshill rd SE13	93	V13
Campshill st SE13	93	U14
Campus rd E17	32	L17
Camrose ave Edg	24	L6
Camrose ave Erith	81	W17
Camrose clo Croy	124	H16
Camrose clo Mord	119	Z8
Camrose st SE2	80	A12
Canada ave N18	17	Z18
Canada cres W3	61	V13
Canada gdns SE13	93	V13
Canada rd W3	61	V13
Canada sq E14	76	D2
Canada way W12	62	K19
Canadian ave SE6	111	R2
Canal app SE8	75	X14
Canal clo E1	63	W11
Canal gro SE15	159	V13
Canal rd E3	63	W11
Canal st SE5	158	F14
Canal wk N1	142	G4
Canal way NW10	61	Z7
Canal way W10	136	H17
Canal way Wem	61	O3
Canal Way wk W10	137	W20
Canberra clo NW4	26	H10
Canberra cres Dag	69	Z1
Canberra rd E6	66	H4
Canberra rd SE7	77	Y17
Canberra rd Bexh	80	J17
Candahar rd SW11	88	J5
Candler st N15	31	R18
Candover st W1	148	B1
Candy st E3	63	Z2
Caney ms NW2	45	O7
Canfield gdns NW6	46	A20
Canfield rd Wdf Grn	35	R2
Canford ave Nthlt	58	D3
Canford clo Enf	7	V9
Canford gdns N Mal	118	A15
Canford rd SW11	89	N12
Canham rd SE25	123	S6
Canham rd W3	74	A5
Canmore gdns SW16	107	W18
Cann Hall rd E11	51	Z12
Canning cres N22	30	E3
Canning cross SE5	91	R5
Canning pas W8	146	A19
Canning pl W8	146	B20
Canning rd E15	64	L5
Canning rd E17	32	K11
Canning rd N5	48	K9
Canning rd Croy	133	U2
Canning rd Har	23	V10
Cannington rd Dag	55	T17
Cannizaro rd SW19	105	N14
Cannon clo SW20	119	N7
Cannon clo Hmptn	100	K15
Cannon dr E14	76	A1
Cannon hill NW6	45	Z14
Cannon hill N14	16	M10
Cannon Hill la SW20	119	O12
Cannon la NW3	46	F10
Cannon la Pnr	22	B14
Cannon pl NW3	46	E10
Cannon pl SE7	78	E13
Cannon rd N14	17	N11
Cannon rd Bexh	98	A3
Cannon st EC4	150	C1
Cannon Street rd E1	151	W5
Cannonbury ave Pnr	22	A19
Canon ave Rom	37	V16
Canon Beck rd SE16	75	R4
Canon rd Brom	126	M5
Canon row SW1	148	K18
Canon st N1	142	B5
Canon Trading est the Wem	43	T12
Canonbie rd SE23	92	C17
Canonbury cres N1	48	K20
Canonbury la N1	48	J19
Canonbury Park north N1	48	L18
Canonbury Park south N1	48	L18
Canonbury pl N1	48	K19
Canonbury rd N1	48	J19
Canonbury rd Enf	8	D5
Canonbury sq N1	48	J19
Canonbury st N1	48	L20
Canonbury vill N1	141	Z1
Canons clo N2	28	G20
Canons clo Edg	12	A18
Canons dr Edg	11	X18
Canons wk Croy	134	F5
Canonsleigh rd Dag	55	S20
Canrobert st E2	143	W10
Cantelowes rd NW1	47	X19
Canterbury ave Ilf	35	R20
Canterbury ave Sid	115	U3
Canterbury clo E6	66	G17
Canterbury clo Beck	111	R20
Canterbury clo Grnf	58	K16
Canterbury cres SW9	90	F8
Canterbury gro SE27	108	F9
Canterbury pl SE17	157	Y7
Canterbury rd E10	33	U20
Canterbury rd NW6	137	T9
Canterbury rd Croy	122	E17
Canterbury rd Felt	100	B6
Canterbury rd Har	22	K15
Canterbury rd Mord	120	B17
Canterbury ter NW6	137	S8
Cantley gdns SE19	123	V1
Cantley gdns Ilf	36	B18
Cantley rd W7	71	Y7
Canton st E14	64	B18
Cantrell rd E3	64	A12
Cantwell rd SE18	78	M19
Canvey st SE1	149	Z13
Cape rd N17	31	X11
Cape yd E1	151	V12
Capel ave Wall	132	D10
Capel clo N20	15	S10
Capel clo Brom	127	T20
Capel ct EC2	150	G5
Capel gdns Ilf	54	L11
Capel gdns Pnr	22	F11
Capel rd E7	52	H11
Capel rd E12	53	N10
Capel rd Barn	15	V1
Capital Business cen Wem	60	G4
Capital Interchange way Brent	73	O13
Capitol Industrial est NW9	25	W10
Capitol way NW9	25	V10
Capland st NW8	138	H16
Caple rd NW10	62	C6
Capper st WC1	140	D19
Capri rd Croy	123	V19
Capstan clo Rom	37	S18
Capstan ride Enf	7	T8
Capstan rd SE8	75	Y10
Capstan sq E14	76	H6
Capstan way SE16	75	X3
Capstone rd Brom	112	B9
Capthorne ave Har	40	A14
Capuchin clo Stan	11	N9
Capworth st E10	51	O3
Caradoc clo W2	145	T4
Caradoc st SE10	76	M14
Caradon way N15	31	O13
Carberry rd SE19	109	T16
Carbery ave W3	73	O5
Carbis clo E4	20	J4
Carbis rd E14	63	Y16
Carbuncle Passage way N17	31	Y6
Carburton st W1	140	A19
Carden rd SE15	92	A8
Cardiff rd W7	71	Y8
Cardiff rd Enf	9	O13
Cardiff st SE18	79	V18
Cardigan gdns Ilf	55	N5
Cardigan rd E3	63	Z5
Cardigan rd SW13	86	G4
Cardigan rd Rich	84	K16
Cardigan st SE11	157	S9
Cardinal ave Kings T	102	J13
Cardinal ave Mord	119	S15
Cardinal Bourne st SE1	158	G3
Cardinal clo Chis	114	G20
Cardinal clo Mord	119	T16
Cardinal clo Wor Pk	128	F8
Cardinal cres N Mal	117	V2
Cardinal pl SW15	87	P9
Cardinal way Har	23	U9
Cardinals wk Hmptn	100	M17
Cardinals way N19	47	X3
Cardine ms SE15	159	W17
Cardington sq Houns	82	A11
Cardington st NW1	140	C13

Name	Pg	Grid
Cardozo rd N7	48	B15
Cardrew ave N12	15	U16
Cardrew clo N12	15	V16
Cardross st W6	74	K8
Cardwell rd N7	48	A12
Cardwell rd SE18	78	H11
Carew clo N7	48	E8
Carew rd N17	31	X8
Carew rd W13	72	D4
Carew rd Mitch	121	O3
Carew rd Th Hth	122	K8
Carew rd Wall	131	V13
Carew st SE5	90	L4
Carey ct Bexh	98	H14
Carey gdns SW8	89	W3
Carey la EC2	150	B5
Carey pl SW1	156	F8
Carey st WC2	149	P5
Carey way Wem	43	U13
Carfax pl SW4	89	X11
Carfax rd Horn	57	V12
Cargill rd SW18	106	C1
Cargreen rd SE25	123	V10
Carholme rd SE23	110	L1
Carisbrook clo Stan	24	G7
Carisbrooke ave Bex	115	V2
Carisbrooke clo Enf	8	G6
Carisbrooke gdns SE15	159	P18
Carisbrooke rd E17	32	J14
Carisbrooke rd Brom	126	M10
Carisbrooke rd Mitch	121	Z10
Carker's la NW5	47	S14
Carleton ave Wall	131	X18
Carleton rd N7	47	X14
Carlile clo E3	63	Z6
Carlingford rd N15	30	H11
Carlingford rd NW3	46	G12
Carlingford rd Mord	119	O16
Carlisle ave EC3	150	M7
Carlisle ave W3	62	A18
Carlisle clo Kings T	117	P1
Carlisle gdns Har	24	H19
Carlisle gdns Ilf	35	P19
Carlisle la SE1	149	R20
Carlisle ms NW8	138	H20
Carlisle pl N11	16	D14
Carlisle pl SW1	156	A3
Carlisle rd E10	51	P5
Carlisle rd N4	48	G2
Carlisle rd NW6	136	L5
Carlisle rd NW9	25	U9
Carlisle rd Hmptn	100	K17
Carlisle rd Rom	39	V16
Carlisle rd Sutt	129	W13
Carlisle st W1	148	E6
Carlos pl W1	147	W9
Carlow st NW1	140	A7
Carlton ave N14	6	K16
Carlton ave Har	24	E10
Carlton ave S Croy	133	R16
Carlton Avenue east Wem	42	F6
Carlton Avenue west Wem	42	A6
Carlton clo NW3	45	Y6
Carlton clo Edg	12	B16
Carlton ct Ilf	36	E10
Carlton cres Sutt	129	S8
Carlton dr SW15	87	R14
Carlton dr Ilf	36	E10
Carlton gdns SW1	148	F13
Carlton gdns W5	60	E18
Carlton gro SE15	159	X20
Carlton hill NW8	137	Z9
Carlton House ter SW1	148	F13
Carlton Park ave SW20	119	O3
Carlton rd E11	52	B3
Carlton rd E12	53	O13
Carlton rd E17	32	J6
Carlton rd N4	48	F1
Carlton rd N11	16	B15
Carlton rd SW14	85	U9
Carlton rd W4	73	Y6
Carlton rd W5	60	D19
Carlton rd Erith	81	V17
Carlton rd N Mal	118	A4
Carlton rd Rom	39	U15
Carlton rd Sid	114	M12
Carlton rd S Croy	133	P15
Carlton rd Well	97	S7
Carlton st SW1	148	E11
Carlton ter E11	34	H14
Carlton ter SE26	110	C8
Carlton Tower pl SW1	155	R1
Carlton vale NW6	137	P10
Carlwell st SW17	106	J14
Carlyle ave Brom	127	N7
Carlyle ave Sthl	58	D19
Carlyle clo N2	28	E18
Carlyle clo NW10	61	Z4
Carlyle gdns Sthl	58	D19
Carlyle pl SW15	87	P9
Carlyle rd E12	53	R12
Carlyle rd SE28	68	E19
Carlyle rd W5	72	E12
Carlyle rd Croy	133	X2
Carlyle sq SW3	154	H12
Carlyon ave Har	40	F11
Carlyon clo Wem	60	K4
Carlyon rd Wem	60	J5
Carmalt gdns SW15	87	N11
Carmelite rd Har	23	N4
Carmelite st EC4	149	V8
Carmelite wk Har	23	N5
Carmelite way Har	23	O6
Carmen st E14	64	E16
Carmichael rd SE25	123	W10
Carminia rd SW17	107	S4
Carnaby st W1	148	C7
Carnac st SE27	109	O8
Carnanton rd E17	33	X5
Carnarvon ave Enf	8	G9
Carnarvon rd E10	33	V17
Carnarvon rd E15	52	B16
Carnarvon rd E18	34	C6
Carnarvon rd Barn	4	E11
Carnation st SE2	80	C13
Carnbrook rd SE3	95	N7
Carnecke gdns SE9	95	S14
Carnegie pl SW19	105	O6
Carnegie st N1	141	O7
Carnforth gdns Horn	57	X14
Carnforth rd SW16	107	W17
Carnoustie dr N1	141	N1
Carnwath rd SW6	87	Z8
Carol st NW1	140	A4
Carolina rd Th Hth	122	K3
Caroline clo N10	29	S8
Caroline clo SW16	108	E8
Caroline clo W2	145	Y10
Caroline clo Croy	133	T8
Caroline clo Islw	71	S20
Caroline gdns E2	142	L11
Caroline pl SW11	89	R5
Caroline pl W2	145	Y9
Caroline Place ms W2	145	Y10
Caroline rd SW19	105	V18
Caroline st E1	63	U18
Caroline ter SW1	155	T6
Carpenter gdns N21	17	W7
Carpenters pl SW4	89	X9
Carpenters rd E15	51	P19
Carr rd E17	33	N6
Carr rd Nthlt	40	J18
Carr st E14	63	X15
Carriage Drive east SW11	155	U16
Carriage Drive north SW11	155	N18
Carriage Drive south SW11	155	W20
Carriage Drive west SW11	155	N18
Carrick dr Ilf	36	B5
Carrick gdns N17	31	R2
Carrick ms SE8	76	B16
Carrill way Belv	80	K10
Carrington ave Houns	82	K14
Carrington clo Croy	124	N16
Carrington rd Rich	85	O11
Carrington sq Har	10	B20
Carrington st W1	147	X14
Carrol clo NW5	47	S13
Carroll clo E15	52	B15
Carron clo E14	64	E16
Carronade pl SE28	79	R8
Carroun rd SW8	157	O18
Carrow rd Dag	55	R20
Carroway la Grnf	59	R8
Carrs la N21	7	Z15
Carshalton gro Sutt	130	G10
Carshalton Park rd Cars	130	L14
Carshalton pl Cars	131	P10
Carshalton rd Mitch	121	O10
Carshalton rd Sutt	130	F12
Carslake rd SW15	86	M15
Carson rd E16	65	U12
Carson rd SE21	109	N3
Carson rd Barn	5	Y15
Carstairs rd SE6	111	U8
Carston clo SE12	94	D13
Carswell clo Ilf	35	O11
Carswell rd SE6	93	U18
Cart la E4	20	L3
Carter clo Rom	38	G1
Carter dr Rom	38	G1
Carter la EC4	149	Y7
Carter pl SE17	158	C11
Carter rd E13	65	V4
Carter rd SW19	106	F15
Carter st SE17	158	A12
Carteret st SW1	148	F19
Carteret way SE8	75	X11
Carterhatch la Enf	8	G4
Carterhatch rd Enf	9	R7
Carters clo Wor Pk	129	P2
Carters Hill clo SE9	112	M1
Carthew rd W6	74	K8
Carthew vill W6	74	K8
Carthusian st EC1	142	A20
Cartier circle E14	76	F3
Carting la WC2	148	M10
Cartmel clo N17	32	A1
Cartmel rd Bexh	98	E1
Cartmell gdns Mord	120	C13
Carton st W1	147	R3
Cartwright gdns WC1	140	J14
Cartwright rd Dag	56	B19
Cartwright st E1	151	B19
Carver rd SE24	90	L15
Carville cres Brent	72	J12
Cary rd E11	52	B11
Carysfort rd N8	29	Y15
Carysfort rd N16	49	U15
Cascade ave N10	29	U12
Casella rd SE14	75	T20
Casewick rd SE27	108	G11
Casimir rd E5	50	C8
Casino ave SE24	91	N12
Caspian st SE5	158	E17
Casselden rd NW10	61	Z1
Cassidy rd SW6	153	T19
Cassilda rd SE2	80	B12
Cassilis rd Twick	84	B14
Cassiobury rd E17	32	G15
Cassland rd E9	50	E19
Cassland rd Th Hth	123	N9
Casslee rd SE6	92	M19
Casson st E1	151	S1
Castellain rd W9	137	X15
Castellane clo Stan	23	X1
Castello ave SW15	86	M13
Castelnau SW13	86	H1
Casterbridge rd SE3	94	G7
Castile rd SE18	78	K10
Castillon rd SE6	112	A5
Castlands rd SE6	110	M5
Castle ave E4	20	K17
Castle ave Epsom	128	H20
Castle clo SW19	105	O6
Castle clo Brom	125	Z7
Castle dr Ilf	35	R18
Castle Hill ave Croy	135	S19
Castle la SW1	156	B1
Castle ms NW1	47	S19
Castle par Epsom	128	G18
Castle rd N12	15	S17
Castle rd NW1	47	S19
Castle rd Dag	68	C3
Castle rd Enf	9	W4
Castle rd Islw	83	V4
Castle rd Nthlt	40	J18
Castle rd Sthl	70	E8
Castle st E6	66	A5
Castle st Kings T	116	K3
Castle way SW19	105	P6
Castle yd N6	47	P1
Castle yd SE1	149	Y12
Castlebar hill W5	60	C15
Castlebar ms W5	60	C13
Castlebar pk W5	60	C13
Castlebar rd W5	60	E15
Castlecombe dr SW19	87	R19
Castlecombe rd SE9	113	P10
Castledine rd SE20	109	Z18
Castleford ave SE9	113	Z1
Castlegate Rich	85	N8
Castlehaven rd NW1	47	T18
Castleleigh ct Enf	8	C16
Castlemaine ave Epsom	128	K19
Castlemaine ave S Croy	133	U12
Castlereagh st W1	147	N4
Castleton ave Bexh	99	N4
Castleton ave Wem	42	J13
Castleton rd E17	33	X7
Castleton rd SE9	113	N10
Castleton rd Ilf	55	O4
Castleton rd Mitch	121	X10
Castletown rd W14	152	M11
Castleview gdns Ilf	35	S18
Castlewood dr SE9	95	V5
Castlewood rd N15	31	X18
Castlewood rd N16	31	X20
Castlewood rd Barn	5	V12
Castor la E14	64	D20
Cat hill Barn	5	Y17
Caterham ave Ilf	35	V8
Caterham rd SE13	93	W8
Catesby st SE17	158	G7
Catford bdy SE6	93	R19
Catford hill SE6	111	N2
Catford rd SE6	93	P19
Cathall rd E11	51	Y8
Cathay st SE16	75	Y18
Cathcart hill N19	47	U10
Cathcart rd SW10	154	A13
Cathcart st NW5	47	S16
Cathedral st SE1	150	E13
Catherine ct N14	6	H17
Catherine gdns Houns	83	P11
Catherine Griffiths ct EC1	141	T16
Catherine gro SE10	93	R1
Catherine pl SW1	148	B20
Catherine rd Rom	39	Y15
Catherine rd Surb	116	G11
Catherine st WC2	149	N7
Catherine Wheel all E1	150	L3
Catherine Wheel yd Brent	72	G18
Cathles rd SW12	89	T17
Cathnor rd W12	74	J6
Catisfield rd Enf	9	V1
Catlin st SE16	159	V10
Catling clo SE23	110	E7
Cato rd SW4	89	Y9
Cato st W1	146	M3
Cator rd SE26	110	G16
Cator rd Cars	131	N11
Cator st SE15	159	O15
Catsey la (Bushey) Wat	10	A2
Catsey wds (Bushey) Wat	10	A2
Cattistock rd SE9	113	S11
Catton st WC1	149	N2
Caulfield rd E6	66	F2
Caulfield rd SE15	92	B4
Causeway the N2	28	H12
Causeway the SW18	88	A11
Causeway the SW19	104	M13
Causeway the Cars	131	O5
Causeway the Sutt	130	D19
Causeway the Tedd	101	W14
Causeyware rd N9	19	O2
Causton rd N6	47	T1
Causton st SW1	156	G7
Cautley ave SW4	89	U14

Cavalier clo Rom	37	V12	Cecil rd Enf	8	A13	Central ave Wall	132	B11	Chalk la Barn	6	A12
Cavalry gdns SW15	87	U13	Cecil rd Har	23	S9	Central ave Well	96	M4	Chalk Pit way Sutt	130	C13
Cavaye pl SW10	154	E12	Cecil rd Houns	83	N6	Central hill SE19	109	N14	Chalk rd E13	65	X14
Cave rd E13	65	W7	Cecil rd Ilf	53	Z11	Central Park ave Dag	56	J10	Chalkhill rd Wem	43	S8
Cave rd Rich	102	C9	Cecil rd Rom	37	Y20	Central Park rd E6	66	A6	Chalklands the Wem	43	V9
Cave st N1	141	R7	Cecil rd Sutt	129	V14	Central pl SE25	123	Y11	Chalkstone clo Well	97	O1
Cavell dr Enf	7	U8	Cecil way Brom	126	E19	Central rd Mord	119	X14	Challice way SW2	90	D20
Cavell rd N17	31	O2	Cecile pk N8	30	A19	Central rd Wem	42	A15	Challin st SE20	110	C20
Cavell st E1	151	Y1	Cecilia clo N2	28	D9	Central rd Wor Pk	128	G1	Challis rd Brent	72	G13
Cavendish ave N3	27	X8	Cecilia rd E8	49	W15	Central sq NW11	27	Z17	Challoner clo N2	28	F8
Cavendish ave NW8	138	G10	Cedar ave Barn	15	W2	Central st EC1	142	A12	Challoner cres W14	153	O11
Cavendish ave W13	59	X15	Cedar ave Enf	9	P7	Central way SE28	79	Z4	Challoner st W14	153	O10
Cavendish ave Erith	81	W17	Cedar ave Rom	37	Z14	Central way Cars	130	K17	Chalsey rd SE4	92	M10
Cavendish ave Har	41	T13	Cedar ave Sid	96	M18	Centre ave W3	73	Z3	Chalton dr N2	28	F17
Cavendish ave Horn	57	Y17	Cedar ave Twick	82	L15	Centre Common rd	114	B16	Chalton st NW1	140	F10
Cavendish ave N Mal	118	H10	Cedar clo SE21	108	M2	Chis			Chamber st E1	151	R8
Cavendish ave Sid	97	N19	Cedar clo E8	49	W15	Centre rd E7	52	G8	Chamberlain cres W	125	R19
Cavendish ave Well	96	L9	Cedar clo SW15	103	Y10	Centre rd E11	52	G8	Wick		
Cavendish ave	34	G3	Cedar clo Cars	131	N13	Centre rd Dag	69	W4	Chamberlain rd N2	28	D8
Wdf Grn			Cedar clo Rom	38	M11	Centre st E2	143	X10	Chamberlain rd N9	18	J9
Cavendish clo N18	19	N15	Cedar copse Brom	127	T3	Centre way E17	33	T3	Chamberlain st NW1	139	P2
Cavendish clo NW6	45	V19	Cedar ct SW19	105	R8	Centre way N9	19	S6	Chamberlain way	116	L19
Cavendish clo NW8	138	G12	Cedar dr N2	28	H13	Centreway NW7	26	G2	Surb		
Cavendish cres Horn	57	Y18	Cedar gdns Sutt	130	D14	Centreway Ilf	54	B7	Chamberlayne rd	136	B2
Cavendish dr E11	51	W3	Cedar gro W5	72	J8	Centric clo NW1	139	W3	NW10		
Cavendish dr Edg	12	A19	Cedar gro Bex	97	V16	Centurion clo N7	48	D19	Chambers gdns N2	28	F5
Cavendish gdns Bark	54	J16	Cedar gro Sthl	58	H14	Centurion way Erith	81	R7	Chambers la NW10	136	B1
Cavendish gdns Ilf	53	W3	Cedar heights Rich	102	K2	Century rd E17	32	J10	Chambers rd N7	48	A12
Cavendish Mews	147	Y1	Cedar Lawn ave Barn	4	F16	Cephas ave E1	63	S11	Chambers st SE16	151	U18
north W1			Cedar mt SE9	113	N2	Cephas st E1	63	P12	Chambord st E2	143	O14
Cavendish Mews	147	Z1	Cedar Park gdns Rom	55	W1	Ceres rd SE18	79	X12	Champion cres SE26	110	H9
south W1			Cedar Park rd Enf	7	Z3	Cerise rd SE15	91	X3	Champion gro SE5	91	R7
Cavendish pl W1	147	Y4	Cedar ri N14	16	C2	Cerne rd Mord	120	C14	Champion hill SE5	91	P7
Cavendish rd E4	20	F20	Cedar rd N17	31	V4	Cester st E2	143	S6	Champion Hill est SE5	91	R9
Cavendish rd N4	30	H18	Cedar rd NW2	45	N11	Ceylon rd W14	152	J3	Champion pk SE5	91	O6
Cavendish rd N18	19	N15	Cedar rd Brom	126	M3	Chadacre ave Ilf	35	U9	Champion rd SE26	110	J9
Cavendish rd NW6	45	T20	Cedar rd Croy	133	P2	Chadacre rd Epsom	128	H14	Champness clo SE27	109	O10
Cavendish rd SW12	89	U15	Cedar rd Enf	7	X3	Chadbourn st E14	64	E15	Champneys clo Sutt	129	U17
Cavendish rd SW19	106	C13	Cedar rd Erith	99	X2	Chadd dr Brom	127	S7	Chance st E1	143	N16
Cavendish rd W4	85	W1	Cedar rd Rom	38	L13	Chadd grn E13	65	T3	Chance st E2	143	N16
Cavendish rd Barn	4	A11	Cedar rd Sutt	130	C15	Chadville gdns Rom	37	W16	Chancel st SE1	149	X13
Cavendish rd Croy	122	J19	Cedar rd Tedd	101	Y13	Chadway Dag	55	V4	Chancellor gdns S	132	J19
Cavendish rd N Mal	118	C10	Cedar Tree gro SE27	108	J12	Chadwell ave Rom	55	R2	Croy		
Cavendish rd Sutt	130	C16	Cedar way NW1	140	F2	Chadwell Heath la	37	S14	Chancellor gro SE21	109	N5
Cavendish sq W1	147	X4	Cedarhurst dr SE9	94	L14	Rom			Chancellor pas E14	76	C3
Cavendish st N1	142	E9	Cedarne rd SW6	153	W19	Chadwell st EC1	141	U11	Chancellors rd W6	152	D11
Cavendish way	125	R20	Cedars the Buck H	21	T5	Chadwick ave E4	20	L12	Chancellors st W6	152	C11
W Wick			Cedars the Tedd	101	X14	Chadwick clo Tedd	101	Z15	Chancelot rd SE2	80	E11
Cavenham gdns Ilf	54	E10	Cedars ave E17	33	O15	Chadwick rd E11	34	B19	Chancery la WC2	149	R3
Caverleigh way	118	H19	Cedars ave Mitch	121	O9	Chadwick rd NW10	62	D2	Chancery la Beck	125	S3
Wor Pk			Cedars clo NW4	27	O9	Chadwick rd SE15	91	U6	Chanctonbury clo	114	A6
Caversham ave N13	17	T10	Cedars ms SW4	89	S10	Chadwick st SW1	156	F3	SE9		
Caversham ave Sutt	129	R3	Cedars rd E15	52	A17	Chadwin rd E13	65	V13	Chanctonbury gdns	129	Z17
Caversham rd N15	30	M12	Cedars rd N21	17	X7	Chadwin rd E13	65	V14	Sutt		
Caversham rd NW5	47	U16	Cedars rd SW4	89	S9	Chaffinch ave Croy	124	F14	Chanctonbury way	14	J14
Caversham rd	116	L4	Cedars rd SW13	86	F5	Chaffinch clo N9	19	S5	N12		
Kings T			Cedars rd W4	73	V15	Chaffinch clo Croy	124	F13	Chandler ave E16	65	S14
Caverswall st SW3	155	U13	Cedars rd Beck	124	K3	Chaffinch rd Beck	124	J1	Chandler clo Hmptn	100	F20
Caverswall st W12	144	B4	Cedars rd Croy	132	B7	Chafford way Rom	37	T14	Chandler st E1	151	X12
Caveside clo Chis	127	W2	Cedars rd Kings T	102	D20	Chagford st NW1	139	P17	Chandlers ms E14	76	A4
Cawdor cres W7	71	Z9	Cedars rd Mord	119	Y8	Chailey ave Enf	8	G7	Chandlers way SW2	90	G19
Cawnpore st SE19	109	T14	Cedarville gdns	108	D16	Chailey st E5	50	D10	Chandlers way Rom	39	S16
Caxton gro E3	64	B7	SW16			Chalcombe rd SE2	80	D8	Chandos ave E17	33	P8
Caxton rd N22	30	E8	Cedric ave Rom	39	R10	Chalcot clo Sutt	129	Y17	Chandos ave N14	16	H10
Caxton rd SW19	106	C13	Cedric rd SE9	114	C6	Chalcot cres NW1	139	R3	Chandos ave N20	15	S5
Caxton rd W12	144	F15	Celadon clo Enf	9	V11	Chalcot gdns NW3	46	L18	Chandos ave W5	72	F10
Caxton st SW1	148	E20	Celandine clo E14	64	B14	Chalcot rd NW1	139	S2	Chandos clo Buck H	21	V7
Caygill clo Brom	126	D9	Celandine dr SE28	80	C3	Chalcot sq NW1	139	S2	Chandos cres Edg	25	O1
Cayton pl EC1	142	E14	Celandine way E15	65	N8	Chalcroft rd SE13	93	Z13	Chandos pl WC2	148	K10
Cayton rd Grnf	59	T6	Celbridge ms W2	145	Y3	Chaldon rd SW6	152	L17	Chandos rd E15	51	W14
Cayton st EC1	142	D13	Celestial gdns SE13	93	Y10	Chale rd SW2	90	A17	Chandos rd N2	28	H8
Cazenove rd E17	33	P5	Celia rd N19	47	V12	Chalfont ave Wem	43	T18	Chandos rd N17	31	S7
Cazenove rd N16	49	U6	Celtic ave Brom	125	Z8	Chalfont ct NW9	26	C11	Chandos rd NW2	44	M15
Cecil ave Bark	54	E19	Celtic st E14	64	F13	Chalfont grn N9	18	F10	Chandos rd NW10	62	A11
Cecil ave Enf	8	G13	Cemetery la SE7	78	E16	Chalfont rd N9	18	F10	Chandos rd Har	23	O16
Cecil ave Wem	42	M16	Cemetery rd E7	52	D13	Chalfont rd SE25	123	V7	Chandos st W1	147	Y3
Cecil ct Barn	4	C10	Cemetery rd N17	31	T2	Chalfont way W13	72	A9	Chandos way NW11	46	A3
Cecil pk Pnr	22	D13	Cemetery rd SE2	80	C19	Chalford rd SE21	109	P8	Channel clo Houns	82	H1
Cecil pl Mitch	121	N11	Cenacle clo NW3	45	Z8	Chalford wdf Wdf Grn	35	N3	Channelsea rd E15	64	K3
Cecil rd E11	52	B8	Centaur st SE1	157	R1	Chalgrove ave Mord	119	Y12	Chant sq E15	64	L1
Cecil rd E13	65	U2	Centenary rd Enf	9	X13	Chalgrove cres Ilf	35	R7	Chant st E15	64	L1
Cecil rd E17	33	O3	Centenary Trading est	9	Y12	Chalgrove gdns N3	27	T10	Chantrey rd SW9	90	D8
Cecil rd N10	29	T7	Enf			Chalgrove rd E9	50	B17	Chantry clo Enf	7	Y4
Cecil rd N14	16	G4	Central ave E11	51	X7	Chalgrove rd N17	31	Z3	Chantry clo Har	25	N16
Cecil rd NW9	26	A10	Central ave N2	28	F7	Chalgrove rd Sutt	130	F17	Chantry la Brom	127	N11
Cecil rd NW10	62	A4	Central ave N9	18	F9	Chalice clo Wall	131	X14	Chantry pl Har	22	K4
Cecil rd SW19	106	A18	Central ave Enf	8	M7	Chalk cres SE12	112	H7	Chantry rd Har	22	K4
Cecil rd W3	61	W15	Central ave Houns	83	N11	Chalk Farm rd NW1	139	X1			
Cecil rd Croy	122	D16	Central ave Pnr	22	D18	Chalk Hill rd W6	152	G7			

Chantry st N1	141	Z6
Chapel clo Dart	99	P12
Chapel ct N2	28	H10
Chapel ct SE1	150	E16
Chapel Farm rd SE9	113	T6
Chapel hill Dart	99	P12
Chapel House st E14	76	E13
Chapel la Pnr	22	A11
Chapel la Rom	55	W1
Chapel mkt N1	141	T8
Chapel pl N1	141	U8
Chapel pl W1	147	X5
Chapel rd SE27	108	K11
Chapel rd W13	72	B2
Chapel rd Bexh	98	E9
Chapel rd Houns	82	L9
Chapel rd Ilf	53	Y9
Chapel rd Twick	84	C19
Chapel side W2	145	X9
Chapel Stones N1	31	V3
Chapel st E15	64	K1
Chapel st NW1	146	K2
Chapel st SW1	147	V20
Chapel st Enf	8	A11
Chapel vw S Croy	134	B15
Chapel wk NW4	26	L13
Chaplin clo SE1	149	V17
Chaplin rd E15	65	O5
Chaplin rd N17	31	V10
Chaplin rd NW2	44	G17
Chaplin rd Dag	55	Z9
Chaplin rd Wem	42	D17
Chapman cres Har	24	L17
Chapman rd E9	50	L18
Chapman rd Belv	81	T15
Chapman rd Croy	122	E19
Chapman st E1	151	W7
Chapman's la SE2	80	H12
Chapmans Park Industrial est NW10	44	E16
Chapone pl W1	148	T6
Chapter clo W4	73	W8
Chapter rd NW2	44	F16
Chapter st SE17	157	Y11
Chapter st SW1	156	F7
Chapter way Hmptn	100	G11
Chara pl W4	73	Y16
Charcroft gdns Enf	9	V17
Chardmore rd N16	49	X4
Chardwell clo E6	66	F16
Charecroft way W12	144	G18
Charford rd E16	65	T15
Chargeable la E13	65	S11
Chargeable st E16	65	S11
Charing Cross rd WC2	148	G5
Charlbert st NW8	138	L9
Charlbury ave Stan	11	T17
Charlbury gdns Ilf	54	L1
Charlbury gro W5	60	E16
Charldane rd SE9	113	Z6
Charlecote gro SE26	110	A6
Charlecote rd Dag	55	Z9
Charlemont rd E6	66	H10
Charles Barry clo SW4	89	V7
Charles clo Sid	115	S9
Charles cres Har	41	R1
Charles Grinling wk SE18	78	J10
Charles rd NW8	138	J9
Charles rd W13	59	Z16
Charles rd Dag	57	N18
Charles rd Rom	37	V20
Charles II st SW1	147	W13
Charles Sevright dr NW7	14	D16
Charles sq N1	142	H14
Charles st E16	77	Z3
Charles st SW13	86	B6
Charles st W1	147	W13
Charles st S Croy	132	L5
Charles st Enf	8	G16
Charles st Houns	82	D4
Charlesfield SE9	112	M7
Charleston st SE17	158	C7
Charleville circ SE26	109	Y12
Charleville rd W14	152	M11
Charlmont rd SW17	106	L14
Charlotte Despard ave SW11	89	P3
Charlotte ms W1	140	D20
Charlotte ms W14	152	L6
Charlotte pl NW9	25	W16
Charlotte pl SW1	156	B6
Charlotte rd EC2	142	K15
Charlotte rd SW13	86	E2
Charlotte rd Dag	56	H18
Charlotte rd Wall	131	V14
Charlotte st W1	140	C20
Charlotte ter N1	141	R7
Charlton Church la SE7	77	Y14
Charlton cres Bark	67	X5
Charlton dene SE7	77	Z19
Charlton Kings rd NW5	47	X15
Charlton la SE7	78	A14
Charlton Park la SE7	78	A20
Charlton Park rd SE7	78	C16
Charlton pl N1	141	W7
Charlton rd N9	19	T1
Charlton rd NW10	62	C3
Charlton rd SE3	77	U18
Charlton rd SE7	77	W17
Charlton rd Har	24	H14
Charlton rd Wem	43	N5
Charlton way SE3	93	Z2
Charlwood Croy	134	L19
Charlwood clo Har	10	G20
Charlwood pl SW1	156	C7
Charlwood rd SW15	87	P9
Charlwood st SW1	156	C9
Charlwood ter SW15	87	P10
Charmian ave Stan	24	G9
Charminster ave SW19	119	Z4
Charminster ct Surb	116	G16
Charminster rd SE9	113	P10
Charminster rd Wor Pk	119	O20
Charmouth rd Well	97	S2
Charnock rd E5	50	A10
Charnwood ave SW19	119	Z4
Charnwood clo N Mal	118	B10
Charnwood dr E18	34	H11
Charnwood gdns E14	76	B10
Charnwood pl N20	15	P10
Charnwood rd SE25	123	P11
Charnwood st E5	49	Z7
Charrington rd S Croy	133	M2
Charsley rd SE6	111	R4
Chart clo Brom	126	B2
Chart st N1	142	F13
Charter ave Ilf	54	F3
Charter cres Houns	82	A9
Charter dr Bex	97	Z18
Charter rd Kings T	117	T5
Charter rd the Wdf Grn	21	N18
Charter sq Kings T	117	T5
Charter way N3	27	V12
Charter way N14	6	J20
Charterhouse ave Wem	42	D13
Charterhouse bldgs EC1	141	Z19
Charterhouse sq EC1	141	Y20
Charterhouse st EC1	149	W2
Charteris rd N4	48	E4
Charteris rd NW6	137	R6
Charteris rd Wdf Grn	34	H1
Charters clo SE19	109	S12
Chartfield ave SW15	86	M14
Chartfield sq SW15	87	P13
Chartham rd SE25	124	A7
Chartley ave NW2	44	B10
Chartley ave Stan	10	J18
Charton clo Belv	81	R16
Chartwell clo SE9	114	D5
Chartwell pl Sutt	129	U7
Charwood SW16	108	F10
Chase the E12	53	N11
Chase the SW4	89	T9
Chase the SW16	108	D17
Chase the SW20	119	S2
Chase the Bexh	98	G7
Chase the Brom	126	H5
Chase the Edg	25	S4
Chase the Pnr	22	E12
Chase the Rom	39	P10
Chase the Rom (Chadwell Heath)	37	Z18
Chase the (Rush Grn) Rom	57	O10
Chase the Stan	10	L19
Chase the Wall	132	A11
Chase Court gdns Enf	7	Y10
Chase Cross rd Rom	38	J2
Chase gdns E4	20	A14
Chase gdns Twick	83	S17
Chase grn Enf	7	Z11
Chase Green ave Enf	7	W9
Chase hill Enf	7	Y10
Chase la Ilf	36	D15
Chase ridings Enf	7	T9
Chase rd N14	6	H16
Chase rd NW10	61	Y13
Chase side N14	6	C17
Chase side Enf	7	Z10
Chase Side ave SW20	119	S2
Chase Side ave Enf	8	A8
Chase Side cres Enf	8	A6
Chase way N14	16	C19
Chasefield rd SW17	107	N10
Chaseley dr W4	73	T13
Chaseley st E14	63	W17
Chasemore gdns Croy	132	G12
Chaseville Park rd N21	7	O17
Chasewood ave Enf	7	W9
Chastilian rd Dart	99	T17
Chatfield rd SW11	88	D8
Chatfield rd Croy	122	J20
Chatham ave Brom	126	G15
Chatham clo NW11	27	Y16
Chatham clo Sutt	119	V19
Chatham pl E9	50	C17
Chatham rd E17	32	J10
Chatham rd SW11	88	M14
Chatham rd Kings T	117	O2
Chatham st SE17	158	E6
Chatsworth pl W5	60	L16
Chatsworth ave NW4	26	M7
Chatsworth ave SW20	119	T2
Chatsworth ave Brom	112	G11
Chatsworth ave Sid	115	S10
Chatsworth ave Wem	43	N16
Chatsworth clo NW4	26	L7
Chatsworth cres Houns	83	O10
Chatsworth dr Enf	18	J1
Chatsworth gdns W3	73	S1
Chatsworth gdns Har	40	K3
Chatsworth gdns N Mal	118	D11
Chatsworth pl Mitch	120	M2
Chatsworth pl Tedd	101	Y10
Chatsworth ri W5	61	N12
Chatsworth rd E5	50	D8
Chatsworth rd E15	52	B15
Chatsworth rd NW2	45	O17
Chatsworth rd W4	73	W17
Chatsworth rd W5	60	M12
Chatsworth rd Croy	133	P8
Chatsworth rd Sutt	129	R10
Chatsworth way SE27	108	K6
Chatterton rd N4	48	J9
Chatterton rd Brom	127	O11
Chatto rd SW11	89	N14
Chaucer ave Rich	85	R6
Chaucer clo N11	16	J16
Chaucer dr SE1	159	O8
Chaucer gdns Sutt	129	Y7
Chaucer grn Croy	124	B17
Chaucer rd E7	52	G18
Chaucer rd E11	34	E18
Chaucer rd E17	33	V6
Chaucer rd SE24	90	G14
Chaucer rd W3	73	W2
Chaucer rd Rom	39	Z1
Chaucer rd Sid	115	U2
Chaucer rd Well	96	J3
Chaucer way SW19	106	F14
Chauncey clo N9	18	J10
Chaundrye clo SE9	95	T16
Cheam Common rd Wor Pk	128	K4
Cheam Park way Sutt	129	R13
Cheam rd (SM1) Sutt	129	U14
Cheam rd (SM2) Sutt	129	P20
Cheam st SE15	92	B7
Cheapside EC2	150	B5
Cheddington rd N18	18	D12
Chedworth clo E16	65	P17
Cheeseman clo Hmptn	100	C15
Cheesemans ter W14	153	O11
Chelford rd Brom	111	W11
Chelmer cres Bark	68	C7
Chelmer rd E9	50	G14
Chelmsford ave Rom	39	O1
Chelmsford clo E6	66	F17
Chelmsford clo W6	152	J12
Chelmsford gdns Ilf	53	S1
Chelmsford rd E11	51	Y3
Chelmsford rd E17	33	N17
Chelmsford rd E18	34	B4
Chelmsford rd N14	16	H3
Chelmsford sq NW10	136	B5
Chelsea bri SW1	155	W13
Chelsea bri SW8	155	W14
Chelsea Bridge rd SW1	155	U10
Chelsea clo NW10	61	Z3
Chelsea clo Edg	25	O7
Chelsea clo Hmptn	101	N14
Chelsea embk SW3	155	O15
Chelsea gdns Sutt	129	U8
Chelsea Harbour dr SW10	88	D1
Chelsea Manor gdns SW3	154	L12
Chelsea Manor st SW3	154	L10
Chelsea Park gdns SW3	154	F13
Chelsea sq SW3	154	H10
Chelsea wf SW10	154	E19
Chelsfield ave N9	19	S1
Chelsfield gdns SE26	110	D7
Chelsham rd SW4	89	Y7
Chelsham rd S Croy	133	O15
Chelsworth dr SE18	79	S17
Cheltenham ave Twick	83	Y19
Cheltenham clo N Mal	117	X7
Cheltenham clo Nthlt	40	J17
Cheltenham gdns E6	66	D7
Cheltenham pl W3	73	U4
Cheltenham pl Har	24	J12
Cheltenham rd E10	33	U19
Cheltenham rd SE15	92	D12
Cheltenham ter SW3	155	P8
Chelverton rd SW15	87	P16
Chelwood gdns Rich	85	R5
Chelwood wk SE4	92	H11
Chenappa clo E13	65	S10
Chenduit way Stan	10	K17
Cheney rd NW1	140	K10
Cheneys rd E11	52	A10
Chenies ms WC1	140	E18
Chenies pl NW1	140	G8
Chenies st WC1	140	F20
Cheniston gdns W8	153	W1
Chepstow clo SW15	87	S14
Chepstow cres W11	145	T8
Chepstow cres Ilf	36	J18
Chepstow gdns Sthl	58	F18
Chepstow pl W2	145	V7
Chepstow ri Croy	133	T5
Chepstow rd W2	145	U3
Chepstow rd W7	71	X7
Chepstow rd Croy	133	S5
Chepstow vill W11	145	R9
Chequer st EC1	142	D18
Chequers la Dag	69	P13
Chequers way N13	17	X15
Cherbury clo SE28	68	K18
Cherbury st N1	142	G10
Cherchefelle ms Stan	11	O16
Cherington rd W7	71	V3
Cheriton ave Brom	126	D13
Cheriton ave Ilf	35	V6
Cheriton clo W5	60	E13

Entry	Page	Ref
Cheriton dr SE18	79	S18
Cheriton sq SW17	107	R4
Cherry clo SW2	90	F18
Cherry clo W5	72	G8
Cherry clo Cars	130	L2
Cherry clo Mord	119	T9
Cherry cres Bren	72	A19
Cherry Garden st SE16	151	W18
Cherry gdns Dag	56	B14
Cherry garth Bren	72	H12
Cherry hill Barn	5	O20
Cherry Hill gdns Croy	132	D8
Cherry Orchard gdns Croy	133	P2
Cherry Orchard rd Croy	123	R20
Cherry rd Enf	9	R3
Cherry st Rom	38	M15
Cherry Tree clo Wem	41	X12
Cherry Tree dr SW16	108	B7
Cherry Tree rd N2	28	L13
Cherry Tree wk Beck	124	M9
Cherry Tree way Stan	11	O17
Cherry wk Brom	126	F20
Cherry Wood way W5	61	O15
Cherrycroft gdns Pnr	22	F1
Cherrydown av E4	19	Z10
Cherrydown clo E4	20	A11
Cherrydown rd Sid	115	W5
Cherrydown wk Rom	38	H6
Cherrywood clo Kings T	103	P18
Cherrywood dr SW15	87	O13
Cherrywood la Mord	119	S8
Chertsey dr Sutt	129	T4
Chertsey rd E11	51	X5
Chertsey rd Ilf	54	E13
Chertsey rd Twick	100	K4
Chertsey rd SW17	107	O12
Chervil ms SE28	80	C3
Cheryls clo SW6	88	A2
Cheseman st SE26	110	B7
Chesfield rd Kings T	102	L18
Chesham av Orp	127	Z14
Chesham clo Rom	38	M11
Chesham cres SE20	124	D2
Chesham ms SW1	155	T1
Chesham pl SW1	155	T2
Chesham rd SE20	124	D3
Chesham rd SW19	106	G14
Chesham rd Kings T	117	P2
Chesham st NW10	43	X10
Chesham st SW1	155	T3
Chesham ter W13	72	A4
Cheshire clo SE4	92	L4
Cheshire clo Mitch	122	A17
Cheshire rd N22	17	R20
Cheshire st E2	143	P17
Chesholm rd N16	49	T9
Cheshunt rd Belv	81	S14
Chesilton rd SW6	87	V1
Chesley gdns E6	66	C7
Chesney cres Croy	135	T16
Chesney st SW11	89	O3
Chesnut est N17	31	W10
Chesnut gro N17	31	W10
Chesnut rd N17	31	W10
Chessington av N3	27	T10
Chessington av Bexh	81	N19
Chessington ct Pnr	22	E13
Chessington Epsom	128	A20
Chessington way W Wick	135	R3
Chesson rd W14	153	O13
Chester av Rich	84	M14
Chester av Twick	100	D2
Chester clo SW1	147	W19
Chester clo SW13	86	K8
Chester Close north NW1	139	Y12
Chester Close south NW1	139	Y13
Chester ct NW1	139	Y13
Chester ct SE5	158	E18
Chester cres E8	49	W16
Chester dr Har	22	F17
Chester gdns Enf	9	N18
Chester gdns Mord	120	C13
Chester gate NW1	139	Y14
Chester ms SW1	147	W20
Chester rd E7	53	N20
Chester rd E11	34	J18
Chester rd E16	65	N11
Chester rd E17	32	G16
Chester rd N9	19	O6
Chester rd N17	31	P9
Chester rd N19	47	R8
Chester rd NW1	139	X13
Chester rd SW19	104	M15
Chester rd Ilf	54	L4
Chester rd Sid	96	J14
Chester row SW1	155	U6
Chester sq SW1	155	V5
Chester Square ms SW1	155	X3
Chester st E2	143	U16
Chester st SW1	147	W20
Chester ter NW1	139	Y13
Chester way SE11	157	U8
Chesterfield gdns W1	147	W13
Chesterfield gro SE22	91	U12
Chesterfield hill W1	147	W13
Chesterfield rd E10	33	U20
Chesterfield rd N3	14	E13
Chesterfield rd W4	73	W16
Chesterfield rd Barn	4	C18
Chesterfield rd Enf	9	V1
Chesterfield st W1	147	W13
Chesterfield wk SE10	93	X1
Chesterfield way SE15	75	P19
Chesterford gdns NW3	46	B13
Chesterford rd E12	53	V16
Chesters the N Mal	104	A20
Chesterton clo Grnf	58	K6
Chesterton rd E13	65	T8
Chesterton rd W10	144	H3
Chesterton ter E13	65	T7
Chesterton ter Kings T	117	O5
Chesthunte rd N17	30	M5
Chestnut all SW6	153	R14
Chestnut ave E7	52	H13
Chestnut ave N8	29	Z14
Chestnut ave Brent	72	H12
Chestnut ave Edg	11	Y19
Chestnut ave Epsom	128	A9
Chestnut ave Hmptn	100	G18
Chestnut ave Horn	57	V17
Chestnut ave Tedd	101	X20
Chestnut ave Wem	42	A14
Chestnut Avenue north E17	33	W13
Chestnut Avenue south E17	33	W14
Chestnut clo N14	6	J17
Chestnut clo SE6	111	R13
Chestnut clo SW16	108	F10
Chestnut clo Cars	130	L1
Chestnut ct SW6	153	R14
Chestnut dr E11	34	E18
Chestnut dr Bexh	97	W3
Chestnut dr Har	23	V2
Chestnut dr Pnr	22	A19
Chestnut glen Horn	57	V17
Chestnut gro SW12	89	O19
Chestnut gro W5	72	H7
Chestnut gro Barn	5	Z18
Chestnut gro Ilf	35	R6
Chestnut gro Islw	83	X11
Chestnut gro Mitch	121	Y11
Chestnut gro N Mal	117	Y6
Chestnut gro S Croy	134	A16
Chestnut gro Wem	42	A14
Chestnut la N20	14	D5
Chestnut ri SE18	79	U15
Chestnut rd SE27	108	K7
Chestnut rd SW20	117	R3
Chestnut rd Kings T	102	J19
Chestnut rd Twick	101	S3
Chestnut wk Wdf Grn	21	S15
Cheston ave Croy	134	J2
Cheswick clo Dart	99	T11
Chesworth clo Erith	99	S3
Chettle ct N8	30	F17
Chetwode rd SW17	107	N6
Chetwynd ave Barn	15	Z5
Chetwynd rd NW5	47	S11
Cheval pl SW7	154	M1
Cheval st E14	76	B7
Chevening rd NW6	136	F9
Chevening rd SE10	77	R14
Chevening rd SE19	109	N16
Chevenings the Sid	115	T7
Cheverton rd N19	47	W3
Chevet st E9	50	H15
Cheviot clo Bexh	99	P4
Cheviot clo Enf	8	C8
Cheviot clo Sutt	130	F20
Cheviot gdns NW2	45	S7
Cheviot gate NW2	45	T6
Cheviot rd SE27	108	G12
Cheviot rd Horn	57	X1
Cheviot way Ilf	36	H14
Chewton rd E17	32	H13
Cheyne ave E18	34	C10
Cheyne ave Twick	100	F3
Cheyne clo NW4	26	L17
Cheyne ct SW3	155	O13
Cheyne gdns SW3	154	M14
Cheyne hill Surb	117	N10
Cheyne ms SW3	154	M14
Cheyne row SW3	154	K14
Cheyne wk N21	7	V16
Cheyne wk NW4	26	M18
Cheyne wk SW3	154	K15
Cheyne wk SW10	154	G17
Cheyne wk Croy	133	Y3
Cheyneys ave Edg	11	W20
Chichele gdns Croy	133	T8
Chichele rd NW2	45	P14
Chicheley gdns Har	22	M2
Chicheley rd Har	23	N1
Chicheley st SE1	149	P16
Chichester clo E6	66	E18
Chichester clo SE3	94	L1
Chichester ct Epsom	128	D19
Chichester ct Stan	24	K9
Chichester gdns Ilf	53	T2
Chichester ms SE27	108	G9
Chichester rd E11	52	A9
Chichester rd N9	18	J4
Chichester rd NW6	137	T9
Chichester rd W2	145	Z1
Chichester rd Croy	133	R7
Chichester rd SW1	156	D11
Chichester way E14	76	J10
Chicksand st E1	151	R2
Chiddingfold N12	14	L11
Chiddingstone ave Bexh	81	P18
Chiddingstone st SW6	87	Y4
Chieveley rd Bexh	98	H10
Chigwell hill E1	151	X10
Chigwell rd E18	34	J9
Chigwell rd Wdf Grn	35	N2
Childebert rd SW17	107	S4
Childeric rd SE14	75	W19
Childerley st SW6	87	R1
Childers st SE8	75	W16
Childs la SE19	109	T16
Child's pl SW5	153	W6
Child's st SW5	153	W6
Childs way NW11	27	W14
Chilham clo Grnf	59	Z6
Chilham clo Bexh	97	W3
Chilham way Brom	126	E17
Chillerton rd SW17	107	N6
Chillingworth rd N7	48	E15
Chilmark gdns N Mal	118	F16
Chilmark rd SW16	121	Y2
Chiltern ave Twick	100	G3
Chiltern ave (Bushey) Wat	10	B1
Chiltern clo Bexh	99	P3
Chiltern clo Croy	133	T6
Chiltern clo Wor Pk	129	N2
Chiltern dene Enf	7	R13
Chiltern dr Surb	117	R14
Chiltern gdns NW2	45	P8
Chiltern gdns Brom	126	D8
Chiltern rd E3	64	C11
Chiltern rd Ilf	36	J14
Chiltern st W1	139	S20
Chilthorne clo SE6	93	N18
Chilton ave W5	72	H10
Chilton gro SE8	75	U11
Chilton rd Rich	85	P7
Chilton st E2	143	R15
Chiltonian Industrial est SE12	94	B16
Chilver st SE10	77	R13
Chilworth gdns Sutt	130	D6
Chilworth ms W2	146	E6
Chilworth st W2	146	D6
Chimes ave N13	17	V15
Chinbrook rd SE12	112	H7
Chine the N10	29	U13
Chine the N21	7	Y16
Chine the Wem	42	C14
Ching ct WC2	148	J6
Chingdale rd E4	21	N11
Chingford ave E4	20	C9
Chingford Hall est E4	19	Y18
Chingford la Wdf Grn	21	P14
Chingford Mount rd E4	20	B17
Chingford rd E4	20	C18
Chingford rd E17	33	P8
Chingley clo Brom	112	A15
Chinnor cres Grnf	58	M7
Chip st SW4	89	W9
Chipka st E14	76	G6
Chippendale st E5	50	F10
Chippenham ave Wem	43	U16
Chippenham gdns NW6	137	T14
Chippenham ms W9	137	T18
Chippenham rd W9	137	T17
Chipping clo Barn	4	F11
Chipstead ave Th Hth	122	J9
Chipstead clo SE19	109	V18
Chipstead gdns NW2	44	K7
Chipstead st SW6	87	Z3
Chisenhale rd E3	63	V5
Chisholm rd Croy	133	S2
Chisholm rd Rich	84	M17
Chislehurst ave N12	28	C1
Chislehurst rd Brom	127	O3
Chislehurst rd Chis	127	V1
Chislehurst rd Rich	84	K14
Chislehurst rd Sid	115	N12
Chislet clo Beck	111	P17
Chisley rd N15	31	R18
Chiswell sq SE3	94	J4
Chiswick bri SW14	85	V5
Chiswick bri W4	85	W4
Chiswick clo Croy	132	C6
Chiswick Common rd W4	73	Z11
Chiswick High rd W4	73	P14
Chiswick la W4	74	C13
Chiswick Lane south W4	74	D15
Chiswick mall W4	74	E15
Chiswick mall W6	74	F14
Chiswick quay W4	85	V2
Chiswick rd N9	18	L8
Chiswick rd W4	73	W12
Chiswick Staithe W4	85	U1
Chiswick vill W4	73	S15
Chitty st W1	140	C20
Chitty's la Dag	55	V4
Chivalry rd SW11	88	J12
Chivers rd E4	20	E12
Choats rd Dag	68	M8
Chobham gdns SW19	105	P4
Chobham rd E15	51	W15
Cholmeley cres N6	47	S1
Cholmeley pk N6	47	S3
Cholmley rd T Ditt	116	A16
Cholmondeley av NW10	62	F5
Choppins ct E1	151	Y13
Choumert gro SE15	91	X5
Choumert rd SE15	91	U6

Chrisp st E14	64	D15
Christ Church rd SW14	85	S12
Christ Church rd Surb	117	N16
Christchurch ave N12	15	P19
Christchurch ave NW6	136	H4
Christchurch ave Har	23	W12
Christchurch ave Tedd	101	X13
Christchurch ave Wem	42	L19
Christchurch clo SW19	106	G19
Christchurch gdns Har	23	Y12
Christchurch grn Wem	42	K19
Christchurch hill NW3	46	F10
Christchurch Industrial cen Har	23	W12
Christchurch la Barn	4	F9
Christchurch pk Sutt	130	C17
Christchurch pas NW3	46	F10
Christchurch pas Barn	4	F10
Christchurch rd N8	29	Z19
Christchurch rd SW2	90	B20
Christchurch rd SW19	106	G19
Christchurch rd Ilf	54	A3
Christchurch rd Sid	114	M9
Christchurch st SW3	155	N13
Christchurch ter SW3	155	O12
Christchurch way SE10	77	N13
Christian flds SW16	108	F19
Christian st E1	151	U5
Christie gdns Rom	37	R20
Christie rd E9	50	H19
Christina clo N4	48	J5
Christina st EC2	142	K17
Christopher ave W7	71	Y8
Christopher clo SE16	75	S5
Christopher clo Sid	96	L14
Christopher gdns Dag	55	W14
Christopher pl NW1	140	G13
Christopher st EC2	142	K17
Chryssell rd SW9	157	U19
Chubworthy st SE14	75	V17
Chudleigh cres Ilf	54	H12
Chudleigh gdns Sutt	130	D5
Chudleigh rd NW6	136	E1
Chudleigh rd SE4	92	M14
Chudleigh rd Twick	83	U16
Chudleigh st E1	63	T16
Chulsa rd SE26	109	Z12
Chumleigh st SE5	158	J13
Church all Croy	122	G19
Church app E21	109	P8
Church ave E4	20	K17
Church ave SW14	85	X9
Church ave Beck	125	O1
Church ave Nthlt	58	D1
Church ave Pnr	22	C19
Church ave Sid	115	O11
Church ave Sthl	70	C8
Church clo N20	15	X11
Church clo Edg	12	J17
Church cres E9	50	E20
Church cres N3	27	V4
Church cres N10	29	R13
Church cres N20	15	W10
Church dr NW9	43	X3
Church dr Har	22	F18
Church Elm la Dag	56	E19
Church end E17	33	S13
Church end NW4	26	K11
Church Farm la Sutt	129	T14
Church gdns W5	72	G6
Church gdns Wem	41	Z12
Church gate SW6	87	T6
Church gro SE13	93	S12
Church gro Kings T	116	E2
Church hill E17	33	P13
Church hill N21	17	R1
Church hill SE18	78	H9
Church hill SW19	105	U13
Church hill Cars	131	N10
Church hill Har	41	U3
Church Hill rd E17	33	S12
Church Hill rd Barn	14	S19
Church Hill rd Surb	116	K12
Church Hill rd Sutt	129	O7
Church la E11	51	Z4
Church la E17	33	S13
Church la N2	28	E10
Church la N8	30	C13
Church la N9	18	J8
Church la N17	31	S4
Church la NW9	43	X1
Church la SW17	107	N13
Church la SW19	119	X1
Church la W5	72	F5
Church la Brom	127	S19
Church la Chis	114	D20
Church la Dag	56	J19
Church la Enf	8	C11
Church la Har	23	V5
Church la Pnr	22	C10
Church la Rom	39	R13
Church la Tedd	101	W13
Church la Wall	131	Y6
Church Manor est SW9	157	U19
Church Manorway SE2	79	Z11
Church Manorway Erith	81	Z7
Church mt N2	28	G16
Church pas Surb	116	J12
Church path N5	48	J14
Church path N12	15	R13
Church path N20	15	R10
Church path NW10	44	C20
Church path SW14	85	Y7
Church path SW19	119	W3
Church path W4	73	W8
Church path W7	71	T2
Church path Croy	132	L3
Church path Mitch	120	H7
Church path Sthl	70	E8
Church pl W5	72	G5
Church pl Mitch	120	J6
Church ri SE23	110	F3
Church rd E10	51	N3
Church rd E12	53	R15
Church rd E17	32	H7
Church rd N6	29	O18
Church rd N17	31	T3
Church rd NW4	26	L12
Church rd NW10	62	A1
Church rd SE19	123	S1
Church rd SW13	86	F3
Church rd (Wimbledon) SW19	105	R13
Church rd W3	73	V4
Church rd W7	59	R20
Church rd Bark	54	B18
Church rd Bexh	98	B9
Church rd Brom	126	E3
Church rd (Shortlands) Brom	125	Z6
Church rd Buck H	21	V5
Church rd Croy	132	K4
Church rd Enf	9	S17
Church rd Erith	81	Z13
Church rd Ilf	36	G19
Church rd Islw	71	T20
Church rd Kings T	117	N3
Church rd Mitch	120	G1
Church rd Nthlt	58	B4
Church rd Rich	84	J10
Church rd (Ham) Rich	102	H9
Church rd Sid	115	O11
Church rd Sthl	70	E8
Church rd Stan	11	O16
Church rd Tedd	101	U10
Church rd Wall	131	W5
Church rd Well	97	P4
Church rd Wor Pk	118	A20
Church row NW3	46	D13
Church row Chis	114	D20
Church st E15	65	N3
Church st E16	78	L4
Church st N9	18	D5
Church st NW8	138	K18
Church st W2	138	G20
Church st W4	74	C16
Church st Croy	132	K5
Church st Dag	56	H19
Church st Enf	8	A12
Church st Epsom	128	F19
Church st Islw	84	A7
Church st Kings T	116	H4
Church st Twick	101	Z1
Church Street est NW8	138	H18
Church Street north E15	65	N2
Church Street pas E15	65	O2
Church Stretton rd Houns	83	O12
Church ter NW4	26	L11
Church ter SE13	93	Z9
Church ter SW8	89	Y4
Church vale N2	28	L8
Church vale SE23	110	E4
Church wk N16	49	R10
Church wk NW2	45	W9
Church wk NW4	26	M11
Church wk SW13	86	F3
Church wk SW15	86	K13
Church wk SW16	121	W4
Church wk SW20	118	M6
Church wk Brent	72	E16
Church way N20	15	V9
Church way Edg	12	D19
Church Yard row SE11	157	Y5
Churchbury clo Enf	8	B20
Churchbury la Enf	8	C11
Churchbury rd SE9	95	N18
Churchbury rd Enf	8	D7
Churchcroft clo SW12	89	P19
Churchdown Brom	111	Z9
Churchfield ave N12	15	S18
Churchfield clo Har	23	N13
Churchfield rd W3	73	W2
Churchfield rd W7	71	T5
Churchfield rd W13	72	C2
Churchfield rd Well	97	O8
Churchfields E18	34	E4
Churchfields rd Beck	124	C4
Churchill ave Har	24	B18
Churchill gdns W3	61	R18
Churchill Gardens est SW1	156	A11
Churchill Gardens rd SW1	155	Z12
Churchill ms Wdf Grn	21	P20
Churchill pl E14	76	E2
Churchill rd E16	65	Y17
Churchill rd NW2	44	J17
Churchill rd NW5	47	T11
Churchill rd Edg	12	B20
Churchill rd S Croy	132	M18
Churchill ter E4	20	B12
Churchill wk E9	50	D15
Churchley rd SE26	110	B9
Churchmead clo Barn	5	W20
Churchmead rd NW10	44	G18
Churchmore rd SW16	107	W20
Churchview rd Twick	101	P3
Churchway NW1	140	G13
Churchwell path E9	50	C15
Churston ave E13	65	W3
Churston clo SW2	108	H2
Churston dr Mord	119	R11
Churston gdns N11	16	H19
Churton pl SW1	156	C7
Churton st SW1	156	C7
Chusan pl E14	63	Z18
Chyngton clo Sid	114	K6
Cibber rd SE23	110	G3
Cicada rd SW18	88	D15
Cicely rd SE15	91	Y3
Cinderford way Brom	112	A10
Cinema par W5	60	M10
Cinnamon row SW11	88	F7
Cinnamon st E1	151	Z14
Cintra pk SE19	109	U17
Circle the NW2	44	B9
Circle the NW7	12	M17
Circle gdns SW19	119	Y5
Circular rd N17	31	V9
Circular way SE18	78	H16
Circus pl EC2	150	G3
Circus rd NW8	138	G20
Circus st SE10	76	G19
Cirencester st W2	137	W20
Cissbury Ring north N12	14	J15
Cissbury Ring south N12	14	J17
Cissbury rd N15	31	P16
Citadel pl SE11	157	N9
Citizen rd N7	48	E12
City Garden row N1	141	Y10
City rd EC1	141	X10
Civic way Ilf	36	D12
Clabon ms SW1	155	O3
Clack st SE16	75	R5
Clacton rd E6	66	A8
Clacton rd E17	32	H17
Clacton rd N17	31	U8
Claigmar gdns N3	27	Z5
Claire ct N12	15	P12
Claire ct Pnr	22	F1
Claire pl E14	76	B8
Clairvale rd Houns	82	A2
Clairview rd SW16	107	T11
Clairville gdns W7	71	U2
Clamp hill Stan	10	D14
Clancarty rd SW6	87	Z5
Clandon clo W3	73	U4
Clandon clo Epsom	128	E14
Clandon gdns N3	27	Y11
Clandon rd Ilf	54	J6
Clandon st SE8	93	P4
Clanricarde gdns W2	145	W10
Clap la Dag	56	H8
Clapham Common North side SW4	89	N11
Clapham Common South side SW4	89	T15
Clapham Common West side SW4	89	N12
Clapham cres SW4	89	X11
Clapham High st SW4	89	X10
Clapham Manor st SW4	89	W7
Clapham Park est SW4	89	Y17
Clapham Park rd SW4	89	X11
Clapham rd SW9	157	R18
Claps Gate la Bark	66	M11
Clapton common E5	49	W1
Clapton Park est E5	50	G12
Clapton sq E5	50	B14
Clapton ter N16	49	X2
Clapton way E5	49	Y10
Clara pl SE18	78	K10
Clare corner SE9	95	Y20
Clare gdns E7	52	E12
Clare gdns W11	145	N6
Clare gdns Bark	54	M18
Clare gdns Stan	11	R16
Clare la N1	142	C1
Clare Lawn ave SW14	85	X14
Clare mkt WC2	149	P6
Clare ms SW6	153	X20
Clare rd E11	33	Y19
Clare rd NW10	44	G19
Clare rd SE14	92	L3
Clare rd Grnf	41	R17
Clare rd Houns	82	D8
Clare st E2	143	X9
Clare way Bexh	97	Y1
Claredale st E2	143	V10
Claremont ave Har	24	B18
Claremont ave N Mal	118	H13
Claremont clo E16	78	K3
Claremont clo N1	141	T11
Claremont cres Dart	99	R10
Claremont gdns Ilf	54	H6
Claremont gdns Surb	116	J11
Claremont gro Wdf Grn	21	Y18
Claremont pk N3	27	T5
Claremont rd E7	52	H15
Claremont rd E11	51	W8
Claremont rd E17	32	J7
Claremont rd N6	29	U20

Name	Page	Grid
Claremont rd NW2	45	N2
Claremont rd W9	137	N10
Claremont rd W13	59	Y13
Claremont rd Barn	5	T1
Claremont rd Brom	127	S10
Claremont rd Croy	123	Y19
Claremont rd Har	23	T8
Claremont rd Horn	39	V19
Claremont rd Surb	116	J14
Claremont rd Tedd	101	W11
Claremont rd Twick	84	C17
Claremont sq N1	141	S10
Claremont st E16	78	K3
Claremont st N18	18	J18
Claremont st SE10	76	F18
Claremont way NW2	44	M4
Clarence ave SW4	89	W18
Clarence ave Brom	127	R8
Clarence ave Ilf	35	V18
Clarence ave N Mal	117	V4
Clarence clo (Bushey) Wat	10	G3
Clarence cres SW4	89	Y17
Clarence cres Sid	115	P8
Clarence gdns NW1	139	Z14
Clarence la SW15	86	B15
Clarence ms E5	50	B14
Clarence pas NW1	140	J10
Clarence pl E5	50	B14
Clarence rd E5	50	A12
Clarence rd E12	53	N14
Clarence rd E16	65	N13
Clarence rd E17	32	G7
Clarence rd N15	31	N14
Clarence rd N22	30	A2
Clarence rd NW6	137	O2
Clarence rd SE9	113	R5
Clarence rd SW19	105	Z15
Clarence rd W4	73	P13
Clarence rd Bexh	97	Y10
Clarence rd Brom	127	P6
Clarence rd Croy	123	O17
Clarence rd Enf	9	P17
Clarence rd Rich	85	O3
Clarence rd Sid	115	P7
Clarence rd Sutt	130	A10
Clarence rd Tedd	101	X16
Clarence rd Wall	131	S12
Clarence st Kings T	116	H3
Clarence st Sthl	70	A7
Clarence ter Houns	82	J10
Clarence wk SW4	90	A4
Clarence way NW1	47	S19
Clarence way est NW1	47	T19
Clarendon clo W2	146	K8
Clarendon cres Twick	101	P7
Clarendon cross W11	144	M11
Clarendon dr SW15	86	M9
Clarendon gdns NW4	26	H9
Clarendon gdns W9	138	C18
Clarendon gdns Ilf	53	V2
Clarendon gdns Wem	42	H11
Clarendon gro NW1	121	N5
Clarendon ms W2	146	K7
Clarendon pl W2	146	K7
Clarendon ri SE13	93	W9
Clarendon rd E11	51	X3
Clarendon rd E17	33	R18
Clarendon rd E18	34	F10
Clarendon rd N8	30	D10
Clarendon rd N15	30	K14
Clarendon rd N18	18	K18
Clarendon rd N22	30	D8
Clarendon rd SW19	106	H18
Clarendon rd W5	60	J10
Clarendon rd W11	144	L7
Clarendon rd Croy	132	K2
Clarendon rd Har	23	T14
Clarendon rd Wall	131	U13
Clarendon st SW1	155	Y10
Clarendon ter W9	138	E17
Clarendon way N21	17	Z1
Claret gdns SE25	123	S8
Clareville gro SW7	154	E7
Clareville st SW7	154	E7
Clarges ms W1	147	X12
Clarges st W1	147	Y13
Claribel rd SW9	90	H4
Clarice way Wall	132	A19
Claridge rd Dag	55	W4
Clarina rd E9	37	V20
Clarissa st E8	143	O3
Clark clo Erith	99	W2
Clark st E1	151	Z3
Clarkes ave Wor Pk	129	P2
Clarks mead (Bushey) Wat	10	B3
Clarks pl EC2	150	K4
Clarks rd Ilf	54	G6
Clarkson rd E16	65	O16
Clarkson st E2	143	W12
Clarksons the Bark	67	P5
Claude rd E10	51	V5
Claude rd E13	65	V2
Claude st E14	76	B11
Claudia pl SW19	105	S2
Claughton rd E13	65	Z6
Clauson ave Nthlt	40	L14
Clave st E1	151	Z13
Claverdale rd SW2	90	D19
Clavering ave SW13	152	A13
Clavering clo Twick	101	X9
Clavering rd E12	53	N5
Claverley gro N3	27	Z3
Claverton st SW1	156	D12
Claxton gro W6	152	H12
Clay ave Mitch	121	S4
Clay hill Enf	8	C1
Clay la Edg	12	C6
Clay la (Bushey) Wat	10	F2
Clay st W1	147	R1
Claybank gro SE13	93	R7
Claybridge rd SE12	112	M10
Claybrook clo N2	28	F9
Claybrook rd W6	152	H13
Claybury bdy Ilf	35	P9
Claybury rd Wdf Grn	35	S1
Claydon dr Croy	132	B9
Clayfarm rd SE9	114	C5
Claygate clo Horn	57	V12
Claygate cres Croy	135	V15
Claygate rd W13	72	A7
Clayhall ave Ilf	35	P9
Clayhill Surb	117	O11
Clayhill cres SE9	113	N10
Claylands pl SW8	157	S16
Claylands rd SW8	157	P15
Claymore clo Mord	119	Y17
Claypole rd E15	64	H6
Clayponds ave Brent	72	J12
Clayponds gdns W5	72	H11
Clayponds la Brent	72	K14
Clays la E15	51	T14
Clays Lane clo E15	51	T15
Clayton ave Wem	42	K20
Clayton clo E6	66	H17
Clayton cres Brent	72	G13
Clayton fld NW9	26	C2
Clayton rd SE15	91	Y3
Clayton rd Islw	83	T9
Clayton rd Rom	56	K3
Clayton st SE11	157	T13
Clayworth clo Sid	97	P15
Cleanthus rd SE18	79	M2
Clearbrook way E1	63	S16
Clearwell dr W9	137	Y7
Cleaveland rd Surb	116	F12
Cleaver sq SE11	157	U10
Cleaver st SE11	157	U10
Cleaverholme clo SE25	123	Z15
Cleeve hill SE23	92	B1
Cleeve Park gdns Sid	115	R5
Clegg st E1	151	Z13
Clegg st E13	65	T5
Clem Attlee ct SW6	153	P15
Clematis st W12	62	F19
Clemence st E14	63	Y16
Clement clo NW6	136	D2
Clement rd SW19	105	S13
Clement rd Beck	124	F4
Clementhorpe rd Dag	55	T18
Clementina rd E10	50	K5
Clementine clo W13	72	A6
Clements ave E16	65	T13
Clement's Inn WC2	149	P6
Clements la EC4	150	G8
Clements la Ilf	53	Z9
Clements pl Brent	72	G13
Clements rd E6	66	F1
Clements rd SE16	159	U3
Clements rd Ilf	54	A9
Clendon way SE18	79	R10
Clenham st SE1	150	B16
Clensham la Sutt	129	Y3
Clenston ms W1	147	R1
Clephane rd N1	49	N17
Clere st EC2	142	H17
Clerkenwell clo EC1	141	V17
Clerkenwell grn EC1	141	V18
Clerkenwell rd EC1	141	S19
Clermont rd E9	63	P2
Cleve rd NW6	45	Z20
Cleve rd Sid	115	W7
Clevedon rd SE20	124	F1
Clevedon rd Kings T	117	P3
Clevedon rd Twick	84	G15
Cleveland ave SW20	119	U3
Cleveland ave W4	74	D11
Cleveland ave Hmptn	100	E17
Cleveland gdns N4	30	L16
Cleveland gdns NW2	45	R6
Cleveland gdns SW13	86	C5
Cleveland gdns W2	146	B6
Cleveland gdns Wor Pk	128	C3
Cleveland ms W1	140	B19
Cleveland Park ave E17	33	O12
Cleveland Park cres E17	33	N12
Cleveland pl SW1	148	D13
Cleveland ri Mord	119	R18
Cleveland rd E18	34	G10
Cleveland rd N1	142	G2
Cleveland rd SW13	86	D5
Cleveland rd W13	59	Y14
Cleveland rd Ilf	54	A9
Cleveland rd Islw	83	Y10
Cleveland rd N Mal	118	A8
Cleveland rd Well	96	L5
Cleveland rd Wor Pk	128	B3
Cleveland row SW1	148	B15
Cleveland sq W2	146	C6
Cleveland st W1	140	A18
Cleveland ter W2	146	C5
Cleveland way E1	63	P12
Cleveley clo SE7	78	C10
Cleveley cres W5	60	L7
Cleves ave Epsom	128	K20
Cleves rd E6	66	B4
Cleves rd Rich	102	E7
Cleves wk Ilf	36	C2
Cleves way Hmptn	100	F18
Clewer cres Har	23	P5
Clichy est E1	63	R15
Clifden rd E5	50	D14
Clifden rd Brent	72	G16
Clifden rd Twick	83	W20
Cliff rd NW1	47	Y17
Cliff ter SE8	93	P5
Cliff vill NW1	47	Y17
Cliff wk E16	65	R13
Cliffe rd S Croy	133	O11
Clifford ave SW14	85	U6
Clifford ave Chis	113	U15
Clifford ave Ilf	35	Z5
Clifford ave Wall	131	V8
Clifford clo Nthlt	58	B4
Clifford dr SW9	90	J10
Clifford gdns NW10	136	E9
Clifford rd E16	65	O12
Clifford rd E17	33	U8
Clifford rd N9	9	R20
Clifford rd SE25	123	W9
Clifford rd Barn	5	O10
Clifford rd Rich	102	H4
Clifford rd Wem	60	F1
Clifford st W1	148	A10
Clifford way NW10	44	D12
Cliffview rd SE13	93	P9
Clifton ave E17	32	G11
Clifton ave N3	27	V4
Clifton ave W12	74	F4
Clifton ave Stan	24	C7
Clifton ave Wem	43	O16
Clifton cres SE15	159	Y18
Clifton est SE15	91	Y3
Clifton gdns N15	31	W18
Clifton gdns NW11	27	X18
Clifton gdns W9	138	B18
Clifton gdns Enf	7	N15
Clifton gro E8	49	X17
Clifton hill NW8	138	A7
Clifton Park ave SW20	119	N4
Clifton pl SE16	75	R4
Clifton pl W2	146	H7
Clifton ri SE14	75	X20
Clifton rd E7	53	O18
Clifton rd E16	65	O14
Clifton rd N3	28	D3
Clifton rd N8	29	X17
Clifton rd N22	29	W4
Clifton rd NW10	62	F7
Clifton rd SE25	123	R9
Clifton rd SW19	105	O16
Clifton rd W9	138	D17
Clifton rd Grnf	59	O11
Clifton rd Har	24	M15
Clifton rd Horn	39	V19
Clifton rd Ilf	36	E19
Clifton rd Islw	83	S4
Clifton rd Kings T	103	O19
Clifton rd Sid	114	H9
Clifton rd Sthl	70	C10
Clifton rd Tedd	101	U10
Clifton rd Wall	131	T11
Clifton rd Well	97	T7
Clifton st EC2	142	J20
Clifton ter N4	48	F5
Clifton vill W9	138	A20
Clifton way SE15	159	Z19
Clifton way Wem	60	K3
Clinch ct E16	65	U15
Cline rd N11	16	H19
Clinger ct N1	142	J7
Clink st SE1	150	E12
Clinton ave Well	96	M10
Clinton rd E3	63	W9
Clinton rd E7	52	F13
Clinton rd N15	31	N13
Clipper way SE13	93	U11
Clipstone ms W1	140	A19
Clipstone rd Houns	82	H7
Clipstone st W1	140	A20
Clissold cres N16	49	N10
Clissold rd N16	49	P9
Clitheroe ave Har	40	F5
Clitheroe rd SW9	90	A5
Clitherow ave W7	71	X7
Clitherow rd Brent	72	C13
Clitterhouse cres NW2	45	N4
Clitterhouse rd NW2	45	N4
Clive ave Dart	99	T17
Clive pas SE21	109	P8
Clive rd SE21	109	O6
Clive rd SW19	106	H16
Clive rd Belv	81	R11
Clive rd Enf	8	J13
Clive rd Rom	39	Z16
Clive rd Twick	101	Y8
Clive way Enf	8	J14
Cliveden clo N12	15	P13
Cliveden pl SW1	155	T6
Cliveden rd SW19	105	V20
Clivedon rd E4	20	M16
Cloak la EC4	150	D8
Clock House rd Beck	124	H7
Clock Tower ms N1	142	C6
Clock Tower pl N7	48	A17
Clock Tower rd Islw	83	W8
Clockhouse ave Bark	66	P2
Clockhouse clo SW19	105	N5
Clockhouse la Rom	38	J1
Cloister gdns SE25	123	Z15
Cloister gdns Edg	12	J15
Cloister rd NW2	45	U8
Cloister rd W3	61	V15
Cloisters the SW9	90	G3
Cloisters ave Brom	127	T12
Clonbrock rd N16	49	R12
Cloncurry st SW6	87	R3

Name	Page	Grid
Clonmel clo Har	41	R5
Clonmell rd Tedd	101	P10
Clonmell rd N17	31	P10
Clonmell rd SW6	153	R20
Clonmore st SW18	105	W1
Clorane gdns NW3	45	X10
Close the N14	16	K8
Close the N20	14	H7
Close the Barn	6	A18
Close the Beck	124	H9
Close the Bex	98	D17
Close the Cars	130	K19
Close the Har	23	O7
Close the Islw	83	P3
Close the Mitch	120	L10
Close the N Mal	117	X4
Close the (Eastcote) Pnr	22	F20
Close the Rich	85	S7
Close the Rom	37	Y17
Close the Sid	115	S11
Close the Sutt	119	V17
Close the (Barnhill rd) Wem	43	W9
Close the Wem (Lyon Park ave)	42	K18
Cloth Fair EC1	149	Z2
Cloth st EC1	150	A1
Clothworkers rd SE18	79	T19
Cloudesdale rd SW17	107	R4
Cloudesley pl N1	141	T7
Cloudesley rd N1	141	T4
Cloudesley rd Bexh	98	C3
Cloudesley rd Erith	99	T2
Cloudesley sq N1	141	T5
Cloudesley st N1	141	U6
Clouston clo Wall	131	Z11
Clova rd E7	52	D16
Clovelly ave NW9	26	C12
Clovelly gdns SE19	109	W20
Clovelly gdns Enf	18	E2
Clovelly gdns Rom	38	H4
Clovelly rd N8	29	Y12
Clovelly rd W4	73	X6
Clovelly rd W5	72	E6
Clovelly rd Bexh	80	L17
Clovelly rd Houns	82	J5
Clovelly way Har	40	D8
Clover clo E11	51	Y7
Clover ms SW3	155	P13
Clover way Wall	121	R20
Cloverdale gdns Sid	96	K16
Clowders rd SE6	110	L6
Clowser clo Sutt	130	E11
Cloyster wd Edg	11	V20
Club Gardens rd Brom	126	G17
Club row E1	143	O16
Club row E1	143	N16
Clunbury ave Sthl	70	D14
Clunbury st N1	142	H9
Cluny ms SW5	153	S7
Cluny pl SE1	158	K1
Cluse ct N1	142	A8
Clutton st E14	64	E14
Clydach rd Enf	8	H12
Clyde circ N15	31	S11
Clyde pl E10	51	R2
Clyde rd N15	31	S12
Clyde rd N22	29	X4
Clyde rd Croy	133	U2
Clyde rd Sutt	129	Z10
Clyde rd Wall	131	V13
Clyde st SE8	75	Z17
Clyde ter SE23	110	D5
Clyde vale SE23	110	D5
Clyde way Rom	39	P3
Clydesdale Enf	9	T15
Clydesdale ave Stan	24	G9
Clydesdale gdns Rich	85	S9
Clydesdale rd W11	145	P5
Clydesdale rd Horn	57	T2
Clyston st SW8	89	W4
Coach & Horses yd W1	148	A9
Coach House la SW19	105	P9
Coach House ms SE20	109	Z18
Coach House ms SE23	92	E17
Coalecroft rd SW15	86	M12
Coate st E2	143	U9
Coates Hill rd Brom	127	X4
Coates rd Borwd	11	T1
Coates wk Brent	72	J15
Cobb st E1	151	N3
Cobbett rd SE9	95	S8
Cobbett rd Twick	100	H1
Cobbett st SW8	157	P20
Cobbetts ave Ilf	35	O16
Cobblers wk E Mol	102	A20
Cobblers wk Hmptn	101	N19
Cobblers wk Kings T	116	C1
Cobblers wk Tedd	101	T19
Cobbold est NW10	44	E18
Cobbold rd NW10	44	D18
Cobbold rd W12	74	C6
Cobb's brk Houns	82	E12
Cobden rd E11	52	A8
Cobden rd SE25	123	Y12
Cobham ave N Mal	118	G11
Cobham clo SW11	88	K15
Cobham clo Brom	127	R17
Cobham clo Wall	131	Z15
Cobham pl Bexh	97	Y12
Cobham rd E17	33	V4
Cobham rd N22	30	J9
Cobham rd Ilf	35	J7
Cobham rd Kings T	117	P2
Cobland rd SE12	112	M10
Coborn rd E3	63	Y7
Coborn st E3	63	Z8
Cobourg rd SE5	159	N14
Cobourg st NW1	156	D4
Coburg clo SW1	156	D4
Coburg cres SW2	108	E2
Coburg gdns Ilf	35	P8
Coburg rd N22	30	D8
Cochrane ms NW8	138	H9
Cochrane rd SW19	105	U18
Cochrane st NW8	138	H9
Cock la EC1	149	X3
Cockayne way SE8	75	X12
Cockfosters rd Barn	5	X1
Cockpit yd WC1	141	O19
Cocks cres N Mal	118	C9
Cockspur ct SW1	148	G12
Cockspur st SW1	148	G12
Code st E1	143	R18
Codling clo E1	151	U13
Codling way Wem	42	F12
Codrington hill SE23	92	J18
Codrington ms W11	145	N7
Cody clo Har	24	H10
Cody clo Wall	131	Z17
Cody rd E16	64	L12
Coe ave SE25	123	X15
Cofers circ Wem	43	T8
Cogan ave E17	32	H3
Coin st SE1	149	T13
Coity rd NW5	47	P17
Coke st E1	151	T4
Colas ms NW6	137	V4
Colbeck ms SW7	154	A7
Colbeck rd Har	41	N1
Colberg pl N16	49	T2
Colborne way Wor Pk	128	L5
Colburn way Sutt	130	F6
Colby rd SE19	109	T12
Colchester ave E12	53	U10
Colchester rd E10	33	U20
Colchester rd E17	33	N19
Colchester rd Edg	25	W1
Cold Blow la SE14	75	T18
Cold Blows Mitch	120	M7
Cold Harbour E14	76	H4
Coldbath sq EC1	141	T17
Coldbath st SE13	93	S4
Coldershaw rd W13	71	Y3
Coldfall ave N10	29	N7
Coldharbour la SW9	90	G10
Coldharbour la Croy	132	G12
Coldharbour way Croy	132	G12
Coldstream gdns SW18	87	U15
Cole clo SE28	80	D3
Cole Park gdns Twick	83	Y14
Cole Park rd Twick	83	Y14
Cole rd Twick	83	Y17
Cole st SE1	150	D19
Colebeck ms N1	48	J19
Colebert ave E1	63	P11
Colebrook clo SW15	87	P18
Colebrook rd SW16	122	B1
Colebrook way N11	16	F16
Colebrooke ave W13	60	A18
Colebrooke dr E11	34	K20
Colebrooke pl N1	141	Y6
Colebrooke row N1	141	W10
Coledale dr Stan	24	C5
Coleford rd SW18	88	C12
Colegrave rd E15	51	W14
Colegrove rd SE15	159	R16
Coleherne ms SW10	153	Y11
Coleherne rd SW10	153	Y10
Colehill gdns SW6	87	S3
Colehill la SW6	87	S3
Coleman clo SE25	123	W4
Coleman rd SE5	158	J17
Coleman rd Belv	81	S10
Coleman rd Dag	56	A19
Coleman st EC2	150	E5
Colemans heath SE9	113	V7
Colenso rd E5	50	D11
Colenso rd Ilf	54	G3
Colepits Wood rd SE9	96	D12
Coleraine rd N8	30	F10
Coleraine rd SE3	77	P17
Coleridge ave E12	53	R16
Coleridge ave Sutt	130	K8
Coleridge clo SW8	89	T5
Coleridge gdns NW6	138	B2
Coleridge la N8	29	Z17
Coleridge rd E17	32	L11
Coleridge rd N4	48	F8
Coleridge rd N8	29	X19
Coleridge rd N12	15	R16
Coleridge rd Croy	124	C16
Coleridge rd Rom	39	Y2
Coleridge sq SW3	59	X18
Coleridge wk NW11	27	X14
Coles cres Har	40	J7
Coles grn (Bushey) Wat	10	B4
Coles Green rd NW2	44	G5
Colesburg rd Beck	124	K5
Coleshill rd Tedd	101	U15
Colestown st SW11	88	K4
Colet clo N13	17	W18
Colet gdns W14	152	H7
Coley st WC1	141	P17
Colfe rd SE23	110	H1
Colin clo NW9	26	B13
Colin clo Croy	134	K5
Colin cres NW9	26	E12
Colin dr NW9	26	E15
Colin gdns NW9	26	E15
Colin Park rd NW9	26	A11
Colin rd NW10	44	F17
Colina ms N15	30	J14
Colina rd N15	30	J14
Colindale ave NW9	25	Z10
Colindale Business pk NW9	25	W9
Colindeep gdns NW4	26	H14
Colindeep la NW9	25	Z11
Colinette rd SW15	86	M11
Colinton rd Ilf	55	S5
Coliston rd SW18	87	Y18
Collamore ave SW18	106	H2
Collapit clo Har	22	L17
College app SE10	76	H16
College ave Har	23	T4
College clo E9	50	C14
College clo N18	18	H16
College clo Har	23	U2
College cres NW3	46	F19
College cross N1	141	V1
College gdns E4	20	D3
College gdns N18	18	J16
College gdns SE21	91	R20
College gdns SW17	106	J4
College gdns Enf	8	B7
College gdns Ilf	35	R15
College gdns N Mal	118	C12
College grn SE19	109	R18
College gro NW1	140	E5
College hill EC4	150	D8
College Hill rd Har	23	T2
College la NW5	47	S12
College ms SW1	156	K1
College Park clo SE13	93	W13
College pl E17	33	Z12
College pl NW1	140	C4
College rd E17	33	U17
College rd N17	18	G20
College rd N21	17	U7
College rd NW10	136	B7
College rd SE19	109	V11
College rd SE21	91	S20
College rd SW19	106	G16
College rd W13	60	A17
College rd Brom	126	E2
College rd Croy	133	O4
College rd Enf	8	C7
College rd Har (Harrow on the Hill)	23	S19
College rd Har (Harrow Weald)	23	S4
College rd Islw	83	V1
College rd Wem	42	H3
College row E9	50	E15
College Slip Brom	126	E2
College st EC4	150	D8
College ter E3	63	X8
College ter N3	27	W6
College vw SE9	113	P3
Collent st E9	50	D18
Colless rd N15	31	V15
Collett rd SE16	159	U2
Collett way Sthl	70	K5
Collier dr Edg	25	P6
Collier Row la Rom	38	J2
Collier Row rd Rom	38	B6
Collier st N1	141	N10
Colliers Water la Th Hth	122	G11
Collindale ave Erith	81	W17
Collindale ave Sid	97	O19
Collingbourne rd W12	74	J1
Collingham gdns SW5	153	Z7
Collingham pl SW5	153	Y6
Collingham rd SW5	153	Z5
Collings clo N22	17	P18
Collingtree rd SE26	110	C9
Collingwood ave N10	29	O11
Collingwood ave Surb	117	W19
Collingwood clo SE20	110	A20
Collingwood clo Twick	82	H17
Collingwood rd E17	33	O18
Collingwood rd N15	31	S12
Collingwood rd Mitch	120	H5
Collingwood rd Sutt	129	W6
Collingwood st E1	143	X16
Collins ave Stan	24	J7
Collins rd N5	48	M11
Collins st SE3	94	B6
Collin's yd N1	141	X5
Collinson st SE1	150	B18
Collinwood ave Enf	9	R12
Collinwood gdns Ilf	35	V15
Colls rd SE15	92	C1
Collyer ave Croy	132	A9
Collyer rd Croy	132	B8
Colman rd E16	65	Y15
Colmer pl Har	23	P2
Colmer rd SW16	108	B19
Colmore ms SE15	92	A2
Colmore rd Enf	9	S14
Colnbrook st SE1	157	W2
Colne rd E5	50	H13
Colne rd N21	18	B3
Colne rd Twick	101	S2
Colne st E13	65	T9
Colney Hatch la N10	29	P2
Colney Hatch la N11	15	Z17

Name	No.	Ref
Cologne rd SW11	88	G10
Colomb st SE10	77	O14
Colombo rd Ilf	54	B2
Colombo st SE1	149	W14
Colonial ave Twick	83	N14
Colonnade WC1	140	K18
Colonnades the W2	145	Z5
Colson rd Croy	133	R2
Colson way SW16	107	V10
Colsterworth rd N15	31	V12
Colston ave Cars	130	L8
Colston clo Cars	130	L9
Colston rd E7	53	O18
Colston rd SW14	85	W10
Coltness cres SE2	80	D13
Colton gdns N17	30	M9
Colton rd Har	23	U14
Columbia ave Edg	25	S4
Columbia ave Wor Pk	118	D18
Columbia ctyd E14	76	A2
Columbia rd E2	143	N13
Columbia rd E13	65	R13
Columbia sq SW14	85	W9
Columbine ave E6	66	D14
Columbine ave S Croy	132	K16
Columbine way SE13	93	U5
Colvestone cres E8	49	U16
Colview ct SE9	113	O2
Colville est N1	142	H5
Colville gdns W11	145	R6
Colville hos W11	145	P5
Colville ms W11	145	S6
Colville rd E11	51	W9
Colville rd E17	32	K8
Colville rd N9	18	M4
Colville rd W3	73	U9
Colville rd W11	145	R6
Colville ter W11	145	P6
Colvin clo SE26	110	C12
Colvin gdns E4	20	H10
Colvin gdns E11	34	J13
Colvin gdns Ilf	36	C3
Colvin rd E6	66	D2
Colvin rd Th Hth	122	F13
Colwell rd SE22	91	U14
Colwith rd W6	152	D15
Colwood gdns SW19	106	G18
Colworth gro SE17	158	C8
Colworth rd E11	33	Z19
Colworth rd Croy	123	X20
Colwyn ave Grnf	59	X6
Colwyn cres Houns	82	M3
Colwyn rd NW2	44	K9
Colyer clo SE9	114	A4
Colyers clo Erith	99	N1
Colyers la Erith	99	M1
Colyton clo Well	97	W1
Colyton rd SE22	92	A14
Colyton way N18	18	J17
Combe ave SE3	77	P18
Combe lo SE7	77	Y16
Combe ms SE3	77	P19
Combedale rd SE10	77	S14
Combemartin rd SW18	87	T19
Comber clo NW2	44	H8
Comber gro SE5	158	B20
Combermere rd SW9	90	C7
Combermere rd Mord	120	B13
Comberton rd E5	50	A6
Combeside SE18	79	Y20
Combwell cres SE2	80	B9
Comely Bank rd E17	33	T14
Comeragh ms W14	152	M10
Comeragh rd W14	152	L11
Comerford rd SE4	92	K11
Comet pl SE8	76	B20
Comet st SE8	76	A20
Commerce rd N22	30	C3
Commerce rd Brent	72	D18
Commerce way Croy	132	D4
Commercial rd E1	151	T5
Commercial rd E14	63	O17
Commercial rd N17	18	F9
Commercial rd N18	18	F17
Commercial st E1	142	M18
Commercial way NW10	61	U7
Commercial way SE15	159	N20
Commerell st SE10	77	N13

Name	No.	Ref
Commodity quay E1	151	P11
Commodore st E1	63	V12
Common the W5	60	K20
Common the Rich	102	F8
Common the Sthl	70	A12
Common the Stan	10	H8
Common rd SW13	86	H7
Common rd Stan	10	D11
Commondale SW15	86	M6
Commonside east Mitch	121	O6
Commonside west Mitch	121	N7
Commonwealth ave W12	62	J20
Commonwealth rd N17	31	Y1
Commonwealth way SE2	80	E13
Community rd E15	51	X15
Community rd Grnf	59	O4
Como rd SE23	110	H3
Como st Rom	39	O13
Compayne gdns NW6	46	A19
Compton ave E6	66	B6
Compton ave N1	48	J19
Compton ave N6	46	J2
Compton clo W13	59	X17
Compton clo Edg	25	U2
Compton ct SE19	109	R13
Compton cres N17	31	N1
Compton cres W4	73	V16
Compton cres Nthlt	58	A1
Compton pl WC1	140	K15
Compton ri Pnr	22	D16
Compton rd N1	48	K18
Compton rd N21	17	U4
Compton rd NW10	136	G13
Compton rd SW19	105	V15
Compton rd Croy	123	Z20
Compton st EC1	141	Y16
Compton ter N1	48	J18
Comreddy clo Enf	7	V4
Comus pl SE17	158	H6
Comyn rd SW11	88	J11
Comyns the (Bushey) Wat	10	B5
Comyns clo E16	65	P13
Comyns rd Dag	56	D20
Conant ms E1	151	T8
Concanon rd SW2	90	C10
Concert Hall app SE1	149	P14
Concord rd W3	61	S12
Concord rd Enf	9	O17
Concorde clo Houns	82	J6
Concorde dr E6	66	G14
Concourse the NW9	26	D5
Condell rd SW8	89	W2
Conder st E14	63	W16
Conderton rd SE5	90	M7
Condover cres SE18	78	M20
Condray pl SW11	154	J20
Conduit rd WC2	148	K8
Conduit la N18	19	O15
Conduit la Croy	133	Z11
Conduit la S Croy	133	W13
Conduit ms W2	146	F7
Conduit pl W2	146	F6
Conduit rd SE18	79	N12
Conduit st W1	148	A8
Conduit way NW10	43	U20
Conewood st N5	48	J10
Coney acre SE21	108	M1
Coney Burrows E4	20	M7
Conference rd SE2	80	G10
Congleton gro SE18	79	O14
Congo rd SE18	79	T13
Congress rd SE2	80	F10
Congreve rd SE9	95	T9
Congreve st SE17	158	K7
Conical corner Enf	7	Z9
Conifer gdns SW16	108	B8
Conifer gdns Enf	8	D20
Conifer gdns Sutt	130	A4
Conifer way Wem	42	H10
Conifers clo Tedd	102	C18
Coniger rd SW6	87	Y4
Coningham ms W12	74	H4
Coningham rd W12	74	J4

Name	No.	Ref
Coningsby cotts W5	72	F6
Coningsby gdns E4	20	E18
Coningsby rd N4	30	H20
Coningsby rd W5	72	F6
Coningsby rd S Croy	132	L20
Conington rd SE13	93	S5
Conisbee ct N14	6	H17
Conisborough cres SE6	111	V6
Coniscliffe rd N13	17	Z11
Coniston ave Bark	67	V1
Coniston ave Grnf	60	B7
Coniston ave Well	96	G8
Coniston clo N20	15	S11
Coniston clo SW20	119	O14
Coniston clo W4	73	V20
Coniston clo Bexh	98	L3
Coniston gdns N9	19	R5
Coniston gdns NW9	25	Y17
Coniston gdns Ilf	35	S13
Coniston gdns Sutt	130	F14
Coniston gdns Wem	42	E3
Coniston rd N10	29	S7
Coniston rd N17	18	J20
Coniston rd Bexh	98	K3
Coniston rd Brom	111	Y14
Coniston rd Croy	123	X18
Coniston rd Twick	82	L16
Coniston way Horn	57	V15
Conistone way N7	48	B19
Conlan st W10	136	L17
Conley rd NW10	44	C19
Connaught ave E4	20	J1
Connaught ave SW14	85	V9
Connaught ave Barn	16	A5
Connaught ave Enf	8	F8
Connaught ave Houns	82	C12
Connaught clo E10	50	G6
Connaught clo W2	146	L7
Connaught clo Enf	8	E9
Connaught Crossing E16	66	A19
Connaught dr NW11	27	Z12
Connaught gdns N10	29	T15
Connaught gdns N13	17	X13
Connaught gdns Mord	120	D10
Connaught la Ilf	54	D7
Connaught ms W2	147	O7
Connaught ms Ilf	54	E7
Connaught pl W2	147	O7
Connaught rd E4	20	L3
Connaught rd E11	51	Y4
Connaught rd E17	33	O16
Connaught rd N4	48	F1
Connaught rd NW10	62	B4
Connaught rd SE18	78	L13
Connaught rd W13	72	A1
Connaught rd Barn	4	D19
Connaught rd Har	23	W5
Connaught rd Ilf	54	E7
Connaught rd N Mal	118	B8
Connaught rd Sutt	130	F4
Connaught rd Tedd	101	P12
Connaught sq W2	147	N6
Connaught st W2	146	L7
Connaught way N13	17	X13
Connell cres W5	61	N10
Connington cres E4	20	K10
Connop rd Enf	9	S2
Connor rd Dag	56	B12
Connor st E9	63	T3
Conolly rd W7	71	T2
Conrad dr Wor Pk	119	N19
Cons st SE1	149	V16
Consfield ave N Mal	118	H11
Consort ms Islw	83	S14
Consort rd SE15	91	Z2
Constable clo NW11	28	B18
Constable cres N15	31	X15
Constable gdns Edg	25	P6
Constable gdns Islw	83	O14
Constable wk SE21	109	T6
Constance cres Brom	126	D19
Constance rd Croy	122	J17
Constance rd Enf	8	E20
Constance rd Sutt	130	E9
Constance rd Twick	82	K18
Constantine rd NW3	46	K13

Name	No.	Ref
Constitution hill SW1	147	W17
Constitution ri SE18	95	X2
Consul ave Dag	69	X10
Content st SE17	158	D6
Convent gdns W5	72	D11
Convent gdns W11	145	N6
Convent hill SE19	108	L16
Convent way Sthl	70	A13
Conway clo Stan	10	L18
Conway cres Grnf	59	V4
Conway cres Rom	37	T20
Conway dr Sutt	130	A15
Conway gdns Enf	8	D3
Conway gdns Mitch	121	Z9
Conway gdns Wem	42	E2
Conway gro W3	61	Z14
Conway ms W1	140	B19
Conway rd N14	17	P10
Conway rd N15	30	K14
Conway rd NW2	44	L7
Conway rd SE18	79	T12
Conway rd SW20	105	N20
Conway rd Felt	100	A12
Conway rd Houns	82	F18
Conway st E13	65	S12
Conway st W1	140	A18
Conyer st E3	63	W7
Conyers rd SW16	107	X12
Cooden clo Brom	112	H18
Cookes clo E11	52	B7
Cookes la Sutt	129	T13
Cookhill rd SE2	80	C7
Cooks clo Rom	38	L4
Cook's Hole rd Enf	7	Y2
Cook's rd E15	64	E6
Cooks rd SE17	157	Y14
Cool Oak la NW9	44	B3
Coolfin rd E16	65	U18
Coolgardie ave E4	20	H17
Coolhurst rd N8	29	W17
Coomassie rd W9	137	O15
Coombe ave Croy	133	T9
Coombe bank Kings T	104	A20
Coombe clo Edg	24	M7
Coombe clo Houns	82	J11
Coombe corner N21	17	W6
Coombe cres Hmptn	100	C17
Coombe dr Kings T	103	Y18
Coombe end Kings T	103	Y19
Coombe gdns SW20	118	G2
Coombe gdns N Mal	118	C9
Coombe Hill glade Kings T	104	C18
Coombe Hill rd Kings T	104	A18
Coombe House chase N Mal	103	Z20
Coombe la SW20	118	F1
Coombe la Croy	134	A11
Coombe Lane west Kings T	117	U1
Coombe lea Brom	127	T7
Coombe Neville Kings T	103	X18
Coombe pk Kings T	103	W12
Coombe ridings Kings T	103	V13
Coombe ri Kings T	117	V1
Coombe rd N22	30	G6
Coombe rd NW10	43	Y8
Coombe rd SE26	109	Z9
Coombe rd W4	74	B14
Coombe rd W13	72	B7
Coombe rd Croy	133	N8
Coombe rd Hmptn	100	D16
Coombe rd Kings T	117	P2
Coombe rd N Mal	118	A3
Coombe rd (Bushey) Wat	10	B1
Coombe wk Sutt	130	A5
Coombe Wood rd Kings T	103	W13
Coombefield clo N Mal	118	B13
Coombehurst clo Barn	5	Z8
Coomber way Croy	121	X17
Coombes rd Dag	69	P3

Coombewood dr Rom	38	D19
Coombs st N1	141	Z10
Coomer ms SW6	153	R15
Coomer pl SW6	153	S15
Coomer rd SW6	153	R15
Cooper av E17	32	H3
Cooper clo SE1	149	V19
Cooper cres Cars	130	M5
Cooper rd NW10	44	F15
Cooper rd Croy	132	H10
Cooper st E16	65	R15
Coopers clo E1	63	R12
Coopers la E10	51	T3
Coopers la NW1	140	G9
Cooper's la SE12	112	G4
Coopers rd SE1	159	P10
Cooper's row EC3	150	M8
Cooper's yd SE19	109	T15
Coopersale rd E9	50	G15
Coote rd Bexh	98	B2
Coote rd Dag	56	C9
Cope pl W8	153	U2
Cope st SE16	75	T10
Copeland dr E14	76	C10
Copeland rd E17	33	S17
Copeland rd SE15	91	Y5
Copeman clo SE26	110	C13
Copenhagen gdns W4	73	X6
Copenhagen pl E14	63	Y17
Copenhagen st N1	140	L5
Copers Cope rd Beck	111	P20
Copland av Wem	42	F15
Copland clo Wem	42	E15
Copland rd Wem	42	J17
Copleston rd SE15	91	V4
Copley clo SE17	157	Z15
Copley clo W7	59	V12
Copley dene Brom	127	N1
Copley pk SW16	108	C15
Copley st E1	11	T15
Coppelia rd SE3	94	C10
Coppen rd Dag	56	B1
Copper Beech clo Ilf	35	W4
Copper Beeches Islw	83	R3
Copper clo SE19	109	V19
Copper Mead clo NW2	44	M9
Copper Mill dr Islw	83	W5
Copper Mill la SW17	106	C10
Copperas st SE8	76	D17
Copperfield ms N18	18	F14
Copperfield rd E3	63	W13
Copperfield SE28	68	G17
Copperfield st SE1	150	A16
Copperfield way Chis	114	C14
Copperfield way Pnr	22	G12
Coppergate clo Brom	112	G20
Coppermill la E17	32	C18
Coppetts clo N12	28	L1
Coppetts rd N10	28	M2
Coppice the Enf	7	W13
Coppice clo SW20	118	M7
Coppice clo Stan	10	H19
Coppice dr SW15	86	H17
Coppice wk N20	14	L9
Coppice way E18	34	C11
Coppies gro N11	16	D14
Copping clo Croy	133	S8
Coppins the Croy	135	S14
Coppins the Har	10	G20
Coppock clo SW11	88	H6
Copse the E4	21	P5
Copse av W Wick	135	R5
Copse clo SE7	77	W17
Copse glade Surb	116	G19
Copse hill SW20	104	F20
Copse hill Sutt	130	B16
Copse vw S Croy	134	G18
Coptefield dr Belv	80	K9
Copthall av EC2	150	F4
Copthall dr NW7	13	U20
Copthall gdns NW7	13	U20
Copthall gdns Twick	101	X1
Copthorne av SW12	89	X20
Coptic st WC1	148	J3
Copwood clo N12	15	U14
Coral clo Rom	37	V11
Coral st SE1	149	U18
Coraline clo Sthl	58	E9

Coralline wk SE2	80	G7
Coram st WC1	140	J17
Coran clo N9	19	T2
Corban rd Houns	82	H8
Corbar clo Barn	5	U5
Corbet clo Wall	131	O1
Corbet ct EC3	150	H7
Corbet pl E1	143	N19
Corbett gro N22	30	A2
Corbett rd E11	34	L11
Corbett rd E17	33	V9
Corbetts la SE16	75	P11
Corbins la Har	40	K9
Corbridge cres E2	143	X7
Corby cres Enf	7	O14
Corby rd NW10	61	X6
Corby way E3	64	B12
Corbylands rd Sid	96	H19
Corbyn st N4	48	B5
Cordelia st E14	64	D17
Cording st E14	64	E15
Cordova rd E3	63	V8
Cordwell rd SE13	93	Y12
Corelli rd SE3	95	R3
Corfe av Har	40	F12
Corfield st E2	143	X14
Corfton rd W5	60	J16
Coriander av E14	64	J8
Corinne rd N19	47	W12
Cork sq E1	151	V13
Cork st W1	148	A10
Cork Street ms W1	148	A10
Cork Tree way E4	19	X15
Corker rd N7	48	D7
Corkran rd Surb	116	J18
Corkscrew hill W Wick	135	V4
Corlett st NW1	146	J1
Cormont rd SE5	90	J2
Cornbury rd Edg	11	V20
Cornelia st N7	48	E19
Corner grn SE3	94	E6
Corner mead NW9	26	D2
Corney rd W4	74	B17
Cornflower la Croy	124	F20
Cornflower ter SE22	91	Z15
Cornford clo Brom	126	F13
Cornford gro SW12	107	T3
Cornhill EC3	150	F6
Cornish ct N9	18	M2
Cornish gro SE20	110	A20
Cornmill la SE13	93	T8
Cornmow dr NW10	44	F13
Cornshaw rd Dag	55	X3
Cornthwaite rd E5	50	C9
Cornwall av E2	63	P9
Cornwall av N3	27	Y2
Cornwall av N22	30	B4
Cornwall av Sthl	58	F14
Cornwall av Well	96	J8
Cornwall clo Bark	54	M19
Cornwall cres W11	144	L7
Cornwall dr Orp	115	T18
Cornwall gdns NW10	44	K19
Cornwall gdns SW7	153	Z3
Cornwall Gardens wk SW7	153	Y3
Cornwall gro W4	74	C15
Cornwall Mews south SW7	154	B3
Cornwall Mews west SW7	153	Y2
Cornwall rd N4	48	F1
Cornwall rd N15	31	O13
Cornwall rd SE1	149	S13
Cornwall rd Croy	132	J3
Cornwall rd Har	22	M17
Cornwall rd Pnr	22	E2
Cornwall rd Sutt	129	M16
Cornwall rd Twick	83	Z20
Cornwall st E1	151	Y8
Cornwall ter NW1	139	R17
Cornwall Terrace ms NW1	139	R18
Cornwallis av N9	19	O7
Cornwallis av SE9	114	E5
Cornwallis gro N9	19	O7
Cornwallis rd E17	32	G13
Cornwallis rd N9	19	O7

Cornwallis rd N19	47	Z6
Cornwallis rd Dag	55	X12
Cornwallis wk SE9	95	U7
Cornwood clo N2	28	F14
Cornwood dr E1	63	P16
Cornworthy rd Dag	55	S15
Corona rd SE12	94	G20
Coronation clo Bex	97	W15
Coronation clo Ilf	36	D13
Coronation dr Horn	57	Y13
Coronation rd E13	65	Z9
Coronation rd NW10	61	N9
Coronation wk Twick	82	G20
Coronet st N1	142	J13
Corporation av Houns	82	A10
Corporation row EC1	141	V16
Corporation st E15	65	N6
Corporation st N7	48	A16
Corrance rd SW2	90	B10
Corri av N14	16	L13
Corrib dr Sutt	130	J11
Corringham ct NW11	45	Z1
Corringham rd NW11	27	X20
Corringham rd Wem	43	P7
Corringway NW11	45	Z2
Corringway W5	61	O15
Corscombe clo Kings T	103	V14
Corsehill st SW16	107	U15
Corsham st N1	142	F13
Corsica st N5	48	J17
Cortayne rd SW6	87	W5
Cortis rd SW15	86	K16
Cortis ter SW15	86	L15
Corunna rd SW8	89	W1
Corunna ter SW8	89	U2
Cosbycote av SE24	90	L13
Cosdach ave Wall	131	W16
Cosedge cres Croy	132	G10
Cosgrove clo N21	17	Y7
Cosmo pl WC1	140	L20
Cosmur clo W12	74	D7
Cossall wk SE15	92	A3
Cosser st SE1	157	S2
Costa st SE15	91	X6
Costons ave Grnf	59	P8
Costons la Grnf	59	O8
Cosway st NW1	138	L20
Cotall st E14	64	B15
Coteford st SW17	107	N10
Cotelands Croy	133	R5
Cotesbach rd E5	50	C9
Cotesmore gdns Dag	55	T13
Cotford rd Th Hth	122	M9
Cotham st SE17	158	D7
Cotherstone rd SW2	90	C20
Cotleigh av Bex	115	W3
Cotleigh rd NW6	45	Y20
Cotleigh rd Rom	39	N18
Cotman clo NW11	28	C17
Cotman clo SW15	87	O15
Cotman gdns Edg	25	O6
Coton rd Well	97	P7
Cotsford av N Mal	117	W12
Cotswold av Bush	10	G1
Cotswold clo Bexh	99	R3
Cotswold clo Kings T	103	U15
Cotswold gdns E6	66	B7
Cotswold gdns NW2	45	P6
Cotswold gdns Ilf	36	E20
Cotswold gate NW2	45	S5
Cotswold grn SW11	88	G2
Cotswold rd Hmptn	100	G14
Cotswold way Enf	7	P11
Cotswold way Wor Pk	129	N2
Cottage av Brom	127	S19
Cottage Field clo Sid	115	U2
Cottage grn SE5	158	H18
Cottage gro SW9	89	Z8
Cottage gro Surb	116	G15
Cottage Homes NW1	13	U14
Cottage Homes Chalet est NW1	13	T13
Cottage pl SW3	154	K2
Cottage st E14	64	E19
Cottenham dr NW9	26	C10
Cottenham dr SW20	104	K18
Cottenham Park rd SW20	104	L19

Cottenham pl SW20	104	K18
Cottenham rd E17	32	M12
Cotterill rd Surb	116	M20
Cottesbrook st SE14	75	V18
Cottesmore ave Ilf	35	V7
Cottesmore gdns W8	153	Z1
Cottingham rd SE20	110	F19
Cottingham rd SW8	157	P20
Cottington clo SE11	157	W8
Cottington Felt	100	J2
Cottington st SE11	157	V8
Cotton ave W3	61	Y17
Cotton hill Brom	111	W9
Cotton row SW11	88	E7
Cotton st E14	64	G18
Cottons app Rom	39	N15
Cottons ct Rom	39	N15
Cottons gdns E2	142	M13
Cottons la SE1	150	H13
Couchmore ave Ilf	35	U8
Coulgate st SE4	92	K7
Coulson clo Dag	55	U2
Coulson st SW3	155	O8
Coulter rd W6	152	A2
Councillor st SE5	158	A20
Counter st SE1	150	J13
Countess rd NW5	47	U14
Countisbury ave Enf	18	G2
Country way Felt	100	A9
County gate SE9	114	D6
County gate Barn	5	O20
County gro SE5	90	L1
County rd E6	66	L15
County rd Th Hth	122	J4
County st SE1	158	C3
Coupland pl SE18	79	P14
Courcy rd N8	30	F9
Courland gro SW8	89	Y3
Courland st SW8	89	Y2
Course the SE9	113	X7
Court the Ruis	40	A12
Court ave Belv	81	O13
Court clo Har	24	J11
Court clo Twick	100	J6
Court clo Wall	131	X17
Court Close ave Twick	100	K6
Court Downs rd Beck	125	P3
Court dr Croy	132	E17
Court dr Stan	11	X14
Court dr Sutt	130	J9
Court Farm ave Epsom	128	A11
Court Farm rd SE9	113	P3
Court Farm rd Nthlt	58	H1
Court House gdns N3	14	M19
Court la SE21	91	R16
Court Lane gdns SE21	91	T17
Court mead Nthlt	58	E8
Court rd SE9	113	S4
Court rd SE25	123	V5
Court rd Sthl	70	D12
Court st E1	143	W20
Court st Brom	126	G2
Court way NW9	26	B11
Court way W3	61	W14
Court way Ilf	36	C10
Court way Twick	83	V19
Court Wood la Croy	134	M20
Court yd SE9	95	U16
Courtauld rd N19	47	Z4
Courtenay ave N6	46	H1
Courtenay ave Har	22	M1
Courtenay ave Sutt	129	Z20
Courtenay dr Beck	125	W5
Courtenay gdns Har	23	N6
Courtenay ms E17	32	K15
Courtenay rd E11	52	C9
Courtenay rd E17	32	G14
Courtenay rd SE20	110	G17
Courtenay rd Wor Pk	129	N5
Courtenay sq SE11	157	S10
Courtenay st SE11	157	S10
Courtfield W5	60	D15
Courtfield ave Har	23	W17
Courtfield cres Har	23	X16
Courtfield gdns SW5	153	Y6
Courtfield gdns W13	59	Z18

Name	No.	Grid
Courtfield ms SW5	154	A6
Courtfield ri W Wick	135	X5
Courtfield st W3	154	B6
Courthill rd SE13	93	U11
Courthope rd NW3	47	N13
Courthope rd SW19	105	S13
Courthope rd Grnf	59	P5
Courthope vill SW19	105	U17
Courthouse rd N12	14	M18
Courtland ave E4	21	P7
Courtland ave NW7	12	M9
Courtland ave Ilf	53	U6
Courtland ave SW16	108	E19
Courtland gro SE28	68	K18
Courtland rd E6	66	D2
Courtlands Rich	85	O12
Courtlands ave SE12	94	H13
Courtlands ave Brom	126	B20
Courtlands ave Hmptn	100	E16
Courtlands ave Rich	85	T3
Courtlands dr Epsom	128	C14
Courtlands rd Surb	117	P17
Courtleet dr Erith	98	J2
Courtleigh ave Barn	5	T2
Courtleigh gdns NW11	27	S14
Courtman rd N17	30	M2
Courtmead clo SE24	91	N16
Courtnell st W2	145	T5
Courtney clo SE19	109	R16
Courtney cres Cars	130	M18
Courtney pl Croy	132	G6
Courtney rd N7	48	F14
Courtney rd SW19	106	J19
Courtney rd Croy	132	G6
Courtrai rd SE23	92	J15
Courtside N8	29	X19
Courtway Wdf Grn	21	Y16
Cousin la EC4	150	E10
Couthurst rd SE3	77	W18
Coval gdns SW14	85	U11
Coval la SW14	85	T11
Coval rd SW14	85	U11
Covelees wall E6	66	L17
Covent gdn WC2	148	M8
Coventry clo E6	66	F17
Coventry clo NW6	137	V7
Coventry rd E1	143	Y17
Coventry rd E2	143	Y15
Coventry rd SE25	123	X9
Coventry rd Ilf	53	Y6
Coventry st W1	148	F10
Coverack clo N14	6	G20
Coverack clo Croy	124	K19
Coverdale clo Stan	11	P15
Coverdale gdns Croy	133	U6
Coverdale rd NW2	45	R19
Coverdale rd W12	144	A15
Coverdales the Bark	67	R5
Coverley clo E1	143	T20
Covert way Barn	5	S7
Coverton rd SW17	106	J11
Covington gdns SW16	108	J19
Covington way SW16	108	D15
Cow la Grnf	59	P7
Cow leaze E6	66	K16
Cowan clo E6	66	E16
Cowbridge la Bark	53	Z20
Cowbridge rd Har	25	N13
Cowcross st EC1	141	W20
Cowden st SE6	111	O9
Cowdenbeath path N1	141	N3
Cowdray way Horn	57	V12
Cowdrey clo Enf	8	D8
Cowdrey ct Dart	99	Z20
Cowdrey rd SW19	106	C14
Cowen ave Har	41	O7
Cowgate rd Grnf	59	R7
Cowick rd SW17	106	M9
Cowings mead Nthlt	40	C19
Cowland ave Enf	9	S13
Cowleaze rd Kings T	116	K1
Cowley la E11	51	Z9
Cowley pl NW4	27	N14
Cowley rd E11	34	G15
Cowley rd SW9	90	G2
Cowley rd SW14	86	A6
Cowley rd W3	74	D4
Cowley rd Ilf	53	U2
Cowley st SW1	156	J2
Cowling clo W11	144	K12
Cowper ave E6	53	P20
Cowper ave Sutt	130	H9
Cowper clo Brom	127	O10
Cowper clo Well	97	O12
Cowper gdns N14	6	F19
Cowper gdns Wall	131	V15
Cowper rd N14	16	E5
Cowper rd N16	49	S14
Cowper rd N18	18	J17
Cowper rd SW19	106	D15
Cowper rd W3	73	X1
Cowper rd W7	59	V19
Cowper rd Belv	81	R11
Cowper rd Brom	127	O10
Cowper rd Kings T	102	M12
Cowper st EC2	142	G15
Cowper ter W10	144	G2
Cowslip rd E18	34	H8
Coxmount rd SE7	78	B12
Cox's wk SE21	109	Y2
Coxwell rd SE18	79	U13
Coxwell rd SE19	109	T17
Crab hill Beck	111	W19
Crabtree ave Rom	37	W12
Crabtree ave Wem	60	L5
Crabtree la SW6	152	E17
Crabtree Manorway north Belv	81	X5
Crabtree Manorway south Belv	81	W8
Craddock rd Enf	8	G12
Craddock st NW5	47	O18
Cradley rd SE9	114	E2
Craig gdns E18	34	D6
Craig Park rd N18	19	N14
Craig rd Rich	102	E9
Craigdale rd Horn	39	U19
Craigen ave Croy	124	A20
Craigerne rd SE3	77	V18
Craigmuir pk Wem	61	O2
Craignair rd SW2	90	E18
Craignish ave SW16	122	D3
Craigs ct SW1	148	J13
Craigton rd SE9	95	T11
Craigweil clo Stan	11	U17
Craigweil dr Stan	11	T16
Crail row SE17	158	G6
Cramer st W1	147	U2
Cramond clo W6	152	J14
Crampton rd SE20	110	C16
Crampton st SE17	158	A8
Cranberry clo Nthlt	58	A5
Cranborne ave Sthl	70	H11
Cranborne rd Bark	67	S2
Cranbourn st WC2	148	H9
Cranbourne ave E11	34	H12
Cranbourne clo SW16	122	A7
Cranbourne gdns NW11	27	U15
Cranbourne rd N10	29	T7
Cranbourne rd E15	51	V12
Cranbourne rd E15	51	V12
Cranbrook clo Brom	126	F15
Cranbrook dr Twick	82	K20
Cranbrook ms E17	32	L15
Cranbrook pk N22	30	E5
Cranbrook ri Ilf	35	U19
Cranbrook rd SE8	93	O3
Cranbrook rd SW19	105	T18
Cranbrook rd W4	74	B13
Cranbrook rd Barn	5	V20
Cranbrook rd Bexh	81	R20
Cranbrook rd Houns	82	D9
Cranbrook rd Ilf	53	X3
Cranbrook rd Th Hth	123	N3
Cranbury rd SW6	88	B5
Crane ave W3	61	X20
Crane ave Islw	83	Y14
Crane clo Dag	56	F18
Crane gro N7	48	G18
Crane mead SE16	75	S12
Crane Park rd Twick	100	J4
Crane rd Twick	101	T1
Crane st SE10	76	K15
Crane way Twick	83	N17
Cranebrook Twick	101	O3
Craneford clo Twick	83	W19
Craneford way Twick	83	T20
Cranes dr Surb	116	L11
Cranes pk Surb	116	M12
Cranes Park ave Surb	116	K10
Cranes Park cres Surb	116	L10
Craneswater pk Sthl	70	F13
Cranfield clo SE27	92	L7
Cranfield dr NW9	26	A3
Cranfield Road east Cars	131	O19
Cranfield Road west Cars	131	N19
Cranford ave N13	17	N15
Cranford clo SW20	104	J20
Cranford la (Heston) Houns	70	A19
Cranford st E1	63	U19
Cranford way N8	30	D14
Cranham rd Horn	39	Z17
Cranhurst rd NW2	44	M16
Cranleigh clo SE20	123	Z2
Cranleigh clo Bex	98	G15
Cranleigh gdns N21	7	T16
Cranleigh gdns SE25	123	T5
Cranleigh gdns Bark	54	E19
Cranleigh gdns Har	24	J16
Cranleigh gdns Kings T	103	N15
Cranleigh gdns Sthl	58	D17
Cranleigh gdns Wall	131	U16
Cranleigh ms SW11	88	K5
Cranleigh rd N15	30	L14
Cranleigh rd SW19	119	X6
Cranleigh st NW1	140	D10
Cranley dr Ilf	36	B20
Cranley gdns N10	29	R13
Cranley gdns N13	17	S9
Cranley gdns SW7	154	E8
Cranley gdns Wall	131	U16
Cranley ms SW7	154	D8
Cranley pl SW7	154	F7
Cranley rd E13	65	V14
Cranley rd Ilf	36	C19
Cranmer ave W13	72	B9
Cranmer clo Mord	119	R15
Cranmer clo Stan	11	S20
Cranmer ct Hmptn	100	K11
Cranmer Farm clo Mitch	120	M10
Cranmer gdns Dag	56	K13
Cranmer rd E7	52	J11
Cranmer rd SW9	157	U18
Cranmer rd Croy	132	K6
Cranmer rd Edg	12	F11
Cranmer rd Hmptn	100	K12
Cranmer rd Kings T	102	K13
Cranmer rd Mitch	121	N10
Cranmer ter SW17	106	G11
Cranmore ave Islw	71	N19
Cranmore rd Brom	112	B7
Cranmore rd Chis	113	V13
Cranmore way N10	29	V13
Cranston clo Houns	82	B5
Cranston est N1	142	G9
Cranston gdns E4	20	D17
Cranston rd SE23	110	H1
Cranswick rd SE16	159	Z10
Crantock rd SE6	111	T4
Cranwell clo E3	64	D12
Cranwich ave N21	18	B1
Cranwich rd N16	31	R20
Cranwood st EC1	142	F14
Cranworth cres E4	20	J6
Cranworth gdns SW9	90	E2
Craster rd SW2	90	D18
Crathie rd SE12	94	J14
Crathorn st SE13	93	U7
Craven ave W5	60	D20
Craven ave Sthl	58	E16
Craven gdns SW19	105	Z13
Craven gdns Bark	67	V7
Craven gdns Ilf	36	E7
Craven hill W2	146	C8
Craven Hill gdns W2	146	B9
Craven Hill ms W2	146	C8
Craven pk NW10	61	Z2
Craven Park ms NW10	62	A2
Craven Park rd N15	31	U19
Craven Park rd NW10	62	B3
Craven pas WC2	148	K12
Craven rd NW10	61	Z3
Craven rd W2	146	E7
Craven rd W5	60	D20
Craven rd Croy	123	Z20
Craven rd Kings T	103	N20
Craven st WC2	148	K12
Craven ter W2	146	E8
Craven wk N16	49	X1
Crawford ave Wem	42	F15
Crawford clo Islw	83	T4
Crawford gdns N13	17	W10
Crawford gdns Nthlt	58	F8
Crawford ms W1	147	O1
Crawford pas EC1	141	T17
Crawford pl W1	146	L3
Crawford rd SE5	90	M3
Crawford st W1	147	N2
Crawley rd E10	51	S4
Crawley rd N22	30	L7
Crawley rd Enf	18	F3
Crawthew gro SE22	91	V11
Cray clo Dart	99	X11
Cray Riverway Dart	99	V12
Cray rd Belv	81	S17
Cray rd Sid	115	T16
Craybrooke rd Sid	115	P10
Craybury end SE9	114	B4
Craydene rd Erith	99	U2
Crayford clo E6	66	C16
Crayford High st Dart	99	R12
Crayford rd N7	47	Z11
Crayford rd Dart	99	U14
Crayford way Dart	99	S13
Crayside Industrial est Dart	99	Z9
Crealock gro Wdf Grn	21	P17
Crealock st SW18	88	C17
Creasey clo Horn	57	Z6
Crebor st SE22	91	Y16
Credenhill st SW16	107	U16
Crediton hill NW6	46	A15
Crediton rd E16	65	T16
Crediton rd NW10	136	F6
Credon rd E13	65	X5
Credon rd SE16	159	Y10
Cree way Rom	39	R3
Creechurch la EC3	150	L6
Creed la EC4	149	Y7
Creek rd SE8	76	A17
Creek rd SE10	76	E17
Creek rd Bark	67	Y9
Creekside SE8	76	C20
Crefeld clo W6	152	K15
Creffield rd W3	61	N20
Creighton ave E6	66	A6
Creighton ave N2	28	J9
Creighton ave N10	29	N8
Creighton rd N17	31	S1
Creighton rd NW6	136	J8
Creighton rd W5	72	F8
Cremer st E2	142	M10
Cremorne rd SW10	154	E18
Crescent the E17	32	K16
Crescent the N11	16	A14
Crescent the NW2	44	K9
Crescent the SW13	86	F4
Crescent the SW19	105	Z7
Crescent the W3	62	A17
Crescent the Barn	5	N10
Crescent the Beck	125	O1
Crescent the Bex	97	V17
Crescent the Croy	123	O13
Crescent the Har	41	O5
Crescent the Ilf	35	W19
Crescent the N Mal	117	W5
Crescent the Sid	114	L9
Crescent the Sthl	70	D5
Crescent the Surb	116	J13
Crescent the Sutt	130	F10
Crescent the Wem	42	A7
Crescent the W Wick	125	Z15
Crescent ave Horn	57	T6
Crescent east Barn	5	S3

Name	Page	Grid
Crescent gdns SW19	105	Z7
Crescent gro SW4	89	W11
Crescent gro Mitch	120	J10
Crescent la SW4	89	V11
Crescent pl SW3	154	L5
Crescent ri N22	29	X3
Crescent ri Barn	5	U14
Crescent rd E4	21	O3
Crescent rd E6	65	Y2
Crescent rd E10	51	R5
Crescent rd E13	65	U3
Crescent rd E18	34	K6
Crescent rd N3	27	W3
Crescent rd N8	29	Y19
Crescent rd N9	18	L5
Crescent rd N11	16	A14
Crescent rd N15	30	J13
Crescent rd N22	29	Y4
Crescent rd SE18	78	M13
Crescent rd SW20	105	O20
Crescent rd Barn	5	V18
Crescent rd Beck	125	S4
Crescent rd Brom	112	F19
Crescent rd Dag	56	G10
Crescent rd Enf	7	W12
Crescent rd Kings T	103	S13
Crescent rd Sid	114	L7
Crescent Stables SW15	87	R12
Crescent way N1	48	D20
Crescent way N12	15	V19
Crescent way SE4	93	N8
Crescent way SW16	108	E16
Crescent west Barn	5	P4
Crescent Wood rd SE26	109	W7
Cresford rd SW6	88	A2
Crespigny rd NW4	26	K17
Cressage clo Sthl	58	G11
Cresset pl SW3	94	C7
Cresset st SW4	89	W9
Cressfield clo NW5	47	P14
Cressida rd N19	47	W3
Cressingham gro Sutt	130	C8
Cressingham rd SE13	93	V7
Cressingham rd Edg	12	L20
Cresswell gdns SW5	154	C9
Cresswell pk SE3	94	C7
Cresswell pl SW10	154	C10
Cresswell rd SE25	123	Y9
Cresswell rd Felt	100	A8
Cresswell rd Twick	84	F15
Cresswell way N21	17	U1
Cressy ct W6	74	J8
Cressy pl E1	63	R14
Cressy rd NW3	46	L13
Crest the N13	17	T13
Crest the NW4	27	U14
Crest the Surb	117	R13
Crest dr Enf	9	R3
Crest rd NW2	44	F8
Crest rd Brom	126	B18
Crest rd S Croy	134	A16
Crestbrook ave N13	17	V9
Crestfield st WC1	140	L11
Creston way Wor Pk	129	P1
Crestway SW15	86	H15
Crestwood way Houns	82	D12
Creswick rd W3	61	S19
Creswick wk NW11	27	W13
Creton st SE18	78	L9
Crewdson rd SW9	157	S18
Crewe pl NW10	62	D8
Crews st E14	76	B10
Crewys rd NW2	45	W6
Crewys rd SE15	92	B5
Crichton ave Wall	131	X10
Crichton rd Cars	130	L15
Cricket grn Mitch	120	L8
Cricket Ground rd Chis	127	Z1
Cricket la Beck	110	J14
Cricketers clo N14	16	G1
Cricketers ct SE11	157	X7
Cricketfield rd E5	50	A13
Cricklade ave SW2	108	B4
Cricklewood bdy NW2	45	N9
Cricklewood la NW2	45	S10
Cridland st E15	65	P3
Crieff ct Tedd	102	D19
Crieff rd SW18	88	E16
Criffel ave SW2	107	Y3
Crimscott st SE1	158	L4
Crimsworth rd SW8	156	G20
Crinan st N1	140	L8
Cringle st SW8	156	C16
Cripplegate st EC2	142	B20
Crisp rd W6	152	C11
Crispen rd Felt	100	B9
Crispian clo NW10	44	C12
Crispin cres Croy	131	Y5
Crispin rd Edg	12	J20
Crispin st E1	151	N2
Cristowe rd SW6	87	V5
Criterion ms N19	47	X6
Crockerton rd SW17	106	L5
Crockham way SE13	113	X10
Crocus fld Barn	4	J19
Croft the NW10	62	D5
Croft the W5	60	J14
Croft the Barn	4	D13
Croft the Houns	70	C18
Croft the Wem	42	C14
Croft ave W Wick	135	V1
Croft clo NW7	13	N11
Croft clo Belv	81	O14
Croft clo Chis	113	U11
Croft gdns W7	71	Y5
Croft Lodge clo Wdf Grn	21	W18
Croft rd SW16	108	G20
Croft rd SW19	106	D19
Croft rd Brom	112	G16
Croft rd Enf	9	V6
Croft rd Sutt	130	H11
Croft st SE8	75	V11
Croft way Sid	114	G7
Croftdown rd NW5	47	R10
Crofters clo Islw	83	R13
Crofters mead Croy	134	M20
Crofters way NW1	140	F3
Crofton ave W4	73	X19
Crofton ave Bex	97	W18
Crofton Park rd SE4	92	K14
Crofton rd E13	65	W10
Crofton rd SE5	91	T2
Crofton ter Rich	84	M9
Crofton way Barn	5	N18
Crofton way Enf	7	U7
Croftongate way SE4	92	J12
Crofts rd Har	23	Y17
Crofts st E1	151	R10
Croftway NW3	45	Y13
Crogsland rd NW1	47	P19
Croham clo S Croy	133	S16
Croham Manor rd S Croy	133	S17
Croham mt S Croy	133	R17
Croham Park ave S Croy	133	T12
Croham rd S Croy	133	O11
Croham Valley rd S Croy	133	W14
Croindene rd SW16	122	B2
Cromartie rd N19	47	Y2
Crombie clo Ilf	35	T16
Crombie rd Sid	114	F2
Cromer rd E10	33	W20
Cromer rd N17	31	X6
Cromer rd SE25	123	Z7
Cromer rd SW17	107	O16
Cromer rd Barn	5	P13
Cromer rd Rom	38	L18
Cromer rd Rom (Chadwell Heath)	37	Z18
Cromer st WC1	140	K14
Cromer Villa rd SW18	87	U16
Cromford rd SW18	87	X13
Cromford way N Mal	117	Z2
Cromlix clo Chis	127	Y2
Crompton st W2	138	E19
Cromwell ave N6	47	T2
Cromwell ave W6	74	J12
Cromwell ave Brom	126	G8
Cromwell ave N Mal	118	C11
Cromwell clo E1	151	T13
Cromwell clo N2	28	F12
Cromwell clo Brom	126	H9
Cromwell cres SW5	153	T5
Cromwell gdns SW7	154	H4
Cromwell ms SW7	154	G4
Cromwell pl N6	47	T3
Cromwell pl SW7	154	G4
Cromwell pl SW14	85	W7
Cromwell rd E7	52	K20
Cromwell rd E17	37	T16
Cromwell rd N3	28	C6
Cromwell rd N10	29	P2
Cromwell rd SW5	153	X5
Cromwell rd SW7	154	D4
Cromwell rd SW9	90	H1
Cromwell rd SW19	105	Z13
Cromwell rd Beck	124	J5
Cromwell rd Croy	123	N17
Cromwell rd Houns	82	F10
Cromwell rd Kings T	116	K2
Cromwell rd Tedd	101	Y15
Cromwell rd Wem	60	J5
Cromwell rd Wor Pk	128	A6
Cromwell st Houns	82	H9
Crondace rd SW6	87	Y3
Crondall st N1	142	H10
Crook Log Bexh	97	W9
Crooke st SE8	75	V13
Crooked Billet SW19	105	N16
Crooked Billet Roundabout E17	33	P3
Crooked Usage N3	27	S10
Crookham rd SW6	87	Y3
Crookston rd SE9	95	W7
Croombs rd E16	65	Y15
Crooms hill SE10	76	J20
Crooms Hill gro SE10	76	H20
Cropley st N1	142	D7
Croppath rd Dag	56	F12
Cropthorne ct W9	138	C14
Crosby clo Felt	100	B8
Crosby ct SE1	150	F17
Crosby rd E7	52	E17
Crosby rd Dag	69	V4
Crosby row SE1	150	F17
Crosby wk E8	49	U18
Crosby wk SW2	90	G18
Cross ave SE10	76	L17
Cross Deep Twick	101	X5
Cross Deep gdns Twick	101	W3
Cross Keys clo W1	147	V3
Cross Lances rd Houns	82	K11
Cross la EC3	150	K10
Cross la N8	30	C11
Cross la Bex	98	C18
Cross rd E4	20	L5
Cross rd N11	16	F15
Cross rd N22	17	U20
Cross rd SW19	105	Y18
Cross rd Croy	123	R20
Cross rd Enf	8	F14
Cross rd Felt	100	B9
Cross rd Har	23	O14
Cross rd (South Harrow) Har	40	J8
Cross rd (Wealdstone) Har	23	Y8
Cross rd Kings T	103	N18
Cross rd Rom	38	F12
Cross rd Rom (Chadwell Heath)	55	T2
Cross rd Sutt	130	G10
Cross st N1	141	Y3
Cross st SW13	86	C6
Cross st Hmptn	101	N20
Cross way the Har	23	U6
Crossbrook rd SE3	95	P6
Crossfield rd N17	30	L10
Crossfield rd NW3	46	H18
Crossfield st SE8	76	B18
Crossford st SW9	90	B5
Crossgate Edg	12	C10
Crossgate Grnf	42	B17
Crossland rd Th Hth	122	H15
Crosslands ave W5	73	N3
Crosslands ave Sthl	70	E14
Crosslet st SE17	158	H6
Crossley st N7	48	E17
Crossmead SE9	113	U2
Crossmead ave Grnf	58	H8
Crossness rd Bark	67	Z9
Crossthwaite ave SE5	91	O11
Crosswall EC3	151	N8
Crossway N12	15	U19
Crossway N16	49	T16
Crossway NW9	26	D14
Crossway SE28	68	E19
Crossway SW20	118	M10
Crossway Dag	55	T10
Crossway Enf	18	D2
Crossway Wdf Grn	21	Z14
Crossway the N22	30	K2
Crossway the SE9	113	O4
Crossway the W13	59	X12
Crossways N21	7	Y20
Crossways S Croy	134	J16
Crossways Sutt	130	F18
Crossways the Houns	70	D20
Crossways the Wem	43	R6
Crossways rd Beck	125	N9
Crossways rd Mitch	121	S6
Croston st E8	143	V4
Crothall clo N13	17	R9
Crouch ave Bark	68	D6
Crouch clo Beck	111	P16
Crouch cft SE9	113	Y6
Crouch End hill N8	29	Z19
Crouch Hall rd N8	29	X18
Crouch hill N4	48	B1
Crouch hill N8	30	A20
Crouch rd NW10	43	Y19
Crouchman clo SE26	109	W8
Crow la Rom	56	C1
Crowborough rd SW17	107	O14
Crowden way SE28	68	G20
Crowder st E1	151	W9
Crowhurst clo SW9	90	G4
Crowland gdns N14	17	N2
Crowland rd N15	31	W16
Crowland rd Th Hth	123	N9
Crowland ter N1	49	N20
Crowland wk Mord	120	C14
Crowlands ave Rom	38	J18
Crowley cres Croy	132	G11
Crowmarsh gdns SE23	92	D20
Crown clo E3	64	A3
Crown clo NW6	46	A16
Crown clo NW7	13	S7
Crown ct SE12	94	H16
Crown dale SE19	108	L14
Crown hill Croy	132	M4
Crown la N14	16	H4
Crown la SW16	108	F14
Crown la Brom	127	O13
Crown la Mord	119	Z8
Crown Lane gdns SW16	108	G13
Crown Lane Spur Brom	127	O14
Crown ms W6	74	F11
Crown Office row EC4	149	T7
Crown pas SW1	148	C14
Crown pl NW5	47	T16
Crown rd N10	29	P2
Crown rd N17	31	W1
Crown rd Enf	9	N13
Crown rd Ilf	36	E13
Crown rd Mord	119	Z8
Crown rd N Mal	117	X1
Crown rd Sutt	129	Z9
Crown rd Twick	84	C17
Crown st SE5	158	C18
Crown st W3	73	T4
Crown st Dag	57	J19
Crown st Har	41	S5
Crown ter Rich	85	N9
Crown wk Wem	43	N9
Crown Woods la SE9	96	B7
Crown Woods la SE18	95	Z4
Crown Woods way SE9	96	E14

Name	Page	Grid		Name	Page	Grid		Name	Page	Grid		Name	Page	Grid
Crown yd Houns	82	M7		Cullum st EC3	150	J7		Curry ri NW7	14	C18		Dagonet gdns Brom	112	E8
Crowndale rd NW1	140	C8		Culmington rd W13	72	D1		Cursitor st EC4	149	S4		Dagonet rd Brom	112	E7
Crownfield ave Ilf	36	G17		Culmington rd S Croy	132	L18		Curtain rd EC2	142	K14		Dahlia gdns Mitch	121	X9
Crownfield rd E15	51	W13		Culmore rd SE15	159	Z19		Curthwaite gdns Enf	6	L15		Dahlia rd SE2	80	D12
Crownhill rd NW10	62	D4		Culmstock rd SW11	89	O13		Curtis dr W3	61	Z17		Dahomey rd SW16	107	U15
Crownhill rd Wdf Grn	35	S2		Culross clo N15	30	L13		Curtis Field rd SW16	108	E9		Daimler way Wall	132	A16
Crownmead way Rom	38	H13		Culross st W1	147	S10		Curtis la Wem	42	J16		Daines clo E12	53	V10
Crownstone rd SW2	90	E14		Culver gro Stan	24	E6		Curtis rd Houns	82	D20		Dainford clo Brom	111	W12
Crowntree clo Islw	71	V17		Culverden rd SW12	107	U5		Curtis rd SE1	158	M5		Dainton clo Brom	112	J20
Crows rd E15	64	L8		Culverhouse gdns SW16	108	C8		Curtis way SE1	159	N4		Daintry clo Har	23	Z13
Crowshott ave Stan	24	D6		Culverlands clo Stan	11	N14		Curve the W12	62	F19		Dairsie rd SE9	95	W8
Crowther ave Brent	72	J12		Culverley rd SE6	93	S20		Curwen rd W12	74	F6		Dairy clo Th Hth	122	M3
Crowther rd SE25	123	X10		Culvers ave Cars	130	L3		Curzon ave Enf	9	U15		Dairy la SE18	78	G12
Crowthorne clo SW18	87	V20		Culvers Retreat Cars	131	N2		Curzon ave Stan	23	X5		Dairy ms SW9	90	B8
Crowthorne rd W10	144	G6		Culvers way Cars	130	M4		Curzon cres NW10	44	B19		Dairy wk SW19	105	S9
Croxden clo Edg	25	O9		Culverstone clo Brom	126	C13		Curzon cres Bark	67	X7		Daisy clo Croy	124	G20
Croxden wk Mord	120	C14		Culvert pl SW11	89	O5		Curzon pl W1	147	V14		Daisy la SW6	87	Y7
Croxford gdns N22	30	K2		Culvert rd N15	31	R16		Curzon rd N10	29	T7		Daisy rd E18	34	H8
Croxford way Rom	56	M4		Culvert rd SW11	89	N4		Curzon rd W5	60	C11		Dalberg rd SW2	90	F12
Croxley grn Orp	115	R20		Culworth st NW8	138	L10		Curzon rd Th Hth	122	K14		Dalberg way SE2	80	J9
Croxley rd W9	137	R13		Cumberland ave NW10	61	T9		Curzon st W1	147	V14		Dalby rd SW18	88	C11
Croxted clo SE21	90	M18		Cumberland ave Well	96	J8		Cut the SE1	149	U17		Dalby st NW5	47	R18
Croxted rd SE21	91	N19		Cumberland cres W14	152	M5		Cutcombe rd SE5	90	M5		Dalcross rd Houns	82	B4
Croxted rd SE24	90	M18		Cumberland dr Bexh	80	M18		Cuthbert gdns SE25	123	S5		Dale ave Edg	24	M5
Croyde ave Grnf	59	N9		Cumberland gdns NW4	27	R6		Cuthbert rd E17	33	V10		Dale ave Houns	82	C7
Croyde clo Sid	96	F19		Cumberland gdns WC1	141	R12		Cuthbert rd Croy	132	J2		Dale clo SE3	94	E7
Croydon gro Croy	122	H20		Cumberland gate W1	147	P8		Cuthbert st W2	138	F19		Dale clo Barn	5	O19
Croydon rd E13	65	S12		Cumberland mkt NW1	139	Z12		Cutler st E1	150	L4		Dale clo Dart	99	U15
Croydon rd SE20	123	Z4		Cumberland Market est NW1	139	Z11		Cutthroat all Rich	102	E4		Dale gdns Wdf Grn	21	V13
Croydon rd Beck	124	F10		Cumberland Mills sq E14	76	J13		Cuxton clo Bexh	97	Y12		Dale Green rd N11	16	F12
Croydon rd Croy	132	A8		Cumberland pk W3	61	X20		Cyclops ms E14	76	B11		Dale gro N12	15	R17
Croydon rd Mitch	121	P10		Cumberland pl NW1	139	X10		Cygnet clo NW10	43	Z16		Dale Park ave Cars	131	N3
Croydon rd Wall	131	U8		Cumberland rd E13	65	V11		Cygnet st E1	143	P17		Dale Park rd SE19	109	N20
Croydon W Wick	135	Z5		Cumberland rd E17	32	J7		Cygnets the Felt	100	B10		Dale rd NW5	47	P14
Croyland rd N9	18	J4		Cumberland rd N9	19	P6		Cynthia st N1	141	R10		Dale rd SE17	157	Z15
Croylands dr Surb	129	J18		Cumberland rd N22	30	D6		Cypress ave Twick	83	N18		Dale rd Dart	99	U16
Crozier ter E9	50	G16		Cumberland rd SE25	124	A13		Cypress pl W1	140	C19		Dale rd Grnf	58	J15
Crucible clo Rom	37	R18		Cumberland rd SW13	86	F1		Cypress rd SE25	123	T4		Dale rd Sutt	129	W10
Crucifix la SE1	150	K16		Cumberland rd W3	61	W20		Cypress rd Har	23	P7		Dale row W11	144	M7
Cruden st N1	141	Y6		Cumberland rd W7	71	W6		Cyprus ave N3	27	T7		Dale st W4	74	A14
Cruikshank rd E15	52	B13		Cumberland rd Brom	126	A8		Cyprus gdns N3	27	T6		Dale vw Erith	99	V4
Cruikshank st WC1	141	S11		Cumberland rd Har	22	K15		Cyprus pl E6	66	K19		Dale View ave E4	20	H8
Crummock gdns NW9	26	A16		Cumberland rd Rich	153	O20		Cyprus rd N3	27	U8		Dale View cres E4	20	G9
Crumpsall st SE2	80	G10		Cumberland rd Stan	25	N11		Cyprus rd N9	18	H7		Dale View gdns E4	20	J9
Crundale ave NW9	25	R16		Cumberland st SW1	155	Y9		Cyprus st E2	63	R7		Dalebury rd SW17	106	L5
Crunden rd S Croy	133	O16		Cumberland ter NW1	139	X10		Cyrena rd SE22	91	V15		Daleham gdns NW3	46	F16
Crusader gdns Croy	133	S6		Cumberland Terrace ms NW1	139	X10		Cyril mans SW11	89	N2		Daleham ms NW3	46	G16
Crusoe rd Erith	81	Z13		Cumberlow ave SE25	123	W7		Cyril rd Bexh	98	A5		Daleside rd SW16	107	S12
Crusoe rd Mitch	106	L18		Cumberton rd N17	31	P5		Cyrus st EC1	141	Y15		Daleview rd N15	31	S19
Crutched Friars EC3	150	L8		Cumbrian ave Bexh	99	R3		Czar st SE8	76	A16		Dalewood gdns Wor Pk	128	K2
Crutchley rd SE6	112	B4		Cumbrian gdns NW2	45	R7						Daley st E9	50	F17
Crystal Palace par SE19	109	U15		Cumming st N1	141	O17		**D**				Daley Thompson way SW8	89	S7
Crystal Palace Park rd SE26	109	X12		Cumnor gdns Epsom	128	H15		Dabbs Hill la Nthlt	40	F17		Dalgarno gdns W10	136	C20
Crystal Palace rd SE22	91	W10		Cumnor rd Sutt	130	E13		Dabin cres SE10	93	T2		Dalgarno way W10	136	D19
Crystal ter SE19	109	O15		Cunard pl EC3	150	L6		Dacca st SE8	75	Z15		Dalgleish st E14	63	X17
Crystal way Dag	55	U3		Cunard rd NW10	61	Y18		Dace rd E3	64	A2		Daling way E3	63	W4
Crystal way Har	23	W14		Cundy rd E16	65	Y18		Dacre ave Ilf	35	Y6		Dalkeith gro Stan	11	V17
Cuba dr Enf	9	P9		Cundy st SW1	155	V7		Dacre clo Grnf	58	L5		Dalkeith rd SE21	90	M20
Cuba st E14	76	A4		Cundy Street est SW1	155	V7		Dacre gdns SE13	93	Z10		Dalkeith rd Ilf	54	C9
Cubitt steps E14	76	B3		Cunliffe rd Wor Pk	128	E8		Dacre pk SE13	94	A8		Dallas rd NW4	26	H20
Cubitt st WC1	141	O14		Cunliffe st SW16	107	V15		Dacre pl SE13	93	Z8		Dallas rd SE26	110	A8
Cubitt st Croy	132	E12		Cunningham clo Rom	37	T16		Dacre rd E11	52	B3		Dallas rd W5	61	N14
Cubitt ter SW4	89	V6		Cunningham clo W Wick	135	R3		Dacre rd E13	65	V3		Dallas rd Sutt	129	U15
Cubitts yd WC2	148	L8		Cunningham pk Har	23	P14		Dacre rd Croy	122	B17		Dallin rd SE18	79	N18
Cuckoo ave W7	59	U11		Cunningham pl NW8	138	F15		Dacre st SW1	148	F20		Dallin rd Bexh	97	X10
Cuckoo dene W7	59	R14		Cunningham rd N15	31	W13		Dacres rd SE23	110	E5		Dalling rd W6	74	J11
Cuckoo Hall la N9	19	P1		Cunnington st W4	73	W10		Dade way Sthl	70	D13		Dallinger rd SE12	94	B17
Cuckoo la W7	59	T19		Cupar rd SW11	89	V1		Daffodil clo Croy	124	G20		Dallington st EC1	141	Y17
Cudas clo Epsom	128	D7		Cupola clo Brom	112	G12		Dafforne rd SW17	107	N7		Dalmain rd SE23	92	F20
Cuddington ave Wor Pk	128	D6		Cureton st SW1	156	H8		Dagenham ave Dag	68	L4		Dalmally rd Croy	123	V19
Cudham st SE6	93	T18		Curlew clo SE28	68	H19		Dagenham rd E10	50	M3		Dalmeny ave N7	47	Y13
Cudworth st E1	143	Y16		Curlew st SE1	151	O16		Dagenham rd Dag	56	J11		Dalmeny ave SW16	122	F4
Cuff cres SE9	95	P17		Curnick's la SE27	108	L11		Dagenham rd Rom	57	O1		Dalmeny clo Wem	42	E17
Culford gdns SW3	155	P7		Curnock est NW1	140	B6		Dagmar ave Wem	42	M13		Dalmeny cres Houns	83	P9
Culford gro N1	49	R19		Curran ave Sid	96	M13		Dagmar gdns NW10	136	F10		Dalmeny rd N7	47	X11
Culford ms N1	49	R17		Curran ave Wall	131	P6		Dagmar rd N4	30	G20		Dalmeny rd Barn	5	S19
Culford rd N1	49	R20		Currey rd Grnf	41	O17		Dagmar rd N22	29	Z4		Dalmeny rd Cars	131	P17
Culgaith gdns Enf	7	N14		Curricle st W3	74	B4		Dagmar rd SE5	91	R3		Dalmeny rd Erith	98	H1
Cullen way NW10	61	W12		Currie Hill clo SW19	105	V10		Dagmar rd SE25	123	R11		Dalmeny rd Wor Pk	128	J6
Culling rd SE16	75	P7						Dagmar rd Dag	56	M19		Dalmeyer rd NW10	44	D16
Cullington clo Har	23	Y13						Dagmar rd Kings T	103	O20		Dalmore rd SE21	108	M4
Cullingworth rd NW10	44	H15						Dagmar rd Sthl	70	B9		Dalrymple rd SE4	92	K12
Culloden rd Enf	7	W9						Dagmar ter N1	141	Y3		Dalston gdns Stan	24	J5
Culloden st E14	64	H17						Dagnall pk SE25	123	R14		Dalston la E8	49	U17
								Dagnall rd SE25	123	R11		Dalton ave Mitch	120	H3
								Dagnall st SW11	89	N4		Dalton st SE27	108	K5
								Dagnan rd SW12	89	T17		Dalwood st SE5	91	S1

Dalyell rd SW9 90 C6
Dame st N1 142 A7
Damer ter SW10 154 D18
Dames rd E7 52 E10
Damien st E1 151 Z3
Damsonwood clo Sthl 70 G9
Dan Leno wk SW6 153 Y19
Danbrook Rd SW16 108 B20
Danbury clo Rom 37 W10
Danbury ms Wall 131 S9
Danbury st N1 141 Y9
Danbury way Wdf Grn 21 Y19
Danby st SE15 91 U7
Dancer rd SW6 87 V3
Dancer rd Rich 85 P7
Dando cres SE3 94 H8
Dandridge clo SE10 77 R13
Dane clo Bex 98 E18
Dane rd N18 19 P12
Dane rd SW19 106 D20
Dane rd W13 72 C1
Dane rd Ilf 54 B16
Dane rd Sthl 70 C1
Dane st WC1 149 O2
Danebury Croy 135 T14
Danebury ave SW15 86 B16
Daneby rd SE6 111 T6
Danecourt gdns Croy 133 V5
Danecroft rd SE24 91 N13
Danehurst gdns Ilf 35 S16
Danehurst st SW6 87 S1
Daneland Barn 6 A17
Danemead gro Nthlt 40 K15
Danemere st SW15 87 N7
Danes gate Har 23 S11
Danes rd Rom 38 K20
Danescombe SE12 94 G20
Danescourt cres Sutt 130 E4
Danescroft NW4 27 P16
Danescroft ave NW4 27 P16
Danescroft gdns NW4 27 R16
Danesdale rd E9 50 J18
Daneswood ave SE6 111 T7
Danethorpe rd Wem 42 F18
Danette gdns Dag 56 D8
Daneville rd SE5 91 N3
Dangan rd E11 34 F18
Daniel Bolt clo E14 64 E14
Daniel clo N18 19 O13
Daniel clo SW17 106 J15
Daniel gdns SE15 159 O16
Daniel pl NW4 26 K20
Daniel rd W5 61 O20
Daniels rd SE15 92 C8
Dansington rd Well 97 O10
Danson cres Well 97 P7
Danson la Well 97 O11
Danson mead Well 97 U8
Danson rd Bex 97 V15
Danson rd Bexh 97 W14
Dante pl SE11 157 Y6
Dante rd SE11 157 X6
Danube st SW3 154 L9
Danvers rd N8 29 X12
Danvers st SW3 154 J15
Daphne gdns E4 20 H10
Daphne st SW18 88 C17
Daplyn st E1 143 S20
D'Arblay st W1 148 D6
Darcy ave Wall 131 V9
Darcy clo N20 15 T8
D'Arcy dr Har 24 H13
D'Arcy gdns Har 23 J13
Darcy rd SW16 121 Z3
D'Arcy rd Sutt 129 O8
Darell Rd Rich 85 P7
Darenth rd N16 49 V1
Darenth rd Well 97 O2
Darfield rd SE4 93 L13
Darfield way W10 144 G7
Darfur st SW15 87 O8
Darien rd SW11 88 H8
Darlan rd SW6 153 R20
Darlaston rd SW19 105 R18
Darley clo Croy 124 H16
Darley dr N Mal 117 Y3
Darley gdns Mord 120 C16
Darley rd N9 18 H4

Darley rd SW11 88 L15
Darling rd SE4 93 O6
Darling row E1 143 Y19
Darlington rd SE27 108 K12
Darlton clo Dart 99 U6
Darmaine clo S Croy 133 N18
Darnley rd E9 50 B18
Darnley rd Wdf Grn 34 G3
Darnley ter W11 144 J13
Darrell rd SE22 91 X13
Darren clo N4 30 D20
Darris clo Hayes 58 B12
Darsley dr SW8 89 Z1
Dart st W10 137 N12
Dartford ave N9 9 R20
Dartford rd 99 W15
(Hextable) Dart
Dartford st SE17 158 C13
Dartmouth clo W11 145 S4
Dartmouth gro SE10 93 V3
Dartmouth hill SE10 93 V2
Dartmouth Park ave 47 T9
NW5
Dartmouth Park hill 47 T4
N19
Dartmouth Park hill 47 U10
NW5
Dartmouth Park rd 47 S11
NW5
Dartmouth pl SE23 110 D5
Dartmouth pl W4 74 B17
Dartmouth rd E16 65 S16
Dartmouth rd NW2 45 O16
Dartmouth rd NW4 26 H18
Dartmouth rd SE26 110 B7
Dartmouth rd Brom 126 F17
Dartmouth row SE10 93 V3
Dartmouth st SW1 148 F19
Dartnell rd Croy 123 U16
Darville rd N16 49 V9
Darwell clo E6 66 J7
Darwin clo N11 16 D11
Darwin dr Sthl 58 K17
Darwin rd N22 30 J5
Darwin rd W5 72 E13
Darwin rd Well 96 L8
Darwin st SE17 158 H5
Daryngton dr Grnf 59 S6
Dashwood clo Bexh 98 F14
Dashwood rd N8 30 C19
Dassett rd SE27 108 K12
Datchelor pl SE5 91 P1
Datchet rd SE6 110 M6
Date st SE17 158 E10
Daubeney gdns N17 30 M1
Daubeney rd E5 50 H12
Daubeney rd N17 30 M1
Dault rd SW18 88 D15
Davenant rd N19 47 Z7
Davenant rd Croy 132 K8
Davenant st E1 151 U1
Davenport clo Tedd 101 Y15
Davenport rd SE6 93 T16
Davenport rd Sid 115 Y4
Daventer dr Stan 23 X1
Daventry ave E17 33 P17
Daventry st NW1 138 L19
Davern clo SE10 77 O12
Davey clo N7 48 E18
Davey rd E9 51 O19
Davey st SE15 159 O15
David ave Grnf 59 S7
David rd Dag 55 Y5
David st E15 51 Y16
Davidge st SE1 149 X19
Davids rd SE23 110 D2
Davids way Ilf 36 G1
Davidson gdns SW8 156 K18
Davidson rd Croy 123 R19
Davidson way Rom 39 S19
Davies clo Croy 123 W15
Davies la E11 52 B5
Davies st W1 147 W7
Davington gdns Dag 55 S15
Davington rd Dag 55 R17
Davis rd W3 74 E4
Davis st E13 65 X7
Davisville rd W12 74 G6
Dawes ave Islw 83 X12

Dawes rd SW6 152 M17
Dawes st SE17 158 F8
Dawlish ave N13 16 M14
Dawlish ave SW18 106 A4
Dawlish ave Grnf 59 Z7
Dawlish dr Ilf 54 J12
Dawlish dr Pnr 22 B16
Dawlish rd E10 51 T5
Dawlish rd N17 31 W9
Dawlish rd NW2 45 R17
Dawn clo Houns 82 C6
Dawnay gdns SW18 106 E4
Dawnay rd SW18 106 E4
Dawpool rd NW2 44 D7
Daws la NW7 13 S16
Dawson ave Bark 67 W2
Dawson clo SE18 79 O12
Dawson gdns Bark 67 Y1
Dawson Heights est 91 Y18
SE22
Dawson pl W2 145 U9
Dawson rd NW2 45 N14
Dawson rd Kings T 117 N6
Dawson st E2 143 P10
Daybrook rd SW19 120 A4
Daylesford av SW15 86 G9
Days la Sid 96 G20
Daysbrook rd SW2 108 C2
Dayton gro SE15 92 D1
De Beauvoir cres N1 142 J4
De Beauvoir est N1 142 J4
De Beauvoir rd N1 142 J4
De Beauvoir sq N1 142 K1
De Bohun ave N14 6 E19
De Crespigny pk SE5 91 O4
De Frene rd SE26 110 G8
De Havilland rd Edg 25 S7
De Havilland rd Wall 132 B16
De Laune st SE17 157 V12
De Luci rd Erith 81 Y13
De Lucy st SE2 80 E10
De Montfort rd SW16 107 Z6
De Morgan rd SW6 88 B7
De Quincey rd N17 31 O3
De Vere gdns W8 146 B18
De Vere gdns Ilf 53 U6
De Walden st W1 147 V2
Deacon rd NW2 44 H16
Deacon rd Kings T 116 M1
Deacon way SE17 158 B4
Deal Porters way 75 S7
SE16
Deal rd SW17 107 O16
Deal st E1 143 T19
Deal's Gateway SE10 93 P2
Dealtry rd SW15 86 M11
Dean Bradley st SW1 156 J3
Dean clo E9 50 D14
Dean ct Wem 42 C8
Dean dr Stan 24 L8
Dean Farrar st SW1 148 G20
Dean gdns E17 33 W11
Dean rd NW2 44 M18
Dean rd Croy 133 O9
Dean rd Hmptn 100 F13
Dean rd Houns 82 L13
Dean Ryle st SW1 156 J4
Dean Stanley st SW1 156 K3
Deans st E7 52 E13
Dean st W1 148 E5
Dean Trench st SW1 156 J3
Dean way Sthl 70 L5
Deancross st E1 151 Z6
Deanery rd N2 28 H12
Deanery rd E15 52 A18
Deanery st W1 147 V13
Deanhill rd SW14 85 U11
Deans bldgs SE17 158 F8
Deans clo W4 73 T16
Deans clo Croy 133 U5
Deans clo Edg 12 N20
Dean's ct EC4 149 Z7
Deans dr N13 17 W18
Dean's Gate clo SE23 110 F7
Deans la Edg 12 H20
Deans ms W1 147 Y3
Deans pl SW1 156 E8
Dean's rd W7 71 W4

Deans rd Sutt 130 A7
Deans way Edg 12 H16
Dean's yd SW1 148 H20
Deansbrook rd Edg 25 S2
Deanscroft ave NW9 43 W5
Deansway N2 28 H12
Deansway N9 18 C9
Dearn gdns Mitch 120 K5
Dearne clo Stan 10 L16
Deason st E15 64 J3
Debnams rd SE16 75 P11
Deborah clo Islw 83 S1
DeBurgh rd SW19 106 D17
Decima st SE1 158 J1
Decoy ave NW11 27 T14
Dee rd Rich 85 N10
Dee st E14 64 H17
Dee way Rom 39 R3
Deeley rd SW8 89 X2
Deena clo W3 61 N17
Deepdale SW19 105 R11
Deepdale ave Brom 126 C10
Deepdene N5 61 N11
Deepdene ave Croy 133 V6
Deepdene clo E11 34 F13
Deepdene ct N21 7 W19
Deepdene gdns SW2 90 C18
Deepdene rd SE5 91 N9
Deepdene rd Well 97 O7
Deepwell clo Islw 83 X2
Deepwood la Grnf 59 R8
Deer Park clo Kings T 103 S18
Deer Park gdns Mitch 120 F8
Deer Park rd SW19 120 D2
Deerbrook rd SE24 108 J1
Deerdale rd SE24 90 L9
Deere ave Rain 57 W19
Deerhurst rd NW2 45 R19
Deerhurst rd SW16 108 C13
Deeside rd SW17 106 F7
Defiant way Wall 132 A16
Defoe ave Rich 73 R20
Defoe clo SW17 106 K15
Defoe rd N16 49 S8
Degema rd Chis 113 Z13
Dehar cres NW9 44 F2
Dekker rd SE21 91 S16
Delafield rd SE7 77 X13
Delaford rd SE16 159 Y10
Delaford st SW6 153 N16
Delamere cres Croy 124 C16
Delamere gdns NW7 12 L17
Delamere rd SW20 119 P1
Delamere rd W5 72 L3
Delamere st W2 137 Z20
Delancey pas NW1 140 A6
Delancey st NW1 139 Y6
Delaware rd W9 137 W15
Delawyk cres SE24 91 N16
Delcombe ave 128 M1
Wor Pk
Delhi rd Enf 18 G3
Delhi st N1 140 L5
Delia st SW18 88 B17
Dell the SE2 80 A14
Dell the SE19 109 U20
Dell the Brent 72 E16
Dell the Wem 42 C14
Dell the Wdf Grn 21 U11
Dell clo E15 64 L3
Dell clo Wall 131 W8
Dell clo Wdf Grn 21 V11
Dell la Epsom 128 G13
Dell rd Enf 9 H7
Dell rd Epsom 128 G13
Dell wk N Mal 118 B6
Dell way W13 60 D16
Dellors clo Barn 4 C15
Dellow clo Ilf 36 E20
Dellow st E1 151 Y8
Dell's ms SW1 156 C7
Dellwood gdns Ilf 35 X11
Delme cres SE3 94 A14
Delmey clo Croy 133 V5
Deloraine st SE8 93 N2
Delorme st W6 152 G15
Delta clo Wor Pk 128 C5
Delta gdns Wor Pk 128 C5
Delta st E2 143 S12

Name	No.	Grid
Delvers mead Dag	56	J12
Delverton rd SE17	157	Y10
Delvino rd SW6	87	Y3
Demesne rd Wall	131	X7
Demeta clo Wat	4	W8
Dempster clo Surb	116	E19
Dempster rd SW18	88	D12
Den clo Beck	125	X8
Den rd Brom	125	Y7
Denberry dr Sid	115	S7
Denbigh clo NW10	62	A1
Denbigh clo W11	145	R8
Denbigh clo Chis	113	U15
Denbigh clo Sutt	129	W10
Denbigh gdns Rich	85	N14
Denbigh ms SW1	156	B7
Denbigh pl SW1	156	B9
Denbigh rd E6	66	B10
Denbigh rd W11	145	R8
Denbigh rd W13	60	C19
Denbigh rd Houns	82	L4
Denbigh rd SW1	58	F17
Denbigh st SW1	156	C7
Denbigh ter W11	145	R8
Denbridge rd Brom	127	U4
Dendy st SW12	107	O1
Dene the W13	60	B14
Dene the Croy	134	F7
Dene the Wem	42	K12
Dene ave Houns	82	E6
Dene ave Sid	97	S19
Dene clo SE4	92	J9
Dene clo Wor Pk	128	D3
Dene gdns Stan	11	S16
Dene rd N11	16	A6
Denehurst gdns NW4	26	M19
Denehurst gdns W3	73	S3
Denehurst gdns Rich	85	R9
Denehurst gdns Twick	83	R20
Denehurst gdns Wdf Grn	21	V13
Denewood Barn	5	S17
Denewood rd N6	28	L19
Denham clo Well	97	T8
Denham cres Mitch	120	M10
Denham dr Ilf	36	B18
Denham rd N20	15	Y9
Denham st SE10	77	S13
Denham way Bark	67	X3
Denholme rd W9	137	R13
Denholme wk Rain	57	U18
Denison clo N2	28	C10
Denison rd SW19	106	G16
Denison rd W5	60	E11
Deniston ave Bex	115	Y2
Denleigh gdns N21	17	T4
Denman dr NW11	27	Y15
Denman Drive north NW11	27	Y15
Denman Drive south NW11	27	Z15
Denman rd SE15	91	U3
Denman st W1	148	E9
Denmark ave SW19	105	S17
Denmark ct Mord	119	Z13
Denmark gdns Cars	131	O6
Denmark gro N1	141	T7
Denmark hill SE5	91	N3
Denmark Hill dr NW9	26	F11
Denmark rd N8	30	E12
Denmark rd NW6	137	R10
Denmark rd SE5	90	L3
Denmark rd SE25	123	Z11
Denmark rd SW19	105	R16
Denmark rd W13	60	C20
Denmark rd Brom	126	H2
Denmark rd Cars	131	N7
Denmark rd Kings T	116	J6
Denmark rd Twick	101	R6
Denmark st E11	51	Z10
Denmark st E13	65	V13
Denmark st N17	31	Z3
Denmark st WC2	148	H5
Denmark wk SE27	108	L10
Denmead rd Croy	122	J20
Dennan rd Surb	116	M20
Denne ter E8	143	P5
Denner rd E4	20	B8
Dennett rd Croy	122	G19
Dennetts gro SE14	92	E3
Dennetts rd SE14	92	E3
Denning ave Croy	132	F10
Denning clo NW8	138	E13
Denning clo Hmptn	100	E14
Denning rd NW3	46	G12
Dennington Park rd NW6	45	Y16
Denningtons the Wor Pk	128	B2
Dennis ave Wem	42	M14
Dennis gdns Stan	11	R15
Dennis la Stan	11	N11
Dennis Park cres SW20	119	S2
Dennis way SW4	89	Y7
Denny clo E6	66	D15
Denny cres SE11	157	U8
Denny gdns Dag	55	S20
Denny rd N9	18	M4
Denny st SE11	157	U9
Densham rd E15	65	N2
Densole clo Beck	110	H20
Densworth gro N9	19	P9
Denton rd N8	30	D16
Denton rd N18	18	F13
Denton rd Dart	99	R20
Denton rd Twick	84	G17
Denton rd Well	80	F18
Denton st SW18	88	B15
Denton way E5	50	G10
Dents rd SW11	88	L16
Denver rd N16	49	R1
Denver rd Dart	99	X18
Denzil rd NW10	44	C15
Deodar rd SW15	87	T9
Depot rd Houns	83	P7
Deptford bdy SE8	93	P1
Deptford bdy SE8	93	O1
Deptford Church st SE8	76	C17
Deptford grn SE8	76	C16
Deptford High st SE8	76	B17
Deptford strand SE8	75	Z11
Deptford wf SE8	75	Y10
Derby ave N12	15	R17
Derby ave Har	23	P5
Derby ave Rom	38	J18
Derby gate SW1	148	K17
Derby hill SE23	110	C4
Derby Hill cres SE23	110	C5
Derby rd E7	53	N19
Derby rd E9	63	S2
Derby rd E18	34	B3
Derby rd N18	19	P15
Derby rd SW14	85	T10
Derby rd SW19	105	Y18
Derby rd Croy	132	K1
Derby rd Enf	9	O16
Derby rd Grnf	58	K3
Derby rd Houns	82	K10
Derby rd Surb	117	O19
Derby rd Sutt	129	W14
Derby st W1	147	W13
Derbyshire st E2	143	T15
Dereham pl EC2	142	L15
Dereham rd Bark	54	L15
Derek ave Wall	131	S7
Derek ave Wem	43	T20
Dericote st E8	143	V4
Derifall clo E6	66	H14
Dering pl Croy	132	M10
Dering rd Croy	132	M9
Dering st W1	147	Y6
Derinton rd SW17	106	M8
Dermody gdns SE13	93	W12
Dermody rd SE13	93	W12
Deronda rd SE24	108	H1
Deroy clo Cars	130	M13
Derrick gdns SE7	77	X9
Derrick rd Beck	124	K8
Derry st W8	145	X19
Dersingham ave E12	53	V11
Dersingham rd NW2	45	T9
Derwent ave N18	18	B15
Derwent ave NW7	12	L17
Derwent ave NW9	26	A15
Derwent ave SW15	104	A9
Derwent ave Barn	15	Y5
Derwent clo Dart	99	Z20
Derwent cres N20	15	S11
Derwent cres Bexh	98	D5
Derwent cres Stan	24	D6
Derwent gdns Ilf	35	S13
Derwent gdns Wem	42	E2
Derwent gro SE22	91	U10
Derwent ri NW9	26	A17
Derwent rd N13	17	P12
Derwent rd SE20	123	Z4
Derwent rd SW20	119	O13
Derwent rd W5	72	D8
Derwent rd Sthl	58	F16
Derwent rd Twick	82	L16
Derwent wk Wall	131	X8
Derwent way Horn	57	Y15
Derwentwater rd W3	73	V2
Desenfans rd SE21	91	S17
Desford rd E16	65	N12
Desmond st SE14	75	W17
Despard rd N19	47	U5
Detling rd Brom	112	E12
Detmold rd E5	50	B6
Devalls clo E6	66	L18
Devana end Cars	131	N5
Devas rd SW20	119	N1
Devas st E3	64	F11
Devenay rd E15	65	P1
Devenish rd SE2	80	C6
Deverell st SE1	158	F3
Devereux rd SW11	89	N16
Deveron way Rom	39	P4
Devizes st N1	142	F5
Devon ave Twick	101	O1
Devon clo N17	31	W9
Devon clo Buck H	21	V6
Devon clo Grnf	60	E4
Devon gdns N4	30	K17
Devon ri N2	28	G14
Devon rd Bark	67	V3
Devon rd Sutt	129	T20
Devon st SE15	159	X15
Devon waye Houns	70	E20
Devoncroft gdns Twick	83	Z19
Devonia gdns N18	17	Z18
Devonia rd N1	141	Y8
Devonport gdns Ilf	35	T18
Devonport rd W12	144	A18
Devonport st E1	63	S17
Devons rd E3	64	C14
Devonshire ave Sutt	130	C17
Devonshire clo E15	52	B13
Devonshire clo N13	17	S12
Devonshire clo W1	139	X20
Devonshire cres NW7	27	P2
Devonshire dr SE10	76	D20
Devonshire gdns N17	17	Z19
Devonshire gdns W4	73	U20
Devonshire gro SE15	159	Y16
Devonshire Hill la N17	17	X19
Devonshire Mews north W1	139	X19
Devonshire Mews south W1	139	W20
Devonshire Mews west W1	139	W19
Devonshire pl NW2	45	X9
Devonshire pl W1	139	W19
Devonshire pl W4	74	B14
Devonshire Place ms W1	139	W19
Devonshire rd E16	65	X17
Devonshire rd E17	33	O18
Devonshire rd N9	19	P5
Devonshire rd N13	17	S13
Devonshire rd N17	17	Z20
Devonshire rd NW7	27	O4
Devonshire rd SE9	113	R4
Devonshire rd SE23	110	D3
Devonshire rd SW19	106	J18
Devonshire rd W4	74	A12
Devonshire rd W5	72	D8
Devonshire rd Bexh	98	A10
Devonshire rd Cars	131	P8
Devonshire rd Croy	123	N16
Devonshire rd Felt	100	B8
Devonshire rd Har	23	P17
Devonshire rd Ilf	36	G20
Devonshire rd (Hatch End) Pnr	22	D3
Devonshire rd Sthl	58	G13
Devonshire rd Sutt	130	E17
Devonshire row EC2	150	K3
Devonshire Row ms W1	139	Y19
Devonshire sq EC2	150	L3
Devonshire sq Brom	126	J8
Devonshire st W1	139	V20
Devonshire st W4	74	B15
Devonshire ter W2	146	D7
Devonshire way Croy	134	H3
Dewar st SE15	91	X8
Dewberry gdns E6	66	C14
Dewberry st E14	64	G15
Dewey rd N1	141	S7
Dewey rd Dag	56	K17
Dewey st SW17	106	M13
Dewhurst rd W14	152	F2
Dewsbury clo Pnr	22	C18
Dewsbury gdns Wor Pk	128	F5
Dewsbury rd NW10	44	F14
Dexter rd Barn	4	B18
Deyncourt rd N17	31	N3
Deyncourt gdns E11	34	L13
D'Eynsford rd SE5	91	O1
Dial wk the W8	145	Z16
Diamond clo Dag	55	U4
Diamond Ruis	40	A12
Diamond st SE15	158	M19
Diamond ter SE10	93	V1
Diana clo E18	34	J5
Diana pl NW1	140	A17
Diana rd E17	33	N9
Diban ave Horn	57	Y12
Dibden st N1	142	A2
Dibdin clo Sutt	129	Y5
Dibdin rd Sutt	129	Y5
Dicey ave NW2	44	M13
Dickens ave N3	28	D4
Dickens clo Rich	102	J4
Dickens dr Chis	114	C14
Dickens est SE1	151	R19
Dickens est SE16	151	R19
Dickens la N18	18	L15
Dickens rd E6	66	B6
Dickens sq SE1	158	C1
Dickens st SW8	89	T5
Dickenson rd N8	30	A20
Dickensons la SE25	123	X12
Dickensons pl SE25	123	Y15
Dickerage la N Mal	117	V2
Dickerage rd Kings T	117	V2
Dickerage rd N Mal	117	V2
Dickson rd SE9	95	S8
Didsbury clo E6	66	H4
Digby cres N4	48	L7
Digby gdns Dag	69	S2
Digby pl Croy	133	V5
Digby rd E9	50	F16
Digby rd Bark	67	X1
Digby st E2	63	R9
Dighton rd SW18	88	C12
Dilhorne clo SE12	112	H6
Dilke st SW3	155	P14
Dillwyn clo SE26	110	J9
Dilton gdns SW15	104	H1
Dimmock dr Grnf	41	R15
Dimond clo E7	52	G13
Dimsdale dr NW9	43	W4
Dimsdale dr Enf	8	J20
Dingle gdns E14	64	C20
Dingley la SW16	107	Y5
Dingley pl EC1	142	C13
Dingley rd EC1	142	A13
Dingwall ave Croy	133	N3
Dingwall gdns NW11	27	X18
Dingwall rd SW18	88	D19
Dingwall rd Cars	130	M19
Dingwall rd Croy	133	O2
Dinmont st E2	143	V9
Dinsdale gdns SE25	123	T11
Dinsdale gdns Barn	5	N18
Dinsdale rd SE3	77	O15
Dinsmore rd SW12	89	T18

Name	No	Grid
Dinton rd SW19	106	G14
Dinton rd Kings T	103	N17
Diploma ave N2	28	J12
Dirleton rd E15	65	P3
Disbrowe rd W6	152	L15
Discovery wk E1	151	X11
Dishforth la NW9	26	A3
Disney pl SE1	150	C17
Disney st SE1	150	C17
Dison clo Enf	9	S6
Disraeli clo SE28	80	E3
Disraeli rd E7	52	F17
Disraeli rd NW10	61	X6
Disraeli rd SW15	87	S11
Disraeli rd W5	72	F3
Diss st E2	143	O11
Distaff la EC4	150	A8
Distillery la W6	152	D11
Distillery rd W6	152	D11
District rd Wem	42	A15
Ditch all SE10	93	S2
Ditchburn st E14	64	H20
Ditchfield rd Hayes	58	B12
Dittisham rd SE9	113	R10
Ditton Grange dr Surb	116	F20
Ditton Hill rd Surb	116	D20
Ditton Reach T Ditt	116	B16
Ditton rd Bexh	97	Y13
Ditton rd Sthl	70	E12
Ditton rd Surb	116	L20
Dixon clo SE	66	H17
Dixon pl W Wick	135	R1
Dixon rd SE14	92	K1
Dixon rd SE25	123	T6
Dixons all SE16	151	X19
Dobbin clo Har	23	Z6
Dobell rd SE9	95	U14
Dobree ave N10	136	A1
Dobson clo NW6	46	F20
Dock Hill ave SE16	75	U4
Dock rd E16	77	R1
Dock rd Brent	72	G18
Dock st E1	151	S8
Dockers Tanner rd E14	76	B10
Dockhead SE1	151	R18
Dockland st E16	78	J4
Dockley rd SE16	159	S2
Doctor Johnson ave SW17	107	S7
Doctors clo SE26	110	C12
Docwra's bldgs N1	49	R16
Dod st E14	64	A17
Dodbrooke rd SE27	108	H8
Doddington gro SE17	157	X12
Doddington pl SE17	157	W13
Dodsley pl N9	19	O11
Dodson st SE1	149	V19
Doel clo SW19	106	C19
Dog Kennel hill SE22	91	S8
Dog la NW10	44	B13
Doggets ct Barn	5	W18
Doggett rd SE6	93	P19
Doherty rd E13	65	T11
Dolben st SE1	149	X14
Dolby rd SW6	87	V5
Dolland st SE11	157	P10
Dollis ave N3	27	V4
Dollis Brook wk Barn	4	E19
Dollis Hill ave NW2	44	L8
Dollis Hill la NW2	44	D11
Dollis pk N3	27	V3
Dollis rd N3	27	W3
Dollis rd NW7	27	T3
Dollis Valley Green wk N20	15	N2
Dollis Valley Green wk Barn	4	F19
Dollis Valley way Barn	4	H17
Dolman rd W4	73	Y12
Dolman st SW4	90	C9
Dolphin app Rom	39	T13
Dolphin clo SE28	68	H17
Dolphin clo Surb	116	H13
Dolphin la E14	64	D20
Dolphin rd Nthlt	58	F5
Dolphin sq SW1	156	D11
Dolphin st Kings T	116	J2
Dombey st WC1	141	N20
Dome Hill pk SE26	109	W10
Domett clo SE5	91	P10
Domfe pl E5	50	C12
Domingo st EC1	142	A17
Dominion rd Croy	123	U16
Dominion rd Sthl	70	C7
Dominion st EC2	150	G1
Domonic dr SE9	114	B7
Domville clo N20	15	T8
Don Phelan clo SE5	91	O1
Don way Rom	39	R2
Donald dr Rom	37	T16
Donald rd E13	65	V3
Donald rd Croy	122	E16
Donaldson rd NW6	137	P6
Donaldson rd SE18	95	Y2
Doncaster dr Nthlt	40	E15
Doncaster gdns Nthlt	40	D15
Doncaster rd N9	19	N3
Doncel ct E4	20	K1
Donegal st N1	141	N10
Doneraile st SW6	87	R3
Dongola rd E13	65	V9
Dongola rd N17	31	R10
Donington ave Ilf	36	C16
Donkey la Enf	8	J8
Donne pl SW3	154	L5
Donne pl Mitch	121	T8
Donne rd Dag	55	T6
Donnefield ave Edg	11	X20
Donnington rd NW10	136	A3
Donnington rd Har	24	F16
Donnington rd Wor Pk	128	G3
Donnybrook rd SW16	107	W18
Donovan ave N10	29	T8
Doon st SE1	149	S13
Doone clo Tedd	101	Y15
Dora rd SW19	105	Y10
Dora st E14	63	Y16
Doran gro SE18	79	U19
Doran mans N2	28	L16
Doran wk E15	64	H1
Dorchester ave N13	17	Y12
Dorchester ave Bex	97	X19
Dorchester ave Har	22	M19
Dorchester clo Nthlt	24	K14
Dorchester clo Orp	115	P19
Dorchester ct N14	16	F1
Dorchester ct SE24	90	M12
Dorchester dr SE24	90	M12
Dorchester gdns E4	20	B14
Dorchester gdns NW11	27	Y12
Dorchester gro W4	74	C15
Dorchester rd Mord	120	B17
Dorchester rd Nthlt	40	L14
Dorchester rd Wor Pk	128	L1
Dorchester way Har	25	N17
Dorcis ave Bexh	97	Z4
Dordrecht rd W3	74	C4
Dore ave E12	53	W15
Dore gdns Mord	120	C16
Doreen ave NW9	43	Y3
Dorell clo Sthl	58	F15
Doria rd SW6	87	W4
Dorian rd Horn	57	X5
Doric way NW1	140	F13
Dorien rd SW20	119	P3
Doris ave Erith	98	J2
Doris rd E7	52	G19
Dorking clo SE8	75	W12
Dorking clo Wor Pk	129	P3
Dorlcote rd SW18	88	H17
Dorman way NW8	138	E3
Dormay st SW18	87	Z12
Dormer clo E15	52	C16
Dormer clo Barn	4	B17
Dormers ave Sthl	58	G17
Dormers ri Sthl	58	L18
Dormers Wells la Sthl	58	H18
Dornberg clo SE3	77	U19
Dorncliffe rd SW6	87	U3
Dornfell st NW6	45	W16
Dornton rd SW12	107	T4
Dornton rd S Croy	133	R12
Dorothy ave Wem	60	L1
Dorothy Evans clo Bexh	98	H9
Dorothy gdns Dag	55	S13
Dorothy rd SW11	88	L8
Dorrington ct SE25	123	S2
Dorrington st EC1	149	T1
Dorrit ms N18	18	F15
Dorrit way Chis	114	D15
Dors clo NW9	43	Y3
Dorset ave Rom	39	O11
Dorset ave Sthl	70	G10
Dorset ave Well	96	L10
Dorset bldgs EC4	149	W7
Dorset clo NW1	139	O19
Dorset dr Edg	12	A19
Dorset est E2	143	O11
Dorset gdns Mitch	122	C9
Dorset ms SW1	155	X1
Dorset pl E15	51	W16
Dorset pl SW1	156	F9
Dorset ri EC4	149	W7
Dorset rd E7	65	Y1
Dorset rd N15	31	P12
Dorset rd N22	30	B5
Dorset rd SE9	113	P4
Dorset rd SW8	156	M17
Dorset rd SW19	105	X20
Dorset rd W5	72	F7
Dorset rd Beck	124	F7
Dorset rd Har	23	O18
Dorset rd Mitch	120	K3
Dorset sq NW1	139	O19
Dorset st W1	147	R2
Dorset way Twick	101	O1
Dorset waye Houns	70	E20
Dorville cres W6	74	J9
Dorville rd SE12	94	D14
Dothill rd SE18	79	S19
Douai gro Hmptn	101	N20
Doughty ms WC1	141	O17
Doughty st WC1	141	O16
Douglas ave E17	33	N4
Douglas ave N Mal	118	K10
Douglas ave Wem	42	K19
Douglas clo Stan	10	M17
Douglas clo Wall	132	B15
Douglas dr Croy	135	N5
Douglas pl E14	76	G12
Douglas rd E4	21	N4
Douglas rd E16	65	T14
Douglas rd N1	48	L19
Douglas rd N22	30	G3
Douglas rd NW6	137	P3
Douglas rd Horn	39	V19
Douglas rd Ilf	37	O19
Douglas rd Kings T	117	T4
Douglas rd Surb	117	N20
Douglas rd Well	97	S3
Douglas st SW1	156	F7
Douglas way SE8	75	Z19
Dounesforth gdns SW18	106	A2
Douro pl W8	146	A20
Douro st E3	64	B5
Douthwaite sq E1	151	V13
Dove app E6	66	C15
Dove ct EC2	150	E6
Dove House gdns E4	20	B8
Dove ms SW5	154	C8
Dove pk Pnr	22	F2
Dove rd N1	49	P18
Dove row E2	143	T7
Dove wk SW1	155	T9
Dovecote ave N22	30	G9
Dovedale ave Har	24	E17
Dovedale ave Ilf	35	W7
Dovedale clo Well	97	N3
Dovedale ri Mitch	106	M18
Dovedale rd SE22	92	A14
Dovedon clo N14	17	N8
Dovehouse mead Bark	67	S6
Dovehouse st SW3	154	H9
Dover clo Rom	38	J8
Dover House rd SW15	86	H9
Dover Park dr SW15	86	K15
Dover rd E12	52	M5
Dover rd N9	19	P8
Dover rd SE19	109	P15
Dover rd Rom	37	Z18
Dover st W1	147	Z10
Dover yd W1	148	A12
Dovercourt ave Th Hth	122	G11
Dovercourt gdns Stan	11	W15
Dovercourt la Sutt	130	C7
Dovercourt rd SE21	91	T17
Dovercourt rd SE22	91	T15
Doverfield rd SW2	90	B17
Doveridge gdns N13	17	W13
Doveton rd S Croy	133	P12
Dowanhill rd SE6	111	W2
Dowdeswell clo SW15	86	B11
Dowding pl Stan	10	M18
Dowding way Horn	57	Z20
Dower ave Wall	131	T19
Dowgate hill EC4	150	E9
Dowland st W10	137	N12
Dowlas st SE5	158	J18
Down end SE18	78	M20
Down Hall rd Kings T	116	H1
Down pl W6	152	A8
Down rd Tedd	102	B16
Down st W1	147	X15
Downage NW4	26	M8
Downalong (Bushey) Wat	10	C5
Downbank ave Bexh	99	O4
Downderry rd Brom	111	Y8
Downe clo Well	80	F18
Downe rd Mitch	121	N3
Downers cotts SW4	89	V9
Downes ct N21	17	T4
Downfield Wor Pk	118	E20
Downfield clo W9	137	W19
Downham clo Rom	38	F1
Downham rd N1	142	E2
Downham way Brom	111	X12
Downhills ave N17	31	O10
Downhills Park rd N17	30	L10
Downhills way N17	30	M6
Downhurst ave NW7	12	K17
Downing clo Har	23	O10
Downing dr Grnf	59	S4
Downing rd Dag	69	R3
Downing st SW1	148	J16
Downings E6	66	K16
Downland clo N20	15	R4
Downleys clo SE9	113	T7
Downman rd SE9	95	S8
Downs the SW20	105	O19
Downs ave Chis	113	T14
Downs ave Pnr	22	D20
Downs Bridge rd Beck	125	X1
Downs hill Beck	111	W20
Downs Park rd E5	49	Z13
Downs Park rd E8	49	V14
Downs rd E5	49	W12
Downs rd Beck	125	S3
Downs rd Enf	8	F14
Downs rd Th Hth	108	L20
Downs vw Islw	83	X1
Downsell rd E15	51	W12
Downsfield rd E17	32	K18
Downshall ave Ilf	36	J19
Downshire hill NW3	46	G13
Downside Twick	101	V6
Downside clo SW19	106	D16
Downside cres NW3	46	H6
Downside cres W13	59	X12
Downside gulf Stan	130	H14
Downsview gdns SE19	108	K19
Downsview rd SE19	108	L19
Downsway the Sutt	133	R7
Downton ave SW2	108	B3
Downtown rd SE16	75	W5

Name	Page	Grid
Downway N12	28	H1
Dowrey st N1	141	T4
Dowsett rd N17	31	V7
Dowson clo SE5	91	P10
Doyce st SE1	150	B16
Doyle clo Erith	99	S2
Doyle gdns NW10	136	A8
Doyle rd SE25	123	X9
D'Oyley st SW1	155	S5
Doynton st N19	47	T7
Draco st SE17	158	A13
Dragmire la Mitch	120	G8
Dragoon rd SE8	75	Y14
Dragor rd NW10	61	X11
Drake cres SE28	68	G17
Drake rd SE4	93	O7
Drake rd Croy	122	D18
Drake rd Har	40	F5
Drake rd Mitch	121	O14
Drake st WC1	149	N1
Drake st Enf	8	B5
Drakefell rd SE4	92	E6
Drakefield rd SW17	107	O6
Drakely ct N5	48	H12
Drakes wk E6	66	H4
Drakewood rd SW16	107	X19
Draper clo Belv	81	R11
Drapers rd E15	51	W13
Drapers rd N17	31	U10
Drapers rd Enf	7	V7
Drappers way SE16	159	V5
Drawdock rd SE10	76	K4
Drawell clo SE18	79	W13
Drax ave SW20	104	F18
Draxmont SW19	105	T15
Dray gdns SW2	90	E13
Draycot rd E11	34	H20
Draycott ave SW3	154	L6
Draycott ave Har	24	C17
Draycott ms SW6	87	V4
Draycott pl SW3	155	O7
Draycott ter SW3	155	P6
Drayford clo W9	137	P16
Drayside ms Sthl	70	D7
Drayson ms W8	145	W18
Drayton ave W13	59	Z19
Drayton Bridge rd W7	59	X19
Drayton Bridge rd W13	59	X18
Drayton clo Houns	82	D12
Drayton gdns N21	17	X2
Drayton gdns SW10	154	C9
Drayton gdns W13	59	Z19
Drayton grn W13	59	Z19
Drayton Green rd W13	60	B20
Drayton gro W13	59	Z19
Drayton pk N5	48	G11
Drayton rd E11	51	Y3
Drayton rd N17	31	S7
Drayton rd NW10	62	D2
Drayton rd W13	60	A18
Drayton rd Croy	132	K3
Dresden clo NW6	46	B17
Dresden rd N19	47	W3
Dressington ave SE4	93	O15
Drew ave NW7	14	E18
Drew gdns Grnf	41	W17
Drew rd E16	78	C3
Drewstead rd SW16	107	X4
Driffield rd E3	63	W5
Drift way Rich	103	P2
Drinkwater rd Har	40	F6
Drive the E4	20	L3
Drive the E17	33	R11
Drive the E18	34	E12
Drive the N3	14	L20
Drive the N6	28	L14
Drive the N11	16	J19
Drive the NW10	62	E2
Drive the NW11	27	S20
Drive the SW16	122	C6
Drive the SW20	104	M18
Drive the W3	61	X17
Drive the Bark	54	L19
Drive the Barn	4	E12
Drive the (New Barnet) Barn	5	R19
Drive the Beck	125	N3
Drive the Bex	97	V16
Drive the Buck H	21	Z3
Drive the Chis	114	J20
Drive the Edg	12	D15
Drive the Enf	8	C6
Drive the Epsom	128	D14
Drive the Erith	81	V18
Drive the Har	22	H20
Drive the Houns	83	O5
Drive the Ilf	35	S18
Drive the Islw	83	R4
Drive the Kings T	103	V19
Drive the Mord	120	E10
Drive the Rom	38	M3
Drive the Sid	115	S8
Drive the Surb	116	J18
Drive the Th Hth	123	O8
Drive the Wem	43	V8
Drive the W Wick	125	W19
Driveway the E17	33	P17
Droitwich clo SE26	109	X8
Dromey gdns Har	23	W1
Dromore rd SW15	87	S16
Dronfield gdns Dag	55	U14
Droop st W10	136	J15
Drover la SE15	159	Y16
Drovers pl SE15	159	Z18
Drovers rd S Croy	133	N12
Druce rd SE21	91	T17
Druid st SE1	150	L16
Druids way Brom	125	Y8
Drumaline ridge r Wor Pk	128	B3
Drummond ave Rom	39	N14
Drummond clo Erith	99	S2
Drummond cres NW1	140	F12
Drummond dr Stan	23	W1
Drummond gate SW1		
Drummond pl Twick	84	A17
Drummond rd E11	34	K18
Drummond rd SE16	159	W1
Drummond rd Croy	132	L3
Drummond rd Rom	38	M13
Drummond st NW1	140	A15
Drummonds the Buck H	21	W8
Drury cres Croy	132	F3
Drury Industrial est NW10	43	W14
Drury la WC2	148	L5
Drury rd Har	41	N1
Drury way NW10	43	X15
Dryad st SW15	87	O16
Dryburgh gdns NW9	25	R10
Dryburgh rd SW15	86	K8
Dryden ave W7	59	V17
Dryden rd SW19	106	C15
Dryden rd Enf	8	F19
Dryden rd Har	23	X5
Dryden rd Well	96	J1
Dryden st WC2	148	L6
Dryfield clo NW10	43	V18
Dryfield rd Edg	12	H19
Dryhill rd Belv	81	O16
Drylands rd N8	30	B17
Drysdale ave E4	20	L2
Drysdale pl N1	142	L12
Drysdale st N1	142	L13
Du Burstow ter W7	71	T4
Du Cane rd W12	144	A5
Du Cros dr Stan	11	T18
Du Cros rd W3	74	A4
Dublin cres E8	143	U3
Ducal st E2	142	P14
Duchess ms W1	147	Y1
Duchess of Bedford's wk W8	145	S18
Duchess st W1	147	Y2
Duchy rd Barn	5	U2
Duchy st SE1	149	U12
Ducie st SW4	90	C10
Duck la W1	148	E7
Duck Lees la Enf	9	W15
Duckett rd N4	30	H17
Duckett st E1	63	U13
Ducketts rd Dart	99	U14
Ducking Stool ct Rom	39	R14
Ducks wk Twick	84	F14
Dudden Hill la NW10	44	C12
Duddington clo SE9	113	O9
Dudley ave Har	24	D10
Dudley dr Mord	119	S20
Dudley gdns W13	72	C5
Dudley gdns Har	41	P5
Dudley rd E17	33	O8
Dudley rd N3	28	A7
Dudley rd NW6	137	N8
Dudley rd SW19	105	Y15
Dudley rd Har	40	M6
Dudley rd Ilf	54	A11
Dudley rd Kings T	116	M5
Dudley rd Rich	85	O5
Dudley rd Sthl	70	A7
Dudley st W2	146	F2
Dudlington rd E5	50	D6
Dudmaston ms SW3	154	H9
Dudsbury rd Dart	99	X15
Dudsbury rd Sid	115	S14
Duff st E14	64	D18
Dufferin ave EC1	142	D17
Dufferin st EC1	142	D18
Duffield clo Har	23	X16
Dufour's pl W1	148	C7
Duke Humphrey rd SE3	94	A3
Duke of Cambridge clo Twick	83	S16
Duke of Edinburgh rd Sutt	130	F4
Duke of Wellington pl SW1	147	V17
Duke of York st SW1	148	D11
Duke rd W4	73	Z12
Duke rd Ilf	36	E13
Duke st SW1	148	C12
Duke st W1	147	V6
Duke st Rich	84	H12
Duke st Sutt	130	F8
Duke Street hill SE1	150	G13
Dukes ave N3	28	A4
Dukes ave N10	29	T10
Dukes ave W4	73	Z14
Dukes ave Edg	11	Z18
Dukes ave Har	22	F19
Dukes ave (Wealdstone) Har	23	S12
Dukes ave Houns	82	B10
Dukes ave Kings T	102	G11
Dukes ave N Mal	118	C7
Dukes ave Nthlt	40	C20
Dukes ave Rich	102	E10
Dukes clo Hmptn	100	E11
Dukes clo Kings T	102	F11
Dukes ct E6	66	K3
Dukes la W8	145	W17
Dukes ms N10	29	T10
Duke's ms W1	147	V5
Dukes pl EC3	150	M5
Dukes rd E6	66	J3
Dukes rd W3	61	P12
Duke's rd WC1	140	G14
Duke's yd W1	147	V8
Dukesthorpe rd SE26	110	F11
Dulford rd SW11	144	K7
Dulka rd SW11	88	M14
Dulverton rd SE9	114	D4
Dulwich common SE21	109	R2
Dulwich Oaks the SE21	109	T7
Dulwich rd SE24	90	H14
Dulwich village SE21	91	R15
Dulwich Wood ave SE19	109	S11
Dulwich Wood pk SE19	109	S10
Dumbarton rd SW2	90	B17
Dumbleton clo Kings T	117	T2
Dumbreck rd SE9	95	V9
Dumont rd N16	49	T8
Dumpton pl NW1	139	T1
Dunbar ave SW16	122	F4
Dunbar ave Beck	124	J8
Dunbar ave Dag	56	E10
Dunbar ct Sutt	130	H11
Dunbar gdns Dag	56	F15
Dunbar rd E7	52	G18
Dunbar rd N22	30	G3
Dunbar rd N Mal	117	W9
Dunbar st SE27	108	K8
Dunblane rd SE9	95	S6
Dunboyne rd NW3	46	M15
Dunbridge st E2	143	T16
Duncan clo Barn	5	R14
Duncan gro W3	62	A17
Duncan rd E8	143	V5
Duncan rd Rich	84	L10
Duncan st N1	141	W8
Duncan ter N1	141	W10
Duncannon st WC2	148	J11
Dunch st E1	151	Y7
Duncombe hill SE23	92	J18
Duncombe rd N19	47	X4
Duncrievie rd SE13	93	Y16
Duncroft SE18	79	V19
Dundalk rd SE4	92	H8
Dundas rd SE15	92	C4
Dundee rd E13	65	V7
Dundee rd SE25	124	A12
Dundee st E1	151	X14
Dundela gdns Wor Pk	128	K10
Dundonald clo E6	66	E16
Dundonald rd NW10	136	F6
Dundonald rd SW19	105	Y19
Dunedin rd E10	51	S10
Dunedin rd Ilf	54	C3
Dunelm gro SE27	108	L8
Dunelm st E1	63	T16
Dunfield gdns SE6	111	T11
Dunfield rd SE6	111	S11
Dunford rd N7	48	D12
Dungarvan ave SW15	86	G9
Dunheved clo Th Hth	122	F14
Dunheved Road north Th Hth	122	G14
Dunheved Road south Th Hth	122	G15
Dunheved Road west Th Hth	122	F14
Dunholme grn N9	18	G10
Dunholme rd N9	18	H11
Dunkeld rd SE25	123	P8
Dunkeld rd Dag	55	T6
Dunkery rd SE9	113	N9
Dunkirk st SE27	108	L9
Dunlace rd E5	50	D13
Dunleary clo Houns	82	F19
Dunley dr Croy	135	S16
Dunloe ave N17	31	P10
Dunloe st E2	143	N10
Dunlop pl SE16	159	R2
Dunmore rd NW6	136	L5
Dunmore rd SW20	119	N1
Dunmow clo Felt	100	A8
Dunmow clo Rom	37	T15
Dunmow rd E15	51	Y13
Dunn mead NW9	26	C2
Dunn st E8	49	U14
Dunningford clo Horn	57	U15
Dunnock clo N9	19	S6
Dunnock rd E6	66	E16
Dunollie rd NW5	47	V14
Dunoon rd SE23	92	D18
Dunraven dr Enf	7	U8
Dunraven rd W12	74	H2
Dunraven st W1	147	S8
Dunsany rd W14	152	F3
Dunsfold way Croy	135	T17
Dunsmure rd N16	49	R2
Dunspring la Ilf	35	Y7
Dunstable ms W1	139	V20
Dunstable rd Rich	84	K11
Dunstall rd SW20	104	L16
Dunstan rd NW11	45	V5

Name	Page	Grid
Dunstans gro SE22	92	A15
Dunstans rd SE22	91	X18
Dunster ave Mord	119	R20
Dunster clo Barn	4	C14
Dunster clo Rom	38	K8
Dunster ct EC3	150	K8
Dunster dr NW9	43	W4
Dunster gdns NW6	137	R1
Dunster way Har	40	C8
Dunsterville way SE1	150	H18
Dunston rd E8	142	M5
Dunston rd SW11	89	P7
Dunston st E8	142	M4
Dunton clo Surb	116	J20
Dunton rd E10	33	R20
Dunton rd SE1	159	N8
Dunton rd Rom	39	P12
Duntshill rd SW18	106	A2
Dunvegan clo SE9	95	V11
Dunwich rd Bexh	98	B1
Dunworth ms W11	145	O5
Dupont rd SW20	119	P3
Dupont st E14	143	T12
Duppas ave Croy	132	J9
Duppas Hill la Croy	132	K7
Duppas Hill rd Croy	132	G8
Duppas Hill ter Croy	132	K7
Duppas rd Croy	132	H7
Dupree rd SE7	77	V13
Dura Den clo Beck	111	S17
Durand clo Cars	120	M20
Durand gdns SW9	90	D2
Durand way NW10	43	U20
Durands wk SE16	75	X4
Durant st E2	143	T12
Durants Park ave Enf	9	S13
Durants rd Enf	9	R13
Durban gdns Dag	56	L20
Durban rd E15	65	N8
Durban rd E17	32	K4
Durban rd N17	18	F19
Durban rd SE27	109	N9
Durban rd Beck	124	K4
Durban rd Ilf	54	H3
Durdans rd Sthl	58	F18
Durell gdns Dag	55	W13
Durell rd Dag	55	W14
Durford cres SW15	104	H1
Durham ave Brom	126	B9
Durham ave Houns	70	F15
Durham hill Brom	112	C9
Durham House st WC2	148	L11
Durham ri SE18	79	R13
Durham rd E12	53	N13
Durham rd E16	65	O12
Durham rd N2	28	L9
Durham rd N7	48	E7
Durham rd N9	18	J7
Durham rd SW20	104	L20
Durham rd W5	72	G9
Durham rd Brom	126	C6
Durham rd Dag	56	K14
Durham rd Har	22	L15
Durham rd Sid	115	R12
Durham st SE11	157	O12
Durham ter W2	145	W4
Durley ave Pnr	22	C19
Durley rd N16	49	S1
Durlston rd E5	49	X7
Durlston rd Kings T	102	J16
Durnford st N15	31	S16
Durning rd SE19	109	P13
Durnsford ave SW19	105	Y4
Durnsford rd N11	29	X3
Durnsford rd SW19	105	Z6
Durrell rd SW6	87	U3
Durrington ave SW20	104	M19
Durrington Park rd SW20	104	M20
Durrington rd E5	50	H13
Dursley clo SE3	94	L4
Dursley gdns SE3	95	N3
Dursley rd SE3	94	L4
Durward st E1	143	V20
Durweston ms W1	147	R1
Durweston st W1	147	P1

Name	Page	Grid
Dury rd Barn	4	H7
Dutch yd SW18	87	Y14
Duthie st E14	76	H1
Dutton st SE10	93	U1
Dutton st SW6	64	B4
Dye House la E3	51	Z5
Dyers Hall rd E11	86	K9
Dyers la SW15	39	Y2
Dyers way Rom	126	B6
Dykes way Brom	11	T1
Dylan clo Borwd	81	T8
Dylan rd Belv	91	P9
Dylways SE5	35	X9
Dymchurch clo Ilf	88	A7
Dymock st SW6	39	T20
Dymoke rd Horn	106	H7
Dymond est SW17	137	N1
Dyne rd NW6	112	L8
Dyneley rd SE12	49	S10
Dynevor rd N16	84	K13
Dynevor rd Rich	45	Y20
Dynevor rd NW6	148	H3
Dyott st WC1	102	F11
Dysart ave Kings T	142	H19
Dysart st EC2	34	A19
Dyson rd E11	52	D18
Dyson rd E15	19	N16
Dysons rd N18		

E

Name	Page	Grid
Eade rd N4	30	K20
Eagans clo N2	28	H10
Eagle ave Rom	37	Z18
Eagle clo Enf	9	R14
Eagle clo Horn	57	Y18
Eagle ct EC1	141	X20
Eagle dr NW9	26	C7
Eagle hill SE19	109	P16
Eagle la E11	34	E13
Eagle ms N1	49	S18
Eagle rd Wem	42	H20
Eagle st WC1	149	O2
Eagle ter Wdf Grn	34	H1
Eagle Wharf rd N1	142	D7
Ealdham sq SE9	94	M11
Ealing grn W5	72	G2
Ealing Park gdns W5	72	D11
Ealing rd Brent	72	G12
Ealing rd Nthlt	58	G1
Ealing rd Wem	42	J17
Ealing village W5	60	K18
Eamont st NW8	138	L8
Eardemont clo Dart	99	U10
Eardley cres SW5	153	V10
Eardley rd SW16	107	W13
Eardley rd Belv	81	T13
Earl ri SE18	79	S12
Earl rd SE1	159	N8
Earl rd SW14	85	W9
Earl st EC2	142	H20
Earldom rd SW15	87	N9
Earle gdns Kings T	102	L17
Earlham gro E7	52	D16
Earlham gro N22	30	D3
Earlham st WC2	148	H7
Earls Court gdns SW5	153	X7
Earls Court rd SW5	153	W7
Earls Court rd W8	153	U4
Earls Court sq SW5	153	W9
Earls cres Har	23	H1
Earls wk Dag	55	P11
Earlsferry way N1	141	N2
Earlsfield rd SW18	106	C2
Earlshall rd SE9	95	U11
Earlsmead Har	40	L12
Earlsmead rd N15	31	V14
Earlsmead rd NW10	136	A11
Earlsthorpe ms SW12	89	O17
Earlsthorpe rd SE26	110	E11
Earlstoke st EC1	141	X13
Earlston gro E9	143	Y5
Earlswood ave Th Hth	122	G13
Earlswood clo SE10	77	N15

Name	Page	Grid
Earlswood gdns Ilf	35	W11
Earlswood st SE10	77	N14
Early ms NW1	139	Y3
Earnshaw st WC2	148	H4
Earsby st W14	153	N5
Easby cres Mord	120	B15
Easeborne rd Dag	55	T15
Easedale dr Horn	57	Y15
Easley's ms W1	147	V4
East Acton la W3	62	C20
East Arbour st E1	53	S16
East ave E12	53	S20
East ave E17	33	R14
East ave Sthl	58	D19
East ave Wall	132	C11
East bank N16	49	S1
East Barnet rd Barn	5	T15
East Churchfield rd W3	73	Y2
East clo W5	61	O12
East clo Barn	6	C14
East clo Grnf	59	O6
East ct Wem	42	E7
East cres N11	16	A12
East cres Enf	8	F16
East Cross Route E3	64	A1
East dr Cars	130	K19
East Dulwich gro SE22	91	T11
East Dulwich rd SE22	91	V10
East End rd N2	28	F11
East End rd N3	27	X7
East End way Pnr	22	C9
East Entrance Dag	69	W6
East Ferry rd E14	76	F11
East gdns SW17	106	J15
East Ham Industrial est E6	66	C12
East Ham Manor way E6	66	J17
East Harding st EC4	149	U5
East Heath rd NW3	46	E9
East hill SW18	88	C13
East hill Wem	43	P5
East Holme Erith	98	M1
East India Dock rd E14	63	X18
East India Dock Wall Rd E14	64	J19
East la SE16	151	T19
East la Kings T	116	H6
East la Wem	42	B10
East Mount st E1	151	X1
East Park clo Rom	37	Y16
East Pier E1	151	W15
East pl SE27	108	L9
East Poultry ave EC1	149	X1
East rd E15	65	S3
East rd N1	142	F12
East rd SW19	106	E16
East rd Barn	16	C4
East rd Edg	25	U3
East rd Enf	9	S3
East rd Kings T	102	K20
East rd Rom (Chadwell Heath)	37	Y14
East rd (Rush Grn) Rom	57	O2
East rd Well	97	P4
East Rochester way SE9	96	E10
East Rochester way Bex	97	X15
East Rochester way Sid	96	K12
East row E11	34	E17
East row W10	136	L17
East Sheen ave SW14	85	Y12
East Smithfield E1	151	P11
East st SE17	158	C10
East st Bark	67	P2
East st Bexh	98	F9
East st Brent	72	D18
East st Brom	126	F3
East Surrey gro SE15	159	O19
East Tenter st E1	151	R6
East vw E4	20	H15

Name	Page	Grid
East vw Barn	4	G9
East wk Barn	16	B3
East way E11	34	H15
East way Brom	126	E17
East way Croy	134	J4
East Woodside Bex	98	A20
Eastbank rd Hmptn	101	N14
Eastbourne ave W3	61	X18
Eastbourne gdns SW14	85	V8
Eastbourne ms W2	146	D5
Eastbourne rd E6	66	K8
Eastbourne rd E15	65	N4
Eastbourne rd N15	31	S19
Eastbourne rd SW17	107	P16
Eastbourne rd W4	73	X16
Eastbourne rd Brent	72	F14
Eastbourne rd Felt	100	A4
Eastbourne ter W2	146	D4
Eastbournia ave N9	19	O10
Eastbrook ave N9	19	R3
Eastbrook ave Dag	56	K11
Eastbrook dr Rom	57	P8
Eastbrook rd SE3	77	X20
Eastbury ave Bark	67	V3
Eastbury ave Enf	8	F5
Eastbury gro W4	74	B15
Eastbury rd E6	66	K13
Eastbury rd Kings T	102	J19
Eastbury rd Rom	38	M17
Eastbury sq Bark	67	Y3
Eastcastle st W1	148	B4
Eastcheap EC3	150	J9
Eastcombe ave SE7	77	U17
Eastcote ave Grnf	41	Y15
Eastcote ave Har	40	L7
Eastcote la Har	40	C12
Eastcote la Nthlt	40	D15
Eastcote Lane north Nthlt	40	G18
Eastcote rd Har	41	N9
Eastcote rd Pnr	22	A15
Eastcote rd Well	96	F6
Eastcote st SW9	90	C5
Eastcroft rd Epsom	128	B17
Eastdown pk SE13	93	X11
Eastern ave E11	34	H18
Eastern ave Ilf	35	U10
Eastern ave Pnr	40	A1
Eastern ave Rom	37	V13
Eastern Avenue east Rom	39	N9
Eastern Avenue west Rom	37	X14
Eastern Gateway Access rd E6	67	N14
Eastern Industrial est E6	81	P5
Eastern rd E13	65	W5
Eastern rd E17	33	V15
Eastern rd N2	28	M11
Eastern rd N22	30	A4
Eastern rd SE4	93	O11
Eastern rd Rom	39	S16
Eastern way SE2	80	J2
Eastern way SE28	80	C5
Eastern way Erith	81	N3
Easternville gdns Ilf	36	C19
Eastfield gdns Dag	56	D13
Eastfield rd E17	33	P12
Eastfield rd N8	30	A11
Eastfield rd Dag	56	C13
Eastfield rd Enf	9	S3
Eastfields rd W3	61	V14
Eastfields rd Mitch	121	P3
Eastgate clo SE28	68	J18
Eastglade Pnr	22	D10
Eastholm NW11	28	B13
Eastlake rd SE5	90	K6
Eastlands cres SE21	91	U17
Eastleigh ave Har	40	J7
Eastleigh clo NW2	44	B10
Eastleigh clo Sutt	130	B18
Eastleigh rd Bexh	98	M6
Eastman rd W3	73	Z4
Eastmead ave Grnf	58	J10
Eastmead clo Brom	127	S3
Eastmearn rd SE21	109	N4
Eastmoor st SE7	78	A10

Eastney rd Croy	122	H20	Ecclestone pl Wem	43	N15	Edison dr Sthl	58	K18	Egerton rd Twick	83	U17
Eastney rd SE10	76	K15	Echo heights E4	20	D5	Edison gro SE18	79	X20	Egerton rd Wem	60	M1
Eastnor rd SE9	114	C2	Eckford st N1	141	S8	Edison rd N8	29	Z18	Egerton ter SW3	154	M3
Easton st WC1	141	S15	Eckstein rd SW11	88	J10	Edison rd Brom	126	E3	Egham clo SW19	105	S4
Eastry ave Brom	126	D15	Eclipse rd E13	65	V14	Edison rd Well	96	K1	Egham clo Sutt	129	R3
Eastry rd Erith	81	T18	Ector rd SE6	111	Z5	Edith gdns Surb	117	S16	Egham cres Sutt	129	R5
Eastside rd NW11	27	U13	Edbrooke rd W9	137	U18	Edith gro SW10	154	C16	Egham rd E13	65	X13
Eastview ave SE18	79	W19	Eddiscombe rd SW6	87	W4	Edith rd E6	53	O20	Eglantine rd SW18	88	C14
Eastville ave NW11	27	V17	Eddy clo Rom	38	G19	Edith rd N11	29	Z2	Egleston rd Mord	120	A16
Eastway E9	50	L17	Eddystone rd SE4	92	J14	Edith rd SE25	123	P13	Eglington st SE17	158	A12
Eastway E10	51	O14	Ede clo Houns	82	E8	Edith rd SW19	106	C15	Eglington rd E4	20	K2
Eastway Mord	119	R11	Eden clo W8	145	V20	Edith rd W14	152	K6	Eglinton hill SE18	79	N19
Eastway Wall	131	U9	Eden clo Wem	60	G4	Edith row SW6	88	B1	Eglinton rd SE18	78	L17
Eastwell clo Beck	110	J19	Eden gro E17	33	S15	Edith st E2	143	R8	Egliston ms SW15	86	M8
Eastwood rd E18	34	F6	Eden gro N7	48	D15	Edith ter SW10	154	C16	Egliston rd SW15	86	M8
Eastwood rd N10	29	O8	Eden Park ave Beck	124	K8	Edith vill W14	153	R9	Eglon ms NW5	139	R2
Eastwood rd Ilf	55	O2	Eden rd E17	33	S14	Edithna st SW9	90	B6	Egmont ave Surb	117	O20
Eastwood st SW16	107	U16	Eden rd SE27	108	K11	Edmansons clo N17	31	T5	Egmont rd N Mal	118	E8
Eatington rd E10	33	W16	Eden rd Beck	124	H8	Edmund rd Mitch	120	J6	Egmont rd Surb	117	O20
Eaton clo SW1	155	T6	Eden rd Croy	133	O8	Edmund rd Well	97	O7	Egmont rd Sutt	130	C18
Eaton clo Stan	11	O13	Eden way Beck	124	M13	Edmund st SE5	158	F17	Egmont st SE14	75	U20
Eaton dr SW9	90	H11	Edenbridge rd E9	63	U1	Edmunds wk N2	28	H13	Egremont rd SE27	108	G8
Eaton dr Kings T	103	R18	Edenbridge rd Enf	8	D20	Edna rd SW20	119	O3	Eighteenth rd	122	A9
Eaton dr Rom	38	G2	Edencourt rd SW16	107	S15	Edna st SW11	88	J3	Mitch		
Eaton gdns Dag	55	Z19	Edendale rd Enf	9	O2	Edric rd SE14	75	S18	Eighth ave E12	53	U11
Eaton gate SW1	155	T5	Edenfield gdns	128	D6	Edrick rd Edg	12	H20	Eileen rd SE25	123	P12
Eaton la SW1	155	Y2	Wor Pk			Edrick wk Edg	12	H20	Eisenhower dr E6	66	E14
Eaton Mews north	155	U3	Edenham way W10	137	O19	Edridge rd Croy	133	N7	Elaine gro NW5	47	O13
SW1			Edenhurst ave SW6	87	U7	Edward ave E4	20	D17	Elam clo SE5	90	K5
Eaton Mews south	155	V4	Edensor gdns W4	74	B19	Edward ave Mord	120	F12	Elam st SE5	90	K4
SW1			Edensor rd W4	74	A19	Edward clo N9	18	H3	Eland rd SW11	89	N7
Eaton Mews west	155	U5	Edenvale rd Mitch	107	P18	Edward clo Hmptn	101	N13	Eland rd Croy	132	H6
SW1			Edenvale st SW6	88	C6	Edward clo Rom	37	Y18	Elba pl SE17	158	D5
Eaton Park rd N13	17	U8	Ederline ave SW16	122	E5	Edward gro Barn	5	U16	Elbe st SW6	88	C4
Eaton pl SW1	155	T4	Edgar rd E3	64	E8	Edward ms NW1	139	Y11	Elberon ave Croy	121	W15
Eaton ri E11	34	L14	Edgar rd Houns	82	E17	Edward pl SE8	75	Z17	Elborough rd SE25	123	X11
Eaton ri W5	60	F14	Edgar rd Rom	37	W20	Edward rd E17	32	F13	Elborough st SW18	105	X1
Eaton rd NW4	26	M15	Edgar rd S Croy	133	O20	Edward rd SE20	110	F17	Elbury dr E16	65	T18
Eaton rd Enf	8	E12	Edgarley ter SW6	87	S2	Edward rd Barn	5	T15	Elcho st SW11	154	L19
Eaton rd Houns	83	R11	Edge hill SE18	78	M15	Edward rd Brom	112	J18	Elcot ave SE15	159	V18
Eaton rd Sid	115	W5	Edge hill SW19	105	O17	Edward rd Chis	114	A13	Elder ave N8	30	A16
Eaton rd Sutt	130	F13	Edge Hill ave N3	27	X11	Edward rd Croy	123	T17	Elder ct	10	F7
Eaton row SW1	155	X2	Edge Hill ct SW19	105	P19	Edward rd Hmptn	101	N13	(Bushey) Wat		
Eaton sq SW1	155	U3	Edge st W8	145	U13	Edward rd Har	23	N10	Elder Oak clo SE20	123	Z1
Eaton ter SW1	155	T5	Edgeborough way	113	N19	Edward st E16	65	S13	Elder rd SE27	108	L11
Eaton Terrace ms	155	T5	Brom			Edward st SE8	76	A17	Elder st E1	142	M19
SW1			Edgebury Chis	113	Z10	Edward st SE14	75	X18	Elder wk N1	141	Z4
Eatons mead E4	20	A8	Edgebury wk Chis	114	B9	Edward Temme ave	65	P1	Elderberry rd W5	72	K7
Eatonville rd SW17	107	N4	Edgecoombe S Croy	134	D17	E15			Elderfield rd E5	50	E13
Ebbisham dr SW8	157	O14	Edgecoombe clo	103	Y18	Edwardes sq W8	153	R3	Elderfield wk E11	34	H14
Ebbisham rd Wor Pk	128	M2	Kings T			Edwards clo Wor Pk	129	P3	Elderslie clo Beck	125	P13
Ebbsfleet rd NW2	45	S13	Edgecot gro N15	31	R15	Edwards la N16	49	R8	Elderslie rd SE9	95	Y13
Ebdon way SE3	94	J9	Edgecote clo W3	73	U4	Edwards ms W1	147	T6	Elderton rd SE26	110	J10
Ebenezer st N1	142	E13	Edgefield ave Bark	54	L20	Edwards rd Belv	81	S10	Eldertree pl Mitch	121	U2
Ebenezer wk SW16	121	U1	Edgehill gdns Dag	56	F15	Edwin ave E6	66	K7	Eldertree way Mitch	121	U2
Ebley clo SE15	159	N15	Edgehill rd W13	60	C15	Edwin clo Bexh	81	O17	Eldon ave Croy	134	D3
Ebner st SW18	88	C12	Edgehill rd Chis	114	B8	Edwin pl Croy	123	R20	Eldon ave Houns	70	G19
Ebor st E1	143	N16	Edgeley rd SW4	89	W6	Edwin rd Edg	12	K20	Eldon gro NW3	46	G14
Ebrington rd Har	24	F18	Edgepoint clo SE27	108	J13	Edwin rd Twick	101	U2	Eldon pk SE25	123	Z8
Ebsworth st SE23	92	G19	Edgewood grn Croy	124	G19	Edwin st E1	63	R11	Eldon rd E17	32	M13
Eburne rd N7	48	B9	Edgewood ave NW4	26	L13	Edwin st E16	65	S14	Eldon rd N9	19	P6
Ebury bri SW1	155	W8	Edgeworth clo NW4	26	G15	Edwina gdns Ilf	35	P16	Eldon rd N22	30	K4
Ebury Bridge est	155	W9	Edgeworth cres NW4	26	G15	Edwyn clo Barn	4	B18	Eldon rd W8	153	Z2
SW1			Edgeworth clo NW4	26	H14	Effie pl SW6	153	V19	Eldon st EC2	150	G1
Ebury Bridge rd SW1	155	V11	Edgeworth rd SE9	94	M10	Effie rd SW6	153	V19	Eldon way NW10	61	T7
Ebury ms SE27	108	K7	Edgeworth rd Barn	5	W13	Effingham clo Sutt	130	B17	Eldonwall Trading est	44	F4
Ebury ms SW5	155	W5	Edgington rd SW16	107	P4	Effingham rd N8	30	G14	NW2		
Ebury Mews east	155	X4	Edgington way Sid	115	U17	Effingham rd SE12	94	B14	Eldred rd Bark	67	U3
SW1			Edgware rd NW2	44	J4	Effingham rd S Croy	122	E18	Eleanor clo SE16	75	T4
Ebury sq SW1	155	V7	Edgware rd NW9	25	W8	Effingham rd Surb	116	C18	Eleanor cres NW7	14	B14
Ebury st SW1	155	U8	Edgware rd W2	146	L1	Effort st SW17	106	J12	Eleanor gdns Barn	4	B17
Eccles rd SW11	88	L9	Edgware way Edg	11	V7	Effra par SW2	90	G13	Eleanor gro SW13	86	C8
Ecclesbourne clo	17	T16	Edgwarebury gdns	12	C15	Effra rd SW2	90	E12	Eleanor rd E8	49	Z18
N13			Edg			Effra rd SW19	105	Z15	Eleanor rd E15	52	D19
Ecclesbourne gdns	17	S16	Edgwarebury la	11	Y2	Egan way SE16	159	Y10	Eleanor rd N11	17	N19
N13			Borwd			Egbert st NW1	139	T3	Eleanor st E3	64	B9
Ecclesbourne rd N1	142	B2	Edgwarebury la	12	B5	Egerton cres SW3	154	L4	Electric ave SW9	90	E9
Ecclesbourne rd	122	L12	Edg			Egerton dr SE10	93	S2	Electric la SW9	90	F10
Th Hth			Edinburgh rd E13	65	V6	Egerton gdns NW4	26	L13	Electric par Surb	116	G15
Eccleston bri SW1	155	Y5	Edinburgh rd E17	33	N16	Egerton gdns NW10	136	C5	Elephant & Castle	157	Z4
Eccleston clo Barn	5	V15	Edinburgh rd N18	18	L15	Egerton gdns SW3	154	L4	SE1		
Eccleston cres Rom	37	P20	Edinburgh rd W7	71	W5	Egerton gdns W13	60	B16	Elephant la SE16	75	P5
Eccleston ms SW1	155	V2	Edinburgh rd Sutt	130	E4	Egerton gdns Ilf	54	L2	Elephant rd SE17	158	A5
Eccleston pl SW1	155	X6	Edington rd SE2	80	E7	Egerton Gardens ms	154	L2	Elers rd W13	72	C7
Eccleston rd W13	71	Y1	Edington rd Enf	9	R9	SW3			Eley rd est N18	19	S15
Eccleston sq SW1	155	Z6	Edis st NW1	139	U3	Egerton pl SW3	154	M3	Eley rd N18	19	R14
Eccleston Square ms	156	A7	Edison ave Horn	57	S5	Egerton rd N16	31	V20	Elf row E1	63	R18
SW1			Edison clo Horn	57	S4	Egerton rd SE25	123	S7	Elfindale rd SE24	90	M13
Eccleston st SW1	155	W3				Egerton rd N Mal	118	E8	Elford clo SE3	94	K9

Street	Pg	Ref
Elfort rd N5	48	H11
Elfrida cres SE6	111	O9
Elfwine rd W7	59	U13
Elgar ave NW10	43	Y17
Elgar ave SW16	122	A5
Elgar ave W5	72	L4
Elgar ave Surb	117	R20
Elgar clo SE8	76	A20
Elgar clo Borwd	11	T1
Elgar st SE16	75	X7
Elgin ave W9	137	S18
Elgin ave Har	24	A8
Elgin cres W11	144	M8
Elgin est W9	137	S18
Elgin ms W11	144	M5
Elgin Mews north W9	138	A13
Elgin Mews south W9	138	A13
Elgin rd N22	29	V6
Elgin rd Croy	133	V2
Elgin rd Ilf	54	J4
Elgin rd Sutt	130	E6
Elgin rd Wall	131	U14
Elham clo Brom	113	N19
Elia st N1	141	X9
Elias pl SW8	157	S16
Elibank rd SE9	95	V10
Elim way E13	65	R10
Eliot bank SE23	110	A4
Eliot dr Har	40	K6
Eliot gdns SW15	86	G11
Eliot hill SE13	93	V5
Eliot pk SE13	93	V5
Eliot pl SE3	93	Z5
Eliot rd Dag	55	X13
Eliot vale SE3	93	Y5
Elizabeth ave N1	142	C3
Elizabeth ave Enf	7	X10
Elizabeth ave Ilf	54	F6
Elizabeth bri SW1	155	X6
Elizabeth clo W9	138	D17
Elizabeth clo Barn	4	B12
Elizabeth clo Rom	38	G4
Elizabeth Clyde clo N15	31	R11
Elizabeth cotts Rich	85	O3
Elizabeth clo SW1	156	G2
Elizabeth est SE17	158	E12
Elizabeth Fry rd E8	143	Y1
Elizabeth gdns W3	74	D4
Elizabeth gdns Stan	11	T17
Elizabeth ms NW3	46	L18
Elizabeth pl N15	31	P12
Elizabeth rd E6	66	A2
Elizabeth rd N15	31	S15
Elizabeth st SW1	155	V5
Elizabeth ter SE9	95	U15
Elizabeth way SE19	109	O18
Elkington rd E13	65	V12
Elkins the Rom	39	R6
Elkstone rd W10	137	P20
Ella rd N8	30	A20
Ellaline rd W6	152	F15
Ellanby cres N18	19	N14
Elland rd SE15	92	D11
Ellement clo Pnr	22	A15
Ellen clo Brom	127	O6
Ellen ct N9	19	P8
Ellen st E1	151	T7
Ellenborough pl SW15	86	G10
Ellenborough rd N22	30	K5
Ellenborough rd Sid	115	X14
Ellenbridge way S Croy	133	T20
Elleray rd Tedd	101	W14
Ellerby st SW6	87	R2
Ellerdale clo NW3	46	D13
Ellerdale rd NW3	46	E14
Ellerdale st SE13	93	R9
Ellerdine rd Houns	83	O11
Ellerker gdns Rich	84	J15
Ellerman ave Twick	100	D2
Ellerslie gdns NW10	62	H2
Ellerslie rd W12	144	A13
Ellerton gdns Dag	68	F1
Ellerton rd SW13	86	G2
Ellerton rd SW18	88	F20
Ellerton rd SW20	104	F17
Ellerton rd Dag	55	T20
Ellerton rd Surb	116	M20
Ellery rd SE19	109	O18
Ellery st SE15	92	A6
Ellesmere ave NW7	12	K10
Ellesmere ave Beck	125	T4
Ellesmere clo E11	34	D16
Ellesmere gdns Ilf	35	S17
Ellesmere gro Barn	4	G16
Ellesmere rd E3	63	W5
Ellesmere rd NW10	44	F14
Ellesmere rd W4	73	X15
Ellesmere rd Grnf	58	M13
Ellesmere rd Twick	84	D15
Ellesmere st E14	64	D16
Ellingfort rd E8	50	A19
Ellingham rd E15	51	X12
Ellingham rd W12	74	H5
Ellington rd N10	29	S13
Ellington rd Houns	82	M5
Ellington st N7	48	F18
Elliot clo E15	51	Z20
Elliot rd NW4	26	J19
Elliot rd Stan	10	M18
Elliott clo Wem	43	O9
Elliott gdns Rom	39	Y3
Elliott rd SW9	157	W20
Elliott rd W4	74	A12
Elliott rd Brom	127	N9
Elliott rd Th Hth	122	K9
Elliott's pl N1	141	Y5
Elliotts row SE11	157	X4
Ellis clo SE9	114	C3
Ellis ct W7	59	V14
Ellis ms SE7	77	X16
Ellis rd Mitch	121	N15
Ellis st SW1	155	S5
Elliscombe rd SE7	77	Y15
Ellisfield dr SW15	86	E18
Ellison gdns Sthl	70	D10
Ellison rd SW13	86	E5
Ellison rd SW16	107	Y17
Ellison rd Sid	114	F2
Ellmore clo Rom	39	Z3
Ellora rd SW16	107	Z13
Ellsworth st E2	143	X12
Elm ave W5	72	L3
Elm bank N14	17	O1
Elm bank Brom	127	N1
Elm Bank gdns SW13	86	C5
Elm clo E11	34	K18
Elm clo NW4	27	O17
Elm clo SW20	118	M9
Elm clo Cars	130	L1
Elm clo Har	22	J19
Elm clo Rom	38	H6
Elm clo S Croy	133	R15
Elm clo Surb	117	W17
Elm clo Twick	100	K5
Elm ct EC4	149	T7
Elm cres W5	72	L4
Elm cres Kings T	116	L2
Elm dr Har	22	J18
Elm Friars wk NW1	140	H1
Elm gdns N2	28	E10
Elm gdns Enf	8	B2
Elm gdns Mitch	121	Y9
Elm grn W3	62	A17
Elm gro N8	30	B9
Elm gro NW2	45	R12
Elm gro SE15	91	W4
Elm gro SW19	105	S18
Elm gro Har	40	H1
Elm gro Kings T	116	L1
Elm gro Sutt	130	B9
Elm gro Wdf Grn	21	R17
Elm Grove par Wall	131	P7
Elm Grove rd SW13	86	H4
Elm Grove rd W5	72	K4
Elm pk SW2	90	D16
Elm pk Stan	11	P16
Elm Park ave N15	31	W16
Elm Park ave Horn	57	V11
Elm Park gdns NW4	27	O16
Elm Park gdns SW10	154	F12
Elm Park la SW3	154	F12
Elm Park mans SW10	154	E13
Elm Park rd E10	50	K4
Elm Park rd N3	27	W2
Elm Park rd N21	17	Y3
Elm Park rd SE25	123	U7
Elm Park rd SW3	154	E13
Elm pl SW7	154	F10
Elm rd E7	52	D18
Elm rd E11	51	W7
Elm rd E17	33	V15
Elm rd N22	30	J4
Elm rd SW14	85	W9
Elm rd Barn	4	G14
Elm rd Beck	124	L3
Elm rd Epsom	128	E15
Elm rd Erith	99	W2
Elm rd Kings T	116	M1
Elm rd N Mal	117	V4
Elm rd Rom	38	H6
Elm rd Sid	115	N10
Elm rd Th Hth	123	N10
Elm rd Wall	131	P1
Elm rd Wem	42	K15
Elm Road west Sutt	130	C11
Elm row NW3	46	E10
Elm st WC1	141	R18
Elm ter NW2	45	X8
Elm ter SE9	95	W15
Elm ter Har	23	R3
Elm Tree clo NW8	138	G12
Elm Tree clo Nthlt	58	B27
Elm Tree rd NW8	138	F13
Elm wk NW3	45	Z7
Elm wk SW20	119	N9
Elm wk Rom	39	W9
Elm way N11	16	C19
Elm way NW10	44	A11
Elm way Wor Pk	128	M5
Elmar rd N15	31	P13
Elmbank ave Barn	4	A14
Elmbank way W7	59	R13
Elmbourne dr Belv	81	U12
Elmbourne rd SW17	107	R8
Elmbridge ave Surb	117	U12
Elmbrook gdns SE9	95	S10
Elmbrook rd Sutt	129	W9
Elmcourt rd SE27	108	J4
Elmcroft ave E11	34	H14
Elmcroft ave N9	9	N19
Elmcroft ave NW11	27	W20
Elmcroft ave Sid	96	M17
Elmcroft clo E11	34	J14
Elmcroft clo W5	60	G16
Elmcroft cres NW11	45	S1
Elmcroft cres Har	22	J11
Elmcroft gdns NW9	25	C11
Elmcroft st E5	50	C11
Elmdale rd N13	17	R16
Elmdene Surb	117	X20
Elmdene clo Beck	124	K13
Elmdene rd SE18	78	M14
Elmdon rd Houns	82	A4
Elmer clo Enf	7	P11
Elmer clo Rain	57	W20
Elmer gdns Edg	25	S1
Elmer gdns Islw	83	R8
Elmer gdns Rain	57	W20
Elmer rd SE6	93	U19
Elmers End rd SE20	124	C2
Elmers End rd Beck	124	F7
Elmers rd SE25	123	Y16
Elmerside rd Beck	124	H8
Elmfield ave N8	30	A15
Elmfield ave Mitch	121	P2
Elmfield ave Tedd	101	X12
Elmfield clo Har	41	S7
Elmfield pk Brom	126	G6
Elmfield rd E4	20	H7
Elmfield rd E17	32	F17
Elmfield rd N2	28	F9
Elmfield rd SW17	107	P3
Elmfield rd Brom	126	F5
Elmfield way S Croy	133	U20
Elmgate gdns Edg	12	K15
Elmgrove cres Har	23	X15
Elmgrove gdns Har	23	X15
Elmgrove rd Croy	124	A19
Elmgrove rd Har	23	V16
Elmhall gdns E11	34	J17
Elmhurst Belv	81	N16
Elmhurst ave N2	28	F10
Elmhurst ave Mitch	107	R19
Elmhurst cres N2	28	F12
Elmhurst dr E18	34	F6
Elmhurst gdns E18	34	G6
Elmhurst rd E7	52	H20
Elmhurst rd N17	31	T7
Elmhurst rd SE9	113	R5
Elmhurst st SW4	89	X7
Elmington clo Bex	98	G17
Elmington est SE5	158	G18
Elmington rd SE5	158	E20
Elmira st SE13	93	T8
Elmlee clo Chis	113	U15
Elmley clo E6	66	E15
Elmley st SE18	79	S12
Elmore clo Wem	60	K6
Elmore rd E11	51	W10
Elmore rd Enf	9	S4
Elmore st N1	49	O20
Elms the SW13	86	D8
Elms ave N10	29	T9
Elms ave NW4	27	O16
Elms ct Wem	41	X13
Elms cres SW4	89	W16
Elms gdns Dag	56	B11
Elms gdns Wem	41	X13
Elms la Wem	41	Z9
Elms ms W2	146	E9
Elms Park ave Wem	41	Y13
Elms rd SW4	89	V13
Elms rd Har	23	S2
Elmscott gdns N21	8	A20
Elmscott rd Brom	112	B12
Elmscroft N8	30	C14
Elmsdale rd E17	32	L12
Elmshaw rd SW15	86	H13
Elmside Croy	135	R14
Elmside rd Wem	43	P9
Elmsleigh ave Har	24	C11
Elmsleigh rd Twick	101	R4
Elmstead ave Chis	113	V13
Elmstead ave Wem	42	K4
Elmstead clo N20	14	L9
Elmstead clo Epsom	128	B12
Elmstead cres Well	80	G17
Elmstead gdns Wor Pk	128	F5
Elmstead glade Chis	113	T14
Elmstead la Chis	113	S18
Elmstead rd Erith	99	P1
Elmstead rd Ilf	54	K6
Elmstone rd SW6	87	X1
Elmsworth ave Houns	82	K4
Elmton way E5	49	Y10
Elmtree rd Tedd	101	U10
Elmwood ave N13	17	O15
Elmwood ave Har	23	Z16
Elmwood clo Epsom	128	G16
Elmwood clo Wall	131	R4
Elmwood ct Wem	41	Z10
Elmwood cres NW9	25	W13
Elmwood dr Bex	97	Y18
Elmwood dr Epsom	128	G16
Elmwood gdns W7	59	T18
Elmwood rd SE24	91	O13
Elmwood rd W4	73	V15
Elmwood rd Croy	122	J18
Elmwood rd Mitch	120	M6
Elmworth gro SE21	109	N5
Elnathan ms W9	137	Y18
Elphinstone rd E17	32	M6
Elphinstone st N5	48	J11
Elrington rd E8	49	X18
Elsa rd Well	97	R4
Elsa st E1	63	V15
Elsdale st E9	50	C18
Elsden ms E2	63	R6
Elsden rd N17	31	U5
Elsenham rd E12	53	V16
Elsenham st SW18	105	V1
Elsham rd E11	52	A11
Elsham rd W14	144	J18
Elsie rd SE22	91	U10

Name	Page	Ref
Elsiedene rd N21	17	Z2
Elsiemaud rd SE4	93	N14
Elsinore rd SE23	110	J2
Elsinore way Rich	85	T7
Elsley rd SW11	88	M7
Elspeth rd SW11	88	M9
Elsrick ave Mord	119	V12
Elstan way Croy	124	J17
Elsted st SE17	158	G7
Elstow clo SE9	95	W13
Elstow gdns Dag	68	L2
Elstow rd Dag	68	L2
Elstree gdns N9	19	N5
Elstree gdns Belv	80	M10
Elstree gdns Ilf	54	B15
Elstree hill Brom	111	Z17
Elstree Hill south Borwd	11	T3
Elswick rd SE13	93	S6
Elswick st SW6	88	C4
Elsworthy ri NW3	138	M1
Elsworthy rd NW3	138	J4
Elsworthy ter NW3	138	M2
Elsynge rd SW18	88	F12
Eltham grn SE9	95	N13
Eltham Green rd SE9	94	M10
Eltham High st SE9	95	T15
Eltham hill SE9	95	O14
Eltham Palace rd SE9	94	L16
Eltham Park gdns SE9	95	X11
Eltham rd SE9	94	L14
Eltham rd SE12	94	E12
Elthiron rd SW6	87	Y2
Elthorne ave W7	71	X6
Elthorne Park rd W7	71	X7
Elthorne rd N19	47	X6
Elthorne rd NW9	25	X20
Elthorne way NW9	25	Y19
Elthruda rd SE13	93	Y16
Eltisley rd Ilf	53	Y12
Elton ave Barn	4	J16
Elton ave Grnf	41	V17
Elton ave Wem	42	C14
Elton clo Kings T	102	E19
Elton pl N16	49	S14
Elton rd Kings T	103	O20
Eltringham st SW18	88	D10
Elvaston ms SW7	154	D2
Elvaston pl SW7	154	B2
Elveden pl NW10	61	P5
Elveden rd NW10	61	P5
Elvendon rd N13	17	N18
Elverson rd SE8	93	S5
Elverton st SW1	156	F14
Elvington grn Brom	126	D11
Elvington la NW9	26	A4
Elvino rd SE26	110	G13
Elvis rd NW2	44	L16
Elwill way Beck	125	U8
Elwin st E2	143	R12
Elwood st N5	48	J10
Elwyn gdns SE12	94	G20
Ely clo Erith	99	T5
Ely clo N Mal	118	E3
Ely gdns Dag	56	L9
Ely pl EC1	149	V2
Ely rd E10	33	U20
Ely rd Croy	123	P11
Elyne rd N4	30	F19
Elystan clo Wall	131	U18
Elystan pl SW3	154	M8
Elystan st SW3	154	K6
Elystan wk N1	141	T6
Emanuel ave W3	61	W18
Emba st SE16	151	V18
Embankment SW15	87	O6
Embankment the Twick	101	Z2
Embankment gdns SW3	155	R13
Embankment pl WC2	148	L13
Embassy ct Sid	115	S8
Embleton rd SE13	93	R8
Embry clo Stan	10	M14
Embry dr Stan	10	M18
Embry way Stan	10	M14
Emden st SW6	88	B2
Emerald clo E16	66	C17
Emerald gdns Dag	56	D5
Emerald st WC1	141	O19
Emerson gdns Har	24	M19
Emerson rd Ilf	35	X20
Emerson st SE1	150	B12
Emerton clo Bexh	97	Z10
Emery Hill st SW1	156	D3
Emery st SE1	149	U20
Emes rd Erith	81	Y18
Emily pl N7	48	G12
Emlyn gdns W12	74	C6
Emlyn rd W12	74	C6
Emma rd E13	65	R7
Emma st E2	143	W8
Emmanuel rd SW12	107	U2
Emmott ave Ilf	36	C16
Emmott clo E1	63	W12
Emmott clo NW11	28	C18
Emms pas Kings T	116	G5
Emperor's gate SW7	154	A4
Empire av N18	17	Y17
Empire ct Wem	43	S10
Empire rd Grnf	60	C3
Empire way Wem	43	O11
Empire Wharf rd E14	76	J12
Empire yd N7	48	A9
Empress ave E4	33	P2
Empress ave E12	52	M7
Empress ave Ilf	53	V7
Empress ave Wdf Grn	34	C2
Empress dr Chis	113	Z14
Empress pl SW6	153	U12
Empress rd SE17	158	C13
Empson st E3	64	F11
Emsworth clo N9	19	P4
Emsworth rd Ilf	36	A6
Emsworth st SW2	108	C4
Emu rd SW8	89	S5
Ena rd SW16	122	A6
Enbrook st W10	136	M15
End way Surb	117	S18
Endale clo Cars	131	N3
Endeavour way SW19	106	A9
Endeavour way Bark	68	A1
Endeavour way Croy	121	Z17
Endell st WC2	148	J5
Enderby st SE10	76	L14
Enderley clo Har	23	S5
Enderley rd Har	23	S5
Endersleigh gdns NW4	26	G14
Endlebury rd E4	20	F7
Endlesham rd SW12	89	O17
Endsleigh gdns WC1	140	F15
Endsleigh gdns Ilf	53	U5
Endsleigh gdns Surb	116	F16
Endsleigh pl WC1	140	G16
Endsleigh rd W13	71	Y1
Endsleigh rd Sthl	70	C10
Endsleigh st WC1	140	F15
Endwell rd SE4	92	J5
Endymion rd N4	48	G1
Endymion rd SW2	90	C16
Enfield rd N1	142	L1
Enfield rd W3	73	S6
Enfield rd Brent	72	H13
Enfield rd Enf	6	L13
Enford st W1	147	N1
Engadine clo Croy	133	T6
Engadine st SW18	105	W1
Engate st SE13	93	U10
Engel pk NW7	14	A20
Engineer clo SE18	78	K16
Engineers way Wem	43	O12
Englands la NW3	46	L18
Englefield clo Croy	122	L16
Englefield rd N1	49	O19
Engleheart rd SE6	93	U20
Englewood rd SW12	89	T15
English grds SE1	150	K14
English st E3	63	Y11
Enid st SE16	151	P20
Enmore ave SE25	123	Y11
Enmore gdns SW14	85	Y13
Enmore rd SE25	123	X12
Enmore rd SW15	87	N12
Enmore rd Sthl	58	H11
Ennerdale ave Horn	57	W15
Ennerdale ave Stan	24	C9
Ennerdale clo (Cheam) Sutt	129	W9
Ennerdale dr NW9	26	A15
Ennerdale gdns Wem	42	E4
Ennerdale rd Bexh	98	E2
Ennerdale rd Rich	85	N5
Ennersdale rd SE13	93	W14
Ennis rd N4	48	F4
Ennis rd SE18	79	R17
Ennismore ave W4	74	C11
Ennismore ave Grnf	41	U16
Ennismore gdns SW7	146	K18
Ennismore Gardens ms SW7	146	J20
Ennismore ms SW7	146	K20
Ennismore st SW7	154	K1
Ensign st E1	151	T9
Enslin rd SE9	95	X17
Ensor ms SW7	154	E9
Enstone rd Enf	9	W10
Enterprise clo Croy	132	E1
Enterprise way NW10	62	F9
Enterprise way SW18	87	Z11
Enterprise way Tedd	101	X14
Enterprize way SE8	75	Y10
Epirus ms SW6	153	T17
Epirus rd SW6	153	S17
Epping clo E14	76	C10
Epping clo Rom	38	H11
Epping New rd Buck H	21	U9
Epping New rd Loug	21	W1
Epping pl N1	48	F18
Epple rd SW6	87	W2
Epsom clo Bexh	98	H8
Epsom clo Nthlt	40	E16
Epsom rd E10	33	U19
Epsom rd Croy	132	F8
Epsom rd Ilf	36	K19
Epsom rd Sutt	119	U17
Epstein rd SE28	80	C3
Epworth rd Islw	72	A20
Epworth st EC2	142	G17
Erasmus st SW1	156	H7
Erconwald st W12	62	D18
Eresby dr Beck	125	P19
Eresby pl NW6	137	U2
Eric clo E7	52	E12
Eric rd E7	52	E12
Eric rd NW10	44	C18
Eric rd Rom	37	X20
Eric st E3	63	X11
Erica gdns Croy	135	P7
Erica st W12	62	H20
Ericcson clo SW18	87	X13
Eridge rd W4	73	Y8
Erin clo Brom	111	Z17
Erindale SE18	79	T18
Erindale ter SE18	79	T17
Erith cres Rom	38	K3
Erith rd Belv	81	T13
Erith rd Bexh	98	H11
Erith rd Erith	98	J2
Erlanger rd SE14	92	F2
Erlesmere gdns W13	71	Y7
Ermine rd N15	31	T17
Ermine rd SE13	93	R8
Ermine side Enf	8	J16
Ermington rd SE9	114	D4
Ernald ave E6	66	E5
Erncroft way Twick	83	W17
Ernest ave SE27	108	K10
Ernest clo Beck	125	N11
Ernest gdns W4	73	T17
Ernest gro Beck	124	M11
Ernest rd Kings T	117	S4
Ernest sq Kings T	117	S4
Ernest st E1	63	T12
Ernle rd SW20	104	L17
Ernshaw pl SW15	87	T13
Erpingham rd SW15	86	M8
Erridge rd SW19	119	X3
Errington rd W9	137	R17
Errol gdns N Mal	118	H10
Errol st EC1	142	D18
Erroll rd Rom	39	U12
Erskine clo Sutt	130	J6
Erskine cres N17	31	Z12
Erskine hill NW11	27	Y14
Erskine ms NW3	139	R1
Erskine rd E17	32	M11
Erskine rd NW3	139	R1
Erskine rd Sutt	130	F7
Erwood rd SE7	78	E13
Esam way SW16	108	G13
Escott gdns SE9	113	S10
Escreet gro SE18	78	J10
Esher ave Rom	38	K18
Esher ave Sutt	129	R6
Esher clo Bex	115	Y2
Esher gdns SW19	105	O4
Esher ms Mitch	121	N6
Esher rd Ilf	54	H8
Esk rd E13	65	V11
Esk way Rom	39	P2
Eskdale ave Nthlt	58	E2
Eskdale clo Wem	42	G6
Eskdale rd Bexh	98	E4
Eskmont ridge SE19	109	R18
Esmar cres NW9	44	F1
Esmeralda rd SE1	159	T7
Esmond rd NW6	137	R5
Esmond rd W4	73	Z9
Esmond st SW15	87	T11
Esparto st SW18	88	B18
Essenden rd Belv	81	R13
Essenden rd S Croy	133	R17
Essendine rd W9	137	U15
Essex ave Islw	83	S8
Essex clo E17	32	H12
Essex clo Mord	119	O16
Essex clo Rom	38	H12
Essex ct SW13	86	D4
Essex gdns N4	30	K17
Essex gro SE19	109	P15
Essex pk N3	15	N19
Essex Park ms W3	74	B4
Essex pl W4	73	X12
Essex rd E4	20	M5
Essex rd E10	33	U17
Essex rd E12	53	S16
Essex rd E17	32	H17
Essex rd E18	34	J7
Essex rd N1	141	Z3
Essex rd NW10	44	C19
Essex rd W3	61	V19
Essex rd W4	73	X12
Essex rd Bark	67	U2
Essex rd Dag	56	K15
Essex rd Enf	8	B14
Essex rd Rom	38	F11
Essex rd Rom (Chadwell Heath)	55	T2
Essex Road south E11	33	X20
Essex st E7	52	F14
Essex st WC2	149	S8
Essex vill W8	145	T19
Essex wf E5	50	E7
Essian st E1	63	W13
Essoldo way Edg	25	N9
Estate way E10	51	N3
Estcourt rd SE25	124	A15
Estcourt rd SW6	153	N17
Este rd SW11	88	J7
Estella ave N Mal	118	K10
Estelle rd NW3	47	N13
Esterbrooke st SW1	156	F7
Esther clo N21	17	U1
Esther rd E11	34	A20
Estreham rd SW16	107	X16
Estridge clo Houns	82	G10
Eswyn rd SW17	106	M11
Etchingham Park rd N3	28	B1
Etchingham rd E15	51	V12

Name			Name			Name			Name			Name		
Eternit wk SW6	87	O2	Everard ave Brom	126	G19	Exeter rd Felt	100	E7	Faber gdns NW4	26	H16	Fairfield gro SE7	78	A15
Etfield gro Sid	115	P12	Everard way Wem	42	J10	Exeter rd Har	40	C5	Fabian rd SW6	153	R17	Fairfield north	116	K3
Ethel rd E16	65	V18	Everdon rd SW13	74	G17	Exeter rd Well	96	J4	Fabian st E6	66	F11	Kings T		
Ethel st SE17	158	B7	Everest pl E14	64	G14	Exeter st WC2	148	M9	Factory la N1	31	V7	Fairfield path Croy	133	P5
Ethelbert gdns Ilf	35	V17	Everest rd SE9	95	T13	Exeter way SE14	75	Y20	Factory pl E14	76	F14	Fairfield pl Kings T	116	L6
Ethelbert clo Brom	126	E5	Everglade strand	26	E5	Exford gdns SE12	112	H2	Factory rd E16	78	D4	Fairfield rd E3	64	B6
Ethelbert rd SW20	119	P1	NW9			Exford rd SE12	112	H3	Factory sq SW16	108	A16	Fairfield rd E17	32	J8
Ethelbert rd Brom	126	E6	Everilda st N1	141	P5	Exhibition rd SW7	144	C9	Factory yd W7	71	T3	Fairfield rd N8	30	A16
Ethelbert rd Erith	81	X18	Evering rd E5	49	Z8	Exhibition rd SW7	154	H4	Fair acres Brom	126	F13	Fairfield rd N18	18	K15
Ethelbert st SW12	107	T2	Evering rd N16	49	U11	Exmoor clo Ilf	36	B5	Fairacre N Mal	118	A7	Fairfield rd W7	71	Y9
Ethelburga st SW11	88	K1	Everington rd N10	29	N6	Exmoor st W10	136	H19	Fairacres SW15	86	F11	Fairfield rd Beck	125	O3
Ethelden rd W12	74	K2	Everington st W6	152	H14	Exmouth mkt EC1	141	T15	Fairacres Croy	134	L20	Fairfield rd Bexh	98	B5
Etheldene ave N10	29	V13	Everitt rd NW10	61	Z9	Exmouth pl E8	143	W2	Fairbairn grn SW9	90	G1	Fairfield rd Brom	112	E18
Etheridge rd NW2	44	M2	Everleigh st N4	48	E4	Exmouth rd E17	32	M16	Fairbanks rd N17	31	W11	Fairfield rd Croy	133	R5
Etherley rd N15	30	M15	Eversfield gdns NW7	13	N20	Exmouth rd Brom	126	G7	Fairbourne rd N17	31	R9	Fairfield rd Ilf	54	A17
Etherow st SE22	91	W17	Eversfield rd Rich	85	N4	Exmouth rd Well	97	S1	Fairbridge rd N19	47	X7	Fairfield rd Kings T	116	K4
Etherstone grn	108	E10	Eversholt st NW1	140	D10	Exmouth st E1	63	R17	Fairbrook clo N13	17	U17	Fairfield rd Sthl	58	D17
SW16			Evershot rd N4	48	C3	Exning rd E16	65	O12	Fairbrook rd N13	17	U17	Fairfield rd Wdf Grn	21	S19
Etherstone rd SW16	108	E11	Eversleigh rd E6	66	B2	Exon st SE17	158	K8	Fairburn ct SW15	87	S13	Fairfield south	116	K5
Ethnard rd SE15	159	V15	Eversleigh rd N3	27	W2	Express dr Ilf	55	R4	Fairby rd SE12	94	H13	Kings T		
Ethronvi rd Bexh	97	Z8	Eversleigh rd SW11	88	M7	Exton cres NW10	43	W20	Faircross ave Bark	54	C17	Fairfield st SW18	88	B12
Etloe rd E10	51	O6	Eversleigh rd Barn	5	R18	Exton gdns Dag	55	V14	Faircross ave Rom	38	M1	Fairfield way Barn	4	L16
Eton ave N12	15	S20	Eversley ave Bexh	99	N4	Exton st SE1	149	T15	Fairdale gdns SW15	86	K9	Fairfield way Epsom	128	A12
Eton ave NW3	46	G20	Eversley ave Wem	43	P6	Eyhurst clo NW2	44	H6	Fairey ave Hayes	68	K9	Fairfield west	116	K4
Eton ave Barn	5	X18	Eversley clo N21	7	P18	Eylewood rd SE27	108	M12	Fairfax ave Epsom	128	J20	Kings T		
Eton ave Houns	70	F16	Eversley cres N21	7	T19	Eynella rd SE22	91	U18	Fairfax gdns SE3	94	M3	Fairfields clo NW9	25	W15
Eton ave N Mal	117	Y11	Eversley cres Islw	83	P3	Eynham rd W12	144	B4	Fairfax pl NW6	138	C1	Fairfields cres NW9	25	W15
Eton ave Wem	42	B13	Eversley cross Bexh	99	R5	Eynsford cres Bex	115	V2	Fairfax rd N8	30	G14	Fairfields rd Houns	82	M8
Eton College rd NW3	47	N19	Eversley mt N21	7	R19	Eynsford rd Ilf	54	J6	Fairfax rd NW6	138	D1	Fairfoot rd E3	64	B11
Eton ct Wem	42	E12	Eversley pk SW19	104	J13	Eynsham dr SE2	80	B11	Fairfax rd W4	74	C9	Fairford ave Bexh	98	M3
Eton Garages NW3	46	K18	Eversley Park rd N21	7	R18	Eynswood dr Sid	115	S13	Fairfax rd Tedd	101	Z16	Fairford ave Croy	124	G13
Eton gro NW9	25	R11	Eversley rd SE7	77	V16	Eyot gdns W6	74	F13	Fairfield ave NW4	26	L19	Fairford clo Croy	124	H12
Eton gro SE13	94	A9	Eversley rd SE19	109	N17	Eyot grn W4	74	E15	Fairfield ave Edg	12	E20	Fairford gdns	128	F4
Eton rd NW3	46	M19	Eversley rd Surb	116	M10	Eyre ct NW8	138	F8	Fairfield ave Twick	100	L1	Wor Pk		
Eton rd Ilf	54	B14	Eversley way Croy	135	N7	Eyre Street hill EC1	141	T18	Fairfield clo N12	15	S14	Fairgreen Barn	5	Y10
Eton st Rich	84	J12	Everthorpe rd SE15	91	U9	Eythorne rd SW9	90	G1	Fairfield clo Epsom	128	A12	Fairgreen east Barn	5	Z10
Eton vill NW3	46	M18	Everton bldgs NW1	140	A14	Ezra st E2	143	R11	Fairfield clo Mitch	106	J19	Fairgreen rd Th Hth	122	K13
Etta st SE8	75	X15	Everton dr Stan	24	L9				Fairfield clo Sid	96	L15	Fairhaven ave Croy	124	E16
Ettrick st E14	64	H16	Everton rd Croy	123	W19				Fairfield clo NW10	62	F4	Fairhazel gdns NW6	138	B1
Etwell pl Surb	116	M14	Evesham ave E17	33	P7	**F**			Fairfield cres Edg	12	E20	Fairholme ave Rom	39	Z13
Eugenia rd SE16	75	R12	Evesham clo Grnf	58	K5				Fairfield dr SW18	88	B13	Fairholme clo N3	27	T12
Eureka rd Kings T	117	O4	Evesham clo Sutt	129	X16	Faber gdns NW4	26	H16	Fairfield dr Grnf	60	F4	Fairholme gdns N3	27	U11
Europa pl EC1	142	B14	Evesham grn Mord	120	A15	Fabian rd SW6	153	R17	Fairfield dr Har	23	N10	Fairholme rd W14	152	M11
Europe rd SE18	78	G8	Evesham rd E15	65	O2	Fabian st E6	66	F11	Fairfield east	116	L4	Fairholme rd Croy	122	H18
Eustace rd E6	66	E8	Evesham rd N11	16	J17	Factory la N1	31	V7	Kings T			Fairholme rd Har	23	V16
Eustace rd SW6	153	T16	Evesham rd Mord	120	B15	Factory pl E14	76	F14	Fairfield gdns N8	30	A16	Fairholme rd Ilf	35	V20
Eustace rd Rom	37	X20	Evesham st W11	144	G10	Factory rd E16	78	D4				Fairholme rd Sutt	129	V13
Euston gro NW1	140	F14	Evesham wk SW9	90	F3	Factory sq SW16	108	A16				Fairholt clo N16	49	R3
Euston rd NW1	140	A17	Evesham way SW11	89	P7	Factory yd W7	71	T3				Fairholt rd N16	49	O3
Euston rd Croy	122	E20	Evesham way Ilf	35	Y10	Fair acres Brom	126	F13				Fairholt st SW7	154	L1
Euston sq NW1	140	F14	Evry rd Sid	115	V15	Fairacre N Mal	118	A7				Fairland rd E15	52	C19
Euston st NW1	140	C15	Ewald rd SW6	87	V5	Fairacres SW15	86	F11				Fairlands ave Buck H	21	U7
Eva rd Rom	37	V20	Ewanrigg ter	21	Y17	Fairacres Croy	134	L20				Fairlands ave Sutt	129	Z2
Evandale rd SW9	90	H4	Wdf Grn			Fairbairn grn SW9	90	G1				Fairlands ave Th Hth	122	D10
Evangelist rd NW5	47	T13	Ewart gro N22	30	E5	Fairbanks rd N17	31	W11				Fairlands ct SE9	95	X16
Evans gro Felt	100	G5	Ewart pl E3	63	Y6	Fairbourne rd N17	31	R9				Fairlawn SE7	77	X18
Evans rd SE6	112	A5	Ewart rd SE23	92	F20	Fairbridge rd N19	47	X7				Fairlawn ave N2	28	K12
Evanston ave E4	33	U3	Ewe clo N7	48	B17	Fairbrook clo N13	17	U17				Fairlawn ave W4	73	W11
Evanston gdns Ilf	35	P18	Ewell bypass Epsom	128	F15	Fairbrook rd N13	17	U17				Fairlawn ave Bexh	97	X5
Eve rd E11	52	Z12	Ewell Court ave	128	F12	Fairburn ct SW15	87	S13				Fairlawn clo N14	6	J20
Eve rd E15	65	N6	Epsom			Fairby rd SE12	94	H13				Fairlawn clo Felt	100	D9
Eve rd N17	31	T9	Ewell Park way	128	F15	Faircross ave Bark	54	C17				Fairlawn clo Kings T	103	U15
Eve rd Islw	83	Z11	Epsom			Faircross ave Rom	38	M1				Fairlawn dr Wdf Grn	34	G1
Evelina rd SE15	92	C6	Ewell rd Surb	116	M17	Fairdale gdns SW15	86	K9				Fairlawn gro W4	73	W11
Evelina rd SE20	110	E19	Ewell rd	116	B18	Fairey ave Hayes	68	K9				Fairlawn pk SE26	110	J11
Eveline Lowe est	159	T3	(Long Ditton) Surb			Fairfax ave Epsom	128	J20				Fairlawn rd SW19	105	V19
SE16			Ewellhurst rd Ilf	35	S7	Fairfax gdns SE3	94	M3				Fairlawns Twick	84	F16
Eveline rd Mitch	120	L2	Ewelme rd SE23	92	D20	Fairfax pl NW6	138	C1				Fairlea pl W5	60	F13
Evelyn ave NW9	25	Y11	Ewen cres SW2	92	F20	Fairfax rd N8	30	G14				Fairlie gdns SE23	92	E19
Evelyn clo Twick	82	J18	Ewer st SE1	150	A15	Fairfax rd NW6	138	D1				Fairlight ave E4	20	J8
Evelyn ct N1	142	F10	Ewhurst ave S Croy	133	U19	Fairfax rd W4	74	C9				Fairlight ave NW10	62	B6
Evelyn Dennington	66	G13	Ewhurst rd SE4	92	M15	Fairfax rd Tedd	101	Z16				Fairlight ave Wdf Grn	21	T20
rd E6			Exbury rd SE6	111	N4	Fairfield ave NW4	26	L19				Fairlight clo E4	20	J8
Evelyn dr Pnr	22	A2	Excelsior clo	117	O5	Fairfield ave Edg	12	E20				Fairlight clo Wor Pk	128	M8
Evelyn gdns SW7	154	E10	Kings T			Fairfield ave Twick	100	L1				Fairlight rd SW17	106	G11
Evelyn gro W5	73	N4	Excelsior gdns SE13	93	U5	Fairfield clo N12	15	S14				Fairlop gdns Ilf	36	C2
Evelyn gro Sthl	58	E16	Exchange sq EC2	142	K20	Fairfield clo Epsom	128	A12				Fairlop rd E11	51	X1
Evelyn rd E17	33	V13	Exchange st Rom	39	R15	Fairfield clo Mitch	106	J19				Fairlop rd Ilf	36	B8
Evelyn rd SW19	106	A14	Exeter clo E6	66	G17	Fairfield clo Sid	96	L15				Fairmead Brom	127	U10
Evelyn rd W4	73	X8	Exeter gdns Ilf	53	S3	Fairfield clo NW10	62	F4				Fairmead clo Brom	127	U9
Evelyn rd Barn	5	Z15	Exeter rd E16	65	T15	Fairfield cres Edg	12	E20				Fairmead clo N Mal	117	Z7
Evelyn rd Rich	84	K8	Exeter rd E17	33	N15	Fairfield dr SW18	88	B13				Fairmead cres Edg	12	H10
Evelyn st SE8	75	X13	Exeter rd N9	19	P9	Fairfield dr Grnf	60	F4				Fairmead gdns Ilf	35	P16
Evelyn ter Rich	84	J8	Exeter rd N14	16	D4	Fairfield dr Har	23	N10				Fairmead rd N19	47	Z10
Evelyn way Wall	131	X7	Exeter rd NW2	45	S15	Fairfield east	116	L4				Fairmead rd Croy	122	E19
Evelyn yd W1	148	F4	Exeter rd SE15	159	O20	Kings T						Fairmile ave SW16	107	X13
Evening hill Beck	111	V19	Exeter rd Croy	123	T18	Fairfield gdns N8	30	A16				Fairmont clo Belv	81	P15
Evenwood clo SW15	87	S14	Exeter rd Dag	56	J17							Fairmount rd SW2	90	D15
			Exeter rd Enf	9	T12									

Name	No	Grid
Fairoak dr SE9	96	E13
Fairoak gdns Rom	39	P8
Fairseat clo (Bushey) Wat	10	E8
Fairthorn rd SE7	77	U13
Fairview ave Wem	42	G17
Fairview clo E17	32	J5
Fairview cres Har	40	H3
Fairview gdns Wdf Grn	34	J3
Fairview rd N15	31	V16
Fairview rd SW16	122	C1
Fairview rd Enf	7	T6
Fairview rd Sutt	130	H12
Fairview way Edg	12	C14
Fairwater ave Well	97	N11
Fairway SW20	118	M6
Fairway Bexh	98	A13
Fairway Wdf Grn	21	Z15
Fairway the N13	17	Z10
Fairway the N14	6	E18
Fairway the NW7	12	K10
Fairway the W3	62	B17
Fairway the Barn	5	O19
Fairway the Brom	127	U11
Fairway the N Mal	117	Z1
Fairway the Nthlt	41	N17
Fairway the Wem	42	C9
Fairway ave NW9	25	T11
Fairway clo NW11	46	C1
Fairway clo Beck	125	X14
Fairway clo Croy	124	H13
Fairway dr Grnf	58	M1
Fairway est Grnf	58	M2
Fairway gdns Ilf	54	C15
Fairways Stan	24	J7
Fairways Tedd	102	F17
Fairweather clo N15	31	R11
Fairweather rd N16	31	X19
Fairwyn rd SE26	110	H8
Fakruddin st E1	143	T17
Falcon ave Brom	127	S8
Falcon clo SE1	149	Z13
Falcon cres Enf	9	T18
Falcon gro SW11	88	J7
Falcon la SW11	88	K9
Falcon rd SW11	88	J6
Falcon rd Enf	9	S17
Falcon st E13	65	S10
Falcon ter SW11	88	K8
Falcon way E11	34	G12
Falcon way E14	76	E10
Falcon way NW9	26	B7
Falcon way Har	24	J16
Falcon way Horn	57	X19
Falconberg ct W1	148	F5
Falconberg ms W1	148	F5
Falconwood ave Well	96	F6
Falconwood par Well	96	J11
Falconwood rd Croy	134	M19
Falcourt clo Sutt	130	A12
Falkirk st N1	142	L10
Falkland ave N3	27	Y2
Falkland ave N11	16	D13
Falkland Park ave SE25	123	S5
Falkland rd N8	30	F13
Falkland rd NW5	47	V15
Falkland rd Barn	4	E9
Falloden way NW11	27	X12
Fallowfield Stan	10	L12
Fallowfield ct Stan	10	L11
Fallsbrook rd SW16	107	T17
Falmer rd E17	33	R10
Falmer rd N15	31	N14
Falmer rd Enf	8	F13
Falmouth ave E4	20	L16
Falmouth clo N22	30	D1
Falmouth clo SE12	94	D13
Falmouth gdns Ilf	35	O12
Falmouth rd SE1	158	C3
Falmouth st E15	51	Y16
Fambridge clo SE26	110	M11
Fambridge rd Dag	56	E2
Fane st W14	153	P12
Fann st EC1	142	A19
Fanshaw st N1	142	J11
Fanshawe ave Bark	54	C18
Fanshawe cres Dag	56	A15
Fanshawe rd Rich	102	E10
Fanthorpe st SW15	87	N7
Faraday ave Sid	115	O5
Faraday clo N7	48	C18
Faraday rd E15	52	C18
Faraday rd SW19	105	Z14
Faraday rd W3	61	W18
Faraday rd W10	136	K20
Faraday rd Sthl	58	K18
Faraday rd Well	97	N7
Faraday way SE18	78	B9
Faraday way Croy	122	D20
Fareham st W1	148	E5
Farewell pl Mitch	120	H2
Faringdon ave Brom	127	X18
Faringford rd E15	64	M1
Farjeon rd SE3	95	N2
Farleigh ave Brom	126	D16
Farleigh pl N16	49	U12
Farleigh rd N16	49	U12
Farley dr Ilf	54	J4
Farley pl SE25	123	X9
Farley rd SE6	93	T17
Farley rd S Croy	133	Z16
Farlington pl SW15	86	J20
Farlow rd SW15	87	N7
Farlton rd SW18	88	C20
Farm ave NW2	45	U10
Farm ave SW16	108	B9
Farm ave Har	22	F20
Farm ave Wem	42	A20
Farm clo Buck H	21	Y12
Farm clo Dag	56	K20
Farm clo Sthl	58	K19
Farm clo Sutt	130	H17
Farm ct NW4	26	H9
Farm dr Croy	134	J3
Farm la N14	6	D20
Farm la SW6	153	U15
Farm la Croy	134	M3
Farm pl W8	145	T13
Farm pl Dart	99	X11
Farm rd N21	17	Y5
Farm rd Edg	12	F18
Farm rd Houns	82	C20
Farm rd Mord	120	B13
Farm rd Sutt	130	G16
Farm st W1	147	W11
Farm vale Bex	98	G16
Farm wk NW11	27	W16
Farm way Buck H	21	Y12
Farm way Wor Pk	128	M6
Farmborough clo Har	41	R2
Farmcote rd SE12	112	F2
Farmdale rd SE10	77	T13
Farmdale rd Cars	130	J17
Farmer rd E10	51	R3
Farmer st W8	145	U12
Farmers rd SE5	157	Z19
Farmfield rd Brom	111	Y13
Farmhouse rd SW16	107	V19
Farmilo rd E17	33	M1
Farmington ave Sutt	130	H5
Farmland wk Chis	113	Z11
Farmlands Enf	7	T6
Farmlands the Nthlt	40	F19
Farmleigh N14	16	G1
Farmstead rd SE6	111	R10
Farmstead rd Har	23	S5
Farmway Dag	55	U9
Farnaby rd SE9	94	M11
Farnaby rd Brom	111	Y19
Farnan ave E17	33	R9
Farnan rd SW16	108	B12
Farnborough ave E17	32	H10
Farnborough ave S Croy	134	G18
Farnborough clo Wem	43	T8
Farnborough cres S Croy	134	J19
Farncombe st SE16	151	V18
Farndale ave N13	17	X9
Farndale Cres Grnf	59	N8
Farnell ms SW5	153	X9
Farnell rd Islw	83	S8
Farnham clo N20	15	R1
Farnham gdns SW20	118	K5
Farnham pl SE1	149	Z14
Farnham rd Ilf	36	M20
Farnham rd Well	97	T4
Farnham Royal SE11	157	P11
Farningham rd N17	31	Y1
Farnley rd E4	20	M2
Farnley rd SE25	123	P9
Faro clo Brom	127	X4
Faroe rd W14	152	J3
Farorna wk Enf	7	T5
Farquhar rd SE19	109	U12
Farquhar rd SW19	105	Y7
Farquharson rd Croy	122	L19
Farr ave Bark	67	Z6
Farr rd Enf	8	B6
Farrance rd Rom	37	Z19
Farrance st E14	64	A17
Farrans ct Har	24	C20
Farrant ave N22	30	G7
Farrant st SE23	110	H4
Farrer ms N8	29	W13
Farrer rd N8	29	W13
Farrer rd Har	24	J14
Farrier rd Nthlt	58	H5
Farrier st NW1	47	U20
Farringdon la EC1	141	U17
Farringdon rd EC1	141	S15
Farringdon st EC4	149	W4
Farrington pl Chis	114	E17
Farrins rents SE16	75	V3
Farrow la SE14	75	R18
Farthing all SE1	151	R18
Farthing flds E1	151	Y12
Farthings the Kings T	103	P20
Farthings clo E4	21	N10
Farwell rd Sid	115	S8
Farwig la Brom	112	D20
Fashion st E1	151	O2
Fashoda rd Brom	127	N9
Fassett rd E8	49	X17
Fassett rd Kings T	116	K8
Fassett sq E8	49	X17
Fauconberg rd W4	73	V16
Faulkner clo Dag	55	W2
Faulkner st SE14	92	E1
Fauna clo Rom	37	U19
Faunce st SE17	157	W12
Favart rd SW6	87	Y2
Faversham ave E4	21	O5
Faversham ave Enf	8	C19
Faversham rd SE6	92	M20
Faversham rd Beck	125	N3
Faversham rd Mord	120	B14
Fawcett clo SW11	88	G6
Fawcett rd NW10	62	C2
Fawcett rd Croy	132	K6
Fawcett st SW10	154	A14
Fawe Park rd SW15	87	V11
Fawe st E14	64	E14
Fawley rd NW6	46	A16
Fawn rd E13	65	Y6
Fawnbrake ave SE24	90	K13
Fawood ave NW10	43	X20
Faygate cres Bexh	98	E13
Faygate rd SW2	108	D5
Fayland ave SW16	107	V12
Fearnley cres Hmptn	100	C14
Fearon st SE10	77	T13
Featherbed la Croy	134	L17
Feathers pl SE10	76	K16
Featherstone ave SE23	110	B5
Featherstone rd NW7	13	W19
Featherstone rd Sthl	70	A8
Featherstone st EC1	142	E16
Featherstone ter Sthl	70	A9
Featley rd SW9	90	H6
Federal rd Grnf	60	E4
Federation rd SE2	80	E12
Felbridge ave Stan	23	Z6
Felbridge clo SW16	108	F9
Felbridge clo Sutt	130	C19
Felbrigge rd Ilf	54	K5
Felday rd SE13	93	R16
Felden clo Pnr	22	C2
Felden st SW6	87	U2
Feldman clo N16	49	X2
Felgate ms W6	74	K11
Felhampton rd SE9	113	Z5
Felhurst cres Dag	56	J11
Felix ave N8	30	A17
Felix rd W13	71	X1
Felix st E2	143	X9
Felixstowe rd N9	18	L11
Felixstowe rd N17	31	U9
Felixstowe rd NW10	136	A11
Felixstowe rd SE2	80	C8
Fell rd Croy	133	N5
Fellbrigg rd SE1	143	Y17
Fellbrook Rich	102	C8
Fellowes rd Cars	130	K4
Fellows ct E2	143	N10
Fellows rd NW3	46	G20
Felltram way SE7	77	T12
Felmersham clo SW4	89	Z11
Felmingham rd SE20	124	C5
Fels ave Dag	56	H9
Fels Farm ave Dag	56	L10
Felsberg rd SW2	90	B17
Felsham rd SW15	87	P9
Felspar clo SE18	79	Y14
Felstead ave Ilf	35	W5
Felstead rd E11	34	G20
Felstead rd Rom	38	L1
Felstead st E9	50	M18
Felsted rd E16	66	A18
Feltham rd Mitch	121	O3
Felton clo Orp	127	Z15
Felton lea Sid	114	K11
Felton rd W13	72	D5
Felton rd Bark	67	W5
Felton st N1	142	G5
Fen ct EC3	150	K8
Fen gro Sid	96	K15
Fen st E16	65	P18
Fencepiece rd Ilf	36	D5
Fenchurch ave EC3	150	K7
Fenchurch bldgs EC3	150	L7
Fenchurch pl EC3	150	L7
Fenchurch st EC3	150	H8
Fendall st SE1	158	M2
Fendyke rd Belv	80	H10
Fenelon pl W14	153	R6
Fenham rd SE15	159	U19
Fenman ct N17	32	A3
Fenman gdns Ilf	55	P3
Fenn clo Brom	112	F16
Fenn st E9	50	E15
Fennel st SE18	78	L17
Fennells mead Epsom	128	C20
Fenner clo SE16	159	Y4
Fenner sq SW11	88	G8
Fenning st SE1	150	H16
Fenstanton ave N12	15	U17
Fentiman rd SW8	156	M15
Fenton clo SW9	90	D4
Fenton clo Chis	113	U12
Fenton rd N17	17	Z20
Fentons ave E13	65	V7
Fenwick clo SE18	78	J17
Fenwick gro SE15	91	X8
Fenwick rd SE15	91	X8
Ferdinand pl NW1	47	R20
Ferdinand st NW1	47	R19
Fergus rd N5	48	J16
Ferguson ave Surb	117	N11
Ferguson clo Brom	125	W6
Ferguson dr W3	61	Z16
Ferme Park rd N4	30	D20
Ferme Park rd N8	30	B16
Fermor rd SE23	110	K1
Fermoy rd W9	137	P18
Fermoy rd Grnf	58	K13
Fern ave Mitch	121	Y8
Fern la Houns	70	D15
Fern st E3	64	C12
Fernbank Buck H	21	V5
Fernbank ave Wem	41	V13
Fernbrook dr Har	40	J1

Fernbrook rd SE13	93	Z15
Ferncliff rd E8	49	X14
Ferncroft ave N12	15	Y18
Ferncroft ave NW3	45	Z11
Ferndale Brom	126	M4
Ferndale ave E17	33	W14
Ferndale ave Houns	82	C7
Ferndale rd E11	52	B6
Ferndale rd N15	31	V16
Ferndale rd SE25	124	A12
Ferndale rd SW4	90	A9
Ferndale rd SW9	90	E8
Ferndale rd Rom	38	L7
Ferndale st E6	66	L19
Ferndale ter Har	23	V13
Fernden way Rom	38	G18
Ferndown cr Pnr	22	A1
Ferndown clo Sutt	130	F15
Ferndown rd SE9	95	N18
Ferney rd Barn	16	C3
Fernhall dr Ilf	35	P16
Fernham rd Th Hth	122	L8
Fernhead rd W9	137	P10
Fernhill ct E17	33	X8
Fernhill gdns Kings T	102	H14
Fernhill st E16	78	H4
Fernholme rd SE15	92	F12
Fernhurst gdns Edg	12	B18
Fernhurst rd SW6	153	N20
Fernhurst rd Croy	123	Z19
Fernlea rd SW12	107	S2
Fernlea rd Mitch	121	O3
Fernleigh clo Croy	132	F9
Fernleigh ct Har	22	L6
Fernleigh ct Wem	42	K5
Fernleigh rd N21	17	U7
Ferns rd E15	52	B18
Fernsbury st WC1	141	S13
Fernshaw rd SW10	154	B15
Fernside NW11	45	Y5
Fernside Buck H	21	U4
Fernside ave NW7	12	L12
Fernside rd SW12	89	N20
Fernthorpe rd SW16	107	V15
Ferntower rd N5	49	N14
Fernwood Croy	134	J20
Fernwood ave SW16	107	Y10
Fernwood ave Wem	42	D16
Fernwood clo Brom	126	K3
Fernwood cres N20	15	Z9
Ferny hill Barn	5	Y3
Ferranti clo E18	78	B9
Ferraro clo Houns	70	G16
Ferrers ave Wall	131	X8
Ferrers rd SW16	107	Y14
Ferrestone rd N8	30	C13
Ferrier st SW18	88	B11
Ferring clo Har	41	N4
Ferrings SE21	109	T6
Ferris ave Croy	134	L6
Ferris rd SE22	91	X11
Ferry app SE18	78	J8
Ferry la N17	31	Y11
Ferry la SW13	74	E17
Ferry la Brent	72	J18
Ferry la Rich	73	N16
Ferry rd SW13	74	G20
Ferry rd Tedd	102	A12
Ferry rd T Ditt	116	A16
Ferry rd Twick	84	B20
Ferry st E14	76	G13
Ferrymead ave Grnf	58	G8
Ferrymead dr Grnf	58	J7
Ferrymead gdns Grnf	58	M7
Ferrymoor Rich	102	B7
Festing rd SW15	87	O7
Festival clo Bex	115	V2
Fetter la EC4	149	U6
Ffinch st SE8	76	A18
Field clo E4	20	C18
Field clo Brom	126	L4
Field clo Buck H	21	Z11
Field ct WC1	149	R1
Field end Nthlt	40	A19
Field end Twick	101	W9
Field End rd Ruis	40	D14
Field la Brent	72	D19
Field la Tedd	101	Y13
Field mead NW7	26	D2
Field mead NW9	26	D2
Field pl N Mal	118	C14
Field rd E7	52	E12
Field rd N17	31	R10
Field rd W6	152	K12
Field st WC1	141	N11
Field way NW10	61	W1
Field way Croy	135	R16
Field way Grnf	58	J4
Fieldend rd SW16	107	V20
Fielders clo Har	41	O5
Fieldfare rd SE28	68	G19
Fieldgate la Mitch	120	K5
Fieldgate st E1	151	T3
Fieldhouse rd SW12	107	W2
Fielding ave Twick	101	N6
Fielding rd W4	73	Z7
Fielding rd W14	144	J20
Fielding st SE17	158	C12
Fieldings the SE23	110	C1
Fields Park cres Rom	37	V15
Fieldsend rd Sutt	129	T11
Fieldside rd Brom	111	X12
Fieldview SW18	106	E1
Fieldway cres N5	48	G16
Fiennes clo Dag	55	T4
Fiesta dr Dag	69	X13
Fife rd E16	65	S15
Fife rd N22	30	K3
Fife rd SW14	85	U13
Fife rd Kings T	116	K2
Fife ter N1	141	O8
Fifield path SE23	110	F6
Fifth ave E12	53	T12
Fifth ave W10	136	K15
Fifth Cross rd Twick	101	P5
Fifth way Wem	43	T11
Figges rd Mitch	107	O18
Filey ave N16	49	W5
Filey clo Sutt	130	E17
Fillebrook ave Enf	8	F8
Fillebrook rd E11	51	Z3
Filmer rd SW6	153	O19
Filston rd Erith	81	W14
Finborough rd SW10	153	Y12
Finborough rd SW17	106	M16
Finch ave SE27	109	N11
Finch clo NW10	43	X16
Finch clo Barn	4	K17
Finch la EC3	150	H6
Finchale rd SE2	80	A8
Finchingfield ave Wdf Grn	34	M1
Finchley ct N3	15	N20
Finchley la NW4	27	N12
Finchley pk N12	15	S12
Finchley pl NW8	138	F8
Finchley rd NW2	45	X10
Finchley rd NW3	138	F3
Finchley rd NW8	138	F3
Finchley rd NW11	27	W18
Finchley way N3	14	K20
Finden rd E7	52	K16
Findhorn st E14	64	H16
Findon clo SW18	87	Y16
Findon clo Har	40	K10
Findon rd N9	18	M5
Findon rd W12	74	H4
Fingal st SE10	77	R13
Finland quay SE16	75	W8
Finland rd SE4	92	H8
Finland st SE16	75	W8
Finlay st SW6	87	R2
Finnis st E2	143	X15
Finnymore rd Dag	56	A20
Finsbury ave EC2	150	H1
Finsbury circ EC2	150	G2
Finsbury cotts N22	30	B2
Finsbury est EC1	141	V15
Finsbury mkt EC2	142	J1
Finsbury Park ave N4	30	L19
Finsbury Park rd N4	48	H6
Finsbury Pavement EC2	150	F1
Finsbury rd N22	30	C2
Finsbury sq EC2	142	G19
Finsbury st EC2	142	F20
Finsbury way Bex	98	C16
Finsen rd SE5	90	M9
Finstock rd W10	144	F4
Finucane gdns Rain	57	X16
Finucane ri (Bushey) Wat	10	A7
Fir gro N Mal	118	E14
Fir rd Felt	100	A13
Fir rd Sutt	119	U20
Fir Tree clo SW16	107	W12
Fir Tree clo W5	60	L16
Fir Tree clo Rom	39	O9
Fir Tree gdns Croy	135	O8
Fir Tree gro Cars	131	N17
Fir Tree rd Houns	82	C11
Fir Tree wk Enf	8	C11
Fir Trees clo SE16	75	W3
Firbank clo E16	66	B13
Firbank clo Enf	7	Y13
Firbank rd SE15	92	B4
Fircroft gdns Har	41	T9
Fircroft rd SW17	106	M5
Fire Bell all Surb	116	L15
Fire Station all Barn	4	G10
Firecrest dr NW3	46	B9
Firhill rd SE6	111	O8
Firs the N20	15	U5
Firs the W5	60	G15
Firs ave N10	29	R11
Firs ave N11	16	A19
Firs ave SW14	85	W11
Firs clo N10	29	R11
Firs clo SE23	92	H20
Firs clo Mitch	121	S2
Firs la N13	17	Z12
Firs la N21	17	Z6
Firs Park ave N21	18	C5
Firs Park gdns N21	18	A5
Firs wk Wdf Grn	21	S15
Firsby ave Croy	134	G1
Firsby rd N16	49	W3
Firscroft N13	17	Z10
Firside gro Sid	114	K2
First ave E12	53	S13
First ave E13	65	T8
First ave E17	33	P14
First ave N18	19	P13
First ave NW4	27	N12
First ave SW14	86	B6
First ave W3	74	D2
First ave W10	137	O16
First ave Bexh	80	H18
First ave Dag	69	V5
First ave Enf	8	F16
First ave Epsom	128	A19
First ave Rom	37	V14
First ave Wem	42	H6
First Cross rd Twick	101	T3
First st SW3	154	M4
First way Wem	43	S13
Firstway SW20	118	L4
Firswood ave Epsom	128	C12
Firth gdns SW6	87	S3
Firtree ave Mitch	121	N3
Firtree clo (Stoneleigh) Epsom	128	E10
Fish Street hill EC3	150	H9
Fisher clo Croy	123	V20
Fisher clo Grnf	58	G8
Fisher rd Har	23	X6
Fisher st E16	65	S13
Fisher st WC1	149	N2
Fisherman clo Rich	102	D10
Fishermans dr SE16	75	U5
Fishermans pl W4	74	D16
Fishers la W4	73	Z11
Fishers way Belv	81	Y3
Fisherton st NW8	138	F17
Fisherton Street est NW8	138	H17
Fishponds rd SW17	106	K10
Fisons rd E16	77	S3
Fitzalan rd N3	27	V10
Fitzalan st SE11	157	T6
Fitzgeorge ave W14	152	L7
Fitzgeorge ave N Mal	103	Z20
Fitzgerald ave SW14	86	B8
Fitzgerald rd E11	34	F17
Fitzgerald rd SW14	85	Y7
Fitzhardinge st W1	147	T5
Fitzhugh gro SW18	88	G16
Fitzjames ave W14	152	M6
Fitzjames ave Croy	133	X4
Fitzjohn ave Barn	4	G17
Fitzjohns ave NW3	46	F18
Fitzmaurice pl W1	147	Y11
Fitzneal st W12	62	D17
Fitzroy clo N6	46	M5
Fitzroy gdns SE19	109	S18
Fitzroy ms W1	140	A18
Fitzroy pk N6	46	M5
Fitzroy rd NW1	139	S4
Fitzroy sq W1	140	A18
Fitzroy st W1	140	A17
Fitzroy yd NW1	139	T3
Fitzstephen rd Dag	55	R13
Fitzwarren gdns N19	47	V3
Fitzwilliam ave Rich	84	M6
Fitzwilliam rd SW4	89	V8
Five acre NW9	26	D6
Five Elms rd Dag	56	B10
Five Ways rd SW9	90	H5
Fiveacre clo Th Hth	122	G15
Fladbury rd N15	31	O18
Fladgate rd E11	34	A18
Flag clo Croy	124	F19
Flambard rd Har	23	Y19
Flamborough st E14	63	V17
Flamingo wk Horn	57	X19
Flamstead rd SE7	78	D14
Flamstead rd Dag	55	U19
Flamsted ave Wem	43	R18
Flanchford rd W12	74	E8
Flanders cres SW17	106	M17
Flanders rd E6	66	G7
Flanders rd W4	74	C10
Flanders way E9	50	E17
Flank st E1	151	S9
Flask wk NW3	46	E12
Flaxen rd E4	20	E11
Flaxley rd Mord	120	A16
Flaxman rd SE5	90	K6
Flaxman ter WC1	140	H14
Flaxton rd SE18	79	U20
Flecker clo Stan	10	J16
Fleece rd Surb	116	D18
Fleeming rd E17	32	M6
Fleet la EC4	149	X5
Fleet rd NW3	46	K14
Fleet st EC4	149	T6
Fleet Street hill E1	143	S18
Fleetwood clo E16	66	B14
Fleetwood gro W3	62	A20
Fleetwood rd NW10	44	F14
Fleetwood rd Kings T	117	T6
Fleetwood sq Kings T	117	U6
Fleming ct W2	146	F1
Fleming ct Croy	132	F12
Fleming mead Mitch	106	K18
Fleming rd SE17	157	Y13
Fleming rd Sthl	58	K17
Fleming way SE28	68	J19
Fleming way Islw	83	V9
Flempton rd E10	50	K3
Fletcher la E10	51	U2
Fletcher rd W4	73	W7
Fletcher st E1	151	U8
Fletchers clo Brom	126	J9
Fletching rd E5	50	C10
Fletching rd SE7	78	A15
Fleur de Lis st E1	142	M19
Fleur gates SW19	87	R20
Flexmere gdns N17	31	R3
Flexmere rd N17	31	R4
Flight app NW9	26	D7
Flimwell clo Brom	111	Z14
Flint st SE17	158	G7
Flintmill cres SE3	95	R6

Name	Page	Ref
Flinton st SE17	158	L8
Flitcroft st WC2	148	H5
Flockton st SE16	151	S19
Flodden rd SE5	157	Z20
Flood st SW3	154	M11
Flood wk SW3	154	L12
Flora clo E14	64	D17
Flora gdns Rom	37	T19
Flora st Belv	81	P14
Floral st WC2	148	L7
Florence ave Enf	7	Y11
Florence ave Mord	120	E13
Florence dr Enf	7	Y10
Florence gdns W4	73	V17
Florence rd E6	65	Z3
Florence rd E13	65	S7
Florence rd N4	48	E1
Florence rd SE2	80	H10
Florence rd SE14	92	A2
Florence rd SW19	105	Z16
Florence rd W4	73	X7
Florence rd W5	60	K20
Florence rd Beck	124	H4
Florence rd Brom	126	F1
Florence rd Kings T	103	N19
Florence rd S Croy	133	N20
Florence rd Sthl	70	A9
Florence st E16	65	P11
Florence st N1	141	X1
Florence st NW4	26	M11
Florence ter SE14	93	N2
Florian ave Sutt	130	G8
Florian rd SW15	87	U10
Florida clo (Bushey) Wat	10	C6
Florida rd Th Hth	108	K20
Florida st E2	143	T14
Floriston clo Stan	24	C4
Floriston gdns Stan	24	C4
Floss st SW15	87	N6
Flower & Dean wk E1	151	P2
Flower la NW7	13	R16
Flower wk the SW7	146	D18
Flowersmead SW17	107	O5
Floyd rd SE7	77	Y13
Fludyer st SE13	93	Z10
Folair way SE16	159	W10
Foley st W1	148	B1
Folgate st E1	142	M19
Foliot st W12	62	D18
Folkestone rd E6	66	L8
Folkestone rd E17	33	R13
Folkestone rd N18	18	K14
Folkington corner N12	14	J17
Follett st E14	64	G18
Folly la E17	19	X19
Folly wall E14	76	H6
Font hills N2	28	D7
Fontaine rd SW16	108	C17
Fontarabia rd SW11	89	P10
Fontayne ave Rom	39	P8
Fontenoy rd SW12	107	T5
Fonteyne gdns Wdf Grn	35	N6
Fonthill clo SE20	123	V3
Fonthill ms N4	48	E5
Fonthill rd N4	48	E5
Fontley way SW15	86	F20
Fontwell clo Har	10	F20
Fontwell clo Nthlt	40	J16
Fontwell dr Brom	127	W12
Football la Har	41	U3
Foots Cray High st Sid	115	V14
Foots Cray la Sid	115	U1
Footscray rd SE9	95	Y17
Footway the SE9	96	D20
Forbes clo Horn	57	Z4
Forbes st E1	151	T7
Forburg rd N16	49	X4
Ford clo Har	23	P20
Ford clo Th Hth	122	K13
Ford end Wdf Grn	21	V19
Ford rd E3	63	X4
Ford rd Dag	56	C20
Ford sq E1	151	Y3
Ford st E3	63	X4
Ford st E16	65	P17
Forde ave Brom	126	K6
Fordel rd SE6	93	W20
Fordham clo Barn	5	V12
Fordham rd Barn	5	V12
Fordham st E1	151	U4
Fordhook ave W5	73	O1
Fordingley rd W9	137	R14
Fordington rd N6	28	M14
Fordmill rd SE6	111	P3
Fords gro N21	17	X5
Fords Park rd E16	65	T16
Fordwych rd NW2	45	S13
Fordyce rd SE13	93	V15
Fordyke rd Dag	56	A5
Fore st EC2	150	D2
Fore st N9	18	K12
Fore st N18	18	J19
Fore Street ave EC2	150	E2
Foreland ct NW4	27	S5
Foreland st SE18	79	S10
Foreshore SE8	75	Y12
Forest the E11	34	A13
Forest app E4	21	N2
Forest app Wdf Grn	21	O1
Forest ave E4	21	O2
Forest clo E11	34	D16
Forest clo Chis	127	W2
Forest clo Wdf Grn	21	V12
Forest ct E4	21	P6
Forest ct E11	34	A12
Forest cft SE23	110	B4
Forest dr E12	53	P11
Forest dr Wdf Grn	33	Z2
Forest Drive E11	33	X20
Forest Drive east E11	51	V1
Forest Edge Buck H	21	Z12
Forest gdns N17	31	U6
Forest gate NW9	26	A14
Forest glade E4	20	M14
Forest glade E11	34	A18
Forest gro E8	49	V19
Forest Hill rd SE22	92	A14
Forest Hill rd SE23	92	C17
Forest la E7	52	F15
Forest la E15	52	A16
Forest Mount rd Wdf Grn	33	X2
Forest ridge Beck	125	O5
Forest ri E17	33	X15
Forest rd E7	52	F11
Forest rd E8	49	U19
Forest rd E11	51	W1
Forest rd E17	32	D12
Forest rd N9	19	N4
Forest rd Erith	99	W3
Forest rd Ilf	36	E6
Forest rd Rich	73	R19
Forest rd Rom	38	G10
Forest rd Sutt	119	X19
Forest rd Wdf Grn	21	S11
Forest side E4	21	O2
Forest side E7	52	G12
Forest side Buck H	21	X4
Forest side Wor Pk	118	D20
Forest st E7	52	F14
Forest vw E4	20	J1
Forest vw E11	50	C1
Forest View ave E10	33	X15
Forest View rd E12	53	P12
Forest View rd E17	33	V4
Forest way Sid	96	F20
Forest way Wdf Grn	21	V12
Forestdale N14	16	K12
Forester rd SE15	92	A14
Foresters clo Wall	131	X17
Foresters cres Bexh	98	G9
Foresters dr E17	33	X13
Foresters dr Wall	131	X15
Forestholme clo SE23	110	C3
Forres gdns NW11	27	X19
Forrest gdns SW16	122	D7
Forset st W1	147	N5
Forstal clo Brom	126	E6
Forster rd E17	32	H18
Forster rd N17	31	U9
Forster rd SW2	89	Z19
Forster rd Beck	124	H7
Forsters clo Rom	38	B18
Forston st N1	142	D8
Forsyte cres SE19	123	S1
Forsyth gdns SE17	157	Y14
Forsyth pl Enf	8	D17
Fort rd SE1	159	R6
Fort rd Nthlt	58	H2
Fort st E1	150	M1
Fort st E16	77	W3
Forterie gdns Ilf	54	M10
Fortescue ave E8	143	X1
Fortescue ave Twick	101	N6
Fortescue rd SW19	106	G19
Fortescue rd Edg	25	X3
Fortess gro NW5	47	U14
Fortess rd NW5	47	U14
Forthbridge rd SW11	89	P10
Fortis clo E16	65	Y17
Fortis grn N2	28	K11
Fortis Green ave N2	29	N11
Fortis Green rd N10	29	P10
Fortismere ave N10	29	P11
Fortnam rd N19	47	Z8
Fortnums acre Stan	10	J18
Fortune Gate rd NW10	62	B2
Fortune Green rd NW6	45	X12
Fortune la Borwd	11	V1
Fortune st EC1	142	C18
Fortune way NW10	62	F9
Fortunes mead Nthlt	40	C19
Forty Acre la E16	65	S15
Forty ave Wem	42	M9
Forty clo Wem	43	N8
Forty hill Enf	8	F3
Forty la Wem	43	S7
Forum way Edg	12	D20
Forumside Edg	12	C19
Forval clo Mitch	120	M12
Forward dr Har	23	X12
Foscote ms W9	137	V19
Foscote rd NW4	26	J17
Foskett rd SW6	87	V5
Foss ave Croy	132	F12
Foss rd SW17	106	F10
Fossdene rd SE7	77	W14
Fossdyke clo Hayes	58	B14
Fosse way W13	59	Y14
Fossil rd SE13	93	P8
Fossington rd Belv	80	J10
Fossway Dag	55	U5
Foster la EC2	150	B5
Foster rd E13	65	T11
Foster rd W3	62	A19
Foster rd W4	73	Y13
Foster st NW4	26	M14
Foster wk NW4	26	M14
Fosters clo E18	34	J5
Fosters clo Chis	113	U13
Fothergill clo E13	65	T5
Fotheringham rd Enf	8	F12
Foubert's pl W1	148	B7
Foulden rd N16	49	U11
Foulis ter SW7	154	G8
Foulser rd SW17	107	N7
Foulsham rd Th Hth	123	N7
Foundry clo SE16	75	V2
Fount st SW8	156	H19
Fountain ct EC4	149	S7
Fountain dr SE19	109	V11
Fountain pl SW9	90	H2
Fountain rd SW17	106	F12
Fountain rd Th Hth	122	L5
Fountain sq SW1	155	Y6
Fountains ave Felt	100	F6
Fountains clo Felt	100	F5
Fountains cres N14	17	N1
Fountayne rd N15	31	Y13
Fountayne rd N16	49	X6
Four Seasons cres Sutt	129	V2
Four Tubs the (Bushey) Wat	10	C1
Fouracres Enf	9	V6
Fourland wk Edg	12	K19
Fournier st E1	151	O1
Fourth ave E12	53	T12
Fourth ave W10	136	L15
Fourth ave Rom	56	M5
Fourth Cross rd Twick	101	P4
Fourth way Wem	43	U11
Fowey ave Ilf	35	P14
Fowey clo E1	151	V12
Fowler clo SW11	88	F8
Fowler rd E7	52	E12
Fowler rd N1	141	Y2
Fowler rd Mitch	121	P2
Fowlers wk W5	60	G11
Fownes st SW11	88	K7
Fox and Knot st EC1	141	Y20
Fox clo E1	63	R11
Fox clo E16	65	S15
Fox hill SE19	109	T18
Fox Hill gdns SE19	109	V19
Fox Hollow dr Bexh	97	W6
Fox House rd Belv	81	W12
Fox la N13	17	O7
Fox la W5	60	K11
Fox rd E16	65	P15
Foxberry rd SE4	92	K9
Foxborough gdns SE4	93	N14
Foxbourne rd SW17	107	P5
Foxbury ave Chis	114	F16
Foxbury clo Brom	112	H16
Foxbury rd Brom	112	G16
Foxcombe Croy	135	S13
Foxcroft rd SE18	95	Z1
Foxearth rd S Croy	134	C20
Foxearth Spur S Croy	134	D19
Foxes dale SE3	94	E9
Foxes dale Brom	125	X6
Foxglove st W12	62	D19
Foxglove way Wall	121	R19
Foxgrove N14	17	N11
Foxgrove ave Beck	111	S19
Foxgrove rd Beck	111	R19
Foxham rd N19	47	W10
Foxhole rd SE9	95	R12
Foxholt gdns NW10	61	V1
Foxhome clo Chis	113	Y16
Foxlands cres Dag	56	K14
Foxlands la Dag	56	L15
Foxlands rd Dag	56	J16
Foxlees Wem	41	Z11
Foxley clo E8	49	W15
Foxley rd SW9	157	V17
Foxley rd Th Hth	122	H9
Foxmead clo Enf	7	R11
Foxmore st SW11	88	L3
Fox's path Mitch	120	H5
Foxwell st SE4	92	J7
Foxwood rd SE3	94	B10
Foyle rd N17	31	Y4
Foyle rd SE3	77	P17
Framfield rd N12	14	K12
Framfield ct Enf	8	E19
Framfield rd N5	48	H14
Framfield rd W7	59	U17
Framfield rd Mitch	107	P20
Framlingham cres SE9	113	S9
Frampton clo Sutt	129	Y17
Frampton Park rd E9	50	C18
Frampton rd Houns	82	B12
Frampton st NW8	138	H17
Francemary rd SE4	93	O12
Frances rd E4	20	C18
Frances st SE18	78	G11
Franche Court rd SW17	106	D7
Francis ave Bexh	98	E5
Francis ave Ilf	54	E6
Francis Barber clo SW16	108	D11

Francis Chichester way SW11	89	P4
Francis gro SW19	105	U16
Francis rd E10	51	U5
Francis rd Croy	122	J16
Francis rd Grnf	60	C5
Francis rd Houns	82	A6
Francis rd Ilf	54	E6
Francis rd Wall	131	W14
Francis st E15	51	Z16
Francis st SW1	156	C5
Francis st Ilf	54	E6
Francis ter N19	47	V9
Franciscan rd SW17	106	M12
Francklyn gdns Edg	12	D9
Francombe gdns Rom	39	X17
Franconia rd SW4	89	W14
Frank Dixon clo SE21	91	S20
Frank Dixon way SE21	109	S1
Frank st E13	65	U12
Frankfurt rd SE24	91	N13
Frankham st SE8	76	B19
Frankland clo SE16	159	Z4
Frankland clo Wdf Grn	21	Y17
Frankland rd E4	20	B15
Frankland rd SW7	154	F2
Franklin clo N20	15	R2
Franklin clo SE27	108	J8
Franklin clo Kings T	117	O5
Franklin cres Mitch	121	V8
Franklin pas SE9	95	S8
Franklin rd SE20	110	D19
Franklin rd Bexh	98	A2
Franklin sq W14	153	R12
Franklin st E3	64	F8
Franklin st N15	31	R19
Franklin way Croy	122	B19
Franklins ms Har	40	M6
Franklin's row SW3	155	R9
Franklyn rd NW10	44	D19
Franks ave N Mal	117	V10
Franlaw cres N13	18	A14
Franmil rd Horn	57	V3
Fransfield gro SE26	110	A8
Frant clo SE20	110	D19
Frant rd Th Hth	122	H11
Franthorne way SE6	111	S6
Fraser clo E6	66	D16
Fraser rd E17	33	T17
Fraser rd N9	18	M10
Fraser rd Erith	81	Y13
Fraser rd Grnf	60	C4
Fraser st W4	74	C4
Frating cres Wdf Grn	21	U19
Frazer clo Rom	57	T1
Frazier st SE1	149	S18
Frean st SE1	159	S1
Freda Corbett clo SE15	159	S17
Frederic st E17	32	J16
Frederica rd E4	20	K2
Frederick clo W2	147	N7
Frederick clo Sutt	129	V10
Frederick cres SW9	157	W20
Frederick cres Enf	9	R8
Frederick gdns Sutt	129	V10
Frederick pl SE18	79	N13
Frederick rd SE17	157	Y12
Frederick rd Sutt	129	W10
Frederick st WC1	141	O13
Frederick ter E8	143	N2
Frederick's pl EC2	150	E6
Fredericks pl N12	15	R13
Frederick's row EC1	141	X11
Freeborne gdns Rain	57	W17
Freedom clo E17	32	G12
Freedom st SW11	88	M4
Freegrove rd N7	48	A15
Freeland pk NW4	27	S6
Freeland rd W5	61	N20
Freeland way Erith	99	V1
Freelands ave S Croy	134	F19
Freelands gro Brom	112	J20
Freelands rd Brom	126	J2
Freeling st N1	141	N2
Freeman clo Nthlt	40	B19
Freeman rd Mord	120	F12
Freemantle ave Enf	9	U16
Freemasons rd E16	65	V14
Freemasons rd Croy	123	R19
Freethorpe clo SE19	109	R20
Freke rd SW11	89	R9
Fremantle rd Belv	81	T12
Fremantle rd Ilf	36	B8
Fremantle st SE17	158	K8
Fremont st E9	143	Z4
French pl E1	142	L15
Frendsbury rd SE4	92	G10
Frensham clo Sthl	58	E10
Frensham dr SW15	104	E6
Frensham dr Croy	135	U17
Frensham rd SE9	114	E5
Frensham st SE15	159	U14
Frere st SW11	88	K4
Fresh Wharf rd Bark	67	N5
Freshfield clo SE13	93	X9
Freshfield dr N14	16	F1
Freshfields Croy	124	L19
Freshford st SW18	106	D6
Freshwater rd SW17	107	P15
Freshwater rd Dag	55	W3
Freshwell ave Rom	37	T14
Freshwood clo Beck	125	R2
Freshwood way Wall	131	U19
Freston gdns Barn	6	B16
Freston pk N3	27	U6
Freston rd W10	144	H11
Freston rd W11	144	H11
Freta rd Bexh	98	B12
Frewin rd SW18	106	G1
Friar ms SE27	108	H8
Friar st EC4	149	Y7
Friars ave N20	15	X12
Friars ave SW15	104	D6
Friars clo N2	28	G12
Friars Gate clo Wdf Grn	21	T13
Friars la Rich	84	F13
Friars mead E14	76	G9
Friars ms SE9	95	W14
Friars Place la W3	61	Z19
Friars rd E6	66	C4
Friars Stile rd Rich	84	K16
Friars wk N14	16	D1
Friars wk SE2	80	K14
Friars way W3	61	Y18
Friars wd Croy	134	J20
Friary clo N12	15	X15
Friary est SE15	159	U15
Friary la Wdf Grn	21	S14
Friary rd N12	15	U14
Friary rd SE15	159	U15
Friary rd W3	61	X17
Friary way N12	15	W14
Friday Hill E4	20	M7
Friday Hill east E4	20	L10
Friday Hill west E4	20	L7
Friday rd Erith	81	Z13
Friday rd Mitch	106	L18
Friday st EC4	150	B7
Friend st EC1	141	W12
Friendly st SE8	93	O3
Friends rd Croy	133	O6
Friern Barnet la N11	15	Y16
Friern Barnet la N20	15	X8
Friern Barnet rd N11	15	Y17
Friern Mount dr N20	15	R2
Friern pk N12	15	S15
Friern rd SE22	91	W18
Friern Watch ave N12	15	S13
Frigate ms SE8	76	B16
Frimley clo SW19	105	T15
Frimley clo Croy	135	V17
Frimley ct Sid	115	T12
Frimley cres Croy	135	V17
Frimley gdns Mitch	120	J6
Frimley rd Ilf	54	J9
Frimley way E1	63	T12
Frimley way Wall	132	B11
Frinton dr Wdf Grn	33	X2
Frinton ms Ilf	35	X18
Frinton rd E6	66	C9
Frinton rd N15	31	T18
Frinton rd SW17	107	P16
Frinton rd Rom	38	D1
Frinton rd Sid	115	Z3
Friston st SW6	88	A6
Frith ct NW7	27	T3
Frith la NW7	14	F20
Frith rd E11	51	V11
Frith rd Croy	132	L3
Frith st W1	148	F6
Fritham clo N Mal	118	A15
Frithville gdns W12	144	C14
Frizlands la Dag	56	G7
Frobisher pas E14	76	C2
Frobisher rd E6	66	H16
Frobisher rd N8	30	F13
Frogley rd SE22	91	V11
Frogmore SW18	87	Y12
Frogmore clo Sutt	129	R7
Frogmore gdns Sutt	129	R7
Frognal NW3	46	D16
Frognal ave Har	23	W13
Frognal ave Sid	115	N13
Frognal clo NW3	46	C14
Frognal ct NW3	46	D16
Frognal gdns NW3	46	D12
Frognal la NW3	46	A14
Frognal pl Sid	115	O15
Frognal ri NW3	46	C10
Frognal way NW3	46	C13
Froissart rd SE9	95	P12
Frome rd N15	30	J10
Frome st N1	142	A8
Fromondes rd Sutt	129	S12
Frostic wk E1	151	R2
Froude st SW8	89	T5
Fry rd E6	66	B1
Fry rd NW10	62	E2
Fryatt rd N17	31	P2
Fryatt st E14	65	N18
Fryent clo NW9	25	P17
Fryent cres NW9	26	A18
Fryent flds NW9	26	B17
Fryent gro NW9	26	A18
Fryent way NW9	25	R18
Frye's bldgs N1	141	U9
Frying Pan all E1	150	M2
Fryston ave Croy	133	Z3
Fuchsia st SE2	80	D13
Fulbeck dr NW9	26	A4
Fulbeck way Har	22	M7
Fulbourne rd E17	33	T3
Fulbourne st E1	151	W1
Fulbrooks ave Wor Pk	118	D20
Fulford rd SE16	151	Y18
Fulham bdy SW6	153	U18
Fulham High st SW6	87	T5
Fulham Palace rd SW6	152	G16
Fulham Palace rd W6	152	E10
Fulham Park gdns SW6	87	U5
Fulham Park rd SW6	87	U4
Fulham rd SW3	154	G10
Fulham rd SW6	153	T19
Fulham rd SW10	154	C14
Fuller rd Dag	55	S10
Fuller st E2	143	S16
Fuller st NW4	26	L11
Fullers ave Wdf Grn	34	D3
Fullers clo Rom	38	K2
Fullers la Rom	38	K2
Fullers rd E18	34	B3
Fullers wd Croy	135	O10
Fullerton rd SW18	88	C13
Fullerton rd Cars	130	J19
Fullerton rd Croy	123	U18
Fullwell ave Ilf	35	U5
Fullwoods ms N1	142	G11
Fulmar ct Surb	116	M14
Fulmar rd Horn	57	Y19
Fulmead st SW6	88	B2
Fulmer clo Hmptn	100	C13
Fulmer rd E16	66	A15
Fulmer way W13	72	B8
Fulready rd E10	33	W16
Fulstone clo Houns	82	D10
Fulthorp rd SE3	94	E5
Fulton ms W2	146	A9
Fulton rd Wem	43	P10
Fulwell Park ave Twick	100	L5
Fulwell rd Tedd	101	P10
Fulwood ave Wem	60	L4
Fulwood gdns Twick	83	X17
Fulwood pl WC1	149	R2
Fulwood wk SW19	105	S1
Furber st W6	74	J9
Furham Feild Pnr	22	J1
Furley rd SE15	159	U18
Furlong clo Wall	131	R1
Furlong rd N7	48	F17
Furmage st SW18	88	B19
Furneaux ave SE27	108	K13
Furner clo Dart	99	T7
Furness rd NW10	62	H5
Furness rd SW6	88	B4
Furness rd Har	40	L2
Furness rd Mord	120	E19
Furness way Horn	57	V15
Furnival st EC4	149	T3
Furrow la E9	50	D16
Fursby ave N3	14	K18
Further acre NW9	26	D7
Further Green rd SE6	94	B20
Furtherfield clo Croy	122	E15
Furze Farm clo Rom	38	A7
Furze la Th Hth	123	N5
Furze st E3	64	C14
Furzedown dr SW17	107	S13
Furzedown rd SW17	107	S11
Furzefield clo Chis	113	Z15
Furzefield rd SE3	77	V18
Fyfield clo Brom	125	Y8
Fyfield rd E17	33	W11
Fyfield rd SW9	90	G7
Fyfield rd Enf	8	D11
Fyfield rd Wdf Grn	34	M1
Fynes st SW1	156	F5

G

Gable clo Dart	99	W14
Gable clo Pnr	22	G2
Gable ct SE26	110	B11
Gables clo SE5	91	R1
Gables clo SE12	112	E3
Gabriel clo Felt	100	A9
Gabriel clo Rom	38	L1
Gabriel st SE23	92	G18
Gabrielle clo Wem	43	N8
Gaddesden ave Wem	43	O17
Gadsbury clo NW9	26	D7
Gage st WC1	140	M20
Gainford st N1	141	S4
Gainsborough ave E12	53	W14
Gainsborough clo Beck	111	N17
Gainsborough gdns NW3	46	G10
Gainsborough gdns NW11	45	V2
Gainsborough gdns Edg	25	O8
Gainsborough gdns Grnf	41	U15
Gainsborough gdns Islw	83	P13
Gainsborough rd E11	52	B1
Gainsborough rd E15	65	N10
Gainsborough rd N12	15	O16
Gainsborough rd W4	74	D10
Gainsborough rd Dag	55	P11
Gainsborough rd N Mal	117	Y16

Gainsborough rd Rich	85	N6
Gainsborough sq Bexh	97	X9
Gainsford rd E7	32	L12
Gainsford st SE1	151	N16
Gairloch rd SE5	91	S4
Gaisford st NW5	47	U17
Gaitskell rd SE9	114	B2
Galahad rd Brom	112	G9
Galata rd SW13	74	F20
Galbraith st E14	76	G7
Galdana ave Barn	5	R11
Gale clo Hmptn	100	C14
Gale clo Mitch	120	G7
Gale st E3	64	C14
Gale st Dag	55	V16
Galeborough ave Wdf Grn	33	X1
Galen pl WC1	148	K2
Galena rd W6	74	K11
Gales gdns E2	143	Y13
Galesbury rd SW18	88	D17
Galgate clo SW19	105	R1
Gallants Farm rd Barn	15	X3
Gallery gdns Nthlt	58	A6
Gallery rd SE21	109	P1
Galleywall rd SE16	159	X6
Gallia rd N5	48	J15
Gallions clo Bark	68	B9
Gallions rd SE7	77	W12
Gallon clo SE7	77	Z12
Gallop the S Croy	134	B16
Gallop the Sutt	130	E18
Gallosson rd SE18	79	V12
Galloway rd W12	74	G3
Gallus clo N21	7	R19
Gallus sq SE3	94	H8
Galpins rd Th Hth	122	A12
Galsworthy ave Rom	37	P20
Galsworthy clo SE28	80	C2
Galsworthy rd NW2	45	T11
Galsworthy rd Kings T	103	S19
Galsworthy ter N16	49	R9
Galton st W10	136	L15
Galva clo Barn	6	B14
Galvani way Croy	122	D20
Galveston rd SW15	87	W13
Galway st EC1	142	D14
Gambetta st SW8	89	T6
Gambia st SE1	149	X15
Gamble ct SW17	106	J7
Games rd Barn	5	Z11
Gamlen rd SW15	87	O9
Gander Green la Sutt	129	X13
Gandhi clo E17	33	P17
Gantshill cres Ilf	35	W16
Gap rd SW19	105	Y12
Garage rd W3	61	F17
Garbrand wk Epsom	128	E20
Garbutt pl W1	147	U1
Gard st EC1	141	Z12
Garden ave Bexh	98	E7
Garden ave Mitch	107	R19
Garden City Edg	12	C19
Garden clo E4	20	A16
Garden clo SE12	112	J7
Garden clo SW15	86	L20
Garden clo Hmptn	100	F13
Garden clo Nthlt	58	B3
Garden clo Wall	132	A12
Garden ct EC4	149	S8
Garden ct Rich	85	N2
Garden la Brom	112	J16
Garden ms W2	145	U10
Garden rd NW8	138	E11
Garden rd SE20	124	D1
Garden rd Brom	112	H18
Garden rd Rich	85	P8
Garden row SE1	157	X2
Garden st E1	63	T15
Garden ter SW1	156	E8
Garden wk EC2	142	J15
Garden wk Beck	124	L2
Garden way NW10	43	X16
Gardeners rd E3	63	U6
Gardenia rd Enf	18	F1
Gardenia way Wdf Grn	21	U18
Gardens the SE22	91	X10
Gardens the Beck	125	V2
Gardens the Har	22	M18
Gardens the Pnr	22	E18
Gardiner ave NW2	44	M14
Gardner clo E11	34	H17
Gardner gro Felt	100	F5
Gardner rd E13	65	V11
Gardnor rd NW3	46	F12
Garendon gdns Mord	119	Z16
Garendon rd Mord	119	Z17
Gareth gro Brom	112	E9
Garfield rd E4	20	L4
Garfield rd E13	65	P12
Garfield rd SW11	89	R9
Garfield rd SW19	106	D14
Garfield rd Enf	9	R15
Garford st E14	64	A20
Garibaldi st SE18	79	V12
Garland rd SE18	79	T20
Garland rd Stan	24	J4
Garlands ct Croy	133	P8
Garlick hill EC4	150	C8
Garlies rd SE23	110	H6
Garlinge rd NW2	45	V18
Garman rd N17	32	B2
Garnault ms EC1	141	U14
Garnault pl EC1	141	U14
Garner rd E17	33	T3
Garner st E2	143	U9
Garnet rd NW10	44	B18
Garnet rd Th Hth	123	N9
Garnet st E1	151	Z10
Garnet wk E6	66	E14
Garnet way E17	32	H4
Garnett clo SE9	95	V8
Garnett rd NW3	46	L14
Garnham st N16	49	U7
Garnies clo SE15	159	O17
Garrad's rd SW16	107	X7
Garrard clo Bexh	98	F7
Garratt clo Croy	132	A8
Garratt la SW17	106	D8
Garratt la SW18	88	B17
Garratt rd Edg	12	D20
Garratt ter SW17	106	J11
Garratts rd (Bushey) Wat	10	B2
Garrett clo W3	61	Y15
Garrett st EC1	142	B17
Garrick ave NW11	27	U19
Garrick clo SW18	88	E12
Garrick clo W5	60	L10
Garrick clo Islw	83	Y9
Garrick clo Rich	84	G12
Garrick cres Croy	133	R4
Garrick dr NW4	27	N8
Garrick dr SE28	79	S9
Garrick pk NW4	27	O8
Garrick rd NW9	26	E18
Garrick rd Grnf	58	L11
Garrick rd Rich	85	R6
Garrick st WC2	148	J8
Garrick way NW4	27	O11
Garrison clo SE18	78	K20
Garry clo Rom	39	R2
Garry way Rom	39	P1
Garside clo Hmptn	100	K16
Garth the Hmptn	100	L14
Garth the Har	25	N18
Garth clo W4	73	X15
Garth clo Kings T	102	M13
Garth clo Mord	119	O17
Garth ct W4	73	X15
Garth rd NW2	45	U8
Garth rd W4	73	X15
Garth rd Kings T	102	L13
Garth rd Mord	119	N16
Garth Road Industrial est Mord	119	O18
Garthorne rd SE23	92	G18
Garthside Rich	102	L11
Garthway N12	15	V19
Gartmoor gdns SW19	105	V2
Gartmore rd Ilf	54	M5
Garton pl SW18	88	C16
Gartons clo Enf	9	R15
Gartons way SW11	88	E8
Garway rd W2	145	X6
Gascoigne gdns Wdf Grn	34	A2
Gascoigne pl E2	143	O13
Gascoigne rd Bark	67	P3
Gascoigne rd Croy	135	W20
Gascony ave NW6	137	T1
Gascoyne dr Dart	99	U6
Gascoyne rd E9	50	G20
Gaselee st E14	76	H1
Gasholder pl SE11	157	R11
Gaskarth rd SW12	89	T17
Gaskarth rd Edg	25	V6
Gaskell rd N6	28	M17
Gaskell st SW4	89	Z4
Gaskin st N1	141	X4
Gaspar ms SW5	153	Z5
Gassiot rd SW17	106	M10
Gassiot way Sutt	130	G6
Gastein rd W6	152	E1
Gaston Bell clo Rich	84	M7
Gaston rd Mitch	121	O6
Gatacker st SE16	159	X2
Gatcombe rd N19	47	Y10
Gate ms SW7	146	L19
Gate st WC2	149	N3
Gateforth st NW8	138	J17
Gatehouse clo Kings T	103	W19
Gateley rd SW9	90	D8
Gatesborough st EC2	142	K16
Gateside rd SW17	106	L7
Gatestone rd SE19	109	S16
Gateway Industrial est NW10	62	E10
Gateways the SW3	155	N8
Gatfield gro Felt	100	G5
Gathorne rd N22	30	E6
Gatliff rd SW1	155	W10
Gatling st SE2	80	A13
Gatting clo Edg	25	V2
Gatton clo Sutt	130	B20
Gatton rd SW17	106	J9
Gatward clo N21	7	V20
Gatward grn N9	18	F7
Gatwick rd SW18	87	V19
Gauden clo SW4	89	X6
Gauden rd SW4	89	X6
Gaunt st SE1	157	Z1
Gauntlet clo Nthlt	40	B19
Gauntlett ct Wem	42	A14
Gauntlett rd Sutt	130	G12
Gautrey rd SE15	92	D4
Gavel st SE17	158	H5
Gavestone cres SE12	94	J20
Gavestone rd SE12	94	H19
Gavin st SE18	79	U11
Gavina clo Mord	120	H12
Gawber st E2	63	R8
Gay clo NW2	44	L15
Gay gdns Dag	56	K13
Gay rd E15	64	J6
Gaydon la NW9	26	A5
Gayfere rd Epsom	128	G12
Gayfere rd Ilf	35	T9
Gayfere st SW1	156	J2
Gayford rd W12	74	E6
Gayhurst rd E8	49	X20
Gaylor rd Nthlt	40	B5
Gaynesford rd SE23	110	F5
Gaysham ave Ilf	35	Y10
Gaysham Hall Ilf	35	Y10
Gayton cres NW3	46	F12
Gayton rd NW3	46	F12
Gayton rd Har	23	W19
Gayville rd SW11	88	M15
Gaywood clo SW2	108	E1
Gaywood rd E17	33	P9
Gaywood st SE1	157	Y2
Gaza st SE17	157	X11
Geariesville gdns Ilf	36	A12
Geary rd NW10	44	G13
Geary st N7	48	D15
GEC est Wem	42	H9
Gedeney rd N17	31	N3
Gedling pl SE1	151	O20
Gee st EC1	142	A16
Geere rd E15	65	P4
Geffrye ct N1	142	M9
Geffrye st E2	143	N10
Geldart rd SE15	159	W19
Geldeston rd E5	49	X8
Gellatly rd SE14	92	E5
Gelsthorpe rd Rom	38	H2
General Gordon pl SE18	78	M10
General Wolfe rd SE10	93	X1
Genesta rd SE18	79	N17
Geneva dr SW9	90	G10
Geneva gdns Rom	37	Y15
Geneva rd Kings T	116	L9
Geneva rd Th Hth	122	L11
Genever clo E4	20	C15
Genista rd N18	19	O16
Genoa ave SW15	87	N13
Genoa rd SE20	124	C1
Genotin rd Enf	8	C12
Gentian row SE13	93	T3
Gentlemans row Enf	8	A11
Geoffrey clo SE5	90	L5
Geoffrey gdns E6	66	D7
Geoffrey rd SE4	92	L7
George Beard rd SE8	75	Y11
George V ave Pnr	22	G9
George V clo Pnr	22	G11
George V way Grnf	60	B2
George Groves rd SE20	123	Y1
George Inn yd SE1	150	E15
George la E18	34	F6
George la SE13	93	T16
George la Brom	126	G19
George rd E4	20	B18
George rd Kings T	103	T18
George rd N Mal	118	E10
George row SE16	151	S19
George sq SW19	119	X6
George st E16	65	P18
George st EC4	150	F7
George st W1	147	N5
George st W7	71	U3
George st Bark	54	B20
George st Croy	133	O4
George st Houns	82	E5
George st Rich	84	H13
George st Rom	39	U18
George st Sthl	70	B11
George st Sutt	130	A11
George Wyver clo SW19	87	S19
George yd EC3	150	H7
George yd W1	147	U8
Georges rd N7	48	E15
Georges sq SW6	153	S14
Georgetown clo SE19	109	R12
Georgette pl SE10	76	H20
Georgeville gdns Ilf	36	A12
Georgia rd N Mal	117	V8
Georgia rd Th Hth	122	A2
Georgian clo Brom	126	G19
Georgian clo Stan	10	L20
Georgian ct Wem	43	R17
Georgian way Har	41	R7
Georgiana st NW1	140	B3
Georgina gdns E2	143	O12
Geraint rd Brom	112	G10
Gerald rd E16	76	H20
Gerald rd SW1	155	V6
Gerald rd Dag	56	B5
Geraldine rd SW18	88	D14
Geraldine rd W4	73	R16

Geraldine st SE11	157	W3
Gerard ave Houns	82	G19
Gerard rd SW13	86	D2
Gerard rd Har	23	Y18
Gerards clo SE16	75	P15
Gerda rd SE9	114	B4
Germander way E15	65	N9
Gernon rd E3	63	V7
Geron way NW2	44	L6
Gerrard pl W1	148	G8
Gerrard rd N1	141	X8
Gerrard st W1	148	G8
Gerrards clo N14	6	H16
Gerridge st SE1	149	U20
Gertrude rd Belv	81	S10
Gertrude st SW10	154	E15
Gervase clo Wem	43	W8
Gervase rd Edg	25	Y5
Gervase st SE15	159	Y17
Ghent st SE6	111	P5
Giant Tree hill (Bushey) Wat	10	B6
Gibbard ms SW19	105	P14
Gibbins rd E15	64	H1
Gibbon rd SE15	92	D5
Gibbon rd W3	62	A19
Gibbon rd Kings T	102	K20
Gibbon wk SW15	86	H11
Gibbons rd NW10	44	A19
Gibbs ave SE19	109	O14
Gibbs clo SE19	109	P14
Gibbs grn W14	153	P9
Gibbs grn Edg	12	J15
Gibbs rd N18	19	P13
Gibbs sq SE19	109	O13
Gibraltar wk E2	143	R14
Gibson clo Islw	83	S8
Gibson gdns N16	49	U7
Gibson rd SE11	157	P6
Gibson rd Dag	55	U3
Gibson rd Sutt	130	A12
Gibson sq N1	141	V3
Gibson st SE10	76	M14
Gibson's hill SW16	108	F19
Gidea ave Rom	39	W9
Gidea clo Rom	39	V9
Gideon clo Belv	81	U10
Gideon rd SW11	89	O7
Giesbach rd N19	47	W6
Giffard rd N18	18	E17
Giffin st SE8	76	B19
Gifford gdns W7	59	R14
Gifford st N1	140	L1
Gift la E15	65	O2
Gilbert gro Edg	25	X4
Gilbert pl WC1	148	K3
Gilbert rd SE11	157	U6
Gilbert rd SW19	106	D18
Gilbert rd Belv	81	R9
Gilbert rd Brom	112	E18
Gilbert rd Rom	39	T13
Gilbert st E15	51	Z13
Gilbert st W1	147	W7
Gilbey rd SW17	106	J11
Gilbourne rd SE18	79	X17
Gilda ave E1	9	W15
Gilda cres N16	49	Y5
Gildea st W1	147	Z2
Gilden cres NW5	47	O16
Giles Coppice SE19	109	T11
Gilkes cres SE21	91	R15
Gilkes pl SE21	91	R16
Gill ave E16	65	T18
Gill st E14	63	Z18
Gillam way Rain	57	X17
Gillan grn (Bushey) Wat	10	A7
Gillender st E3	64	G11
Gillender st E14	64	G11
Gillespie rd N5	48	G10
Gillett ave E6	66	D5
Gillett rd Th Hth	123	N9
Gillett st N16	49	T16
Gillham ter N17	18	K20
Gillian Park rd Sutt	119	V19
Gillian st SE13	93	R12
Gillies st NW5	47	R15
Gillingham ms SW1	156	A5
Gillingham rd NW2	45	S9
Gillingham row SW1	156	B5
Gillingham st SW1	156	A5
Gillison wk SE16	159	V1
Gillman dr E15	65	O3
Gillum clo Barn	15	Z4
Gilmore rd SE13	93	W9
Gilmore way E15	85	Z10
Gilpin ave SW14	85	V10
Gilpin clo Mitch	120	J3
Gilpin cres N18	18	J16
Gilpin cres Twick	82	K17
Gilpin rd E5	50	H11
Gilroy clo Rain	57	U18
Gilsland rd Th Hth	123	O9
Gilstead rd SW6	88	B4
Gilston rd SW10	154	D12
Gilton rd SE6	112	A6
Giltspur st EC1	149	Y4
Gipsy hill SE19	109	S11
Gipsy la SW15	86	H9
Gipsy rd SE27	108	L11
Gipsy rd Well	97	W6
Gipsy Road gdns SE27	108	M11
Giralda clo E16	66	A15
Giraud st E14	64	D16
Girdlers rd W14	152	H4
Girdlestone wk N19	47	U7
Girdwood rd SW18	87	T19
Gironde rd SW6	153	R18
Girton ave NW9	25	P11
Girton clo Nthlt	40	M19
Girton gdns Croy	135	N5
Girton rd SE26	110	F12
Girton rd Nthlt	40	M18
Gisburn rd N8	30	D13
Given Wilson wk E13	65	P7
Gladbeck way Enf	7	X15
Gladding rd E12	53	O11
Glade the N21	17	P1
Glade the SE7	77	Y19
Glade the Brom	127	O4
Glade the Croy	124	F12
Glade the Epsom	128	H13
Glade the Ilf	35	T4
Glade the Sutt	129	T19
Glade the W Wick	135	S6
Glade the Wdf Grn	21	U11
Glade gdns Croy	124	J17
Glade la Sthl	70	J5
Gladeside N21	17	P1
Gladeside Croy	124	F18
Gladesmore rd N15	31	U18
Gladeswood rd Belv	81	U10
Gladiator st SE23	92	J17
Glading ter N16	49	U10
Gladioli clo Hmptn	100	G15
Gladsmuir rd N19	47	V4
Gladsmuir rd Barn	4	G9
Gladstone ave E12	53	S19
Gladstone ave N22	30	F7
Gladstone ave Twick	83	P20
Gladstone ms SE20	110	C19
Gladstone Park gdns NW2	44	J10
Gladstone pl E3	63	Z5
Gladstone pl Barn	4	D13
Gladstone rd SW19	105	X19
Gladstone rd W4	73	X9
Gladstone rd Buck H	21	X5
Gladstone rd Croy	123	P17
Gladstone rd Kings T	117	R6
Gladstone rd Sthl	70	B7
Gladstone st SE1	157	W2
Gladstone ter SE27	108	M11
Gladstone ter SW8	89	T1
Gladstone way Har	23	U10
Gladwell rd N8	30	C18
Gladwell rd Brom	112	G15
Gladwyn rd SW15	87	P7
Gladys rd NW6	45	Y19
Glamis pl E1	63	S19
Glamis rd E1	63	R20
Glamis way Nthlt	40	M18
Glamorgan clo Mitch	122	A7
Glamorgan rd Kings T	102	E19
Glanfield rd Beck	124	M9
Glanleam rd Stan	11	T13
Glanville rd SW2	90	B14
Glanville rd Brom	126	J7
Glasbrook ave Twick	100	E2
Glasbrook rd SE9	95	O17
Glaserton rd N16	49	T2
Glasford st SW17	106	M15
Glasgow rd E13	65	V6
Glasgow rd N18	18	M15
Glasgow ter SW1	156	A11
Glass st E2	143	Y15
Glass yd SE18	78	K8
Glasse clo W13	59	Y19
Glasshill st SE1	149	Y17
Glasshouse flds E1	63	T19
Glasshouse st W1	148	D10
Glasshouse wk SE11	156	M9
Glasslyn rd N8	29	W17
Glassmill la Brom	126	D4
Glastonbury rd N9	119	Z16
Glastonbury rd NW6	45	W16
Glaucus st E3	64	D13
Glazbury rd W14	152	L7
Glazebrook clo SE21	109	O3
Glazebrook rd Tedd	101	V17
Glebe the SE3	94	A7
Glebe the SW16	107	Z9
Glebe the Wor Pk	118	D19
Glebe ave Enf	7	W11
Glebe ave Har	24	K10
Glebe ave Mitch	120	H4
Glebe ave Wdf Grn	21	S20
Glebe ct W7	59	R20
Glebe ct Stan	11	R16
Glebe cres NW4	27	N11
Glebe cres Har	24	K11
Glebe gdns N Mal	118	B17
Glebe la Har	24	J13
Glebe path Mitch	120	L7
Glebe pl SW3	154	K12
Glebe rd E8	49	U20
Glebe rd N3	28	E4
Glebe rd N8	30	C14
Glebe rd NW10	44	F18
Glebe rd SW13	86	F3
Glebe rd Cars	131	N14
Glebe rd Dag	56	J19
Glebe rd Stan	11	R16
Glebe rd Sutt	129	T18
Glebe side Twick	83	W16
Glebe st W4	73	Z13
Glebe way Felt	100	H7
Glebe way W Wick	135	V2
Glebelands Dart	99	T10
Glebelands ave E18	34	F8
Glebelands ave Ilf	36	F19
Glebeway Wdf Grn	21	V16
Gledhow gdns SW5	154	B8
Gledstanes rd W14	152	M11
Gleed ave (Bushey) Wat	10	C7
Glegg pl SW15	87	P9
Glen the Croy	134	G4
Glen the Enf	7	X13
Glen the Pnr	22	C20
Glen the Sthl	70	E13
Glen the Wem	42	H12
Glen Albyn rd SW19	105	R4
Glen cres Wdf Grn	21	V19
Glen gdns Croy	132	H7
Glen Mill Hmptn	100	F12
Glen ri Wdf Grn	21	V19
Glen rd E13	65	X11
Glen rd E17	32	M15
Glen Road end Wall	131	S19
Glen wk Islw	83	S13
Glena mt Sutt	130	D8
Glenaffric ave E14	76	A12
Glenalmond rd Har	24	K12
Glenalvon way SE18	78	D10
Glenarm rd E5	50	C13
Glenavon rd E15	52	A19
Glenbow rd Brom	112	A11
Glenbrook north Enf	7	R13
Glenbrook rd NW6	45	X16
Glenbrook south Enf	7	R14
Glenbuck rd Surb	116	H15
Glenburnie rd SW17	106	L7
Glencairn dr W5	60	C13
Glencairn rd SW16	108	A18
Glencairne clo E16	66	B14
Glencoe ave Ilf	54	G2
Glencoe dr Dag	56	F11
Glencoe rd Hayes	58	A14
Glendale ave N22	17	S20
Glendale ave Edg	12	B12
Glendale ave Rom	37	T20
Glendale dr SW19	105	W13
Glendale gdns Wem	42	H5
Glendale ms Beck	125	T2
Glendale rd Erith	81	Z11
Glendale way SE28	80	H1
Glendall st SW9	90	C9
Glendarvon st SW15	87	P7
Glendish rd N17	31	Z5
Glendor gdns NW7	12	M13
Glendower pl SW7	154	G8
Glendower rd E4	20	K5
Glendower rd SW14	85	Y8
Glendown rd SE2	80	A20
Glendun rd W3	62	B20
Gleneagle rd SW16	107	X14
Gleneagles Stan	11	O20
Gleneldon ms SW16	107	Z10
Gleneldon rd SW16	107	Z10
Glenelg rd SW2	90	A12
Glenesk rd SE9	95	X7
Glenfarg rd SE6	93	W20
Glenfield rd SW12	107	W2
Glenfield rd W13	72	B5
Glenfield ter W13	72	A4
Glenfinlas way SE5	157	Y17
Glenforth st SE10	77	P13
Glengall gro E14	76	F8
Glengall rd NW6	137	P5
Glengall rd SE15	159	P12
Glengall rd Bexh	98	A8
Glengall rd Edg	12	E10
Glengall rd Wdf Grn	21	U19
Glengall ter SE15	159	P13
Glengarnock ave E14	76	H12
Glengarry rd SE22	91	T13
Glenham dr Ilf	36	A16
Glenhill clo N3	27	Y6
Glenhouse rd SE9	95	W12
Glenhurst ave NW5	47	R12
Glenhurst ri SE19	108	M19
Glenhurst rd N12	15	U15
Glenhurst rd Brent	72	E15
Glenilla rd NW3	46	H16
Glenister Park rd SW16	107	X18
Glenister rd SE10	77	P13
Glenister st E16	78	L4
Glenlea rd SE9	95	V12
Glenloch rd NW3	46	J16
Glenloch rd Enf	9	R8
Glenluce rd SE3	77	T18
Glenlyon rd SE9	95	X12
Glenmere ave NW7	13	T20
Glenmore rd NW3	46	J17
Glenmore rd Well	96	C4
Glenmore way Bark	68	B7
Glennie rd SE27	108	F8
Glenny rd Bark	54	C18
Glenorchy clo Hayes	58	C14
Glenparke rd E7	52	H17
Glenrosa st SW6	88	C4
Glenrose st Sid	115	R11
Glenroy st W12	144	B4
Glensdale rd SE4	92	M8
Glenshiel rd SE9	95	X12
Glentham gdns SW13	74	K15
Glentham rd SW13	74	H16
Glenthorne ave Croy	124	B20
Glenthorne clo Sutt	119	Y20
Glenthorne gdns Ilf	35	Y11
Glenthorne gdns Sutt	119	Y19

Name	Page	Ref
Glenthorne rd E17	32	H15
Glenthorne rd N11	16	A15
Glenthorne rd W6	152	B6
Glenthorne rd Kings T	116	M8
Glenthorpe rd Mord	119	P12
Glenton rd SE13	93	Z10
Glenton way Rom	39	P1
Glentworth st NW1	139	P17
Glenure rd SE9	95	Y13
Glenview SE2	80	J16
Glenview rd Brom	127	O4
Glenville ave Enf	8	A4
Glenville gro SE8	75	Z19
Glenville ms SW18	87	Z19
Glenville rd Kings T	103	O20
Glenwood ave NW9	44	A3
Glenwood clo Har	23	W15
Glenwood dr Rom	39	V14
Glenwood gdns Ilf	35	V15
Glenwood gro NW9	43	V4
Glenwood rd N15	30	K15
Glenwood rd NW7	13	O10
Glenwood rd SE6	111	N1
Glenwood rd Epsom	128	G14
Glenwood rd Houns	83	P8
Glenwood way Croy	124	F16
Gliddon rd W14	152	K8
Glimpsing grn Erith	81	N8
Globe Pond rd SE16	75	V3
Globe rd E1	63	S11
Globe rd E2	63	P7
Globe rd Horn	39	W18
Globe rd Wdf Grn	21	Z18
Globe st SE1	150	D20
Globe yd W1	147	X7
Glossop rd S Croy	133	P19
Gloster rd N Mal	118	A9
Gloucester ave NW1	139	S1
Gloucester ave Sid	114	J5
Gloucester ave Well	96	L12
Gloucester circ SE10	76	H19
Gloucester clo NW10	43	X20
Gloucester ct EC3	150	L10
Gloucester ct Rich	73	O20
Gloucester cres NW1	139	W3
Gloucester dr N4	48	J5
Gloucester dr NW11	27	Y13
Gloucester gdns NW1	27	U20
Gloucester gdns W2	146	A4
Gloucester gdns Barn	6	C15
Gloucester gdns Ilf	35	S20
Gloucester gdns Sutt	130	B2
Gloucester gate NW1	139	W7
Gloucester gro Edg	25	Y4
Gloucester Grove est SE15	158	L16
Gloucester ms W2	146	D6
Gloucester Mews west W2	146	C6
Gloucester pl NW1	139	O17
Gloucester pl W1	147	R2
Gloucester Place ms W1	147	R2
Gloucester rd E10	51	N2
Gloucester rd E11	34	K15
Gloucester rd E12	53	U10
Gloucester rd E17	32	F6
Gloucester rd N17	31	P8
Gloucester rd N18	18	G15
Gloucester rd SW7	154	C3
Gloucester rd W3	73	X4
Gloucester rd W5	72	E6
Gloucester rd Barn	5	O16
Gloucester rd Belv	81	P13
Gloucester rd Croy	123	R15
Gloucester rd Dart	99	Z17
Gloucester rd Enf	8	A3
Gloucester rd Hmptn	100	K19
Gloucester rd Har	22	K15
Gloucester rd Houns	82	A11
Gloucester rd Kings T	117	R4
Gloucester rd Rich	73	P18
Gloucester rd Rom	39	S18
Gloucester rd Tedd	101	T13
Gloucester rd Twick	101	N1
Gloucester sq E2	143	R6
Gloucester sq W2	146	J7
Gloucester st SW1	156	A10
Gloucester ter W2	145	Y4
Gloucester wk W8	145	V16
Gloucester way EC1	141	V14
Glover dr N18	19	P18
Glover rd Pnr	22	A17
Glycena rd SW11	89	N8
Glyn ave Barn	5	T13
Glyn clo SE25	123	R2
Glyn clo Epsom	128	F20
Glyn dr Sid	115	S10
Glyn rd E5	50	F10
Glyn rd Enf	9	P14
Glyn rd Wor Pk	129	O4
Glyn st SE11	157	N11
Glynde ms SW3	155	N3
Glynde rd Bexh	97	Y8
Glynde st SE4	92	M15
Glyndon rd SE18	79	R12
Glynfield rd NW10	62	B1
Glynne rd N22	30	G8
Glynwood dr SE23	110	D5
Goat la Enf	8	H2
Goat rd Mitch	121	N16
Goat st SE1	151	N16
Goat wf Brent	72	J17
Goaters all SW6	153	P18
Gobions ave Rom	39	N1
Godalming ave Wall	132	B11
Godbold rd E15	65	N10
Goddard rd Beck	124	G9
Godfrey ave Nthlt	58	A3
Godfrey ave Twick	83	R18
Godfrey hill SE18	78	E11
Godfrey rd SE18	78	F11
Godfrey st SW3	154	M9
Godfrey way Houns	82	D19
Goding st SE11	156	M11
Godley rd SW18	106	F1
Godliman st EC4	149	Z7
Godman rd SE15	91	Z6
Godolphin clo N13	17	W18
Godolphin pl W3	61	Z20
Godolphin rd W12	74	K4
Godric cres Croy	135	X20
Godson rd Croy	132	F6
Godstone rd Sutt	130	E8
Godstone rd Twick	84	A17
Godstow rd SE2	80	F6
Godwin clo N1	142	C9
Godwin rd E7	52	J12
Godwin rd Brom	126	L7
Goffers rd SE3	93	Y3
Goidel clo Wall	131	Z8
Golborne gdns W10	137	N18
Golborne ms W10	144	L1
Golborne rd W10	144	M1
Gold hill Edg	12	M19
Gold la Edg	12	L19
Golda clo Barn	4	D18
Goldbeaters gro Edg	13	N20
Goldcliff clo Mord	119	Z16
Goldcrest clo SE28	68	F19
Goldcrest ms W5	60	G14
Goldcrest way Croy	135	W19
Golden la EC1	142	B17
Golden Lane est EC1	142	B18
Golden Manor W7	71	T1
Golden sq W1	148	C9
Golders clo Edg	12	F15
Golders gdns NW11	45	U2
Golders Green cres NW11	45	W2
Golders Green rd NW11	27	S18
Golders Manor dr NW11	27	R19
Golders Park clo NW11	45	Z5
Golders ri NW4	27	O14
Golders way NW11	45	W2
Goldfinch rd SE28	79	U6
Goldhawk rd W6	74	F10
Goldhawk rd W12	144	B19
Goldhurst ter NW6	137	Y1
Golding st E1	151	V7
Goldington cres NW1	140	E7
Goldington st NW1	140	F7
Goldman clo E2	143	S16
Goldney rd W9	137	U18
Goldsborough cres E4	20	F8
Goldsborough rd SW8	156	G20
Goldsdown clo Enf	9	V9
Goldsdown rd Enf	9	U9
Goldsmid st SE18	79	V15
Goldsmith ave E12	53	S17
Goldsmith ave NW9	26	B17
Goldsmith ave W3	61	X19
Goldsmith ave Rom	56	E2
Goldsmith clo W3	73	Z1
Goldsmith clo Har	40	J4
Goldsmith la NW9	25	U13
Goldsmith rd E10	51	P4
Goldsmith rd E17	32	G7
Goldsmith rd N11	15	Y16
Goldsmith rd SE15	91	X1
Goldsmith rd W3	73	X1
Goldsmith st EC2	150	B5
Goldsmith's row E2	143	T9
Goldsmith's sq E2	143	U7
Goldsworthy gdns SE16	75	R12
Goldwell rd Th Hth	122	D8
Goldwin clo SE14	92	D1
Golf clo Stan	24	C1
Golf Club dr Kings T	103	Z18
Golf rd W5	61	N16
Golf rd Brom	127	X6
Golf side Twick	101	S7
Golfe rd Ilf	54	E10
Golfside clo N20	15	V11
Golfside clo N Mal	118	B4
Goliath clo Wall	132	A17
Gollogly ter SE7	77	Y15
Gomer gdns Tedd	101	Y14
Gomer pl Tedd	101	Y14
Gomm rd SE16	75	P8
Gomshall ave Wall	132	A11
Gondar gdns NW6	45	V14
Gonson pl SE8	76	C17
Gonson st SE8	76	D17
Gonston clo SW19	105	S5
Gonville cres Nthlt	40	L18
Gonville rd Th Hth	122	E12
Goodall rd E11	51	V10
Goodenough rd SW19	105	U18
Goodge pl W1	148	C1
Goodge st W1	148	D1
Goodhall st NW10	62	C9
Goodhart pl E14	63	W19
Goodhart way W Wick	125	Z17
Goodhew rd Croy	123	W15
Gooding clo N Mal	117	W10
Goodinge clo N7	47	Z16
Goodman cres SW2	107	Z3
Goodman rd E10	51	U2
Goodmans ct wem	42	H13
Goodman's Stile E1	151	S5
Goodmans yd E1	151	X4
Goodmayes ave Ilf	55	N3
Goodmayes la Ilf	55	O5
Goodmayes rd Ilf	55	O5
Goodrich rd SE22	91	V15
Goods way NW1	140	J9
Goodson rd NW10	44	C20
Goodway gdns E14	64	J16
Goodwin clo Mitch	120	G6
Goodwin dr Sid	115	X4
Goodwin gdns Croy	132	J13
Goodwin rd N9	19	S6
Goodwin rd W12	74	H6
Goodwin rd Croy	132	J11
Goodwin st N4	48	F7
Goodwood ave Enf	9	P1
Goodwood clo Mord	119	Y10
Goodwood clo Stan	11	S17
Goodwood dr Nthlt	40	F18
Goodwood rd SE14	75	W20
Goodwyn ave NW7	13	O16
Goodwyns vale N10	29	R5
Goodyers gdns NW4	27	O16
Goosander way SE28	79	S8
Gooseley la E6	66	K8
Gophir la EC4	150	F9
Gopsall st N1	142	G6
Gordon ave E4	20	L18
Gordon ave SW14	86	A9
Gordon ave Horn	57	T5
Gordon ave Stan	10	J20
Gordon ave Twick	83	Z13
Gordon clo N19	47	U5
Gordon cres Croy	123	T19
Gordon gdns Edg	25	T7
Gordon gro SE5	90	J6
Gordon hill Enf	7	Y5
Gordon House rd NW5	47	R12
Gordon pl W8	145	W17
Gordon rd E4	21	N3
Gordon rd E11	34	F19
Gordon rd E15	51	V12
Gordon rd E18	34	H4
Gordon rd N3	24	W1
Gordon rd N9	19	N7
Gordon rd N11	29	Y1
Gordon rd SE15	92	A4
Gordon rd W4	13	U16
Gordon rd W5	60	D19
Gordon rd W13	60	B19
Gordon rd Bark	67	V4
Gordon rd Beck	124	L7
Gordon rd Belv	81	Y10
Gordon rd Cars	130	M15
Gordon rd Enf	8	A7
Gordon rd Har	23	T10
Gordon rd Houns	82	M9
Gordon rd Ilf	54	E8
Gordon rd Kings T	116	M2
Gordon rd Rich	85	O6
Gordon rd Rom	38	B17
Gordon rd Sid	96	H14
Gordon rd Sthl	70	C11
Gordon rd Surb	117	N19
Gordon sq WC1	140	F17
Gordon st E13	65	T10
Gordon st WC1	140	E15
Gordon way Barn	4	J13
Gordonbrock rd SE4	93	O12
Gordondale rd SW19	105	Z4
Gore ct NW9	25	P16
Gore rd E9	63	R3
Gore rd SW20	118	M4
Gore st SW7	154	D1
Gorefield pl NW6	137	U8
Goresbrook rd Dag	68	E3
Goresbrook village Dag	68	D3
Gorham pl W11	144	K10
Goring clo Rom	38	J4
Goring rd N11	17	N19
Goring rd Dag	57	N18
Goring st EC3	150	L5
Goring way Grnf	59	N7
Gorleston rd N15	31	O14
Gorleston st W14	152	M6
Gorman rd SE18	78	H11
Gorringe Park ave Mitch	107	N17
Gorse rd SW17	107	P13
Gorse rd Croy	135	P6
Gorseway Rom	57	O5
Gorst rd NW10	61	Y11
Gorst rd SW11	88	L16
Gorsuch pl E2	143	N11
Gorsuch st E2	143	N11
Gosberton rd SW12	89	N20
Gosfield rd Dag	56	F5
Gosfield st W1	148	A1
Gosford gdns Ilf	35	U15
Goslett yd WC2	148	G5
Gosling clo Grnf	58	G8
Gosling way SW9	90	F1

Gospatrick rd N17	30	L2
Gosport rd E17	32	M15
Gossage rd SE18	79	T14
Gosset st E2	143	P13
Gosshill rd Chis	127	X3
Gossington clo Chis	114	A11
Gosterwood st SE8	75	W15
Gostling rd Twick	100	J1
Goston gdns Th Hth	122	F7
Goswell rd EC1	141	W10
Gothic rd Twick	101	R4
Goudhurst rd Brom	112	B12
Gough rd E15	52	B13
Gough rd Enf	8	M8
Gough sq EC4	149	V5
Gough st WC1	141	P16
Gould rd Twick	101	S2
Gould ter E8	50	B16
Goulston st E1	151	O4
Goulton rd E5	50	B13
Gourley pl N15	31	S17
Gourley st N15	31	S16
Gourock rd SE9	95	X13
Govan st E2	143	U6
Govier clo E15	65	O1
Gowan ave SW6	87	S2
Gowan rd NW10	44	J19
Gower ct WC1	140	E16
Gower ms WC1	148	G1
Gower pl WC1	140	D16
Gower rd E7	52	G18
Gower rd Islw	71	W17
Gower st WC1	140	E17
Gower's wk E1	151	S5
Gowland pl Beck	124	L5
Gowlett rd SE15	91	X8
Gowrie rd SW11	89	P9
Grace ave Bexh	98	C4
Grace clo SE9	113	O8
Grace clo Edg	25	U3
Grace Jones clo E8	49	W19
Grace rd Croy	122	L16
Grace st E3	64	F9
Gracechurch st EC3	150	H8
Gracedale rd SW16	107	T13
Gracefield gdns SW16	108	A8
Grace's all E1	151	T9
Graces ms SE5	91	R4
Graces rd SE5	91	R4
Gradient the SE26	109	W11
Graeme rd Enf	8	C8
Graemesdyke ave SW14	85	U9
Grafton clo W13	59	Y17
Grafton clo Houns	100	C1
Grafton clo Wor Pk	128	B5
Grafton cres NW1	47	S18
Grafton gdns N4	30	L17
Grafton gdns Dag	56	A5
Grafton ms W1	140	B18
Grafton Park rd Wor Pk	128	B4
Grafton pl NW1	140	G14
Grafton rd NW5	47	P14
Grafton rd W3	61	V19
Grafton rd Croy	132	H1
Grafton rd Dag	56	A5
Grafton rd Enf	7	P10
Grafton rd Har	23	O16
Grafton rd N Mal	118	B8
Grafton rd Wor Pk	128	A6
Grafton sq SW4	89	V8
Grafton st W1	147	Z10
Grafton ter NW5	47	N16
Grafton way W1	140	A19
Grafton way WC1	140	D17
Graham ave W13	72	B7
Graham ave Mitch	121	O1
Graham clo Croy	135	N3
Graham gdns Surb	116	K19
Graham rd E8	49	Y17
Graham rd E13	65	T10
Graham rd N15	30	H10
Graham rd NW4	26	J18
Graham rd SW19	105	W18
Graham rd W4	73	X7
Graham rd Bexh	98	D9
Graham rd Hmptn	100	F9

Graham rd Har	23	S9
Graham rd Mitch	121	O2
Graham st N1	141	Y9
Graham ter SW1	155	U7
Grahame Park est NW9	26	B4
Grahame Park way NW7	13	P20
Grahame Park way NW9	26	E4
Grainger rd N22	30	L5
Grainger rd Islw	83	W6
Grainger way Rom	39	W18
Gramer clo E11	51	Y7
Grampian gdns NW2	45	S4
Granard ave SW15	86	K14
Granard rd SW12	88	M18
Granary st NW1	140	F5
Granby bldgs SE11	157	O7
Granby rd SE9	95	U6
Granby st E2	143	P16
Granby ter NW1	140	A10
Grand ave EC1	149	Y1
Grand ave N10	29	O12
Grand ave Surb	117	U16
Grand ave Wem	43	P15
Grand Avenue east Wem	43	S16
Grand Depot rd SE18	78	K13
Grand dr SW20	118	M4
Grand Parade ms SW15	87	T12
Grand Union cres E8	143	U2
Grand Union Industrial est NW10	61	S5
Granden rd SW16	122	B4
Grandison rd SW11	89	N12
Grandison rd Wor Pk	128	M4
Granfield st SW11	88	H2
Grange the N20	15	S5
Grange the SE1	159	N1
Grange the SW19	105	P14
Grange the Croy	134	L3
Grange the Wem	61	O1
Grange ave N12	15	P16
Grange ave N20	14	E3
Grange ave SE25	123	R3
Grange ave Barn	15	Y4
Grange ave Stan	24	C7
Grange ave Twick	101	U4
Grange clo Edg	12	J16
Grange clo Houns	70	D15
Grange clo Sid	115	N6
Grange clo Wdf Grn	21	S20
Grange cres SE28	68	G18
Grange dr Chis	113	S15
Grange Farm clo Har	41	N5
Grange gdns N14	16	L5
Grange gdns NW3	46	B10
Grange gdns SE25	123	R3
Grange gdns Pnr	22	C11
Grange gro N1	48	K17
Grange hill SE25	123	R3
Grange hill Edg	12	J16
Grange la SE21	109	T5
Grange mans Epsom	128	E18
Grange ms SE10	76	J19
Grange pk W5	72	K2
Grange Park ave N21	7	X20
Grange Park pl SW20	104	J17
Grange Park rd E10	51	S6
Grange Park rd Th Hth	123	N8
Grange pl NW6	137	T2
Grange pl SE16	159	R3
Grange rd E10	51	P4
Grange rd E13	65	P9
Grange rd E17	32	H16
Grange rd N6	29	N19
Grange rd N17	18	K20
Grange rd N18	18	K19
Grange rd NW10	44	K19
Grange rd SE1	158	L2
Grange rd SW13	86	F3
Grange rd W4	73	U13
Grange rd W5	72	G2
Grange rd Edg	12	M20

Grange rd (Greenhill) Har	23	X17
Grange rd (Roxeth) Har	41	P7
Grange rd Ilf	54	A11
Grange rd Kings T	116	K6
Grange rd S Croy	133	N20
Grange rd Sthl	70	B4
Grange rd Sutt	129	X17
Grange rd Th Hth	123	O9
Grange vale Sutt	130	B16
Grange View rd N20	15	S5
Grange wk SE1	158	M2
Grange way N12	15	O13
Grange yd SE1	159	N2
Grangecliffe gdns SE25	123	R3
Grangecourt rd N16	49	R3
Grangehill rd SE9	95	V10
Grangehill rd SE6	111	O5
Grangemill way SE6	111	O5
Grangeway NW6	137	T1
Grangeway the N21	7	W18
Grangeway gdns Ilf	35	S15
Grangewood la Beck	110	M16
Grangewood st E6	66	A2
Granham gdns N9	18	H9
Granite st SE18	79	Y13
Granleigh rd E11	51	Z7
Gransden ave E8	50	A20
Gransden rd W12	74	E6
Grant clo N14	16	G2
Grant pl Croy	123	V20
Grant rd SW11	88	H9
Grant rd Croy	123	V19
Grant rd Har	23	V9
Grant st E13	65	S10
Grant st N1	141	T8
Grant way Islw	71	Y18
Grantbridge st N1	141	W8
Grantchester clo Har	41	W9
Grantham clo Edg	11	W9
Grantham rd SW9	38	B19
Grantham pl W1	147	W15
Grantham rd E12	53	W11
Grantham rd SW9	90	B5
Grantham rd W4	74	B18
Grantley st E1	63	T10
Grantock rd E17	33	X5
Granton rd SW16	107	V20
Granton rd Ilf	55	N4
Granton rd Sid	115	T14
Grants clo NW7	27	N1
Grantully rd W9	137	W14
Granville ave N9	19	P10
Granville ave Houns	82	G13
Granville clo Croy	133	R4
Granville ct N1	108	C20
Granville gdns W5	73	O2
Granville gro SE13	93	V8
Granville ms Sid	115	O9
Granville pk SE13	93	V7
Granville pl N12	28	E2
Granville pl W1	147	SC9
Granville rd E17	34	J8
Granville rd E18	33	R17
Granville rd N4	30	D19
Granville rd N12	15	P20
Granville rd N13	17	P18
Granville rd N22	30	J5
Granville rd NW2	45	V6
Granville rd NW6	137	T10
Granville rd SW18	87	V18
Granville rd SW19	105	Y19
Granville rd Barn	4	B12
Granville rd Ilf	53	Y5
Granville rd Sid	115	O8
Granville rd Well	97	U7
Granville sq WC1	141	R14
Granville st WC1	141	R13
Grape st WC2	148	K4
Graphite sq SE11	157	N9
Grasdene rd SE18	80	B18
Grasmere ave SW15	103	Z10
Grasmere ave SW19	119	Z6

Grasmere ave W3	61	X19
Grasmere ave Houns	82	J16
Grasmere ave Wem	42	E1
Grasmere ct N22	17	P19
Grasmere gdns Har	23	Y7
Grasmere gdns Ilf	35	T14
Grasmere rd E13	65	T5
Grasmere rd N10	29	S5
Grasmere rd N17	18	J19
Grasmere rd SE25	124	A13
Grasmere rd SW16	108	C12
Grasmere rd Bexh	98	J3
Grasmere rd Brom	112	B19
Grass pk N3	27	U5
Grassington rd Sid	115	N10
Grassmount SE23	109	X11
Grassway Wall	131	V9
Grasvenor ave Barn	4	M18
Gratton dr W14	152	K3
Gratton ter NW2	45	O10
Gravel hill N3	27	W7
Gravel hill Bexh	98	G13
Gravel hill Croy	134	E13
Gravel Hill clo Bexh	98	H14
Gravel la E1	151	N4
Gravel Pit la SE9	96	C12
Gravel rd Twick	101	S2
Gravelwood clo Chis	114	B7
Graveney gro SE20	110	C19
Graveney rd SW17	106	J10
Gravesend rd W12	74	G1
Gray ave Dag	56	C4
Gray gdns Rain	57	V16
Gray st SE1	149	V18
Grayham cres N Mal	117	Y10
Grayham rd N Mal	117	Y10
Grayland clo Brom	127	O2
Grayling rd N16	49	P6
Gray's Inn pl WC1	149	R1
Gray's Inn rd WC1	141	N13
Gray's Inn sq WC1	149	S1
Grayscroft rd SW16	107	X18
Grayshott rd SW11	89	N6
Grayswood gdns SW20	118	K5
Grazebrook rd N16	49	O7
Grazeley clo Bexh	98	L12
Grazeley ct SE19	109	S11
Great Brownings SE21	109	V9
Great Bushey dr N20	15	O4
Great Cambridge rd N9	18	G3
Great Cambridge rd N17	31	O2
Great Cambridge rd N18	18	A15
Great Cambridge rd Enf	18	G3
Great Castle st W1	148	A5
Great Central st NW1	139	O20
Great Central way NW10	43	V13
Great Chapel st W1	148	S15
Great Chertsey rd W4	85	W3
Great Chertsey rd Felt	100	G6
Great Church la W6	152	G8
Great College st SW1	156	J1
Great Cross ave SE10	76	M20
Great Cullings Rom	57	R6
Great Cumberland ms W1	147	P6
Great Cumberland pl W1	147	P5
Great Dover st SE1	150	D18
Great Eastern rd E15	51	X19
Great Eastern st EC2	142	J15
Great Elms rd Brom	126	L9
Great fld NW9	26	C4
Great George st SW1	148	H18
Great Guildford st SE1	150	A13
Great Harry dr SE9	113	W8
Great James st WC1	141	O19
Great Marlborough st W1	148	B7
Great Maze Pond SE1	150	G16

Name	Page	Grid
Great New st EC4	149	U5
Great North rd N2	28	K14
Great North rd N6	28	K14
Great North rd Barn	4	J3
Great North way NW4	26	K6
Great Ormond st WC1	141	N19
Great Percy st WC1	141	P13
Great Peter st SW1	156	G2
Great Portland st W1	139	Y19
Great Pulteney st W1	148	D8
Great Queen st WC2	148	G3
Great Russell st WC1	148	G3
Great St Helens EC3	150	J5
Great St Thomas Apostle EC4	150	C8
Great Scotland yd SW1	148	J13
Great Smith st SW1	156	H1
Great Spilmans SE22	91	S14
Great strand NW9	26	E6
Great Suffolk st SE1	149	Y14
Great Sutton st EC1	141	Y18
Great Swan all EC2	150	F4
Great Titchfield st W1	139	Z19
Great Tower st EC3	150	K9
Great Trinity la EC4	150	C8
Great West rd W4	73	T14
Great West rd W6	74	H13
Great West rd Brent	72	A18
Great West rd Hours	82	A4
Great West rd Islw	71	T19
Great Western Industrial pk Sthl		
Great Western rd W9	137	R19
Great Winchester st EC2	150	H4
Great Windmill st W1	148	E8
Greatdown rd W7	59	V13
Greatfield clo E6	66	G11
Greatfield clo N19	47	V11
Greatfield clo SE3	93	O11
Greatfields rd Bark	67	T4
Greatorex st E1	151	T1
Greatwood Chis	113	W17
Greaves pl SW17	106	H11
Grecian cres SE19	108	J15
Greek st W1	148	G6
Greek yd WC2	148	J9
Green the E4	20	H4
Green the E11	34	H19
Green the E15	52	B18
Green the N9	18	L8
Green the N14	16	K9
Green the N21	17	U3
Green the SW19	105	P13
Green the W3	62	B16
Green the Bexh	98	E2
Green the Brom	126	E18
Green the Cars	131	O9
Green the Croy	134	M19
Green the Houns	70	G16
Green the Mord	119	R10
Green the N Mal	117	X5
Green the Orp	115	R17
Green the Rich	84	G12
Green the Sid	115	N11
Green the Sthl	70	C7
Green the Sutt	130	A7
Green the Twick	101	T3
Green the Well	96	G10
Green the Wdf Grn	21	U15
Green acres Croy	135	U6
Green Arbour ct EC1	149	X4
Green ave NW7	12	M12
Green ave W13	72	C8
Green bank E1	151	Y14
Green bank N12	15	P13
Green clo NW9	25	W17
Green clo NW11	28	C20
Green clo Brom	125	Z5
Green clo Cars	130	M3
Green clo Felt	100	B12
Green dale SE22	91	S13
Green Dragon ct SE1	150	F13
Green Dragon la N21	7	S17
Green Dragon la Brent	72	K14
Green Dragon yd E1	151	R2
Green dr Sthl	70	J2
Green hill Buck H	21	X4
Green Hundred rd SE15	159	U14
Green la NW4	27	P14
Green la SE9	95	Y20
Green la SE20	110	E19
Green la SW16	108	C19
Green la W7	71	S6
Green la Chis	113	Z11
Green la Dag	55	Y6
Green la Edg	11	Z12
Green la Felt	100	A12
Green la Har	41	U10
Green la Ilf	54	E8
Green la Mord	119	Y14
Green la N Mal	117	X11
Green la Stan	11	N13
Green la Th Hth	122	H1
Green la Wor Pk	128	G1
Green Lane gdns Th Hth	122	L3
Green las N4	30	K19
Green las N8	30	H11
Green las N13	17	S16
Green las N16	49	N12
Green las N21	17	W7
Green las Epsom	128	B18
Green Man la W13	71	Z1
Green Moor link N21	17	W2
Green pl Dart	99	S12
Green Pond clo E17	32	K9
Green Pond rd E17	32	J9
Green rd N14	6	D19
Green rd N20	15	S9
Green st E7	52	J16
Green st E13	65	Y2
Green st W1	147	S8
Green st Enf	9	P9
Green vale W5	60	M16
Green vale Bexh	97	X13
Green Verges Stan	11	T20
Green wk NW4	27	P14
Green wk SE1	158	J3
Green wk Dart	99	S12
Green wk Sthl	70	G14
Green wk the E4	20	H4
Green way SE9	95	N13
Green way Brom	127	R13
Green Wrythe cres Cars	130	K1
Green Wrythe la Cars	120	G15
Greenacre clo Barn	4	J3
Greenacre wk N14	16	M10
Greenacres SE9	95	X16
Greenacres (Bushey) Wat	10	D8
Greenacres clo Stan	11	N20
Greenaway gdns NW3	46	A13
Greenbank ave Wem	41	Y14
Greenbank clo E4	20	G7
Greenbank cres NW4	27	S12
Greenbay rd SE7	78	B19
Greenberry st NW8	138	K10
Greenbrook ave Barn	5	S6
Greencoat pl SW1	156	D5
Greencoat row SW1	156	D3
Greencourt ave Croy	134	B2
Greencourt ave Edg	25	S5
Greencourt gdns Croy	134	A1
Greencrest pl NW2	44	H10
Greencroft clo E6	66	C15
Greencroft gdns Enf	8	E11
Greencroft rd Houns	82	D3
Greenend rd W4	74	A6
Greenfield ave Surb	117	T16
Greenfield gdns NW2	45	U9
Greenfield gdns Dag	68	H2
Greenfield rd E1	151	U3
Greenfield rd N15	31	S15
Greenfield rd Dag	68	H2
Greenfield way Har	22	J10
Greenford ave W7	59	S12
Greenford ave Sthl	58	E20
Greenford gdns Grnf	58	L8
Greenford rd Grnf	59	P8
Greenford rd Har	41	V12
Greenford rd Sthl	59	N19
Greenford rd Sutt	130	A10
Greengate Grnf	42	B17
Greengate st E13	65	V7
Greenhalgh wk N2	28	D14
Greenham clo SE1	149	T19
Greenham rd N10	29	P6
Greenheys dr E18	34	D9
Greenhill NW3	46	F13
Greenhill SE18	78	G13
Greenhill Sutt	130	D4
Greenhill Wem	43	U6
Greenhill gdns Nthlt	58	D7
Greenhill gro E12	53	R13
Greenhill pk Barn	5	O17
Greenhill pk NW10	62	A4
Greenhill rd NW10	62	A4
Greenhill rd Har	23	U17
Greenhill ter SE18	78	G13
Greenhill ter Nthlt	58	E7
Greenhill way Nthlt	23	S18
Greenhill way Wem	43	T6
Greenhill's rents EC1	149	X1
Greenhithe clo Sid	96	G18
Greenholm rd SE9	95	Y13
Greenhurst rd SE27	108	G12
Greening st SE2	80	F10
Greenland quay SE16	75	U10
Greenland rd NW1	140	A3
Greenland rd Barn	4	A18
Greenland st NW1	140	A4
Greenlaw gdns N Mal	118	E16
Greenlaw st SE18	78	H9
Greenlea Trading pk SW19	106	G19
Greenleaf clo SW2	90	F18
Greenleaf rd E6	65	Z3
Greenleaf rd E17	32	M10
Greenleafe dr Ilf	35	Z10
Greenman st N1	142	A2
Greenmoor rd Enf	9	R8
Greenoak way SW19	105	O8
Greenock rd SW16	107	W20
Greenock rd W3	73	U9
Green's end SE18	78	M10
Greenside clo N20	15	T9
Greenside rd W12	74	H7
Greenside rd Croy	122	H17
Greenstead ave Wdf Grn	21	Y20
Greenstead clo Wdf Grn	21	Y19
Greenstead gdns SW15	86	H14
Greenstead gdns Wdf Grn	21	Y19
Greenstone ms E11	34	E18
Greenvale SE9	95	U11
Greenview ave Beck	124	K14
Greenview ave Croy	124	H15
Greenway N14	16	M8
Greenway N20	14	K7
Greenway SW20	118	L9
Greenway Chis	113	Y12
Greenway Dag	55	V5
Greenway Har	24	K16
Greenway Pnr	22	E19
Greenway Wall	131	V9
Greenway Wdf Grn	21	Y15
Greenway the NW9	25	V7
Greenway the Har	23	U5
Greenway the Houns	82	D9
Greenway ave E17	33	W12
Greenway clo N4	49	N7
Greenway clo N11	16	C19
Greenway clo N20	14	L8
Greenway clo NW9	25	X8
Greenway gdns NW9	25	X8
Greenway gdns Croy	134	L7
Greenway gdns Grnf	58	J9
Greenway gdns Har	23	U6
Greenways Beck	125	P4
Greenwell st W1	139	Z19
Greenwich Church st SE10	76	H16
Greenwich High rd SE10	76	F19
Greenwich Industrial est SE7	77	V12
Greenwich Park st SE10	76	L16
Greenwich South st SE10	76	G20
Greenwich View pl E14	76	D9
Greenwood ave Dag	56	J11
Greenwood ave Enf	9	V6
Greenwood clo Mord	119	S10
Greenwood clo Sid	115	O4
Greenwood clo (Bushey) Wat	10	E3
Greenwood dr E4	20	J16
Greenwood gdns N13	17	V9
Greenwood gdns Ilf	36	C3
Greenwood la Hmptn	103	L13
Greenwood pk Kings T	104	B17
Greenwood rd E8	49	Y16
Greenwood rd Croy	122	K16
Greenwood rd Islw	83	V7
Greenwood rd Mitch	121	X7
Greenwood ter NW10	61	Y4
Greer rd Har	23	O4
Greet st SE1	149	V15
Gregor ms SE3	77	T20
Gregory cres SE9	95	O19
Gregory pl W8	145	X17
Gregory rd Rom	37	V13
Gregory rd Sthl	70	H8
Greig clo N8	30	A15
Greig ter SE17	157	Z13
Grena gdns Rich	85	N11
Grena rd Rich	85	O11
Grenaby ave Croy	123	O18
Grenaby rd Croy	123	O18
Grenada rd SE7	77	V12
Grenade st E14	63	Z19
Grenadier st E16	78	H4
Grendon gdns Wem	43	P6
Grendon st NW8	138	K16
Grenfell ave Horn	57	T3
Grenfell gdns Har	24	J20
Grenfell rd W11	144	J9
Grenfell rd Mitch	107	N17
Grennell clo Sutt	130	F4
Grennell rd Sutt	130	E2
Grenoble gdns N13	17	S18
Grenville clo N3	27	U6
Grenville clo Surb	117	V20
Grenville gdns Wdf Grn	34	K2
Grenville ms SW7	154	C6
Grenville ms Hmptn	100	K12
Grenville pl NW7	12	L16
Grenville pl SW7	154	B4
Grenville rd N19	48	A4
Grenville st WC1	140	L18
Gresham ave N20	15	Y12
Gresham clo Bex	98	A16
Gresham dr Rom	37	P16
Gresham gdns NW11	45	T4
Gresham rd E6	66	H7
Gresham rd E16	65	W17
Gresham rd NW10	43	Z16
Gresham rd SE25	123	X10
Gresham rd SW9	90	F8
Gresham rd Beck	124	H4
Gresham rd Edg	12	A19
Gresham rd Hmptn	100	G14

Name	Page	Grid
Gresham rd Houns	83	N1
Gresham st EC2	150	C4
Gresham way SW19	105	Z6
Gresley rd N19	47	W2
Gresse st W1	148	F3
Gressenhall rd SW18	87	V17
Gresswell clo Sid	115	O7
Greswell st SW6	87	P2
Gretton rd N1	31	T2
Greville clo Twick	84	A18
Greville pl NW6	137	Y8
Greville rd E17	33	V13
Greville rd NW6	137	X7
Greville rd Rich	85	N15
Greville st EC1	149	V1
Grey clo NW11	28	C17
Grey Eagle st E1	143	O19
Greycoat pl SW1	156	E2
Greycoat st SW1	156	E3
Greycot rd Beck	111	O13
Greyhound hill NW4	26	H10
Greyhound la SW16	107	Y17
Greyhound rd N17	31	T11
Greyhound rd NW10	136	A11
Greyhound rd W6	152	G14
Greyhound rd W14	152	M12
Greyhound rd Sutt	130	C11
Greyhound ter SW16	107	V20
Greyhound way Dart	99	R14
Greystead rd SE23	92	C18
Greystoke ave Pnr	22	H9
Greystoke gdns W5	60	L11
Greystoke gdns Enf	6	M14
Greystone ave Har	24	D18
Greystone gdns Ilf	36	C6
Greyswood st SW16	107	S15
Grierson rd SE23	92	G17
Griffin clo NW10	44	K16
Griffin Manor way SE28	79	U9
Griffin rd E17	31	R7
Griffin rd SE18	79	T14
Griffiths clo Wor Pk	128	K4
Griffiths rd SW19	105	Z17
Griggs app Ilf	54	B6
Griggs pl SE1	158	L2
Griggs rd E10	33	V19
Grilse clo N9	19	N12
Grimsby st E2	143	P17
Grimsdyke rd Pnr	22	D1
Grimshaw clo N6	47	O1
Grimston rd SW6	87	V5
Grimwade ave Croy	133	X6
Grimwood rd Twick	83	X18
Grindal st SE1	149	S19
Grinling pl SE8	76	A17
Grinstead rd SE8	75	W14
Grittleton ave Wem	43	T18
Grittleton rd W9	137	T16
Grizedale ter SE23	110	A3
Grocer's Hall ct EC2	150	E6
Groom cres SW18	88	F19
Groom pl SW1	147	V20
Groombridge clo Well	97	O13
Groombridge rd E9	50	F20
Groomfield clo SW17	107	O10
Grosmont rd SE18	79	Y15
Grosse way SW15	86	K17
Grosvenor ave N5	48	L16
Grosvenor ave SW14	87	T17
Grosvenor ave Cars	131	N14
Grosvenor ave Har	22	L19
Grosvenor ave Rich	84	J13
Grosvenor cotts SW1	155	T5
Grosvenor ct N14	16	H1
Grosvenor cres NW9	25	R13
Grosvenor cres SW1	147	U19
Grosvenor Crescent ms SW1	147	T18
Grosvenor est SW1	156	G5
Grosvenor gdns E6	66	A8
Grosvenor gdns N10	29	V3
Grosvenor gdns N14	6	K15
Grosvenor gdns NW2	45	N16
Grosvenor gdns NW11	27	U17
Grosvenor gdns SW1	155	X1
Grosvenor gdns SW14	86	A9
Grosvenor gdns Kings T	102	H15
Grosvenor gdns Wall	131	U16
Grosvenor gdns Wdf Grn	21	U19
Grosvenor Gardens Mews north SW1	155	X2
Grosvenor hill SW19	105	S15
Grosvenor hill W1	147	X9
Grosvenor pk SE5	158	A16
Grosvenor Park rd E17	33	P16
Grosvenor pl SW1	147	W19
Grosvenor Rise east E17	33	S15
Grosvenor rd E6	66	B3
Grosvenor rd E7	52	B18
Grosvenor rd E10	51	U4
Grosvenor rd E11	34	G16
Grosvenor rd N3	27	W1
Grosvenor rd N9	19	N4
Grosvenor rd N10	29	S5
Grosvenor rd SE25	123	W8
Grosvenor rd SW1	156	C13
Grosvenor rd W4	73	T14
Grosvenor rd W7	71	Y3
Grosvenor rd Belv	81	R15
Grosvenor rd Bexh	97	X14
Grosvenor rd Brent	72	H17
Grosvenor rd Dag	56	C3
Grosvenor rd Houns	82	E8
Grosvenor rd Ilf	54	B8
Grosvenor rd Rich	84	J13
Grosvenor rd Rom	57	N2
Grosvenor rd Sthl	70	E8
Grosvenor rd Twick	83	X20
Grosvenor rd Wall	131	R13
Grosvenor rd W Wick	135	S2
Grosvenor sq W1	147	U8
Grosvenor st W1	147	W8
Grosvenor ter SE5	158	A16
Grosvenor Wharf rd E14	76	J12
Grote's bldgs SE3	94	A5
Grote's pl SE3	94	A5
Groton rd SW18	106	B3
Grotto pas W1	147	U1
Grotto rd Twick	101	W4
Grove the E15	51	Z17
Grove the N3	27	X3
Grove the N4	48	D1
Grove the N6	47	O3
Grove the N8	29	Z15
Grove the N13	17	T15
Grove the N14	6	H16
Grove the NW9	25	Y15
Grove the NW11	27	T20
Grove the W5	72	G2
Grove the Bexh	97	W10
Grove the Edg	12	F14
Grove the Enf	7	U9
Grove the Grnf	58	M16
Grove the Islw	83	S3
Grove the Sid	115	Z10
Grove the Tedd	101	Y11
Grove the W Wick	135	T7
Grove ave N3	27	Y2
Grove ave N10	29	V8
Grove ave W7	59	T17
Grove ave Pnr	22	C14
Grove ave Sutt	129	Y13
Grove ave Twick	101	W1
Grove clo SE23	92	G20
Grove clo Felt	100	A10
Grove clo Kings T	116	M9
Grove cotts SW3	154	M13
Grove ct SE3	94	G1
Grove cres E18	34	D7
Grove cres NW9	25	W12
Grove cres SE5	91	R5
Grove cres Felt	100	B10
Grove cres Kings T	116	J7
Grove Crescent rd E15	51	Y18
Grove end E18	34	B6
Grove End rd NW8	138	F9
Grove Farm Industrial est Mitch	120	L13
Grove footpath Surb	116	K10
Grove gdns E15	51	Z19
Grove gdns NW4	26	G14
Grove gdns NW8	138	L14
Grove gdns Dag	56	K10
Grove gdns Enf	9	T4
Grove gdns Tedd	101	Y10
Grove Green rd E11	51	V9
Grove Hall ct NW8	138	D12
Grove hill E18	34	C7
Grove hill Har	41	U1
Grove Hill rd SE5	91	S7
Grove Hill rd Har	23	U20
Grove House rd N8	30	A13
Grove la SE5	91	R6
Grove la Kings T	116	K8
Grove Market pl SE9	95	T15
Groves ms W6	152	C1
Grove pk E11	34	J15
Grove pk NW9	25	X11
Grove pk SE5	91	S6
Grove Park ave E4	33	P3
Grove Park bri W4	73	V19
Grove Park gdns W4	73	V18
Grove Park rd N15	31	S13
Grove Park rd SE9	112	M7
Grove Park rd W4	73	V18
Grove Park ter W4	73	U18
Grove pas E2	143	X8
Grove pl NW3	46	F10
Grove pl W3	73	V3
Grove pl Bark	67	O2
Grove rd E3	63	U4
Grove rd E4	20	F11
Grove rd E11	52	C2
Grove rd E17	33	R17
Grove rd E18	34	B6
Grove rd N11	16	F15
Grove rd N12	15	T16
Grove rd N15	31	R16
Grove rd NW2	44	M17
Grove rd SW13	86	D4
Grove rd SW19	106	D18
Grove rd W3	73	W3
Grove rd W5	72	H1
Grove rd Barn	5	V11
Grove rd Belv	81	P16
Grove rd Bexh	98	L11
Grove rd Brent	72	F14
Grove rd Edg	12	C18
Grove rd Houns	82	G10
Grove rd Islw	83	U3
Grove rd Mitch	121	P6
Grove rd Pnr	22	D14
Grove rd Rich	84	M16
Grove rd Rom	37	S20
Grove rd Surb	116	G12
Grove rd Sutt	129	X15
Grove rd Th Hth	122	E9
Grove rd Twick	101	R8
Grove Road west Enf	9	R1
Grove st N18	18	H17
Grove st SE8	75	X10
Grove ter NW5	47	N15
Grove ter Tedd	101	Y10
Grove vale SE22	91	T10
Grove vale Chis	113	W15
Grove vill E14	76	F18
Grovebury rd SE2	80	E5
Grovedale rd N19	47	X5
Groveland ave SW16	108	F12
Groveland rd Beck	124	L6
Groveland way N Mal	117	R4
Grovelands clo SE5	91	R5
Grovelands clo Har	40	K10
Grovelands ct N14	16	K3
Grovelands rd N13	17	R12
Grovelands rd N15	31	X17
Grovelands rd Orp	115	O19
Groveside clo W3	61	R15
Groveside clo Cars	130	K2
Groveside rd E4	21	O10
Groveway SW9	90	E3
Groveway Dag	55	V11
Groveway Wem	43	U14
Grovewood Rich	85	O3
Grummant rd SE15	91	V2
Grundy st E14	64	D18
Gruneisen rd N3	28	A1
Guardian clo Horn	57	Y5
Gubyon ave SE24	90	K13
Guernsey clo Houns	70	J20
Guernsey gro SE24	90	L18
Guernsey rd E11	51	W5
Guibal rd SE12	94	G20
Guild rd SE7	78	C15
Guildersfield rd SW16	108	A18
Guildford gro SE10	93	S1
Guildford rd E6	66	F17
Guildford rd E17	33	V4
Guildford rd SW8	156	L20
Guildford rd Croy	123	O14
Guildford rd Ilf	54	J7
Guildford way Wall	132	B10
Guildhouse st SW1	156	A6
Guildown ave N12	15	N12
Guildsway E17	32	K4
Guilford ave Surb	116	M12
Guilford pl WC1	141	N18
Guilford st WC1	140	K19
Guilsborough clo NW10	62	A1
Guinness clo E9	63	V1
Guinness sq SE1	158	K4
Guinness Trust est N16	49	T3
Guinness Trust est SW9	90	J11
Guion rd SW6	87	W4
Gulliver clo Nthlt	58	D3
Gulliver rd Sid	114	G5
Gulliver st SE16	75	X7
Gumleigh rd W5	72	D11
Gumley gdns Islw	83	X7
Gun st E1	150	M1
Gundulph rd Brom	126	L7
Gunmakers la E3	63	X3
Gunner la SE18	78	K14
Gunners gro E4	20	F10
Gunners rd SW18	106	G3
Gunnersbury ave W3	73	P8
Gunnersbury ave W5	73	M1
Gunnersbury cres W3	73	P6
Gunnersbury dr W5	73	N6
Gunnersbury gdns W3	73	P6
Gunnersbury la W3	73	R6
Gunning st SE18	79	V11
Gunstor rd N16	49	S11
Gunter gro SW10	154	B16
Gunter gro Edg	25	Y3
Gunterstone rd W14	152	L8
Gunthorpe st E1	151	P3
Gunton rd E5	50	B8
Gunton rd SW17	107	P16
Gunwhale clo SE16	75	T4
Gurdon rd SE7	77	U14
Gurnell gro W13	59	X11
Gurney clo E17	32	F4
Gurney clo Bark	53	Z18
Gurney cres Croy	122	E20
Gurney dr N2	28	E14
Gurney rd E15	51	Z14
Gurney rd Cars	131	N7
Guthrie st SW3	154	J9
Gutter la EC2	150	B4
Guy rd Wall	131	Z6
Guy st SE1	150	G18
Guyscliff rd SE13	93	T13
Gwalior rd SW15	87	R9
Gwendolen ave SW15	87	O12
Gwendolen clo SW15	87	O13
Gwendoline ave E13	65	W3
Gwendwr rd W14	152	M8
Gwillim clo Sid	97	P14
Gwydor rd Beck	124	G8
Gwydyr rd Brom	126	D6
Gwyn clo SW6	154	A20
Gwynne ave Croy	124	F16
Gwynne rd SW11	88	G4
Gylcote clo SE5	91	P11

Name	Page	Grid
Gyles pk Stan	24	E3
Gyllyngdune gdns Ilf	54	L8

H

Name	Page	Grid
Ha-Ha rd SE18	78	J16
Haarlem rd W14	152	F3
Haberdasher pl N1	142	H11
Haberdasher st N1	142	G12
Hackbridge grn Wall	131	O2
Hackbridge Park gdns Cars	131	N3
Hackbridge rd Wall	131	O2
Hackford rd SW9	157	S20
Hackington cres Beck	111	P14
Hackney rd E2	143	N13
Hadden rd SE28	79	U8
Hadden way Grnf	41	R17
Haddington rd Brom	111	Y8
Haddo st SE10	76	F17
Haddon clo Enf	8	K19
Haddon clo N Mal	118	C11
Haddon gro Sid	96	M18
Haddon rd Sutt	130	A10
Haddonfield SE8	75	T11
Hadleigh rd N9	18	M1
Hadleigh st E2	63	R10
Hadley clo N21	7	U19
Hadley common Barn	4	K8
Hadley gdns W4	73	Y14
Hadley gdns Sthl	70	D14
Hadley grn Barn	4	G9
Hadley Green rd Barn	4	H8
Hadley Green west Barn	4	G8
Hadley gro Barn	4	F9
Hadley Highstone Barn	4	H6
Hadley ridge Barn	4	G10
Hadley rd Barn (New Barnet)	5	N9
Hadley rd Belv	81	P9
Hadley rd Enf	6	B3
Hadley rd Mitch	121	X9
Hadley st NW1	47	S18
Hadley way N21	7	U20
Hadlow pl SE19	109	X17
Hadlow rd Sid	115	P9
Hadlow rd Well	80	F18
Hadrian est E2	143	U10
Hadrian st SE10	76	M13
Hadrians ride Enf	8	H15
Hadyn Park rd W12	74	F5
Hafer rd SW11	88	L10
Hafton rd SE6	112	A2
Haggard rd Twick	84	A19
Haggerston rd E8	143	N1
Hague st E2	143	V14
Haig rd Stan	11	R17
Haig Road east E13	65	Y7
Haig Road west E13	65	Y8
Haigville gdns Ilf	36	A12
Hailey rd Erith	81	T5
Haileybury ave Enf	8	H19
Hailsham ave SW2	108	D5
Hailsham clo Surb	116	H17
Hailsham dr Har	23	R9
Hailsham rd SW17	107	R16
Haimo rd SE9	95	O12
Hainault Gore Rom	38	A17
Hainault rd E11	51	U3
Hainault rd Rom	38	L8
Hainault rd Rom (Chadwell Heath)	38	C17
Hainault rd (Hainault) Rom	37	P1
Hainault st SE9	114	A2
Hainault st Ilf	54	B7
Hainford clo SE4	92	G10
Hainthorpe rd SE27	108	H8
Halberd ms E5	50	A5
Halbutt gdns Dag	56	B10
Halbutt st Dag	56	B12
Halcomb st N1	142	K6
Halcot ave Bexh	98	G12
Halcrow st E1	151	Y2
Haldan rd E4	20	H20
Haldane clo N10	29	R1
Haldane pl SW18	88	B20
Haldane rd E6	66	C8
Haldane rd SE28	68	J20
Haldane rd SW6	153	S16
Haldane rd Sthl	58	M18
Haldon rd SW18	87	W15
Hale the E4	33	W2
Hale the N17	31	X11
Hale clo E4	20	G9
Hale clo Edg	12	J16
Hale dr NW7	12	H18
Hale End rd E4	20	J19
Hale End rd E17	33	W3
Hale End rd Wdf Grn	33	W3
Hale gdns N17	31	X11
Hale gdns W3	73	P1
Hale Grove gdns NW7	12	M15
Hale la NW7	12	L16
Hale la Edg	12	L16
Hale rd E6	66	D12
Hale rd N17	31	X10
Hale st E14	64	D19
Hale wk W7	59	T15
Halefield rd N17	31	Z5
Hales st SE8	76	B20
Halesowen rd Mord	120	A18
Halesworth rd SE13	93	R7
Haley rd NW4	27	N19
Half acre Brent	72	F16
Half Acre rd W7	71	T2
Half Moon ct EC1	150	A6
Half Moon cres N1	141	R7
Half Moon la SE24	90	L15
Half Moon st W1	147	Y13
Halford rd E10	33	W16
Halford rd SW6	153	T16
Halford rd Rich	84	J13
Halfway st Sid	96	F18
Haliburton rd Twick	83	Z12
Halidon clo E9	50	D15
Halifax rd Enf	8	A7
Halifax rd Grnf	58	K3
Halifax st SE26	110	A8
Halifield dr Belv	80	M9
Haling Down pas S Croy	132	L20
Haling gro S Croy	132	M17
Haling Park gdns S Croy	132	K14
Haling Park rd S Croy	132	K12
Haling rd S Croy	133	O13
Halkin arc SW1	147	S20
Halkin ms SW1	147	S20
Halkin pl SW1	155	S1
Halkin st SW1	147	V19
Hall the SE3	94	E8
Hall clo W5	60	J15
Hall ct Tedd	101	X12
Hall dr SE26	110	C11
Hall dr W7	59	U16
Hall Farm clo Stan	11	O12
Hall Farm dr Twick	83	P17
Hall gdns E4	19	Z14
Hall gate NW8	138	E13
Hall la E4	19	X15
Hall la NW4	26	H6
Hall pl W2	138	F19
Hall Place cres Bex	98	M14
Hall rd E6	66	H2
Hall rd E15	51	Y11
Hall rd NW8	138	C14
Hall rd Islw	83	P14
Hall rd Rom	37	V19
Hall rd Wall	131	T19
Hall st EC1	141	Y12
Hall st N12	15	R16
Hall vw SE9	113	N5
Hallam clo Chis	113	U13
Hallam gdns Pnr	22	C2
Hallam ms W1	139	Y20
Hallam rd N15	30	K13
Hallam st W1	139	Y19
Halley gdns SE13	93	Y10
Halley rd E7	52	K18
Halley rd E12	53	P16
Halley st E14	63	W14
Hallfield est W2	146	A6
Halliford st N1	142	D1
Halliwell rd SW2	90	C14
Halliwick rd N10	29	O5
Hallmead rd Sutt	130	A6
Hallowell ave Croy	131	Z7
Hallowell clo Mitch	121	P6
Hallside rd Enf	8	G4
Hallsville rd E16	65	P17
Hallswelle rd NW11	27	V15
Hallywell cres E6	66	H14
Halons rd SE9	95	X17
Halpin pl SE17	158	H7
Halsbrook rd SE3	95	N6
Halsbury clo Stan	11	O14
Halsbury rd W12	74	H2
Halsbury Road east Nthlt	41	N13
Halsbury Road west Nthlt	40	L13
Halsey st SW3	155	O5
Halsham cres Bark	54	K16
Halsmere rd SE5	90	K1
Halstead ct N1	142	F11
Halstead gdns N21	18	B5
Halstead rd E11	34	G15
Halstead rd N21	18	A5
Halstead rd Enf	8	F13
Halstead rd Erith	99	R1
Halston clo SW11	88	L15
Halstow rd NW10	136	G13
Halstow rd SE10	77	S14
Halt Robin rd Belv	81	T10
Halton rd N1	141	Y3
Ham the Brent	72	E19
Ham clo Rich	102	D7
Ham Farm rd Rich	102	H9
Ham Gate ave Rich	102	H8
Ham Park rd E7	52	F19
Ham Park rd E15	52	B20
Ham ridings Rich	102	M12
Ham st Rich	102	C2
Ham vw Croy	124	J16
Hambalt rd SW4	89	V14
Hamble st SW6	88	B6
Hambleden pl SE21	109	T2
Hambledon gdns SE25	123	V7
Hambledon rd SW18	87	V19
Hambledown rd Sid	96	G19
Hambleton clo Wor Pk	129	N2
Hambridge way SW2	90	G19
Hambro ave Brom	126	F20
Hambro rd SW16	107	Y14
Hambrook rd SE25	123	Z7
Hambrough rd Sthl	70	B4
Hamden cres Dag	56	G9
Hameway E6	66	J10
Hamfrith rd E15	52	C17
Hamilton ave N9	18	K1
Hamilton ave Ilf	36	A14
Hamilton ave Rom	39	N8
Hamilton ave Sutt	129	S2
Hamilton clo N17	31	W10
Hamilton clo NW8	138	F15
Hamilton clo Barn	5	Y14
Hamilton clo Stan	10	H9
Hamilton ct W5	60	M19
Hamilton ct W9	138	A12
Hamilton cres N13	17	U14
Hamilton cres Har	40	F9
Hamilton cres Houns	82	K14
Hamilton gdns NW8	138	D11
Hamilton pk N5	48	K13
Hamilton Park west N5	48	J13
Hamilton pl W1	147	W15
Hamilton rd E15	65	N10
Hamilton rd E17	32	J8
Hamilton rd N2	28	D10
Hamilton rd N9	18	K2
Hamilton rd NW10	44	G14
Hamilton rd NW11	45	S2
Hamilton rd SE27	109	O9
Hamilton rd SW19	106	B18
Hamilton rd W4	74	A7
Hamilton rd W5	60	L19
Hamilton rd Barn	5	X13
Hamilton rd Bexh	98	A4
Hamilton rd Brent	72	G15
Hamilton rd Har	23	U15
Hamilton rd Ilf	53	Z12
Hamilton rd Rom	39	Y15
Hamilton rd Sid	114	M9
Hamilton rd Sthl	70	E2
Hamilton rd Th Hth	123	N6
Hamilton rd Twick	101	U1
Hamilton sq SE1	150	G17
Hamilton ter NW8	138	A9
Hamilton way N3	14	K20
Hamilton way N13	17	V14
Hamilton way Wall	131	V19
Hamlea clo SE12	94	E12
Hamlet the SE5	91	P7
Hamlet clo Rom	38	D2
Hamlet gdns W6	74	G11
Hamlet rd SE19	109	W18
Hamlet rd Rom	38	D2
Hamlet sq NW2	45	R8
Hamlets way E3	63	Y11
Hamlyn clo Edg	11	W10
Hamlyn gdns SE19	109	R19
Hammelton rd Brom	112	E20
Hammers la NW7	13	U16
Hammersmith bri SW13	152	A12
Hammersmith Bridge rd W6	152	B10
Hammersmith bdy W6	152	D7
Hammersmith Flyover W6	152	D9
Hammersmith gro W6	144	B19
Hammersmith rd W14	152	J6
Hammond ave Mitch	121	S4
Hammond clo Barn	4	G17
Hammond rd Enf	9	N9
Hammond rd Sthl	70	C8
Hammond st NW5	47	U17
Hamonde clo Edg	12	E8
Hampden ave Beck	124	K4
Hampden clo NW1	140	G9
Hampden Gurney st W1	147	O6
Hampden la N17	31	W4
Hampden rd N8	30	F12
Hampden rd N10	29	P2
Hampden rd N17	31	X4
Hampden rd Beck	124	J4
Hampden rd Har	23	O4
Hampden rd Kings T	117	R5
Hampden rd Rom	38	J1
Hampden way N14	16	E5
Hampshire Hog la W6	74	J12
Hampshire rd N22	30	D1
Hampshire st NW5	47	U17
Hampson way SW8	157	O20
Hampstead clo SE28	80	C2
Hampstead gdns NW11	27	X19
Hampstead grn NW3	46	J14
Hampstead gro NW3	46	D9
Hampstead High st NW3	46	E12
Hampstead Hill gdns NW3	46	H13
Hampstead la N6	46	M2
Hampstead la NW3	46	F3
Hampstead rd NW1	140	B11
Hampstead sq NW3	46	E10
Hampstead way NW11	47	W16
Hampton clo NW6	137	T13
Hampton clo SW20	104	M18
Hampton Court E Mol	116	A5
Hampton Court rd Kings T	116	A5
Hampton la Felt	100	C10
Hampton ri Har	24	K19
Hampton rd E4	19	V15
Hampton rd E7	52	G14
Hampton rd E11	51	Y5

Name	Page	Grid
Hampton rd Croy	123	N15
Hampton rd Ilf	54	A13
Hampton rd Tedd	101	P12
Hampton rd Twick	101	R8
Hampton rd Wor Pk	128	H3
Hampton Road east Felt	100	E8
Hampton Road west Felt	100	B6
Hampton st SE1	157	Z6
Hamshades clo Sid	114	M6
Hanah ct SW19	105	O18
Hanameel st E16	77	V3
Hanbury ms N1	142	B6
Hanbury rd N17	31	Z7
Hanbury rd W3	73	T6
Hanbury st E1	143	O20
Hancock rd E3	64	F8
Hancock st SE19	109	O15
Hand ct WC1	149	P2
Handcroft rd Croy	122	J18
Handel clo Edg	11	L18
Handel st WC1	140	K16
Handel way Edg	12	C20
Handen rd SE12	94	C14
Handforth rd SW9	157	S18
Handley rd E9	63	S2
Handowe clo NW4	26	H12
Handside clo Wor Pk	129	P1
Handsworth ave E4	20	J19
Handsworth rd N17	31	P10
Handtrough way Bark	67	N5
Hanford clo SW18	105	Y1
Hanford row SW19	104	M14
Hanger grn W5	61	O11
Hanger la W5	60	K7
Hanger Vale la W3	61	O15
Hanger Vale la W5	61	N16
Hanger View way W3	61	O16
Hankey pl SE1	150	F19
Hankins la NW7	13	N10
Hanley rd N4	48	A5
Hannah clo NW10	43	W12
Hannah ms Wall	131	V16
Hannell rd SW6	152	L18
Hannibal rd E1	63	R13
Hannibal way Croy	132	C14
Hannington rd SW4	89	T8
Hanover clo Rich	73	P19
Hanover clo Sutt	129	U8
Hanover dr Chis	114	B11
Hanover gdns SW11	157	S15
Hanover gdns Ilf	36	B2
Hanover gate NW1	138	M14
Hanover pk SE15	91	X3
Hanover rd N15	31	W13
Hanover rd NW10	136	C3
Hanover rd SW19	106	E17
Hanover sq W1	147	Z6
Hanover st W1	147	Z7
Hanover st Croy	132	K6
Hanover ter NW1	139	N14
Hanover ter Islw	83	Z1
Hanover Terrace ms NW1	139	N15
Hanover way Bexh	97	X8
Hans cres SW1	147	O20
Hans pl SW1	155	P1
Hans rd SW3	155	N1
Hans st SW1	155	P2
Hansard ms W14	144	J18
Hansart way Enf	7	U7
Hanselin clo Stan	10	K17
Hansha dr Edg	25	Y4
Hansler rd SE22	91	V13
Hansol rd Bexh	97	Z12
Hanson clo SW12	89	T19
Hanson gdns Sthl	70	C5
Hanson st W1	148	A1
Hanway pl W1	148	F4
Hanway rd W7	59	R16
Hanway st W1	148	F4
Hanworth rd Hmptn	100	D10
Hanworth rd Houns	82	D20
Hanworth ter Houns	82	K10
Hanworth Trading est Felt	100	B7
Hapgood clo Grnf	41	P15
Harben rd NW6	46	E19
Harberson rd E15	65	P3
Harberson rd SW12	89	S20
Harberton rd N19	47	V4
Harbet rd N18	19	U16
Harbet rd W2	146	J2
Harbex clo Bex	98	G18
Harbinger rd E14	76	D12
Harbledown rd SW6	87	X1
Harbord st SW6	87	P1
Harborough ave Sid	96	J19
Harborough rd SW16	108	D10
Harbour ave SW10	88	D2
Harbour Exchange sq E14	76	E6
Harbour rd SE5	90	L6
Harbridge ave SW15	86	F18
Harbury rd Cars	130	H19
Harbut rd SW11	88	F11
Harcombe rd N16	49	S9
Harcourt ave Edg	12	H12
Harcourt ave Sid	97	T16
Harcourt clo Islw	83	Y6
Harcourt fld Wall	131	T9
Harcourt rd E15	65	P5
Harcourt rd N22	29	X4
Harcourt rd SE4	92	K9
Harcourt rd SW19	105	Y19
Harcourt rd Bexh	98	A9
Harcourt rd Th Hth	122	E14
Harcourt rd Wall	131	S9
Harcourt st W1	146	M1
Harcourt ter SW10	154	A11
Hardcastle clo Croy	123	W14
Hardcourts clo W Wick	135	S7
Hardel ri SW2	108	H3
Hardens Manorway SE7	78	B9
Harders rd SE15	91	Z3
Hardie clo NW10	43	X15
Hardie rd Dag	56	K10
Harding clo SE17	158	A14
Harding rd Bexh	98	A4
Hardinge rd N18	18	E17
Hardinge st E1	63	R18
Hardings la SE20	110	E16
Hardman rd SE7	77	U13
Hardman rd Kings T	116	L3
Hardwick clo Stan	11	R16
Hardwick grn W13	60	B14
Hardwick st EC1	141	U14
Hardwicke ave Houns	82	H1
Hardwicke rd N13	17	N18
Hardwicke rd W4	73	X11
Hardwicke rd Rich	102	C9
Hardwicke st Bark	67	P4
Hardwicks way SW18	87	Z14
Hardwidge st SE1	150	J17
Hardy clo SE16	75	U5
Hardy rd SE3	77	R18
Hardy rd SW19	106	C18
Hardy way Enf	7	U6
Hare & Billet rd SE3	93	W3
Hare Hall la Rom	39	Z12
Hare row E2	143	X7
Hare st SE18	78	K9
Hare wk N1	142	L9
Harecastle clo Hayes	58	B10
Harecourt rd N1	48	L17
Haredale rd SE24	90	M11
Haredon clo SE23	92	E18
Harefield clo Enf	7	U4
Harefield ms SE4	92	K7
Harefield rd N8	29	X15
Harefield rd SE4	92	L8
Harefield rd SW16	108	D19
Harefield rd Sid	115	W6
Haresfield rd Dag	56	F18
Harewood ave NW1	138	M17
Harewood ave Nthlt	58	C1
Harewood clo Nthlt	58	D1
Harewood dr Ilf	35	T7
Harewood pl W1	147	Z6
Harewood rd SW19	106	K16
Harewood rd Islw	71	W20
Harewood rd S Croy	133	S13
Harewood row NW1	138	M20
Harewood ter Sthl	70	F11
Harfield gdns SE5	91	R7
Harford clo E4	20	E2
Harford rd E4	20	E2
Harford st E1	63	V13
Harford wk N2	28	H14
Hargood clo Har	24	L18
Hargood rd SE3	94	L3
Hargrave pk N19	47	U7
Hargrave pl N7	47	X16
Hargrave rd N19	47	W7
Hargwyne st SW9	90	C7
Haringey pk N8	30	A18
Haringey pas N4	30	J17
Haringey pas N8	30	G11
Haringey rd N8	30	A14
Harkett clo Har	23	V7
Harland ave Croy	133	W5
Harland ave Sid	114	E6
Harland rd SE12	94	F20
Harlech rd N14	17	O11
Harlequin ave Brent	71	Z17
Harlequin clo Islw	83	S14
Harlequin rd Tedd	102	B17
Harlescott rd SE15	92	F11
Harlesden gdns NW10	62	D3
Harlesden la NW10	62	F4
Harlesden rd NW10	62	G4
Harley clo Wem	42	G16
Harley cres Har	23	R12
Harley gdns SW10	154	D11
Harley gro E3	63	Z8
Harley pl W1	147	X2
Harley rd NW3	138	J2
Harley rd NW10	62	B6
Harley rd Har	23	R12
Harley st W1	139	W19
Harleyford Brom	112	K20
Harleyford rd SE11	157	N12
Harleyford st SE11	157	S15
Harlington rd Bexh	98	A8
Harlow rd N13	18	A10
Harman ave Wdf Grn	21	P20
Harman clo E4	20	L14
Harman clo NW2	45	U10
Harman dr NW2	45	T11
Harman dr Sid	96	L16
Harman rd Enf	8	G16
Harmony clo NW11	27	T15
Harmony clo Wall	131	Z19
Harmood gro NW1	47	R20
Harmood pl NW1	47	R19
Harmood st NW1	47	R19
Harmsworth st SE17	157	W12
Harmsworth way N20	14	J5
Harness st SE28	79	Z6
Harold ave Belv	81	O14
Harold pl SE11	157	S11
Harold rd E4	20	F12
Harold rd E11	52	A4
Harold rd E13	65	Y3
Harold rd N8	30	B14
Harold rd N15	31	V14
Harold rd NW10	61	X9
Harold rd SE19	109	P18
Harold rd Sutt	130	G9
Harold rd Wdf Grn	34	G4
Haroldstone rd E17	32	G15
Harp la EC3	150	K10
Harp rd W7	59	U12
Harpenden rd E12	52	K6
Harpenden rd SE27	108	J5
Harper rd E6	66	G17
Harper rd SE1	150	B20
Harpley sq E1	63	S10
Harpour rd Bark	54	C18
Harpsden st SW11	89	O3
Harpur ms WC1	141	N20
Harpur st WC1	141	N20
Harraden rd SE3	94	L2
Harrier clo Horn	57	Y18
Harrier ms SE28	79	T7
Harrier rd NW9	26	B7
Harrier way E6	66	G15
Harriers clo W5	60	J20
Harriers clo E8	143	R4
Harriet gdns Croy	133	Y2
Harriet st SW1	147	R19
Harriet wk SW1	147	R18
Harriet way (Bushey) Wat	10	D2
Harringay gdns N8	30	J13
Harringay rd N15	30	J12
Harrington clo Croy	131	Z4
Harrington gdns SW7	154	A7
Harrington hill E5	50	B4
Harrington rd E11	52	A3
Harrington rd SE25	123	Z10
Harrington sq NW1	140	B10
Harrington st NW1	140	A10
Harrington way SE18	78	B8
Harriott clo SE10	77	P12
Harris clo Enf	7	W6
Harris clo Houns	82	G3
Harris rd Bexh	98	A2
Harris rd Dag	56	B16
Harris st E17	50	L2
Harris st SE5	158	H18
Harrison rd Dag	56	G18
Harrison st WC1	140	M14
Harrisons ri Croy	132	J5
Harrold rd Dag	55	R14
Harrow ave Enf	8	H20
Harrow cres Rom	39	Z3
Harrow dr N9	18	G4
Harrow Fields gdns Har	41	V9
Harrow la E14	64	F20
Harrow Manorway SE2	80	G3
Harrow pk Har	41	U6
Harrow pl E1	150	M4
Harrow rd E6	66	E2
Harrow rd E11	52	A9
Harrow rd NW10	136	E14
Harrow rd W2	146	G1
Harrow rd Bark	67	W2
Harrow rd Cars	130	J12
Harrow rd Ilf	53	D13
Harrow rd Wem	43	O15
Harrow vw Har	23	N7
Harrow View rd W5	60	C11
Harrow Weald pk Har	10	D18
Harroway rd SW11	88	G5
Harrowby st W1	146	M4
Harrowdene clo Wem	42	F13
Harrowdene gdns Tedd	101	Z16
Harrowdene rd Wem	42	G10
Harrowes Meade Edg	12	D10
Harrowgate rd E9	50	H19
Hart gro W5	73	P3
Hart gro Sthl	58	H14
Hart st EC3	150	L8
Harte rd Houns	82	F5
Hartfield cres SW19	105	V17
Hartfield gro SE20	110	B20
Hartfield rd SW19	105	W17
Hartfield ter E3	64	B7
Hartford ave Har	24	A10
Hartford rd Bex	98	F16
Hartham clo N7	48	B15
Hartham clo Islw	83	Y2
Hartham rd N7	48	A15
Hartham rd N17	31	U6
Hartham rd Islw	83	X3
Harting rd SE9	113	R8
Hartington clo Har	71	T12
Hartington ct W4	73	U19
Hartington rd E16	65	V17
Hartington rd E17	32	H18
Hartington rd SW8	156	K19
Hartington rd W4	73	U19
Hartington rd W13	60	B20
Hartington rd Sthl	70	B7
Hartington rd Twick	84	B17
Hartismere rd SW6	153	R17
Hartlake rd E9	50	G18
Hartland clo Edg	12	D8

Name	Pg	Ref
Hartland dr Edg	12	C9
Hartland rd E15	52	B20
Hartland rd N11	15	Z16
Hartland rd NW1	47	R20
Hartland rd NW6	137	O7
Hartland rd Hmptn	100	K10
Hartland rd Horn	57	W7
Hartland rd Islw	83	Z7
Hartland rd Mord	119	Z18
Hartland way Croy	134	H3
Hartland way Mord	119	W17
Hartlands clo Bex	98	D16
Hartley ave E6	66	D4
Hartley ave NW7	13	R16
Hartley clo NW7	13	R17
Hartley clo Brom	127	V4
Hartley rd E11	52	D3
Hartley rd Croy	122	K17
Hartley rd Well	80	G19
Hartley st E2	63	S7
Harton clo Brom	113	N20
Harton rd N9	18	N8
Harton st SE8	93	O2
Harts gro Wdf Grn	21	T17
Harts la SE14	92	H1
Harts la Bark	53	Z19
Hartsbourne ave (Bushey) Wat	10	B8
Hartsbourne clo (Bushey) Wat	10	C8
Hartsbourne rd (Bushey) Wat	10	C7
Hartshorn gdns E6	66	K10
Hartslock dr SE2	80	H4
Hartsmead rd SE9	113	U3
Hartsway Enf	9	O14
Hartswood grn (Bushey) Wat	10	B7
Hartswood rd W12	74	D6
Hartsworth clo E13	65	R6
Hartville rd SE18	79	W11
Hartwell dr E4	20	G19
Hartwell st E8	49	U17
Harvard la W4	73	U15
Harvard rd SE13	93	V14
Harvard rd W4	73	T14
Harvard rd Islw	83	T2
Harvard wk Horn	57	V12
Harvel cres SE2	80	K15
Harvesters clo Islw	83	R12
Harvey gdns SE7	77	Z12
Harvey rd E11	52	B3
Harvey rd N8	30	C14
Harvey rd SE5	91	O1
Harvey rd Houns	82	E19
Harvey rd Ilf	24	A15
Harvey st N1	142	H5
Harveys la Rom	57	O5
Harvill rd Sid	115	Y13
Harvist rd NW6	136	G11
Harwich la EC2	142	L20
Harwood ave Brom	126	G3
Harwood ave Mitch	120	K6
Harwood clo Wem	42	G11
Harwood rd SW6	153	V19
Harwood ter SW6	88	A1
Hascombe ter SE5	91	O4
Haselbury rd N9	18	F8
Haselbury rd N18	18	E14
Haseley end SE23	92	D20
Haselrigge rd SW4	89	Z11
Haseltine rd SE26	110	L10
Haselwood dr Enf	7	W13
Haskard rd Dag	55	W13
Hasker st SW3	154	M4
Haslam ave Sutt	119	T19
Haslam clo N1	48	H19
Haslemere ave NW4	27	U16
Haslemere ave SW18	106	A4
Haslemere ave W7	71	Y9
Haslemere ave W13	72	A8
Haslemere ave Barn	15	Y5
Haslemere ave Mitch	120	E4
Haslemere clo Hmptn	100	E12
Haslemere clo Wall	132	A12
Haslemere gdns N3	27	U11
Haslemere rd N8	29	Z20
Haslemere rd N21	17	V7
Haslemere rd Bexh	98	C5
Haslemere rd Ilf	54	K5
Haslemere rd Th Hth	122	J11
Hasler clo SE28	68	E19
Hasluck gdns Barn	5	P18
Hassard st E2	143	P10
Hassendean rd SE3	77	V18
Hassett rd E9	50	G17
Hassocks clo SE26	110	A6
Hassocks rd SW16	121	W1
Hassop rd NW2	45	O11
Hassop wk SE9	113	R9
Hasted rd SE7	78	B12
Hastings ave Ilf	36	C13
Hastings clo SE15	159	S19
Hastings clo Barn	5	R13
Hastings rd N11	16	J16
Hastings rd N17	31	O9
Hastings rd W13	60	B20
Hastings rd Brom	127	S19
Hastings rd Croy	123	U20
Hastings st WC1	140	J14
Hastoe clo Hayes	58	A11
Hatch the Enf	9	T7
Hatch gro Rom	38	A13
Hatch la E4	20	L12
Hatch pl Kings T	103	N12
Hatch rd SW16	122	A3
Hatcham Park ms SE14	92	G1
Hatcham Park rd SE14	92	F1
Hatcham rd SE15	75	P16
Hatchard rd N19	47	Z6
Hatchcroft NW4	26	H11
Hatcliffe clo SE3	94	B8
Hatcliffe st SE10	75	S19
Hatfield clo SE14	75	S19
Hatfield clo Ilf	36	A9
Hatfield clo Mitch	120	E9
Hatfield mead Mord	119	X12
Hatfield rd E15	52	B14
Hatfield rd W4	73	Z5
Hatfield rd W13	71	Y3
Hatfield rd Dag	56	A20
Hatfields SE1	149	V13
Hathaway clo Stan	10	K17
Hathaway cres E12	53	A22
Hathaway gdns W13	59	X14
Hathaway gdns Rom	37	W16
Hathaway rd Croy	122	K19
Hatherleigh clo Mord	119	Y9
Hatherley cres Sid	115	O5
Hatherley gdns E6	66	B17
Hatherley gdns N8	30	A18
Hatherley gro W2	145	Y5
Hatherley rd E17	33	N12
Hatherley rd Rich	85	N3
Hatherley rd Sid	115	O9
Hatherley st SW1	156	D6
Hathern gdns SE9	113	W10
Hatherop rd Hmptn	100	D17
Hathorne clo SE15	92	B4
Hathway st SE15	92	E6
Hatley ave Ilf	36	C13
Hatley clo N11	15	Y15
Hatley rd N4	48	E8
Hattersfield clo Belv	81	P11
Hatton clo SE18	79	S19
Hatton gdn EC1	141	U19
Hatton gdns Mitch	120	L20
Hatton pl EC1	141	U19
Hatton rd Croy	122	G19
Hatton st NW8	138	G18
Hatton wall EC1	141	T19
Haunch of Venison yd W1	147	Y7
Havana rd Rom	39	R17
Havana rd SW19	105	Z5
Havannah st E14	76	B6
Havant rd E17	33	U10
Havelock pl Har	23	U19
Havelock rd N17	31	Y7
Havelock rd SW19	106	C12
Havelock rd Belv	81	P12
Havelock rd Brom	126	L8
Havelock rd Croy	133	V2
Havelock rd Dart	99	Z16
Havelock rd Har	23	T9
Havelock rd Sthl	70	C8
Havelock st N1	140	M4
Havelock st Ilf	54	A7
Havelock ter SW8	155	Z20
Havelock wk SE23	110	D3
Haven the Rich	85	R7
Haven clo SE9	113	T7
Haven clo SW19	105	P6
Haven clo Sid	115	S16
Haven grn W5	60	G18
Haven la W5	60	J18
Haven pl W5	60	H19
Haven st NW1	139	Y1
Havenhurst ri Enf	7	U9
Havenwood Wem	43	U8
Haverfield gdns Rich	73	P18
Haverfield rd E3	63	V8
Haverford way Edg	25	O5
Haverhill rd SW12	107	V1
Havering dr Rom	39	P12
Havering gdns Rom	37	V16
Havering rd Rom	38	M9
Havering st E1	63	S18
Havering way Bark	68	D7
Haversham clo SE9	84	G17
Haversham pl SE19	108	J16
Haverstock hill NW3	46	K16
Haverstock rd NW5	47	N15
Haverstock st N1	141	Z10
Havil st SE5	158	J19
Hawarden gro SE24	90	L18
Hawarden hill NW2	44	G10
Hawarden rd E17	32	F13
Hawbridge rd E11	51	W3
Hawes la W Wick	125	V19
Hawes rd N18	18	M18
Hawes rd Brom	112	G20
Hawes st N1	141	Y2
Hawgood st E3	64	C14
Hawke Park rd N22	30	K9
Hawke rd SE19	109	R14
Hawker clo Wall	132	B17
Hawkes rd Mitch	106	L20
Hawkesbury rd SW15	86	J13
Hawkesfield rd SE23	110	K5
Hawkesley clo Twick	101	X9
Hawkhurst rd SW16	107	Y20
Hawkhurst way N Mal	117	X11
Hawkhurst way W Wick	135	R2
Hawkins clo Har	23	P20
Hawkins clo Tedd	102	B16
Hawkridge clo Rom	37	U19
Hawks rd Kings T	117	N5
Hawksbrook la Beck	125	R14
Hawkshead rd NW10	44	D20
Hawkshead rd W4	74	B7
Hawkslade rd SE15	92	E13
Hawksley rd N16	49	R9
Hawksmoor ms E1	151	W8
Hawksmoor st W6	152	H15
Hawksmouth E4	20	F3
Hawkstone rd SE16	75	R11
Hawkwood mt E5	50	A3
Hawlands dr Pnr	40	B1
Hawley clo Hmptn	100	D15
Hawley cres NW1	139	Y2
Hawley rd NW1	47	T20
Hawley st NW1	47	S20
Hawstead rd SE6	93	R16
Hawsted Buck H	21	W3
Hawthorn ave N13	17	N15
Hawthorn ave Cars	131	P16
Hawthorn ave Th Hth	121	H1
Hawthorn clo Hmptn	100	G13
Hawthorn ct Rich	85	S3
Hawthorn dr Har	22	F19
Hawthorn gdns W5	72	H8
Hawthorn gro SE20	110	A19
Hawthorn gro Enf	8	C4
Hawthorn Hatch Brent	72	C19
Hawthorn ms NW7	27	S5
Hawthorn pl Erith	81	Z14
Hawthorn rd N8	29	Y17
Hawthorn rd N18	18	G17
Hawthorn rd NW10	44	H19
Hawthorn rd Bexh	98	C12
Hawthorn rd Brent	72	B20
Hawthorn rd Sutt	130	H13
Hawthorn rd Wall	131	R16
Hawthorn way N9	18	F9
Hawthorne ave Har	24	A17
Hawthorne ave Mitch	120	G3
Hawthorne clo N1	49	S17
Hawthorne clo Brom	127	T7
Hawthorne Farm ave Nthlt	58	C3
Hawthorne gro NW9	25	W20
Hawthorne rd E17	33	O10
Hawthorne rd Brom	127	S7
Hawthorns Wdf Grn	21	S10
Hawthorns the Epsom	128	F16
Hawtrey rd NW3	138	J1
Hay clo E15	52	B20
Hay Currie st E14	64	F16
Hay hill W1	147	Z11
Hay la NW9	25	W13
Hay st E2	143	U7
Hayburn way Horn	57	U3
Haycroft gdns NW10	62	H4
Haycroft rd SW2	90	B13
Hayday rd E16	65	S14
Hayden way Rom	38	L7
Haydens pl W11	145	N5
Haydns ms W3	61	W18
Haydock ave Nthlt	40	F17
Haydock grn Nthlt	40	G17
Haydon clo NW9	25	W14
Haydon clo Enf	8	D18
Haydon Park rd SW19	105	Z12
Haydon st EC3	151	O7
Haydons rd SW19	106	B12
Hayes chase W Wick	125	Y15
Hayes cres NW11	27	V15
Hayes cres Sutt	129	P7
Hayes dr Rain	57	Y20
Hayes hill Brom	125	Z20
Hayes Hill rd Brom	126	B20
Hayes la Beck	125	U8
Hayes la Brom	126	J10
Hayes Mead rd Brom	126	A20
Hayes pl NW1	138	M19
Hayes rd Brom	126	F8
Hayes st Brom	126	H19
Hayes way Beck	125	U8
Hayes Wood ave Brom	126	H19
Hayesford Park dr Brom	126	D12
Haygarth pl SW19	105	R14
Haygreen clo Kings T	103	T16
Hayland clo NW9	25	Y13
Hayles st SE11	157	X3
Haylett gdns Kings T	116	H10
Haymarket SW1	148	F11
Haymer gdns Wor Pk	128	H5
Haymerle rd SE15	159	S15
Haymill clo Grnf	59	V8
Hayne rd Beck	124	L3
Hayne st EC1	141	Z20
Haynes clo N17	32	A1
Haynes clo SE3	94	A8
Haynes la SE19	109	S16
Haynes rd Wem	42	K19
Haynt wk SW20	119	T6
Hay's la SE1	150	H13
Hay's ms W1	147	X11
Haysleigh gdns SE20	123	Y4

Name	Page	Grid
Haysoms clo Rom	39	P13
Hayter rd SW2	90	B12
Hayward clo SW19	106	B19
Hayward clo Dart	99	O13
Hayward gdns SW15	87	N16
Hayward rd N20	15	R8
Hayward's pl EC1	141	W17
Haywood rd Brom	127	O8
Hayworth clo Enf	9	W9
Hazel clo N13	18	A11
Hazel clo Brent	72	C18
Hazel clo Croy	124	F19
Hazel clo Horn	57	Y10
Hazel clo Mitch	121	Z9
Hazel clo Twick	83	O18
Hazel dr Erith	99	Y1
Hazel gdns Edg	12	E13
Hazel gro SE26	110	G11
Hazel gro Rom	37	Y9
Hazel gro Wem	60	K4
Hazel Grove est SE26	110	G10
Hazel la Rich	102	J4
Hazel la NW10	136	A13
Hazel rd Erith	99	X2
Hazel wk Brom	127	X16
Hazel way E4	19	Y17
Hazelbank rd SE6	111	X5
Hazelbourne rd SW12	89	T16
Hazelbrouck gdns Ilf	36	F1
Hazelbury rd SW19	119	Z3
Hazelbury grn N9	18	F12
Hazelbury la N9	18	F11
Hazeldean rd NW10	61	Z1
Hazeldene rd Ilf	55	R5
Hazeldene rd Well	97	T5
Hazeldon rd SE4	92	J13
Hazelgreen clo N21	17	X4
Hazelhurst Beck	125	W2
Hazelhurst rd SW17	106	E9
Hazell cres Rom	38	G3
Hazellville rd N19	47	X1
Hazelmere clo Nthlt	58	E5
Hazelmere dr Nthlt	58	F6
Hazelmere rd NW6	137	S4
Hazelmere rd Nthlt	58	F5
Hazelmere wk Nthlt	58	E5
Hazelmere way Brom	126	E15
Hazeltree la Nthlt	58	C9
Hazelwood ave Mord	120	B9
Hazelwood clo W5	72	K4
Hazelwood clo Har	22	J13
Hazelwood ct NW10	43	Y9
Hazelwood cres N13	17	U12
Hazelwood cres W10	137	N17
Hazelwood cft Surb	116	K14
Hazelwood la N13	17	T12
Hazelwood rd E17	32	H15
Hazelwood rd Enf	8	H18
Hazlebury rd SW6	88	A4
Hazledean rd Croy	133	P4
Hazledene rd W4	73	V16
Hazlemere gdns Wor Pk	118	H20
Hazlewell rd SW15	86	M12
Hazlitt rd W14	152	K3
Head st E1	63	T16
Headcorn rd N17	31	U2
Headcorn rd Brom	112	D12
Headcorn rd Th Hth	122	D9
Headfort pl SW1	147	V19
Headington rd SW18	106	E3
Headlam rd SW4	89	X17
Headlam st E1	143	Y18
Headley app Ilf	35	Y17
Headley ave Wall	132	D10
Headley ct SE26	110	B12
Headley dr Croy	135	S17
Headley dr Ilf	35	Z17
Head's ms W11	145	U6
Headstone dr Har	23	N17
Headstone gdns Har	23	N12
Headstone la Har	22	K2
Headstone rd Har	23	S16
Headway the Epsom	128	D20
Heald st SE14	93	N1
Healey st NW1	47	S18
Hearn st EC2	142	K18
Hearne rd W4	73	P15
Hearnville rd SW12	107	O1
Heath ave Bexh	80	K17
Heath brow NW3	46	D8
Heath clo NW11	46	A2
Heath clo W5	61	O12
Heath clo Rom	39	W9
Heath dr NW3	45	Z13
Heath dr SW20	119	N8
Heath dr Sutt	130	C19
Heath gdns Twick	101	V2
Heath Hurst rd NW3	46	H13
Heath la SE3	93	Y5
Heath mead SW19	105	O6
Heath Park rd Brom	127	P5
Heath Park rd Rom	39	X15
Heath ri Brom	126	D14
Heath ri SW8	89	T6
Heath rd Dart	99	U17
Heath rd Har	23	N20
Heath rd Houns	82	L11
Heath rd Rom	55	X1
Heath rd Th Hth	122	M6
Heath rd Twick	101	V2
Heath side NW3	46	G11
Heath st NW3	46	E10
Heath View clo N2	28	E11
Heath View clo N2	28	D12
Heath vill SE18	79	X15
Heath way Erith	98	L2
Heatham pk Twick	83	V20
Heathbourne rd (Bushey) Wat	10	H5
Heathclose ave Dart	99	Y19
Heathclose rd Dart	99	X20
Heathcote ave Ilf	35	U6
Heathcote gro E4	20	F10
Heathcote rd Twick	84	C15
Heathcote st WC1	141	N15
Heathcroft NW11	46	C2
Heathcroft W5	61	N12
Heathdale ave Houns	82	B8
Heathdene rd SW16	108	C18
Heathdene rd Wall	131	R17
Heathedge SE26	110	A5
Heather ave Rom	39	O6
Heather clo E6	66	L18
Heather clo SW8	89	S7
Heather clo Hmptn	100	F20
Heather clo Islw	83	R12
Heather clo Rom	39	O5
Heather dr Dart	99	V18
Heather dr Enf	7	W7
Heather dr Rom	39	P6
Heather gdns NW11	27	S18
Heather gdns Rom	39	O6
Heather gdns Sutt	129	X15
Heather glen Rom	39	O7
Heather Park dr Wem	61	R2
Heather rd NW2	44	E7
Heather rd SE12	112	F3
Heather wk Edg	12	F15
Heather way Rom	39	O5
Heather way S Croy	134	F19
Heather way Stan	10	J19
Heatherbank SE9	95	V5
Heatherbank Chis	127	Y3
Heatherbank clo Dart	99	R16
Heatherdale clo Kings T	103	R16
Heatherdene clo Mitch	120	H10
Heatherley dr Ilf	35	T10
Heatherset gdns SW16	108	C19
Heatherside rd Sid	115	V6
Heatherwood clo E12	52	K7
Heathfield E4	20	G9
Heathfield Chis	114	C16
Heathfield ave SW18	88	G17
Heathfield clo E16	66	A13
Heathfield dr Mitch	106	J20
Heathfield gdns NW11	27	P19
Heathfield gdns SW18	88	F15
Heathfield gdns W4	73	W14
Heathfield la Chis	114	B14
Heathfield north Twick	83	V18
Heathfield pk NW2	44	M19
Heathfield rd SW18	88	F16
Heathfield rd W3	73	S6
Heathfield rd Bexh	98	B11
Heathfield rd Brom	112	D18
Heathfield rd Croy	133	N10
Heathfield south Twick	83	V18
Heathfield sq SW18	88	G19
Heathfield ter SE18	79	W16
Heathfield ter W4	73	W13
Heathfield vale S Croy	134	G19
Heathfields ct Houns	82	C12
Heathgate NW11	28	A18
Heathland rd N16	49	R3
Heathlands clo Twick	101	V3
Heathlands ri Dart	99	Y17
Heathlands way Houns	82	C13
Heathlee rd SE3	94	C10
Heathlee rd Dart	99	R16
Heathley end Chis	114	C15
Heathmans rd SW6	87	W2
Heaths clo Enf	8	D9
Heathside Houns	82	C13
Heathside ave Bexh	98	A3
Heathstan rd W12	62	H18
Heathurst rd S Croy	133	R10
Heathview ave Dart	99	S17
Heathview clo SW19	105	O3
Heathview cres Dart	99	X20
Heathview dr SE2	80	H16
Heathview gdns SW15	86	L19
Heathview rd Th Hth	122	F9
Heathville rd N19	48	A2
Heathwall st SW11	88	M7
Heathway SE3	77	S20
Heathway Croy	134	M4
Heathway Dag	56	D9
Heathway Wdf Grn	21	Z15
Heathwood gdns SE7	78	D13
Heaton ave Rom	39	Z1
Heaton Grange rd Rom	39	U6
Heaton rd SE15	91	Y6
Heaton rd Mitch	107	O18
Heavitree rd SE18	79	R15
Hebdon rd SW17	106	K7
Heber rd NW2	45	O13
Heber rd SE22	91	V15
Hebron rd W6	152	A2
Hecham clo E17	32	H6
Heckfield pl SW6	153	T19
Hector st SE18	79	U12
Heddington gro N7	48	C14
Heddon clo Islw	83	Y9
Heddon Court ave Barn	6	B15
Heddon rd Barn	5	Z16
Heddon st W1	148	B9
Hedge hill Enf	7	W6
Hedge la N13	17	X11
Hedgeley Ilf	35	T13
Hedgeley st SE12	94	E19
Hedgemans rd Dag	55	W20
Hedgemans way Dag	55	Z19
Hedgerley gdns Grnf	58	M7
Hedgers gro E9	50	H18
Hedgewood gdns Ilf	35	W14
Hedingham clo N1	142	A2
Hedingham rd Dag	55	R16
Hedley rd Twick	82	G18
Heene rd Enf	8	B7
Heigham rd E6	66	C2
Heighton gdns Croy	132	J11
Heights the SE7	77	Z14
Heights the Nthlt	58	A2
Heights clo SW20	104	K19
Heiron st SE17	157	Z14
Helby rd SW4	89	Y17
Helder gro SE12	94	D19
Helder st S Croy	133	O14
Heldmann clo Hours	83	R10
Helen clo Dart	99	Z18
Helena clo Barn	5	U1
Helena clo Wall	132	B17
Helena rd E13	65	S7
Helena rd E17	33	N16
Helena rd NW10	44	J14
Helena rd W5	60	H13
Helen's pl E2	63	P8
Helenslea ave NW11	45	X4
Helix gdns SW2	90	D15
Helix rd SW2	90	E15
Hellings st E1	151	U14
Helme clo SW19	105	V12
Helmet row EC1	142	C15
Helmsdale clo Rom	39	R1
Helmsdale rd SW16	107	W20
Helmsdale rd Rom	39	R1
Helmsley pl E8	143	X1
Helston clo Pnr	22	E3
Helvetia st SE6	110	L5
Hemans st SW8	156	H18
Hemberton rd SW9	90	A7
Hemery rd Grnf	41	P14
Heming rd Edg	12	E20
Hemingford rd N1	141	R5
Hemingford rd Sutt	129	N9
Hemington ave N11	15	Y16
Hemlock rd W12	62	E20
Hemming st E1	143	V17
Hemp wk SE17	158	G6
Hempstead clo Buck H	21	S7
Hempstead rd E17	33	X8
Hemstal rd NW6	45	Y19
Hemswell dr NW9	26	A4
Hemsworth ct N1	142	J7
Hemsworth st N1	142	J7
Hemus pl SW3	154	L10
Henchman st W12	62	D17
Hendale ave NW4	26	H10
Henderson clo NW10	43	W16
Henderson clo Horn	57	Z5
Henderson dr NW8	138	G15
Henderson rd E7	52	K17
Henderson rd N9	18	M4
Henderson rd SW18	88	H18
Henderson rd Croy	123	N14
Hendham rd SW17	106	K4
Hendon ave N3	27	T5
Hendon la N3	27	R11
Hendon Park row NW11	27	V17
Hendon rd N9	18	L7
Hendon way NW2	45	R2
Hendon way NW4	26	L17
Hendon Wood la NW7	13	S1
Hendre rd SE1	158	L7
Hendren clo Grnf	41	R15
Hendrick ave SW12	89	N18
Heneage st E1	151	R1
Henfield clo N19	47	W5
Henfield clo Bex	98	F15
Henfield rd SW19	119	U1
Hengelo gdns Mitch	120	F10
Hengist rd SE12	94	J18
Hengist rd Erith	81	W19
Hengist way Brom	125	Y9
Hengrave rd SE23	92	E17
Hengrove ct Bex	115	Z1
Henley ave Sutt	129	S4
Henley clo Grnf	59	O6
Henley clo Islw	83	V3
Henley ct N14	16	G3
Henley dr SE1	159	P4
Henley dr Kings T	104	C17
Henley gdns Rom	37	Z14
Henley rd E16	78	H5
Henley rd N18	19	D13
Henley rd NW10	136	D3
Henley rd Ilf	54	B13
Henley st SW11	89	P4
Hennel clo SE23	110	E7
Henniker gdns E6	66	C8
Henniker ms SW3	154	E12
Henniker rd E15	51	X15

Henning st SW11	88	J3
Henningham rd N17	31	O4
Henrietta ms WC1	140	L15
Henriston ave N8	30	A15
Henrietta pl W1	147	X5
Henrietta st E15	51	V15
Henrietta st WC2	148	L9
Henriques st E1	151	U5
Henry Cooper way SE9	113	N8
Henry Darlot dr NW7	14	C17
Henry Dickens ct W11	144	J11
Henry Jackson rd SW15	87	O8
Henry rd E6	66	E5
Henry rd N4	48	K5
Henry rd Barn	5	U16
Henry st Brom	112	J20
Henry's ave Wdf Grn	21	O17
Henry's wk Ilf	36	D1
Henryson rd SE4	93	N13
Hensford gdns SE26	110	A9
Henshall st N1	49	P18
Henshaw st SE17	158	E5
Henshawe rd Dag	55	X8
Henslowe rd SE22	91	Y14
Henson ave NW2	44	M14
Henson path Har	24	G11
Henstridge pl NW8	138	J7
Henty wk SW15	86	J14
Henville rd Brom	126	K2
Henwick rd SE9	95	P8
Hepple clo Islw	84	A5
Hepplestone clo SW15	86	K16
Hepscott rd E9	51	N19
Hepworth gdns Bark	55	N14
Hepworth SW16	108	B19
Herald gdns Wall	131	S4
Herald st E2	143	Z15
Herald's ct SE11	157	V6
Herald's pl SE11	157	V6
Herbal hill EC1	141	U18
Herbert cres SW1	155	P1
Herbert gdns NW10	136	A9
Herbert gdns W4	73	T17
Herbert rd E12	53	R13
Herbert rd E17	32	L20
Herbert rd N11	17	N20
Herbert rd N15	31	V15
Herbert rd NW9	26	F19
Herbert rd SE18	78	K19
Herbert rd SW19	105	W18
Herbert rd Bark	98	A5
Herbert rd Brom	127	P11
Herbert rd Ilf	54	H6
Herbert rd Kings T	116	M7
Herbert rd Sthl	70	E2
Herbert st E13	65	U7
Herbert st NW5	47	O16
Herbert ter SE18	78	M18
Herbrand st WC1	140	J16
Hercules SE1	157	R3
Hercules st N7	48	B10
Hereford ave Barn	15	Z6
Hereford gdns Ilf	35	S20
Hereford gdns Pnr	22	B15
Hereford gdns Twick	101	N2
Hereford ms W2	145	W6
Hereford pl SE14	75	Y19
Hereford Retreat SE15	159	S16
Hereford rd E11	34	J15
Hereford rd W2	145	V4
Hereford rd W3	61	U19
Hereford rd W5	72	E8
Hereford sq SW7	154	D7
Hereford st E2	143	T15
Herent dr Ilf	35	S11
Hereward gdns N13	17	U17
Hereward rd SW17	106	L9
Herga ct Har	41	U8
Herga rd Har	23	W12
Heriot ave E4	20	A8
Heriot rd NW4	27	N15
Heriots clo Stan	10	M12
Heritage vw Har	41	X8
Herlwyn gdns SW17	106	L9

Hermes st N1	141	S10
Hermes way Wall	131	Z16
Hermiston ave N8	30	A15
Hermit pl NW6	137	W5
Hermit rd E16	65	P10
Hermit st EC1	141	W12
Hermitage the SE23	110	C1
Hermitage the SW13	86	E3
Hermitage the Rich	84	J13
Hermitage clo E18	34	D13
Hermitage clo Enf	7	W9
Hermitage ct E18	34	E12
Hermitage gdns NW2	45	X9
Hermitage la NW2	45	W9
Hermitage la Croy	123	W16
Hermitage rd N4	30	K20
Hermitage rd N15	31	O17
Hermitage rd SE19	109	N17
Hermitage st W2	146	F2
Hermitage wk E18	34	D12
Hermitage wall SE1	151	U14
Hermitage way Stan	23	Y4
Hermon hill E11	34	F15
Herndon rd SW18	88	C13
Herne clo NW10	43	Y16
Herne hill SE24	90	L14
Herne Hill rd SE24	90	L8
Herne ms N18	18	L14
Herne pl SE24	90	J14
Heron clo E17	32	L6
Heron clo NW10	44	B18
Heron clo Buck H	21	T4
Heron ct Brom	126	L10
Heron cres Sid	114	H8
Heron Flight ave SE2	57	X19
Heron hill Belv	81	R13
Heron ms Ilf	53	Y7
Heron pl SE16	75	X2
Heron quay E14	76	B3
Heron rd SE24	90	L10
Heron rd Croy	133	T2
Heron rd Twick	84	A11
Herondale ave SW18	106	G2
Herongate rd E12	52	L6
Heron's pl Islw	84	A8
Heronsforde SW13	60	D16
Heronsgate Edg	12	D17
Heronslea dr Stan	11	W15
Heronway Wdf Grn	21	Z14
Herrick rd N5	48	L9
Herrick st SW1	156	H4
Herries st W10	136	M10
Herringham rd SE7	77	Z9
Hersant clo NW10	62	H2
Herschell rd SE23	92	K19
Hersham clo SW15	86	H20
Hertford ave SW14	85	Z12
Hertford clo Barn	5	T11
Hertford pl W1	140	B19
Hertford rd N1	142	L3
Hertford rd N2	28	J9
Hertford rd N9	18	L8
Hertford rd Bark	53	Y20
Hertford rd Barn	5	S11
Hertford rd Enf	9	P13
Hertford rd Ilf	36	H18
Hertford st W1	147	X13
Hertford way Mitch	121	Z10
Hertslet rd N7	48	C10
Hertsmere rd E14	76	A1
Hervey clo N3	27	Y4
Hervey Park rd E17	32	J12
Hervey rd SE3	94	J1
Hesketh pl W11	144	K9
Hesketh rd E7	52	E10
Heslop rd SW12	107	N1
Hesper ms SW5	153	Y8
Hesperus cres E14	76	D12
Hessel rd W13	71	Z6
Hessel st E1	151	V5
Hester rd N18	18	K17
Hester rd SW11	154	L18
Hestercombe ave SW6	87	T3

Heston ave Houns	70	C18
Heston Grange la Houns	70	D17
Heston rd Houns	70	G17
Heston st SE14	93	N2
Hetherington rd SW4	90	A10
Hetley gdns SE19	109	U18
Hetley rd W12	74	J4
Heton gdns NW4	26	H12
Hevelius clo SE10	77	O13
Hever cft SE9	113	X11
Hever gdns Brom	127	W5
Heverham rd SE18	79	V11
Heversham rd Bexh	98	E4
Hewer st W10	136	H20
Hewett clo Stan	11	O14
Hewett rd Dag	55	V14
Hewett st EC2	142	K17
Hewish rd N18	18	D13
Hewitt ave N22	30	H8
Hewitt rd N8	30	G15
Hewlett rd E3	63	W5
Hexagon the N6	47	N4
Hexal rd SE6	111	Z6
Hexham gdns Islw	71	Z19
Hexham rd SE27	108	L4
Hexham rd Barn	5	O13
Hexham rd Mord	119	Z19
Heybourne rd N17	32	A1
Heybridge ave SW16	108	B17
Heybridge dr Ilf	36	E9
Heybridge way E10	50	K2
Heyford ave SW8	156	M17
Heyford ave SW20	119	W7
Heyford rd Mitch	120	K3
Heygate st SE17	158	B6
Heynes rd Dag	55	U11
Heysham la NW3	46	B10
Heysham rd N15	31	P19
Heythrop st SW18	105	W1
Heywood ave NW9	26	A4
Heyworth rd E5	50	A11
Heyworth rd E15	52	B13
Hibbert rd E17	50	L2
Hibbert rd Har	23	W7
Hibbert st SW11	88	E9
Hibernia gdns Houns	82	H11
Hibernia rd Houns	82	H9
Hichisson rd SE15	92	E12
Hickin clo SE7	78	A11
Hickling rd Ilf	54	A14
Hickman ave E4	20	G17
Hickman clo E16	66	A15
Hickman rd Rom	37	U20
Hickmore wk SW4	89	W7
Hickory clo N9	18	J3
Hicks ave Grnf	59	S7
Hicks clo SW11	88	H6
Hicks st SE8	75	V13
Hidcote gdns SW20	118	J5
Hide pl SW1	156	F7
Hide rd Har	23	P13
High Beech S Croy	133	T16
High Beeches Sid	115	Z12
High bri SE10	76	K14
High Broom cres W Wick	125	S18
High Cedar dr SW20	104	L18
High Coombe pl Kings T	103	X17
High Cross rd N17	31	W11
High dr N Mal	117	W1
High Elms Wdf Grn	21	S16
High gro SE18	79	T20
High gro Brom	126	M1
High Holborn WC1	148	L4
High la W7	59	R16
High Lawns Har	41	T8
High Level dr SE26	109	W10
High mead Har	23	U15
High mead W Wick	135	Y3
High Meadow cres NW9	25	X16
High Meads rd E16	66	A16
High mt NW4	26	G18
High Oaks Enf	7	N4
High Park ave Rich	85	P3
High Park rd Rich	85	R3

High path SW19	106	B20
High pt SE9	114	A7
High rd E18	34	E7
High rd N2	28	H8
High rd N11	16	E15
High rd N12	15	R12
High rd N15	31	U19
High rd N17	31	V2
High rd N20	15	P1
High rd N22	30	E7
High rd (Willesden) NW10	44	D17
High rd Buck H	21	V9
High rd (Harrow Weald) Har	23	S2
High rd Ilf	54	D7
High rd Loug	21	Y2
High rd Rom	55	T1
High rd (Bushey) Wat	10	D6
High rd Wem	42	K15
High rd Wdf Grn	34	D1
High Road Leyton E10	33	S19
High Road Leyton E15	51	V11
High Road Leytonstone E11	51	Z12
High Road Leytonstone E15	51	Z12
High st E11	34	E15
High st E13	65	T6
High st E15	64	H4
High st E17	32	K15
High st N8	30	A12
High st N14	16	K6
High st NW7	13	X15
High st (Harlesden) NW10	62	D5
High st SE20	110	C17
High st (South Norwood) SE25	123	W8
High st (Colliers Wd) SW19	106	G17
High st (Wimbledon) SW19	105	P13
High st W3	73	U3
High st W5	72	G1
High st Barn	4	G11
High st Beck	125	O2
High st Brent	72	E19
High st Brom	126	E2
High st Cars	131	O10
High st Chis	113	Z14
High st Croy	132	M5
High st Edg	12	B18
High st (Ponders End) Enf	9	P16
High st (Ewell) Epsom	128	F20
High st Hmptn	101	O14
High st Har	41	T5
High st (Wealdstone) Har	23	T6
High st Houns	82	K8
High st Ilf	36	C9
High st Kings T	116	H6
High st Kings T (Hampton Wick)	116	F1
High st N Mal	118	B7
High st Pnr	22	B11
High st Rom	39	P15
High st Sthl	70	F2
High st Sutt	130	E8
High st (Cheam) Sutt	129	T15
High st Tedd	101	X13
High st Th Hth	123	O9
High st (Whitton) Twick	83	N19
High st Wem	43	N12
High st W Wick	135	R1
High Street ms SW19	105	S13
High Street north E6	66	E2
High Street north E12	53	R14
High Street south E6	66	F4
High Tor clo Brom	112	G19
High Trees SW2	108	F1
High Trees Barn	5	X15
High Trees Croy	124	J19

Name	Page	Grid
High View clo SE19	123	U4
High View rd E18	34	B8
High View rd Sid	115	R9
High Worple Har	40	E3
Higham Hill rd E17	32	H5
Higham pl E17	32	J9
Higham rd N17	31	N10
Higham rd Wdf Grn	21	S19
Higham Station ave E4	20	C19
Higham st E17	32	J9
Highams Lodge Business cen E17	32	G10
Highams Park Industrial est E4	20	G18
Highbanks clo Well	80	C20
Highbarrow rd Croy	123	W19
Highbridge rd Bark	66	M2
Highbrook rd SE3	95	N7
Highbury ave Th Hth	122	H4
Highbury clo N Mal	117	W10
Highbury clo W Wick	135	S4
Highbury cres N5	48	H15
Highbury est N5	48	H15
Highbury gdns Ilf	54	H6
Highbury gra N5	48	K12
Highbury gro N5	48	K14
Highbury hill N5	48	G10
Highbury ms N7	48	G16
Highbury New pk N5	48	M10
Highbury pk N5	48	K11
Highbury pl N5	48	H17
Highbury quadrant N5	48	K10
Highbury rd SW19	105	T13
Highbury Station rd N1	48	G18
Highbury ter N5	48	J15
Highbury Terrace ms N5	48	H15
Highclere rd N Mal	117	Y7
Highclere st SE26	110	H10
Highcliffe dr SW15	86	D16
Highcliffe gdns Ilf	35	R16
Highcombe SE7	77	W16
Highcombe clo SE9	113	P2
Highcroft NW9	26	A14
Highcroft ave Wem	61	O2
Highcroft gdns NW11	27	V18
Highcroft rd N19	48	A2
Highdaun dr N6	122	C8
Highdown Wor Pk	128	B2
Highdown rd SW15	86	J15
Highfield ave NW9	25	W15
Highfield ave NW11	27	P20
Highfield ave Erith	81	W17
Highfield ave Grnf	41	U14
Highfield ave Pnr	22	C16
Highfield ave Wem	42	L8
Highfield clo NW9	25	W15
Highfield clo Surb	116	E20
Highfield ct N14	6	H19
Highfield dr Brom	126	B8
Highfield dr Epsom	128	D14
Highfield dr W Wick	135	T4
Highfield gdns NW11	27	R19
Highfield hill SE19	109	P18
Highfield rd N21	17	X6
Highfield rd NW11	27	T18
Highfield rd W3	61	U14
Highfield rd Bexh	98	C13
Highfield rd Brom	127	T9
Highfield rd Islw	83	V2
Highfield rd Surb	117	U17
Highfield rd Sutt	130	J11
Highfield rd Wdf Grn	35	R2
Highfields gdns N6	47	N4
Highgate ave N6	29	S20
Highgate clo N6	47	P2
Highgate High st N6	47	P3
Highgate hill N19	47	T4
Highgate NW5	47	P9
Highgate wk SE23	110	C3
Highgate West hill N6	47	P3
Highgrove clo Chis	113	S20
Highgrove rd Dag	55	T14
Highland ave W7	59	T16
Highland ave Dag	56	K9
Highland cotts Wall	131	T10
Highland cft Beck	111	R14
Highland rd SE19	109	S14
Highland rd Bexh	98	F12
Highland rd Brom	112	B20
Highlands the Edg	25	T6
Highlands ave W3	61	V20
Highlands clo Houns	82	K3
Highlands gdns Ilf	53	T3
Highlands heath SW15	86	M20
Highlands rd Barn	4	M15
Highlea clo NW9	26	B3
Highlever rd W10	144	C1
Highmead SE18	79	X19
Highmead cres Wem	43	N20
Highmore rd SE3	77	N18
Highshore rd SE15	91	W3
Highstone ave E11	34	E19
Highview ave Edg	12	G14
Highview ave Wall	132	C11
Highview gdns N3	27	S11
Highview gdns N11	16	H17
Highview gdns Edg	12	H15
Highview rd SE19	109	P16
Highview rd W13	59	Y15
Highway the E1	151	V10
Highway the E14	63	S20
Highway the Stan	23	X3
Highway the Sutt	130	E18
Highwood ave N12	15	R13
Highwood gdns Ilf	35	U14
Highwood gro NW7	12	M15
Highwood hill NW7	13	S9
Highwood rd N19	47	Z9
Highworth rd N11	16	L17
Hilary ave Mitch	121	O5
Hilary clo SW6	153	X18
Hilary clo Erith	98	J2
Hilary rd W12	62	E18
Hilbert rd Sutt	129	P7
Hilda rd E6	53	O20
Hilda rd E16	65	O11
Hildenborough gdns Brom	112	B14
Hildenlea pl Brom	125	Y4
Hildreth st SW12	107	R1
Hildyard rd SW6	153	U14
Hiley rd NW10	136	B11
Hilgrove rd NW6	138	D1
Hiliary gdns Stan	24	E8
Hill brow Brom	113	P20
Hill brow Dart	99	U16
Hill clo NW2	44	J10
Hill clo NW11	27	Z18
Hill clo Chis	113	Y12
Hill clo Har	41	T10
Hill clo Stan	11	O14
Hill cres N20	15	N7
Hill cres Har	23	Y16
Hill cres Surb	117	N11
Hill cres Wor Pk	129	N4
Hill Crest Sid	97	P19
Hill Crest gdns N3	27	S12
Hill dr NW9	43	U4
Hill dr SW16	122	C6
Hill Farm rd W10	136	E20
Hill gro Rom	39	P9
Hill House clo N21	17	T2
Hill House rd SW16	108	C13
Hill path SW16	108	D13
Hill ri N9	9	N19
Hill ri NW11	28	C13
Hill ri SE23	110	B2
Hill ri Grnf	59	N2
Hill ri Rich	84	H14
Hill rd N10	29	N6
Hill rd NW8	138	D10
Hill rd Cars	130	K14
Hill rd Har	23	Y16
Hill rd Mitch	107	S20
Hill rd Pnr	22	A16
Hill rd Sutt	130	B12
Hill rd Wem	42	A8
Hill st W1	147	V12
Hill st Rich	84	G13
Hill Top NW11	28	B12
Hill View dr Well	96	G5
Hill View gdns NW9	25	Z15
Hill View rd Twick	83	Y16
Hillary ri Barn	4	L13
Hillary rd Sthl	70	G7
Hillbeck clo SE15	159	Z16
Hillbeck way Grnf	59	P3
Hillborough clo SW19	106	C19
Hillbrook rd SW17	107	N8
Hillbrow N Mal	118	E7
Hillbrow rd Brom	111	Z17
Hillbury ave Har	24	C16
Hillbury rd SW17	107	S7
Hillcote ave SW16	108	E19
Hillcourt ave N12	15	N18
Hillcourt rd SE22	91	Z17
Hillcrest N21	17	V1
Hillcrest N6	29	P20
Hillcrest ave NW11	27	V14
Hillcrest ave Edg	12	F13
Hillcrest clo SE26	109	X11
Hillcrest clo Beck	124	L13
Hillcrest gdns NW2	44	F10
Hillcrest rd E17	33	Y7
Hillcrest rd E18	34	D6
Hillcrest rd W3	73	S3
Hillcrest rd W5	60	L13
Hillcrest rd Brom	112	E12
Hillcrest rd Dart	99	S18
Hillcrest rd Horn	39	W20
Hillcrest vw Beck	124	K14
Hillcroft ave Pnr	22	E19
Hillcroft cres W5	60	J16
Hillcroft cres Wem	43	N12
Hillcroft rd E6	66	L14
Hillcroome rd Sutt	130	G13
Hillcross ave Mord	119	P14
Hilldale rd Sutt	129	W9
Hilldown rd SW16	108	B18
Hilldown rd Brom	126	B19
Hilldrop cres N7	47	Y15
Hilldrop la N7	47	Y15
Hilldrop rd N7	47	X14
Hilldrop rd Brom	112	G15
Hillend SE18	95	Y3
Hillersdon ave SW13	86	F4
Hillersdon ave Edg	12	A15
Hillery clo SE17	158	G6
Hillfield ave N8	30	B15
Hillfield ave NW9	26	B14
Hillfield ave Mord	120	H14
Hillfield ave Wem	42	L19
Hillfield clo Har	23	N13
Hillfield ct NW3	46	J16
Hillfield pk N10	29	S15
Hillfield pk N21	17	S11
Hillfield rd NW6	45	W15
Hillfield rd Hmptn	100	D19
Hillfoot ave Rom	38	K5
Hillfoot rd Rom	38	K5
Hillgate pl SW12	89	S17
Hillgate pl W8	145	T13
Hillgate st W8	145	T12
Hilliards ct E1	151	Z13
Hillier clo Barn	5	N19
Hillier gdns Croy	132	G11
Hillier rd SW11	89	N15
Hilliers la Croy	131	Z7
Hillingdon rd Bexh	98	K6
Hillingdon st SE5	157	X16
Hillingdon st SE17	158	A14
Hillington gdns Wdf Grn	35	O7
Hillside clo Mord	119	T9
Hillside clo Wdf Grn	21	Y16
Hillside cres Enf	8	B2
Hillside cres Har	40	M5
Hillside dr Edg	12	B17
Hillside est N15	31	U19
Hillside gdns E17	33	X9
Hillside gdns N6	29	R19
Hillside gdns SW2	108	E4
Hillside gdns Barn	4	E14
Hillside gdns Edg	12	A13
Hillside gdns Har	42	L11
Hillside gdns Wall	131	V17
Hillside gro N14	16	K3
Hillside gro NW7	13	T20
Hillside rd N15	31	T20
Hillside rd SW2	108	E5
Hillside rd W5	60	K15
Hillside rd Brom	126	B5
Hillside rd Croy	132	J9
Hillside rd Dart	99	V16
Hillside rd Sthl	58	F11
Hillside rd Surb	117	O11
Hillside rd Sutt	129	V17
Hillsleigh rd W8	145	S13
Hillstowe st E5	50	E8
Hilltop Sutt	119	U18
Hilltop gdns NW4	26	K6
Hilltop rd NW6	45	Z19
Hilltop way Stan	10	M11
Hillview SW20	104	K19
Hillview ave Har	24	J15
Hillview cres Ilf	35	U18
Hillview gdns NW4	27	P12
Hillview gdns Har	22	H11
Hillview rd NW7	14	B14
Hillview rd Chis	113	X12
Hillview rd Pnr	22	D1
Hillview rd Sutt	130	E5
Hillway N6	47	P5
Hillway NW9	44	A2
Hillworth rd SW2	90	F19
Hilly Fields cres SE4	93	N9
Hillyard rd W7	59	T13
Hillyard st SW9	90	E2
Hillyfield E17	32	H8
Hilsea st E5	50	C11
Hilton ave N12	15	V17
Himley rd SW17	106	L14
Hinchcliffe clo Wall	132	C16
Hinckler clo Wall	132	B18
Hinckley rd SE15	91	W9
Hind cres Erith	81	Z17
Hind gro E14	64	B17
Hinde st W1	147	U4
Hindes rd Har	23	R16
Hindhead clo N16	49	S3
Hindhead gdns Nthlt	58	B3
Hindhead way Wall	132	A10
Hindmans rd SE22	91	X13
Hindmans way Dag	69	N12
Hindmarsh clo E1	151	U18
Hind rd E5	50	A15
Hindsley pl SE23	110	E3
Hinkler rd Har	24	G10
Hinksey path SE2	80	J7
Hinstock rd SE18	79	P18
Hinton ave Houns	82	A10
Hinton clo SE9	113	S2
Hinton rd N18	18	D14
Hinton rd SE24	90	K8
Hinton rd Wall	131	V14
Hippodrome pl W11	144	L11
Hiroshima wk SE7	77	W9
Hitcham rd E17	50	L2
Hitchin sq E3	63	X5
Hither Green la SE13	93	V12
Hitherfield rd SW16	108	E6
Hitherfield rd Dag	55	Z6
Hitherwell dr Har	23	O4
Hitherwood dr SE19	109	U10
Hive clo (Bushey) Wat	10	D7
Hive rd (Bushey) Wat	10	D7
Hoadly rd SW16	107	X6
Hobart clo N20	15	N7
Hobart rd Dag	55	Z13
Hobart rd Th Hth	123	N7
Hobart pl SW1	155	X1

Name	Page	Grid
Hobart pl Rich	84	M17
Hobart rd Dag	55	X12
Hobart rd Ilf	36	C7
Hobart rd NW Pk	128	J5
Hobbayne rd W7	59	R16
Hobbes wk SW15	86	J14
Hobbs grn N2	28	E10
Hobbs rd SE27	109	N11
Hobday st E14	64	D16
Hobill wk E16	116	M15
Hoblands end Chis	114	H15
Hobury st SW10	154	E15
Hocker st E2	143	N14
Hockley ave E6	66	D5
Hocroft ave NW2	45	U10
Hocroft rd NW2	45	V10
Hocroft wk NW2	45	W9
Hodder dr Grnf	59	W6
Hoddesdon rd Belv	81	S15
Hodford rd NW11	45	W5
Hodgkin clo SE28	68	K19
Hodnet gro SE16	75	S10
Hodson clo Har	40	E9
Hoe la Enf	8	J4
Hoe st E17	33	O12
Hofland rd W14	152	J1
Hog Hill rd Rom	38	C2
Hogan ms W2	146	E1
Hogan way E5	49	Y7
Hogarth clo E16	66	A13
Hogarth clo W5	60	L13
Hogarth ct SE19	109	V11
Hogarth cres SW19	120	G2
Hogarth cres Croy	122	M18
Hogarth gdns Houns	70	G9
Hogarth hill NW11	27	W14
Hogarth la W4	74	A15
Hogarth rd SW5	153	W7
Hogarth rd Edg	25	U6
Hogarth Roundabout W4	74	C15
Holbeach gdns Sid	96	J16
Holbeach rd SE6	93	P18
Holbeck row SE15	159	U18
Holbein ms SW1	155	S8
Holbein pl SW1	155	T8
Holberton gdns NW10	62	J8
Holborn EC1	149	U2
Holborn circ EC1	149	V3
Holborn pl WC1	149	O3
Holborn rd E13	65	W13
Holborn Viaduct EC1	149	W3
Holbrook clo N19	47	T5
Holbrook clo Enf	8	J4
Holbrook la Chis	114	F18
Holbrook rd E15	65	P5
Holbrook way Brom	127	L14
Holbrooke pl Rich	84	H14
Holburne clo SE3	94	K13
Holburne gdns SE3	95	N3
Holburne rd SE3	94	L13
Holcombe hill NW7	13	T10
Holcombe rd N17	31	X9
Holcombe rd Ilf	53	X2
Holcombe st W6	74	K12
Holcote clo Belv	81	N9
Holcroft rd E9	50	D20
Holden ave N12	15	O15
Holden ave NW9	43	W4
Holden rd N12	15	N15
Holden st SW11	89	O6
Holdenby rd SE4	92	J13
Holdenhurst ave N12	28	C2
Holderness way SE27	108	K13
Holdernesse rd SW17	107	N6
Holders Hill ave NW4	27	P8
Holders Hill circ NW7	27	S2
Holders Hill cres NW4	27	R9
Holders Hill dr NW4	27	R7
Holders Hill gdns NW4	27	R7
Holders Hill rd NW4	27	O8
Holders Hill rd NW4	27	O8
Holdgate st SE7	78	A9
Holford pl WC1	141	R12
Holford rd NW3	46	E10
Holford st WC1	141	S12
Holgate ave SW11	88	F8
Holgate gdns Dag	56	E16
Holgate rd Dag	56	D16
Holland ave SW20	104	E20
Holland ave Sutt	129	Y18
Holland clo Barn	15	U1
Holland clo Stan	11	N15
Holland dr SE23	110	H7
Holland gdns W14	152	M1
Holland gro SW9	157	V19
Holland pk W11	145	N15
Holland Park ave W11	144	J16
Holland Park ave Ilf	36	J17
Holland Park gdns W14	144	L15
Holland Park ms W11	145	N15
Holland Park rd W14	153	P2
Holland rd E6	66	J2
Holland rd E15	65	N8
Holland rd NW10	62	H4
Holland rd SE25	123	Y11
Holland rd W14	144	K18
Holland rd Wem	42	F18
Holland st SE1	149	Y12
Holland st W8	145	V18
Holland Villas rd W14	144	K14
Holland wk N19	47	U8
Holland wk W8	145	S17
Holland wk Stan	11	N15
Hollands the Wor Pk	128	D1
Hollar rd N16	49	U10
Hollen st W1	148	E5
Holles clo Hmptn	100	H14
Holles st W1	147	Y5
Holley rd W3	74	C5
Hollickwood ave N12	15	Y19
Hollidge way Dag	56	G19
Hollies ave Sid	114	K3
Hollies clo SW16	108	G16
Hollies clo Twick	101	V4
Hollies end NW7	13	X15
Hollies rd W5	72	D11
Holligrave rd Brom	112	F20
Hollingbourne ave Bexh	98	C1
Hollingbourne gdns W13	60	A15
Hollingbourne rd SE24	90	M13
Hollingsworth rd Croy	134	A15
Hollington cres N Mal	118	E16
Hollington rd E6	66	F9
Hollington rd N17	31	X6
Hollingworth rd Orp	127	Z16
Hollman gdns SW16	108	J16
Hollow the Wdf Grn	21	N13
Holloway rd E6	66	H9
Holloway rd E11	51	Y10
Holloway rd N7	48	A9
Holloway rd N19	47	W6
Holloway st Houns	82	L7
Holly ave Stan	24	K8
Holly Bush hill NW3	46	D10
Holly Bush la Hmptn	100	E18
Holly clo NW10	44	A20
Holly clo Felt	100	A13
Holly clo Wall	131	T18
Holly cres Beck	124	M13
Holly cres Wdf Grn	20	L20
Holly dr E4	20	F3
Holly Farm rd Sthl	70	A13
Holly gro NW9	25	W20
Holly gro SE15	91	W4
Holly gro Pnr	22	C5
Holly gro (Bushey) Wat		
Holly Hedge ter SE13	93	W12
Holly hill N21	7	P19
Holly hill NW3	46	D11
Holly Hill rd Belv	81	V13
Holly Hill rd Erith	81	V13
Holly Lodge gdns N6	47	O5
Holly pk N3	27	X10
Holly pk N4	48	B1
Holly Park est N4	48	C1
Holly Park gdns N3	27	X10
Holly Park rd N11	16	B15
Holly Park rd W7	71	V1
Holly rd E11	34	D20
Holly rd Hmptn	100	M15
Holly rd Houns	82	L9
Holly rd Twick	101	X2
Holly st E8	143	P1
Holly View clo NW4	26	H17
Holly wk NW3	46	D12
Holly way Mitch	121	Y8
Hollybank clo Hmptn	100	G13
Hollybrake clo Chis	114	E18
Hollybush clo E11	34	E15
Hollybush clo Har	23	U3
Hollybush gdns E2	143	Y12
Hollybush hill E11	34	D19
Hollybush pl E2	143	Y12
Hollybush rd Kings T	102	L13
Hollybush st E13	65	W7
Hollybush wk SW9	90	H11
Hollycroft ave NW3	45	Z10
Hollycroft ave Wem	42	M8
Hollydale rd SE15	92	B3
Hollydene SE15	91	Z1
Hollydown way E11	51	Y9
Hollyfield ave N11	15	Z17
Hollyfield rd Surb	117	N18
Hollymead Cars	130	M7
Hollymount clo SE10	93	U2
Hollytree clo SW19	105	P2
Hollywood ms SW10	154	B12
Hollywood rd E4	19	X16
Hollywood rd SW10	154	C13
Hollywood way Wdf Grn	20	K20
Holm Oak clo SW15	87	V15
Holm Oak ms SW4	89	Z14
Holm wk SE3	94	F6
Holman rd SW11	88	F5
Holmbridge gdns Enf	9	T13
Holmbrook dr NW4	27	R15
Holmbury ct SW17	106	M7
Holmbury ct SW19	106	H17
Holmbury gro Croy	134	L17
Holmbury pk Brom	113	R18
Holmbury vw E5	50	A3
Holmbush rd SW15	87	S15
Holmcroft way Brom	127	U13
Holmdale gdns NW4	27	P15
Holmdale rd NW6	45	Y15
Holmdale rd Chis	114	B12
Holmdale ter N15	31	T20
Holmdene ave NW7	13	U19
Holmdene ave SE24	90	M13
Holmdene ave Har	22	J10
Holmdene clo Beck	125	U5
Holme Lacey rd SE12	94	B17
Holme rd E6	66	E2
Holme way Stan	0	J19
Holmead rd SW6	153	Z18
Holmebury clo (Bushey) Wat		
Holmes ave E17	32	L9
Holmes ave NW7	14	F17
Holmes pl SW10	154	D12
Holmes rd NW5	47	T16
Holmes rd SW19	106	E18
Holmes rd Twick	101	W5
Holmes ter SE1	149	T17
Holmesdale ave SW14	85	U9
Holmesdale clo SE25	123	V7
Holmesdale rd N6	29	T20
Holmesdale rd SE25	123	V8
Holmesdale rd Bexh	97	X5
Holmesdale rd Croy	123	O11
Holmesdale rd Rich	85	N2
Holmesdale rd Tedd	102	D17
Holmesley rd SE23	92	H15
Holmewood gdns SW2	90	C19
Holmewood rd SE25	123	T7
Holmewood rd SW2	90	B19
Holmfield ave NW4	27	P15
Holmhurst rd Belv	81	W13
Holmleigh rd N16	49	T3
Holmsdale gro Bexh	99	R6
Holmshaw clo SE26	110	J9
Holmside rd SW12	89	P16
Holmsley clo N Mal	118	C16
Holmstall ave Edg	25	U9
Holmwood clo Har	22	M9
Holmwood clo Nthlt	40	K17
Holmwood clo Sutt	129	P18
Holmwood gdns N3	27	Y8
Holmwood gdns Wall	131	S14
Holmwood gro NW7	12	L17
Holmwood rd Ilf	54	J7
Holmwood rd Sutt	129	O19
Holmwood vill SE7	77	U13
Holne chase N2	28	E17
Holne chase Mord	119	W15
Holness rd E15	52	C19
Holroyd rd SW15	87	N12
Holstein way Erith	80	L8
Holstock rd Ilf	54	B8
Holsworth clo Har	22	M15
Holsworthy sq WC1	141	R18
Holt the Wall	131	U8
Holt clo N10	29	O13
Holt clo SE28	68	E19
Holt rd E16	78	E3
Holt rd Wem	42	C9
Holton st E1	63	T11
Holtwhite ave Enf	7	V7
Holtwhites hill Enf	7	V5
Holwell pl Pnr	22	A13
Holwood pl SW4	89	X11
Holybourne ave SW15	86	G20
Holyhead clo E3	64	C9
Holyoak rd SE11	157	X6
Holyoake ct SE16	75	X5
Holyoake wk N2	28	C11
Holyoake wk W5	60	E11
Holyport rd SW6	152	E17
Holyrood ave Har	40	C12
Holyrood gdns Edg	25	S9
Holyrood rd Barn	5	S20
Holyrood st SE1	150	K15
Holywell clo SE3	77	T16
Holywell la EC2	142	K17
Holywell row EC2	142	J18
Home clo Cars	130	M4
Home clo Nthlt	58	E8
Home gdns Dag	56	K10
Home mead Stan	24	F3
Home Park rd SW19	105	U10
Home Park wk Kings T	116	H10
Homer rd SW11	88	J4
Homecroft rd N22	30	K3
Homecroft rd SE26	110	E12
Homefarm rd W7	59	U17
Homefield ave Ilf	36	H16
Homefield clo NW10	43	X19
Homefield gdns N2	28	G10
Homefield gdns Mitch	120	E3
Homefield pk Sutt	130	A18
Homefield rd SW19	105	R14
Homefield rd W4	74	D12
Homefield rd Brom	126	K2
Homefield rd Edg	12	L20
Homefield rd Wem	42	A12
Homefield st N1	142	K10
Homeland dr Sutt	130	A20
Homelands dr SE19	109	S19
Homeleigh rd SE15	92	F12
Homemead rd Brom	127	V11
Homemead rd Croy	121	W15
Homer clo Bexh	98	K3
Homer dr E14	76	B11
Homer rd E9	50	J18
Homer rd Croy	124	G15
Homer row W1	146	M2
Homer st W1	146	M2
Homersham rd Kings T	117	R2
Homerton gro E9	50	F15
Homerton High st E9	50	F16
Homerton rd E9	50	J15
Homerton row E9	50	D15
Homerton ter E9	50	D17

Name	Page	Ref
Homesdale clo E11	34	E15
Homesdale rd Brom	127	N6
Homesfield NW11	27	Y14
Homestall rd SE22	92	C12
Homestead the N11	16	E13
Homestead Paddock N14	6	F17
Homestead pk NW2	44	E10
Homestead rd SW6	153	P18
Homestead rd Dag	56	B7
Homewillow clo N21	7	W18
Homewood cres Chis	114	H16
Honduras st EC1	142	B17
Honeybourne rd NW6	45	Z15
Honeybrook rd SW12	89	V18
Honeyman clo NW6	45	P19
Honeypot clo NW9	25	O12
Honeypot la NW9	25	O12
Honeypot la Stan	24	G2
Honeysett rd N17	31	V7
Honeysuckle gdns Croy	124	F19
Honeywell rd SW11	88	L15
Honeywood rd NW10	62	D7
Honeywood rd Islw	83	Y11
Honeywood wk Cars	131	N10
Honister clo Stan	24	C3
Honister gdns Stan	24	C3
Honister pl Stan	24	B3
Honiton rd NW6	137	P7
Honiton rd Rom	39	N18
Honiton rd Well	96	K4
Honley rd SE6	93	T18
Honor Oak pk SE23	92	D17
Honor Oak ri SE23	92	D17
Honor Oak rd SE23	110	B2
Hood ave N14	6	E19
Hood ave SW14	85	W13
Hood clo Croy	132	K1
Hood rd SW20	104	E19
Hood wk Rom	38	H4
Hoodcote gdns N21	17	W2
Hook the Barn	5	U19
Hook Farm rd Brom	127	N13
Hook la Well	96	K12
Hook wk Edg	12	K20
Hookers rd E17	32	F10
Hooking grn Har	22	J14
Hooks Hall dr Dag	56	M9
Hookstone way Wdf Grn	35	N2
Hoop la NW11	45	W1
Hooper rd E16	65	T17
Hooper st E1	151	S6
Hooper's ct SW3	147	O18
Hope clo SE12	112	H7
Hope clo Sutt	130	D11
Hope pk Brom	112	D19
Hope st SW11	88	F8
Hopedale rd SE7	77	V17
Hopefield ave NW6	136	M7
Hopetown st E1	151	R2
Hopewell st SE5	158	F19
Hopewell yd SE5	158	G19
Hopgood st W12	144	C15
Hopkins st W1	148	E7
Hopkinsons pl NW1	139	S3
Hoppers rd N13	17	U9
Hoppers rd N21	17	U4
Hoppett rd E4	21	N8
Hopping la N1	48	K18
Hoppingwood ave N Mal	118	B5
Hopton gdns SE1	149	Y12
Hopton gdns N Mal	118	G14
Hopton rd SW16	107	Z12
Hopton st SE1	149	Y12
Hopwood rd SE17	158	G13
Horace ave Rom	56	M4
Horace rd E7	52	H12
Horace rd Ilf	36	B9
Horace rd Kings T	116	M7
Horatio st E2	143	R10
Horatius way Croy	132	C13
Horbury cres W11	145	S11
Horbury ms W11	145	S11
Horder rd SW6	87	T3
Horizon way SE7	77	W12
Horley clo Bexh	98	D13
Horley rd SE9	113	R9
Hormead rd W9	137	P19
Horn la SE10	77	T11
Horn la W3	61	W17
Horn la Wdf Grn	21	T19
Horn Park clo SE12	94	H14
Horn Park la SE12	94	H14
Hornbeam clo SE11	157	S5
Hornbeam clo Nthlt	40	F15
Hornbeam cres Brent	72	C18
Hornbeam gro E4	21	O9
Hornbeam la Bexh	98	J5
Hornbeam ter Cars	120	H19
Hornbeam wk Rich	103	N7
Hornbeam way Brom	127	X16
Hornbeams ri N11	16	C19
Hornbuckle clo Har	41	P7
Hornby clo NW3	46	H20
Horncastle clo SE12	94	F18
Horncastle rd SE12	94	G18
Hornchurch rd Horn	57	X3
Horndean clo SW15	86	H20
Horndon clo Rom	38	M4
Horndon grn Rom	38	L4
Horndon rd Rom	38	M6
Horne way SW15	86	M5
Horner la Mitch	120	G4
Hornfair rd SE7	77	Z17
Hornford way Rom	57	R2
Horniman dr SE23	110	B1
Horning clo SE9	113	S9
Horns rd Ilf	36	D14
Hornsey la N6	47	T4
Hornsey Lane est N19	47	W1
Hornsey Lane gdns N6	47	U2
Hornsey Park rd N8	30	E9
Hornsey ri N19	47	Y1
Hornsey Rise gdns N19	47	Z1
Hornsey rd N7	48	E11
Hornsey rd N19	48	A5
Hornsey st N7	48	D14
Hornshay st SE15	75	R17
Hornton pl W8	145	W19
Hornton st W8	145	U15
Horsa clo Wall	132	B17
Horsa rd SE12	94	K18
Horsa rd Erith	81	W19
Horse Fair Kings T	116	H3
Horse Guards ave SW1	148	K15
Horse Guards rd SW1	148	G14
Horse leaze E6	66	L17
Horse ride SW1	148	F14
Horse Shoe cres Nthlt	58	G5
Horse Shoe yd W1	147	Y8
Horsebridges clo Dag	69	N3
Horsecroft rd Edg	25	Y1
Horseferry pl SE10	76	F16
Horseferry rd E14	63	V19
Horseferry rd SW1	156	F3
Horsell rd N5	48	F15
Horselydown la SE1	151	N16
Horsenden ave Grnf	41	U14
Horsenden cres Grnf	41	V15
Horsenden Lane north Grnf	41	T17
Horsenden Lane south Grnf	59	Z3
Horseshoe clo E14	76	G13
Horseshoe clo NW2	44	J6
Horseshoe la N20	14	C4
Horsfeld gdns SE9	95	P12
Horsfeld rd SE9	95	P12
Horsford rd SW2	90	C13
Horsham ave N12	15	Y16
Horsham rd Bexh	98	D14
Horsley dr Croy	135	U17
Horsley rd E4	20	H8
Horsley st SE17	158	E13
Hortensia rd SW10	154	B16
Horticultural pl W4	73	X13
Horton ave NW2	45	T12
Horton rd E8	49	Z18
Horton st SE13	93	S6
Hortus rd E4	20	H6
Hortus rd Sthl	70	D6
Hosack rd SW17	107	N3
Hoser ave SE12	112	F3
Hosier la EC1	149	X3
Hoskins clo E16	65	Z17
Hoskins st SE10	76	L14
Hospital Bridge rd Twick	82	J18
Hospital la Islw	83	V13
Hospital rd E9	50	E15
Hospital rd Houns	82	G9
Hotham rd SW15	87	N9
Hotham rd SW19	106	D18
Hotham st E15	64	M2
Hothfield pl SE16	75	R8
Hotspur rd Nthlt	58	G6
Hotspur st SE11	157	S8
Houblon rd Rich	84	L12
Houghton clo Hmptn	100	B15
Houghton rd WC2	149	P7
Houlder cres Croy	132	H13
Houndsden rd N21	17	R1
Houndsditch EC3	150	L4
Houndsfield rd N9	18	M3
Hounslow ave Houns	82	L13
Hounslow gdns Houns	82	L13
Hounslow rd (Hanworth) Felt	100	B4
Hounslow rd Twick	82	L15
Houston rd SE23	110	J5
Hove ave E17	32	L16
Hove gdns Sutt	130	C1
Hoveden rd NW2	45	R14
Hoveton rd SE28	68	F18
Howard ave Bex	97	U20
Howard clo N11	16	B8
Howard clo NW2	45	S11
Howard clo W3	61	S16
Howard clo Hmptn	100	M17
Howard clo (Bushey) Wat	10	G2
Howard ms N5	48	K12
Howard rd E6	66	H6
Howard rd E11	52	A9
Howard rd E17	33	P10
Howard rd N15	31	T18
Howard rd N16	49	P13
Howard rd NW2	45	P13
Howard rd SE20	110	C20
Howard rd Bark	67	T4
Howard rd Brom	112	E19
Howard rd Ilf	53	Z12
Howard rd Islw	83	V7
Howard rd N Mal	118	C7
Howard rd Sthl	58	L17
Howard rd Surb	116	M14
Howard st T Ditt	116	B16
Howard wk N2	28	E12
Howards Crest clo Beck	125	V5
Howards la SW15	86	L12
Howards rd E13	65	T8
Howarth rd SE2	80	C13
Howberry clo Edg	11	V20
Howberry rd Edg	11	V19
Howberry rd Stan	11	V19
Howberry rd Th Hth	123	N2
Howbury la Erith	99	W3
Howbury rd SE15	92	C7
Howcroft cres N3	27	Y1
Howcroft la Grnf	59	R8
Howden rd SE25	123	U5
Howden st SE15	91	W7
Howe clo Rom	38	F5
Howell clo Rom	37	W16
Howell wk SE1	157	Z6
Howes st N3	27	Y9
Howgate rd SW14	85	X8
Howick pl SW1	156	C7
Howie st SW11	154	K19
Howitt rd NW3	46	K16
Howland Mews east W1	140	D19
Howland st W1	140	C20
Howland way SE16	75	W6
Howletts rd SE24	91	N15
Howley pl W2	138	D20
Howley rd Croy	132	K5
Hows st E2	142	M7
Howsman rd SW13	74	F17
Howson rd SE4	92	K11
Howson ter Rich	84	J15
Howton pl (Bushey) Wat	10	C5
Hoxton mkt N1	142	J14
Hoxton sq N1	142	J13
Hoxton st N1	142	J6
Hoy st E16	65	P18
Hoylake gdns Mitch	121	V6
Hoylake rd W3	62	B18
Hoyland clo SE15	159	V18
Hoyle rd SW17	106	J12
Hubbard rd SE27	108	M9
Hubbard st E15	64	M4
Hubbinet Industrial est Rom	38	L10
Hubert gro SW9	90	B8
Hubert rd E6	66	B8
Huddart st E3	64	A14
Huddleston rd N7	47	V10
Huddlestone rd E7	52	D11
Huddlestone rd NW2	44	K17
Hudson pl SE18	79	P13
Hudson rd Bexh	98	B5
Hudson's pl SW1	156	A5
Hugh ms SW1	155	Z6
Hugh pl SW1	156	F5
Hugh st SW1	155	Z6
Hughan rd E15	51	Y14
Hughenden ave Har	24	C14
Hughenden rd Wor Pk	118	H17
Hughendon ter E15	51	V11
Hugo gdns Rain	57	V18
Hugo rd N19	47	V12
Hugon rd SW6	88	A7
Huguenot pl SW18	88	D13
Hull clo SE16	75	U4
Hull st EC1	142	B13
Hullbridge ms N1	142	E3
Hulse ave Bark	54	F17
Hulse ave Rom	38	H4
Hulverston clo Sutt	130	A20
Humber rd NW2	44	K6
Humber rd SE3	77	P16
Humberstone rd E13	65	Y10
Humbolt rd W6	152	L14
Humes ave W7	71	U7
Humphrey clo Ilf	35	U5
Humphrey st SE1	159	O9
Humphries clo Dag	56	B11
Hundred acre NW9	26	D6
Hungerford ave Grnf	20	G4
Hungerford bri SE1	149	N13
Hungerford bri WC2	149	N13
Hungerford la WC2	148	L13
Hungerford rd N7	47	Z16
Hungerford st E1	151	Y5
Hunsdon clo Dag	56	A18
Hunsdon rd SE14	75	S18
Hunston rd Mord	120	A20
Hunt rd Sthl	70	G7
Hunt st W11	144	H12
Hunter clo SE1	158	H2
Hunter rd SW20	104	M20
Hunter rd Ilf	54	A15
Hunter rd Th Hth	123	O6
Hunter st WC1	140	L15
Hunter wk E13	65	T5
Hunters the Beck	111	T19
Hunters clo SW12	107	O2
Hunters gro Har	24	E12
Hunters Hall rd Dag	56	F12
Hunters sq Dag	56	E12
Hunters way Croy	133	T8
Hunting Gate clo Enf	7	U4
Hunting Gate ms Sutt	130	B6
Huntingdon clo Mitch	122	A8
Huntingdon gdns W4	73	W18

Name		
Huntingdon gdns Wor Pk	128	M6
Huntingdon rd N2	28	J10
Huntingdon rd N9	19	R6
Huntingdon st E16	65	R18
Huntingdon st N1	141	O1
Huntingfield Croy	134	M17
Huntingfield rd SW15	86	H13
Huntings rd Dag	56	F18
Huntley st WC1	140	D18
Huntley way SW20	118	F4
Huntly rd SE25	123	T8
Hunton st E1	143	S19
Hunt's clo SE3	94	F5
Hunts la E15	64	F7
Hunts mead Enf	9	U10
Hunts Slip rd SE21	109	S6
Huntsman st SE17	158	H7
Huntsmead clo Chis	113	T19
Huntspill st SW17	106	E8
Hurley la Grnf	58	K16
Hurlingham gdns SW6	87	V7
Hurlingham rd SW6	87	U6
Hurlingham rd Bexh	81	P20
Hurlingham sq SW6	87	Z8
Hurlock st N5	48	J9
Hurlstone rd SE25	123	R11
Huron rd SW17	107	P5
Hurren clo SE3	93	Z6
Hurry clo E15	65	N1
Hurst ave E4	20	B11
Hurst ave N6	29	V19
Hurst clo E4	20	B11
Hurst clo NW11	28	A17
Hurst clo Brom	126	D20
Hurst clo Nthlt	40	E16
Hurst la SE2	80	J15
Hurst ri Barn	4	L11
Hurst rd E17	33	R10
Hurst rd N21	17	U5
Hurst rd Bex	115	Y2
Hurst rd Croy	133	O10
Hurst rd Erith	98	L1
Hurst rd Sid	115	O4
Hurst Springs Bex	115	Z2
Hurst st SE24	90	J15
Hurst View rd S Croy	133	S16
Hurst way S Croy	133	S15
Hurstbourne gdns Bark	54	G17
Hurstbourne rd SE23	110	K2
Hurstcourt rd Sutt	129	Z2
Hurstdene ave Brom	126	C20
Hurstdene gdns N15	31	T20
Hurstfield Brom	126	F11
Hurstleigh gdns Ilf	35	V5
Hurstmead ct Edg	12	F12
Hurstway wk W11	144	H9
Hurstwood ave E18	34	J12
Hurstwood ave Bex	115	Z1
Hurstwood ave Bexh	99	R5
Hurstwood ave Erith	99	R5
Hurstwood dr Brom	127	V7
Hurstwood rd NW11	27	U13
Huson clo NW3	46	J20
Husseywell cres Brom	126	E20
Hutchings st E14	76	A6
Hutchings wk NW11	28	B13
Hutchinson ter Wem	42	H10
Hutton clo Wdf Grn	21	V17
Hutton gdns Har	23	O1
Hutton gro N12	15	P17
Hutton la Har	23	O1
Hutton row Edg	25	U1
Hutton st EC4	149	V7
Hutton wk Har	23	N1
Huxbear st SE4	92	M13
Huxley clo Nthlt	58	C4
Huxley dr Rom	55	P2
Huxley gdns NW10	61	N7
Huxley pl N13	17	X12
Huxley rd E10	51	U8
Huxley rd N18	18	B12
Huxley rd Well	96	L8
Huxley st W10	136	K15
Hyacinth clo Hmptn	100	F14
Hyacinth rd SW15	104	H1

Name		
Hyde the NW9	26	C16
Hyde clo E13	4	G11
Hyde ct N20	15	U9
Hyde cres NW9	26	C16
Hyde la SW11	88	J1
Hyde Park ave N21	18	A6
Hyde Park corner W1	147	U17
Hyde Park cres W2	146	K6
Hyde Park gdns N21	18	A6
Hyde Park gdns W2	146	H9
Hyde Park gate SW7	146	C18
Hyde Park Gate ms SW7	146	C20
Hyde Park sq W2	146	K7
Hyde Park Square ms W2	146	K7
Hyde Park st W2	146	L7
Hyde rd N1	142	H6
Hyde rd Bexh	98	D5
Hyde rd Rich	76	A18
Hyde vale SE10	76	H20
Hyde wk Mord	119	Z17
Hyde way N9	18	G8
Hydefield clo N21	18	B5
Hydefield ct N9	18	E7
Hydeside gdns N9	18	G8
Hydethorpe ave N9	18	G8
Hydethorpe rd SW12	107	U1
Hyland clo Horn	57	Z1
Hyland way Horn	39	Z19
Hylands rd E17	33	Y8
Hylton st SE18	79	X11
Hyndewood SE23	110	E7
Hyndman st E15	159	W14
Hynton rd Dag	55	U7
Hyrst dene S Croy	132	K10
Hyson rd SE16	159	Y8
Hythe ave Bexh	81	N20
Hythe clo N18	18	L14
Hythe path Th Hth	123	P5
Hythe rd NW10	62	E10
Hythe rd Th Hth	123	O4
Hyver hill NW7	12	M1

I

Name		
Ibbotson ave E16	65	R16
Iberian ave Wall	131	Y8
Ibis la W4	85	V3
Ibscott clo Dag	56	K18
Ibsley gdns SW15	104	G1
Ibsley way Barn	5	X15
Iceland rd E3	64	B3
Ickburgh rd E5	49	Z9
Ickleton rd SE9	113	S10
Icknield dr Ilf	36	A6
Ickworth Park rd E17	32	J12
Ida rd N15	31	O14
Ida st E14	64	F17
Iden clo Brom	126	A6
Idlecombe rd SW17	107	O14
Idmiston rd E15	52	C14
Idmiston rd SE27	108	L6
Idmiston sq Wor Pk	118	E19
Idol la EC3	150	J9
Idonia st SE8	76	A19
Iffley rd W6	152	A1
Ifield rd SW10	153	Y13
Ightham rd Erith	81	S19
Ilbert st W10	136	J14
Ilchester gdns W2	145	X8
Ilchester pl W14	145	P20
Ilchester rd Dag	55	R14
Ildersley gro SE21	109	P5
Ilderton rd SE16	159	Y9
Ilex rd NW10	44	C18
Ilex way SW16	108	F13
Ilford hill Ilf	53	X9
Ilford la Ilf	53	Z10
Ilfracombe gdns Rom	55	P2
Ilfracombe rd Brom	112	B7
Iliffe st SE17	157	Z9
Iliffe yd SE17	157	Z9
Ilkley clo SE19	109	P16
Ilkley rd E16	65	X15
Illingworth clo Mitch	120	G7

Name		
Illingworth way Enf	8	E15
Ilmington rd Har	24	F17
Ilminster gdns SW11	88	K9
Imber clo N14	16	J1
Imber st N1	142	F5
Imperial clo Har	22	G19
Imperial College rd SW7	154	E2
Imperial dr Har	40	F2
Imperial gdns Mitch	121	S7
Imperial ms E6	66	A6
Imperial rd N22	30	A4
Imperial rd SW6	88	C2
Imperial sq SW6	88	B1
Imperial st E3	64	G9
Imperial way Chis	114	C10
Imperial way Croy	132	D14
Imperial way Har	24	L18
Inca dr SE9	95	Y19
Inchmery rd SE6	111	S3
Inchwood Croy	135	S8
Independent pl E8	49	V14
Inderwick rd N8	30	C15
India st EC3	151	N7
India way W12	62	J19
Indus rd SE7	77	Z20
Ingal rd E13	65	T12
Ingate pl SW8	89	T2
Ingatestone rd E12	52	K5
Ingatestone rd SE25	123	Z10
Ingatestone rd Wdf Grn	34	G1
Ingelow rd SW8	89	R5
Ingersoll rd W12	74	K3
Ingersoll rd Enf	9	S3
Ingestre pl W1	148	D7
Ingestre rd E7	52	F11
Ingestre rd NW5	47	S12
Ingham clo S Croy	134	E19
Ingham rd NW6	45	X13
Ingham rd S Croy	134	E19
Ingle clo Pnr	22	C11
Inglebert st EC1	141	T12
Ingleborough st SW9	90	E4
Ingleby dr Har	41	R8
Ingleby rd N7	48	A9
Ingleby rd Dag	56	G18
Ingleby rd Ilf	53	Z4
Ingleby way Chis	113	Y13
Ingleby way Wall	131	W18
Ingledew rd SE18	79	U13
Inglehurst gdns Ilf	35	T15
Inglemere rd SE23	110	E6
Inglemere rd Mitch	107	N17
Ingleside clo Beck	111	O18
Ingleside gro SE3	77	R17
Inglethorpe st SW6	152	H20
Ingleton ave Well	97	O12
Ingleton rd N18	18	K19
Ingleton rd Cars	130	J19
Ingleton st SW9	90	F4
Ingleway N12	15	V19
Inglewood Croy	134	J20
Inglewood clo E14	76	C10
Inglewood copse Brom	127	T4
Inglewood rd NW6	45	Y16
Inglewood rd Bexh	98	M9
Inglis rd W5	61	N19
Inglis rd Croy	123	W20
Inglis st SE5	90	K2
Ingram ave NW11	46	C1
Ingram clo SE11	157	P5
Ingram clo Stan	11	R17
Ingram rd N2	28	K13
Ingram rd Th Hth	108	L20
Ingram way Grnf	59	P4
Ingrave rd Rom	39	P13
Ingrave st SW11	88	H7
Ingress st W4	74	B13
Inigo Jones rd SE7	78	C18
Inkerman rd NW5	47	S17
Inks grn E4	20	F16
Inman rd NW10	62	A2
Inman rd SW18	88	D20
Inmans row Wdf Grn	21	T14
Inner circle NW1	139	T13
Inner Park rd SW19	105	O1
Inner Temple la EC4	149	T7

Name		
Innes clo SW20	119	T5
Innes gdns SW15	86	K16
Inniskilling rd E13	65	Z7
Inskip clo E10	51	R7
Inskip rd Dag	55	X5
Institute pl E8	49	Z16
Instone clo Wall	132	B16
Insurance st WC1	141	T13
Integer gdns E11	51	W1
Inveraray pl SE18	79	T15
Inverclyde gdns Rom	37	V14
Inveresk gdns Wor Pk	128	E7
Inverforth rd N11	16	F17
Inverine rd SE7	77	W14
Invermore pl SE18	79	P11
Inverness ave Enf	8	F15
Inverness gdns W8	145	W15
Inverness ms W2	145	Z8
Inverness pl W2	145	Z9
Inverness rd N18	18	M15
Inverness rd Houns	82	F10
Inverness rd Wor Pk	129	O1
Inverness rd Sthl	70	C11
Inverness st NW1	139	X4
Inverness ter W2	145	Z6
Inverton rd SE15	92	E11
Invicta clo Chis	113	X12
Invicta gro Nthlt	58	D9
Invicta rd SE3	77	U18
Inville rd SE17	158	G11
Inwood clo Croy	134	J2
Inwood rd Houns	82	L11
Inworth st SW11	88	J4
Ion sq E2	143	T10
Iona clo SE6	93	N18
Ipswich rd SW17	107	R16
Ireland yd EC4	149	Y7
Irene rd SW6	87	Y3
Iris ave Bex	98	A14
Iris clo Croy	124	F19
Iris clo Surb	116	M18
Iris cres Bexh	81	P17
Iris way E4	19	Z19
Irkdale ave Enf	8	H5
Iron Mill la Dart	99	R11
Iron Mill pl Dart	99	T11
Iron Mill rd SW18	88	B16
Ironmonger la EC2	150	D6
Ironmonger row EC1	142	B13
Irons way Rom	38	L2
Irvine ave Har	24	A10
Irvine clo N20	15	W8
Irving rd W14	152	H1
Irving st WC2	148	H10
Irving way NW9	26	E17
Irwin ave SE18	79	W18
Irwin gdns NW10	136	A6
Isabel st SW9	90	E2
Isabella st SE1	149	W15
Isambard ms E14	76	H19
Isbell gdns Rom	39	R1
Isham rd SW16	122	A13
Isis clo SW15	86	L9
Isis st SW18	106	D4
Island rd SE18	79	O17
Island rd Mitch	106	L18
Isledon rd N7	48	F9
Islehurst clo Chis	127	Y2
Islington grn N1	141	W6
Islington High st N1	141	W8
Islington Park st N1	48	G20
Islip gdns Edg	12	K20
Islip gdns Nthlt	40	C20
Islip Manor rd Nthlt	40	D19
Islip st NW5	47	U16
Ismailia rd E7	52	H19
Isom clo E13	65	X10
Ivanhoe dr Har	24	B8
Ivanhoe rd SE5	91	T7
Ivatt pl W14	153	R11
Ivatt way N17	30	K10
Ive Farm clo E10	51	P6
Ive Farm la E10	51	O6
Iveagh ave NW10	61	P5
Iveagh clo E9	63	U2
Iveagh clo NW10	61	P4
Ivedon rd Well	97	U5

Iveley rd SW4	89	V6
Ivere dr Barn	5	N18
Iverhurst clo Bexh	97	X12
Iverna ct W8	145	W20
Iverna gdns W8	153	W1
Ivers way Croy	135	S17
Iverson rd NW6	45	V19
Ives gdns Rom	39	U14
Ives rd E16	64	M14
Ives st SW3	154	M6
Ivestor ter SE23	92	C18
Ivimey rd E2	143	U13
Ivinghoe clo Enf	8	D7
Ivinghoe rd Dag	55	R15
Ivinghoe rd (Bushey) Wat	10	B2
Ivor gro SE9	114	A1
Ivor pl NW1	139	O17
Ivor st NW1	47	U20
Ivory sq SW11	88	E8
Ivorydown Brom	112	E10
Ivy clo Har	40	L12
Ivy gdns N8	30	A18
Ivy gdns Mitch	121	Y7
Ivy la Houns	82	D10
Ivy rd E16	65	T17
Ivy rd E17	33	P19
Ivy rd N14	16	J2
Ivy rd NW2	44	M12
Ivy rd SE4	92	L11
Ivy rd Houns	82	L11
Ivy st N1	142	J8
Ivy wk Dag	55	Z18
Ivybridge clo Twick	83	Y17
Ivybridge est Islw	83	W14
Ivybridge la WC2	148	M10
Ivychurch la SE17	158	M9
Ivydale rd SE15	92	E7
Ivydale rd Cars	131	N3
Ivyday gro SW16	108	C8
Ivydene clo Sutt	130	D9
Ivyhouse rd Dag	55	W18
Ivymount rd SE27	108	G8
Ixworth pl SW3	154	K8
Izane rd Bexh	98	B11

J

Jack Cornwell st E12	53	W12
Jack Walker ct N5	48	J12
Jacklin grn Wdf Grn	21	S14
Jackman ms NW10	44	A10
Jackman st E8	143	V5
Jackson rd N7	48	E12
Jackson rd Bark	67	U4
Jackson rd Barn	5	V20
Jackson rd Brom	127	U20
Jackson st SE18	78	K16
Jackson way Sthl	70	K4
Jacksons la N6	29	R20
Jacob st SE1	151	R17
Jacobs clo Dag	56	H11
Jacob's Well ms W1	147	U3
Jade clo E16	66	B17
Jade clo Dag	55	U3
Jaffray rd SE27	108	K10
Jaffray rd Brom	127	N9
Jaggard way SW12	88	M20
Jago clo SE18	79	R16
Jago wk SE5	158	F19
Jamaica rd SE1	151	R19
Jamaica rd SE16	151	U20
Jamaica rd Th Hth	122	J14
Jamaica st E1	63	S15
James ave NW2	44	M14
James ave Dag	56	D5
James clo Rom	39	X14
James Collins clo W9	137	O17
James ct N1	142	C2
James Dudson ct NW10	43	V7
James gdns N22	30	K2
James la E10	33	W20
James la E11	33	Z18
James pl N17	31	V3
James rd Dart	99	V17
James st W1	147	V5
James st WC2	148	L7
James st Bark	54	C20
James st Enf	8	H16
James st Houns	83	O7
James yd E4	20	J18
Jameson st W8	145	U12
James's cotts Rich	73	O19
Jamestown rd NW1	139	W3
Jane st E1	151	X5
Janet st E14	76	B7
Janeway pl SE16	151	V19
Janeway st SE16	151	V19
Jansen wk SW11	88	F9
Janson clo NW10	44	A8
Janson rd E15	51	Z14
Jansons rd N15	31	S11
Japan cres N4	48	C2
Japan rd Rom	37	X19
Jarrett clo SW2	108	H2
Jarrow clo Mord	120	A12
Jarrow rd N17	31	Z12
Jarrow rd SE16	75	P12
Jarrow rd Rom	37	U18
Jarrow way E9	50	K13
Jarvis clo Barn	4	C18
Jarvis rd S Croy	133	O14
Jasmine gdns Croy	135	P7
Jasmine gdns Har	40	H7
Jasmine gro SE20	110	B20
Jason wk SE9	113	W9
Jasper clo Enf	9	R3
Jasper pas SE19	109	U14
Jasper rd E16	66	C18
Jasper rd SE19	109	U14
Jasper wk N1	142	E11
Javelin way Nthlt	58	A10
Jay gdns Chis	113	V10
Jay ms SW7	146	E19
Jaycroft Enf	7	U6
Jebb av SW2	90	B16
Jebb st E3	64	C7
Jedburgh rd E13	65	X8
Jedburgh st SW11	89	R10
Jeddo rd W12	74	D5
Jefferson clo W13	72	B8
Jefferson clo Ilf	36	A15
Jefferys rd SW4	89	Z4
Jefferys rd Enf	9	X11
Jefferys st NW1	47	U20
Jeffs clo Hmptn	100	L14
Jeffs rd Sutt	129	W9
Jeken rd SE9	94	M11
Jelf rd SW2	90	G12
Jellicoe gdns Stan	10	L18
Jellicoe rd N17	31	O2
Jengar clo Sutt	130	B8
Jenkins la E6	66	L7
Jenkins la Bark	67	N6
Jenkins rd E13	65	X12
Jenner clo W3	61	Y15
Jenner rd SW13	74	J17
Jenner rd N16	49	W9
Jennett rd Croy	132	F5
Jennifer rd Brom	112	D6
Jennings rd SE22	91	V15
Jennings way Barn	4	A12
Jenningtree way Belv	81	Y5
Jenson way SE19	109	U18
Jenton ave Bexh	97	Z3
Jephson rd E7	52	L19
Jephtha rd SW18	87	X16
Jeppos la Mitch	120	L10
Jeremiah st E14	64	D18
Jeremys grn N18	19	O12
Jermyn st SW1	148	B12
Jerningham ave Ilf	35	Y6
Jerningham rd SE14	92	H1
Jerome cres NW8	138	J16
Jerome st E1	143	N19
Jerrard st SE13	93	S7
Jersey ave Stan	24	C8
Jersey par Houns	82	K1
Jersey rd E11	51	W5
Jersey rd E16	65	X16
Jersey rd SW17	107	R17
Jersey rd W7	71	Y6
Jersey rd Houns	82	L2
Jersey rd Ilf	54	A13
Jersey rd Islw	71	N19
Jersey rd Rain	57	X20
Jersey st E2	143	X13
Jervis ct W1	147	Z6
Jerviston gdns SW16	108	F14
Jesmond ave Wem	43	O17
Jesmond rd Croy	123	X17
Jesmond way Stan	11	Y15
Jessam ave E5	49	Z4
Jessamine rd W7	71	U3
Jesse rd E10	51	T5
Jessica rd SW18	88	E15
Jessop ave Sthl	70	E11
Jessops way Croy	121	V15
Jetstar way Nthlt	58	A9
Jevington way SE12	112	J3
Jewel rd E17	33	O10
Jewry st EC3	151	N6
Jew's row SW18	88	B10
Jews wk SE26	110	B9
Jeymer ave NW2	44	L16
Jeymer dr Grnf	58	L4
Jeypore rd SW18	88	D17
Jillian clo Hmptn	100	H18
Jim Bradley clo SE18	78	K11
Joan cres SE9	95	O20
Joan gdns Dag	55	Z5
Joan rd Dag	55	Z5
Joan st SE1	149	W15
Jocelyn rd Rich	84	K8
Jockey's flds WC1	141	P20
Jodrell rd E3	63	Z2
Johanna st SE1	149	T18
John Adam st WC2	148	L11
John Ashby clo SW2	90	A15
John Bradshaw rd N14	16	M4
John Burns dr Bark	67	W1
John Campbell rd N16	49	T15
John Carpenter st EC4	149	V8
John Deed Industrial est Mitch	120	L14
John Felton rd SE16	151	S18
John Fisher st E1	151	S9
John Gooch dr Enf	7	V7
John Groom's est Edg	12	J13
John Islip st SW1	156	H9
John McKenna wk SE16	159	V1
John Newton ct Well	97	S8
John Parker clo Dag	56	H19
John Penn st SE13	93	S3
John Perrin pl Har	24	L20
John Princes st W1	147	Z10
John Roll way SE16	159	U1
John Ruskin st SE5	157	X18
John Spencer sq N1	48	J18
John st E15	65	P4
John st SE25	123	Y9
John st WC1	141	P19
John st Enf	8	G16
John st Houns	82	C4
John Wilson st SE18	78	J9
John Woolley clo SE13	93	Z9
Johns ave NW4	26	M12
Johns la Mord	120	D13
John's ms WC1	141	P19
John's ter Croy	123	R20
Johnson clo E8	143	T3
Johnson rd Brom	127	O12
Johnson rd Croy	123	N17
Johnson st E1	63	R18
Johnsons clo Cars	131	N4
Johnson's pl SW1	156	C11
Johnsons way NW10	61	S11
Johnston rd Wdf Grn	21	S17
Johnstone rd E6	66	H10
Joiner st SE1	150	G14
Jollys la Har	41	P4
Jolly's la Hayes	58	A13
Jonathan st SE11	157	O8
Jones rd E13	65	W13
Jonquil gdns Hmptn	100	F15
Jonson clo Mitch	121	T8
Joram way SE16	159	X10
Jordan clo Dag	56	G11
Jordan rd Grnf	60	C2
Jordans clo Islw	83	U3
Joseph ave W3	61	X17
Joseph Powell clo SW12	89	U16
Joseph st E3	63	Z13
Josephine ave SW2	90	D14
Joshua st E14	64	G16
Joubert st SW11	88	M4
Jowett st SE15	159	P18
Joyce ave N18	18	H17
Joydon dr Rom	37	R18
Joyners clo Dag	56	B11
Jubilee ave E4	20	H17
Jubilee ave Rom	38	H17
Jubilee ave Twick	83	N20
Jubilee clo NW9	25	Y18
Jubilee clo Rom	38	H16
Jubilee cres E14	76	H9
Jubilee cres N9	18	K4
Jubilee dr Ruis	40	B12
Jubilee gdns Sthl	58	G16
Jubilee pl SW3	154	M9
Jubilee rd Grnf	60	A2
Jubilee rd Sutt	129	R16
Jubilee st E1	63	P14
Jubilee way SW19	120	B2
Jubilee way Sid	115	O5
Judd st WC1	140	J13
Jude st E16	65	P18
Juer st SW11	154	M19
Julia gdns Bark	68	K5
Julian ave W3	61	U20
Julian clo Barn	4	M11
Julian hill Har	41	U7
Julian pl E14	76	E13
Julien rd W5	72	E9
Junction app SW11	88	J9
Junction ms W2	146	K3
Junction pl W2	146	J3
Junction rd E13	65	W5
Junction rd N9	18	K6
Junction rd N17	31	X10
Junction rd N19	47	V10
Junction rd W5	72	F11
Junction rd Har	23	S19
Junction rd Rom	39	T13
Junction rd S Croy	133	N13
Junction Road east Rom	55	Z1
Junction Road west Rom	37	Y20
Junction wf N1	142	A9
Juniper clo Wem	43	O15
Juniper gdns SW16	121	U1
Juniper la E6	66	E15
Juniper rd Ilf	53	Y11
Juniper st E1	63	P19
Juno way SE14	75	T15
Jupiter way N7	48	D17
Jupp rd E15	64	J1
Jupp Road west E15	64	J2
Justice wk SW3	154	J15
Justin clo Brent	72	H19
Justin rd E4	19	Z20
Jute la Enf	9	X10
Jutland rd E13	65	U12
Jutland rd SE6	93	T20
Jutsums av Rom	38	H19
Jutsums la Rom	38	H18
Juxon clo Har	22	L5
Juxon st SE11	157	P4

K

Kale rd Erith	80	L6
Kambala rd SW11	88	H6
Kangley Bridge rd SE26	110	L10
Karen ct Brom	126	C1
Karoline gdns Grnf	59	P5
Kashgar rd SE18	79	Y12
Kashmir rd SE7	78	A18
Kassala rd SW11	88	M2

Name	Page	Ref
Katella Trading est Bark	67	V7
Katharine st Croy	133	N5
Katherine gdns SE9	95	O12
Katherine gdns Ilf	36	C1
Katherine rd E6	66	B3
Katherine rd E7	52	L16
Kathleen ave W3	61	W13
Kathleen ave Wem	60	K1
Kathleen rd SW11	88	M8
Kay rd SW9	90	C6
Kay st E2	143	U8
Kay st E15	64	K1
Kay st Well	97	R2
Kayemoor rd Sutt	130	H16
Kean st WC2	149	N6
Keats ave Rom	39	Y3
Keats clo SE1	159	O7
Keats clo SW19	106	F15
Keats gro NW3	46	H12
Keats pl EC2	150	F2
Keats rd Belv	81	X8
Keats rd Well	96	K2
Keats way Croy	124	D15
Keats way Grnf	58	J15
Keble clo Nthlt	41	O15
Keble st SW17	106	E9
Kechill gdns Brom	126	F18
Kedleston wk E2	143	Y11
Keedonwood rd Brom	112	A11
Keel clo SE16	75	U4
Keeley rd Croy	132	L3
Keeley st WC2	149	N5
Keeling rd SE9	95	N13
Keely clo Barn	5	X16
Keemor clo SE18	78	K18
Keens rd Croy	132	M8
Keens yd N1	48	J18
Keep the SE3	94	E5
Keep the Kings T	102	M17
Keetons rd SE16	151	V20
Keevil dr SW19	87	R19
Keighley clo N7	48	A13
Keightley dr SE9	114	D2
Keildon rd SW1	88	M11
Keir Hardie way Bark	68	A1
Keith gro W12	74	G4
Keith rd E17	32	M5
Keith rd Bark	67	T5
Kelbrook rd SE3	95	R6
Kelby path SE9	114	A8
Kelceda clo NW2	44	H5
Kelfield gdns W10	144	E4
Kell st SE1	149	Y20
Kelland rd E13	65	T10
Kellaway rd SE3	94	M4
Kellerton rd SE13	93	Z13
Kellett rd SW2	90	F11
Kelling gdns Croy	122	J17
Kellino st SW17	106	M10
Kellner rd SE28	79	X8
Kelly rd NW7	14	E18
Kelly st NW1	47	T18
Kelly way Rom	37	Z17
Kelman clo SW4	89	Y5
Kelmore gro SE22	91	X10
Kelmscott clo E17	32	L6
Kelmscott gdns W12	74	G7
Kelmscott rd SW11	88	L14
Kelross rd N5	48	K12
Kelsall clo SE3	94	J4
Kelsey la Beck	125	O5
Kelsey Park ave Beck	125	R5
Kelsey Park rd Beck	125	P3
Kelsey st E2	143	V15
Kelsey way Beck	125	N6
Kelso pl W8	153	Y2
Kelso rd Cars	120	E18
Kelston rd Ilf	36	A6
Kelvedon clo Kings T	103	O16
Kelvedon rd SW6	153	R20
Kelvin ave N13	17	R18
Kelvin ave Tedd	101	U15
Kelvin cres Har	10	F20
Kelvin dr Twick	84	C15
Kelvin gdns Sthl	58	G17
Kelvin gro SE26	110	A7
Kelvin Industrial est Grnf	58	L2
Kelvin rd N5	48	K13
Kelvin rd Well	96	M7
Kelvington clo Croy	124	J16
Kelvington rd SE15	92	E13
Kember st N1	141	N1
Kemble rd N17	31	W5
Kemble rd SE23	110	G1
Kemble rd Croy	132	H5
Kemble st WC2	149	N6
Kemerton rd SE5	90	L8
Kemerton rd Beck	125	T4
Kemerton rd Croy	123	V18
Kemeys st E9	50	H16
Kemnal rd Chis	114	D18
Kemp gdns Croy	122	L16
Kemp rd Dag	55	W4
Kempe rd NW6	136	G10
Kemplay rd NW3	46	G12
Kemps gdns SE13	93	V13
Kempsford gdns SW5	153	V10
Kempsford rd SE11	157	V7
Kempshott rd SW16	107	Z17
Kempson rd SW6	153	W20
Kempt st SE18	78	K17
Kempthorne rd SE8	75	X11
Kempton ave Nthlt	40	H17
Kempton clo Erith	81	Y16
Kempton rd E6	66	F3
Kempton wk Croy	124	J15
Kemsing clo Bex	98	A17
Kemsing clo Th Hth	122	M9
Kemsing rd SE10	77	S14
Ken way Wem	43	W8
Kenbury st SE5	90	L4
Kenchester clo SW8	156	L19
Kencot way Erith	81	P6
Kendal ave N18	18	B13
Kendal ave W3	61	R12
Kendal ave Bark	67	V2
Kendal clo SW9	157	W18
Kendal clo Wdf Grn	21	R8
Kendal cft Horn	57	W15
Kendal gdns N18	18	B13
Kendal gdns Sutt	130	D3
Kendal par N18	18	B14
Kendal pl SW15	87	U13
Kendal rd NW10	44	G13
Kendal st W2	146	M6
Kendale rd Brom	111	Z13
Kendall ave Beck	124	H3
Kendall ave S Croy	133	O20
Kendall pl W1	147	T3
Kendall rd Beck	124	H3
Kendall rd Islw	83	X6
Kender st SE14	75	R20
Kendoa rd SW4	89	Z10
Kendon clo E11	34	J16
Kendra Hall rd S Croy	132	J17
Kendrey gdns Twick	83	S17
Kendrick ms SW7	154	F6
Kendrick pl SW7	154	F6
Kenelm clo Har	41	Y8
Kenerne dr Barn	4	D16
Keniford rd SW12	89	T18
Kenilworth ave E17	33	P9
Kenilworth ave SW19	105	X12
Kenilworth ave Har	40	D12
Kenilworth cres Enf	8	E4
Kenilworth gdns SE18	95	Z4
Kenilworth gdns Ilf	54	L5
Kenilworth gdns Sthl	58	F9
Kenilworth rd E3	63	V6
Kenilworth rd NW6	137	R3
Kenilworth rd SE20	110	E20
Kenilworth rd W5	72	J3
Kenilworth rd Edg	12	G9
Kenilworth rd Epsom	128	F13
Kenley ave NW9	26	A5
Kenley clo Bex	98	F19
Kenley clo Th Hth	122	J9
Kenley rd SW19	119	W4
Kenley rd Kings T	117	T3
Kenley rd Twick	84	A16
Kenley wk W11	144	L11
Kenley wk Sutt	129	O9
Kenlor rd SW17	106	G16
Kenmare dr Mitch	106	M18
Kenmare gdns N13	17	X14
Kenmare rd Th Hth	122	E15
Kenmere rd Well	97	T5
Kenmont gdns NW10	62	J8
Kenmore ave Har	23	Z13
Kenmore gdns Edg	25	T6
Kenmore rd Har	24	G10
Kenmure rd E8	50	A16
Kennard rd E15	64	J1
Kennard rd N11	15	Z16
Kennard st E16	78	G3
Kennard st SW11	89	O3
Kennedy ave Enf	9	R19
Kennedy clo E13	65	T7
Kennedy rd W7	59	T13
Kennedy rd Bark	67	V4
Kennet clo SW11	88	F9
Kennet rd W9	137	P17
Kennet rd Dart	99	X8
Kennet rd Islw	83	V7
Kennet sq Mitch	120	H1
Kennet st E1	151	T12
Kennet Wharf la EC4	150	C9
Kenneth ave Ilf	53	Y11
Kenneth cres NW2	44	L15
Kenneth gdns Stan	10	L19
Kenneth rd Rom	55	X1
Kennett dr Hayes	58	B14
Kenning ter N1	142	J5
Kenninghall rd E5	49	X10
Kenninghall rd N18	19	O15
Kennings way SE11	157	V10
Kennington grn SE11	157	T12
Kennington gro SE11	157	P12
Kennington la SE11	157	P11
Kennington Oval SE11	157	P14
Kennington Park gdns SE11	157	W14
Kennington Park pl SE11	157	V12
Kennington Park rd SE11	157	V12
Kennington rd SE1	157	T2
Kennington rd SE11	157	T9
Kenny rd NW7	14	F17
Kennylands rd Ilf	37	O1
Kensal rd W10	136	J16
Kensington ave E12	53	S19
Kensington ave Th Hth	122	F2
Kensington Church ct W8	145	X18
Kensington Church st W8	145	V14
Kensington Church wk W8	145	W17
Kensington ct W8	145	Z19
Kensington Court pl W8	145	Z20
Kensington dr Wdf Grn	35	P6
Kensington gdns Ilf	53	U5
Kensington Gardens sq W2	145	X6
Kensington gate W8	146	C20
Kensington Gore SW7	146	E18
Kensington Hall gdns W14	153	P9
Kensington High st W8	153	R2
Kensington High st W14	153	N4
Kensington mall W8	145	V12
Kensington Palace gdns W8	145	W11
Kensington Park gdns W11	145	P10
Kensington Park ms W11	145	O6
Kensington Park rd W11	145	O7
Kensington pl W8	145	U13
Kensington rd SW7	146	H18
Kensington rd W8	146	A18
Kensington rd Nthlt	58	G8
Kensington rd Rom	38	L18
Kensington sq W8	145	Y19
Kensington ter S Croy	133	O18
Kent ave W13	60	A13
Kent ave Dag	69	T12
Kent ave Well	96	M12
Kent clo Mitch	122	B8
Kent dr Barn	6	D15
Kent dr Tedd	101	S12
Kent gdns W13	60	B13
Kent Gate way Croy	134	M15
Kent House la Beck	110	K14
Kent House rd SE26	110	H12
Kent pas NW1	139	N15
Kent rd N21	18	B2
Kent rd W4	73	W9
Kent rd Dag	56	J15
Kent rd Kings T	116	H6
Kent rd Rich	73	P19
Kent rd W Wick	135	T1
Kent st E2	143	P7
Kent st E13	65	X9
Kent ter NW1	139	N15
Kent View gdns Ilf	54	H7
Kentford way Nthlt	58	A4
Kentish bldgs SE1	150	E16
Kentish rd Belv	81	S11
Kentish Town rd NW1	139	Z3
Kentish Town rd NW5	47	T20
Kentish way Brom	126	G5
Kentmere rd SE18	79	W12
Kenton ave Har	23	V20
Kenton ave Sthl	58	H20
Kenton gdns Har	24	E14
Kenton la Har	10	H19
Kenton Park ave Har	24	F14
Kenton Park clo Har	24	E14
Kenton Park cres Har	24	E13
Kenton Park rd Har	24	E13
Kenton rd E9	50	F18
Kenton rd Har	23	W20
Kenton st WC1	140	K16
Kentwode grn SW13	74	G18
Kenver ave N12	15	T20
Kenward rd SE9	94	M13
Kenway Rom	38	J6
Kenway rd SW5	153	W7
Kenwood ave N14	6	L17
Kenwood clo NW3	46	F3
Kenwood dr Beck	125	U6
Kenwood gdns E18	34	H9
Kenwood gdns Ilf	35	X13
Kenwood rd N6	29	N17
Kenwood rd N9	18	L6
Kenworthy rd E9	50	H16
Kenwyn dr NW2	44	C8
Kenwyn rd SW4	89	Y10
Kenwyn rd SW20	118	M1
Kenya rd SE7	78	A20
Kenyngton pl Har	24	D16
Kenyon st SW6	152	H20
Keogh rd E15	52	A17
Kepler rd SW4	90	A10
Keppel rd E6	66	F1
Keppel rd Dag	55	Y11
Keppel row SE1	150	B14
Keppel st WC1	140	G20
Kerbela st E2	143	S16
Kerbey st E14	64	E18
Kerfield cres SE5	91	O3
Kerfield pl SE5	91	P3
Kerrison pl W5	72	H3
Kerrison rd E15	64	J3
Kerrison rd SW11	88	J6
Kerrison rd W5	72	H3
Kerry ave Stan	11	T13
Kerry clo E16	65	V17
Kerry ct Stan	11	T14
Kersey gdns SE9	113	R9
Kersfield rd SW15	87	R16
Kershaw clo SW18	88	E16
Kershaw rd Dag	56	F8
Kersley ms SW11	88	L3
Kersley rd N16	49	T8

Kersley st SW11	88	L3
Kerswell clo N15	31	R16
Kerwick clo N7	48	B19
Keslake rd NW6	136	G10
Kessock clo N17	31	Z15
Keston clo N18	18	C12
Keston clo Well	80	F19
Keston rd N17	31	O11
Keston rd SE15	91	W8
Keston rd Th Hth	122	E14
Kestrel ave E6	66	D15
Kestrel ave SE24	90	L13
Kestrel clo NW9	26	B6
Kestrel clo N10	43	Y16
Kestrel clo Horn	57	Y19
Kestrel way Croy	135	X19
Keswick ave SW15	104	A13
Keswick ave SW19	119	V4
Keswick clo Sutt	130	D8
Keswick gdns Ilf	35	R14
Keswick gdns Wem	42	J13
Keswick ms W5	72	J3
Keswick rd SW15	87	T13
Keswick rd Bexh	98	D3
Keswick rd Twick	82	M16
Keswick rd W Wick	135	Z2
Kett gdns SW2	90	E12
Kettering st SW17	107	U16
Kettlebaston rd E10	50	K4
Kevelioc rd N17	31	N5
Kew bri Brent	73	O15
Kew bri Rich	73	O16
Kew Bridge ct W4	73	O15
Kew Bridge rd Brent	73	N15
Kew cres Sutt	129	U6
Kew Foot rd Rich	84	J9
Kew Gardens rd Rich	73	O17
Kew grn Rich	73	N17
Kew Meadows path Rich	85	S2
Kew rd Rich	84	J10
Key clo E1	143	Z19
Keyes rd NW2	45	R14
Keymer rd SW2	108	D5
Keynes clo N2	29	N11
Keynsham ave Wdf Grn	21	N14
Keynsham gdns SE9	95	P13
Keynsham rd SE9	95	P13
Keynsham rd Mord	120	A19
Keynsham rd Mord	120	A19
Keyse rd SE1	159	O4
Keystone cres N1	140	M10
Keyworth pl SE1	157	Y1
Keyworth st SE1	149	Y20
Kezia st SE8	75	V14
Khama rd SW17	106	J10
Khartoum rd E13	65	V9
Khartoum rd SW17	106	G10
Khartoum rd Ilf	54	A15
Khyber rd SW11	88	J6
Kibworth st SW8	157	O19
Kidbrooke gdns SE3	94	F3
Kidbrooke gro SE3	94	G2
Kidbrooke la SE9	95	S11
Kidbrooke Park clo SE3	94	H3
Kidbrooke Park rd SE3	94	G1
Kidbrooke way SE3	94	K6
Kidd pl SE7	78	E12
Kidderminster pl Croy	122	K19
Kidderminster rd Croy	122	K19
Kidderpore ave NW3	45	Z12
Kidderpore gdns NW3	45	Z12
Kidlington way NW9	26	A5
Kidron way E9	63	P2
Kiffen st EC2	142	H17
Kilberry clo Islw	83	R6
Kilburn High rd NW6	137	U3
Kilburn la W9	136	K11
Kilburn Park rd NW6	137	U15
Kilburn pl NW6	137	V5
Kilburn Priory NW6	137	X7
Kilburn vale NW6	137	W5
Kildare rd E16	65	T14
Kildare ter W2	145	V4
Kildoran rd SW2	90	A13
Kildowan rd Ilf	55	N4
Kilgour rd SE23	92	H15
Kilkie st SW6	88	C5
Killarney rd SW18	88	D16
Killearn rd SE6	111	W1
Killester gdns Wor Pk	128	L10
Killick st N1	141	N8
Killieser ave SW2	108	A4
Killip clo E16	65	R16
Killowen ave Nthlt	41	N14
Killowen rd E9	50	E19
Killyon rd SW8	89	W5
Kilmaine rd SW6	152	M20
Kilmarnock gdns Dag	55	U10
Kilmarsh rd W6	152	B5
Kilmartin ave SW16	122	E6
Kilmartin rd Ilf	55	O7
Kilmartin way Horn	57	Y16
Kilmington rd SW13	74	G16
Kilmorey gdns Twick	84	A12
Kilmorey rd Twick	84	A11
Kilmorie rd SE23	110	J1
Kiln pl NW5	47	P13
Kilner st E14	64	B15
Kilpatrick way Hayes	58	C15
Kilravock st W10	136	M14
Kilsby wk Dag	55	R19
Kilvinton dr Enf	8	C2
Kimball gdns SW6	87	S2
Kimber rd SW18	87	Y19
Kimberley ave E6	66	D5
Kimberley ave SE15	92	B6
Kimberley ave Ilf	54	G2
Kimberley ave Rom	38	J19
Kimberley gdns N4	30	J16
Kimberley gdns Enf	8	G12
Kimberley rd E4	20	M4
Kimberley rd E11	51	X5
Kimberley rd E16	65	O11
Kimberley rd E17	32	K4
Kimberley rd N17	31	X7
Kimberley rd N18	19	N17
Kimberley rd NW6	137	N3
Kimberley rd SW9	90	B6
Kimberley rd Beck	124	G3
Kimberley rd Croy	122	K14
Kimberley way E4	21	N5
Kimble cres (Bushey) Wat	10	A2
Kimble rd SW19	106	G14
Kimbolton clo SE12	94	D17
Kimmeridge gdns SE9	113	S9
Kimmeridge rd SE9	113	R10
Kimpton Industrial est Sutt	129	V3
Kimpton rd SE5	91	O1
Kimpton rd Sutt	129	V5
Kinburn st SE16	75	S4
Kincaid rd SE15	159	W19
Kinch gro Har	24	L20
Kinder clo SE28	68	H20
Kinder st E1	151	W6
Kinfauns rd SW2	108	G5
Kinfauns rd Ilf	55	O4
King Alfred ave SE6	111	P10
King & Queen st SE17	158	D8
King Arthur clo SE15	75	P20
King Charles cres Surb	116	N17
King Charles rd Surb	116	M13
King Charles st SW1	148	H17
King David la E1	63	P19
King Edward ms SW13	86	G2
King Edward rd E10	51	U3
King Edward rd E17	32	H10
King Edward rd Barn	4	L13
King Edward rd Rom	39	T17
King Edward st EC1	149	Z4
King Edward wk SE1	157	U1
King Edwards gdns W3	73	R3
King Edwards gro Tedd	102	C16
King Edwards rd E9	143	Y3
King Edwards rd N9	18	M2
King Edwards rd Bark	67	S3
King Edward's rd Enf	9	U14
King gdns Croy	132	H10
King George ave E16	66	A17
King George ave Ilf	36	F16
King George clo Rom	38	L10
King George VI ave Mitch	121	N9
King George sq Rich	85	N16
King George st SE10	76	H20
King Georges dr Sthl	58	E14
King Harolds way Bexh	80	J19
King Henry st N16	49	S15
King Henry's dr Croy	135	T20
King Henry's rd NW3	138	J1
King Henrys rd Kings T	117	T6
King Henry's wk N1	49	R16
King James st SE1	149	Y19
King John ct EC2	142	L16
King John st E1	63	U15
King John's wk SE9	113	O2
King sq EC1	142	A14
King st E13	65	S12
King st EC2	150	D6
King st N2	28	F8
King st N17	31	U3
King st SW1	148	C14
King st W3	73	U3
King st W6	152	B7
King st WC2	148	K8
King st Rich	84	G13
King st Sthl	70	C9
King st Twick	101	Y2
King William st EC4	150	G10
King William wk SE10	76	H16
Kingaby gdns Rain	57	W19
Kingcup clo Croy	124	F19
Kingdon rd NW6	45	Y17
Kingfield rd W5	60	H10
Kingfield st E14	76	H11
Kingfisher clo SE28	68	G19
Kingfisher dr Rich	102	C9
Kingfisher st E6	66	E14
Kingfisher way NW10	43	Y16
Kingham clo SW18	88	C18
Kingham clo W11	144	K16
Kinghorn st EC1	149	Z1
Kinglake st SE17	158	J11
Kingly st W1	148	B8
Kings Arbour Sthl	70	B14
Kings Arms yd EC2	150	E5
Kings ave N10	29	P9
Kings ave N21	17	W4
King's ave SW4	89	Z12
King's ave SW12	89	Y20
Kings ave W5	60	H16
Kings ave Brom	112	B16
Kings ave Cars	130	K18
Kings ave Grnf	58	J15
Kings ave Houns	82	L2
Kings ave N Mal	118	C8
Kings ave Rom	38	C17
Kings ave Wdf Grn	21	W18
Kings Bench st SE1	149	Y17
Kings Bench wk EC4	149	U7
Kings clo E10	51	S2
Kings clo NW4	27	R13
Kings clo Dart	99	P11
Kings College rd NW3	46	H19
Kings ct E13	65	W4
Kings cres N4	48	L8
King's Cross rd WC1	141	P14
Kings dr Edg	11	Z14
Kings dr Surb	117	P16
Kings dr Tedd	101	P14
Kings dr T Ditt	116	A16
Kings dr Wem	43	T4
Kings Farm ave Rich	85	O10
Kings gdns NW6	137	V2
Kings gdns Ilf	54	E3
King's Garth ms SE23	110	C4
Kings gro SE15	159	Y20
Kings gro Rom	39	V16
Kings Hall rd Beck	110	L18
Kings Head hill E4	20	F13
Kings Head yd SE1	150	F14
Kings Highway SE18	79	W16
Kings Keep Kings T	116	K10
Kings la Sutt	130	H12
Kings ms SW4	89	Z13
King's ms WC1	141	R19
King's Orchard SE9	95	S16
King's pas E11	52	A1
Kings pas Kings T	116	G4
Kings pl SE1	150	B19
Kings pl Buck H	21	Z8
Kings Ride gate Rich	85	P11
Kings rd E4	20	J5
Kings rd E6	65	Z3
Kings rd E11	51	Z1
King's rd N17	31	U3
Kings rd N18	18	L15
King's rd N22	30	E4
Kings rd NW10	44	J20
Kings rd SE25	123	Y6
King's rd SW1	155	V4
King's rd SW3	154	G14
Kings rd SW10	154	A19
Kings rd SW14	85	Z9
Kings rd SW19	105	X16
Kings rd W5	60	H15
Kings rd Barn	4	A12
Kings rd Har	40	D7
Kings rd Kings T	102	J19
Kings rd Mitch	121	P5
Kings rd Rich	84	L15
Kings rd Rom	39	V16
Kings rd Surb	116	D20
Kings rd Tedd	101	R12
Kings rd Twick	84	C16
King's Scholars' pas SW1	156	B3
King's ter NW1	140	B6
Kings wk Kings T	102	H20
Kings way Har	23	T12
Kingsand rd SE12	112	F23
Kingsash rd Hayes	58	A11
Kingsbridge ave W3	73	N5
Kingsbridge cres Sthl	58	D15
Kingsbridge rd W10	144	E3
Kingsbridge rd Bark	67	U6
Kingsbridge rd Mord	119	P16
Kingsbridge rd Sthl	70	D12
Kingsbury circ NW9	25	O15
Kingsbury rd N1	49	S17
Kingsbury rd NW9	25	T15
Kingsbury ter N1	49	S16
Kingsbury Trading est NW9	25	X18
Kingsclere clo SW15	86	F18
Kingscliffe gdns SW19	105	U3
Kingscote rd W4	73	Y9
Kingscote rd Croy	124	A19
Kingscote rd N Mal	117	Y7
Kingscote st EC4	149	W8
Kingscourt rd SW16	107	Y7
Kingscroft rd NW2	45	U17
Kingsdale gdns W11	144	H16
Kingsdale rd SE18	79	W18
Kingsdale rd SE20	110	F19
Kingsdown ave W3	62	B19
Kingsdown ave W13	72	C5
Kingsdown ave S Croy	132	K20
Kingsdown clo W10	144	H6
Kingsdown rd E11	52	A10
Kingsdown rd N19	47	Z7
Kingsdown rd Sutt	129	S12

Name		
Kingsdown way Brom	126	E16
Kingsdowne rd Surb	116	L18
Kingsfield ave Har	22	L14
Kingsfield rd Har	41	S2
Kingsford ave Wall	132	B17
Kingsford st NW5	46	M15
Kingsgate Wem	43	V8
Kingsgate ave N3	27	Y11
Kingsgate clo Bexh	97	Y1
Kingsgate pl NW6	137	T2
Kingsgate rd NW6	137	U2
Kingsgate rd Kings T	116	J2
Kingsground SE9	95	P18
Kingshill ave Har	24	B11
Kingshill ave Wor Pk	118	H17
Kingshill dr Har	24	A8
Kingshold rd E9	63	R1
Kingsholm gdns SE9	95	P10
Kingshurst rd SE12	94	G19
Kingsland grn E8	49	T17
Kingsland High st E8	49	T17
Kingsland rd E2	142	L13
Kingsland rd E8	142	M2
Kingsland rd E13	65	Y9
Kingslawn clo SW15	86	K12
Kingsleigh pl Mitch	120	M7
Kingsleigh wk Brom	126	C10
Kingsley ave W13	59	Y16
Kingsley ave Houns	83	N4
Kingsley ave Sthl	70	G1
Kingsley ave Sutt	130	H9
Kingsley clo N2	28	C15
Kingsley clo Dag	56	G12
Kingsley gdns E4	20	C15
Kingsley ms W8	153	Z2
Kingsley pl N6	47	R1
Kingsley rd E7	52	G20
Kingsley rd E17	33	U8
Kingsley rd N13	17	V13
Kingsley rd NW6	137	R3
Kingsley rd SW19	106	B12
Kingsley rd Croy	122	F20
Kingsley rd Har	40	M11
Kingsley rd Houns	83	N6
Kingsley rd Ilf	36	C4
Kingsley rd Pnr	22	E13
Kingsley st SW11	89	N6
Kingsley way N2	28	C15
Kingsley Wood dr SE9	113	U7
Kingslyn cres SE19	123	R2
Kingsman st SE18	78	H9
Kingsmead Barn	4	L13
Kingsmead Rich	85	N16
Kingsmead ave N9	19	N5
Kingsmead ave NW9	43	Y2
Kingsmead ave Mitch	121	W5
Kingsmead ave Rom	39	S17
Kingsmead ave Wor Pk	128	J4
Kingsmead clo Sid	115	N5
Kingsmead clo Tedd	102	A16
Kingsmead dr Nthlt	40	F20
Kingsmead est E9	50	K13
Kingsmead rd SW2	108	F5
Kingsmead way E9	50	K13
Kingsmere pk NW9	43	U4
Kingsmere rd SW19	105	R4
Kingsmill gdns Dag	56	C16
Kingsmill rd Dag	56	C16
Kingsmill ter NW8	138	G8
Kingsnympton pk Kings T	103	T17
Kingspark ct E18	34	E9
Kingsridge SW19	105	S4
Kingsthorpe rd SE26	110	F11
Kingston ave Sutt	129	T7
Kingston bri Kings T	116	G3
Kingston clo Nthlt	58	E2
Kingston clo Rom	37	Y9
Kingston clo Tedd	102	B16
Kingston cres Beck	124	M1
Kingston gdns Croy	134	A4
Kingston Hall rd Kings T	116	H5
Kingston hill Kings T	103	R19
Kingston Hill ave Rom	37	Z8
Kingston la Tedd	101	Z13
Kingston pl Har	10	H20
Kingston rd N9	18	L7
Kingston rd SW15	104	J2
Kingston rd SW19	119	V2
Kingston rd SW20	119	N3
Kingston rd Barn	5	U17
Kingston rd Epsom	128	A10
Kingston rd Ilf	54	A12
Kingston rd Kings T	117	S6
Kingston rd N Mal	117	Y9
Kingston rd Rom	39	U13
Kingston rd Sthl	70	D6
Kingston rd Tedd	102	A12
Kingston sq SE19	109	P12
Kingston vale SW15	103	Y10
Kingstown st NW1	139	S4
Kingsway N12	15	R17
Kingsway SW14	85	T8
Kingsway WC2	149	N5
Kingsway Croy	132	D12
Kingsway Enf	9	N16
Kingsway N Mal	118	L10
Kingsway Wem	42	K12
Kingsway Wdf Grn	21	Y15
Kingsway cres Har	22	M13
Kingsway Industrial est N18	19	U18
Kingsway rd Sutt	129	S16
Kingswear rd NW5	47	S8
Kingswood ave NW6	136	L5
Kingswood ave Belv	81	O9
Kingswood ave Brom	125	Y8
Kingswood ave Hmptn	100	K16
Kingswood ave Houns	82	D3
Kingswood ave Th Hth	122	G13
Kingswood clo N20	15	N1
Kingswood clo SW8	156	L19
Kingswood clo Enf	8	F15
Kingswood clo Surb	116	K16
Kingswood dr SE19	109	T10
Kingswood dr Cars	131	N1
Kingswood est SE21	109	T9
Kingswood pk N3	27	U6
Kingswood pl SE13	94	A9
Kingswood rd SE20	110	C16
Kingswood rd SW2	90	A18
Kingswood rd SW19	105	W19
Kingswood rd W4	73	V9
Kingswood rd Brom	125	Y8
Kingswood rd Ilf	55	N3
Kingswood way Wall	132	A10
Kingsworth clo Beck	124	H11
Kingsworthy clo Kings T	117	N5
Kingthorpe rd NW10	43	Y19
Kingthorpe ter NW10	43	Y19
Kingwell rd Barn	5	U2
Kingwood rd SW6	152	L20
Kinlet rd SE18	96	B1
Kinloch dr NW9	43	Z1
Kinloch st N7	48	D10
Kinloss gdns N3	27	V11
Kinloss rd Cars	120	D19
Kinnaird ave W4	73	U20
Kinnaird ave Brom	112	D17
Kinnaird clo Brom	112	D16
Kinnear rd W12	74	D5
Kinnerton Place north SW1	147	S18
Kinnerton Place south SW1	147	S18
Kinnerton st SW1	147	S19
Kinnerton yd SW1	147	S19
Kinnoul rd W6	152	L13
Kinross ave Wor Pk	128	F3
Kinross clo Edg	12	F9
Kinross clo Har	24	L16
Kinsale rd SE15	91	Y8
Kintyre clo SW16	122	E5
Kinveachy gdns SE7	78	D13
Kinver rd SE26	110	D9
Kipling dr SW19	106	F14
Kipling est SE1	150	H18
Kipling rd Bexh	97	Z2
Kipling st SE1	150	G18
Kippington dr SE9	113	O2
Kirby clo Epsom	128	D12
Kirby gro SE1	150	J17
Kirby la SE18	79	P16
Kirby st EC1	141	U20
Kirchen rd W13	72	B1
Kirk la SE18	79	P16
Kirk rd E17	33	N18
Kirkdale SE26	110	A4
Kirkdale rd E11	52	A2
Kirkham rd E6	66	E16
Kirkham st SE18	79	V17
Kirkland ave Ilf	35	W7
Kirkland clo Sid	96	H15
Kirkland wk E8	49	U18
Kirkleas rd Surb	116	K19
Kirklees rd Dag	55	T16
Kirklees rd Th Hth	122	E11
Kirkley rd SW19	105	Z20
Kirkly clo S Croy	133	T20
Kirks pl E14	63	Y15
Kirkside rd SE3	77	T16
Kirkstall ave N17	31	O12
Kirkstall gdns SW2	107	Z1
Kirkstall rd SW2	107	Z2
Kirksted rd Mord	120	A19
Kirkstone way Brom	112	A17
Kirkton rd N15	31	S14
Kirkwall pl E2	63	R8
Kirkwood rd SE15	92	A4
Kirn rd W13	72	B1
Kirtley rd SE26	110	K9
Kirtling st SW8	156	C16
Kirton clo W4	73	Y12
Kirton gdns E2	143	P13
Kirton rd E13	65	Y5
Kirton wk Edg	25	W2
Kirwyn way SE5	157	Z17
Kitcat ter E3	64	B8
Kitchener rd E7	52	H18
Kitchener rd E17	33	S3
Kitchener rd N2	28	H11
Kitchener rd N17	31	R10
Kitchener rd Dag	123	N6
Kitchener rd Th Hth	123	N6
Kitley gdns SE19	123	U1
Kitson rd SE5	158	D16
Kitson rd SW13	86	F3
Kitson wk Edg	25	W2
Kitto rd SE14	92	E6
Kitts End rd Barn	4	F1
Kiver rd N19	47	Z6
Klea ave SW4	89	V15
Knapdale clo SE23	110	A4
Knapmill rd SE6	111	P4
Knapmill way SE6	111	R5
Knapp clo NW10	44	C16
Knapp rd E3	64	B12
Knaresborough pl SW5	153	X5
Knatchbull rd NW10	61	Z2
Knatchbull rd SE5	90	J4
Knebworth ave E17	33	O4
Knebworth rd N16	49	S11
Knee hill SE2	80	G10
Knee Hill cres SE2	80	G11
Kneller gdns Islw	83	P15
Kneller rd SE4	92	J10
Kneller rd N Mal	118	A17
Kneller rd Twick	82	M15
Knighten st E1	151	V14
Knightland rd E5	49	Z5
Knighton clo Rom	38	M18
Knighton clo S Croy	132	J18
Knighton clo Wdf Grn	21	W13
Knighton la Buck H	21	V9
Knighton Park rd SE26	110	G12
Knighton rd E7	52	F11
Knighton rd Rom	38	M18
Knightrider st EC4	149	Z7
Knights ave W5	72	L6
Knights ct Kings T	116	K5
Knights Hill SE27	108	J14
Knights Hill sq SE27	108	K9
Knights la N9	18	L10
Knights pk Kings T	116	K6
Knights rd E16	77	U4
Knights rd Stan	11	S13
Knights wk SE11	157	W7
Knightsbridge SW1	147	S17
Knightsbridge SW7	154	L18
Knightsbridge gdns Rom	39	O16
Knightsbridge grn SW1	147	O18
Knightswood clo Edg	12	G8
Knightwood cres N Mal	118	B14
Knivet rd SW6	153	T16
Knobs Hill rd E15	64	D2
Knockholt rd SE9	95	N12
Knole the SE9	113	W10
Knole clo Croy	124	C14
Knole gate Sid	114	J6
Knole rd Dart	99	X18
Knoll the W13	60	D15
Knoll the Beck	125	R2
Knoll dr N14	16	C2
Knoll rd SW18	88	C14
Knoll rd Bex	98	D18
Knoll rd Sid	115	S10
Knollmead Surb	117	X20
Knolls clo Wor Pk	128	J5
Knollys clo SW16	108	G6
Knollys rd SW16	108	E7
Knottisford st E2	63	S8
Knotts Green rd E10	33	T18
Knowle ave Bexh	81	N18
Knowle clo SW9	90	F6
Knowle clo Twick	101	U2
Knowles Hill cres SE13	93	W14
Knowles wk SW4	89	W7
Knowlton grn Brom	126	D12
Knowsley ave Sthl	70	J3
Knowsley rd SW11	88	L5
Knox rd E7	52	D18
Knox st W1	147	O1
Kohat rd SW19	106	C12
Kossuth st SE10	76	M13
Kotree way SE1	159	U7
Kramer ms SW5	153	W10
Kreisel wk Rich	73	N16
Kuala gdns SW16	108	D20
Kylemore clo E6	66	B5
Kylemore rd NW6	45	Y19
Kymberley rd Har	23	S18
Kyme rd Horn	39	U19
Kynance gdns Stan	24	D5
Kynance ms SW7	154	A2
Kynance pl SW7	154	B2
Kynaston ave N16	49	S9
Kynaston ave Th Hth	122	L12
Kynaston clo Har	23	S1
Kynaston cres Th Hth	122	M11
Kynaston rd N16	49	S9
Kynaston rd Brom	112	F13
Kynaston rd Enf	8	C6
Kynaston rd Th Hth	122	M11
Kynaston wd Har	23	R1
Kynock rd N18	19	S14
Kyrle rd SW11	89	O15
Kyverdale rd N16	49	W2

L

Name		
Laburnum ave N9	18	F8
Laburnum ave N17	18	B20
Laburnum ave Horn	57	V8
Laburnum ave Sutt	130	J7
Laburnum clo E4	19	Z18
Laburnum clo N11	16	C19
Laburnum clo SE15	75	O20
Laburnum ct Stan	11	R14
Laburnum gdns N21	17	Z7
Laburnum gdns Croy	124	E19
Laburnum gro N21	17	Y7
Laburnum gro NW9	25	N20
Laburnum gro Houns	82	F10
Laburnum gro N Mal	117	X4

Laburnum gro Sthl	58	F12
Laburnum rd SW19	106	E18
Laburnum rd Mitch	121	P4
Laburnum st E2	142	M6
Laburnum way Brom	127	Y17
Lacebark clo Sid	96	M19
Lacey clo N9	18	L8
Lacey dr Edg	11	Y13
Lacey wk E3	64	A6
Lackington st EC2	142	G20
Lacock clo SW19	106	D16
Lacon rd SE22	91	W11
Lacy rd SW15	87	P9
Ladas rd SE27	108	L11
Ladbroke cres W11	144	L6
Ladbroke gdns W11	145	O9
Ladbroke gro W10	136	H15
Ladbroke gro W11	144	M5
Ladbroke rd W11	145	N13
Ladbroke rd Enf	8	H18
Ladbroke sq W11	145	P11
Ladbroke ter W11	145	R11
Ladbroke wk W11	145	R12
Ladbrook clo Pnr	22	E16
Ladbrook rd SE25	123	P8
Ladbrooke cres Sid	115	X8
Ladderstile ride Kings T	103	U14
Ladderswood way N11	16	G16
Lady Booth rd Kings T	116	J4
Lady Hay Wor Pk	128	D2
Lady Margaret rd N19	47	V12
Lady Margaret rd NW5	47	V15
Lady Margaret rd Sthl	58	E20
Lady Somerset rd NW5	47	S13
Ladycroft rd SE13	93	R8
Ladycroft wk Stan	24	G5
Ladygrove Croy	134	G20
Ladysmith ave E6	66	D5
Ladysmith ave Ilf	54	G1
Ladysmith rd E16	65	O10
Ladysmith rd N17	31	W7
Ladysmith rd N18	19	N17
Ladysmith rd SE9	95	X17
Ladysmith rd Enf	8	F12
Ladysmith rd Har	23	T8
Ladywell rd SE13	93	O12
Ladywell st E15	65	P4
Lafone st SE1	151	O16
Lagado ms SE16	75	T3
Laings ave Mitch	120	L2
Lainlock pl Houns	82	L3
Lainson st SW18	87	X19
Lairdale clo SE21	90	L20
Laitwood rd SW12	107	T1
Lake the (Bushey) Wat	10	B4
Lake ave Brom	112	F15
Lake dr (Bushey) Wat	10	B7
Lake gdns Dag	56	E15
Lake gdns Rich	102	B6
Lake gdns Wall	131	R7
Lake House rd E11	52	E9
Lake ri Rom	39	T8
Lake rd SW19	105	V13
Lake rd Croy	134	L2
Lake rd Rom	37	W13
Lake vw Edg	11	Z17
Lakedale rd SE18	79	V16
Lakefield rd N22	30	J8
Lakehall gdns Th Hth	122	J13
Lakehall rd Th Hth	122	J13
Lakehurst rd Epsom	128	A12
Lakeland clo Har	10	C18
Lakenheath N14	16	H16
Laker pl SW15	87	U15
Lakeside W13	60	D16
Lakeside Beck	125	S5
Lakeside Enf	6	L14
Lakeside ave Ilf	35	N13
Lakeside clo SE25	123	W4
Lakeside clo Sid	97	U14
Lakeside cres Barn	6	A18
Lakeside rd N13	17	P12
Lakeside rd W14	144	F20
Lakeside way Wem	43	O12
Lakeview ct SW19	105	T5
Lakeview rd SE27	108	J13
Lakeview rd Well	97	P10
Lakis clo NW3	46	E11
Laleham ave NW7	12	L10
Laleham rd SE6	93	U16
Lalor st SW6	87	T3
Lamb la E8	143	X1
Lamb st E1	143	N20
Lamb wk SE1	151	K19
Lambarde ave SE9	113	X10
Lamberhurst rd SE27	108	G11
Lamberhurst rd Dag	56	A4
Lambert ave Rich	85	S8
Lambert rd E16	65	V17
Lambert rd N12	15	S17
Lambert rd SW2	90	B14
Lambert st N1	141	S2
Lamberts pl Croy	123	P20
Lamberts rd Surb	116	L13
Lambeth bri SE1	156	M4
Lambeth bri SW1	156	L4
Lambeth High st SE1	157	N6
Lambeth hill EC4	150	B8
Lambeth Palace rd SE1	157	N3
Lambeth rd SE1	157	P3
Lambeth rd Croy	122	H19
Lambeth wk SE11	157	S4
Lamble st NW5	47	O14
Lambley rd Dag	55	R18
Lambolle pl NW3	46	K18
Lambolle rd NW3	46	J18
Lambourn clo W7	71	V7
Lambourn rd SW4	89	T7
Lambourne ave SW19	105	W9
Lambourne gdns E4	20	B7
Lambourne gdns Bark	67	Y1
Lambourne gdns Enf	8	G8
Lambourne gro Kings T	117	T3
Lambourne rd E11	51	W2
Lambourne rd Bark	67	W1
Lambourne rd Ilf	54	J6
Lambrook ter SW6	87	S2
Lamb's bldgs EC1	142	E18
Lamb's Conduit st WC1	141	N16
Lamb's meadow Wdf Grn	35	N7
Lambs ms N1	141	X6
Lamb's pas EC1	142	E19
Lambs wk Enf	7	Z9
Lambscroft ave SE9	113	N7
Lambton pl W11	145	S7
Lambton rd N19	48	A4
Lambton rd SW20	118	L1
Lamerock rd Brom	112	C9
Lamerton st Ilf	36	A6
Lamerton st SE8	76	B17
Lamford clo N17	18	C20
Lamington st W6	74	K10
Lamlash st SE11	157	X4
Lammas ave Mitch	121	O4
Lammas grn SE26	109	Z6
Lammas Park gdns W5	72	E4
Lammas Park rd W5	72	F4
Lammas rd E9	63	U1
Lammas rd E10	50	H5
Lammas rd Rich	102	E11
Lammermoor rd SW12	89	T19
Lamont rd SW10	154	F15
Lamont Road pas SW10	154	F15
Lamorbey clo Sid	114	K3
Lamorna gro Stan	24	G5
Lampard gro N16	49	V4
Lampern sq E2	143	U11
Lampeter sq W6	152	L15
Lampmead rd SE12	94	B12
Lamport clo SE18	78	G10
Lampton ave Houns	82	J3
Lampton House clo SW19	105	P10
Lampton Park rd Houns	82	K6
Lampton rd Houns	82	K4
Lanacre ave NW9	25	Z4
Lanark clo W5	60	E13
Lanark pl W9	138	D17
Lanark rd W9	137	Z11
Lanark sq E14	76	E8
Lanbury rd SE15	92	F11
Lancaster ave E18	34	H12
Lancaster ave SE27	108	K5
Lancaster ave SW19	105	R12
Lancaster ave Bark	67	V1
Lancaster ave Barn	5	S3
Lancaster ave Mitch	122	A11
Lancaster clo N1	142	L2
Lancaster clo N17	31	W3
Lancaster clo SE27	108	K5
Lancaster clo Brom	126	B9
Lancaster clo Kings T	102	H13
Lancaster ct SW6	153	S19
Lancaster dr NW3	46	H18
Lancaster gdn SW19	105	S12
Lancaster gdns W13	72	C4
Lancaster gdns Kings T	102	H13
Lancaster gate W2	146	C10
Lancaster gro NW3	46	H18
Lancaster ms W2	146	D8
Lancaster pk Rich	84	J14
Lancaster pl SW19	105	R13
Lancaster pl WC2	149	O9
Lancaster pl Twick	83	Z17
Lancaster rd E7	52	G20
Lancaster rd E11	52	A7
Lancaster rd E17	32	G7
Lancaster rd N4	48	F1
Lancaster rd N11	16	L18
Lancaster rd N18	18	H16
Lancaster rd NW10	44	F14
Lancaster rd SE25	123	V5
Lancaster rd SW19	105	R13
Lancaster rd W11	144	K7
Lancaster rd Barn	5	T15
Lancaster rd Enf	8	B5
Lancaster rd Nthlt	40	M16
Lancaster rd Sthl	70	B1
Lancaster st SE1	149	X18
Lancaster ter W2	146	F9
Lancaster wk W2	146	E12
Lance rd Har	41	N2
Lancefield st W10	137	O15
Lancell st N16	49	T8
Lancelot ave Wem	42	G12
Lancelot cres Wem	42	G12
Lancelot gdns Barn	16	B2
Lancelot pl SW7	147	N19
Lancelot rd Well	97	O9
Lancelot rd Wem	42	H13
Lancey clo SE7	78	C10
Lanchester rd N6	29	N15
Lancing gdns N9	18	H5
Lancing rd W13	60	B20
Lancing rd Croy	122	E16
Lancing rd Ilf	36	E19
Lancing st NW1	140	F13
Landcroft rd SE22	91	V14
Landells rd SE22	91	V17
Landford rd SW15	86	M8
Landgrove rd SW19	105	Y11
Landmann way SE14	75	T15
Landon pl SW1	155	P1
Landons clo E14	76	H2
Landor rd SW9	89	Z8
Landor wk W12	74	F5
Landra gdns N21	7	V19
Landridge rd SW6	87	U4
Landrock rd N8	30	B18
Landscape rd Wdf Grn	34	H2
Landseer ave E12	53	W14
Landseer clo SW19	120	E2
Landseer clo Edg	25	R6
Landseer clo Horn	57	Z3
Landseer rd N19	48	A8
Landseer rd Enf	8	J17
Landseer rd N Mal	117	Z17
Landseer rd Sutt	129	Y14
Landstead rd SE18	79	T19
Lane the NW8	138	A9
Lane the SE3	94	F7
Lane app NW7	14	F17
Lane clo NW2	44	J9
Lane end Bexh	98	G7
Lane gdns (Bushey) Wat	10	G3
Lanercost clo SW2	108	G3
Lanercost gdns N14	16	M1
Lanercost rd SW2	108	G3
Laneside Chis	114	B12
Laneside Edg	12	H16
Laneside ave Dag	56	D2
Lanfranc rd E3	63	W6
Lanfrey pl W14	153	P11
Lang st E1	63	P11
Langbourne ave N6	47	O8
Langbrook rd SE3	95	O6
Langcroft clo Cars	130	M6
Langdale ave Mitch	120	M6
Langdale clo SE17	158	B13
Langdale clo SW14	85	T9
Langdale cres Bexh	98	F1
Langdale gdns Horn	57	X15
Langdale rd SE10	76	F19
Langdale rd Th Hth	122	F9
Langdale st E1	151	V6
Langdon ct NW10	62	A3
Langdon cres E6	66	K5
Langdon dr NW9	43	V3
Langdon Park rd N6	47	U1
Langdon pl SW14	85	V7
Langdon rd E6	66	K4
Langdon rd Brom	126	H7
Langdon rd Mord	120	D13
Langdon Shaw Sid	114	K12
Langdon wk Mord	120	D12
Langford clo E8	49	X14
Langford clo N15	31	R18
Langford clo NW8	138	D8
Langford cres Barn	5	Z13
Langford grn SE5	91	R8
Langford pl NW8	138	D9
Langford pl Sid	115	O7
Langford rd SW6	88	B4
Langford rd Barn	5	Y13
Langford rd Wdf Grn	21	Z20
Langham dr Rom	37	P18
Langham gdns N21	7	U16
Langham gdns W13	60	C19
Langham gdns Edg	12	J20
Langham gdns Rich	102	E9
Langham gdns Wem	42	D7
Langham House clo Rich	102	F9
Langham pl N15	30	J10
Langham pl W1	147	Z3
Langham pl N15	30	H10
Langham rd SW20	119	N2
Langham rd Edg	12	J19
Langham rd Tedd	102	A13
Langham st W1	147	Z2
Langhedge clo N18	18	H18
Langhedge la N18	18	H18
Langhedge Lane Industrial est N18	18	H19
Langholm clo SW12	89	Y19
Langhorne rd Dag	56	E19
Langland cres Stan	24	H7
Langland dr Pnr	22	B1
Langland gdns NW3	46	B15
Langland gdns Croy	134	L3
Langler rd NW10	136	E11
Langley ave Surb	116	H20
Langley ave Wor Pk	129	O2
Langley ct SE9	95	X17
Langley ct WC2	148	K7
Langley cres E11	34	K19
Langley cres Dag	68	H1
Langley cres Edg	12	J11
Langley dr E11	34	J20
Langley dr W3	73	T4
Langley gdns Brom	126	L9
Langley gdns Dag	68	H1

Name	No.	Grid
Langley gro N Mal	118	A3
Langley la SW8	156	M13
Langley pk NW7	13	N18
Langley Park rd Sutt	130	D12
Langley rd SW19	119	W1
Langley rd Beck	124	H9
Langley rd Islw	83	X3
Langley rd Surb	116	K18
Langley rd Well	80	F17
Langley st WC2	148	K7
Langley way W Wick	125	X19
Langmead dr (Bushey) Wat	10	E4
Langmore ct Bexh	97	X8
Langroyd rd SW17	106	M5
Langside ave SW15	86	G10
Langside cres N14	16	L11
Langthorn ct EC2	150	F3
Langthorne rd E11	51	V9
Langthorne st SW6	152	G19
Langton ave E6	66	K9
Langton ave N20	15	S2
Langton clo WC1	141	P15
Langton ri SE23	92	A18
Langton rd NW2	44	M10
Langton rd SW9	157	X19
Langton rd Har	22	M2
Langton st SW10	154	D16
Langton way Croy	133	T7
Langtry rd NW8	137	X5
Langtry rd Nthlt	58	A5
Langwood chase Tedd	102	E16
Lanhill rd W9	137	T15
Lanier rd SE13	93	W15
Lankaster gdns N2	28	F5
Lankers dr Har	22	F17
Lankton clo Beck	125	T2
Lannoy rd SE9	114	B1
Lanrick rd E14	64	L16
Lanridge rd SE2	80	J9
Lansbury ave N18	18	C17
Lansbury ave Bark	68	A1
Lansbury ave Rom	37	Z16
Lansbury clo NW10	43	W16
Lansbury rd Enf	9	S6
Lansdell rd Mitch	121	O4
Lansdown rd Sid	115	P6
Lansdowne ave Bexh	80	H19
Lansdowne clo SW20	105	O19
Lansdowne cres W11	145	N9
Lansdowne dr E8	143	U1
Lansdowne gdns SW8	156	K20
Lansdowne gro NW10	44	B13
Lansdowne hill SE27	108	J7
Lansdowne la SE7	78	A14
Lansdowne ms SE7	78	A14
Lansdowne pl SE1	158	G2
Lansdowne pl SE19	109	U17
Lansdowne ri W11	144	M10
Lansdowne rd E4	20	B9
Lansdowne rd E11	52	C7
Lansdowne rd E17	33	N17
Lansdowne rd E18	34	F7
Lansdowne rd N3	27	X1
Lansdowne rd N10	29	V7
Lansdowne rd N17	31	W5
Lansdowne rd SW20	105	N18
Lansdowne rd W11	145	O13
Lansdowne rd Brom	112	G18
Lansdowne rd Croy	133	N2
Lansdowne rd Har	23	T20
Lansdowne rd Houns	82	K7
Lansdowne rd Ilf	54	K1
Lansdowne rd Stan	11	S20
Lansdowne ter WC1	140	M17
Lansdowne wk W11	145	N12
Lansdowne way SW8	89	Z2
Lansdowne Wood clo SE27	108	J6
Lant st SE1	150	B17
Lantern clo SW15	86	G10
Lantern clo Wem	42	H15
Lanvanor rd SE15	92	B5
Lapford clo W9	137	P15
Lapse Wood wk SE23	109	Z3
Lapstone gdns Har	24	E18
Lara clo SE13	93	V16
Larbert rd SW16	107	U19
Larch ave W3	74	A3
Larch clo N11	16	B20
Larch clo SW12	107	S3
Larch dr W4	73	P12
Larch gro Sid	114	M2
Larch rd NW2	45	N11
Larch Tree way Croy	135	P7
Larches the N13	17	Y12
Larches ave SW14	85	X10
Larchwood rd SE9	114	A4
Larcom st SE17	158	B7
Larcombe clo Croy	133	T9
Larden rd W3	74	B4
Larissa st SE17	158	H8
Lark row E2	143	Z6
Larkbere rd SE26	110	J10
Larken dr (Bushey) Wat	10	A4
Larkfield ave Har	24	C10
Larkfield rd Rich	84	K10
Larkfield rd Sid	114	K8
Larkhall la SW4	89	Z4
Larkhall ri SW4	89	W6
Larkhill ter SE18	78	J20
Larks gro Bark	54	J20
Larksfield gro Enf	9	N6
Larkshall cres E4	20	H14
Larkshall rd E4	20	J14
Larkspur clo E6	66	D13
Larkspur clo N17	31	O2
Larkswood clo Erith	99	X1
Larkswood rd E4	20	C14
Larkway clo NW9	25	Z13
Larnach rd W6	152	F15
Larpent ave SW15	86	L13
Larwood clo Grnf	41	P15
Lascelles ave Har	41	P1
Lascelles clo E11	51	X7
Lascotts rd N22	17	P19
Lassa rd SE9	95	T14
Lassell st SE10	76	L14
Latchett rd E18	34	J5
Latchmere clo Rich	102	L12
Latchmere la Kings T	102	M13
Latchmere rd SW11	88	M7
Latchmere rd Kings T	102	K17
Lateward rd Brent	72	H17
Latham clo E6	66	E16
Latham clo Twick	83	X18
Latham rd Bexh	98	D12
Latham rd Twick	83	X18
Lathams way Croy	132	C1
Lathkill clo Enf	18	J1
Lathom rd E6	66	F1
Latimer ave E6	66	G3
Latimer clo Wor Pk	128	K8
Latimer pl W10	144	D4
Latimer rd E7	52	J11
Latimer rd N15	31	S18
Latimer rd SW19	106	A16
Latimer rd W10	144	D5
Latimer rd Barn	5	N10
Latimer rd Tedd	101	V12
Latona rd SE15	159	R15
Latymer rd N9	18	G4
Latymer way N9	18	D8
Laud st SE11	157	N10
Laud st Croy	132	L7
Lauderdale dr Rich	102	G6
Lauderdale rd W9	137	X15
Laughton rd Nthlt	58	A4
Launcelot rd Brom	112	E10
Launcelot st SE1	149	S18
Launceston gdns Grnf	60	D2
Launceston pl W8	154	B1
Launceston rd Grnf	60	C3
Launch st E14	76	F7
Laundry rd W6	152	L15
Laura clo E11	34	K15
Laura clo Enf	8	E17
Laura pl E5	50	B12
Lauradale rd N2	29	N12
Laurel ave Twick	101	V1
Laurel Bank rd Enf	8	A5
Laurel clo Sid	115	O6
Laurel cres Croy	135	O7
Laurel cres Rom	57	P5
Laurel dr N21	17	T2
Laurel gdns E4	20	D2
Laurel gdns NW7	12	L11
Laurel gdns W7	71	T3
Laurel gdns Houns	82	A11
Laurel gro SE20	110	C18
Laurel gro SE26	110	G11
Laurel pk Har	23	W2
Laurel rd SW13	86	F5
Laurel rd SW20	104	H20
Laurel rd Hmptn	101	P13
Laurel st E8	49	V18
Laurel vw N12	15	N11
Laurel way E18	34	D12
Laurel way N20	14	M8
Laurence ms W12	74	F6
Laurence Pountney hill EC4	150	F8
Laurence Pountney la EC4	150	F7
Laurie gro SE14	92	K1
Laurie rd W7	59	T14
Laurie wk Rom	39	S14
Laurier rd NW5	47	S10
Laurier rd Croy	123	U17
Laurino pl (Bushey) Wat	10	B8
Lauriston rd E9	63	T2
Lauriston rd SW19	105	O15
Lausanne rd N8	30	F13
Lausanne rd SE15	92	D3
Lavell st N16	49	P12
Lavender ave NW9	43	V3
Lavender ave Mitch	120	J2
Lavender ave Wor Pk	129	N6
Lavender clo SW3	154	J15
Lavender clo Cars	131	R9
Lavender gdns SW11	88	M10
Lavender gdns Enf	7	X4
Lavender gro E8	143	R1
Lavender gro Mitch	120	L2
Lavender hill SW11	88	K9
Lavender hill Enf	7	U5
Lavender pl Ilf	53	Z16
Lavender ri SE16	75	V1
Lavender rd SW11	88	G7
Lavender rd Cars	131	R10
Lavender rd Croy	122	C15
Lavender rd Enf	8	C5
Lavender rd Sutt	130	F8
Lavender Sweep SW11	88	L10
Lavender vale Wall	131	X13
Lavender wk Mitch	120	M9
Lavender way Croy	124	F15
Lavengro rd SE27	108	M4
Lavenham rd SW18	105	X3
Lavernock rd Bexh	98	F5
Lavers rd N16	49	T9
Laverstoke gdns SW15	86	F19
Laverton ms SW5	153	Y7
Laverton pl SW5	153	Y7
Lavidge rd SE9	113	S5
Lavina gro N1	141	N8
Lavington rd W13	72	C3
Lavington rd Croy	132	C7
Lavington st SE1	149	Z14
Law st SE1	150	D1
Lawdons gdns Croy	132	K9
Lawford clo Wall	131	Z18
Lawford rd N1	142	J2
Lawford rd NW5	47	U19
Lawford rd W4	73	W18
Lawless st E14	64	E19
Lawley rd N14	16	E2
Lawley st E5	50	D12
Lawn clo N9	18	H3
Lawn clo Brom	112	J17
Lawn clo N Mal	118	A5
Lawn cres Rich	85	O4
Lawn Farm gro Rom	37	Y11
Lawn gdns W7	71	T2
Lawn House clo E14	76	G5
Lawn la SW8	156	M14
Lawn rd NW3	46	L16
Lawn rd Beck	110	M18
Lawn ter SE3	94	B7
Lawns the E4	20	C16
Lawns the SE3	94	B7
Lawns the SE19	123	O1
Lawns the Sid	115	S10
Lawns the Sutt	129	T17
Lawnside SE3	94	C11
Lawnsway Rom	38	L1
Lawrence ave E12	53	W13
Lawrence ave E17	32	G4
Lawrence ave N13	17	W14
Lawrence ave NW7	13	P12
Lawrence ave N Mal	117	Z16
Lawrence bldgs N16	49	U8
Lawrence Campe clo N20	15	U9
Lawrence clo E3	64	A7
Lawrence clo N15	31	R11
Lawrence ct NW7	13	O15
Lawrence cres Dag	56	G9
Lawrence cres Edg	25	R8
Lawrence gdns NW7	13	S10
Lawrence hill E4	20	B7
Lawrence la EC2	150	D6
Lawrence rd E6	66	C2
Lawrence rd E13	65	V3
Lawrence rd N15	31	S12
Lawrence rd N18	18	M14
Lawrence rd SE25	123	V9
Lawrence rd W5	72	F10
Lawrence rd Hmptn	100	E18
Lawrence rd Rich	102	E9
Lawrence rd Rom	39	Y16
Lawrence st E16	65	R15
Lawrence st NW7	13	R15
Lawrence st SW3	154	K14
Lawrie Park ave SE26	110	B11
Lawrie Park cres SE26	110	B13
Lawrie Park gdns SE26	110	A10
Lawrie Park rd SE26	110	B15
Lawson clo E16	65	Z16
Lawson clo SW19	105	O8
Lawson rd Enf	9	O6
Lawson rd Sthl	58	F12
Lawton rd E3	63	W10
Lawton rd E10	51	T4
Lawton rd Barn	5	T12
Laxcon clo NW10	43	X14
Laxley clo SE5	157	Y18
Laxton pl NW1	139	Z15
Layard rd SE16	159	Y4
Layard rd Enf	8	H5
Layard rd Th Hth	123	O3
Laycock st N1	48	G19
Layer gdns W3	61	P20
Layfield clo NW4	44	K1
Layfield cres NW4	44	J1
Layfield rd NW4	44	J1
Layhams rd W Wick	135	Y7
Laymarsh clo Belv	81	P9
Laymead clo Nthlt	40	A19
Laystall st EC1	141	S18
Layton cres Croy	132	H11
Layton rd N1	141	U7
Layton rd Brent	72	G15
Layton rd Houns	82	L9
Laytons bldgs SE1	150	D17
Le May ave SE12	112	H6
Lea Bridge rd E5	50	C9
Lea Bridge rd E10	50	L3
Lea Bridge rd E17	33	V16
Lea gdns Wem	42	L13
Lea Hall rd E10	51	P3
Lea rd Enf	8	B5
Lea rd Sthl	70	B11
Lea vale Dart	99	N11
Lea Valley rd E4	20	C1
Lea Valley rd Enf	9	U15
Lea Valley Viaduct E4	19	V16
Lea Valley Viaduct N18	19	T16
Leabank clo Har	41	T9
Leabank sq E9	51	N17
Leabank vw N15	31	X17
Leabourne rd N16	31	W19
Leacroft ave SW12	88	M18
Leadale ave E4	20	A9

Name	Page	Grid
Leadale rd N15	31	X18
Leadale rd N16	31	X18
Leadenhall st EC3	150	J6
Leader ave E12	53	X15
Leadings the Wem	43	V9
Leaf gro SE27	108	F12
Leafield clo SW16	108	J16
Leafield rd SW20	119	W5
Leafield rd Sutt	129	Y4
Leafy Oak rd SE12	112	L9
Leafy way Croy	133	T4
Leagrave st E5	50	D8
Leahurst rd SE13	93	X13
Leake ct SE1	149	P17
Leake st SE1	149	S18
Lealand rd N15	31	U17
Leamington ave E17	33	P16
Leamington ave Brom	112	K12
Leamington ave Mord	119	T9
Leamington clo E12	53	T15
Leamington clo Brom	112	K11
Leamington clo Houns	83	O12
Leamington cres Har	40	C10
Leamington gdns Ilf	54	L6
Leamington pk W3	61	X15
Leamington Road vill W11	145	R2
Leamore st W6	152	A6
Leamouth rd E6	66	D15
Leamouth rd E14	64	L17
Leander ct SE8	93	O2
Leander rd SW2	90	E15
Leander rd Nthlt	58	G7
Leander rd Th Hth	122	D10
Learoyd gdns E6	66	J18
Leas dale SE9	113	W8
Leas grn Chis	114	L15
Leaside ave N10	29	O11
Leaside rd E5	50	B5
Leasowes rd E10	51	O3
Leathart clo Horn	57	Z19
Leather Bottle la Belv	80	M10
Leather clo Mitch	121	P4
Leather gdns E15	65	N4
Leather la EC1	141	T19
Leatherbottle grn Erith	81	O8
Leatherhead clo N16	49	T3
Leathermarket st SE1	150	J18
Leathsail rd Har	40	L10
Leathwaite rd SW11	88	M11
Leathwell rd SE8	93	S5
Leaveland clo Beck	125	O9
Leaver gdns Grnf	59	R7
Leavesden rd Stan	10	M19
Leaway E10	50	G5
Lebanon gdns SW18	87	X14
Lebanon pk Twick	84	B20
Lebanon rd SW18	87	X14
Lebanon rd Croy	133	T2
Lebrun sq SE3	94	H9
Lechmere app Wdf Grn	34	M7
Lechmere ave Wdf Grn	35	N6
Lechmere rd NW2	44	K17
Leckford rd SW18	106	E3
Leckwith ave Bexh	80	L16
Lecky st SW7	154	F9
Leconfield ave SW13	86	D9
Leconfield rd N5	49	N13
Leda ave Enf	9	S4
Leda rd SE18	78	G8
Ledbury est SE15	159	V16
Ledbury Mews north W11	145	T7
Ledbury Mews west W11	145	S8
Ledbury rd W11	145	S4
Ledbury rd Croy	123	N10
Ledbury st SE15	159	V17
Ledrington rd SE19	109	W16
Ledway dr Wem	42	M1
Lee ave Rom	37	Y19
Lee bri SE13	93	V8
Lee Church st SE13	94	A10
Lee clo E17	32	F5
Lee Conservancy rd E9	50	L14
Lee grn SE12	94	D12
Lee High rd SE12	94	B11
Lee High rd SE13	93	W9
Lee pk SE3	94	B10
Lee Park way N9	19	V9
Lee Park way N18	19	U15
Lee rd NW7	27	R2
Lee rd SE3	94	C9
Lee rd SW19	120	B1
Lee rd Enf	8	K19
Lee rd Grnf	60	D3
Lee st E8	142	M3
Lee ter SE3	93	Z8
Lee Valley Trading est N18	19	T17
Lee vw Enf	7	W5
Leechcroft ave Sid	96	L14
Leechcroft rd Wall	131	R7
Leecroft rd Barn	4	E16
Leeds pl N4	48	D5
Leeds st N18	18	K16
Leefern rd W12	74	H6
Leegate SE12	94	D12
Leeke st WC1	141	N11
Leeland ter W13	71	Z3
Leeland way NW10	44	C12
Leerdam dr E14	76	H8
Lees the Croy	134	M3
Lees pl W1	147	T8
Leeside Barn	4	F17
Leeside cres NW11	27	T17
Leeside rd N17	19	N19
Leeson rd SE24	90	G12
Leeward gdns SW19	105	U14
Leeway SE8	75	Y13
Leeway clo Pnr	22	D2
Lefevre wk E3	64	A4
Lefroy rd W12	74	C5
Legard rd N5	48	J10
Legatt rd SE9	95	N13
Leggatt rd E15	64	H6
Legge st SE13	93	T13
Leghorn rd NW10	62	F6
Leghorn rd SE18	79	T14
Legion clo N1	48	G19
Legion ct Mord	119	Y14
Legion rd Grnf	59	O5
Legon ave Rom	56	M4
Leicester ave Mitch	122	A9
Leicester gdns Ilf	36	J20
Leicester pl WC2	148	G9
Leicester rd E11	34	J15
Leicester rd N2	28	K10
Leicester rd NW10	43	Z20
Leicester rd Barn	5	N16
Leicester rd Croy	123	T18
Leicester sq WC2	148	G9
Leicester st WC2	148	G9
Leigh ave Ilf	35	N14
Leigh clo N Mal	117	X8
Leigh ct Har	41	S5
Leigh cres Croy	135	T17
Leigh gdns NW10	136	E8
Leigh Hunt st SE1	150	B17
Leigh Orchard clo SW16	108	C8
Leigh pl Well	97	O4
Leigh rd E6	53	W19
Leigh rd E10	51	V1
Leigh rd N5	48	J13
Leigh rd Houns	83	P11
Leigh st WC1	140	K15
Leigham ave SW16	108	A7
Leigham Court rd SW16	108	B5
Leigham dr Islw	71	U19
Leigham vale SW2	108	H4
Leigham vale SW16	108	J7
Leighton ave E12	53	X15
Leighton ave Pnr	22	B9
Leighton clo Edg	25	R7
Leighton cres NW5	47	W15
Leighton gdns NW10	136	A7
Leighton gro NW5	47	W15
Leighton pl NW5	47	V15
Leighton rd NW5	47	W15
Leighton rd W13	71	Z6
Leighton rd Enf	8	H17
Leighton rd Har	23	O7
Leighton Street east Croy	122	H20
Leinster ave SW14	85	V9
Leinster gdns W2	146	B6
Leinster ms W2	146	C9
Leinster pl W2	146	A7
Leinster rd N10	29	T13
Leinster sq W2	145	W7
Leinster ter W2	146	B9
Leith clo NW9	43	Y5
Leith rd N22	30	H3
Leithcote gdns SW16	108	C9
Lelitia clo E8	143	S4
Leman st E1	151	R6
Lemark clo Stan	11	R17
Lemna rd E11	52	B2
Lemonwell ct SE9	96	B14
Lemsford clo N15	31	X17
Lena gdns W6	152	D2
Lena Kennedy clo E4	20	F18
Lenelby rd Surb	117	P20
Lenham rd SE12	94	B11
Lenham rd Bexh	81	O17
Lenham rd Sutt	130	C10
Lenham rd Th Hth	123	P4
Lennard rd SE20	110	E15
Lennard rd Beck	110	L17
Lennard rd Brom	127	U20
Lennard rd Croy	122	L19
Lennon rd NW2	44	M16
Lennox clo Rom	39	T19
Lennox gdns NW10	44	E12
Lennox gdns SW1	155	N3
Lennox gdns Croy	132	K9
Lennox gdns Ilf	53	T3
Lennox Gardens ms SW1	155	N3
Lennox rd E17	33	N18
Lennox rd N4	48	E6
Lens rd E7	65	Y1
Lensbury way SE2	80	J7
Lenthall pl SW7	154	C5
Lenthall rd E8	49	W20
Lenthorp rd SE10	77	P12
Lentmead rd Brom	112	C7
Lenton st SE18	79	S10
Lenville way SE16	159	V10
Leo st SE15	159	Y17
Leof cres SE6	111	R12
Leominster rd Mord	120	E14
Leominster wk Mord	120	D13
Leonard ave Mord	120	E12
Leonard ave Rom	56	M4
Leonard rd E4	20	B18
Leonard rd E7	52	E13
Leonard rd N9	18	J11
Leonard rd SW16	107	U20
Leonard st E16	78	E3
Leonard st EC2	142	G16
Leontine clo SE15	159	T18
Leopold ave SW19	105	W12
Leopold rd E17	33	O16
Leopold rd N2	28	G9
Leopold rd N18	19	O16
Leopold rd NW10	62	C1
Leopold rd W5	73	N2
Leopold st E3	63	Z14
Leppoc rd SW4	89	X13
Leroy st SE1	158	J3
Lescombe clo SE23	110	K7
Lescombe rd SE23	110	K7
Lesley clo Bex	98	H18
Leslie gdns Sutt	129	Z16
Leslie gro Croy	123	R20
Leslie Park rd Croy	123	S20
Leslie rd E11	51	V12
Leslie rd E16	65	V18
Leslie rd N2	28	G10
Lessar ave SW4	89	U14
Lessing st SE23	92	H17
Lessingham ave SW17	106	M9
Lessingham ave Ilf	35	V9
Lessington ave Rom	38	K18
Lessness ave Bexh	80	J18
Lessness pk Belv	81	O12
Lessness rd Mord	120	E13
Lester ave E15	65	N10
Leswin rd N16	49	U10
Leswin pl N16	49	U10
Letchford gdns NW10	62	H8
Letchford ter Har	22	K4
Letchworth clo Brom	126	F12
Letchworth dr Brom	126	F12
Letchworth st SW17	106	M10
Lethbridge clo SE13	93	U3
Lett rd E15	64	J2
Letterstone rd SW6	153	N18
Lettice st SW6	87	V3
Lettsom st SE5	91	R4
Lettsom wk E13	65	S5
Leucha rd E17	32	H16
Levana clo SW19	105	R2
Levehurst way SW4	90	A4
Leven rd E14	64	H15
Levendale rd SE23	110	K4
Lever st EC1	141	Z14
Leverett st SW3	154	M6
Leverholme gdns SE9	113	W9
Leverson st SW16	107	V16
Leverton st NW5	47	U15
Levett gdns Ilf	54	K11
Levett rd Bark	54	H18
Levine gdns Bark	68	K5
Lewes clo Nthlt	40	H18
Lewes rd N12	15	W17
Lewes rd Brom	127	N3
Lewesdon clo SW19	105	P2
Leweston pl N16	49	V1
Lewgars ave NW9	25	W18
Lewin rd SW14	85	Z9
Lewin rd SW16	107	X15
Lewin rd Bexh	98	A11
Lewis ave E17	33	O4
Lewis cres NW10	43	X16
Lewis gdns N2	28	K9
Lewis gro SE13	93	V9
Lewis rd Mitch	120	G4
Lewis rd Sid	115	U6
Lewis rd Sthl	70	C5
Lewis rd Sutt	130	B7
Lewis rd Well	97	U7
Lewis st NW1	47	S19
Lewisham High st SE13	93	U6
Lewisham hill SE13	93	V6
Lewisham pk SE13	93	T13
Lewisham rd SE13	93	T3
Lewisham st SW1	148	F19
Lewisham way SE14	92	L1
Lexden dr Rom	37	P18
Lexden rd W3	73	T2
Lexden rd Mitch	121	W8
Lexham gdns W8	153	V4
Lexham Gardens ms W8	153	Y4
Lexham ms W8	153	V4
Lexington st W1	148	D7
Lexington way Barn	4	C15
Lexton gdns SW12	107	Y1
Ley st Ilf	54	A7
Leybourne ave W13	72	D5
Leyborne pk Rich	85	O1
Leybourne clo Brom	126	E13
Leybourne rd E11	52	D4
Leybourne rd NW1	47	S19
Leybourne rd NW9	25	P15
Leyburn clo E17	33	T13
Leyburn gdns Croy	133	S3
Leyburn gro N18	18	K18
Leyburn rd N18	18	L18
Leycroft gdns Erith	99	Y2
Leyden st E1	151	N3
Leyes rd E16	65	Y2
Leyfield Wor Pk	128	B1
Leyland ave Enf	9	V7

Leyland gdns Wdf Grn	21	Y16	Lillie yd SW6	153	U12	Lincoln rd Har	22	E16	Lingfield rd Wor Pk	128	M6
Leyland rd SE12	94	D12	Lillieshall rd SW4	89	T8	Lincoln rd Mitch	122	A11	Lingham st SW9	90	B5
Leylang rd SE14	75	T19	Lillington Gardens est SW1	156	D7	Lincoln rd N Mal	117	V6	Lingholm way Barn	4	C15
Leys the N2	28	D12	Lilliput ave Nthlt	58	D3	Lincoln rd Sid	115	R12	Lings Coppice SE21	109	O3
Leys the Har	24	L18	Lilliput rd Rom	57	O1	Lincoln rd Wem	62	G18	Lingwell rd SW17	106	K7
Leys ave Dag	69	Y3	Lily clo W14	152	K7	Lincoln rd Wor Pk	118	H19	Lingwood gdns Islw	71	T18
Leys clo Har	23	S14	Lily gdns Wem	60	E6	Lincoln st E11	51	Y8	Lingwood rd E5	31	X20
Leys gdns Barn	6	B16	Lily pl EC1	141	V20	Lincoln st SW3	155	P7	Linhope st NW1	139	N17
Leys Road east Enf	9	W5	Lily rd E17	33	P19	Lincoln way Enf	8	M16	Link the W3	61	S16
Leys Road west Enf	9	V5	Lilyville rd SW6	87	V1	Lincolns the NW7	13	S9	Link the Enf	9	W5
Leysdown ave Bexh	98	K11	Limbourne ave Dag	56	C1	Lincoln's Inn flds WC2	149	O4	Link the Nthlt	40	D16
Leysdown rd SE9	113	S5	Limburg rd SW11	88	L10	Lincombe rd Brom	112	C7	Link the Wem	42	E4
Leysfield rd W12	74	H7	Lime clo E1	151	U13	Lind rd Sutt	130	E10	Link la Wall	131	Y14
Leyspring rd E11	52	D3	Lime clo Brom	127	S8	Lind st SE8	93	P4	Link rd N11	16	A12
Leyswood dr Ilf	36	G14	Lime clo Cars	130	L2	Lindal cres Enf	7	O15	Link rd Dag	69	U6
Leythe rd W3	73	W6	Lime clo Har	23	X6	Lindal rd SE4	92	L14	Link rd Wall	131	O1
Leyton gra E10	51	P5	Lime clo Rom	38	K14	Lindbergh rd Wall	131	Z16	Link st E9	50	D16
Leyton Green rd E10	33	T19	Lime ct Mitch	120	G4	Linden ave NW10	136	F11	Link way Brom	127	R16
Leyton Park rd E10	51	U8	Lime gro N20	14	G4	Linden ave Enf	8	L5	Link way Dag	55	U11
Leyton rd E15	51	W15	Lime gro W12	144	B16	Linden ave Houns	82	K12	Linkfield Brom	126	E14
Leyton rd SW19	106	E18	Lime gro N Mal	117	Y6	Linden ave Th Hth	122	H9	Linkfield rd Islw	83	V4
Leyton way E11	34	C20	Lime gro Sid	96	L15	Linden clo N14	6	H19	Linklea clo NW9	26	B3
Leytonstone rd E15	52	Z13	Lime gro Twick	83	X17	Linden clo Stan	11	N16	Links the E17	32	J13
Leywick st E15	65	N5	Lime rd Rich	85	N10	Linden ct W12	144	B13	Links ave Mord	119	Y8
Liardet st SE14	75	W17	Lime st E17	32	H12	Linden cres Grnf	41	V17	Links ave Rom	39	Z8
Liberia rd N5	48	J16	Lime st EC3	150	J8	Linden cres Kings T	117	N5	Links dr N20	14	M5
Liberty the Rom	39	R15	Lime Street pas EC3	150	J7	Linden cres Wdf Grn	21	U18	Links gdns SW16	108	F18
Liberty ave SW19	120	E2	Lime Tree gro Croy	134	L6	Linden gdns W2	145	V10	Links rd NW2	44	D7
Liberty ms SW12	89	S16	Lime Tree pl Mitch	121	T2	Linden gdns W4	73	Z13	Links rd SW17	107	N16
Liberty st SW9	90	E2	Lime Tree rd Houns	82	K1	Linden gdns Enf	8	L4	Links rd W3	61	P17
Libra rd E3	63	Z5	Lime Tree wk E7	7	Y3	Linden gro SE15	92	A8	Links rd W Wick	135	V1
Libra rd E13	65	S5	Lime Tree wk (Bushey) Wat	10	F6	Linden gro SE26	110	E16	Links rd Wdf Grn	21	S16
Library pl E1	151	X8	Limeharbour E14	76	F6	Linden gro N Mal	118	A7	Links side Enf	7	S11
Library st SE1	149	X19	Limehouse Causeway E14	63	Z20	Linden Lawns Wem	42	M13	Links vw N3	27	V2
Lichfield gdns Rich	84	K12	Limehouse Fields est E14	63	W15	Linden leas W Wick	135	W2	Links View clo Stan	10	M20
Lichfield gro N3	27	Z6	Limerick clo SW12	89	V19	Linden ms W2	145	U11	Links View rd Croy	135	O5
Lichfield rd E3	63	X8	Limerston st SW10	154	D13	Linden rd N10	29	T13	Links View rd Hmptn	101	O11
Lichfield rd E6	66	B10	Limes the W2	145	V10	Linden rd N11	16	A7	Links way Beck	125	P14
Lichfield rd NW2	45	S11	Limes ave E11	34	K14	Linden rd N15	30	L12	Linkside N12	14	K17
Lichfield rd Dag	55	N12	Limes ave N12	15	R12	Linden rd Hmptn	100	G19	Linkside N Mal	118	B4
Lichfield rd Rich	85	N2	Limes ave NW7	13	N18	Linden st Rom	39	O14	Linkside clo Enf	7	S12
Lichfield rd Wdf Grn	21	N14	Limes ave NW11	27	T20	Linden way N14	6	H19	Linkside gdns Enf	7	S11
Lidbury rd N1	14	E18	Limes ave SE20	110	A19	Lindenfield Chis	127	Y3	Linksway NW4	27	P7
Lidcote gdns SW9	90	E5	Limes ave SW13	86	C5	Lindens the N12	15	U16	Linkway N4	30	M20
Liddell clo Har	24	H11	Limes ave Cars	130	L1	Lindens the W4	85	V1	Linkway SW20	118	K8
Liddell gdns NW10	136	D7	Limes ave Croy	132	E6	Lindens the Croy	135	U13	Linkway the Barn	4	M19
Liddell rd NW6	45	X17	Limes ave the N11	16	F16	Lindeth clo Stan	11	P19	Linley cres Rom	38	K9
Lidding rd Har	24	H15	Limes gdns SW18	87	X17	Lindfield gdns NW3	46	C14	Linley rd N17	31	T6
Liddington rd E15	65	P3	Limes gro SE13	93	V10	Lindfield rd W5	60	D11	Linnell clo N11	27	Z19
Liddon rd E13	65	U10	Limes pl Croy	123	O16	Lindfield rd Croy	123	V16	Linnell dr NW11	27	Z20
Liddon rd Brom	126	M6	Limes rd Beck	125	T3	Lindfield st E14	64	B17	Linnell rd SE5	91	S4
Liden clo E17	50	K2	Limes rd Croy	123	O16	Lindisfarne rd SW20	104	G19	Linnet clo SE28	68	F20
Lidfield rd N16	49	O13	Limes wk SE15	92	B10	Lindisfarne rd Dag	55	U8	Linnet ms SW12	89	O18
Lidiard rd SW18	106	E3	Limes wk W5	72	H7	Lindisfarne way E9	52	K12	Linnett clo E4	20	H13
Lidlington pl NW1	140	C9	Limesdale gdns Edg	25	V7	Lindley rd est SE15	159	T17	Linom rd SW4	90	A11
Lidyard rd N19	47	V5	Limesford rd SE15	92	E13	Lindley rd E10	51	T5	Linscott rd E5	50	C13
Liffler rd SE18	79	U13	Limestone wk Erith	80	K9	Lindley st E1	151	Z1	Linsdell rd Bark	67	O4
Lifford st SW15	87	P10	Limetree clo SW2	108	D2	Lindo st SE15	92	E5	Linsey st SE16	159	T3
Lightcliffe rd N13	17	U13	Limewood clo W13	60	C16	Lindore rd SW11	88	L11	Linslade clo Houns	82	C12
Lightermans rd E14	76	C6	Limewood rd Erith	81	Y19	Lindores rd Cars	120	D19	Linstead ct SE9	96	H16
Lightfoot rd N8	30	A14	Limpsfield ave SW19	105	P3	Lindrop st SW6	88	C4	Linstead st NW6	45	X19
Lightley clo Wem	60	L2	Limpsfield ave Th Hth	122	E13	Lindsay dr Har	24	K18	Linstead way SW18	105	S18
Ligonier st E2	143	N15	Linacre rd NW2	44	K17	Lindsay rd Hmptn	100	L11	Linthorpe ave Wem	42	F17
Lilac ave E10	19	Y17	Linberry wk SE8	75	X11	Lindsay rd Wor Pk	128	K3	Linthorpe rd N16	49	T2
Lilac gdns W5	72	H7	Linchmere rd SE12	94	D19	Lindsay sq SW1	156	G10	Linthorpe rd Barn	5	V11
Lilac gdns Croy	135	O6	Lincoln ave N14	16	G9	Lindsell st SE10	93	T1	Linton clo Well	97	P3
Lilac gdns Rom	57	P3	Lincoln ave SW19	105	O7	Lindsey clo Brom	127	P8	Linton gdns E6	66	D17
Lilac pl SE11	157	O7	Lincoln ave Rom	57	O5	Lindsey clo Mitch	122	B9	Linton gro SE27	108	L11
Lilac st W12	62	G19	Lincoln ave Twick	100	L3	Lindsey ms N1	8	N20	Linton rd Bark	54	B20
Lilburne gdns SE9	95	S14	Lincoln clo Erith	99	T4	Lindsey rd Dag	55	S12	Linton st N1	142	D5
Lilburne rd SE9	95	S14	Lincoln clo Grnf	58	M3	Lindsey st EC1	149	Z1	Linver rd SW6	87	X4
Lilburne wk NW10	43	U19	Lincoln clo Har	22	E16	Lindum rd Tedd	102	D18	Linwood clo SE5	91	U5
Lile cres W7	59	U15	Lincoln cres Enf	8	F15	Lindway SE27	108	J13	Linzee rd N8	29	Z12
Lilestone st NW8	138	K17	Lincoln gdns Ilf	53	S1	Lindwood clo E6	66	F16	Lion clo SE4	93	O16
Lilford rd SE5	90	H4	Lincoln ms NW6	137	N3	Linford st E17	33	V11	Lion Gate gdns Rich	84	M6
Lilian Barker clo SE12	94	G13	Lincoln ms SE21	109	N3	Linford st SW8	89	U2	Lion rd E6	66	G15
Lilian Board way Grnf	41	P14	Lincoln rd E7	53	O18	Ling rd E16	65	U13	Lion rd N9	18	K8
Lilian clo N16	49	R10	Lincoln rd E13	65	V12	Ling rd Erith	81	Y18	Lion rd Bexh	98	A10
Lilian gdns Wdf Grn	34	J4	Lincoln rd N2	28	K11	Lingards rd SE13	93	V11	Lion rd Croy	122	M13
Lilian rd SW16	121	V1	Lincoln rd SE25	123	Z7	Lingey clo Sid	114	L3	Lion rd Twick	101	V1
Lillechurch rd Dag	55	S17	Lincoln rd Enf	8	D15	Lingfield ave Kings T	116	M9	Lion way Brent	72	F18
Lilleshall rd Mord	120	F14	Lincoln rd Erith	99	U5	Lingfield clo Enf	8	E18	Lion Wharf rd Islw	84	A8
Lilley la NW7	12	M16	Lincoln rd Felt	100	D7	Lingfield cres SE9	96	E10	Lionel gdns SE9	95	O13
Lillian ave W3	73	P6				Lingfield gdns N9	19	N2	Lionel ms W10	136	K20
Lillian rd SW13	74	H15				Lingfield rd SW19	105	R14	Lionel rd SE9	95	O13
Lillie rd SW6	152	H15							Lionel rd Brent	72	J8
									Lions clo SE9	112	M8

Liphook clo Horn	57	U13
Liphook cres SE23	92	B19
Lisbon ave Twick	100	M5
Lisburne rd NW3	46	M13
Lisford st SE15	91	V1
Lisgar ter W12	153	O6
Liskeard clo Chis	114	D16
Liskeard gdns SE3	94	F2
Lisle st WC2	148	G9
Lismore clo Islw	83	X5
Lismore rd N17	31	O11
Lismore rd S Croy	133	R15
Lissenden gdns NW5	47	P11
Lisson Green est NW8	138	K14
Lisson gro NW1	138	M19
Lisson gro NW8	138	G15
Lisson st NW1	138	K20
Lister clo W3	61	Z15
Lister clo Mitch	106	J20
Lister gdns N18	17	Z16
Lister ms N7	48	D11
Lister rd E11	52	B5
Liston rd N17	31	W5
Liston rd SW4	89	V8
Liston way Wdf Grn	34	L2
Listowel clo SW9	157	U18
Listowel rd Dag	56	E8
Listria pk N16	49	T6
Litchfield ave E15	51	Z18
Litchfield ave Mord	119	W16
Litchfield gdns NW10	44	G18
Litchfield rd Sutt	130	C9
Litchfield rd WC2	148	H8
Litchfield way NW11	28	C15
Lithos rd NW3	46	C16
Little acre Beck	125	P7
Little Albany st NW1	139	Z15
Little Argyll st W1	148	A6
Little Birches Sid	114	H5
Little Boltons the SW10	154	A10
Little Britain EC1	149	Z2
Little Brownings SE23	110	A4
Little Bury st N9	18	C4
Little Bushey la (Bushey) Wat	10	C1
Little Cedars N12	15	P12
Little Chester st SW1	147	W20
Little College st SW1	156	K2
Little ct W Wick	135	Z4
Little Dean's yd SW1	156	J1
Little Dimocks SW12	107	T4
Little Dorrit ct SE1	150	C16
Little Ealing la W5	72	E10
Little Edward st NW1	139	Y11
Little Essex st WC2	149	S7
Little Friday rd E4	20	M8
Little Gearies Ilf	35	Z13
Little George st SW1	148	J18
Little grn Rich	84	H11
Little heath SE7	78	E14
Little heath Rom	37	R14
Little Heath rd Bexh	98	A1
Little Ilford la E12	53	U11
Little Marlborough st W1	148	B6
Little Moss la Pnr	22	C6
Little New st EC4	149	V4
Little Newport st WC2	148	H8
Little Park dr Felt	100	A4
Little Park gdns Enf	8	A11
Little Portland st W1	148	A4
Little Potters (Bushey) Wat	10	D2
Little Queens rd Tedd	101	V15
Little Redlands Brom	127	R3
Little rd Croy	123	R19
Little Russell st WC1	148	K3
Little St James's st SW1	148	B15
Little St Leonards SW14	85	W7
Little Sanctuary SW1	148	H19
Little Smith st SW1	156	H1
Little Somerset st E1	151	O6
Little strand NW9	26	E6
Little Titchfield st W1	148	A3
Little Trinity la EC4	150	C8
Littlebrook clo Croy	124	G15
Littlebury rd SW4	89	X8
Littlecombe SE7	77	W16
Littlecombe clo SW15	87	R15
Littlecote clo SW19	87	R18
Littlecroft SE9	95	W7
Littledale SE2	80	B18
Littlefield clo N19	47	V11
Littlefield rd Edg	25	V1
Littlegrove Barn	5	X20
Littleheath rd S Croy	133	Z18
Littlejohn rd W7	59	V16
Littlemede SE3	113	V7
Littlemoor rd Ilf	54	F10
Littlemore rd SE2	80	B6
Littlers clo SW19	120	E1
Littlestone clo Beck	111	P16
Littleton ave E4	21	O5
Littleton cres Har	41	X7
Littleton rd Har	41	X8
Littleton st SW18	106	D5
Littlewood SE13	93	V15
Littlewood clo W13	72	B8
Livermere rd E8	143	O3
Liverpool gro SE17	158	D11
Liverpool rd E10	33	V17
Liverpool rd E16	65	N14
Liverpool rd N1	141	V1
Liverpool rd N7	48	F16
Liverpool rd N5	48	F10
Liverpool rd Kings T	103	P17
Liverpool rd Th Hth	123	N7
Liverpool st EC2	150	K3
Livesey pl SE15	159	T18
Livingstone rd E15	64	H4
Livingstone rd E17	33	R18
Livingstone rd N13	17	N18
Livingstone rd Houns	83	N9
Livingstone rd Sthl	58	A20
Livingstone rd Th Hth	123	N5
Livonia st W1	148	D6
Lizard st EC1	142	D15
Lizban st SE3	77	W19
Llanelly rd NW2	45	W8
Llanover rd SE18	78	K18
Llanover rd Wem	42	G10
Llanthony rd Mord	120	F13
Llanvanor rd NW2	45	W6
Llewellyn st SE16	151	T18
Lloyd ave SW16	122	B2
Lloyd Baker st WC1	141	R15
Lloyd Park ave Croy	133	U9
Lloyd rd E6	66	F4
Lloyd rd E17	32	G13
Lloyd rd Dag	56	C19
Lloyd rd Wor Pk	129	O5
Lloyd sq WC1	141	S13
Lloyd st WC1	141	S12
Lloyd's ave EC3	150	M7
Lloyds pl SE3	94	A5
Lloyd's row EC1	141	V13
Lloyds way Beck	124	K12
Loampit hill SE13	93	P6
Loampit vale SE13	93	T7
Loanda clo E8	143	N3
Loats rd SW2	90	A15
Lobelia clo E6	66	D14
Locarno rd W3	73	W3
Locarno rd Grnf	59	O10
Lochaber rd SE13	93	Z11
Lochaline st W6	152	E12
Lochan clo Hayes	58	A12
Lochinvar st SW12	89	R19
Lochmere clo Erith	81	V17
Lochnagar st E14	64	H14
Lock chase SE3	94	B8
Lock rd Rich	102	D9
Locke clo Rain	57	U19
Lockesfield pl E14	76	F12
Lockesley sq Surb	116	G16
Locket rd Har	23	U8
Lockfield ave Enf	9	X8
Lockhart clo N7	48	C17
Lockhart st E3	63	Z13
Lockhurst st E5	50	F11
Lockie pl SE25	123	X6
Lockington rd SW8	89	T1
Lockmead rd N15	31	X17
Lockmead rd SE13	93	V7
Locks la Mitch	121	N2
Lockside E14	63	X19
Locksley st E14	63	Y15
Locksmeade rd Rich	102	D10
Lockwood sq SE16	159	W1
Lockwood clo SE26	110	G10
Lockwood wk Rom	39	R15
Lockwood way E17	32	F7
Lockyer st SE1	150	G18
Loddiges rd E9	50	C19
Loder st SE15	75	P20
Lodge ave SW14	86	A8
Lodge ave Croy	132	E6
Lodge ave Dag	68	B3
Lodge ave Har	24	J14
Lodge ave Rom	39	V11
Lodge clo N18	18	A16
Lodge clo Edg	12	B18
Lodge clo Islw	84	A1
Lodge clo Wall	131	O1
Lodge dr N13	17	T13
Lodge gdns Beck	124	M12
Lodge hill Ilf	35	S12
Lodge hill Well	80	D20
Lodge la N12	15	P15
Lodge la Bex	97	V14
Lodge la Croy	135	O14
Lodge la Rom	38	E2
Lodge pl Sutt	130	B10
Lodge rd NW4	26	M13
Lodge rd NW8	138	H15
Lodge rd Brom	112	K18
Lodge rd Croy	122	K15
Lodge rd Wall	131	S10
Lodge vill Wdf Grn	21	P20
Lodgehill Park clo Har	40	L6
Lodore gdns NW9	26	A15
Lodore st E14	64	G17
Loftie st SE16	151	U18
Lofting rd N1	141	R1
Loftus rd W12	144	A12
Logan clo Enf	9	T7
Logan clo Houns	82	D8
Logan pl W8	153	T5
Logan rd N9	19	O8
Logan rd Wem	42	J6
Loggetts the SE21	109	R6
Logs hill Chis	113	S18
Logs Hill clo Chis	113	S20
Lolesworth clo E1	151	O2
Lollard st SE11	157	R5
Loman st SE1	149	Z16
Lomas clo Croy	135	U17
Lomas st E1	143	V20
Lombard ave Enf	9	R6
Lombard ave Ilf	54	H5
Lombard Business pk SW19	120	B2
Lombard la EC4	149	U7
Lombard rd N11	17	F16
Lombard rd SW11	88	F5
Lombard rd SW19	120	B2
Lombard st EC3	150	G7
Lombard wall SE7	77	V9
Lombardy pl W2	145	Y10
Lomond clo N15	31	S14
Lomond clo Wem	43	N20
Lomond gro SE5	158	E18
Loncroft rd SE5	158	M13
Londesborough rd N16	49	S11
London bri EC4	150	G11
London bri SE1	150	G12
London Bridge st SE1	150	G14
London Fields East side E8	143	W2
London Fields West side E8	49	Y19
London Industrial pk E6	66	K13
London la E8	50	A20
London la Brom	112	C17
London rd E13	65	S6
London rd SE1	157	X1
London rd SE23	110	C2
London rd Bark	66	M2
London rd Brent	72	C20
London rd Brom	112	C17
London rd Croy	122	K19
London rd Dart	99	N12
London rd Enf	8	C12
London rd Epsom	128	H17
London rd Har	41	T7
London rd Houns	83	N7
London rd Islw	83	Y3
London rd Kings T	116	M3
London rd Mitch	120	J10
London rd Mitch (Mitcham junct)	121	P16
London rd Mord	119	X13
London rd Rom	38	E18
London rd Stan	11	U14
London rd Sutt	128	M9
London rd Th Hth	122	G13
London rd Twick	83	Y14
London rd Wall	131	S3
London rd Wem	42	K15
London Stile W4	73	P14
London st EC3	150	L7
London st W2	146	F5
London wall EC2	150	C3
Long acre WC2	148	J8
Long Deacon rd E4	20	M5
Long dr W3	62	A16
Long dr Grnf	58	L4
Long dr Ruis	40	A10
Long Elmes Har	22	L4
Long fld NW9	26	C3
Long Hedges Houns	82	H2
Long la EC1	149	Z1
Long la N2	28	F9
Long la N3	28	A3
Long la SE1	150	E18
Long la Bexh	80	K20
Long la Croy	124	B16
Long Leys E4	20	F19
Long mead NW9	26	D4
Longmeadow NW5	47	X15
Long Meadow clo W Wick	125	U18
Long Pond rd SE3	93	Z3
Long Reach ct Bark	67	T6
Long Reach rd Bark	67	X11
Long rd SW4	89	T10
Longs st E2	143	N12
Long wk SE1	158	L1
Long wk SE18	78	M15
Long wk SE13	86	C5
Long wk N Mal	117	W5
Long yd WC1	141	N18
Longacre pl Cars	131	P14
Longacre rd E17	33	W4
Longbeach rd SW11	89	N9
Longberrys NW2	45	V9
Longboat row Sthl	58	D17
Longbridge rd Bark	54	E18
Longbridge rd Dag	55	N12
Longbridge way SE13	93	U12
Longcroft SE9	113	V8
Longcrofte rd Edg	24	H1
Longdown rd SE6	111	O9
Longfellow rd E17	32	M19
Longfellow la Wor Pk	128	H2
Longfellow way SE1	159	P7
Longfield Brom	112	D20
Longfield ave E17	32	H13
Longfield ave NW7	26	G2
Longfield ave W5	60	F19
Longfield ave Enf	9	P1
Longfield ave Horn	57	P11
Longfield ave Wall	131	P1
Longfield ave Wem	42	K5
Longfield cres SE26	110	C6
Longfield dr SW14	85	T12
Longfield dr Mitch	106	J20

Longfield est SE1	159	P6
Longfield rd W5	60	F18
Longfield st SW18	87	X20
Longfield wk W5	60	E18
Longford ave Sthl	58	J20
Longford clo Hmptn	100	G10
Longford gdns Sutt	130	E5
Longford rd Twick	100	J2
Longford st MW1	139	Z16
Longhayes ave Rom	37	X11
Longheath gdns Croy	124	E12
Longhill rd SE6	111	X5
Longhope clo SE15	158	M16
Longhurst rd SE13	93	Y13
Longhurst rd Croy	124	B15
Longland dr N20	15	N10
Longlands ct W11	145	R8
Longlands ct Mitch	121	R1
Longlands Park cres Sid	114	H5
Longlands rd Sid	114	H7
Longleat rd Enf	8	F18
Longleigh la SE2	80	E15
Longleigh la Bexh	80	H17
Longley ave Wem	61	N5
Longley rd SE13	106	J14
Longley rd Croy	122	H18
Longley rd Har	23	P14
Longley st SE1	159	S6
Longley way NW2	45	N10
Longmead Chis	127	Y3
Longmead dr Sid	115	V4
Longmead rd SW17	106	L11
Longmeadow rd Sid	114	G2
Longmoore st SW1	156	B6
Longmore ave Barn	5	R18
Longnor rd E1	63	U10
Longridge la Sthl	58	L19
Longridge rd W5	153	T7
Longshaw rd E4	20	L11
Longshore SE8	75	Y11
Longstaff cres SW18	87	Z17
Longstaff rd SW18	87	Z17
Longstone ave NW10	62	E1
Longstone rd SW17	107	S13
Longthornton rd SW16	121	W3
Longton ave SE26	109	X9
Longton gro SE26	109	Z11
Longview way Rom	38	M5
Longville rd SE11	157	X5
Longwood SW15	86	H17
Longwood gdns Ilf	35	U14
Longworth clo SE28	68	K18
Loning the NW9	26	C12
Loning the Enf	9	P2
Lonsdale ave E6	66	B10
Lonsdale ave Rom	38	J17
Lonsdale ave Wem	42	L15
Lonsdale clo E6	66	D10
Lonsdale clo SE9	113	N8
Lonsdale clo Pnr	22	C3
Lonsdale cres Ilf	35	Y18
Lonsdale dr Enf	6	K14
Lonsdale gdns Th Hth	122	C8
Lonsdale pl N1	141	U2
Lonsdale rd E11	34	D20
Lonsdale rd NW6	137	N7
Lonsdale rd SE25	123	Z8
Lonsdale rd SW13	86	D2
Lonsdale rd W4	74	D10
Lonsdale rd W11	145	P7
Lonsdale rd Bexh	98	C6
Lonsdale sq N1	141	U2
Loobert rd N15	31	T11
Looe gdns Ilf	36	A9
Loop rd Chis	114	B16
Lopen rd N18	18	E14
Loraine clo Enf	9	P16
Loraine rd N7	48	D12
Loraine rd W4	73	T17
Lord ave Ilf	35	T12
Lord Chancellor wk Kings T	103	X20
Lord gdns Ilf	35	T12
Lord Hills bri W2	145	Y3
Lord Hills rd W2	137	Y20
Lord Napier pl W6	74	G13
Lord North st SW1	156	J2
Lord Roberts ms SW6	153	X19
Lord Roberts ter SE18	78	L14
Lord st E16	78	E3
Lord Warwick st SE18	78	G9
Lorden wk E2	143	R13
Lord's clo SE21	108	M3
Lords clo Felt	100	C5
Lordship gro N16	49	P7
Lordship la N17	31	N6
Lordship la N22	30	F6
Lordship la SE22	91	V13
Lordship Lane est SE22	91	X20
Lordship pk N16	49	N6
Lordship pl SW3	154	K14
Lordship rd N16	49	R7
Lordship rd Nthlt	40	B20
Lordship ter N16	49	P8
Lordsmead rd N17	31	S5
Lorenzo st WC1	141	O11
Loretto gdns Har	24	J13
Lorian clo N12	15	N13
Loring rd N20	15	W8
Loring rd Islw	83	V4
Loris rd W6	152	D2
Lorn rd SW9	90	E3
Lorne ave Croy	124	G17
Lorne clo NW8	138	L15
Lorne gdns E11	34	K13
Lorne gdns W11	144	J16
Lorne gdns Croy	124	G16
Lorne rd E7	52	K11
Lorne rd E17	33	N16
Lorne rd N4	48	E3
Lorne rd Har	23	V8
Lorraine pk Har	23	T2
Lorrimore rd SE17	157	Y14
Lorrimore sq SE17	157	Z12
Losberne way SE16	159	V10
Lothair rd W5	72	F6
Lothair Road north N4	30	J19
Lothair Road south N4	30	H20
Lothbury EC2	150	F5
Lothian clo Wem	41	Z11
Lothian rd SW9	157	Y20
Lothrop st W10	136	L13
Lots rd SW10	154	B18
Loubet st SW17	106	M15
Loudoun ave Ilf	36	A14
Loudoun rd NW8	138	D2
Lough rd N7	48	D16
Loughborough est SW9	90	G7
Loughborough pk SW9	90	J9
Loughborough rd SW9	90	F4
Loughborough st SE11	157	R10
Louisa st E1	63	S13
Louise rd E15	52	A17
Louisville rd SW17	107	O6
Louvaine rd SW11	88	G11
Lovage app E4	66	F15
Lovat clo NW2	44	B10
Lovat wk Houns	70	B19
Lovatt clo Edg	12	F17
Love la EC2	150	C4
Love la N17	31	U1
Love la SE18	78	L11
Love la SE25	124	A7
Love la Bex	98	C17
Love la Mitch	120	J7
Love la Mord	119	Z18
Love la Pnr	22	B10
Love la Sutt	129	T13
Love wk SE5	91	O4
Loveday rd W13	72	C4
Lovegrove st SE1	159	U12
Lovegrove wk E14	76	G3
Lovekyn clo Kings T	116	L3
Lovel ave Well	96	M5
Lovelace ave Brom	127	X15
Lovelace gdns Bark	55	N13
Lovelace gdns Surb	116	G17
Lovelace grn SE9	95	U8
Lovelace rd SE21	108	L3
Lovelace rd Barn	11	W2
Lovelace rd Surb	116	F18
Lovelinch clo SE15	75	R16
Lovell pl SE16	75	W7
Lovell rd Rich	102	E7
Lovell rd Sthl	58	J17
Lovell wk Rain	57	V16
Loveridge rd NW6	45	W18
Lovers wk N3	14	J20
Lovers wk NW7	14	G18
Lovers wk SE10	76	M18
Lovers' wk W1	147	T13
Lovett dr Cars	120	E18
Lovett way NW10	43	W14
Low Cross Wood la SE21	109	U7
Low Hall clo E4	20	C3
Low Hall la E17	32	J18
Lowbrook rd Ilf	53	Z12
Lowden rd N9	19	N4
Lowden rd SE24	90	K12
Lowden rd Sthl	58	B20
Lowe ave E16	65	U15
Lowell st E14	63	X17
Lowen rd Rain	69	Z6
Lower Addiscombe rd Croy	123	R19
Lower Addison gdns W14	144	K18
Lower Belgrave st SW1	155	W2
Lower Boston rd W7	71	T4
Lower Broad st Dag	69	S3
Lower Camden Chis	113	U19
Lower Clapton rd E5	50	B11
Lower Common south SW15	86	L8
Lower Coombe st Croy	132	L7
Lower Downs rd SW20	105	P20
Lower George st Rich	84	H12
Lower Gravel rd Brom	127	T20
Lower Green west Mitch	120	K7
Lower Grosvenor pl SW1	155	Y1
Lower Grove rd Rich	85	O15
Lower Hall la E4	19	V15
Lower Ham rd Kings T	102	H13
Lower James st W1	148	D9
Lower John st W1	148	D9
Lower Kenwood ave Enf	6	M16
Lower Lea Crossing E14	64	L19
Lower Maidstone rd N11	16	H17
Lower mall W6	152	A10
Lower Mardyke ave Rain	69	Y7
Lower Marsh SE1	149	T16
Lower Marsh la Kings T	117	N9
Lower Merton ri NW3	138	L1
Lower Morden la Mord	119	O15
Lower Mortlake rd Rich	84	K9
Lower Park rd N11	16	G17
Lower Park rd Belv	81	T9
Lower Richmond rd SW14	85	T7
Lower Richmond rd SW15	86	L7
Lower rd SE16	75	R9
Lower rd Belv	81	X9
Lower rd Har	41	P5
Lower rd Sutt	130	E10
Lower Sloane st SW1	155	S7
Lower sq Islw	84	A7
Lower Station rd (Crayford) Dart	99	R16
Lower strand NW9	26	E7
Lower Sydenham Industrial est SE26	110	L12
Lower Teddington rd Kings T	116	F2
Lower ter NW3	46	D10
Lower Thames st EC3	150	H10
Lower Tub (Bushey) Wat	10	C1
Loweswater clo Wem	42	G6
Lowfield rd NW6	45	X19
Lowfield rd W3	61	V16
Lowick rd Har	23	T14
Lowlands gdns Rom	38	H17
Lowlands rd Har	23	S19
Lowman rd N7	48	D12
Lowndes clo SW1	155	U2
Lowndes pl SW1	155	U2
Lowndes sq SW1	147	R19
Lowndes st SW1	155	S1
Lowood st E1	151	Z9
Lowry cres Mitch	120	J3
Lowshoe la Rom	38	F4
Lowth rd SE5	90	M3
Lowther dr Enf	6	M13
Lowther gdns SW7	146	G20
Lowther hill SE23	92	J19
Lowther rd E17	32	H7
Lowther rd SW13	86	E2
Lowther rd Kings T	103	N20
Lowther rd Stan	24	M9
Loxford ave E6	66	B6
Loxford la Ilf	54	B16
Loxford rd Bark	54	A17
Loxham rd E4	20	D20
Loxham st WC1	140	M13
Loxley clo SE26	110	F12
Loxley rd SW18	106	G1
Loxley rd Hmptn	100	E11
Loxton rd SE23	110	G3
Loxwood rd N17	31	S10
Lubbock rd Chis	113	T18
Lubbock st SE14	75	S20
Lucan pl SW3	154	L6
Lucan rd Barn	4	F10
Lucas ave E13	65	X3
Lucas ave Har	40	G5
Lucas rd SE20	110	D16
Lucas sq NW11	27	Y17
Lucas st SE8	93	N3
Lucerne clo N13	17	N12
Lucerne gro E17	33	X14
Lucerne ms W8	145	V13
Lucerne rd N5	48	J11
Lucerne rd Th Hth	122	K11
Lucey clo SE16	159	S3
Lucien rd SW17	107	O10
Lucien rd SW19	105	Z4
Lucknow st SE18	79	V18
Lucorn clo SE12	94	D17
Luctons ave Buck H	21	X3
Lucy cres W3	61	V13
Lucy gdns Dag	56	A10
Luddesdon rd Erith	81	S18
Ludford clo NW9	26	A6
Ludford clo Croy	132	H7
Ludgate bdy EC4	149	X7
Ludgate circ EC4	149	W6
Ludgate ct EC4	149	X6
Ludgate hill EC4	149	Y6
Ludgate sq EC4	149	Y6
Ludlow clo Har	40	F12
Ludlow rd W5	60	F10
Ludlow st EC1	142	A16
Ludlow way N2	28	C12
Ludovick wk SW15	86	C10
Ludwick ms SE14	75	W18
Luffield rd SE2	80	E8
Luffman rd SE12	112	K7
Lugard rd SE15	92	A4
Luke st EC2	142	H17
Lukin cres E4	20	J11

Lukin st E1	63	R18
Lullingstone clo Orp	115	P17
Lullingstone cres Orp	115	O18
Lullingstone rd Belv	81	P15
Lullington garth N12	14	G16
Lullington garth Brom	112	A18
Lullington rd SE20	109	X18
Lullington rd Dag	55	Y19
Lulworth ave Houns	70	M20
Lulworth ave Wem	42	D1
Lulworth clo Har	40	D8
Lulworth cres Mitch	120	J4
Lulworth dr Pnr	22	A20
Lulworth gdns Har	40	C7
Lulworth rd SE9	113	P5
Lulworth rd SE15	92	B5
Lulworth rd Well	96	L5
Lumley clo Belv	81	T15
Lumley gdns Sutt	129	T12
Lumley rd Sutt	129	S13
Lumley st W1	147	V7
Luna rd Th Hth	123	N7
Lunham rd SE19	109	S15
Lupin clo SW2	108	H4
Lupin clo Croy	124	F19
Lupton clo SE12	112	H8
Lupton st NW5	47	U13
Lupus st SW1	155	Z12
Luralda gdns E14	76	J13
Lurgan ave W6	152	H13
Lurline gdns SW11	89	R1
Luscombe ct Brom	125	Z4
Luscombe way SW8	156	K17
Lushington rd NW10	62	J6
Lushington rd SE6	111	P11
Lushington ter E8	49	Y15
Luther clo Edg	12	H8
Luther King clo E17	32	J19
Luther rd Tedd	101	V13
Luton pl SE10	76	H20
Luton rd E17	32	K9
Luton rd Sid	115	T6
Luton st NW8	138	H18
Lutton ter NW3	46	E11
Luttrell ave SW15	86	L13
Lutwyche rd SE6	110	K4
Luxborough st W1	139	T19
Luxemburg gdns W6	152	F5
Luxfield rd SE9	113	R2
Luxford st SE16	75	S11
Luxmore st SE4	92	M3
Luxor st SE5	90	K6
Lyal rd E3	63	X6
Lyall ave SE21	109	T8
Lyall ms SW1	155	T2
Lyall Mews west SW1	155	T3
Lyall st SW1	155	T3
Lycett pl W12	74	G4
Lyconby gdns Croy	124	K18
Lydd clo Sid	114	J8
Lydd rd Bexh	81	P18
Lydden ct SE9	96	G16
Lydden gro SW18	88	A19
Lydden rd SW18	88	A20
Lydeard rd E6	53	U20
Lydford rd N15	31	R16
Lydford rd NW2	45	O18
Lydford rd W9	137	R15
Lydhurst ave SW2	108	D5
Lydney clo SE15	158	L17
Lydney clo SW19	105	T3
Lydon rd SW4	89	U8
Lydstep rd Chis	113	Y11
Lyford rd SW18	88	H19
Lygon pl SW1	155	X2
Lyham clo SW2	90	A16
Lyham rd SW2	90	A13
Lyme Farm rd SE12	94	G11
Lyme rd Well	97	S3
Lyme st NW1	140	B2
Lymer ave SE19	109	V11
Lymescote gdns Sutt	129	Y4
Lyminge clo Sid	114	L8
Lyminge gdns SW18	106	J2

Lymington ave N22	30	F8
Lymington clo SW16	121	X3
Lymington gdns Epsom	128	D11
Lymington rd NW6	46	B16
Lymington rd Dag	55	X3
Lympstone gdns SE15	159	U17
Lynbridge gdns N13	17	W14
Lynbrook clo SE15	158	K17
Lyncroft ave Pnr	22	A15
Lyncroft gdns NW6	45	Z14
Lyncroft gdns W13	72	D4
Lyncroft gdns Houns	83	N13
Lyndale NW2	45	W11
Lyndale ave NW2	45	W10
Lyndale clo SE3	77	P17
Lyndhurst ave N12	15	Y17
Lyndhurst ave NW7	13	O19
Lyndhurst ave SW16	121	V13
Lyndhurst ave Sthl	70	K2
Lyndhurst ave Surb	117	U20
Lyndhurst ave Twick	100	E1
Lyndhurst clo NW10	43	Z8
Lyndhurst clo Bexh	98	H7
Lyndhurst clo Croy	133	U6
Lyndhurst dr E10	51	V1
Lyndhurst dr N Mal	118	C16
Lyndhurst gdns N3	27	U4
Lyndhurst gdns NW3	46	G14
Lyndhurst gdns Bark	54	H17
Lyndhurst gdns Enf	8	D15
Lyndhurst gdns Ilf	36	E19
Lyndhurst gro SE15	91	T4
Lyndhurst rd E4	33	V2
Lyndhurst rd N18	18	K14
Lyndhurst rd N22	17	S20
Lyndhurst rd NW3	46	G14
Lyndhurst rd Bexh	98	H6
Lyndhurst rd Grnf	58	K10
Lyndhurst rd Th Hth	122	F10
Lyndhurst sq SE15	91	V3
Lyndhurst ter NW3	46	F14
Lyndhurst way SE15	91	V2
Lyndhurst way Sutt	129	Z18
Lyndon ave Sid	96	L13
Lyndon ave Wall	131	P6
Lyndon rd Belv	81	T10
Lyne cres E17	32	K4
Lyneham wk E5	50	H14
Lynett rd Dag	55	X5
Lynette ave SW4	89	U15
Lynford clo Edg	25	V3
Lynford gdns Edg	12	E11
Lynford gdns Ilf	54	M6
Lynmere rd Well	97	R5
Lynmouth ave Enf	8	H20
Lynmouth ave Mord	119	P16
Lynmouth gdns Grnf	60	C2
Lynmouth gdns Houns	82	A1
Lynmouth rd E17	32	H17
Lynmouth rd N2	29	N11
Lynmouth rd N16	49	V4
Lynmouth rd Grnf	60	C3
Lynn clo Har	23	P8
Lynn rd SW12	89	T17
Lynn rd Ilf	36	E20
Lynn st Enf	8	B5
Lynne way NW10	44	A19
Lynscott way S Croy	132	H20
Lynsted clo Bexh	98	G12
Lynsted clo Brom	126	L3
Lynsted gdns SE9	95	O9
Lynton ave N12	15	T12
Lynton ave NW9	26	D12
Lynton ave W13	59	Y17
Lynton ave Rom	38	F5
Lynton clo Islw	83	X11
Lynton cres Ilf	35	Z19
Lynton gdns N11	16	J20
Lynton gdns Enf	18	F3
Lynton mead N20	14	M10
Lynton rd E4	20	E16
Lynton rd N8	29	Z16
Lynton rd NW6	137	P7
Lynton rd SE1	159	O6
Lynton rd W3	61	R19
Lynton rd Croy	122	F16

Lynton rd Har	40	D6
Lynton rd N Mal	117	Y12
Lynwood clo E18	34	K4
Lynwood clo Har	40	C9
Lynwood dr Wor Pk	128	G3
Lynwood gdns Croy	132	E9
Lynwood gdns Sthl	58	E16
Lynwood gro N21	17	O4
Lynwood rd SW17	106	M8
Lynwood rd W5	60	J2
Lyon Industrial est Bark	67	W6
Lyon Meade Stan	24	F5
Lyon Park ave Wem	42	K18
Lyon rd SW19	120	D2
Lyon rd Har	23	V19
Lyon rd Rom	39	T20
Lyon st N1	141	N1
Lyon way Grnf	59	T3
Lyons pl NW8	138	F17
Lyons wk W14	152	L5
Lyonsdown ave Barn	5	R19
Lyonsdown rd Barn	5	P19
Lyric dr Grnf	58	L11
Lyric rd SW13	86	D3
Lysander gro N19	47	W6
Lysander rd Croy	132	D14
Lysia st SW6	152	G18
Lysias rd SW12	89	R17
Lysons wk SW15	86	H12
Lytchet rd Brom	112	G17
Lytchet way Enf	9	P5
Lytchgate clo S Croy	133	T17
Lytcott gro SE22	91	T13
Lytham gro W5	60	L8
Lytham st SE17	158	E11
Lyttelton clo NW3	138	K1
Lyttelton rd E10	51	T9
Lyttelton rd N2	28	E14
Lyttleton rd N8	30	F10
Lytton ave N13	17	V8
Lytton ave Enf	9	X2
Lytton clo N2	28	E17
Lytton clo Nthlt	40	E20
Lytton gdns Wall	131	X7
Lytton gro SW15	87	R14
Lytton rd E11	33	Z20
Lytton rd Barn	5	R13
Lytton rd Pnr	22	B3
Lytton rd Rom	39	Z16
Lyveden rd SE3	77	V18
Lyveden rd SW17	106	L16

M

Maberley cres SE19	109	W19
Maberley rd SE19	123	W1
Maberley rd Beck	124	F6
Mabledon pl WC1	140	H13
Mablethorpe rd SW6	152	K18
Mabley st E9	50	J15
Macaret clo N20	15	P2
Macaulay rd E6	66	C5
Macaulay rd SW4	89	T8
Macaulay sq SW4	89	T9
Macaulay ms SE13	93	V3
Macbean st SE18	78	L9
Macbeth st W6	152	K8
Macclesfield bri NW1	139	N8
Macclesfield rd EC1	142	A12
Macclesfield rd SE25	124	B12
Macclesfield st W1	148	G8
Macdonald ave Dag	56	J10
Macdonald rd E7	52	E13
Macdonald rd E17	33	U7
Macdonald rd N11	16	A16
Macdonald rd N19	47	V6
Macduff rd SW11	89	R1
Mace clo E1	151	W12
Mace st E2	63	S7
MacFarlane la Islw	71	X16
Macfarlane rd W12	144	C14
Macfarren pl NW1	139	V18
Macgregor rd E16	65	Z14
Machell rd SE15	92	C7

Mackay rd SW4	89	T7
Mackennal st NW8	138	L8
Mackenzie rd N7	48	D17
Mackenzie rd Beck	124	D5
Mackeson rd NW3	46	L13
Mackie rd SW2	90	F19
Mackintosh la E9	50	F16
Macklin st WC2	148	M4
Macks rd SE16	159	T5
Mackworth st NW1	140	A11
Maclean rd SE23	92	H16
Macleod st SE17	158	C12
Maclise rd W14	152	L3
Macoma rd SE18	79	S17
Macoma ter SE18	79	S17
Macquarie way E14	76	E12
Macroom rd W9	137	S12
Maddams st E3	64	D13
Maddison clo Tedd	101	W16
Maddock way SE17	157	Y15
Maddocks clo Sid	115	Y14
Maddox st W1	147	Z8
Madeira ave Brom	112	A18
Madeira gro Wdf Grn	21	X19
Madeira rd E11	51	Y5
Madeira rd N13	17	W12
Madeira rd SW16	108	A12
Madeira rd Mitch	121	N9
Madeley rd W5	60	H18
Madeline rd SE20	109	X19
Madison cres Bexh	80	G19
Madison gdns Bexh	80	H19
Madison gdns Brom	126	D7
Madras pl N7	48	F16
Madras rd Ilf	53	Z12
Madrid rd SW13	86	G1
Madrigal la SE5	157	Y18
Madron st SE17	158	L8
Mafeking ave E6	66	C5
Mafeking ave Brent	72	J16
Mafeking ave Ilf	54	G2
Mafeking rd E16	65	P11
Mafeking rd N17	31	X8
Mafeking rd Enf	8	G12
Magdala ave N19	47	U6
Magdala rd Islw	83	Z8
Magdala rd S Croy	133	O16
Magdalen rd SW18	106	C3
Magdalen st SE1	150	K15
Magdalene gdns E6	66	J11
Magee st SE11	157	T14
Magnaville rd (Bushey) Wat	10	G3
Magnin clo E8	143	T4
Magnolia clo Kings T	103	U16
Magnolia ct Har	24	M20
Magnolia ct Rich	85	S2
Magnolia pl SW4	89	Z12
Magnolia pl W5	60	H13
Magnolia rd W4	73	T17
Magnolia st Wdf Grn	34	A1
Magpie clo Enf	8	K4
Magpie Hall clo Brom	127	S16
Magpie Hall la Brom	127	R17
Magpie Hall rd (Bushey) Wat	10	F7
Maguire dr Rich	102	E10
Maguire st SE1	151	P16
Mahogany clo SE16	75	W3
Mahon clo Enf	8	H5
Maida ave E4	20	D3
Maida ave W2	138	C20
Maida rd Belv	81	T8
Maida vale W9	137	Y8
Maida Vale rd Dart	99	X14
Maida way E4	20	E3
Maiden Erlegh ave Bex	97	Z20
Maiden la NW1	140	H1
Maiden la SE1	150	D13
Maiden la WC2	148	L9
Maiden la Dart	99	W7
Maiden rd E15	52	A19
Maidenstone hill SE10	93	U2
Maidstone ave Rom	38	K7
Maidstone bldgs SE1	150	D15

Name	Page	Grid
Maidstone rd N11	16	J18
Maidstone rd Sid	115	W15
Mail Coach yd N1	142	L11
Main ave Enf	8	S16
Main rd Rom	39	S13
Main rd Sid	114	H7
Main st Felt	100	A12
Mainridge rd Chis	113	X11
Maisemore st SE15	159	T16
Maitland clo SE16	76	F20
Maitland clo Houns	82	D7
Maitland Park rd NW3	47	N17
Maitland Park vill NW3	47	N16
Maitland rd E15	52	B18
Maitland rd SE26	110	E15
Majendie rd SE18	79	S13
Majestic way Mitch	121	N5
Major rd E15	51	W14
Major rd SE16	151	V20
Makepeace ave N6	47	O7
Makepeace rd Nthlt	58	B5
Makins st SW3	154	M7
Malabar st E14	76	B6
Malam gdns E14	64	D19
Malan sq Rain	57	Y17
Malbrook rd SW15	86	L11
Malcolm ct Stan	11	S17
Malcolm cres NW4	26	G17
Malcolm dr Surb	116	J20
Malcolm pl E2	63	P10
Malcolm rd E1	63	P11
Malcolm rd SE20	110	C17
Malcolm rd SE25	123	X15
Malcolm rd SW19	105	T16
Malcolm way E11	34	E14
Malden ave SE25	124	A7
Malden ave Grnf	41	S16
Malden cres NW1	47	P18
Malden Green ave Wor Pk	118	E19
Malden hill N Mal	118	C8
Malden Hill gdns N Mal	118	E8
Malden pk N Mal	118	D14
Malden rd NW5	47	N15
Malden rd N Mal	118	C11
Malden rd Sutt	129	O7
Malden rd Wor Pk	118	E19
Malden way N Mal	117	X16
Maldon clo N1	142	B3
Maldon clo SE5	91	R7
Maldon rd N9	18	H10
Maldon rd W3	61	W20
Maldon rd Rom	38	K20
Maldon rd Wall	131	T10
Maldon wk Wdf Grn	21	Y19
Malet pl WC1	140	F18
Malet st WC1	140	F19
Maley ave SE27	108	K3
Malford gro E18	34	D12
Malfort rd SE5	91	T7
Malham rd SE23	110	F1
Mall the N14	16	M9
Mall the SW1	148	C17
Mall the SW14	85	V13
Mall the W5	60	H19
Mall the Croy	132	M2
Mall the Har	24	M20
Mall the Surb	116	F13
Mall rd W6	152	A10
Mallard clo E9	50	M17
Mallard clo Barn	5	U20
Mallard clo Twick	82	G17
Mallard pl Twick	101	Y8
Mallard wk NW9	43	V2
Mallard way Wall	131	V19
Mallards rd Wdf Grn	34	J1
Mallet dr Nthlt	40	E15
Mallet rd SE13	93	X16
Malling clo Croy	124	C14
Malling gdns Mord	120	D14
Malling way Brom	126	D17
Mallinson rd SW11	88	L12
Mallinson rd Croy	131	Z5
Mallord st SW3	154	H13
Mallory clo SE4	92	H9
Mallory gdns Barn	16	B2
Mallory st NW8	138	L17
Mallow mead NW7	27	T2
Mallow st EC1	142	F15
Malmains clo Beck	125	W10
Malmains way Beck	125	U9
Malmesbury rd E3	63	Y8
Malmesbury rd E16	65	O14
Malmesbury rd E18	34	D6
Malmesbury rd Mord	120	D17
Malmesbury ter E16	65	P14
Malpas rd E8	50	A16
Malpas rd SE4	92	K6
Malpas rd Dag	55	W18
Malt st SE1	159	S12
Malta rd E10	51	N2
Malta st EC1	141	X15
Maltby dr Enf	8	M2
Maltby rd SE1	151	N19
Maltings ms Sid	115	O6
Maltings pl SW6	88	C3
Malton ms W10	144	L4
Malton rd W10	144	K5
Malton st SE18	79	W17
Maltravers st WC2	149	R8
Malvern ave E4	33	W1
Malvern ave Bexh	80	M20
Malvern ave Har	42	K5
Malvern clo SE20	123	Y4
Malvern clo W10	145	O1
Malvern clo Mitch	121	V7
Malvern dr Ilf	54	L13
Malvern dr Wdf Grn	21	X14
Malvern gdns NW2	45	V6
Malvern gdns NW6	137	R10
Malvern gdns Har	24	L11
Malvern ms NW6	137	T13
Malvern pl NW6	137	R11
Malvern rd E6	66	C3
Malvern rd E8	143	S2
Malvern rd E11	52	B6
Malvern rd N8	30	E10
Malvern rd N17	31	W9
Malvern rd NW6	137	S11
Malvern rd Hmptn	100	H19
Malvern rd Horn	39	V19
Malvern rd Th Hth	122	G10
Malvern ter N1	141	S3
Malvern ter N9	18	J5
Malvern way W13	60	B14
Malwood rd SW12	89	S17
Malyons rd SE13	93	P15
Malyons ter SE13	93	R12
Manaton clo SE15	92	A6
Manaton cres Sthl	58	G16
Manbey gro E15	51	Z17
Manbey Park rd E15	51	Z17
Manbey st E15	52	A18
Manborough ave E6	66	H9
Manbre rd W6	152	D13
Manchester dr W10	136	K18
Manchester gro E14	76	F13
Manchester rd E14	76	H9
Manchester rd N15	31	P18
Manchester rd Th Hth	123	N6
Manchester sq W1	147	U4
Manchester st W1	147	T2
Manchuria rd SW11	89	P15
Manciple st SE1	150	F19
Mandalay rd SW4	89	V14
Mandela clo NW10	43	W20
Mandela rd E16	65	U18
Mandela st NW1	140	C4
Mandela st SW9	157	T20
Mandela way SE1	158	K5
Mandeville clo SE3	77	R20
Mandeville clo SW20	105	T19
Mandeville pl W1	147	V4
Mandeville rd N14	16	F9
Mandeville rd Islw	83	X5
Mandeville rd Nthlt	40	J18
Mandeville st E5	50	H10
Mandrake rd SW17	106	L5
Mandrell rd SW2	90	A13
Manette st W1	148	G6
Manfred rd SW15	87	V13
Manger rd N7	48	A17
Mangold way Erith	80	K8
Manilla st E14	76	B5
Manister rd SE2	80	B7
Manley ct N16	49	U9
Manley st NW1	139	T3
Mannin rd Rom	37	R20
Manning gdns Har	24	H20
Manning rd E17	32	H14
Manning rd Dag	56	E19
Manningford clo EC1	141	X12
Manningtree clo SW19	105	T1
Manningtree st E1	151	S4
Mannock rd N22	30	J9
Manns clo Islw	83	W12
Manns rd Edg	12	C18
Manoel rd Twick	100	M6
Manor ave SE4	92	M6
Manor ave Nthlt	40	D20
Manor clo NW9	25	S14
Manor clo SE28	68	G18
Manor clo Barn	4	F13
Manor clo Dag	57	O18
Manor clo (Crayford) Dart	99	O10
Manor clo Rom	39	W16
Manor clo Wor Pk	118	C20
Manor Cottages app N2	28	D7
Manor ct SW6	88	B2
Manor Court rd W7	71	S1
Manor cres Surb	117	O15
Manor dr N14	16	F3
Manor dr N20	15	X10
Manor dr NW7	12	M16
Manor dr Epsom	128	C14
Manor dr Surb	117	O14
Manor dr Wem	43	N11
Manor dr the Wor Pk	118	B20
Manor Drive north N Mal	117	Y16
Manor Drive north Wor Pk	118	A19
Manor est SE16	159	W6
Manor Farm dr E4	21	N9
Manor Farm rd Th Hth	122	F3
Manor Farm rd Wem	60	F7
Manor flds SW15	87	O15
Manor gdns N7	48	B9
Manor gdns SW20	119	V3
Manor gdns W3	73	R11
Manor gdns Hmptn	100	L19
Manor gdns Rich	85	O10
Manor gdns S Croy	133	U14
Manor gate Nthlt	40	B20
Manor gro SE15	75	P17
Manor gro Beck	125	R3
Manor gro Rich	85	O9
Manor Hall ave NW4	27	N7
Manor Hall dr NW4	27	O8
Manor House dr NW6	136	H1
Manor House way Islw	84	A7
Manor la SE12	94	B15
Manor la SE13	94	A12
Manor la Sutt	130	C10
Manor Lane ter SE13	93	Z12
Manor ms NW6	137	W7
Manor ms SE4	93	N4
Manor mt SE23	110	C1
Manor pk SE13	93	Y11
Manor pk Rich	85	N10
Manor Park cres Edg	12	C19
Manor Park dr Har	22	E8
Manor Park gdns Edg	12	C18
Manor Park rd E12	53	P13
Manor Park rd N2	28	E9
Manor Park rd NW10	62	C4
Manor Park rd Chis	114	D20
Manor Park rd Sutt	130	D11
Manor Park rd W Wick	125	S20
Manor pl SE17	157	Z10
Manor pl Mitch	121	V7
Manor pl Sutt	130	B10
Manor rd E10	51	O1
Manor rd E15	64	M8
Manor rd E16	65	N14
Manor rd E17	32	J6
Manor rd N16	49	P5
Manor rd N17	31	Y3
Manor rd N22	17	O20
Manor rd SE25	123	X8
Manor rd SW20	119	U3
Manor rd W13	59	Y20
Manor rd Bark	54	L19
Manor rd Barn	4	F13
Manor rd Beck	125	R2
Manor rd Bex	98	H20
Manor rd Dag	56	L18
Manor rd Dart	99	P18
Manor rd Enf	8	A7
Manor rd Har	23	X18
Manor rd Loug	21	X1
Manor rd Mitch	121	U9
Manor rd Rich	85	O11
Manor rd Rom (Chadwell Heath)	39	W15
Manor rd Sid	114	M6
Manor rd Sutt	129	U17
Manor rd Tedd	102	A11
Manor rd Twick	101	O3
Manor rd Wall	131	T11
Manor rd W Wick	135	R2
Manor Road north Wall	131	R8
Manor sq Dag	55	V6
Manor vale Brent	72	D14
Manor vw N3	28	A7
Manor way E4	20	K12
Manor way NW9	26	A11
Manor way SE3	94	C10
Manor way Beck	125	P4
Manor way Bex	98	E20
Manor way Bexh	98	M8
Manor way Brom	127	S15
Manor way Har	22	J12
Manor way Mitch	121	U8
Manor way S Croy	133	T13
Manor way Wor Pk	118	C20
Manor way the Wall	131	T8
Manorbrook SE3	94	C9
Manordene rd SE28	68	H18
Manorgate rd Kings T	117	P1
Manorhall gdns E10	51	P4
Manorside Barn	4	F14
Manorside clo SE2	80	H10
Manorway Enf	18	D1
Manorway Wdf Grn	21	Z16
Manresa rd SW3	154	J11
Mansard Beeches SW17	107	R13
Mansard clo Horn	57	V6
Manse rd N16	49	V11
Mansel gro E17	33	O4
Mansel rd SW19	105	U15
Mansell rd W3	73	Y4
Mansell rd Grnf	58	K14
Mansell st E1	151	O6
Mansergh clo SE18	78	E19
Mansfield ave N15	31	O12
Mansfield ave Barn	6	A18
Mansfield clo N9	8	L20
Mansfield hill E4	20	D4
Mansfield ms W1	147	X2
Mansfield rd E11	34	H18
Mansfield rd E17	32	L13
Mansfield rd NW3	46	M14
Mansfield rd W3	61	T12
Mansfield rd Ilf	53	X5
Mansfield rd S Croy	133	O15
Mansfield st W1	147	Y2
Mansford st E2	143	U10
Manship rd Mitch	107	O20
Mansion gdns NW3	46	B9
Mansion House pl EC4	150	F7
Manson ms SW7	154	E6
Manson pl SW7	154	F6
Mansted gdns Rom	55	U1
Manston ave Sthl	70	G11

Name	Page	Grid
Manston clo SE20	124	D1
Manston way Horn	57	Z19
Manstone rd NW2	45	S15
Manthorp st SE18	79	R13
Mantilla rd SW17	107	P10
Mantle rd SE4	92	J7
Mantlet clo SW16	107	W17
Manton ave W7	71	Y5
Manton rd SE2	80	A11
Mantus rd E1	63	P10
Manville gdns SW17	107	R5
Manville rd SW17	107	R5
Manwood rd SE4	92	M14
Manwood st E16	78	H4
Manygates SW12	107	T3
Mape st E2	143	V16
Mapesbury rd NW2	45	S17
Maple ave E4	19	Y17
Maple ave W3	74	B3
Maple ave Har	40	L8
Maple clo N16	31	Y18
Maple clo SW4	89	Y15
Maple clo Hmptn	100	D15
Maple clo Horn	57	Z10
Maple clo Mitch	121	S1
Maple ct N Mal	117	Z7
Maple cres Sid	97	N15
Maple gdns Edg	26	B2
Maple gro Brent	43	W1
Maple gro W5	72	G7
Maple gro Brent	72	B18
Maple gro Sthl	58	F13
Maple Leaf Dr Sid	114	K2
Maple ms NW6	137	X8
Maple ms SW16	108	D13
Maple pl W1	140	C19
Maple rd E11	34	A18
Maple rd SE20	124	B1
Maple rd Surb	116	G15
Maple st W1	140	B19
Maple st Rom	38	L13
Mapledale ave Croy	133	Y4
Mapledene rd E8	49	W20
Maplehurst clo Kings1	116	J9
Mapleleafe gdns Ilf	35	Z11
Maples pl E1	143	Y20
Maplestead rd SW2	90	D19
Maplestead rd Dag	68	C3
Maplethorpe rd Th Hth	122	H10
Mapleton clo Brom	126	E13
Mapleton cres SW18	88	A16
Mapleton cres Enf	9	P2
Mapleton rd E4	20	G12
Mapleton rd SW18	87	Z16
Mapleton rd Enf	9	O9
Maplin clo N21	7	R18
Maplin rd E16	65	U17
Maplin st E3	63	Y10
Maran way Erith	80	K6
Marban rd W9	137	O12
Marble Arch W1	147	O18
Marble clo W3	73	S4
Marble Hill clo Twick	84	B18
Marble Hill gdns Twick	84	B18
Marble quay E1	151	R12
Marbrook ct SE12	112	K7
March rd Twick	83	X18
Marchant rd E11	51	Y8
Marchbank rd W14	153	R12
Marchmont rd Wall	131	U19
Marchmont rd Rich	84	M14
Marchmont st WC1	140	K16
Marchwood clo SE5	158	L19
Marchwood cres W5	60	F16
Marcia rd SE1	158	L7
Marcilly rd SW18	88	F12
Marco rd W6	152	B3
Marcon pl E8	49	Z16
Marconi way Sthl	58	K18
Marcus st E15	65	O3
Marcus Garvey way SE24	90	G11
Marcus rd Dart	99	W18
Marcus st E15	65	O3
Marcus st SW18	88	B15
Mardale dr NW9	25	Z16
Mardell rd Croy	124	F12
Marden ave Brom	126	D15
Marden cres Bex	98	L13
Marden cres Croy	122	E15
Marden rd N17	31	R8
Marden rd Croy	122	E15
Mardon st E14	63	X15
Mare st E8	143	Y5
Marechal Niel ave Sid	114	F7
Mares fld Croy	133	S5
Maresfield gdns NW3	46	E15
Margaret ave E4	20	F1
Margaret rd N16	49	V4
Margaret rd Barn	5	U15
Margaret rd Bex	97	X15
Margaret rd Rom	39	Z15
Margaret st W1	147	Z5
Margaret way Ilf	35	P17
Margaretta ter SW3	154	L12
Margaretting rd E12	52	M5
Margery Park rd E7	52	E17
Margery rd Dag	55	X8
Margery st WC1	141	S15
Margin dr SW19	105	P11
Margravine gdns W6	152	H10
Margravine rd W6	152	G11
Marham gdns SW18	106	J2
Marham gdns Mord	120	D14
Maria ter E1	63	S13
Maria Theresa clo N Mal	117	Z12
Marian ct Sutt	129	Z15
Marian pl E2	143	V7
Marian rd SW16	121	V1
Marian sq E2	143	V7
Marian st E2	143	W8
Marian way NW10	62	D1
Maricas ave Har	23	P3
Mariette way Wall	132	A18
Marigold all SE1	149	W11
Marigold rd N17	32	B3
Marigold st SE16	151	W20
Marigold way Croy	124	F20
Marina app Hayes	58	C15
Marina ave N Mal	118	J13
Marina clo Brom	126	D6
Marina dr Well	96	H5
Marina gdns Rom	38	J17
Marine dr SE18	78	G15
Marine st SE16	159	S1
Marinefield rd SW6	88	B4
Mariner gdns Rich	102	C8
Marion clo Ilf	36	D5
Marion gro Wdf Grn	21	N15
Marion rd NW7	13	T16
Marion rd Th Hth	123	N11
Marischal rd SE13	93	W8
Maritime st E3	63	Z12
Marius rd SW17	107	N3
Marjorie gro SW11	89	N10
Mark clo Bexh	97	Z1
Mark clo Sthl	70	J1
Mark la EC3	150	L9
Mark st E15	51	Z20
Mark st EC2	142	H16
Market hill SE18	78	L8
Market la Edg	25	V6
Market link Rom	39	P14
Market ms W1	147	W14
Market pl N2	28	H11
Market pl NW11	28	C14
Market pl SE16	159	V5
Market pl W1	148	B5
Market pl Bexh	98	E10
Market pl Brent	72	F18
Market pl Kings1	116	H4
Market pl Rom	39	R14
Market rd N7	47	Z19
Market rd Rich	85	P8
Market sq Brom	126	F3
Market st E6	66	G5
Market st SE18	78	L11
Markfield gdns E4	20	D1
Markfield rd N15	31	X14
Markham sq SW3	155	N9
Markham st SW3	155	N9
Markhole clo Hmptn	100	E19
Markhouse ave E17	32	K17
Markhouse rd E17	32	K16
Markmanor ave E17	32	K20
Marks rd Rom	38	L16
Marksbury ave Rich	85	R6
Markwell clo SE26	110	A9
Markyate rd Dag	55	S16
Marl rd SW18	88	C10
Marlands rd Ilf	35	S10
Marlborough ave E8	143	S5
Marlborough ave N14	16	G9
Marlborough ave Edg	12	F10
Marlborough bldgs SW3	154	M5
Marlborough clo SE17	157	Z6
Marlborough clo SW19	106	H17
Marlborough cres W4	73	Z9
Marlborough dr Ilf	35	S10
Marlborough gdns N20	15	Z11
Marlborough Gate ho W2	146	F9
Marlborough gro SE1	159	T12
Marlborough hill NW8	138	E6
Marlborough hill Har	23	R14
Marlborough la SE7	77	Y17
Marlborough Park ave Sid	97	N19
Marlborough pl NW8	138	B9
Marlborough rd E4	20	C19
Marlborough rd E7	52	K19
Marlborough rd E18	34	G8
Marlborough rd N9	18	J6
Marlborough rd N19	47	Y7
Marlborough rd N22	30	B1
Marlborough rd SW1	148	D15
Marlborough rd SW19	106	H16
Marlborough rd W4	73	V12
Marlborough rd W5	72	H4
Marlborough rd Bexh	97	W6
Marlborough rd Brom	126	M9
Marlborough rd Dag	55	R13
Marlborough rd Hmptn	100	G15
Marlborough rd Islw	72	A20
Marlborough rd Rich	84	L15
Marlborough rd Rom	38	F17
Marlborough rd S Croy	132	M16
Marlborough rd Sutt	129	Z4
Marlborough rd SW3	154	L8
Marlborough yd N19	47	Y7
Marler rd SE23	110	L2
Marley ave Bexh	80	J17
Marley clo Grnf	58	G7
Marlingdene clo Hmptn	100	G16
Marloes clo Wem	42	F12
Marloes rd W8	153	W2
Marlow clo SE20	124	B6
Marlow cres Twick	83	V16
Marlow dr Sutt	129	R4
Marlow rd E6	66	G9
Marlow rd SE20	124	A6
Marlow rd Sthl	70	E8
Marlow way SE16	75	T4
Marlowe clo Chis	114	D16
Marlowe clo Ilf	36	D5
Marlowe gdns SE9	95	X15
Marlowe rd E17	33	U12
Marlowe sq Mitch	121	U8
Marlowe way Croy	132	A2
Marlowes the NW8	138	F5
Marlowes the Dart	99	N11
Marlton st SE10	77	R13
Marmadon rd SE18	79	X10
Marmion app E4	20	A12
Marmion ave E4	19	Y13
Marmion clo E4	20	A12
Marmion rd SW11	89	P10
Marmont rd SE15	159	U20
Marmora rd SE22	92	B16
Marne ave N11	16	D13
Marne ave Well	96	M8
Marne st W10	136	M13
Marney rd SW11	89	O10
Marnham ave NW2	45	S11
Marnham cres Grnf	58	K8
Marnock rd SE4	92	K13
Maroons way SE6	111	P11
Marquess est N1	49	N18
Marquess rd N1	49	O18
Marquis clo Wem	61	O1
Marquis rd N4	48	E3
Marquis rd N22	17	R20
Marquis rd NW1	47	Z18
Marrick clo SW15	86	H9
Marrilyne ave Enf	9	Y2
Marriots clo NW9	26	D19
Marriott rd E15	64	M2
Marriott rd N4	48	C4
Marriott rd N10	28	M5
Marriott rd Barn	4	D13
Marryat pl SW19	105	S10
Marryat rd SW19	105	P13
Marsala rd SE13	93	S11
Marsden rd N9	19	N8
Marsden rd SE15	91	V18
Marsden st NW5	47	O18
Marsh ave Mitch	121	N3
Marsh clo NW7	13	R10
Marsh dr NW9	26	D18
Marsh Farm rd Twick	101	V2
Marsh Green rd Dag	69	S3
Marsh hill E9	50	H15
Marsh la E10	51	N5
Marsh la N17	32	B4
Marsh la NW7	13	N11
Marsh la Stan	11	T18
Marsh rd Pnr	22	B11
Marsh rd Wem	60	H7
Marsh wall E14	76	B4
Marshall clo Houns	82	E12
Marshall rd N17	31	P3
Marshall st W1	148	C7
Marshalls clo N11	16	E12
Marshalls dr Rom	39	P9
Marshall's gro SE18	78	E13
Marshalls pl SE16	159	P2
Marshalls rd Rom	39	N13
Marshall's rd Sutt	130	A9
Marshalsea rd SE1	150	B16
Marsham clo Chis	113	Z13
Marsham st SW1	156	H2
Marshbrook clo SE3	95	N7
Marshfield st E14	76	G8
Marshgate la E15	64	D2
Marshgate path SE18	79	P9
Marsland clo SE17	157	Z11
Marston ave Dag	56	D7
Marston clo NW6	46	D20
Marston clo Dag	56	E8
Marston rd Ilf	35	R5
Marston rd Tedd	102	B14
Marston way SE19	108	K18
Marsworth ave Pnr	22	A3
Marsworth clo Hayes	58	B14
Martaban rd N16	49	T6
Martell rd SE21	109	N7
Martello st E8	50	A20
Martello ter E8	143	X1
Marten rd E17	33	P6
Martens ave Bexh	98	J10
Martens clo Bexh	98	K10
Martha ct E2	143	Y8
Martha rd E15	52	B16
Martha st E1	151	Z7
Marthorne cres Har	23	R7
Martin Bowes rd SE9	95	U6
Martin cres Croy	132	E1

Martin Dale Industrial est Enf	8	M10
Martin dene Bexh	98	B13
Martin dr Nthlt	40	E15
Martin gdns Dag	55	V13
Martin gro Mord	119	X7
Martin la EC4	150	G9
Martin ri Bexh	98	B13
Martin rd Dag	55	V12
Martin way SW20	119	R5
Martin way Mord	119	T7
Martinbridge Trading est Enf	8	M14
Martindale SW14	85	V12
Martindale rd SW12	89	T19
Martindale rd Houns	82	B7
Martineau rd N5	48	H13
Martingales clo Rich	102	G7
Martins mt Barn	4	M13
Martins rd Brom	126	B3
Martins wk N10	29	N4
Martley dr N17	35	Z16
Marton clo SE6	111	O7
Marton rd N16	49	S8
Marvels clo SE12	112	J5
Marvels la SE12	112	J5
Marville rd SW6	153	O20
Marwell clo Rom	39	X17
Marwood clo Well	97	P8
Marwood way SE16	159	V10
Mary Adelaide clo SW15	104	A8
Mary Ann gdns SE8	76	B18
Mary clo Stan	25	N11
Mary Datchelor clo SE5	91	P1
Mary Gardener dr SE9	113	T4
Mary Peters dr Grnf	41	P14
Mary pl W11	144	K10
Mary Rose clo Hmptn	100	H20
Mary Rose mall E6	66	H15
Mary Rose way N20	15	U4
Mary Seacole clo E8	143	N5
Mary st N1	142	C5
Mary ter NW1	140	A6
Maryatt ave Har	40	J6
Marybank SE18	78	G10
Maryland pk E15	52	A16
Maryland rd E15	51	Y15
Maryland rd N22	17	S20
Maryland sq E15	52	A15
Maryland st E15	51	Y16
Marylands rd W9	137	V19
Marylebone Flyover NW1	146	J1
Marylebone Flyover W2	146	J1
Marylebone High st W1	139	U20
Marylebone la W1	147	V4
Marylebone ms W1	147	W2
Marylebone pas W1	148	C4
Marylebone rd NW1	139	O20
Marylebone st W1	147	V1
Marylee way SE11	157	R8
Maryon gro SE7	78	E11
Maryon rd SE7	78	D11
Maryon rd SE7	78	D10
Mary's ter Twick	83	Y19
Masbro rd W14	152	H2
Mascalls ct SE7	77	X17
Mascalls rd SE7	77	X17
Mascotte rd SW15	87	R9
Mascotts clo NW2	44	L10
Masefield ave Sthl	58	H19
Masefield ave Stan	10	J17
Masefield clo Erith	99	U3
Masefield cres N14	6	G19
Masefield gdns E6	66	J11
Mashie rd W3	62	B17
Mashiters hill Rom	39	N4
Mashiters wk Rom	39	R8
Maskall clo SW2	108	G2
Maskell rd SW17	106	C7
Maskelyn clo SW11	88	K1
Mason clo E16	65	S19
Mason clo SE16	159	V9
Mason clo Bexh	98	G8
Mason rd Wdf Grn	21	N14
Mason st SE17	158	H5
Masons ave Croy	133	N7
Masons ave Har	23	V11
Masons ct Wem	43	P7
Masons Green la W3	61	P12
Masons hill SE18	79	N12
Masons hill Brom	126	H8
Masons pl Mitch	106	L20
Mason's yd SW1	148	C13
Massinger st SE17	158	J6
Massingham st E1	63	S11
Mast House ter E14	76	B12
Master Gunner pl SE18	78	D20
Masterman rd E6	66	C9
Masters st E1	63	U14
Mastmaker rd E14	76	C6
Maswell Park cres Houns	82	M12
Maswell Park rd Houns	82	L13
Matcham rd E11	52	B9
Matchless dr SE18	78	K20
Matfield clo Brom	126	E13
Matfield rd Belv	81	S16
Matham gro SE22	91	U11
Matheson rd W14	153	O6
Mathews Park ave E15	52	C19
Matilda st N1	141	P5
Matlock clo SE24	91	N11
Matlock cres Sutt	129	T7
Matlock gdns Sutt	129	T10
Matlock pl Sutt	129	T9
Matlock rd E10	33	U18
Matlock st E14	63	V16
Matlock way N Mal	117	V1
Matrimony pl SW8	89	V5
Matthew clo W10	136	G19
Matthew ct Mitch	121	Y11
Matthew Parker st SW1	148	G19
Matthews ave E6	66	K7
Matthews rd Grnf	41	R15
Matthews st SW11	88	M4
Matthias rd N16	49	P14
Mattison rd N4	30	G17
Mattock la W5	72	F1
Mattock la W13	72	B2
Maud gdns E13	65	R5
Maud gdns Bark	67	Y6
Maud rd E10	51	U10
Maud rd E13	65	R4
Maud st E16	65	P15
Maude rd E17	32	J14
Maude rd SE5	91	R3
Maude ter E17	32	J14
Maudslay rd SE9	95	U7
Maulden rd W7	71	V4
Maunsel st SW1	156	F5
Maurice ave N22	30	K7
Maurice Brown clo NW7	14	C17
Maurice st W12	62	J18
Maurice wk NW11	28	C13
Mauritius rd SE10	77	N12
Maury rd N16	49	W8
Mavelstone clo Brom	113	R20
Mavelstone rd Brom	113	P20
Maverton rd E3	64	B4
Mavis ave Epsom	128	B11
Mavis clo Epsom	128	C10
Mawbey pl SE1	159	P10
Mawbey rd SE1	159	P11
Mawbey st SW8	156	K19
Mawney clo Rom	38	H8
Mawney rd Rom	38	J7
Mawson clo SW20	119	T14
Maxey gdns Dag	56	A11
Maxey rd SE18	79	P10
Maxey rd Dag	55	Y13
Maxfield clo N20	15	R2
Maxilla wk W10	144	J6
Maxim rd N21	7	U18
Maxim rd Dart	99	R13
Maxted pk Har	41	T1
Maxted rd SE15	91	W6
Maxwell rd SW6	153	Y19
Maxwell rd Well	96	M9
Maxwelton av NW7	12	L16
Maxwelton clo NW7	12	L16
May gdns Wem	60	E7
May rd E4	20	A18
May rd E13	65	U5
May rd Twick	101	T1
May st W14	153	P11
May Tree la Stan	10	K20
May wk E13	65	U5
Maya rd N2	28	D12
Mayall rd SE24	90	H12
Maybank ave E18	34	J6
Maybank ave Wem	41	X14
Maybank rd E18	34	J5
Maybells Commercial est Bark	68	J5
Mayberry pl Surb	117	N17
Maybourne clo SE26	110	B14
Maybury gdns NW10	44	H19
Maybury ms N6	47	V1
Maybury rd E13	65	Y12
Maybury rd Bark	67	Z6
Maybury st SW17	106	H13
Maychurch clo Stan	24	G3
Maycross ave Mord	119	V8
Mayday gdns SE3	95	R5
Mayday rd Th Hth	122	H15
Mayerne rd SE9	95	P13
Mayes rd N22	30	J7
Mayesbrook rd Bark	67	Y3
Mayesbrook rd Dag	55	R9
Mayesbrook rd Ilf	55	O8
Mayesford rd Rom	37	U20
Mayeswood rd SE12	112	L8
Mayfair ave Bexh	97	X3
Mayfair ave Ilf	53	V6
Mayfair ave Rom	37	X18
Mayfair ave Wor Pk	118	F19
Mayfair clo Beck	111	S20
Mayfair clo Surb	116	L20
Mayfair gdns N17	18	A19
Mayfair gdns Wdf Grn	21	T20
Mayfair ms NW1	139	R1
Mayfair pl W1	147	Z13
Mayfair ter N14	16	K3
Mayfield Bexh	98	B8
Mayfield ave N12	15	S13
Mayfield ave N14	16	A3
Mayfield ave W4	74	B12
Mayfield ave W13	72	B6
Mayfield ave Har	24	B16
Mayfield ave Wdf Grn	21	T20
Mayfield clo E8	49	U19
Mayfield clo SW4	89	Z13
Mayfield cres N9	9	N18
Mayfield cres Th Hth	122	C10
Mayfield dr Pnr	22	E12
Mayfield gdns NW4	27	O18
Mayfield gdns W7	59	R16
Mayfield rd E4	20	H7
Mayfield rd E8	143	N2
Mayfield rd E13	65	P13
Mayfield rd E17	32	H7
Mayfield rd N8	30	D16
Mayfield rd SW19	105	W20
Mayfield rd W3	61	S19
Mayfield rd W12	74	C5
Mayfield rd Belv	81	X10
Mayfield rd Brom	127	R11
Mayfield rd Dag	55	T5
Mayfield rd Enf	9	T9
Mayfield rd S Croy	133	P20
Mayfield rd Sutt	130	G14
Mayfield rd Th Hth	122	C10
Mayfields Wem	43	O5
Mayfields clo Wem	43	O6
Mayflower rd SW9	90	A8
Mayflower st SE16	75	P5
Mayford clo SW12	88	M20
Mayford clo Beck	124	F7
Mayford rd SW12	88	M20
Maygood st N1	141	R7
Maygreen cres Horn	57	V2
Maygrove rd NW6	45	V18
Mayhew clo E4	20	A10
Mayhill rd SE7	77	V17
Mayhill rd Barn	4	E18
Maylands ave Horn	57	Y13
Maylands dr Sid	115	W8
Maynard clo SW6	154	A20
Maynard rd E17	33	T15
Mayo rd NW10	44	B18
Mayo rd Croy	123	N12
Mayola rd E5	50	D11
Mayow rd SE23	110	G6
Mayow rd SE26	110	F11
Mayplace ave Dart	99	V9
Mayplace clo Bexh	98	H8
Mayplace la SE18	79	N19
Mayplace Road east Bexh	98	H9
Mayplace Road west Bexh	98	F10
Maypole cres Ilf	36	E1
Mays Hill rd Brom	126	A5
Mays la E4	20	J7
Mays la Barn	13	V2
Maysoule rd SW11	88	F10
Mayswood gdns Dag	56	L17
Mayton st N7	48	C10
Maytree clo Edg	12	H9
Maytree wk SW2	108	G4
Mayville rd E11	51	Y7
Mayville rd Ilf	53	Z14
Maywood clo Beck	111	R18
Maze hill SE3	77	N17
Maze hill SE10	76	M16
Maze rd Rich	73	P18
Mazenod ave NW6	137	U2
McAdam dr Enf	7	W8
McAuley clo SE1	157	S1
McAuley clo SE9	95	Y13
McCall clo SW4	89	Z4
McCall cres SE7	78	D14
McDermott clo SW11	88	H6
McDermott rd SE15	91	X6
McDowall rd SE5	90	L2
McDowall clo E16	65	S15
McEntee ave E17	32	H4
McEwan way E15	64	L2
McGrath rd E15	52	C16
McGregor rd W11	145	P3
McIntosh clo Rom	39	P10
McIntosh clo Wall	132	A16
McIntosh rd Rom	39	P9
McKay rd SW20	104	L17
McKellar clo (Bushey) Wat	10	B7
McKerrell rd SE15	91	Y3
McLeod rd SE2	80	C12
McLeod's ms SW7	154	A4
McMillan st SE8	76	B17
McNeil rd SE5	91	R5
Mead the N2	28	D7
Mead the W13	60	B14
Mead the Beck	125	U2
Mead the Wall	131	Y14
Mead the W Wick	135	X1
Mead clo Har	23	R4
Mead clo Rom	39	W7
Mead ct NW9	25	X16
Mead cres E4	20	H12
Mead cres Sutt	130	J8
Mead gro Rom	37	Y9
Mead pl E9	50	D18
Mead pl Croy	132	K1
Mead Plat NW10	43	X17
Mead rd Chis	114	B14
Mead rd Edg	12	B20
Mead rd Rich	102	E8
Mead row SE1	157	T1
Mead way Brom	126	B14
Mead way Croy	134	K2
Meadcroft SE11	157	V14
Meade clo W4	73	R16
Meadfield Edg	12	E7
Meadfoot rd SW16	107	V19
Meadlands dr Rich	102	F4

Name	Page	Grid
Meadow the Chis	114	B14
Meadow ave Croy	124	F14
Meadow bank N21	7	R20
Meadow clo E4	20	D6
Meadow clo SE6	111	O12
Meadow clo SW20	119	N9
Meadow clo Barn	4	H19
Meadow clo Chis	113	Z12
Meadow clo Enf	9	V4
Meadow clo Houns	82	G17
Meadow clo Nthlt	58	H5
Meadow clo Rich	102	J2
Meadow dr N10	29	R9
Meadow dr NW4	26	L2
Meadow gdns Edg	12	G18
Meadow garth NW10	43	W19
Meadow hill N Mal	118	A14
Meadow ms SW8	157	O16
Meadow pl SW8	156	M18
Meadow rd SW8	157	N17
Meadow rd SW19	106	D19
Meadow rd Bark	54	M20
Meadow rd Brom	126	A2
Meadow rd Dag	56	B17
Meadow rd Felt	100	A4
Meadow rd Pnr	22	A14
Meadow rd Rom	56	K3
Meadow rd Sthl	58	F20
Meadow rd Sutt	130	J10
Meadow row SE1	158	B3
Meadow vw Sid	97	P17
Meadow View rd Th Hth	122	H13
Meadow wk E18	34	E12
Meadow wk Dag	56	B17
Meadow wk Epsom	128	B15
Meadow wk Wall	131	R5
Meadow way NW9	25	Z14
Meadow way Wem	42	H12
Meadow way the Har	23	T5
Meadow waye Houns	70	B18
Meadowbank NW3	139	O2
Meadowbank SE3	94	D8
Meadowbank Surb	116	M13
Meadowbank clo SW6	152	E19
Meadowbank rd NW9	43	X1
Meadowcourt rd SE3	94	D11
Meadowcroft Brom	127	V7
Meadowcroft rd N13	17	U9
Meadowside SE9	94	L11
Meadowside rd Sutt	129	T20
Meadowview SE6	111	N11
Meadowview rd Epsom	128	B19
Meads the Edg	12	L19
Meads the Sutt	129	R6
Meads la Ilf	36	J20
Meads rd N22	30	H8
Meads rd Enf	9	W6
Meadvale rd W5	60	B11
Meadvale rd Croy	123	V16
Meadway N14	16	L8
Meadway NW11	28	B18
Meadway SW20	119	N9
Meadway Barn	4	J14
Meadway Beck	125	V2
Meadway Ilf	54	J11
Meadway Rom	39	V7
Meadway Twick	101	P1
Meadway Wdf Grn	21	Y15
Meadway the SE3	93	Y6
Meadway clo NW11	27	Z19
Meadway clo Barn	4	K12
Meadway gate NW11	27	Z19
Meaford way SE20	110	A18
Meanley rd E12	53	S13
Meard st W1	148	F7
Meath rd E15	65	O5
Meath rd Ilf	54	D9
Meath st SW11	89	T1
Mechanics path SE8	76	B19
Mecklenburgh pl WC1	141	N17
Mecklenburgh sq WC1	141	N15
Mecklenburgh st WC1	141	N15
Medburn st NW1	140	F8
Medcalf rd Enf	9	Z1
Medcroft gdns SW14	85	U10
Medebourne clo SE3	94	F7
Medesenge way N13	17	V18
Medfield st SW15	86	H19
Median rd E5	50	C14
Medina gro N7	48	E8
Medina rd N7	48	E8
Medland clo Wall	121	P20
Medlar clo Nthlt	58	A5
Medlar st SE5	158	C20
Medora rd SW2	90	E17
Medora rd Rom	39	N13
Medusa rd SE6	93	R16
Medway clo Croy	124	C14
Medway clo Ilf	54	D15
Medway dr Grnf	59	W6
Medway gdns Wem	41	Y13
Medway rd E3	63	W6
Medway rd Dart	99	V9
Medway st SW1	156	F3
Medwin st SW4	90	C9
Meerbrook rd SE3	94	M8
Meeson rd E15	65	P2
Meeson st E5	50	H13
Meeting House la SE15	159	W20
Meetinghouse all E1	151	X13
Mehetabel rd E9	50	C16
Melancholy wk Rich	102	F4
Melanda clo Chis	113	U14
Melanie clo Bexh	97	Y1
Melba way SE13	93	T3
Melbourne ave N13	17	R18
Melbourne ave W13	71	Z3
Melbourne ave Pnr	22	K9
Melbourne clo Wall	131	U12
Melbourne ct SE20	109	Y19
Melbourne gdns Rom	37	Y14
Melbourne gro SE22	91	T10
Melbourne ms SE6	93	U18
Melbourne ms SW9	90	F3
Melbourne pl WC2	149	P7
Melbourne rd E6	66	H4
Melbourne rd E10	51	R1
Melbourne rd E17	32	K12
Melbourne rd SW19	119	Z1
Melbourne rd Ilf	54	A3
Melbourne rd Tedd	102	F15
Melbourne rd Wall	131	T12
Melbourne way Enf	8	H19
Melbury ave Sthl	70	J9
Melbury clo Chis	113	T16
Melbury ct W8	153	S1
Melbury dr SE5	158	K19
Melbury gdns SW20	104	K20
Melbury rd W14	153	O1
Melbury rd Har	25	O16
Melbury ter NW1	139	N18
Melcombe gdns Har	25	N17
Melcombe pl NW1	139	N19
Melcombe st NW1	139	P19
Meldrum rd Ilf	55	O8
Melfield gdns SE6	111	T11
Melford av Bark	54	J17
Melford rd E6	66	G10
Melford rd E11	51	Z7
Melford rd E17	32	K13
Melford rd SE22	91	Y20
Melford rd Ilf	54	F7
Melfort ave Th Hth	122	K7
Melfort rd Th Hth	122	H5
Melgund rd N5	48	G15
Melina pl NW8	138	E13
Melina rd W12	74	J5
Melior pl SE1	150	J16
Melior rd SE1	150	H16
Meliot rd SE6	111	Y5
Meller clo Croy	131	Z5
Melling st SE18	79	W17
Mellish clo Bark	67	X4
Mellish gdns Wdf Grn	21	T17
Mellish st E14	158	B7
Mellison rd SW17	106	L13
Mellitus st W12	62	D16
Mellows rd Ilf	35	V9
Mellows rd Wall	131	X12
Mells cres SE9	113	T11
Melody rd SW18	88	D13
Melon pl W8	145	W16
Melon rd SE15	91	W1
Melrose ave N22	30	J4
Melrose ave NW2	44	K14
Melrose ave SW16	122	E6
Melrose ave SW19	105	W5
Melrose ave Grnf	58	L6
Melrose ave Mitch	107	R18
Melrose ave Twick	82	L19
Melrose clo SE12	112	G1
Melrose clo Grnf	58	K6
Melrose dr Sthl	70	G1
Melrose gdns W6	152	D1
Melrose gdns Edg	25	T8
Melrose gdns N Mal	117	Z8
Melrose rd SW13	86	D3
Melrose rd SW18	87	U17
Melrose rd SW19	119	Y2
Melrose rd W3	73	U8
Melrose rd Pnr	22	F13
Melrose ter W6	144	D20
Melsa rd Mord	120	D14
Meltham way SE16	159	X10
Melthorpe gdns SE3	95	P1
Melton st SW7	154	G6
Melton gdns Rom	57	T1
Melton st NW1	140	E15
Melville ave SW20	104	F19
Melville ave Grnf	41	W16
Melville ave S Croy	133	V13
Melville gdns N13	17	V17
Melville rd E17	32	M11
Melville rd NW10	43	Y20
Melville rd SW13	86	F2
Melville rd Rom	38	H3
Melville rd Sid	115	U5
Melville rd SE20	110	C20
Melyn clo N7	47	W13
Memorial ave E15	65	N8
Memorial clo Houns	70	E18
Mendip clo SE26	110	C10
Mendip clo Wor Pk	129	N2
Mendip dr NW2	45	R7
Mendip rd SW11	88	E8
Mendip rd Bexh	99	P2
Mendip rd Horn	57	W2
Mendip rd Ilf	36	H15
Mendora rd SW6	153	O16
Menelik rd NW2	45	T13
Menlo gdns SE19	109	N19
Menotti st E2	143	V16
Mentmore clo Har	24	E18
Mentmore ter E8	143	X2
Meon ct Islw	83	S5
Meon rd W3	73	W5
Meopham rd Mitch	121	U2
Mepham cres Har	23	N1
Mepham gdns Har	23	N2
Mepham st SE1	149	R15
Merantun way SW19	120	B1
Merbury clo SE13	93	W13
Merbury rd SE28	79	U4
Mercator rd SE13	93	X9
Mercer st WC2	148	J6
Merceron st E1	143	X19
Mercers clo SE10	77	P12
Mercers pl W6	152	E4
Mercers rd N19	47	X11
Merchant st E3	64	A9
Merchiston rd SE6	111	W3
Merchland rd SE9	114	D2
Mercia gro SE13	93	V9
Mercier rd SW15	87	S13
Mercury gdns Rom	39	T15
Mercury way SE14	75	T15
Mercy ter SE13	93	S12
Mere clo SW15	87	R18
Mere end Croy	124	G18
Merebank la Croy	132	D10
Meredith ave NW2	45	N14
Meredith st E13	65	T10
Meredith st EC1	141	W15
Meredyth rd SW13	86	G4
Meretone clo SE4	92	H9
Merevale cres Mord	120	D15
Mereway rd Twick	101	S2
Merewood clo Brom	127	W3
Merewood rd Bexh	98	J4
Mereworth clo Brom	126	C12
Mereworth dr SE18	79	O20
Meriden clo Brom	113	O19
Meriden clo Ilf	36	C4
Meridian rd SE7	78	B18
Meridian Trading est SE7	77	W10
Meridian way N9	19	U3
Meridian way N18	19	P18
Meridian way Enf	9	U20
Merifield rd SE9	94	M10
Merivale rd SW15	87	T9
Merivale rd Har	41	O1
Merlewood dr Chis	127	U1
Merley ct NW9	43	X2
Merlin clo Croy	133	S7
Merlin cres Edg	25	N4
Merlin gdns Brom	112	E8
Merlin gro Beck	124	M10
Merlin gro Ilf	36	B1
Merlin rd E12	53	N7
Merlin rd Well	97	O10
Merlin Road north Well	97	N9
Merlin st WC1	141	T14
Merlins ave Har	40	F8
Mermaid ct SE1	150	E16
Merredene st SW2	90	D17
Merrick rd Sthl	70	D6
Merrick sq SE1	150	D20
Merridene N21	7	W19
Merrielands cres Dag	69	P5
Merrilands rd Wor Pk	128	M1
Merrilees rd Sid	96	H20
Merriman rd SE3	94	M1
Merrington rd SW6	153	U13
Merrion ave Stan	11	T14
Merritt rd SE4	92	L13
Merrivale N14	6	J18
Merrivale ave Ilf	35	O14
Merrow rd Sutt	129	O19
Merrow st SE17	158	D12
Merrow wk SE17	158	H10
Merrow way Croy	135	V15
Merrydown way Chis	127	T2
Merryfield SE3	94	D5
Merryfield gdns Stan	11	S17
Merryhill clo E4	20	D2
Merryhills ct N14	6	G16
Merryhills dr Enf	6	L14
Mersey rd E17	32	M9
Mersham dr NW9	25	R16
Mersham pl SE20	110	B20
Mersham rd Th Hth	123	N5
Merten rd Rom	38	A20
Merthyr ter SW13	74	K16
Merton ave W4	74	D11
Merton ave Nthlt	41	N15
Merton Hall gdns SW20	105	T20
Merton Hall rd SW19	105	T20
Merton High st SW19	106	B19
Merton Industrial pk SW19	120	C1
Merton la N6	47	N6
Merton mans SW20	119	P5
Merton ri NW3	46	J19
Merton rd SE25	123	W12
Merton rd SW18	87	Y15
Merton rd SW19	106	A13
Merton rd Bark	67	Z1
Merton rd Enf	8	A4
Merton rd Har	41	N3
Merton rd Ilf	36	K20
Merttins rd SE15	92	F12
Mervan rd SW2	90	F11
Mervyn ave SE9	114	C6
Mervyn rd W13	72	A8
Messaline ave W3	61	X18
Messent rd SE9	94	M12
Messeter pl SE9	95	W15
Messina ave NW6	137	T1
Meteor st SW11	89	P10

Meteor way Wall	132	A17
Metheringham way NW9	26	A5
Methley st SE11	157	U10
Methuen clo Edg	25	P1
Methuen pk N10	29	T9
Methuen rd Belv	81	W10
Methuen rd Bexh	98	B11
Methuen rd Edg	25	P2
Methwold rd W10	136	F20
Mews the N1	142	C4
Mews the Ilf	35	O17
Mews pl Wdf Grn	21	T13
Mews st E1	151	S12
Mexfield rd SW15	87	W13
Meyer gro Enf	8	K3
Meyer rd Erith	81	Z17
Meymott st SE1	149	W14
Meynell cres E9	50	E20
Meynell gdns E9	50	E20
Meynell rd E9	50	F19
Meyrick rd NW10	44	F17
Meyrick rd SW11	88	H8
Micawber st N1	142	B11
Michael Gaynor clo W7	71	X3
Michael rd E11	52	B4
Michael rd SE25	123	R7
Michael rd SW6	88	B1
Michaels clo SE13	93	Z9
Micheldever rd SE12	94	C15
Michelham gdns Twick	101	X6
Michleham down N12	14	K13
Mickleham gdns Sutt	129	S13
Mickleham way Croy	135	X17
Micklethwaite rd SW6	153	V15
Midas Metropolitan Industrial est the Wor Pk	119	N19
Middle dene NW7	12	M11
Middle fld NW8	138	F3
Middle la N8	29	Z16
Middle la N8	101	W14
Middle Park ave SE9	95	N16
Middle path Har	41	R5
Middle rd E13	65	S7
Middle rd SW16	121	W4
Middle rd Barn	5	V19
Middle rd Har	41	P5
Middle row W10	136	K17
Middle st EC1	150	A1
Middle Temple la EC4	149	T7
Middle way SW16	121	X4
Middle way Erith	80	L8
Middle way the Har	23	V6
Middlefield gdns Ilf	36	A19
Middlefield W13	60	B13
Middlefields Croy	134	H20
Middleham gdns N18	18	K18
Middleham rd N18	18	K19
Middlesborough rd N18	18	L18
Middlesex Business cen the Sthl	70	F5
Middlesex st E4	74	E12
Middlesex rd Mitch	122	A11
Middlesex st E1	150	M3
Middleton ave E4	19	Z12
Middleton ave Grnf	59	R16
Middleton ave Sid	115	T14
Middleton clo E4	19	Z11
Middleton dr SE16	75	T5
Middleton gdns Ilf	36	A19
Middleton gro N7	47	Z15
Middleton ms N7	47	Z15
Middleton rd E8	142	M1
Middleton rd Cars	120	F16
Middleton rd Mord	120	A15
Middleton st E2	143	W12
Middleton way SE13	93	Y9
Middleway NW11	28	B16
Midfield ave Bexh	98	L8
Midfield way Orp	115	S20
Midford pl W1	140	C18
Midholm NW11	28	A13
Midholm Wem	43	R5
Midholm clo NW11	28	A12
Midholm rd Croy	134	J4
Midhope st WC1	140	L13
Midhurst ave N10	29	O11
Midhurst ave Croy	122	G17
Midhurst clo Horn	57	V13
Midhurst hill Bexh	98	E13
Midhurst rd W13	71	Z6
Midland pl E14	76	G14
Midland rd E10	51	U2
Midland rd NW1	140	H10
Midland ter NW2	45	O10
Midland ter NW10	62	B11
Midleton rd N Mal	117	V5
Midlothian rd E3	63	X13
Midmoor rd SW12	107	V1
Midmoor rd SW19	105	R20
Midstrath rd NW10	44	B12
Midsummer ave Houns	82	D11
Midway Sutt	119	V17
Midwood clo NW2	44	J9
Miers clo E6	66	L2
Mighell ave Ilf	35	P14
Milborne gro SW10	154	D12
Milborne st E9	50	D19
Milbourne cres SE12	94	B17
Milcote st SE1	149	X19
Mildenhall rd E5	50	B11
Mildmay ave N1	49	O16
Mildmay gro N1	49	O16
Mildmay pk N1	49	P15
Mildmay rd N1	49	P15
Mildmay rd Rom	38	K14
Mildmay st N1	49	P17
Mildred ave Nthlt	40	L15
Mile end the E17	32	G6
Mile End pl E1	63	T11
Mile End rd E1	143	Z20
Mile End rd E3	63	O13
Miles pl NW1	138	J20
Miles rd N8	30	B11
Miles rd Mitch	120	H6
Miles st SW8	156	K14
Miles way N20	15	X8
Milespit hill NW7	13	Y16
Milestone clo Sutt	130	F15
Milestone rd SE19	109	V16
Milfoil st W12	62	G19
Milford clo SE2	81	N16
Milford gdns Edg	25	P2
Milford gdns Wem	42	G13
Milford gro Sutt	130	D8
Milford la WC2	149	R8
Milford ms SW16	108	D8
Milford rd W13	72	A3
Milford rd Sthl	58	H20
Milk st E16	78	M3
Milk st EC2	150	C5
Milk st Brom	112	H14
Milk yd E1	75	P1
Milkwell yd SE5	91	N3
Milkwood rd SE24	90	K9
Mill clo Cars	131	P3
Mill corner Barn	4	H6
Mill ct E10	51	U10
Mill Farm cres Houns	100	C1
Mill gdns SE26	110	A8
Mill Green rd Mitch	121	N17
Mill Hill circ NW7	13	R15
Mill Hill gro W3	73	U3
Mill Hill rd SW13	86	G6
Mill Hill rd W3	73	T4
Mill la NW6	45	U16
Mill la SE18	78	L14
Mill la Cars	131	N9
Mill la Croy	132	E6
Mill la Epsom	128	E18
Mill la Rom (Chadwell Heath)	37	Y19
Mill la Wdf Grn	21	R17
Mill Mead Industrial cen N17	32	A8
Mill Mead rd N17	32	A11
Mill pl Dart	99	X11
Mill pl Kings T	116	L5
Mill Plat Islw	83	Y6
Mill Plat ave Islw	83	Y6
Mill ridge Edg	12	B17
Mill rd E16	77	W3
Mill rd SW19	106	E19
Mill rd Erith	81	X20
Mill rd Ilf	53	X8
Mill rd Twick	101	O4
Mill row N1	142	L6
Mill Shot clo SW6	152	E20
Mill st SE1	151	P18
Mill st W1	148	A8
Mill st Kings T	116	L5
Mill Trading est the NW10	61	W9
Mill vale Brom	126	D4
Millais gdns Edg	25	P7
Millais rd E11	51	V12
Millais rd Enf	8	J16
Millais rd N Mal	118	A16
Millbank SW1	156	K3
Millbank way SE12	94	E14
Millbourne rd Felt	100	C10
Millbrook ave Well	96	F9
Millbrook gdns Rom	39	S6
Millbrook gdns Rom (Chadwell Heath)	38	A17
Millbrook rd N9	18	M5
Millbrook rd SW9	90	H8
Millender wk SE16	75	R11
Miller rd SW19	106	G15
Miller rd Croy	122	E20
Miller st NW1	140	A7
Miller's ave E8	49	L14
Millers clo NW7	13	V12
Millers st W4	74	F14
Millers Green clo Enf	7	V11
Miller's ter E8	49	U14
Millers way W6	144	E18
Millet rd Grnf	58	L8
Millfield ave E17	32	J4
Millfield la N6	46	M5
Millfield pl N6	47	O7
Millfield rd Edg	25	W7
Millfield rd Houns	82	D20
Millfields est E5	50	G9
Millfields est E5	50	C11
Millgrove st SW11	89	O3
Millharbour E14	76	D7
Millhaven clo Rom	37	S18
Millhouse pl SE27	108	K11
Millicent rd E10	50	M2
Milligan st E14	63	Z20
Milling rd Edg	25	Z1
Millman ms WC1	141	N18
Millman st WC1	141	O18
Millmark gro SE14	92	K5
Millmarsh la Enf	9	X8
Millpond est SE16	151	X19
Mills ct EC2	142	K15
Mills gro E14	64	C15
Mills gro NW4	27	O11
Mills row W4	73	X11
Millside Cars	131	N2
Millside rd Islw	84	A6
Millson clo N20	15	U8
Millstream rd SE1	151	O19
Millway NW7	13	N14
Millway gdns Nthlt	40	E18
Millwood rd Houns	82	M13
Millwood st W10	144	J2
Milman rd NW6	136	K9
Milmans st SW10	154	G15
Milne Feild Pnr	22	H1
Milne gdns SE9	95	R13
Milner dr Twick	83	P19
Milner pl N1	141	V3
Milner rd E15	65	N9
Milner rd SW19	106	A20
Milner rd Dag	55	T7
Milner rd Kings T	116	H7
Milner rd Mord	120	F12
Milner rd Th Hth	123	N6
Milner sq N1	141	V2
Milner st SW3	155	O4
Milnthorpe rd W4	73	X16
Milo rd SE22	91	U16
Milson rd W14	152	H1
Milton ave E6	66	B1
Milton ave N6	47	U1
Milton ave NW9	25	U10
Milton ave NW10	61	X3
Milton ave Barn	4	J15
Milton ave Croy	123	P18
Milton ave Horn	57	U6
Milton ave Sutt	130	H7
Milton clo N2	28	E17
Milton clo SE1	159	O7
Milton clo Sutt	130	H6
Milton ct EC2	142	E20
Milton Court rd SE14	75	X17
Milton cres Ilf	36	B20
Milton gro N11	16	J15
Milton gro N16	49	R13
Milton pk N6	47	U1
Milton pl N7	48	E15
Milton rd E17	33	O12
Milton rd N6	47	V1
Milton rd N15	30	J11
Milton rd NW7	13	T15
Milton rd SE24	90	H14
Milton rd SW14	85	X8
Milton rd SW19	106	D15
Milton rd W3	73	X1
Milton rd W7	59	V20
Milton rd Belv	81	S12
Milton rd Croy	123	P19
Milton rd Hmptn	100	H19
Milton rd Har	23	U13
Milton rd Mitch	107	P17
Milton rd Rom	39	V17
Milton rd Sutt	129	Y7
Milton rd Wall	131	W14
Milton rd Well	96	K1
Milton st EC2	142	E20
Milverton gdns Ilf	54	L5
Milverton rd NW6	136	D1
Milverton st SE11	157	T11
Milverton way SE9	113	Y9
Milward st E1	151	Y1
Mimosa st SW6	87	V2
Mina rd SE17	158	L11
Mina rd SW19	105	Z20
Minard rd SE6	93	Z19
Minchenden cres N14	16	J10
Mincing la EC3	150	K8
Minden rd Sutt	129	U3
Minehead rd SW16	108	D14
Minehead rd Har	40	F9
Minera ms SW1	155	U5
Mineral st SE18	79	U12
Minerva clo SW9	157	U18
Minerva rd NW10	61	X10
Minerva rd Kings T	116	M4
Minerva st E2	143	W9
Minet ave NW10	62	A5
Minet gdns NW10	62	A5
Minet rd SW9	90	J4
Minford gdns W14	144	F18
Ming st E14	64	B20
Ministry way SE9	113	T3
Minniedale Surb	117	N11
Minories EC3	151	N6
Minshull pl Beck	111	P19
Minshull st SW8	89	X3
Minson rd E9	63	U2
Minstead gdns SW15	86	D18
Minstead way N Mal	118	A15
Minster dr Croy	133	S8
Minster rd NW2	45	T15
Minster rd Brom	112	H17
Minstrel gdns Surb	117	N10
Mint rd Wall	131	S10
Mint st SE1	150	B17
Mint wk Croy	132	M5
Mintern clo N13	17	X11
Mintern st N1	142	G8
Minterne ave Sthl	70	G10
Minterne rd Har	25	O16
Mirabel rd SW6	153	P17
Miranda clo W3	61	N17
Miranda rd N19	47	W4

Name	Page	Grid
Mirfield st SE7	78	A9
Miriam rd SE18	79	U13
Missenden gdns Mord	120	E14
Mission gro E17	32	K14
Mitcham Industrial est Mitch	107	R20
Mitcham la SW16	107	T16
Mitcham pk Mitch	120	K10
Mitcham rd E6	66	E8
Mitcham rd SW17	106	L12
Mitcham rd Croy	122	A15
Mitcham rd Ilf	36	L20
Mitchell clo SE2	80	F12
Mitchell clo Belv	81	W9
Mitchell rd N13	17	X15
Mitchell st EC1	142	B15
Mitchell wk E6	66	F15
Mitchell way NW10	43	V18
Mitchell way Brom	126	F1
Mitchellbrook way NW10	43	Y17
Mitchison rd N1	49	O18
Mitchley rd N17	31	W9
Mitford rd N19	48	B6
Mitre the E14	63	Z18
Mitre clo Brom	126	D3
Mitre clo Sutt	130	E17
Mitre ct EC4	149	U6
Mitre rd E15	65	N5
Mitre rd SE1	149	V17
Mitre sq EC3	150	M6
Mitre st EC3	150	M6
Mitre way NW10	136	A20
Moat the N Mal	118	A1
Moat cres N3	28	A9
Moat cft Well	97	T7
Moat dr Har	23	O13
Moat Farm rd Nthlt	40	E18
Moat la Erith	99	W3
Moat pl SW9	90	D6
Moat pl W3	61	T16
Moatside Enf	9	S13
Moberley rd SW4	89	Y17
Model Farm clo SE9	113	R6
Moelwyn Hughes ct N7	47	Y15
Moelyn ms Har	23	Y15
Moffat gdns Mitch	120	H17
Moffat rd N13	17	O18
Moffat st SE17	106	L9
Moffat rd Th Hth	123	N4
Mogden la Islw	83	U13
Moiety rd E14	76	A6
Moir clo S Croy	133	W20
Moira clo N17	31	R6
Moira rd SE9	95	U9
Moland mead SE16	75	S12
Molescroft SE9	114	B6
Molesey dr Sutt	129	T5
Molesford rd SW6	87	Y3
Molesworth st SE13	93	U9
Mollison ave Enf	9	W16
Mollison dr Wall	131	Z17
Mollison way Edg	25	P8
Molly Huggins clo SW12	89	V20
Molyneux st W1	146	M3
Mona rd SE15	92	E4
Mona st E16	65	P14
Monarch dr E16	66	A15
Monarch ms SW16	108	H13
Monarch rd Belv	81	T9
Monastery gdns Enf	8	B8
Monck st SW1	156	G2
Monclar rd SE5	91	R9
Moncorvo clo SW7	146	J19
Moncrieff clo E6	66	D17
Moncrieff st SE15	91	Y4
Monega rd E7	52	K18
Monega rd E12	53	P16
Monfitchet E6	66	M17
Monier rd E3	64	A1
Monivea rd Beck	110	M19
Monk dr E16	65	S18
Monk st SE18	78	K10
Monkfrith ave N14	6	E20
Monkfrith clo N14	16	D1
Monkfrith way N14	16	C3
Monkhams ave Wdf Grn	21	U15
Monkhams dr Wdf Grn	21	V15
Monkhams la Wdf Grn	21	T15
Monkleigh rd Mord	119	T7
Monks ave Barn	5	S19
Monks clo SE2	80	J11
Monks clo Enf	7	Y9
Monks clo Har	40	J7
Monks Orchard rd Beck	125	P16
Monks pk Wem	43	T19
Monks Park gdns Wem	43	T19
Monks rd Enf	7	X7
Monks way NW11	27	V13
Monks way Beck	125	O13
Monksdene gdns Sutt	130	B5
Monkswell ct N10	29	R3
Monkswood gdns Ilf	35	X11
Monkton rd Well	96	L4
Monkton st SE11	157	U6
Monkville ave NW11	27	V13
Monkwell sq EC2	150	C2
Monmouth ave E18	34	J11
Monmouth ave Kings T	102	F19
Monmouth clo Mitch	122	B9
Monmouth clo Well	97	N9
Monmouth pl W2	145	W6
Monmouth rd E6	66	G10
Monmouth rd N9	19	N8
Monmouth rd W2	145	W6
Monmouth rd Dag	56	B15
Monmouth st WC2	148	J6
Monnery rd N19	47	V9
Monnow rd SE1	159	T6
Monoux gro E17	33	N4
Monro gdns Har	23	S1
Monroe cres Enf	9	N6
Monroe dr SW14	85	T13
Mons way Brom	127	S14
Monsell rd N4	48	J8
Monson rd NW10	62	H6
Monson rd SE14	75	T19
Montacute rd SE6	92	L19
Montacute rd Croy	135	T20
Montacute rd Mord	120	F15
Montacute rd (Bushey) Wat	10	G2
Montagu cres N18	19	N14
Montagu gdns N18	19	N13
Montagu gdns Wall	131	V10
Montagu mans W1	147	R1
Montagu Mews north W1	147	P2
Montagu Mews south W1	147	P4
Montagu Mews west W1	147	P4
Montagu pl W1	147	P2
Montagu pl N9	19	P10
Montagu rd N18	19	O15
Montagu rd NW4	26	G18
Montagu row W1	147	R1
Montagu sq W1	147	P3
Montagu st W1	147	O1
Montague ave SE4	93	N10
Montague ave W7	71	V4
Montague clo SE1	150	F12
Montague gdns W3	61	P19
Montague pl WC1	148	H1
Montague rd E8	49	W15
Montague rd E11	52	C8
Montague rd N8	30	C15
Montague rd N15	31	W11
Montague rd SW19	105	Z18
Montague rd W7	71	V4
Montague rd W13	60	C17
Montague rd Croy	122	J20
Montague rd Houns	83	K7
Montague rd Rich	84	K15
Montague rd Sthl	70	B10
Montague sq SE15	75	R20
Montague st EC1	150	A3
Montague st WC1	148	K1
Montague waye Sthl	70	A9
Montalt rd Wdf Grn	21	O14
Montana rd SW17	107	O8
Montana rd SW20	119	N1
Montbelle rd SE9	113	Z8
Montcalm clo Brom	126	F15
Montcalm rd SE7	78	A18
Montclare st E2	143	O15
Monteagle ave Bark	54	D18
Monteagle way SE15	92	A7
Montefiore st SW8	89	S6
Monteith rd E3	63	Y3
Montem rd SE23	92	K20
Montem rd N Mal	118	A8
Montem st N4	48	C4
Montenotte rd N8	29	W16
Montford pl SE11	157	S11
Montfort pl SW19	87	R20
Montgomery clo Mitch	122	B9
Montgomery clo Sid	96	J14
Montgomery rd W4	73	V10
Montgomery rd Edg	12	A19
Montholme rd SW11	88	M16
Monthope rd E1	151	S2
Montolieu gdns SW15	86	L12
Montpelier ave W5	60	E15
Montpelier ave Bex	97	W19
Montpelier gdns E6	66	B8
Montpelier gdns Rom	55	U1
Montpelier gro NW5	47	V14
Montpelier pl SW7	146	L20
Montpelier ri NW11	45	S1
Montpelier ri Wem	42	F4
Montpelier rd N3	28	C5
Montpelier rd SE15	159	Y20
Montpelier rd W5	60	F14
Montpelier rd Sutt	130	E9
Montpelier row SE3	94	C5
Montpelier row Twick	84	C18
Montpelier sq SW7	146	M19
Montpelier st SW7	146	M20
Montpelier ter SW7	146	L19
Montpelier vale SE3	94	B5
Montpelier wk SW7	146	L20
Montpelier way NW11	45	S1
Montrave rd SE20	110	D17
Montreal pl WC2	149	O8
Montreal rd Ilf	54	B1
Montrell rd SW2	108	A1
Montrose ave NW6	136	M8
Montrose ave Edg	25	Z3
Montrose ave Sid	97	O19
Montrose ave Twick	82	K19
Montrose ave Well	96	F8
Montrose clo Well	96	K7
Montrose clo Wdf Grn	21	S12
Montrose ct SW7	146	H19
Montrose cres N12	15	P20
Montrose cres Wem	42	J16
Montrose gdns Mitch	121	N5
Montrose gdns Sutt	130	B4
Montrose pl SW1	147	U19
Montrose rd SW1	147	U19
Montrose way SE23	110	E2
Montserrat ave Wdf Grn	33	X2
Montserrat clo SE19	109	P12
Montserrat rd SW15	87	S10
Monument gdns SE13	93	V13
Monument st EC3	150	H9
Monument way N17	31	V11
Monza st E1	75	P1
Moodkee st SE16	75	P7
Moody st E1	63	T9
Moon la Barn	4	H12
Moon st N1	141	W4
Moor la EC2	150	E1
Moor pl EC2	150	F2
Moor st W1	148	G7
Moorcroft rd SW16	107	Z6
Moorcroft way Pnr	22	A15
Moordown SE18	95	X2
Moore clo SW14	85	W8
Moore clo Mitch	121	S4
Moore cres Dag	68	C3
Moore Park rd SW6	153	W20
Moore rd SE19	108	K14
Moore st SW3	155	O5
Moorefield rd N17	31	U8
Moorehead way SE3	94	G8
Mooreland rd Brom	112	D19
Moorfield av W5	60	H11
Moorfield rd Enf	9	P6
Moorfields EC2	150	F1
Moorgate EC2	150	F2
Moorgate pl EC2	150	F3
Moorhouse rd W2	145	T5
Moorhouse rd Har	24	G10
Moorings the SE28	68	E20
Moorland clo Rom	38	H3
Moorland clo Twick	82	G18
Moorland rd SW9	90	J10
Moorlands ave NW7	13	X19
Moormead dr Epsom	128	B11
Moorside rd Brom	112	A7
Moot ct NW9	25	P16
Mora rd NW2	44	M11
Mora st EC1	142	C13
Morant st E14	64	C19
Morat st SW9	90	E1
Moravian pl SW10	154	G16
Moravian st E2	63	R7
Moray clo Rom	39	P2
Moray ms N7	48	D6
Moray rd N4	48	C6
Moray way Rom	39	O2
Mordaunt gdns Dag	55	Z20
Mordaunt rd NW10	61	Z4
Mordaunt st SW9	90	C8
Morden clo SE13	93	U4
Morden gdns Grnf	41	X15
Morden gdns Mitch	120	H10
Morden Hall rd Mord	120	C8
Morden hill SE13	93	U4
Morden la SE13	93	U3
Morden rd SE3	94	F4
Morden rd SW19	106	B20
Morden rd Mitch	120	G9
Morden rd Rom	38	A20
Morden Road ms SE3	94	E5
Morden st SE13	93	S3
Morden way Sutt	119	Y18
Morden Wharf rd SE10	76	M9
Mordon rd Ilf	36	L20
Mordred rd SE6	111	Z5
More clo E16	65	Z6
More clo W14	152	J7
Morecambe gdns Stan	11	U14
Morecambe st SE17	158	D8
Morecombe clo Kings T	103	T17
Moree way N18	18	J14
Moreland clo NW11	46	C3
Moreland st EC1	141	Y13
Moreland way E4	20	F9
Morella rd SW12	88	M18
Moremead rd SE6	111	O10
Morena st SE6	93	R18
Moresby ave Surb	117	T19
Moresby rd E5	49	Z4
Moresby wk SW8	89	U16
Moreton ave Islw	83	S1
Moreton clo E5	50	S5
Moreton clo N15	31	P18
Moreton clo NW7	13	Z20
Moreton pl SW1	156	D9
Moreton rd N15	31	P17
Moreton rd S Croy	133	P12
Moreton rd Wor Pk	128	H3
Moreton st SW1	156	D9
Moreton ter SW1	156	D9
Moreton Terrace Mews north SW1		

Moreton Terrace Mews south SW1	156	C9
Morgan ave E17	33	Y13
Morgan clo Dag	69	S1
Morgan rd N7	48	F15
Morgan rd W10	145	O1
Morgan rd Brom	112	E18
Morgan st E3	63	X9
Morgan st E16	65	R14
Morgans la SE1	150	K14
Moriarti clo N7	48	A11
Morie st SW18	88	B12
Morieux rd E10	50	L4
Moring rd SW17	107	P10
Morkyns wk SE21	109	R6
Morland ave Croy	123	S19
Morland ave Dart	99	Z14
Morland clo Hmptn	100	E13
Morland clo NW10	120	K7
Morland gdns NW10	61	Y2
Morland gdns Sthl	70	L3
Morland ms N1	141	U1
Morland rd E17	32	G16
Morland rd SE20	110	G17
Morland rd Croy	123	S20
Morland rd Dag	69	T1
Morland rd Har	24	K14
Morland rd Ilf	53	Y6
Morland rd Sutt	130	E13
Morley ave E4	33	W2
Morley ave N18	18	L14
Morley ave N22	30	G7
Morley cres Edg	12	H9
Morley Crescent east Stan	24	F8
Morley Crescent west Stan	24	F9
Morley hill Enf	8	B4
Morley rd E10	51	U5
Morley rd E15	65	P5
Morley rd SE13	93	U11
Morley rd Bark	67	S4
Morley rd Rom	37	Z17
Morley rd Sutt	119	V20
Morley rd Twick	84	F16
Morley st SE1	149	U19
Morna rd SE5	91	N3
Morning la E9	50	B17
Morningside rd Wor Pk	128	L4
Mornington ave W14	153	O7
Mornington ave Brom	126	M7
Mornington ave Ilf	35	W20
Mornington clo Wdf Grn	21	S13
Mornington cres NW1	140	A9
Mornington gro E3	64	B9
Mornington ms SE5	90	L1
Mornington pl NW1	140	A9
Mornington rd E4	20	J2
Mornington rd E11	52	C3
Mornington rd SE8	75	Z19
Mornington rd Grnf	58	K13
Mornington rd Wdf Grn	21	P12
Mornington st NW1	139	W8
Mornington ter NW1	139	Y7
Mornington wk Rich	102	F9
Morocco st SE1	150	J19
Morpeth gro E9	63	S3
Morpeth rd E9	63	S3
Morpeth st E2	63	S3
Morpeth ter SW1	156	C4
Morrab gdns Ilf	54	K8
Morrell clo Barn	5	R11
Morris ave E12	53	T15
Morris gdns SW18	87	X17
Morris pl N4	48	F6
Morris rd E14	64	E14
Morris rd E15	51	Z12
Morris rd Dag	56	C7
Morris rd Islw	83	V8
Morris st E1	151	Y7
Morrish rd SW2	90	A19

Morrison ave N17	31	S10
Morrison rd Bark	68	L5
Morrison st SW11	89	O7
Morse clo E13	65	S9
Morshead rd W9	137	W14
Morson rd Enf	9	V20
Morston gdns SE9	113	T11
Morten clo SW4	89	Y16
Morteyne rd N17	31	P4
Mortham st E15	64	L14
Mortimer clo NW2	45	W8
Mortimer clo SW16	107	X4
Mortimer cres NW6	137	Y5
Mortimer dr Enf	8	D18
Mortimer est NW6	137	X6
Mortimer mkt WC1	140	D18
Mortimer pl NW6	137	X6
Mortimer rd E6	66	G9
Mortimer rd N1	142	K2
Mortimer rd NW10	136	C12
Mortimer rd W13	60	C17
Mortimer rd Mitch	120	L2
Mortimer sq W11	144	H11
Mortimer st W1	148	A3
Mortlake clo Croy	132	B6
Mortlake dr Mitch	120	H1
Mortlake High st SW14	85	X6
Mortlake rd E16	65	W16
Mortlake rd Ilf	54	B13
Mortlake rd Rich	73	O19
Morton cres N14	16	J12
Morton gdns Wall	131	V10
Morton ms SW5	153	Y6
Morton pl SE1	157	S2
Morton rd E15	65	O2
Morton rd N1	142	C2
Morton rd Mord	120	G12
Morton way N14	16	H11
Morval rd SW2	90	F13
Morvale clo Belv	81	P11
Morven rd SW17	106	L7
Morville st E3	64	A6
Morwell st WC1	148	G3
Moscow pl W2	145	Y8
Moscow rd W2	145	W9
Moselle ave N22	30	F7
Moselle clo N8	30	B11
Moselle st N17	31	V1
Moss clo E1	151	U1
Moss clo Pnr	22	D8
Moss gdns S Croy	134	F18
Moss Hall cres N12	15	P19
Moss Hall gro N12	15	O19
Moss la Pnr	22	B6
Moss la Rom	39	T18
Moss rd Dag	56	F19
Mossborough clo N12	15	O18
Mossbury rd SW11	88	K9
Mossdown clo Belv	81	T12
Mossford clo Ilf	35	Z8
Mossford grn Ilf	36	B9
Mossford la Ilf	36	A8
Mossford st E3	63	X11
Mosslea rd SE20	110	C17
Mosslea rd Brom	127	O12
Mossop st SW3	154	M6
Mossville gdns Mord	119	V7
Mostyn ave Wem	43	N14
Mostyn gdns NW10	136	F11
Mostyn gro E3	64	A6
Mostyn rd SW9	90	G3
Mostyn rd SW19	119	W1
Mostyn rd Edg	25	Z2
Mosul way Brom	127	S16
Motcomb st SW1	147	S20
Motspur pk N Mal	118	D15
Mottingham gdns SE9	113	O2
Mottingham la SE9	112	L1
Mottingham la SE12	94	L20
Mottingham rd N9	19	S1
Mottingham rd SE9	113	R3
Mottisfont rd SE2	80	A9
Moulins rd E9	63	S1
Moulton ave Houns	82	C4
Mound the SE9	113	W8
Moundfield rd N16	31	W19

Mount the N20	15	S8
Mount the N Mal	118	E7
Mount the Wem	43	U7
Mount the Wor Pk	128	K9
Mount Adon pk SE22	91	X19
Mount Angelus rd SW15	86	E18
Mount Ararat rd Rich	84	K13
Mount Ash rd SE26	110	A7
Mount ave E4	20	C12
Mount ave W5	60	E15
Mount ave Sthl	58	G18
Mount clo W5	60	E15
Mount clo Barn	6	B15
Mount clo Brom	113	R20
Mount clo Cars	131	P20
Mount ct W Wick	135	Z3
Mount Culver ave Sid	115	X15
Mount dr Bexh	97	Z13
Mount dr Har	22	E14
Mount dr Wem	43	V6
Mount Echo ave E4	20	E5
Mount Echo dr E4	20	E5
Mount Ephraim la SW16	107	X7
Mount Ephraim rd SW16	107	Y6
Mount gdns SE26	109	Z6
Mount gro Edg	12	K11
Mount Mills EC1	141	X20
Mount Nod rd SW16	108	C7
Mount pk Cars	131	P20
Mount Park ave Har	41	S7
Mount Park ave S Croy	132	K20
Mount Park cres W5	60	G17
Mount Park rd W5	60	G14
Mount Park rd Har	41	S10
Mount Pleasant SE27	108	M9
Mount Pleasant WC1	141	S18
Mount Pleasant Barn	5	X13
Mount Pleasant Wem	60	K2
Mount Pleasant cres N4	48	D2
Mount Pleasant hill E5	50	C6
Mount Pleasant la E5	50	A8
Mount Pleasant rd E17	32	J6
Mount Pleasant rd N17	31	S6
Mount Pleasant rd NW10	136	D3
Mount Pleasant rd SE13	93	T15
Mount Pleasant rd W5	60	E12
Mount Pleasant rd N Mal	117	V5
Mount Pleasant vill N4	30	C20
Mount Pleasant wk Bex	98	L14
Mount rd NW2	44	L8
Mount rd NW4	26	G19
Mount rd SW19	105	Z4
Mount rd Barn	5	W15
Mount rd Bexh	97	X13
Mount rd Dag	56	D3
Mount rd Dart	99	U15
Mount rd Felt	100	B6
Mount rd Mitch	120	G3
Mount rd N Mal	117	X6
Mount row W1	147	W10
Mount Stewart ave Har	24	G20
Mount st W1	147	T11
Mount ter E1	151	V2
Mount Vernon NW3	46	D11
Mount vw NW7	12	M11
Mount vw Enf	7	X1
Mount View rd E4	20	J3
Mount View rd N4	30	B20
Mount View rd NW9	25	Y14
Mount vill SE27	108	J7
Mount way Cars	131	R20
Mountacre clo SE26	109	W9
Mountague pl E14	64	F19

Mountbatten clo SE18	79	U17
Mountbatten clo SE19	109	S13
Mountbel rd Stan	23	Y5
Mountcombe clo Surb	116	J17
Mountearl gdns SW16	108	C6
Mountfield rd E6	66	H7
Mountfield rd N3	27	W9
Mountfield rd W5	60	H18
Mountford st E1	151	S4
Mountfort ter N1	141	S1
Mountgrove rd N5	48	K8
Mounthurst rd Brom	126	C18
Mountington Park clo Har	24	G18
Mountjoy clo SE2	80	D5
Mounts Pond rd SE3	93	W5
Mountsfield ct SE13	93	W15
Mountside Stan	23	X4
Movers la Bark	67	U3
Mowatt clo N19	47	Y5
Mowbray rd NW6	45	S19
Mowbray rd SE19	109	V20
Mowbray rd Barn	5	R15
Mowbray rd Edg	12	D12
Mowbray rd Rich	102	D7
Mowbrays clo Rom	38	L6
Mowbrays rd Rom	38	K6
Mowlem st E2	143	Z7
Mowlem Trading est N17	19	R20
Mowll st SW9	157	S19
Moxon clo E13	65	P6
Moxon st W1	147	U1
Moxon st Barn	4	H12
Moye clo E2	143	T7
Moyers rd E10	51	V2
Moylan rd W6	152	M15
Moyne pl NW10	61	R7
Moyser rd SW16	107	S15
Mozart st W10	137	O14
Muchelney rd Mord	120	E15
Mud la W5	60	H13
Mudlarks way SE7	77	U9
Mudlarks way SE10	77	R7
Muggeridge rd Dag	56	G12
Muir rd E5	49	Z10
Muir st E16	78	F3
Muirdown ave SW14	85	X10
Muirfield W3	62	C17
Muirfield cres E14	76	D8
Muirkirk rd SE6	111	V1
Mulberry clo E4	20	C7
Mulberry clo SE7	78	A16
Mulberry clo SE22	91	X14
Mulberry clo NW4	26	M11
Mulberry clo NW3	105	H10
Mulberry clo Barn	5	U14
Mulberry clo Nthlt	58	A5
Mulberry ct Bark	54	L19
Mulberry cres Brent	72	C19
Mulberry la Croy	133	V2
Mulberry ms Wall	131	U13
Mulberry st E1	151	T3
Mulberry wk SW3	154	G12
Mulberry way E18	34	J6
Mulberry way Belv	81	Z5
Mulberry way Ilf	36	C13
Mulgrave rd NW10	44	E13
Mulgrave rd SW6	153	P14
Mulgrave rd W5	60	H10
Mulgrave rd Croy	133	O7
Mulgrave rd Har	41	Y8
Mulgrave rd Sutt	129	V16
Mulholland clo Mitch	121	T3
Mulkern rd N19	47	Y3
Muller rd SW4	89	Z17
Mullet gdns E2	143	U11
Mullins path SW14	85	Y7
Mullion clo Har	22	K3
Mulready st NW8	138	K18
Multon rd SW18	88	G20
Mulvaney way SE1	150	G18
Mumford ct EC2	150	D5
Muncaster rd SW11	89	N12

Name	Page	Grid
Muncies ms SE6	111	V3
Mund st W14	153	P10
Mundania rd SE22	92	B15
Munday rd E16	65	T19
Munden st W14	152	L6
Mundford rd E5	50	C6
Mundon gdns Ilf	54	E4
Mundy st N1	142	K13
Mungo Park clo (Bushey) Wat	10	B7
Mungo Park rd Rain	57	W17
Munnings gdns Islw	83	P14
Munro dr N11	16	H19
Munro ms W10	136	M20
Munro ter SW10	154	F16
Munster ave Houns	82	B12
Munster ct Tedd	102	E15
Munster gdns N13	17	Y13
Munster rd SW6	152	L17
Munster rd Tedd	102	C16
Munster sq NW1	139	Z15
Munton rd SE17	158	D5
Murchison ave Bex	97	Y19
Murchison rd E10	51	T7
Murdock clo E16	65	R16
Murdock st SE15	159	X14
Murfett clo SW19	105	R5
Muriel st N1	141	P8
Murillo rd SE13	93	Y11
Murphy st SE1	149	S19
Murray ave Brom	126	J6
Murray ave Houns	82	K14
Murray gro N1	142	D11
Murray ms NW1	47	X19
Murray rd SW19	105	P15
Murray rd W5	72	D12
Murray rd Rich	102	C5
Murray sq E16	65	U18
Murray st NW1	47	W19
Mursell est SW8	90	C1
Musard rd W6	152	L13
Musbury st E1	63	P16
Muschamp rd SE15	91	V8
Muschamp rd Cars	130	K3
Muscovy st EC3	150	L9
Museum st WC1	148	K3
Musgrave clo Barn	5	R5
Musgrave cres SW6	153	V20
Musgrave rd Islw	83	V2
Musgrove rd SE14	92	G3
Muston rd E5	50	A6
Muswell ave N10	29	S5
Muswell hill N10	29	U11
Muswell Hill bdy N10	29	S11
Muswell Hill pl N10	29	T12
Muswell Hill rd N6	29	R18
Muswell Hill rd N10	29	R14
Muswell ms N10	29	S9
Muswell rd N10	29	S9
Mutrix rd NW6	137	V3
Mutton pl NW1	47	R18
Muybridge rd N Mal	117	V5
Myatt rd SW9	157	X20
Myatt's Fields south SW9	90	G5
Mycenae rd SE3	77	S17
Myddelton ave Enf	8	F3
Myddelton clo Enf	8	G5
Myddelton gdns N21	17	X2
Myddelton pk N20	15	Y10
Myddelton pas EC1	141	U12
Myddelton rd N8	30	B11
Myddelton sq EC1	141	U11
Myddelton st EC1	141	U15
Myddelton rd N22	30	D1
Myers la SE14	75	T16
Mylis clo SE26	110	A9
Mylne st EC1	141	T11
Myra st SE2	80	A12
Myrdle st E1	151	V4
Myrna clo Mitch	106	K18
Myron pl SE13	93	W8
Myrtle clo Barn	16	A5
Myrtle clo Erith	99	S1
Myrtle gdns W7	71	T3
Myrtle gro Enf	8	C3
Myrtle gro N Mal	117	W4
Myrtle rd E6	66	E3
Myrtle rd E17	32	K18
Myrtle rd N13	18	A10
Myrtle rd W3	73	X2
Myrtle rd Croy	135	P6
Myrtle rd Hmptn	100	M16
Myrtle rd Houns	82	M6
Myrtle rd Ilf	54	A7
Myrtle rd Sutt	130	D10
Myrtle wk N1	142	J10
Myrtledene rd SE2	80	A12
Mysore rd SW11	89	N9
Myton rd SE21	109	N7

N

Name	Page	Grid
Nadine st SE7	77	Y15
Nagle clo E17	33	X8
Nags Head la Well	97	R7
Nags Head rd Enf	9	R14
Nairn st E14	64	H15
Nairne gro SE24	91	P12
Namton dr Th Hth	122	C9
Nan Clark's la NW7	13	S7
Nankin st E14	64	C18
Nansen rd SW11	89	P9
Nant rd NW2	45	W6
Nant st E2	143	Y12
Nantes clo SW18	88	D11
Nantes pas E1	143	N20
Napier ave E14	76	C13
Napier ave SW6	87	V6
Napier clo SE8	75	Z18
Napier clo W14	153	N1
Napier clo Horn	57	Z4
Napier gro N1	142	D9
Napier pl W14	153	O2
Napier rd E6	66	J4
Napier rd E11	51	Z11
Napier rd E15	65	O5
Napier rd N17	31	S10
Napier rd NW10	62	J7
Napier rd SE25	123	Z10
Napier rd W14	153	N2
Napier rd Belv	81	P12
Napier rd Brom	126	J9
Napier rd Enf	9	U17
Napier rd Islw	83	Y11
Napier rd S Croy	133	O16
Napier rd Wem	42	H16
Napier ter N1	141	W2
Napoleon rd E5	49	Z10
Napoleon rd Twick	84	B17
Narbonne ave SW4	89	U14
Narborough st SW6	88	A5
Narcissus rd NW6	45	X15
Naresby Fold Stan	11	S19
Narford rd E5	49	Y8
Narrow st E14	63	V19
Narrow way Brom	127	S15
Nascot st W12	144	B5
Naseby clo NW6	46	E19
Naseby clo Islw	83	U2
Naseby rd SE19	109	P15
Naseby rd Dag	56	F9
Naseby rd Ilf	35	T5
Nash grn Brom	112	F16
Nash pl E14	76	C3
Nash rd N9	19	P7
Nash rd SE4	92	H12
Nash rd Rom	37	V12
Nash st NW1	139	Y13
Nasmyth st W6	74	J8
Nassau rd SW13	86	D2
Nassau st W1	148	B2
Nassington rd NW3	46	L12
Natal rd N11	16	M18
Natal rd SW16	107	X14
Natal rd Ilf	53	Z13
Natal rd Th Hth	123	N7
Nathan way SE28	79	U10
Nathaniel clo E1	151	P2
Nathans rd Wem	42	E4
Naval row E14	64	H19
Navarino gro E8	49	Y17
Navarino rd E8	49	Y16
Navarre rd E6	66	E5
Navarre st E2	143	N15
Navestock clo E4	20	H12
Navestock cres Wdf Grn	34	L2
Navy st SW4	89	X7
Naylor gro Enf	9	T17
Naylor rd N20	15	P8
Naylor rd SE15	159	W17
Nazrul st E2	142	M11
Neal ave Sthl	58	F10
Neal st WC2	148	J6
Nealden st SW9	90	C7
Neale clo N2	28	D11
Neal's yd WC2	148	J6
Near acre NW9	26	D5
Neasden clo NW10	44	B14
Neasden la NW10	44	A10
Neasden Lane north NW10	43	X8
Neasham rd Dag	55	R16
Neate st SE5	158	H14
Neath gdns Mord	120	D16
Neathouse pl SW1	156	A4
Neatscourt rd E6	66	C15
Nebraska st SE1	150	D19
Neckinger SE16	159	P1
Neckinger est SE16	159	P1
Neckinger st SE1	151	R19
Nectarine way SE13	93	S3
Needham rd W11	145	U6
Needham ter NW2	45	O10
Needleman st SE16	75	S6
Neeld cres NW4	26	J16
Neeld cres Wem	43	P16
Nelgarde rd E6	93	P19
Nella rd W6	152	F14
Nelldale rd SE16	159	Z6
Nello James gdns SE27	109	O9
Nelson clo Croy	132	J1
Nelson clo Rom	38	G5
Nelson gdns E2	143	U12
Nelson gdns Houns	82	H16
Nelson Grove rd SW19	106	B20
Nelson Mandela clo N10	29	O7
Nelson Mandela rd SE3	94	L7
Nelson pas EC1	142	C13
Nelson pl N1	141	Y10
Nelson pl W3	73	U2
Nelson pl Sid	115	N10
Nelson rd E4	20	C20
Nelson rd E11	34	G14
Nelson rd N8	30	C15
Nelson rd N9	19	N9
Nelson rd N15	31	S12
Nelson rd SE10	76	H17
Nelson rd SW19	106	C18
Nelson rd Belv	81	P13
Nelson rd Brom	126	M9
Nelson rd Enf	9	T18
Nelson rd Har	41	S3
Nelson rd Houns	82	G15
Nelson rd N Mal	117	V13
Nelson rd Sid	115	O10
Nelson rd Stan	11	R18
Nelson sq SE1	149	X16
Nelson st E1	151	W4
Nelson st E6	66	G5
Nelson st E16	65	P19
Nelson ter N1	141	Y10
Nelson's row SW4	89	X10
Nemoure rd W3	61	V20
Nene gdns Felt	100	D6
Nepaul rd SW11	88	J6
Nepean st SW15	86	H17
Neptune rd Har	23	O19
Neptune st SE16	75	P7
Nesbit clo SE3	93	Z6
Nesbit rd SE9	95	O10
Nesbitts all Barn	4	G11
Nesham st E1	151	T11
Ness st SE16	159	S2
Nesta rd Wdf Grn	21	O18
Nestor ave N21	7	W19
Nether clo N3	27	Y1
Nether st N3	27	X3
Nether st N12	15	R17
Netheravon rd W7	71	V2
Netheravon Road north W4	74	E12
Netheravon Road south W4	74	D15
Netheravon rd W5	72	F8
Netherby gdns Enf	6	M14
Netherby rd SE23	92	C17
Nethercourt ave N13	14	L18
Netherfield gdns Bark	54	F19
Netherfield rd N12	15	O16
Netherford rd SW4	89	V5
Netherhall gdns NW3	46	E15
Netherhall way NW3	46	D16
Netherlands rd Barn	5	T19
Netherleigh clo N6	47	U4
Netherpark dr Rom	39	S7
Netherton gro SW10	154	C14
Netherton rd N15	31	O19
Netherton rd Twick	84	A14
Netherwood pl W14	144	F20
Netherwood rd W14	144	F20
Netherwood st NW6	45	W19
Netley clo Croy	135	V16
Netley clo Sutt	129	P11
Netley gdns Mord	120	D17
Netley rd E17	32	M15
Netley rd Brent	72	J15
Netley rd Ilf	36	D15
Netley rd Mord	120	D17
Netley st NW1	140	A14
Nettlecombe clo Sutt	130	B20
Nettleden ave Wem	43	P17
Nettlefold pl SE27	108	J8
Nettleton rd SE14	92	G1
Nettlewood rd SW16	107	Y19
Neuchatel rd SE6	110	L4
Nevada st SE10	76	H18
Nevern pl SW5	153	V7
Nevern rd SW5	153	U7
Nevern sq SW5	153	U7
Nevill rd N16	49	S9
Neville ave N Mal	103	Z20
Neville clo E11	52	D9
Neville clo NW1	140	G9
Neville clo NW6	137	S10
Neville clo SE15	159	T20
Neville clo W3	73	W4
Neville clo Barn	82	J3
Neville clo Sid	114	M9
Neville dr N2	28	D18
Neville gdns Dag	55	W8
Neville Gill clo SW18	87	Z15
Neville pl N22	30	D4
Neville rd E7	65	U2
Neville rd NW6	137	S10
Neville rd W5	60	F10
Neville rd Croy	123	P17
Neville rd Dag	55	W8
Neville rd Ilf	36	C4
Neville rd Kings T	117	R3
Neville rd Rich	102	D6
Neville st SW7	154	G9
Neville ter SW7	154	G9
Neville wk Cars	120	J18
Nevin dr E4	20	F5
Nevis rd SW17	107	O3
New Barn st E13	65	U11
New Barns ave Mitch	121	X10
New Bond st W1	147	X6
New Brent st NW4	26	M14
New Bridge st EC4	149	X7
New Broad st EC2	150	H3
New bdy W5	60	G20
New Burlington ms W1	148	B9
New Burlington pl W1	148	A8
New Burlington st W1	148	B9
New Butt la SE8	76	B20
New Cavendish st W1	147	W2
New Change EC4	150	B6
New Charles st EC1	141	Y12
New Church rd SE5	158	E17
New City rd E13	65	Y8
New clo SW19	120	E5

New clo Felt	100	A11
New Compton st WC2	148	H6
New ct EC4	149	S7
New Coventry st W1	148	G10
New Cross rd SE14	75	R19
New end W3	46	E11
New End sq NW3	46	F11
New Farm ave Brom	126	E8
New Fetter la EC4	149	U4
New Goulston st E1	151	N4
New Heston rd Houns	70	D18
New Inn pas WC2	149	P7
New Inn st EC2	142	L15
New Inn yd EC2	142	L16
New Kent rd SE1	158	A3
New King st SE8	76	A16
New Kings rd SW6	87	U6
New London st EC3	150	L8
New Lydenburgh st SE7	77	Z9
New Mount st E15	64	K2
New North pl EC2	142	J17
New North rd N1	142	B2
New North rd Ilf	36	D1
New North st WC1	141	N20
New Oak rd N2	28	E8
New Orleans wk N19	47	Y1
New Oxford st WC1	148	H4
New Park ave N13	17	Z11
New Park clo Nthlt	40	B18
New Park rd SW2	107	Y1
New Plaistow rd E15	65	N3
New Quebec st W1	147	R5
New ride SW7	146	M17
New River cres N13	17	V11
New River wk N1	48	M18
New rd E1	151	V2
New rd E4	20	C13
New rd N8	29	Z16
New rd N9	18	L9
New rd N17	31	U3
New rd N22	30	L4
New rd NW7	27	S2
New rd (Barnet gate) NW7	13	S1
New rd SE2	80	H10
New rd Brent	72	H15
New rd Dag	69	S4
New rd Felt	100	B11
New rd Har	41	V12
New rd Houns	82	K11
New rd Ilf	54	J6
New rd Kings T	103	P18
New rd Mitch	121	O19
New rd Rain	69	Y7
New rd Rich	102	F9
New rd Well	97	P6
New row WC2	148	J9
New sq WC2	149	R5
New st EC2	150	L3
New Street hill Brom	112	H13
New Street sq EC4	149	U4
New Trinity rd N2	28	F8
New Union clo E14	76	H7
New Union st EC2	150	E1
New Wanstead E11	34	D18
New Way rd NW9	26	B13
New Wharf rd N1	140	M7
New Zealand way W12	62	K20
Newark cres NW10	61	X9
Newark Knok E6	66	K16
Newark rd S Croy	133	O15
Newark st E1	151	V3
Newark way NW4	26	H11
Newbolt ave Sutt	129	O10
Newbolt rd Stan	10	J17
Newborough grn N Mal	117	Y9
Newburgh rd W3	73	V1
Newburgh st W1	148	C7
Newburn st SE11	157	P10
Newbury ave Enf	9	X2
Newbury clo Nthlt	40	D17

Newbury gdns Epsom	128	D8
Newbury rd E4	20	H20
Newbury rd Brom	126	E7
Newbury rd Ilf	36	G18
Newbury st EC1	150	A1
Newbury way Nthlt	40	C17
Newby clo Enf	8	F9
Newby pl E14	64	F19
Newby st SW8	89	T6
Newcastle clo EC4	149	W4
Newcastle pl W2	146	H1
Newcastle row EC1	141	V17
Newcombe gdns SW16	108	B8
Newcombe pk NW7	13	O16
Newcombe pk Wem	61	N2
Newcombe st W8	145	V12
Newcomen rd E11	52	C8
Newcomen rd SW11	88	G8
Newcomen st SE1	150	E16
Newcourt st NW8	138	K10
Newell st E14	63	Y18
Newent clo SE15	158	K16
Newent clo Cars	120	L20
Newfield clo Hmptn	100	G20
Newfield ri NW2	44	J8
Newgale gdns Edg	24	M3
Newgate Croy	123	N19
Newgate clo Felt	100	C5
Newgate st EC1	149	Z4
Newham way E6	66	B12
Newham way E16	65	S14
Newhams row SE1	150	L19
Newhaven gdns SE9	95	N9
Newhaven rd SE25	123	P11
Newhouse ave Rom	37	X10
Newhouse clo N Mal	118	B18
Newhouse wk Mord	120	C17
Newick clo Bex	98	G15
Newick rd E5	50	B11
Newing grn Brom	113	O18
Newington Barrow way N7	48	C8
Newington Butts SE1	157	Y6
Newington Butts SE11	157	Y7
Newington Causeway SE1	157	Z3
Newington grn N16	49	O14
Newington Green rd N1	49	O17
Newland ct Wem	43	P7
Newland dr Enf	9	N6
Newland gdns W13	71	Z6
Newland rd N8	30	A10
Newland st E16	78	T3
Newlands the Wall	131	W18
Newlands clo Edg	11	W10
Newlands clo Sthl	70	B13
Newlands clo Wem	42	E16
Newlands ct SE9	95	X16
Newlands pk SE26	110	E15
Newlands pl Barn	4	C16
Newlands quay E1	63	P20
Newlands rd SW16	122	C4
Newlands ri Wdf Grn	21	R9
Newlands wd Croy	134	L20
Newling clo E6	66	H17
Newlyn gdns Har	40	D2
Newlyn rd N17	31	U5
Newlyn rd Barn	4	G15
Newlyn rd Well	96	K5
Newman pas W1	148	D3
Newman rd E13	65	V10
Newman rd E17	32	G14
Newman rd Brom	126	G2
Newman rd Croy	122	D19
Newman st W1	148	D2
Newman yd W1	148	D4
Newman's ct EC3	150	H6
Newmans la Surb	116	H14
Newman's row WC2	149	P3
Newmans way Barn	5	S7
Newmarket ave Nthlt	40	J15
Newminster rd Mord	120	D16

Newnham clo Nthlt	40	M16
Newnham clo Th Hth	122	L4
Newnham gdns Nthlt	41	N16
Newnham rd N22	30	E3
Newnham ter SE1	149	S20
Newnham way Har	24	L14
Newnhams clo Brom	127	V7
Newton clo N4	49	N2
Newport pl WC2	148	H8
Newport rd E10	51	V6
Newport rd E17	32	J13
Newport rd SW13	86	H1
Newport st SE11	157	O6
Newquay cres Har	40	C6
Newquay rd SE6	111	S4
Newry rd Twick	84	A12
Newsam ave N15	31	O14
Newstead rd SE12	94	B18
Newstead wk Cars	120	D18
Newstead way SW19	105	R8
Newton ave N10	29	R3
Newton ave W3	73	V5
Newton gro W4	74	A9
Newton rd E15	51	Y14
Newton rd N15	31	W14
Newton rd NW2	44	M11
Newton rd SW19	105	U19
Newton rd W2	145	W5
Newton rd Har	23	T6
Newton rd Islw	83	V5
Newton rd Well	97	N8
Newton rd Wem	42	M20
Newton st WC2	148	M4
Newton way N18	17	Z16
Newtown st SW11	89	S2
Niagara ave W5	72	D10
Nibthwaite rd Har	23	S15
Nichol clo N14	16	K4
Nichol la Brom	112	G17
Nicholas clo Grnf	58	L5
Nicholas gdns W5	72	G4
Nicholas la EC4	150	G7
Nicholas rd E1	63	R12
Nicholas rd Dag	56	C8
Nicholay rd N19	47	Y4
Nicholes rd Houns	82	G11
Nicholl st E2	143	T6
Nichols grn W5	60	J13
Nicholson dr (Bushey) Wat	10	A6
Nicholson rd Croy	123	V20
Nicholson st SE1	149	X14
Nickleby clo SE28	68	F18
Nicola clo Har	23	R6
Nicola clo S Croy	132	L15
Nicoll pl NW4	26	K19
Nicoll rd NW10	62	B6
Nicosia rd SW18	88	J13
Niederwald rd SE26	110	H9
Nigel ms Ilf	53	Z11
Nigel Playfair ave W6	74	J12
Nigel rd E7	52	M15
Nigel rd SE15	91	X7
Nigeria rd SE7	77	Z19
Nightingale ave E4	20	M15
Nightingale clo E4	20	L12
Nightingale clo W4	73	V17
Nightingale clo Cars	131	O3
Nightingale est E5	49	Y10
Nightingale gro SE13	93	X13
Nightingale la E11	34	H14
Nightingale la N8	29	Z12
Nightingale la SW4	89	S16
Nightingale la SW12	88	L20
Nightingale la Brom	126	L4
Nightingale la Rich	84	K18
Nightingale pl SE18	78	K15
Nightingale rd E5	49	Z9
Nightingale rd N9	9	Y4
Nightingale rd N22	30	A3
Nightingale rd NW10	62	E8
Nightingale rd W7	71	V2
Nightingale rd Cars	131	N5
Nightingale rd Hmptn	100	H13

Nightingale sq SW12	89	O19
Nightingale vale SE18	78	K16
Nightingale wk SW4	89	R15
Nightingale way E6	66	E13
Nile rd E13	65	Y7
Nile st N1	142	D12
Nile ter SE15	159	O11
Nimmo dr (Bushey) Wat	10	D3
Nimrod rd SW16	107	R15
Nine Acres clo E12	53	S14
Nine Elms la SW8	156	F15
Nineteenth rd Mitch	122	A9
Nithdale rd SE18	79	N18
Niton clo Barn	4	C18
Niton rd Rich	85	P7
Niton st SW6	152	G17
Nobel rd N18	19	S15
Noble st EC2	150	B3
Noel Park rd N22	30	F8
Noel rd E6	66	D12
Noel rd N1	141	X8
Noel rd W3	61	R17
Noel st W1	148	D6
Nolan way E5	49	Y11
Nolton pl Edg	25	N5
Nonsuch wk Sutt	129	P20
Nora gdns NW4	27	P12
Nora ter Har	41	T4
Norbiton ave Kings T	117	R3
Norbiton Common rd Kings T	117	U5
Norbiton rd E14	63	Y17
Norbroke st W12	62	D18
Norburn st W10	144	K2
Norbury ave SW16	122	D1
Norbury ave Houns	83	P12
Norbury ave Th Hth	122	H4
Norbury clo SW16	108	G20
Norbury Court rd SW16	122	A5
Norbury cres SW16	122	D1
Norbury cross SW16	121	Z5
Norbury gdns Rom	37	V16
Norbury gro NW7	13	O10
Norbury hill SW16	108	G19
Norbury ri SW16	122	A5
Norbury rd E4	20	A15
Norbury rd Th Hth	123	N5
Norcombe gdns Har	24	E17
Norcott rd N16	49	X8
Norcroft gdns SE22	91	W17
Norcutt rd Twick	101	U1
Norfolk ave N13	17	V19
Norfolk ave N15	31	U18
Norfolk clo N2	28	H10
Norfolk clo N13	17	X19
Norfolk clo Barn	6	C14
Norfolk clo Twick	84	B15
Norfolk cres W2	146	K4
Norfolk cres Sid	96	J18
Norfolk gdns Bexh	98	C1
Norfolk House rd SW16	107	Y7
Norfolk pl W2	146	H5
Norfolk pl Well	97	N5
Norfolk rd E6	66	H3
Norfolk rd E17	32	G6
Norfolk rd NW8	138	H6
Norfolk rd NW10	44	B20
Norfolk rd SW19	106	J17
Norfolk rd Bark	67	U1
Norfolk rd Barn	4	M11
Norfolk rd Dag	56	J15
Norfolk rd Enf	9	N18
Norfolk rd Har	22	L16
Norfolk rd Ilf	54	H4
Norfolk rd Rom	38	L18
Norfolk rd Th Hth	122	M6
Norfolk row SE1	157	O4
Norfolk sq W2	146	G5
Norfolk Square ms W2	146	H6
Norfolk st E7	52	F14
Norfolk ter W6	152	K12
Norgrove st SW12	89	P20
Norhyrst ave SE25	123	U5
Norland pl W11	144	M14
Norland rd W11	144	H14

Name	No.	Ref
Norland sq W11	144	M14
Norlands cres Chis	127	Z1
Norley vale SW15	104	H2
Norlington rd E10	51	V3
Norlington rd E11	51	X5
Norman ave N22	30	K4
Norman ave Felt	100	C4
Norman ave Sthl	58	C19
Norman ave Twick	84	C18
Norman clo Rom	38	J6
Norman gro E3	63	X6
Norman rd E6	66	H10
Norman rd E11	51	Y7
Norman rd N15	31	V15
Norman rd SE10	76	E19
Norman rd SW19	106	D17
Norman rd Belv	81	U8
Norman rd Horn	57	X1
Norman rd Ilf	54	A16
Norman rd Sutt	129	X10
Norman rd Th Hth	122	J12
Norman st EC1	142	B15
Norman way N14	16	M9
Norman way W3	61	T15
Normanby clo SW15	87	V13
Normanby rd NW10	44	E13
Normand ms W14	153	N13
Normand rd W14	153	N12
Normandy ave Barn	4	H14
Normandy rd SW9	90	F2
Normandy ter E16	65	V18
Normandy way Erith	99	P2
Normanhurst ave Bexh	97	W3
Normanhurst dr Twick	84	A14
Normanhurst rd SW2	108	D4
Normans clo NW10	43	X18
Normans mead NW10	43	X17
Normansfield ave Tedd	102	E19
Normanshire ave E4	20	F13
Normanshire dr E4	20	C14
Normanton ave SW19	105	X5
Normanton pk E4	21	N7
Normanton rd S Croy	133	R12
Normanton st SE23	110	G4
Normington clo SW16	108	E11
Norrice lea N2	28	F16
Norris st SW1	148	F11
Norris way Dart	99	V6
Norroy rd SW15	87	P11
Norrys clo Barn	5	Z15
Norrys rd Barn	5	Z15
Norseman clo Ilf	55	S3
Norstead pl SW15	104	G3
North Access rd E17	32	G18
North acre NW9	26	B5
North Acton rd NW10	61	Y7
North Audley st W1	147	T7
North ave N18	18	L13
North ave W13	60	B15
North ave Cars	131	N17
North ave Har	22	M18
North ave Rich	85	O3
North ave Sthl	58	E20
North bank NW8	138	J15
North Birkbeck rd E11	51	X10
North Carriage dr W2	146	L9
North Circular rd E4	19	W16
North Circular rd E18	34	J6
North Circular rd N3	27	X12
North Circular rd N12	28	B8
North Circular rd N13	17	T16
North Circular rd NW2	44	D6
North Circular rd NW10	60	L8
North Circular rd NW11	27	P19
North clo Bexh	97	W10
North clo Dag	69	T4
North clo Mord	119	T8
North colonnade E14	76	C2
North Common rd W5	60	L20
North Countess rd E17	32	L9
North ct W1	140	C20
North Cray rd Sid	115	Y15
North cres N3	27	V8
North cres WC1	140	E20
North Cross rd SE22	91	V12
North Cross rd Ilf	36	B13
North dene NW7	12	M10
North dene Houns	82	J2
North dr SW16	107	U9
North dr Houns	83	O5
North end NW3	46	C5
North end Buck H	21	X3
North end Croy	132	L2
North End ave NW3	46	D5
North End cres W14	153	O7
North End rd NW11	45	Y3
North End rd SW6	153	S14
North End rd W14	152	M5
North End rd Wem	43	S10
North End way NW3	46	D7
North Flockton st SE16	151	S17
North gdns SW19	106	G17
North glade the Bex	98	B20
North Gower st NW1	140	C15
North gro N6	47	P2
North gro N15	31	O16
North hill N6	29	N17
North Hill ave N6	29	N17
North Hyde la Houns	70	D17
North Hyde la Sthl	70	A13
North la Tedd	101	V14
North Lodge clo SW15	87	P14
North ms WC1	141	P18
North pk SE9	95	U16
North pas SW18	87	Y12
North Peckham est SE15	159	N17
North pl Mitch	106	L17
North pl Tedd	101	V15
North Pole rd W10	144	B3
North ride W2	146	L9
North rd N6	47	P2
North rd N7	47	Z17
North rd N9	18	M3
North rd SE18	79	W10
North rd SW19	106	D16
North rd W5	72	G9
North rd Belv	81	U7
North rd Brent	72	K15
North rd Brom	112	H20
North rd Dart	99	U17
North rd Edg	25	T4
North rd Ilf	54	H6
North rd Rich	85	O7
North rd Rom	37	Y16
North rd Sthl	58	G18
North rd Surb	116	H14
North rd W Wick	135	S1
North row W1	147	R8
North sq NW11	27	Z17
North st E13	65	V6
North st NW4	27	N14
North st SW4	89	U7
North st Bark	54	A19
North st Bexh	98	E9
North st Brom	126	E2
North st Cars	130	M6
North st Islw	83	Y6
North st Rom	39	N12
North Street pas E13	65	W5
North Tenter st E1	151	P6
North ter SW3	154	K4
North vw SW19	104	L12
North vw W5	60	E11
North vw Ilf	37	O1
North View cres NW10	44	D13
North View dr Wdf Grn	35	N8
North View rd N8	29	Y11
North vill NW1	47	X18
North wk Croy	135	T13
North way N9	19	S6
North way N11	16	G19
North way NW9	25	S10
North way Mord	119	T8
North Wharf rd W2	146	F3
North Woolwich rd E16	77	W3
North Worple way SW14	85	X7
Northall rd Bexh	98	K6
Northampton gro N1	49	N16
Northampton pk N1	49	N16
Northampton rd EC1	141	U17
Northampton rd Croy	133	X3
Northampton rd Enf	9	X15
Northampton sq EC1	141	X14
Northampton st N1	48	L20
Northanger rd SW16	107	Z16
Northbank rd E17	33	T6
Northborough rd SW16	121	X6
Northbourne Brom	126	F16
Northbourne rd SW4	89	Z12
Northbrook rd SE13	93	Y12
Northbrook rd Barn	4	E19
Northbrook rd Croy	123	O12
Northbrook rd Ilf	53	W8
Northburgh st EC1	141	Y17
Northchurch SE17	158	G9
Northchurch rd N1	142	J1
Northchurch rd Wem	43	O17
Northchurch ter N1	142	J1
Northcliffe clo Wor Pk	128	B6
Northcliffe dr N20	14	H6
Northcote ave W5	60	J20
Northcote ave Islw	83	X13
Northcote ave Sthl	58	C20
Northcote ave Surb	117	N15
Northcote ms SW11	88	K11
Northcote rd E17	32	H14
Northcote rd NW10	62	B1
Northcote rd SW11	88	K11
Northcote rd Croy	123	O15
Northcote rd N Mal	117	Y8
Northcote rd Sid	114	H9
Northcote rd Twick	83	Z13
Northcott ave N22	30	A4
Northcroft rd W13	72	A5
Northcroft rd Epsom	128	A17
Northdene gdns N15	31	T19
Northdown gdns Ilf	36	H14
Northdown rd Horn	57	Y1
Northdown rd Well	97	R5
Northdown st N1	141	N10
Northend rd Erith	99	T2
Northern ave N9	18	F9
Northern Relief rd Bark	54	B19
Northern rd E13	65	W4
Northern Service rd Barn	4	F11
Northernhay wk Mord	119	T10
Northey st E14	63	X19
Northfield ave W5	72	D9
Northfield ave W13	72	B2
Northfield clo Brom	127	R1
Northfield gdns Dag	56	C12
Northfield rd E6	53	V19
Northfield rd N16	49	T1
Northfield rd W13	72	B5
Northfield rd Barn	5	W10
Northfield rd Dag	56	C11
Northfield rd Enf	9	O18
Northfields SW18	87	X11
Northfields Industrial est Wem	61	P3
Northfields rd W3	61	U14
Northgate dr NW9	26	A17
Northiam N12	14	K12
Northiam st E9	143	Y6
Northington st WC1	141	P19
Northlands st SE5	90	M6
Northolm Edg	12	N13
Northolme gdns Edg	25	R3
Northolme rd N5	48	K11
Northolt gdns Grnf	41	W15
Northolt Industrial est Nthlt	58	K1
Northolt rd Har	40	L12
Northover Brom	112	D6
Northport st N1	142	H6
Northspur rd Sutt	129	X5
Northstead rd SW2	108	G5
Northumberland all EC3	150	M7
Northumberland ave E12	52	L4
Northumberland ave WC2	148	J12
Northumberland ave Enf	9	N4
Northumberland ave Islw	83	W1
Northumberland ave Well	96	G9
Northumberland gdns N9	18	H9
Northumberland gdns Islw	71	Z19
Northumberland gdns Mitch	121	Z11
Northumberland gro N17	31	Z2
Northumberland pk N17	18	J20
Northumberland pk Erith	81	X19
Northumberland pl W2	145	U5
Northumberland pl Rich	84	H14
Northumberland rd E6	66	F16
Northumberland rd E17	33	O20
Northumberland rd Barn	5	P20
Northumberland rd Har	22	E14
Northumberland st WC2	148	K12
Northumberland way Erith	98	L2
Northumbria st E14	64	C16
Northway NW7	26	G1
Northway NW11	27	Z17
Northway Wall	131	V9
Northway circ NW7	12	M13
Northway cres NW7	12	M13
Northway rd SE5	90	L8
Northway rd Croy	123	U15
Northwest pl N1	141	U8
Northwick ave Har	23	T18
Northwick circle Har	24	D17
Northwick clo NW8	138	F16
Northwick Park rd Har	23	X17
Northwick ter NW8	138	F16
Northwick wk Har	41	V2
Northwold est E5	49	Y6
Northwold rd E5	49	Y7
Northwold rd N16	49	U7
Northwood ave Horn	57	W11
Northwood gdns N12	15	T16
Northwood gdns Grnf	41	W15
Northwood gdns Ilf	35	X12
Northwood pl Erith	81	N8
Northwood rd SE23	110	K1
Northwood rd Cars	131	O15
Northwood rd Th Hth	122	K3
Norton ave Surb	117	T17
Norton clo E4	20	B15
Norton clo Enf	9	N18
Norton Folgate E1	142	L20
Norton gdns SW16	122	A3
Norton rd E10	50	M3
Norton rd Dag	57	O18
Norton rd Wem	42	G17
Norval rd Wem	42	A6
Norway gate SE16	75	W7
Norway st SE10	76	F16
Norwich pl Bexh	98	F11
Norwich rd E7	52	E16

Name	Page	Grid
Norwich rd Dag	69	T6
Norwich rd Grnf	58	L3
Norwich rd Th Hth	122	M7
Norwich st EC4	149	T4
Norwich wk Edg	25	W2
Norwood ave Rom	57	O2
Norwood ave Wem	60	M4
Norwood clo Sthl	70	G12
Norwood dr Har	22	F18
Norwood gdns Sthl	70	D10
Norwood Green rd Sthl	70	H12
Norwood High st SE27	108	K8
Norwood Park rd SE27	109	N12
Norwood rd SE24	90	K18
Norwood rd SE27	108	J3
Norwood rd Sthl	70	F11
Notley st SE5	158	F18
Notre Dame est SW4	89	V12
Notson rd SE25	124	A10
Notting Barn rd W10	136	F18
Notting Hill gate W11	145	T12
Nottingham ave E16	65	Y15
Nottingham ct WC2	148	K6
Nottingham pl W1	139	U19
Nottingham rd E10	33	V18
Nottingham rd SW17	106	L2
Nottingham rd Islw	83	V5
Nottingham rd S Croy	132	L10
Nottingham st W1	139	T20
Nova ms Sutt	119	T19
Nova rd Croy	122	K19
Novar rd SE9	114	B2
Novello st SW6	87	Y2
Nowell rd SW13	74	H16
Nower hill Pnr	22	E12
Noyna rd SW17	107	N6
Nuding clo SE13	93	P8
Nugent rd N19	48	A4
Nugent rd SE25	123	T6
Nugent ter NW8	138	C10
Nugents pk Pnr	22	C3
Nuneaton rd Dag	55	Y20
Nunhead cres SE15	91	Z8
Nunhead grn SE15	92	B7
Nunhead gro SE15	92	B8
Nunhead la SE15	92	A8
Nunhead pas SE15	91	Y8
Nunnington clo SE9	113	S7
Nunns rd Enf	8	A8
Nupton dr Barn	4	A18
Nursery ave Bexh	98	C6
Nursery ave Croy	134	F3
Nursery clo SW15	87	P12
Nursery clo Croy	134	E4
Nursery clo Enf	9	T5
Nursery clo Rom	37	W19
Nursery clo Wdf Grn	21	U10
Nursery gdns Enf	9	T6
Nursery la E7	52	G16
Nursery la W10	144	C1
Nursery rd E9	50	C17
Nursery rd N2	28	G4
Nursery rd N14	16	G2
Nursery rd SW9	90	D9
Nursery rd (Merton) SW19	120	A2
Nursery rd (Wimbledon) SW19	105	S19
Nursery rd Sutt	130	D9
Nursery rd Th Hth	123	O10
Nursery row Barn	4	F10
Nursery st N17	31	U2
Nursery wk NW4	26	L9
Nursery wk Rom	39	O20
Nurstead rd Erith	81	T19
Nutbourne st W10	136	L12
Nutbrook st SE15	91	W8
Nutbrowne rd Dag	69	R3
Nutcroft rd SE15	159	W18
Nutfield clo N18	18	J18
Nutfield clo Cars	130	K6
Nutfield gdns Ilf	36	M6
Nutfield rd E15	51	V11
Nutfield rd NW2	44	F8
Nutfield rd SE22	91	V12
Nutfield rd Th Hth	122	H8
Nutford pl W1	147	N5
Nuthatch gdns SE28	79	T6
Nuthurst ave SW2	108	D4
Nutley ter NW3	46	L16
Nutmeg la E14	64	J18
Nutt gro Edg	11	U7
Nutt st SE15	159	P17
Nuttall st N1	142	L7
Nutter la E11	34	K17
Nutwell st SW17	106	K13
Nuxley rd Belv	81	R16
Nyanza st SE18	79	U18
Nylands ave Rich	85	P3
Nymans gdns SW20	118	J5
Nynehead st SE14	75	W18
Nyon gro SE6	110	L5
Nyton clo N19	47	Z4

O

Name	Page	Grid
Oak ave N8	29	Z13
Oak ave N10	29	S2
Oak ave N17	18	C20
Oak ave Croy	135	P1
Oak ave Enf	7	P4
Oak ave Hmptn	100	B12
Oak ave Houns	70	A20
Oak bank Croy	135	V14
Oak clo N14	16	D3
Oak clo Dart	99	S11
Oak clo Sutt	130	D4
Oak Cottage clo SE6	112	B2
Oak cres E16	65	O14
Oak gdns Croy	135	P2
Oak gdns Edg	25	V6
Oak gro NW2	45	R12
Oak gro W Wick	135	V2
Oak Grove rd SE20	124	C2
Oak Hall rd E11	34	J19
Oak Hill Wdf Grn	33	X1
Oak Hill ave NW3	46	A12
Oak Hill clo Wdf Grn	33	X2
Oak Hill cres Wdf Grn	33	Y2
Oak Hill gdns Wdf Grn	34	B4
Oak Hill pk NW3	46	B11
Oak Hill Park ms NW3	46	C12
Oak Hill way NW3	46	C11
Oak la E14	63	Y19
Oak la N2	28	F7
Oak la N11	16	M19
Oak la Islw	83	U9
Oak la Twick	83	Z19
Oak la Wdf Grn	21	R13
Oak Lodge dr W Wick	125	S18
Oak Park gdns SW19	87	P20
Oak rd W5	60	H19
Oak rd Erith (Northumberland Heath)	81	X20
Oak rd (Slade Grn) Erith	99	X3
Oak rd N Mal	117	X3
Oak row SW16	121	V3
Oak st Rom	38	K14
Oak Tree clo W5	60	E17
Oak Tree clo Stan	24	C2
Oak Tree dell NW9	25	X16
Oak Tree dr N20	15	O5
Oak Tree gdns Brom	112	K12
Oak Tree rd NW8	138	J13
Oak village NW5	47	P13
Oak way N14	16	D2
Oak way W3	74	A3
Oak way Croy	124	G13
Oakbank gro SE24	90	L13
Oakbrook clo Brom	112	J9
Oakbury rd SW6	88	B5
Oakcombe clo N Mal	104	A20
Oakcroft rd SE13	93	W6
Oakdale ave Har	24	K15
Oakdale rd E7	52	J20
Oakdale rd E11	51	W7
Oakdale rd E18	34	J8
Oakdale rd N4	31	N19
Oakdale rd SE15	92	E6
Oakdale rd SW16	108	B12
Oakden st SE11	157	U5
Oakdene ave Chis	113	W13
Oakdene ave Erith	81	X17
Oakdene clo Horn	39	Y18
Oakdene clo Pnr	22	E1
Oakdene dr Surb	117	W19
Oakdene ms Sutt	119	U19
Oakdene pk N3	14	J20
Oakenshaw clo Surb	116	L17
Oakes clo E6	66	H17
Oakeshott ave N6	47	O6
Oakey la SE1	157	T1
Oakfield E4	20	C16
Oakfield ave Har	24	B10
Oakfield clo N Mal	118	E12
Oakfield ct N8	30	A20
Oakfield gdns N18	18	D14
Oakfield gdns SE19	109	T12
Oakfield gdns Beck	125	P13
Oakfield gdns Cars	120	L20
Oakfield gdns Grnf	59	P10
Oakfield rd E6	66	D3
Oakfield rd N3	28	A5
Oakfield rd N4	30	E18
Oakfield rd N14	17	O8
Oakfield rd SE20	110	A19
Oakfield rd SW19	105	R7
Oakfield rd Croy	122	M19
Oakfield rd Ilf	54	A8
Oakfield st SW10	154	B13
Oakfields rd NW11	27	T17
Oakford rd NW5	47	U12
Oakham clo SE6	110	M5
Oakham dr Brom	126	D10
Oakhampton rd NW7	27	P3
Oakhill Surb	116	K16
Oakhill ave Pnr	22	B6
Oakhill ct E11	34	J18
Oakhill ct SW19	105	P18
Oakhill cres Surb	116	L16
Oakhill dr Surb	116	L17
Oakhill gro Surb	116	J16
Oakhill path Surb	116	K15
Oakhill pl SW15	87	X12
Oakhill rd SW15	87	U12
Oakhill rd SW16	122	B2
Oakhill rd Beck	125	T4
Oakhill rd Surb	116	K16
Oakhill rd Sutt	130	B7
Oakhouse rd Bexh	98	F12
Oakhurst ave Barn	15	V1
Oakhurst ave Bexh	80	M20
Oakhurst clo E17	33	Z12
Oakhurst clo Ilf	36	B5
Oakhurst clo Tedd	101	T13
Oakhurst gdns E4	21	P5
Oakhurst gdns E17	33	Z12
Oakhurst gdns Bexh	80	M20
Oakhurst gro SE22	91	X10
Oakington ave Har	40	G2
Oakington ave Wem	42	M9
Oakington Manor dr Wem	43	O15
Oakington rd W9	137	V17
Oakington way N8	30	A19
Oakland way Epsom	128	A13
Oaklands N21	17	R7
Oaklands Twick	82	M19
Oaklands ave N9	9	N20
Oaklands ave Islw	71	W16
Oaklands ave Rom	39	S11
Oaklands ave Sid	96	K18
Oaklands ave Th Hth	122	F8
Oaklands ave W Wick	135	S5
Oaklands clo Bexh	98	C13
Oaklands est SW4	89	V17
Oaklands Park ave Ilf	54	D6
Oaklands pl SW4	89	W11
Oaklands rd N20	14	H2
Oaklands rd NW2	45	P12
Oaklands rd SW14	85	X8
Oaklands rd W7	71	W6
Oaklands rd Bexh	98	B11
Oaklands rd Brom	112	B17
Oaklands way Wall	131	W17
Oaklea pas Kings T	116	H6
Oakleafe gdns Ilf	35	Z10
Oakleigh ave N20	15	V6
Oakleigh ave Edg	25	T6
Oakleigh clo N20	16	A10
Oakleigh ct Barn	5	W19
Oakleigh ct Edg	25	V7
Oakleigh cres N20	15	X9
Oakleigh gdns N20	15	S5
Oakleigh gdns Edg	12	A15
Oakleigh ms N20	15	S6
Oakleigh Park ave Chis	127	X2
Oakleigh Park north N20	15	U6
Oakleigh Park south N20	15	V3
Oakleigh Road north N20	15	T6
Oakleigh Road south N11	16	C12
Oakleigh way Mitch	121	S2
Oakley ave W5	61	O19
Oakley ave Bark	54	M19
Oakley ave Croy	132	C9
Oakley clo E4	20	H11
Oakley clo E6	66	E17
Oakley clo Islw	83	R2
Oakley cres EC1	141	Y10
Oakley dr SE9	114	E2
Oakley gdns N8	30	C15
Oakley gdns SW3	154	M13
Oakley pk Bex	97	T19
Oakley pl SE1	159	O11
Oakley rd N1	49	O19
Oakley rd SE25	124	A11
Oakley rd Brom	127	R20
Oakley rd Har	23	S17
Oakley sq NW1	140	D9
Oakley st SW3	154	K12
Oakmead ave Brom	126	F16
Oakmead gdns Edg	12	L13
Oakmead pl Mitch	120	J1
Oakmead rd SW12	107	R2
Oakmead rd Croy	121	X15
Oakmere rd SE2	80	A16
Oakridge dr N2	28	H10
Oakridge rd Brom	111	X11
Oaks the N12	15	O13
Oaks the SE18	79	O15
Oaks ave SE19	109	R11
Oaks ave Felt	100	A4
Oaks ave Rom	38	L8
Oaks ave Wor Pk	128	K6
Oaks gro E4	20	M8
Oaks la Croy	134	A8
Oaks la Ilf	36	H17
Oaks rd Croy	133	Z10
Oaks way Cars	131	N17
Oaksford ave SE26	109	Z8
Oakshade rd Brom	111	Y9
Oakshaw rd SW18	88	C19
Oakthorpe rd N13	17	S15
Oaktree ave N13	17	V10
Oakview gro Croy	124	K19
Oakview rd SE6	111	R12
Oakway SW20	119	N10
Oakway Brom	125	X4
Oakways SE9	95	Z16
Oakwood Wall	131	T20
Oakwood ave N14	16	L2
Oakwood ave Beck	125	U3
Oakwood ave Brom	126	H7
Oakwood ave Mitch	120	H3
Oakwood ave Sthl	58	H20
Oakwood clo N14	6	J20
Oakwood clo Chis	113	V16
Oakwood ct W14	145	O20
Oakwood cres N21	7	O18
Oakwood cres Grnf	42	A17
Oakwood dr SE19	109	P14
Oakwood dr Bexh	98	M10
Oakwood dr Edg	12	H18
Oakwood gdns Ilf	54	L7
Oakwood gdns Sutt	129	Z4

Name	Pg	Ref
Oakwood la W14	145	O20
Oakwood Park rd N14	16	L1
Oakwood pl Croy	122	F16
Oakwood rd NW11	27	Z14
Oakwood rd Croy	104	H20
Oakwood rd Croy	122	F15
Oakwood vw N14	16	L1
Oakworth rd W10	144	E1
Oat la EC2	150	B3
Oates clo Brom	125	X6
Oatland ri E17	32	H8
Oatlands rd Enf	9	R6
Oban rd E13	65	Z10
Oban rd SE25	123	P8
Oban st E14	64	K16
Oberstein rd SW11	88	G11
Oborne clo SE24	90	K14
Observatory gdns W8	145	U17
Observatory rd SW14	85	V11
Occupation la SE18	95	Z1
Occupation la W5	72	G10
Occupation rd SE17	158	B9
Occupation rd W13	72	B4
Ocean st E1	63	U14
Ockenden rd N1	49	O19
Ockham dr Orp	115	P18
Ockley rd SW16	107	Z9
Ockley rd Croy	122	C18
Octavia clo Mitch	120	H11
Octavia rd Islw	83	U6
Octavia st SW11	88	J3
Octavius st SE8	76	A19
Odessa rd E7	52	C11
Odessa rd NW10	62	H6
Odessa st SE16	75	Y7
Odger st SW11	88	M4
Offenham rd SE9	113	U9
Offerton rd SW4	89	W8
Offham slope N12	14	J16
Offley rd SW9	157	T17
Offord clo N17	18	K20
Offord rd N1	48	D20
Offord st N1	48	D20
Ogilby st SE18	78	F12
Oglander rd SE15	91	U9
Ogle st W1	148	B1
Oglethorpe rd Dag	56	D8
Ohio rd E13	65	P12
Okeburn rd SW17	107	O12
Okehampton clo N12	15	T15
Okehampton cres Well	97	S1
Okehampton rd NW10	136	E6
Olaf st W11	144	G11
Old Bailey EC4	149	X6
Old Barge House all SE1	149	U11
Old Barn clo Sutt	129	T17
Old Barn way Bexh	99	T4
Old Barrack yd SW1	147	T18
Old Bethnal Green rd E2	143	X11
Old Bond st W1	148	A9
Old Bridge clo Nthlt	58	H5
Old Bridge st Kings T	116	G3
Old Broad st EC2	150	H5
Old Bromley rd Brom	111	X11
Old Brompton rd SW5	153	W11
Old Brompton rd SW7	154	D8
Old bldgs WC2	149	S4
Old Burlington st W1	148	A9
Old Castle st E1	151	O4
Old Cavendish st W1	147	Y5
Old Chelsea ms SW3	154	J15
Old Church la NW9	43	X7
Old Church la Grnf	59	Z8
Old Church la Stan	10	M13
Old Church rd E1	63	T17
Old Church rd E4	20	C12
Old Church st SW3	154	G10
Old Compton st W1	148	F8
Old Cote dr Houns	70	G17
Old Court pl W8	145	X17
Old Deer Park gdns Rich	84	K8
Old Devonshire rd SW12	89	S20
Old Dock clo Rich	73	P17
Old Dover rd SE3	77	U19
Old Farm ave N14	16	H1
Old Farm ave Sid	114	F2
Old Farm clo Houns	82	E9
Old Farm rd N2	28	G4
Old Farm rd Hmptn	100	D16
Old Farm Road east Sid	114	M3
Old Farm Road west Sid	114	L4
Old Fold clo Barn	4	G6
Old Fold la Barn	4	G6
Old Fold vw Barn	4	A11
Old Ford rd E2	143	Z11
Old Ford rd E3	63	U5
Old Forge clo Stan	10	M13
Old Forge ms W12	74	J5
Old Forge rd Enf	8	G3
Old Forge way Sid	115	R11
Old Gloucester st WC1	148	M1
Old Hall clo Pnr	22	C5
Old Hall dr Pnr	22	B4
Old hill Chis	127	W2
Old Homesdale rd Brom	126	L8
Old House clo SW19	105	S12
Old Jamaica rd SE16	159	S1
Old James st SE15	91	Z7
Old Jewry EC2	150	E6
Old Kent rd SE1	159	K6
Old Kent rd SE15	159	Y16
Old Kenton la NW9	25	T15
Old Lodge pl Twick	84	B15
Old Lodge way Stan	10	L16
Old Malden la Wor Pk	128	A4
Old Manor dr Islw	83	O15
Old Manor way Bexh	99	N5
Old Manor way Chis	113	T12
Old Manor yd SW5	153	W8
Old Marylebone rd NW1	146	L3
Old ms Har	23	S16
Old Mill ct E18	34	K9
Old Mill la W6	74	H13
Old Mill rd SE18	79	S16
Old Montague st E1	151	R2
Old Nichol st E2	143	N16
Old North st WC1	149	N1
Old Oak Common la NW10	62	B12
Old Oak Common la W3	62	C14
Old Oak la NW10	62	C9
Old Oak rd W3	62	D20
Old Orchard the NW3	46	L12
Old Palace la Rich	84	E12
Old Palace rd Croy	132	K5
Old Palace yd SW1	148	K20
Old Palace yd Rich	84	F12
Old Paradise st SE11	157	O5
Old Park ave SW12	89	O16
Old Park ave Enf	7	Z12
Old Park gro Enf	7	Y15
Old Park la W1	147	W15
Old Park ms Houns	70	F20
Old Park ridings N21	7	X20
Old Park rd N13	17	R13
Old Park rd SE2	80	B14
Old Park rd Enf	7	W11
Old Park Road south Enf	7	W14
Old Park vw Enf	7	V11
Old Perry st Chis	114	G16
Old Pye st SW1	156	F1
Old Quebec st W1	147	R7
Old Queen st SW1	148	F18
Old Rectory gdns Edg	12	D18
Old rd SE13	94	A11
Old rd Dart	98	M12
Old rd Enf	9	P5
Old Royal Free pl N1	141	U5
Old Royal Free sq N1	141	V5
Old School clo SW19	119	Y3
Old School clo Beck	124	H3
Old Schools la Epsom	128	D19
Old Seacoal la EC4	149	X5
Old South Lambeth rd SW8	156	M17
Old sq WC2	149	S4
Old st E13	65	X4
Old st EC1	142	A17
Old Swan yd Cars	130	M3
Old town SW4	89	V8
Old town Croy	132	K6
Old Tram yd SE18	79	V12
Old Woolwich rd SE10	76	K15
Old York rd SW18	88	B12
Oldberry rd Edg	12	M19
Oldborough rd Wem	42	D7
Oldbury pl W1	139	U19
Oldbury rd Enf	8	L8
Oldchurch ri Rom	39	P20
Oldchurch rd Rom	39	P19
Oldfield circ Nthlt	41	O16
Oldfield clo Brom	127	U9
Oldfield clo Grnf	41	T16
Oldfield clo Stan	10	M15
Oldfield Farm gdns Grnf	59	P4
Oldfield gro SE16	75	T11
Oldfield Lane north Grnf	59	P3
Oldfield Lane south Grnf	59	N10
Oldfield ms N6	47	V2
Oldfield pk Brom	127	W8
Oldfield rd N16	49	S8
Oldfield rd NW10	44	C19
Oldfield rd SW19	105	S15
Oldfield rd W3	74	D5
Oldfield rd Bexh	97	Z5
Oldfield rd Brom	127	T8
Oldfield rd Hmptn	100	D19
Oldfields rd Sutt	129	V7
Oldham ter W3	73	V4
Oldhill st N16	49	W5
Oldridge rd SW12	89	P19
Oldstead rd Brom	111	W10
O'Leary sq E1	63	P13
Olga st E3	63	W7
Olinda rd N16	31	V19
Oliphant st W10	136	K12
Olive rd E13	65	Z9
Olive rd NW2	44	L12
Olive rd W5	72	H8
Olive st Rom	39	N14
Oliver ave SE25	123	U8
Oliver clo E10	51	R7
Oliver clo W4	73	S16
Oliver gdns E6	66	E15
Oliver gro SE25	123	V8
Oliver rd E10	51	R7
Oliver rd E17	33	V14
Oliver rd N Mal	117	W4
Oliver rd Sutt	130	F9
Olivers yd EC1	142	G17
Ollerton grn E3	63	Z2
Ollerton rd N11	16	K16
Olley clo Wall	132	A16
Ollgar clo W12	74	E3
Olliffe st E14	76	J9
Olmar st SE1	159	S13
Olney rd SE17	158	A14
Olron cres Bexh	97	X14
Olven rd SE18	79	R18
Olveston wk Cars	120	G15
Olyffe ave Well	97	O3
Olyffe dr Beck	111	U20
Olympia ms W2	145	Z10
Olympia way W14	152	M3
Olympic Industrial est Wem	43	S11
Olympic way Grnf	58	L4
Olympic way Wem	43	R12
Oman ave NW2	44	L13
O'Meara st SE1	150	C15
Omega pl N1	140	M10
Ommaney rd SE14	92	G3
Ondine rd SE15	91	V9
One Tree clo SE23	92	D16
Onega gate SE16	75	V8
Ongar clo Rom	37	U14
Ongar rd SW6	153	U13
Onra rd E17	33	O20
Onslow ave Rich	84	K14
Onslow clo E4	20	J8
Onslow cres Chis	127	Z2
Onslow dr Sid	115	W6
Onslow gdns E18	34	K9
Onslow gdns N10	29	R15
Onslow gdns N21	7	U16
Onslow gdns SW7	154	F8
Onslow gdns Wall	131	U16
Onslow Mews east SW7	154	G7
Onslow Mews west SW7	154	F8
Onslow rd Croy	122	E18
Onslow rd N Mal	118	F9
Onslow rd Rich	84	L15
Onslow sq SW7	154	G7
Onslow st EC1	141	U19
Ontario st SE1	157	Y2
Opal clo E16	66	C17
Opal ms Ilf	54	A7
Opal st SE11	157	W8
Openshaw rd SE2	80	D11
Openview SW18	106	E2
Ophir ter SE15	91	W3
Orange Hill rd Edg	25	V1
Orange st WC2	148	G11
Orange yd W1	148	G6
Orangery the Rich	102	E4
Orangery la SE9	95	U14
Orb st SE17	158	F7
Orbain rd SW6	152	M19
Orbel st SW11	88	H3
Orchard the N14	6	G17
Orchard the N21	8	B18
Orchard the NW11	27	X16
Orchard the SE3	93	Y4
Orchard the W4	73	Z10
Orchard the Epsom	128	D16
Orchard the Houns	83	O5
Orchard ave N3	27	X10
Orchard ave N14	16	H1
Orchard ave N20	15	U8
Orchard ave Belv	81	N16
Orchard ave Croy	134	J2
Orchard ave Houns	70	C19
Orchard ave Mitch	121	O19
Orchard ave N Mal	118	C5
Orchard ave Sthl	70	C2
Orchard clo E4	20	B14
Orchard clo E11	34	H13
Orchard clo NW2	42	F10
Orchard clo SE23	92	C16
Orchard clo SW20	118	M8
Orchard clo W10	145	N1
Orchard clo Bexh	97	Z2
Orchard clo Edg	11	Y18
Orchard clo Surb	116	B19
Orchard clo Wat	10	D4
Orchard clo Wem	60	K2
Orchard cres Edg	12	H17
Orchard cres Enf	8	G6
Orchard dr SE3	93	Y4
Orchard dr Edg	12	Z15
Orchard gdns Sutt	129	Y10
Orchard gate NW9	26	A12
Orchard gate Grnf	42	C17
Orchard gro SE20	109	Y17
Orchard gro Croy	123	J17
Orchard gro Edg	25	R4
Orchard gro Har	25	N15
Orchard hill Cars	131	N10
Orchard hill Dart	99	P12
Orchard la Wdf Grn	21	Y12
Orchard ms N1	142	G2
Orchard pl E14	65	N18
Orchard pl N17	31	V2
Orchard ri Croy	124	K19

Name	Page	Grid
Orchard ri Kings T	103	V20
Orchard ri Rich	85	S11
Orchard Rise east Sid	96	K13
Orchard Rise west Sid	96	H13
Orchard rd N6	29	T20
Orchard rd SE18	79	U11
Orchard rd Barn	4	G14
Orchard rd Belv	81	S12
Orchard rd Brent	72	F15
Orchard rd Brom	112	L20
Orchard rd Dag	69	T3
Orchard rd Enf	9	R18
Orchard rd Hmptn	100	F17
Orchard rd Houns	82	F12
Orchard rd Kings T	116	K5
Orchard rd Mitch	121	O19
Orchard rd Rich	85	P8
Orchard rd Rom	38	G6
Orchard rd Sid	114	J9
Orchard rd Sutt	129	Z10
Orchard rd Twick	83	Z14
Orchard rd Well	97	R6
Orchard st E17	32	H12
Orchard st W1	147	T6
Orchard way Beck	124	K12
Orchard way Croy	124	K19
Orchard way Enf	8	D11
Orchard way Sutt	130	G7
Orchardleigh ave Enf	9	O8
Orchardmede N21	8	B19
Orchardson st NW8	138	G18
Orchid clo E6	66	D13
Orchid la N14	16	G3
Orchid st W12	62	G20
Orde Hall st WC1	141	N19
Ordell rd E3	64	A7
Ordnance cres SE10	76	M6
Ordnance hill NW8	138	G5
Ordnance ms NW8	138	H8
Ordnance rd E16	65	O13
Ordnance rd SE18	78	J17
Oregano dr E14	64	K18
Oregon ave E12	53	T11
Orestes ms NW6	45	X15
Orford gdns Twick	101	V5
Orford rd E17	33	P16
Orford rd E18	34	H10
Organ la E4	20	H7
Oriel clo Mitch	121	Y8
Oriel ct NW3	46	E12
Oriel gdns Ilf	35	U11
Oriel rd E9	50	G17
Oriel way Nthlt	40	L19
Orient st SE11	157	W4
Orient way E5	50	F10
Oriental rd E16	78	B2
Oriole way SE28	68	D19
Orissa rd SE18	79	V13
Orkney st SW11	89	G13
Orlando rd SW4	89	U8
Orleans rd SE19	109	P16
Orleans rd Twick	84	C18
Orleston ms N7	48	G17
Orleston rd N7	48	F17
Orley Farm rd Har	41	S10
Orlop st SE10	76	M14
Ormanton rd SE26	109	Y11
Orme la W2	145	Y10
Orme Court ms W2	145	Y10
Orme la W2	145	X10
Orme rd Kings T	117	U4
Orme sq W2	145	Y10
Ormeley rd SW12	89	S20
Ormerod gdns Mitch	121	P3
Ormiston gro W12	74	J3
Ormiston rd SE10	77	S14
Ormond ave Hmptn	100	J20
Ormond clo WC1	140	M20
Ormond cres Hmptn	100	K20
Ormond dr Hmptn	100	L19
Ormond ms WC1	140	M19
Ormond rd N19	48	B3
Ormond rd Rich	84	H14
Ormond yd SW1	148	D12
Ormonde gdns SW4	155	P11
Ormonde pl SW1	155	U7
Ormonde ri Buck H	21	Y5
Ormonde rd SW14	85	U9
Ormonde ter NW8	139	O5
Ormsby gdns Grnf	59	N7
Ormsby pl N16	49	U10
Ormsby st E2	143	N9
Ormside st SE15	75	P16
Ornan rd NW3	46	J15
Orpen wk N16	49	T11
Orpheus st SE5	91	N3
Orpington gdns N18	18	D11
Orpington rd N21	17	V5
Orpwood clo Hmptn	100	D14
Orsett st SE11	157	P9
Orsett ter W2	146	B4
Orsett ter Wdf Grn	34	L3
Orsman rd N1	142	L5
Orton st E1	151	T14
Orville rd SW11	88	G4
Orwell rd E13	65	Y4
Osbaldeston rd N16	49	W7
Osbert st SW1	156	E7
Osberton st SE12	94	E13
Osborn clo E8	143	T4
Osborn gdns NW7	27	O2
Osborn la SE23	92	K20
Osborn st E1	151	R3
Osborn ter SE3	94	D11
Osborne clo Beck	124	J9
Osborne gdns Th Hth	122	M4
Osborne gro E17	32	L14
Osborne gro N4	48	F4
Osborne pl Sutt	130	F12
Osborne rd E7	52	G15
Osborne rd E9	50	M16
Osborne rd E10	51	T8
Osborne rd N4	48	E3
Osborne rd N13	17	U11
Osborne rd NW2	44	N17
Osborne rd W3	73	S7
Osborne rd Belv	81	O15
Osborne rd Buck H	21	V6
Osborne rd Dag	56	C14
Osborne rd Enf	9	V9
Osborne rd Horn	39	Z18
Osborne rd Houns	82	E8
Osborne rd Kings T	102	K18
Osborne rd Sthl	58	M17
Osborne rd Th Hth	122	L3
Osborne sq Dag	56	C13
Oscar st SE8	93	N3
Oseney cres NW5	47	W16
O'Shea gro E3	63	Y3
Osidge la N14	16	B6
Osier st E1	63	S12
Osier way E10	51	R8
Osier way Mitch	120	L12
Osiers rd SW18	87	V11
Oslac rd SE6	111	S12
Oslo st NW8	138	K10
Oslo sq SE16	75	X7
Osman rd N9	18	K11
Osman rd W6	152	D1
Osmond clo Har	41	O6
Osmond gdns Wall	131	V11
Osmund st W12	62	D16
Osnaburgh st NW1	139	Z16
Osnaburgh ter NW1	139	Y17
Osney wk Cars	120	H14
Osprey clo E6	66	D15
Osprey clo E11	34	G12
Osprey ms Enf	9	O17
Ospringe clo SE20	110	D19
Ospringe ct SE9	96	G16
Ospringe rd NW5	47	U13
Ossian rd N4	30	C20
Ossington bldgs W1	147	U1
Ossington st W2	145	W10
Ossory rd SE1	159	S12
Ossulston st NW1	140	F10
Ossulton way N2	28	D12
Ostade rd SW2	90	D18
Osten ms SW7	153	Z3
Osterley ave Islw	71	P19
Osterley ct Islw	83	O1
Osterley cres Islw	83	U1
Osterley gdns Th Hth	122	L3
Osterley la Islw	71	N13
Osterley la Sthl	70	H13
Osterley Park rd Sthl	70	D7
Osterley Park View rd W7	71	U6
Osterley rd N16	49	S11
Osterley rd Islw	71	S20
Ostliffe rd N13	17	X15
Oswald clo Sthl	70	C2
Oswald st E5	50	G10
Osward Croy	134	M20
Osward pl N9	18	M8
Osward rd SW17	107	N3
Oswin st SE11	157	Y4
Oswyth rd SE5	91	S4
Otford clo Bex	98	G16
Otford clo Brom	127	X6
Otford cres SE4	92	K15
Othello clo SE11	157	W9
Otis st E3	64	G8
Otley dr Ilf	35	Z17
Otley rd E16	65	Y16
Otley ter E5	50	E8
Ottawa gdns Dag	56	M20
Otter rd Grnf	59	N12
Otterbourne rd E4	20	K11
Otterbourne rd Croy	132	K3
Otterburn gdns Islw	71	Y19
Otterburn st SW17	107	N15
Otterden st SE6	111	N8
Otto clo SE26	110	A6
Otto st SE17	157	X14
Oulton cres Bark	54	K17
Oulton rd N15	31	R15
Ouseley rd SW12	107	N2
Outer circle NW1	139	O8
Outgate rd NW10	44	D20
Outram pl N1	140	L4
Outram rd E6	66	C2
Outram rd N22	29	X4
Outram rd Croy	133	W2
Outwich st EC3	150	K4
Oval the E2	143	X8
Oval the Sid	97	N18
Oval pl SW8	157	P18
Oval rd NW1	139	W3
Oval rd Croy	133	P2
Oval Road north Dag	69	U3
Oval Road south Dag	69	U5
Oval way SE11	157	P11
Overbrae Beck	111	P14
Overbrook wk Edg	25	P1
Overbury ave Beck	125	T5
Overbury rd N15	31	O19
Overbury st E5	50	G11
Overcliff rd SE13	93	P8
Overcourt clo Sid	97	R15
Overdale ave N Mal	117	X3
Overdale rd W5	72	D8
Overdown rd SE6	111	P10
Overhill rd SE22	91	Z17
Overhill way Beck	125	W12
Overlea rd E5	49	X1
Overmead Sid	96	E19
Overstand clo Beck	125	P11
Overstone gdns Croy	124	K17
Overstone rd W6	152	B5
Overton clo NW10	43	V18
Overton clo Islw	83	V3
Overton dr E11	52	G2
Overton dr Rom	55	U2
Overton rd E10	50	J2
Overton rd N14	6	M17
Overton rd SE2	80	G8
Overton rd SW9	90	G4
Overton rd Sutt	129	Y15
Overton Road east SE2	80	K8
Overtons yd Croy	132	L5
Ovesdon ave Har	40	D5
Ovett clo SE19	109	T16
Ovex clo E14	76	H7
Ovington gdns SW3	154	M2
Ovington ms SW3	154	M2
Ovington sq SW3	154	M2
Ovington st SW3	155	N4
Owen clo SE28	80	F2
Owen rd N13	17	Y15
Owen st EC1	141	V11
Owen way NW10	43	W16
Owenite st SE2	80	E11
Owen's ct EC1	141	W11
Owen's row EC1	141	W11
Owens way SE23	92	J19
Owgan clo SE5	158	H19
Ox la Epsom	128	G20
Oxberry ave SW6	87	T4
Oxendon st SW1	148	F10
Oxenford st SE15	91	U8
Oxenpark ave Wem	42	L1
Oxestalls rd SE8	75	W13
Oxford ave SW20	119	S2
Oxford ave Houns	70	G15
Oxford clo N9	19	N7
Oxford clo Mitch	121	U7
Oxford ct EC4	150	E8
Oxford cres N Mal	117	Y14
Oxford gdns N20	15	T6
Oxford gdns N21	18	A2
Oxford gdns W4	73	S15
Oxford gdns W10	144	E5
Oxford gate W6	152	J5
Oxford rd E15	51	Y18
Oxford rd N4	48	F3
Oxford rd N9	19	N7
Oxford rd NW6	137	W8
Oxford rd SE19	109	O15
Oxford rd SW15	87	T11
Oxford rd W5	60	H20
Oxford rd Cars	130	J14
Oxford rd Enf	9	N17
Oxford rd Har	23	O18
Oxford rd (Wealdstone) Har	23	W11
Oxford rd Ilf	54	C13
Oxford rd Sid	115	S13
Oxford rd Tedd	101	R13
Oxford rd Wall	131	U12
Oxford rd Wdf Grn	21	Z15
Oxford Road north W4	73	S13
Oxford Road south W4	73	S15
Oxford sq W2	146	L6
Oxford st W1	147	S7
Oxford wk Sthl	70	E3
Oxgate gdns NW2	44	K8
Oxgate la NW2	44	J6
Oxhawth cres Brom	127	X13
Oxleas E6	66	M16
Oxleas clo Well	96	F6
Oxleay rd Har	40	F4
Oxleigh clo N Mal	118	B11
Oxley clo SE1	159	P8
Oxleys rd NW2	44	K10
Oxlow la Dag	56	B12
Oxonian st SE22	91	U10
Oxtoby way SW16	121	X2
Ozolins way E16	65	S17

P

Name	Page	Grid
Pace pl E1	151	X6
Pacific rd E16	65	T16
Packington sq N1	142	A6
Packington st N1	141	Y5
Packmores rd SE9	96	F14
Padbury ct E2	143	P15
Paddenswick rd W6	74	H8
Paddington clo Hayes	58	A11
Paddington grn W2	146	G1
Paddington st W1	147	S1
Paddock clo SE3	94	G6
Paddock clo SE26	110	E9
Paddock clo Nthlt	58	H5
Paddock clo Wor Pk	128	B1
Paddock gdns SE19	109	T16
Paddock rd NW2	44	H8
Paddock rd Bexh	98	A11
Paddock rd Ruis	40	A9
Paddock way Chis	114	F19
Paddocks the Barn	5	Z12
Paddocks the Wem	43	T7
Paddocks clo Har	44	K12
Padfield rd SE5	90	L7
Padnall rd Rom	37	W10

Name		
Padstow rd Enf	7	W7
Padua rd SE20	110	C20
Pagden st SW8	89	T1
Page clo Dag	55	Z14
Page clo Hmptn	100	B14
Page clo Har	25	N19
Page cres Croy	132	H11
Page Green rd N15	31	W15
Page Green ter N15	31	V16
Page Heath la Brom	127	O6
Page Heath vill Brom	127	O6
Page meadow NW7	13	V20
Page st NW7	13	V20
Page st SW1	156	G5
Pageant ave NW9	26	A3
Pageant wk Croy	133	S6
Pagehurst rd Croy	123	Z17
Pages hill N10	29	R7
Pages la N10	29	R8
Pages wk SE1	158	K5
Paget ave Sutt	130	G7
Paget clo Hmptn	101	O10
Paget la Islw	83	S9
Paget pl Kings T	103	V14
Paget ri SE18	78	L18
Paget rd N16	49	P4
Paget rd Ilf	53	Z13
Paget ter SE18	78	L17
Pagitts gro Barn	5	N6
Pagnell st SE14	75	X19
Pagoda ave Rich	84	M8
Pagoda gdns SE3	93	X5
Paignton rd N15	31	S19
Paines clo Pnr	22	C10
Paines la Pnr	22	A5
Pains clo Mitch	121	T4
Painters rd Ilf	36	L9
Paisley rd N22	30	K3
Paisley rd Cars	120	G19
Pakeman st N7	48	D10
Pakenham st WC1	141	P15
Palace ave W8	145	Z17
Palace ct W2	145	X10
Palace ct Har	24	J18
Palace Court gdns N10	29	U8
Palace Garden ms W8	145	W12
Palace Gardens ter W8	145	W14
Palace gate W8	146	B18
Palace Gates rd N22	29	Y6
Palace grn W8	145	Y17
Palace grn Croy	134	M17
Palace gro SE19	109	V18
Palace gro Brom	126	G2
Palace ms E17	33	N13
Palace ms SW1	155	V7
Palace pl SW1	148	A20
Palace rd N8	29	Y15
Palace rd N11	29	Z2
Palace rd SE19	109	W17
Palace rd SW2	108	D1
Palace rd Brom	126	H1
Palace rd Kings T	116	H10
Palace rd Ruis	40	A11
Palace Road est SW2	108	E2
Palace sq SE19	109	V17
Palace st SW1	148	A20
Palace vw SE12	112	F4
Palace vw Brom	126	H6
Palace vw Croy	134	L2
Palace View rd E4	20	E15
Palamos rd E10	51	O3
Palatine rd N16	49	T12
Palermo rd NW10	62	H7
Palestine gro SW19	120	F11
Palewell Common dr SW14	85	Z12
Palewell pk SW14	85	X12
Palfrey pl SW8	157	P19
Palgrave ave Sthl	58	G20
Palgrave rd W12	74	D8
Palliser rd W14	152	L10
Palm ave Sid	115	X15
Palm gro W5	72	J7
Palm rd Rom	38	L16
Palmar cres Bexh	98	E6
Palmar rd Bexh	98	D6
Palmeira rd Bexh	97	W7
Palmer ave Sutt	128	M9
Palmer clo Houns	82	F1
Palmer clo W Wick	135	X4
Palmer cres Kings T	116	J5
Palmer gdns Barn	4	B17
Palmer pl N7	48	F16
Palmer rd E13	65	X12
Palmer rd Dag	55	V3
Palmer st SW1	148	E20
Palmers la Enf	9	O5
Palmers rd E2	63	U7
Palmers rd N11	16	H16
Palmers rd SW14	85	W8
Palmers rd SW16	122	C3
Palmerston cres N13	17	R16
Palmerston cres SE18	79	R17
Palmerston rd E7	52	H16
Palmerston rd E17	32	K11
Palmerston rd N22	30	C2
Palmerston rd NW6	45	W19
Palmerston rd SW14	85	V11
Palmerston rd SW19	105	Y17
Palmerston rd W3	73	V7
Palmerston rd Buck H	21	W6
Palmerston rd Cars	131	N7
Palmerston rd Har	23	V11
Palmerston rd Sutt	130	E10
Palmerston rd Th Hth	123	N11
Palmerston rd Twick	83	V16
Palmerston way SW8	155	Z20
Pamber st W10	144	F5
Pampisford rd S Croy	132	J20
Pancras la EC4	150	D7
Pancras rd NW1	140	F7
Pandora rd NW6	45	Y16
Panfield ms Ilf	35	X18
Panfield rd SE2	80	A8
Pangbourne ave W10	144	E1
Pangbourne dr Stan	11	V15
Panmuir rd SW20	118	K1
Panmure clo N5	48	J12
Panmure rd SE26	109	Z7
Pannard pl Sthl	58	L19
Pansy gdns W12	62	G20
Pantiles the NW11	27	W14
Pantiles the Bexh	81	P19
Pantiles the Brom	127	S7
Pantiles the (Bushey) Wat	10	D3
Panton st SW1	148	G11
Papillons wk SE3	94	F6
Papworth gdns N7	48	E16
Papworth way SW2	90	F19
Parade the SW11	155	R16
Parade ms SE27	108	H3
Paradise pas N7	48	E16
Paradise rd Rich	84	J13
Paradise rd SW4	90	A4
Paradise row E2	143	Y13
Paradise st SE16	151	X19
Paradise wk SW3	155	P13
Paragon the SE3	94	D4
Paragon gro Surb	116	M14
Paragon pl SE3	94	C4
Paragon rd E9	50	C18
Parbury rd SE23	92	H16
Parchmore rd Th Hth	122	K4
Parchmore way Th Hth	122	K4
Pardon st EC1	141	Y17
Pardoner st SE1	158	G15
Parfett st E1	151	V4
Parfrey st W6	152	E13
Parham dr Ilf	35	Z16
Paris gdn SE1	149	W13
Parish Gate dr Sid	96	G15
Parish la SE20	110	E16
Parish ms SE20	110	F18
Park the N6	29	P19
Park the NW11	46	A4
Park the SE19	109	T18
Park the SE23	110	B3
Park the W5	72	G3
Park the Cars	131	N12
Park the Sid	114	M11
Park app Well	97	R9
Park ave E6	66	J4
Park ave E15	51	Z18
Park ave N3	28	B4
Park ave N13	17	T12
Park ave N18	18	J13
Park ave N22	30	B6
Park ave NW2	44	K16
Park ave NW10	60	M7
Park ave NW11	46	A4
Park ave SW14	85	Y11
Park ave Bark	54	C17
Park ave Barn	5	S18
Park ave Brom	112	C17
Park ave Cars	131	O13
Park ave Enf	8	C17
Park ave Houns	82	J15
Park ave Ilf	53	Y5
Park ave Mitch	107	S18
Park ave Sthl	70	E4
Park ave W Wick	135	U2
Park ave Wdf Grn	21	V16
Park Avenue east Epsom	128	G14
Park Avenue north N8	29	Y12
Park Avenue north NW10	44	K13
Park Avenue rd N17	32	A2
Park Avenue south N8	29	X14
Park Avenue west Epsom	128	F15
Park boul Rom	39	T5
Park chase Wem	42	M11
Park clo E9	63	R2
Park clo NW2	44	H10
Park clo NW10	61	N9
Park clo SW1	147	O18
Park clo W4	73	Z15
Park clo W14	145	S20
Park clo Cars	131	O13
Park clo Har	23	T3
Park clo Houns	83	N13
Park clo Kings T	116	E1
Park clo Wem	42	L14
Park cres N3	28	C2
Park cres W1	139	X19
Park cres Enf	8	C15
Park cres Erith	81	Y17
Park cres Har	23	T4
Park cres Horn	39	V20
Park cres Twick	83	O20
Park Crescent Mews east W1	139	Y18
Park Crescent Mews west W1	139	W19
Park cft Edg	25	W4
Park dale N11	16	L19
Park dr N21	7	Y19
Park dr NW11	46	A4
Park dr SE7	78	D15
Park dr SW14	85	Z11
Park dr W3	73	R8
Park dr Dag	56	L9
Park dr Har	22	G20
Park dr Rom	39	O12
Park Drive clo SE7	78	E15
Park end NW3	46	J12
Park end Brom	112	C20
Park End Rd Rom	39	R12
Park Farm clo N2	28	D11
Park Farm rd Brom	127	N2
Park Farm rd Kings T	102	L17
Park Garden pl W2	146	M5
Park gdns NW9	25	U11
Park gdns Erith	81	Z12
Park gdns Kings T	103	O14
Park gate N2	28	G10
Park gate N21	17	P2
Park gate W5	60	F13
Park gro E15	65	T3
Park gro N11	29	Y2
Park gro Bexh	98	K11
Park gro Edg	12	A16
Park Grove rd E11	51	Z7
Park Hall rd N2	28	K12
Park Hall rd SE21	109	N6
Park hill SE23	110	B3
Park hill SW4	89	Y12
Park hill W5	60	H15
Park hill Brom	127	S9
Park hill Cars	130	L12
Park hill Rich	85	N16
Park Hill clo Cars	130	L13
Park Hill ri Croy	133	T3
Park Hill rd Brom	125	Y4
Park Hill rd Croy	133	R3
Park Hill rd Sid	114	G7
Park Hill rd Wall	131	S15
Park House gdns Twick	84	D14
Park la E15	64	J2
Park la N9	18	F12
Park la N17	31	Z2
Park la W1	147	M8
Park la Cars	131	P10
Park la Croy	133	N7
Park la Har	40	J9
Park la Horn	39	V19
Park la (Elm Pk) Horn	57	Z17
Park la Rich	84	H11
Park la Rom (Chadwell Heath)	37	W19
Park la Sutt	129	S15
Park la Tedd	101	V16
Park la Wem	42	L13
Park Lane clo N17	31	X2
Park Lawns Wem	42	L13
Park mead Har	40	K10
Park mead Sid	97	R14
Park ms SE24	90	K14
Park Nook gdns Enf	8	B1
Park par NW10	62	E5
Park pl E14	76	A2
Park pl SW1	148	B13
Park pl W3	73	R10
Park pl W5	72	H3
Park pl Hmptn	100	M16
Park pl Wem	43	N13
Park Place vill W2	138	D19
Park ridings N8	30	E9
Park ri SE23	92	J20
Park ri Har	23	T5
Park Rise rd SE23	110	J1
Park rd E6	65	Z2
Park rd E10	51	O5
Park rd E12	52	K5
Park rd E15	65	S3
Park rd E17	32	M15
Park rd N2	28	H9
Park rd N8	29	X14
Park rd N11	29	Z1
Park rd N14	16	L3
Park rd N15	30	J14
Park rd N18	18	J13
Park rd NW1	139	O16
Park rd NW4	26	H20
Park rd NW8	138	L13
Park rd NW9	43	Y1
Park rd NW10	62	A2
Park rd SE25	123	S8
Park rd SW19	106	H17
Park rd W4	73	W19
Park rd W7	59	X19
Park rd Barn	4	H13
Park rd (New Barnet) Barn	5	U14
Park rd Beck	110	L17
Park rd Brom	126	G2
Park rd Chis	114	A14
Park rd Hmptn	100	L11
Park rd Houns	82	L13

Park rd Ilf	54	E8
Park rd Islw	84	A2
Park rd Kings T	103	N12
Park rd Kings T (Hampton Wick)	116	E2
Park rd N Mal	117	Z10
Park rd Rich	84	M15
Park rd Surb	117	N14
Park rd Sutt	129	T14
Park rd Tedd	101	X16
Park rd Twick	84	E14
Park rd Wall	131	T11
Park rd (Hackbridge) Wall	131	R4
Park rd Wem	42	K17
Park Road east W3	73	U5
Park Road north W3	73	U5
Park Road north W4	73	Z15
Park row SE10	76	K15
Park Royal rd NW10	61	W11
Park side Sutt	129	S15
Park Square east NW1	139	Y17
Park Square ms NW1	139	W17
Park Square west NW1	139	W17
Park st SE1	150	A12
Park st W1	147	S7
Park st Croy	133	N4
Park st Tedd	101	U14
Park ter Wor Pk	128	F1
Park vw N21	17	P2
Park vw W3	61	W14
Park vw N Mal	118	F6
Park vw Pnr	22	F3
Park vw Wem	43	T14
Park View clf Ilf	36	H19
Park View cres N11	16	E13
Park View gdns NW4	27	O17
Park View rd N3	28	B4
Park View rd N17	31	Y7
Park View rd NW10	44	E12
Park View rd W5	60	K14
Park View rd Sthl	70	G2
Park View rd Well	97	S8
Park Village east NW1	139	X7
Park Village west NW1	139	X8
Park vill Rom	37	X19
Park wk SW10	154	E13
Park way N20	15	Y13
Park way NW11	27	T15
Park way Edg	25	U5
Park way Enf	7	S9
Park way Ilf	54	K10
Park west W2	146	M5
Park West pl W2	146	M5
Parkcroft rd SE12	94	C18
Parkdale rd SE18	79	U15
Parke rd SW13	86	F1
Parker ms WC2	148	L5
Parker rd Croy	132	M8
Parker st E16	78	D2
Parker st WC2	148	L5
Parkers row SE1	151	R18
Parkfield ave SW14	86	A10
Parkfield ave Har	22	M6
Parkfield ave Nthlt	58	A6
Parkfield clo Edg	12	E19
Parkfield clo Nthlt	58	B5
Parkfield cres Har	23	N8
Parkfield cres Ruis	40	B8
Parkfield dr Nthlt	58	A6
Parkfield gdns Har	22	L9
Parkfield rd NW10	44	H19
Parkfield rd SE14	92	L1
Parkfield rd Har	41	N9
Parkfield rd Nthlt	58	A6
Parkfield st N1	141	V8
Parkfield way Brom	126	C19
Parkfields SW15	86	M10
Parkfields ave NW9	43	Z2
Parkfields ave SW20	118	J2
Parkfields rd Kings T	103	N13
Parkgate SE3	94	D9
Parkgate ave Barn	5	P5
Parkgate cres Barn	5	P7
Parkgate gdns SW14	85	X14
Parkgate rd SW11	154	L19
Parkgate rd Wall	131	R10
Parkham st SW11	88	H2
Parkhill rd E4	20	H3
Parkhill rd NW3	46	M17
Parkhill rd Bex	98	A18
Parkhill wk NW3	46	M16
Parkholme rd E8	49	W18
Parkhouse st SE5	158	G17
Parkhurst rd E12	53	W13
Parkhurst rd E17	32	J14
Parkhurst rd N7	48	A12
Parkhurst rd N11	16	C15
Parkhurst rd N17	31	W6
Parkhurst rd N22	17	R20
Parkhurst rd Bex	98	D19
Parkhurst rd Sutt	130	F7
Parkland ave Rom	39	S8
Parkland gdns SW19	105	P1
Parkland rd N22	30	D7
Parkland rd Wdf Grn	34	G2
Parkland wk N4	48	E1
Parkland wk N6	29	T19
Parkland wk N10	29	S13
Parklands clo SW14	85	V13
Parklands dr N3	27	S11
Parklands rd SW16	107	T12
Parklands way Wor Pk	128	B4
Parklea clo NW9	84	J10
Parkleigh rd SW19	120	A3
Parkleys Rich	102	H10
Parkmead SW15	86	J16
Parkmead gdns NW7	13	R18
Parkmore clo Wdf Grn	21	S14
Parkshot Rich	84	J10
Parkside N3	28	A3
Parkside NW2	44	H10
Parkside NW7	13	T19
Parkside SW19	105	O9
Parkside Buck H	21	V6
Parkside Hmptn	101	O13
Parkside Sid	115	S5
Parkside ave SW19	105	O12
Parkside ave Bexh	99	N6
Parkside ave Brom	127	R9
Parkside ave Rom	39	N10
Parkside cres Surb	117	N13
Parkside cres Bexh	99	P5
Parkside dr Edg	12	C12
Parkside gdns SW19	105	O10
Parkside gdns Barn	16	A4
Parkside rd Belv	81	W10
Parkside rd Houns	82	J12
Parkside way Har	22	L14
Parkstead rd SW15	86	J13
Parkstone ave N18	18	F17
Parkstone rd E17	33	U9
Parkthorne clo Har	22	K19
Parkthorne dr Har	22	J18
Parkthorne rd SW12	89	X15
Parkview rd SE9	113	Z3
Parkview rd Croy	123	Y19
Parkville rd SW6	153	O18
Parkway N14	16	M7
Parkway NW1	139	X5
Parkway SW20	119	O8
Parkway Croy	135	T20
Parkway Erith	81	N7
Parkway Rom	39	U6
Parkway Wdf Grn	21	T15
Parkwood N20	16	A11
Parkwood Beck	111	P19
Parkwood ms N6	29	R18
Parkwood rd SW19	105	N14
Parkwood rd Islw	83	W2
Parliament hill NW3	46	K12
Parliament sq SW1	148	J18
Parliament st SW1	148	K18
Parma cres SW11	88	L10
Parmiter st E2	143	Y9
Parnell clo Edg	12	G12
Parnell rd E3	63	Z3
Parolles rd N19	47	W4
Paroma rd Belv	81	R9
Parr clo N9	19	N12
Parr rd E6	66	B4
Parr rd Stan	24	H4
Parr st N1	142	E7
Parrs clo S Croy	133	O19
Parrs pl Hmptn	100	J19
Parry ave E6	66	G18
Parry clo Epsom	128	H16
Parry pl SE18	79	N10
Parry rd SE25	123	S7
Parry rd W10	137	N13
Parry st SW8	156	L13
Parsifal rd NW6	45	Y14
Parsloes ave Dag	55	X12
Parson st NW4	27	N11
Parsonage gdns Enf	8	A8
Parsonage la Enf	8	A8
Parsonage Manorway Belv	81	S17
Parsonage st E14	76	H12
Parsons cres Edg	12	C9
Parsons grn SW6	87	X3
Parsons Green la SW6	87	X1
Parsons gro Edg	12	C10
Parson's mead Croy	122	K20
Parsons rd E13	65	X7
Parthenia rd SW6	87	Y2
Partingdale la NW7	14	B16
Partington clo N19	47	Y3
Partridge clo E16	66	B15
Partridge grn SE9	113	W7
Partridge rd Hmptn	100	F15
Partridge rd Sid	114	G8
Partridge sq E6	66	F13
Partridge way N22	30	B3
Parvin st SW8	89	X2
Pascal st SW8	156	H17
Pascoe rd SE13	93	X13
Pasley clo SE17	158	A11
Pasquier rd E17	32	K10
Passey pl SE9	95	U15
Passfield dr E14	64	E13
Passmore gdns N11	16	K20
Passmore st SW1	155	T8
Pasteur clo NW9	26	B8
Pasteur gdns N18	17	X17
Paston cres SE12	94	J18
Pastor st SE11	157	Y5
Pasture clo Wem	42	B9
Pasture rd SE6	112	B2
Pasture rd Dag	56	B14
Pasture rd Wem	42	A7
Pastures the N20	14	H4
Patcham ct Sutt	130	C19
Patcham ter SW8	89	S1
Pater st W8	153	U2
Paternoster row EC4	150	A5
Path the SW19	106	A20
Pathfield rd SW16	107	Y16
Patience rd SW11	88	J6
Patio clo SW4	89	X15
Patmore st SW8	89	V1
Patmos rd SW9	157	W20
Paton clo E3	64	C8
Patricia ct Well	80	C20
Patrick Connolly gdns E3	64	E9
Patrick pas SW11	88	J4
Patrick rd E13	65	Z9
Patriot sq E2	143	Z10
Patrol pl SE6	93	S17
Patshull rd NW5	47	V18
Patten rd SW18	88	J19
Pattenden rd SE6	110	M2
Patterdale clo Brom	112	B16
Patterdale rd SE15	75	P18
Patterson ct SE19	109	U17
Patterson rd SE19	109	U16
Pattison rd NW2	45	X9
Paul gdns Croy	133	U4
Paul st E15	64	L2
Paul st EC2	142	H18
Paulet rd SE5	90	K4
Paulhan rd Har	24	F12
Paulin dr N21	17	U2
Pauline cres Twick	101	N1
Paultons sq SW3	154	H14
Paultons st SW3	154	H14
Pauntley st N19	47	V5
Paveley dr SW11	154	J19
Paveley st NW8	138	L10
Pavement the SW4	89	V10
Pavement ms Rom	37	V20
Pavement sq Croy	123	X19
Pavet clo Dag	56	G17
Pavilion rd SW1	147	P20
Pavilion way Edg	25	U1
Pawleyne clo SE20	110	D19
Pawsey clo E13	65	U2
Pawson's rd Croy	122	L15
Paxford rd Wem	42	A7
Paxton clo Rich	85	N4
Paxton pl SE27	109	R10
Paxton rd N17	31	W2
Paxton rd SE23	110	H6
Paxton rd W4	74	A16
Paxton rd Brom	112	F18
Paxton ter SW1	155	Z12
Payne rd E3	64	E7
Payne st SE8	75	Z18
Paynell ct SE3	94	A7
Paynesfield ave SW14	85	Z9
Paynesfield rd (Bushey) Wat	10	H3
Peabody ave SW1	155	Y10
Peabody clo SE10	93	S1
Peabody est N17	31	R5
Peabody est SE24	90	K19
Peabody est W6	152	D11
Peabody est W10	136	D19
Peabody hill SE21	90	K20
Peabody Hill est SE21	108	K1
Peabody sq SE1	149	W20
Peace clo N14	6	F17
Peace gro Wem	43	U8
Peach rd W10	136	J12
Peaches clo Sutt	129	S17
Peachum rd SE3	77	R16
Peacock st SE17	157	Z8
Peacock yd SE17	157	Z7
Peak the SE26	110	D8
Peak hill SE26	110	D9
Peak Hill ave SE26	110	C10
Peak Hill gdns SE26	110	D10
Peaketon ave Ilf	35	O14
Peal gdns W13	59	Y10
Pear clo NW9	25	Y13
Pear clo SE14	75	W19
Pear pl SE1	149	T17
Pear Tree ct EC1	141	U17
Pear Tree st EC1	142	A15
Pearcefield ave SE23	110	C2
Pearcroft rd E11	51	W7
Peardon st SW8	89	T6
Pearesswood gdns Stan	24	H5
Pearfield rd SE23	110	H6
Pearl clo E6	66	J17
Pearl rd E17	33	O10
Pearl st E1	151	Z12
Pearman st SE1	149	U20
Pears rd Houns	83	N8
Pearscroft ct SW6	88	B3
Pearscroft rd SW6	88	B3
Pearson st E2	142	M8
Peartree clo Erith	99	N2
Peartree clo Mitch	105	K5
Peartree gdns Dag	55	R13
Peartree gdns Rom	38	G6
Peartree la E1	151	R20
Peartree rd Enf	8	E11
Peary pl E2	63	R8
Pease clo Horn	57	Z19
Peatfield clo Sid	114	H7
Pebworth rd Har	41	X7
Peckarmans wd SE26	109	W6
Peckett sq N5	48	K12

Peckford pl SW9	90	F6
Peckham gro SE15	158	L18
Peckham High st SE15	91	X2
Peckham Hill st SE15	159	S19
Peckham Park rd SE15	159	S19
Peckham rd SE5	91	T2
Peckham rd SE15	91	U2
Peckham Rye SE15	91	Y9
Peckham Rye SE22	91	Y9
Peckwater st NW5	47	V16
Pedlars wk N7	48	B16
Pedley st E1	143	R18
Pedro st E5	50	G10
Peek cres SW19	105	P12
Peel clo E4	20	D8
Peel clo N9	18	L10
Peel dr NW9	26	E11
Peel dr Ilf	35	S9
Peel gro E2	63	P7
Peel pas W8	145	U14
Peel pl Ilf	35	R8
Peel prec NW6	137	T10
Peel rd E18	34	B6
Peel rd NW6	137	S11
Peel rd Har	23	V10
Peel rd Wem	42	F9
Peel st W8	145	V13
Peerless st EC1	142	E14
Pegamoid rd N18	19	P11
Pegasus ct Kings T	116	H7
Pegasus pl SE11	157	T12
Pegley gdns SE12	112	G4
Pegwell st SE38	79	U18
Pekin st E14	64	C18
Peldon ct Rich	85	N11
Pelham ave Bark	67	X3
Pelham clo SE5	91	T6
Pelham cres SW7	154	J6
Pelham pl SW7	154	J6
Pelham rd E18	34	H9
Pelham rd N15	31	U13
Pelham rd N22	30	F7
Pelham rd SW19	105	X18
Pelham rd Beck	124	D3
Pelham rd Bexh	98	E8
Pelham rd Ilf	54	F7
Pelham st SW7	154	J6
Pelican est SE15	91	U2
Pelier st SE17	158	C13
Pelinore rd SE6	111	Z5
Pellant rd SW6	152	M16
Pellatt gro N22	30	E5
Pellatt rd SE22	91	V14
Pellerin rd N16	49	S14
Pelling st E14	64	A17
Pellipar clo N13	17	T1
Pellipar gdns SE18	78	F12
Pelly rd E13	65	T3
Pelter st E2	143	N12
Pelton rd SE10	76	M13
Pembar ave E17	32	H11
Pember rd NW10	136	F13
Pemberton gdns N19	47	W8
Pemberton gdns Rom	37	Z16
Pemberton rd N4	30	G16
Pemberton row EC4	149	U5
Pemberton ter N19	47	V8
Pembridge ave Twick	100	D2
Pembridge cres W11	145	S9
Pembridge gdns W2	145	U10
Pembridge ms W11	145	T8
Pembridge pl W2	145	U8
Pembridge rd W11	145	U9
Pembridge sq W2	145	U9
Pembridge vill W11	145	U8
Pembroke ave Enf	9	N4
Pembroke ave Har	24	A9
Pembroke ave Surb	117	T12
Pembroke clo SW1	147	U18
Pembroke clo Erith	81	Z12
Pembroke gdns W8	153	R4

Pembroke gdns Dag	56	G10
Pembroke Gardens clo W8	153	S3
Pembroke ms N10	29	R3
Pembroke ms W8	153	T3
Pembroke pl W8	153	T2
Pembroke pl Edg	25	R2
Pembroke rd E6	66	G14
Pembroke rd E17	33	R15
Pembroke rd N8	30	A12
Pembroke rd N10	29	R3
Pembroke rd N13	18	A11
Pembroke rd N15	31	V15
Pembroke rd SE25	123	R10
Pembroke rd W8	153	T5
Pembroke rd Brom	126	M5
Pembroke rd Erith	81	Y13
Pembroke rd Grnf	58	L10
Pembroke rd Ilf	54	L4
Pembroke rd Mitch	121	O15
Pembroke rd Wem	42	H10
Pembroke sq W8	153	T4
Pembroke st N1	140	M2
Pembroke studios W8	153	R4
Pembroke vill W8	153	T4
Pembroke vill Rich	84	F11
Pembroke wk W8	153	T4
Pembury ave Wor Pk	118	H18
Pembury clo Brom	126	D17
Pembury cres Sid	115	Y5
Pembury pl E5	49	Z15
Pembury rd E5	50	A14
Pembury rd N17	31	V4
Pembury rd SE25	123	Y9
Pembury rd Bexh	80	M18
Pemdevon rd Croy	122	H18
Pemell clo E1	63	S10
Pempath pl Wem	42	F6
Penally pl N1	142	F4
Penang st E1	151	Y12
Penarth st SE15	75	P16
Penberth rd SE6	111	V3
Penbury rd Sthl	70	D12
Pencombe ms W11	145	S8
Pencraig way SE15	159	W15
Penda rd Erith	81	W18
Pendarves rd SW20	118	M1
Pendennis rd N17	31	O10
Pendennis rd SW16	108	A8
Penderel rd Houns	82	H12
Penderry ri SE6	111	W4
Penderyn way N7	47	Z12
Pendle rd SW16	107	T14
Pendlestone rd E17	33	P17
Pendragon rd Brom	112	D7
Pendragon wk NW9	26	B17
Pendrell rd SE4	92	H6
Pendrell st SE18	79	T17
Penerley rd SE6	111	S1
Penfold clo Croy	132	G7
Penfold la Bex	115	W3
Penfold pl NW1	138	J20
Penfold rd N9	19	S4
Penfold st NW1	138	J20
Penfold st NW8	138	G18
Penford gdns SE9	95	N9
Penford st SE5	90	J4
Pengarth rd Bex	97	X14
Penge la SE20	110	E17
Penge rd E13	65	X2
Penge rd SE25	123	X7
Penhall rd SE7	78	A10
Penhill rd Bex	97	U17
Penhurst rd Ilf	36	A2
Penifather la Grnf	59	R7
Peniston rd SW16	108	A17
Penketh dr Har	41	P9
Penmon rd SE2	80	C8
Penn clo Grnf	58	M7
Penn clo Har	24	C13
Penn gdns Chis	127	Z3
Penn gdns Rom	38	E1
Penn la Bex	97	X15
Penn rd N7	48	B14
Penn st N1	142	G5
Pennack rd SE15	159	P15
Pennant ms W8	153	X4

Pennant ter E17	32	M6
Pennard rd W12	144	C17
Penner clo SW19	105	S5
Pennethorne clo E9	63	P3
Pennethorne rd SE15	159	V19
Pennine dr NW2	45	P7
Pennine la NW2	45	S6
Pennine way Bexh	99	P3
Pennington st E1	151	U10
Penny rd NW10	61	T8
Pennycroft Croy	134	H20
Pennyfields E14	64	B19
Pennyroyal ave E6	66	K18
Penpoll rd E8	50	A17
Penpool la Well	97	S8
Penrhyn ave E17	33	N5
Penrhyn cres E17	33	P4
Penrhyn cres SW14	85	W10
Penrhyn gro E17	33	N5
Penrhyn rd Kings T	116	J8
Penrith clo SW15	87	T14
Penrith clo Beck	125	R1
Penrith cres Rain	57	X16
Penrith rd N15	31	O15
Penrith rd N Mal	117	Z9
Penrith rd Th Hth	122	M3
Penrith st SW16	107	V15
Penrose gro SE17	158	A11
Penrose st SE17	158	B10
Penry st SE1	158	M7
Penryn st NW1	140	F8
Pensbury pl SW8	89	V4
Pensbury st SW8	89	V4
Pensford ave Rich	85	R4
Penshurst ave Sid	97	O16
Penshurst gdns Edg	12	E16
Penshurst grn Brom	126	C13
Penshurst rd E9	63	T1
Penshurst rd N17	31	U2
Penshurst rd Bexh	98	C2
Penshurst rd Th Hth	122	J11
Penshurst way Sutt	129	Y18
Penstock footpath N22	30	B10
Pentire rd E17	33	W5
Pentland clo NW11	45	S8
Pentland gdns SW18	88	C15
Pentland pl Nthlt	58	B4
Pentland st SW18	88	C16
Pentlands clo Mitch	121	S7
Pentlow st SW15	87	N6
Pentney rd E4	20	J5
Pentney rd SW12	107	V1
Penton gro N1	141	T9
Penton pl SE17	157	Y8
Penton ri WC1	141	P12
Penton st N1	141	S9
Pentonville rd N1	141	P10
Pentrich ave Enf	8	K3
Pentridge st SE15	159	N19
Pentyre ave N18	18	B15
Penwerris ave Islw	71	N9
Penwith rd SW18	105	Z3
Penwortham rd SW16	107	U15
Penylan pl Edg	25	R2
Penywern rd SW5	153	W9
Penzance pl W11	144	L12
Penzance st W11	144	L13
Peony gdns W12	62	G19
Peploe rd NW6	136	J10
Pepper clo E6	66	H19
Pepper st E14	76	D7
Pepper st SE1	150	A16
Peppermint clo Croy	122	A16
Pepys cres Barn	4	A16
Pepys rd SE14	92	G2
Pepys rd SW20	119	N3
Pepys st EC3	150	L9
Perceval ave NW3	46	H15
Perch st E8	49	V13
Percival ct N17	18	H20
Percival gdns Rom	37	V19
Percival rd SW14	85	V12
Percival rd Enf	8	J13
Percival st EC1	141	X15

Percy circ WC1	141	P12
Percy gdns Enf	9	T16
Percy gdns Islw	84	A6
Percy gdns Wor Pk	118	A19
Percy ms W1	148	E3
Percy rd E11	33	Z20
Percy rd E16	65	N14
Percy rd N12	15	R16
Percy rd N21	18	A2
Percy rd NW6	137	U20
Percy rd SE20	124	E1
Percy rd SE25	123	W11
Percy rd W12	74	G6
Percy rd Bexh	97	Z6
Percy rd Dag	69	R11
Percy rd Hmptn	100	F17
Percy rd Ilf	37	N20
Percy rd Islw	83	Z10
Percy rd Mitch	121	O18
Percy rd Rom	38	H9
Percy rd Twick	100	K3
Percy st W1	148	E3
Percy way Twick	100	M1
Percy yd WC1	141	P13
Peregrine clo NW10	43	Z16
Peregrine ct SW16	108	C10
Peregrine gdns Croy	134	J2
Peregrine way SW19	104	M17
Perham rd W14	153	N12
Peridot st E6	66	E14
Perifield SE21	109	N1
Perimeade rd Grnf	60	E5
Periton rd SE9	95	N11
Perivale gdns W13	60	A11
Perivale gra Grnf	59	Y8
Perivale Industrial pk Grnf	60	A5
Perivale la Grnf	59	X9
Perkins clo Wem	42	A14
Perkin's rents SW1	156	G2
Perkins rd Ilf	36	E15
Perks clo SE3	93	Z6
Perpins rd SE9	96	G17
Perran rd SW2	108	H3
Perran wk Brent	72	K15
Perrers rd W6	74	J10
Perrin rd Wem	42	A11
Perrins la NW3	46	E13
Perrin's wk NW3	46	D13
Perry ave W3	61	Z16
Perry hill SE6	110	L5
Perry How Wor Pk	118	C20
Perry mead Enf	7	X7
Perry ri SE23	110	H6
Perry st Chis	114	G16
Perry st Dart	99	R8
Perry vale SE23	110	D3
Perryfield way NW9	26	E19
Perryfield way Rich	102	C6
Perrymans Farm rd Ilf	36	E17
Perrymead st SW6	87	Z3
Perryn rd SE16	151	V20
Perryn rd W3	73	Y1
Perrys pl W1	148	E4
Persant rd SE6	111	Y6
Perseverance pl SW9	157	U19
Pershore clo Ilf	36	A15
Pershore gro Cars	120	G15
Pert clo N10	16	D20
Perth ave NW9	43	Z1
Perth clo SW20	118	F3
Perth rd E10	50	K4
Perth rd E13	65	W7
Perth rd N4	48	F4
Perth rd N22	30	J4
Perth rd Bark	67	T5
Perth rd Beck	125	U4
Perth rd Ilf	35	X17
Perth ter Ilf	54	D1
Perwell ave Har	40	E4
Peter ave NW10	44	K19
Peter st W1	148	E8
Peterboat clo SE10	77	N10
Peterborough gdns Ilf	35	S20

Peterborough ms SW6	87	X4	Phipps Bridge rd Mitch	120	G6	Pine rd N11	16	A7	Plaxtol clo Brom	126	L2
Peterborough rd E10	33	V16	Phipps Hatch la Enf	7	Z2	Pine rd NW2	45	O11	Plaxtol rd Erith	81	T18
Peterborough rd SW6	87	Y5	Phipp's ms SW1	155	X4	Pine st EC1	141	T16	Playfield ave Rom	38	J4
Peterborough rd Cars	120	H14	Phoebeth rd SE4	93	P12	Pine wk Surb	117	P13	Playfield cres SE22	91	T13
Peterborough rd Har	41	U3	Phoenix clo W Wick	135	Y2	Pinefield clo E14	64	B19	Playfield rd Edg	25	X6
Peterborough vill SW6	88	A2	Phoenix pl WC1	141	R16	Pines the N14	6	H16	Playford rd N4	48	E6
			Phoenix rd NW1	140	E12	Pines the Wdf Grn	21	S10	Playgreen way SE6	111	O8
Petergate SW11	88	D10	Phoenix rd SE20	110	D16	Pines rd Brom	127	R3	Playground clo Beck	124	G4
Peters clo Dag	55	V4	Phoenix st WC2	148	H6	Pinewood ave Sid	114	H2			
Peters clo Stan	11	U18	Phyllis ave N Mal	118	J12	Pinewood clo Croy	134	H6	Playhouse yd EC4	149	X7
Peters clo Well	96	H4	Physic pl SW3	155	P13	Pinewood gro W5	60	E17	Pleasance the SW15	86	J11
Peters path SE26	109	Z9	Picardy Manorway Belv	81	V8	Pinewood rd SE2	80	H16	Pleasance rd SW15	86	J12
Petersfield clo N18	17	Y16				Pinewood rd Brom	126	G8	Pleasant gro Croy	134	M5
Petersfield ri SW15	86	J20	Picardy rd Belv	81	S13	Pinfold rd SW16	108	A9	Pleasant pl N1	141	Z2
Petersfield rd W3	73	W5	Picardy st Belv	81	T9	Pinkham way N11	16	C20	Pleasant row NW1	139	Z5
Petersham clo Rich	102	H3	Piccadilly W1	147	X15	Pinley gdns Dag	68	C2	Pleasant way Wem	60	F5
Petersham clo Sutt	129	X12	Piccadilly circ W1	148	E10	Pinnacle hill Bexh	98	J11	Plender st NW1	140	B6
Petersham la SW7	154	C1	Pickard st EC1	141	Z12	Pinnacle Hill north Bexh	98	J9	Pleshey rd N7	47	W13
Petersham ms SW7	154	C2	Pickering ave E6	66	K7				Plesman way SW1	132	A18
Petersham pl SW7	154	C2	Pickering ms W2	145	Y5	Pinnell pl SE9	95	O11	Plevna cres N15	31	S17
Petersham rd Rich	84	J17	Pickering st N1	141	Z3	Pinnell rd SE9	95	O11	Plevna rd N9	18	L10
Peterstone rd SE2	80	D6	Pickets clo (Bushey) Wat	10	E4	Pinner ct Pnr	22	G13	Plevna st E14	76	G7
Peterstow clo SW19	105	T3				Pinner gro Pnr	22	C14	Pleydell ave SE19	109	V17
Petherton rd N5	49	N12	Pickets st SW12	89	R18	Pinner Park ave Har	22	L8	Pleydell ave W6	74	E9
Petley rd W6	152	E15	Pickett cft Stan	24	F5	Pinner Park gdns Har	23	O8	Pleydell st EC4	149	U6
Peto pl NW1	139	Y17	Picketts Lock la N9	19	R7	Pinner rd Pnr	22	J14	Plimsoll clo E14	64	D18
Petrie clo NW2	45	T17	Pickford clo Bexh	97	Z5	Pinner vw Har	23	N11	Plimsoll rd N4	48	G8
Pett clo Horn	57	Z6	Pickford la Bexh	97	Z5	Pintail clo E6	66	D15	Plough ct EC3	150	H8
Pett st SE18	78	D9	Pickford rd Bexh	97	Z9	Pintail rd Wdf Grn	34	J1	Plough la SE22	91	V17
Pettits boul Rom	39	S5	Pickford wf N1	142	A10	Pinto way SE3	94	H10	Plough la SW17	106	D10
Pettits clo Rom	39	P7	Pickhurst grn Brom	126	B17	Pioneer way W12	144	B6	Plough la SW19	106	B12
Pettits la Rom	39	R6	Pickhurst la Brom	126	B17	Piper clo N7	48	C16	Plough la Pur	132	B19
Pettits Lane north Rom	39	N4	Pickhurst la W Wick	126	A12	Piper rd Kings T	117	O5	Plough la Wall	132	A11
			Pickhurst mead Brom	126	B18	Piper's gdns Croy	124	H17	Plough Lane clo Wall	131	Z10
Pettits pl Dag	56	D16	Pickhurst pk Brom	126	A11	Pipers grn NW9	25	W16			
Pettits rd Dag	56	E15	Pickhurst ri W Wick	125	V19	Pipers Green la Edg	11	W10	Plough pl EC4	149	U4
Pettiward clo SW15	86	L10	Pickwick clo Houns	82	C13	Pipewell rd Cars	120	H15	Plough rd SW11	88	B8
Pettley gdns Rom	39	O16	Pickwick ms N18	18	F14	Pippin clo Croy	124	L19	Plough st E1	151	R5
Pettman cres SE28	79	S9	Pickwick pl Har	41	T1	Piquet rd SE20	124	C4	Plough ter SW11	88	G10
Petts hill Nthlt	40	K16	Pickwick rd SE21	91	R18	Pirbright cres Croy	135	V15	Plough way SE16	75	U10
Pettsgrove ave Wem	42	E14	Pickwick st SE1	150	B18	Pirbright rd SW18	105	W1	Plough yd EC2	142	L18
Petty France SW1	148	D20	Pickwick way Chis	114	C14	Pirie clo SE5	91	P7	Ploughmans clo NW1	140	E3
Petworth clo Nthlt	40	F20	Pickworth clo SW8	156	L19	Pirie st E16	77	W3			
Petworth gdns SW20	118	J5	Picton pl W1	147	V6	Pitcairn rd Mitch	106	M17	Ploughmans end Islw	83	R13
Petworth rd N12	15	X17	Picton st SE5	158	F19	Pitchford st E15	64	L1			
Petworth rd Bexh	98	D13	Piedmont rd SE18	79	U14	Pitfield cres SE28	80	A3	Plover way SE16	75	W8
Petworth st SW11	88	K2	Pier rd E16	78	J5	Pitfield st N1	142	H14	Plowman clo N18	18	C16
Petworth way Horn	57	U13	Pier st E14	76	H10	Pitfield way NW10	43	V17	Plowman way Dag	55	V3
Petyt pl SW3	154	J15	Pier ter SW18	88	B9	Pitfield way Enf	9	P5	Plum garth Brent	72	H12
Petyward SW3	154	M6	Pier way SE28	79	R7	Pitfold clo SE12	94	G17	Plum la SE18	79	N20
Pevensey ave N11	16	K17	Piermont pl Brom	127	P2	Pitfold rd SE12	94	G16	Plumbers row E1	151	T3
Pevensey ave Enf	8	D7	Piermont rd SE22	91	Z14	Pitlake Croy	132	K2	Plummer la Mitch	120	M2
Pevensey clo Islw	71	N19	Pierrepoint rd W3	61	U20	Pitman st SE5	158	A18	Plummer rd SW4	89	X18
Pevensey rd E7	52	D11	Pigeon la Hmptn	100	G11	Pitsea st E1	63	U18	Plumpton clo Nthlt	40	G16
Pevensey rd SW17	106	G10	Piggot st E14	64	A17	Pitshanger la W5	60	B12	Plumpton way Cars	130	K6
Pevensey rd Felt	101	A3	Pike clo Brom	112	H13	Pitt cres SW19	105	Z10	Plumstead Common rd SE18	78	L15
Peveril dr Tedd	101	R12	Pikestone clo Hayes	58	B12	Pitt rd Har	41	N7			
Pewsey clo E4	20	A16	Pilgrim hill SE27	108	L8	Pitt rd Th Hth	122	M12	Plumstead High st SE18	79	V11
Peyton pl SE10	76	G19	Pilgrim st EC4	149	X7	Pitt st SE15	91	V1			
Phelp st SE17	158	F12	Pilgrimage st SE1	150	E19	Pitt st W8	145	V17	Plumstead rd SE18	79	P10
Phene st SW3	154	L13	Pilgrims clo N13	17	R14	Pittman gdns Ilf	54	C16	Plumtree clo Wall	131	X16
Philbeach gdns SW5	153	T8	Pilgrims clo Nthlt	41	N15	Pitt's Head ms W1	147	V14	Plumtree ct EC4	149	V3
			Pilgrims clo SE3	94	F2	Pittsmead ave Brom	126	F18	Plymouth rd E16	65	T15
Philchurch pl E1	151	U7	Pilgrim's la NW3	46	G12	Pittville gdns SE25	123	X6	Plymouth rd Brom	112	J20
Philip ave Rom	57	N3	Pilgrims ri Barn	5	X16	Pixley st E14	63	Z16	Plymouth wf E14	76	K11
Philip gdns Croy	134	K2	Pilgrims way N19	47	X3	Pixton way Croy	134	M20	Plympton ave NW6	137	N2
Philip la N15	31	O12	Pilgrims way S Croy	133	V12	Plaistow gro E15	65	P4	Plympton rd NW6	45	V20
Philip st E13	65	S12				Plaistow gro Brom	112	G18	Plympton st NW8	138	K18
Philip wk SE15	91	Y7	Pilgrim's way Wem	43	T4	Plaistow la Brom	112	H18	Plymstock rd Well	80	G20
Philipot path SE9	95	V15	Pilkington rd SE15	91	Z5	Plaistow Park rd E13	65	V5	Pocklington clo NW9	26	A6
Philippa gdns SE9	95	N12	Pimlico rd SW1	155	U8	Plaistow rd E15	65	R5			
Phillimore gdns NW10	136	A5	Pimlico wk N1	142	J11	Plane st SE26	109	Z8	Pocock st SE1	149	X17
			Pinchin st E1	151	U8	Plantagenet gdns Rom	55	W2	Podmore rd SW18	88	C11
Phillimore gdns W8	145	T20	Pincott rd SW19	106	C20				Poets rd N5	49	N14
Phillimore Gardens clo W8	145	T20	Pincott rd Bexh	98	E12	Plantagenet pl Rom	55	X2	Poets way Har	23	U14
			Pindar st EC2	142	J20	Plantagenet rd Barn	5	P14	Point clo SE10	93	V2
Phillimore pl W8	145	T19	Pindock ms W9	137	Z17	Plantain pl SE1	150	F17	Point hill SE10	76	H20
Phillimore wk W8	145	U20	Pine ave E15	51	Y14	Plantation the SE3	94	F5	Point Pleasant SW18	87	X10
Phillipp st N1	142	L6	Pine ave W Wick	125	R20	Plantation rd Erith	99	W1	Pointalls clo N3	28	D6
Phillips clo Dart	99	Y15	Pine clo N14	16	H2	Plashet gro E6	65	Y2	Pointers clo E14	76	D14
Philpot la EC3	150	H9	Pine clo Stan	11	N12	Plashet rd E13	65	U2	Pointers cotts Rich	102	D5
Philpot sq SW6	88	A8	Pine coombe Croy	134	F9	Plassy rd SE6	93	S20	Poland st W1	148	C5
Philpot st E1	151	X4	Pine gdns Surb	117	P16	Platina st EC2	142	G17	Pole Hill rd E4	20	G3
Phineas Pett rd SE9	95	S7	Pine gro N4	48	B6	Plato rd SW2	90	A10	Polebrook rd SE3	94	M6
Phipp st EC2	142	K17	Pine gro N20	14	J5	Platt the SW15	87	R8	Polecroft la SE6	110	L4
Phipps Bridge rd SW19	120	E3	Pine gro SW19	105	U13	Platt st NW1	140	F9	Polesden gdns SW20	118	H5
			Pine ridge Cars	131	P20	Platt's la NW3	45	Y11	Polesworth rd Dag	55	Y19
						Platts rd Enf	9	S6	Pollard clo E16	65	S19

Pollard clo N7 48 D13
Pollard rd N20 15 W8
Pollard rd Mord 120 H12
Pollard row E2 143 U12
Pollard st E2 143 U13
Pollard wk Sid 115 U15
Pollards cres SW16 122 B7
Pollards Hill east SW16 122 D6
Pollards Hill north SW16 122 B6
Pollards Hill south SW16 122 B7
Pollards Hill west SW16 122 C7
Pollards Wood rd SW16 122 A5
Pollen st W1 148 A7
Pollitt dr NW8 138 G15
Polsted rd SE6 92 M19
Polthorne gro SE18 79 R10
Polworth rd SW16 108 A13
Polygon the SW4 89 V9
Polygon rd NW1 140 E11
Polytechnic st SE18 78 L10
Pomell way E1 151 P4
Pomeroy st SE14 75 R20
Pond clo SE3 94 D5
Pond Cottage la W Wick 135 P1
Pond cotts SE21 109 S3
Pond Hill gdns Sutt 129 S13
Pond mead SE21 91 P15
Pond pl SW3 154 K7
Pond rd E15 64 M5
Pond rd SE3 94 D4
Pond sq N6 47 P3
Pond st NW3 46 H14
Pond way Tedd 102 E16
Ponder st N7 48 C19
Pondfield rd Brom 126 A20
Pondfield rd Dag 56 H14
Ponler st E1 151 V7
Ponsard rd NW10 62 J8
Ponsford st E9 50 E16
Ponsonby pl SW1 156 H9
Ponsonby rd SW15 86 J19
Ponsonby ter SW1 156 H9
Pont st SW1 155 O2
Pont Street ms SW1 155 O2
Pontefract rd Brom 112 D13
Ponton rd SW8 156 F18
Pontypool pl SE1 149 W17
Pool clo Beck 111 P14
Pool rd Har 41 P2
Poole Court rd Houns 82 B4
Poole rd E9 50 E19
Poole st N1 142 F6
Pooles bldgs EC1 141 S18
Pooles la SW10 154 B19
Pooles la Dag 69 N4
Pooles pk N4 48 F7
Poolmans st SE16 75 T5
Poolsford rd NW9 26 B13
Pope rd Brom 127 N12
Pope st SE1 150 M19
Popes ave Twick 101 U3
Popes dr N3 27 Y3
Pope's gro Croy 134 L5
Popes gro Twick 101 U5
Popes la W5 72 G9
Popes rd SW9 90 F8
Popham clo Felt 100 D7
Popham rd N1 142 A5
Popham st N1 142 A4
Poplar ave Mitch 121 N1
Poplar ct SW19 105 Z11
Poplar gdns N Mal 117 Z5
Poplar gro N11 16 A20
Poplar gro W6 104 D19
Poplar gro N Mal 117 Z5
Poplar gro Wem 43 X9
Poplar High st E14 64 E20
Poplar mt Belv 81 W10
Poplar pl SE28 80 G1
Poplar pl W2 145 Y9
Poplar rd SE24 90 L9
Poplar rd SW19 119 Y2

Poplar rd Sutt 119 U20
Poplar Road south SW19 119 Y6
Poplar st Rom 38 K13
Poplar wk SE24 90 L10
Poplar wk Croy 132 M2
Poplar way Ilf 36 D13
Poplars the N14 6 F17
Poplars ave NW2 44 M18
Poplars rd E17 33 S18
Poppins ct EC4 149 W6
Poppleton rd E11 34 A19
Poppy clo Wall 121 R19
Poppy la Croy 124 D18
Porch way N20 15 Z10
Porchester gdns W2 145 Y8
Porchester Gardens ms W2 146 A7
Porchester mead Beck 111 P15
Porchester ms W2 145 Z4
Porchester pl W2 146 L6
Porchester rd W2 145 Y4
Porchester rd Kings T 117 S3
Porchester sq W2 145 Z4
Porchester ter W2 146 B9
Porchester Terrace north W2 146 A4
Porcupine clo SE9 113 S4
Porden rd SW2 90 D11
Porlock ave Har 41 N4
Porlock rd W10 136 J19
Porlock rd Enf 18 F2
Porlock st SE1 150 F17
Porrington clo Chis 113 W20
Port cres E13 65 V12
Portal clo SE27 108 G6
Portchester clo SE5 91 N10
Portcullis Lodge rd Enf 8 B10
Portelet rd E1 63 S10
Porten rd W14 152 K2
Porter rd E6 66 H17
Porter st SE1 150 C13
Porter st W1 139 S20
Porters ave Dag 55 R18
Portersfield rd Enf 8 D15
Porteus rd W2 146 E1
Portgate clo W9 137 P16
Porthcawe rd SE26 110 K10
Porthkerry ave Well 97 O10
Portia way E3 49 Y12
Portinscale rd SW15 87 T14
Portland ave N16 49 U2
Portland ave N Mal 118 D16
Portland ave Sid 97 O17
Portland clo Rom 37 Y15
Portland cres SE9 113 R5
Portland cres Grnf 58 L13
Portland cres Stan 24 J7
Portland gdns N4 30 K18
Portland gdns Rom 37 X15
Portland gro SW8 90 C2
Portland ms W1 148 D6
Portland pl W1 139 Y19
Portland ri N4 48 K4
Portland rd N15 31 T14
Portland rd SE9 113 R4
Portland rd SE25 123 X8
Portland rd W11 144 L9
Portland rd Brom 112 H1
Portland rd Kings T 116 M7
Portland rd Mitch 120 K4
Portland rd Sthl 70 D8
Portland sq E1 151 W13
Portland st SE17 158 E9
Portland ter Rich 85 V3
Portman ave SW14 85 Y9
Portman clo W1 147 O3
Portman dr Wdf Grn 35 O8
Portman gdns NW9 25 X8
Portman gate NW1 138 L18
Portman Mews south W1 147 S6
Portman pl E2 63 R10
Portman rd Kings T 117 N4
Portman sq W1 147 S5
Portman st W1 147 S6
Portmeadow wk SE2 80 J5

Portnall rd W9 137 P17
Portnoi clo Rom 39 N6
Portobello rd W10 136 K20
Portobello rd W11 145 O5
Portpool la EC1 141 S20
Portree clo SE13 30 D2
Portree st E14 64 L16
Portsdown ave NW11 27 V19
Portsdown ms NW11 27 W18
Portsea pl W2 147 N6
Portslade rd SW8 89 V4
Portsmouth rd SW15 86 L19
Portsmouth rd Kings T 116 H9
Portsmouth st WC2 149 O5
Portsoken st E1 151 O8
Portugal gdns Twick 100 M5
Portugal st WC2 149 P5
Portway E15 65 P2
Portway gdns SE18 78 B20
Post la Twick 101 P1
Post Office way SW8 156 F16
Postern grn Enf 7 U10
Postway ms Ilf 54 A8
Potier st SE1 158 G2
Pott st E2 143 Y14
Potter clo Mitch 121 S4
Potterne clo SW19 87 P19
Potters clo Croy 124 J20
Potters gro N Mal 117 V10
Potters la SW16 107 X15
Potters la Barn 4 M14
Potters rd Barn 5 N13
Pottery la W11 144 L11
Pottery rd Brent 72 K16
Pottery st SE16 151 W18
Poulett gdns Twick 101 X2
Poulett rd E6 66 G5
Poulton ave Sutt 130 H6
Poulton clo E8 49 Z16
Poultry EC2 150 E6
Pound clo Surb 116 D19
Pound la NW10 44 F18
Pound Park rd SE7 78 B12
Pound pl SE9 95 W15
Pound st Cars 130 L11
Pountney rd SW11 89 O9
Powder Mill la Twick 82 E20
Powell clo Edg 11 Z17
Powell clo Wall 131 Z16
Powell gdns Dag 56 D12
Powell rd E5 50 A10
Powell rd Buck H 21 Z3
Powell's wk W4 74 C16
Power rd W4 73 P12
Powers ct Twick 84 G18
Powerscroft rd E5 50 C13
Powerscroft rd Sid 115 T16
Powis gdns NW11 45 U2
Powis gdns W11 145 R4
Powis ms W11 145 S4
Powis pl WC1 140 M19
Powis rd E3 64 E9
Powis sq W11 145 S5
Powis st SE18 78 L9
Powis ter W11 145 R4
Powlett pl NW1 47 R19
Pownall gdns Houns 82 L10
Pownall rd E8 143 R5
Pownall rd Houns 82 L10
Powster rd Brom 112 G11
Powys clo Bexh 80 K17
Powys la N13 16 M14
Powys la N14 16 M12
Poynders gdns SW4 89 V18
Poynders rd SW4 89 W17
Poynings rd N19 47 U9
Poynings way N12 14 K17
Poyntell cres Chis 114 F20
Poynter rd Enf 8 J16
Poynton rd N17 31 X6
Poyntz rd SW11 88 M5
Poyser st E2 143 Y10
Praed st W2 146 G5
Pragel st E13 65 X7
Pragnell rd SE12 112 G13
Prague pl SW2 90 A14

Prah rd N4 48 H7
Prairie st SW8 89 R5
Pratt ms NW1 140 A5
Pratt st NW1 140 B5
Pratt wk SE11 157 P4
Prayle gro NW2 45 O3
Prebend gdns W4 74 D9
Prebend st N1 142 D6
Prendergast rd SE3 94 A6
Prentis rd SW16 107 Y9
Prentiss ct SE7 78 A12
Presburg rd N Mal 118 B11
Prescelly pl Edg 25 N5
Prescot st E1 151 P8
Prescott ave Orp 127 Z15
Prescott clo SW16 108 A17
Prescott pl SW4 89 X9
President dr E1 151 X11
President st EC1 142 A13
Press rd NW10 43 Z9
Prestbury rd E7 52 L20
Prestbury sq SE9 113 U9
Preston ave E4 20 J19
Preston clo SE1 158 J6
Preston clo Twick 101 S6
Preston dr E11 34 L16
Preston dr Bexh 97 W3
Preston dr Epsom 128 C13
Preston gdns NW10 44 C18
Preston gdns Enf 9 X1
Preston gdns Ilf 35 S19
Preston hill Har 42 K1
Preston pl NW2 44 H18
Preston pl Rich 84 L13
Preston rd E11 34 A19
Preston rd SE19 108 J15
Preston rd SW20 104 F19
Preston rd Har 42 K1
Preston rd Wem 42 K5
Preston waye Har 42 J3
Prestons rd E14 76 H4
Prestwick clo Sthl 70 B14
Prestwood ave Har 24 B13
Prestwood clo SE18 80 A18
Prestwood clo Har 24 C13
Prestwood gdns Croy 122 M16
Prestwood st N1 142 C10
Pretoria ave E17 32 H12
Pretoria clo N17 18 G20
Pretoria cres E4 20 H6
Pretoria rd E4 20 H5
Pretoria rd E11 51 X4
Pretoria rd E16 65 O11
Pretoria rd N17 18 G19
Pretoria rd SW16 107 X15
Pretoria rd Ilf 53 Z14
Pretoria rd Cars 38 H8
Pretoria Road north N18 18 G18
Prevost rd N11 16 B7
Price clo NW7 14 E18
Price clo SW17 106 M8
Price rd Croy 132 J10
Price way Hmptn 100 C15
Price's st SE1 149 Y14
Pricklers Hill Barn 5 O18
Priddy's yd Croy 132 M4
Prideaux pl W3 61 Z19
Prideaux pl WC1 141 R13
Prideaux rd SW9 90 A7
Pridham rd Th Hth 123 N10
Priest Park ave Har 40 J6
Priestfield rd SE23 110 J7
Priestlands Park rd Sid 114 L6
Priestley gdns Rom 37 P18
Priestley rd Mitch 121 P3
Priestley way E17 32 F9
Priestley way NW2 44 G4
Priests ave Rom 39 N7
Priests bri SW14 86 C9
Prima rd SW9 157 T16
Primrose ave Enf 8 D5
Primrose ave Rom 37 P20
Primrose clo SE6 111 V11
Primrose clo Har 40 D10
Primrose clo Wall 121 R19
Primrose gdns NW3 46 K17

Primrose hill EC4	149	V7
Primrose Hill rd NW3	139	N1
Primrose Hill studios NW1	139	S4
Primrose la Croy	134	C1
Primrose rd E10	51	R4
Primrose rd E18	34	H7
Primrose st EC2	142	K20
Primrose way Wem	60	F6
Primula st W12	62	F18
Prince Albert rd NW1	138	L11
Prince Albert rd NW8	139	R6
Prince Arthur ms NW3	46	E13
Prince Arthur rd NW3	46	E14
Prince Charles dr NW4	44	M1
Prince Charles rd SE3	94	C1
Prince Charles way Wall	131	S5
Prince Consort rd SW7	146	E20
Prince Edward rd E9	51	N18
Prince George ave N14	6	J15
Prince George rd N16	49	S13
Prince George's ave SW20	119	N3
Prince George's rd SW19	106	G20
Prince Henry rd SE7	78	B19
Prince Imperial rd SE18	95	V1
Prince Imperial rd Chis	114	A19
Prince John rd SE9	95	R14
Prince of Wales dr SW8	155	Y20
Prince of Wales dr SW11	155	W20
Prince of Wales footpath Enf	9	U1
Prince of Wales rd E16	65	Y18
Prince of Wales rd NW5	47	O18
Prince of Wales rd SE3	94	C3
Prince of Wales rd Sutt	130	F3
Prince of Wales ter W4	74	A13
Prince of Wales ter W8	146	A19
Prince Regent la E13	65	X11
Prince Regent la E16	65	X16
Prince Regent rd Houns	82	M7
Prince rd SE25	123	S11
Prince Rupert rd SE9	95	T10
Prince st SE8	75	Z16
Princedale rd W11	144	M13
Princelet st E1	143	O20
Princes ave N3	27	Z3
Princes ave N10	29	R10
Princes ave N13	17	S3
Princes ave N22	29	Y4
Princes ave NW9	25	O14
Princes ave W3	73	R7
Princes ave Cars	130	L18
Princes ave Grnf	58	L16
Princes ave Wdf Grn	21	W15
Princes clo NW9	25	P13
Princes clo SW4	89	U8
Princes clo Edg	12	C16
Princes clo Sid	115	V7
Princes clo Tedd	101	R10
Princes ct Wem	42	K14
Princes dr Har	23	T11
Princes gdns SW7	146	K20
Princes gdns W3	61	P14
Princes gdns W5	60	D12
Princes gate SW7	146	K18
Princes Gate ms SW7	154	H1
Princes la N10	29	R11
Princes ms W2	145	W9
Princes pk Rain	57	X20
Princes Park ave NW11	27	S18
Princes pl W11	144	L13
Princes Plain Brom	127	S18
Princes ri SE13	93	V5
Princes rd N18	19	P12
Princes rd SE20	110	F16
Princes rd SW14	85	Z8
Princes rd SW19	105	X16
Princes rd W13	72	C2
Princes rd Buck H	21	X7
Princes rd Dart	99	W15
Princes rd Ilf	36	E12
Princes rd Kings T	103	P19
Princes rd Rich	84	M12
Princes rd (Kew) Rich	85	O1
Princes rd Rom	39	V16
Princes rd Tedd	101	P11
Princes sq W2	145	W8
Princes st EC2	150	F5
Princes st N17	18	E20
Princes st W1	147	Z6
Princes st Bexh	98	B8
Princes st Sutt	130	F9
Princes ter E13	65	W4
Princes way SW19	87	R19
Princes way Buck H	21	Y8
Princes way Croy	132	E12
Princes way Ruis	40	B12
Princess ave Wem	42	L5
Princess cres N4	48	J6
Princess May rd N16	49	S13
Princess rd NW1	139	U3
Princess rd NW6	137	T10
Princess rd Croy	122	L15
Princess st SE1	157	Y3
Princethorpe rd SE26	110	F11
Princeton st WC1	149	O1
Pringle gdns SW16	107	U10
Printer st EC4	149	V5
Printing House yd E2	142	M13
Priolo rd SE7	77	X15
Prior ave Sutt	130	H16
Prior Bolton st N1	48	K18
Prior rd Ilf	53	X9
Prior st SE10	76	G20
Prioress rd SE27	108	H8
Prioress st SE1	158	H2
Priors cft E17	32	K9
Priors mead Enf	8	E5
Priory the SE3	94	D9
Priory ave E4	19	Z10
Priory ave E17	33	O15
Priory ave N8	29	Y12
Priory ave W4	74	B10
Priory ave Sutt	129	P9
Priory ave Wem	41	X12
Priory clo E4	20	A10
Priory clo E18	34	E4
Priory clo N3	27	W5
Priory clo N14	6	F17
Priory clo N20	14	G3
Priory clo Beck	124	J7
Priory clo Chis	127	V2
Priory clo Stan	10	J10
Priory clo (Sudbury) Wem	41	X12
Priory ct E17	32	L8
Priory ct SW8	89	Z2
Priory ct (Bushey) Wat	10	B4
Priory Court est E17	32	M7
Priory cres SE19	109	N18
Priory cres Sutt	129	P9
Priory cres Wem	41	Y10
Priory dr SE2	80	K14
Priory dr Stan	10	H9
Priory Field dr Edg	12	G13
Priory gdns N6	29	T18
Priory gdns SW13	86	C8
Priory gdns Hmptn	100	E19
Priory gdns Wem	41	X11
Priory Green est N1	141	O9
Priory gro SW8	89	Z3
Priory hill Wem	41	Y12
Priory la SW15	86	B15
Priory la Rich	73	R19
Priory ms SW8	89	Z2
Priory pk SE3	94	C9
Priory Park rd NW6	137	P4
Priory Park rd Wem	41	Y12
Priory rd E6	66	A5
Priory rd N8	29	X13
Priory rd NW6	137	X4
Priory rd SW19	106	F18
Priory rd W4	73	Y8
Priory rd Croy	122	F18
Priory rd Bark	54	E20
Priory rd Hmptn	100	D19
Priory rd Houns	83	N13
Priory rd Rich	73	P18
Priory rd Sutt	129	P10
Priory st E3	64	F8
Priory ter NW6	137	X4
Priory vw (Bushey) Wat	10	F3
Priory wk SW10	154	C11
Priory way Har	22	J12
Priter rd SE16	159	T2
Private rd Enf	8	C16
Probert rd SW2	90	G12
Probyn rd SW2	108	H4
Procter st WC1	149	N2
Progress Business pk the Croy	132	D3
Progress way N22	30	F4
Progress way Croy	132	D3
Progress way Enf	8	L18
Promenade the W4	86	B3
Promenade Approach rd W4	74	B19
Prospect clo SE26	110	A9
Prospect clo Belv	81	S12
Prospect clo Houns	82	E3
Prospect cres Twick	83	N16
Prospect hill E17	33	S12
Prospect pl E1	75	P7
Prospect pl N2	28	H12
Prospect pl Brom	126	H7
Prospect pl Rom	38	K7
Prospect ring N2	28	H11
Prospect rd NW2	45	W9
Prospect rd Barn	4	M15
Prospect rd Surb	116	D15
Prospect rd Wdf Grn	21	Y18
Prospect st SE16	151	Y20
Prospect vale SE18	78	E10
Prospero rd N19	47	W4
Prothero gdns NW4	26	K14
Prothero rd SW6	153	O16
Prout gro NW10	44	C13
Prout rd E5	50	B9
Providence ct W1	147	U8
Providence pl Rom	38	B6
Providence yd E2	143	R11
Provost est N1	142	F11
Provost rd NW3	47	N19
Provost st N1	142	F13
Prowse ave (Bushey) Wat	10	A8
Prowse pl NW1	140	A1
Pruden clo N14	16	J7
Prusom st E1	151	Z12
Pudding la EC3	150	H9
Pudding Mill la E15	64	F4
Puddle Dock EC4	149	V8
Pulborough rd SW18	87	V19
Pulford rd N15	31	P18
Pulham ave N2	28	E11
Puller rd Barn	4	E10
Pulleyns ave E6	66	E8
Pullman ct SW2	108	B11
Pullman gdns SW15	87	N15
Pulross rd SW9	90	C9
Pulteney clo E3	63	Y4
Pulteney rd E18	34	G10
Pulteney ter N1	141	R5
Pulton pl SW6	153	U19
Puma ct E1	143	O20
Pump all Brent	72	H18
Pump ct EC4	149	T7
Pump la SE14	75	R18
Pump Pail north Croy	132	L7
Pumping Station rd W4	74	C18
Pundersons gdns E2	143	X12
Purbeck ave N Mal	118	E15
Purbeck dr NW2	45	R5
Purbeck rd Horn	57	X1
Purbrook st SE1	150	M20
Purcell cres SW6	152	K16
Purcell rd Grnf	58	K13
Purcell st N1	142	J9
Purcells ave Edg	12	B15
Purchese st NW1	140	G9
Purdy st E3	64	D11
Purland clo Dag	56	B4
Purland rd SE28	79	Z7
Purley ave NW2	45	T7
Purley clo Ilf	35	X7
Purley pl N1	48	H20
Purley rd N9	18	D10
Purley rd S Croy	133	N18
Purley way Croy	122	D19
Purneys rd SE9	95	N9
Purrett rd SE18	79	Y14
Purser's Cross rd SW6	87	W2
Pursewardens clo W13	72	D2
Pursley rd NW7	26	H1
Purves rd NW10	136	A11
Putney bri SW6	87	T7
Putney bri SW15	87	S8
Putney Bridge app SW6	87	T7
Putney Bridge rd SW15	87	U10
Putney common SW15	86	M7
Putney heath SW15	86	M17
Putney Heath la SW15	87	P17
Putney High st SW15	87	R10
Putney hill SW15	87	P15
Putney Park ave SW15	86	H9
Putney Park la SW15	86	H10
Pycroft way N9	18	J12
Pyecombe corner N12	14	J14
Pylbrook rd Sutt	129	Z6
Pylon way Croy	132	B1
Pymers mead SE21	109	N1
Pymmes clo N13	17	O17
Pymmes clo N17	31	Z5
Pymmes Gardens north N9	18	H11
Pymmes Gardens south N9	18	H11
Pymmes Green rd N11	16	F12
Pymmes rd N13	17	O18
Pymms Brook dr Barn	5	W13
Pynham clo SE2	80	C9
Pynnacles clo Stan	11	O15
Pyrland rd N5	49	N15
Pyrland rd Rich	85	N16
Pyrmont gro SE27	108	H7
Pyrmont rd W4	73	P16
Pytchley cres SE19	108	M16
Pytchley rd SE22	91	T9

Q

Quadrant the SW20	119	T1
Quadrant the Bexh	98	K19
Quadrant the Rich	84	J12
Quadrant the Sutt	130	C14
Quadrant arc Rom	39	R15
Quadrant gro NW5	47	N16
Quadrant rd Rich	84	H12
Quadrant rd Th Hth	122	K9
Quaggy wk SE3	94	E10
Quainton st NW10	43	X10
Quaker la Sthl	70	H7
Quaker st E1	143	N18
Quakers course NW9	26	C5
Quakers la Islw	83	Z1
Quakers wk N21	8	A19
Quality ct WC2	149	S4

Name	Page	Grid
Quantock dr Wor Pk	129	N3
Quantock gdns NW2	45	P7
Quarr rd Cars	120	H15
Quarrendon st SW6	87	Z4
Quarry Park rd Sutt	129	W13
Quarry ri Sutt	129	V14
Quarry rd SW18	88	E15
Quarter Mile la E10	51	R12
Quarterdeck the E14	76	B6
Quebec ms W1	147	R5
Quebec rd Ilf	54	A1
Quebec way SE16	75	U6
Queen Adelaide rd SE20	110	D17
Queen Anne ave N15	31	U15
Queen Anne ave Brom	126	C6
Queen Anne ms W1	147	Y3
Queen Anne rd E9	50	F19
Queen Anne st W1	147	W3
Queen Anne's clo Twick	101	R8
Queen Anne's gdns W4	74	B9
Queen Annes gdns W5	72	J5
Queen Annes gdns Enf	8	E19
Queen Anne's gdns Mitch	120	L6
Queen Anne's gate SW1	148	F19
Queen Anne's gate Bexh	97	X8
Queen Anne's gro W4	74	A8
Queen Annes gro W5	72	K5
Queen Annes gro Enf	18	C2
Queen Annes pl Enf	8	F18
Queen Caroline st W6	152	D8
Queen Elizabeth gdns Mord	119	Y9
Queen Elizabeth rd E17	32	J10
Queen Elizabeth rd Kings T	116	M3
Queen Elizabeth st SE1	151	N16
Queen Elizabeth wk SW13	86	H2
Queen Elizabeth wk Wall	131	Y8
Queen Elizabeths clo N16	49	N6
Queen Elizabeths dr N14	16	M5
Queen Elizabeths dr Croy	135	W20
Queen Elizabeths wk N16	49	O6
Queen Margarets gro N1	49	R15
Queen Mary ave Mord	119	O12
Queen Mary clo Rom	39	T18
Queen Mary rd SE19	108	K14
Queen Mary's ave Cars	130	L17
Queen sq WC1	140	L19
Queen st EC4	150	D8
Queen st N17	18	F19
Queen st W1	147	X12
Queen st Bexh	98	A9
Queen st Croy	132	M7
Queen st Rom	39	O17
Queen Street pl EC4	150	D9
Queen Victoria ave Wem	42	G20
Queen Victoria st EC4	149	Y8
Queenborough gdns Chis	114	D16
Queenborough gdns Ilf	35	X12
Queenhithe EC4	150	C9
Queens acre Sutt	129	R16
Queens ave N3	28	D3
Queens ave N10	29	P10
Queens ave N20	15	U8
Queen's ave N21	17	X6
Queens ave Grnf	58	L16
Queens ave Stan	24	C9
Queens ave Wdf Grn	21	W16
Queen's circ SW8	155	X19
Queens clo Edg	12	C16
Queens Club gdns W14	152	M13
Queens ct SE23	110	B3
Queens cres NW5	47	O18
Queens cres Rich	85	N12
Queens dr E10	51	P1
Queens dr N4	48	J6
Queens dr W3	61	O17
Queen's dr Surb	117	R15
Queen's Elm sq SW3	154	G10
Queens gdns NW4	27	N16
Queens gdns W2	146	C7
Queens gdns W5	60	D13
Queen's gdns Houns	82	B2
Queen's gate SW7	146	D19
Queen's Gate gdns SW7	154	C3
Queen's Gate ms SW7	146	D20
Queen's Gate pl SW7	154	D2
Queen's Gate Place ms SW7	154	D3
Queen's Gate ter SW7	154	D1
Queen's gro NW8	138	F6
Queen's Grove ms NW8	138	F6
Queens Grove rd E4	20	L4
Queen's Head st N1	141	Y5
Queens Head yd SE1	150	E15
Queens la N10	29	S10
Queens ms W2	145	Y8
Queens par N11	15	Y17
Queens Park ct W10	136	J14
Queens pl Mord	119	Z9
Queens ride SW13	86	H8
Queen's ride Rich	85	S20
Queens ri Rich	84	M15
Queens rd E11	51	Z2
Queens rd E13	65	W4
Queen's rd E17	32	L18
Queens rd N3	28	D5
Queens rd N9	19	N9
Queen's rd N11	17	N20
Queens rd NW4	26	M16
Queens rd SE14	92	D2
Queens rd SE15	92	B2
Queens rd SW14	85	Z8
Queens rd SW19	105	X15
Queens rd W5	60	J16
Queens rd Barn	4	C12
Queens rd Beck	124	J4
Queens rd Brom	126	G3
Queens rd Buck H	21	W7
Queens rd Chis	114	A14
Queens rd Croy	122	K14
Queens rd Enf	8	E12
Queens rd Hmptn	100	K10
Queens rd Houns	82	J7
Queens rd Kings T	103	R18
Queens rd Mitch	120	F5
Queens rd Mord	119	Z8
Queens rd N Mal	118	E10
Queens rd Rich	84	L18
Queens rd Sthl	70	A7
Queens rd Tedd	101	W16
Queens rd Twick	83	X20
Queens rd Wall	131	S10
Queen's rd Well	97	P3
Queens Road west E13	65	U5
Queen's row SE17	158	E12
Queens ter E13	65	X4
Queen's ter NW8	138	F7
Queens ter Islw	83	Z9
Queens wk E4	20	J4
Queens wk NW9	43	W5
Queen's wk SW1	148	A14
Queens wk W5	60	D12
Queens wk Har	23	S12
Queens way NW4	27	N15
Queens Well ave N20	15	X12
Queen's Wood rd N10	29	T17
Queens yd WC1	140	D19
Queensberry Mews west SW7	154	F5
Queensberry pl SW7	154	F4
Queensberry way SW7	154	G5
Queensborough ms W2	146	A9
Queensborough pas W2	146	A8
Queensborough ter W2	146	A9
Queensbridge pk Islw	83	S14
Queensbridge rd E2	143	R8
Queensbridge rd E8	143	R1
Queensbury rd NW9	43	X2
Queensbury rd Wem	60	L6
Queensbury Station par Edg	25	N9
Queensbury st N1	142	C2
Queenscourt Wem	42	K11
Queenscroft rd SE9	95	P14
Queensdale cres W11	144	H13
Queensdale pl W11	144	K13
Queensdale rd W11	144	H15
Queensdale wk W11	144	L14
Queensdown rd E5	50	A12
Queensland ave N18	18	A18
Queensland ave SW19	106	A20
Queensland pl N7	48	F13
Queensland rd N7	48	F13
Queensmead NW8	138	G3
Queensmead rd Brom	126	B4
Queensmere clo SW19	105	O6
Queensmere rd SW19	105	O5
Queensmill rd SW6	152	G19
Queensthorpe rd SE26	110	C2
Queenstown rd SW8	155	X19
Queensville rd SW12	89	X19
Queensway W2	145	Y5
Queensway Croy	132	D13
Queensway Enf	9	O15
Queenswood ave E17	33	O15
Queenswood ave Hmptn	100	K15
Queenswood ave Houns	82	E4
Queenswood ave Th Hth	122	H12
Queenswood ave Wall	131	X10
Queenswood gdns E11	52	G5
Queenswood pk N3	27	T6
Queenswood rd SE23	110	G8
Queenswood rd Sid	96	K14
Quemerford rd N7	48	C14
Quentin pl SE13	94	A8
Quentin rd SE13	94	A8
Quernmore clo Brom	112	E15
Quernmore rd N4	30	E19
Quernmore rd Brom	112	E15
Querrin st SW6	88	C5
Quex ms NW6	137	U4
Quex rd NW6	137	U3
Quick rd W4	74	A14
Quick st N1	141	X10
Quicks rd SW19	106	B17
Quickswood NW3	46	K20
Quilp st SE1	150	B16
Quilter st E2	143	R12
Quinta dr Barn	4	A18
Quintin ave SW20	119	U2
Quinton clo Beck	125	V7
Quinton clo Wall	131	S8
Quinton st SW18	106	D5
Quixley st E14	64	J20
Quorn rd SE22	91	T9

R

Name	Page	Grid
Rabbits rd E12	53	S11
Rabournmead dr Nthlt	40	C15
Raby rd N Mal	117	Z8
Racton rd SW6	153	S15
Radbourne ave W5	72	E10
Radbourne cres E17	33	W5
Radbourne rd SW12	89	W19
Radcliffe ave NW10	62	F5
Radcliffe ave Enf	8	A4
Radcliffe gdns Cars	130	J18
Radcliffe rd N21	17	X4
Radcliffe rd Croy	133	U3
Radcliffe rd Har	23	X7
Radcliffe sq SW15	87	P15
Radcot st SE11	157	V11
Raddington rd W10	145	N2
Radfield way Sid	96	F18
Radford rd SE13	93	V15
Radford way Bark	67	Y8
Radipole rd SW6	87	V1
Radland rd E16	65	S17
Radlet ave SE26	110	B6
Radlett pl NW8	138	K5
Radley ave Ilf	54	M12
Radley gdns Har	24	L13
Radley ms W8	153	W4
Radley rd N17	31	T6
Radleys la E18	34	E7
Radleys mead Dag	56	G17
Radlix rd E10	51	O4
Radnor ave Har	23	S14
Radnor ave Well	97	P13
Radnor clo Chis	114	H16
Radnor clo Mitch	122	B10
Radnor cres SE18	79	Z18
Radnor cres Ilf	35	U16
Radnor gdns Enf	8	E5
Radnor gdns Twick	101	V3
Radnor ms W2	146	H6
Radnor pl W2	146	J5
Radnor rd NW6	136	L5
Radnor rd SE15	159	S17
Radnor rd Har	23	R14
Radnor rd Twick	101	W2
Radnor st EC1	142	C15
Radnor ter W14	153	O4
Radnor wk SW3	155	N10
Radnor wk Croy	124	K16
Radnor way NW10	61	S10
Radstock ave Har	24	A11
Radstock st SW11	154	K18
Raeburn ave Surb	117	S20
Raeburn clo NW11	28	C18
Raeburn clo Kings T	102	F19
Raeburn rd Edg	25	O6
Raeburn rd Sid	96	J16
Raeburn st SW2	90	B11
Rafford way Brom	126	H4
Raft rd SW18	87	Y12
Raggleswood Chis	113	X20
Raglan clo Houns	82	D13
Raglan ct S Croy	132	K10
Raglan ct Wem	43	O11
Raglan rd E17	33	V15
Raglan rd SE18	79	O13
Raglan rd Belv	81	P12
Raglan rd Brom	126	M10
Raglan rd Enf	18	F1
Raglan st NW5	47	T17
Raglan ter Har	41	K13
Raglan way Nthlt	41	N17
Ragley clo W3	73	V4
Raider clo Rom	38	F4
Railey ms NW5	47	U14
Railshead rd Twick	84	A10
Railton rd SE24	90	G11
Railway app SE1	150	G13
Railway app Har	23	V12
Railway app Wall	131	T13
Railway ave SE16	75	R5
Railway ms E3	64	A9

Railway ms W10	144	L5	Randle rd Rich	102	F10	Ravens clo Enf	8	D9	Ravensworth rd SE9	113	T8
Railway pas Tedd	101	X15	Randlesdown rd	111	N9	Ravens way SE12	94	E12	Ravent rd SE11	157	P6
Railway pl Belv	81	T8	SE6			Ravensbourne ave	111	X17	Ravey st EC2	142	J15
Railway rd Tedd	101	V10	Randolph ave W9	137	Z12	Brom			Ravine gro SE18	79	V16
Railway side SW13	86	C7	Randolph clo Bexh	98	K7	Ravensbourne gdns	60	A15	Rawlings st SW3	155	N6
Railway st N1	140	L9	Randolph clo	103	W13	W13			Rawlins clo N3	27	S9
Railway st Rom	55	T2	Kings T			Ravensbourne gdns	35	X3	Rawlins clo S Croy	134	K17
Railway ter SE13	93	R12	Randolph cres W9	138	B17	Ilf			Rawnsley ave	120	H11
Rainborough clo	43	V17	Randolph gdns	137	X9	Ravensbourne pk	93	N17	Mitch		
NW10			NW6			SE6			Rawson st SW11	89	R2
Rainbow ave E14	76	D13	Randolph gro Rom	37	T16	Ravensbourne Park	92	M18	Rawstone pl EC1	141	W12
Rainbow st SE5	158	J18	Randolph ms W9	138	D18	cres SE6			Rawstorne st EC1	141	W12
Raine st E1	151	Y12	Randolph rd E17	33	S15	Ravensbourne pl	93	S3	Ray gdns Bark	68	A6
Rainham clo SE9	96	G16	Randolph rd W9	138	C18	SE13			Ray gdns Stan	11	P15
Rainham clo SW11	88	K15	Randolph st NW1	140	C1	Ravensbourne rd SE6	92	K20	Ray Lodge rd	21	Z18
Rainham rd NW10	136	E13	Randon clo Har	22	K6	Ravensbourne rd	126	E6	Wdf Grn		
Rainham rd Rain	57	T20	Ranelagh ave SW6	87	V6	Brom			Ray st EC1	141	U18
Rainham Road north	56	G7	Ranelagh ave SW13	86	H5	Ravensbourne rd	99	V7	Ray Street bri EC1	141	U18
Dag			Ranelagh bri W2	146	A2	Dart			Raydean rd Barn	4	M17
Rainham Road south	56	J12	Ranelagh clo Edg	12	C13	Ravensbourne rd	84	D15	Raydon st N19	47	T7
Dag			Ranelagh dr Edg	12	B13	Twick			Raydons gdns Dag	56	A13
Rainhill way E3	64	C8	Ranelagh dr Twick	84	C12	Ravensbury ave	120	E12	Raydons rd Dag	55	Z14
Rainsborough ave	75	V12	Ranelagh gdns E11	34	L15	Mord			Rayfield clo Brom	127	R15
SE8			Ranelagh gdns SW6	87	U7	Ravensbury gro	120	F10	Rayford ave SE12	94	C19
Rainsford clo Stan	11	R14	Ranelagh gdns W4	73	U18	Mitch			Rayleas clo SE18	95	Z2
Rainsford rd NW10	61	S7	Ranelagh gdns W6	74	E9	Ravensbury la Mitch	120	F10	Rayleigh ave Tedd	101	T16
Rainsford st W2	146	J4	Ranelagh gdns Ilf	53	V3	Ravensbury path	120	G9	Rayleigh clo N13	18	A10
Rainsford way Horn	57	V3	Ranelagh gdns SW1	155	V8	Mitch			Rayleigh ct Kings T	117	O3
Rainton rd SE7	77	U13	Ranelagh ms W5	72	G5	Ravensbury rd	105	Z4	Rayleigh ri S Croy	133	S14
Rainville rd W6	152	D15	Ranelagh pl N Mal	118	A11	SW18			Rayleigh rd N13	18	A10
Raith ave N14	16	L11	Ranelagh rd E6	66	J4	Ravensbury ter	106	B3	Rayleigh rd SW19	119	V1
Raleigh ave Wall	131	X8	Ranelagh rd E11	51	Z11	SW18			Rayleigh rd Wdf Grn	21	X19
Raleigh clo NW4	26	L15	Ranelagh rd E15	65	O5	Ravenscar rd Brom	111	Z10	Raymead NW4	27	N1
Raleigh ct Wall	131	T15	Ranelagh rd N17	31	T9	Ravenscourt ave W6	74	H11	Raymead ave	122	G11
Raleigh dr N20	15	X10	Ranelagh rd N22	30	C5	Ravenscourt gdns	74	F10	Th Hth		
Raleigh dr Surb	117	W20	Ranelagh rd NW10	62	D6	W6			Raymere gdns SE18	79	U18
Raleigh gdns Mitch	120	L5	Ranelagh rd SW1	156	C10	Ravenscourt pk W6	74	G10	Raymond ave E18	34	C9
Raleigh rd N8	30	F12	Ranelagh rd W5	72	G5	Ravenscourt pl W6	74	J11	Raymond ave W13	71	Z8
Raleigh rd SE20	110	E18	Ranelagh rd Sthl	70	A2	Ravenscourt rd W6	74	H10	Raymond bldgs WC1	141	P20
Raleigh rd Enf	8	B14	Ranelagh rd Wem	42	H16	Ravenscourt sq W6	74	F8	Raymond clo SE26	110	C11
Raleigh rd Rich	85	N8	Ranfurly rd Sutt	129	Z2	Ravenscraig rd N11	16	F13	Raymond rd E13	65	Y2
Raleigh rd Sthl	70	B12	Rangefield rd Brom	111	Z11	Ravenscroft ave	27	V20	Raymond rd SW19	105	T16
Raleigh st N1	141	Y6	Rangemoor rd N15	31	V15	NW11			Raymond rd Beck	124	H10
Raleigh way N14	16	M4	Rangers rd E4	21	R2	Ravenscroft ave	42	L3	Raymond rd Ilf	54	E1
Ralston st SW3	155	O11	Rangers rd Loug	21	T1	Wem			Raymouth rd SE16	159	Y5
Ram pas Kings T	116	G5	Rangers sq SE10	93	W1	Ravenscroft clo E16	65	T14	Rayne ct E18	34	C12
Ram pl E9	50	D17	Rangeworth pl Sid	114	M6	Ravenscroft pk Barn	4	D12	Rayners clo Wem	42	G14
Ram st SW18	88	A13	Rankin clo NW9	26	C10	Ravenscroft rd E16	65	U14	Rayners la Har	40	F4
Rama ct Har	41	T7	Ranleigh gdns Bexh	81	P9	Ravenscroft rd W4	73	W10	Rayners la Pnr	22	D14
Ramac Industrial est	77	U11	Ranmoor clo Har	23	R13	Ravenscroft rd Beck	124	D4	Rayners rd SW15	87	R13
SE7			Ranmoor gdns Har	23	S13	Ravenscroft st E2	143	P10	Raynes ave E11	52	L1
Ramac way SE7	77	U13	Ranmore ave Croy	133	V7	Ravensdale ave N12	15	S14	Raynham ave N18	18	L18
Rambler clo SW16	107	U10	Ranmore rd Sutt	129	P20	Ravensdale gdns	109	P19	Raynham rd N18	18	K15
Ramilies clo SW2	90	A14	Rannoch rd W6	152	E14	SE19			Raynham rd W6	74	J10
Ramillies pl W1	148	B6	Rannock ave NW9	43	Z2	Ravensdale rd N16	31	V20	Raynham ter N18	18	K16
Ramillies rd NW7	13	O9	Ranston rd NW1	138	K19	Ravensdale rd Houns	82	B7	Raynor clo Sthl	70	D3
Ramillies rd W4	73	Z9	Ranulf rd NW2	45	N11	Ravensdon st SE11	157	U11	Raynor pl N1	142	C2
Ramillies rd Sid	97	R15	Ranwell st E3	63	X4	Ravensfield clo Dag	55	Y12	Raynton clo Har	40	C3
Ramillies st W1	148	B5	Ranworth clo Erith	99	S4	Ravensfield gdns	128	B10	Rays av N18	19	O14
Rampart st E1	151	W6	Ranworth rd N9	19	O8	Epsom			Rays rd N18	19	O14
Rampayne st SW1	156	F9	Raphael ave Rom	39	S8	Ravenshaw st NW6	45	W16	Rays rd W Wick	125	V18
Rampton clo E4	20	A10	Raphael st SW7	147	N19	Ravenshill Chis	127	Y2	Reachview clo NW1	140	C1
Rams gro Rom	38	A12	Rasper rd N20	15	S9	Ravenshurst ave	26	M12	Reading la E8	50	A18
Ramsay pl Har	41	S4	Rastell ave SW2	107	X3	NW4			Reading rd Nthlt	40	L14
Ramsay rd E7	52	A12	Ratcliff rd E7	52	K9	Ravenside clo N18	19	S17	Reading rd Sutt	130	E12
Ramsay rd W3	73	W7	Ratcliffe Cross st E1	63	U18	Ravenslea rd SW12	88	M19	Reading way NW7	14	D16
Ramscroft clo N9	18	D3	Ratcliffe la E14	63	V18	Ravensmead rd	111	X18	Reapers clo NW1	140	F4
Ramsdale rd SW17	107	P13	Rathbone pl W1	148	E4	Brom			Reardon path E1	151	X14
Ramsden dr Rom	38	F2	Rathbone st E16	65	P16	Ravenstone rd N8	30	E10	Reardon st E1	151	X12
Ramsden rd N11	16	A16	Rathbone st W1	148	D2	Ravenstone st SW12	107	R2	Reaston st SE14	75	S19
Ramsden rd SW12	89	O16	Rathcoole ave N8	30	D14	Ravenswood Bex	115	Z1	Reckitt rd W4	74	A14
Ramsey clo NW9	26	E18	Rathcoole gdns N8	30	D15	Ravenswood ave	135	U1	Record st SE15	75	P15
Ramsey clo Grnf	41	O15	Rathfern rd SE6	110	M2	W Wick			Recovery st SW17	106	J12
Ramsey rd Th Hth	122	E14	Rathgar ave W13	72	C4	Ravenswood ct	103	U16	Recreation ave Rom	38	L16
Ramsey st E2	143	U15	Rathgar clo N3	27	V6	Kings T			Recreation rd SE26	110	E9
Ramsey way N14	16	H3	Rathmell dr SW4	89	X16	Ravenswood cres	40	D6	Recreation rd Brom	126	B3
Ramsgate st E8	49	V17	Rathmore rd SE7	77	W13	Har			Recreation rd Sid	114	J7
Ramsgill app Ilf	36	K14	Rattray rd SW2	90	F11	Ravenswood cres	125	T20	Recreation rd Sthl	70	A10
Ramsgill dr Ilf	36	L13	Raul rd SE15	91	Y3	W Wick			Recreation way	121	Z8
Ramulis dr Hayes	58	A12	Raveley st NW5	47	U12	Ravenswood gdns	83	U2	Mitch		
Rancliffe gdns SE9	95	R10	Raven clo NW9	26	L19	Islw			Rector st N1	142	B5
Rancliffe rd E6	66	E7	Raven rd E18	34	K6	Ravenswood rd E17	33	T14	Rectory clo E4	20	B10
Randall ave NW2	44	C7	Raven row E1	151	Y1	Ravenswood rd	89	T19	Rectory clo N3	27	W5
Randall clo SW11	88	J1	Ravenet st SW11	89	S2	SW12			Rectory clo SW20	118	M5
Randall clo Erith	81	Z17	Ravenhill rd E13	65	Y5	Ravenswood rd Croy	132	Z4	Rectory clo Dart	99	S11
Randall pl SE10	76	F18	Ravenna rd SW15	87	P12	Ravensworth rd	62	K7	Rectory clo Sid	115	R10
Randall rd SE11	157	N8	Ravenor Park rd Grnf	58	K8	NW10			Rectory clo Stan	11	O17
Randall row SE11	157	N8	Ravens clo Brom	126	C5				Rectory cres E11	34	K18
Randell's rd N1	140	L3							Rectory Farm rd Enf	7	R3

Name	Page	Grid
Rectory Field cres SE7	77	X18
Rectory gdns N8	30	A12
Rectory gdns SW4	89	V7
Rectory gdns Nthlt	58	F2
Rectory grn Beck	124	M2
Rectory gro SW4	89	V7
Rectory gro Croy	132	J4
Rectory gro Hmptn	100	D10
Rectory la SW17	107	O14
Rectory la Edg	12	D18
Rectory la Sid	115	R10
Rectory la Stan	11	O17
Rectory la Surb	116	C20
Rectory la Wall	131	W7
Rectory Orchard SW19	105	T11
Rectory Park ave Nthlt	58	D8
Rectory pl SE18	78	J11
Rectory rd E12	53	V16
Rectory rd E17	33	R12
Rectory rd N16	49	V8
Rectory rd SW13	86	H4
Rectory rd W3	73	U2
Rectory rd Beck	125	N2
Rectory rd Dag	56	G19
Rectory rd Sthl	70	E9
Rectory rd Sutt	129	Z7
Rectory sq E1	63	T14
Reculver ms N18	18	L14
Reculver rd SE16	75	S13
Red Anchor clo SW3	154	J14
Red Barracks rd SE18	78	G11
Red hill Chis	113	Y13
Red House la Bexh	97	Y11
Red House rd Croy	121	Y14
Red Lion clo SE17	158	D13
Red Lion hill N2	28	F8
Red Lion la SE18	95	W2
Red Lion rd Surb	117	P20
Red Lion row SE17	158	D14
Red Lion sq WC1	149	N1
Red Lion st WC1	149	O1
Red Lion st Rich	84	H13
Red Lodge rd W Wick	125	V19
Red path E9	50	L17
Red pl W1	147	T8
Red Post hill SE21	91	Y6
Red Post hill SE24	91	N11
Redan pl W2	145	Y6
Redan st W14	152	G1
Redan ter SE5	90	K5
Redberry gro SE26	110	C6
Redbourne ave N3	27	Z4
Redbridge gdns SE5	158	L20
Redbridge Lane east Ilf	35	O17
Redbridge Lane west E11	34	J19
Redburn st SW3	155	N12
Redcar clo Nthlt	40	K16
Redcar st SE5	158	A19
Redcastle clo E1	63	P19
Redchurch st E2	142	M16
Redcliffe gdns SW10	153	Z11
Redcliffe gdns Ilf	53	V3
Redcliffe ms SW10	154	A11
Redcliffe pl SW10	154	B14
Redcliffe rd SW10	154	C12
Redcliffe sq SW10	153	Y12
Redcliffe st SW10	153	Z12
Redclose ave Mord	119	Y12
Redclyffe rd E6	65	Z3
Redcroft rd Sthl	58	M18
Redcross way SE1	150	C16
Reddings the NW7	13	R11
Reddings clo NW7	13	S12
Reddins rd SE15	159	S16
Reddons rd Beck	110	H17
Rede pl W2	145	V7
Redesdale gdns Islw	71	X19
Redesdale st SW3	155	N12
Redfern ave Houns	82	G19
Redfern rd NW10	62	B1
Redfern rd SE6	93	V19
Redfield la SW5	153	W5
Redford ave Th Hth	122	E10
Redford ave Wall	131	Z13
Redgate ter SW15	87	R15
Redgrave clo Croy	123	W15
Redgrave rd SW15	87	P9
Redhill dr Edg	25	U8
Redhill st NW1	139	Y11
Redington gdns NW3	46	A11
Redington rd NW3	46	B12
Redlands rd Enf	9	V6
Redlands way SW2	90	C19
Redlaw way SE16	159	U10
Redleaf clo Belv	81	R16
Redlees clo Islw	83	X11
Redman's rd E1	63	R14
Redmead la E1	151	T13
Redmore rd W6	74	J10
Redpoll way Erith	80	K7
Redriff rd SE16	75	V8
Redriff rd Rom	38	J7
Redriffe rd E13	65	R4
Redroofs clo Beck	111	R20
Redruth rd E9	63	S3
Redstart clo E6	66	D14
Redston rd N8	29	W12
Redvers rd N22	30	F6
Redvers st N1	142	L11
Redwald rd E5	50	G12
Redway dr Twick	83	N17
Redwood clo SE16	75	W4
Redwood way Barn	4	B16
Redwoods SW15	104	G2
Reece ms SW7	154	F6
Reed clo E16	65	T15
Reed clo SE12	94	F13
Reed Pond wk Rom	39	U6
Reed rd N17	31	W8
Reede rd Dag	56	E17
Reede way Dag	56	H16
Reedham clo N17	32	A12
Reedham st SE15	91	W6
Reedholm vill N16	49	P12
Reedworth st SE11	157	U7
Reenglass rd Stan	11	V13
Rees gdns Croy	123	V15
Rees st N1	142	D5
Reesland clo E12	53	W16
Reets Farm clo NW9	26	B17
Reeves ave NW9	43	X1
Reeves corner Croy	132	K4
Reeves ms W1	147	U11
Reeves rd E3	64	D10
Reeves rd SE18	78	L17
Reform row N17	31	W7
Reform st SW11	88	M4
Regal clo E1	151	U1
Regal clo W5	60	H15
Regal ct N18	18	J15
Regal cres Wall	131	S5
Regal way Har	24	H17
Regan way N1	142	J9
Regarth ave Rom	39	R18
Regency clo W5	60	K17
Regency clo Hmptn	100	E11
Regency ct Enf	8	C17
Regency cres NW4	27	R7
Regency ms NW10	44	H18
Regency ms Beck	111	U19
Regency ms Islw	83	S14
Regency st SW1	156	G7
Regency wk Croy	124	K15
Regency way Bexh	97	X8
Regent clo N12	15	R17
Regent clo Har	24	J18
Regent gdns Ilf	36	M19
Regent pl W1	148	C9
Regent pl Croy	123	U20
Regent rd SE24	90	J14
Regent rd Surb	117	O12
Regent sq E3	64	D9
Regent sq WC1	140	M14
Regent sq Belv	81	U11
Regent st NW10	136	H14
Regent st SW1	148	E11
Regent st W1	147	Z4
Regent st W4	73	P15
Regents ave N13	17	S16
Regents Bridge gdns SW8	156	M16
Regents clo S Croy	133	S13
Regents ms NW8	138	D9
Regents pk NW1	139	R10
Regents Park est NW1	139	Z14
Regents Park rd N3	27	V11
Regents Park rd NW1	139	R1
Regents Park ter NW1	139	X4
Regent's pl SE3	94	E4
Regents row E8	143	U5
Regina clo Barn	4	B11
Regina rd N4	48	D4
Regina rd SE25	123	Y7
Regina rd W13	71	Z3
Regina ter W13	72	A3
Reginald rd E7	52	E19
Reginald rd SE8	76	B20
Reginald sq SE8	76	B20
Regis rd NW5	47	S15
Regnart bldgs NW1	140	D15
Reidhaven rd SE18	79	V11
Reigate ave Sutt	129	Y2
Reigate rd Brom	112	D6
Reigate rd Ilf	54	K7
Reigate way Wall	132	B10
Reighton rd E5	49	Y8
Relay rd W12	144	E11
Relf rd SE15	91	X6
Relko gdns Sutt	130	G11
Rembrandt clo E14	76	J9
Rembrandt rd SE13	93	Z11
Rembrandt rd Edg	25	P6
Remington rd E6	66	D16
Remington rd N15	31	P17
Remington st N1	141	Y10
Remnant st WC2	149	N4
Rempstone ms N1	142	G8
Remus rd E3	64	A1
Rendlesham clo Brom	126	M1
Rendlesham rd E5	49	X11
Rendlesham rd Enf	7	X4
Renforth st SE16	75	R6
Renfrew clo E6	66	J19
Renfrew rd SE11	157	W6
Renfrew rd Houns	82	A4
Renfrew rd Kings T	103	U17
Renmuir st SW17	106	M15
Rennell st SE13	93	U8
Renness rd E17	32	J11
Rennets clo SE9	96	G13
Rennets Wood rd SE9	96	F13
Rennie est SE16	159	Y7
Rennie st SE1	149	W12
Renown clo Croy	132	J2
Renown clo Rom	38	F4
Rensburg rd E17	32	F16
Renshaw clo Belv	81	P16
Renters ave NW4	27	N19
Renwick rd Bark	68	E12
Rephidim st SE1	158	H2
Replingham rd SW18	105	W1
Reporton rd SW6	152	M20
Repository rd SE18	78	H15
Repton ave Rom	39	W10
Repton ave Wem	42	E12
Repton clo Cars	130	J13
Repton ct Beck	111	S20
Repton dr Rom	39	W11
Repton gdns Rom	39	X11
Repton gro Ilf	35	V4
Repton rd Har	25	N13
Repton st E14	63	W16
Repulse clo Rom	38	G3
Reservoir rd N14	6	G16
Reservoir rd SE4	92	H5
Restell clo SE3	77	O16
Reston pl SW7	146	B19
Restons cres SE9	96	E15
Restormel clo Houns	82	H12
Retford st N1	142	L10
Retingham way E4	20	E8
Retreat the NW9	25	X14
Retreat the Har	40	J1
Retreat the Surb	116	M15
Retreat the Th Hth	123	O8
Retreat the Wor Pk	128	K4
Retreat clo Har	24	F15
Retreat pl E9	50	D18
Retreat rd Rich	84	G13
Revell ri SE18	79	X17
Revell rd Kings T	117	U12
Revell rd Sutt	129	V13
Revelon rd SE4	92	H8
Revelstoke rd SW18	105	Y4
Reventlow rd SE9	114	B2
Reverdy rd SE1	159	S6
Reverend clo Har	40	K9
Revesby rd Cars	120	H16
Review rd NW2	44	D7
Review rd Dag	69	U4
Rewell st SW6	154	A19
Rewley rd Cars	120	G16
Rex clo Rom	38	J2
Rex pl W1	147	U11
Reydon ave E11	34	K17
Reynard clo Brom	127	V5
Reynard dr SE19	109	U18
Reynardson rd N17	31	N2
Reynolds ave E12	53	Y15
Reynolds ave Rom	37	U20
Reynolds clo NW11	46	A2
Reynolds clo SW19	120	G2
Reynolds clo Cars	131	N1
Reynolds dr Edg	25	P8
Reynolds pl SE3	77	W19
Reynolds pl SE15	92	D12
Reynolds rd W4	73	W7
Reynolds rd N Mal	117	Z17
Reynolds way Croy	133	T7
Rheidol ms N1	142	A7
Rheidol ter N1	141	Z7
Rheingold way Wall	132	A19
Rheola clo N17	31	W5
Rhoda st E2	143	O15
Rhodes ave N22	29	U5
Rhodes Moorhouse ct Mord	119	Y15
Rhodesia rd E11	51	X6
Rhodesia rd SW9	90	B6
Rhodeswell rd E14	63	X14
Rhondda gro E3	63	X9
Rhyl rd Grnf	59	X6
Rhyl st NW5	47	P17
Rhys ave N11	16	L20
Rialto rd Mitch	121	R3
Ribblesdale ave Nthlt	40	V19
Ribblesdale rd N8	30	D13
Ribblesdale rd SW16	107	S15
Ribchester ave Grnf	59	W8
Ricardo st E14	64	D17
Ricards rd SW19	105	W12
Rich la SW5	153	X10
Richard clo SE18	78	E11
Richard Foster clo E17	32	L20
Richard st E1	151	W6
Richards ave Rom	38	L17
Richards clo Har	23	X16
Richards clo (Bushey) Wat	10	C2
Richards pl E17	33	O11
Richards pl SW3	154	M4
Richardson clo E8	143	N4
Richardson rd E15	64	M6
Richardson's ms W1	140	M13
Richbell pl WC1	141	O20
Richborne ter SW8	157	O17
Richborough rd NW2	45	R13
Riches rd Ilf	54	B7
Richfield rd (Bushey) Wat	10	B3
Richford rd E15	65	P3
Richford st W6	144	B19
Richlands ave Epsom	128	H10
Richmond ave E4	20	K15
Richmond ave N1	141	O4
Richmond ave NW10	44	L18
Richmond ave SW20	119	U2

Richmond bri Rich	84	G14
Richmond bldgs W1	148	E6
Richmond clo E17	32	M18
Richmond cres E4	20	K16
Richmond cres N1	141	R3
Richmond cres N9	18	L4
Richmond gdns NW4	26	H14
Richmond gdns Har	10	H20
Richmond grn Croy	132	B6
Richmond gro N1	141	X1
Richmond hill Rich	84	J15
Richmond Hill ct Rich	84	J15
Richmond ms W1	148	E7
Richmond Park heights Kings T	103	W11
Richmond Park rd SW14	85	W12
Richmond Park rd Kings T	102	K19
Richmond pl SE18	79	P11
Richmond rd E4	20	K5
Richmond rd E7	52	J15
Richmond rd E8	49	U19
Richmond rd E11	51	W6
Richmond rd N11	17	N20
Richmond rd N15	31	S19
Richmond rd SW20	118	H1
Richmond rd W5	72	J5
Richmond rd Barn	5	P17
Richmond rd Croy	132	A6
Richmond rd Ilf	54	B8
Richmond rd Islw	83	Z9
Richmond rd Kings T	102	G10
Richmond rd Rom	39	T18
Richmond rd Th Hth	122	H7
Richmond rd Twick	84	B19
Richmond st E13	65	U6
Richmond way E11	52	F6
Richmond way W12	144	H18
Richmond way W14	144	H20
Richmount gdns SE3	94	G8
Rickard clo NW4	26	H13
Rickard clo SW2	108	E1
Rickett st W6	153	V12
Rickman st E1	63	R10
Rickyard path SE9	95	S10
Ridding la Grnf	41	V15
Riddons rd SE12	112	L7
Ride the Brent	72	C13
Ride the Enf	9	K2
Rideout st SE18	78	F12
Rider clo Sid	96	H15
Ridgdale st E3	64	C7
Ridge the Bex	98	C17
Ridge the Surb	117	O12
Ridge the Twick	83	P19
Ridge ave N21	17	Z2
Ridge ave Dart	99	T15
Ridge clo NW4	27	P8
Ridge clo NW9	25	Z13
Ridge Crest Enf	7	S5
Ridge hill NW11	45	T3
Ridge rd N8	30	D19
Ridge rd N21	18	A4
Ridge rd NW2	45	W8
Ridge rd Mitch	107	S17
Ridge rd Sutt	129	S1
Ridge way Dart	99	T16
Ridge way Felt	100	A7
Ridgebrook rd SE3	94	M9
Ridgemont gdns Edg	12	J14
Ridgemount ave Croy	134	G2
Ridgemount gdns Enf	7	V9
Ridgeview clo Barn	4	C19
Ridgeview rd N20	15	P11
Ridgeway Wdf Grn	21	Z14
Ridgeway the E4	20	E7
Ridgeway the N3	28	A2
Ridgeway the N11	15	Y14
Ridgeway the N14	17	O7
Ridgeway the NW7	13	U11
Ridgeway the NW9	25	Z13
Ridgeway the NW11	45	T2
Ridgeway the W3	73	P7

Ridgeway the Croy	132	D7
Ridgeway the Enf	7	O1
Ridgeway the Har	22	E15
Ridgeway the (Kenton) Har	24	C19
Ridgeway the (Gidea Pk) Rom	39	W12
Ridgeway the Stan	11	P19
Ridgeway the Sutt	130	G17
Ridgeway ave Barn	5	Y20
Ridgeway dr Brom	112	H10
Ridgeway east Sid	96	K13
Ridgeway gdns N6	47	W1
Ridgeway gdns Ilf	35	S14
Ridgeway rd SW9	90	J8
Ridgeway rd Islw	71	T20
Ridgeway Road north Islw	71	T18
Ridgeway west Sid	96	H12
Ridgewell clo Dag	69	V2
Ridgewell rd E16	65	Z14
Ridgmount gdns WC1	140	F19
Ridgmount pl WC1	148	F1
Ridgmount rd SW18	88	B14
Ridgmount st WC1	140	F20
Ridgway SW19	105	N18
Ridgway gdns SW19	105	P17
Ridgway pl SW19	105	T16
Riding the NW11	45	V2
Riding House st W1	148	A3
Ridings the W5	60	M11
Ridings the Surb	117	R12
Ridings ave N21	7	X15
Ridings clo N6	47	V2
Ridler rd Enf	8	F4
Ridley ave W13	72	B8
Ridley clo Rom	39	Z3
Ridley rd E7	52	L11
Ridley rd E8	49	V16
Ridley rd NW10	62	G5
Ridley rd SW19	106	A17
Ridley rd Brom	126	D6
Ridley rd Well	97	P2
Ridsdale rd SE20	109	Z19
Riefield rd SE9	96	D10
Riesco dr Croy	134	D14
Riffel rd NW2	44	M15
Rifle pl SE11	157	U12
Rifle pl W11	144	H12
Rifle st E14	64	E15
Rigault rd SW6	87	U5
Rigby clo Croy	132	F5
Rigby ms Ilf	53	Y7
Rigeley rd NW10	62	H8
Rigg app E10	50	H5
Rigge pl SW4	89	Y11
Riggindale rd SW16	107	X12
Riley rd SE1	150	M20
Riley rd Enf	9	R4
Riley st SW10	154	F16
Rinaldo rd SW12	89	S19
Ring the W2	146	K9
Ring clo Brom	112	J18
Ringcroft st N7	48	F16
Ringers rd Brom	126	E6
Ringford rd SW18	87	X15
Ringmer ave SW6	87	T3
Ringmer gdns N19	48	A6
Ringmer pl N21	8	B17
Ringmer way Brom	127	T11
Ringmore ri SE23	92	B18
Ringslade rd N22	30	D6
Ringstead rd SE6	93	S18
Ringstead rd Sutt	130	H10
Ringway N11	16	G18
Ringway Sthl	70	A14
Ringwold clo Beck	110	H19
Ringwood ave N2	29	N9
Ringwood ave Croy	122	B17
Ringwood gdns SW15	104	G3
Ringwood rd E17	32	L17
Ringwood way N21	17	V4
Ringwood way Hmptn	100	H10
Ripley clo Brom	127	T11
Ripley clo Croy	135	U15

Ripley gdns SW14	85	Z7
Ripley gdns Sutt	130	C9
Ripley ms E11	33	Z20
Ripley rd E16	65	Y16
Ripley rd Belv	81	R10
Ripley rd Enf	7	V4
Ripley rd Hmptn	100	F18
Ripley rd Ilf	54	K7
Ripley vill W5	60	E17
Ripon clo Nthlt	40	J16
Ripon gdns Ilf	35	R20
Ripon rd N9	19	N2
Ripon rd N17	31	O11
Ripon rd SE18	78	M17
Ritches rd N15	30	C9
Rippersley rd Well	97	N2
Ripple rd Bark	67	S3
Ripple rd Dag	69	P4
Rippleside Industrial est Bark	68	D4
Ripplevale gro N1	141	R2
Rippolson rd SE18	79	Y13
Risborough dr Wor Pk	118	H17
Risborough st SE1	149	Z16
Risdon st SE16	75	R6
Rise the E11	34	E15
Rise the N13	17	T14
Rise the NW7	13	S20
Rise the NW10	43	Z11
Rise the Bex	97	T20
Rise the Dart	99	U11
Rise the Edg	12	E15
Rise the Grnf	41	Y15
Rise Park boul Rom	39	S5
Risebridge rd Rom	39	V6
Risedale rd Bexh	98	J6
Riseldine rd SE23	92	H16
Risinghill st N1	141	R9
Risingholme clo Har	23	T5
Risingholme rd Har	23	T6
Risings the E17	33	X12
Risley ave N17	30	M4
Rita rd SW8	157	N16
Ritchie rd Croy	124	A15
Ritchie st N1	141	U7
Ritchings ave E17	32	J12
Ritherdon rd SW17	107	P5
Ritson rd E8	49	W17
Ritter st SE18	78	J17
Rivaz pl E9	50	D17
Rivenhall gdns E18	34	C12
River ave N13	17	V10
River bank N21	17	Z2
River clo E11	34	L18
River clo Surb	116	G11
River Front Enf	8	D12
River gdns Cars	131	O4
River Grove pk Beck	125	N1
River la Rich	84	H20
River Meads ave Twick	100	J6
River Park gdns Brom	111	X18
River Park rd N22	30	D6
River pl N1	142	A1
River Reach Tedd	102	E14
River rd Bark	67	W6
River Road Business pk Bark	67	X9
River st EC1	141	T12
River ter W6	152	B11
River View gdns Twick	101	W5
River way SE10	77	P7
River way Epsom	128	A12
River way Twick	100	J5
Riverbank way Brent	72	D16
Rivercourt rd W6	74	J12
Riverdale gdns Twick	84	E14
Riverdale rd SE18	79	X13
Riverdale rd Bex	98	A17
Riverdale rd Erith	81	V15
Riverdale rd Felt	100	C9
Riverdale rd Twick	84	E15
Riverdene Edg	12	J11
Riverdene rd Ilf	53	Y10

Riverhead clo E17	32	E6
Riverholme dr Epsom	128	A19
Rivermead clo Tedd	102	C14
Riversdale rd N5	48	K10
Riversdale rd Rom	38	G1
Riversfield rd Enf	8	E10
Riverside NW4	44	J1
Riverside SE7	77	X8
Riverside Twick	102	A1
Riverside clo E5	50	D5
Riverside clo W7	59	U12
Riverside clo Kings T	116	H9
Riverside clo Wall	131	S6
Riverside dr W4	73	Z20
Riverside dr Mitch	120	J11
Riverside dr Rich	102	D4
Riverside gdns W6	74	K12
Riverside gdns Enf	8	A9
Riverside gdns Wem	60	K6
Riverside Industrial est Bark	68	B8
Riverside Industrial est Enf	9	W20
Riverside rd E15	64	J6
Riverside rd N15	31	X18
Riverside rd SW17	106	B9
Riverside rd Sid	115	Z6
Riverside wk SE1	149	O15
Riverside wk Bex	97	U20
Riverside wk Islw	83	T9
Riverton clo W9	137	P15
Riverview gdns SW13	152	A13
Riverview gro W4	73	T18
Riverview pk SE6	111	N4
Riverview rd W4	73	T18
Riverway N13	17	T15
Rivington ave Wdf Grn	35	N7
Rivington ct NW10	62	F4
Rivington cres NW7	26	C2
Rivington pl EC2	142	L14
Rivington st EC2	142	J15
Rivington wk E8	143	T4
Rivulet rd N17	30	K1
Rixsen rd E12	53	S15
Roach rd E3	51	O20
Roads jn N19	48	B6
Roan st SE10	76	F18
Robb rd Stan	10	M19
Robert Adam st W1	147	T4
Robert clo W9	138	D18
Robert Dashwood way SE17	158	A7
Robert Lowe clo SE14	75	U19
Robert Owen ho SW6	87	R1
Robert st E16	78	L4
Robert st NW1	139	Z13
Robert st SE18	79	S13
Robert st WC2	148	M11
Roberta st E2	143	T13
Roberton dr Brom	126	L2
Roberts clo SE9	114	D2
Roberts clo Rom	39	Z3
Roberts clo Sutt	129	R16
Robert's pl EC1	141	U17
Roberts rd E17	33	R4
Roberts rd NW7	14	E17
Roberts rd Belv	81	T14
Roberts st Croy	132	M6
Robertsbridge rd Cars	120	D19
Robertson rd E15	64	H3
Robertson st SW8	89	S6
Robin clo NW7	13	N10
Robin clo Hmptn	100	C13
Robin clo Rom	39	N1
Robin ct SE16	159	R4
Robin cres E6	66	C14
Robin gro N6	47	O5
Robin gro Brent	72	E16
Robin gro Har	25	O19
Robin Hill dr Chis	113	S15
Robin Hood dr Har	23	V2
Robin Hood la E14	64	H19

Robin Hood la SW15	104	A11
Robin Hood la Bexh	98	A12
Robin Hood la Sutt	129	Y11
Robin Hood rd SW19	104	K12
Robin Hood way SW15	104	B8
Robin Hood way SW20	104	B14
Robin Hood way Grnf	41	W17
Robina clo Bexh	97	Y10
Robinhood clo Mitch	121	W8
Robinhood la Mitch	121	W7
Robins ct SE12	112	L7
Robinson clo Horn	57	Z20
Robinson rd E2	63	P6
Robinson rd SW17	106	H15
Robinson rd Dag	56	D11
Robinson's clo W13	59	Z15
Robinwood pl SW15	103	Y9
Robsart st SW9	90	E4
Robson ave NW10	62	H1
Robson clo E6	66	D17
Robson clo Enf	7	V9
Robson rd SE27	108	K7
Roch ave Edg	25	N6
Rochdale rd E17	33	N20
Rochdale rd SE2	80	C13
Roche rd SW16	122	B1
Roche wk Cars	120	F16
Rochelle clo SW11	88	F11
Rochelle st E2	143	O15
Rochester ave E13	65	X4
Rochester ave Brom	126	H4
Rochester clo SW16	108	B18
Rochester clo Enf	8	F6
Rochester clo Sid	97	R14
Rochester dr Bex	98	C15
Rochester gdns Croy	133	S6
Rochester gdns Ilf	53	T2
Rochester ms NW1	47	V19
Rochester pl NW1	47	U19
Rochester rd NW1	47	U19
Rochester rd Cars	131	N8
Rochester row SW1	156	D6
Rochester sq NW1	47	W20
Rochester st SW1	156	E3
Rochester ter NW1	47	U19
Rochester wk SE1	150	E13
Rochester way SE3	94	L6
Rochester way SE9	95	V11
Rochester way Dart	99	O19
Rochester Way Relief rd SE3	94	J3
Rochester Way Relief rd SE9	95	V12
Rochford ave Rom	37	T14
Rochford clo E6	66	B5
Rochford st NW5	47	T19
Rochford way Croy	121	Z14
Rock ave SW14	85	Z8
Rock gdns Dag	56	G15
Rock Grove way SE16	159	V4
Rock hill SE26	109	V10
Rock st N4	48	H7
Rockbourne rd SE23	110	E2
Rockells pl SE22	92	B16
Rockford ave Grnf	60	A7
Rockhall rd NW2	45	O13
Rockhampton clo SE27	108	F9
Rockhampton rd SE27	108	F9
Rockhampton rd S Croy	133	R15
Rockingham ave Horn	39	Z19
Rockingham clo SW15	86	C10
Rockingham est SE1	158	B2
Rockingham st SE1	158	A2
Rockland rd SW15	87	T11
Rocklands dr Stan	24	C8
Rockley rd W14	144	F18
Rockmount rd SE18	79	T14
Rockmount rd SE19	109	P16
Rocks la SW13	86	D8
Rockwell rd Dag	56	G15
Rockwells gdns SE19	109	T11
Rockwood pl W12	144	D17
Rocliffe st N1	141	Y10
Rocombe cres SE23	92	C19

Rocque la SE3	94	D6
Rodborough rd NW11	45	W3
Roden ct N6	47	W1
Roden gdns Croy	123	R16
Roden st N7	48	C10
Roden st Ilf	53	Y10
Rodenhurst rd SW4	89	W17
Roderick rd NW3	46	M13
Roding Lane north Wdf Grn	35	O8
Roding Lane south Ilf	35	O17
Roding Lane south Wdf Grn	35	O9
Roding ms E1	151	U12
Roding rd E5	50	G13
Roding rd E6	66	L14
Rodmarton st W1	147	R2
Rodmell clo Hayes	58	B12
Rodmell slope N12	14	J15
Rodmill la SW2	90	B19
Rodney clo Croy	132	K1
Rodney clo N Mal	118	A11
Rodney ct W9	138	D15
Rodney pl E17	32	K6
Rodney pl SE17	158	D4
Rodney pl SW19	106	C20
Rodney rd E11	34	H14
Rodney rd SE17	158	E6
Rodney rd Mitch	120	J5
Rodney rd N Mal	118	A11
Rodney rd Twick	82	H17
Rodney st N1	141	P10
Rodney way Rom	38	G4
Rodway rd SW15	86	H18
Rodway rd Brom	112	H20
Rodwell pl Edg	12	C19
Rodwell rd SE22	91	V14
Roe end NW9	25	V12
Roe grn NW9	25	W14
Roe la NW9	25	U12
Roe way Wall	132	B15
Roebourne way E16	78	J4
Roebuck la N17	21	Y3
Roedean ave Enf	9	P4
Roedean clo Enf	9	P5
Roedean cres SW15	86	A14
Roehampton clo SW15	86	G11
Roehampton dr Chis	114	D17
Roehampton gate SW15	86	B15
Roehampton High st SW15	86	H18
Roehampton la SW15	86	G14
Roehampton vale SW15	104	B7
Roffey st E14	76	F6
Roger st WC1	141	P18
Rogers gdns Dag	56	F15
Rogers rd E16	65	R17
Rogers rd SW17	106	H9
Rogers rd Dag	56	F16
Rojack rd SE23	110	E1
Rokeby gdns Wdf Grn	34	F3
Rokeby pl SW20	104	K18
Rokeby rd SE4	92	M4
Rokeby st E15	64	L3
Rokesby clo Well	96	G5
Rokesby pl Wem	42	F16
Rokesly ave N8	30	A14
Roland gdns SW7	154	D8
Roland rd E17	33	W14
Roland way SE17	158	G12
Roland way Wor Pk	128	E2
Roles gro Rom	37	X12
Rolfe clo Barn	5	X15
Roll gdns Ilf	35	X15
Rollesby way SE28	68	F18
Rolleston ave Orp	127	Z15
Rolleston rd S Croy	133	O17
Rollins st SE15	75	R16
Rollit cres Houns	82	H13
Rolls bldgs EC4	149	T5
Rolls Park ave E4	20	C17
Rolls Park rd E4	20	D16
Rolls rd SE1	159	O8
Rollscourt ave SE24	90	L13

Rolt st SE8	75	W16
Rolvenden gdns Brom	113	O19
Rolvenden pl N17	31	Y3
Rom cres Rom	57	S2
Rom Valley way Rom	39	R19
Roma Read clo SW15	86	H20
Roma rd E17	32	J10
Roman ri SE19	109	P14
Roman rd E2	143	Z13
Roman rd E3	63	W6
Roman rd E6	66	C12
Roman rd N10	29	R2
Roman rd W4	74	C10
Roman rd Ilf	54	B16
Roman sq SE28	80	B3
Roman way N7	48	C17
Roman way Croy	132	H1
Roman way Dart	99	R13
Roman way Enf	8	J16
Romanhurst ave Brom	126	A10
Romanhurst gdns Brom	125	Z9
Romany gdns E17	32	H4
Romany gdns Sutt	119	X18
Romberg rd SW17	107	O8
Romborough gdns SE13	93	U13
Romborough way SE13	93	T13
Romero sq SE3	94	L10
Romeyn rd SW16	108	D7
Romford rd E7	52	J16
Romford rd E12	53	O14
Romford rd E15	52	C18
Romford rd Rom	37	Z1
Romford st E1	151	V3
Romilly rd N4	48	H8
Romilly st W1	148	G8
Rommany rd SE27	109	O10
Romney clo N17	31	Z4
Romney clo NW11	46	C4
Romney clo SE14	75	R20
Romney clo Har	40	J1
Romney dr Brom	113	N19
Romney dr Har	22	J20
Romney gdns Bexh	98	C1
Romney rd SE10	76	J17
Romney rd N Mal	117	Y16
Romney st SW1	156	H3
Romola rd SE24	108	H1
Romsey gdns Dag	68	K2
Romsey rd W13	71	Z1
Romsey rd Dag	68	J2
Rona rd NW3	47	O13
Ronald ave E15	65	O10
Ronald clo Beck	124	M10
Ronalds rd N5	48	F15
Ronalds rd Brom	112	F20
Ronaldstone rd Sid	96	J15
Ronart st Har	23	W9
Rondu rd NW2	45	S14
Roneo corner Horn	57	T3
Ronver rd SE12	94	D20
Rood la EC3	150	J8
Rook clo Horn	57	X20
Rookery clo NW9	26	C15
Rookery cres Dag	56	J20
Rookery dr Chis	127	W1
Rookery la Brom	127	N15
Rookery rd SW4	89	U11
Rookfield av N10	29	U12
Rookfield clo N10	29	V12
Rookstone rd SW17	106	L13
Rookwood ave N Mal	118	F9
Rookwood ave Wall	131	X8
Rookwood gdns E4	21	P6
Rookwood rd N16	31	W20
Roosevelt way Dag	57	O18
Rope st SE16	75	W9
Rope Walk gdns E1	151	V5
Rope Yard Rails SE18	78	M8

Ropemaker rd SE16	75	W7
Ropemaker st EC2	142	E20
Roper la SE1	150	L17
Roper st SE9	95	V15
Roper way Mitch	121	P3
Ropers ave E4	20	G16
Ropery st E3	63	Y12
Ropley st E2	143	S10
Rosaline rd SW6	152	M18
Rosamond st SE26	109	Z7
Rosary clo Houns	82	B4
Rosary gdns SW7	154	C7
Rosaville rd SW6	153	O19
Roscoe st EC1	142	B18
Roscoff clo Edg	25	U3
Rose all SE1	150	B12
Rose & Crown yd SW1	148	D13
Rose ave E18	34	J7
Rose ave Mitch	106	M20
Rose ave Mord	120	D11
Rose Bates dr NW9	25	O13
Rose Garden clo Edg	11	Y18
Rose gdns W5	72	H7
Rose gdns Sthl	58	H12
Rose glen NW9	25	X11
Rose glen Rom	57	P4
Rose hill Sutt	130	B5
Rose la Rom	37	X10
Rose Lawn (Bushey) Wat	10	A5
Rose wk Surb	117	T11
Rose wk W Wick	135	V3
Rose way SE12	94	F14
Roseacre clo W13	60	B13
Roseacre rd Well	97	S9
Rosebank SE20	110	A17
Rosebank clo N12	15	V15
Rosebank gdns E3	63	X6
Rosebank gro E17	32	L10
Rosebank rd E17	33	P18
Rosebank rd W7	71	U6
Rosebank vill E17	33	O13
Rosebank way W3	61	X15
Roseberry gdns N4	30	K17
Roseberry pl E8	49	U18
Roseberry st SE16	159	W7
Rosebery ave E12	53	S17
Rosebery ave E17	141	S19
Rosebery ave N17	31	X6
Rosebery ave Har	40	C11
Rosebery ave N Mal	118	C5
Rosebery ave Sid	96	H18
Rosebery ave Th Hth	123	N3
Rosebery clo Mord	119	O16
Rosebery gdns N8	30	A16
Rosebery gdns W13	59	Z17
Rosebery gdns Sutt	130	B8
Rosebery ms N10	29	U6
Rosebery rd N9	18	K9
Rosebery rd N10	29	U6
Rosebery rd SW2	89	Z16
Rosebery rd Houns	83	O14
Rosebery rd Kings T	117	S4
Rosebery rd Sutt	129	W14
Rosebery sq Kings T	117	S4
Rosebine ave Twick	83	N19
Rosebury rd SW6	88	B6
Rosecourt rd Croy	122	C16
Rosecroft ave NW3	45	Z9
Rosecroft gdns NW2	44	G10
Rosecroft gdns Twick	83	R20
Rosecroft rd Sthl	58	H12
Rosecroft wk Wem	42	G15
Rosedale clo Stan	11	O20
Rosedale gdns Dag	68	D1
Rosedale rd E7	52	M16
Rosedale rd Dag	68	D1
Rosedale rd Epsom	128	F12
Rosedale rd Rich	84	J9
Rosedale rd Rom	38	L8
Rosedene NW6	136	H3
Rosedene ave SW16	108	D7
Rosedene ave Croy	122	B17
Rosedene ave Grnf	58	H8
Rosedene ave Mord	119	Y12

Rosedene gdns Ilf	35	Y12	Rossdale rd SW15	87	N9	Routh st E6	66	H14	Royal clo Ilf	36	M20
Rosedene ter E10	51	S6	Rosse ms SE3	94	H1	Routledge clo N19	47	Z5	Royal clo Wor Pk	128	B3
Rosedew rd W6	152	F14	Rossendale st E5	49	Z6	Rowallan rd SW6	152	K19	Royal College st NW1	140	B1
Rosefield gdns E14	64	B19	Rossendale way NW1	140	D2	Rowan ave E4	19	Z18	Royal cres W11	144	J15
Rosehatch ave Rom	37	X10	Rossetti rd SE16	159	X8	Rowan clo SW16	121	V1	Royal cres Ruis	40	B11
Roseheath rd Houns	82	E12	Rossignol gdns Cars	131	O3	Rowan clo W5	72	L6	Royal Crescent ms W11	144	J15
Rosehill ave Sutt	120	C19	Rossindel rd Houns	82	H12	Rowan clo N Mal	118	A4	Royal hill SE10	76	G20
Rosehill gdns Grnf	41	W15	Rossington st E5	49	Y7	Rowan clo Wem	41	Z10	Royal Hospital rd SW3	155	O14
Rosehill gdns Sutt	130	B2	Rossiter rd SW12	107	S1	Rowan cres SW16	121	V2	Royal London est the N17	18	L20
Rosehill Park west Sutt	130	C1	Rossland clo Bexh	98	G12	Rowan dr NW9	26	G10	Royal Mint ct EC3	151	P9
Rosehill rd SW18	88	C15	Rosslyn ave E4	21	O7	Rowan gdns Croy	133	V5	Royal Mint pl E1	151	R9
Roseleigh ave N5	48	J13	Rosslyn ave SW13	86	C8	Rowan rd SW16	121	W1	Royal Mint st E1	151	P9
Roseleigh clo Twick	84	G17	Rosslyn ave Barn	5	W20	Rowan rd W6	152	G6	Royal Naval pl SE14	75	Y19
Rosemary ave N3	28	A7	Rosslyn ave Dag	56	C1	Rowan rd Bexh	97	Z8	Royal Oak pl SE22	92	A16
Rosemary ave N9	19	N5	Rosslyn cres Har	23	V13	Rowan rd Brent	72	C20	Royal Oak rd E8	49	Z19
Rosemary ave Enf	8	D4	Rosslyn cres Wem	42	J11	Rowan ter W6	152	F6	Royal Oak rd Bexh	98	C12
Rosemary ave Houns	82	A6	Rosslyn hill NW3	46	H14	Rowan wk N2	28	E17	Royal Opera arc SW1	148	F12
Rosemary ave Rom	39	T10	Rosslyn rd E17	33	U13	Rowan way Rom	37	V10	Royal Orchard clo SW18	87	S17
Rosemary dr E14	64	K18	Rosslyn rd Bark	54	E20	Rowans the N13	17	Y11	Royal par SE3	94	B5
Rosemary dr Ilf	35	O16	Rosslyn rd Twick	84	D16	Rowantree clo N21	18	C4	Royal par W5	60	L10
Rosemary la SW14	85	W7	Rossmore rd NW1	138	L18	Rowantree rd N21	18	C4	Royal par Chis	114	D18
Rosemary pl N1	142	F4	Rosswood gdns Wall	131	U14	Rowantree rd Enf	7	W8	Royal Parade ms Chis	114	D19
Rosemary rd SE15	159	P18	Rostella rd SW17	106	G10	Rowanwood ave Sid	114	M1	Royal pl SE10	76	H20
Rosemary rd SW17	106	C8	Rostrevor ave N15	31	U19	Rowben clo N20	15	N5	Royal rd E16	65	Z18
Rosemary rd Well	96	M3	Rostrevor gdns Sthl	70	B14	Rowberry clo SW6	152	E20	Royal rd SE17	157	W13
Rosemead NW9	44	F1	Rostrevor rd SW6	87	U1	Rowcross st SE1	159	O10	Royal rd Sid	115	W6
Rosemead ave Wem	42	L15	Rostrevor rd SW19	105	X13	Rowdell rd Nthlt	58	G3	Royal rd Tedd	101	R11
Rosemont ave N12	15	R18	Rotary st SE1	149	X20	Rowden rd E4	20	C20	Royal Route Wem	43	O13
Rosemont rd NW3	46	C17	Rothbury gdns Islw	71	Y20	Rowden rd Beck	124	K1	Royal st SE1	149	P20
Rosemont rd W3	61	S19	Rothbury rd E9	51	N19	Rowditch la SW11	89	O5	Royal Victor pl E3	63	T6
Rosemont rd Rich	84	L16	Rothbury wk N17	31	Y2	Rowdon ave NW10	44	K20	Roycraft ave Bark	67	X6
Rosemont rd Wem	60	J3	Rotherfield rd Cars	131	P10	Rowdown cres Croy	135	Y20	Roycraft clo Bark	67	X6
Rosemoor st SW3	155	N6	Rotherfield st N1	142	C1	Rowdowns rd Dag	69	P3	Roycroft clo E18	34	H4
Rosemount dr Brom	127	U8	Rotherhill ave SW16	107	Y16	Rowe gdns Bark	67	Z6	Roycroft clo SW2	108	G2
Rosemount rd W13	59	Z16	Rotherhithe New rd SE16	159	W11	Rowe la E9	50	C15	Roydene st SE18	79	V15
Rosenau cres SW11	88	L3	Rotherhithe Old rd SE16	75	S10	Rowe wk Har	40	H9	Royle clo Rom	39	Y16
Rosenau rd SW11	88	L1	Rotherhithe st SE16	75	R4	Rowena cres SW11	88	J5	Royle cres W13	59	Y12
Rosendale rd SE21	108	M2	Rotherhithe Tunnel E1	75	S1	Rowfant rd SW17	107	O2	Royston ave E4	20	C17
Rosendale rd SE24	90	L18	Rotherhithe Tunnel app E14	63	V19	Rowhill rd E5	50	B12	Royston ave Sutt	130	H5
Roseneath ave N21	17	V4	Rotherhithe Tunnel app SE16	75	P6	Rowington clo W2	137	Y20	Royston ave Wall	131	Y8
Roseneath rd SW11	89	O16	Rothermere rd Croy	132	E12	Rowland ave Har	24	D11	Royston ct Rich	85	N1
Roseneath wk Enf	8	D14	Rotherwick hill W5	61	U13	Rowland ct E16	65	P11	Royston gdns Ilf	35	N19
Rosens wk Edg	12	F11	Rotherwick rd NW11	45	Y2	Rowland Hill ave N17	18	A20	Royston par Ilf	35	O19
Rosenthal rd SE6	93	T17	Rotherwood clo SW20	105	S20	Rowland Hill st NW3	46	J14	Royston rd SE20	124	F1
Rosenthorpe rd SE15	92	E12	Rotherwood rd SW15	87	O7	Rowlands ave Pnr	22	K1	Royston rd Dart	99	S16
Roserton st E14	76	G6	Rothery st N1	141	X4	Rowlands clo N6	29	O19	Royston rd Rich	84	L14
Rosery the Croy	124	E14	Rothesay ave SW20	119	T2	Rowlands clo NW7	26	F1	Royston st E2	63	R7
Rosethorn clo SW12	89	W19	Rothesay ave Grnf	41	O18	Rowlands rd Dag	56	C7	Roystons the Surb	117	S11
Rosetta clo SW8	156	L19	Rothesay ave Rich	85	S9	Rowley ave Sid	97	P19	Rozel rd SW4	89	U6
Roseveare rd SE12	112	M9	Rothesay rd SE25	123	S10	Rowley gdns N4	48	L1	Rubens st SE6	110	M5
Roseville ave Houns	82	G13	Rothsay rd E7	52	L19	Rowley Industrial est W3	73	T8	Ruberoid rd Enf	9	Y10
Rosevine rd SW20	118	M2	Rothsay st SE1	158	J2	Rowley rd N15	30	M16	Ruby rd E17	33	O10
Roseway SE21	91	P17	Rothschild rd W4	73	V10	Rowley way NW8	138	A4	Ruby st SE15	159	W13
Rosewood ave Grnf	41	Y16	Rothschild st SE27	108	K10	Rowlls rd Kings T	117	O5	Ruby Triangle SE15	159	W13
Rosewood ave Horn	57	X15	Rothwell gdns Dag	68	G2	Rowney gdns Dag	55	S18	Ruckholt clo E10	51	S10
Rosewood clo Sid	115	T6	Rothwell rd Dag	68	F2	Rowney rd Dag	55	S18	Ruckholt rd E10	51	P13
Rosewood ct Brom	112	M20	Rothwell st NW1	139	R3	Rowntree rd Twick	101	S1	Rucklidge ave NW10	62	F6
Rosewood gdns SE13	93	T4	Rotten row SW1	147	N16	Rowse clo E15	64	H2	Ruddstreet clo SE18	79	O12
Rosewood gro Sutt	130	E2	Rotten row SW7	147	N16	Rowsley ave NW4	26	M9	Rudland rd Bexh	98	H7
Rosewood sq W12	62	G18	Rotterdam dr E14	76	H8	Rowstock gdns N7	47	Z16	Rudloe rd SW12	89	V18
Rosher clo E15	64	J1	Rouel rd SE16	159	S2	Rowton rd SE18	79	P18	Rudolph pl E13	65	R6
Rosina st E9	50	E16	Rougemont ave Mord	119	X15	Roxborough ave Har	41	S1	Rudolph rd NW6	137	W9
Roskell rd SW15	87	O7	Round grn Croy	124	G18	Roxborough ave Islw	71	W19	Rudyard gro NW7	12	J18
Roslin rd W3	73	T7	Round hill SE26	110	B5	Roxborough pk Har	23	S20	Ruffetts the S Croy	134	A17
Roslin way Brom	112	G14	Roundaway rd Ilf	35	T5	Roxborough rd Har	23	R16	Ruffetts clo S Croy	133	Z16
Roslyn clo Mitch	120	G3	Roundhay clo SE23	110	E5	Roxbourne clo Nthlt	40	A19	Rufford clo Har	23	Z18
Roslyn gdns Rom	39	S6	Roundhedge way Enf	7	S3	Roxburgh rd SE27	108	H12	Rufford st N1	140	L3
Roslyn rd N15	31	P14	Roundhill dr Enf	7	P15	Roxby pl SW6	153	V12	Rufus clo Ruis	40	A9
Rosmead rd W11	144	M8	Roundtable rd Brom	112	D6	Roxeth Green ave Har	40	K8	Rufus st N1	142	K14
Rosoman pl EC1	141	U15	Roundtree rd Wem	42	B15	Roxeth gro Har	40	L11	Rugby ave N9	18	H4
Rosoman st EC1	141	U14	Roundway the N17	30	M5	Roxeth hill Har	41	S6	Rugby ave Grnf	41	S17
Ross ave NW7	14	F17	Roundwood Chis	127	Y4	Roxley rd SE13	93	T16	Rugby ave Wem	42	C14
Ross ave Dag	56	B5	Roundwood rd NW10	44	C18	Roxton gdns Croy	135	N12	Rugby clo Har	23	S14
Ross clo Har	10	A20	Rounton rd E3	64	C11	Roxwell rd W12	74	G5	Rugby gdns Dag	55	T19
Ross par Wall	131	T13	Roupell rd SW2	108	D1	Roxwell rd Bark	68	B6	Rugby rd NW9	25	S12
Ross rd SE25	123	P8	Roupell st SE1	149	V14	Roxwell way Wdf Grn	21	Z20	Rugby rd W4	74	A6
Ross rd Dart	99	W17	Rousden st NW1	140	C1	Roxy ave Rom	37	T20	Rugby rd Dag	55	R19
Ross rd Twick	100	L3	Rouse gdns SE21	109	S9	Roy gdns Ilf	36	K14	Rugby rd Islw	83	U14
Ross rd Wall	131	U13	Routh rd SW18	88	H20	Roy gro Hmptn	100	K14	Rugby rd Twick	83	U15
Ross way SE9	95	S7				Roy sq E14	63	X20	Rugby st WC1	141	N19
Rossall clo Horn	39	X19				Royal Albert Dock Spine rd E16	66	E19	Ruislip clo Grnf	58	K11
Rossall cres NW10	60	M9				Royal ave SW3	155	N9	Ruislip rd Grnf	58	G9
Rossdale Sutt	130	J10				Royal ave Wor Pk	128	B4	Ruislip rd Nthlt	58	A8
Rossdale dr N9	9	O20				Royal circ SE27	108	H6	Ruislip Road east W7	59	X11
Rossdale dr NW9	43	V4									

Name		
Ruislip Road east W13	59	X11
Ruislip Road east Grnf	59	O12
Ruislip st SW17	106	M9
Rum clo E1	151	Z10
Rumbold rd SW6	153	Z19
Rumsey clo Hmptn	100	E15
Rumsey rd SW9	90	E7
Runbury circ NW9	43	Z6
Runcorn clo N17	31	Z13
Runcorn pl W11	144	K9
Rundell cres NW4	26	J16
Runnel fld Har	41	T10
Runnymede SW19	120	E1
Runnymede clo Twick	82	L17
Runnymede ct Croy	133	U4
Runnymede cres SW16	107	Z20
Runnymede gdns Grnf	59	S6
Runnymede gdns Twick	82	L17
Runnymede rd Twick	82	L15
Rupert ave Wem	42	L16
Rupert gdns SW9	90	J6
Rupert rd N19	47	Y9
Rupert rd NW6	137	R9
Rupert rd W4	74	B9
Rupert st W1	148	E8
Rural clo Horn	57	Z5
Rural wk SW16	107	T17
Ruscoe rd E16	65	P17
Rush Green gdns Rom	56	L3
Rush Green rd Rom	56	J4
Rush Grove st SE18	78	H12
Rush Hill rd SW11	89	P8
Rusham rd SW12	89	N17
Rushbrook cres E17	33	N5
Rushbrook rd SE9	114	B4
Rushcroft rd E4	33	P1
Rushcroft rd SW2	90	E10
Rushden clo SE19	109	P19
Rushden gdns NW7	14	A18
Rushden gdns Ilf	35	W8
Rushdene SE2	80	H9
Rushdene ave Barn	15	X3
Rushdon clo Rom	39	X16
Rushen wk Cars	120	G19
Rushett clo T Ditt	116	B19
Rushett rd T Ditt	116	B19
Rushey clo N Mal	117	X10
Rushey grn SE6	93	S18
Rushey hill Enf	7	R15
Rushey mead SE4	93	P14
Rushford rd SE4	92	M16
Rushgrove ave NW9	26	C15
Rushmead E2	143	V13
Rushmead Rich	102	C8
Rushmead clo Croy	133	U8
Rushmore clo Brom	127	R7
Rushmore rd E5	50	C12
Rusholme ave Dag	56	E9
Rusholme gro SE19	109	T11
Rusholme rd SW15	87	R17
Rushout ave Har	24	A18
Rushton st N1	142	F8
Rushworth ave NW4	26	H10
Rushworth gdns NW4	26	G11
Rushworth st SE1	149	Y17
Ruskin ave E12	53	S17
Ruskin ave Rich	73	R20
Ruskin ave Well	97	N6
Ruskin clo NW11	28	A18
Ruskin dr Well	97	N6
Ruskin dr Wor Pk	128	L2
Ruskin gdns W5	60	F11
Ruskin gdns Har	25	N13
Ruskin gdns Rom	39	Y3
Ruskin gro Well	97	N6
Ruskin rd N17	31	V4
Ruskin rd Belv	81	R11
Ruskin rd Cars	131	P11
Ruskin rd Croy	132	K3
Ruskin rd Islw	83	V8
Ruskin rd Sthl	58	A20
Ruskin wk N9	18	K7
Ruskin wk SE24	90	M14
Ruskin wk Brom	127	T14
Ruskin way SW19	120	F2
Rusland Park rd Har	23	T14
Rusper clo NW2	44	M10
Rusper clo Stan	11	S14
Rusper rd N22	30	K8
Rusper rd Dag	55	U18
Russell ave N22	30	G8
Russell clo NW10	43	V20
Russell clo SE7	77	X20
Russell clo Beck	125	T6
Russell clo Bexh	98	E9
Russell clo Dart	99	X9
Russell ct SW1	148	C14
Russell gdns N20	15	X7
Russell gdns NW11	27	T19
Russell gdns W14	144	L20
Russell gdns Rich	102	C5
Russell Gardens ms W14	144	K20
Russell gro NW7	13	N14
Russell gro SW9	157	V20
Russell Kerr clo W4	73	X19
Russell la N20	15	X8
Russell rd E4	19	X14
Russell rd E10	33	R19
Russell rd E16	65	U16
Russell rd E17	32	L11
Russell rd N8	29	Y17
Russell rd N13	17	O18
Russell rd N15	31	S16
Russell rd N20	15	W7
Russell rd NW9	26	E18
Russell rd SW19	105	X17
Russell rd W14	153	N3
Russell rd Buck H	21	W6
Russell rd Enf	8	G3
Russell rd Mitch	120	K6
Russell rd Nthlt	41	N14
Russell rd Twick	83	V17
Russell sq WC1	140	J19
Russell st WC2	148	M8
Russell way Sutt	129	Z11
Russell's footpath SW16	108	B12
Russet dr Croy	124	J20
Russets clo E4	20	J12
Russett way SE13	93	T4
Russia ct EC2	150	C5
Russia Dock rd SE16	75	W3
Russia la E2	143	P6
Russia row EC2	150	C5
Russia wk SE16	75	V5
Rust sq SE5	158	D17
Rusthall ave W4	73	Z7
Rusthall clo Croy	124	C14
Rustic ave SW16	107	T17
Rustic pl Wem	42	F11
Rustington wk Mord	119	W17
Ruston ave Surb	117	S18
Ruston ms W11	144	K5
Ruston st E3	63	Z3
Rutford rd SW16	108	A12
Ruth clo Stan	24	M12
Rutherford clo Sutt	130	F13
Rutherford st SW1	156	F5
Rutherford way (Bushey) Wat	10	E5
Rutherford way Wem	43	R11
Rutherglen rd SE2	80	A16
Rutherwyke clo Epsom	128	G14
Ruthin rd SE3	77	T16
Ruthven st E9	63	T2
Rutin clo NW9	26	A18
Rutland ave Sid	97	N19
Rutland clo SW14	85	U7
Rutland clo Bex	115	W3
Rutland dr Mord	119	W16
Rutland dr Rich	102	J1
Rutland gdns N4	30	L17
Rutland gdns SW7	146	L18
Rutland gdns W13	59	Y15
Rutland gdns Croy	133	T9
Rutland gdns Dag	55	T14
Rutland gate SW7	146	L18
Rutland gate Belv	81	U13
Rutland gate Brom	126	D9
Rutland gro W6	152	A10
Rutland ms NW8	138	A6
Rutland pk NW2	45	N18
Rutland pk SE6	110	M5
Rutland pl EC1	141	Z19
Rutland pl (Bushey) Wat	10	D5
Rutland rd E7	53	N19
Rutland rd E9	63	S3
Rutland rd E11	34	J14
Rutland rd E17	33	O18
Rutland rd SW19	106	J17
Rutland rd Har	23	N18
Rutland rd Ilf	54	A11
Rutland rd Sthl	58	G12
Rutland rd Twick	101	P5
Rutland st SW7	154	L11
Rutland wk SE6	110	M4
Rutley clo SE17	157	W14
Rutlish rd SW19	105	Y20
Rutter gdns Mitch	120	E10
Rutts the (Bushey) Wat	10	D4
Rutts ter SE14	92	E3
Ruvigny gdns SW15	87	P7
Ruxley clo Sid	115	Y15
Ruxley Corner Industrial est Sid	115	W15
Ryalls ct N20	16	A11
Ryan clo SE3	94	K10
Ryan dr Brent	71	Z17
Rycroft way N17	31	V10
Rycuilf sq SE3	94	D4
Rydal clo NW4	27	R5
Rydal cres Grnf	60	B8
Rydal dr Bexh	98	D4
Rydal gdns NW9	26	B15
Rydal gdns SW15	104	B12
Rydal gdns Houns	82	L15
Rydal gdns Wem	42	E3
Rydal rd SW16	107	X11
Rydal way Enf	9	R18
Ryde pl Twick	84	F15
Ryde Vale rd SW12	107	U3
Ryder clo Brom	112	J13
Ryder gdns Rain	57	U18
Ryder st SW1	148	C13
Ryder st SW1	148	C12
Ryder yd SW1	148	C12
Ryders ter NW8	138	B8
Rydon st N1	142	D4
Rydons clo SE9	95	P8
Rydston clo N7	48	B19
Rye the N14	16	J1
Rye clo Bex	98	H15
Rye Hill pk SE15	92	C10
Rye la SE15	91	X4
Rye pas SE15	91	Y7
Rye rd SE15	92	E11
Rye wk SW15	87	P14
Rye way Edg	12	B19
Ryecotes mead SE21	109	T1
Ryecroft ave Ilf	35	Z6
Ryecroft ave Twick	82	L20
Ryecroft rd SE13	93	V13
Ryecroft rd SW16	108	G14
Ryecroft st SW6	88	A3
Ryedale SE22	91	Z16
Ryefield rd SE19	108	M15
Ryelands cres SE12	94	K16
Ryfold rd SW19	105	Y7
Ryhope rd N11	16	F12
Ryland rd NW5	47	S17
Rylandes rd NW2	44	F8
Rylett cres W12	74	E7
Rylett rd W12	74	F8
Rylston rd N13	18	A12
Rylston rd SW6	153	O15
Rymer rd Croy	123	T18
Rymer st SE24	90	K15
Rymill st E16	78	J4
Rysbrack st SW3	147	O20

S

Sabine rd SW11	88	M7
Sable st N1	48	J20
Sach rd E5	50	A6
Sackville ave Brom	126	E20
Sackville clo Har	41	O10
Sackville est SW16	108	B7
Sackville gdns Ilf	53	U3
Sackville st W1	129	Y18
Sackville st W1	148	C10
Saddlescombe way N12	14	K16
Sadler clo Mitch	120	L4
Saffron ave E14	64	J19
Saffron clo NW11	27	V17
Saffron hill EC1	141	U19
Saffron rd Rom	38	M6
Saffron st EC1	141	U20
Sage st E1	151	Z8
Saigasso clo E16	66	A18
Sail st SE11	157	R4
Sainfoin rd SW17	107	R5
Sainsbury rd SE19	109	S12
St Agathas dr Kings T	103	N16
St Agathas gro Cars	120	L19
St Agnes clo E9	63	P3
St Agnes pl SE11	157	V16
St Aidans rd SE22	91	Z15
St Aidans rd W13	72	C6
St Alban's ave E6	66	J9
St Alban's ave W4	73	Y6
St Albans clo NW11	45	Y4
St Albans cres N22	30	F5
St Albans cres Wdf Grn	34	E3
St Alban's gdns Tedd	101	Z12
St Albans gro W8	154	A1
St Albans gro Cars	120	K18
St Albans la NW11	45	Y3
St Albans ms W2	138	H20
St Alban's pl N1	141	W5
St Alban's rd NW5	47	P9
St Albans rd NW10	62	A3
St Alban's rd Barn	4	B2
St Albans rd Ilf	54	K4
St Alban's rd Kings T	102	K16
St Alban's rd Sutt	129	U9
St Albans rd Wdf Grn	34	E2
St Albans rd SW1	148	F11
St Albans ter W6	152	K12
St Alfege pas SE10	76	G17
St Alfege rd SE7	78	B15
St Alphage gdns EC2	150	D2
St Alphage wk Edg	25	W7
St Alphege rd N9	19	O1
St Alphonsus rd SW4	89	W11
St Amunds clo SE6	111	O10
St Andrew st EC4	109	V3
St Andrews ave Horn	57	V14
St Andrews ave Wem	41	Y12
St Andrew's clo N12	15	P13
St Andrew's clo NW2	44	J10
St Andrew's clo Islw	83	S1
St Andrews clo Stan	24	E6
St Andrew's clo der Stan	24	E6
St Andrew's gro N16	49	P3
St Andrew's hill EC4	149	Y7
St Andrew's ms N16	49	S3
St Andrews ms SE3	77	S18
St Andrews pl NW1	139	Y16
St Andrews rd E13	65	W10
St Andrews rd E17	32	G8
St Andrews rd N9	19	R2
St Andrews rd NW9	43	X5
St Andrews rd NW11	27	V19
St Andrew's rd W3	62	B17
St Andrews rd W7	71	T5
St Andrews rd W14	152	M12
St Andrews rd Cars	130	K5
St Andrews rd Croy	132	M8
St Andrews rd Enf	8	C11
St Andrews rd Ilf	53	U1
St Andrews rd Rom	39	O17
St Andrews rd Sid	115	X7
St Andrews rd Surb	116	G14
St Andrews sq W11	144	K6
St Andrews sq Surb	116	G14
St Andrews way E3	64	E12
St Anne's clo N6	47	P8
St Annes gdns NW10	60	M8

Entry	Page	Grid
St Annes rd E11	51	W5
St Anne's rd Wem	42	H15
St Ann's Bark	67	R3
St Ann's cres SW18	88	C15
St Ann's gdns NW5	47	N17
St Ann's hill SW18	88	B14
St Ann's la SW1	156	G1
St Ann's Park rd SW18	88	D16
St Ann's pas SW13	86	C7
St Anns rd N18	18	H6
St Anns rd N15	30	J15
St Ann's rd SW13	86	D3
St Anns rd W11	144	H10
St Ann's rd Har	23	T18
St Ann's st SW1	156	G1
St Ann's ter NW8	138	H8
St Anns vill W11	144	J14
St Anns way S Croy	132	K15
St Anselm's pl W1	147	W7
St Anthonys ave Wdf Grn	21	X20
St Anthonys clo E1	151	S13
St Antony's rd E7	52	G19
St Arvans clo Croy	133	T5
St Asaph rd SE4	92	E7
St Aubyn's ave SW19	105	U12
St Aubyns ave Hous	82	G14
St Aubyn's rd SE19	109	U16
St Audrey ave Bexh	98	F5
St Augustine's ave W5	60	L7
St Augustines ave Brom	127	R12
St Augustines ave S Croy	132	L15
St Augustines ave Wem	42	K10
St Augustines rd NW1	47	X20
St Augustine's rd Belv	81	P10
St Austell clo Edg	25	N7
St Austell rd SE13	93	V4
St Awdry's rd Bark	67	T2
St Barnabas clo Beck	125	U4
St Barnabas rd E17	33	O18
St Barnabas Mitch	107	O18
St Barnabas rd Wdf Grn	34	J4
St Barnabas st SW1	155	V8
St Barnabas ter E9	50	F15
St Bartholomews clo SE26	110	B10
St Bartholomew's rd E6	66	F5
St Benet's gro Cars	120	D18
St Benet's pl EC3	151	N5
St Bernard's clo SE27	109	O9
St Bernard's rd E6	66	C4
St Blaise ave Brom	126	H3
St Botolph st EC3	151	N5
St Bride st EC4	149	W5
St Brides ave Edg	24	M5
St Catherines rd E4	20	B8
St Chads gdns Rom	37	Z20
St Chads pl WC1	140	M12
St Chads rd Rom	37	Y20
St Chad's st WC1	140	L12
St Charles pl W10	144	K2
St Charles sq W10	136	J20
St Christopher's clo Islw	83	S2
St Christophers gdns Th Hth	122	F7
St Christophers ms Wall	131	V11
St Clair dr Wor Pk	128	J6
St Clair rd E13	65	W7
St Claire clo Ilf	35	U7
St Clair's rd Croy	133	S3
St Clare st EC3	151	O7
St Clements heights SE26	109	W8
St Clement's la WC2	149	P6
St Clements st N1	48	E19
St Clements st N7	48	E19
St Cloud rd SE27	109	N9
St Crispins clo NW3	46	J13
St Crispin's clo Sthl	58	F16
St Cross st EC1	141	U20
St Cuthberts gdns Pnr		
St Cuthberts rd NW2	45	U17
St Cyprian's st SW17	106	L10
St Davids clo Wem	43	V10
St Davids clo W Wick	125	S18
St Davids dr Edg	24	M4
St Davids pl NW4	26	J20
St Denis rd SE27	109	N10
St Dionis rd SW6	87	W3
St Donatts rd SE14	92	K2
St Dunstans ave W3	61	Y20
St Dunstans gdns W3	61	Y19
St Dunstan's hill EC3	150	K10
St Dunstan's hill Sutt	129	U8
St Dunstan's la EC3	150	J9
St Dunstans la Twick	82	L18
St Dunstan's rd E7	52	K16
St Dunstans rd SE25	123	V8
St Dunstans rd W6	152	F11
St Dunstans rd W7	71	T6
St Edmunds clo NW8	139	O6
St Edmunds dr Stan	23	Y4
St Edmund's la Twick	82	L18
St Edmunds rd N9	18	J3
St Edmunds rd Ilf	35	V19
St Edmunds ter NW8	138	M7
St Edwards clo NW11	27	X19
St Edwards way Rom	39	O15
St Egberts way E4	20	G4
St Elmo rd W12	74	E4
St Elmos rd SE16	75	V5
St Erkenwald rd Bark	67	S2
St Ermin's hill SW1	148	F20
St Ervans rd W10	137	N20
St Faiths clo Enf	7	Z4
St Faith's rd SE21	108	J2
St Fillans rd SE6	93	V20
St Francis rd SE22	91	S10
St Gabriels rd NW2	45	O15
St Georges ave E7	52	J19
St Georges ave N7	47	W12
St Georges ave NW9	25	X12
St Georges ave W5	72	F5
St Georges ave Sthl	70	D1
St Georges circ SE1	149	W20
St Georges clo NW11	27	U18
St Georges clo Wem	41	Z9
St Georges ct E6	66	G10
St George's dr SW1	155	Y7
St Georges flds W2	146	L7
St Georges Industrial est N17	30	K1
St Georges ms NW1	139	P2
St Georges rd E7	52	H19
St Georges rd E10	51	U9
St Georges rd N9	18	L10
St Georges rd N13	17	R9
St Georges rd NW11	27	V18
St Georges rd SE1	157	W2
St George's rd SW19	105	V16
St Georges rd W4	73	Z5
St George's rd W7	71	W3
St Georges rd Beck	125	R1
St Georges rd Dag	55	Z14
St Georges rd Enf	8	G3
St George's rd Felt	100	A10
St George's rd Ilf	53	U1
St George's rd Kings T	103	O19
St Georges rd Mitch	121	S6
St Georges rd Rich	85	N8
St George's rd Sid	115	X15
St Georges rd Twick	84	C14
St Georges rd Wall	131	R11
St Georges Road west Brom	127	S2
St Georges sq E7	52	J19
St Georges sq SE8	75	Y10
St George's sq SW1	156	E9
St George's Square ms SW1	156	F11
St Georges ter NW1	139	P2
St Georges wk Croy	133	N4
St Georges way SE15	158	J15
St Gerards clo SW4	89	U13
St German's pl SE3	94	E2
St Germans rd SE23	92	J20
St Giles ave Dag	56	J19
St Giles clo Dag	56	J19
St Giles High st WC2	148	H5
St Giles pas WC2	148	H6
St Giles rd SE5	158	H20
St Gothard rd SE27	109	O9
St Helena rd SE16	75	S11
St Helena st WC1	141	S13
St Helens gdns W10	144	F2
St Helens pl EC3	150	K5
St Helens rd SW16	122	D2
St Helen's rd W13	72	C1
St Helen's rd Erith	80	K5
St Helens rd Ilf	35	V19
St Helier ave Mord	120	C17
St Heliers ave Hous	82	G14
St Heliers rd E10	33	T19
St Hildas clo NW6	136	H2
St Hilda's rd SW13	74	J16
St Ivians dr Rom	39	S6
St James ave E2	63	S6
St James ave N20	15	W11
St James ave W13	71	Y3
St James ave Beck	124	J6
St James ave Sutt	129	X10
St James clo N20	15	W11
St James clo SE18	79	O13
St James clo N Mal	118	D12
St James gdns SW11	144	K13
St James gdns Wem	60	J1
St James gro SW11	88	M4
St James ms E14	76	H9
St James rd E15	52	C15
St James rd Cars	130	L5
St James rd Mitch	107	P19
St James rd Surb	116	H14
St James rd Sutt	129	X10
St James st W6	152	C11
St James's SE14	92	J1
St James's ave Hmptn	100	M12
St James's ct SW1	156	C1
St James's cres SW9	90	G7
St James's dr SW17	88	L20
St James's la N10	29	T12
St James's mkt SW1	148	F11
St James's pk Croy	122	M17
St James's pl SW1	148	B14
St James's rd SE1	159	U1
St James's rd SE16	159	U1
St James's rd Croy	122	K18
St James's rd Hmptn	100	L13
St James's rd Kings T	116	J5
St James's row EC1	141	V17
St James's sq SW1	148	D12
St James's st E17	32	J15
St James's st SW1	148	B12
St James's Terrace ms NW8	139	N7
St James's wk EC1	141	W17
St Joans rd N9	18	L6
St John Fisher rd Erith	80	L7
St John st EC1	141	V10
St Johns ave N11	15	Z17
St John's ave NW10	62	D3
St John's ave SW15	87	O12
St John's Church rd E9	50	C15
St Johns clo Wem	42	J14
St Johns ct Buck H	21	X5
St John's ct Islw	83	V5
St John's cres SW9	90	F7
St Johns dr SW18	106	A1
St Johns est N1	142	H10
St Johns gdns W11	145	N11
St Johns gro N19	47	W8
St John's hill SW11	88	H11
St John's Hill gro SW11	88	F10
St John's la EC1	141	X19
St John's ms W11	145	T6
St John's pk SE3	77	S20
St John's path EC1	141	W19
St John's pl EC1	141	W19
St Johns rd E4	20	E12
St Johns rd E6	66	E4
St Johns rd E16	65	S16
St Johns rd E17	33	S8
St Johns rd N15	31	R19
St Johns rd NW11	27	V19
St John's rd SE20	110	D17
St Johns rd SW11	88	K10
St Johns rd SW19	105	S17
St John's rd Bark	67	V4
St Johns rd Cars	130	K5
St Johns rd Croy	132	J5
St Johns rd Felt	100	C10
St Johns rd Har	23	V18
St Johns rd Ilf	36	G20
St John's rd Islw	83	U4
St John's rd Kings T	116	F2
St John's rd N Mal	117	V7
St John's rd Rich	84	K10
St Johns rd Sid	115	P10
St Johns rd Sthl	70	B8
St John's rd Sutt	129	Z3
St Johns rd Well	97	R8
St John's rd Wem	42	H12
St John's sq EC1	141	X18
St Johns ter E7	52	J16
St Johns ter SE18	79	R15
St Johns ter W10	136	J15
St Johns ter Enf	8	B1
St Johns vale SE8	93	P5
St Johns vill N19	47	X6
St Johns way N19	47	W5
St John's Wood ct NW8	138	G15
St John's Wood High st NW8	138	J10
St John's Wood pk NW8	138	G4
St John's Wood rd NW8	138	F15
St John's Wood ter NW8	138	K8
St Josephs clo W10	145	N1
St Josephs dr Sthl	70	D3
St Joseph's gro NW4	26	J13
St Josephs rd N9	19	N3
St Joseph's vale SE3	93	X6
St Jude st N16	49	S16
St Jude's rd E2	143	Y10
St Julian's clo SW16	108	F11
St Julian's Farm rd SE27	108	F10
St Julian's rd NW6	137	S3
St Katharines prec NW1	139	W9
St Katharine's way E1	151	O11
St Katharines rd Erith	80	K5
St Keverne rd SE9	113	S10
St Kilda rd N16	71	Z4
St Kilda's rd N16	49	P5
St Kildas rd Har	23	T17
St Kitts ter SE19	109	R12
St Laurence clo NW6	136	J6
St Lawrence clo Edg	24	M1
St Lawrence ter W10	144	L12
St Lawrence way SW9	90	G3
St Leonards ave E4	20	L17
St Leonards ave Har	24	C14
St Leonard's clo Well	97	O8
St Leonard's gdns Bark	82	B1
St Leonards gdns Ilf	54	C16
St Leonards rd E14	64	F15
St Leonards rd NW10	61	Z22
St Leonard's rd SW14	85	U8
St Leonards rd W13	60	D19
St Leonards rd Croy	132	H6
St Leonards rd Surb	116	G12
St Leonard's rd T Ditt	116	A16
St Leonards sq NW5	47	P18
St Leonards sq Surb	116	G12
St Leonards st E3	64	E8
St Leonard's ter SW3	155	P10

Name	Pg	Ref
St Leonards wk SW16	108	C18
St Leonards way Horn	57	Z4
St Loo ave SW3	155	N13
St Louis rd SE27	109	N10
St Loys rd N17	31	U9
St Luke's ave SW4	89	Y10
St Lukes ave Enf	8	B3
St Luke's ave Ilf	54	A14
St Lukes clo SE25	124	A14
St Lukes ms W11	145	P4
St Lukes rd W11	145	R3
St Lukes sq E16	65	R18
St Luke's st SW3	154	L9
St Luke's yd W9	137	O10
St Malo ave N9	19	O10
St Margarets Bark	67	R3
St Margarets ave N15	30	J12
St Margarets ave N20	15	R6
St Margaret's ave Har	40	M8
St Margarets ave Sid	114	F7
St Margaret's ave Sutt	129	T7
St Margaret's ct SE1	150	D15
St Margarets cres SW15	86	L13
St Margaret's dr Twick	84	B12
St Margarets gro SE18	79	O15
St Margarets gro Twick	83	Z15
St Margaret's rd E12	52	M7
St Margarets rd N17	31	S9
St Margaret's rd NW10	136	B11
St Margarets rd SE4	92	L10
St Margarets rd W7	71	T6
St Margarets rd Beck	124	F9
St Margarets rd Edg	12	E17
St Margarets rd Twick	84	A12
St Margarets sq SE4	92	M11
St Margaret's st SW1	148	K19
St Margaret's ter SE18	79	P14
St Mark st E1	151	P6
St Marks clo W11	144	K6
St Mark's clo Barn	5	N12
St Mark's gro SW10	154	A16
St Marks pl W11	144	M6
St Marks ri E8	49	V15
St Marks rd SE25	123	Y8
St Mark's rd W5	72	K2
St Marks rd W7	71	T5
St Marks rd W10	136	F20
St Marks rd W11	144	L6
St Marks rd Brom	126	G7
St Marks rd Enf	8	H16
St Marks rd Mitch	121	O4
St Marks rd Tedd	102	C18
St Marks sq NW1	139	T5
St Martins ave E6	66	A6
St Martin's clo NW1	140	A4
St Martins clo Enf	8	M4
St Martins rd N9	108	G1
St Martin's la WC2	148	J10
St Martin's pl WC2	148	J11
St Martins rd N9	19	N8
St Martin's rd SW9	90	D4
St Martin's st WC2	148	H10
St Martins way SW17	106	C8
St Martin's-le-Grand EC1	150	A5
St Mary Abbots pl W8	153	R3
St Mary at hill EC3	150	J10
St Mary ave Wall	131	R6
St Mary Axe EC3	150	K6
St Mary rd E17	33	P14
St Mary st SE18	78	J9
St Marychurch st SE16	19	P5
St Marys Bark	67	S4
St Marys app E12	53	U15
St Mary's ave E11	34	H19
St Mary's ave N3	27	T6
St Mary's ave Brom	126	A6
St Mary's ave Sthl	70	J12
St Mary's ave Tedd	101	W16
St Marys clo Epsom	128	F18
St Mary's ct SE7	66	G10
St Mary's ct SE7	78	B19
St Marys cres NW4	26	K11
St Marys cres Islw	71	S19
St Mary's gdns SE11	157	U5
St Mary's gate W8	153	X3
St Mary's gro SW13	48	K18
St Mary's gro SW13	86	K8
St Mary's gro W4	73	U17
St Mary's gro Rich	85	N10
St Marys mans W2	138	E20
St Mary's ms NW6	137	X2
St Marys path N1	141	Y4
St Mary's pl W5	72	G5
St Mary's pl W8	153	Y3
St Marys rd E10	51	U8
St Mary's rd E13	65	U5
St Marys rd N9	19	O3
St Marys rd NW10	62	C2
St Marys rd NW11	27	S20
St Mary's rd SE15	92	C3
St Mary's rd SE25	123	S7
St Mary's rd (Wimbledon) SW19	105	T12
St Mary's rd W5	72	G5
St Mary's rd Barn	15	Y3
St Marys rd Islw	54	D7
St Marys rd Surb	116	G14
St Marys rd (Long Ditton) Surb	116	E18
St Mary's rd Wor Pk	128	C4
St Marys sq W2	146	F1
St Marys ter W2	138	E20
St Marys vw Har	24	D15
St Mary's wk SE11	157	U5
St Matthew st SW1	156	F2
St Matthews ave Surb	116	L19
St Matthew's dr Brom	127	U6
St Matthew's rd SW2	90	E14
St Matthews rd W5	72	K3
St Matthew's row E2	143	S15
St Matthias clo NW9	26	D14
St Maur rd SW6	87	W2
St Merryn clo SE18	79	T18
St Michaels ave N9	19	R2
St Michael's ave Wem	43	R17
St Michael's clo N3	27	V7
St Michaels clo N12	15	V15
St Michaels clo Brom	127	R6
St Michaels clo Wor Pk	128	C3
St Michaels cres Pnr	22	B18
St Michaels gdns W10	144	L3
St Michael's rd NW2	44	L12
St Michael's rd SW9	90	C4
St Michaels rd Croy	132	M1
St Michaels rd Wall	131	V13
St Michaels rd Well	97	R8
St Michaels ter N22	30	J3
St Mildred's ct EC2	150	F6
St Mildreds rd SE12	94	B19
St Nicholas Glebe SW17	107	O14
St Nicholas la Chis	127	S1
St Nicholas rd SE18	79	Z12
St Nicholas rd Sutt	130	B12
St Nicholas st SE8	93	N3
St Nicholas way Sutt	130	A11
St Ninian's ct N20	15	Z11
St Norbert grn SE4	92	J9
St Norbert rd SE4	92	G12
St Olaf's rd SW6	152	M19
St Olaves rd E6	66	J2
St Olave's wk SW16	121	W4
St Oswald's pl SE11	157	O10
St Oswald's rd SW16	108	H20
St Oswulf st SW1	156	H7
St Pancras way NW1	140	C1
St Paul st N1	142	A6
St Paul's ave NW2	44	L17
St Paul's ave SE16	75	U1
St Pauls ave Har	25	N12
St Paul's churchyard EC4	149	Z6
St Paul's clo SE7	78	A14
St Paul's clo W5	72	L4
St Pauls clo Cars	120	J19
St Pauls clo Houns	82	C6
St Paul's ct W14	152	J7
St Pauls Cray rd Chis	114	E19
St Pauls cres NW1	140	G1
St Pauls dr E15	51	X16
St Paul's pl N1	49	O17
St Pauls ri N13	17	V18
St Pauls rd N1	48	K17
St Paul's rd N17	31	Y3
St Paul's rd Bark	67	O3
St Paul's rd Brent	72	G17
St Paul's rd Erith	81	X19
St Paul's rd Rich	84	M8
St Paul's rd Th Hth	122	M7
St Paul's Shrubbery N1	49	N17
St Pauls sq Brom	126	D3
St Pauls st E3	63	Y15
St Paul's ter SE17	157	Y12
St Pauls way E3	63	Z15
St Pauls way N3	28	A2
St Paul's Wood hill Orp	115	O20
St Peter's ave E17	33	Y12
St Peters ave N18	18	L14
St Peters clo E2	143	U11
St Peters clo Chis	114	F18
St Peters clo Ilf	36	J13
St Peters clo (Bushey) Wat	10	C4
St Peter's ct NW4	27	N15
St Peters ct SE4	93	N6
St Peter's gdns SE27	108	F8
St Peter's gro W6	74	G12
St Peter's pl W9	137	W17
St Peters rd N9	19	O6
St Peter's rd W6	74	G12
St Peters rd Croy	133	O8
St Peters rd Kings T	117	O4
St Peters rd Sthl	58	G15
St Peters rd Twick	84	C12
St Peter's sq E2	143	U10
St Peter's sq W6	74	F12
St Peters st N1	141	Y6
St Peter's st S Croy	133	O11
St Peters ter SW6	153	N19
St Peter's vill W6	74	F12
St Peter's way N1	142	L1
St Peters way W5	60	H14
St Petersburgh ms W2	145	X9
St Petersburgh pl W2	145	X9
St Philip sq SW8	89	S4
St Philip st SW8	89	S6
St Philip's ave Wor Pk	128	J3
St Philip's rd E8	49	X18
St Philip's rd Surb	116	H14
St Philip's way N1	142	C5
St Quentin rd Well	96	M7
St Quintin ave W10	144	C2
St Quintin gdns W10	144	C2
St Quintin rd E13	65	W7
St Raphael's way NW10	43	W16
St Regis clo N10	29	S6
St Ronan's clo Barn	5	T3
St Ronans cres Wdf Grn	34	E1
St Rule st SW8	89	U5
St Saviour's est SE1	151	N20
St Saviour's rd SW2	90	C14
St Saviours rd Croy	122	K15
St Silas pl NW5	47	P18
St Silas Street est NW5	47	O17
St Simon's ave SW15	87	N13
St Stephens ave E17	33	T16
St Stephens ave W12	74	K4
St Stephens ave W13	60	A16
St Stephens clo E17	33	S16
St Stephens clo NW8	138	L5
St Stephens clo Sthl	58	G16
St Stephens cres W2	145	V4
St Stephens cres Th Hth	122	F7
St Stephens Garden est W2	145	S4
St Stephens gdns W2	145	U3
St Stephen's gdns Twick	84	D17
St Stephens gro SE13	93	V7
St Stephens ms W2	145	U3
St Stephens rd E6	65	X4
St Stephens rd E6	65	Y1
St Stephens rd W13	60	B16
St Stephen's rd Barn	4	B16
St Stephens rd Enf	9	S1
St Stephens rd Houns	82	H15
St Stephens ter SW8	157	N19
St Stephen's wk SW7	154	B4
St Swithin's la EC4	150	F8
St Swithun's rd SE13	93	W14
St Thomas ct Bex	98	E18
St Thomas dr Pnr	22	C4
St Thomas gdns Ilf	54	C16
St Thomas rd E16	65	S16
St Thomas rd N14	16	M3
St Thomas rd Belv	81	X6
St Thomas st SE1	150	G14
St Thomas's gdns NW5	47	O17
St Thomas's pl E9	50	B20
St Thomas's rd N4	48	H9
St Thomas's rd NW10	62	B3
St Thomas's rd W4	73	U17
St Thomas's sq E9	50	B19
St Thomas's way SW6	153	P17
St Ursula gro Pnr	22	A17
St Ursula rd Sthl	58	H16
St Vincent clo SE27	108	J12
St Vincent rd Twick	82	M17
St Vincent st W1	147	U2
St Wilfrid's rd Barn	5	R17
St Winifreds rd Tedd	102	B15
St Winifride's ave E12	53	V15
Saints dr E7	53	N14
Salamanca pl SE11	157	N7
Salamanca st SE11	157	N7
Salcombe dr Mord	119	P20
Salcombe dr Rom	38	C19
Salcombe gdns NW7	13	Z20
Salcombe rd E17	51	N1
Salcott rd SW11	88	K13
Salcott rd Croy	132	B7
Sale pl W2	146	K3
Salehurst clo Har	24	L15
Salehurst rd SE4	92	L17
Salem pl Croy	132	L6
Salem rd W2	145	Y8
Salford rd SW2	107	Y3
Salisbury ave N3	27	U9
Salisbury ave Bark	54	D20
Salisbury ave Sutt	129	V15
Salisbury clo SE17	158	F6
Salisbury clo Wor Pk	128	C5
Salisbury ct EC4	149	V6
Salisbury gdns SW19	105	T18
Salisbury ms SW6	153	O18
Salisbury pl SW9	157	Y19
Salisbury pl W1	139	O20
Salisbury rd E4	20	C11
Salisbury rd E7	52	E18
Salisbury rd E10	51	V7
Salisbury rd E12	53	P14
Salisbury rd E17	33	U16
Salisbury rd N4	30	J16
Salisbury rd N9	18	J9
Salisbury rd N22	30	H5
Salisbury rd SE25	123	Y16
Salisbury rd SW19	105	T18
Salisbury rd W13	72	A6
Salisbury rd Barn	4	E11
Salisbury rd Bex	98	E20
Salisbury rd Brom	127	R11
Salisbury rd Cars	130	M14
Salisbury rd Dag	56	H19
Salisbury rd Enf	9	Z1

Name	Page	Grid
Salisbury rd Har	23	R15
Salisbury rd Ilf	54	J5
Salisbury rd N Mal	117	Z10
Salisbury rd Rich	84	L10
Salisbury rd Rom	39	Z15
Salisbury rd Sthl	70	C10
Salisbury rd Wor Pk	128	A7
Salisbury sq EC4	149	V6
Salisbury st NW8	138	J18
Salisbury st W3	73	W4
Salisbury ter SE15	92	D7
Salisbury wk N19	47	U6
Salmen rd E13	65	R7
Salmon la E14	63	W17
Salmon rd Belv	81	T14
Salmon st NW9	43	U5
Salmons rd N9	18	K5
Salop rd E17	32	G17
Saltash clo Sutt	129	V9
Saltash rd Ilf	36	E1
Saltash rd Well	97	U2
Saltcoats rd W4	74	A6
Saltcroft clo Wem	43	S4
Salter rd SE16	75	S4
Salter st E14	64	A19
Salter st NW10	62	F10
Salterford rd SW17	107	P14
Salters hill SE19	109	O13
Salters rd E17	33	Y13
Salters rd W10	136	F18
Salterton rd N7	48	B9
Saltoun rd SW2	90	E11
Saltram clo N15	31	V11
Saltram cres W9	137	R11
Saltwell st E14	64	C19
Salusbury rd NW6	136	M4
Salvia gdns Grnf	59	Y5
Salvin rd SW15	87	O8
Salway clo Wdf Grn	34	E2
Salway rd E15	51	Y19
Sam Bartram clo SE7	77	Z13
Samantha clo E17	32	L20
Sambruck ms SE6	111	S3
Samels ct W6	74	G13
Samford st NW8	138	J18
Samos rd SE20	124	B3
Sampson ave Barn	4	D17
Sampson st E1	151	V14
Samson st E13	65	X7
Samuel clo E8	143	R4
Samuel clo SE14	75	T17
Samuel clo SE18	78	F10
Samuel Johnson clo SW16	108	E9
Samuel Lewis Trust dwellings SW3	154	K7
Samuel Lewis Trust dwellings SW6	153	V17
Samuel st SE18	78	F10
Sancroft clo NW2	44	K10
Sancroft rd Har	23	X7
Sancroft rd Stan	11	T17
Sancroft st SE11	157	S9
Sanctuary the Bex	97	W17
Sanctuary st SE1	150	C17
Sandal rd N18	18	K17
Sandal rd N Mal	118	A10
Sandal st E15	64	M3
Sandale clo N16	49	O10
Sandall clo W5	60	K11
Sandall rd NW5	47	W18
Sandall rd W5	60	J11
Sandalwood clo E1	63	W12
Sandbach pl SE18	79	P13
Sandbourne ave SW19	120	A3
Sandbourne rd SE4	92	H4
Sandbrook clo NW7	12	M18
Sandbrook rd N16	49	R9
Sandby grn SE9	95	S8
Sandell st SE1	149	T16
Sanders clo Hmptn	100	M13
Sanders la NW7	13	Z20
Sanderson clo NW5	47	S13
Sanderstead ave NW2	45	S7
Sanderstead clo SW12	89	V18
Sanderstead rd E10	50	J3
Sanderstead rd S Croy	133	N17
Sandfield gdns Th Hth	122	K6
Sandfield pas Th Hth	122	L5
Sandfield rd Th Hth	122	K7
Sandford ave N22	30	K3
Sandford clo E6	66	F11
Sandford ct N16	49	S3
Sandford rd E6	66	F9
Sandford rd Bexh	97	Z9
Sandford rd Brom	112	G8
Sandgate la SW18	106	J2
Sandgate rd Well	80	F18
Sandgate st SE15	159	V13
Sandhills Wall	131	Y8
Sandhurst ave Har	22	L18
Sandhurst ave Surb	117	S17
Sandhurst clo NW9	25	O10
Sandhurst clo S Croy	133	T19
Sandhurst dr Ilf	54	M12
Sandhurst rd N9	9	R20
Sandhurst rd NW9	25	P10
Sandhurst rd SE6	111	V1
Sandhurst rd Bex	97	W14
Sandhurst rd Sid	114	M7
Sandhurst way S Croy	133	T18
Sandiford rd Sutt	129	U3
Sandilands Croy	133	W3
Sandilands rd SW6	88	A3
Sandison st SE15	91	W6
Sandland st WC1	149	P2
Sandling ri SE9	113	W7
Sandlings the N22	30	H8
Sandmere rd SW4	90	A9
Sandown ave Dag	56	K17
Sandown dr Cars	131	O19
Sandown rd SE25	124	A11
Sandown way Nthlt	40	B20
Sandpit pl SE7	78	E13
Sandpit rd Brom	111	Z13
Sandpits rd Croy	134	F8
Sandpits rd Rich	102	H3
Sandra clo N22	30	L5
Sandra clo Houns	82	L14
Sandridge clo Har	23	U12
Sandringham ave SW20	119	T2
Sandringham clo Enf	8	E8
Sandringham cres Har	22	L20
Sandringham dr Well	96	G5
Sandringham gdns N8	30	B18
Sandringham gdns N12	15	T19
Sandringham gdns Ilf	36	D10
Sandringham rd E7	52	K16
Sandringham rd E8	49	U15
Sandringham rd E10	33	X19
Sandringham rd N22	30	L8
Sandringham rd NW2	44	J17
Sandringham rd NW11	45	S2
Sandringham rd Bark	54	K18
Sandringham rd Brom	112	G13
Sandringham rd Nthlt	40	H20
Sandringham rd Th Hth	123	N12
Sandringham rd Wor Pk	128	H5
Sandrock pl Croy	134	F8
Sandrock rd SE13	93	P7
Sand's End la SW6	88	B1
Sandstone rd SE12	112	H5
Sandtoft rd SE7	77	V16
Sandwell cres NW6	45	Z17
Sandwich st WC1	140	J14
Sandy Hill rd SE18	78	M13
Sandy Hill rd Wall	131	V19
Sandy la Kings T	102	C20
Sandy la Mitch	121	P1
Sandy la Orp	115	X20
Sandy la Rich	102	E5
Sandy la Sid	115	X17
Sandy la Sutt	129	T15
Sandy la Tedd	101	Y17
Sandy Lane north Wall	131	X15
Sandy Lane south Wall	31	V20
Sandy ridge Chis	113	W15
Sandy way Croy	134	K5
Sandycombe rd Rich	85	O7
Sandycombe rd Twick	84	D17
Sandycroft SE2	80	A16
Sandyhill rd Ilf	53	Z12
Sandymount ave Stan	11	T15
Sandys row E1	150	M2
Sanford st SE14	75	V16
Sanford ter N16	49	V8
Sanford wk SE14	75	V16
Sangley rd SE6	93	S20
Sangley rd SE25	123	T8
Sans wk EC1	141	V17
Sansom rd E11	52	B8
Sansom st SE5	158	G20
Santley st SW4	90	B10
Santos rd SW18	87	X13
Sapphire clo E6	66	J17
Sapphire clo Dag	55	U3
Sapphire rd SE8	75	W12
Sara ct Beck	125	T1
Saracen clo Croy	123	O13
Saracen st E14	64	B18
Sarah st N1	142	L12
Saratoga rd E5	50	D11
Sardinia st WC2	149	O5
Sarita clo Har	23	P6
Sark clo Houns	70	H20
Sark wk E16	65	W16
Sarre rd NW2	45	V14
Sarsen ave Houns	82	F4
Sarsfeld rd SW12	106	M3
Sarsfield rd Grnf	60	C5
Sartor rd SE15	92	E11
Satanita clo E16	66	A16
Satchell mead NW9	26	D3
Satchwell st E2	143	R14
Saunders Ness rd E14	76	J12
Saunders rd SE18	79	X14
Saunderton rd Wem	42	B15
Saunton rd Horn	57	W5
Savage gdns E6	66	H18
Savage gdns EC3	150	M8
Savernake rd N9	8	L20
Savernake rd NW3	47	N12
Savile row N Mal	118	B13
Savile gdns Croy	133	V4
Savile row W1	148	B9
Savill gdns SW20	118	H5
Savill row Wdf Grn	21	R17
Saville rd E16	78	D3
Saville rd W4	73	X8
Saville rd Rom	38	B19
Saville rd Twick	101	W2
Saville row N9	9	S9
Savona clo SW19	105	R17
Savona st SW8	156	B18
Savoy clo Edg	12	C15
Savoy hill WC2	149	N10
Savoy pl WC2	148	M11
Savoy row WC2	149	N10
Savoy steps WC2	149	N10
Savoy st WC2	149	N10
Savoy way WC2	149	N10
Sawkins clo SW19	105	R4
Sawley rd W12	74	F1
Sawtry clo Cars	120	H18
Sawyer st SE1	150	A16
Sawyers clo Dag	56	K17
Sawyer's hill Rich	84	M19
Sawyers Lawn W13	59	Y17
Saxby rd SW2	90	A18
Saxham rd Bark	67	W5
Saxlingham rd E4	20	L11
Saxon ave Felt	100	C3
Saxon clo Surb	116	J15
Saxon dr W3	61	S15
Saxon rd E3	63	X6
Saxon rd E6	66	F12
Saxon rd N22	30	J4
Saxon rd SE25	123	O12
Saxon rd Brom	112	D18
Saxon rd Ilf	54	A16
Saxon rd Sthl	70	C1
Saxon rd Wem	43	V9
Saxon wk Sid	115	T14
Saxon way N14	6	J19
Saxonbury clo Mitch	120	F6
Saxonbury gdns Surb	116	E19
Saxton clo SE13	93	X9
Sayes Court st SE8	75	Z15
Scala st W1	148	D1
Scales rd N17	31	W17
Scampston ms W10	144	H5
Scandrett st E1	151	W15
Scarborough rd E11	51	X4
Scarborough rd N4	48	G2
Scarborough rd N9	19	P1
Scarborough st E1	151	P7
Scarbrook rd Croy	132	L6
Scarle rd Wem	42	H17
Scarlet rd SE6	111	Z6
Scarsbrook rd SE3	95	O6
Scarsdale pl W8	153	X1
Scarsdale rd Har	40	M10
Scarsdale vill W8	153	U3
Scarth rd SW13	86	F6
Scawen rd SE8	75	V13
Scawfell st E2	143	R9
Scaynes link N12	14	K15
Sceptre rd E2	63	R9
Scholars rd E4	20	J6
Scholars rd SW12	107	U1
Scholefield rd N19	47	Y5
Scholes cres SW2	108	H1
School House la Tedd	102	C19
School la SE23	110	A4
School la Kings T	116	F2
School la Pnr	22	B12
School la Well	97	S7
School pas Kings T	117	N4
School pas Sthl	70	F1
School rd E12	53	T13
School rd NW10	61	Z12
School rd Chis	114	C20
School rd Dag	69	T2
School rd Hmptn	100	M14
School rd Houns	83	N7
School rd Kings T	116	F2
School Road ave Hmptn	100	M14
School way N12	15	S12
Schoolhouse la E1	63	T19
Schoolway N12	15	V18
Schoolway Dag	55	T9
Schubert rd SW15	87	W13
Sclater st E1	143	O17
Scoresby st SE1	149	X15
Scorton ave Grnf	59	Y6
Scot gro Pnr	22	A1
Scotch common W13	60	A13
Scoter clo Wdf Grn	34	J1
Scotland grn N17	31	W6
Scotland Green rd Enf	9	T16
Scotland Green Road north Enf	9	V15
Scotland pl SW1	148	K13
Scotland rd Buck H	21	Y6
Scotsdale clo Sutt	129	T16
Scotsdale rd SE12	94	J14
Scotswood st EC1	141	V16
Scott clo SW16	122	C2
Scott cres Har	40	K5
Scott Ellis gdns NW8	138	F14
Scott Farm clo T Ditt	116	A20
Scott Lidgett cres SE16	151	T19
Scott st E1	143	W17
Scotts ave Brom	125	X3
Scotts dr Hmptn	100	K17
Scotts la Brom	125	X3
Scotts rd E10	51	U4

Name	Page	Ref
Scotts rd W12	144	A18
Scotts rd Brom	112	E19
Scott's yd EC4	150	E8
Scoulding rd E16	65	S16
Scout app NW10	44	A12
Scout way NW7	12	M13
Scovell rd SE1	150	A19
Scrattons ter Bark	68	J4
Scriven st E8	143	P3
Scrooby st SE6	93	R17
Scrubs la NW10	62	H9
Scrubs la W10	144	A1
Scrutton clo SW12	89	X19
Scrutton st EC2	142	J17
Scudamore la NW9	25	U11
Scutari rd SE22	92	B14
Scylla rd SE15	91	Y7
Seabright st E2	143	W14
Seabrook dr W Wick	135	Z3
Seabrook gdns Rom	56	F1
Seabrook rd Dag	55	W9
Seacoal la EC4	149	X6
Seacole clo W3	61	Y16
Seacourt rd SE2	80	J5
Seafield rd N11	16	K15
Seaford rd E17	33	R11
Seaford rd N15	31	P14
Seaford rd W13	72	A2
Seaford rd Enf	8	E13
Seaford st WC1	140	M14
Seaforth ave N Mal	118	J12
Seaforth cres N5	48	M15
Seaforth gdns N21	17	S3
Seaforth gdns Epsom	128	D8
Seaforth gdns Wdf Grn	21	Y16
Seager pl E3	63	Y14
Seagrave rd SW6	153	U12
Seagry rd E11	34	G20
Seal st E8	49	V13
Searle pl N4	48	D4
Searles clo SW11	154	L19
Searles rd SE1	158	F4
Sears st SE5	158	E17
Seasprite clo Nthlt	58	A8
Seaton ave Ilf	54	J14
Seaton clo E13	65	U12
Seaton clo SE11	157	V9
Seaton clo SW15	86	L20
Seaton clo Twick	83	O16
Seaton pl NW1	140	A16
Seaton rd Dart	99	W18
Seaton rd Mitch	120	J4
Seaton rd Twick	83	O16
Seaton rd Well	80	F20
Seaton rd Wem	60	K5
Seaton st N18	18	L17
Sebastian st EC1	141	Y14
Sebastopol rd N9	18	K12
Sebbon st N1	141	Y1
Sebert rd E7	52	H14
Sebright rd Barn	4	D10
Secker cres Har	22	M5
Secker st SE1	149	T14
Second ave E12	53	S13
Second ave E13	65	T8
Second ave E17	33	P15
Second ave N18	19	P12
Second ave NW4	27	O12
Second ave SW14	86	A6
Second ave W3	74	D3
Second ave W10	137	N16
Second ave Dag	69	V4
Second ave Enf	8	G16
Second ave Rom	37	U15
Second ave Wem	42	H6
Second Cross rd Twick	101	S3
Second way Wem	43	T12
Sedan way SE17	158	J8
Sedcombe clo Sid	115	S10
Sedcote rd Enf	9	T16
Sedding st SW1	155	S6
Seddon rd Mord	120	G13
Seddon st WC1	141	O15
Sedge rd N17	32	C1
Sedgebrook rd SE3	95	P6
Sedgecombe ave Har	24	E16
Sedgeford rd W12	74	E1
Sedgehill rd SE6	111	P11
Sedgemere ave N2	28	D10
Sedgemere rd SE2	80	H8
Sedgemoor dr Dag	56	F11
Sedgeway SE6	112	B2
Sedgewood clo Brom	126	C17
Sedgmoor pl SE5	158	K19
Sedgwick rd E10	51	T7
Sedgwick st E9	50	F16
Sedleigh rd SW18	87	W15
Sedlescombe rd SW6	153	T14
Seeley dr SE21	109	T10
Seelig ave NW9	44	F1
Seely rd SW17	107	O15
Seething la EC3	150	L9
Seething Wells la Surb	116	E15
Sefton ave NW7	12	K17
Sefton ave Har	23	P6
Sefton rd Croy	123	Z20
Sefton st SW15	86	M6
Segal clo SE23	92	J19
Sekforde st EC1	141	W16
Selbie ave NW10	44	D15
Selborne ave E12	53	W11
Selborne ave Bex	97	Y20
Selborne gdns NW4	26	G13
Selborne gdns Grnf	59	Y5
Selborne rd E17	32	M15
Selborne rd N14	17	O9
Selborne rd N22	30	C5
Selborne rd Croy	133	T7
Selborne rd Ilf	53	W7
Selborne rd N Mal	118	A4
Selborne rd Sid	115	R10
Selby clo E6	66	D16
Selby clo Chis	113	W15
Selby gdns Sthl	58	G12
Selby grn Cars	120	L16
Selby rd E11	52	A10
Selby rd E13	65	W13
Selby rd N17	18	E20
Selby rd SE20	123	Z3
Selby rd W5	60	C11
Selby rd Cars	120	K16
Selby st E1	143	U18
Selden rd SE15	92	D5
Selhurst New rd SE25	123	R14
Selhurst pl SE25	123	R15
Selhurst rd N9	18	C10
Selhurst rd SE25	123	R14
Selinas la Dag	56	B2
Selkirk dr Erith	99	S1
Selkirk rd SW17	106	J10
Selkirk rd Twick	100	M3
Sellers Hall clo N3	27	X2
Sellincourt rd SW17	106	K13
Sellindge clo Beck	110	M19
Sellon ms SE11	157	O6
Sellons ave NW10	62	E3
Sellwood dr Barn	4	C17
Selsdon ave S Croy	133	P13
Selsdon clo Rom	38	K3
Selsdon clo Surb	116	K12
Selsdon Park rd S Croy	134	G20
Selsdon rd E11	34	F20
Selsdon rd E13	65	Y4
Selsdon rd NW2	44	E7
Selsdon rd SE27	108	H8
Selsdon rd S Croy	133	N10
Selsdon Road Industrial est Croy	133	P16
Selsdon way E14	76	E9
Selsey cres Well	97	V1
Selsey st E14	64	B14
Selvage la NW7	12	K15
Selwood pl SW7	154	F9
Selwood rd Croy	133	Z2
Selwood rd Sutt	119	V19
Selworthy clo E11	34	E16
Selworthy rd SE6	110	L7
Selwyn ave E4	20	F20
Selwyn ave Ilf	36	J17
Selwyn ave Rich	84	L9
Selwyn clo Houns	82	C9
Selwyn cres Well	97	P9
Selwyn rd E3	63	X7
Selwyn rd E13	65	U4
Selwyn rd NW10	43	Z20
Selwyn rd N Mal	117	Y11
Semley pl SW1	155	W7
Semley rd SW16	122	A3
Senate st SE15	92	E6
Seneca rd Th Hth	122	L10
Senga rd Wall	131	O1
Senhouse rd Sutt	129	O6
Senior st W2	137	X20
Senlac rd SE12	112	H2
Sennen rd Enf	18	G2
Sennen wk SE9	113	S7
Senrab st E1	63	T17
Sentinel clo Nthlt	58	C10
Sentinel sq NW4	27	N14
September way Stan	11	P19
Sequoia rd (Bushey) Wat	10	C6
Serbin clo E10	51	V2
Serjeants Inn EC4	149	U6
Serle st WC2	149	R5
Serpentine rd W2	147	O14
Serviden dr Brom	113	N20
Setchell way SE1	159	N4
Seton gdns Dag	55	U20
Settles st E1	151	U3
Settrington rd SW6	88	A5
Seven acres Cars	130	J4
Seven Kings rd Ilf	54	K5
Seven Sisters rd N4	48	J4
Seven Sisters rd N7	48	E8
Seven Sisters rd N15	31	O20
Sevenoaks clo Bexh	98	J10
Sevenoaks rd SE4	92	K15
Sevenoaks way Orp	115	T19
Sevenoaks way Sid	115	S18
Seventh ave E12	53	U12
Severn ave Rom	39	Z9
Severn dr Enf	8	L1
Severn way NW10	44	D15
Severnake clo E14	76	C10
Severus rd SW11	88	K10
Seville st SW1	147	R18
Sevington rd NW4	26	J17
Sevington st W9	137	W17
Seward rd W7	71	Y4
Seward rd Beck	124	G4
Seward st EC1	142	A15
Sewardstone rd E2	63	P5
Sewardstone rd E4	20	D3
Sewdley st E5	50	E10
Sewell rd SE2	80	A7
Sewell st E13	65	U8
Sextant ave E14	76	J10
Seymer rd Rom	39	N11
Seymour ave N17	31	W7
Seymour ave Epsom	128	K20
Seymour ave Mord	119	P16
Seymour clo Pnr	22	D4
Seymour gdns SE4	92	H7
Seymour gdns Ilf	53	U4
Seymour gdns Surb	117	N13
Seymour gdns Twick	84	A19
Seymour ms W1	147	T5
Seymour pl SE25	123	Z10
Seymour pl W1	147	N1
Seymour rd E4	20	D4
Seymour rd E6	66	A4
Seymour rd E10	50	L3
Seymour rd N3	28	B1
Seymour rd N8	30	G16
Seymour rd N9	19	O8
Seymour rd SW18	87	W17
Seymour rd SW19	105	P5
Seymour rd W4	73	W10
Seymour rd Cars	131	O11
Seymour rd Hmptn	101	N12
Seymour rd Kings T	116	F1
Seymour rd Mitch	121	O18
Seymour st W1	147	P6
Seymour st W2	147	N7
Seymour ter SE20	123	Z2
Seymour vill SE20	123	Z1
Seymour wk SW10	154	C12
Seyssel st E14	76	H11
Shaa rd W3	73	Y1
Shacklegate la Tedd	101	T10
Shackleton clo SE23	110	B4
Shackleton rd Sthl	58	E20
Shacklewell grn E8	49	V13
Shacklewell la E8	49	U15
Shacklewell rd N16	49	V12
Shacklewell row E8	49	V13
Shacklewell st E2	143	P15
Shad Thames SE1	151	O15
Shadbolt clo Wor Pk	128	D3
Shadwell dr Nthlt	58	D8
Shadwell pl E1	151	Z7
Shady Bush clo (Bushey) Wat	10	B2
Shaef way Tedd	101	Z17
Shafter rd Dag	56	K17
Shaftesbury ave W1	148	E9
Shaftesbury ave WC2	148	H7
Shaftesbury ave Barn	5	R12
Shaftesbury ave Enf	9	S9
Shaftesbury ave Har	40	M3
Shaftesbury ave (Kenton) Har	24	H17
Shaftesbury ave Sthl	70	G10
Shaftesbury ms W8	153	U3
Shaftesbury rd E4	20	K5
Shaftesbury rd E7	52	L20
Shaftesbury rd E10	51	P5
Shaftesbury rd E17	33	R17
Shaftesbury rd N18	18	F18
Shaftesbury rd N19	48	A3
Shaftesbury rd Beck	125	N4
Shaftesbury rd Cars	120	G17
Shaftesbury rd Rich	84	J9
Shaftesbury st N1	142	E19
Shaftesbury way Twick	101	R6
Shaftesburys the Bark	67	P5
Shafto ms SW1	155	P3
Shafton rd E9	63	T2
Shakespeare ave N11	16	J16
Shakespeare ave NW10	61	X2
Shakespeare cres E12	53	U16
Shakespeare cres NW10	61	Y3
Shakespeare dr Har	25	N19
Shakespeare gdns N2	28	M12
Shakespeare rd E17	32	G8
Shakespeare rd N3	27	Y3
Shakespeare rd NW7	13	T14
Shakespeare rd SE24	90	H14
Shakespeare rd W3	73	W1
Shakespeare rd W7	59	V20
Shakespeare rd Bexh	97	Y19
Shakespeare rd Rom	39	V17
Shakespeare wk N16	49	R13
Shalcomb st SW10	154	E15
Shaldon dr Mord	119	S12
Shaldon rd Edg	24	M6
Shalfleet dr W10	144	G8
Shalimar gdns W3	61	U19
Shalimar rd W3	61	U19
Shallons rd SE9	113	Z9
Shalston vill Surb	116	M15
Shalstone rd SW14	85	T7
Shamrock rd Croy	122	D14
Shamrock st SW4	89	W7
Shamrock way N14	16	E5
Shand st SE1	150	K16
Shandon rd SW4	89	V15
Shandy st E1	63	U13
Shanklin rd N8	29	Y17
Shanklin rd N15	31	X13
Shannon clo Sthl	70	A13
Shannon gro SW9	90	D9
Shannon pl NW8	138	L8
Shannon way Beck	111	R16
Shap cres Cars	120	L19
Shapland way N13	17	R16
Shardcroft ave SE24	90	K13
Shardeloes rd SE14	92	K6
Sharnbrooke clo Well	97	T8

Sharon clo Surb	116	F19
Sharon gdns E9	63	P2
Sharon rd W4	73	Y13
Sharon rd Enf	9	W7
Sharpleshall st NW1	139	R2
Sharpness clo Hayes	58	B14
Sharratt st SE15	75	R16
Sharsted st SE17	157	W12
Shaw ave Bark	68	L5
Shaw clo SE28	80	E3
Shaw clo Horn	57	Z4
Shaw clo (Bushey) Wat	10	E7
Shaw gdns Bark	68	L5
Shaw rd Brom	112	B8
Shaw rd Enf	9	T6
Shaw sq E17	32	K4
Shaw way Wall	131	Z16
Shawbrooke rd SE9	94	M13
Shawbury rd SE22	91	V12
Shawfield pk Brom	127	O3
Shawfield st SW3	154	M11
Shaws cotts SE23	110	H6
Shaxton cres Croy	135	U20
Shearing dr Cars	120	D17
Shearling way N7	48	A16
Shearman rd SE3	94	B9
Shearwood cres Dart	99	V6
Sheaveshill ave NW9	26	B13
Sheen Common dr Rich	85	R11
Sheen ct Rich	85	R9
Sheen Court rd Rich	85	R9
Sheen Gate gdns SW14	85	V10
Sheen gro N1	141	S4
Sheen la SW14	85	X7
Sheen pk Rich	84	K12
Sheen rd Rich	84	L11
Sheen wd SW14	85	V12
Sheendale rd Rich	84	M9
Sheenewood SE26	110	B10
Sheep la E8	143	W6
Sheep Walk ms SW19	105	R15
Sheepcote la SW11	88	L5
Sheepcote rd Har	23	W18
Sheepcotes rd Rom	37	Y13
Sheephouse way N Mal	117	Y19
Sheerwater rd E16	66	B14
Sheffield st WC2	149	O6
Sheffield ter W8	145	V15
Sheila rd Rom	38	G1
Shelbourne clo Pnr	22	D11
Shelbourne rd N17	31	Z6
Shelburne rd N7	48	D11
Shelbury clo Sid	115	N8
Shelbury rd SE22	92	B14
Sheldon ave N6	46	K2
Sheldon ave Ilf	35	Y7
Sheldon clo SE12	94	H14
Sheldon rd N18	18	F14
Sheldon rd NW2	45	P13
Sheldon rd Bexh	98	B3
Sheldon rd Dag	55	Z20
Sheldon st Croy	132	L7
Sheldrake pl W8	145	S17
Sheldrick clo SW19	120	F3
Shelduck clo NW9	26	A7
Shelford pl N16	49	O10
Shelford ri SE19	109	T19
Shelford rd Barn	4	A19
Shelgate rd SW11	88	L12
Shell clo Brom	127	T15
Shell rd SE13	93	R7
Shelley ave E12	53	R18
Shelley ave Grnf	59	P8
Shelley ave Horn	57	U5
Shelley clo Edg	12	B14
Shelley clo Grnf	59	P9
Shelley cres Sthl	58	F18
Shelley dr Well	96	J2
Shelley gdns Wem	42	D8
Shelley way SW19	106	F14
Shellgrove est N16	49	T15
Shellness rd E5	50	A14
Shellwood rd SW11	88	M6
Shelmerdine clo E3	64	A14
Shelton rd SW19	105	Y20
Shelton st WC2	148	J7
Shenfield rd Wdf Grn	34	H2
Shenfield st N1	142	L10
Shenley rd SE5	91	T2
Shenley rd Houns	82	B2
Shenstone clo Dart	98	M11
Shepherd mkt W1	147	X13
Shepherd st W1	147	W14
Shepherdess pl N1	142	D12
Shepherdess wk N1	142	C8
Shepherds Bush grn W12	144	D17
Shepherds Bush mkt W12	144	C18
Shepherds Bush pl W12	144	G16
Shepherds Bush rd W6	144	E18
Shepherds clo Rom	37	W14
Shepherds hill N6	29	S19
Shepherds la E9	50	E16
Shepherds la Dart	99	X20
Shepherds pl W1	147	T8
Shepherds wk NW2	44	F6
Shepherds wk NW3	46	F14
Shepherds wk (Bushey) Wat	10	D7
Shepherds way S Croy	134	E17
Shepley clo Cars	131	O5
Shepperton rd N1	142	D3
Sheppey gdns Dag	55	S19
Sheppey rd Dag	55	R20
Sherard rd SE9	95	S13
Sheraton st W1	148	E6
Sherborne ave Enf	9	P7
Sherborne ave Sthl	70	G10
Sherborne gdns NW9	25	P10
Sherborne gdns W13	60	B15
Sherborne la EC4	150	F8
Sherborne rd Sutt	129	X2
Sherborne st N1	142	E3
Sherboro rd N15	31	U17
Sherbourne cres Cars	120	J17
Sherbrook gdns N21	17	X2
Sherbrooke clo Bexh	98	D9
Sherbrooke rd SW6	152	M19
Shere rd Ilf	35	Y16
Sheredan rd E4	20	L16
Sherfield gdns SW15	86	C16
Sheridan ct Houns	82	C13
Sheridan cres Chis	127	Z2
Sheridan gdns Har	24	F19
Sheridan rd E7	52	D10
Sheridan rd E12	53	T16
Sheridan rd SW19	119	V2
Sheridan rd Belv	81	S10
Sheridan rd Bexh	97	Z7
Sheridan rd Rich	102	D7
Sheridan st E1	151	Z6
Sheridan wk Beck	124	L1
Sheringham ave E12	53	V11
Sheringham ave N14	6	K17
Sheringham ave Rom	38	L19
Sheringham ave Twick	100	F2
Sheringham dr Bark	54	M14
Sheringham rd N7	48	E17
Sheringham rd SE20	124	B5
Sherington ave Pnr	22	H1
Sherington rd SE7	77	V17
Sherland rd Twick	83	X20
Sherman rd Brom	126	G1
Shernhall st E17	33	T9
Sherrard rd E7	52	K17
Sherrard rd E12	53	P16
Sherrards way Barn	4	M17
Sherrick Green rd NW10	44	J15
Sherriff rd NW6	45	Z19
Sherrin rd E10	51	P11
Sherringham ave N17	31	W6
Sherrock gdns NW4	26	H11
Sherwin rd SE14	92	F3
Sherwood ave E18	34	H11
Sherwood ave SW16	107	W19
Sherwood ave Grnf	41	U16
Sherwood clo SW13	86	K8
Sherwood clo W13	72	A3
Sherwood clo Bex	97	U16
Sherwood gdns E14	76	C11
Sherwood gdns Bark	54	E19
Sherwood Park ave Sid	97	O17
Sherwood Park rd Mitch	121	V8
Sherwood Park rd Sutt	129	Z11
Sherwood rd NW4	26	M10
Sherwood rd SW19	105	V19
Sherwood rd Croy	123	Z18
Sherwood rd Hmptn	100	M11
Sherwood rd Har	40	M7
Sherwood rd Ilf	36	D14
Sherwood rd Well	96	H6
Sherwood st N20	15	S10
Sherwood st W1	148	D9
Sherwood ter N20	15	T10
Sherwood way W Wick	135	T3
Shetland rd E3	63	Z6
Shield dr Brent	71	Z17
Shieldhall st SE2	80	F11
Shifford path SE23	110	G6
Shillibeer pl W1	146	M1
Shillingford st N1	141	Y2
Shillitoe rd N13	17	X15
Shinfield st W12	144	C5
Shinglewell rd Erith	81	S19
Shinners clo SE25	123	X11
Ship and Mermaid row SE1	150	H17
Ship la SW14	85	W6
Ship st SE8	93	O2
Shipka rd SW12	107	S1
Shipman rd E16	65	W18
Shipman rd SE23	110	G4
Shipton clo Dag	55	W9
Shipton st E2	143	R11
Shipwright rd SE16	75	W6
Shirburn clo SE23	92	D20
Shirbutt st E14	64	D19
Shirebrook rd SE3	95	O6
Shirehall clo NW4	27	P17
Shirehall gdns NW4	27	P17
Shirehall la NW4	27	P17
Shirehall pk NW4	27	O19
Shires the Rich	102	K11
Shirland ms W9	137	R15
Shirland rd W9	137	P14
Shirley ave Bex	97	V20
Shirley ave Croy	134	C1
Shirley ave Sutt	130	H8
Shirley ave Sutt (Cheam)	129	U20
Shirley Church rd Croy	134	E4
Shirley clo E17	33	T14
Shirley clo Houns	82	M14
Shirley cres Beck	124	H10
Shirley dr Houns	82	M13
Shirley gdns W7	71	X2
Shirley gdns Bark	54	G17
Shirley gro N9	19	S2
Shirley gro SW11	89	P8
Shirley heights Wall	131	U20
Shirley Hills rd Croy	134	F8
Shirley House dr SE7	77	Y18
Shirley Oaks rd Croy	134	F2
Shirley Park rd Croy	124	B19
Shirley rd E15	52	B20
Shirley rd W4	73	Z6
Shirley rd Croy	124	A18
Shirley rd Enf	7	Z12
Shirley rd Sid	114	H7
Shirley rd Wall	131	U19
Shirley st E16	65	P17
Shirley way Croy	134	J5
Shirlock rd NW3	47	N13
Shobden rd N17	31	O5
Shoe la EC4	149	V4
Shoebury rd E6	53	U19
Shoot Up hill NW2	45	T16
Shooters ave Har	24	E12
Shooter's hill SE18	95	X3
Shooter's hill Well	96	C4
Shooter's Hill rd SE3	77	X20
Shooter's Hill rd SE10	93	X2
Shooter's Hill rd SE18	95	R1
Shooters rd Enf	7	V5
Shore clo Hmptn	100	C14
Shore gro Felt	100	F5
Shore pl E9	63	P1
Shore rd E9	63	P1
Shoreditch High st E1	142	M14
Shoreham clo Bex	115	W2
Shoreham clo Croy	124	C13
Shoreham way Brom	126	D16
Shorncliffe rd SE1	158	M10
Shorndean st SE6	93	V20
Shorne clo Sid	97	S15
Shornefield clo Brom	127	W5
Shornells way SE2	80	E13
Shorrolds rd SW6	153	R18
Short gate N12	14	J12
Short Hedges Houns	82	J3
Short rd E11	51	Z6
Short rd E15	64	K2
Short rd W4	74	A16
Short st SE1	149	V16
Short wall E15	64	H8
Short way N12	15	X18
Short way SE9	95	R8
Short way Twick	83	N19
Shortcroft rd Epsom	128	E16
Shortcrofts rd Dag	56	B17
Shorter st E1	151	O9
Shortland rd E10	33	R20
Shortlands W6	152	G7
Shortlands clo N18	18	C12
Shortlands gdns Brom	126	B2
Shortlands gro Brom	125	X5
Shortlands rd Brom	125	X7
Shortlands rd Kings T	103	N18
Shorts cft NW9	25	U12
Shorts gdns WC2	148	K5
Shorts rd Cars	130	K10
Shotfield Wall	131	T14
Shottendane rd SW6	87	X1
Shottery clo SE9	113	S6
Shottfield ave SW14	86	A9
Shouldham st W1	147	N3
Shrapnel clo SE18	78	E18
Shrapnel rd SE9	95	U8
Shrewsbury ave SW14	85	X11
Shrewsbury ave Har	24	K12
Shrewsbury cres NW10	61	Y4
Shrewsbury la SE18	95	Z3
Shrewsbury ms W2	145	T3
Shrewsbury rd E7	53	N15
Shrewsbury rd N11	16	J17
Shrewsbury rd W2	145	T3
Shrewsbury rd Beck	124	K6
Shrewsbury rd Cars	120	E14
Shrewton rd SW17	106	M17
Shroffold rd Brom	112	A9
Shropshire clo Mitch	122	B10
Shropshire pl WC1	140	E19
Shropshire rd N22	30	C1
Shroton st NW1	138	L19
Shrubberies the E18	34	F6
Shrubbery clo N1	142	B5
Shrubbery gdns N21	17	W3
Shrubbery rd N9	18	K11
Shrubbery rd SW16	108	A10
Shrubbery rd Sthl	70	F1

Shrubland gro	128	L6
Wor Pk		
Shrubland rd E8	143	R3
Shrubland rd E10	33	P20
Shrubland rd E17	33	N15
Shrublands ave Croy	135	O7
Shrublands clo N20	15	U19
Shrublands clo SE26	110	C8
Shurland ave Barn	5	U19
Shurland gdns SE15	159	P17
Shuttle clo Sid	96	K20
Shuttle rd Dart	99	W8
Shuttle st E1	143	R18
Shuttlemead Bex	98	B17
Shuttleworth rd SW11	88	J4
Sibella rd SW4	89	Y6
Sibley clo Bexh	97	Z13
Sibley gro E12	53	S20
Sibthorp rd Mitch	120	M4
Sibthorpe rd SE12	94	K18
Sibton rd Cars	120	J17
Sidbury st SW6	87	S1
Sidcup bypass Orp	115	Y19
Sidcup bypass Sid	114	G8
Sidcup High st Sid	115	N9
Sidcup hill Sid	115	N12
Sidcup Hill gdns Sid	115	T14
Sidcup pl Sid	115	N12
Sidcup rd SE9	94	L19
Sidcup rd SE12	94	K14
Sidcup Technology	115	W14
cen Sid		
Siddons rd N17	31	X5
Siddons rd SE23	110	H5
Siddons rd Croy	132	H5
Side rd E17	32	L15
Sidewood rd SE9	114	E1
Sidford pl SE1	157	R2
Sidings the E11	51	V3
Sidmouth ave Islw	83	T4
Sidmouth rd E10	51	U8
Sidmouth rd NW2	136	B1
Sidmouth rd SE15	91	V1
Sidmouth rd Well	80	F19
Sidmouth st WC1	141	N15
Sidney ave N13	17	R17
Sidney gdns Brent	72	F16
Sidney gro EC1	141	X10
Sidney rd E7	52	F10
Sidney rd N22	30	C1
Sidney rd SE25	123	W11
Sidney rd SW9	90	D5
Sidney rd Beck	124	J3
Sidney rd Har	23	O10
Sidney rd Twick	84	A16
Sidney sq E1	63	P15
Sidney st E1	143	Z20
Sidworth st E8	143	Y2
Siebert rd SE3	77	T17
Siemens rd E18	28	C8
Sigdon rd E8	49	Y15
Signmakers yd NW1	139	Z5
Silbury ave Mitch	120	J1
Silbury st N1	142	F13
Silchester rd W10	144	H7
Silecroft rd Bexh	98	F2
Silex st SE1	149	Y18
Silk clo SE12	94	E14
Silk Mills path SE13	93	U6
Silk st EC2	142	D20
Silkfield rd NW9	26	C15
Silkstream rd Edg	25	W5
Silsoe rd N22	30	D8
Silver Birch ave E4	19	Z17
Silver Birch clo N11	16	B20
Silver clo SE14	75	V19
Silver clo Har	23	P1
Silver cres W4	73	T12
Silver la W Wick	135	W3
Silver rd W12	144	F11
Silver Spring clo	81	W16
Erith		
Silver st N18	18	C14
Silver st Enf	8	D12
Silver wk SE16	75	X3
Silver way Rom	38	G11
Silvercliffe gdns	5	W14
Barn		
Silverdale SE26	110	D11
Silverdale Enf	7	O15
Silverdale ave Ilf	36	J17
Silverdale clo W7	71	U2
Silverdale clo Nthlt	40	E15
Silverdale clo Sutt	129	V8
Silverdale dr SE9	113	P5
Silverdale dr Horn	57	Y15
Silverdale rd E4	20	K19
Silverdale rd Bexh	98	G6
Silverhall st Islw	83	Z7
Silverholme clo Har	42	J1
Silverland st E16	78	H3
Silverleigh rd Th Hth	122	C9
Silvermere rd SE6	93	P16
Silverst clo Nthlt	40	L18
Silverston way Stan	11	S19
Silverthorn gdns E4	20	C7
Silverthorne rd SW8	89	T4
Silverton rd W6	152	F16
Silvertown way E16	65	O16
Silvertree la Grnf	59	R8
Silverwood clo Beck	111	N17
Silvester rd SE22	91	V14
Silwood st SE16	75	S13
Simla clo SE14	75	V17
Simmons clo N20	15	X6
Simmons la E4	20	K9
Simmons rd SE18	78	L12
Simmons way N20	15	W7
Simms clo Cars	130	J4
Simms rd SE1	159	T7
Simnel rd SE12	94	H18
Simon clo W11	145	S9
Simonds rd E10	51	O6
Simone clo Brom	127	P1
Simons wk E15	51	X16
Simpson rd Houns	82	E17
Simpson rd Rain	57	U18
Simpson rd Rich	102	D9
Simpson st SW11	88	H5
Simpsons rd E14	64	E20
Simpsons rd Brom	126	F7
Sims clo Rom	39	U14
Sinclair ct Beck	111	O19
Sinclair dr Sutt	130	A19
Sinclair gdns W14	144	H19
Sinclair gro NW11	27	R19
Sinclair rd E4	19	X16
Sinclair rd W14	144	J19
Sinclare clo Enf	8	H5
Singapore rd W13	71	Y2
Singer st EC2	142	H15
Singleton clo SW17	106	L17
Singleton clo Croy	122	L16
Singleton rd Dag	56	C16
Singleton Scarp N12	14	L15
Sinnott rd E17	32	G3
Sion rd Twick	84	A20
Sir Alexander clo W3	74	C2
Sir Alexander rd W3	74	D1
Sirdar rd N22	30	J9
Sirdar rd W11	144	J9
Sirdar rd Mitch	107	N16
Sise la EC4	150	D7
Sisley rd Bark	67	W3
Sispara gdns SW18	87	V15
Sissinghurst rd Croy	123	Y17
Sister Mabel's way	159	S18
SE15		
Sisters ave SW11	89	N9
Sistova rd SW12	107	T1
Sisulu pl SW9	90	G7
Sittingbourne ave Enf	8	C19
Sitwell gro Stan	10	H16
Siviter rd Dag	56	H19
Siviter way Dag	56	H19
Siward rd N17	31	O5
Siward rd SW17	106	C7
Siward rd Brom	126	J7
Sixth ave E12	53	T12
Sixth ave W10	136	J15
Sixth Cross rd Twick	100	M6
Skardu rd NW2	45	S14
Skeena hill SW18	87	S19
Skeffington rd E6	66	F2
Skelbrook st SW18	106	C4
Skelgill rd SW15	87	V11
Skelley rd E15	52	C20
Skelton rd E7	52	G19
Skeltons la E10	51	S2
Skelwith rd W6	152	E14
Skerne rd Kings T	102	H20
Sketchley gdns SE16	75	S13
Sketty rd Enf	8	F11
Skiers st E15	64	M3
Skiffington clo SW2	90	G20
Skinner ct E2	143	Y8
Skinner pl SW1	155	T7
Skinner st EC1	141	V15
Skinners la EC4	150	D8
Skinners la Houns	82	J1
Skinner's row SE10	93	R2
Skipsey ave E6	66	H10
Skipton rd SE1	157	Z2
Skipworth rd E9	63	R2
Sky Peals rd	33	W3
Wdf Grn		
Slade the SE18	79	V16
Slade gdns Erith	99	V1
Slade Green rd Erith	99	X1
Sladebrook rd SE3	95	O6
Sladedale rd SE18	79	V15
Slades clo Enf	7	T11
Slades dr Chis	114	C9
Slades gdns Enf	7	T9
Slades hill Enf	7	T10
Slades ri Enf	7	T11
Slagrove pl SE13	93	R13
Slaidburn st SW10	154	D16
Slaithwaite rd SE13	93	V11
Sleaford st SW8	156	C18
Slingsby pl WC2	148	J7
Slippers pl SE16	159	Y2
Sloane ave SW3	154	L6
Sloane Court east	155	S9
SW3		
Sloane Court west	155	S9
SW3		
Sloane gdns SW1	155	S7
Sloane sq SW1	155	S6
Sloane st SW1	147	P18
Sloane ter SW1	155	S5
Sloane wk Croy	124	K15
Slocum clo SE28	68	F20
Slough la NW9	25	V16
Sly st E1	151	W5
Smallberry ave Islw	83	X5
Smallbrook ms W2	146	E7
Smalley clo N16	49	V8
Smallwood rd SW17	106	F12
Smarden clo Belv	81	S13
Smarden gro SE9	113	U9
Smart st E2	63	T8
Smart's pl WC2	148	L4
Smeaton rd SW18	87	X19
Smeaton st E1	151	V13
Smedley st SW4	89	Y5
Smedley st SW8	89	Y4
Smeed rd E3	64	A1
Smiles pl SE13	93	U4
Smith clo SE16	75	T3
Smith sq SW1	156	J3
Smith st SW3	155	O10
Smith st Surb	116	M15
Smith ter SW3	155	N11
Smithfield st EC1	149	X3
Smithies rd SE2	80	D11
Smith's ct W1	148	E9
Smiths way NW2	44	F6
Smith's yd Croy	133	N5
Smithson rd N17	31	O3
Smithwood clo	105	R3
SW19		
Smithy st E1	63	P14
Smock wk Croy	122	M16
Smugglers way	88	A11
SW18		
Smyrks rd SE17	158	L10
Smyrna rd NW6	137	U1
Smythe st E14	64	E19
Snakes la Barn	6	H15
Snakes Lane east	21	X18
Wdf Grn		
Snakes Lane west	21	T17
Wdf Grn		
Snaresbrook dr Stan	11	W14
Snaresbrook rd E11	33	Z13
Snarsgate st W10	144	C3
Sneath ave NW11	27	U20
Snells pk N18	18	H18
Sneyd rd NW2	44	M13
Snow hill EC1	149	W3
Snow Hill ct EC1	149	Y3
Snowbury rd SW6	88	B5
Snowden st EC2	142	J19
Snowdon dr NW9	26	B17
Snowdown clo SE20	124	E1
Snowsfields SE1	150	G17
Snowshill rd E12	53	R14
Snowy Fielder waye	84	B5
Islw		
Soames st SE15	91	U8
Soames wk N Mal	118	A2
Socket la Brom	126	G16
Soho sq W1	148	F5
Soho st W1	148	F5
Solebay st E1	63	W12
Solent rd NW6	45	X15
Soley ms WC1	141	S12
Solna ave SW15	86	M14
Solna rd N21	18	A2
Solomon's pas SE15	92	A10
Solon New rd SW4	90	A10
Solon rd SW2	90	A10
Solway clo Houns	82	C7
Solway rd N22	30	H4
Solway rd SE22	91	X10
Somaford gro Barn	5	V19
Somali rd NW2	45	U13
Somerby rd Bark	54	E20
Somercoates clo Barn	5	X11
Somerfield rd N4	48	J7
Somerford gro N16	49	V13
Somerford gro N17	31	Y2
Somerford st E1	143	W17
Somerford way SE16	75	W6
Somerhill ave Sid	97	P19
Somerhill rd Well	97	R5
Somerleyton rd SW9	90	G10
Somers clo NW1	140	F9
Somers cres W2	146	K6
Somers ms W2	146	J5
Somers pl SW2	90	C17
Somers rd E17	32	M13
Somers rd SW2	90	C17
Somersby gdns Ilf	35	T15
Somerset ave SW20	118	J3
Somerset ave Well	96	L12
Somerset clo N Mal	118	B13
Somerset clo	34	G4
Wdf Grn		
Somerset est SW11	88	H1
Somerset gdns N6	47	R1
Somerset gdns	93	R6
SE13		
Somerset gdns	122	D6
SW16		
Somerset gdns	101	U12
Tedd		
Somerset rd E17	33	O17
Somerset rd N17	31	V10
Somerset rd N18	18	G16
Somerset rd NW4	26	M13
Somerset rd SW19	105	O8
Somerset rd W4	73	X7
Somerset rd W13	72	C3
Somerset rd Barn	5	O16
Somerset rd Brent	72	F17
Somerset rd Har	22	M17
Somerset rd Kings T	117	N5
Somerset rd Sthl	58	F16
Somerset rd Tedd	101	U12
Somerset sq W14	145	N19
Somerset waye	70	A18
Houns		
Somersham rd Bexh	98	A5
Somerton ave Rich	85	S8
Somerton rd NW2	45	S9
Somerton rd SE15	92	A10
Somertrees ave	112	H5
SE12		
Somervell rd Har	40	D14
Somerville SE20	110	G17
Somerville rd Rom	37	U18
Sondes st SE17	158	F12
Sonia ct Har	23	V19
Sonia gdns N12	15	P13

Name	No.	Ref.
Sonia gdns NW10	44	D12
Sonia gdns Houns	70	G20
Sonning gdns Hmptn	100	C16
Sonning rd SE25	123	X16
Soper clo E4	20	A15
Sophia rd E16	51	R2
Sophia rd E16	65	V16
Sopwith way Kings T	116	K2
Sorrel clo SE28	80	C3
Sorrel wk Rom	39	T10
Sorrell clo SE14	75	V19
Sorrell gdns E6	66	D13
Sorrento rd Sutt	130	A6
Sotheby rd N5	48	K11
Sotheran clo E8	143	U4
Sotheron rd SW6	153	Z20
Soudan rd SW11	88	M2
Souldern rd W14	152	H3
South Access rd E17	32	H19
South acre NW9	26	C7
South Africa rd W12	144	A10
South Audley st W1	147	U10
South ave E4	20	E1
South ave Cars	131	N17
South ave Rich	85	O4
South ave Sthl	58	D20
South Avenue gdns Sthl	58	D20
South bank Chis	114	B8
South bank Surb	116	K15
South Bank ter Surb	116	K15
South Birkbeck rd E11	51	X11
South Black Lion la W6	74	F13
South Bolton gdns SW5	154	A10
South Carriage dr SW1	147	P17
South Carriage dr SW7	147	P17
South clo N6	29	R17
South clo Barn	4	H11
South clo Bexh	97	W11
South clo Dag	69	T4
South clo Pnr	40	E1
South clo Twick	100	H7
South colonnade E14	76	C2
South Countess rd E17	32	L10
South cres WC1	148	F2
South Cross rd Ilf	36	B14
South Croxted rd SE21	109	P6
South dene NW7	12	M11
South Ealing rd W5	72	G11
South Eastern ave N9	18	G10
South Eaton pl SW1	155	V10
South Eden Park rd Beck	125	R16
South Edwardes sq W8	153	S3
South end W8	145	Y20
South End clo NW3	46	K13
South End rd NW3	46	J13
South End rd Horn	57	Z18
South End rd Rain	57	Y20
South End row NW3	153	Y1
South Esk rd E7	52	K19
South gdns SW19	106	G18
South Gipsy rd Well	97	V8
South gro E17	32	L16
South gro N6	47	P3
South gro N15	31	P16
South Hill Chis	113	T17
South Hill ave Har	41	O9
South Hill gro Har	41	T11
South Hill pk NW3	46	K12
South Hill rd Brom	125	Z7
South Island pl SW9	157	R19
South Lambeth pl SW8	156	M12
South Lambeth rd SW8	156	M15
South la Kings T	116	H6
South la N Mal	117	X9
South Lane west N Mal	117	X9
South Lodge ave Mitch	121	Z8
South Lodge cres Enf	6	L14
South Lodge dr N14	6	K14
South mead NW9	26	E4
South mead Epsom	128	C16
South meadows Wem	42	L14
South Molton la W1	147	W7
South Molton rd E16	65	U16
South Molton st W1	147	W7
South Norwood hill SE25	123	S1
South Oak rd SW16	108	D10
South par SW3	154	G10
South par W4	73	Y10
South Park cres SE6	112	B1
South Park cres Ilf	54	G8
South Park dr Ilf	54	H8
South Park gro N Mal	117	V10
South Park Hill rd S Croy	133	P11
South Park ms SW6	88	A6
South Park rd SW19	105	W16
South Park rd Ilf	54	F8
South Park ter Ilf	54	G10
South pl EC2	150	G1
South pl Enf	9	R16
South pl Surb	116	M16
South Place ms EC2	150	G1
South rd N9	18	L5
South rd SE23	110	E4
South rd SW19	106	E16
South rd W5	72	G10
South rd Edg	25	U4
South rd Felt	100	A13
South rd Hmptn	100	D16
South rd Rom (Chadwell Heath)	37	Y17
South rd Rom (Little Heath)	37	T15
South rd Sthl	70	D4
South rd Twick	101	R8
South row SE3	94	D4
South Sea st SE16	75	X8
South side W6	74	D9
South Side common SW19	105	O15
South sq NW11	27	Z18
South sq WC1	149	S1
South st W1	147	U12
South st Brom	126	F2
South st Enf	9	R17
South st Islw	83	Y7
South st Rain	69	Z7
South st Rom	39	R15
South Tenter st E1	151	P7
South ter SW7	154	K5
South ter Surb	116	L14
South vale SE19	109	S16
South vale Har	41	U11
South vw Brom	126	K4
South View dr E18	34	J10
South View rd N8	29	Y11
South vill NW1	47	Y18
South vw W Wick	135	Z6
South way N9	19	S7
South way Brom	126	E17
South way Croy	134	J6
South way Har	22	H14
South way Wem	43	O14
South Western rd Twick	84	A16
South Wharf rd W2	146	G3
South Woodford to Barking Relief rd E6	53	S3
South Woodford to Barking Relief rd E11	35	N16
South Woodford to Barking Relief rd E12	53	S3
South Woodford to Barking Relief rd E18	35	N16
South Woodford to Barking Relief rd Bark	66	M2
South Woodford to Barking Relief rd Ilf	35	N16
South Worple way SW14	85	X8
Southall pl SE1	150	E18
Southam st W10	137	N19
Southampton bldgs WC2	149	S3
Southampton pl WC1	148	M3
Southampton rd NW5	46	M14
Southampton row WC1	140	K19
Southampton st WC2	148	M9
Southampton way SE5	158	F17
Southbank T Ditt	116	B17
Southborough clo Surb	116	H20
Southborough la Brom	127	R13
Southborough rd E9	63	S2
Southborough rd Brom	127	S6
Southborough rd Surb	116	J20
Southbourne Brom	126	F18
Southbourne ave NW9	25	X8
Southbourne clo Pnr	22	C20
Southbourne cres NW4	27	S12
Southbourne gdns SE12	94	H13
Southbourne gdns Ilf	54	B15
Southbridge pl Croy	132	L8
Southbridge rd Croy	132	L8
Southbridge way Sthl	70	C6
Southbrook ms SE12	94	D16
Southbrook rd SE12	94	C15
Southbrook rd SW16	122	A1
Southbury ave Enf	8	N15
Southbury rd Enf	8	C12
Southchurch rd E6	66	G7
Southcombe st W14	152	L5
Southcote ave Surb	117	S18
Southcote rd E17	32	G14
Southcote rd N19	47	V12
Southcote rd SE25	124	A13
Southcroft ave Well	96	J7
Southcroft ave W Wick	135	U4
Southcroft rd SW16	107	S16
Southcroft rd SW17	107	O14
Southdean gdns SW19	105	U3
Southdown ave W7	71	X8
Southdown cres Har	40	M5
Southdown cres Ilf	36	G15
Southdown dr SW20	105	O19
Southdown rd SW20	119	P1
Southdown rd Cars	131	O19
Southdown rd Horn	57	Y1
Southend clo SE9	95	Z15
Southend cres SE9	95	Y15
Southend la SE6	111	R11
Southend la SE26	110	L9
Southend rd E6	53	T20
Southend rd E17	33	W3
Southend rd E18	34	B6
Southend rd Beck	111	P17
Southend rd Wdf Grn	35	N7
Southern ave SE25	123	V6
Southern gro E3	63	Y10
Southern rd E13	65	W6
Southern rd N2	28	L12
Southern row W10	136	K17
Southern st N1	141	N9
Southern way Rom	38	F18
Southerngate way SE14	75	V19
Southerton rd W6	152	B4
Southey rd N15	31	S15
Southey rd SW9	90	E1
Southey rd SW19	105	Z18
Southey st SE20	110	E18
Southfield Barn	4	B19
Southfield cotts W7	71	W5
Southfield gdns Twick	101	V9
Southfield rd N17	31	T8
Southfield rd W4	73	X6
Southfield rd Enf	9	O18
Southfields NW4	26	H8
Southfields ct SW19	105	T2
Southfields rd SW18	87	X16
Southgate circ N14	16	K5
Southgate gro N1	142	G1
Southgate rd N1	142	G4
Southholme clo SE19	109	T20
Southill rd Chis	113	S17
Southill st E14	64	E17
Southland rd SE18	79	Y18
Southland way Houns	83	P13
Southlands gro Brom	127	R7
Southlands rd Brom	126	M11
Southly clo Sutt	129	Y6
Southmead rd SW19	87	S20
Southmoor way E9	50	M16
Southold ri SE9	113	V8
Southolm st SW11	89	S2
Southover N12	14	K11
Southover Brom	112	E11
Southport rd SE18	79	T11
Southridge pl SW20	105	O18
Southsea rd Kings T	116	J9
Southspring Sid	96	F19
Southvale rd SE3	94	A6
Southview ave NW10	44	D14
Southview clo Bex	98	B17
Southview cres Ilf	35	Z19
Southview gdns Wall	131	V17
Southview rd Brom	111	X9
Southville SW8	89	Y2
Southville rd T Ditt	116	A19
Southwark bri EC4	150	C10
Southwark bri SE1	150	C11
Southwark Bridge rd SE1	149	Z20
Southwark gro SE1	150	A14
Southwark Park rd SE16	159	S5
Southwark pl Brom	127	U8
Southwark st SE1	149	X12
Southwater clo E14	63	Y16
Southwater clo Beck	111	S18
Southway N20	14	M6
Southway NW7	26	G2
Southway NW11	28	A17
Southway SW20	119	N10
Southway Wall	131	V9
Southwell ave Nthlt	40	H17
Southwell gdns SW7	154	B14
Southwell Grove rd E11	51	Z8
Southwell rd SE5	90	L7
Southwell rd Croy	122	F15
Southwell rd Har	24	H18
Southwest rd E11	51	Y3
Southwick ms W2	146	J5
Southwick pl W2	146	K7
Southwick st W2	146	J5
Southwold dr Bark	55	N14
Southwold rd E5	50	B7
Southwold rd Bex	98	H17
Southwood ave N6	29	R20
Southwood ave Kings T	103	W20
Southwood clo Brom	127	V9
Southwood clo Wor Pk	129	P1
Southwood dr Surb	117	X19
Southwood gdns Ilf	35	Z13
Southwood la N6	47	P2
Southwood Lawn rd N6	29	R20
Southwood rd SE9	113	Z4
Southwood rd SE28	80	D3
Sovereign clo E1	151	Y10

Name	Page	Ref
Sovereign clo W5	60	D14
Sovereign ms E2	142	M9
Sovereign pk NW10	61	T10
Sowerby clo SE9	95	T14
Sowrey ave Rain	57	V17
Spa clo SE25	123	R2
Spa hill SE19	123	O1
Spa rd SE16	159	N3
Spafield st EC1	141	T15
Spalding rd NW4	27	N19
Spalding rd NW17	107	S13
Spanby rd E3	64	B12
Spaniards clo NW11	46	E3
Spaniards end NW3	46	E3
Spaniards rd NW3	46	D8
Spanish pl W1	147	U3
Spanish rd SW18	88	E12
Sparkbridge rd Har	23	T13
Sparks clo W3	61	X17
Sparrow clo Hmptn	100	B14
Sparrow Farm rd Epsom	128	H9
Sparrow grn Dag	56	H8
Sparrows Herne (Bushey) Wat	10	A3
Sparrows la SE9	96	C20
Sparsholt rd N19	48	C3
Sparsholt rd Bark	67	V3
Sparta st SE10	93	T3
Spear ms SW5	153	V7
Spearman st SE18	78	K17
Spears rd N19	48	A4
Speart la Houns	70	B19
Spedan clo NW3	46	C10
Speedy pl WC1	140	K13
Speke rd Th Hth	123	N4
Spekehill SE9	113	V8
Speldhurst clo Brom	126	E13
Speldhurst rd E9	63	O18
Speldhurst rd W4	73	Y7
Spelman st E1	151	S1
Spencer ave N13	17	P19
Spencer clo N3	27	X6
Spencer clo NW10	61	N8
Spencer clo Wdf Grn	21	Y17
Spencer dr N2	28	D18
Spencer gdns SW14	85	V12
Spencer hill SW19	105	V17
Spencer Hill rd SW19	105	T17
Spencer ms W6	152	K13
Spencer pk SW18	88	F13
Spencer pl Croy	123	R17
Spencer ri NW5	47	T11
Spencer rd E6	66	C2
Spencer rd E17	33	U6
Spencer rd N8	30	D15
Spencer rd N11	16	D13
Spencer rd N17	31	Y5
Spencer rd SW18	88	G12
Spencer rd SW20	118	K2
Spencer rd W3	73	W1
Spencer rd W4	73	W19
Spencer rd Brom	112	B18
Spencer rd Har	23	T6
Spencer rd Ilf	54	M3
Spencer rd Islw	83	O2
Spencer rd Mitch	121	P6
Spencer rd (Beddington) Mitch	121	N18
Spencer rd S Croy	133	S11
Spencer rd Twick	101	T6
Spencer rd Wem	42	D6
Spencer st EC1	141	O13
Spencer wk SW15	87	O10
Spenser gro N16	49	R13
Spenser rd SE24	90	H14
Spenser st SW1	156	D1
Spensley wk N16	49	P8
Speranza st SE18	79	X13
Sperling rd N17	31	U8
Spert st E14	63	V19
Spey st E14	64	F15
Spey way Rom	39	P2
Speyside N14	6	G20
Spezia rd NW10	62	G6
Spicer clo SW9	90	J5
Spiers clo N Mal	118	E13
Spigurnell rd N17	31	N5
Spikes Bridge rd Sthl	58	C18
Spilsby clo NW9	26	B6
Spindlewood gdns Croy	133	R8
Spindrift ave E14	76	D11
Spinel clo SE18	79	Z14
Spinnells rd Har	40	D3
Spinney the N21	17	S2
Spinney the SW16	107	W7
Spinney the Barn	5	O9
Spinney the Sid	115	Z11
Spinney the Stan	11	X14
Spinney the Sutt	129	N9
Spinney the Wem	41	Y10
Spinney clo N Mal	118	A12
Spinney gdns SE19	109	V13
Spinney gdns Dag	56	A14
Spinney Oak Brom	127	S3
Spinneys the Brom	127	T3
Spital sq E1	142	L20
Spital st E1	143	R19
Spital yd E1	142	L20
Spondon rd N15	31	X13
Spooner wk Wall	131	Z11
Sportsbank st SE6	93	U20
Spottons gro N17	30	M3
Spout hill Croy	135	O12
Spratt Hall rd E11	34	E17
Spray la Twick	83	S16
Spray st SE18	79	N10
Sprimont pl SW3	155	N8
Spring Bridge rd W5	60	G19
Spring clo Barn	4	B16
Spring clo Dag	55	W2
Spring Close la Sutt	129	T13
Spring Court rd Enf	7	S4
Spring gdns SW1	148	H13
Spring gdns Horn	57	Z12
Spring gdns Rom	38	K17
Spring gdns Wall	131	V12
Spring gdns Wdf Grn	34	K1
Spring gro W4	73	O15
Spring gro Mitch	121	P1
Spring Grove cres Houns	82	M2
Spring Grove rd Houns	82	L2
Spring Grove rd Islw	83	S3
Spring Grove rd Rich	85	N13
Spring hill E5	49	Y2
Spring hill SE26	110	D10
Spring Lake Stan	11	N13
Spring la E5	50	B3
Spring la SE25	124	A15
Spring ms W1	147	R1
Spring Park ave Croy	134	G3
Spring Park rd N4	48	M2
Spring Park rd Croy	134	G3
Spring pl NW5	47	R16
Spring st W2	146	F6
Spring st Epsom	128	D20
Spring vale Bexh	98	J9
Spring Villa rd Edg	25	P1
Springall st SE15	159	X19
Springbank N21	7	P20
Springbank rd SE13	93	Y15
Springbourne ct Beck	111	V20
Springcroft ave N2	28	L11
Springdale rd N16	49	O12
Springfield E5	49	Z3
Springfield (Bushey) Wat	10	C4
Springfield ave N10	29	V11
Springfield ave SW20	119	U5
Springfield ave Hmptn	100	J15
Springfield clo N12	15	N16
Springfield clo Stan	10	L10
Springfield dr Ilf	36	B16
Springfield gdns E5	50	A3
Springfield gdns NW9	25	Z15
Springfield gdns W Wick	135	S2
Springfield gdns Wdf Grn	34	M2
Springfield gro SE7	77	Y17
Springfield la NW6	137	W6
Springfield mt NW9	26	A15
Springfield ri SE26	109	Z8
Springfield rd E4	20	H6
Springfield rd E6	53	V19
Springfield rd E15	65	O8
Springfield rd E17	32	K18
Springfield rd N11	16	F16
Springfield rd N15	31	W12
Springfield rd NW8	138	A6
Springfield rd SE26	110	B13
Springfield rd SW19	105	W13
Springfield rd W7	71	U2
Springfield rd Bexh	98	H9
Springfield rd Brom	127	U9
Springfield rd Har	23	T18
Springfield rd Kings T	116	K8
Springfield rd Tedd	101	Y13
Springfield rd Th Hth	108	L20
Springfield rd Twick	82	J20
Springfield rd Wall	131	R12
Springfield rd Well	97	P6
Springfield wk NW6	137	X6
Springhill clo SE5	91	Q4
Springhurst clo Croy	134	L8
Springpark dr Beck	125	V5
Springpond rd Dag	56	A14
Springrice rd SE13	107	W14
Springvale ave Brent	72	H12
Springvale ter W14	152	H2
Springwater clo SE18	95	W2
Springwell ave NW10	62	E4
Springwell rd SW16	108	E11
Springwell rd Houns	82	A2
Springwood cres Edg	12	K7
Springwood way Rom	39	W15
Sprowston ms E7	52	F16
Sprowston rd E7	52	F15
Spruce ct W4	73	X5
Spruce ct W5	72	K7
Spruce Hills rd E17	33	T8
Sprucedale gdns Croy	134	F8
Sprucedale gdns Wall	131	Z20
Sprules rd SE4	92	J5
Spur rd N15	31	O12
Spur rd SW1	148	B18
Spur rd Bark	67	P8
Spur rd Edg	11	Y12
Spur rd Islw	84	A1
Spurgeon ave SE19	109	O19
Spurgeon rd SE19	109	O19
Spurgeon st SE1	158	E2
Spurling rd SE22	91	V10
Spurling rd Dag	56	C17
Spurstowe ter E8	49	Z16
Square the W6	152	D10
Square the Cars	131	O10
Square the Ilf	53	X1
Square the Rich	84	H12
Square the Wdf Grn	21	S17
Squarey st SW17	106	E8
Squires la N3	28	B6
Squires ct SW19	105	X9
Squires mt NW3	46	F9
Squires Wood dr Chis	113	S19
Squirrels the SE13	93	X8
Squirrels the Pnr	22	E11
Squirrels clo N12	15	P12
Squirrels grn Wor Pk	128	E2
Squirrels Heath ave Rom	39	Y10
Squirries st E2	143	U13
Stable clo Ntholt	58	G5
Stable way W10	144	E7
Stable yd SW1	148	B16
Stable Yard rd SW1	148	B15
Stables the Buck H	21	Y2
Stables ms SE27	108	M13
Stables way SE11	157	T10
Stacey ave N18	19	R13
Stacey clo E10	33	W16
Stacey st WC2	148	H6
Stackhouse st SW3	147	P20
Stadium rd NW2	44	L2
Stadium rd SE18	78	F17
Stadium way Dart	99	R14
Stadium way Wem	43	O13
Staff st EC1	142	G14
Staffa rd E10	50	G3
Stafford clo N14	6	H16
Stafford clo NW6	137	T13
Stafford clo Sutt	129	T14
Stafford Cross Industrial est Croy	132	D12
Stafford gdns Croy	132	E10
Stafford pl SW1	148	A20
Stafford pl Rich	84	M18
Stafford rd E3	63	Y6
Stafford rd E7	53	N19
Stafford rd NW6	137	T11
Stafford rd Croy	132	F9
Stafford rd Har	23	O3
Stafford rd N Mal	117	V6
Stafford rd Sid	114	J8
Stafford rd Wall	131	U14
Stafford st W1	148	A11
Stafford ter W8	145	U19
Staffordshire st SE15	91	Y1
Stag clo Edg	25	U6
Stag la NW9	25	U9
Stag la SW15	104	E6
Stag la Buck H	21	V7
Stag la Edg	25	U6
Stag pl SW1	156	A1
Stags way Islw	71	V18
Stainbank rd Mitch	121	S5
Stainby rd N15	31	W11
Stainer st SE1	150	H15
Staines ave Sutt	129	R4
Staines rd Houns	82	A12
Staines rd Ilf	54	D14
Staines rd Twick	100	J7
Staines wk Sid	115	U15
Stainforth rd E17	33	P13
Stainforth rd Ilf	36	G20
Staining la EC2	150	B4
Stainmore clo Chis	114	F20
Stainsby pl E14	64	B16
Stainsby rd E14	64	B16
Stainton rd SE6	93	W16
Stainton rd Enf	9	R5
Stalbridge st NW1	138	L19
Stalham st SE16	159	Y3
Stambourne way SE19	109	T19
Stambourne way W Wick	135	V5
Stamford Brook ave W6	74	E9
Stamford Brook rd W6	74	D9
Stamford clo N15	31	X14
Stamford clo Har	23	T1
Stamford clo Sthl	70	H1
Stamford clo W6	74	F10
Stamford dr Brom	126	D9
Stamford gdns Dag	68	G1
Stamford Grove east N16	49	W3
Stamford Grove west N16	49	W3
Stamford hill N16	49	U3
Stamford Hill est N16	49	V3
Stamford rd E6	66	D3
Stamford rd N1	49	T19
Stamford rd N15	31	W14
Stamford rd Dag	68	D2
Stamford st SE1	149	U13
Stamp pl E2	143	O11
Stanard clo N16	31	T20
Stanborough clo Hmptn	100	E14
Stanborough rd Houns	83	R6
Stanbridge pl N21	17	X7
Stanbridge rd SW15	87	N8
Stanbrook rd SE2	80	D6

Name	Page	Ref	Name	Page	Ref	Name	Page	Ref	Name	Page	Ref
Stanbury rd SE15	92	B3	Stanley pas NW1	140	J9	Stapleton rd SW17	107	O7	Station rd SW13	86	E4
Stancroft NW9	26	A14	Stanley rd E4	20	L4	Stapleton rd Bexh	81	O19	Station rd SW19	106	D20
Standard Industrial est E16	78	G5	Stanley rd E10	33	R19	Stapley rd Belv	81	R15	Station rd W5	61	N17
			Stanley rd E12	53	R16	Stapylton rd Barn	4	E12	Station rd W7 (Hanwell)	71	U2
Standard pl EC2	142	L14	Stanley rd E15	64	J4	Star & Garter hill	84	L20			
Standard rd NW10	61	X10	Stanley rd E18	34	C6	Rich			Station rd Barn	5	N16
Standard rd Belv	81	S14	Stanley rd N2	28	G11	Star hill Dart	99	P12	Station rd Belv	81	U9
Standard rd Bexh	97	Z10	Stanley rd N9	18	G6	Star la E16	65	N12	Station rd Bexh	98	A6
Standard rd Enf	9	W1	Stanley rd N10	29	R2	Star rd W14	153	P12	Station rd Brom	126	A3
Standard rd Houns	82	D8	Stanley rd N11	16	L17	Star rd Islw	83	R5	(Shortlands)		
Standen rd SW18	87	X20	Stanley rd N15	30	K13	Star st E16	65	R13	Station rd Cars	131	N8
Standfield gdns Dag	56	F16	Stanley rd SW14	85	T11	Star st W2	146	K3	Station rd Croy (East Croydon)	133	P3
Standfield rd Dag	56	F16	Stanley rd SW19	105	Y17	Star yd WC2	149	S5			
Standish rd W6	74	G12	Stanley rd W3	73	U7	Starboard way E14	76	C8	Station rd Croy (West Croydon)	132	L1
Stane clo SW19	106	B19	Stanley rd Brom	126	K8	Starch House la Ilf	36	E6			
Stane way SE18	78	C20	Stanley rd Cars	131	O16	Starcross st NW1	140	C14	Station rd Dart (Crayford)	99	T18
Stanfield rd E3	63	X7	Stanley rd Croy	122	F16	Starfield rd W12	74	G6			
Stanford clo Hmptn	100	E15	Stanley rd Enf	8	F12	Starkleigh way SE16	159	Y10	Station rd Edg	12	D19
Stanford clo Rom	38	G18	Stanley rd Har	40	M7	Starling clo Buck H	21	U5	Station rd Enf	7	Y11
Stanford pl SE17	158	K7	Stanley rd Houns	82	M9	Starling ms SE28	79	T6	Station rd Har	23	V13
Stanford rd N11	16	A16	Stanley rd Ilf	54	E7	Starts hill rd Orp	166	N10	Station rd Har (North Harrow)	22	J16
Stanford rd SW16	121	X3	Stanley rd Mitch	107	P18	Statham gro N16	49	N10			
Stanford rd W8	153	Z2	Stanley rd Mord	119	Z8	Statham gro N18	18	E15	Station rd Houns	82	K11
Stanford st SW1	156	E7	Stanley rd Sid	115	O8	Station app N11	16	D16	Station rd Ilf	53	Z8
Stanford way SW16	121	W4	Stanley rd Sthl	58	B20	Station app N12	15	N14	Station rd Ilf (Barkingside)	36	F11
Stangate gdns Stan	11	O14	Stanley rd Sutt	130	A15	(Woodside Pk)					
Stanger rd SE25	123	Y10	Stanley rd Tedd	101	U13	Station app N16	49	U6	Station rd Kings T (Hampton Wick)	116	F1
Stanham pl Dart	99	X11	Stanley rd Twick	101	R7	(Stoke Newington)					
Stanhope ave N3	27	W10	Stanley rd Wem	43	N16	Station app NW10	62	D8	Station rd N Mal (Motspur Pk)	118	J13
Stanhope ave Brom	126	E20	Stanley sq Cars	131	N19	Station app SE9 (Mottingham)	113	T2			
Stanhope ave Har	23	P4	Stanley st SE8	75	Z19				Station rd Rom (Chadwell Heath)	55	W2
Stanhope gdns N4	30	K18	Stanley ter NW1	48	A7	Station app SE26	110	D11			
Stanhope gdns N6	29	U19	Stanleycroft clo Islw	83	S3	Station app SW6	87	U6	Station rd Sid	115	N4
Stanhope gdns NW7	13	P17	Stanmer st SW11	88	K3	Station app SW16	107	Y13	Station rd Tedd	101	X14
Stanhope gdns SW7	154	D5	Stanmore gdns Rich	85	N7	Station app W7	71	T1	Station rd Twick	83	W20
Stanhope gdns Ilf	53	T4	Stanmore gdns Sutt	130	D7	Station app Bexh	97	Z6	Station rd W Wick	125	V20
Stanhope gate W1	147	V13	Stanmore hill Stan	10	L11	Station app Bexh (Barnehurst)	98	J5	Station Road north Belv	81	U8
Stanhope gro Beck	124	M12	Stanmore rd E11	52	C4						
Stanhope Mews east SW7	154	E4	Stanmore rd N15	30	K12	Station app Chis	127	W2	Station st E15	51	W20
			Stanmore rd Belv	81	Y11	Station app Chis (Elmstead Wds)	113	S16	Station st E16	78	M4
Stanhope Mews south SW7	154	D6	Stanmore rd Rich	84	M7				Station ter NW10	136	E10
			Stanmore st N1	141	N4	Station app Dart	99	S15	Station ter SE5	90	M22
Stanhope Mews west SW7	154	C5	Stanmore ter Beck	125	P3	Station app Grnf	59	O1	Station vw Grnf	59	P2
			Stannard rd E8	49	W17	Station app Har	23	U20	Station way Buck H (Roding Valley)	21	Z12
Stanhope Park rd Grnf	59	N10	Stannary pl SE11	157	U12	Station app Ilf	36	E11			
			Stansfield rd E6	66	B15	Station app Kings T	117	R2	Station yd Twick	83	X20
Stanhope pl W2	147	N7	Stansfield rd SW9	90	D7	Station app Pnr	22	B11	Staunton rd Kings T	102	L16
Stanhope rd E17	33	R15	Stansgate rd Dag	56	E8	Station app Rich	85	O1	Staunton st SE8	75	Z16
Stanhope rd N6	47	W1	Stanstead clo Brom	126	D13	Station app Sid	115	O4	Stave Yard rd SE16	75	V2
Stanhope rd N12	15	S16	Stanstead Manor Sutt	129	Z13	Station app S Croy	133	P20	Staveley clo N7	48	B13
Stanhope rd Barn	4	B18				Station app Well	96	M6	Staveley clo SE15	92	B1
Stanhope rd Bexh	98	A4	Stanstead rd E11	34	H15	Station app Wem	42	C17	Staveley gdns W4	85	Y1
Stanhope rd Cars	131	O17	Stanstead rd SE23	110	E2	Station Approach rd W4	73	W19	Staveley rd W4	73	W17
Stanhope rd Croy	133	S7	Stansted cres Bex	115	W2				Staverton rd NW2	44	L19
Stanhope rd Dag	56	B7	Stanswood gdns SE5	158	L13	Station ave Epsom	128	B20	Stavordale rd N5	48	H12
Stanhope rd Grnf	59	N14				Station ave N Mal	118	C7	Stavordale rd Cars	120	D19
Stanhope rd Sid	115	N8	Stanthorpe rd SW16	107	Z11	Station ave Rich	85	O2	Stayners rd E1	63	S12
Stanhope row W1	147	W14	Stanton ave Tedd	101	T14	Station clo N3	27	Z6	Stayton rd Sutt	129	X5
Stanhope st NW1	140	A11	Stanton clo Epsom	129	O1	Station clo Hmptn	100	J20	Stead st SE17	158	E17
Stanhope ter W2	146	H8	Stanton rd SW13	86	D4	Station cres N15	31	N13	Steadfast rd Kings T	116	H2
Stanier clo W14	153	R11	Stanton rd SW20	119	O2	Station cres SE3	77	T15	Stean st E8	143	N3
Stanlake ms W12	144	B14	Stanton rd Croy	122	L19	Station cres Wem	42	B16	Stebbing way Bark	68	B6
Stanlake rd W12	144	A14	Stanton st SE15	91	W1	Station est Beck	124	G8	Stebondale st E14	76	H12
Stanlake vill W12	144	B14	Stanton way SE26	110	L9	Station gdns W4	73	W20	Stedham pl WC1	148	J3
Stanley ave Beck	125	V5	Stanway gdns W3	73	P1	Station gro Wem	42	K16	Steed clo Horn	57	Y6
Stanley ave Dag	56	C2	Stanway gdns Edg	12	G17	Station par N14	45	N17	Steedman st SE17	158	A6
Stanley ave Grnf	58	M3	Stanway st N1	142	K8	Station par W3	61	R17	Steeds rd N10	28	M5
Stanley ave N Mal	118	F11	Stanwick rd W14	153	O7	Station par Bark	54	D20	Steele rd E11	51	Z11
Stanley ave Rom	39	W14	Stanworth st SE1	151	O19	Station par Rich	85	O2	Steele rd N17	31	T9
Stanley ave Wem	60	L1	Stapenhill rd Wem	42	A9	Station pas E18	34	H8	Steele rd NW10	61	X6
Stanley clo SW8	157	N15	Staple Inn bldgs WC1	149	S3	Station pl N4	48	G6	Steele rd W4	73	X8
Stanley clo Rom	39	X11	Staple st SE1	150	G19	Station ri SE27	108	J3	Steele rd Islw	83	Z11
Stanley clo Wem	42	K20	Staplefield clo SW2	108	B1	Station rd E4 (Chingford)	20	K4	Steeles Mews north NW3	46	M18
Stanley cres W11	145	P9	Staplefield clo Pnr	22	A1						
Stanley gdns NW2	45	N16	Stapleford ave Ilf	36	H16	Station rd E7	52	E12	Steeles Mews south NW3	46	M18
Stanley gdns SW17	107	O16	Stapleford clo E4	20	G11	Station rd E10	51	V10			
Stanley gdns W3	74	A4	Stapleford clo SW19	87	S19	Station rd E12	53	P13	Steeles rd NW3	46	M19
Stanley gdns W11	145	P9	Stapleford clo Kings T	117	P5	Station rd E17	32	K17	Steel's la E1	63	R17
Stanley gdns Wall	131	U15				Station rd N3	27	V5	Steep hill SW16	107	Z8
Stanley Gardens ms W11	145	P8	Stapleford rd Wem	42	G20	Station rd N11	16	E16	Steep hill Croy	133	R8
			Stapleford way Bark	68	D8	Station rd N17	31	X11	Steeple clo SW6	87	T6
Stanley Gardens rd Tedd	101	T11	Staplehurst rd SE13	93	Y14	Station rd N19	47	V10	Steeple clo SW19	105	T11
			Staplehurst rd Cars	130	J17	Station rd N21	17	V4	Steeple ct E1	143	Y17
Stanley gro SW8	89	R5	Staples clo SE16	75	V2	Station rd N22	30	B6	Steeplestone clo N18	17	Z16
Stanley gro Croy	122	F15	Staples Corner Business pk NW2	44	H5	Station rd NW4	26	F19	Steerforth st SW18	106	C5
Stanley Park dr Wem	60	M2				Station rd NW7	13	O17	Steers Mead Mitch	120	L1
Stanley Park rd Cars	130	K17	Stapleton cres Rain	57	X19	Station rd NW10	62	D6	Steers way SE16	75	W6
Stanley Park rd Wall	131	T15	Stapleton gdns Croy	132	G10	Station rd SE20	110	C15	Stella rd SW17	107	N15
			Stapleton Hall rd N4	48	D2	Station rd SE25 (Norwood junct)	123	W9	Stellman clo E5	49	X10

Stembridge rd SE20	124	A4	
Stephan clo E8	143	U4	
Stephen ave Rain	57	V17	
Stephen ms W1	148	F3	
Stephen rd Bexh	98	L8	
Stephen st W1	148	F3	
Stephendale rd SW6	88	C4	
Stephen's rd E15	65	O4	
Stephenson rd W7	59	V16	
Stephenson rd Twick	82	G18	
Stephenson st E16	64	M11	
Stephenson st NW10	62	C9	
Stephenson way NW1	140	D15	
Stepney Causeway E1	63	T18	
Stepney grn E1	63	S14	
Stepney High st E1	63	U15	
Stepney way E1	151	W2	
Sterling ave Bark	12	A12	
Sterling pl W5	72	J10	
Sterling rd Enf	8	A4	
Sterling st SW7	146	L20	
Sterling way N18	18	B14	
Sterndale rd W14	152	F2	
Sterne st W12	144	F16	
Sternhall la SE15	91	Y6	
Sternhold ave SW2	107	X3	
Sterry cres Dag	56	D14	
Sterry dr Epsom	128	A8	
Sterry gdns Dag	56	E17	
Sterry rd Bark	67	X3	
Sterry rd Dag	56	E12	
Sterry st SE1	150	E18	
Steucers la SE23	92	K20	
Steve Biko la SE6	111	P11	
Stevedale rd Well	97	U5	
Stevenage rd E6	53	W18	
Stevenage rd SW6	152	E19	
Stevens ave E9	50	D17	
Stevens clo Beck	111	P16	
Stevens clo Hmptn	100	D14	
Stevens grn (Bushey) Wat	10	B6	
Stevens rd Dag	55	S7	
Stevens st SE1	150	M20	
Stevenson clo SE16	159	V9	
Steventon rd W12	74	F1	
Steward st E1	150	M1	
Stewards wk Rom	39	R15	
Stewart clo NW9	25	W18	
Stewart clo Chis	114	A11	
Stewart clo Hmptn	100	C14	
Stewart E15	51	W13	
Stewart st E14	76	H6	
Stewart's gro SW3	154	J8	
Stewart's rd SW8	156	A19	
Stewartsby clo N18	17	Y16	
Steyne rd W3	73	T2	
Steyning gro SE9	113	T12	
Steynings way N12	14	K17	
Steynton ave Bex	115	X3	
Stickland rd Belv	81	T10	
Stickleton clo Grnf	58	K10	
Stile Hall gdns W4	73	P14	
Stilecroft gdns Wem	42	A10	
Stiles clo Brom	127	U13	
Stillingfleet rd SW13	74	G18	
Stillington st SW1	156	C4	
Stillness rd SE23	92	J17	
Stilton cres NW10	43	X20	
Stirling clo SW16	121	W2	
Stirling rd E13	65	V7	
Stirling rd E17	32	H9	
Stirling rd N17	31	X5	
Stirling rd N22	30	H4	
Stirling rd SW9	90	A6	
Stirling rd W3	73	T8	
Stirling rd Har	23	V8	
Stirling rd Twick	82	J20	
Stirling Road path E17	32	G9	
Stirling wk N Mal	117	V11	
Stirling wk Surb	117	T15	
Stirling way Croy	122	A17	
Stiven cres Har	40	E10	
Stock Orchard cres N7	48	C14	
Stock Orchard st N7	48	C15	
Stock st E13	65	T7	
Stockbury rd Croy	124	C14	

Stockdale rd Dag	56	B6	
Stockdove way Grnf	59	V9	
Stockfield rd SW16	108	E6	
Stockholm rd SE16	75	R15	
Stockhurst clo SW15	87	O5	
Stockingswater la Enf	9	X10	
Stockland rd Rom	39	N18	
Stockport rd SW16	121	X1	
Stocksfield rd E17	33	V10	
Stockton gdns N17	30	M2	
Stockton gdns NW7	13	N10	
Stockton rd N17	30	L3	
Stockton rd N18	18	L18	
Stockwell ave SW9	90	E8	
Stockwell clo Brom	126	G4	
Stockwell gdns SW9	90	C3	
Stockwell Gardens est SW9	90	B4	
Stockwell grn SW9	90	C6	
Stockwell la SW9	90	C5	
Stockwell Park cres SW9	90	D4	
Stockwell Park est SW9	90	E6	
Stockwell Park rd SW9	90	D2	
Stockwell Park wk SW9	90	E7	
Stockwell rd SW9	90	D5	
Stockwell st SE10	76	H18	
Stodart rd SE20	124	C1	
Stofield gdns SE9	113	N7	
Stoford clo SW19	87	S20	
Stoke pl NW10	62	D9	
Stoke rd Kings T	103	W18	
Stokenchurch st SW6	87	Z3	
Stokes rd E6	66	D11	
Stokes rd Croy	124	G15	
Stokesley st W12	62	E17	
Stoll clo NW2	45	N10	
Stonard rd N13	17	U9	
Stonard rd Dag	55	S13	
Stondon pk SE23	92	J17	
Stone bldgs WC2	149	R3	
Stone clo SW4	89	V6	
Stone clo Dag	56	C8	
Stone Hall rd N21	17	S1	
Stone Park ave Beck	125	O9	
Stone pl Wor Pk	128	G2	
Stone rd Brom	126	C11	
Stone st Croy	132	E12	
Stonebridge pk NW10	43	Y20	
Stonebridge rd N15	31	T16	
Stonebridge way Wem	43	T18	
Stonechat sq E6	66	E14	
Stonecot clo Sutt	119	T20	
Stonecot hill Sutt	119	T20	
Stonecroft rd Erith	81	X20	
Stonecroft way Croy	122	B17	
Stonecutter st EC4	149	W4	
Stonefield clo Bexh	98	E8	
Stonefield clo Ruis	40	A14	
Stonefield st N1	141	U4	
Stonefield way Ruis	40	B13	
Stonegrove Edg	11	Y14	
Stonegrove gdns Edg	11	Y15	
Stonehall ave Ilf	35	R19	
Stoneham rd N11	16	J17	
Stonehill clo SW14	85	Y13	
Stonehill rd SW14	85	X13	
Stonehill rd W4	73	R13	
Stonehills ct SE21	109	T7	
Stonehorse rd Enf	9	R16	
Stonehouse st SW4	89	W9	
Stoneleigh ave Enf	9	N4	
Stoneleigh ave Wor Pk	128	G5	

Stoneleigh cres Epsom	128	F10	
Stoneleigh Park ave Croy	124	G14	
Stoneleigh Park rd Epsom	128	E13	
Stoneleigh pl W11	144	H10	
Stoneleigh rd N17	31	V9	
Stoneleigh rd Cars	120	J17	
Stoneleigh rd Ilf	35	S11	
Stoneleigh st W11	144	H10	
Stonells rd SW11	88	M15	
Stonenest st N4	48	D4	
Stoney la E1	150	M5	
Stoney la SE19	109	T16	
Stoney st SE1	150	E13	
Stoneyard la E14	64	D20	
Stoneycroft clo SE12	94	D18	
Stoneydown E17	32	G13	
Stoneydown ave E17	32	H12	
Stoneyfields gdns Edg	12	K13	
Stoneyfields la Edg	12	J15	
Stonhouse st SW4	89	W9	
Stonor rd W14	153	P7	
Stopford rd E13	65	T3	
Stopford rd SE17	157	Z10	
Store rd E16	78	J5	
Store st E15	51	Y16	
Store st WC1	148	F1	
Storers quay E14	76	K11	
Storey rd E17	32	M14	
Storey rd N6	29	N18	
Storey st E16	78	L4	
Storey's gate SW1	148	H19	
Stories ms SE5	91	R6	
Stork rd E7	52	E18	
Storks rd SE16	159	V2	
Storksmead rd Edg	26	A11	
Stormont rd N6	46	L2	
Stormont rd SW11	89	P19	
Storrington rd Croy	123	V10	
Story st N1	141	N2	
Stothard pl EC2	142	L20	
Stothard st E1	63	R11	
Stoughton ave Sutt	129	R11	
Stoughton clo SE11	157	P7	
Stoughton clo SW15	104	H1	
Stour ave Sthl	70	H9	
Stour rd E3	64	B1	
Stour rd Dag	56	F7	
Stour rd Dart	99	W8	
Stourcliffe st W1	147	O5	
Stourhead clo SW19	87	R18	
Stourhead gdns SW20	118	H5	
Stourton ave Felt	100	D9	
Stow cres E17	32	K3	
Stowage SE8	76	C17	
Stowe gdns N9	18	J5	
Stowe pl N15	31	S11	
Stowe rd W12	74	K6	
Stox mead Har	23	P4	
Stracey rd E7	52	F13	
Stracey rd NW10	61	Z3	
Strachan pl SW19	104	M16	
Stradbroke gro Ilf	35	R9	
Stradbroke rd N5	48	M12	
Stradella rd SE24	90	L16	
Strafford ave Ilf	35	X8	
Strafford rd W3	73	V6	
Strafford rd Barn	4	E10	
Strafford rd Houns	82	F8	
Strafford rd Twick	84	A19	
Strafford st E14	76	B5	
Strahan rd E3	63	W7	
Straight the Sthl	70	A6	
Straightsmouth SE10	76	G18	
Strait rd E6	66	E19	
Strand WC2	148	K11	
Strand on the grn W4	73	O15	
Strand pl N18	18	D14	
Strand School app W4	73	R16	
Strandfield clo SE18	79	W13	
Strangways ter W14	153	P2	

Stranraer way N1	140	M2	
Stratfield Park clo N21	17	V2	
Stratford ave W8	153	W3	
Stratford clo Bark	68	A1	
Stratford clo Dag	56	K20	
Stratford ct N Mal	117	Y8	
Stratford gro SW15	87	R10	
Stratford pl W1	147	W6	
Stratford rd E13	65	S4	
Stratford rd W8	153	V4	
Stratford rd Sthl	70	A11	
Stratford rd Th Hth	122	G8	
Stratford vill NW1	47	W20	
Strath ter SW11	88	H11	
Strathan clo SW18	87	U16	
Strathaven rd SE12	94	J15	
Strathblaine rd SW11	88	H12	
Strathbrook rd SW16	108	C19	
Strathcona rd Wem	42	F6	
Strathdale SW16	108	D12	
Strathdon dr SW17	106	F8	
Strathearn ave Twick	100	L2	
Strathearn pl W2	146	J7	
Strathearn rd SW19	105	Y12	
Strathearn rd Sutt	129	Z10	
Stratheden rd SE3	77	T20	
Strathfield gdns Bark	54	F18	
Strathleven rd SW2	90	B13	
Strathmore gdns N3	28	A6	
Strathmore gdns W8	145	V13	
Strathmore gdns Edg	25	T6	
Strathmore gdns Horn	57	U5	
Strathmore rd SW19	105	Y6	
Strathmore rd Croy	123	N17	
Strathmore rd Tedd	101	S9	
Strathnairn st SE1	159	T6	
Strathray gdns NW3	46	H19	
Strathville rd SW18	105	Z3	
Strathyre ave SW16	122	E7	
Stratton ave Enf	8	C1	
Stratton ave Wall	131	X20	
Stratton clo SW19	119	X3	
Stratton clo Bexh	97	Z7	
Stratton clo Edg	12	A20	
Stratton clo Houns	82	F3	
Stratton dr Bark	54	J15	
Stratton gdns Sthl	58	F17	
Stratton rd SW19	119	X4	
Stratton rd Bexh	98	A8	
Stratton st W1	147	Z12	
Strattondale st E14	76	G8	
Strauss rd W4	73	Y6	
Strawberry Hill Twick	101	V8	
Strawberry Hill clo Twick	101	V8	
Strawberry Hill rd Twick	101	V7	
Strawberry la Cars	131	N5	
Strawberry vale N2	28	F5	
Strawberry vale Twick	101	X6	
Streakes Field rd NW2	44	G5	
Stream la Edg	12	E17	
Streamway Belv	81	R16	
Streamdale SE2	80	C17	
Streamside clo N9	18	G6	
Streamside clo Brom	126	F9	
Streatfield ave E6	66	G3	
Streatfield rd Har	24	D11	
Streatham clo SW16	108	B6	
Streatham Common north SW16	108	A14	
Streatham Common south SW16	108	A16	
Streatham ct SW16	108	A6	
Streatham High rd SW16	107	Z11	
Streatham hill SW2	108	A4	
Streatham pl SW2	90	A19	
Streatham rd Mitch	121	N2	
Streatham st WC1	148	J3	
Streatham vale SW16	107	V20	

Streathbourne rd SW17	107	P5
Streatley pl NW3	46	E11
Streatley rd NW6	137	P1
Streeters la Wall	131	Y6
Streetfield ms SE3	94	F6
Streimer rd E15	64	J6
Strelley way W3	62	A19
Stretton rd Croy	123	S17
Stretton rd Rich	102	D5
Strickland row SW18	88	F19
Strickland st SE8	93	P3
Stride rd E13	65	R7
Strode clo N10	16	C20
Strode rd N17	31	S8
Strode rd NW10	44	H18
Strode rd SW6	152	K17
Strone rd E7	52	K18
Strone rd E12	53	R17
Strone way Hayes	58	B12
Strongbow cres SE9	95	U13
Strongbow rd SE9	95	U13
Strongbridge clo Har	40	H3
Stronsa rd W12	74	D5
Strood ave Rom	57	N4
Stroud cres SW15	104	F6
Stroudes clo Wor Pk	118	C18
Stroudley wk E3	64	D8
Strouts pl E2	143	N11
Strutton grd SW1	156	F2
Strype st E1	151	N3
Stuart ave NW9	44	F2
Stuart ave W5	73	N4
Stuart ave Brom	126	F20
Stuart ave Har	40	E10
Stuart cres N22	30	E5
Stuart cres Croy	134	M7
Stuart Evans clo Well	97	U7
Stuart gro Tedd	101	U12
Stuart pl Mitch	106	L20
Stuart rd NW6	137	U13
Stuart rd SE15	92	D11
Stuart rd SW19	105	Y6
Stuart rd W3	73	V1
Stuart rd Bark	67	V2
Stuart rd Barn	15	Y3
Stuart rd Har	23	W8
Stuart rd Rich	102	C6
Stuart rd Th Hth	123	N9
Stuart rd Well	97	R2
Stubbs dr SE16	159	X9
Stucley pl NW1	139	Y2
Stucley rd Houns	70	M20
Studd st N1	141	W4
Studdridge st SW6	87	Y5
Studholme ct NW3	45	Z13
Studholme st SE15	159	X19
Studland clo Sid	114	U7
Studland rd SE26	110	E14
Studland rd W7	90	R7
Studland rd Kings T	102	K16
Studland st W6	74	J12
Studley ave E4	20	J20
Studley clo E5	50	H15
Studley ct Sid	115	S12
Studley dr Ilf	35	P18
Studley est SW4	90	A3
Studley Grange rd W7	71	U7
Studley rd E7	52	H18
Studley rd SW4	90	A3
Studley rd Dag	68	K1
Stukeley rd E7	65	W1
Stukeley st WC2	148	L4
Stumps Hill la Beck	111	P15
Sturdy rd SE15	92	A6
Sturge ave E17	33	S6

Sturge st SE1	150	A17
Sturgeon rd SE17	158	A11
Sturges fld Chis	114	E16
Sturgess ave NW4	26	J20
Sturrock clo N15	31	O14
Sturry st E14	64	E18
Sturt st N1	142	C10
Stutfield st E1	151	U7
Styles gdns SW9	90	J6
Styles way Beck	125	U10
Sudbourne rd SW2	90	D12
Sudbrook gdns Rich	102	J7
Sudbrook la Rich	102	J3
Sudbrooke rd SW12	89	N17
Sudbury ave Wem	42	F10
Sudbury Court dr Har	41	X9
Sudbury Court rd Har	41	X10
Sudbury cres Brom	112	E14
Sudbury cres Wem	42	B14
Sudbury cft Wem	41	X11
Sudbury gdns Croy	133	T7
Sudbury Heights ave Grnf	41	W14
Sudbury hill Har	41	V9
Sudbury Hill clo Wem	41	X11
Sudbury rd Bark	54	L14
Sudeley st N1	141	Y10
Sudlow rd SW18	87	Y12
Sudrey st SE1	150	A18
Suez ave Grnf	59	W6
Suez rd Enf	9	W13
Suffield rd E4	20	F12
Suffield rd N15	31	U15
Suffield rd SE20	124	B5
Suffolk ct Ilf	36	J17
Suffolk la EC4	150	F9
Suffolk Park rd E17	32	J12
Suffolk pl SW1	148	G12
Suffolk rd E13	65	S10
Suffolk rd N15	31	P17
Suffolk rd NW10	44	B20
Suffolk rd SE25	123	W8
Suffolk rd SW13	74	E20
Suffolk rd Bark	67	T1
Suffolk rd Dag	56	J15
Suffolk rd Enf	9	N17
Suffolk rd Har	22	E17
Suffolk rd Ilf	36	J18
Suffolk rd Sid	115	T15
Suffolk rd Wor Pk	128	E3
Suffolk st E7	52	F13
Suffolk st SW1	148	G11
Sugar House la E15	64	G6
Sugden rd SW11	89	O10
Sugden rd T Ditt	116	B20
Sugden way Bark	67	Z5
Sulgrave gdns W6	144	E19
Sulgrave rd W6	144	E19
Sulina rd SW2	90	A19
Sulivan ct SW6	87	Y6
Sulivan rd SW6	87	Z8
Sullivan ave E16	66	A14
Sullivan clo SW11	88	H7
Sullivan rd SE11	157	V5
Sullivan way Borwd	11	T1

Summerlee ave N2	28	L11
Summerlee gdns N2	28	L13
Summerley st SW18	106	C4
Summers clo Sutt	129	Z17
Summers clo Wem	43	T4
Summers la N12	15	U20
Summers row N12	15	X18
Summers st EC1	141	T18
Summersby rd N6	29	R17
Summerstown SW17	106	D8
Summerton way SE28	68	J18
Summerville gdns Sutt	129	V14
Summerwood rd Islw	83	W13
Summit ave NW9	25	Y15
Summit clo N14	16	G7
Summit clo NW9	25	Z14
Summit clo Edg	25	R2
Summit dr Wdf Grn	35	O7
Summit est N16	49	W2
Summit rd E17	33	T13
Summit rd Nthlt	58	H1
Summit way N14	16	F8
Summit way SE19	109	T19
Sumner gdns Croy	122	H20
Sumner pl SW7	154	G6
Sumner Place ms SW7	154	G7
Sumner rd SE15	159	P14
Sumner rd Croy	122	H19
Sumner rd Har	41	N1
Sumner Road south Croy	132	G1
Sumner st SE1	149	Z13
Sumpter clo NW3	46	E18
Sun ct EC3	150	H6
Sun clo Erith	99	V5
Sun la SE3	77	W20
Sun pas SE16	159	S1
Sun rd W14	153	P11
Sun st EC2	142	H20
Sun Street pas EC2	150	J2
Sunbeam rd NW10	61	X11
Sunbury ave NW7	12	L15
Sunbury gdns NW7	12	K15
Sunbury la SW11	88	G1
Sunbury rd Sutt	129	R5
Suncroft pl SE26	110	C7
Sundale ave S Croy	134	F20
Sunderland ct SE22	91	X20
Sunderland rd SE23	110	G5
Sunderland rd W5	72	G8
Sunderland ter W2	145	W5
Sunderland way E12	53	O6
Sundew ave W12	62	F20
Sundial ave SE25	123	V5
Sundorne rd SE7	77	X14
Sundridge ave Brom	127	N1
Sundridge ave Chis	113	S18
Sundridge ave Well	96	G6
Sundridge rd Croy	123	W19
Sunfields pl SE3	77	V19
Sunkist way Wall	131	Z19
Sunland ave Bexh	98	A11
Sunleigh rd Wem	60	K2
Sunley gdns Grnf	59	Y4
Sunningdale N14	16	L15
Sunningdale ave W3	62	C18
Sunningdale ave Bark	67	S2
Sunningdale ave Felt	100	B5
Sunningdale clo Stan	10	M20
Sunningdale gdns NW9	25	V16
Sunningdale rd Brom	127	R10
Sunningdale rd Sutt	129	W8
Sunningfields cres NW4	26	K8
Sunningfields rd NW4	26	K8
Sunninghill rd SE13	93	R6
Sunny bank SE25	123	X7
Sunny cres NW10	61	V1
Sunny Gardens rd NW4	26	L7

Sunny hill NW4	26	J10
Sunny Nook gdns S Croy	133	O13
Sunny rd the Enf	9	U6
Sunny vw NW9	25	Y14
Sunny way N12	15	W20
Sunnycroft rd SE25	123	X8
Sunnycroft rd Houns	82	K5
Sunnycroft rd Sthl	58	H13
Sunnydale gdns NW7	12	M18
Sunnydale rd SE12	94	H12
Sunnydene ave E4	20	L15
Sunnydene gdns Wem	42	D18
Sunnydene st SE26	110	H10
Sunnyfield NW7	13	R12
Sunnyhill rd SW16	108	A9
Sunnyhurst clo Sutt	129	Y6
Sunnymead ave Mitch	121	W5
Sunnymead rd NW9	25	X20
Sunnymead rd SW15	86	J13
Sunnymede ave Epsom	128	A18
Sunnymede dr Ilf	35	Z14
Sunnyside NW2	45	W8
Sunnyside dr E4	20	G3
Sunnyside rd E10	51	O3
Sunnyside rd N19	47	X1
Sunnyside rd W5	72	F3
Sunnyside rd Ilf	54	D8
Sunnyside rd Tedd	101	R10
Sunnyside Road east N9	18	J11
Sunnyside Road north N9	18	J11
Sunnyside Road south N9	18	J11
Sunray ave SE24	91	P12
Sunray ave Brom	127	S14
Sunrise clo Felt	100	E7
Sunset ave E4	20	E4
Sunset ave Wdf Grn	21	P13
Sunset gdns SE25	123	T3
Sunset rd SE5	91	N10
Sunset vw Barn	4	E9
Sunshine way Mitch	120	M3
Sunwell clo SE15	92	A3
Surbiton cres Kings T	116	J10
Surbiton Hall clo Kings T	116	J10
Surbiton Hill pk Surb	116	M13
Surbiton Hill rd Surb	116	K11
Surbiton rd Kings T	116	J9
Surlingham clo SE28	68	J19
Surr st N7	48	A15
Surrendale pl W9	137	W18
Surrey Canal rd SE14	75	U15
Surrey Canal rd SE15	75	R15
Surrey cres W4	73	R13
Surrey gdns N4	30	L19
Surrey gro SE17	158	K10
Surrey gro Sutt	130	F5
Surrey la SW11	88	J2
Surrey Lane est SW11	88	J2
Surrey ms SE27	109	R10
Surrey mt SE23	110	B2
Surrey Quays rd SE16	75	P8
Surrey rd SE15	92	E12
Surrey rd Bark	67	U2
Surrey rd Dag	56	J14
Surrey rd Har	22	M17
Surrey rd W Wick	135	S1
Surrey row SE1	149	X17
Surrey sq SE17	158	K9
Surrey st E13	65	X9
Surrey st WC2	149	P8
Surrey st Croy	132	M4
Surrey ter SE17	158	K8
Surrey Water rd SE16	75	U3
Surridge gdns SE19	109	O16
Susan clo Rom	38	J11
Susan rd SE3	94	J5
Susan wd Chis	127	Y1

Name		
Susannah st E14	64	F18
Sussex ave Islw	83	S7
Sussex clo N19	48	A6
Sussex clo Ilf	35	U17
Sussex clo N Mal	118	B9
Sussex cres Nthlt	40	G17
Sussex gdns N4	30	L17
Sussex gdns N6	28	M16
Sussex gdns W2	146	H6
Sussex Mews west W2	146	G8
Sussex pl NW1	139	O15
Sussex pl W2	146	H7
Sussex pl W6	152	C9
Sussex pl Erith	81	V19
Sussex pl N Mal	118	B8
Sussex ring N12	14	L16
Sussex rd E6	66	K4
Sussex rd Cars	130	L15
Sussex rd Erith	81	V19
Sussex rd Har	22	L16
Sussex rd N Mal	118	B9
Sussex rd Sid	115	R13
Sussex rd S Croy	133	O13
Sussex rd W Wick	135	T1
Sussex sq W2	146	H8
Sussex st E13	65	W9
Sussex st SW1	155	Z10
Sussex wk SW9	90	H10
Sussex way N7	48	C8
Sussex way N19	47	Z4
Sussex way Barn	6	D16
Sutcliffe clo NW11	28	B15
Sutcliffe rd SE18	79	V17
Sutcliffe rd Well	97	U5
Sutherland ave W9	137	V19
Sutherland ave W13	60	A18
Sutherland ave Well	96	G10
Sutherland clo Barn	4	F14
Sutherland ct NW9	25	S14
Sutherland dr SW19	120	F2
Sutherland gdns SW14	86	B8
Sutherland gdns Wor Pk	118	J19
Sutherland gro SW18	87	U16
Sutherland gro Tedd	101	U13
Sutherland pl W2	145	U5
Sutherland rd E17	32	G8
Sutherland rd N9	18	L4
Sutherland rd N17	31	X3
Sutherland rd W4	74	A16
Sutherland rd W13	59	Z18
Sutherland rd Belv	81	T8
Sutherland rd Croy	122	G19
Sutherland rd Enf	9	S18
Sutherland rd Sthl	58	D17
Sutherland Road path E17	32	G9
Sutherland row SW1	155	Y9
Sutherland sq SE17	158	B12
Sutherland st SW1	155	X9
Sutherland wk SE17	158	C11
Sutlej rd SE7	77	J18
Sutterton st N7	48	C19
Sutton arc Sutt	130	B12
Sutton clo Beck	125	S1
Sutton Common rd Sutt	119	U18
Sutton ct W4	73	V16
Sutton Court rd E13	65	Y9
Sutton Court rd W4	73	W18
Sutton Court rd Sutt	130	C13
Sutton cres Barn	4	D16
Sutton dene Houns	82	J3
Sutton est SW3	154	L8
Sutton est W10	136	C20
Sutton gdns Croy	123	W12
Sutton gro Sutt	130	G10
Sutton Hall rd Houns	70	G20
Sutton la W4	73	W13
Sutton la Houns	82	E7
Sutton Lane south W4	73	V14
Sutton Park rd Sutt	130	A13
Sutton pl E9	50	C16
Sutton rd E13	65	R11
Sutton rd E17	32	F6
Sutton rd N10	29	P5
Sutton rd Bark	67	W5
Sutton rd Houns	82	G1
Sutton row W1	148	G5
Sutton sq E9	50	C15
Sutton sq Houns	82	E2
Sutton st E1	63	P18
Sutton way W10	136	B20
Sutton way Houns	82	F2
Sutton's way EC1	142	D19
Swaby rd SW18	106	D2
Swaffield rd SW18	88	C18
Swain rd Th Hth	122	M11
Swains la N6	47	P3
Swains rd SW17	106	L17
Swainson rd W4	74	D4
Swaisland dr Dart	99	S13
Swaisland rd Dart	99	Z15
Swale rd Dart	99	W9
Swallands rd SE6	111	O7
Swallow clo SE14	92	E3
Swallow dr NW10	43	Y16
Swallow pl W1	148	A6
Swallow st E6	66	F14
Swallow st W1	148	C11
Swallowdale S Croy	134	G20
Swallowfield rd SE7	77	X14
Swan app E6	66	D15
Swan clo Croy	123	R17
Swan clo Felt	100	B10
Swan dr NW9	26	A7
Swan la EC4	150	F10
Swan la N20	15	R9
Swan la Dart	99	T20
Swan mead SE1	158	J3
Swan ms SW9	90	D3
Swan pl SW13	86	E4
Swan rd SE16	75	R4
Swan rd SE18	78	B9
Swan rd Felt	100	A11
Swan rd Sthl	58	K17
Swan st SE1	150	C20
Swan st Islw	84	A7
Swan wk SW3	155	P13
Swan wk Rom	39	R14
Swan way Enf	9	S8
Swanage rd E4	33	U2
Swanage rd SW18	88	D16
Swanbridge rd Bexh	98	G3
Swandon way SW18	88	B11
Swanfield st E2	143	O15
Swanley rd Well	97	T3
Swanscombe rd W4	74	B13
Swanscombe rd W11	144	H14
Swansea rd Enf	9	P13
Swanton gdns SW19	105	R1
Swanton rd Erith	81	U18
Swaton rd E3	64	C11
Swaylands rd Belv	81	T16
Swaythling clo N18	19	N13
Sweden gate SE16	75	W9
Swedenborg gdns E1	151	V9
Sweeney cres SE1	151	P19
Sweet Briar grn N9	18	G11
Sweet Briar gro N9	18	G11
Sweet Briar wk N18	18	F14
Sweets way N20	15	T9
Swete st E13	65	U7
Sweyn pl SE3	94	G5
Swift clo Har	40	K6
Swift rd Felt	100	A9
Swift rd Sthl	70	F8
Swift st SW6	87	U2
Swiftsden way Brom	112	A14
Swinbrook rd W10	136	M20
Swinburne cres Croy	124	C16
Swinburne rd SW15	86	H11
Swinderby rd Wem	42	J17
Swindon clo Ilf	54	A2
Swindon st W12	144	A13
Swinfield clo Felt	100	A8
Swinford gdns SW9	90	H7
Swingate la SE18	79	W16
Swinnerton st E9	50	J16
Swinton clo Wem	43	T5
Swinton pl WC1	141	O13
Swinton st WC1	141	N13
Swiss ter NW6	46	F20
Swithland gdns SE9	113	W9
Swyncombe ave W5	72	B12
Swynford gdns NW4	26	H13
Sybil ms N4	30	J19
Sybourn st E17	50	M2
Sycamore ave W5	72	H8
Sycamore ave Sid	96	M15
Sycamore clo N9	18	J12
Sycamore clo Barn	5	U18
Sycamore clo Cars	130	M9
Sycamore clo Nthlt	58	C4
Sycamore gdns W6	144	A20
Sycamore gdns Mitch	120	H4
Sycamore gro NW9	43	W1
Sycamore gro SE6	93	U17
Sycamore gro SE20	109	Y19
Sycamore gro N Mal	118	A5
Sycamore hill N11	16	C19
Sycamore rd SW19	104	M15
Sycamore rd Tedd	102	F14
Sycamore st EC1	142	A17
Sycamore way Th Hth	122	F11
Sydenham ave SE26	110	A13
Sydenham clo Rom	39	T11
Sydenham cotts SE12	112	K5
Sydenham hill SE23	109	Z2
Sydenham hill SE26	109	W11
Sydenham Hill est SE26	109	Y7
Sydenham pk SE26	110	B8
Sydenham Park rd SE26	110	C6
Sydenham ri SE23	110	A3
Sydenham rd SE26	110	F11
Sydenham rd Croy	133	N2
Sydmons ct SE23	92	C18
Sydner ms N16	49	U11
Sydner rd N16	49	U11
Sydney clo SW3	154	H7
Sydney gro NW4	26	M15
Sydney ms SW3	154	J7
Sydney pl SW7	154	J7
Sydney rd N8	30	F12
Sydney rd N10	29	R5
Sydney rd SE2	80	J8
Sydney rd SW20	119	P3
Sydney rd W13	71	Z3
Sydney rd Bexh	97	X11
Sydney rd Enf	8	B12
Sydney rd Ilf	36	C8
Sydney rd Rich	84	K11
Sydney rd Sid	114	J10
Sydney rd Sutt	129	Y9
Sydney rd Tedd	101	U13
Sydney rd Wdf Grn	21	S14
Sydney st SW3	154	J8
Sylvan ave N3	27	Z7
Sylvan ave N22	30	E1
Sylvan ave NW7	13	P18
Sylvan ave Rom	38	C17
Sylvan gdns Surb	116	G19
Sylvan gro SE15	159	Z16
Sylvan hill SE19	109	T20
Sylvan rd E7	52	G17
Sylvan rd E11	34	F14
Sylvan rd E17	33	O15
Sylvan rd SE19	109	U20
Sylvan wk Brom	127	T7
Sylvan way Dag	55	R10
Sylverdale rd Croy	132	J5
Sylvester ave Chis	113	T16
Sylvester rd E8	50	A17
Sylvester rd E17	32	M20
Sylvester rd N2	28	E6
Sylvester rd Wem	42	E14
Sylvestrus clo Kings T	117	P2
Sylvia gdns Wem	43	S20
Symes ms NW1	140	A7
Symons st SW3	155	R7
Syon Gate way Brent	72	A19
Syon la Islw	71	U15
Syon Park gdns Islw	71	W18

T

Name		
Tabard Garden est SE1	150	G19
Tabard st SE1	150	E18
Tabernacle st EC2	142	G18
Tableer ave SW4	89	W12
Tabley rd N7	47	Z11
Tabor gdns Sutt	129	U15
Tabor gro SW19	105	U17
Tabor rd W6	152	A2
Tachbrook est SW1	156	G11
Tachbrook ms SW1	156	B5
Tachbrook st SW1	156	C7
Tack ms SE4	93	N6
Tadema rd SW10	154	D18
Tadmor st W12	144	F15
Tadworth ave N Mal	118	D11
Tadworth rd NW2	44	F7
Taeping st E14	76	E10
Taffy's How Mitch	120	K5
Taft way E3	64	F8
Tait rd Croy	123	R17
Takeley clo Rom	38	M6
Talacre rd NW5	47	R18
Talbot ave N2	28	F11
Talbot clo N15	31	V13
Talbot ct EC3	150	H8
Talbot cres NW4	26	G15
Talbot gdns Ilf	55	N6
Talbot pl SE3	93	Z3
Talbot rd E6	66	H5
Talbot rd E7	52	F11
Talbot rd N6	29	O18
Talbot rd N15	31	V13
Talbot rd N22	29	W6
Talbot rd W2	145	U4
Talbot rd W11	145	P5
Talbot rd W13	71	Y1
Talbot rd Cars	131	O11
Talbot rd Dag	56	C18
Talbot rd Har	23	Z10
Talbot rd Islw	83	Z10
Talbot rd Sthl	70	C10
Talbot rd Th Hth	123	P9
Talbot rd Twick	101	V1
Talbot rd Wem	42	G16
Talbot sq W2	146	G6
Talbot yd SE1	150	E15
Talfourd pl SE15	91	U3
Talfourd rd SE15	91	U2
Talgarth rd W6	152	D8
Talgarth rd W14	152	K9
Talgarth wk NW9	26	B16
Talisman clo Ilf	55	S3
Talisman sq SE26	109	W9
Talisman way Wem	42	L9
Tall Elms clo Brom	126	C11
Tall Trees SW16	122	C8
Tallack clo Har	23	U3
Tallack rd E10	51	N3
Tallis gro SE7	77	W16
Tallis st EC4	149	V8
Tallis vw NW10	43	Z17
Talma gdns Twick	83	T17
Talma rd SW2	90	G11
Talmage clo SE23	92	D20
Talman gro Stan	11	T18
Talwin st E3	64	E10
Tamar st SE7	78	D9
Tamar way N17	31	W9
Tamarind pl E1	151	T11
Tamarisk sq W12	62	E20
Tamesis gdns Wor Pk	128	B2
Tamworth ave Wdf Grn	21	N18
Tamworth la Mitch	121	R4
Tamworth pk Mitch	121	T8
Tamworth pl Croy	132	L3
Tamworth rd Croy	132	K4
Tamworth st SW6	153	U14
Tancred rd N4	30	J19
Tanfield ave NW2	44	C11
Tanfield rd Croy	132	L8

Entry	Pg	Ref
Tangier rd Rich	85	S9
Tanglebury clo Brom	127	T9
Tanglewood clo Croy	134	D5
Tanglewood clo Stan	10	F9
Tangley gro SW15	86	E17
Tangley Park rd Hmptn	100	E13
Tangmere way NW9	26	B6
Tankerton st SW1	140	L13
Tankerville rd SW16	107	Y17
Tankridge rd NW2	44	K7
Tanner st SE1	151	O18
Tanner st Bark	54	B18
Tanners End la N18	18	E14
Tanners hill SE8	93	N3
Tanners la Ilf	36	C10
Tannery clo Beck	124	E11
Tannery clo Dag	56	G8
Tannsfield rd SE26	110	E13
Tanswell est SE1	149	U18
Tanswell st SE1	149	T18
Tansy clo E6	66	L18
Tant ave E16	65	P16
Tantallon rd SW12	89	O20
Tantony gro Rom	37	X10
Tanza rd NW3	46	L11
Tapestry clo Sutt	130	A17
Taplow st N1	142	C10
Tapp st E1	143	X17
Tappesfield rd SE15	92	C7
Tapster st Barn	4	G12
Tarbert rd SE22	91	T12
Tariff rd N17	18	L19
Tarleton gdns SE23	110	A3
Tarling clo Sid	115	R8
Tarling rd E16	65	R19
Tarling rd N2	28	E6
Tarling st E1	151	Z6
Tarn st SE1	158	A2
Tarnbank Enf	7	O15
Tarnwood pk SE9	95	U20
Tarragon gro SE26	110	E14
Tarrant pl W1	147	N2
Tarrington clo SW16	107	X8
Tarry la SE8	75	W11
Tarver rd SE17	157	Y10
Tarves way SE10	76	E18
Tash pl N11	16	E16
Tasker rd NW3	46	M15
Tasman rd SW9	90	A8
Tasmania ter N18	18	A18
Tasso rd W6	152	L13
Tatam rd NW10	43	X19
Tate rd E16	78	F3
Tate rd Sutt	129	X12
Tatnell rd SE23	92	H16
Tattersall clo SE9	95	S13
Tatton cres N16	31	V20
Tatum st SE17	158	H7
Taunton ave SW20	118	J4
Taunton ave Houns	82	Z2
Taunton clo Bexh	99	O6
Taunton clo Sutt	129	X1
Taunton dr Enf	7	S11
Taunton ms NW1	139	O18
Taunton pl NW1	139	O18
Taunton rd SE12	94	A13
Taunton rd Grnf	58	K2
Taunton way Stan	24	K9
Tavern la SW9	90	G4
Taverner sq N5	48	L12
Tavistock ave E17	32	G10
Tavistock ave Grnf	59	Z6
Tavistock clo N16	49	T15
Tavistock cres W11	145	O2
Tavistock cres Mitch	107	Z3
Tavistock gdns Ilf	54	J12
Tavistock gate Croy	123	N20
Tavistock gro Croy	123	N18
Tavistock ms E18	34	F11
Tavistock pl E18	34	F11
Tavistock pl N14	16	E12
Tavistock pl WC1	140	J16
Tavistock rd E7	52	B11
Tavistock rd E15	52	B20
Tavistock rd E18	34	E10
Tavistock rd N4	31	N18
Tavistock rd NW10	62	C5
Tavistock rd W11	145	O3
Tavistock rd Brom	126	D8
Tavistock rd Cars	130	H1
Tavistock rd Croy	123	N20
Tavistock rd Edg	25	O4
Tavistock rd Well	97	T1
Tavistock sq WC1	140	G16
Tavistock st WC2	148	M9
Tavistock ter N19	47	Z9
Tavistock wk Cars	120	H20
Taviton st WC1	140	F15
Tavy bri SE2	80	H7
Tawney rd SE28	68	D20
Tawny way SE16	75	T10
Tay way Rom	39	T4
Tayben ave Twick	83	U17
Taybridge rd SW11	89	R8
Tayburn clo E14	64	G17
Taylor ave Rich	85	S4
Taylor clo Hmptn	101	O12
Taylor clo Rom	38	E1
Taylor ct E15	51	U14
Taylor rd Mitch	106	L18
Taylor rd Wall	131	R11
Taylors clo Sid	114	K8
Taylors grn W3	62	B16
Taylors la NW10	44	A20
Taylors la SE26	109	Z9
Taylors la Barn	4	G5
Taymount ri SE23	110	B3
Tayport clo N1	140	M1
Tayside dr Edg	12	F9
Taywood rd Nthlt	58	E9
Teak clo SE16	75	W4
Teal clo E16	66	B15
Teale st E2	143	U8
Teasel clo Croy	124	E20
Teasel way E15	65	N8
Tebworth rd N17	31	U3
Tedder clo S Croy	134	E17
Teddington pk Tedd	101	W12
Teddington Park rd Tedd	101	W11
Tedworth gdns SW3	155	N11
Tedworth sq SW3	155	O11
Tee the W3	62	A16
Tees ave Grnf	59	U6
Teesdale ave Islw	83	Z2
Teesdale clo E2	143	V9
Teesdale gdns SE25	123	R2
Teesdale gdns Islw	83	Z2
Teesdale rd E11	34	B20
Teesdale st E2	143	V10
Teevan clo Croy	123	Y17
Teevan rd Croy	123	Y18
Teignmouth clo SW4	89	X11
Teignmouth clo Edg	25	N7
Teignmouth gdns Grnf	59	X7
Teignmouth rd NW2	45	N16
Teignmouth rd Well	97	T4
Telegraph ms Ilf	55	O2
Telegraph hill	86	L17
Telegraph st EC2	150	F4
Telephone pl SW6	153	S13
Telfer clo W3	73	V4
Telferscot rd SW12	107	W1
Telford ave SW2	107	X3
Telford rd N11	16	J17
Telford rd SE9	113	D5
Telford rd W10	136	K20
Telford rd Sthl	58	K19
Telford rd Twick	82	G18
Telford rd SW1	156	A12
Telford way W3	62	B15
Telford way Hayes	58	B14
Telham rd E6	66	J7
Tell gro SE22	91	U11
Tellson ave SE18	95	P1
Temeraire st SE16	75	R5
Temperley rd SW12	89	P18
Tempest way Rain	57	W17
Templar dr SE28	68	J18
Templar pl Hmptn	100	G17
Templar st SE5	90	J3
Templars ave NW11	27	W18
Templars cres N3	27	X8
Templars dr Har	10	B19
Temple ave EC4	149	U8
Temple ave N20	15	U2
Temple ave Croy	134	L4
Temple ave Dag	56	D2
Temple clo N3	27	V8
Temple clo SE28	79	R7
Temple Fortune hill NW11	27	X16
Temple Fortune la NW11	27	W17
Temple gdns N21	17	W8
Temple gdns NW11	27	V17
Temple gdns Dag	55	W8
Temple gro NW11	27	X18
Temple gro Enf	7	W10
Temple la EC4	149	U7
Temple Mead clo Stan	11	N19
Temple Mill la E15	51	P13
Temple pl WC2	149	R9
Temple rd N8	30	C13
Temple rd NW2	44	M11
Temple rd W4	73	V9
Temple rd W5	72	F9
Temple rd Croy	133	O8
Temple rd Houns	82	L15
Temple rd Rich	85	N6
Temple Sheen SW14	85	U11
Temple Sheen rd SW14	85	T11
Temple st E2	143	W9
Temple way Sutt	130	G6
Temple West ms SE11	157	X3
Templecombe rd E9	143	Z3
Templecombe way Mord	119	S12
Templehof ave NW2	44	M1
Templeman rd W7	59	V4
Templemead clo W3	62	A18
Templeton ave E4	20	C12
Templeton clo SE19	123	P2
Templeton pl SW5	153	U6
Templeton rd N15	31	O17
Templewood W13	60	B13
Templewood ave NW3	46	A10
Templewood gdns NW3	46	A10
Tempsford clo Enf	7	Y12
Temsford clo Har	22	M7
Tenbury clo E7	53	N15
Tenbury ct SW2	89	Z20
Tenby ave Har	24	B8
Tenby clo N15	31	V13
Tenby clo Rom	37	Z19
Tenby gdns Nthlt	58	B9
Tenby rd E17	32	H14
Tenby rd Edg	25	N5
Tenby rd Enf	9	P12
Tenby rd Rom	37	Z19
Tenby rd Well	97	V1
Tench st E1	151	W14
Tenda rd SE16	159	W7
Tendring way Rom	37	T15
Tenham ave SW2	107	X3
Tenison way SE1	149	R14
Tenniel clo W2	146	A7
Tennis st SE1	150	E17
Tennison rd SE25	123	U10
Tenniswood rd Enf	8	D6
Tennyson ave E11	52	G1
Tennyson ave E12	53	R19
Tennyson ave NW9	25	V10
Tennyson ave N Mal	118	K12
Tennyson ave Twick	101	W2
Tennyson clo Well	96	J2
Tennyson rd E10	51	S5
Tennyson rd E15	52	A20
Tennyson rd E17	32	M17
Tennyson rd NW6	137	P3
Tennyson rd NW7	13	T15
Tennyson rd SE20	110	F17
Tennyson rd SW19	106	D14
Tennyson rd W7	59	V20
Tennyson rd Houns	82	M4
Tennyson st SW8	89	S6
Tennyson way Horn	57	V5
Tensing rd Sthl	70	G8
Tent st E1	143	W17
Tentelow la Sthl	70	J11
Tenter grd E1	151	N2
Tenterden clo NW4	27	O10
Tenterden clo SE9	113	T10
Tenterden dr NW4	27	P10
Tenterden gdns NW4	27	P11
Tenterden gdns Croy	123	Y17
Tenterden gro NW4	27	O10
Tenterden rd N17	31	U2
Tenterden rd Croy	123	Y17
Tenterden rd Dag	56	B6
Tenterden st W1	147	Y7
Teresa ms E17	33	P12
Terling clo E11	52	C9
Terling rd Dag	56	E5
Terminus st E1	155	Z3
Terrace the NW6	137	T3
Terrace the SW13	86	B5
Terrace the Wdf Grn	21	S18
Terrace gdns SW13	86	C4
Terrace la Rich	84	K16
Terrace rd E9	50	E20
Terrace rd E13	65	U4
Terrace wk Dag	56	A15
Terrapin rd SW17	107	S6
Terrick rd N22	30	A5
Terrick st W12	62	K18
Terrilands Pnr	22	D10
Terront rd N15	30	M14
Testerton wk W11	144	H9
Tetcott rd SW10	154	B18
Tetherdown N10	29	P9
Tetterby way SE16	159	V10
Tetty way Brom	126	E4
Teversham la SW8	90	B1
Teviot clo Well	97	R2
Teviot st E14	64	F13
Tewkesbury ave SE23	92	A20
Tewkesbury ave Pnr	22	C17
Tewkesbury gdns NW9	25	T10
Tewkesbury rd N15	31	O19
Tewkesbury rd W13	71	Y1
Tewkesbury rd Cars	120	G19
Tewkesbury ter N11	16	H18
Tewson rd SE18	79	W14
Teynham ave Enf	8	C19
Teynham grn Brom	126	E11
Teynton ter N17	30	M5
Thackeray ave N17	31	W7
Thackeray clo SW19	105	R18
Thackeray clo Har	40	H4
Thackeray dr Rom	55	O2
Thackeray rd E6	66	C5
Thackeray rd SW8	89	S5
Thackeray st W8	145	Y20
Thakeham clo SE26	110	A11
Thalia clo SE10	76	L16
Thame rd SE16	75	U4
Thames ave SW10	88	E2
Thames ave Dag	69	T13
Thames ave Grnf	59	V6
Thames bank SW14	85	W5
Thames rd E16	78	A3
Thames rd W4	73	S16
Thames rd Bark	67	W8
Thames rd Dart	99	W7
Thames side Kings T	116	H2
Thames st SE10	76	F16
Thames st Kings T	116	H3
Thames vill W4	85	U2
Thamesbank pl SE28	68	D20
Thamesgate clo Rich	102	C10
Thameshill ave Rom	38	L7
Thameside Tedd	102	F17
Thameside Industrial est E16	78	C4
Thameside wk SE28	68	A18
Thamesmere dr SE28	68	A20
Thamesvale clo Houns	82	H6
Thane vill N7	48	E9
Thanescroft gdns Croy	133	T6

Name	Page	Grid
Thanet pl Croy	133	N7
Thanet rd Bex	98	E19
Thanet st WC1	140	J14
Thanington ct SE9	96	H15
Thant clo E10	51	T10
Tharp rd Wall	131	X12
Thatcham gdns N20	15	R2
Thatchers way Islw	83	P13
Thatches gro Rom	37	Z12
Thavies Inn EC1	149	V4
Thaxted pl SW20	105	O18
Thaxted SE9	114	B6
Thaxton rd W14	153	R12
Thayer st W1	147	V3
Thayers Farm rd Beck	124	J1
Theatre st SW11	88	M8
Theberton st N1	141	W4
Theed st SE1	149	T14
Thelma gdns SE3	95	P2
Thelma gro Tedd	101	X14
Theobald cres Har	22	M5
Theobald rd E17	51	N1
Theobald rd Croy	132	H3
Theobald st SE1	158	E3
Theobalds ave N12	15	R13
Theobald's rd WC1	141	O20
Theodore rd SE13	93	W15
Therapia la Croy	121	X17
Therapia rd SE22	92	B16
Theresa rd W6	74	G12
Thermopylae gate E14	76	E12
Theseus wk N1	141	Y10
Thesiger rd SE20	110	G17
Thessaly rd SW8	156	B18
Thetford clo N13	17	X19
Thetford gdns Dag	68	L2
Thetford rd Dag	68	L1
Thetford rd N Mal	117	Y14
Thetis ter Rich	73	O17
Theydon gro Wdf Grn	21	Y19
Theydon rd E5	50	C5
Theydon st E17	50	L1
Thicket cres Sutt	130	E9
Thicket gro Dag	55	V17
Thicket rd SE20	109	Y18
Thicket rd Sutt	130	E10
Third ave E12	53	S12
Third ave E13	65	U9
Third ave E17	33	P15
Third ave W3	74	D3
Third ave W10	136	L12
Third ave Dag	69	V4
Third ave Enf	8	H16
Third ave Rom	37	U17
Third ave Wem	42	G6
Third Cross rd Twick	101	R3
Third way Wem	43	U13
Thirleby rd SW1	156	C3
Thirleby rd Edg	25	X4
Thirlmere ave Grnf	60	C8
Thirlmere gdns Wem	42	E4
Thirlmere ri Brom	112	B16
Thirlmere rd N10	29	T5
Thirlmere rd SW16	107	X11
Thirlmere rd Bexh	98	K3
Thirsk clo Nthlt	40	J17
Thirsk rd SE25	123	P8
Thirsk rd SW11	89	O9
Thirsk rd Mitch	107	O18
Thistle gro SW10	154	C10
Thistlebrook SE2	80	F7
Thistlecroft gdns Stan	24	F5
Thistledene ave Har	40	C10
Thistlemead Chis	127	Y3
Thistlewaite rd E5	50	B10
Thistlewood clo N7	48	D6
Thistleworth clo Islw	71	P19
Thomas Baines rd SW11	88	G9
Thomas Darby ct W11	144	K6
Thomas Doyle st SE1	157	X1
Thomas la SE6	93	P19
Thomas More st E1	151	S11
Thomas More way N2	28	C9
Thomas pl W8	153	Y3
Thomas rd E14	64	B15
Thomas st SE18	78	L10
Thomas à Beckett clo Wem	41	W11
Thompson ave Rich	85	S6
Thompson clo Ilf	54	C7
Thompson rd SE22	91	V16
Thompson rd Dag	56	C10
Thompson's ave SE5	158	A17
Thomson cres Croy	122	E20
Thomson rd Har	23	U9
Thorburn sq SE1	159	S6
Thorburn way SW19	120	E2
Thoresby st N1	142	B11
Thorkhill gdns T Ditt	116	A20
Thorkhill rd T Ditt	116	A20
Thorn ave (Bushey) Wat	10	A5
Thorn clo Brom	127	X14
Thorn clo Nthlt	58	E8
Thornaby gdns N18	18	M18
Thornbury ave Islw	71	P20
Thornbury rd SW2	89	Z16
Thornbury rd Islw	71	R18
Thornby rd E5	50	C10
Thorncliffe rd SW2	89	Z17
Thorncliffe rd Sthl	70	D13
Thorncombe rd SE22	91	T12
Thorncroft Horn	39	Z16
Thorncroft rd Sutt	130	A10
Thorncroft st SW8	156	J19
Thorndean st SW18	106	C5
Thorndene ave N11	16	A6
Thorndike clo SW10	154	C18
Thorndike st SW1	156	E8
Thorndon gdns Epsom	128	B10
Thorne clo E11	51	Z11
Thorne clo E16	65	S16
Thorne clo Erith	81	W16
Thorne pas SW13	86	B6
Thorne rd SW8	156	K20
Thorne st SW13	86	B6
Thorneloe gdns Croy	132	G12
Thornes clo Beck	125	U7
Thornet Wood rd Brom	127	W7
Thorney cres SW11	154	H19
Thorney Hedge rd W4	73	S11
Thorney st SW1	156	K4
Thornfield ave NW7	27	S3
Thornfield rd W12	144	A17
Thornford rd SE13	93	V14
Thorngate rd W9	137	W17
Thorngrove rd E13	65	X2
Thornham gro E15	51	W16
Thornham st SE10	76	F17
Thornhaugh st WC1	140	H19
Thornhill ave SE18	79	W19
Thornhill Bridge wf N1	141	N6
Thornhill cres N1	141	O1
Thornhill gdns E10	51	S7
Thornhill gdns Bark	54	J20
Thornhill gro N1	141	N2
Thornhill rd E10	51	R7
Thornhill rd N1	141	T1
Thornhill rd Croy	122	M17
Thornhill sq N1	141	O2
Thornlaw rd SE27	108	G11
Thornley dr Har	40	L7
Thornsbeach rd SE6	111	U1
Thornsett pl SE20	124	A4
Thornsett rd SE20	123	Z4
Thornsett rd SW18	106	B3
Thornside Edg	12	D20
Thornton ave SW2	107	Y2
Thornton ave W4	74	B11
Thornton ave Croy	122	C15
Thornton dene Beck	125	O4
Thornton gdns SW12	107	X1
Thornton hill SW19	105	S17
Thornton pl W1	147	P1
Thornton rd E11	51	X6
Thornton rd N18	19	S12
Thornton rd SW12	89	W19
Thornton rd SW14	85	Y9
Thornton rd SW19	105	R16
Thornton rd Barn	4	E12
Thornton rd Belv	81	U10
Thornton rd Brom	112	G12
Thornton rd Cars	120	F20
Thornton rd Ilf	53	Y12
Thornton rd Th Hth	122	E13
Thornton row Th Hth	122	G11
Thornton st SW9	90	F4
Thornton way NW11	28	B16
Thorntons Farm ave Rom	56	M5
Thorntree rd SE7	78	B14
Thornville st SE8	93	N3
Thornwood clo E18	34	K7
Thornwood rd SE13	94	A13
Thorogood gdns E15	52	A16
Thorold rd N22	30	A1
Thorold rd Ilf	53	Z7
Thorparch rd SW8	156	H20
Thorpe cres E17	32	M6
Thorpe Hall rd E17	33	V5
Thorpe rd E6	66	F3
Thorpe rd E7	52	D11
Thorpe rd E17	33	T6
Thorpe rd N15	31	T19
Thorpe rd Bark	54	E20
Thorpe rd Kings T	102	K18
Thorpebank rd W12	74	G2
Thorpedale gdns Ilf	35	Y12
Thorpedale rd N4	48	B5
Thorpewood ave SE26	110	A5
Thorsden way SE19	109	S11
Thorverton rd NW2	45	S10
Thoydon rd E3	63	V7
Thrale rd SW16	107	U11
Thrale st SE1	150	C14
Thrawl st E1	151	P2
Threadneedle st EC2	150	F6
Three Colt st E14	63	Z18
Three Colts la E2	143	Y16
Three corners Bexh	98	J5
Three Cups yd WC1	149	P1
Three Kings rd Mitch	121	N6
Three Kings yd W1	147	W8
Three Mill la E3	64	G8
Three Oak la SE1	151	O17
Threshers pl W11	144	K9
Thriffwood SE26	110	E8
Throckmorten rd E16	65	W18
Throgmorton ave EC2	150	G4
Throgmorton st EC2	150	G5
Throwley clo SE2	80	F7
Throwley rd Sutt	130	B12
Throwley way Sutt	130	B9
Thrupp clo Mitch	121	T4
Thrush grn Har	22	G13
Thrush st SE17	158	A9
Thurbarn rd SE6	111	S12
Thurland rd SE16	159	T1
Thurlby clo Har	23	Y19
Thurlby rd SE27	108	H10
Thurlby rd Wem	42	H18
Thurleigh ave SW12	89	P16
Thurleigh rd SW12	88	L17
Thurleston ave Mord	119	R11
Thurlestone ave N12	15	Y18
Thurlestone ave Ilf	54	K13
Thurlestone rd SE27	108	G8
Thurloe clo SW7	154	J4
Thurloe gdns Rom	39	S18
Thurloe pl SW7	154	J4
Thurloe sq SW7	154	J5
Thurloe st SW7	154	H5
Thurlow clo E4	20	F19
Thurlow gdns Wem	42	H16
Thurlow hill SE21	108	L2
Thurlow Park rd SE21	108	K3
Thurlow rd NW3	46	G14
Thurlow rd W7	71	Y6
Thurlow st SE17	158	K11
Thurlow ter NW5	47	N16
Thursland rd Sid	115	Y14
Thursley cres Croy	135	W17
Thursley gdns SW19	105	P5
Thursley rd SE9	113	T8
Thurso st SW17	106	G10
Thurstan rd SW20	104	J17
Thurston rd SE13	93	S6
Thurston rd Sthl	58	F18
Thurtle rd E2	143	P7
Thwaite clo Erith	81	Y17
Thyra gro N12	15	O19
Tibbatts rd E3	64	D11
Tibbets clo SW19	105	P2
Tibbet's ride SW15	87	O18
Tiber gdns N1	140	M6
Ticehurst clo Orp	115	O19
Ticehurst rd SE23	110	J5
Tickford clo SE2	80	F5
Tidal Basin rd E16	65	R20
Tidenham gdns Croy	133	T6
Tideswell rd SW15	87	N11
Tideswell rd Croy	135	N6
Tideway clo Rich	102	C10
Tidey st E3	64	C13
Tidford rd Well	96	K4
Tidworth rd E3	64	B10
Tierney rd SW2	108	A1
Tiger la Brom	126	H8
Tiger way E5	49	Z11
Tilbrook rd SE3	94	M8
Tilbury clo SE15	159	P16
Tilbury rd E6	66	G6
Tilbury rd E10	51	T2
Tildesley rd SW15	86	L15
Tile Kiln la N6	47	U2
Tile Kiln la N13	17	Y16
Tilehurst rd SW18	106	F1
Tilehurst rd Sutt	129	S11
Tileyard rd N7	47	Z20
Tilford ave Croy	135	U18
Tilford gdns SW19	105	P2
Tilia rd E5	50	B13
Tiller rd E14	76	B8
Tillett clo NW10	43	V18
Tillett way E2	143	T12
Tilling rd NW2	44	L3
Tillingbourne gdns N3	27	W11
Tillingham way N12	14	M13
Tillman st E1	151	Y7
Tilloch st N1	141	N1
Tillotson rd N9	18	F7
Tillotson rd Har	22	K2
Tillotson rd Ilf	53	W1
Tilney ct EC1	142	D16
Tilney dr Buck H	21	U8
Tilney gdns N1	49	P18
Tilney rd Dag	56	C18
Tilney st W1	147	V13
Tilson gdns SW2	89	Z18
Tilson rd N17	31	Y5
Tilt Yard app SE9	95	T17
Tilton st SW6	153	N15
Tiltwood the W3	61	X19
Timber clo Chis	127	X2
Timber Mill way SW4	89	X7
Timber Pond rd SE16	75	U5
Timber Slip dr Wall	131	Y20
Timber st EC1	142	A17
Timbercroft Epsom	128	A8
Timbercroft la SE18	79	U17
Timberdene NW4	27	R6
Timberdene ave Ilf	36	B5
Timberland rd E1	151	Y6
Timberwharf rd N16	31	X18
Times sq Sutt	130	B11
Tindal st SW9	157	Y20
Tinderbox all SW14	85	Z6
Tinsley rd E1	63	S14
Tintagel cres SE22	91	U10
Tintagel dr Stan	11	W14
Tintern ave NW9	25	T10

Tintern clo SW15 87 S14
Tintern clo SW19 106 D17
Tintern gdns N14 17 N2
Tintern rd N22 30 L5
Tintern rd Cars 130 G1
Tintern st SW4 90 B10
Tintern way Har 40 K2
Tinto rd E16 65 T13
Tinworth st SE11 156 M8
Tippetts clo Enf 7 Z7
Tipthorpe rd SW11 89 O8
Tipton dr Croy 133 S8
Tiptree clo E4 20 G12
Tiptree cres Ilf 35 X8
Tiptree dr Enf 8 C14
Tiptree est Ilf 35 X9
Tirlemont rd S Croy 132 L16
Tirrell rd Croy 122 M15
Tisbury rd SW16 121 Z4
Tisdall pl SE17 158 H7
Titchborne row W2 146 L6
Titchfield rd NW8 139 N7
Titchfield rd Cars 120 F20
Titchfield rd Enf 9 V1
Titchfield wk Cars 120 H18
Titchwell rd SW18 88 G20
Tite st SW3 155 O12
Tithe Barn clo
  Kings T 117 N2
Tithe clo NW7 26 G3
Tithe Farm ave Har 40 G9
Tithe Farm clo Har 40 G8
Tithe wk NW7 26 F3
Titian ave (Bushey)
  Wat 10 E3
Titley clo E4 20 B16
Titmuss ave SE28 68 D20
Titmuss st W12 144 N19
Tiverton ave Ilf 35 X9
Tiverton dr SE9 114 B1
Tiverton rd N15 31 O18
Tiverton rd N18 18 E17
Tiverton rd NW10 136 H6
Tiverton rd Edg 24 M8
Tiverton rd Houns 82 M5
Tiverton rd Wem 60 K5
Tiverton st SE1 158 A2
Tivoli gdns SE18 78 D10
Tivoli rd N8 29 Y16
Tivoli rd SE27 108 L13
Tivoli rd Houns 82 B11
Tobin clo NW3 46 K20
Toby la E1 63 V11
Tokenhouse yd EC2 150 F5
Tokyngton ave Wem 43 O18
Toland sq SW15 86 G14
Toley ave Wem 42 K2
Tollbridge clo W10 137 N17
Tollesbury gdns Ilf 36 D9
Tollet st E1 63 S11
Tollgate dr SE21 109 T5
Tollgate gdns NW6 137 W8
Tollgate rd E6 66 B14
Tollgate rd E16 65 Z14
Tollington pk N4 48 C7
Tollington pl N4 48 C5
Tollington rd N7 48 D11
Tollington way N7 48 B8
Tolmers sq NW1 140 C15
Tolpuddle st N1 141 S8
Tolsford rd E5 50 A15
Tolson rd Islw 84 B9
Tolverne rd SW20 118 M2
Tolworth gdns
  Rom 37 X15
Tom Cribb rd SE28 79 R9
Tom Mann clo Bark 67 W4
Tomlins gro E3 64 B9
Tomlins Orchard
  Bark 67 P4
Tomlinson clo E2 143 P14
Tomlinson clo W4 73 S13
Tompion st EC1 141 X14
Tomswood hill Ilf 36 A1
Tonbridge cres Har 24 K11
Tonbridge st WC1 140 K13
Tonfield rd Sutt 119 V20
Tonge clo Beck 125 P12
Tonsley hill SW18 88 B12

Tonsley pl SW18 88 B13
Tonsley rd SW18 88 B13
Tonsley st SW18 88 B12
Tonstall rd Mitch 121 O3
Tooke clo Pnr 22 A3
Took's ct EC4 149 T4
Tooley st SE1 150 H14
Toorack rd Har 23 P7
Tooting Bec gdns
  SW16 107 Y10
Tooting Bec rd
  SW16 107 V9
Tooting Bec rd
  SW17 107 O7
Tooting gro SW17 106 J12
Tooting High st
  SW17 106 J14
Tootswood rd Brom 125 Z11
Top House ri E4 20 H2
Top pk Beck 125 Y11
Topham sq N17 30 M4
Topham st EC1 141 T17
Topiary sq Rich 84 M7
Topp wk NW2 44 L7
Topsfield rd N8 29 Z15
Topsham rd SW17 107 N7
Tor gdns W8 145 U16
Tor rd Well 97 U1
Torbay rd NW6 137 O2
Torbay rd Har 40 D2
Torbridge clo Edg 24 L2
Torbrook clo Bex 97 Z16
Torcross dr SE23 110 C5
Tormead clo Sutt 129 Z13
Tormount rd SE18 79 U15
Toronto rd E11 51 X12
Toronto rd Ilf 54 A3
Torquay gdns Ilf 35 P13
Torquay st W2 145 W2
Torr rd SE20 110 F18
Torre wk Cars 120 H20
Torrens rd E15 52 B17
Torrens rd SW2 90 C13
Torrens sq E15 52 B17
Torrens st EC1 141 V10
Torriano ave NW5 47 X16
Torriano cotts NW5 47 W15
Torridge gdns SE15 92 B10
Torridge rd Th Hth 122 K11
Torridon rd SE6 93 Y19
Torridon rd SE13 93 Z18
Torrington ave N12 15 V16
Torrington dr Har 40 K11
Torrington gdns N11 16 J19
Torrington gdns
  Grnf 60 D2
Torrington gro N12 15 W15
Torrington pk N12 15 S15
Torrington pl E1 151 V13
Torrington pl WC1 140 E19
Torrington rd E18 34 F11
Torrington rd Dag 56 C3
Torrington rd Grnf 60 D3
Torrington sq WC1 140 G19
Torrington way
  Mord 119 Y16
Torver rd Har 23 U13
Torwood rd SW15 86 H14
Tothill st SW1 148 F19
Totnes rd Well 80 E20
Totnes wk N2 28 G14
Tottenhall rd N13 17 S18
Tottenham Court rd
  W1 140 C17
Tottenham Green
  east N15 31 V12
Tottenham la N8 30 A16
Tottenham ms W1 148 C1
Tottenham rd N1 R18
Tottenham st W1 148 C1
Totterdown st SW17 106 M11
Totteridge common
  N20 13 X7
Totteridge grn N20 14 K8
Totteridge la N20 14 L6
Totteridge village
  N20 14 H6
Totternhoe clo Har 24 E15
Totton rd Th Hth 122 G7

Toulmin st SE1 150 B18
Toulon st SE5 158 A18
Tournay rd SW6 153 S16
Toussaint wk SE16 159 V1
Tovil clo SE20 123 Z3
Towcester rd E3 64 F12
Tower bri E1 151 O13
Tower bri SE1 151 N14
Tower Bridge app E1 151 O12
Tower Bridge rd SE1 158 J3
Tower clo SE20 109 Z17
Tower Gardens rd
  N17 31 P5
Tower Hamlets rd E7 52 D13
Tower Hamlets rd
  E17 33 O10
Tower hill EC3 151 N10
Tower ms E17 33 O13
Tower ri Rich 84 K8
Tower rd NW10 44 G20
Tower rd Belv 81 Y12
Tower rd Bexh 98 F10
Tower rd Twick 101 V6
Tower Royal EC4 150 D7
Tower st WC2 148 J7
Tower vw Croy 124 G18
Towers rd Pnr 22 B3
Towers rd Sthl 58 H10
Towfield rd Felt 100 D4
Town the Enf 8 C12
Town Court path N4 48 M3
Town Hall Approach
  rd N15 31 U2
Town hall ave W4 73 X13
Town Hall rd SW11 89 N9
Town meadow Brent 72 H7
Town quay Bark 67 N3
Town rd N9 19 N8
Towney mead Nthlt 58 E7
Townhlm cres W7 71 V7
Townley ct E15 52 C18
Townley rd SE22 91 S14
Townley rd Bexh 98 B14
Townley st SE17 158 D8
Townmead rd SW6 88 B7
Townmead rd Rich 85 T4
Townsend ave N14 16 M13
Townsend Industrial
  est SW10 61 X5
Townsend la NW9 25 Z18
Townsend rd N15 31 V16
Townsend rd Sthl 70 A4
Townsend st SE17 158 H6
Townsend yd N6 47 R3
Townshend clo Sid 115 S16
Townshend est
  NW8 138 K7
Townshend rd NW8 138 K6
Townshend rd Chis 127 O8
Townshend rd Rich 84 M11
Townshend ter Rich 84 M10
Towton rd SE27 108 M5
Toynbec clo Chis 114 A11
Toynbee rd SW20 119 R1
Toynbee st E1 151 O2
Toyne way N6 28 M6
Tracey ave NW2 44 L14
Tradescant rd SW8 156 M18
Trading Estate rd
  NW10 61 V11
Trafalgar ave N17 18 E20
Trafalgar ave SE15 159 P11
Trafalgar ave
  Wor Pk 119 P20
Trafalgar Business
  cen SW18 67 Y11
Trafalgar gdns E1 63 U13
Trafalgar gro SE10 76 L16
Trafalgar pl E11 34 F13
Trafalgar pl N18 18 K16
Trafalgar rd SE10 76 L15
Trafalgar rd SW19 106 C17
Trafalgar rd Twick 101 R5
Trafalgar sq WC2 148 H11
Trafalgar st SE17 158 F10
Trafalgar way E14 76 F2
Trafalgar way Croy 132 K3
Trafford clo E15 51 T15
Trafford rd Th Hth 122 E11

Tramway ave E15 51 Y19
Tramway ave N9 19 O2
Tramway path 120 M11
  Mitch
Tranby pl E9 50 G14
Tranmere rd N9 18 G3
Tranmere rd SW18 106 D3
Tranmere rd Twick 82 L19
Tranquil vale SE3 94 A5
Transept st NW1 146 L2
Transom sq E14 76 E12
Transport ave Brent 72 A14
Tranton rd SE16 159 V1
Traps la N Mal 118 A3
Travers clo E17 32 F4
Travers rd N7 48 E9
Treacy clo (Bushey) 10 B6
  Wat
Treadgold st W11 144 H10
Treadway st E2 143 W9
Treaty st N1 141 N5
Trebeck st W1 147 X13
Trebovir rd SW5 153 V8
Treby st E3 63 Y12
Tredegar rd E3 63 Y7
Tredegar rd N11 29 Y2
Tredegar sq E3 63 Y9
Tredegar ter E3 63 Y8
Trederwen rd E8 143 U3
Tredown rd SE26 110 D13
Tredwell clo Brom 127 P9
Tredwell rd SE27 108 H11
Tree clo Rich 102 H2
Tree rd E16 65 Y17
Treen ave SW13 86 D8
Treetops clo SE2 81 N13
Treeview clo SE19 109 T19
Treewall gdns Brom 112 H10
Trefgarne rd Dag 56 F7
Trefil wk N7 48 B12
Trefoil rd SW18 88 E14
Tregaron ave N8 30 A19
Tregaron gdns 118 B8
  N Mal
Tregarvon rd SW11 89 P10
Tregenna ave Har 40 G11
Tregenna clo N14 6 H17
Trego rd E9 51 N20
Tregothnan rd SW9 90 A7
Tregunter rd SW10 154 A12
Trehearn rd Ilf 36 E1
Treherne rd SW14 85 Z8
Treherne st SW17 107 R8
Trehurst st E5 50 J14
Trelawn rd E10 51 V10
Trelawn rd SW2 90 F13
Trelawney rd Ilf 36 D2
Treloar gdns SE19 109 O16
Tremadoc rd SW4 89 Y9
Tremaine clo SE4 93 O6
Tremaine rd SE20 124 A4
Trematon pl Tedd 102 F17
Tremlett gro N19 47 U8
Tremlett ms N19 47 U9
Trenance gdns Ilf 54 M9
Trenchard clo Stan 11 N19
Trenchard st SE10 76 L15
Trenchold st SW8 156 K15
Trenholme clo SE20 110 A18
Trenholme rd SE20 110 A18
Trenholme ter SE20 110 A18
Trenmar gdns NW10 62 J8
Trent ave W5 72 E7
Trent gdns N14 6 E19
Trent rd SW2 90 C13
Trent rd Buck H 21 V5
Trent way Wor Pk 128 M5
Trentham st SW18 105 X1
Trentwood side Enf 7 R10
Treport st SW18 88 B18
Tresco clo Brom 111 Z16
Tresco gdns Ilf 54 M7
Tresco rd SE15 92 B9
Trescoe gdns Har 40 C2
Tresham cres NW8 138 L15
Tresham rd Bark 67 X1
Tressell clo N1 141 X1
Tressillian cres SE4 93 O7
Tressillian rd SE4 92 M10

Treswell rd Dag	69	N2
Tretawn gdns NW7	13	O12
Tretawn pk NW7	13	O12
Trevanion rd W14	153	N8
Treve ave Har	41	P2
Trevelyan ave E12	53	U13
Trevelyan cres Har	24	H20
Trevelyan gdns NW10	136	C5
Trevelyan rd E15	52	B13
Trevelyan rd SW17	106	J14
Treveris st SE1	149	X14
Treverton st W10	136	J19
Treville st SW15	86	J18
Treviso rd SE23	110	G3
Trevithick st SE8	76	B15
Trevone gdns Pnr	22	C17
Trevor clo Barn	5	V18
Trevor clo Brom	126	D18
Trevor clo Islw	83	W12
Trevor gdns Edg	25	Y4
Trevor pl SW7	146	M18
Trevor rd SW19	105	T19
Trevor rd Edg	25	Y5
Trevor rd Wdf Grn	34	G1
Trevor sq SW7	147	N19
Trevor st SW7	147	N18
Trevose rd E17	33	W4
Trewince rd SW20	118	M2
Trewint st SW18	106	C4
Trewsbury rd SE26	110	G12
Triandra way Hayes	58	A13
Triangle the Kings T	117	V4
Triangle pl SW4	89	X10
Triangle rd E8	143	X3
Trident st SE16	75	U10
Trigon rd SW8	157	R16
Trilby rd SE23	110	G4
Trimmer wk Brent	72	K16
Trinder gdns N19	48	B3
Trinder rd N19	48	B2
Trinder rd Barn	4	A15
Tring ave W5	73	N2
Tring ave Sthl	58	E16
Tring ave Wem	43	P18
Tring clo Ilf	36	D16
Trinidad gdns Dag	69	Z1
Trinity ave N2	28	F10
Trinity ave Enf	8	H18
Trinity Church pas SW13	74	K17
Trinity Church rd SW13	74	K17
Trinity Church sq SE1	150	C20
Trinity clo E11	51	Z6
Trinity clo SE13	93	W12
Trinity clo Houns	82	B9
Trinity clo S Croy	133	T19
Trinity cotts Rich	85	N9
Trinity ct N1	142	J3
Trinity ct SE7	78	B11
Trinity cres SW17	107	N5
Trinity gdns E16	65	P13
Trinity gdns SW9	90	D10
Trinity gro SE10	93	T2
Trinity ms W10	144	H5
Trinity pl Bexh	98	B10
Trinity ri SW2	90	J20
Trinity rd N2	28	F9
Trinity rd N22	30	A2
Trinity rd SW18	88	F14
Trinity rd SW19	105	Z14
Trinity rd Ilf	36	B9
Trinity rd Rich	85	N9
Trinity rd Sthl	70	A4
Trinity sq EC3	150	M9
Trinity st E16	65	S15
Trinity st SE1	150	C19
Trinity st Enf	7	Z8
Trinity way E4	19	Z20
Trinity way W3	62	C20
Trio pl SE1	150	C19
Tristan sq SE3	94	A8
Tristram clo E17	33	X9
Tristram rd Brom	112	D9
Triton sq NW1	140	A16
Tritton ave Croy	132	A7
Tritton rd SE21	109	O8
Triumph rd E6	66	G16
Trojan way Croy	132	E4
Troon st E1	63	V16
Trosley rd Belv	81	S17
Trossachs rd SE22	91	T12
Trothy rd SE1	159	T6
Trott rd N10	29	N3
Trott st SW11	88	H3
Troughton rd SE7	77	X13
Troutbeck rd SE14	92	H2
Trouville rd SW4	89	V16
Trowbridge rd E9	50	M18
Trowlock ave Tedd	102	E15
Trowlock way Tedd	102	F16
Troy ct SE18	79	N11
Troy rd SE19	109	P16
Troy town SE15	91	X7
Truesdale rd E6	66	G17
Trulock rd N17	31	X1
Truman clo Edg	25	U1
Truman's rd N16	49	T14
Trump st EC2	150	D6
Trumpers way W7	71	V7
Trumpington rd E7	52	C11
Trundle st SE1	150	B17
Trundlers way (Bushey) Wat	10	E5
Trundleys rd SE8	75	U12
Trundleys ter SE8	75	T12
Truro gdns Ilf	53	S1
Truro rd E17	32	M14
Truro rd N22	30	A2
Truro st NW5	47	O19
Truslove rd SE27	108	H12
Trussley rd W6	152	C2
Trust wk SE21	108	K1
Trustons gdns Horn	57	W2
Tryfan clo Ilf	35	P15
Tryon st SW3	155	O8
Tuam rd SE18	79	S17
Tubbs rd NW10	62	E7
Tuck rd Rain	57	W18
Tudor ave Hmptn	100	H16
Tudor ave Rom	39	X10
Tudor ave Wor Pk	128	J6
Tudor clo N6	47	U2
Tudor clo NW3	46	J16
Tudor clo NW7	13	V20
Tudor clo NW9	43	W6
Tudor clo Chis	127	U1
Tudor clo Dart	99	Y16
Tudor clo Sutt	129	R13
Tudor clo Wall	131	W17
Tudor clo Wdf Grn	21	V15
Tudor ct E17	32	K20
Tudor Court north Wem	43	R15
Tudor Court south Wem	43	R16
Tudor cres Enf	7	Y4
Tudor dr Kings T	102	H11
Tudor dr Mord	119	P15
Tudor dr Rom	39	W11
Tudor est NW10	61	S8
Tudor gdns NW9	43	W7
Tudor gdns SW13	86	C8
Tudor gdns W3	61	R15
Tudor gdns Rom	39	W12
Tudor gdns Twick	101	W1
Tudor gdns W Wick	135	Z6
Tudor gro E9	143	Z2
Tudor pl W1	148	F4
Tudor pl Mitch	106	K19
Tudor rd E4	20	L19
Tudor rd E6	65	Z4
Tudor rd E9	143	Y3
Tudor rd N9	19	O2
Tudor rd SE19	109	U18
Tudor rd SE25	124	B13
Tudor rd Bark	67	Y2
Tudor rd Barn	4	M11
Tudor rd Beck	125	T6
Tudor rd Hmptn	100	H18
Tudor rd Har	23	P7
Tudor rd Houns	83	P10
Tudor rd Kings T	103	P18
Tudor rd Sthl	70	B1
Tudor st EC4	149	W7
Tudor wk Bex	97	Z15
Tudor way N14	16	L4
Tudor way W3	73	O6
Tudor Well clo Stan	11	P17
Tudway rd SE3	94	K9
Tufnell Park rd N7	47	Z11
Tufnell Park rd N19	47	V11
Tufton rd E4	20	A13
Tufton st SW1	156	J3
Tugela rd Croy	123	O15
Tugela st SE6	110	M5
Tuilerie st E2	143	S9
Tulip clo Croy	124	E20
Tulip clo Hmptn	100	F15
Tulse clo Beck	125	U7
Tulse hill SW2	90	F18
Tulse Hill est SW2	90	F16
Tulsemere rd SE27	108	M4
Tummons gdns SE25	123	S3
Tunis rd W12	144	A13
Tunley rd NW10	62	A2
Tunley rd SW17	107	O3
Tunmarsh la E13	65	X9
Tunnaleys E6	66	K16
Tunnel ave SE10	76	L6
Tunnel gdns N11	29	W1
Tunstall rd SW9	90	E9
Tunstall rd Croy	133	T1
Tunstall wk Brent	72	J15
Tunstock way Belv	81	N9
Tunworth clo NW9	25	W19
Tunworth cres SW15	86	C17
Turenne clo SW18	88	E11
Turin rd N9	19	P2
Turin st E2	143	S13
Turkey Oak clo SE19	109	S20
Turk's Head yd EC1	141	W19
Turks row SW3	155	S9
Turle rd N4	48	C5
Turle rd SW16	121	Z2
Turlewray clo N4	48	C5
Turley clo E15	65	N3
Turnage rd Dag	55	Y5
Turnberry quay E14	76	E8
Turnchapel ms SW4	89	R8
Turner ave N15	31	R14
Turner ave Mitch	106	M20
Turner ave Twick	101	O7
Turner clo NW11	28	B18
Turner dr NW11	28	B19
Turner rd E17	33	U11
Turner rd Edg	24	L7
Turner rd N Mal	117	Z16
Turner st E1	151	W4
Turner st E16	65	P17
Turners Meadow way Beck	124	L2
Turners rd E3	63	Y15
Turners way Croy	132	F3
Turners wd NW11	46	D3
Turneville rd W14	153	O12
Turney rd SE21	90	M20
Turnham Green ter W4	74	B12
Turnham Green Terrace ms W4	74	B11
Turnham rd SE4	92	H12
Turnmill st EC1	141	V19
Turnpike clo SE8	75	Z19
Turnpike la N8	30	F11
Turnpike la Sutt	130	D11
Turnpike link Croy	133	S4
Turnstone clo E13	65	S9
Turpentine la SW1	155	Y10
Turpin ave Rom	38	E1
Turpin way Wall	131	T16
Turpington clo Brom	127	R16
Turpington la Brom	127	R17
Turquand st SE17	158	C7
Turret gro SW4	89	U7
Turton rd Wem	42	J15
Turville st E2	143	O15
Tuscan rd SE18	79	T14
Tuskar st SE10	76	M15
Tuttlebee la Buck H	21	U7
Tweed way Rom	39	O2
Tweedale ct E15	51	T14
Tweedale rd Cars	120	F20
Tweedmouth rd E13	65	V6
Tweedy rd Brom	126	D1
Twelvetrees cres E3	64	F10
Twentyman clo Wdf Grn	21	U15
Twickenham bri Twick	84	D14
Twickenham clo Croy	132	C6
Twickenham gdns Grnf	41	X15
Twickenham gdns Har	23	T2
Twickenham rd E11	51	W6
Twickenham rd Felt	100	F8
Twickenham rd Islw	83	Y5
Twickenham rd Rich	84	H10
Twickenham rd Tedd	101	Y10
Twickenham Trading est Twick	83	V15
Twilley st SW18	88	A19
Twine ct E1	151	Z8
Twineham grn N12	14	M13
Twining ave Twick	101	O6
Twinn rd NW7	14	F18
Twisden rd NW5	47	S11
Twybridge way NW10	43	W20
Twyford Abbey rd NW10	60	M9
Twyford av N2	28	L10
Twyford ave W3	61	R19
Twyford cres W3	73	R2
Twyford rd Cars	120	F19
Twyford rd Har	40	K2
Twyford rd Ilf	54	C14
Twyford st N1	141	N4
Tyas rd E16	65	O13
Tybenham rd SW19	119	X5
Tyberry rd Enf	9	O10
Tyburn la Har	41	U1
Tyers gate SE1	150	K18
Tyers st SE11	157	O11
Tyers ter SE11	157	O10
Tyeshurst clo SE2	81	N14
Tylecroft rd SW16	121	Z4
Tylehurst gdns Ilf	54	C14
Tyler clo E2	143	N7
Tyler st SE10	77	O15
Tylers gate Har	24	L18
Tylers path Cars	131	N8
Tylney ave SE19	109	U12
Tylney rd E7	52	K11
Tylney rd Brom	127	N4
Tyndale la N1	48	J20
Tyndall rd E10	51	U7
Tyndall rd Well	96	L8
Tyneham rd SW11	89	P6
Tynemouth dr Enf	8	L13
Tynemouth rd N15	31	W12
Tynemouth rd Mitch	107	O18
Tynemouth st SW6	88	C4
Type st E2	63	T6
Tyrawley rd SW6	88	A1
Tyrell clo Har	41	T12
Tyrell ct Cars	130	M8
Tyrell sq Mitch	120	J2
Tyron way Sid	114	J11
Tyrone rd E6	66	H7
Tyrrel way NW9	26	E20
Tyrrell ave Well	97	R13
Tyrrell rd SE22	91	X11
Tyrwhitt rd SE4	93	O8
Tysoe st EC1	141	T15
Tyson rd SE23	92	D19
Tyssen pas E8	49	U17
Tyssen rd N16	49	U9
Tyssen st E8	49	V17
Tyssen st N1	142	K9
Tytherton rd N19	47	X10

U

Uamvar st E14	64	E13
Uckfield gro Mitch	107	P20
Uckfield rd Enf	9	U1

Name	Page	Grid
Udall st SW1	156	D6
Udney Park rd Tedd	101	Z13
Uffington rd NW10	62	H3
Uffington rd SE27	108	G9
Ufford clo Har	22	L2
Ufford rd Har	22	L2
Ufford st SE1	149	V17
Ufton rd N1	142	H2
Ujima ct SW16	108	B10
Ullathorne rd SW16	107	U11
Ulleswater rd N14	17	O12
Ullin st E14	64	F15
Ullswater clo SW15	103	Y10
Ullswater cres SW15	103	Z9
Ullswater rd SE27	108	J5
Ullswater rd SW13	74	G19
Ullswater way Horn	57	W15
Ulster gdns N13	17	Y13
Ulundi rd SE3	77	O16
Ulva rd SW15	87	P12
Ulverscroft rd SE22	91	W13
Ulverston rd E17	33	X7
Ulverstone rd SE27	108	J5
Ulysses rd NW6	45	W14
Umberston st E1	151	V5
Umbria st SW15	86	G17
Umfreville rd N4	30	H18
Undercliff rd SE13	93	P7
Underhill Barn	4	K16
Underhill rd SE22	91	X14
Underhill st NW1	139	Z5
Underne ave N14	16	F8
Undershaft EC3	150	K6
Undershaw rd Brom	112	B8
Underwood Croy	135	U13
Underwood the SE9	113	V5
Underwood rd E1	143	T19
Underwood rd Wdf Grn	35	N2
Underwood row N1	142	D12
Underwood st N1	142	D11
Undine rd E14	76	E11
Undine st SW17	106	M12
Uneeda dr Grnf	59	R3
Union ct EC2	150	J4
Union dr E1	63	W11
Union gro SW8	89	X5
Union rd N11	16	L17
Union rd SW4	89	Z5
Union rd SW8	89	X4
Union rd Brom	127	O11
Union rd Croy	123	N17
Union rd Nthlt	58	H6
Union rd Wem	42	J17
Union sq N1	142	B6
Union st E15	64	J4
Union st SE1	149	V15
Union st Barn	4	E13
Union st Kings T	116	H4
Union wk E2	142	M12
Unity way SE18	78	A8
University clo NW7	26	D1
University rd SW19	106	G16
University st WC1	140	D18
Unwin clo SE15	159	S16
Unwin rd Islw	83	U7
Upbrook ms W2	146	D7
Upcerne rd SW10	154	C19
Upchurch clo SE20	110	B19
Upcroft ave Edg	12	H15
Upfield Croy	133	Z5
Upfield rd W7	59	V13
Uphall rd Ilf	54	A15
Upham Park rd W4	74	C11
Uphill dr NW7	13	O15
Uphill dr NW9	25	W16
Uphill gro NW7	13	P13
Uphill rd NW7	13	O11
Upland rd E13	65	S11
Upland rd SE22	91	X12
Upland rd Bexh	98	B7
Upland rd S Croy	133	N12
Upland rd Sutt	130	H13
Uplands Beck	125	O5
Uplands ave E17	32	F8
Uplands clo SW14	85	T13
Uplands end Wdf Grn	35	P1
Uplands Park rd Enf	7	U9
Uplands rd N8	30	E16
Uplands rd Barn	16	C5
Uplands rd Rom	37	V10
Uplands rd Wdf Grn	35	P2
Uplands Trading est E17	32	F8
Uplands way N21	7	T16
Upney la Bark	54	J16
Upnor way SE17	158	M9
Uppark dr Ilf	36	D18
Upper Abbey rd Belv	81	S10
Upper Addison gdns W14	144	J17
Upper Belgrave st SW1	155	V1
Upper Berkeley st W1	147	P5
Upper Beulah hill SE19	109	R20
Upper Brighton rd Surb	116	H16
Upper Brockley rd SE4	92	L6
Upper Brook st W1	147	S9
Upper Butts Brent	72	E17
Upper Cavendish ave N3	27	X9
Upper Cheyne row SW3	154	J14
Upper Clapton rd E5	49	Y4
Upper Elmers End rd Beck	124	J10
Upper Green east Mitch	120	M5
Upper Green west Mitch	120	M5
Upper Grosvenor st W1	147	S10
Upper Grotto rd Twick	101	V4
Upper grd SE1	149	R13
Upper gro SE25	123	V9
Upper Grove rd Belv	81	O16
Upper Ham rd Rich	102	H10
Upper Harley st NW1	139	W17
Upper Holly Hill rd Belv	81	V13
Upper James st W1	148	D8
Upper John st W1	148	C8
Upper mall W6	74	H13
Upper Marsh SE1	149	P20
Upper Montagu st W1	139	O20
Upper Mulgrave rd Sutt	129	T17
Upper North st E14	64	C15
Upper Park rd N11	16	G16
Upper Park rd NW3	46	L16
Upper Park rd Belv	81	U12
Upper Park rd Brom	112	K20
Upper Park rd Kings T	103	P16
Upper Phillimore gdns W8	145	T19
Upper Rainham rd Horn	57	U4
Upper Richmond rd SW15	86	C9
Upper Richmond Road west SW14	85	T10
Upper rd E13	65	S6
Upper rd Wall	131	Z12
Upper St Martin's la WC2	148	J8
Upper Selsdon rd S Croy	133	T17
Upper Shirley rd Croy	134	D4
Upper st N1	141	V9
Upper Sutton la Houns	82	G1
Upper Tachbrook st SW1	156	C6
Upper Teddington rd Kings T	102	E19
Upper ter NW3	46	C10
Upper Thames st EC4	149	X9
Upper Tollington pk N4	48	E4
Upper Tooting pk SW17	106	M4
Upper Tooting rd SW17	106	L11
Upper Town rd Grnf	58	J12
Upper Tulse hill SW2	90	C17
Upper Vernon rd Sutt	130	F11
Upper Walthamstow rd E17	33	W12
Upper Wickham la Well	97	P6
Upper Wimpole st W1	139	W20
Upper Woburn pl WC1	140	G15
Upperton rd Sid	114	L12
Upperton Road west E13	65	Y9
Uppingham ave Stan	24	C5
Upsdell ave N13	17	S18
Upstall st SE5	90	K3
Upton ave E7	52	G20
Upton clo Bex	98	C15
Upton gdns Har	24	C16
Upton la E7	65	T2
Upton Park rd E7	52	J20
Upton rd N18	18	M16
Upton rd SE18	79	R17
Upton rd Bex	98	B15
Upton rd Bexh	97	Z9
Upton rd Houns	82	H8
Upton rd Th Hth	123	N2
Upton Road south Bex	98	C16
Upway N12	15	V20
Upwood rd SE12	94	F15
Upwood rd SW16	122	B2
Urlwin st SE5	158	C15
Urmston dr SW19	105	S1
Ursula st SW11	88	J3
Urswick rd E9	50	C15
Urswick rd Dag	68	K1
Usborne ms SW8	157	P17
Usher rd E3	64	A5
Usk rd SW11	88	E9
Usk st E2	63	S8
Utopia village NW1	139	T3
Uvedale rd Dag	56	F8
Uvedale rd Enf	8	B16
Uverdale rd SW10	154	D19
Uxbridge rd W3	73	P2
Uxbridge rd W5	73	O2
Uxbridge rd W7	71	S3
Uxbridge rd W12	144	B15
Uxbridge rd W13	72	C1
Uxbridge rd Felt	100	A5
Uxbridge rd Hmptn	100	G9
Uxbridge rd Har	10	D20
Uxbridge rd Kings T	116	G10
Uxbridge rd Pnr	22	B4
Uxbridge rd Sthl	70	K2
Uxbridge rd Stan	10	L17
Uxbridge st W8	145	U12
Uxendon cres Wem	42	K3
Uxendon hill Wem	42	M3

V

Name	Page	Grid
Valan leas Brom	126	A7
Valance ave E4	21	O6
Vale the N10	29	P4
Vale the N14	16	M3
Vale the NW11	45	R8
Vale the SW3	154	G13
Vale the W3	73	Y4
Vale the Croy	134	G3
Vale the Houns	70	A17
Vale the Wdf Grn	34	F2
Vale clo W9	138	B13
Vale ct W9	138	C13
Vale cres SW15	104	B9
Vale cft Pnr	22	B15
Vale dr Barn	4	J15
Vale end SE22	91	T9
Vale gro N4	30	M20
Vale gro W3	73	Y4
Vale la W3	61	P15
Vale of Health NW3	46	E8
Vale ri NW11	45	W4
Vale rd E7	52	H17
Vale rd N4	30	L20
Vale rd Brom	127	W2
Vale rd Epsom	128	E8
Vale rd Mitch	121	X8
Vale rd Sutt	130	A8
Vale rd Wor Pk	128	E5
Vale row N5	48	J9
Vale Royal N7	140	K1
Vale st SE27	109	O8
Vale ter N4	30	L19
Valence ave Dag	55	W3
Valence circ Dag	55	X10
Valence Wood rd Dag	55	X9
Valencia rd Stan	11	R14
Valentine ave Bex	115	Y3
Valentine pl SE1	149	W17
Valentine rd E9	50	E19
Valentine rd Har	40	L10
Valentine row SE1	149	W18
Valentines rd Ilf	53	Z4
Valeswood rd Brom	112	C14
Valetta gro E13	65	S5
Valetta rd W3	74	B5
Valette st E9	50	B18
Valiant clo Rom	38	F6
Valiant way E6	66	F15
Vallance rd E1	143	U20
Vallance rd E2	143	U14
Vallance rd N22	29	V6
Vallentin rd E17	33	U12
Valley ave N12	15	V14
Valley clo Dart	99	U15
Valley dr NW9	25	R18
Valley Fields cres Enf	7	T8
Valley gdns SW19	106	G17
Valley gdns Wem	42	L20
Valley gro SE7	77	Y13
Valley ms Twick	101	X3
Valley rd SW16	108	C13
Valley rd Belv	81	W11
Valley rd Brom	126	A4
Valley rd Dart	99	U15
Valley rd Erith	81	Z11
Valley rd Orp	115	R19
Valley side E4	20	B7
Valley vw Barn	4	E18
Valley wk Croy	134	D2
Valleyfield rd SW16	108	D12
Valliere rd NW10	62	H8
Valliers Wood rd Sid	114	G2
Vallis way W13	65	Y13
Valmar rd SE5	90	M3
Valnay st SW17	106	M12
Valognes ave E17	32	H3
Valonia gdns SW18	87	W15
Vambery rd SE18	79	P16
Van Dyck ave N Mal	117	Z17
Vanbrugh clo E16	66	A15
Vanbrugh flds SE3	77	O18
Vanbrugh hill SE3	77	O16
Vanbrugh hill SE10	77	O15
Vanbrugh pk SE3	77	O19
Vanbrugh Park rd SE3	77	R18
Vanbrugh Park Road west SE3	77	P18
Vanbrugh rd W4	73	Z8
Vanbrugh ter SE3	94	D1
Vancouver rd SE23	110	J3
Vancouver rd Edg	25	S3
Vancouver rd Rich	102	E11
Vanderbilt rd SW18	106	B1
Vandome clo E16	65	V18
Vandon st SW1	148	D20
Vandy st EC2	142	J19
Vandyke clo SW15	87	P17
Vandyke cross SE9	95	P14
Vane clo NW3	46	F13

Name	No	Ref
Vane clo Har	24	M19
Vane st SW1	156	D5
Vanessa clo Belv	81	T13
Vanguard clo Croy	132	J1
Vanguard clo Rom	38	G7
Vanguard st SE8	93	O2
Vanguard way Wall	132	A17
Vanoc gdns Brom	112	E8
Vansittart rd E7	52	D12
Vansittart st SE14	75	X18
Vanston pl SW6	153	T17
Vant rd SW17	106	M13
Varcoe rd SE16	159	Y11
Varden clo W3	61	Y16
Varden st E1	151	W4
Vardens rd SW11	88	H11
Vardon clo N3	27	T4
Varley par NW9	26	B13
Varley rd E16	65	X16
Varley way Mitch	120	G4
Varna rd SW6	153	N18
Varndell st NW1	140	A12
Vartry rd N15	31	S19
Vassall rd SW9	157	U20
Vauban st SE16	159	P2
Vaughan ave NW4	26	G15
Vaughan ave W6	74	E10
Vaughan gdns Ilf	53	U2
Vaughan rd E15	52	C18
Vaughan rd SE5	90	L6
Vaughan rd Har	23	N20
Vaughan rd T Ditt	116	B17
Vaughan rd Well	96	M5
Vaughan way E1	151	U10
Vauxhall bri SE1	156	K11
Vauxhall bri SW1	156	J10
Vauxhall Bridge rd SW1	156	C6
Vauxhall gdns S Croy	132	M15
Vauxhall Gardens est SE11	157	P10
Vauxhall gro SW8	157	N13
Vauxhall st SE11	157	P8
Vauxhall st SE11	157	N10
Vawdrey clo E1	63	P13
Veals mead Mitch	106	K20
Vectis gdns SW17	107	R16
Veda rd SE13	93	P11
Vega rd (Bushey) Wat	10	A2
Vellicoe rd E13	65	U11
Vellum dr Cars	131	O7
Venables clo Dag	56	H11
Venables st NW8	138	H19
Vencourt pl W6	74	H12
Venetia rd N4	30	J19
Venetia rd W5	72	F7
Venetian rd SE5	91	N5
Venn st SW4	89	W9
Venner rd SE26	110	D14
Venners clo Bexh	99	P4
Ventnor ave Stan	24	B5
Ventnor dr N20	14	M10
Ventnor gdns Bark	54	H16
Ventnor rd SE14	75	U19
Ventnor rd Sutt	130	A18
Venture clo Bex	97	Z18
Venue st E14	64	F13
Venus rd SE18	78	G8
Vera ave N21	7	T17
Vera rd SW6	87	T2
Verbena gdns W6	74	F13
Verdant la SE6	112	A1
Verdayne ave Croy	134	G2
Verdun rd SE18	80	A18
Verdun rd SW13	74	F17
Vere st W1	147	X5
Vereker rd W14	153	N10
Verity clo W11	144	K7
Vermont rd SE19	109	R16
Vermont rd SW18	88	B16
Vermont rd Sutt	130	A5
Verney gdns Dag	55	Y13
Verney rd Dag	55	Z11
Verney rd SE16	159	V12
Verney st NW10	43	Y10
Verney way SE16	159	W11
Vernham rd SE18	79	O17
Vernon ave E12	53	T13
Vernon ave SW20	119	O3
Vernon ave Wdf Grn	21	U20
Vernon ct Stan	24	A3
Vernon cres Barn	6	B18
Vernon dr Stan	23	Y3
Vernon ms W14	152	M6
Vernon pl WC1	148	L2
Vernon ri WC1	141	P12
Vernon ri Grnf	41	P15
Vernon rd E3	63	Z6
Vernon rd E11	52	A4
Vernon rd E15	52	A20
Vernon rd E17	32	M14
Vernon rd N8	30	G10
Vernon rd SW14	85	Y8
Vernon rd Ilf	54	K5
Vernon rd Sutt	130	E11
Vernon st W14	152	L6
Veroan rd Bexh	97	Y5
Veronica gdns SW16	121	U2
Veronica rd SW17	107	S5
Veronique gdns Ilf	36	B15
Verran rd SW12	89	R20
Versailles rd SE20	109	X19
Verulam ave E17	32	K19
Verulam rd Grnf	58	J11
Verulam st WC1	141	S20
Verwood rd Har	22	M8
Vespan rd W12	74	F5
Vesta rd SE4	92	H5
Vestris rd SE23	110	G4
Vestry ms SE5	91	R3
Vestry rd E17	33	R14
Vestry rd SE5	91	S2
Vestry st N1	142	F12
Vevey st SE6	110	L5
Veysey gdns Dag	56	D8
Viaduct the E18	34	F7
Viaduct pl E2	143	W14
Viaduct st E2	143	W15
Vian st SE13	93	T7
Vibart gdns SW2	90	D19
Vicarage ave SE3	77	T20
Vicarage clo Erith	81	Y17
Vicarage clo Nthlt	58	F2
Vicarage cres SW11	88	G4
Vicarage dr SW14	85	X13
Vicarage dr Bark	67	R1
Vicarage Farm rd Houns	82	B5
Vicarage gdns W8	145	W15
Vicarage gdns Mitch	120	J7
Vicarage gate W8	145	W15
Vicarage gro SE5	91	P1
Vicarage la E6	66	G9
Vicarage la E15	52	B19
Vicarage la Epsom	128	G19
Vicarage la Ilf	54	D4
Vicarage pk SE18	79	R14
Vicarage path N8	47	Z1
Vicarage rd E10	51	P1
Vicarage rd E15	52	B20
Vicarage rd N17	31	X3
Vicarage rd NW4	26	G19
Vicarage rd SE18	79	P14
Vicarage rd SW14	85	Y12
Vicarage rd Croy	132	G5
Vicarage rd Dag	56	G19
Vicarage rd Horn	57	X4
Vicarage rd Kings T	116	H2
Vicarage rd Kings T (Hampton Wick)	116	D1
Vicarage rd Tedd	101	X12
Vicarage rd Twick	101	X16
Vicarage rd (Whitton) Twick	82	M16
Vicarage rd Wdf Grn	35	S2
Vicarage way NW10	43	Z10
Vicarage way Har	40	H1
Vicars Bridge clo Wem	60	K5
Vicars clo E9	143	Z6
Vicars clo E15	65	T3
Vicars clo Enf	8	F9
Vicars hill SE13	93	R10
Vicars Moor la N21	17	V2
Vicars Oak rd SE19	109	S15
Vicars rd NW5	47	O14
Vicars wk Dag	55	R10
Viceroy clo N2	28	J11
Viceroy rd SW8	90	A1
Vickers way Houns	82	D13
Victor gro Wem	42	L20
Victor rd NW10	62	K7
Victor rd SE20	110	F17
Victor rd Har	23	N11
Victor rd Tedd	101	T11
Victoria ave E6	66	B2
Victoria ave EC2	150	L2
Victoria ave N3	27	W5
Victoria ave Barn	5	U15
Victoria ave Houns	82	F13
Victoria ave Surb	116	F16
Victoria ave Wall	131	P6
Victoria ave Wem	43	S18
Victoria clo Barn	5	V15
Victoria cotts Rich	85	O3
Victoria ct Wem	43	R17
Victoria cres N15	31	R16
Victoria cres SE19	109	R15
Victoria cres SW19	105	W17
Victoria Dock rd E16	65	T19
Victoria dr SW19	87	P19
Victoria embk EC4	149	T9
Victoria embk SW1	148	L16
Victoria embk WC2	148	M12
Victoria gdns W11	145	S11
Victoria gdns Houns	82	A2
Victoria gro N12	15	T15
Victoria gro W8	154	B1
Victoria Grove ms W2	145	W10
Victoria Industrial est NW10	62	B9
Victoria la Barn	4	H14
Victoria ms NW6	137	T4
Victoria ms SW4	89	S10
Victoria Park rd E9	63	P9
Victoria Park sq E2	63	P8
Victoria ri SW4	89	S9
Victoria rd E4	21	N4
Victoria rd E13	65	T6
Victoria rd E17	33	T7
Victoria rd E18	34	H8
Victoria rd N4	48	D2
Victoria rd N9	18	J9
Victoria rd N15	31	W14
Victoria rd N18	18	H15
Victoria rd N22	29	V5
Victoria rd NW4	27	N13
Victoria rd NW6	137	O8
Victoria rd NW7	13	R15
Victoria rd NW10	62	A12
Victoria rd SW14	85	Y7
Victoria rd W3	61	Y13
Victoria rd W5	60	C14
Victoria rd W8	146	A18
Victoria rd Bark	54	B17
Victoria rd Barn	5	T14
Victoria rd Bexh	98	E12
Victoria rd Brom	127	P13
Victoria rd Chis	113	X13
Victoria rd Dag	56	J14
Victoria rd Kings T	117	N4
Victoria rd Mitch	106	J19
Victoria rd Rom	39	S17
Victoria rd Ruis	40	B12
Victoria rd Sid	114	M8
Victoria rd Sthl	70	D9
Victoria rd Surb	116	H14
Victoria rd Sutt	130	F12
Victoria rd Tedd	101	X16
Victoria rd Twick	84	A18
Victoria sq SW1	155	Y1
Victoria st E15	51	Z20
Victoria st SW1	156	C2
Victoria st Belv	81	P14
Victoria ter N4	48	F3
Victoria ter Har	41	S4
Victoria vill Rich	85	N9
Victoria way SE7	77	V13
Victorian gro N16	49	T10
Victorian rd N16	49	T10
Victors dr Hmptn	100	C15
Victors way Barn	4	H12
Victory ave Mord	120	E12
Victory pl SE17	158	D5
Victory rd SW19	106	C18
Victory way SE16	75	W6
Victory way Rom	38	G6
Vienna clo Ilf	35	P8
View the SE2	81	N13
View clo N6	29	N20
View clo Har	23	P12
View rd N6	28	M20
Viewfield clo Har	42	J1
Viewfield rd SW18	87	V16
Viewfield rd Bex	97	T20
Viewland rd SE18	79	X14
Viga rd N21	7	V19
Vigilant clo SE26	109	X10
Vignoles rd Rom	56	E1
Vigo st W1	148	B10
Viking clo E3	63	X7
Viking rd Sthl	58	C19
Viking way Erith	81	Z8
Villa rd SW9	90	F6
Villa st SE17	158	G10
Villacourt rd SE18	80	A18
Village the SE7	78	A16
Village clo E4	20	H16
Village Green rd Dart	99	V11
Village ms NW9	43	X5
Village rd N3	27	S6
Village rd Enf	18	C1
Village row Sutt	129	Y16
Village way NW10	43	Z11
Village way SE21	91	O15
Village way Beck	125	N4
Village way Pnr	40	C1
Village Way east Har	40	F1
Villas rd SE18	79	R12
Villiers ave Surb	116	M12
Villiers ave Twick	100	E2
Villiers clo E10	51	P6
Villiers clo Surb	117	N9
Villiers gro Sutt	129	R19
Villiers path Surb	116	L12
Villiers rd NW2	44	G16
Villiers rd Beck	124	F4
Villiers rd Islw	83	S4
Villiers rd Kings T	116	M9
Villiers rd Sthl	70	F4
Villiers st WC2	148	K11
Vincam clo Twick	82	H18
Vince st EC1	142	G14
Vincent clo SE16	75	W5
Vincent clo Barn	5	N10
Vincent clo Brom	126	J10
Vincent clo Sid	114	G2
Vincent gdns NW2	44	E9
Vincent rd E4	20	K20
Vincent rd N15	30	L13
Vincent rd N22	30	G6
Vincent rd SE18	79	N11
Vincent rd W3	73	V8
Vincent rd Croy	123	S18
Vincent rd Dag	68	L1
Vincent rd Islw	83	P3
Vincent rd Kings T	117	P5
Vincent rd Wem	61	N1
Vincent row Hmptn	100	M14
Vincent sq SW1	156	E4
Vincent st E16	65	R16
Vincent st SW1	156	F6
Vincent ter N1	141	X9
Vine clo Surb	117	N14
Vine clo Sutt	130	C6
Vine ct E1	151	U2
Vine ct Har	24	K17
Vine gdns Ilf	54	B14
Vine hill EC1	141	S18
Vine la SE1	150	L15
Vine pl Houns	82	J10
Vine rd SW13	86	E8
Vine st EC3	151	N7
Vine st W1	148	D11
Vine st Rom	38	M14
Vine Street bri EC1	141	V18
Vine yd SE1	150	C17
Vinegar all E17	33	S12
Vinegar st E1	151	X13

Street	No	Grid
Vineries the N14	6	H18
Vineries the Enf	8	E10
Vineries bank NW7	13	X16
Vineries clo Dag	56	D16
Vines ave N3	28	A4
Viney bank Croy	134	L19
Viney rd SE13	93	S8
Vineyard the Rich	84	J14
Vineyard ave NW7	27	S2
Vineyard clo SE6	111	N2
Vineyard hill rd SW19	105	X10
Vineyard path SW14	85	X7
Vineyard row Kings T	116	D1
Vineyard wk EC1	141	T16
Vining st SW9	90	F10
Vintners pl EC4	150	C9
Viola ave SE2	80	D12
Viola sq W12	62	E19
Violet ave Enf	8	C3
Violet clo Wall	121	R20
Violet gdns Croy	132	J12
Violet hill NW8	138	C10
Violet la Croy	132	J13
Violet rd E3	64	D12
Violet rd E17	33	P19
Violet rd E18	34	H6
Violet st E2	143	Y15
Virgil pl W1	147	N1
Virgil st SE1	157	R1
Virginia clo N Mal	117	V8
Virginia gdns Ilf	36	D7
Virginia rd E2	143	N14
Virginia rd Th Hth	122	H1
Virginia st E1	151	U10
Viscount dr E6	66	G14
Viscount st EC1	142	B19
Vista the SE9	95	P18
Vista ave Enf	9	T8
Vista dr Ilf	35	O16
Vista way Har	24	J17
Vivian ave NW4	26	H17
Vivian ave Wem	43	P15
Vivian gdns Wem	43	O15
Vivian rd E3	63	O5
Vivian sq SE15	91	Z7
Vivian way N2	28	G14
Vivienne clo Twick	84	F17
Voce rd SE18	79	T20
Voewood clo N Mal	118	D14
Volta way Croy	122	C20
Voltaire rd SW4	89	X8
Voluntary pl E11	34	E18
Vorley rd N19	47	V7
Voss ct SW16	108	A16
Voss st E2	143	U14
Vulcan clo Wall	132	C17
Vulcan gate Enf	7	U9
Vulcan rd SE4	92	L5
Vulcan ter SE4	92	L5
Vulcan way N7	48	D17
Vyne the Bexh	98	J8
Vyner rd W3	61	Z20
Vyner st E2	143	Y7

W

Street	No	Grid
Wadding st SE17	158	D7
Waddington rd E15	51	X16
Waddington st E15	51	X17
Waddington way SE19	108	L19
Waddon clo Croy	132	G5
Waddon Court rd Croy	132	E7
Waddon Marsh way Croy	132	D1
Waddon New rd Croy	132	J4
Waddon Park ave Croy	132	F8
Waddon rd Croy	132	F6
Waddon way Croy	132	F14
Wade rd E16	65	Z18
Wades gro N21	17	U2
Wades hill N21	7	U19
Wades la Tedd	101	Y13

Street	No	Grid
Wades pl E14	64	D19
Wadeson st E2	143	Y7
Wadeville ave Rom	38	A19
Wadeville clo Belv	81	S15
Wadham ave E17	33	S2
Wadham gdns NW3	138	K2
Wadham gdns Grnf	41	O17
Wadham rd E17	33	S3
Wadham rd SW15	91	X7
Wadhurst clo SE20	123	Z4
Wadhurst rd SW8	156	C20
Wadhurst rd W4	73	Y9
Wadley rd E11	33	Z20
Wadsworth clo Enf	9	S17
Wadsworth clo Grnf	60	D7
Wadsworth rd Grnf	60	B6
Wager st E3	63	Y13
Waghorn rd E13	65	X4
Waghorn rd Har	24	H10
Waghorn st SE15	91	X7
Wagner st SE15	75	P18
Wagtail clo NW9	26	A6
Wainfleet ave Rom	38	L8
Wainford clo SW19	87	P20
Wainwright gro Islw	83	S11
Waite Davies rd SE12	94	D20
Waite st SE15	159	O13
Wakefield gdns SE19	109	S18
Wakefield gdns Ilf	35	P20
Wakefield ms WC1	140	L15
Wakefield rd N11	16	M17
Wakefield rd N15	31	V15
Wakefield rd Rich	84	H13
Wakefield st E6	66	C4
Wakefield st N18	18	K17
Wakefield st WC1	140	L15
Wakeham st N1	49	O18
Wakehams hill Pnr	22	E10
Wakehurst rd SW11	88	K14
Wakelin rd E15	65	N6
Wakeling rd W7	59	W15
Wakeling st E14	63	V17
Wakeman rd NW10	136	D13
Wakemans Hill ave NW9	25	Y15
Wakering rd Bark	54	C19
Wakley st EC1	141	X11
Walberswick st SW8	156	M19
Walbrook EC4	150	E7
Walburgh st E1	151	X7
Walcorde ave SE17	158	C7
Walcot rd Enf	9	Y8
Walcot sq SE11	157	U4
Walcott st SW1	156	D6
Waldeck gro SE27	108	H7
Waldeck rd N15	30	K12
Waldeck rd SW14	85	W7
Waldeck rd W4	73	P15
Waldeck rd W13	60	B18
Waldegrave gdns Twick	101	W5
Waldegrave pk Twick	101	V9
Waldegrave rd N8	30	G10
Waldegrave rd SE19	109	V18
Waldegrave rd W5	61	N18
Waldegrave rd Brom	127	S11
Waldegrave rd Dag	55	T6
Waldegrave rd Tedd	101	W11
Waldegrave rd Twick	101	W8
Waldegrove Croy	133	U7
Waldemar ave SW6	87	T3
Waldemar ave W13	72	D3
Waldemar rd SW19	105	X12
Walden ave N13	17	Z13
Walden ave Chis	113	V10
Walden ave Rain	69	Z7
Walden clo Belv	81	O13
Walden gdns Th Hth	122	D8
Walden rd N17	31	O5
Walden rd Chis	113	T14
Walden st E1	151	W3
Walden way NW7	14	D19
Walden way Ilf	36	H1

Street	No	Grid
Waldenshaw rd SE23	110	C2
Waldo clo SW4	89	V12
Waldo pl Mitch	106	K19
Waldo rd NW10	62	H8
Waldo rd Brom	127	N7
Waldorf clo S Croy	132	K18
Waldram cres SE23	110	D2
Waldram Park rd SE23	110	E3
Waldrist way Erith	81	P6
Waldron gdns Brom	125	X7
Waldron ms SW3	154	H13
Waldron rd SW18	106	D5
Waldron rd Har	41	T4
Waldronhyrst S Croy	132	K9
Waldrons the Croy	132	K9
Waleran clo Stan	10	K17
Walerand rd SE13	93	V6
Wales ave Cars	130	J12
Wales Farm rd W3	61	Y15
Waley rd E1	63	V14
Walfield av N20	15	O1
Walford rd N16	49	T11
Walfrey gdns Dag	56	A19
Walham gro SW6	153	T17
Walham ri SW19	105	S14
Walham yd SW6	153	T17
Walkden rd Chis	113	X11
Walker clo N11	16	H14
Walker clo SE18	79	O11
Walker clo W7	71	S4
Walker clo Dart	99	T7
Walker clo Hmptn	100	D15
Walkers ct E8	49	X18
Walkers pl SW15	87	R9
Walkerscroft mead SE21	109	N2
Walkley rd Dart	99	Z14
Walks the N2	28	H10
Wall End rd E6	66	J1
Wall st N1	49	P19
Wallace clo SE28	68	J20
Wallace cres Cars	130	M11
Wallace rd N1	48	M16
Wallbutton rd SE4	92	H5
Wallcote ave NW2	45	P3
Wallenger ave Rom	39	Z10
Waller rd SE14	92	E2
Wallers clo Dag	69	N3
Wallflower st W12	62	E20
Wallgrave rd SW5	153	W6
Wallingford ave W10	144	E3
Wallington rd Ilf	36	M20
Wallis clo SW11	88	F8
Wallis rd E9	51	N19
Wallis rd Sthl	58	K17
Wallorton gdns SW14	85	Z10
Wallwood rd E11	51	X2
Wallwood st E14	63	Z15
Walm la NW2	45	O16
Walmar clo Barn	5	U4
Walmer clo E4	20	D8
Walmer clo Rom	38	H8
Walmer gdns W13	71	Z6
Walmer pl W1	147	N1
Walmer rd W11	144	K8
Walmer ter SE18	79	P11
Walmgate rd Grnf	60	B4
Walmington Fold N12	14	K18
Walnut clo Cars	130	L12
Walnut clo Ilf	36	D12
Walnut flds Epsom	128	D18
Walnut gdns E15	51	Y13
Walnut gro Enf	8	C17
Walnut ms Sutt	130	D17
Walnut Tree clo SW13	86	D1
Walnut Tree clo Chis	114	D20
Walnut Tree rd SE10	77	O15
Walnut Tree rd Brent	72	K16
Walnut Tree rd Dag	55	Y7
Walnut Tree rd Houns	70	F17
Walnut Tree wk SE11	157	S4
Walpole ave Rich	84	M5

Street	No	Grid
Walpole cres Tedd	101	V13
Walpole gdns W4	73	V13
Walpole gdns Twick	101	U5
Walpole pl Tedd	101	V14
Walpole rd E6	65	Z1
Walpole rd E17	32	K12
Walpole rd E18	34	B6
Walpole rd (Downhills way) N17	30	M9
Walpole rd (Lordship la) N17	30	M6
Walpole rd SW19	106	G15
Walpole rd Brom	127	N12
Walpole rd Croy	133	N2
Walpole rd Surb	116	J16
Walpole rd Tedd	101	V13
Walpole rd Twick	101	T4
Walpole st SW3	155	P9
Walrond ave Wem	42	L16
Walsham clo N16	49	W2
Walsham clo SE28	68	H19
Walsham rd SE14	92	E4
Walsingham gdns Epsom	128	C9
Walsingham rd E5	49	Y9
Walsingham rd Enf	8	B15
Walsingham rd Mitch	121	N11
Walsingham wk Belv	81	T16
Walter st E2	63	T9
Walter ter E1	63	U16
Walter wk Edg	12	J19
Walters rd SE25	123	T10
Walters rd Enf	9	S15
Walters way SE23	92	E17
Walterton rd W9	137	R18
Waltham ave NW9	25	R18
Waltham clo Dart	99	V15
Waltham dr Edg	25	P8
Waltham Park way E17	33	N3
Waltham rd Cars	120	G18
Waltham rd Sthl	70	B8
Waltham way E4	19	Y12
Walthamstow ave E4	19	X17
Walthamstow Business cen E17	33	U7
Waltheof ave N17	31	N5
Waltheof gdns N17	31	N3
Walton ave Har	40	D14
Walton ave N Mal	118	D10
Walton ave Sutt	129	V6
Walton clo NW2	44	K7
Walton clo SW8	156	L17
Walton clo Har	23	R12
Walton cres Har	40	E12
Walton dr NW10	43	Z17
Walton dr Har	23	R13
Walton gdns W3	61	T15
Walton gdns Wem	42	J6
Walton grn Croy	135	T18
Walton pl SW3	155	O1
Walton rd E12	53	W11
Walton rd E13	65	Y5
Walton rd N15	31	W14
Walton rd Har	23	R11
Walton rd Rom	38	D2
Walton rd Sid	115	T5
Walton st SW3	154	L5
Walton st Enf	8	B5
Walton way W3	61	T15
Walton way Mitch	121	V9
Walworth pl SE17	158	C10
Walworth rd SE17	158	B8
Walwyn ave Brom	127	N8
Wanborough dr SW15	104	J1
Wandle bank SW19	106	F17
Wandle bank Croy	132	A6
Wandle Side Croy	106	K4
Wandle rd Croy	132	M7
Wandle rd (Waddon) Croy	132	A6
Wandle rd Mord	120	E10
Wandle rd Wall	131	R4
Wandle side Croy	132	E6
Wandle side Wall	131	R6
Wandle way SW18	106	A1
Wandle way Mitch	120	L11

Wandon rd SW6	154	A18
Wandsworth bri SW18	88	C9
Wandsworth Bridge rd SW6	88	A3
Wandsworth common (North side) SW18	88	E13
Wandsworth common (West side) SW18	88	E13
Wandsworth High st SW18	87	Z14
Wandsworth Plain SW18	87	Z13
Wandsworth rd SW8	156	H20
Wanless rd SE24	90	L8
Wanley rd SE5	91	P10
Wanlip rd E13	65	W11
Wannock gdns Ilf	36	A1
Wansbeck rd E9	51	N20
Wansdown pl SW6	153	W18
Wansey st SE17	158	B7
Wansford rd Wdf Grn	34	K3
Wanstead clo Brom	126	L3
Wanstead la Ilf	35	P19
Wanstead Park ave E12	53	N7
Wanstead Park rd Ilf	35	R20
Wanstead pl E11	34	F17
Wanstead rd Brom	126	L3
Wansunt rd Bex	98	L20
Wantage rd SE12	94	C13
Wantz rd Dag	56	G12
Wapping Dock st E1	151	Z14
Wapping High st E1	151	T14
Wapping la E1	151	Y10
Wapping wall E1	75	P2
Warbank la Kings T	104	C19
Warbeck rd W12	144	A15
Warberry rd N22	30	D6
Warboys cres E4	20	H17
Warboys rd Kings T	103	U15
Warburton clo Har	10	B18
Warburton rd E8	143	X3
Warburton rd Twick	100	J1
Warburton ter E17	33	S7
Ward clo Erith	81	Z17
Ward rd E15	64	J2
Ward rd N19	47	V11
Wardalls gro SE14	75	R19
Wardell clo NW7	26	B2
Wardell fld NW9	26	C3
Warden ave Har	40	D4
Warden rd NW5	47	R17
Wardens gro SE1	150	A15
Wardle st E9	50	F15
Wardo ave SW6	87	S2
Wardour ms W1	148	E6
Wardour st W1	148	D5
Wards rd Ilf	54	E1
Wareham clo Houns	82	J10
Waremead rd Ilf	35	Y15
Warepoint dr SE28	79	T4
Warfield rd NW10	136	G14
Warfield rd Hmptn	100	K20
Wargrave ave N15	31	U18
Wargrave rd Har	40	M10
Warham rd N4	30	G16
Warham rd Har	23	V7
Warham rd S Croy	132	J11
Warham st SE5	157	Y18
Waring rd Sid	115	T14
Waring st SE27	108	L9
Warkworth gdns Islw	71	Y19
Warkworth rd N17	31	P3
Warland rd SE18	79	T19
Warley ave Dag	56	C2
Warley rd N9	19	R6
Warley rd Ilf	35	Y4
Warley rd Wdf Grn	34	H2
Warley st E2	63	S9
Warlingham rd Th Hth	122	J9
Warlock rd W9	137	R15
Warlters clo N7	48	B12
Warlters rd the N7	48	B11
Warltersville rd N19	48	A1

Warminster gdns SE25	123	X4
Warminster rd SE25	123	W5
Warminster way Mitch	121	T2
Warndon st SE16	75	S11
Warneford rd Har	24	H11
Warneford st E9	143	Z4
Warner ave Sutt	129	S3
Warner clo NW9	26	F20
Warner pl E2	143	T10
Warner rd E17	32	J13
Warner rd N8	29	X12
Warner rd SE5	90	L3
Warner rd Brom	112	C18
Warner st EC1	141	T18
Warner yd EC1	141	T18
Warners la Kings T	102	G11
Warners path	21	T16
Wdf Grn		
Warnham Court rd Cars	130	M16
Warnham rd N12	15	V16
Warple way W3	74	A4
Warren the E12	53	S12
Warren the Cars	130	G20
Warren the Houns	70	D20
Warren ave Brom	111	Z18
Warren ave Rich	85	T9
Warren ave S Croy	134	F18
Warren clo N9	19	T3
Warren clo SE21	90	L19
Warren clo Wem	42	H6
Warren cres N9	18	J3
Warren Cutting Kings T	103	X17
Warren dr Grnf	58	M11
Warren dr Horn	57	V11
Warren dr the E11	52	L1
Warren Drive north Surb	117	T20
Warren Drive south Surb	117	V20
Warren la SE18	78	M8
Warren la Stan	10	K9
Warren ms W1	140	A18
Warren pk Kings T	103	X16
Warren Park rd Sutt	130	H13
Warren Pond rd E4	21	P4
Warren ri N Mal	103	Y20
Warren rd E4	20	G7
Warren rd E10	51	V9
Warren rd E11	34	K18
Warren rd NW2	44	D8
Warren rd SW19	106	H16
Warren rd Bexh	98	E12
Warren rd Croy	123	T20
Warren rd Ilf	36	E14
Warren rd Kings T	103	V14
Warren rd Sid	115	T8
Warren rd Twick	83	O17
Warren rd (Bushey) Wat	10	B6
Warren st W1	140	A18
Warren ter Rom	37	X14
Warren wk SE7	77	Z6
Warren way NW7	14	F18
Warrender rd N19	47	V17
Warrens Shawe la Edg	12	F6
Warriner gdns SW11	89	O2
Warrington cres W9	138	C20
Warrington gdns W9	138	A18
Warrington rd Croy	132	X6
Warrington rd Har	23	T15
Warrington sq Dag	55	X7
Warrior sq E12	53	W11
Warspite rd SE18	78	C8
Warton rd E15	64	G1
Warwall E6	66	L17
Warwick ave W2	138	C20
Warwick ave W9	137	Y17
Warwick ave Edg	12	G10
Warwick ave Har	40	D12
Warwick clo Barn	5	V16
Warwick clo Bex	98	D20
Warwick clo Hmptn	100	M17

Warwick clo (Bushey) Wat	10	G2
Warwick ct SE15	91	X6
Warwick ct WC1	149	R2
Warwick cres W2	146	B1
Warwick dene W5	72	L3
Warwick dr SW15	86	J9
Warwick est W2	145	Y1
Warwick gdns N4	30	L16
Warwick gdns W14	153	R4
Warwick gdns Ilf	54	A4
Warwick gro E5	49	Z5
Warwick gro Surb	116	M16
Warwick House st SW1	148	G13
Warwick la EC4	149	Y5
Warwick pl W5	72	H4
Warwick pl W9	138	B20
Warwick Place north SW1	156	A7
Warwick rd E4	20	A16
Warwick rd E11	34	J15
Warwick rd E12	53	R15
Warwick rd E15	52	D18
Warwick rd E17	32	K6
Warwick rd N11	16	L19
Warwick rd N18	18	F14
Warwick rd SE20	124	A6
Warwick rd SW5	153	U8
Warwick rd W5	72	G4
Warwick rd W14	153	P4
Warwick rd Barn	5	O15
Warwick rd Kings T	102	E20
Warwick rd N Mal	117	U6
Warwick rd Sid	115	R12
Warwick rd Sthl	70	E8
Warwick rd Sutt	130	D10
Warwick rd Th Hth	122	E7
Warwick rd Twick	101	U1
Warwick rd Well	97	T8
Warwick row SW1	156	A1
Warwick sq EC4	149	Y5
Warwick sq SW1	156	A8
Warwick Square ms SW1	156	A7
Warwick st W1	148	C9
Warwick ter SE18	79	T15
Warwick way SW1	155	Y8
Warwick yd EC1	142	C18
Warwickshire path SE8	75	Z18
Washington ave E12	53	T11
Washington rd E18	34	C7
Washington rd SW13	74	G19
Washington rd Kings T	117	O4
Washington rd Wor Pk	128	J2
Wastdale rd SE23	92	G20
Wat Tyler rd SE10	93	V4
Watcombe cotts Rich	73	P17
Watcombe rd SE25	123	Z11
Water gdns Stan	11	O19
Water la E15	52	A17
Water la SE14	75	R18
Water la Ilf	54	J10
Water la Kings T	116	H2
Water la Rich	84	G13
Water la Twick	101	Z2
Water rd Wem	61	O4
Water st WC2	149	R8
Water Tower hill Croy	133	R8
Waterbank rd SE6	111	T8
Waterbeach rd Dag	55	U16
Waterbeck la NW4	27	N16
Watercress pl N1	142	K2
Waterdale rd SE2	80	A17
Waterden rd E15	51	O14
Waterer ri Wall	131	Y15
Waterfall clo N14	16	H10
Waterfall cotts SW19	106	H15
Waterfall rd N11	16	F14
Waterfall rd N14	16	H10
Waterfall rd SW19	106	H15
Waterfall ter SW17	106	J14
Waterfield clo SE28	80	C2

Waterfield clo Belv	81	T7
Waterfield gdns SE25	123	R10
Waterford rd SW6	153	X19
Watergate EC4	149	W8
Watergate st SE8	76	B16
Watergate wk WC2	148	L12
Waterhall ave E4	20	M2
Waterhall clo E17	32	G3
Waterhouse clo E16	66	A14
Waterhouse clo W6	152	H8
Waterloo bri SE1	149	O11
Waterloo bri WC2	149	O11
Waterloo clo E9	50	D15
Waterloo gdns E2	63	P5
Waterloo gdns Rom	39	O17
Waterloo pas NW6	137	S1
Waterloo pl SW1	148	F13
Waterloo rd E6	65	Z1
Waterloo rd E10	51	O2
Waterloo rd NW2	44	H6
Waterloo rd SE1	149	U17
Waterloo rd Ilf	36	B7
Waterloo rd Rom	39	P17
Waterloo rd Sutt	130	F11
Waterloo ter N1	141	W2
Waterlow rd N19	47	U4
Waterman st SW15	87	R8
Waterman way E1	151	W12
Waterman's clo Kings T	102	J18
Watermans wk SE16	75	V6
Watermead rd SE6	111	T10
Watermead way N17	31	Y11
Watermill clo Rich	102	D8
Watermill la N18	18	D16
Watermill way SW19	106	E20
Watermill way Felt	100	F5
Waters gdns Dag	56	E16
Waters rd SE6	111	Y7
Waters rd Kings T	117	S5
Waters sq Kings T	117	S5
Watersfield way Edg	24	H1
Waterside Dart	99	S12
Waterside clo SE16	151	U19
Waterside clo Bark	55	N12
Waterside clo Nthlt	58	F8
Waterside pl NW1	139	U3
Waterside rd Sthl	70	G7
Waterside way SW17	106	D11
Watersmeet way SE28	68	H17
Waterson st E2	142	M12
Watersplash clo Kings T	116	J6
Waterworks la E5	50	E8
Waterworks rd SW2	90	B15
Waterworks yd Croy	132	M5
Watery la SW20	119	V3
Watery la Sid	115	S17
Wates way Mitch	120	M15
Wateville rd N17	31	N5
Watford bypass Borwd	11	O2
Watford clo SW11	88	K1
Watford rd E16	65	T14
Watford rd Har	41	Y3
Watford rd Wem	42	A11
Watford way NW4	26	H6
Watford way NW7	13	N13
Watkin rd Wem	43	S10
Watkinson rd N7	48	C17
Watling ave Edg	25	V5
Watling ct EC4	150	C7
Watling Farm clo Stan	11	R4
Watling gdns NW2	45	U17
Watling st EC4	150	C7
Watling st Bexh	98	J11
Watlington gro SE26	110	H11
Watney rd SW14	85	V6
Watney st E1	151	Z7
Watneys rd Mitch	121	X13
Watson ave E6	53	W20
Watson ave Sutt	129	T3
Watson clo SW19	106	K16

Name	Page	Grid
Watson st E13	65	V5
Watsons ms W1	146	L3
Watsons rd N22	30	D6
Watson's st SE8	76	A20
Watsons yd NW2	44	F5
Wattisfield rd E5	50	C9
Watts gro E3	64	C13
Watts la Chis	114	A20
Watts la Tedd	101	Y12
Watts st E1	151	X13
Watts way SW7	154	H1
Wauthier clo N13	17	V14
Wavel ms N8	29	Y13
Wavel ms NW6	137	W2
Wavel pl SE26	109	W11
Wavell dr Sid	96	J15
Wavendon ave W4	73	X14
Waveney ave SE15	92	A9
Waveney clo E1	151	U12
Waverley ave E4	19	Y14
Waverley ave E17	33	W10
Waverley ave Surb	117	U14
Waverley ave Sutt	130	B4
Waverley ave Twick	82	E20
Waverley ave Wem	43	N16
Waverley clo E18	34	L6
Waverley clo Brom	127	O12
Waverley cres SE18	79	S14
Waverley gdns E6	66	E15
Waverley gdns Bark	67	U7
Waverley gdns Ilf	36	D8
Waverley gro N3	27	R9
Waverley Industrial pk Har	23	P9
Waverley pl N4	48	J5
Waverley pl NW8	138	F8
Waverley rd E17	33	V10
Waverley rd E18	34	L6
Waverley rd N8	29	Z19
Waverley rd N17	31	Z1
Waverley rd SE18	79	R13
Waverley rd SE25	124	A8
Waverley rd Enf	7	X12
Waverley rd Epsom	128	H13
Waverley rd Har	40	C2
Waverley rd Sthl	58	H20
Waverley wk W2	145	U1
Waverley way Cars	130	K15
Waverton st W1	147	W12
Wavertree rd SW2	108	B2
Wavertree rd E18	34	G6
Wavertree rd SW2	108	B2
Waxlow cres Sthl	58	G17
Waxlow rd NW10	61	Y6
Waxwell clo Pnr	22	A7
Waxwell la Pnr	22	A9
Wayfarer rd Sthl	58	B9
Wayfield link SE9	96	F16
Wayford st SW11	88	K6
Wayland ave E8	49	Y15
Waylands mead Beck	125	S1
Wayleave the SE28	80	D1
Waylett pl SE27	108	J6
Waylett pl Wem	42	F11
Waynflete ave Croy	132	J7
Waynflete sq W10	144	G7
Waynflete SW18	106	D4
Wayside NW11	45	T4
Wayside SW14	85	W12
Wayside clo N14	6	J19
Wayside clo Rom	39	T9
Wayside ct Twick	84	D15
Wayside ct Wem	43	O9
Wayside gdns SE9	113	U10
Wayside gdns Dag	56	D14
Wayside gro SE9	113	U11
Wayside ms Ilf	35	X17
Weald the Chis	113	V15
Weald clo SE16	159	W9
Weald la Har	23	O6
Weald ri Har	23	V3
Weald way Rom	38	G18
Wealdstone rd Sutt	129	V4
Weale rd E4	20	L9
Wear pl E2	143	W13
Weardale gdns Enf	8	C6
Weardale rd SE13	93	Y11
Wearside rd SE13	93	T11
Weatherley clo E3	64	A13
Weaver st E1	143	S18
Weaver wk SE27	108	K10
Weavers clo Islw	83	U9
Weavers way NW1	140	E3
Webb gdns E13	65	T10
Webb pl NW10	62	D9
Webb rd SE3	77	P16
Webb st SE1	158	K2
Webber row SE1	149	V18
Webber st SE1	149	U17
Webbs rd SW11	88	L11
Webbscroft rd Dag	56	H11
Webster gdns W5	72	G3
Webster rd E11	51	V10
Webster rd SE16	159	U3
Wedderburn rd NW3	46	G15
Wedderburn rd Bark	67	U3
Wedgewood way SE19	108	M17
Wedlake st W10	137	N17
Wedmore ave Ilf	35	X4
Wedmore gdns N19	47	X8
Wedmore ms N19	47	Z8
Wedmore rd Grnf	59	R9
Wedmore st N19	47	Y9
Weech rd NW6	45	X12
Weedington rd NW5	47	O14
Weekley sq SW11	88	G9
Weigall rd SE12	94	F11
Weighouse st W1	147	V7
Weighton rd Har	23	R4
Weihurst gdns Sutt	130	H12
Weimar st SW15	87	S9
Weir st SW12	89	V19
Weir Hall ave N18	18	C18
Weir Hall gdns N18	18	B15
Weir Hall rd N17	18	C20
Weir Hall rd N18	18	C17
Weir rd SW12	89	U20
Weir rd SW19	106	B9
Weir rd Bex	98	G19
Weirdale ave N20	15	Z7
Weir's pas NW1	140	H13
Weiss rd SW15	87	P8
Welbeck ave Brom	112	G10
Welbeck ave Sid	115	N1
Welbeck clo N12	15	T15
Welbeck clo Epsom	128	F17
Welbeck clo N Mal	112	C12
Welbeck rd E6	66	A8
Welbeck rd Barn	5	V19
Welbeck rd Cars	130	H1
Welbeck rd Har	40	K2
Welbeck rd Sutt	130	G3
Welbeck st W1	147	V2
Welbeck way N1	147	W4
Welby st SE5	90	K3
Weld pl N11	16	F17
Welfare rd E15	52	B20
Welford pl SW19	105	S11
Welham rd SW16	107	T15
Welham rd SW17	107	P13
Welhouse rd Cars	130	J2
Well app Barn	4	A16
Well clo SW16	108	D11
Well clo Ruis	40	B9
Well ct EC4	150	D7
Well gro N20	15	S4
Well Hall rd SE9	95	T10
Well la SW14	85	U12
Well rd NW3	46	F10
Well rd Barn	4	A16
Well st E9	143	Z1
Well st E15	51	Z16
Well wk NW3	46	G10
Wellacre rd Har	24	C18
Wellan clo Well	97	R14
Welland gdns Grnf	59	W7
Welland ms E1	151	V12
Welland st SE10	76	G16
Wellands clo Brom	127	U3
Wellclose sq E1	151	T9
Wellclose gdns Har	23	T16
Weller st SE1	150	B17
Wellers ct NW1	140	K10
Wellesley ave W6	74	H8
Wellesley ct W9	138	B12
Wellesley Court rd Croy	133	N3
Wellesley cres Twick	101	T5
Wellesley gro Croy	133	N3
Wellesley pl NW1	140	F13
Wellesley rd E11	34	G15
Wellesley rd E17	33	O18
Wellesley rd N22	30	F6
Wellesley rd NW5	47	O15
Wellesley rd W4	73	P14
Wellesley rd Croy	132	M1
Wellesley rd Har	23	T16
Wellesley rd Ilf	53	Y6
Wellesley rd Sutt	130	C14
Wellesley rd Twick	101	S6
Wellesley st E1	63	S15
Wellesley ter N1	142	C12
Wellfield ave N10	29	S9
Wellfield rd SW16	108	B10
Wellfield wk SW16	108	E11
Wellgarth Grnf	42	A18
Wellgarth rd NW11	46	B3
Wellhouse la Barn	4	B13
Wellhouse rd Beck	125	N9
Welling High st Well	97	P7
Welling way SE9	96	D8
Welling way Well	96	H7
Wellington ave E4	20	C8
Wellington ave N9	19	N9
Wellington ave N15	31	W18
Wellington ave Houns	82	F13
Wellington ave Pnr	22	E4
Wellington ave Sid	97	O16
Wellington ave Wor Pk	128	M7
Wellington bldgs SW1	155	V11
Wellington clo W11	145	T6
Wellington clo Dag	56	K20
Wellington ct NW8	138	G39
Wellington cres N Mal	117	W7
Wellington dr Dag	56	L20
Wellington gdns SE7	77	X15
Wellington gdns Twick	101	Y10
Wellington ms SE22	91	Y10
Wellington Park Industrial est NW2	44	F5
Wellington pas E11	34	F15
Wellington pl N2	28	K14
Wellington pl NW8	138	H11
Wellington rd E6	66	H4
Wellington rd E7	52	D13
Wellington rd E10	50	H3
Wellington rd E11	34	G14
Wellington rd E17	32	J11
Wellington rd NW8	138	H10
Wellington rd NW10	136	G14
Wellington rd SW19	105	Z5
Wellington rd W5	72	D9
Wellington rd Belv	81	P12
Wellington rd Bex	97	W14
Wellington rd Brom	126	L9
Wellington rd Croy	122	J18
Wellington rd Enf	8	E15
Wellington rd Hmptn	101	O12
Wellington rd Har	23	S9
Wellington rd Pnr	22	D3
Wellington rd Twick	101	P9
Wellington Road north Houns	82	E7
Wellington Road south Houns	82	E10
Wellington row E2	143	R13
Wellington sq SW3	155	O9
Wellington st SE18	78	J12
Wellington st WC2	148	M7
Wellington st Bark	67	P2
Wellington ter E1	151	W11
Wellington way E3	64	A9
Wellmeadow rd SE6	112	A1
Wellmeadow rd SE13	93	Y11
Wellmeadow rd W7	71	Y11
Wellow wk Cars	130	G1
Wells the N14	16	L3
Wells dr NW9	43	X5
Wells gdns Dag	56	H16
Wells gdns Ilf	35	R20
Wells gdns Rain	57	U17
Wells House rd NW10	62	B13
Wells ms W1	148	C3
Wells Park rd SE26	109	Y8
Wells ri NW8	139	O6
Wells rd W12	144	C19
Wells rd Brom	127	U3
Wells st W1	148	B2
Wells ter N4	48	F6
Wells way SE5	158	H13
Wells way SW7	154	E1
Wellside clo Barn	4	A15
Wellsmoor gdns Brom	127	W5
Wellsprings cres Wem	43	U9
Wellstead ave N9	19	S3
Wellstead rd E6	66	J7
Wellwood rd Ilf	55	N2
Welsford st SE1	159	S8
Welsh clo E13	65	S10
Welshpool st E8	143	V4
Weltje rd W6	74	H12
Welton rd SE18	79	U20
Wembley Commercial cen Wem	42	F7
Wembley Hill rd Wem	42	L10
Wembley Park Business cen Wem	43	T10
Wembley Park dr Wem	42	M11
Wembley rd Hmptn	100	F19
Wembley way Wem	43	U17
Wemborough rd Stan	24	C3
Wembury rd N6	47	T1
Wemyss rd SE3	94	C5
Wendela ct Har	41	T8
Wendell rd W12	74	C7
Wendling rd Sutt	130	F2
Wendon st E3	64	A3
Wendover dr N Mal	118	E15
Wendover rd NW10	62	D6
Wendover rd SE9	95	O8
Wendover rd Brom	126	J8
Wendover way Well	97	O12
Wendy clo Enf	8	H19
Wendy way Wem	60	K3
Wenlock rd N1	142	B9
Wenlock rd Edg	12	G20
Wenlock st N1	142	D10
Wennington rd E3	63	U6
Wensley ave Wdf Grn	34	E1
Wensley clo SE9	95	U16
Wensley rd N18	19	N18
Wensleydale ave Ilf	35	S8
Wensleydale gdns Hmptn	100	J18
Wensleydale pas Hmptn	100	J19
Wensleydale rd Hmptn	100	H16
Wentland clo SE6	111	Y5
Wentland rd SE6	111	Y5
Wentworth ave N3	15	N20
Wentworth clo N3	15	N20
Wentworth clo Mord	119	X17
Wentworth cres SE15	159	T20
Wentworth dr Dart	99	W16
Wentworth gdns N13	17	W11
Wentworth hill Wem	43	N2
Wentworth pk N3	27	Z2
Wentworth pl Stan	11	N20
Wentworth rd E12	53	O13
Wentworth rd NW11	27	U18
Wentworth rd Barn	4	C10
Wentworth rd Croy	122	F18
Wentworth rd Sthl	70	A12
Wentworth st E1	151	N3
Wentworth way Pnr	22	A13

Name	Page	Grid
Wenvoe ave Bexh	98	G5
Wernbrook st SE18	79	R16
Werndee rd SE25	123	Y10
Werneth Hall rd Ilf	35	U10
Werrington st NW1	140	D10
Werter rd SW15	87	S11
Wesley ave NW10	61	X8
Wesley ave Houns	82	C4
Wesley clo N7	48	E7
Wesley clo SE17	157	Y8
Wesley clo Har	41	N6
Wesley rd E10	51	U2
Wesley st W1	147	V1
Wesleyan pl NW5	47	R12
Wessex ave SW19	119	Z5
Wessex clo Ilf	36	J18
Wessex clo Kings T	117	S2
Wessex dr Erith	99	S4
Wessex dr Pnr	22	B1
Wessex gdns NW11	45	T3
Wessex la Grnf	59	R7
Wessex st E2	63	P10
Wessex way NW11	45	T2
West Arbour st E1	63	S16
West ave N3	14	L19
West ave NW4	27	O15
West ave Pnr	22	D18
West ave Sthl	58	D20
West ave Wall	132	B11
West Avenue rd E17	33	P13
West bank N16	49	S1
West bank Bark	67	N3
West bank Enf	7	Y9
West Barnes la SW20	118	K4
West Barnes la N Mal	118	J13
West Carriage dr W2	146	J11
West Central st WC1	148	K4
West Chantry Har	22	K4
West clo N9	18	H10
West clo (Cockfosters) Barn	6	C14
West clo Grnf	59	N6
West clo Wem	43	N4
West cotts NW6	45	Y15
West ct Wem	42	E8
West Cromwell rd SW5	153	T6
West Cromwell rd W14	153	O8
West Cross Route W10	144	F10
West Cross Route W11	144	G11
West Cross way Brent	72	A17
West dr SW16	107	U10
West dr Har	10	C18
West dr Sutt	129	R20
West Drive gdns Har	10	C20
West Eaton pl SW1	155	T4
West Eaton Place ms SW1	155	T4
West Ella rd NW10	62	A1
West End ave E10	33	W16
West End ave Pnr	22	A12
West End la NW6	137	V5
West End la Barn	4	C13
West End la Pnr	22	A14
West End rd Sthl	70	B4
West gdns E1	151	Z10
West gdns SW17	106	H15
West gate W5	60	K8
West Green rd N15	30	J12
West gro SE10	93	W2
West gro Wdf Grn	21	Z10
West Halkin st SW1	155	S1
West Hall rd Rich	85	S3
West Hallowes SE9	113	P1
West Ham la E15	64	M1
West Harding st EC4	149	S5
West Heath ave NW11	45	Y5
West Heath clo NW3	45	Y9
West Heath dr NW11	45	Y4
West Heath gdns NW3	45	X8
West Heath rd NW3	45	Y7
West Heath rd SE2	80	H17
West Heath rd Dart	99	U16
West Hendon bdy NW9	26	E18
West hill SW15	87	P18
West hill SW18	87	X14
West hill Har	41	S5
West hill S Croy	133	T18
West hill Wem	42	M4
West Hill ct N6	47	O8
West Hill pk N6	47	N6
West Hill rd SW18	87	V15
West Hill way N20	15	N5
West Holme Erith	98	L2
West House clo SW19	105	S1
West India ave E14	76	A2
West India Dock rd E14	64	A19
West la SE16	151	X18
West Lodge ave W3	73	P3
West mead Epsom	128	B14
West ms N17	19	N20
West pk SE9	113	R3
West Park ave Rich	85	R2
West Park clo Rom	37	Y16
West Park rd Rich	85	P2
West Pier E1	151	V15
West pl SW19	104	M12
West Poultry ave EC1	149	W2
West Quarters W12	62	F17
West Quay dr Hayes	58	B15
West Ridge gdns Grnf	58	M7
West rd E15	65	R3
West rd N17	18	M19
West rd SW3	155	R12
West rd SW4	89	Y13
West rd W5	60	J14
West rd Barn	16	B4
West rd Kings T	103	W20
West rd Rom (Chadwell Heath)	37	Y18
West rd (Rush Grn) Rom	57	N2
West row W10	136	J17
West Sheen vale Rich	84	M9
West Side common SW19	104	M13
West Smithfield EC1	149	W2
West sq SE11	157	W4
West st E2	143	Y10
West st E11	51	Z8
West st WC2	148	H7
West st Bexh	98	A8
West st Brent	72	D18
West st Brom	126	E2
West st Cars	130	L7
West st Croy	132	M7
West st Har	41	R4
West st Sutt	130	B11
West Street la Cars	130	M9
West Temple Sheen SW14	85	U11
West Tenter st E1	151	P7
West vw NW4	26	M14
West View cres N9	18	D2
West wk W5	60	J15
West wk Barn	16	B3
West Warwick pl SW1	156	A7
West way N18	18	C14
West way NW10	43	Z11
West way Croy	134	H3
West way Edg	12	G18
West way Houns	82	D1
West way W Wick	125	Y15
West Way gdns Croy	134	G3
West Woodside Bex	97	Z20
Westacott clo N19	47	Y4
Westbank rd Hmptn	100	M16
Westbeech rd N22	30	G9
Westbere dr Stan	11	U15
Westbere rd NW2	45	T13
Westbourne ave W3	61	X18
Westbourne ave Sutt	129	S2
Westbourne bri W2	146	A2
Westbourne cres W2	146	E8
Westbourne dr SE23	110	E3
Westbourne gdns W2	145	X4
Westbourne gro W2	145	W6
Westbourne gro W11	145	P8
Westbourne Grove ms W11	145	T7
Westbourne Grove ter W2	145	X5
Westbourne Park rd W2	145	X4
Westbourne Park rd W11	145	N5
Westbourne Park vill W2	145	X3
Westbourne rd N7	48	D17
Westbourne rd SE26	110	E15
Westbourne rd Bexh	80	L19
Westbourne rd Croy	123	V15
Westbourne rd W2	146	F8
Westbourne ter W2	146	D5
Westbourne Terrace ms W2	146	C4
Westbourne Terrace rd W2	146	A1
Westbridge rd SW11	154	K20
Westbrook ave Hmptn	100	E17
Westbrook clo Barn	5	U11
Westbrook cres Barn	5	U11
Westbrook rd SE3	94	H2
Westbrook rd Houns	70	E18
Westbrook rd Th Hth	123	O2
Westbrook sq Barn	5	T11
Westbrooke cres Well	97	U6
Westbrooke rd Sid	114	F5
Westbrooke rd Well	97	R6
Westbury ave N22	30	H10
Westbury ave Sthl	58	G11
Westbury ave Wem	42	K19
Westbury gro N12	14	M18
Westbury la Buck H	21	X7
Westbury rd E7	52	J16
Westbury rd E17	33	N12
Westbury rd N11	17	N19
Westbury rd N12	14	M17
Westbury rd SE20	124	E1
Westbury rd W5	60	K18
Westbury rd Bark	67	S2
Westbury rd Brom	127	O1
Westbury rd Buck H	21	Y6
Westbury rd Croy	123	O15
Westbury rd Felt	100	A3
Westbury rd Ilf	53	V7
Westbury rd N Mal	117	Z10
Westbury rd Wem	42	K20
Westbury st SW8	89	V5
Westbury ter E7	52	J17
Westchester dr NW4	27	O9
Westcombe ave Croy	122	B16
Westcombe dr Barn	4	L16
Westcombe hill SE3	77	T18
Westcombe hill SE10	77	T14
Westcombe Park rd SE3	77	N18
Westcoombe ave SW20	118	E1
Westcote rd SW16	107	V13
Westcott clo N15	31	U18
Westcott clo Brom	127	S11
Westcott clo Croy	135	T19
Westcott cres W7	59	U16
Westcott rd SE17	157	X13
Westcroft clo NW2	45	S12
Westcroft clo Enf	9	R3
Westcroft gdns Mord	119	U8
Westcroft rd Cars	131	P9
Westcroft rd Wall	131	P9
Westcroft sq W6	74	F11
Westcroft way NW2	45	S12
Westdale rd SE18	78	M16
Westdean ave SE12	112	K2
Westdean clo SW18	88	B14
Westdown rd E15	51	U12
Westdown rd SE6	93	N19
Westerfield rd N15	31	T15
Westergate rd SE2	80	M15
Westerham ave N9	18	C11
Westerham dr Sid	97	S15
Westerham rd E10	33	S14
Westerley cres SE26	110	M12
Western ave NW11	27	P19
Western ave W3	61	X14
Western ave W5	60	G9
Western ave Dag	56	L17
Western ave Grnf	58	K4
Western ave Nthlt	58	B1
Western gdns W5	61	O19
Western Gateway E16	65	T20
Western la SW12	89	O18
Western rd E13	65	X5
Western rd E17	33	V15
Western rd N2	28	M11
Western rd N22	30	C8
Western rd NW10	61	V11
Western rd SW9	90	G8
Western rd SW19	120	G1
Western rd W5	72	H1
Western rd Mitch	120	H1
Western rd Rom	39	R16
Western rd Sthl	70	A9
Western rd Sutt	129	Y12
Western Trading est NW10	61	T11
Western way SE28	79	U7
Western way Barn	4	M20
Westerville gdns Ilf	36	B20
Westferry circ E14	76	A2
Westferry rd E14	76	A4
Westfield clo Enf	9	V11
Westfield clo Sutt	129	V8
Westfield dr Har	24	H13
Westfield gdns Har	24	G13
Westfield la Har	24	G14
Westfield pk Pnr	22	F1
Westfield rd NW7	12	M10
Westfield rd W13	72	A4
Westfield rd Beck	124	M3
Westfield rd Bexh	98	L6
Westfield rd Croy	132	J3
Westfield rd Dag	56	B13
Westfield rd Mitch	120	L5
Westfield rd Surb	116	F13
Westfield rd Sutt	129	U9
Westfield st SE18	78	C9
Westfields SW13	86	D7
Westfields ave SW13	86	C7
Westfields rd W3	61	U14
Westgate rd SE25	124	A9
Westgate rd Beck	125	T2
Westgate st E8	143	X4
Westgate ter SW10	153	Z12
Westglade ct Har	24	F15
Westgrove la SE10	93	W2
Westhay gdns SW14	85	U12
Westholm NW11	28	A13
Westhorne ave SE9	95	P11
Westhorne ave SE12	94	E18
Westhorpe gdns NW4	27	O10
Westhorpe rd SW15	87	N8
Westhurst dr Chis	114	A11
Westlake clo N13	17	T10
Westland pl N1	142	E12
Westlands ter SW12	89	U17
Westlea rd W7	71	X8
Westleigh ave SW15	86	M14
Westleigh dr Brom	127	R2
Westleigh gdns Edg	25	R5
Westmead SW15	86	J17
Westmead rd Sutt	130	F10
Westmere dr NW7	12	K10
Westminster ave Th Hth	122	H13
Westminster bri SE1	149	N18
Westminster bri SW1	148	L18
Westminster Bridge rd SE1	149	R19
Westminster clo Ilf	36	E8

Name	Page	Grid
Westminster clo Tedd	101	Y11
Westminster dr N13	17	N16
Westminster gdns E4	21	N5
Westminster gdns Bark	67	U6
Westminster gdns Ilf	36	D8
Westminster rd N9	19	N5
Westminster rd W7	71	U3
Westminster rd Sutt	130	F2
Westmoat clo Beck	111	U19
Westmoor gdns Enf	9	T7
Westmoor rd Enf	9	T9
Westmoor st SE7	78	A10
Westmoreland ave Well	96	H9
Westmoreland dr Sutt	130	B18
Westmoreland pl SW1	155	Y10
Westmoreland pl W5	60	G13
Westmoreland rd NW9	25	O11
Westmoreland rd SE17	158	D13
Westmoreland rd SW13	86	F2
Westmoreland rd Brom	126	A12
Westmoreland st W1	147	V1
Westmoreland ter SW1	155	Y10
Westmorland clo E12	53	O5
Westmorland rd E17	33	O19
Westmorland rd Har	22	L16
Westmorland way Mitch	121	Z10
Westmount rd SE9	95	V6
Westoe rd N9	19	N8
Weston dr Stan	24	A5
Weston gdns Islw	83	S3
Weston grn Dag	56	A11
Weston gro Brom	112	D19
Weston pk N8	30	A17
Weston pk Kings T	116	K3
Weston ri WC1	141	P11
Weston rd W4	73	V9
Weston rd Brom	112	D19
Weston rd Dag	56	A11
Weston rd Enf	8	C7
Weston st SE1	150	H19
Weston wk E8	143	Z1
Westover clo Sutt	130	A20
Westover hill NW3	45	Z7
Westover rd SW18	88	E17
Westow hill SE19	109	T15
Westow st SE19	109	T16
Westpoint Trading est W3	61	S13
Westpole ave Barn	6	C14
Westport rd E13	65	V13
Westport st E1	63	U17
Westrow SW15	87	N15
Westrow dr Bark	54	L19
Westrow gdns Ilf	54	M8
Westside NW4	26	H6
Westview clo NW10	44	D14
Westview clo W7	59	T17
Westview dr Wdf Grn	35	N7
Westville rd W12	74	H5
Westville rd T Ditt	116	A18
Westward rd E4	19	X17
Westward way Har	24	J19
Westway NW7	26	G2
Westway SW20	118	L7
Westway W2	145	U1
Westway W10	144	L4
Westway W12	144	D6
Westway clo SW20	118	K7
Westways Epsom	128	E8
Westwell rd SW16	107	Z16
Westwick gdns W14	144	F19
Westwood ave Har	40	L12
Westwood clo Brom	127	P6
Westwood gdns SW13	86	C9
Westwood hill SE26	109	W11
Westwood la Sid	97	N14
Westwood la Well	96	L7
Westwood pk SE23	110	B1
Westwood rd E16	77	V3
Westwood rd SW13	86	D8
Westwood rd Ilf	54	M3
Wetheral dr Stan	24	C5
Wetherby clo Nthlt	40	J16
Wetherby gdns SW5	154	A8
Wetherby pl SW7	154	C7
Wetherby rd Enf	7	Z4
Wetherden st E17	50	L1
Wetherell rd E9	63	U3
Wetherill rd N10	29	R4
Wexford rd SW12	88	M19
Weybourne st SW18	106	C5
Weybridge rd Th Hth	122	G10
Weydown clo SW19	105	S2
Weyhill rd E1	151	T4
Weyland rd Dag	56	B9
Weyman rd SE3	94	M2
Weymouth ave NW7	13	N15
Weymouth ave W5	72	E7
Weymouth ct Sutt	129	Z17
Weymouth ms W1	147	X1
Weymouth st W1	147	V1
Weymouth ter E2	143	P9
Weymouth wk Stan	10	L20
Whadcote st N4	48	F7
Whalebone ave Rom	38	B17
Whalebone gro Rom	38	A18
Whalebone Lane north Rom	37	Z1
Whalebone Lane south Dag	56	B1
Whalebone Lane south Rom	38	A19
Wharf la Twick	101	Y2
Wharf pl E2	143	V6
Wharf rd E15	64	K2
Wharf rd N1	142	A9
Wharf rd Enf	9	V18
Wharf Road Industrial est Enf	9	V18
Wharf st E16	64	M15
Wharfdale rd N1	140	L8
Wharfedale gdns Th Hth	122	D8
Wharfedale st SW10	153	X11
Wharfside rd E16	65	N16
Wharncliffe dr Sthl	71	R3
Wharncliffe gdns SE25	123	R5
Wharncliffe rd SE25	123	R4
Wharton clo NW10	44	D17
Wharton rd Brom	126	H1
Wharton st WC1	141	P3
Whateley rd SE20	110	G17
Whateley rd SE22	91	V13
Whatley ave SW20	119	P6
Whatman rd SE23	92	C19
Wheatfield way Kings T	116	J5
Wheatfields Enf	9	V7
Wheathill rd SE20	123	Z5
Wheatlands Houns	70	H16
Wheatley clo NW4	26	G7
Wheatley gdns N9	18	D9
Wheatley la Islw	83	V8
Wheatley st W1	147	V2
Wheatsheaf clo Nthlt	40	B16
Wheatsheaf la SW6	152	E18
Wheatsheaf la SW8	156	L18
Wheatsheaf rd Rom	39	T18
Wheatsheaf ter SW6	153	R19
Wheatstone rd W10	136	L20
Wheel Farm dr Dag	56	C19
Wheelers cross Bark	67	S6
Wheelwright st N7	48	C19
Whelan way Wall	131	Y6
Wheler st E1	143	N19
Whellock rd W4	74	A7
Whernside clo SE28	80	H1
Whetstone clo N20	15	T7
Whetstone pk WC2	149	C4
Whetstone rd SE3	94	M4
Whewell rd N19	48	A7
Whidborne st SE8	93	P5
Whidborne st WC1	140	L13
Whimbrel clo SE28	68	F19
Whinchat rd SE28	79	S8
Whinfell clo SW16	107	X11
Whinyates rd SE9	95	R8
Whipps Cross rd E11	33	X15
Whiskin st EC1	141	V14
Whisperwood clo Har	23	U3
Whistler gdns Edg	25	O7
Whistler st N5	48	H13
Whistlers ave SW11	154	H20
Whiston rd E2	142	M7
Whitbread clo N17	31	W4
Whitbread rd SE4	92	K11
Whitburn rd SE13	93	T11
Whitby ave NW10	61	S8
Whitby gdns NW9	25	R10
Whitby gdns Sutt	130	F2
Whitby rd SE18	78	G11
Whitby rd Har	41	N10
Whitby rd Ruis	40	A9
Whitby rd Sutt	130	F3
Whitby st E1	143	N16
Whitcher clo SE14	75	V17
Whitcher pl NW1	47	V19
Whitchurch ave Edg	24	M1
Whitchurch clo Edg	11	Z19
Whitchurch gdns Edg	11	Z19
Whitchurch la Edg	24	G2
Whitchurch rd W11	144	H9
Whitcomb st WC2	148	G11
White acre NW9	26	C6
White Adder way E14	76	E11
White Church la E1	151	S4
White City clo W12	144	C10
White City rd W12	144	A8
White Conduit st N1	141	T8
White gdns Dag	56	E17
White Gate gdns Har	23	U1
White Hart la N17	30	K1
White Hart la N22	30	E4
White Hart la NW10	44	D17
White Hart la SW13	86	B6
White Hart la Rom	39	S10
White Hart rd SE18	79	W11
White Hart st SE11	157	U9
White Hart yd SE1	150	F14
White Horse hill Chis	113	V9
White Horse la E1	63	T12
White Horse la E1	63	V15
White Horse rd E6	66	G7
White Horse st W1	147	Y14
White House dr Stan	11	T14
White Kennet st E1	150	M4
White Lion hill EC4	149	Z9
White Lion st N1	141	U9
White lo SE19	108	K17
White Lodge clo N2	28	H19
White Lodge clo Sutt	130	E16
White Oak dr Beck	125	V4
White Orchards N20	14	H3
White Orchards Stan	10	K17
White Post la E9	51	O19
White rd E15	52	B19
White Swan ms W4	74	B15
Whitear wk E15	51	X16
Whitebarn la Dag	69	T3
Whitebeam ave Brom	127	W17
Whitebeam clo SW9	157	R20
Whitebutts rd Ruis	40	A10
Whitechapel High st E1	151	O5
Whitechapel rd E1	151	S3
Whitecote rd Sthl	58	M18
Whitecroft clo Beck	125	W8
Whitecroft way Beck	125	V11
Whitecross st EC1	142	C16
Whitecross st EC2	142	D20
Whitefield ave NW2	45	N2
Whitefield clo SW15	87	T16
Whitefoot la Brom	111	U9
Whitefoot ter Brom	112	B7
Whitefriars ave Har	23	S7
Whitefriars dr Har	23	S7
Whitefriars st EC4	149	V6
Whitehall SW1	148	J14
Whitehall ct SW1	148	K14
Whitehall gdns E4	20	L6
Whitehall gdns SW1	148	K15
Whitehall gdns W3	73	R3
Whitehall gdns W4	73	T16
Whitehall la Buck H	21	U8
Whitehall la Erith	99	U3
Whitehall pk N19	47	V3
Whitehall Park rd W4	73	T16
Whitehall pl SW1	148	K14
Whitehall rd E4	20	M7
Whitehall rd W7	71	Y6
Whitehall rd Brom	127	P11
Whitehall rd Har	23	T20
Whitehall rd Th Hth	122	F13
Whitehall rd Wdf Grn	21	S10
Whitehall st N17	31	V2
Whitehaven clo Brom	126	E9
Whitehaven st NW8	138	K19
Whitehead clo N18	18	C15
Whitehead clo SW18	88	C18
Whitehead's gro SW3	154	M8
Whitehill rd Dart	99	W14
Whitehorn gdns Croy	134	A2
Whitehorse la SE25	123	P9
Whitehorse rd SE1	157	V1
Whitehorse rd Croy	123	N18
Whitehouse way N14	16	F9
Whiteledges W13	60	D17
Whitelegg rd E13	65	P6
Whiteley rd SE19	109	P12
Whiteleys cotts W14	153	P8
Whiteleys way Felt	100	G7
Whiteoak gdns Sid	96	L20
Whiteoaks la Grnf	59	R7
Whites ave Ilf	36	G17
Whites dr Brom	126	C16
Whites grds SE1	150	L18
White's row E1	151	N2
White's sq SW4	89	Y10
Whitestile rd Brent	72	E13
Whitethorn gdns Enf	8	B16
Whitethorn st E3	64	B13
Whitfield pl W1	140	B17
Whitfield rd E6	65	Z1
Whitfield rd SE3	93	Y3
Whitfield rd Bexh	81	O18
Whitfield st W1	140	B17
Whitford gdns Mitch	120	M6
Whitgift ave S Croy	132	K12
Whitgift st SE11	157	N6
Whitgift st Croy	132	M6
Whiting ave Bark	54	A20
Whitings rd Barn	4	A18
Whitings rd E6	66	J13
Whitland rd Cars	130	H1
Whitley rd N17	31	T6
Whitlock dr SW19	87	T20
Whitman rd E3	63	W10
Whitmead clo S Croy	133	R13
Whitmore clo N11	16	F16
Whitmore gdns NW10	136	D8
Whitmore rd N1	142	J5
Whitmore rd Beck	124	L5
Whitmore rd Har	40	L2
Whitnell way SW15	87	N14
Whitney ave Ilf	35	N13
Whitney rd E10	51	R1
Whitney wk SW16	115	Y16
Whitstable clo Beck	124	M1
Whitta rd E12	53	O11
Whittaker rd Sutt	129	V5
Whittaker st SW1	155	T7
Whittell gdns SE26	110	C8
Whittingstall rd SW6	87	V2
Whittington ave EC3	150	J7
Whittington rd N22	30	A1

Name	Page	Grid
Whittington way Pnr	22	B16
Whittle clo Sthl	58	K17
Whittlebury clo Cars	131	N17
Whittlesea rd Har	23	N3
Whittlesey st SE1	149	T14
Whitton Avenue east Grnf	41	W15
Whitton Avenue west Grnf	41	R16
Whitton Avenue west Nthlt	40	L15
Whitton clo Grnf	42	C18
Whitton dene Houns	82	L14
Whitton dene Islw	83	O14
Whitton dr Grnf	41	Z17
Whitton Manor rd Islw	83	O14
Whitton rd Houns	82	L10
Whitton rd Twick	82	L10
Whitton wk E3	64	A8
Whitton waye Houns	82	J15
Whitwell rd E13	65	T10
Whitworth pl SE18	79	N12
Whitworth rd SE18	78	K18
Whitworth rd SE25	123	T7
Whitworth st SE10	77	N13
Whorlton rd SE15	91	Z8
Whymark av N22	30	H10
Whytecroft Houns	70	A19
Whyteville rd E7	52	H17
Wick la E3	64	A2
Wick rd E9	50	J18
Wick rd Tedd	102	C18
Wickers Oake SE19	109	U11
Wickersley rd SW11	89	P5
Wicket the Croy	135	O12
Wicket rd Grnf	59	Y8
Wickford st E1	63	P11
Wickford way E17	32	E12
Wickham ave Croy	134	H7
Wickham ave Sutt	128	M10
Wickham chase W Wick	125	X19
Wickham clo Enf	9	O10
Wickham clo N Mal	118	C13
Wickham Court rd W Wick	135	V2
Wickham cres W Wick	135	V3
Wickham gdns SE4	92	L8
Wickham la SE2	79	Z14
Wickham ms SE4	92	M6
Wickham rd E4	33	U1
Wickham rd SE4	92	L9
Wickham rd Beck	125	S3
Wickham rd Croy	134	E3
Wickham st SE11	157	O9
Wickham st Well	96	J5
Wickham way Beck	125	T8
Wickliffe ave N3	27	T8
Wickliffe gdns Wem	43	S19
Wicklow st WC1	141	O12
Wicks clo SE9	113	N9
Wickwood st SE5	90	K6
Widdecombe ave Har	40	B7
Widdenham rd N7	48	C13
Widdin st E15	64	L1
Wide way Mitch	121	Y7
Widecombe gdns Ilf	35	S12
Widecombe rd SE9	113	S8
Widecombe way N2	28	F14
Widegate st E1	150	L2
Widley rd W9	137	V15
Widmore Lodge rd Brom	127	O4
Widmore rd Brom	126	F3
Wigeon path SE28	79	T7
Wiggington av Wem	43	R19
Wiggins mead NW9	26	D2
Wightman rd N4	30	G20
Wightman rd N8	30	E12
Wigley rd Felt	100	A2
Wigmore pl W1	147	X3
Wigmore rd Cars	121	V12
Wigmore st W1	147	T5
Wigram rd E11	34	K18
Wigram sq E17	33	V8
Wigston rd E13	65	W10
Wigton gdns Stan	24	J5
Wigton rd E17	32	L4
Wilberforce rd N4	48	H6
Wilberforce rd NW9	26	F17
Wilberforce way SW19	105	O15
Wilbraham pl SW1	155	S5
Wilbury way N18	18	B16
Wilby ms W11	145	R12
Wilcox clo SW8	156	L18
Wilcox rd SW8	156	J18
Wilcox rd Sutt	130	A9
Wilcox rd Tedd	101	S10
Wild ct WC2	149	N5
Wild Goose dr SE14	92	D3
Wild Hatch NW11	27	Z19
Wild st WC2	148	M6
Wildcroft gdns Edg	11	U19
Wildcroft rd SW15	87	N18
Wilde clo E8	143	T4
Wilde pl N13	17	V18
Wilde pl SW18	88	G19
Wilderness rd Chis	114	A17
Wilderton rd N16	49	T2
Wildfell rd SE6	93	R17
Wild's rents SE1	158	H1
Wildwood clo SE12	94	D18
Wildwood gro NW3	46	C5
Wildwood ri NW11	46	E3
Wildwood rd NW11	28	C18
Wilford clo Enf	8	B12
Wilfred st SW1	148	C20
Wilfrid gdns W3	61	V13
Wilkes st E1	143	O20
Wilkin st NW5	47	R17
Wilkins clo Mitch	106	K20
Wilkinson rd E16	65	Y16
Wilkinson st SW8	157	N19
Wilks pl N1	142	K9
Will Crooks gdns SE9	94	M9
Willan rd N17	31	P8
Willard st SW8	89	S7
Willcott rd W3	73	S3
Willenhall ave Barn	5	P20
Willenhall rd SE18	78	M14
Willersley ave Sid	114	K2
Willersley clo Sid	96	L20
Willes rd NW5	47	S17
Willesden la NW2	45	P19
Willesden la NW6	137	N1
Willet way SE16	159	X10
Willett rd Th Hth	122	F12
William Barefoot dr SE9	113	V9
William Booth rd SE20	109	X20
William Carey way Har	23	U19
William clo Rom	38	M5
William Covell clo Enf	7	S3
William IV st WC2	148	J10
William gdns SW15	86	K12
William ms SW1	147	R18
William Morley clo E6	66	A3
William Morris clo E17	32	L9
William rd NW1	140	A15
William rd SW19	105	T19
William rd Sutt	130	E10
William st E10	33	T19
William st N17	31	V1
William st SW1	147	R18
William st Bark	54	B20
William st Cars	130	L6
Williams ave E17	32	L5
Williams bldgs E2	63	P10
Williams clo N8	29	Y19
Williams gro N22	30	E4
William's la SW14	85	V6
Williams la Mord	120	E13
Williams rd W13	71	Z1
Williams st N1	30	B12
Williams ter Croy	132	F13
Williamson rd N4	30	K19
Williamson st N7	48	B12
Williamson way NW7	14	F18
Willifield way NW11	27	W14
Willingale clo Wdf Grn	21	Z19
Willingdon rd N22	30	H8
Willingham ter NW5	47	V15
Willingham way Kings T	117	P6
Willington rd SW9	90	A8
Willis ave Sutt	130	H15
Willis rd E15	65	P5
Willis rd Croy	122	M17
Willis rd Erith	81	Z11
Willis st E14	64	F17
Willmore end SW19	120	A2
Willoughby ave Croy	132	C9
Willoughby la N17	19	N18
Willoughby Park rd N17	32	A1
Willoughby rd N8	30	H12
Willoughby rd NW3	46	F12
Willoughby rd Kings T	103	N20
Willoughby rd Twick	84	F15
Willoughby st WC1	148	J3
Willoughby way SE7	77	U10
Willow ave SW13	86	E6
Willow ave Sid	97	N15
Willow bank SW6	87	T7
Willow bank Rich	102	C6
Willow Bridge rd N1	48	L18
Willow clo Bex	98	B16
Willow clo Brent	72	E17
Willow clo Brom	127	U13
Willow clo Erith	99	W3
Willow clo Horn	57	Z10
Willow clo Th Hth	122	H14
Willow ct Edg	11	Y13
Willow dene (Bushey) Wat	10	G3
Willow dr Barn	4	F15
Willow end N20	14	L8
Willow end Surb	116	K20
Willow gdns Houns	82	G3
Willow gro Chis	113	X16
Willow la Mitch	120	M14
Willow Lane Industrial est Mitch	121	N14
Willow mt Croy	133	T7
Willow pl SW1	156	C5
Willow rd NW3	46	H11
Willow rd W5	72	K6
Willow rd Enf	8	D11
Willow rd Erith	99	X2
Willow rd N Mal	117	V8
Willow rd Rom	37	Z17
Willow rd Wall	131	T16
Willow st E4	20	K3
Willow st EC2	142	J15
Willow st Rom	38	L12
Willow Tree wk Brom	126	J2
Willow vale W12	74	H2
Willow vale Chis	113	Y16
Willow vw SW19	120	F2
Willow wk E17	32	L14
Willow wk N2	28	F17
Willow wk N15	30	J12
Willow wk N21	7	P20
Willow wk SE1	158	L3
Willow wk Sutt	129	W5
Willow way N3	28	A3
Willow way SE26	110	B8
Willow way Epsom	128	A12
Willow way Twick	100	K5
Willow Wood cres SE25	123	S14
Willowbrook rd SE15	159	P16
Willowbrook rd Sthl	70	F9
Willowcourt ave Har	24	B16
Willowdene clo Twick	82	M18
Willowhayne gdns Wor Pk	129	N7
Willowmead clo W5	60	G13
Willows ave Mord	120	B12
Willrose cres SE2	80	E12
Wills cres Houns	82	K15
Wills gro NW7	13	U16
Wilman gro E8	49	Y20
Wilmar gdns W Wick	125	R20
Wilmer clo Kings T	103	N13
Wilmer cres Kings T	103	O13
Wilmer gdns N1	142	K7
Wilmer Lea clo E15	64	J2
Wilmer way N14	16	L15
Wilmington ave W4	73	X19
Wilmington gdns Bark	54	F18
Wilmington sq WC1	141	T15
Wilmington st WC1	141	T14
Wilmot clo N2	28	E6
Wilmot clo SE15	159	T19
Wilmot pl NW1	47	U19
Wilmot rd E10	51	R7
Wilmot rd N17	31	O9
Wilmot rd Cars	130	M11
Wilmot rd Dart	99	X14
Wilmot st E2	143	X14
Wilmount st SE18	78	M11
Wilna rd SW18	88	C19
Wilsham st W11	144	J12
Wilshaw st SE14	93	N1
Wilsmere dr Har	23	U1
Wilsmere dr Nthlt	40	C16
Wilson ave Mitch	106	K19
Wilson clo Wem	25	N20
Wilson dr Wem	42	M1
Wilson gdns Har	22	M20
Wilson gro SE16	151	V19
Wilson rd E6	66	A7
Wilson rd SE5	91	R3
Wilson rd Ilf	53	V1
Wilson st E17	33	T14
Wilson st EC2	150	G1
Wilson st N21	17	V3
Wilsons pl E14	63	X17
Wilsons rd W6	152	H10
Wilstone clo Hayes	58	A10
Wilthorne gdns Dag	56	J20
Wilton ave W4	74	B14
Wilton cres SW1	147	S19
Wilton cres SW19	105	V20
Wilton dr Rom	38	M2
Wilton gro SW19	105	W20
Wilton gro N Mal	118	D13
Wilton ms SW1	155	W1
Wilton Park ct SE18	78	J20
Wilton pl SW1	147	S18
Wilton rd N10	29	P6
Wilton rd SE2	80	G10
Wilton rd SW1	156	A3
Wilton rd SW19	106	K17
Wilton rd Barn	5	Y13
Wilton row SW1	147	T18
Wilton sq N1	142	E4
Wilton st SW1	155	W1
Wilton ter SW1	147	T20
Wilton vill N1	142	D5
Wilton way E8	49	Y18
Wiltshire clo SW3	155	N6
Wiltshire gdns N4	30	L18
Wiltshire gdns Twick	101	O2
Wiltshire rd SW9	90	G8
Wiltshire rd Th Hth	122	G7
Wiltshire row N1	142	F5
Wilverley cres N Mal	118	C16
Wimbart rd SW2	90	D18
Wimbledon bri SW19	105	V16
Wimbledon Hill rd SW19	105	T14
Wimbledon Park est SW19	105	U2
Wimbledon Park rd SW18	87	X17
Wimbledon Park rd SW19	105	T5
Wimbledon Park side SW19	105	O4
Wimbledon rd SW17	106	E9
Wimbolt st E2	143	S11
Wimborne ave Sthl	70	F11
Wimborne clo SE12	94	C13
Wimborne clo Buck H	21	X7

Name	Ref1	Ref2
Wimborne clo	129	N1
Wor Pk		
Wimborne dr NW9	25	P10
Wimborne dr Pnr	22	A20
Wimborne gdns	60	C15
W13		
Wimborne rd N9	18	J7
Wimborne rd N17	31	S7
Wimborne way	124	G8
Beck		
Wimbourne st N1	142	E8
Wimpole clo	117	O4
Kings T		
Wimpole ms W1	147	W1
Wimpole st W1	147	X3
Winans wk SW9	90	F5
Wincanton cres	40	J14
Nthlt		
Wincanton gdns Ilf	35	Z8
Wincanton rd SW18	87	V18
Winchcomb gdns	95	P8
SE9		
Winchcombe rd Cars	130	H3
Winchelsea ave Bexh	81	O20
Winchelsea clo	87	P14
SW15		
Winchelsea rd E7	52	E11
Winchelsea rd N17	31	T11
Winchelsea rd NW10	61	Z3
Winchelsey ri S Croy	133	U14
Winchendon rd SW6	87	V1
Winchendon rd Tedd	101	R10
Winchester ave NW6	136	M3
Winchester ave NW9	25	O10
Winchester ave	70	F16
Houns		
Winchester clo E6	66	F18
Winchester clo SE17	157	Y6
Winchester clo Brom	126	C6
Winchester clo Enf	8	E18
Winchester clo	103	U17
Kings T		
Winchester pk Brom	126	B7
Winchester pl N6	47	T3
Winchester rd E4	33	V2
Winchester rd N6	47	T2
Winchester rd N9	18	J4
Winchester rd NW3	138	H1
Winchester rd Bexh	97	W4
Winchester rd Brom	126	C7
Winchester rd Felt	100	D7
Winchester rd Har	24	L12
Winchester rd Ilf	54	D9
Winchester rd Twick	84	A16
Winchester sq SE1	150	E13
Winchester st SW1	155	Y9
Winchester st W3	73	W4
Winchester wk SE1	150	E13
Winchfield clo Har	24	E7
Winchfield rd SE26	110	J11
Winchmore Hill rd	16	K4
N14		
Winchmore Hill rd	17	P1
N21		
Winckley clo Har	25	N15
Wincott st SE11	157	U6
Wincrofts dr SE9	96	F10
Windborough rd	131	O17
Cars		
Windermere ave N3	27	X11
Windermere ave	136	M6
NW6		
Windermere ave	120	A7
SW19		
Windermere ave	57	X13
Horn		
Windermere ave	42	E2
Wem		
Windermere gdns Ilf	35	S16
Windermere rd N10	29	S5
Windermere rd N19	47	W7
Windermere rd	104	A11
SW15		
Windermere rd	121	X2
SW16		
Windermere rd W5	72	D7
Windermere rd Bexh	98	J4
Windermere rd Croy	123	V19
Windermere rd Sthl	58	F13

Name	Ref1	Ref2
Windermere rd	135	Z3
W Wick		
Winders rd SW11	88	H4
Windfield clo SE26	110	E10
Windham ave Croy	135	X20
Windham rd Rich	85	N7
Winding way Dag	55	U8
Winding way Har	41	S11
Windlass pl SE8	75	X12
Windlesham gro	105	P1
SW19		
Windley clo SE23	110	C4
Windmill clo Surb	116	C19
Windmill dr SW4	89	S14
Windmill gdns Enf	7	S10
Windmill gro Croy	122	M16
Windmill hill NW3	46	C10
Windmill hill Enf	7	W11
Windmill la E15	51	X17
Windmill la Grnf	59	N16
Windmill la Islw	71	U14
Windmill la Sthl	71	N5
Windmill la Surb	116	C17
Windmill la (Bushey)	10	E6
Wat		
Windmill ri Kings T	103	S17
Windmill rd N18	18	C14
Windmill rd SW18	88	F16
Windmill rd SW19	104	L6
Windmill rd W4	74	A12
Windmill rd W5	72	D10
Windmill rd Brent	72	F16
Windmill rd Croy	122	L17
Windmill rd Hmptn	100	L13
Windmill rd Mitch	121	U12
Windmill row SE11	157	T10
Windmill st W1	148	E2
Windmill st (Bushey)	10	F4
Wat		
Windmill wk SE1	149	U14
Windover ave NW9	25	Z12
Windrush clo SW11	88	G9
Windrush clo W4	85	V1
Windrush la SE23	110	F6
Windsor ave E17	33	T10
Windsor ave SW19	120	D2
Windsor ave Edg	12	P17
Windsor ave N Mal	117	W11
Windsor ave Sutt	129	S7
Windsor clo N3	27	U7
Windsor clo SE27	108	L10
Windsor clo Brent	72	A17
Windsor clo Chis	114	A11
Windsor ct N14	16	H3
Windsor cres Har	40	G11
Windsor cres Wem	43	S9
Windsor dr Barn	5	Y17
Windsor dr Dart	99	X16
Windsor gdns W9	137	T20
Windsor gdns Croy	132	B6
Windsor gro SE27	108	L10
Windsor pl SW1	156	D4
Windsor rd E4	20	E12
Windsor rd E7	52	H15
Windsor rd E10	51	S8
Windsor rd E11	52	F5
Windsor rd N3	27	T8
Windsor rd N7	48	B9
Windsor rd N13	17	U11
Windsor rd N17	31	X1
Windsor rd NW2	44	J17
Windsor rd W5	60	H20
Windsor rd Barn	4	D19
Windsor rd Bexh	97	Y11
Windsor rd Dag	55	Z9
Windsor rd Har	23	O4
Windsor rd Ilf	54	A12
Windsor rd	102	K18
Kings T		
Windsor rd Rich	85	O5
Windsor rd Sthl	70	E8
Windsor rd Tedd	101	R11
Windsor rd Th Hth	122	K4
Windsor rd	128	H3
Wor Pk		
Windsor st N1	141	Z5
Windsor ter N1	142	C11
Windsor wk SE5	91	N7
Windsor way W14	152	J5

Name	Ref1	Ref2
Windspoint dr SE15	159	V15
Windus rd N16	49	V5
Windus wk N16	49	V5
Windy ridge	127	R1
Brom		
Windyridge clo	105	R11
SW19		
Wine clo E1	151	Z11
Wine Office ct EC4	149	V5
Winforton st SE10	93	U1
Winfrith rd SW18	88	C20
Wingate cres Croy	121	Z14
Wingate rd W6	74	J8
Wingate rd Ilf	54	A14
Wingate rd Sid	115	U14
Wingate Trading est	31	W1
N17		
Wingfield rd E15	51	Z13
Wingfield rd E17	33	S15
Wingfield rd	103	O15
Kings T		
Wingfield st SE15	91	W7
Wingford rd SW2	90	A16
Wingmore rd SE24	90	L8
Wingrave rd W6	152	E15
Wingrove rd SE6	112	A5
Winifred gro SW11	89	N10
Winifred rd SW19	105	Y20
Winifred rd Dag	56	A4
Winifred rd Dart	99	Y14
Winifred rd Hmptn	100	G10
Winifred st E16	78	G4
Winkfield rd E13	65	V7
Winkfield rd N22	30	G4
Winkley st E2	143	V11
Winlaton rd Brom	111	Y10
Winmill rd Dag	56	B10
Winn Common rd	79	X15
SE18		
Winn rd SE12	94	G20
Winnett st W1	148	F8
Winnington clo N2	28	F18
Winnington rd N2	46	F2
Winnington rd Enf	9	P1
Winns ave E17	32	K9
Winns ms N15	31	S13
Winns ter E17	33	N8
Winsbeach E17	33	X8
Winscombe cres W5	60	G12
Winscombe st N19	47	T8
Winscombe way	10	M16
Stan		
Winsford rd SE6	110	L6
Winsham gro SW11	89	O14
Winslade rd SW2	90	B12
Winslade ms W2	146	G5
Winsland st W2	146	F5
Winsley st W1	148	B5
Winslow gro E4	20	M8
Winslow W6	152	D13
Winslow way Felt	100	A7
Winsor ter E6	66	J15
Winstanley rd SW11	88	G8
Winstead gdns Dag	56	L14
Winston ave NW9	44	A1
Winston clo Har	10	H19
Winston clo Rom	38	J13
Winston ct Har	22	K3
Winston rd N16	49	P14
Winston wk W4	73	X9
Winston way Ilf	53	Z9
Winter ave E6	66	E3
Winter Box wk Rich	84	M11
Winterbourne rd SE6	92	L20
Winterbourne rd Dag	55	T6
Winterbourne rd	122	F8
Th Hth		
Winterbrook rd SE24	90	M16
Winterfold clo SW19	105	S4
Wintergreen clo E6	66	D14
Winters rd T Ditt	116	B16
Winterstoke rd SE6	110	M1
Winterton pl SW10	154	E13
Winterwell rd SW2	90	B13
Winthorpe rd SW15	87	T11
Winthrop st E1	143	X20
Winton ave N11	29	V2
Winton clo N9	19	T2
Winton gdns Edg	25	N1

Name	Ref1	Ref2
Winton way SW16	108	F13
Wisbeach rd Croy	123	P12
Wisborough rd	133	U20
S Croy		
Wisdons clo Dag	56	H5
Wise la NW7	13	U16
Wise rd E15	64	J3
Wiseman rd E10	51	O5
Wiseton rd SW17	106	L1
Wishart rd SE3	95	O3
Wisley rd SW11	89	N14
Wisley rd Orp	115	O18
Wisteria rd SE13	93	X11
Witan st E2	143	Y15
Witham rd SE20	124	C6
Witham rd W13	72	A15
Witham rd Dag	56	F15
Witham rd Islw	83	R3
Witham rd Rom	39	Y14
Witherby clo Croy	133	T10
Witherfield way	159	Y10
SE16		
Witherington rd N5	48	G15
Withers mead NW9	26	D3
Witherston way SE9	113	W5
Withy mead E4	20	K10
Withycombe rd	87	O20
SW19		
Witley cres Croy	135	U15
Witley gdns Sthl	70	D10
Witley rd N19	47	W7
Witney path SE23	110	G6
Wittenham way E4	20	K10
Wittersham rd Brom	112	C13
Wivenhoe clo SE15	91	Z6
Wivenhoe ct Houns	82	E9
Wivenhoe rd Bark	68	A5
Wiverton rd SE26	110	D15
Wix rd Dag	68	K2
Wixs la SW4	89	R8
Woburn ave Horn	57	W13
Woburn pl WC1	140	J17
Woburn rd Cars	130	J2
Woburn rd Croy	123	N20
Woburn sq WC1	140	G18
Woffington clo	102	D20
Kings T		
Woking clo SW15	86	D10
Woldham rd Brom	126	L8
Wolfe clo Brom	126	F14
Wolfe cres SE7	78	B13
Wolfe cres SE16	75	T6
Wolferton rd E12	53	V12
Wolffram clo SE13	93	Z12
Wolfington rd SE27	108	H9
Wolftencroft clo	88	H6
SW11		
Wollaston clo SE1	158	A6
Wolmer clo Edg	12	E12
Wolmer gdns Edg	12	C9
Wolseley ave SW19	105	Y5
Wolseley gdns W4	73	T15
Wolseley rd E7	52	H19
Wolseley rd N8	29	Y16
Wolseley rd N22	30	C5
Wolseley rd W4	73	W10
Wolseley rd Har	23	T9
Wolseley rd Mitch	121	O17
Wolseley rd Rom	57	N2
Wolseley st SE1	151	R18
Wolsey ave E6	66	K9
Wolsey ave E17	32	M10
Wolsey clo SW20	104	J17
Wolsey clo Houns	83	N11
Wolsey clo Kings T	117	T1
Wolsey clo Sthl	71	N7
Wolsey clo Wor Pk	128	F8
Wolsey cres Croy	135	T20
Wolsey cres Mord	119	U17
Wolsey dr Kings T	102	J13
Wolsey gro Edg	25	Y1
Wolsey ms NW5	47	U17
Wolsey rd N1	49	R15
Wolsey rd Enf	9	N8
Wolsey rd Hmptn	100	M14
Wolsey st E1	151	Z2
Wolsley clo Dart	99	R13
Wolstonbury N12	14	K16
Wolvercote rd SE2	80	H6

Name	Page	Grid
Wolverley st E2	143	W13
Wolverton ave Kings T	117	R1
Wolverton gdns W5	73	N1
Wolverton gdns W6	152	F6
Wolverton rd Stan	11	P20
Wolverton way N14	6	J17
Wolves la N13	17	V18
Wolves la N22	30	G2
Womersley rd N8	30	C18
Wonersh way Sutt	129	P19
Wonford clo Kings T	104	B20
Wontner clo N1	142	A2
Wontner rd SW17	107	N3
Wood clo E2	143	S16
Wood clo NW9	43	Z2
Wood clo Har	41	P2
Wood dr Chis	113	R15
Wood End ave Har	40	M12
Wood End clo Nthlt	41	O14
Wood End gdns Nthlt	41	N14
Wood End la Nthlt	40	L16
Wood End rd Har	41	R12
Wood End way Nthlt	41	N15
Wood la N6	29	R18
Wood la NW9	43	X2
Wood la W12	144	B5
Wood la Dag	55	V12
Wood la Horn	57	W16
Wood la Islw	71	T16
Wood la Stan	10	M12
Wood la Wdf Grn	21	O14
Wood Lodge gdns Brom	113	P18
Wood Lodge la W Wick	135	U5
Wood ride Barn	5	T5
Wood st E16	65	W18
Wood st E17	33	V9
Wood st EC2	150	C5
Wood st W4	74	B14
Wood st Barn	4	C13
Wood st Kings T	116	H3
Wood st Mitch	121	N18
Wood vale N10	29	U15
Wood vale SE23	109	Z2
Wood Vale est SE23	92	B17
Woodall rd Enf	9	U18
Woodbank rd Brom	112	C7
Woodbastwick rd SE26	110	G14
Woodberry ave N21	17	U7
Woodberry ave Har	22	L14
Woodberry cres N10	29	S9
Woodberry down W4	48	L2
Woodberry Down est N4	48	M1
Woodberry gdns N12	15	P19
Woodberry gro N4	48	L1
Woodberry gro N12	15	R18
Woodberry way E4	20	H4
Woodberry way N12	15	P20
Woodbine clo Twick	101	P5
Woodbine gro SE20	110	B19
Woodbine gro Enf	8	C2
Woodbine la Wor Pk	128	L6
Woodbine pl E11	34	G18
Woodbine rd Sid	96	H20
Woodbine ter E9	50	D17
Woodbines ave Kings T	116	H8
Woodborough rd SW15	86	K11
Woodbourne ave SW16	107	X8
Woodbourne gdns Wall	131	T17
Woodbridge clo N7	48	D7
Woodbridge clo NW2	44	H8
Woodbridge st Bark	54	K16
Woodbridge st EC1	141	W16
Woodbrook rd SE2	80	B17
Woodburn clo NW4	27	R17
Woodbury clo E11	34	H14
Woodbury clo Croy	133	W3
Woodbury Park rd W13	60	B12
Woodbury rd E17	33	R12
Woodbury st SW17	106	K13
Woodchester sq W2	137	W20
Woodchurch clo Sid	114	G7
Woodchurch dr Brom	113	O18
Woodchurch rd NW6	137	W1
Woodclyffe dr Chis	127	X2
Woodcock ct Har	42	J2
Woodcock Dell ave Har	42	F1
Woodcock hill Har	24	E15
Woodcombe cres SE23	110	D1
Woodcote ave NW7	13	Z18
Woodcote ave Horn	57	W11
Woodcote ave Th Hth	122	J10
Woodcote ave Wall	131	R18
Woodcote clo Enf	9	R19
Woodcote clo Kings T	103	N14
Woodcote grn Wall	131	U20
Woodcote ms Wall	131	U13
Woodcote pl SE27	108	K12
Woodcote rd E11	52	E1
Woodcote rd Wall	131	U16
Woodcroft N21	17	S6
Woodcroft SE9	113	U6
Woodcroft Grnf	41	Z17
Woodcroft ave NW7	13	O20
Woodcroft ave Stan	23	X3
Woodcroft rd Th Hth	122	H13
Woodedge clo E4	21	O5
Woodend SE19	108	L14
Woodend Sutt	130	C3
Woodend the Wall	131	S20
Woodend gdns Enf	7	N15
Woodend rd E17	33	U6
Wooder gdns E7	52	E13
Wooderson clo SE25	123	S9
Woodfall ave Barn	4	J15
Woodfall dr Dart	99	S10
Woodfall rd N4	48	E5
Woodfall st SW3	155	O10
Woodfarrs SE5	91	P11
Woodfield ave NW9	26	B14
Woodfield ave SW16	107	Y5
Woodfield ave W5	60	F12
Woodfield ave Cars	131	O15
Woodfield ave Wem	42	E10
Woodfield clo SE19	108	M17
Woodfield clo Enf	8	E14
Woodfield cres W5	60	F12
Woodfield dr Barn	16	A4
Woodfield dr Rom	39	Y12
Woodfield gdns W9	137	S20
Woodfield gdns N Mal	118	D12
Woodfield gro SW16	107	Y6
Woodfield la SW16	107	X6
Woodfield pl W9	137	S19
Woodfield ri (Bushey) Wat	10	D2
Woodfield rd W5	60	F12
Woodfield rd W9	137	R19
Woodfield way N11	16	J20
Woodford ave Ilf	35	P9
Woodford Bridge rd Ilf	35	N8
Woodford New rd E17	33	Z12
Woodford New rd E18	34	B3
Woodford pl Wem	42	J4
Woodford rd E7	52	G12
Woodford rd E18	34	E13
Woodford Trading est Wdf Grn	35	N8
Woodger rd W12	144	D18
Woodget clo E6	66	D16
Woodgrange ave N12	15	R14
Woodgrange ave W5	73	O2
Woodgrange ave Enf	8	K19
Woodgrange ave Har	24	F15
Woodgrange clo Har	24	G15
Woodgrange gdns Enf	8	L19
Woodgrange rd E7	52	G14
Woodhall ave SE21	109	U6
Woodhall ave Pnr	22	A6
Woodhall dr SE21	109	U6
Woodhall dr Pnr	22	A4
Woodham ct E18	34	C13
Woodham rd SE6	111	T7
Woodhaven gdns Ilf	36	B12
Woodhayes rd SW19	104	M17
Woodheyes rd NW10	43	Z16
Woodhill SE18	78	E10
Woodhill cres Har	24	G19
Woodhouse ave Grnf	59	W5
Woodhouse clo Grnf	59	W4
Woodhouse gro E12	53	P18
Woodhouse rd E11	52	B9
Woodhouse rd N12	15	T18
Woodhurst rd SE2	80	A13
Woodhurst rd W3	73	W1
Woodington clo SE9	95	W16
Woodison st E3	63	W13
Woodknoll dr Chis	127	T1
Woodland clo NW9	25	W17
Woodland clo SE19	109	T14
Woodland clo Epsom	128	B15
Woodland clo Wdf Grn	21	V10
Woodland cres SE10	76	M15
Woodland gdns N10	29	R14
Woodland gdns Islw	83	T7
Woodland gro SE10	77	N15
Woodland hill SE19	109	T14
Woodland ri N10	29	R14
Woodland ri Grnf	41	Z17
Woodland rd E4	20	H5
Woodland rd N11	16	E16
Woodland rd SE19	109	T13
Woodland rd Th Hth	122	G10
Woodland ter SE7	78	C12
Woodland wk NW3	46	K15
Woodland way N21	17	T8
Woodland way NW7	13	P18
Woodland way SE2	80	J11
Woodland way Croy	124	H20
Woodland way Mitch	107	P18
Woodland way Mord	119	V9
Woodland way W Wick	135	S8
Woodland way Wdf Grn	21	V10
Woodlands NW11	27	S17
Woodlands SW20	119	N9
Woodlands Har	22	F13
Woodlands the N14	16	E5
Woodlands the SE13	93	X18
Woodlands the SE19	108	M18
Woodlands the Islw	83	V6
Woodlands the Wall	131	R19
Woodlands ave E11	52	G4
Woodlands ave N3	28	C3
Woodlands ave W3	73	T3
Woodlands ave N Mal	117	W2
Woodlands ave Rom	37	Z19
Woodlands ave Sid	114	H1
Woodlands ave Wor Pk	128	F2
Woodlands clo NW11	27	S15
Woodlands clo Brom	127	U4
Woodlands dr Stan	10	J18
Woodlands gro Islw	83	T6
Woodlands Park rd N15	30	K15
Woodlands Park rd SE10	77	N15
Woodlands rd E11	52	Z6
Woodlands rd E17	33	V10
Woodlands rd N9	19	O4
Woodlands rd SW13	86	D8
Woodlands rd Bexh	97	Z6
Woodlands rd Brom	127	R4
Woodlands rd Enf	8	A4
Woodlands rd Har	23	V15
Woodlands rd Ilf	54	B9
Woodlands rd Islw	83	R7
Woodlands rd Rom	39	T10
Woodlands rd Sthl	70	A3
Woodlands rd Surb	116	G19
Woodlands st SE13	93	Y18
Woodlands way SW15	87	U12
Woodlawn clo SW15	87	U14
Woodlawn cres Twick	100	J4
Woodlawn dr Felt	100	A4
Woodlawn rd SW6	152	F17
Woodlea dr Brom	126	A12
Woodlea rd N16	49	R8
Woodleigh ave N12	15	X18
Woodleigh gdns SW16	108	A8
Woodman st E16	78	K4
Woodmans ms W12	144	A3
Woodmansterne rd SW16	107	W19
Woodmansterne rd Cars	130	K19
Woodmere SE9	95	T20
Woodmere ave Croy	124	G18
Woodmere clo SW11	124	G17
Woodmere gdns Croy	124	E18
Woodmere way Beck	125	W11
Woodnook rd SW16	107	T11
Woodpecker clo N9	8	M19
Woodpecker mt Croy	134	K19
Woodpecker rd SE14	75	W18
Woodpecker rd SE28	68	F20
Woodquest ave SE24	90	K13
Woodridge clo Enf	7	U7
Woodridings ave Pnr	22	E4
Woodridings clo Pnr	22	D2
Woodriffe rd E11	33	Y20
Woodrow SE18	78	F12
Woodrow clo Grnf	60	B1
Woodrow ct N17	32	A2
Woodrush way Rom	37	W13
Woods ms W1	147	S9
Woods pl SE1	158	K2
Woods rd SE15	91	Z2
Woodseer st E1	143	P19
Woodsford sq W14	144	M16
Woodshire rd Dag	56	J10
Woodside NW11	27	Y15
Woodside SW19	105	U15
Woodside Buck H	21	L8
Woodside ave N6	28	M15
Woodside ave N10	29	P13
Woodside ave N12	15	P14
Woodside ave SE25	124	C23
Woodside ave Chis	114	B13
Woodside ave Wem	60	K2
Woodside clo Bexh	99	O9
Woodside clo Stan	11	N15
Woodside clo Surb	117	U19
Woodside clo Wem	60	L2
Woodside ct N12	15	O13
Woodside Court rd Croy	123	Y18
Woodside cres Sid	114	J7
Woodside end Wem	60	L4
Woodside gdns E4	20	E17
Woodside gdns N17	31	T8
Woodside Grange rd N12	15	O14
Woodside grn SE25	123	Y16
Woodside gro N12	15	R11
Woodside la N12	15	P11
Woodside la Bex	117	O14
Woodside pk SE25	123	Z13
Woodside Park ave E17	33	X14
Woodside Park rd N12	15	R14
Woodside pl Wem	60	L3
Woodside rd E13	65	X11
Woodside rd N22	30	F1
Woodside rd SE25	123	Z16
Woodside rd Bexh	99	N10
Woodside rd Brom	127	R11

Street	Page	Grid
Woodside rd Kings T	102	J18
Woodside rd N Mal	117	Z4
Woodside rd Sid	114	H8
Woodside rd Sutt	130	C7
Woodside rd Wdf Grn	21	S13
Woodside way Croy	124	B15
Woodside way Mitch	121	U1
Woodsome rd NW5	47	R10
Woodspring rd SW19	105	T4
Woodstead gro Edg	11	Y19
Woodstock ave NW11	45	T1
Woodstock ave W13	71	Z8
Woodstock ave Islw	83	X12
Woodstock ave Sthl	58	F9
Woodstock ave Sutt	119	V18
Woodstock clo Bex	98	C20
Woodstock clo Stan	24	L8
Woodstock ct SE12	94	E17
Woodstock cres N9	8	M19
Woodstock gdns Beck	111	S19
Woodstock gdns Ilf	55	N6
Woodstock gro W12	144	H17
Woodstock ms W1	147	V1
Woodstock ri SW1	119	U19
Woodstock rd E7	52	K20
Woodstock rd E17	33	W7
Woodstock rd N4	48	G4
Woodstock rd NW11	45	V2
Woodstock rd W4	74	B9
Woodstock rd Cars	131	P11
Woodstock rd Croy	133	O7
Woodstock rd) (Bushey)Wat	10	G2
Woodstock rd Wem	60	L2
Woodstock st W1	147	X6
Woodstock ter E14	64	E19
Woodstock way Mitch	121	T2
Woodstone ave Epsom	128	G12
Woodsyre SE26	109	V9
Woodthorpe rd SW15	86	K11
Woodtree clo NW4	27	N6
Woodvale ave SE25	123	U5
Woodvale wk SE27	108	L12
Woodview ave E4	20	G12
Woodview clo N4	30	K20
Woodview clo SW15	103	Y9
Woodville SE3	94	J1
Woodville clo SE12	94	F13
Woodville clo Tedd	101	Y10
Woodville gdns W5	60	J17
Woodville gdns Ilf	35	Z11
Woodville gro Well	97	N7
Woodville rd E11	52	C3
Woodville rd E17	32	K14
Woodville rd E18	34	J7
Woodville rd N16	49	R15
Woodville rd NW6	137	S7
Woodville rd NW11	27	S20
Woodville rd W5	60	H18
Woodville rd Barn	5	N10
Woodville rd Mord	119	Y8
Woodville rd Rich	102	C7
Woodville rd Th Hth	123	O7
Woodville SE18	78	E11
Woodward ave NW4	26	G16
Woodward gdns Dag	55	T20
Woodward gdns Stan	10	J20
Woodward rd Dag	55	R20
Woodwarde rd SE22	91	S16
Woodway cres Har	23	Z17
Woodwell st SW18	88	E12
Woodyard clo NW5	47	R15
Woodyard la SE21	91	S19
Woodyates rd SE12	94	E16
Wool rd SW20	104	K16
Woolacombe rd SE3	94	K5
Wooler st SE17	158	F10
Woolf clo SE28	80	D3
Woollaston rd N4	30	H19
Woolmead ave NW9	44	F2
Woolmer gdns N18	18	L17
Woolmer rd N18	18	L16
Woolmore st E14	64	G19
Woolneigh st SW6	88	A6
Woolstaplers way SE16	159	S4
Woolston clo E17	32	F6
Woolstone rd SE23	110	H5
Woolwich Church st SE18	78	G9
Woolwich common SE18	78	J17
Woolwich High st SE18	78	K8
Woolwich Industrial est SE28	79	X7
Woolwich Manor way E16	66	H12
Woolwich New rd SE18	78	M11
Woolwich rd SE2	80	J15
Woolwich rd SE7	77	O14
Woolwich rd Belv	81	P14
Woolwich rd Bexh	98	F6
Wooster gdns E14	64	J17
Woosters ms Har	23	N10
Wootton gro N3	27	Y6
Wootton st SE1	149	U15
Worbeck rd SE20	124	B3
Worcester ave N17	31	X1
Worcester clo Croy	135	N4
Worcester clo Mitch	121	R5
Worcester cres NW7	13	O9
Worcester cres Wdf Grn	21	X15
Worcester gdns Grnf	41	O18
Worcester gdns Ilf	35	S20
Worcester gdns Wor Pk	128	C4
Worcester pl EC4	150	C9
Worcester rd E12	53	T11
Worcester rd E17	32	F6
Worcester rd SW19	105	W14
Worcester rd Sutt	129	X16
Worcesters ave Enf	8	K2
Wordsworth ave E12	53	R19
Wordsworth ave E18	34	C9
Wordsworth ave Grnf	59	P8
Wordsworth dr Sutt	129	O10
Wordsworth rd N16	49	S13
Wordsworth rd SE1	159	O7
Wordsworth rd SE20	110	E17
Wordsworth rd Hmptn	100	E10
Wordsworth rd Wall	131	W15
Wordsworth rd Well	96	J2
Wordsworth wk NW11	27	W14
Worfield st SW11	154	M19
Worgan st SE11	157	O9
Worland rd E15	52	A19
World's End est SW10	154	E17
Worlds End la N21	7	S17
Worlds End la Enf	7	S13
World's End pas SW10	154	F16
Worlidge st W6	152	C9
Worlingham rd SE22	91	W10
Wormholt rd W12	74	G3
Wormwood st EC2	150	J4
Wornington rd W10	136	L19
Woronzow rd NW8	138	H5
Worple ave SW19	105	R19
Worple ave Islw	83	Y13
Worple clo Har	40	E3
Worple rd SW20	118	M3
Worple rd Islw	83	Y11
Worple Road ms SW19	105	U15
Worple st SW14	85	Z7
Worple way Har	40	E3
Worple way Rich	84	L12
Worship st EC2	142	G1
Worslade rd SW17	106	F11
Worsley Bridge rd SE26	110	M10
Worsley Bridge rd Beck	111	O17
Worsley rd E11	52	A11
Worsopp dr SW4	89	W12
Worthing rd Houns	70	D17
Worthington rd Surb	117	N20
Wortley rd E6	66	A1
Wortley rd Croy	122	F16
Worton gdns Islw	83	P4
Worton rd Islw	83	R10
Worton way Islw	83	O3
Wotton rd NW2	44	M10
Wotton rd SE8	75	Z17
Wouldham rd E16	65	O17
Wragby rd E11	52	A10
Wrampling pl N9	18	L6
Wrangthorn wk Croy	132	F9
Wray ave Ilf	35	X10
Wray cres N4	48	B6
Wray rd Sutt	129	V20
Wrayfield rd Sutt	129	R7
Wraysbury clo Houns	82	C13
Wrekin rd SE18	79	R18
Wren ave NW2	45	N13
Wren ave Sthl	70	E10
Wren clo E16	65	R16
Wren cres (Bushey) Wat	10	A4
Wren gdns Dag	55	W14
Wren gdns Horn	57	T5
Wren Landing E14	76	B2
Wren path SE28	79	T8
Wren rd SE5	91	O2
Wren rd Dag	55	V14
Wren rd Sid	115	T9
Wren st WC1	141	P16
Wrentham ave NW10	136	F8
Wrenthorpe rd Brom	111	Z10
Wrexham rd E3	64	C7
Wricklemarsh rd SE3	94	H3
Wrigglesworth st SE14	75	S19
Wrights clo SE13	93	W11
Wrights clo Dag	56	H11
Wrights la W8	145	W20
Wrights rd E3	63	Y5
Wrights rd SE25	123	S6
Wrights row Wall	131	R9
Wrights wk SW14	85	Y7
Wrotham rd NW1	140	D1
Wrotham rd W13	72	C2
Wrotham rd Barn	4	E9
Wrottesley rd NW10	62	G4
Wrottesley rd SE18	79	O17
Wroughton rd SW11	89	N14
Wroughton ter NW4	26	L12
Wroxall rd Dag	55	U16
Wroxham gdns N11	29	W2
Wroxton rd SE15	92	B5
Wrythe grn Cars	130	L6
Wrythe Green rd Cars	130	L6
Wrythe la Cars	120	D19
Wulfstan st W12	62	D16
Wyatt Park rd SW2	108	B3
Wyatt rd E7	52	G18
Wyatt rd N5	48	K9
Wyatt rd Dart	99	T6
Wyatts la E17	33	U10
Wybert st NW1	140	A15
Wyborne way NW10	43	V20
Wyburn ave Barn	4	G10
Wyche gro S Croy	133	N18
Wycherley clo SE3	77	P19
Wycherley cres Barn	5	N18
Wychwood ave Edg	11	U19
Wychwood ave Th Hth	122	L6
Wychwood clo Edg	11	U19
Wychwood gdns Ilf	35	V13
Wyclif st EC1	141	W14
Wycliffe clo Well	96	K2
Wycliffe rd SW11	89	P5
Wycliffe rd SW19	106	B16
Wycombe gdns NW11	45	W5
Wycombe pl SW18	88	C15
Wycombe rd N17	31	Y5
Wycombe rd Ilf	35	U16
Wycombe rd Wem	61	R3
Wydehurst rd Croy	123	Z18
Wydell clo Mord	119	O16
Wydeville Manor rd SE12	112	H9
Wye st SW11	88	G6
Wyemead cres E4	20	M7
Wyfold rd SW6	152	L20
Wyhill wk Dag	56	K19
Wyke clo Islw	71	W17
Wyke gdns W7	71	X9
Wyke rd E3	64	A1
Wyke rd SW20	119	N3
Wykeham grn Dag	55	U17
Wykeham hill Wem	43	N3
Wykeham ri N20	14	F5
Wykeham rd NW4	26	L14
Wykeham rd Har	24	A12
Wyld way Wem	43	T18
Wyldes clo NW11	46	C4
Wyldfield gdns N9	18	H7
Wyleu st SE23	92	H18
Wylie rd Sthl	70	H8
Wyllen clo E1	143	Z18
Wymering rd W9	137	V14
Wymond st SW15	87	N7
Wynan rd E14	76	D13
Wynaud ct N22	17	P19
Wyncham ave Sid	114	J2
Wynchgate N14	16	L5
Wynchgate N21	17	O2
Wynchgate Har	23	U1
Wyncroft clo Brom	127	U7
Wyndale ave NW9	25	R17
Wyndcliff rd SE7	77	W15
Wyndcroft clo Enf	7	W12
Wyndham clo Sutt	129	Y18
Wyndham cres N19	47	U10
Wyndham cres Houns	82	F15
Wyndham est SE5	158	B17
Wyndham ms W1	147	O2
Wyndham pl W1	147	O2
Wyndham rd E6	66	A1
Wyndham rd SE5	157	Z19
Wyndham rd W13	72	A7
Wyndham rd Barn	15	Z5
Wyndham rd Kings T	103	N17
Wyndham st W1	147	O1
Wyneham rd SE24	91	N14
Wynell rd SE23	110	G6
Wynford pl Belv	81	S16
Wynford rd N1	141	O8
Wynford way SE9	113	U6
Wynndale rd E18	34	H4
Wynne rd SW9	90	F5
Wynns ave Sid	96	M14
Wynnstay gdns W8	153	V13
Wynter st SW11	88	B20
Wynton gdns SE25	123	T19
Wynton pl W3	61	T16
Wynyard ter SE11	157	R10
Wynyatt st EC1	141	W13
Wyre gro Edg	12	F11
Wyresdale cres Grnf	59	W8
Wythburn pl W1	147	O5
Wythens wk SE9	95	Y15
Wythenshawe rd Dag	56	F9
Wythes clo Brom	127	T3
Wythes rd E16	78	D3
Wythfield rd SE9	95	T15
Wyvenhoe rd Har	40	M10
Wyvil rd SW8	156	K16
Wyvis st E14	64	E14

Y

Street	Page	Grid
Yabsley st E14	76	H2
Yalding rd SE16	159	S4
Yale clo Houns	82	D12
Yale way Horn	57	V12
Yarborough rd SW19	120	F1
Yardley st WC1	141	S14
Yarmouth cres N17	31	Z15

Yarmouth pl W1	147	X14	Yew Tree rd W12	62	F20	York rd N11	16	L18	Yorkshire clo N16	49	T10

Yarmouth pl W1 147 X14
Yarnton way SE2 80 H6
Yarnton way Erith 80 M7
Yarrow cres E6 66 C14
Yateley st SE18 78 B9
Yates ct NW2 45 P18
Yeading ave Har 40 B4
Yeames clo W13 59 Y18
Yeate st N1 142 F1
Yeatman rd N6 29 N18
Yeldham rd W6 152 E10
Yellow Hammer ct NW9 26 B6
Yelverton rd SW11 88 G5
Yenston clo Mord 119 Z16
Yeo st E3 64 D14
Yeoman clo SE27 108 H8
Yeoman rd Nthlt 40 B20
Yeoman st SE8 75 V10
Yeoman's row SW3 154 M2
Yeomans way Enf 9 O9
Yeomans yd E1 151 R8
Yerbury rd N19 47 Y9
Yester dr Chis 113 S19
Yester pk Chis 113 V16
Yester rd Chis 113 S19
Yew gro NW2 45 R13
Yew Tree clo N21 17 U3
Yew Tree clo Well 97 N2
Yew Tree clo Wor Pk 118 B20
Yew Tree gdns Rom 39 O15
Yew Tree gdns Rom (Chadwell Heath) 37 Z14

Yew Tree rd W12 62 F20
Yew Tree wk Houns 82 E14
Yew wk Har 41 T4
Yewdale clo Brom 112 A16
Yewfield rd NW10 44 D19
Yewtree clo N22 29 U5
Yewtree rd Beck 124 L5
Yoakley rd N16 49 R6
Yolande gdns SE9 95 R14
Yonge pk N4 48 F8
York ave SW14 85 W12
York ave W7 71 U2
York ave Sid 114 J4
York ave Stan 24 B5
York bri NW1 139 T17
York bldgs WC2 148 L11
York clo E6 66 F18
York clo Mord 120 A9
York gate N14 17 N1
York gate NW1 139 U18
York gro SE15 92 C1
York hill SE27 108 J6
York Hill est SE27 108 J6
York House pl W8 145 X17
York ms Ilf 53 X8
York pl SW11 88 E7
York pl Dag 56 K16
York pl Ilf 53 Y8
York ri NW5 47 S9
York rd E4 20 A17
York rd E7 52 E18
York rd E10 51 T9
York rd E17 32 G16

York rd N11 16 L18
York rd N18 18 M18
York rd N21 18 B2
York rd SE1 149 P16
York rd SW11 88 E9
York rd SW19 106 C15
York rd W3 61 X16
York rd W5 72 E8
York rd Barn 5 S15
York rd Brent 72 F14
York rd Croy 122 G16
York rd Houns 82 K8
York rd Ilf 53 W8
York rd Kings T 103 N19
York rd Sutt 129 X14
York rd Tedd 101 T11
York sq E14 63 V17
York st W1 147 N1
York st Bark 67 O4
York st Mitch 121 O18
York st Twick 101 Z1
York ter Enf 7 Z4
York ter Erith 98 J1
York Terrace east NW1 139 V18
York Terrace west NW1 139 T18
York way N1 140 L9
York way N7 140 K1
York way N20 15 Y10
York way Felt 100 D7
York Way ct N1 140 M6
Yorkland ave Well 96 K8

Yorkshire clo N16 49 T10
Yorkshire gdns N18 19 N17
Yorkshire Grey pl NW3 46 D12
Yorkshire rd E14 63 W17
Yorkshire rd Mitch 121 Z11
Yorkton st E2 143 S9
Young rd E16 65 Y16
Young st W8 145 Y18
Youngmans clo Enf 7 Z5
Young's bldgs EC1 142 C16
Youngs rd Ilf 36 D17
Yoxley app Ilf 36 C18
Yoxley dr Ilf 36 C17
Yukon rd SW12 89 T18
Yuletide clo NW10 44 A19
Yunus Khan clo E17 33 O17

Z

Zampa rd SE16 75 P14
Zander ct E2 143 U11
Zangwill rd SE3 95 P2
Zealand rd E3 63 V5
Zennor rd SW12 89 U20
Zenoria st SE22 91 V10
Zermatt rd Th Hth 122 L16
Zetland st E14 64 F14
Zion pl Th Hth 123 O10
Zion rd Th Hth 123 O10
Zoar st SE1 150 A13
Zoffany st N19 47 Y6

This is index is also available on floppy disk with

THE BARTHOLOMEW INDEXMASTER

The index to street or place names on a map or atlas is a vital part of the overall map information. It enables the user to locate the grid square in which the place they are looking for is situated.

All too often however the position of the index can create problems. It is usually printed on the reverse side of the map so that when the product is laid out flat on a table or mounted on the wall the index is no longer visible.

In street atlases, the index often has to be printed in very small text to fit within the space allowed, so it can be difficult to read. Then of course it is always possible to misread an entry particularly when there are twenty 'Station Roads' or 'High Streets'!....there is no doubt reading an index can be a painstaking and often frustrating routine.

IndexMaster is a piece of software available from Bartholomew which enables streets on the map to be located quickly using the home or office personal computer.

The software can be 'bundled' on disk with the index for any street map or atlas from the Nicholson and Bartholomew range. When it is loaded onto a PC, the user can simply type in the street or place name required and it will be highlighted on the screen with its grid reference in seconds.....no more searching, squinting and frustration.

Besides being able to find rapidly any streets in the index, with IndexMaster, it is possible to add additional locations. For instance, a taxi company might like to add their own choice of popular destinations in a variety of colours, for example pubs in green, hospitals in red and police stations in blue. There are many ways of customising the index to individual specifications.

IndexMaster, which is simple to install and operate, runs under Microsoft Windows 3.0 and higher, on all IBM and 100% compatible PCs.

For further details contact
Department EP, Bartholomew, Cheltenham:

Telephone - (0242) 512748
Fax - (0242) 222725

LONDON INFORMATION

LONDON TRANSPORT

London Transport	**148 E 20**
Travel Information Centre	

St James's Park Underground Station SW1. 071-222 1234. For enquiries on London Transport buses, London Underground and Docklands Light Railway routes, fares and times of running. Other travel information centres at these Underground stations:

Euston	**140 D 13**
Heathrow Airport	
King's Cross	**140 K 10**
Oxford Circus	**148 A 6**
Piccadilly Circus	**148 E 10**
Victoria	**155 Z 3**

Underground
London Underground tube trains run *05.30–00.15 Mon–Sat, 07.30–23.30 Sun.* Weekly, monthly, quarterly or annual Travelcards provide considerable savings. Travelcards can be used on both the Underground and buses.

Buses
London Transport buses run *06.00–24.00 Mon–Sat, 07.30–23.00 Sun.* They tend to be slower, especially in the rush hours, but more pleasant and you see so much more. They cover the whole of Greater London. Many routes now have night bus services, with a greatly extended service to the suburbs as well. Consult *Buses for Night Owls* for night buses, available from London Transport and British Rail travel information centres.

BRITISH RAIL

Booking centre for rail travel in Britain, rail and sea journeys to the Continent and Ireland, motorail and rail package holidays and tours. Several languages spoken.

British Travel Centre	**148 F 11**

4–12 Regent St SW1. British Rail trains generally run *06.00–24.00 Mon–Sat, 07.00–22.30 Sun.*

Blackfriars	**149 X 8**

Queen Victoria St EC4. 071-928 5100. Serves south and south east London suburbs. *Closed Sat & Sun.*

Cannon Street	**150 E 8**

Cannon St EC4. 071-928 5100. Serves south east London suburbs, Kent, East Sussex. *Closed Sat & Sun.*

Charing Cross	**148 K 12**

Strand WC2. 071-928 5100. Serves south east London suburbs, Kent. Trains from here go over Hungerford Bridge.

City Thameslink	**149 U 3**

New Bridge St EC1. 071-928 5100 Serves south and south east London suburbs. *Closed Sat & Sun.*

Euston	**140 E 14**

Euston Rd NW1. 071-387 7070. Fast trains to Birmingham, Manchester, Liverpool, Glasgow, Inverness, Northampton, Holyhead, Crewe. Suburban line to Watford.

Fenchurch Street	**150 L 8**

Railway Pl, Fenchurch St EC3. 071-928 5100. Trains to Tilbury and Southend.

King's Cross	**140 K 10**

Euston Rd N1. 071-278 2477. Fast trains to Leeds, York, Newcastle, Edinburgh, Aberdeen.

Liverpool Street	**150 K 2**

Liverpool St EC2. 071-283 7171. suburbs. Fast trains to Cambridge, Colchester, Norwich, Harwich Docks.

London Bridge   *150 H 14*
Borough High St SE1. 071-928 5100.
Serves south and south east London
suburbs, Kent, Sussex, East Surrey.

Marylebone   *139 N 19*
Boston Pl NW1. 071-387 7070.
Suburban lines to Amersham, High
Wycombe, Banbury, Aylesbury.

Moorgate   *150 E 2*
Moorgate EC2. 071-278 2477.
Suburban services to Welwyn Garden
City, Hertford.

Paddington   *146 E 5*
Praed St W2. 071-262 6767. Fast trains
to Bath, Bristol, Cardiff, Hereford,
Swansea, Reading, Swindon, Devon,
Cornwall.

St Pancras   *140 J 11*
Euston Rd NW1. Information 071-387
7070. Fast trains to Nottingham,
Leicester, Sheffield, Derby. Suburban
services to Luton, Bedford, St Albans.

Victoria   *155 Z 4*
Terminus Pl SW1. 071-928 5100.
Serves south and south east London
suburbs, Kent, Sussex, East Surrey.
Fast trains to Brighton. 'Gatwick
Express' *every 15 mins from 05.30–
22.00, every 30 mins from 22.00–24.00,
every hour from 24.00–05.30.*

Waterloo   *149 S 17*
York Rd SE1. Information 071-928 5100.
Serves south west London suburbs,
west Surrey, Hampshire, Dorset. Fast
trains to Portsmouth, Southampton,
Bournemouth. There is also a separate
station, Waterloo East, where all trains
from Charing Cross stop.

THAMESLINE RIVERBUS

Waterjet propelled catamaran service
between Chelsea Harbour Pier and
Greenwich Pier with eight stops in
between, including Cadogan Pier,
Charing Cross Pier for Embankment,
Festival Pier for Waterloo and South
Bank, Swan Lane Pier for the City,
London Bridge City Pier for London
Bridge, St Katharine's Pier for the
Tower, and Canary Wharf Pier for

Docklands. There is also a connecting
minibus service from Canary Wharf
Pier to London City Airport. Boats
run Mon - Fri at 20 minute intervals
between 07.00 - 20.00. On Sat & Sun
boats run every 30 minutes between
11.00 - 16.30.

COACHES

Green Line Coaches
Enquiries: 081-668 7261. These are
express buses run by the London
Country Bus company. Most run from
central London to outlying areas,
departing from Eccleston Bridge,
Victoria or Regent Street. There is a
special service, route 747, from
Gatwick to Heathrow and Luton
airports. Services generally run every
hour. Green Line can be used for
travel within central London but the
bus stops are quite far apart and the
fares are high for short journeys.

Victoria Coach Station   *155 W 6*
164 Buckingham Palace Rd SW1.
071-730 0202. The main provincial
coach companies operate from here,
travelling all over Britain and the
Continent. Booking necessary.

AIRPORTS

London City Airport   *78 E 2*
King George V Dock,
Silvertown E16. 071-474 5555

London Gatwick Airport
West Sussex. (0293) 535353

London Heathrow Airport
Hounslow, Middx. 081-759 4321.

London Stansted Airport
Stansted, Essex. (0279) 680500.

Luton Airport
Luton, Beds. (0582) 405100.

Southend Airport
Southend-on-Sea, Essex. (0702)
340201.